BOOKS FOR THE ENTHUSIAST

WORLD AIRLINE COLOURS
of yesteryear

This new addition to the popular World Airline Colours series takes a nostalgic look at colour schemes and airliners of yesteryear, with coverage of 100 airlines and over 40 different aircraft types. Entries include: BOAC/BKS/Monarch/Cunard Eagle Britannias, BEA Vanguard/Herald, BUA Carvair/VC-10, Eagle Airways Viking, Autair Ambassador, Dan Air DC-7/1-11/707/Comet, BMA Argonaut, BAF Carvair, Laker 707/DC-10, TMAC DC-7/CL-44, BEA Airtours Comet, Euravia L-049, BKS Trident, Cambrian DC-3/1-11, Aer Turas Bristol 170/DC-4/DC-7, Aer Lingus F-27, Lufthansa/Flying Tigers C-46s, Iberia/Varig/National/BOAC/Eastern Super Constellations, Northeast Viscount, TWA Starliner, Aeroflot Tu-104, SAS/TMA/UTA/Balair/Kar Air/SAM/Pan Am/Sabena DC-6s, plus many others.

148 full colour illustrations - casebound.

AIRLINES & AIRLINERS
VC10

The second in a new series of airliner monographs featuring quality photographic coverage and comprehensive operational/production histories. All VC10 operators illustrated, including BOAC, Nigeria Airways and MEA etc., plus many derelict/damaged aircraft - some rarely seen or photographed. Approximately 50 illustrations in colour and mono record the VC10's history from beginning to end.

AIRLINES & AIRLINERS
VANGUARD

Recently published, the third issue in the Airlines & Airliners series is dedicated to the Vickers Vanguard, with full operational/production histories and quality photographic coverage. Operators illustrated include BEA, Invicta, TCA, Air Canada, Merpati Nusantara, EAS, Air Gabon, Air Bridge, Air Trader, Thor Air Cargo, Air Viking, ICS, British Airways, plus many others.

WORLD AIRLINE COLOURS
VOLUME 1

Last published in 1985 as the first in the original four-volume series, this new and completely updated edition follows the established format with coverage of 148 of the world's major airlines. Full colour photographic coverage focuses on many new generation types such as the Boeing 747-400, McDonnell Douglas MD-11, Airbus A320, and the CFM-powered Boeing 737 family etc., most of which were still at the development stage when the original World Airline Colours 1 was published. This new volume also features many newly-created airlines such as Tajik Air and Moscow Airways etc.

148 full colour illustrations - casebound
To be published May/June 1994

CIVIL
Aircraft Markings

ALAN J. WRIGHT

IAN ALLAN Publishing

Contents

This forty-fifth edition published 1994

ISBN 0 7110 2129 5

Published by Ian Allan Ltd, Shepperton, Surrey;
and printed in Great Britain by Ian Allan Printing Ltd,
Coombelands House, Addlestone, Surrey KT15 1HY.

Front cover: G-AYWI, BN-2A MK III-J Trilander of Aurigny Air Services, since sold. *Austin J. Brown (AJB)*
Rear cover, top: PP-VMQ, Douglas DC-10-30. *AJB*
Rear cover, bottom: G-BYAD, Boeing 767-204ER of Britannia at Manchester. *AJB*

Introduction

The 'G' prefixed four letter registration system was adopted in 1919 after a short-lived spell of about three months with serial numbers beginning at K-100. Until July 1928 the UK allocations were in the G-Exxx range, but as a result of further International agreements, this series was ended at G-EBZZ, the replacement being G-Axxx. From this point the registrations were issued in a reasonably orderly manner through to G-AZZZ, reached in July 1972. There were two exceptions. To avoid possible confusion with signal codes, the G-AQxx sequence was omitted, while G-AUxx was reserved for Australian use originally. In recent years however, an individual request for a mark in the latter range has been granted by the Authorities.

Although the next logical sequence was started at G-Bxxx, it was not long before the strictly applied rules relating to aircraft registration began to be relaxed. Permission was readily given for personalised marks to be issued incorporating virtually any four letter combination, while re-registration has also become a common feature, a practice almost unheard of in the past. In this book, where this has taken place at some time, the previous UK civil identity appears in parenthesis after the owner's/operator's name. An example of this is One-Eleven G-BBMG which originally carried G-AWEJ.

Some aircraft have also been allowed to wear military markings without displaying their civil identity. In this case the serial number actually carried is shown in parenthesis after the type's name. For example Mosquito G-ASKH flies as RR299 in RAF colours. As an aid to the identification of these machines, a military conversion list is provided.

Other factors caused a sudden acceleration in the number of registrations allocated by the Civil Aviation Authority in the early 1980s. The first surge came with the discovery that it was possible to register plastic bags and other items even less likely to fly, on payment of the standard fee. This erosion of the main register was checked in early 1982 by the issue of a special sequence for such devices commencing at G-FYAA. Powered hang-gliders provided the second glut of allocations as a result of the decision that these types should be officially registered. Although a few of the early examples penetrated the normal in-sequence register, the vast majority were given marks in other special ranges, this time G-MBxx, G-MGxx, G-MJxx, G-MMxx, G-MNxx, G-MTxx, G-MVxx, G-MWxx, G-MYxx and G-MZxx. At first it was common practice for microlights to ignore the requirement to carry their official identity. However the vast majority now display their registration somewhere on the structure, the size and position depending on the dimensions of the component to which it is applied.

Throughout the UK section of this book, there are many instances where the probable base of the aircraft has been included. This is positioned at the end of the owner/operator details preceded by an oblique stroke. It must of course be borne in mind that changes do take place and that no attempt has been made to record the residents at the many private strips. The base of airline aircraft has been given as the company's headquarter's airport, although frequently aircraft are outstationed for long periods.

Non-airworthy preserved aircraft are shown with a star after the type.

The three-letter codes used by airlines to prefix flight numbers are included for those carriers appearing in the book. Radio frequencies for the larger airfields/airports are also listed.

Acknowledgements

Once again thanks are extended to the Registration Department of the Civil Aviation Authority for its assistance and allowing access to its files. The comments and amendments flowing from Wal Gandy have as always proved of considerable value, while Richard Lawsey, Howard Curtis, Bob Elliott, Kenneth Nimbley and Anthony Smith also contributed useful facts. The help given by numerous airlines or their information agencies has been much appreciated. The work of A. S. Wright and C. P. Wright during the update of this edition must not go unrecorded, since without it, deadlines would probably become impossible. **AJW**

International Civil Aircraft Markings

A2-	Botswana	OB-	Peru
A3-	Tonga	OD-	Lebanon
A5-	Bhutan	OE-	Austria
A6-	United Arab Emirates	OH-	Finland
A7-	Qatar	OK-	Czech Republic & Slovakia
A9C-	Bahrain	OO-	Belgium
A40-	Oman	OY-	Denmark
AP-	Pakistan	P-	Korea (North)
B-	China/Taiwan	P2-	Papua New Guinea
BNMAU-	Mongolia	P4-	Aruba
C-F, C-G	Canada	PH-	Netherlands
C2-	Nauru	PJ-	Netherlands Antilles
C3	Andora	PK-	Indonesia and West Irian
C5-	Gambia	PP-, PT-	Brazil
C6-	Bahamas	PZ-	Surinam
C9-	Mozambique	RA-	Russia
CC-	Chile	RDPL-	Laos
CN-	Morocco	RP-	Philippine Republic
CP-	Bolivia	S2-	Bangladesh
CS-	Portugal	S5-	Slovenia
CU-	Cuba	S7-	Seychelles
CX-	Uruguay	S9-	São Tomé
D-	Germany	SE-	Sweden
D2-	Angola	SP-	Poland
D4-	Cape Verde Islands	ST-	Sudan
D6-	Comores Islands	SU-	Egypt
DQ-	Fiji	SX-	Greece
EC-	Spain	T2-	Tuvalu
EI-	Republic of Ireland	T3-	Kiribati
EK-	Armenia	T7-	San Marino
EL-	Liberia	TC-	Turkey
EP-	Iran	TF-	Iceland
ER-	Moldova	TG-	Guatemala
ES-	Estonia	TI-	Costa Rica
ET-	Ethiopia	TJ-	United Republic of Cameroon
EW-	Belarus	TL-	Central African Republic
EY-	Tajikistan	TN-	Republic of Congo (Brazzaville)
EZ-	Turkmenistan	TR-	Gabon
F-	France, Colonies and Protectorates	TS-	Tunisia
G-	United Kingdom	TT-	Chad
GR-	Georgia	TU-	Ivory Coast
H4-	Solomon Islands	TY-	Benin
HA-	Hungary	TZ-	Mali
HB-	Switzerland and Liechtenstein	UK-	Uzbekistan
HC-	Ecuador	UR-	Ukraine
HH-	Haiti	V2-	Antigua
HI-	Dominican Republic	V3-	Belize
HK-	Colombia	V5-	Namibia
HL-	Korea (South)	V8-	Brunei
HP-	Panama	VH-	Australia
HR-	Honduras	VN-	Vietnam
HS-	Thailand	VP-F	Falkland Islands
HV-	The Vatican	VP-LA	Anguilla
HZ-	Saudi Arabia	VP-LM	Montserrat
I-	Italy	VP-LV	Virgin Islands
J2-	Djibouti	VQ-T	Turks & Caicos Islands
J3-	Grenada	VR-B	Bermuda
J5-	Guinea Bissau	VR-C	Cayman Islands
J6-	St Lucia	VR-G	Gibraltar
J7-	Dominica	VR-H	Hong Kong
J8-	St Vincent	VT-	India
JA-	Japan	XA-, XB-,	
JY-	Jordan	XC-,	Mexico
LN-	Norway	XT-	Burkina Faso
LV-	Argentine Republic	XU-	Kampuchea
LX-	Luxembourg	XY-	Myanmar
LY-	Lithuania	YA-	Afghanistan
LZ-	Bulgaria	YI-	Iraq
MT-	Mongolia	YJ-	Vanuatu
N-	United States of America	YK-	Syria

YL-	Latvia	5V-	Togo
YN-	Nicaragua	5W-	Western Samoa (Polynesia)
YR-	Romania	5X-	Uganda
YS-	El Salvador	5Y-	Kenya
YU-	Yugoslavia	6O-	Somalia
YV-	Venezuela	6V-	Senegal
Z-	Zimbabwe	6Y-	Jamaica
ZA-	Albania	7O-	Yemen
ZK-	New Zealand	7P-	Lesotho
ZP-	Paraguay	7Q-	Malawi
ZS-	South Africa	7T-	Algeria
3A-	Monaco	8P-	Barbados
3B-	Mauritius	8Q-	Maldives
3C-	Equatorial Guinea	8R-	Guyana
3D-	Swaziland	9A-	Croatia
3X-	Guinea	9G-	Ghana
4K	Azerbaijan	9H-	Malta
4R-	Sri Lanka	9J-	Zambia
4U-	United Nations Organisation	9K-	Kuwait
4X-	Israel	9L-	Sierra Leone
5A-	Libya	9M-	Malaysia
5B-	Cyprus	9N-	Nepal
5H-	Tanzania	9Q-	Zaïre
5N-	Nigeria	9U-	Burundi
5R-	Malagasy Republic (Madagascar)	9V-	Singapore
5T-	Mauritania	9XR-	Rwanda
5U-	Niger	9Y-	Trinidad and Tobago

Aircraft Type Designations & Abbreviations

(eg PA-28 Piper Type 28)

A.	Beagle, Auster	G.C.	Globe
AA-	American Aviation, Grumman American	GY	Gardan
		H	Helio
AB	Agusta-Bell	HM.	Henri Mignet
AG	American General	HP.	Handley Page
AS	Aérospatiale	HR.	Robin
A.S.	Airspeed	H.S.	Hawker Siddeley
ATI	Aero Trasporti Italiani	IL	Ilyushin
A.W.	Armstrong Whitworth	IMCO	Intermountain Manufacturing Co
B.	Blackburn, Bristol Boeing, Beagle	J.	Auster
		L.	Lockheed
BAC	British Aircraft Corporation	L.A.	Luton
BAe	British Aerospace	M.	Miles, Mooney
BAT	British Aerial Transport	MBB	Messerschmitt-Bölkow-Blohm
B.K.	British Klemm	MJ	Jurca
BN	Britten-Norman	M.S.	Morane-Saulnier
Bo	Bolkow	NA	North American
Bu	Bucker	P.	Hunting (formerly Percival), Piaggio
CAARP	Co-operative des Ateliers Aer de la Région Parisienne	PA-	Piper
		PC.	Pilatus
CCF	Canadian Car & Foundry Co	QAC	Quickie Aircraft Co
C.H.	Chrislea	R.	Rockwell
CHABA	Cambridge Hot-Air Ballooning Association	RAFGSA	Royal Air Force Gliding & Soaring Association
CLA	Comper	S.	Short, Sikorsky
CP.	Piel	SA., SE, SO.	Sud-Aviation, Aérospatiale, Scottish Aviation
D.	Druine		
DC-	Douglas Commercial	SC	Short
D.H.	de Havilland	SCD	Side Cargo Door
D.H.C.	de Havilland Canada	Soc	Society
DR.	Jodel (Robin-built)	S.R.	Saunders-Roe, Stinson
EMB	Embraer	ST	SOCATA
EoN	Elliotts of Newbury	T.	Tipsy
EP	Edgar Percival	TB	SOCATA
F.	Fairchild, Fokker	Tu	Tupolev
FFA	Flug und Fahrzeugwerke AG	UH.	United Helicopters (Hiller)
FH	Fairchild-Hiller	UTA	Union de Transports Aérien
G.	Grumman	V.	Vickers-Armstrongs, BAC
GA	Gulfstream American	V.S.	Vickers-Supermarine
G.A.L.	General Aircraft	WAR	War Aircraft Replicas
		W.S.	Westland
		Z.	Zlin

9

British Civil Aircraft Registrations

Reg.	Type (†False registration)	Owner or Operator	Notes
G-EACN	BAT BK23 Bantam (K123) ★	Shuttleworth Collection/O. Warden	
G-EAGA	Sopwith Dove	R. H. Reeves	
G-EASD	Avro 504L	AJD Engineering Ltd	
G-EASQ	Bristol Babe (replica) (BAPC87) ★	Bomber County Museum/Hemswell	
G-EAVX	Sopwith Pup (B1807)	K. A. M. Baker	
G-EBHX	D.H.53 Humming Bird	Shuttleworth Collection/O. Warden	
G-EBIA	RAF SE-5A (F904)	Shuttleworth Collection/O. Warden	
G-EBIB	RAF SE-5A ★	Science Museum/S. Kensington	
G-EBIC	RAF SE-5A (F938) ★	RAF Museum	
G-EBIR	D.H.51	Shuttleworth Collection/O. Warden	
G-EBJE	Avro 504K (E449)★	RAF Museum	
G-EBJG	Parnall Pixie III ★	Midland Aircraft Preservation Soc	
G-EBJO	ANEC II ★	Shuttleworth Collection/O. Warden	
G-EBKY	Sopwith Pup (N6181)	Shuttleworth Collection/O. Warden	
G-EBLV	D.H.60 Cirrus Moth	British Aerospace/Hatfield	
G-EBMB	Hawker Cygnet I ★	RAF Museum	
G-EBNV	English Electric Wren	Shuttleworth Collection/O. Warden	
G-EBQP	D.H.53 Humming Bird (J7326)★	Russavia Collection	
G-EBWD	D.H.60X Hermes Moth	Shuttleworth Collection/O. Warden	
G-EBXU	D.H.60X Moth Seaplane	D. E. Cooper-Maguire	
G-EBZM	Avro 594 Avian IIIA ★	Greater Manchester Museum of Science & Technology	
G-EBZN	D.H.60X Moth	J. Hodgkinson (G-UAAP)	
G-AAAH	D.H.60G Gipsy Moth (replica) (BAPC 168) ★	Hilton Hotel/Gatwick	
G-AAAH	D.H.60G Gipsy Moth *Jason* ★	Science Museum/S. Kensington	
G-AACN	H.P.39 Gugnunc ★	Science Museum/Wroughton	
G-AADR	D.H.60GM Moth	H. F. Moffatt	
G-AAHI	D.H.60G Moth	N. J. W. Reid	
G-AAHY	D.H.60M Moth	M. E. Vaisey	
G-AAIN	Parnall Elf II	Shuttleworth Collection/O. Warden	
G-AAMX	D.H.60GM Moth	R. J. Parkhouse	
G-AAMY	D.H.60M Moth	R. M. Brooks	
G-AAMZ	D.H.60G Moth	C. C. & J. M. Lovell	
G-AANG	Blériot XI	Shuttleworth Collection/O. Warden	
G-AANH	Deperdussin Monoplane	Shuttleworth Collection/O. Warden	
G-AANI	Blackburn Monoplane	Shuttleworth Collection/O. Warden	
G-AANJ	L.V.G.-C VI (7198/18)	Shuttleworth Collection/O. Warden	
G-AANL	D.H.60M Moth	D. & P. Ellis	
G-AANM	Bristol 96A F.2B (D7889)	Aero Vintage Ltd	
G-AANO	D.H.60GMW Moth	A. W. & M. E. Jenkins	
G-AANV	D.H.60G Moth	R. I. Souch	
G-AAOK	Curtiss Wright Travel Air 12Q	Shipping & Airlines Ltd/Biggin Hill	
G-AAOR	D.H.60G Moth (EM-01)	J. A. Pothecary/Shoreham	
G-AAPZ	Desoutter I (mod.)	Shuttleworth Collection/O. Warden	
G-AAUP	Klemm L.25-1A	J. I. Cooper	
G-AAVJ	D.H.60GMW Moth	Glidegold Ltd/Booker	
G-AAWO	D.H.60G Gipsy Moth	N. J. W. Reid & L. A. Fenwick	
G-AAXK	Klemm L.25-1A	C. C. Russell-Vick (*stored*)	
G-AAYX	Southern Martlet	Shuttleworth Collection/O. Warden	
G-AAZP	D.H.80A Puss Moth	R. P. Williams	
G-ABAA	Avro 504K (H2311) ★	Greater Manchester Museum of Science & Technology	
G-ABAG	D.H.60G Moth	Shuttleworth Collection/O. Warden	
G-ABDA	D.H.60G-III Moth Major	I. M. Castle	
G-ABDW	D.H.80A Puss Moth (VH-UQB) ★	Museum of Flight/E. Fortune	
G-ABDX	D.H.60G Moth	M. D. Souch	
G-ABEE	Avro 594 Avian IVM (Sports) ★	Aeroplane Collection Ltd	
G-ABEV	D.H.60G Moth	Wessex Aviation & Transport Ltd	
G-ABLM	Cierva C.24 ★	Mosquito Aircraft Museum	
G-ABLS	D.H.80A Puss Moth	R. C. F. Bailey	
G-ABMR	Hart 2 (J9941)★	RAF Museum	
G-ABNT	Civilian C.A.C.1 Coupe	Shipping & Airlines Ltd/Biggin Hill	
G-ABNX	Redwing 2	J. Pothecary (*stored*)	
G-ABOI	Wheeler Slymph ★	Midland Air Museum	
G-ABOX	Sopwith Pup (N5195)	Museum of Army Flying/Middle Wallop	

Notes	Reg.	Type	Owner or Operator
	G-ABSD	D.H.60G Moth	M. E. Vaisey
	G-ABTC	CLA.7 Swift	P. Channon (*stored*)
	G-ABUS	CLA.7 Swift	R. C. F. Bailey
	G-ABUL†	D.H.82A Tiger Moth ★	F.A.A. Museum (G-AOXG)/Yeovilton
	G-ABUU	CLA.7 Swift	H. B. Fox
	G-ABVE	Arrow Active 2	J. D. Penrose
	G-ABWP	Spartan Arrow	R. E. Blain/Barton
	G-ABXL	Granger Archaeopteryx ★	Shuttleworth Collection/O. Warden
	G-ABYN	Spartan Three Seater II	J. D. Souch
	G-ABZB	D.H.60G-III Moth Major	R. E. & B. A. Ogden
	G-ACAA	Bristol 96A F.2B (D8084)	Patina Ltd/Duxford
	G-ACBH	Blackburn B.2 ★	R. Coles
	G-ACCB	D.H.83 Fox Moth	E. A. Gautrey
	G-ACDA	D.H.82A Tiger Moth	R. J. Biddle
	G-ACDC	D.H.82A Tiger Moth	Tiger Club Ltd/Headcorn
	G-ACDD	D.H.83 Fox Moth	—
	G-ACDJ	D.H.82A Tiger Moth	P. Henley & J. K. Moorhouse
	G-ACEJ	D.H.83 Fox Moth	J. I. Cooper
	G-ACET	D.H.84 Dragon	M. C. Russell
	G-ACGT	Avro 594 Avian IIIA ★	Yorkshire Light Aircraft Ltd/Leeds
	G-ACIT	D.H.84 Dragon ★	Science Museum/Wroughton
	G-ACLL	D.H.85 Leopard Moth	D. C. M. & V. M. Stiles
	G-ACMA	D.H.85 Leopard Moth	S. J. Filhol/Sherburn
	G-ACMD	D.H.82A Tiger Moth	J. A. Pothecary/Shoreham
	G-ACMN	D.H.85 Leopard Moth	H. D. Labouchere
	G-ACOJ	D.H.85 Leopard Moth	Aviation Heritage Ltd
	G-ACOL	D.H.85 Leopard Moth	M. J. Abbott
	G-ACSP	D.H.88 Comet	Saltair Ltd/Staverton
	G-ACSS	D.H.88 Comet	Shuttleworth Collection *Grosvenor House*/ Hatfield
	G-ACTF	CLA.7 Swift ★	Brooklands Museum of Aviation/ Weybridge
	G-ACUS	D.H.85 Leopard Moth	T. P. A. Norman/Panshanger
	G-ACUU	Cierva C.30A (HM580)★	G. S. Baker/Duxford
	G-ACUX	S.16 Scion (VH-UUP) ★	Ulster Folk & Transport Museum
	G-ACVA	Kay Gyroplane★	Glasgow Museum of Transport
	G-ACWM	Cierva C.30A ★	International Helicopter Museum/ Weston-s-Mare
	G-ACWP	Cierva C.30A (AP507) ★	Science Museum
	G-ACXB	D.H.60G-III Moth Major	D. F. Hodgkinson
	G-ACXE	B.K.L-25C Swallow	J. C. Wakeford
	G-ACYK	Spartan Cruiser III ★	Museum of Flight (front fuselage)/ E. Fortune
	G-ACZE	D.H.89A Dragon Rapide	Wessex Aviation & Transport Ltd (G-AJGS)/Henstridge
	G-ADAH	D.H.89A Dragon Rapide ★	Greater Manchester Museum of Science & Technology
	G-ADEV	Avro 504K (H5199)	Shuttleworth Collection (G-ACNB)/ O. Warden
	G-ADFO	Blackburn B-2 ★	R. Cole
	G-ADFV	Blackburn B-2 ★	Humberside Aircraft Preservation Soc
	G-ADGP	M.2L Hawk Speed Six	R. I. Souch
	G-ADGT	D.H.82A Tiger Moth	D. R. & Mrs M. Wood
	G-ADGV	D.H.82A Tiger Moth	K. J. Whitehead
	G-ADHA	D.H.83 Fox Moth	Wessex Aviation & Transport Ltd
	G-ADHD	D.H.60G-III Moth Major	M. E. Vaisey
	G-ADIA	D.H.82A Tiger Moth	M. F. W. B. Maunsell/Goodwood
	G-ADJJ	D.H.82A Tiger Moth	J. M. Preston
	G-ADKC	D.H.87B Hornet Moth	L. E. Day/Carlisle
	G-ADKK	D.H.87B Hornet Moth	C. P. B. Horsley & R. G. Anniss
	G-ADKL	D.H.87B Hornet Moth	A. de Cadenet
	G-ADKM	D.H.87B Hornet Moth	L. V. Mayhead
	G-ADLY	D.H.87B Hornet Moth	Glidegold Ltd/Booker
	G-ADMT	D.H.87B Hornet Moth	Memorex Telex Ltd/White Waltham
	G-ADMW	M.2H Hawk Major (DG590) ★	Museum of Army Flying/Middle Wallop
	G-ADND	D.H.87B Hornet Moth	Shuttleworth Collection/O. Warden
	G-ADNE	D.H.87B Hornet Moth	Aviation Heritage Ltd
	G-ADNL	M.5 Sparrowhawk	K. D. Dunkerley
	G-ADNZ	D.H.82A Tiger Moth	C. A. Pullan
	G-ADOT	D.H.87B Hornet Moth ★	Mosquito Aircraft Museum
	G-ADPC	D.H.82A Tiger Moth	N. J. Baker & J. Beattie

13

Notes	Reg.	Type	Owner or Operator
	G-ADPJ	B.A.C. Drone	N. H. Ponsford
	G-ADPR	P.3 Gull	Shuttleworth Collection *Jean*/O. Warden
	G-ADPS	B.A. Swallow 2	Wessex Aviation & Transport Ltd
	G-ADRA	Pietenpol Air Camper	A. J. Mason
	G-ADRC	K. & S. Jungster J-1	J. J. Penney & L. R. Williams
	G-ADRG†	Mignet HM.14 (replica) (BAPC77) ★	Stratford Aircraft Collection
	G-ADRR	Aeronca C.3	D. S. Morgan
	G-ADRY†	Mignet HM.14 (replica) (BAPC29) ★	Brooklands Museum of Aviation/ Weybridge
	G-ADSK	D.H.87B Hornet Moth	R. G. Grocott
	G-ADUR	D.H.87B Hornet Moth	Wessex Aviation & Transport Ltd
	G-ADWJ	D.H.82A Tiger Moth	C. R. Hardiman
	G-ADWO	D.H.82A Tiger Moth (BB807)	Wessex Aviation Soc
	G-ADXS	Mignet HM.14 ★	Thameside Aviation Museum/E. Tilbury
	G-ADXT	D.H.82A Tiger Moth	R. G. Hanauer/Goodwood
	G-ADYS	Aeronca C.3	B. C. Cooper
	G-AEBB	Mignet HM.14 ★	Shuttleworth Collection/O. Warden
	G-AEBJ	Blackburn B-2	British Aerospace PLC/Brough
	G-AEDB	B.A.C. Drone 2	M. C. Russell
	G-AEDT	D.H.90 Dragonfly	Wessex Aviation & Transport Ltd
	G-AEDU	D.H.90 Dragonfly	T. P. A. Norman
	G-AEEG	M.3A Falcon	Skysport Engineering Ltd
	G-AEEH	Mignet HM.14 ★	RAF Museum/St Athan
	G-AEFG	Mignet HM.14 (BAPC75) ★	N. H. Ponsford
	G-AEFT	Aeronca C.3	G-AEFT Group/Yeovil
	G-AEGV	Mignet HM.14 ★	Midland Aircraft Preservation Soc
	G-AEHM	Mignet HM.14 ★	Science Museum/Wroughton
	G-AEJZ	Mignet HM.14 (BAPC120) ★	Bomber County Museum/Hemswell
	G-AEKR	Mignet HM.14 (BAPC121) ★	S. Yorks Aviation Soc
	G-AEKV	Kronfeld Drone ★	Brooklands Museum of Aviation/ Weybridge
	G-AELO	D.H.87B Hornet Moth	D. E. Wells
	G-AEML	D.H.89 Dragon Rapide	Proteus Holdings Ltd
	G-AENP	Hawker Hind (K5414) (BAPC78)	Shuttleworth Collection/O. Warden
	G-AEOA	D.H.80A Puss Moth	P. & A. Wood/O. Warden
	G-AEOF†	Mignet HM.14 (BAPC22) ★	Aviodome/Schiphol, Holland
	G-AEOF	Rearwin 8500	Shipping & Airlines Ltd/Biggin Hill
	G-AEOH	Mignet HM.14 ★	Midland Air Museum
	G-AEPH	Bristol F.2B (D8096)	Shuttleworth Collection/O. Warden
	G-AERV	M.11A Whitney Straight ★	Ulster Folk & Transport Museum
	G-AESB	Aeronca C.3	D. S. & I. M. Morgan
	G-AESE	D.H.87B Hornet Moth	J. G. Green/Redhill
	G-AESZ	Chilton D.W.1	R. E. Nerou
	G-AETA	Caudron G.3 (3066) ★	RAF Museum
	G-AEUJ	M.11A Whitney Straight	R. E. Mitchell
	G-AEVS	Aeronca 100	A. J. E. Smith
	G-AEVZ	B. A. Swallow 2	J. R. H. Ealand
	G-AEXD	Aeronca 100	Mrs M. A. & R. W. Mills
	G-AEXF	P.6 Mew Gull	J. D. Penrose/Old Warden
	G-AEXT	Dart Kitten II	A. J. Hartfield
	G-AEXZ	Piper J-2 Cub	Mrs M. & J. R. Dowson/Leicester
	G-AEYY	Martin Monoplane ★	Martin Monoplane Syndicate/Hatfield
	G-AEZF	S.16 Scion 2 ★	Southend Historic Aircraft Soc
	G-AEZJ	P.10 Vega Gull	R. A. J. Spurrell/White Waltham
	G-AEZX	Bucker Bu133C Jungmeister	A. J. E. Ditheridge
	G-AFAP†	C.A.S.A. C.352L ★	Aerospace Museum/Cosford
	G-AFAX	B. A. Eagle 2	J. G. Green
	G-AFBS	M.14A Hawk Trainer ★	G. D. Durbridge-Freeman (G-AKKU)/ Duxford
	G-AFCL	B. A. Swallow 2	A. M. Dowson/O. Warden
	G-AFDO	Piper J-3F-60 Cub	R. Wald
	G-AFDX	Hanriot HD.1 (75) ★	RAF Museum
	G-AFEL	Monocoupe 90A	Daryll Group
	G-AFFD	Percival Q-6 ★	B. D. Greenwood
	G-AFFH	Piper J-2 Cub	M. J. Honeychurch
	G-AFFI	Mignet HM.14 (replica) (BAPC76) ★	Yorkshire Air Museum/Elvington
	G-AFGC	B. A. Swallow 2	G. E. Arden
	G-AFGD	B. A. Swallow 2	A. T. Williams & ptnrs/Shobdon
	G-AFGE	B. A. Swallow 2	G. R. French

G-AEML, D.H.89 Dragon Rapide. *Alan J. Wright (AJW)*

15

Notes	Reg.	Type	Owner or Operator
	G-AFGH	Chilton D.W.1.	M. L. & G. L. Joseph
	G-AFGI	Chilton D.W.1.	J. E. McDonald
	G-AFGM	Piper J-4A Cub Coupé	A. J. P. Marshall/Carlisle
	G-AFGZ	D.H.82A Tiger Moth	M. R. Paul (G-AMHI)
	G-AFHA	Mosscraft M.A.1. ★	C. V. Butler
	G-AFIN	Chrislea Airguard ★	Aeroplane Collection Ltd
	G-AFIR	Luton LA-4 Minor	A. J. Mason
	G-AFIU	Parker C.A.4 Parasol (LA-3 Minor)★	Aeroplane Collection Ltd/Warmingham
	G-AFJA	Watkinson Dingbat ★	K. Woolley
	G-AFJB	Foster-Wikner G.M.1. Wicko (DR613) ★	K. Woolley
	G-AFJR	Tipsy Trainer 1	M. E. Vaisey (*Stored*)
	G-AFJU	M.17 Monarch ★	Museum of Flight/E. Fortune
	G-AFJV	Mosscraft MA.2	C. V. Butler
	G-AFLW	M.17 Monarch	N. I. Dalziel/Biggin Hill
	G-AFNG	D.H.94 Moth Minor	T. E. G. Buckett
	G-AFNI	D.H.94 Moth Minor	B. M. Welford
	G-AFOB	D.H.94 Moth Minor	Wessex Aviation & Transport Ltd
	G-AFOJ	D.H.94 Moth Minor	Mosquito Aircraft Museum
	G-AFPN	D.H.94 Moth Minor	J. W. & A. R. Davy/Carlisle
	G-AFPR	D.H.94 Moth Minor	J. A. Livett
	G-AFRZ	M.17 Monarch	R. E. Mitchell (G-AIDE)
	G-AFSC	Tipsy Trainer 1	R. V. & M. H. Smith
	G-AFSV	Chilton D.W.1A	R. Nerou
	G-AFSW	Chilton D.W.2 ★	R. I. Souch
	G-AFTA	Hawker Tomtit (K1786)	Shuttleworth Collection/O. Warden
	G-AFTN	Taylorcraft Plus C2	Leicestershire County Council Museums
	G-AFUP	Luscombe 8A Silvaire	Trust Me Airtours
	G-AFVE	D.H.82 Tiger Moth (T7230)	P. A. Shaw & M. R. Paul
	G-AFVN	Tipsy Trainer 1	D. F. Lingard
	G-AFWH	Piper J-4A Cub Coupé	J. R. Edwards & D. D. Smith
	G-AFWI	D.H.82A Tiger Moth	E. Newbigin
	G-AFWT	Tipsy Trainer 1	J. S. Barker/Redhill
	G-AFYD	Luscombe 8E Silvaire	J. D. Iliffe
	G-AFYO	Stinson H.W.75	R. N. Wright
	G-AFZA	Piper J-4A Cub Coupé	J. R. Joiner & M. L. Ryan
	G-AFZE	Heath Parasol	K. C. D. St Cyrien
	G-AFZK	Luscombe 8A Silvaire	M. G. Byrnes
	G-AFZL	Porterfield CP.50	P. G. Lucas & S. H. Sharpe/ White Waltham
	G-AFZN	Luscombe 8A Silvaire	A. L. Young/Henstridge
	G-AGAT	Piper J-3F-50 Cub	G. S. Williams
	G-AGBN	G.A.L.42 Cygnet 2 ★	Museum of Flight/E. Fortune
	G-AGEG	D.H.82A Tiger Moth	T. P. A. Norman
	G-AGFT	Avia FL.3	P. A. Smith
	G-AGHY	D.H.82A Tiger Moth	P. Groves
	G-AGIV	Piper J-3C-65 Cub	P. C. & F. M. Gill
	G-AGJG	D.H.89A Dragon Rapide	M. J. & D. J. T. Miller/Duxford
	G-AGLK	Auster 5D	L. Colliver/Shoreham
	G-AGMI	Luscombe 8A Silvaire	Ebork Ltd
	G-AGNJ	D.H.82A Tiger Moth	B. P. Borsberry & ptnrs
	G-AGNV	Avro 685 York 1 (TS798) ★	Aerospace Museum/Cosford
	G-AGOH	J/1 Autocrat	Leicestershire County Council Museums
	G-AGOS	R.S.4 Desford Trainer (VZ728)	Museum of Flight/E. Fortune
	G-AGOY	M.48 Messenger 3 (U-0247)	P. A. Brooks
	G-AGPG	Avro 19 Srs 2 ★	Brenzett Aviation Museum
	G-AGPK	D.H.82A Tiger Moth	P. D. Castle
	G-AGRU	V.498 Viking 1A ★	Brooklands Museum of Aviation/Weybridge
	G-AGSH	D.H.89A Dragon Rapide 6	Venom Jet Promotions Ltd/Bournemouth
	G-AGTM	D.H.89A Dragon Rapide 6	Russavia Ltd
	G-AGTO	J/1 Autocrat	M. J. Barnett & D. J. T. Miller/Duxford
	G-AGTT	J/1 Autocrat	R. Farrer
	G-AGVG	J/1 Autocrat	S. J. Riddington/Leicester
	G-AGVN	J/1 Autocrat	R. J. Hirst
	G-AGVV	Piper J-3C-65 Cub	P. R. Lewis
	G-AGXN	J/1N Alpha	I. R. Walters/Cranwell
	G-AGXT	J/1N Alpha ★	Nene Valley Aircraft Museum
	G-AGXU	J/1N Alpha	R. J. Guess/Sibson
	G-AGXV	J/1 Autocrat	B. S. Dowsett
	G-AGYD	J/1N Alpha	P. D. Hodson
	G-AGYH	J/1N Alpha	W. R. V. Marklew

16

Reg.	Type	Owner or Operator	Notes
G-AGYK	J/1 Autocrat	Autocrat Syndicate	
G-AGYL	J/1 Autocrat ★	Military Vehicle Conservation Group	
G-AGYT	J/1N Alpha	P. J. Barrett	
G-AGYU	DH.82A Tiger Moth (DE208)	A. Grimshaw	
G-AGYY	Ryan ST.3KR	G-AGYY Group/Sandown	
G-AGZZ	D.H.82A Tiger Moth	G. P. P. Shea-Simonds/Netheravon	
G-AHAL	J/1N Alpha	Wickenby Flying Club Ltd	
G-AHAM	J/1 Autocrat	P. J. Stock/Goodwood	
G-AHAN	D.H.82A Tiger Moth	A. J. Clarry & S. F. Bancroft/Redhill	
G-AHAP	J/1 Autocrat	V. H. Bellamy	
G-AHAU	J/1 Autocrat	B. W. Webb	
G-AHAV	J/1 Autocrat	C. J. Freeman/Headcorn	
G-AHBL	D.H.87B Hornet Moth	Dr Ursula H. Hamilton	
G-AHBM	D.H.87B Hornet Moth	P. A. & E. P. Gliddon	
G-AHCK	J/1N Alpha	Skegness Air Taxi Service Ltd	
G-AHCL	J/1N Alpha	Electronic Precision Ltd (G-OJVC)	
G-AHCR	Gould-Taylorcraft Plus D Special	D. E. H. Balmford & D. R. Shepherd/Dunkeswell	
G-AHEC	Luscombe 8A Silvaire	Luscombe EC Group	
G-AHED	D.H.89A Dragon Rapide (RL962) ★	RAF Museum Storage & Restoration Centre/Cardington	
G-AHGD	D.H.89A Dragon Rapide	R. Jones	
G-AHGW	Taylorcraft Plus D (LB375)	C. V. Butler/Coventry	
G-AHGZ	Taylorcraft Plus D	M. Pocock	
G-AHHH	J/1 Autocrat	H. A. Jones/Norwich	
G-AHHP	J/1N Alpha	D. J. Hutcheson (G-SIME)	
G-AHHT	J/1N Alpha	A. C. Barber & N. J. Hudson	
G-AHHU	J/1N Alpha ★	L. A. Groves & I. R. F. Hammond	
G-AHIP	Piper J-3C-65 Cub	R. T. & D. H. Tanner	
G-AHIZ	D.H.82A Tiger Moth	C.F.G. Flying Ltd/Cambridge	
G-AHKX	Avro 19 Srs 2	British Aerospace PLC/Woodford	
G-AHKY	Miles M.18 Series 2 ★	Museum of Flight/E. Fortune	
G-AHLI	Auster 3	G. A. Leathers	
G-AHLK	Auster 3	E. T. Brackenbury/Leicester	
G-AHLT	D.H.82A Tiger Moth	R. C. F. Bailey	
G-AHMJ	Cierva C.30A (K4235) ★	Shuttleworth Collection/O. Warden	
G-AHMN	D.H.82A Tiger Moth (N6985)	Museum of Army Flying/Middle Wallop	
G-AHNH	Bucker Bu181 Bestmann	R. A. Anderson	
G-AHNR	Taylorcraft BC-12D	M. L. Balding & J. M. Oakins/Biggin Hill	
G-AHOO	D.H.82A Tiger Moth	G. W. Bisshopp	
G-AHRI	D.H.104 Dove 1 ★	Newark Aviation Museum	
G-AHRO	Cessna 140	R. H. Screen/Kidlington	
G-AHSA	Avro 621 Tutor (K3215)	Shuttleworth Collection/O. Warden	
G-AHSD	Taylorcraft Plus D	A. Tucker	
G-AHSO	J/1N Alpha	W. P. Miller	
G-AHSP	J/1 Autocrat	N. J. Hudson & A. C. Barber	
G-AHSS	J/1N Alpha	Felthorpe Auster Group	
G-AHST	J/1N Alpha	C. H. Smith	
G-AHTE	P.44 Proctor V	D. K. Tregilgas	
G-AHTW	A.S.40 Oxford (V3388) ★	Skyfame Collection/Duxford	
G-AHUF	D.H.82A Tiger Moth	D. S. & I. M. Morgan	
G-AHUG	Taylorcraft Plus D	D. Nieman	
G-AHUI	M.38 Messenger 2A ★	Berkshire Aviation Group	
G-AHUJ	M.14A Hawk Trainer 3 (R1914)	—	
G-AHUN	Globe GC-1B Swift	R. J. Hamlett	
G-AHUV	D.H.82A Tiger Moth	W. G. Gordon	
G-AHVU	D.H.82A Tiger Moth (T6313)	Foley Farm Flying Group	
G-AHVV	D.H.82A Tiger Moth	R. Jones	
G-AHWJ	Taylorcraft Plus D (LB294)	Museum of Army Flying/Middle Wallop	
G-AHXE	Taylorcraft Plus D (LB312)	J. Pothecary/Shoreham	
G-AIBE	Fulmar II (N1854) ★	F.A.A. Museum/Yeovilton	
G-AIBH	J/1N Alpha	M. J. Bonnick	
G-AIBM	J/1 Autocrat	D. G. Greatrex	
G-AIBR	J/1 Autocrat	A. A. Marshall	
G-AIBW	J/1N Alpha	W. E. Bateson/Blackpool	
G-AIBX	J/1 Autocrat	Wasp Flying Group	
G-AIBY	J/1 Autocrat	D. Morris/Sherburn	
G-AICX	Luscombe 8A Silvaire	R. V. Smith/Henstridge	
G-AIDL	D.H.89A Dragon Rapide 6	Snowdon Mountain Aviation Ltd	
G-AIDS	D.H.82A Tiger Moth	K. D. Pogmore & T. Dann	
G-AIEK	M.38 Messenger 2A (RG333)	J. Buckingham	

Notes	Reg.	Type	Owner or Operator
	G-AIFZ	J/1N Alpha	C. P. Humphries
	G-AIGD	J/1 Autocrat	R. B. Webber & P. K. Pike
	G-AIGF	J/1N Alpha	A. R. C. Mathie
	G-AIGT	J/1N Alpha	P. R. & J. S. Johnson
	G-AIGU	J/1N Alpha	N. K. Geddes
	G-AIIH	Piper J-3C-65 Cub	J. A. de Salis
	G-AIJI	J/1N Alpha ★	C. J. Baker
	G-AIJM	Auster J/4	N. Huxtable
	G-AIJR	Auster J/4	Shakespeare Flying Group
	G-AIJS	Auster J/4 ★	stored
	G-AIJT	Auster J/4 srs 100	Aberdeen Auster Flying Group
	G-AIJZ	J/1 Autocrat	stored
	G-AIKE	Auster 5	C. J. Baker
	G-AIPR	Auster J/4	MPM Flying Group/Booker
	G-AIPV	J/1 Autocrat	W. P. Miller
	G-AIPW	J/1 Autocrat	B. Hillman
	G-AIRC	J/1 Autocrat	R. C. Tebbett
	G-AIRI	D.H.82A Tiger Moth	E. R. Goodwin (stored)
	G-AIRK	D.H.82A Tiger Moth	R. C. Teverson & ptnrs
	G-AISA	Tipsy B Srs 1	J. W. Thomson & R. P. Aston
	G-AISC	Tipsy B Srs 1	Wagtail Flying Group
	G-AISS	Piper J-3C-65 Cub	K. W. Wood & F. Watson
	G-AIST	V.S.300 Spitfire IA (AR213)	Proteus Holdings Ltd/Goodwood
	G-AISX	Piper J-3C-65 Cub	V. Luck
	G-AITB	A.S.10 Oxford (MP425) ★	Newark Air Museum
	G-AIUA	M.14A Hawk Trainer 3	P. A. Brook
	G-AIUL	D.H.89A Dragon Rapide 6	I. Jones
	G-AIXA	Taylorcraft Plus D	A. A. & M. J. Copse
	G-AIXD	D.H.82A Tiger Moth	Sark International Airways/Guernsey
	G-AIXJ	D.H.82A Tiger Moth	D. Green
	G-AIXN	Benes-Mraz M.1c Sokol	P. Knott
	G-AIYG	SNCAN Stampe SV-4B	J. F. Hopkins/Old Sarum
	G-AIYR	D.H.89A Dragon Rapide	Clacton Aero Club (1988) Ltd/Duxford
	G-AIYS	D.H.85 Leopard Moth	Wessex Aviation & Transport Ltd
	G-AIZE	F.24W Argus 2 ★	RAF Museum/Henlow
	G-AIZF	D.H.82A Tiger Moth ★	stored
	G-AIZG	V.S. Walrus 1 (L2301) ★	F.A.A. Museum/Yeovilton
	G-AIZU	J/1 Autocrat	C. J. & J. G. B. Morley
	G-AJAC	J/1N Alpha	N. J. Mortimore & H. A. Bridgman
	G-AJAD	Piper J-3C-65 Cub	R. A. D. Wilson & D. J. Morris
	G-AJAE	J/1N Alpha	M. G. Stops
	G-AJAJ	J/1N Alpha	R. B. Lawrence
	G-AJAM	J/2 Arrow	D. A. Porter
	G-AJAO	Piper J-3C-65 Cub	G. M. Perfect & M. Stow
	G-AJAP	Luscombe 8A Silvaire	R. J. Thomas
	G-AJAS	J/1N Alpha	C. J. Baker
	G-AJCP	D.31 Turbulent	B. R. Pearson
	G-AJDW	J/1 Autocrat	D. R. Hunt
	G-AJDY	J/1 Autocrat	Truck Panels Ltd
	G-AJEB	J/1N Alpha ★	Aeroplane Collection Ltd/Warmingham
	G-AJEE	J/1 Autocrat	A. R. C. De Albanoz/Bournemouth
	G-AJEH	J/1N Alpha	J. T. Powell-Tuck
	G-AJEI	J/1N Alpha	W. P. Miller
	G-AJEM	J/1 Autocrat	J. C. Greenslade
	G-AJES	Piper J-3C-65 Cub (330485)	D. Silsbury
	G-AJGJ	Auster 5 (RT486)	S. C. Challis
	G-AJHJ	Auster 5	stored
	G-AJHS	D.H.82A Tiger Moth	S. R. N. Higgins/Holland
	G-AJHU	D.H.82A Tiger Moth	M. E. R. Coghlan
	G-AJIH	J/1 Autocrat	T. Boyd & A. H. Diver
	G-AJIS	J/1N Alpha	K. J. Slattery
	G-AJIT	J/1 Kingsland Autocrat	A. J. Kay
	G-AJIU	J/1 Autocrat	W. Greenhalgh & Son Ltd/Doncaster
	G-AJIW	J/1N Alpha	Millair Services Ltd
	G-AJJP	Jet Gyrodyne (XJ389) ★	Aerospace Museum/Cosford
	G-AJJS	Cessna 120	Robhurst Flying Group
	G-AJJT	Cessna 120	J. S. Robson
	G-AJJU	Luscombe 8E Silvaire	L. C. Moon
	G-AJKB	Luscombe 8E Silvaire	A. F. Hall & P. S. Hatwell/Ipswich
	G-AJOA	D.H.82A Tiger Moth (T5424)	F. P. Le Coyte
	G-AJOC	M.38 Messenger 2A ★	Ulster Folk & Transport Museum
	G-AJOE	M.38 Messenger 2A	Cotswold Aircraft Restoration Group

Reg.	Type	Owner or Operator	Notes
G-AJON	Aeronca 7AC Champion	A. Biggs & J. L. Broad/Booker	
G-AJOV†	Sikorsky S-51 ★	Aerospace Museum/Cosford	
G-AJOZ	F.24W Argus 2 ★	Lincolnshire Aviation Museum	
G-AJPI	F.24R-41a Argus 3 (314887)	M. R. Keen/Liverpool	
G-AJPZ	J/1 Autocrat ★	Wessex Aviation Soc	
G-AJRB	J/1 Autocrat	S. C. Luck/Sywell	
G-AJRC	J/1 Autocrat	S. Maycock	
G-AJRE	J/1 Autocrat (Lycoming)	T. A. Hodges	
G-AJRH	J/1N Alpha	Museum of Science & Industry/Coalville	
G-AJRS	M.14A Hawk Trainer 3 (P6382)	Shuttleworth Collection/O. Warden	
G-AJTW	D.H.82A Tiger Moth (N6965)	J. A. Barker	
G-AJUD	J/1 Autocrat	C. L. Sawyer	
G-AJUE	J/1 Autocrat	P. H. B. Cole	
G-AJUL	J/1N Alpha	M. J. Crees	
G-AJVE	D.H.82A Tiger Moth	R. W. J. Foster	
G-AJWB	M.38 Messenger 2A	P. G. Lee	
G-AJXC	Auster 5	J. E. Graves	
G-AJXV	Auster 4 (NJ695)	B. A. Farries/Leicester	
G-AJXY	Auster 4	P. D. Lowdon	
G-AJYB	J/1N Alpha	P. J. Shotbolt	
G-AKAA	Piper J-3C-65 Cub	G. J. C. Ball	
G-AKAT	M.14A Magister (T9738)	A. J. E. Smith	
G-AKAZ	Piper J-3C-65 Cub (HL-6⅞)	AKAZ Group	
G-AKBM	M.38 Messenger 2A ★	Bristol Plane Preservation Unit	
G-AKBO	M.38 Messenger 2A	B. du Cros	
G-AKDN	D.H.C. 1A Chipmunk 10	D. S. Backhouse	
G-AKEL	M.65 Gemini 1A ★	Ulster Folk & Transport Museum	
G-AKER	M.65 Gemini 1A ★	Berkshire Aviation Group	
G-AKEZ	M.38 Messenger 2A (RG333)	P. G. Lee	
G-AKGD	M.65 Gemini 1A ★	Berkshire Aviation Group	
G-AKGE	M.65 Gemini 3C ★	Ulster Folk & Transport Museum	
G-AKHP	M.65 Gemini 1A	P. G. Lee	
G-AKHZ	M.65 Gemini 7 ★	Berkshire Aviation Group	
G-AKIB	Piper J-3C-90 Cub (480015)	M. C. Bennett	
G-AKIF	D.H.89A Dragon Rapide	Airborne Taxi Services Ltd/Booker	
G-AKIN	M.38 Messenger 2A	R. Spiller & Sons/Sywell	
G-AKIU	P.44 Proctor V	J. N. Sharman	
G-AKKB	M.65 Gemini 1A	J. Buckingham	
G-AKKH	M.65 Gemini 1A	M. C. Russell	
G-AKKR	M.14A Magister (T9707) ★	Greater Manchester Museum of Science & Technology	
G-AKKY	M.14A Hawk Trainer 3 (L6906) (BAPC44) ★	Berkshire Aviation Group/Woodley	
G-AKLW	SA.6 Sealand 1 ★	Ulster Folk & Transport Museum	
G-AKOE	D.H.89A Dragon Rapide 4	J. E. Pierce/Chirk	
G-AKOT	Auster 5 ★	C. J. Baker	
G-AKOW	Auster 5 (TJ569) ★	Museum of Army Flying/Middle Wallop	
G-AKPF	M.14A Hawk Trainer 3 (V1075)	P. A. Brook/Shoreham	
G-AKPI	Auster 5 (NJ703)	B. H. Hargrave/Doncaster	
G-AKRA	Piper J-3C-65 Cub	W. R. Savin	
G-AKSY	Auster 5	Aerofab Flying Group	
G-AKSZ	Auster 5	A. R. C. Mathie	
G-AKTH	Piper J-3C-65 Cub	A. L. Wickens	
G-AKTI	Luscombe 8A Silvaire	N. C. W. N. Lester	
G-AKTK	Aeronca 11AC Chief	R. W. Marshall & ptnrs	
G-AKTM	Luscombe 8F Silvaire	B. Bayley	
G-AKTN	Luscombe 8A Silvaire ·	R. G. Morris	
G-AKTO	Aeronca 7AC Champion	D. C. Murray	
G-AKTP	PA-17 Vagabond	L. A. Maynard	
G-AKTR	Aeronca 7AC Champion	C. & G. Fielder	
G-AKTS	Cessna 120	J. Greenaway & J. J. Boon/Popham	
G-AKTT	Luscombe 8A Silvaire	S. J. Charters	
G-AKUE	D.H.82A Tiger Moth	D. F. Hodgkinson	
G-AKUF	Luscombe 8A Silvaire	A. G. Palmer	
G-AKUG	Luscombe 8A Silvaire	P. & L. A. Groves	
G-AKUH	Luscombe 8E Silvaire	I. M. Bower	
G-AKUI	Luscombe 8E Silvaire	J. A. Pothecary	
G-AKUJ	Luscombe 8E Silvaire	P. R. Edwards	
G-AKUK	Luscombe 8A Silvaire	Leckhampstead Flying Group	
G-AKUL	Luscombe 8A Silvaire	E. A. Taylor	
G-AKUM	Luscombe 8F Silvaire	R. J. Willies	
G-AKUN	Piper J-3F-65 Cub	W. A. Savin	

19

Notes	Reg.	Type	Owner or Operator
	G-AKUO	Aeronca 11AC Chief	KUO Flying Group/White Waltham
	G-AKUP	Luscombe 8E Silvaire	R. J. Williams
	G-AKUR	Cessna 140	P. Power & L. P. Z. Yelland
	G-AKUW	C.H.3 Super Ace	D. R. Bean
	G-AKVF	C.H.3 Super Ace	P. V. B. Longthorp/Bodmin
	G-AKVM	Cessna 120	N. Wise & S. Walker
	G-AKVN	Aeronca 11AC Chief	S. R. Napthen & J. Moore
	G-AKVO	Taylorcraft BC-12D	R. J. Whybrow & S. R. Roberts
	G-AKVP	Luscombe 8A Silvaire	R. M. Shipp
	G-AKVZ	M.38 Messenger 4B	Shipping & Airlines Ltd/Biggin Hill
	G-AKWS	Auster 5-160	J. E. Homewood
	G-AKWT	Auster 5 ★	Loughborough & Leicester Aircraft Preservation Soc
	G-AKXP	Auster 5	F. E. Telling & G. R. Attwell
	G-AKXS	D.H.82A Tiger Moth	P. A. Colman
	G-AKZN	P.34A Proctor 3 (Z7197) ★	RAF Museum/St Athan
	G-ALAH	M.38 Messenger 4A (RH377) ★	RAF Museum/Henlow
	G-ALAX	D.H.89A Dragon Rapide ★	Durney Aeronautical Collection/Andover
	G-ALBJ	Auster 5	P. N. Elkington
	G-ALBK	Auster 5	S. J. Wright & Co (Farmers) Ltd
	G-ALBN	Bristol 173 (XF785) ★	RAF Museum/Henlow
	G-ALCK	P.34A Proctor 3 (LZ766) ★	Skyfame Collection/Duxford
	G-ALCS	M.65 Gemini 3C ★	*Stored*
	G-ALCU	D.H.104 Dove 2 ★	Midland Air Museum/Coventry
	G-ALDG	HP.81 Hermes 4 ★	Duxford Aviation Soc (Fuselage only)
	G-ALEH	PA-17 Vagabond	A. D. Pearce/Redhill
	G-ALFA	Auster 5	H&B Auster Group
	G-ALFM	D.H.104 Devon C.2	C. Charalambous
	G-ALFT	D.H.104 Dove 6 ★	Snowdon Mountain Aviation Museum
	G-ALFU	D.H.104 Dove 6 ★	Duxford Aviation Soc
	G-ALGA	PA-15 Vagabond	M. J. Markey/Biggin Hill
	G-ALIJ	PA-17 Vagabond	Popham Flying Group/Popham
	G-ALIW	D.H.82A Tiger Moth	D. I. M. Geddes & F. Curry/Booker
	G-ALJF	P.34A Proctor 3	J. F. Moore/Biggin Hill
	G-ALJL	D.H.82A Tiger Moth	C. G. Clarke
	G-ALLF	Slingsby T.31A Kirby Prefect	N. J. Churcher
	G-ALNA	D.H.82A Tiger Moth	R. F. Harvey
	G-ALND	D.H.82A Tiger Moth (N9191)	J. T. Powell-Tuck
	G-ALNV	Auster 5 ★	*stored*
	G-ALOD	Cessna 140	J. R. Stainer
	G-ALRH	EoN Type 8 Baby (AST)	P. D. Moran/Chipping
	G-ALRI	D.H.82A Tiger Moth (T5672)	Wessex Aviation & Transport Ltd
	G-ALSP	Bristol 171 (WV783) Sycamore ★	RN Fleetlands Museum
	G-ALSS	Bristol 171 (WA576) Sycamore ★	E. Fortune
	G-ALST	Bristol 171 (WA577) Sycamore ★	N.E. Aircraft Museum/Usworth
	G-ALSW	Bristol 171 (WT933) Sycamore ★	Newark Air Museum
	G-ALSX	Bristol 171 (G-48-1) Sycamore ★	International Helicopter Museum/ Weston-s-Mare
	G-ALTO	Cessna 140	J. P. Bell
	G-ALTW	D.H.82A Tiger Moth ★	A. Mangham
	G-ALUC	D.H.82A Tiger Moth	D. R. & M. Wood
	G-ALVP	D.H.82A Tiger Moth ★	V. & R. Wheele (*stored*)
	G-ALWB	D.H.C.1 Chipmunk 22A	M. L. & J. M. Soper/Perth
	G-ALWF	V.701 Viscount ★	Viscount Preservation Trust *RMA Sir John Franklin*/Duxford
	G-ALWS	D.H.82A Tiger Moth	C. J. Weaver
	G-ALWW	D.H.82A Tiger Moth	D. E. Findon
	G-ALXT	D.H.89A Dragon Rapide ★	Science Museum/Wroughton
	G-ALXZ	Auster 5-150	B. J. W. Thomas & R. A. E. Witheridge
	G-ALYB	Auster 5 (RT520)★	S. Yorks Aircraft Preservation Soc
	G-ALYG	Auster 5D	A. L. Young/Henstridge
	G-ALYW	D.H.106 Comet 1 ★	RAF Exhibition Flight (*fuselage converted to Nimrod*)
	G-ALZE	BN-1F ★	M. R. Short/Southampton Hall of Aviation
	G-ALZO	A.S.57 Ambassador★	Duxford Aviation Soc
	G-AMAW	Luton LA-4 Minor	R. H. Coates
	G-AMBB	D.H.82A Tiger Moth	J. Eagles
	G-AMCA	Dakota 3	Air Atlantique Ltd/Coventry
	G-AMCK	D.H.82A Tiger Moth	D. L. Frankel
	G-AMCM	D.H.82A Tiger Moth	G. C. Masterton
	G-AMDA	Avro 652A Anson 1 (N4877)★	Skyfame Collection/Duxford

Reg.	Type	Owner or Operator	Notes
G-AMEN	PA-18 Super Cub 95	A. Lovejoy & W. Cook	
G-AMHF	D.H.82A Tiger Moth	Wavendon Social Housing Ltd	
G-AMHJ	Dakota 6	Air Atlantique Ltd/Coventry	
G-AMIU	D.H.82A Tiger Moth	R. & Mrs J. L. Jones	
G-AMKU	J/1B Aiglet	P. G. Lipman	
G-AMLZ	P.50 Prince 6E ★	J. F. Coggins/Coventry	
G-AMMS	J/5F Aiglet Trainer	A. J. Large	
G-AMNN	D.H.82A Tiger Moth	M. Thrower/Shoreham	
G-AMOG	V.701 Viscount ★	Aerospace Museum/Cosfor	
G-AMPG	PA-12 Super Cruiser	R. Simpson	
G-AMPI	SNCAN Stampe SV-4C	J. Hewett	
G-AMPO	Dakota 4	Air Atlantique Ltd/Coventry	
G-AMPY	Dakota 4	Air Atlantique Ltd/Coventry	
G-AMPZ	Dakota 4	Air Atlantique Ltd/Coventry	
G-AMRA	Dakota 6	Air Atlantique Ltd/Coventry	
G-AMRF	J/5F Aiglet Trainer	A. I. Topps/E. Midlands	
G-AMRK	G.37 Gladiator I (N2308)	Shuttleworth Collection/O. Warden	
G-AMSG	SIPA 903	S. W. Markham	
G-AMSV	Dakota 4	Air Atlantique Ltd/Coventry	
G-AMTA	J/5F Aiglet Trainer	N. H. T. Cottrell	
G-AMTD	J/5F Aiglet Trainer	Leicestershire Aero Club Ltd	
G-AMTK	D.H.82A Tiger Moth	S. W. McKay & M. E. Vaisey	
G-AMTM	J/1 Autocrat	R. Stobo & D. Clewley (G-AJUJ)	
G-AMTV	D.H.82A Tiger Moth	K. J. Slattery	
G-AMUF	D.H.C.1 Chipmunk 21	Redhill Tailwheel Flying Club Ltd	
G-AMUI	J/5F Aiglet Trainer	D. P. Copse	
G-AMVD	Auster 5	R. F. Tolhurst	
G-AMVP	Tipsy Junior	A. R. Wershat	
G-AMVS	D.H.82A Tiger Moth	J. T. Powell-Tuck	
G-AMXT	D.H.104 Sea Devon C.20	W. Gentle & P. C. Gill	
G-AMYA	Zlin Z.381	D. M. Fenton	
G-AMYD	J/5L Aiglet Trainer	G. H. Maskell	
G-AMYJ	Dakota 6	Air Atlantique Ltd/Coventry	
G-AMYL	PA-17 Vagabond	P. J. Penn-Sayers/Shoreham	
G-AMZI	J/5F Aiglet Trainer	J. F. Moore/Biggin Hill	
G-AMZT	J/5F Aiglet Trainer	D. Hyde & J. W. Saull/Cranfield	
G-AMZU	J/5F Aiglet Trainer	J. A. Longworth & ptnrs	
G-ANAF	Dakota 3	Air Atlantique Ltd/Coventry	
G-ANAP	D.H.104 Dove 6 ★	Brunel Technical College/Lulsgate	
G-ANCF	B.175 Britannia 308 ★	R. Hargreaves	
G-ANCS	D.H.82A Tiger Moth (R4907)	P. G. Wright	
G-ANCX	D.H.82A Tiger Moth	D. R. Wood/Biggin Hill	
G-ANDE	D.H.82A Tiger Moth	The Vintage Aeroplane Co Ltd	
G-ANDM	D.H.82A Tiger Moth	J. G. Green	
G-ANDP	D.H.82A Tiger Moth	A. H. Diver	
G-ANDX	D.H.104 Devon C.2 (XG496) ★	Solway Aviation Soc/Carlisle	
G-ANEC	D.H.82A Tiger Moth ★	(stored)	
G-ANEF	D.H.82A Tiger Moth (T5493)	RAF College Flying Club Co Ltd/Cranwell	
G-ANEH	D.H.82A Tiger Moth	P. L. Gaze	
G-ANEL	D.H.82A Tiger Moth	Chauffair Ltd	
G-ANEM	D.H.82A Tiger Moth	P. J. Benest (stored)	
G-ANEN	D.H.82A Tiger Moth	M. D. Souch	
G-ANEW	D.H.82A Tiger Moth	A. L. Young	
G-ANEZ	D.H.82A Tiger Moth	C. D. J. Bland & T. S. Warren/Sandown	
G-ANFC	D.H.82A Tiger Moth	H. J. Jauncey/Rochester	
G-ANFH	Westland S-55 ★	International Helicopter Museum/ Weston-s-Mare	
G-ANFI	D.H.82A Tiger Moth (DE623)	G. P. Graham	
G-ANFL	D.H.82A Tiger Moth	R. P. Whitby & ptnrs	
G-ANFM	D.H.82A Tiger Moth	S. A. Brook & ptnrs/Booker	
G-ANFP	D.H.82A Tiger Moth ★	Mosquito Aircraft Museum	
G-ANFU	Auster 5 (NJ719)★	N.E. Aircraft Museum	
G-ANFV	D.H.82A Tiger Moth (DF155)	R. A. L. Falconer	
G-ANFW	D.H.82A Tiger Moth	G. M. Fraser/Denham	
G-ANGK	Cessna 140A	D. W. Munday	
G-ANHK	D.H.82A Tiger Moth	J. D. Iliffe	
G-ANHR	Auster 5	C. G. Winch	
G-ANHS	Auster 4	Tango Uniform Group	
G-ANHU	Auster 4	D. J. Baker (stored)	
G-ANHX	Auster 5D	D. J. Baker	
G-ANHZ	Auster 5 (TW384)	D. W. Pennell	
G-ANIE	Auster 5 (TW467)	S. J. Partridge	

Notes	Reg.	Type	Owner or Operator
	G-ANIJ	Auster 5D (TJ672)	M. Pocock & R. Eastmann
	G-ANIS	Auster 5	J. Clarke-Cockburn
	G-ANJA	D.H.82A Tiger Moth (N9389)	J. J. Young
	G-ANJD	D.H.82A Tiger Moth	H. J. Jauncey (stored)/Rochester
	G-ANJK	D.H.82A Tiger Moth	A. D. Williams
	G-ANJV	W.S.55 Whirlwind 3 (VR-BET)★	International Helicopter Museum/ Weston-s-Mare
	G-ANKK	D.H.82A Tiger Moth (T5854)	Halfpenny Green Tiger Group
	G-ANKL	D.H.82A Tiger Moth	M. D. Souch
	G-ANKT	D.H.82A Tiger Moth (T6818)	Shuttleworth Collection/O. Warden
	G-ANKZ	D.H.82A Tiger Moth (N6466)	R. Stephens
	G-ANLD	D.H.82A Tiger Moth	K. Peters
	G-ANLH	D.H.82A Tiger Moth	Wessex Aviation & Transport Ltd
	G-ANLS	D.H.82A Tiger Moth	P. A. Gliddon
	G-ANLU	Auster 5	S. C. Challis & G. Guinn
	G-ANLW	W.B.1. Widgeon (MD497) ★	Wilkie Museum Collection/Blackpool
	G-ANLX	D.H.82A Tiger Moth	B. J. Borsberry & ptnrs
	G-ANMO	D.H.82A Tiger Moth	E. Lay
	G-ANMV	D.H.82A Tiger Moth (T7404)	J. W. Davy/Cardiff
	G-ANMY	D.H.82A Tiger Moth	D. J. Elliott
	G-ANNB	D.H.82A Tiger Moth	Cormack (Aircraft Services) Ltd
	G-ANNG	D.H.82A Tiger Moth	P. F. Walter
	G-ANNI	D.H.82A Tiger Moth	A. R. Brett
	G-ANNK	D.H.82A Tiger Moth	P. J. Wilcox/Cranfield
	G-ANNN	D.H.82A Tiger Moth	T. Pate
	G-ANOA	Hiller UH-12A ★	Redhill Technical College
	G-ANOD	D.H.82A Tiger Moth	P. G. Watson
	G-ANOH	D.H.82A Tiger Moth	N. Parkhouse/White Waltham
	G-ANOK	SAAB S.91C Safir ★	A. F. Galt & Co (stored)
	G-ANOM	D.H.82A Tiger Moth	P. R. & A. L. Williams
	G-ANON	D.H.82A Tiger Moth (T7909)	A. C. Mercer/Sherburn
	G-ANOO	D.H.82A Tiger Moth	R. K. Packman
	G-ANOR	D.H.82A Tiger Moth (T6991)	C. L. Keith-Lucas & Aero Vintage Ltd
	G-ANOV	D.H.104 Dove 6 ★	Museum of Flight/E. Fortune
	G-ANPE	D.H.82A Tiger Moth	I. E. S. Huddleston (G-IESH)
	G-ANPK	D.H.82A Tiger Moth	The D. & P. Group
	G-ANPP	P.34A Proctor 3	C. P. A. & J. Jeffrey
	G-ANRF	D.H.82A Tiger Moth	C. D. Cyster
	G-ANRM	D.H.82A Tiger Moth	Clacton Aero Club (1988) Ltd & A. B. Cutting
	G-ANRN	D.H.82A Tiger Moth	J. J. V. Elwes
	G-ANRP	Auster 5 (TW439)	A. Brier
	G-ANRS	V.372 Viscount ★	Wales Aircraft Museum/Cardiff
	G-ANRX	D.H.82A Tiger Moth ★	Mosquito Aircraft Museum
	G-ANSM	D.H.82A Tiger Moth	J. L. Bond
	G-ANTE	D.H.82A Tiger Moth	T. I. Sutton & B. J. Champion/Chester
	G-ANTK	Avro 685 York ★	Duxford Aviation Soc
	G-ANTS	D.H.82A Tiger Moth (N6532)	J. G. Green
	G-ANUO	D.H.114 Heron 2D	Avtech Ltd/Biggin Hill
	G-ANUW	D.H.104 Dove 6 ★	(stored)/Stansted
	G-ANWB	D.H.C.1 Chipmunk 21	G. Briggs/Blackpool
	G-ANWO	M.14A Hawk Trainer 3 ★	P. A. Brook
	G-ANXB	D.H.114 Heron 1B ★	Newark Air Museum
	G-ANXC	J/5R Alpine	C. J. Repek & ptnrs
	G-ANXR	P.31C Proctor 4 (RM221)	L. H. Oakins/Biggin Hill
	G-ANYP	P.31C Proctor 4 (NP184)	R. A. Anderson
	G-ANZJ	P.31C Proctor 4 (NP303) ★	A. Hillyard
	G-ANZT	Thruxton Jackaroo	D. J. Neville & P. A. Dear
	G-ANZU	D.H.82A Tiger Moth	P. A. Jackson
	G-ANZZ	D.H.82A Tiger Moth	D. L. Frankel
	G-AOAA	D.H.82A Tiger Moth	R. C. P. Brookhouse
	G-AOAR	P.31C Proctor 4 (NP181) ★	Historic Aircraft Preservation Soc
	G-AOBG	Somers-Kendall SK.1 ★	stored
	G-AOBH	D.H.82A Tiger Moth	P. Nutley
	G-AOBJ	D.H.82A Tiger Moth (DE970)	D. H. R. Jenkins
	G-AOBO	D.H.82A Tiger Moth	P. A. Brook
	G-AOBU	P.84 Jet Provost	T. J. Manna
	G-AOBV	J/5P Autocar	P. E. Champney (stored)
	G-AOBX	D.H.82A Tiger Moth	P. G. Watson
	G-AOCP	Auster 5 ★	C. J. Baker (stored)
	G-AOCR	Auster 5D	J. M. Edis
	G-AOCU	Auster 5	S. J. Ball/Leicester

22

Reg.	Type	Owner or Operator	Notes
G-AODA	Westland S-55 Srs 3 ★	International Helicopter Museum/ Weston-s-Mare	
G-AODT	D.H.82A Tiger Moth	A. H. Warminger	
G-AOEH	Aeronca 7AC Champion	R. P. Clark	
G-AOEI	D.H.82A Tiger Moth	C.F.G. Flying Ltd/Cambridge	
G-AOEL	D.H.82A Tiger Moth ★	Museum of Flight/E. Fortune	
G-AOES	D.H.82A Tiger Moth	A. Twemlow & G. A. Cordery	
G-AOET	D.H.82A Tiger Moth	Venom Jet Promotions Ltd/Bournemouth	
G-AOEX	Thruxton Jackaroo	A. T. Christian	
G-AOFE	D.H.C.1 Chipmunk 22A (WB702)	E. J. F. McEntee	
G-AOFM	J/5P Autocar	N. P. Beaumont	
G-AOFS	J/5L Aiglet Trainer	P. N. A. Whitehead	
G-AOGA	M.75 Aries ★	Irish Aviation Museum (stored)	
G-AOGE	P.34A Proctor 3	N. I. Dalziel/Biggin Hill	
G-AOGI	D.H.82A Tiger Moth	W. J. Taylor	
G-AOGR	D.H.82A Tiger Moth (T6099)	M. I. Edwards	
G-AOGV	J/5P Alpine	R. E. Heading	
G-AOHL	V.802 Viscount ★	British World Airlines Ltd (Cabin Trainer)/ Southend	
G-AOHM	V.802 Viscount	British World Airlines Ltd Viscount Sir George Edwards/Southend	
G-AOHY	D.H.82A Tiger Moth	C. R. & S. A. Hardiman/Shobdon	
G-AOHZ	J/5P Autocar	A. D. Hodgkinson	
G-AOIL	D.H.82A Tiger Moth	T. C. Lawless	
G-AOIM	D.H.82A Tiger Moth	C. R. Hardiman/Shobdon	
G-AOIR	Thruxton Jackaroo	L. H. Smith	
G-AOIS	D.H.82A Tiger Moth	V. B. & R. G. Wheele/Shoreham	
G-AOIY	J/5G Autocar	C. N. Towers	
G-AOJC	V.802 Viscount (fuselage only) ★	Wales Aircraft Museum/Cardiff	
G-AOJH	D.H.83C Fox Moth	R. M. Brooks	
G-AOJJ	D.H.82A Tiger Moth (DF128)	E. Lay	
G-AOJK	D.H.82A Tiger Moth	P. A. de Courcy Swoffer	
G-AOJS	D.H.C.1 Chipmunk 22A	R. H. Cooper	
G-AOJT	D.H.106 Comet 1 ★	Mosquito Aircraft Museum	
G-AOKH	P.40 Prentice 1	J. F. Moore/Biggin Hill	
G-AOKL	P.40 Prentice 1 (VS610)	G-AOKL Flying Group	
G-AOKO	P.40 Prentice 1 ★	J. F. Coggins/Coventry	
G-AOKZ	P.40 Prentice 1 (VS623) ★	Midland Air Museum	
G-AOLK	P.40 Prentice 1	Hilton Aviation Ltd/Southend	
G-AOLU	P.40 Prentice 1 (VS356) ★	P. Morris	
G-AORB	Cessna 170B	Eaglescott Parachute Centre	
G-AORG	D.H.114 Heron 2	Duchess of Brittany (Jersey) Ltd	
G-AORW	D.H.C.1 Chipmunk 22A	R. C. McCarthy	
G-AOSF	D.H.C.1 Chipmunk 22	D. Mercer	
G-AOSK	D.H.C.1 Chipmunk 22	A. M. S. Cullen	
G-AOSO	D.H.C.1 Chipmunk 22	Earl of Suffolk & Berkshire & J. Hoerner	
G-AOSU	D.H.C.1 Chipmunk 22 (Lycoming)	RAFGSA/Bicester	
G-AOSY	D.H.C.1 Chipmunk 22 (WB585)	Franbrave Ltd	
G-AOTD	D.H.C.1 Chipmunk 22 (WB588)	Shuttleworth Collection/O. Warden	
G-AOTF	D.H.C.1 Chipmunk 23 (Lycoming)	RAFGSA/Bicester	
G-AOTI	D.H.114 Heron 2D	Avtech Ltd/Biggin Hill	
G-AOTK	D.53 Turbi	The T. K. Flying Group/Hatfield	
G-AOTR	D.H.C.1 Chipmunk 22	Ulster Chipmunk Group/Newtownards	
G-AOTY	D.H.C.1 Chipmunk 22A (WG472)	P. D. Harrison	
G-AOUJ	Fairey Ultra-Light ★	International Helicopter Museum/ Weston-s-Mare	
G-AOUO	D.H.C.1 Chipmunk 22 (Lycoming)	RAFGSA/Bicester	
G-AOUP	D.H.C.1 Chipmunk 22	G-AOUP Flying Group/St Just	
G-AOUR	D.H.82A Tiger Moth ★	Ulster Folk & Transport Museum	
G-AOVF	B.175 Britannia 312F ★	Aerospace Museum/Cosford	
G-AOVT	B.175 Britannia 312F ★	Duxford Aviation Soc	
G-AOVW	Auster 5	B. Marriott/Cranwell	
G-AOXN	D.H.82A Tiger Moth	S. L. G. Darch	
G-AOYN	V.806 Viscount	British World Airlines Ltd/Southend	
G-AOYP	V.806 Viscount	British World Airlines Ltd/Southend	
G-AOYR	V.806 Viscount	British World Airlines Ltd/Southend	
G-AOZH	D.H.82A Tiger Moth (K2572)	V. B. & R. G. Wheele/Shoreham	
G-AOZL	J/5Q Alpine	E. A. Taylor/Southend	
G-AOZP	D.H.C.1 Chipmunk 22	M. Darlington	
G-AOZU	D.H.C.1 Chipmunk 22A	R. H. Cooper	
G-APAA	J/5R Alpine ★	L. A. Groves (stored)	
G-APAF	Auster 5 (TW511)	J. E. Allen (G-CMAL)	

Notes	Reg.	Type	Owner or Operator
	G-APAH	Auster 5	D. J. Wilson & J. R. Kimberley
	G-APAL	D.H.82A Tiger Moth (N6847)	P. S. & R. A. Chapman
	G-APAM	D.H.82A Tiger Moth	R. P. Williams
	G-APAO	D.H.82A Tiger Moth	F. J. Longe
	G-APAP	D.H.82A Tiger Moth	R. A. Slade
	G-APAS	D.H.106 Comet 1XB ★	Aerospace Museum/Cosford
	G-APBE	Auster 5	C. W. Wilkinson/Panshanger
	G-APBI	D.H.82A Tiger Moth (EM903)	R. Devaney & ptnrs/Audley End
	G-APBO	D.53 Turbi	R. C. Hibberd
	G-APBW	Auster 5	N. Huxtable
	G-APCB	J/5Q Alpine	A. A. Beswick & I. A. Freeman
	G-APCC	D.H.82A Tiger Moth	L. J. Rice/Henstridge
	G-APDB	D.H.106 Comet 4 ★	Duxford Aviation Soc
	G-APEG	V.953C Merchantman ★	Airport Fire Service/E. Midlands
	G-APEJ	V.953C Merchantman ★	Hunting Cargo Airlines Ltd *Ajax*
	G-APEM	V.953C Merchantman	Hunting Cargo Airlines Ltd/ DHL *Agamemnon*
	G-APEP	V.953C Merchantman	Hunting Cargo Airlines Ltd *Superb*
	G-APES	V.953C Merchantman	Hunting Cargo Airlines Ltd *Swiftsure*
	G-APET	V.953C Merchantman ★	Hunting Cargo Airlines Ltd (*stored*)
	G-APEY	V.806 Viscount	British World Airlines Ltd/Southend
	G-APFA	D.54 Turbi	A. Eastelow & F. J. Keitch/Dunkeswell
	G-APFG	Boeing 707-436 ★	*Cabin water spray tests*/Cardington
	G-APFJ	Boeing 707-436 ★	Aerospace Museum/Cosford
	G-APFU	D.H.82A Tiger Moth	Mithril Racing Ltd/Goodwood
	G-APGL	D.H.82A Tiger Moth	K. A. Broomfield
	G-APHV	Avro 19 Srs 2 (VM360) ★	Museum of Flight/E. Fortune
	G-APIE	Tipsy Belfair B	P. A. Smith
	G-APIH	D.H.82A Tiger Moth (R5086)	C. R. Kirby
	G-APIK	J/1N Alpha	N. D. Voce
	G-APIM	V.806 Viscount ★	Brooklands Museum of Aviation/ Weybridge
	G-APIT	P.40 Prentice 1 (VR192) ★	WWII Aircraft Preservation Soc/Lasham
	G-APIU	P.40 Prentice 1 ★	J. F. Coggins/Coventry
	G-APIY	P.40 Prentice 1 (VR249) ★	Newark Air Museum
	G-APIZ	D.31 Turbulent	M. J. Whatley/Booker
	G-APJB	P.40 Prentice 1 (VR259) ★	City Airways/Coventry
	G-APJJ	Fairey Ultra-light ★	Midland Aircraft Preservation Soc
	G-APJO	D.H.82A Tiger Moth	D. R. & M. Wood
	G-APJZ	J/1N Alpha	P. G. Lipman
	G-APKH	D.H.85 Leopard Moth	R. G. Grocott (G-ACGS)
	G-APKM	J/1N Alpha	D. E. A. Huggins
	G-APKN	J/1N Alpha	Felthorpe Auster Group
	G-APKY	Hiller UH-12B	D. A. George (*stored*)
	G-APLG	J/5L Aiglet Trainer	G. R. W. Brown
	G-APLK	Miles M.100 Student 2	A. S. Topen (G-MIOO)/Cranfield
	G-APLO	D.H.C.1 Chipmunk 22A (WD379)	Lindholme Aircraft Ltd/Jersey
	G-APLU	D.H.82A Tiger Moth	The Intrepid Flying Group
	G-APMB	D.H.106 Comet 4B ★	Gatwick Handling Ltd (*ground trainer*)
	G-APMH	J/1U Workmaster	R. E. Neal & E. R. Stevens/Leicester
	G-APML	Dakota 6	Air Atlantique Ltd/Coventry
	G-APMM	D.H.82A Tiger Moth (K2568)	R. K. J. Hadlow
	G-APMX	D.H.82A Tiger Moth	G. A. Broughton
	G-APMY	PA-23 Apache 160 ★	NE Wales Institute of Higher Education (*instructional airframe*)/Clwyd
	G-APNJ	Cessna 310 ★	Chelsea College/Shoreham
	G-APNS	Garland-Bianchi Linnet	Paul Penn-Sayers Model Services Ltd
	G-APNT	Currie Wot	J. W. Salter
	G-APNZ	D.31 Turbulent	Tiger Club (1990) Ltd/Headcorn
	G-APOD	Tipsy Belfair	L. F. Potts
	G-APOI	Saro Skeeter Srs 8 ★	Wilkie Museum Collection/Blackpool
	G-APOL	D.31 Turbulent	A. Gregori & S. Tinker
	G-APPA	D.H.C.1 Chipmunk 22	I. R. Young/Glasgow
	G-APPL	P.40 Prentice 1	S. J. Saggers/Biggin Hill
	G-APPM	D.H.C.1 Chipmunk 22	Freston Aviation Ltd
	G-APRF	Auster 5	D. R. Slade
	G-APRJ	Avro 694 Lincoln B.2 ★	Aces High Ltd/North Weald
	G-APRL	AW.650 Argosy 101 ★	Midland Air Museum
	G-APRR	Super Aero 45	R. H. Jowett
	G-APRS	SA. Twin Pioneer 3	Bravo Aviation Ltd (G-BCWF)
	G-APRT	Taylor JT.1 Monoplane	J. P. Leigh
	G-APSA	Douglas DC-6A	Instone Air Line Ltd/Coventry
	G-APSR	J/1U Workmaster	D. & K. Aero Services Ltd/Shobdon

Reg.	Type	Owner or Operator	Notes
G-APTP	PA-22 Tri-Pacer 150	Contest (Ralph & Susan Chesters) Ltd	
G-APTR	J/1N Alpha	C. J. & D. J. Baker	
G-APTU	Auster 5	G-APTU Flying Group	
G-APTW	W.B.1 Widgeon ★	Cornwall Aero Park/Helston	
G-APTY	Beech G.35 Bonanza	G. E. Brennand & ptnrs	
G-APTZ	D.31 Turbulent	F. R. Hutchings	
G-APUD	Bensen B.7M (modified) ★	Greater Manchester Museum of Science & Technology	
G-APUE	L.40 Meta Sokol	S. E. & M. J. Aherne	
G-APUK	J/1 Autocrat	P. L. Morley	
G-APUP	Sopwith Pup (replica) (N5182) ★	RAF Museum/Hendon	
G-APUR	PA-22 Tri-Pacer 160	P. J. Hewitt	
G-APUW	J/5V-160 Autocar	Anglia Auster Syndicate	
G-APUY	D.31 Turbulent	C. Jones & ptnrs/Barton	
G-APUZ	PA-24 Comanche 250	P. A. Brook	
G-APVF	Putzer Elster B (97+04)	B. W. Griffiths & J. Prest	
G-APVG	J/5L Aiglet Trainer	C. M. Daggett/Cranfield	
G-APVN	D.31 Turbulent	R. Sherwin/Shoreham	
G-APVS	Cessna 170B	N. Simpson	
G-APVU	L.40 Meta Sokol	S. E. & M. J. Aherne	
G-APVZ	D.31 Turbulent	M. J. A. Trudgill	
G-APWA	HPR-7 Herald 101 ★	Museum of Berkshire Aviation/Woodley	
G-APWJ	HPR-7 Herald 201 ★	Duxford Aviation Soc	
G-APWN	WS-55 Whirlwind 3 ★	Midland Air Museum	
G-APWY	Piaggio P.166 ★	Science Museum/Wroughton	
G-APWZ	EP.9 Prospector	Prospector Flying Group	
G-APXJ	PA-24 Comanche 250	T. Wildsmith/Netherthorpe	
G-APXM	PA-22 Tri-Pacer 160	R. J. Chinn	
G-APXR	PA-22 Tri-Pacer 160	A. Troughton	
G-APXT	PA-22 Tri-Pacer 150 (modified)	J. W. & I. Daniels	
G-APXU	PA-22 Tri-Pacer 125	Medway Aircraft Preservation Soc Ltd	
G-APXW	EP.9 Prospector ★	Museum of Army Flying/Middle Wallop	
G-APXX	D.H.A.3 Drover 2 (VH-FDT) ★	WWII Aircraft Preservation Soc/Lasham	
G-APXY	Cessna 150	Merlin Flying Club Ltd/Hucknall	
G-APYB	Tipsy T.66 Nipper 3	B. O. Smith	
G-APYD	D.H.106 Comet 4B ★	Science Museum/Wroughton	
G-APYG	D.H.C.1 Chipmunk 22	E. J. I. Musty & P. A. Colman	
G-APYI	PA-22 Tri-Pacer 135	G. K. Hare/Fenland	
G-APYN	PA-22 Tri-Pacer 160	W. D. Stephens	
G-APYT	Champion 7FC Tri-Traveller	B. J. Anning	
G-APYW	PA-22 Tri-Pacer 150	Fiddian Ltd	
G-APZJ	PA-18 Super Cub 150	Southern Sailplanes	
G-APZK	PA-18 Super Cub 95	R. E. Knapton/Bicester	
G-APZL	PA-22 Tri-Pacer 160	R. T. Evans	
G-APZR	Cessna 150 ★	Engine test-bed/Biggin Hill	
G-APZS	Cessna 175A	G. A. Nash/Booker	
G-APZX	PA-22 Tri-Pacer 150	Applied Signs Ltd	
G-ARAI	PA-22 Tri-Pacer 160	T. Richards & G. C. Winters	
G-ARAM	PA-18 Super Cub 150	Clacton Aero Club (1988) Ltd	
G-ARAN	PA-18 Super Cub 150	A. P. Docherty/Redhill	
G-ARAO	PA-18 Super Cub 95 (607327)	R. T. Bennett & N. Tyler	
G-ARAS	Champion 7EC Traveller	Clipgate Flying Group	
G-ARAT	Cessna 180C	Eaglescott Parachute Centre	
G-ARAU	Cessna 150	S. Lynn/Sibson	
G-ARAW	Cessna 182C Skylane	P. Channon	
G-ARAX	PA-22 Tri-Pacer 150	S. J. Kew/Booker	
G-ARAZ	D.H.82A Tiger Moth	S. G. North	
G-ARBE	D.H.104 Dove 8	M. Whale & M. W. A. Lunn	
G-ARBG	Tipsy T.66 Nipper 2	J. Horovitz & J. McLeod	
G-ARBM	J/1B Aiglet	B. V. Nabbs & C. Chaddock	
G-ARBN	PA-23 Apache 160	H. Norden & H. J. Liggins	
G-ARBO	PA-24 Comanche 250	D. M. Harbottle & I. S. Graham/Goodwood	
G-ARBP	Tipsy T.66 Nipper 2	F. W. Kirk	
G-ARBS	PA-22 Tri-Pacer 160 (tailwheel)	S. D. Rowell	
G-ARBV	PA-22 Tri-Pacer 150	Oaksey Pacers	
G-ARBZ	D.31 Turbulent	J. Mickleburgh & C. J. Wilkins	
G-ARCC	PA-22 Tri-Pacer 150	Popham Flying Group/Popham	
G-ARCF	PA-22 Tri-Pacer 150	M. M. Mason	
G-ARCH	Cessna 310D ★	Instructional airframe/Perth	
G-ARCS	Auster D6/180	E. A. Matty/Shobdon	
G-ARCT	PA-18 Super Cub 95	M. J. Kirk	
G-ARCV	Cessna 175A	R. Francis & C. Campbell	

Notes	Reg.	Type	Owner or Operator
	G-ARCW	PA-23 Apache 160	D. R. C. Reeves
	G-ARCX	AW Meteor 14 ★	Museum of Flight/E. Fortune
	G-ARDB	PA-24 Comanche 250	R. A. Sareen/Booker
	G-ARDD	CP.301C1 Emeraude	R. M. Shipp
	G-ARDE	D.H.104 Dove 6	R. J. H. Small/North Weald
	G-ARDG	EP.9 Prospector ★	Museum of Army Flying/Middle Wallop
	G-ARDJ	Auster D.6/180	RN Aviation (Leicester Airport) Ltd
	G-ARDO	Jodel D.112	W. R. Prescott
	G-ARDP	PA-22 Tri-Pacer 150	G. M. Jones
	G-ARDS	PA-22 Caribbean 150	A. C. Donaldson & C. I. Lavery
	G-ARDT	PA-22 Tri-Pacer 160	M. Henderson
	G-ARDV	PA-22 Tri-Pacer 160	B. R. Griffiths
	G-ARDY	Tipsy T.66 Nipper 2	P. R. Teager
	G-ARDZ	Jodel D.140A	M. J. Wright
	G-AREA	D.H.104 Dove 8 ★	Mosquito Aircraft Museum
	G-AREB	Cessna 175B Skylark	R. J. Postlethwaite & ptnrs/Wellesbourne
	G-AREF	PA-23 Aztec 250 ★	Southall College of Technology
	G-AREH	D.H.82A Tiger Moth	T. Pate
	G-AREI	Auster 3 (MT438)	J. A. Vetch
	G-AREL	PA-22 Caribbean 150	H. H. Cousins/Fenland
	G-AREO	PA-18 Super Cub 150	DRA (Farnborough) Gliding Club Ltd
	G-ARET	PA-22 Tri-Pacer 160	D. T. Daniels
	G-AREV	PA-22 Tri-Pacer 160	Spatrek Ltd/Barton
	G-AREX	Aeronca 15AC Sedan	R. J. Middleton-Turnbull & P. Lowndes
	G-AREZ	D.31 Turbulent	J. St. Clair-Quentin/Shobdon
	G-ARFB	PA-22 Caribbean 150	C. T. Woodward & ptnrs
	G-ARFD	PA-22 Tri-Pacer 160	J. K. Cook
	G-ARFG	Cessna 175A Skylark	R. J. Fray/Sibson
	G-ARFH	PA-24 Comanche 250	L. M. Walton
	G-ARFI	Cessna 150A	J. H. Fisher
	G-ARFL	Cessna 175B Skylark	D. J. Mason
	G-ARFN	Cessna 150A ★	Instructional airframe/Perth
	G-ARFO	Cessna 150A	Moray Flying Club Ltd
	G-ARFT	Jodel DR. 1050	R. Shaw
	G-ARFV	Tipsy T.66 Nipper 2	C. G. Stone/Biggin Hill
	G-ARGB	Auster 6A ★	C. Baker (stored)
	G-ARGG	D.H.C.1 Chipmunk 22 (WD305)	Willpower Garage Ltd
	G-ARGO	PA-22 Colt 108	B. E. Goodman/Liverpool
	G-ARGV	PA-18 Super Cub 150	Deeside Gliding Club (Aberdeenshire) Ltd/Aboyne
	G-ARGY	PA-22 Tri-Pacer 160	G. K. Hare (G-JEST)
	G-ARGZ	D.31 Turbulent	J. C. Mansell
	G-ARHB	Forney F-1A Aircoupe	A. V. Rash & D. R. Wickes
	G-ARHC	Forney F-1A Aircoupe	A. P. Gardner/Elstree
	G-ARHF	Forney F-1A Aircoupe	Disabled Flying Group
	G-ARHI	PA-24 Comanche 180	W. H. Entress/Swansea
	G-ARHL	PA-23 Aztec 250	J. J. Freeman & Co Ltd/Headcorn
	G-ARHM	Auster 6A	D. Hollowell & ptnrs/Finmere
	G-ARHN	PA-22 Caribbean 150	D. B. Furniss & A. Munro/Doncaster
	G-ARHP	PA-22 Tri-Pacer 160	W. Wardle
	G-ARHR	PA-22 Caribbean 150	A. Milton & S. D. Kent
	G-ARHT	PA-22 Caribbean 150 ★	Moston Technical College
	G-ARHU	PA-22 Tri-Pacer 160	B. L. Newbold & H. Streets
	G-ARHW	D.H.104 Dove 8	Glidegold Ltd/Booker
	G-ARHX	D.H.104 Dove 8 ★	—/Booker
	G-ARHZ	D.62 Condor	Condor Hotel Zulu Group/Andrewsfield
	G-ARID	Cessna 172B	L. M. Edwards
	G-ARIE	PA-24 Comanche 250	Zendair Ltd
	G-ARIF	Ord-Hume O-H.7 Minor Coupé	N. H. Ponsford
	G-ARIH	Auster 6A (TW591)	India Hotel Ltd
	G-ARIK	PA-22 Caribbean 150	C. J. Berry
	G-ARIL	PA-22 Caribbean 150	K. Knight
	G-ARIM	D.31 Turbulent	R. W. L. Breckell
	G-ARIV	Cessna 172B	G-ARIV Flying Group
	G-ARJB	D.H.104 Dove 8 ★	J. C. Bamford (stored)
	G-ARJC	PA-22 Colt 108	F. W. H. Dulles
	G-ARJE	PA-22 Colt 108	Touchdown Aviation Ltd
	G-ARJF	PA-22 Colt 108	M. J. Collins
	G-ARJH	PA-22 Colt 108	G. P. A. Elborough
	G-ARJR	PA-23 Apache 160G ★	Instructional airframe/Kidlington
	G-ARJS	PA-23 Apache 160G	Bencray Ltd/Blackpool
	G-ARJT	PA-23 Apache 160G	Hiveland Ltd
	G-ARJU	PA-23 Apache 160G	Chantaco Ltd/Biggin Hill

Reg.	Type	Owner or Operator	Notes
G-ARJV	PA-23 Apache 160G	Economic Insulations Ltd	
G-ARJW	PA-23 Apache 160G	*stored*/Bristol	
G-ARJZ	D.31 Turbulent	N. H. Jones	
G-ARKG	J/5G Autocar	C. M. Milborrow	
G-ARKJ	Beech N35 Bonanza	T. Cust	
G-ARKK	PA-22 Colt 108	A. T. J. Hyatt	
G-ARKM	PA-22 Colt 108	B. V. & E. A. Howes/Earls Colne	
G-ARKN	PA-22 Colt 108	R. A. & N. L. E. Dupee	
G-ARKP	PA-22 Colt 108	C. J. & J. Freeman/Headcorn	
G-ARKR	PA-22 Colt 108	B. J. M. Montegut	
G-ARKS	PA-22 Colt 108	R. A. Nesbitt-Dufort	
G-ARLG	Auster D.4/108	Auster D4 Group	
G-ARLK	PA-24 Comanche 250	M. Walker & C. Robinson	
G-ARLO	A.61 Terrier 1 ★	*stored*	
G-ARLP	A.61 Terrier 1	Gemini Flying Group	
G-ARLR	A.61 Terrier 2	M. J. Breeze	
G-ARLU	Cessna 172B Skyhawk ★	*Instructional airframe*/Irish AC	
G-ARLV	Cessna 172B Skyhawk	P. D. Lowdon	
G-ARLW	Cessna 172B Skyhawk ★	*(spares' source)*/Barton	
G-ARLX	Jodel D.140B	Shipping & Airlines Ltd/Biggin Hill	
G-ARLZ	D.31A Turbulent	R. S. Hatwell & A. F. Hall	
G-ARMA	PA-23 Apache 160G ★	*Instructional airframe*/Kidlington	
G-ARMB	D.H.C.1 Chipmunk 22A (WB660)	Red Baron Aviation Ltd/Shipdham	
G-ARMC	D.H.C.1 Chipmunk 22A (WB703)	John Henderson Children's Trust	
G-ARMD	D.H.C.1 Chipmunk 22A ★	K. & L. Aero Services (*stored*)	
G-ARMF	D.H.C.1 Chipmunk 22A	Chipmunk G-BCIO Syndicate	
G-ARMG	D.H.C.1 Chipmunk 22A	Chipmunk Preservation Group Ltd/ Wellesbourne	
G-ARML	Cessna 175B Skylark	R. C. Convine	
G-ARMN	Cessna 175B Skylark ★	Southall College of Technology	
G-ARMO	Cessna 172B Skyhawk	G. M. Jones	
G-ARMR	Cessna 172B Skyhawk	Sunsaver Ltd/Barton	
G-ARMZ	D.31 Turbulent	J. E. M. B. Millns	
G-ARNB	J/5G Autocar	R. F. Tolhurst	
G-ARND	PA-22 Colt 108	E. J. Clarke	
G-ARNE	PA-22 Colt 108	T. D. L. Bowden/Shipdham	
G-ARNG	PA-22 Colt 108	S. S. Delwarte/Shoreham	
G-ARNI	PA-22 Colt 108	P. R. Monk & A. C. Savage	
G-ARNJ	PA-22 Colt 108	Colt Flying Group	
G-ARNK	PA-22 Colt 108 (tailwheel)	G. K. Hare	
G-ARNL	PA-22 Colt 108	J. A. & J. A. Dodsworth/White Waltham	
G-ARNO	A.61 Terrier 1	*(stored)*	
G-ARNP	A.109 Airedale	S. W. & M. Isbister	
G-ARNY	Jodel D.117	D. J. Lockett	
G-ARNZ	D.31 Turbulent	N. J. Mathias	
G-AROA	Cessna 172B Skyhawk	D. E. Partridge	
G-AROE	Aero 145	Gooney Bird Trading Ltd	
G-AROF	L.40 Meta-Sokol	G. D. H. Crawford	
G-AROJ	A.109 Airedale ★	D. J. Shaw (*stored*)	
G-AROM	PA-22 Colt 108	J. R. Colthurst	
G-ARON	PA-22 Colt 108	R. W. Curtis	
G-AROO	Forney F-1A Aircoupe	W. J. McMeekan/Newtownards	
G-AROW	Jodel D.140B	Cubair Ltd/Redhill	
G-AROY	Boeing Stearman A.75N.1	W. A. Jordan	
G-ARPH	H.S.121 Trident 1C ★	Aerospace Museum, Cosford	
G-ARPK	H.S.121 Trident 1C ★	Manchester Airport Authority	
G-ARPL	H.S.121 Trident 1C ★	BAA Airport Fire Service/Edinburgh	
G-ARPN	H.S.121 Trident 1C ★	BAA Airport Fire Service/Aberdeen	
G-ARPO	H.S.121 Trident 1C ★	CAA Fire School/Teesside	
G-ARPP	H.S.121 Trident 1C ★	BAA Airport Fire Service/Glasgow	
G-ARPV	H.S.121 Trident 1C ★	Aerospace Museum (*cockpit*)/Cosford	
G-ARPW	H.S.121 Trident 1C ★	CAA Fire School/Teesside	
G-ARPX	H.S.121 Trident 1C ★	Airwork Services Ltd/Perth	
G-ARPZ	H.S.121 Trident 1C ★	RFD Ltd/Dunsfold	
G-ARRD	Jodel DR.1050	C. M. Fitton	
G-ARRE	Jodel DR.1050	A. Luty & M. P. Edwards/Barton	
G-ARRF	Cessna 150A	Electrical Engineering Services	
G-ARRL	J/1N Alpha	G. N. Smith & C. Webb	
G-ARRM	Beagle B.206-X ★	Shoreham Airport Museum	
G-ARRS	CP.301A Emeraude	E. H. Booker	
G-ARRT	Wallis WA-116-1	K. H. Wallis	
G-ARRU	D.31 Turbulent	N. C. Lowes	
G-ARRX	Auster 6A	J. E. D. Mackie	

Notes	Reg.	Type	Owner or Operator
	G-ARRY	Jodel D.140B	Fictionview Ltd
	G-ARRZ	D.31 Turbulent	C. I. Jefferson
	G-ARSB	Cessna 150A	B. T. White/Andrewsfield
	G-ARSG	Roe Triplane Type IV replica	Shuttleworth Collection/O. Warden
	G-ARSJ	CP.301-C2 Emeraude	R. J. Lewis
	G-ARSL	A.61 Terrier 2	R. A. Hutchinson & P. T. M. Hardy
	G-ARSU	PA-22 Colt 108	W. H. & D. Gough
	G-ARSW	PA-22 Colt 108	Sierra Whisky Flying Group/Sibson
	G-ARSX	PA-22 Tri-Pacer 160	S. Hutchinson
	G-ARTD	PA-23 Apache 160	Dr. D. A. Jones
	G-ARTG	Hiller UH-12C ★	White Hart Inn/Stockbridge
	G-ARTH	PA-12 Super Cruiser	R. I. Souch & B. J. Dunford
	G-ARTJ	Bensen B.8 ★	Museum of Flight/E. Fortune
	G-ARTL	D.H.82A Tiger Moth (T7281)	P. A. Jackson
	G-ARTT	M.S.880B Rallye Club	R. N. Scott
	G-ARTW	Cessna 150B ★	Instructional airframe/Perth
	G-ARTX	Cessna 150B ★	Instructional airframe/Perth
	G-ARTY	Cessna 150B ★	Instructional airframe/Perth
	G-ARTZ	McCandless M.4 Gyrocopter	W. E. Partridge (stored)
	G-ARUG	J/5G Autocar	D. P. H. Hulme/Biggin Hill
	G-ARUH	Jodel DR.1050	PFA Group/Denham
	G-ARUI	A.61 Terrier	A. C. Ladd
	G-ARUL	Cosmic Wind	P. G. Kynsey
	G-ARUO	PA-24 Comanche 180	Uniform Oscar Group/Elstree
	G-ARUV	CP.301A Emeraude	J. Tanswell
	G-ARUY	J/1N Alpha	Gullwing Aviation Ltd
	G-ARUZ	Cessna 175C Skylark	Cardiff Skylark Group
	G-ARVM	V.1101 VC10 ★	Aerospace Museum/Cosford
	G-ARVO	PA-18 Super Cub 95	Deltair Ltd
	G-ARVS	PA-28 Cherokee 160	Skyscraper Ltd/Stapleford
	G-ARVT	PA-28 Cherokee 160	Red Rose Aviation Ltd/Liverpool
	G-ARVU	PA-28 Cherokee 160	D. J. Hockings/Biggin Hill
	G-ARVV	PA-28 Cherokee 160	G. E. Hopkins
	G-ARVZ	D.62B Condor	P. A. Silcox
	G-ARWB	D.H.C.1 Chipmunk 22 (WK611)	L. J. Willcocks
	G-ARWH	Cessna 172C Skyhawk ★	—
	G-ARWO	Cessna 172C Skyhawk	J. P. Stafford
	G-ARWR	Cessna 172C Skyhawk	The Devanha Flying Group Ltd/Aberdeen
	G-ARWS	Cessna 175C Skylark	E. N. Skinner
	G-ARXD	A.109 Airedale	D. Howden
	G-ARXG	PA-24 Comanche 250	I. M. Callier
	G-ARXH	Bell 47G	A. B. Searle
	G-ARXP	Luton LA-4A Minor	W. C. Hymas
	G-ARXT	Jodel DR.1050	CJM Flying Group
	G-ARXU	Auster 6A (VF526)	The A Team
	G-ARXW	M.S.885 Super Rallye	Bond Glen Flying Club Ltd/Dunnamanagh
	G-ARXX	M.S.880B Rallye Club	P. S. E. Clifton
	G-ARYB	H.S.125 Srs 1★	British Aerospace PLC/Hatfield
	G-ARYC	H.S.125 Srs 1 ★	The Mosquito Aircraft Museum
	G-ARYD	Auster AOP.6 (WJ358) ★	Museum of Army Flying/Middle Wallop
	G-ARYF	PA-23 Aztec 250B	I. J. T. Branson/Biggin Hill
	G-ARYH	PA-22 Tri-Pacer 160	Filtration (Water Treatment Engineers) Ltd
	G-ARYI	Cessna 172C	J. Rhodes
	G-ARYK	Cessna 172C	L. S. & K. Johnson/Ipswich
	G-ARYR	PA-28 Cherokee 180	G-ARYR Flying Group
	G-ARYS	Cessna 172C Skyhawk	Guildbrook Associates Ltd
	G-ARYV	PA-24 Comanche 250	Ilford Business Machines Ltd
	G-ARYZ	A.109 Airedale	Rutland Aviation
	G-ARZB	Wallis WA-116 Srs 1	K. H. Wallis
	G-ARZE	Cessna 172C ★	Parachute jump trainer/Cockerham
	G-ARZM	D.31 Turbulent	Tiger Club (1990) Ltd/Headcorn
	G-ARZN	Beech N35 Bonanza	D. W. Mickleburgh/Leicester
	G-ARZP	A.109 Airedale	G. B. O'Neill (stored)/Booker
	G-ARZW	Currie Wot	J. H. Blake
	G-ARZX	Cessna 150B	P. H. Slade
	G-ASAA	Luton LA-4A Minor	J. W. Cudby
	G-ASAI	A.109 Airedale	K. R Howden & ptnrs
	G-ASAJ	A.61 Terrier 2 (WE569)	G-ASAJ Flying Group
	G-ASAK	A.61 Terrier 2	Rochford Hundred Flying Group/Southend
	G-ASAL	SAL Bulldog 120	British Aerospace PLC/Prestwick
	G-ASAM	D.31 Turbulent	Tiger Club (1990) Ltd/Headcorn
	G-ASAN	A.61 Terrier 2	D. R. Godfrey

Reg.	Type	Owner or Operator	Notes
G-ASAT	M.S.880B Rallye Club	M. Cutovic	
G-ASAU	M.S.880B Rallye Club	T. C. & R. Edwards	
G-ASAX	A.61 Terrier 2	P. G. & F. M. Morris	
G-ASAZ	Hiller UH-12E4	Pan-Air Ltd	
G-ASBA	Currie Wot	M. A. Kaye	
G-ASBB	Beech 23 Musketeer	D. Silver/Southend	
G-ASBH	A.109 Airedale	D. T. Smollett	
G-ASBY	A.109 Airedale	M. R. H. Wheatley & R. K. Wilson	
G-ASCC	Beagle E.3 AOP Mk 11	Old Training Plane Co	
G-ASCM	Isaacs Fury II (K2050)	M. M. Ward	
G-ASCU	PA-18A Super Cub 150	Farm Aviation Services Ltd	
G-ASCZ	CP.301A Emeraude	J. O. R. Penman/France	
G-ASDF	Edwards Gyrocopter ★	B. King	
G-ASDK	A.61 Terrier 2	M. L. Rose	
G-ASDL	A.61 Terrier 2	C. E. Mason	
G-ASDO	Beech 95-A55 Baron ★	No 2498 Sqn ATC/Jersey	
G-ASDY	Wallis WA-116/F	K. H. Wallis	
G-ASEA	Luton LA-4A Minor	G. C. Jones	
G-ASEB	Luton LA-4A Minor	S. R. P. Harper	
G-ASEG	A.61 Terrier (VF548)	R. S. O. B. Evans & J. P. P. A. Midgley	
G-ASEO	PA-24 Comanche 250	Planetalk Ltd	
G-ASEP	PA-23 Apache 235	Arrowstate Ltd/Denham	
G-ASEU	D.62A Condor	W. M. Grant	
G-ASFA	Cessna 172D	APS Worldwide/Cranfield	
G-ASFD	L-200A Morava	M. Emery/Bournemouth	
G-ASFK	J/5G Autocar	R. W. & M. Struth	
G-ASFL	PA-28 Cherokee 180	D. F. Ranger/Popham	
G-ASFR	Bo.208A1 Junior	S. T. Dauncey	
G-ASFX	D.31 Turbulent	E. F. Clapham & W. B. S. Dobie	
G-ASGC	V.1151 Super VC10 ★	Duxford Aviation Soc	
G-ASHB	Cessna 182F	Sport Parachute Centre Ltd/Tilstock	
G-ASHD	Brantly B-2A ★	International Helicopter Museum/ Weston-s-Mare	
G-ASHH	PA-23 Aztec 250	Leicestershire Thread & Trimming Manufacturers Ltd/Sibson	
G-ASHS	SNCAN Stampe SV-4B	Three Point Flying Ltd	
G-ASHT	D.31 Turbulent	C. W. N. Huke	
G-ASHU	PA-15 Vagabond	G. J. Romanes	
G-ASHV	PA-23 Aztec 250B	R. J. Ashley & G. O'Gorman	
G-ASHX	PA-28 Cherokee 180	Powertheme Ltd/Barton	
G-ASIB	Cessna F.172D	G-ASIB Flying Group	
G-ASII	PA-28 Cherokee 180	T. R. Hart & Natocars Ltd	
G-ASIJ	PA-28 Cherokee 180	Precision Products Ltd & D. Beadle	
G-ASIL	PA-28 Cherokee 180	J. Dickenson & C. D. Powell	
G-ASIS	Jodel D.112	E. F. Hazel	
G-ASIT	Cessna 180	A. & P. A. Wood	
G-ASIY	PA-25 Pawnee 235	RAFGSA/Bicester	
G-ASJC	BAC One-Eleven 201AC	British World Airlines Ltd/Southend	
G-ASJL	Beech H.35 Bonanza	A. Littlejohns & C. B. Ranald	
G-ASJM	PA-30 Twin Comanche 160 ★	Via Nova Ltd (stored)	
G-ASJO	Beech B.23 Musketeer	S. Boon/Sandown	
G-ASJV	V.S.361 Spitfire IX (MH434)	Nalfire Aviation Ltd/Duxford	
G-ASJY	GY-80 Horizon 160	A. H. Wooffindin	
G-ASJZ	Jodel D.117A	P. J. & M. Edwards	
G-ASKC	D.H.98 Mosquito 35 (TA719) ★	Skyfame Collection/Duxford	
G-ASKH	D.H.98 Mosquito T.3 (RR299)	British Aerospace PLC/Chester	
G-ASKJ	A.61 Terrier 1 (VX926)	N. K. & M. D. Freestone	
G-ASKK	HPR-7 Herald 211 ★	Norwich Aviation Museum	
G-ASKL	Jodel D.150A	J. M. Graty	
G-ASKP	D.H.82A Tiger Moth	Tiger Club (1990) Ltd/Headcorn	
G-ASKS	Cessna 336 Skymaster	N. Foulds	
G-ASKT	PA-28 Cherokee 180	A. Mattacks & T. Hood	
G-ASKV	PA-25 Pawnee 235	Southdown Gliding Club Ltd	
G-ASLH	Cessna 182F	R. W. Boote	
G-ASLK	PA-25 Pawnee 235	Bristol Gliding Club (Pty) Ltd/Nympsfield	
G-ASLL	Cessna 336 ★	stored/Bournemouth	
G-ASLR	Agusta-Bell 47J-2	N. M. G. Pearson	
G-ASLV	PA-28 Cherokee 235	Sackville Flying Group	
G-ASLX	CP.301A Emeraude	T. J. Caton	
G-ASMA	PA-30 Twin Comanche 160 C/R	B. D. Glynn/Redhill	
G-ASME	Bensen B.8M	K. Brogden	
G-ASMF	Beech D.95A Travel Air	M. J. A. Hornblower	
G-ASMJ	Cessna F.172E	Mike Juliet Group/Audley End	

Notes	Reg.	Type	Owner or Operator
	G-ASML	Luton LA-4A Minor	Fenland Strut Flying Group
	G-ASMM	D.31 Tubulent	G. E. Arthur
	G-ASMO	PA-23 Apache 160G ★	Aviation Enterprises/Fairoaks
	G-ASMS	Cessna 150A	M. B. & G. T. Cocks
	G-ASMT	Fairtravel Linnet 2	A. F. Cashin
	G-ASMU	Cessna 150D	Telepoint Ltd/Barton
	G-ASMV	CP.1310-C3 Super Emeraude	P. F. D. Waltham/Leicester
	G-ASMW	Cessna 150D	Yorkshire Light Aircraft Ltd/Leeds
	G-ASMY	PA-23 Apache 160H	R. D. & E. Forster
	G-ASMZ	A.61 Terrier 2 (VF516)	R. C. Burden
	G-ASNB	Auster 6A (VX118)	M. J. Miller & G. Hengeveld
	G-ASNC	D.5/180 Husky	Peterborough & Spalding Gliding Club/ Boston
	G-ASND	PA-23 Aztec 250	Sky Leisure Aviation Ltd/Shoreham
	G-ASNF	Ercoupe 415CD	C. R. Weldon
	G-ASNH	PA-23 Aztec 250B	J. Hoerner & The Earl of Suffolk & Berkshire
	G-ASNI	CP.1310-C3 Super Emeraude	D. Chapman
	G-ASNK	Cessna 205	Justgold Ltd
	G-ASNN	Cessna 182F ★	*(parachute jump trainer)*/Tilstock
	G-ASNU	H.S.125 Srs. 1	Flintgrange Ltd
	G-ASNW	Cessna F.172E	J. A. Gibbs
	G-ASOC	Auster 6A	J. A. Rayment/Hinton-in-the-Hedges
	G-ASOH	Beech 95-B55A Baron	GMD Group
	G-ASOI	A.61 Terrier 2	N. K. & C. M. Geddes
	G-ASOK	Cessna F.172E	Okay Flying Group/Denham
	G-ASOM	A.61 Terrier 2	J. E. Tootell (G-JETS)
	G-ASON	PA-30 Twin Comanche 160	Follandbeech Ltd
	G-ASOO	PA-30 Twin Comanche 160	K. H. Acketts
	G-ASOP	Sopwith F.1 Camel (B6291)	A. J. E. Ditheridge
	G-ASOX	Cessna 205A	Border Parachute Centre
	G-ASPF	Jodel D.120	T. J. Bates
	G-ASPI	Cessna F.172E	Icarus Flying Group/Rochester
	G-ASPK	PA-28 Cherokee 140	Westward Airways (Lands End) Ltd/St Just
	G-ASPP	Bristol Boxkite (replica)	Shuttleworth Collection/O. Warden
	G-ASPS	Piper J-3C-90 Cub	A. J. Chalkley/Blackbushe
	G-ASPU	D.31 Turbulent	I. MacLennan
	G-ASPV	D.H.82A Tiger Moth	B. S. Charters/Shipdham
	G-ASRB	D.62B Condor	T. J. McRae & H. C. Palmer/Shoreham
	G-ASRC	D.62B Condor	J. Knight
	G-ASRF	Jenny Wren	G. W. Gowland (*stored*)
	G-ASRH	PA-30 Twin Comanche 160	Island Aviation & Travel Ltd
	G-ASRI	PA-23 Aztec 250B ★	Graham Collins Associates Ltd
	G-ASRK	A.109 Airedale ★	R. K. Wilson & M. R. H. Wheatley
	G-ASRO	PA-30 Twin Comanche 160	D. W. Blake
	G-ASRR	Cessna 182G	J. A. Rees
	G-ASRT	Jodel D.150	P. Turton
	G-ASRW	PA-28 Cherokee 180	R. J. Keyte
	G-ASSE	PA-22 Colt 108	J. B. King/Goodwood
	G-ASSF	Cessna 182G Skylane	Burbage Farms Ltd/Lutterworth
	G-ASSM	H.S.125 Srs 1/522 ★	Science Museum/S. Kensington
	G-ASSP	PA-30 Twin Comanche 160	P. H. Tavener
	G-ASSS	Cessna 172E	D. H. N. Squires & P. R. March/Bristol
	G-ASST	Cessna 150D	F. R. H. Parker
	G-ASSU	CP.301A Emeraude	R. W. Millward (*stored*)/Redhill
	G-ASSV	Kensinger KF	C. I. Jefferson
	G-ASSW	PA-28 Cherokee 140	W. G. R. Wunderlich/Biggin Hill
	G-ASTA	D.31 Turbulent	R. N. Steel
	G-ASTH	Mooney M.20C ★	E. L. Martin (*stored*)
	G-ASTI	Auster 6A	M. Pocock
	G-ASTL	Fairey Firefly 1 (DK431) ★	Skyfame Collection/Duxford
	G-ASTP	Hiller UH-12C ★	International Helicopter Museum/ Weston-s-Mare
	G-ASTV	Cessna 150D (tailwheel) ★	*stored*
	G-ASUB	Mooney M.20E Super 21	P. K. Pemberton
	G-ASUD	PA-28 Cherokee 180	S. J. Rogers & M. N. Petchey
	G-ASUE	Cessna 150D	D. Huckle/Panshanger
	G-ASUG	Beech E18S ★	Museum of Flight/E. Fortune
	G-ASUI	A.61 Terrier 2	K. W. Chigwell & D. R. Lee
	G-ASUL	Cessna 182G Skylane	Blackpool & Fylde Aero Club Ltd
	G-ASUP	Cessna F.172E	GASUP Air/Cardiff
	G-ASUR	Dornier Do 28A-1	Sheffair Ltd
	G-ASUS	Jurca MJ.2B Tempete	D. G. Jones/Coventry
	G-ASVG	CP.301B Emeraude	K. R. Jackson

Reg.	Type	Owner or Operator	Notes
G-ASVM	Cessna F.172E	GATRL Flying Group	
G-ASVN	Cessna U.206 Super Skywagon	L. Rawson	
G-ASVO	HPR-7 Herald 214	Channel Express (Air Services) Ltd/ Bournemouth	
G-ASVP	PA-25 Pawnee 235	Aquila Gliding Club Ltd	
G-ASVZ	PA-28 Cherokee 140	J. H. Mitchell & A. W. Parker	
G-ASWB	A.109 Airedale	Lawson Engineering	
G-ASWH	Luton LA-5A Major	J. T. Powell-Tuck	
G-ASWJ	Beagle 206 Srs 1 (8449M) ★	RAF Halton	
G-ASWL	Cessna F.172F	Bagby Aviation Flying Group	
G-ASWN	Bensen B.8M	D. R. Shepherd	
G-ASWP	Beech A.23 Musketeer	J. Holdon & G. Benet	
G-ASWW	PA-30 Twin Comanche 160	D. M. White	
G-ASWX	PA-28 Cherokee 180	A. F. Dadds	
G-ASXC	SIPA 901	M. K. Dartford & M. Cookson	
G-ASXD	Brantly B.2B	Lousada PLC	
G-ASXI	Tipsy T.66 Nipper 3	P. F. J. Wells	
G-ASXJ	Luton LA-4A Minor	J. S. Allison/Halton	
G-ASXR	Cessna 210	A. Schofield	
G-ASXS	Jodel DR.1050	R. A. Hunter	
G-ASXU	Jodel D.120A	G. W. Worley & D. J. Buffham	
G-ASXX	Avro 683 Lancaster 7 (NX611) ★	Lincolnshire Aviation Heritage Centre/ E. Kirkby	
G-ASXY	Jodel D.117A	P. A. Davies & ptnrs/Cardiff	
G-ASXZ	Cessna 182G Skylane	P. M. Robertson/Perth	
G-ASYD	BAC One-Eleven 670	British Aerospace	
G-ASYG	A.61 Terrier 2	G. Rea	
G-ASYJ	Beech D.95A Travel Air	Crosby Aviation (Jersey) Ltd	
G-ASYK	PA-30 Twin Comanche 160	M. S. Harvell	
G-ASYP	Cessna 150E	Henlow Flying Group	
G-ASYW	Bell 47G-2	Bristow Helicopters Ltd	
G-ASYZ	Victa Airtourer 100	N. C. Grayson	
G-ASZB	Cessna 150E	W. A. Smale/Exeter	
G-ASZD	Bo 208A2 Junior	A. J. Watson & ptnrs/O. Warden	
G-ASZE	A.61 Terrier 2	P. J. Moore	
G-ASZJ	S.C.7 Skyvan 3A-100	GEC Marconi Ltd/Luton	
G-ASZR	Fairtravel Linnet	H. C. D. & F. J. Garner	
G-ASZS	GY.80 Horizon 160	J. M. B. Duncan	
G-ASZU	Cessna 150E	T. H. Milburn	
G-ASZV	Tipsy T.66 Nipper 2	R. L. Mitcham/Elstree	
G-ASZX	A.61 Terrier 1	C. A. Bailey	
G-ATAF	Cessna F.172F	S. Lancashire Flyers Ltd	
G-ATAG	Jodel DR. 1050	T. M. Dawes-Gamble	
G-ATAI	D.H.104 Dove 8	L. A. Wootton/France	
G-ATAS	PA-28 Cherokee 180	E. J. Titterrell	
G-ATAT	Cessna 150E	The Derek Pointon Group (stored)	
G-ATAU	D.62B Condor	M. A. Peare/Redhill	
G-ATAV	D.62C Condor	R. W. H. Watson & K. J. Gallagher	
G-ATBG	Nord 1002 (NJ-C11)	L. M. Walton	
G-ATBH	Aero 145	P. D. Aberbach	
G-ATBI	Beech A.23 Musketeer	R. F. G. Dent/Staverton	
G-ATBJ	Sikorsky S-61N	British International Helicopters	
G-ATBL	D.H.60G Moth	J. M. Greenland	
G-ATBP	Fournier RF-3	K. McBride	
G-ATBS	D.31 Turbulent	D. R. Keene & J. A. Lear	
G-ATBU	A.61 Terrier 2	P. R. Anderson	
G-ATBW	Tipsy T.66 Nipper 2	Stapleford Nipper Group	
G-ATBX	PA-20 Pacer 135	G. D. & P. M. Thomson	
G-ATBZ	W.S.58 Wessex 60 ★	International Helicopter Museum/ Weston-s-Mare	
G-ATCC	A.109 Airedale	J. F. Moore & ptnrs/Biggin Hill	
G-ATCD	D.5/180 Husky	Oxford Flying & Gliding Group/Enstone	
G-ATCE	Cessna U.206	J. Fletcher & D. Hickling/Langar	
G-ATCJ	Luton LA-4A Minor	R. M. Sharphouse	
G-ATCL	Victa Airtourer 100	A. D. Goodall	
G-ATCN	Luton LA-4A Minor	J. C. Gates & C. Neilson	
G-ATCR	Cessna 310 ★	ITD Aviation Ltd/Denham	
G-ATCU	Cessna 337	University of Cambridge	
G-ATCX	Cessna 182H Skylane	K. J. Fisher/Bodmin	
G-ATDA	PA-28 Cherokee 160	S. A. Vale/Basle	
G-ATDB	Nord 1101 Noralpha	J. W. Hardie	
G-ATDN	A.61 Terrier 2 (TW641)	S. J. Saggers/Biggin Hill	

Notes	Reg.	Type	Owner or Operator
	G-ATDO	Bo 208C Junior	H. Swift
	G-ATEF	Cessna 150E	Swans Aviation
	G-ATEG	Cessna 150E	S. A. Seshie
	G-ATEK	H.S. 748 Srs 2B	STH Sales Ltd
	G-ATEM	PA-28 Cherokee 180	Chiltern Valley Aviation Ltd
	G-ATEP	EAA Biplane ★	E. L. Martin (*stored*)/Guernsey
	G-ATES	PA-32 Cherokee Six 260 ★	*Parachute jump trainer*/Ipswich
	G-ATET	PA-30 Twin Comanche 160	R. Marsden & P. E. T. Price
	G-ATEV	Jodel DR. 1050	R. A. Smith
	G-ATEW	PA-30 Twin Comanche 160	Air Northumbria Group/Newcastle
	G-ATEX	Victa Airtourer 100	Medway Victa Group
	G-ATEZ	PA-28 Cherokee 140	J. A. Burton/E. Midlands
	G-ATFD	Jodel DR. 1050	V. Usher
	G-ATFF	PA-23 Aztec 250C	Neatspin Ltd
	G-ATFG	Brantly B.2B ★	Museum of Flight/E. Fortune
	G-ATFK	PA-30 Twin Comanche 160	D. J. Crinnon/White Waltham
	G-ATFM	Sikorsky S-61N	British International Helicopters
	G-ATFR	PA-25 Pawnee 150	R. R. Harris
	G-ATFU	D.H.85 Leopard Moth	A. de Cadenet
	G-ATFV	Agusta-Bell 47J-2A	Alexander Warren & Co Ltd
	G-ATFW	Luton LA-4A Minor	C. W. Uldale
	G-ATFX	Cessna F.172G	Isabella Properties Ltd
	G-ATFY	Cessna F.172G	H. Cowan
	G-ATGE	Jodel DR.1050	J. R. Roberts
	G-ATGH	Brantly B.2B	Helihire Ltd
	G-ATGN	Thorn Coal Gas balloon	British Balloon Museum
	G-ATGO	Cessna F.172G	P. J. Spedding & M. Johnston
	G-ATGP	Jodel DR.1050	Madley Flying Group
	G-ATGY	GY.80 Horizon	P. W. Gibberson/Birmingham
	G-ATGZ	Griffiths GH-4 Gyroplane	G. Griffiths
	G-ATHA	PA-23 Apache 235 ★	Brunel Technical College/Bristol
	G-ATHD	D.H.C.1 Chipmunk 22 (WP971)	Spartan Flying Group Ltd/Denham
	G-ATHF	Cessna 150F ★	Lincolnshire Aircraft Museum
	G-ATHK	Aeronca 7AC Champion	N. S. Chittenden
	G-ATHM	Wallis WA-116 Srs 1	Wallis Autogyros Ltd
	G-ATHN	Nord 1101 Noralpha ★	E. L. Martin (*stored*)/Guernsey
	G-ATHR	PA-28 Cherokee 180	Britannia Airways Ltd/Luton
	G-ATHT	Victa Airtourer 115	H. C. G. Munroe
	G-ATHU	A.61 Terrier 1	J. A. L. Irwin
	G-ATHV	Cessna 150F	P. Cooper
	G-ATHX	Jodel DR. 100A	I. M. Hursey
	G-ATHZ	Cessna 150F	E. & R. D. Forster
	G-ATIA	PA-24 Comanche 260	L. A. Brown
	G-ATIC	Jodel DR.1050	R. J. Major
	G-ATID	Cessna 337	M. R. Tarrant/Bourn
	G-ATIE	Cessna 150F ★	*Parachute jump trainer*/Chetwynd
	G-ATIG	HPR-7 Herald 214	Nordic Oil Services Ltd/Aberdeen
	G-ATIN	Jodel D.117	D. R. Upton & J. G. Kay/Barton
	G-ATIR	AIA Stampe SV-4C	N. M. Bloom
	G-ATIS	PA-28 Cherokee 160	P. J. Fydelor
	G-ATIZ	Jodel D.117	R. Frith & ptnrs
	G-ATJA	Jodel DR.1050	Bicester Flying Group
	G-ATJC	Victa Airtourer 100	Aviation West Ltd
	G-ATJG	PA-28 Cherokee 140	Defence Research Agency/Thurleigh
	G-ATJL	PA-24 Comanche 260	M. J. Berry & T. R. Quinn/Blackbushe
	G-ATJM	Fokker Dr.1 (replica) (152/17)	R. Lamplough/Duxford
	G-ATJN	Jodel D.119	R. F. Bradshaw
	G-ATJR	PA-E23 Aztec 250C	S. Lightbown
	G-ATJT	GY.80 Horizon 160	N. Huxtable
	G-ATJV	PA-32 Cherokee Six 260	SMK Engineers Ltd
	G-ATKF	Cessna 150F	B. V. & L. J. Mayo
	G-ATKH	Luton LA-4A Minor	H. E. Jenner
	G-ATKI	Piper J-3C-65 Cub	J. H. Allistone/Booker
	G-ATKS	Cessna F.172G	D. P. Marshall-Andrew
	G-ATKT	Cessna F.172G	P. J. Megson
	G-ATKU	Cessna F.172G	Heatherlake Ltd
	G-ATKX	Jodel D.140C	A. J. White & G. A. Piper/Biggin Hill
	G-ATKZ	Tipsy T.66 Nipper 2	M. W. Knights
	G-ATLA	Cessna 182J Skylane	Shefford Transport Engineers Ltd/Luton
	G-ATLB	Jodel DR.1050/M1	La Petit Oiseau Syndicate/Sherburn
	G-ATLC	PA-23 Aztec 250C ★	Alderney Air Charter Ltd (*stored*)
	G-ATLG	Hiller UH-12B	Bristow Helicopters Ltd
	G-ATLM	Cessna F.172G	Air Fotos Aviation Ltd/Newcastle

Reg.	Type	Owner or Operator	Notes
G-ATLP	Bensen B.8M	C. D. Julian	
G-ATLT	Cessna U-206A	Army Parachute Association/Netheravon	
G-ATLV	Jodel D.120	L. S. Thorne	
G-ATLW	PA-28 Cherokee 180	R. D. Masters	
G-ATMC	Cessna F.150F	C. J. & E. J. Leigh	
G-ATMG	M.S.893 Rallye Commodore 180	D. R. Wilkinson & T. Coldwell	
G-ATMH	D.5/180 Husky	Devon & Somerset Gliding Club Ltd	
G-ATMI	H.S.748 Srs 2A	Emerald Airways Ltd/Liverpool	
G-ATMJ	H.S.748 Srs 2A	Emerald Airways Ltd/Liverpool	
G-ATML	Cessna F.150F	B. A. Pickers	
G-ATMM	Cessna F.150F	C. H. Mitchell & R. Felton	
G-ATMT	PA-30 Twin Comanche 160	D. H. T. Bain/Newcastle	
G-ATMU	PA-23 Apache 160G	P. K. Martin & R. W. Harris	
G-ATMW	PA-28 Cherokee 140	Bencray Ltd/Blackpool	
G-ATMX	Cessna F.150F	N. E. Binner	
G-ATMY	Cessna 150F	C. F. Read/Doncaster	
G-ATNB	PA-28 Cherokee 180	R. F. Hill	
G-ATNE	Cessna F.150F	J. & S. Brew	
G-ATNJ	Cessna F.150F ★	*Instructional airframe*/Perth	
G-ATNK	Cessna F.150F	Pegasus Aviation Ltd	
G-ATNL	Cessna F.150F	S. M. Kemp & ptnrs	
G-ATNV	PA-24 Comanche 260	B. S. Reynolds & P. R. Fortescue/Bourn	
G-ATNX	Cessna F.150F	P. Jenkins	
G-ATOA	PA-23 Apache 160G	K. White	
G-ATOD	Cessna F.150F	E. Watson & ptnrs/St Just	
G-ATOE	Cessna F.150F	Kesh Flyers Group/Enniskillen	
G-ATOF	Cessna F-150F ★	*Instructional airframe*/Perth	
G-ATOG	Cessna F-150F ★	*Instructional airframe*/Perth	
G-ATOH	D.62B Condor	L. S. Thorne	
G-ATOI	PA-28 Cherokee 140	O. & E. Flying Ltd/Stapleford	
G-ATOJ	PA-28 Cherokee 140	Firefly Aviation Ltd/Glasgow	
G-ATOK	PA-28 Cherokee 140	ILC Flying Group	
G-ATOL	PA-28 Cherokee 140	L. J. Nation & G. Alford	
G-ATOM	PA-28 Cherokee 140	R. W. Mason/Kidlington	
G-ATON	PA-28 Cherokee 140	R. G. Walters	
G-ATOO	PA-28 Cherokee 140 ★	*Instructional airframe*/Moston Centre	
G-ATOP	PA-28 Cherokee 140	P. R. Coombs/Blackbushe	
G-ATOR	PA-28 Cherokee 140	D. Palmer & V. G. Whitehead	
G-ATOS	PA-28 Cherokee 140	E. Alexander	
G-ATOT	PA-28 Cherokee 180	Totair Flying Group	
G-ATOU	Mooney M.20E Super 21	M20 Flying Group	
G-ATOY	PA-24 Comanche 260 ★	Museum of Flight/E. Fortune	
G-ATOZ	Bensen B.8M	J. Jordan	
G-ATPD	H.S.125 Srs 1B	Aeromedicare Ltd/Bournemouth	
G-ATPN	PA-28 Cherokee 140	M. F. Hatt & ptnrs/Southend	
G-ATPT	Cessna 182J Skylane	Western Models Ltd/Redhill	
G-ATPV	JB.01 Minicab	I. A. J. Lappin	
G-ATRA	LET L.13 Blanik	Blanik Sydincate	
G-ATRC	Beech B.95A Travel Air	P. J. Simmons	
G-ATRG	PA-18 Super Cub 150	Lasham Gliding Soc Ltd	
G-ATRI	Bo 208C Junior	Chertwood Ltd	
G-ATRK	Cessna F.150F	J. Rees & F. Doncaster	
G-ATRL	Cessna F.150F	A. A. W. Stevens	
G-ATRO	PA-28 Cherokee 140	390th Flying Group	
G-ATRR	PA-28 Cherokee 140	Marnham Investments Ltd	
G-ATRW	PA-32 Cherokee Six 260	Moxley & Frankl Ltd	
G-ATRX	PA-32 Cherokee Six 260	J. W. Stow	
G-ATSI	Bo 208C Junior	M. R. Reynolds & B. A. Riseborough	
G-ATSL	Cessna F.172G	D. Le Cheminant/Guernsey	
G-ATSM	Cessna 337A	Landscape & Ground Maintenance	
G-ATSR	Beech M.35 Bonanza	Bonanza International Ltd	
G-ATSX	Bo 208C Junior	R. J. C. Campbell & M. H. Goley	
G-ATSY	Wassmer WA41 Super Baladou IV	Baladou Flying Group	
G-ATTB	Wallis WA-116-1 (XR944)	D. A. Wallis	
G-ATTD	Cessna 182J Skylane	K. M. Brennan & ptnrs	
G-ATTF	PA-28 Cherokee 140	D. H. Fear	
G-ATTG	PA-28 Cherokee 140	Arrow Air Services Engineering Ltd/ Shipdham	
G-ATTI	PA-28 Cherokee 140	D. J. Skidmore	
G-ATTK	PA-28 Cherokee 140	G-ATTK Flying Group/Southend	
G-ATTM	Jodel DR.250-160	R. W. Tomkinson	
G-ATTR	Bo 208C Junior 3	S. Luck	
G-ATTV	PA-28 Cherokee 140	G-ATTV Group	

Notes	Reg.	Type	Owner or Operator
	G-ATTX	PA-28 Cherokee 180	IPAC Aviation Ltd
	G-ATTY	PA-32 Cherokee Six 260	F. J. Wadia
	G-ATUB	PA-28 Cherokee 140	R. H. Partington & M. J. Porter
	G-ATUD	PA-28 Cherokee 140	E. J. Clempson
	G-ATUF	Cessna F.150F	A. R. Hawes/Ipswich
	G-ATUG	D.62B Condor	HMW Aviation
	G-ATUH	Tipsy T.66 Nipper 1	D. G. Spruce
	G-ATUI	Bo 208C Junior	A. W. Wakefield
	G-ATUL	PA-28 Cherokee 180	H. M. Synge
	G-ATVF	D.H.C.1 Chipmunk 22 (Lycoming)	RAFGSA/Dishforth
	G-ATVK	PA-28 Cherokee 140	JRB Aviation Ltd/Southend
	G-ATVL	PA-28 Cherokee 140	White Waltham Airfield Ltd
	G-ATVO	PA-28 Cherokee 140	D. L. Claydon
	G-ATVP	F.B.5 Gunbus (2345) ★	RAF Museum/Hendon
	G-ATVS	PA-28 Cherokee 180	Markel Aviation
	G-ATVW	D.62B Condor	J. P. Coulter & J. Chidley/Panshanger
	G-ATVX	Bo 208C Junior	G. & G. E. F. Warren
	G-ATWA	Jodel DR.1050	Jodel Syndicate
	G-ATWB	Jodel D.117	Andrewsfield Whisky Bravo Group
	G-ATWE	M.S.892A Rallye Commodore	D. I. Murray
	G-ATWJ	Cessna F.172F	C. J. & J. Freeman/Headcorn
	G-ATWR	PA-30 Twin Comanche 160B	Lubair (Transport Services) Ltd/ E. Midlands
	G-ATXA	PA-22 Tri-Pacer 150	R. C. Teverson
	G-ATXD	PA-30 Twin Comanche 160B	Jet Heritage Ltd/Bournemouth
	G-ATXF	GY-80 Horizon 150	D. C. Hyde
	G-ATXJ	H.P.137 Jetstream 300 ★	British Aerospace (*display mock-up*)/ Prestwick
	G-ATXM	PA-28 Cherokee 180	D. J. Bates
	G-ATXN	Mitchell-Proctor Kittiwake	D. W. Kent
	G-ATXO	SIPA 903	D. Hillam/Sherburn
	G-ATXZ	Bo 208C Junior	M. W. Hurst
	G-ATYM	Cessna F.150G	J. F. Perry & Co
	G-ATYN	Cessna F.150G	J. S. Grant
	G-ATYS	PA-28 Cherokee 180	R. V. Waite
	G-ATZA	Bo 208C Junior	Skyward Services Ltd/Jersey
	G-ATZG	AFB2 gas balloon	Flt Lt S. Cameron *Aeolis*
	G-ATZK	PA-28 Cherokee 180	Austen Associates Partnership
	G-ATZM	Piper J-3C-65 Cub	R. W. Davison
	G-ATZS	Wassmer WA41 Super Baladou IV	G. R. Outwin & D. P. Bennett
	G-ATZY	Cessna F.150G	J. Easson/Edinburgh
	G-ATZZ	Cessna F.150G	Meganair/Southend
	G-AVAA	Cessna F.150G	L. J. Cook
	G-AVAK	M.S.893A Rallye Commodore 180	W. K. Anderson (*stored*)/Perth
	G-AVAP	Cessna F.150G	D. G. Kipling/Southend
	G-AVAR	Cessna F.150G	J. A. Rees & F. Doncaster
	G-AVAU	PA-30 Twin Comanche 160B	L. Batin/Fairoaks
	G-AVAW	D.62B Condor	Avato Flying Group
	G-AVAX	PA-28 Cherokee 180	J. J. Parkes
	G-AVBG	PA-28 Cherokee 180	G-AVBG Flying Group/White Waltham
	G-AVBH	PA-28 Cherokee 180	T. R. Smith (Agricultural Machinery) Ltd
	G-AVBP	PA-28 Cherokee 140	Bristol & Wessex Aeroplane Club
	G-AVBS	PA-28 Cherokee 180	Piper Aircraft Club/St Just
	G-AVBT	PA-28 Cherokee 180	J. F. Mitchell
	G-AVBZ	Cessna F.172H	M. Byl
	G-AVCE	Cessna F.172H	Doncaster Aero Club Ltd
	G-AVCM	PA-24 Comanche 260	F. Smith & Sons Ltd/Stapleford
	G-AVCS	A.61 Terrier 1	A. S. Topen/Cranfield
	G-AVCT	Cessna F.150G	M. L. Biggs/Shobdon
	G-AVCU	Cessna F.150G	M. Hussain
	G-AVCV	Cessna 182J Skylane	University of Manchester Institute of Science & Technology/Woodford
	G-AVCX	PA-30 Twin Comanche 160B	T. Barge
	G-AVCY	PA-30 Twin Comanche 160B	R. C. Pugsley/Cardiff
	G-AVDA	Cessna 182K Skylane	F. W. Ellis & M. C. Burnett
	G-AVDF	Beagle Pup 100 ★	Beagle Owners Club
	G-AVDG	Wallis WA-116 Srs 1	K. H. Wallis
	G-AVDT	Aeronca 7AC Champion	D. Cheney & J. G. Woods
	G-AVDV	PA-22 Tri-Pacer 150 (tailwheel)	S. C. Brooks/Slinfold
	G-AVDW	D.62B Condor	Druine Condor G-AVDW Group
	G-AVDY	Luton LA-4A Minor	P. J. Manifold & M. J. Nairn
	G-AVEB	Morane MS 230 (157)	T. McG. Leaver

Reg.	Type	Owner or Operator	Notes
G-AVEC	Cessna F.172H	W. H. Ekin (Engineering) Co Ltd	
G-AVEF	Jodel D.150	Tiger Club (1990) Ltd/Headcorn	
G-AVEH	SIAI-Marchetti S.205	Bob Crowe Aircraft Sales Ltd	
G-AVEM	Cessna F.150G	G-AVEM Flying Group	
G-AVEN	Cessna F.150G	N. J. Budd/Aberdeen	
G-AVEO	Cessna F.150G	Meganair/Southend	
G-AVER	Cessna F.150G	E. Atherton	
G-AVEU	Wassmer WA.41 Baladou IV	G. J. Richardson	
G-AVEX	D.62B Condor	Cotswold Roller Hire Ltd/Long Marston	
G-AVEY	Currie Super Wot	A. Eastelow/Dunkeswell	
G-AVEZ	HPR-7 Herald 210 ★	Rescue Trainer/Norwich	
G-AVFB	H.S.121 Trident 2E ★	Duxford Aviation Soc	
G-AVFE	H.S.121 Trident 2E ★	Belfast Airport Authority	
G-AVFG	H.S.121 Trident 2E ★	Ground handling trainer/Heathrow	
G-AVFH	H.S.121 Trident 2E ★	Mosquito Aircraft Museum (Fuselage only)	
G-AVFK	H.S.121 Trident 2E ★	Metropolitan Police Training Centre/ Hounslow	
G-AVFM	H.S.121 Trident 2E ★	Brunel Technical College/Bristol	
G-AVFP	PA-28 Cherokee 140	M. Howells	
G-AVFR	PA-28 Cherokee 140	VFR Flying Group/Newtownards	
G-AVFS	PA-32 Cherokee Six 300	A. S. Janes	
G-AVFU	PA-32 Cherokee Six 300	Ashley Gardner Flying Club Ltd	
G-AVFX	PA-28 Cherokee 140	D. J. Young & H. Weldon	
G-AVFZ	PA-28 Cherokee 140	G-AVFZ Flying Group	
G-AVGA	PA-24 Comanche 260	Conram Aviation/Biggin Hill	
G-AVGC	PA-28 Cherokee 140	P. A. Hill	
G-AVGD	PA-28 Cherokee 140	S. & G. W. Jacobs	
G-AVGE	PA-28 Cherokee 140	H. H. T. Wolf	
G-AVGH	PA-28 Cherokee 140	Phoenix Aviation Services Ltd	
G-AVGI	PA-28 Cherokee 140	D. G. Smith & C. D. Barden	
G-AVGK	PA-28 Cherokee 180	Golf Kilo Flying Group	
G-AVGP	BAC One-Eleven 408EF	Maersk Air Ltd/British Airways/Birmingham	
G-AVGV	Cessna F.150G	Bagby Aviation Flying Group	
G-AVGY	Cessna 182K Skylane	Clifford F. Cross (Wisbech) Ltd/Fenland	
G-AVGZ	Jodel DR.1050	D. C. Webb	
G-AVHH	Cessna F.172H	M. J. Mann & J. Hickinbotom	
G-AVHL	Jodel DR.105A	Jodel G-AVHL Flying Group	
G-AVHM	Cessna F.150G	A. G. Wintle & J. Knight/Elstree	
G-AVHN	Cessna F.150F ★	Brunel Technical College/Bristol	
G-AVHT	Auster AOP.9 (WZ711)	M. Somerton-Rayner/Middle Wallop	
G-AVHY	Fournier RF.4D	J. Connelly	
G-AVIA	Cessna F.150G	Cheshire Air Training School (Merseyside) Ltd/Liverpool	
G-AVIB	Cessna F.150G	Group India Bravo	
G-AVIC	Cessna F.172H	Pembrokeshire Air Ltd/Haverfordwest	
G-AVID	Cessna 182J	J. Rolston & G. McGuinness	
G-AVIE	Cessna F.172H	M. P. Parker	
G-AVII	AB-206A JetRanger	Bristow Helicopters Ltd	
G-AVIL	Alon A.2 Aircoupe (VX147)	M. J. Close	
G-AVIN	M.S.880B Rallye Club	G. I. J. Thomson/Norwich	
G-AVIP	Brantly B.2B	P. J. Troy-Davies	
G-AVIS	Cessna F.172H	R. T. Jones/Rochester	
G-AVIT	Cessna F.150G	Shropshire Aero Club Ltd/Sleap	
G-AVIZ	Scheibe SF.25A Motorfalke	D. C. Pattison & D. A. Wilson	
G-AVJE	Cessna F.150G	G-AVJE Syndicate	
G-AVJF	Cessna F.172H	J. A. & G. M. Rees	
G-AVJG	Cessna 337B	Alderney Air Charter	
G-AVJI	Cessna F.172H	M. A. Kempson	
G-AVJJ	PA-30 Twin Comanche 160B	A. H. Manser	
G-AVJK	Jodel DR.1050/M1	G. Wylde	
G-AVJO	Fokker E.III (replica) (422-15)	Bianchi Aviation Film Services Ltd	
G-AVJV	Wallis WA-117 Srs 1	K. H. Wallis (G-ATCV)	
G-AVJW	Wallis WA-118 Srs 2	K. H. Wallis (G-ATPW)	
G-AVKB	MB.50 Pipistrelle	B. H. Pickard	
G-AVKD	Fournier RF-4D	Lasham RF4 Group	
G-AVKE	Gadfly HDW.1 ★	International Helicopter Museum/ Weston-s-Mare	
G-AVKG	Cessna F.172H	P. E. P. Sheppard	
G-AVKI	Slingsby T.66 Nipper 3	J. Fisher	
G-AVKJ	Slingsby T.66 Nipper 3	L. B. Clark	
G-AVKK	Slingsby T.66 Nipper 3	C. Watson	
G-AVKL	PA-30 Twin Comanche 160B	C. Matthews	
G-AVKN	Cessna 401	Law Leasing Ltd	

Notes	Reg.	Type	Owner or Operator
	G-AVKP	A.109 Airedale	D. R. Williams
	G-AVKR	Bo 208C Junior	C. W. Grant
	G-AVKY	Hiller UH-12E	Agricopters Ltd/Chilbolton
	G-AVKZ	PA-23 Aztec 250C	Tindon Ltd/Little Snoring
	G-AVLB	PA-28 Cherokee 140	M. Wilson
	G-AVLC	PA-28 Cherokee 140	F. C. V. Hopkins/Swansea
	G-AVLD	PA-28 Cherokee 140	WLS Flying Group/White Waltham
	G-AVLE	PA-28 Cherokee 140	Video Security Services/Tollerton
	G-AVLF	PA-28 Cherokee 140	G. H. Hughesdon
	G-AVLG	PA-28 Cherokee 140	R. Friedlander & D. C. Raymond
	G-AVLH	PA-28 Cherokee 140	Menai Flying Group
	G-AVLI	PA-28 Cherokee 140	J. V. White
	G-AVLJ	PA-28 Cherokee 140	J. G. P. Weatherlake
	G-AVLN	B.121 Pup 2	C. A. Thorpe
	G-AVLO	Bo 208C Junior	J. A. Webb & K. F. Barnard/Popham
	G-AVLR	PA-28 Cherokee 140	Group 140/Panshanger
	G-AVLT	PA-28 Cherokee 140	R. W. Harris & ptnrs/Southend
	G-AVLU	PA-28 Cherokee 140	London Transport (CRS) Sports Association Flying Club/Fairoaks
	G-AVLW	Fournier RF-4D	N. M. Groome
	G-AVLY	Jodel D.120A	N. V. de Candole
	G-AVMA	GY-80 Horizon 180	B. R. Hildick
	G-AVMB	D.62B Condor	J. C. Mansell
	G-AVMD	Cessna 150G	Bagby Aviation Flying Group
	G-AVMF	Cessna F. 150G	J. F. Marsh
	G-AVMH	BAC One-Eleven 510ED	European Aircharter Ltd
	G-AVMI	BAC One-Eleven 510ED	European Aircharter Ltd
	G-AVMJ	BAC One-Eleven 510ED	European Aviation Ltd
	G-AVMK	BAC One-Eleven 510ED	European Aircharter Ltd
	G-AVML	BAC One-Eleven 510ED	European Aviation Ltd
	G-AVMM	BAC One-Eleven 510ED	European Aviation Ltd
	G-AVMN	BAC One-Eleven 510ED	European Aviation Ltd
	G-AVMO	BAC One-Eleven 510ED ★	Aerospace Museum/Cosford
	G-AVMO	BAC One-Eleven 510ED	European Aircharter Ltd
	G-AVMR	BAC One-Eleven 510ED	European Aviation Ltd
	G-AVMS	BAC One-Eleven 510ED	European Aviation Ltd
	G-AVMT	BAC One-Eleven 510ED	Air Bristol/Filton
	G-AVMU	BAC One-Eleven 510ED ★	Duxford Aviation Soc
	G-AVMV	BAC One-Eleven 510ED	European Aviation Ltd
	G-AVMW	BAC One-Eleven 510ED	Air Bristol/Filton
	G-AVMX	BAC One-Eleven 510ED	European Aviation Ltd
	G-AVMY	BAC One-Eleven 510ED	European Aviation Ltd
	G-AVMZ	BAC One-Eleven 510ED	European Aviation Ltd
	G-AVNC	Cessna F.150G	J. Turner
	G-AVNE	W.S.58 Wessex Mk 60 Srs 1 ★	International Helicopter Museum/ Weston-s-Mare
	G-AVNN	PA-28 Cherokee 180	B. Andrews & C. S. Mitchell
	G-AVNO	PA-28 Cherokee 180	Allister Flight Ltd/Stapleford
	G-AVNP	PA-28 Cherokee 180	R. W. Harris & ptnrs
	G-AVNR	PA-28 Cherokee 180	R. R. Livingstone
	G-AVNS	PA-28 Cherokee 180	November Sierra Flying Group
	G-AVNU	PA-28 Cherokee 180	O. Durrani
	G-AVNW	PA-28 Cherokee 180	Len Smith's School & Sports Ltd
	G-AVNX	Fournier RF-4D	Nymphsfield RF-4 Group
	G-AVNY	Fournier RF-4D	V. S. E. Norman/Staverton
	G-AVNZ	Fournier RF-4D	Shipping & Airlines Ltd/Biggin Hill
	G-AVOA	Jodel DR.1050	D. A. Willies/Cranwell
	G-AVOH	D.62B Condor	D. F. Ranger/Popham
	G-AVOM	Jodel DR.221	M. A. Mountford/Headcorn
	G-AVOO	PA-18 Super Cub 150	London Gliding Club Ltd/ Dunstable
	G-AVOZ	PA-28 Cherokee 180	J. R. Winning/Booker
	G-AVPC	D.31 Turbulent	S. A. Sharp
	G-AVPD	D.9 Bebe	S. W. McKay (stored)
	G-AVPH	Cessna F.150G	W. Lancashire Aero Club/Woodvale
	G-AVPI	Cessna F.172H	R. W. Cope
	G-AVPJ	D.H.82A Tiger Moth	C. C. Silk
	G-AVPK	M.S.892A Rallye Commodore	B. A. Bridgewater/Halfpenny Green
	G-AVPM	Jodel D.117	J. Houghton/Brighton
	G-AVPN	HPR-7 Herald 213	Channel Express (Air Services) Ltd/ Bournemouth
	G-AVPO	Hindustan HAL-26 Pushpak	J. A. Rimell
	G-AVPR	PA-30 Twin Comanche 160B	J. O. Coundley
	G-AVPS	PA-30 Twin Comanche 160B	J. M. Bisco/Staverton

Reg.	Type	Owner or Operator	Notes
G-AVPT	PA-18 Super Cub 150	Tiger Club (1990) Ltd/Headcorn	
G-AVPV	PA-28 Cherokee 180	MLP Aviation Ltd/Elstree	
G-AVRK	PA-28 Cherokee 180	J. Gama	
G-AVRP	PA-28 Cherokee 140	T. Hiscox	
G-AVRS	GY-80 Horizon 180	Air Venturas Ltd	
G-AVRT	PA-28 Cherokee 140	Star Aviation Trust Group/Stapleford	
G-AVRU	PA-28 Cherokee 180	G-AVRU Partnership/Clacton	
G-AVRW	GY-20 Minicab	Kestrel Flying Group/Tollerton	
G-AVRY	PA-28 Cherokee 180	Brigfast Ltd/Blackbushe	
G-AVRZ	PA-28 Cherokee 180	Mantavia Group Ltd	
G-AVSA	PA-28 Cherokee 180	G-AVSA Flying Group	
G-AVSB	PA-28 Cherokee 180	White House Garage Ashford Ltd	
G-AVSC	PA-28 Cherokee 180	Medidata Ltd	
G-AVSD	PA-28 Cherokee 180	Landmate Ltd	
G-AVSE	PA-28 Cherokee 180	Yorkshire Aeroplane Club Ltd/Leeds	
G-AVSF	PA-28 Cherokee 180	Monday Club/Blackbushe	
G-AVSI	PA-28 Cherokee 140	CR Aviation Ltd	
G-AVSP	PA-28 Cherokee 180	Devon School of Flying/Dunkeswell	
G-AVSR	D.5/180 Husky	A. L. Young	
G-AVSW	AB-206B JetRanger	Nash Group Ltd	
G-AVSZ	AB-206B JetRanger	Glenair Helicopters Ltd	
G-AVTC	Slingsby T.66 Nipper 3	M. K. Field	
G-AVTJ	PA-32 Cherokee Six 260	L. P. Marsh/Sandown	
G-AVTK	PA-32 Cherokee Six 260	Aeroclub Montagnana SNC	
G-AVTP	Cessna F.172H	W. Murphy	
G-AVTT	Ercoupe 415D	Wright's Farm Eggs Ltd/Andrewsfield	
G-AVTV	M.S.893A Rallye Commodore	D. B. Meeks	
G-AVUD	PA-30 Twin Comanche 160B	F. M. Aviation/Biggin Hill	
G-AVUG	Cessna F.150H	Skyways Flying Group/Netherthorpe	
G-AVUH	Cessna F.150H	G-AVUH Group	
G-AVUL	Cessna F.172H	R. Bilson & R. D. Turner	
G-AVUS	PA-28 Cherokee 140	R. Groat/Glasgow	
G-AVUT	PA-28 Cherokee 140	Bencray Ltd/Blackpool	
G-AVUU	PA-28 Cherokee 140	A. Jahanfar & ptnrs/Southend	
G-AVUZ	PA-32 Cherokee Six 300	Ceesix Ltd/Jersey	
G-AVVC	Cessna F.172H	J. S. M. Cattle	
G-AVVE	Cessna F.150H ★	R. Windley (stored)	
G-AVVI	PA-30 Twin Comanche 160B	H. E. Boulter & D. G. Bligh	
G-AVVJ	M.S.893A Rallye Commodore	Herefordshire Gliding Club Ltd/ Shobdon	
G-AVVL	Cessna F.150H	N. E. Sams/Cranfield	
G-AVVO	Avro 652A Anson 19 (VL348) ★	Newark Air Museum	
G-AVVX	Cessna F.150H	Hatfield Flying Club	
G-AVWA	PA-28 Cherokee 140	M. Jarrett	
G-AVWD	PA-28 Cherokee 140	M. P. Briggs	
G-AVWE	PA-28 Cherokee 140	W. C. C. Meyer (stored)/Biggin Hill	
G-AVWG	PA-28 Cherokee 140	Bencray Ltd/Blackpool	
G-AVWH	PA-28 Cherokee 140	G-OHOG Flying Ltd	
G-AVWI	PA-28 Cherokee 140	L. M. Veitch	
G-AVWJ	PA-28 Cherokee 140	M. J. Steer/Biggin Hill	
G-AVWL	PA-28 Cherokee 140	P. J. Pratt/Dunkeswell	
G-AVWM	PA-28 Cherokee 140	P. E. Preston & ptnrs/Southend	
G-AVWN	PA-28R Cherokee Arrow 180	Vawn Air Ltd/Jersey	
G-AVWO	PA-28R Cherokee Arrow 180	P. D. Cahill/Biggin Hill	
G-AVWR	PA-28R Cherokee Arrow 180	S. J. French & ptnrs/Exeter	
G-AVWT	PA-28R Cherokee Arrow 180	Cloud Base Aviation Group	
G-AVWU	PA-28R Cherokee Arrow 180	Arrow Flyers Ltd	
G-AVWV	PA-28R Cherokee Arrow 180	Strathtay Flying Group	
G-AVWY	Fournier RF-4D	B. Houghton	
G-AVXA	PA-25 Pawnee 235	S. Wales Gliding Club Ltd	
G-AVXC	Slingsby T.66 Nipper 3	D. S. T. Eggleton	
G-AVXD	Slingsby T.66 Nipper 3	D. A. Davidson	
G-AVXF	PA-28R Cherokee Arrow 180	JDR Arrow Group	
G-AVXI	H.S.748 Srs 2A	Civil Aviation Authority/Teesside	
G-AVXJ	H.S.748 Srs 2A	Civil Aviation Authority/Teesside	
G-AVXW	D.62B Condor	A. J. Cooper/Rochester	
G-AVXY	Auster AOP.9 (XK417) ★	R. Windley (on rebuild)/Leicester	
G-AVXZ	PA-28 Cherokee 140 ★	ATC Hayle (instructional airframe)	
G-AVYB	H.S.121 Trident 1E-140 ★	SAS training airframe/Hereford	
G-AVYE	H.S.121 Trident 1E-140 ★	Test airframe/Hatfield	
G-AVYK	A.61 Terrier 3	A. R. Wright/Booker	
G-AVYL	PA-28 Cherokee 180	Cherokee G-AVYL Flying Group	
G-AVYM	PA-28 Cherokee 180	Carlisle Aviation (1985) Ltd/Crosby	
G-AVYP	PA-28 Cherokee 140	T. D. Reid (Braids) Ltd/Newtownards	

Notes	Reg.	Type	Owner or Operator
	G-AVYR	PA-28 Cherokee 140	D.R. Flying Club Ltd/Staverton
	G-AVYS	PA-28R Cherokee Arrow 180	D. H. Saunders/Ipswich
	G-AVYT	PA-28R Cherokee Arrow 180	E. J. Booth & B. D. Tipler
	G-AVYV	Jodel D.120	A. J. Sephton
	G-AVZB	Aero Z-37 Cmelak ★	Science Museum/Wroughton
	G-AVZI	Bo 208C Junior	C. F. Rogers
	G-AVZM	B.121 Pup 1	ARAZ Group/Elstree
	G-AVZN	B.121 Pup 1	E. M. Lewis & C. A. Homewood
	G-AVZO	B.121 Pup 1 ★	Thameside Aviation Museum/E. Tilbury
	G-AVZP	B.121 Pup 1	T. A. White
	G-AVZR	PA-28 Cherokee 180	Lincoln Aero Club Ltd/Sturgate
	G-AVZU	Cessna F.150H	R. D. & E. Forster/Swanton Morley
	G-AVZV	Cessna F.172H	E. M. & D. S. Lightbown
	G-AVZW	EAA Biplane Model P	R. G. Maidment & G. R. Edmundson/Goodwood
	G-AVZX	M.S.880B Rallye Club	A. F. K. Horne
	G-AWAA	M.S.880B Rallye Club	P. A. Cairns/Dunkeswell
	G-AWAC	GY-80 Horizon 180	R. D. Harper
	G-AWAD	Beech 95-D55 Baron	M. Gardner
	G-AWAH	Beech 95-D55 Baron	B. J. S. Grey
	G-AWAJ	Beech 95-D55 Baron	Standard Hose Ltd/Leeds
	G-AWAT	D.62B Condor	Tarwood Ltd/Redhill
	G-AWAU	Vickers F.B.27A Vimy (replica) (F8614) ★	Bomber Command Museum/Hendon
	G-AWAW	Cessna F.150F ★	Science Museum/S. Kensington
	G-AWAZ	PA-28R Cherokee Arrow 180	A. & A. A. Buckley
	G-AWBA	PA-28R Cherokee Arrow 180	March Flying Group/Stapleford
	G-AWBB	PA-28R Cherokee Arrow 180	M. D. Parker & J. Lowe
	G-AWBC	PA-28R Cherokee Arrow 180	Anglo Aviation (UK) Ltd
	G-AWBE	PA-28 Cherokee 140	B. E. Boyle
	G-AWBH	PA-28 Cherokee 140	R. C. A. Mackworth
	G-AWBJ	Fournier RF-4D	J. M. Adams
	G-AWBL	BAC One-Eleven 416EK	Maersk Air Ltd/British Airways/Birmingham
	G-AWBM	D.31 Turbulent	A. D. Pratt
	G-AWBN	PA-30 Twin Comanche 160B	Stourfield Investments Ltd/Jersey
	G-AWBP	Cessna 182L Skylane	Xaxanaka Aviation Ltd/Thruxton
	G-AWBS	PA-28 Cherokee 140	P. Baker/White Waltham
	G-AWBT	PA-30 Twin Comanche 160B ★	Instructional airframe/Cranfield
	G-AWBU	Morane-Saulnier N (replica) (MS.824)	Personal Plane Services Ltd/Booker
	G-AWBV	Cessna 182L Skylane	Tindon Ltd
	G-AWBW	Cessna F.172H ★	Brunel Technical College/Bristol
	G-AWBX	Cessna F.150H	D. F. Ranger
	G-AWCM	Cessna F.150H	Cheshire Air Training School (Merseyside) Ltd/Liverpool
	G-AWCN	Cessna FR.172E	Cubair Ltd/Redhill
	G-AWCP	Cessna F.150H (tailwheel)	C. E. Mason/Shobdon
	G-AWDA	Slingsby T.66 Nipper 3	J. A. Cheesebrough
	G-AWDD	Slingsby T.66 Nipper 3	P. F. J. Wells
	G-AWDI	PA-23 Aztec 250C	(stored)
	G-AWDO	D.31 Turbulent	R. N. Crosland
	G-AWDP	PA-28 Cherokee 180	B. H. & P. M. Illston/Shipdham
	G-AWDR	Cessna FR.172E	B. A. Wallace
	G-AWDU	Brantly B.2B	G. E. J. Redwood
	G-AWEF	SNCAN Stampe SV-4B	Tiger Club (1990) Ltd/Headcorn
	G-AWEI	D.62B Condor	M. J. Steer
	G-AWEL	Fournier RF-4D	A. B. Clymo/Halfpenny Green
	G-AWEM	Fournier RF-4D	B. J. Griffin/Wickenby
	G-AWEP	Ord-Hume JB-01 Minicab	J. A. Stewart & S. N. Askey
	G-AWER	PA-23 Aztec 250C	H. McC. Clarke/Ronaldsway
	G-AWET	PA-28 Cherokee 180	Broadland Flying Group Ltd/ Shipdham
	G-AWEV	PA-28 Cherokee 140	Norflight Ltd
	G-AWEX	PA-28 Cherokee 140	R. Badham
	G-AWEZ	PA-28R Cherokee Arrow 180	T. R. Leighton & ptnrs
	G-AWFB	PA-28R Cherokee Arrow 180	Luke Aviation Ltd/Bristol
	G-AWFC	PA-28R Cherokee Arrow 180	K. A. Goodchild/Southend
	G-AWFD	PA-28R Cherokee Arrow 180	D. J. Hill
	G-AWFF	Cessna F.150H	Shobdon Aircraft Maintenance
	G-AWFJ	PA-28R Cherokee Arrow 180	K. Barr
	G-AWFK	PA-28R Cherokee Arrow 180	Steepletone Products Ltd
	G-AWFN	D.62B Condor	R. James
	G-AWFO	D.62B Condor	T. A. Major

Reg.	Type	Owner or Operator	Notes
G-AWFP	D.62B Condor	Blackbushe Flying Club	
G-AWFR	D.31 Turbulent	J. R. Froud	
G-AWFT	Jodel D.9 Bebe	W. H. Cole	
G-AWFW	Jodel D.117	F. H. Greenwell	
G-AWFZ	Beech A23 Musketeer	R. Sweet & B D. Corbett	
G-AWGA	A.109 Airedale ★	stored/Sevenoaks	
G-AWGD	Cessna F.172H	Aero Marine Technology Ltd	
G-AWGJ	Cessna F.172H	J. & C. J. Freeman/Headcorn	
G-AWGK	Cessna F.150H	G. R. Brown/Shoreham	
G-AWGM	Arkle Kittiwake 2	M. K. Field	
G-AWGN	Fournier RF-4D	R. H. Ashforth/Staverton	
G-AWGP	Cessna T.210H	S. Harcourt/Elstree	
G-AWGR	Cessna F.172H	P. A. Hallam	
G-AWGZ	Taylor JT.1 Monoplane	R. L. Sambell	
G-AWHB	C.A.S.A. 2-111D (6J+PR) ★	Aces High Ltd/North Weald	
G-AWHV	Rollason Beta B.2A	J. W. Hart	
G-AWHX	Rollason Beta B.2	S. G. Jones	
G-AWHY	Falconar F.11-3	J. R. Riley-Gale (G-BDPB)	
G-AWIF	Brookland Mosquito 2	—/Husbands Bosworth	
G-AWII	V.S.349 Spitfire VC (AR501)	Shuttleworth Collection/O. Warden	
G-AWIO	Brantly B.2B	M. J. Owen (G-OBPG)	
G-AWIP	Luton LA-4A Minor	J. Houghton	
G-AWIR	Midget Mustang	K. E. Sword/Leicester	
G-AWIT	PA-28 Cherokee 180	Manco Ltd	
G-AWIV	Airmark TSR.3	D. J. & F. M. Nunn	
G-AWIW	SNCAN Stampe SV-4B	R. E. Mitchell	
G-AWIY	PA-23 Aztec 250C	B. Anderson/Newtownards	
G-AWJE	Slingsby T.66 Nipper 3	T. Mosedale	
G-AWJF	Slingsby T.66 Nipper 3	R. Wilcock/Shoreham	
G-AWJI	M.S.880B Rallye Club	D. V. Tyler/Southend	
G-AWJV	D.H.98 Mosquito TT Mk 35 (TA634) ★	Mosquito Aircraft Museum	
G-AWJX	Zlin Z.526 Akrobat	Aerobatics International Ltd	
G-AWJY	Zlin Z.526 Akrobat	Elco Manufacturing Co	
G-AWKB	M.J.5 Sirocco F2/39	G. D. Claxton	
G-AWKD	PA-17 Vagabond	A. T. & M. R. Dowie/ White Waltham	
G-AWKM	B.121 Pup 1	D. M. G. Jenkins/Swansea	
G-AWKO	B.121 Pup 1	Bustard Flying Club Ltd	
G-AWKP	Jodel DR.253	D. A. Hood	
G-AWKT	M.S.880B Rallye Club	J. Strain/Portadown	
G-AWKX	Beech A65 Queen Air ★	(Instructional airframe)/Shoreham	
G-AWLA	Cessna F.150H	Royal Artillery Aero Club Ltd/Middle Wallop	
G-AWLE	Cessna F.172H	H. Mendelssohn & H. I. Shott	
G-AWLF	Cessna F.172H	Gannet Aviation Ltd/Belfast	
G-AWLG	SIPA 903	S. W. Markham	
G-AWLI	PA-22 Tri-Pacer 150	J. S. Lewery/Shoreham	
G-AWLO	Boeing Stearman E.75	N. D. Pickard/Shoreham	
G-AWLP	Mooney M.20F	Petratek Ltd	
G-AWLR	Slingsby T.66 Nipper 3	C. F. O'Neill	
G-AWLS	Slingsby T.66 Nipper 3	Stapleford Nipper Group	
G-AWLZ	Fournier RF-4D	E. V. Goodwin & C. R. Williamson	
G-AWMD	Jodel D.11	G. E. Valler	
G-AWMF	PA-18 Super Cub 150 (modified)	Booker Gliding Club Ltd	
G-AWMI	Glos-Airtourer 115	Airtourer Group 86/Cardiff	
G-AWMK	AB-206B JetRanger	Bristow Helicopters Ltd	
G-AWMM	M.S.893A Rallye Commodore 180	D. P. & S. White	
G-AWMN	Luton LA-4A Minor	C. F. O'Neill	
G-AWMP	Cessna F.172H	R. J. D. Blois	
G-AWMR	D.31 Turbulent	C. F. Kennedy	
G-AWMT	Cessna F.150H	R. V. Grocott/Sleap	
G-AWMZ	Cessna F.172H ★	Parachute jump trainer/Cark	
G-AWNA	Boeing 747-136	British Airways Colliford Lake	
G-AWNB	Boeing 747-136	British Airways Llangorse Lake	
G-AWNC	Boeing 747-136	British Airways Lake Windermere	
G-AWNE	Boeing 747-136	British Airways Derwent Water	
G-AWNF	Boeing 747-136	British Airways Blagdon Water	
G-AWNG	Boeing 747-136	British Airways Rutland Water	
G-AWNH	Boeing 747-136	British Airways Devoke Water	
G-AWNJ	Boeing 747-136	British Airways Bassenthwaite Lake	
G-AWNL	Boeing 747-136	British Airways Ennerdale Water	
G-AWNM	Boeing 747-136	British Airways Ullswater	
G-AWNN	Boeing 747-136	British Airways Loweswater	
G-AWNO	Boeing 747-136	British Airways Grafham Water	

Notes	Reg.	Type	Owner or Operator
	G-AWNP	Boeing 747-136	British Airways *Hanningfield Water*
	G-AWNT	BN-2A Islander	Aerofilms Ltd/Elstree
	G-AWOA	M.S.880B Rallye Club	M. Craven & ptnrs/Barton
	G-AWOE	Aero Commander 680E	J. M. Houlder/Elstree
	G-AWOF	PA-15 Vagabond	J. K. Davies
	G-AWOH	PA-17 Vagabond	The High Flatts Flying Group
	G-AWOT	Cessna F.150H	J. M. Montgomerie & J. Ferguson
	G-AWOU	Cessna 170B	S. Billington/Denham
	G-AWOX	W.S.58 Wessex 60 ★	International Helicopter Museum/ Weston-s-Mare
	G-AWPH	P.56 Provost T.1	J. A. D. Bradshaw
	G-AWPJ	Cessna F.150H	W. J. Greenfield
	G-AWPN	Shield Xyla	M. J. Herlihy
	G-AWPP	Cessna F.150H	Croxley Flying Group/Denham
	G-AWPS	PA-28 Cherokee 140	K. J. Steele & D. J. Hewitt
	G-AWPU	Cessna F.150J	Lancashire Aero Club/Barton
	G-AWPW	PA-12 Super Cruiser	J. E. Davies/Sandown
	G-AWPY	Bensen B.8M	J. Jordan
	G-AWPZ	Andreasson BA-4B	J. M. Vening
	G-AWRK	Cessna F.150J	Southern Strut Flying Group/Shoreham
	G-AWRL	Cessna F.172H	B. Welsh
	G-AWRS	Avro 19 Srs. 2 ★	N. E. Aircraft Museum
	G-AWRY	P.56 Provost T.1 (XF836)	Slymar Aviation & Services Ltd
	G-AWRZ	Bell 47G-5	Hammond Aerial Spraying Ltd
	G-AWSA	Avro 652A Anson 19 (VL349) ★	Norfolk & Suffolk Aviation Museum
	G-AWSD	Cessna F.150J	British Skysports *(stored)*
	G-AWSL	PA-28 Cherokee 180D	Fascia Ltd/Southend
	G-AWSM	PA-28 Cherokee 235	S. J. Green
	G-AWSN	D.62B Condor	J. Leader
	G-AWSP	D.62B Condor	R. Q. & A. S. Bond/Wellesbourne
	G-AWSS	D.62C Condor	G. Bruce/Inverness
	G-AWST	D.62B Condor	P. L. Clements
	G-AWSV	Skeeter 12 (XM553)	Maj. M. Somerton-Rayner/Middle Wallop
	G-AWSW	D.5/180 Husky (XW635)	RAF College Flying Club/Cranwell
	G-AWTA	Cessna E.310N	Heliscott Ltd
	G-AWTJ	Cessna F.150J	B. L. Wratten & D. G. Williams
	G-AWTL	PA-28 Cherokee 180D	D. M. Bailey
	G-AWTS	Beech A.23 Musketeer	M. Gardner
	G-AWTV	Beech A.23 Musketeer	A. Johnston/Blackbushe
	G-AWTW	Beech 95-B55 Baron	R. W. Davies/Staverton
	G-AWTX	Cessna F.150J	R. D. & E. Forster
	G-AWUB	GY-201 Minicab	H. P. Burrill
	G-AWUE	Jodel DR.1050	S. Bichan
	G-AWUG	Cessna F.150H	J. Easson/Edinburgh
	G-AWUH	Cessna F.150H	H. D. Hounsell
	G-AWUJ	Cessna F.150H	W. Lawton/Doncaster
	G-AWUL	Cessna F.150H	Alderquest Ltd
	G-AWUN	Cessna F.150H	D. King
	G-AWUO	Cessna F.150H	Air Fenland Ltd
	G-AWUS	Cessna F.150J	Recreational Flying Centre (Popham) Ltd
	G-AWUT	Cessna F.150J	S. J. Black/Leeds
	G-AWUU	Cessna F.150J	D. G. Burden
	G-AWUW	Cessna F.172H	B. Stewart
	G-AWUX	Cessna F.172H	D. K. Brian & ptrs
	G-AWUZ	Cessna F.172H	G. F. Burling
	G-AWVA	Cessna F.172H	Barton Air Ltd
	G-AWVB	Jodel D.117	Gower Taildraggers/Swansea
	G-AWVC	B.121 Pup 1	J. H. Marshall & J. J. West
	G-AWVE	Jodel DR.1050/M1	E. A. Taylor/Southend
	G-AWVF	P.56 Provost T.1 (XF877)	Hunter Wing Ltd/Bournemouth
	G-AWVG	AESL Airtourer T.2	C. J. Schofield
	G-AWVN	Aeronca 7AC Champion	W. S. & W. A. Bowker/Rush Green
	G-AWVZ	Jodel D.112	D. C. Stokes
	G-AWWE	B.121 Pup 2	J. M. Randle/Coventry
	G-AWWF	B.121 Pup 1	R. B. Sandell
	G-AWWI	Jodel D.117	J. C. Hatton
	G-AWWM	GY-201 Minicab	J. S. Brayshaw
	G-AWWN	Jodel DR.1051	T. W. M. Beck & ptnrs
	G-AWWO	Jodel DR.1050	Whiskey Oscar Group/Barton
	G-AWWP	Aerosport Woody Pusher III	M. S. Bird & R. D. Bird
	G-AWWT	D.31 Turbulent	P. J. Simpson
	G-AWWU	Cessna FR.172F	Westward Airways (Lands End) Ltd
	G-AWWW	Cessna 401	Air Charter & Travel Ltd

Reg.	Type	Owner or Operator	Notes
G-AWXA	Cessna 182M	P. Cannon	
G-AWXR	PA-28 Cherokee 180D	R. Farrer	
G-AWXS	PA-28 Cherokee 180D	Rayhenro Flying Group/Shobdon	
G-AWXU	Cessna F.150J	Howe Aviation Group	
G-AWXY	M.S.885 Super Rallye	Sussex Spraying Services Ltd/Shoreham	
G-AWXZ	SNCAN Stampe SV-4C	Personal Plane Services Ltd/Booker	
G-AWYB	Cessna FR.172F	C. W. Larkin/Southend	
G-AWYF	G.159 Gulfstream 1	Ford Motor Co Ltd/Stansted	
G-AWYJ	B.121 Pup 2	H. C. Taylor	
G-AWYL	Jodel DR.253B	M. J. McRobert	
G-AWYO	B.121 Pup 1	B. R. C. Wild/Popham	
G-AWYS	BAC One-Eleven 501EX	Maersk Air/British Airways/Birmingham	
G-AWYX	M.S.880B Rallye Club	J. M. L. Edwards/Exeter	
G-AWYY	T.57 Camel replica (B6401) ★	F.A.A. Museum/Yeovilton	
G-AWZE	H.S.121 Trident 3B ★	*Instructional airframe*/Heathrow	
G-AWZI	H.S.121 Trident 3B ★	Surrey Fire Brigade (*instructional airframe*)/ Reigate	
G-AWZJ	H.S.121 Trident 3B ★	British Airports Authority/Prestwick	
G-AWZK	H.S.121 Trident 3B ★	*Ground trainer*/Heathrow	
G-AWZM	H.S.121 Trident 3B ★	Science Museum/Wroughton	
G-AWZN	H.S.121 Trident 3B ★	Cranfield	
G-AWZO	H.S.121 Trident 3B ★	British Aerospace PLC/Hatfield	
G-AWZP	H.S.121 Trident 3B ★	Greater Manchester Museum of Science & Technology (*nose only*)	
G-AWZR	H.S.121 Trident 3B ★	CAA Fire School/Teesside	
G-AWZU	H.S.121 Trident 3B ★	BAA Airport Fire Service/Stansted	
G-AWZX	H.S.121 Trident 3B ★	BAA Airport Fire Services/Gatwick	
G-AWZZ	H.S.121 Trident 3B ★	Airport Fire Services/Birmingham	
G-AXAB	PA-28 Cherokee 140	Bencray Ltd/Blackpool	
G-AXAK	M.S.880B Rallye Club	R. L. & C. Stewart	
G-AXAN	D.H.82A Tiger Moth (EM720)	M. E. Carrell	
G-AXAO	Omega 56 balloon	P. D. Furlong	
G-AXAS	Wallis WA-116T	K. H. Wallis (G-AVDH)	
G-AXAT	Jodel D.117A	P. S. Wilkinson	
G-AXAU	PA-30 Twin Comanche 160C	Bartcourt Ltd (*derelict*)/Bournemouth	
G-AXAX	PA-23 Aztec 250D	Air Navigation & Trading Ltd/Blackpool	
G-AXBF	D.5/180 Husky	C. H. Barnes	
G-AXBH	Cessna F.172H	R. A. C. Hoppenbrouwers	
G-AXBJ	Cessna F.172H	Bravo Juliet Group/Leicester	
G-AXBW	D.H.82A Tiger Moth (T5879)	R. Venning	
G-AXBZ	D.H.82A Tiger Moth	D. H. McWhir	
G-AXCA	PA-28R Cherokee Arrow 200	M. D. & J. E. M. Williams	
G-AXCG	Jodel D.117	Charlie Golf Group/Andrewsfield	
G-AXCI	Bensen B.8M ★	Loughborough & Leicester Aircraft Museum	
G-AXCL	M.S.880B Rallye Club	P. P. Loucas/Andrewsfield	
G-AXCM	M.S.880B Rallye Club	J. R. Hammett	
G-AXCN	M.S.880B Rallye Club	J. E. Compton	
G-AXCX	B.121 Pup 2	L. A. Pink	
G-AXCY	Jodel D.117	C. L. Betts & ptnrs/Shoreham	
G-AXDB	Piper J-3C-65 Cub	J. R. Wraight	
G-AXDC	PA-23 Aztec 250D	N. J. Lilley/Bodmin	
G-AXDI	Cessna F.172H	M. F. & J. R. Leusby/Conington	
G-AXDK	Jodel DR.315	Delta Kilo Flying Group/Sywell	
G-AXDM	H.S.125 Srs 400B	GEC Ferranti Defence Systems Ltd/ Edinburgh	
G-AXDN	BAC-Sud Concorde 01 ★	Duxford Aviation Soc	
G-AXDU	B.121 Pup 2	J. R. Clegg	
G-AXDV	B.121 Pup 1	C. N. G. Hobbs & J. J. Teagle	
G-AXDW	B.121 Pup 1	Cranfield Institute of Technology	
G-AXDY	Falconar F-11	J. Nunn	
G-AXDZ	Cassutt Racer Srs IIIM	A. Chadwick/Little Staughton	
G-AXEB	Cassutt Racer Srs IIIM	G. E. Horder/Redhill	
G-AXED	PA-25 Pawnee 235	Wolds Gliding Club Ltd/Pocklington	
G-AXEH	B.121 Pup ★	Museum of Flight/E. Fortune	
G-AXEI	Ward Gnome ★	Lincolnshire Aviation Museum	
G-AXEO	Scheibe SF.25B Falke	R. Cassidy & W. P. Stephen	
G-AXEV	B.121 Pup 2	D. S. Russell	
G-AXFG	Cessna 337D	Cumbria Constabulary/Carlisle	
G-AXFH	D.H.114 Heron 1B/C	(*stored*)/Southend	
G-AXFN	Jodel D.119	M. C. Lee & A. M. Westley	
G-AXGC	M.S.880B Rallye Club	Ian Richard Transport Services Ltd	

Notes	Reg.	Type	Owner or Operator
	G-AXGE	M.S.880B Rallye Club	R. P. Loxton
	G-AXGG	Cessna F.150J	G. L. Carpenter & S. C. May
	G-AXGP	Piper J-3C-65 Cub	W. K. Butler
	G-AXGR	Luton LA-4A Minor	B. Thomas
	G-AXGS	D.62B Condor	B. W. Haston
	G-AXGV	D.62B Condor	R. J. Wrixon
	G-AXGZ	D.62B Condor	J. Evans
	G-AXHA	Cessna 337A	G. Evans
	G-AXHC	SNCAN Stampe SV-4C	D. L. Webley
	G-AXHE	BN-2A Islander	NW Parachute Centre Ltd/Cark
	G-AXHI	M.S.880B Rallye Club	J. M. Whittard (stored)/Sandown
	G-AXHO	B.121 Pup 2	L. W. Grundy/Stapleford
	G-AXHP	Piper J-3C-65 Cub	P. J. Acreman
	G-AXHR	Piper J-3C-65 Cub (329601)	G-AXHR Cub Group
	G-AXHS	M.S.880B Rallye Club	B. & A. Swales
	G-AXHT	M.S.880B Rallye Club	D. E. Guck
	G-AXHV	Jodel D.117A	D. M. Cashmore
	G-AXHX	M.S.892A Rallye Commodore	D. W. Weever
	G-AXIA	B.121 Pup 1	Cranfield Institute of Technology
	G-AXIE	B.121 Pup 2	G. A. Ponsford/Goodwood
	G-AXIF	B.121 Pup 2	T. G. Hiscock & R. G. Knapp
	G-AXIG	B.125 Bulldog 104	George House (Holdings) Ltd
	G-AXIO	PA-28 Cherokee 140B	White Waltham Airfield Ltd
	G-AXIR	PA-28 Cherokee 140B	J. E. T. Lock
	G-AXIT	M.S.893A Rallye Commodore 180	T. J. Price
	G-AXIW	Scheibe SF.25B Falke	M. B. Hill
	G-AXIX	Glos-Airtourer 150	J. C. Wood
	G-AXIY	Bird Gyrocopter ★	Motor Museum/Chudleigh
	G-AXJB	Omega 84 balloon	Southern Balloon Group
	G-AXJH	B.121 Pup 2	J. S. Chillingworth
	G-AXJI	B.121 Pup 2	Cole Aviation Ltd/Southend
	G-AXJJ	B.121 Pup 2	Bumpf Group
	G-AXJN	B.121 Pup 2	D. M. Jenkins & D. F. Jenvey/Shoreham
	G-AXJO	B.121 Pup 2	J. A. D. Bradshaw
	G-AXJR	Scheibe SF.25B Falke	D. R. Chatterton
	G-AXJV	PA-28 Cherokee 140B	Mona Aviation Ltd
	G-AXJX	PA-28 Cherokee 140B	Patrolwatch Ltd
	G-AXJY	Cessna U-206D	B. W. Wells
	G-AXKH	Luton LA-4A Minor	M. E. Vaisey
	G-AXKI	Jodel D.9 Bebe	M. R. M. Welch
	G-AXKJ	Jodel D.9 Bebe	C. C. Gordon & R. M. Lee
	G-AXKO	Westland-Bell 47G-4A	Alan Mann Helicopters Ltd/Fairoaks
	G-AXKR	Westland Bell 47G-4A	F. C. Owen
	G-AXKS	Westland-Bell 47G-4A ★	Museum of Army Flying/Middle Wallop
	G-AXKW	Westland-Bell 47G-4A	A. C. Watson
	G-AXKX	Westland Bell 47G-4A	Alan Mann Helicopters Ltd/Fairoaks
	G-AXKY	Westland Bell 47G-4A	A. M. Parkes
	G-AXLG	Cessna 310K	Smiths (Outdrives) Ltd
	G-AXLI	Slingsby T.66 Nipper 3	N. J. Arthur/Finmere
	G-AXLS	Jodel DR.105A	E. Gee/Southampton
	G-AXLZ	PA-18 Super Cub 95	J. C. Quantrell/Shipdham
	G-AXMA	PA-24 Comanche 180	Tegrel Products Ltd/Newcastle
	G-AXMB	Slingsby T.7 Motor Cadet 2	I. G. Smith/Langar
	G-AXMD	Omega O-56 balloon ★	British Balloon Museum
	G-AXMN	J/5B Autocar	A. Phillips
	G-AXMP	PA-28 Cherokee 180	T. M. P. Tomsett
	G-AXMW	B.121 Pup 1	DJP Engineering (Knebworth) Ltd
	G-AXMX	B.121 Pup 2	Susan A. Jones/Cannes
	G-AXNJ	Wassmer Jodel D.120	Clive Flying Group/Sleap
	G-AXNL	B.121 Pup 1	Northamptonshire School of Flying Ltd/ Sywell
	G-AXNM	B.121 Pup 1	J. & F. E. Green
	G-AXNN	B.121 Pup 2	Gabrielle Aviation Ltd/Shoreham
	G-AXNP	B.121 Pup 2	J. W. Ellis
	G-AXNR	B.121 Pup 2	P. A. Jackson
	G-AXNS	B.121 Pup 2	Derwent Aero/Netherthorpe
	G-AXNW	SNCAN Stampe SV-4C	C. S. Grace
	G-AXNX	Cessna 182M	Cast High Ltd
	G-AXNZ	Pitts S.1C Special	W. A. Jordan
	G-AXOG	PA-E23 Aztec 250D	R. W. Diggens/Denham
	G-AXOH	M.S.894 Rallye Minerva	Bristol Cars Ltd/White Waltham
	G-AXOI	Jodel D.9 Bebe	D. G. Garner
	G-AXOJ	B.121 Pup 2	Pup Flying Group

Reg.	Type	Owner or Operator	Notes
G-AXOL	Currie Wot	R. G. Boyes	
G-AXOR	PA-28 Cherokee 180D	Oscar Romeo Aviation Ltd	
G-AXOS	M.S.894A Rallye Minerva	D. R. C. Bell	
G-AXOT	M.S.893 Rallye Commodore 180	P. Evans & J. C. Graves	
G-AXOZ	B.121 Pup 1	R. J. Ogborn	
G-AXPB	B.121 Pup 1	M. J. K. Seary	
G-AXPF	Cessna F.150K	D. R. Marks/Denham	
G-AXPG	Mignet HM-293	W. H. Cole (*stored*)	
G-AXPM	B.121 Pup 1	P. A. Teichman	
G-AXPN	B.121 Pup 2	D. J. Elbourn & ptnrs	
G-AXPZ	Campbell Cricket	W. R. Partridge	
G-AXRC	Campbell Cricket	K. W. Hayr	
G-AXRL	PA-28 Cherokee 160	T. W. Clark/Headcorn	
G-AXRO	PA-30 Twin Comanche 160C	S. M. Bogdiukiewicz/Staverton	
G-AXRR	Auster AOP.9 (XR241)	The Aircraft Restoration Co/Duxford	
G-AXRT	Cessna FA.150K (tailwheel)	J. K. Horne	
G-AXRU	Cessna FA.150K	Arrival Enterprises Ltd	
G-AXSC	B.121 Pup 1	T. R. Golding & C. Spencer	
G-AXSD	B.121 Pup 1	A. C. Townend	
G-AXSF	Nash Petrel	Nash Aircraft Ltd/Lasham	
G-AXSG	PA-28 Cherokee 180	J. Montgomery	
G-AXSI	Cessna F.172H	R. I. Chantry & A. J. G. Davis (G-SNIP)	
G-AXSM	Jodel DR.1051	K. D. Doyle	
G-AXSR	Brantly B.2B	S. Lee (G-ROOF)	
G-AXSV	Jodel DR.340	Leonard F. Jollye Ltd	
G-AXSW	Cessna FA.150K	Furness Aviation Ltd/Walney Island	
G-AXSZ	PA-28 Cherokee 140B	Kilo Foxtrot Group/Sandown	
G-AXTA	PA-28 Cherokee 140B	G-AXTA Syndicate	
G-AXTC	PA-28 Cherokee 140B	B. Mellor & J. Hutchinson	
G-AXTD	PA-28 Cherokee 140B	N. Robinson	
G-AXTH	PA-28 Cherokee 140B	W. London Aero Services Ltd/ White Waltham	
G-AXTI	PA-28 Cherokee 140B	London Transport (CRS) Sports Association Flying Club/Fairoaks	
G-AXTJ	PA-28 Cherokee 140B	A. P. Merrifield/Stapleford	
G-AXTL	PA-28 Cherokee 140B	Jenrick Flying Group	
G-AXTO	PA-24 Comanche 260	J. L. Wright	
G-AXTP	PA-28 Cherokee 180	E. R. Moore/Elstree	
G-AXTX	Jodel D.112	T. J. Price	
G-AXTZ	B.121 Pup 1	R. S. & A. D. Kent	
G-AXUA	B.121 Pup 1	F. R. Blennerhassett & ptnrs	
G-AXUB	BN-2A Islander	Headcorn Parachute Club	
G-AXUC	PA-12 Super Cruiser	J. J. Bunton	
G-AXUE	Jodel DR.105A	L. Lewis	
G-AXUF	Cessna FA.150K	A. D. McLeod	
G-AXUI	H.P.137 Jetstream 1	Cranfield Institute of Technology	
G-AXUJ	J/1 Autocrat	R. G. Earp & J. W. H. Lee/Sibson	
G-AXUK	Jodel DR.1050	North Oxford Flying Co	
G-AXUM	H.P.137 Jetstream 1	Cranfield Institute of Technology	
G-AXUW	Cessna FA.150K	Coventry Air Training School	
G-AXVB	Cessna F.172H	C. Gabbitas/Staverton	
G-AXVK	Campbell Cricket	L. W. Harding	
G-AXVM	Campbell Cricket	D. M. Organ	
G-AXVN	McCandless M.4	W. R. Partridge	
G-AXVS	Jodel DR.1050	D. T. J. Harwood	
G-AXVV	Piper J-3C-65 Cub	J. D. MacCarthy	
G-AXVW	Cessna F.150K	F. & H. (Aircraft) Ltd/Sibson	
G-AXWA	Auster AOP.9 (XN437)	M. L. & C. M. Edwards/Biggin Hill	
G-AXWB	Omega 65 balloon	A. Robinson & M. J. Moore *Ezekiel*	
G-AXWH	BN-2A Islander	Midland Parachute Centre Ltd	
G-AXWR	BN-2A Islander	Isles of Scilly Skybus Ltd/St Just	
G-AXWT	Jodel D.11	R. C. Owen	
G-AXWV	Jodel DR.253	J. R. D. Bygraves/O. Warden	
G-AXWZ	PA-28R Cherokee Arrow 200	E. J. M. Kroes	
G-AXXV	D.H.82A Tiger Moth (DE992)	C. N. Wookey & S. G. Jones	
G-AXXW	Jodel D.117	A. Szep/Netherthorpe	
G-AXYK	Taylor JT.1 Monoplane	T. W. M. Beck & M. J. Smith	
G-AXYY	WHE Airbuggy	R. A. A. Chiles	
G-AXYZ	WHE Airbuggy	W. B. Lumb	
G-AXZA	WHE Airbuggy	C. Verlaan/Holland	
G-AXZB	WHE Airbuggy	D. R. C. Pugh	
G-AXZD	PA-28 Cherokee 180E	M. D. & V. A. Callaghan	
G-AXZF	PA-28 Cherokee 180E	E. P. C. & W. R. Rabson/Southampton	

Notes	Reg.	Type	Owner or Operator
	G-AXZK	BN-2A Islander	Factultra Ltd
	G-AXZM	Slingsby T.66 Nipper 3	G. R. Harlow
	G-AXZO	Cessna 180	Cessna 180 Group
	G-AXZP	PA-E23 Aztec 250D	D. J. Skidmore
	G-AXZT	Jodel D.117	N. Batty
	G-AXZU	Cessna 182N	S. E. Bradney
	G-AYAA	PA-28 Cherokee 180E	Alpha-Alpha Ltd
	G-AYAB	PA-28 Cherokee 180E	J. A. & J. C. Cunningham
	G-AYAC	PA-28R Cherokee Arrow 200	Fersfield Flying Group
	G-AYAJ	Cameron O-84 balloon	E. T. Hall
	G-AYAL	Omega 56 balloon ★	British Balloon Museum
	G-AYAN	Slingsby Motor Cadet III	A. Nelson
	G-AYAR	PA-28 Cherokee 180E	D. M. Markscheffel/Stapleford
	G-AYAT	PA-28 Cherokee 180E	AYAT Flying Group
	G-AYAU	PA-28 Cherokee 180E	Tiarco Ltd
	G-AYAV	PA-28 Cherokee 180E	Tee Tee Aviation Ltd/Biggin Hill
	G-AYAW	PA-28 Cherokee 180E	R. C. Pendle & M. J. Rose
	G-AYBD	Cessna F.150K	F. A. Fox/Southampton
	G-AYBG	Scheibe SF.25B Falke	D. J. Rickman
	G-AYBO	PA-23 Aztec 250D	Twinguard Aviation Ltd/Elstree
	G-AYBP	Jodel D.112	G-AYBP Group
	G-AYBR	Jodel D.112	D. H. Nourish
	G-AYBV	Chasle YC-12 Tourbillon	B. A. Mills
	G-AYCC	Campbell Cricket	D. J. M. Charity
	G-AYCE	CP.301C Emeraude	R. A. Austin/Bodmin
	G-AYCF	Cessna FA.150K	E. J. Atkins/Popham
	G-AYCG	SNCAN Stampe SV-4C	N. Bignall/Booker
	G-AYCJ	Cessna TP.206D	H. O. Holm/Bournemouth
	G-AYCN	Piper J-3C-65 Cub	W. R. & B. M. Young
	G-AYCO	CEA DR.360	G. T. Birks & T. M. Curry/Booker
	G-AYCP	Jodel D.112	D. J. Nunn
	G-AYCT	Cessna F.172H	Charlie Tango Flying Group
	G-AYDG	M.S.894A Rallye Minerva	Rallye Minerva Group
	G-AYDI	D.H.82A Tiger Moth	R. B. Woods & ptnrs
	G-AYDR	SNCAN Stampe SV-4C	A. J. Mcluskie
	G-AYDV	Coates SA.II-1 Swalesong	J. R. Coates/Rush Green
	G-AYDW	A.61 Terrier 2	A. Topen/Cranfield
	G-AYDX	A.61 Terrier 2	D. G. Roberts
	G-AYDY	Luton LA-4A Minor	T. Littlefair & N. Clark
	G-AYDZ	Jodel DR.200	L. J. Cudd & C. A. Bailey
	G-AYEB	Jodel D.112	M. A. Watts
	G-AYEC	CP.301A Emeraude	R. S. Needham
	G-AYED	PA-24 Comanche 260	G. N. Snell
	G-AYEE	PA-28 Cherokee 180E	D. J. Beale
	G-AYEF	PA-28 Cherokee 180E	S. R. J. Attwood
	G-AYEG	Falconar F-9	B. E. Trinder
	G-AYEH	Jodel DR.1050	R. G. Hallam
	G-AYEI	PA-31 Turbo Navajo	Stewart McDonald & Co
	G-AYEJ	Jodel DR.1050	J. M. Newbold
	G-AYEN	Piper J-3C-65 Cub	P. Warde & C. F. Morris
	G-AYET	M.S.892A Rallye Commodore 150	R. N. Jones
	G-AYEV	Jodel DR.1050	L. G. Evans/Headcorn
	G-AYEW	Jodel DR.1051	Taildragger Group/Halfpenny Green
	G-AYEY	Cessna F.150K	W. J. Moyse
	G-AYFA	SA Twin Pioneer 3	Flight One Ltd/Shobdon
	G-AYFC	D.62B Condor	K. Knight
	G-AYFD	D.62B Condor	B. G. Manning
	G-AYFE	D.62C Condor	D. I. H. Johnstone & W. T. Barnard
	G-AYFF	D.62B Condor	A. F. S. Caldecourt
	G-AYFG	D.62C Condor	W. A. Braim
	G-AYFJ	M.S.880B Rallye Club	Rallye FJ Group
	G-AYFP	Jodel D.140	S. K. Minocha/Sherburn
	G-AYFT	PA-39 Twin Comanche 160 C/R	G. A. Barber/Blackbushe
	G-AYFV	Crosby BA-4B	A. R. C. Mathie/Norwich
	G-AYGA	Jodel D.117	R. L. E. Horrell
	G-AYGB	Cessna 310Q ★	*Instructional airframe*/Perth
	G-AYGC	Cessna F.150K	Alpha Aviation Group/Barton
	G-AYGD	Jodel DR.1051	P. J. Pengilly
	G-AYGE	SNCAN Stampe SV-4C	The Hon A. M. J. Rothschild/Booker
	G-AYGG	Jodel D.120	G-AYGG Group
	G-AYGK	BN-2A Islander	Pathcircle Ltd/Langar
	G-AYGX	Cessna FR.172G	A. Douglas & J. K. Brockley

Reg.	Type	Owner or Operator	Notes
G-AYHA	AA-1 Yankee	Elstree Emus Flying Group	
G-AYHI	Campbell Cricket	J. F. MacKay/Inverness	
G-AYHX	Jodel D.117A	L. J. E. Goldfinch	
G-AYHY	Fournier RF-4D	P. M. & S. M. Wells	
G-AYIA	Hughes 369HS ★	G. D. E. Bilton/Sywell	
G-AYIF	PA-28 Cherokee 140C	The Hare Flying Group/Elstree	
G-AYIG	PA-28 Cherokee 140C	Snowdon Mountain Aviation Ltd	
G-AYII	PA-28R Cherokee Arrow 200	Devon Growers Ltd & A. L. Bacon/Exeter	
G-AYIJ	SNCAN Stampe SV-4B	K. B. Palmer/Headcorn	
G-AYIT	D.H.82A Tiger Moth	Ulster Tiger Group/Newtownards	
G-AYJA	Jodel DR.1050	G. I. Doake	
G-AYJB	SNCAN Stampe SV-4C	F. J. M. & J. P. Esson/Middle Wallop	
G-AYJD	Alpavia-Fournier RF-3	E. Shouler	
G-AYJP	PA-28 Cherokee 140C	RAF Brize Norton Flying Club Ltd	
G-AYJR	PA-28 Cherokee 140C	RAF Brize Norton Flying Club Ltd	
G-AYJW	Cessna FR.172G	S. Walsh & I. J. A. Charleton	
G-AYJY	Isaacs Fury II	A. V. Francis	
G-AYKA	Beech 95-B55A Baron	Walsh Bros (Tunnelling) Ltd/Elstree	
G-AYKD	Jodel DR.1050	S. D. Morris	
G-AYKF	M.S.880B Rallye Club	F. A. Lemon	
G-AYKJ	Jodel D.117A	Juliet Group/Shoreham	
G-AYKK	Jodel D.117	D. M. Whitham	
G-AYKL	Cessna F.150L	M. A. Judge	
G-AYKS	Leopoldoff L-7	W. B. Cooper	
G-AYKT	Jodel D.117	G. Wright/Sherburn	
G-AYKW	PA-28 Cherokee 140C	T. A. Hird	
G-AYKX	PA-28 Cherokee 140C	Robin Flying Group	
G-AYKZ	SAI KZ-8	R. E. Mitchell/Coventry	
G-AYLA	Glos-Airtourer 115	R. E. Parker	
G-AYLB	PA-39 Twin Comanche 160 C/R	Penny (Mechanical Services) Ltd	
G-AYLE	M.S.880B Rallye Club	G-AYLE Syndicate	
G-AYLF	Jodel DR.1051	Sicile Group	
G-AYLL	Jodel DR.1050	B. R. Cornes	
G-AYLP	AA-1 Yankee	D. Nairn & E. Y. Hawkins	
G-AYLV	Jodel D.120	M. R. Henham	
G-AYLX	Hughes 269C	R. Evans	
G-AYME	Fournier RF-5	R. D. Goodger/Biggin Hill	
G-AYMG	HPR-7 Herald 213	Jet Heritage Ltd/Bournemouth	
G-AYMK	PA-28 Cherokee 140C	The Piper Flying Group	
G-AYMO	PA-23 Aztec 250C	Supreme Windows	
G-AYMP	Currie Wot Special	H. F. Moffatt	
G-AYMR	Lederlin 380L Ladybug	J. S. Brayshaw	
G-AYMT	Jodel DR.1050	Merlin Flying Club Ltd/Hucknall	
G-AYMU	Jodel D.112	M. R. Baker	
G-AYMV	Western 20 balloon	G. F. Turnbull	
G-AYMW	Bell 206A JetRanger 2	Dollar Air Services Ltd/Coventry	
G-AYMZ	PA-28 Cherokee 140C	T. H. & M. G. Weetman/Prestwick	
G-AYNA	Currie Wot	J. M. Lister	
G-AYND	Cessna 310Q	Source Premium & Promotional Consultants Ltd/Fairoaks	
G-AYNF	PA-28 Cherokee 140C	W. S. Bath	
G-AYNJ	PA-28 Cherokee 140C	Lion Flying Group Ltd/Elstree	
G-AYNN	Cessna 185B Skywagon	Bencray Ltd/Blackpool	
G-AYNP	W.S.55 Whirlwind Srs 3	Bristow Helicopters	
G-AYOM	Sikorsky S-61N Mk 2	British International Helicopters	
G-AYOW	Cessna 182N Skylane	A. T. Jay	
G-AYOY	Sikorsky S-61N Mk 2	British International Helicopters	
G-AYOZ	Cessna FA.150L	Exavia Ltd/Exeter	
G-AYPD	Beech 95-B55A Baron	F. Sherwood & Sons (Transport) Ltd	
G-AYPE	Bo 209 Monsun	Papa Echo Ltd/Biggin Hill	
G-AYPG	Cessna F.177RG	D. Davies	
G-AYPH	Cessna F.177RG	W. J. D. Tollett	
G-AYPI	Cessna F.177RG	Cardinal Aviation Ltd/Guernsey	
G-AYPJ	PA-28 Cherokee 180	Mona Aviation Ltd	
G-AYPM	PA-18 Super Cub 95	J. A. Cook	
G-AYPO	PA-18 Super Cub 95	A. W. Knowles	
G-AYPR	PA-18 Super Cub 95	D. G. Holman & J. E. Burrell	
G-AYPS	PA-18 Super Cub 95	Tony Dyer Television	
G-AYPT	PA-18 Super Cub 95	D. Adcock	
G-AYPU	PA-28R Cherokee Arrow 200	Alpine Ltd/Jersey	
G-AYPV	PA-28 Cherokee 140D	Ashley Gardner Flying Club Ltd	
G-AYPZ	Campbell Cricket	A. Melody	
G-AYRF	Cessna F.150L	D. T. A. Rees	

Notes	Reg.	Type	Owner or Operator
	G-AYRG	Cessna F.172K	W. I. Robinson
	G-AYRH	M.S.892A Rallye Commodore 150	J. D. Watt
	G-AYRI	PA-28R Cherokee Arrow 200	E. P. Van Mechelen & Delta Motor Co (Windsor) Sales Ltd/White Waltham
	G-AYRO	Cessna FA.150L Aerobat	Thruxton Flight Centre
	G-AYRS	Jodel D.120A	Claybourns Garage Ltd
	G-AYRT	Cessna F.172K	K. W. J. & A. B. L. Hayward
	G-AYRU	BN-2A-6 Islander	Joint Service Parachute Centre/ Netheravon
	G-AYSA	PA-23 Aztec 250C	N. Parkinson & W. Smith
	G-AYSB	PA-30 Twin Comanche 160C	R. K. Double/Booker
	G-AYSD	Slingsby T.61A Falke	G-AYSD Flying Group
	G-AYSH	Taylor JT.1 Monoplane	C. J. Lodge
	G-AYSJ	Bücker Bü133 Jungmeister (LG+01)	Patina Ltd/Duxford
	G-AYSK	Luton LA-4A Minor	Luton Minor Group
	G-AYSX	Cessna F.177RG	C. P. Heptonstall
	G-AYSY	Cessna F.177RG	Horizon Flyers Ltd/Denham
	G-AYTJ	Cessna 207 Super Skywagon	Foxair/Perth
	G-AYTN	Cameron O-65 balloon	P. G. Hall & R. F. Jessett *Prometheus*
	G-AYTR	CP.301A Emeraude	G. N. Hopcraft
	G-AYTT	Phoenix PM-3 Duet	H. E. Jenner
	G-AYTV	MJ.2A Tempete	D. Perry
	G-AYTY	Bensen B.8	J. H. Wood & J. S. Knight
	G-AYUA	Auster AOP.9 (XK416) ★	A. S. Topen *(stored)*
	G-AYUB	CEA DR.253B	D. J. Brook
	G-AYUH	PA-28 Cherokee 180F	G-AYUH Group
	G-AYUI	PA-28 Cherokee 180	Ansair Aviation Ltd/Andrewsfield
	G-AYUJ	Evans VP-1	T. N. Howard
	G-AYUM	Slingsby T.61A Falke	Hereward Flying Group/Sibson
	G-AYUN	Slingsby T.61A Falke	C. W. Vigar & R. J. Watts
	G-AYUP	Slingsby T.61A Falke	Cranwell Gliding Club
	G-AYUR	Slingsby T.61A Falke	R. Hanningan & R. Lingard
	G-AYUS	Taylor JT.1 Monoplane	R. R. McKinnon
	G-AYUT	Jodel DR.1050	R. Norris
	G-AYUV	Cessna F.172H	Snowdon Mountain Aviation Ltd/ Caernarfon
	G-AYUW	BAC One-Eleven 476FM★	AIM Aviation Ltd *(cabin water spray tests)*/ Bournemouth
	G-AYVO	Wallis WA120 Srs 1	K. H. Wallis
	G-AYVP	Woody Pusher	J. R. Wraight
	G-AYVT	Brochet MB.84 ★	Dunelm Flying Group *(stored)*
	G-AYWA	Avro 19 Srs 2 ★	Strathallan Aircraft Collection
	G-AYWD	Cessna 182N	Chartec Ltd
	G-AYWE	PA-28 Cherokee 140	N. Roberson
	G-AYWH	Jodel D.117A	D. Kynaston & J. Deakin
	G-AYWM	Glos-Airtourer Super 150	The Star Flying Group/Staverton
	G-AYWT	AIA Stampe SV-4C	B. K. Lecomber/Denham
	G-AYXP	Jodel D.117A	G. N. Davies
	G-AYXS	SIAI-Marchetti S205-18R	J. J. Barnett/Old Sarum
	G-AYXT	W.S. 55 Whirlwind Srs 2 (XK940)	Wilkie Museum Collection/Blackpool
	G-AYXU	Champion 7KCAB Citabria	Norfolk Gliding Club Ltd/Tibenham
	G-AYXV	Cessna FA.150L	Wreck/Popham
	G-AYXX	Evans VP-1	J. S. Penny/Doncaster
	G-AYYK	Slingsby T.61A Falke	Cornish Gliding & Flying Club Ltd/ Perranporth
	G-AYYL	Slingsby T.61A Falke	C. Wood
	G-AYYO	Jodel DR.1050/M1	Bustard Flying Club Ltd/Old Sarum
	G-AYYT	Jodel DR.1050/M1	Echo November Flight
	G-AYYU	Beech C23 Musketeer	P. Peck
	G-AYYW	BN-2A Islander	RN & R. Marines Sport Parachute Association/Dunkeswell
	G-AYYX	M.S.880B Rallye Club	J. Turnbull & P. W. Robinson
	G-AYYY	M.S.880B Rallye Club	T. W. Heffer/Elstree
	G-AYZE	PA-39 Twin Comanche 160 C/R	J. E. Palmer/Staverton
	G-AYZH	Taylor JT.2 Titch	P. J. G. Goddard
	G-AYZJ	W.S. 55 Whirlwind Srs 2 (XM685) ★	Newark Air Museum
	G-AYZK	Jodel DR.1050/M1	D. G. Hesketh & D. Lees
	G-AYZN	PA-23 Aztec 250D	D. J. Sewell/Nigeria
	G-AYZS	D.62B Condor	P. E. J. Huntley & M. N. Thrush
	G-AYZU	Slingsby T.61A Falke	The Falcon Gliding Group/Enstone
	G-AYZW	Slingsby T.61A Falke	J. A. Dandie & R. J. M. Clement

Reg.	Type	Owner or Operator	Notes
G-AZAB	PA-30 Twin Comanche 160B	T. W. P. Sheffield/Humberside	
G-AZAD	Jodel DR.1051	Cawdor Flying Group/Inverness	
G-AZAJ	PA-28R Cherokee Arrow 200B	J. McHugh & ptnrs/Stapleford	
G-AZAV	Cessna 337F	J. R. Surbey	
G-AZAW	GY-80 Horizon 160	E. P. Sadler	
G-AZAZ	Bensen B.8M ★	F.A.A. Museum/Yeovilton	
G-AZBA	T.66 Nipper 3	Nipper Aerobatic Flying Group	
G-AZBB	MBB Bo 209 Monsun 160FV	G. N. Richardson/Staverton	
G-AZBC	PA-39 Twin Comanche 160 C/R	H. G. Orchin	
G-AZBE	Glos-Airtourer Super 150	BE Flying Group/Staverton	
G-AZBI	Jodel D.150	F. M. Ward	
G-AZBK	PA-23 Aztec 250E	Vulcan Aviation Ltd	
G-AZBL	Jodel D.9 Bebe	J. Hill	
G-AZBN	AT-16 Harvard IIB (FT391)	Swaygate Ltd/Shoreham	
G-AZBU	Auster AOP.9	K. H. Wallis	
G-AZBY	W.S.58 Wessex 60 Srs 1 ★	International Helicopter Museum/Weston-s-Mare	
G-AZBZ	W.S.58 Wessex 60 Srs 1 ★	International Helicopter Museum/Weston-s-Mare	
G-AZCB	SNCAN Stampe SV-4C	M. J. Cowburn/Redhill	
G-AZCK	B.121 Pup 2	D. R. Newell	
G-AZCL	B.121 Pup 2	E. G. A. Prance	
G-AZCP	B.121 Pup 1	Pup Group 87/Elstree	
G-AZCT	B.121 Pup 1	Northamptonshire School of Flying Ltd	
G-AZCU	B.121 Pup 1	A. A. Harris	
G-AZCV	B.121 Pup 2	N. R. W. Long/Elstree	
G-AZCZ	B.121 Pup 2	L. & J. M. Northover	
G-AZDA	B.121 Pup 1	G. H. G. Bishop/Shoreham	
G-AZDD	MBB Bo 209 Monsun 150FF	Double Delta Flying Group/Biggin Hill	
G-AZDE	PA-28R Cherokee Arrow 200B	Electro-Motion UK (Export) Ltd/E. Midlands	
G-AZDF	Cameron O-84 balloon	K. L. C. M. Busemeyer	
G-AZDG	B.121 Pup 2	D. J. Sage/Coventry	
G-AZDK	Beech 95-B55 Baron	C. C. Forrester	
G-AZDX	PA-28 Cherokee 180F	M. Cowan	
G-AZDY	D.H.82A Tiger Moth	J. B. Mills	
G-AZEE	M.S.880B Rallye Club	J. Shelton	
G-AZEF	Jodel D.120	J. R. Legge	
G-AZEG	PA-28 Cherokee 140D	Ashley Gardner Flying Club Ltd	
G-AZEU	B.121 Pup 2	P. Tonkin & R. S. Kinman	
G-AZEV	B.121 Pup 2	G. P. Martin/Shoreham	
G-AZEW	B.121 Pup 2	K. Cameron	
G-AZEY	B.121 Pup 2	R. Hodgson	
G-AZFA	B.121 Pup 2	K. F. Plummer	
G-AZFC	PA-28 Cherokee 140D	M. L. Hannah/Blackbushe	
G-AZFF	Jodel D.112	C. R. Greenaway	
G-AZFI	PA-28R Cherokee Arrow 200B	G-AZFI Ltd/Sherburn	
G-AZFM	PA-28R Cherokee Arrow 200B	Linco (Holdings) Ltd	
G-AZFP	Cessna F.177RG	Allen Aviation Ltd/Goodwood	
G-AZFR	Cessna 401B	Westair Flying Services Ltd/Blackpool	
G-AZFZ	Cessna 414	Redapple Ltd/Fairoaks	
G-AZGA	Jodel D.120	D. H. Pattison	
G-AZGC	SNCAN Stampe SV-4C (No 120)	V. Lindsay	
G-AZGE	SNCAN Stampe SV-4A	M. R. L. Astor/Booker	
G-AZGF	B.121 Pup 2	K. Singh	
G-AZGI	M.S.880B Rallye Club	B. McIntyre	
G-AZGJ	M.S.880B Rallye Club	P. Rose	
G-AZGL	M.S.894A Rallye Minerva	The Cambridge Aero Club Ltd	
G-AZGY	CP.301B Emeraude	J. R. Riley-Gale	
G-AZGZ	D.H.82A Tiger Moth (NM181)	F. R. Manning	
G-AZHB	Robin HR.100-200	C. & P. P. Scarlett/Sywell	
G-AZHC	Jodel D.112	J. A. Summer & A. Burton/Netherthorpe	
G-AZHD	Slingsby T.61A Falke	J. Sentance	
G-AZHH	SA 102.5 Cavalier	D. W. Buckle	
G-AZHI	Glos-Airtourer Super 150	H. J. Douglas/Biggin Hill	
G-AZHJ	S.A. Twin Pioneer Srs 3	Prestwick Pioneer Preservation Soc Ltd	
G-AZHK	Robin HR.100/200B	D. J. Sage (G-ILEG)	
G-AZHR	Piccard Ax6 balloon	G. Fisher	
G-AZHT	Glos-Airtourer T.3	Aviation West Ltd/Glasgow	
G-AZHU	Luton LA-4A Minor	W. Cawrey/Netherthorpe	
G-AZIB	ST-10 Diplomate	Diplomate Group	
G-AZID	Cessna FA.150L	Exeter Flying Club Ltd	
G-AZII	Jodel D.117A	J. S. Brayshaw	

Notes	Reg.	Type	Owner or Operator
	G-AZIJ	Jodel DR.360	Rob Airway Ltd/Guernsey
	G-AZIK	PA-34-200 Seneca II	Xaxanaka Aviation Ltd
	G-AZIL	Slingsby T.61A Falke	D. W. Savage
	G-AZIO	SNCAN Stampe SV-4C (Lycoming) ★	/Booker
	G-AZIP	Cameron O-65 balloon	Dante Balloon Group *Dante*
	G-AZJC	Fournier RF-5	W. St. G. V. Stoney/Italy
	G-AZJE	Ord-Hume JB-01 Minicab	J. B. Evans/Sandown
	G-AZJI	Western O-65 balloon	W. Davison *Peek-a-Boo*
	G-AZJN	Robin DR.300/140	Wright Farm Eggs Ltd
	G-AZJV	Cessna F.172L	J. A. & A. J. Boyd/Cardiff
	G-AZJY	Cessna FRA.150L	G. Firbank
	G-AZJZ	PA-23 Aztec 250E	Gatherton Ltd
	G-AZKC	M.S.880B Rallye Club	L. J. Martin/Redhill
	G-AZKE	M.S.880B Rallye Club	B. S. Rowden & W. L. Rogers
	G-AZKK	Cameron O-56 balloon	Gemini Balloon Group *Gemini*
	G-AZKN	Robin HR.100/200	Wonderful Flying Circus
	G-AZKO	Cessna F.337F	Crispair Aviation Services Ltd
	G-AZKP	Jodel D.117	J. Lowe
	G-AZKR	PA-24 Comanche 180	S. McGovern
	G-AZKS	AA-1A Trainer	M. D. Henson
	G-AZKW	Cessna F.172L	J. C. C. Wright
	G-AZKZ	Cessna F.172L	R. D. & E. Forster/Swanton Morley
	G-AZLE	Boeing N2S-5 Kaydet	Air Farm Flyers
	G-AZLF	Jodel D.120	M. S. C. Ball
	G-AZLH	Cessna F.150L	P. T. W. Sheffield
	G-AZLL	Cessna FRA.150L	Air Service Training Ltd/Perth
	G-AZLN	PA-28 Cherokee 180F	Liteflite Ltd/Kidlington
	G-AZLO	Cessna F.337F	*Stored*/Bourn
	G-AZLV	Cessna 172K	B. L. F. Karthaus
	G-AZLY	Cessna F.150L	Cleveland Flying School Ltd/Tees-side
	G-AZLZ	Cessna F.150L	G-AZLZ Group
	G-AZMB	Bell 47G-3B	Helitech (Luton) Ltd
	G-AZMC	Slingsby T.61A Falke	Essex Gliding Club Ltd
	G-AZMD	Slingsby T.61C Falke	R. A. Rice
	G-AZMF	BAC One-Eleven 530FX	–
	G-AZMH	Morane-Saulnier M.S.500 (7A+WN)	Wessex Aviation & Transport Ltd
	G-AZMJ	AA-5 Traveler	R. T. Love/Bodmin
	G-AZMN	Glos-Airtourer T.5	W. Crozier & I. Young/Glasgow
	G-AZMX	PA-28 Cherokee 140 ★	NE Wales Institute of Higher Education (*Instructional airframe*)/Clwyd
	G-AZMZ	M.S.893A Rallye Commodore 150	P. J. Wilcox/Cranfield
	G-AZNK	SNCAN Stampe SV-4A	P. D. Jackson
	G-AZNL	PA-28R Cherokee Arrow 200D	P. L. Buckley Ltd
	G-AZNO	Cessna 182P	M&D Aviation/Bournemouth
	G-AZOA	MBB Bo 209 Monsun 150FF	R. P. Wilson
	G-AZOB	MBB Bo 209 Monsun 150FF	G. N. Richardson/Staverton
	G-AZOE	Glos-Airtourer 115	R. J. Zukowski
	G-AZOF	Glos-Airtourer Super 150	Cirrus Flying Group/Denham
	G-AZOG	PA-28R Cherokee Arrow 200D	J. G. Collins/Cambridge
	G-AZOL	PA-34-200 Seneca II	St Bridgets Aviation Ltd & ptnrs
	G-AZOR	MBB Bo 105D	Bond Helicopters Ltd/Bourn
	G-AZOS	Jurca MJ.5-F1 Sirocco	O. R. B. Dixon/Barton
	G-AZOT	PA-34-200 Seneca II	M. R. C. Smerald
	G-AZOU	Jodel DR.1051	Horsham Flying Group/Slinfold
	G-AZOZ	Cessna FRA.150L	Seawing Flying Club Ltd/Southend
	G-AZPA	PA-25 Pawnee 235	Black Mountain Gliding Co Ltd
	G-AZPC	Slingsby T.61C Falke	M. F. Cuming
	G-AZPF	Fournier RF-5	R. Pye/Blackpool
	G-AZPH	Craft-Pitts S-1S Special ★	Science Museum/London
	G-AZPV	Luton LA-4A Minor	G. D. S. Rumble
	G-AZRA	MBB Bo 209 Monsun 150FF	Alpha Flying Ltd/Denham
	G-AZRD	Cessna 401B	Morbaine Ltd
	G-AZRH	PA-28 Cherokee 140D	Joseph Carter & Sons (Jersey) Ltd
	G-AZRK	Fournier RF-5	Thurleigh Flying Group
	G-AZRL	PA-18 Super Cub 95	B. J. Stead
	G-AZRM	Fournier RF-5	A. R. Dearden & R. Speer/Shoreham
	G-AZRN	Cameron O-84 balloon	C. A. Butter & J. J. T. Cooke
	G-AZRP	Glos-Airtourer 115	B. F. Strawford
	G-AZRR	Cessna 310Q	Routarrow Ltd/Norwich
	G-AZRS	PA-22 Tri-Pacer 150	T. W. R. Case
	G-AZRV	PA-28R Cherokee Arrow 200B	Designed for Sound Ltd
	G-AZRW	Cessna T.337C	R. C. Frazle/Southend

Reg.	Type	Owner or Operator	Notes
G-AZRX	GY-80 Horizon 160	Horizon Flying Group	
G-AZRZ	Cessna U.206F	M. E. Bolton	
G-AZSA	Stampe et Renard SV-4B	J. K. Faulkner/Biggin Hill	
G-AZSC	AT-16 Harvard IIB	Machine Music Ltd/Fairoaks	
G-AZSD	Slingsby T.29B Motor Tutor	R. G. Boynton	
G-AZSF	PA-28R Cherokee Arrow 200D	W. T. Northorpe & R. J. Mills/Coventry	
G-AZSH	PA-28R Cherokee Arrow 180	C. & G. Clarke	
G-AZSN	PA-28R Cherokee Arrow 200	Jetstream Air Couriers Ltd/Bristol	
G-AZSU	H.S.748 Srs 2A	Euroair Transport Ltd	
G-AZSW	B.121 Pup 1	Northamptonshire School of Flying Ltd/ Swell	
G-AZSZ	PA-23 Aztec 250D	Strata Surveys Ltd	
G-AZTA	MBB Bo 209 Monsun 150FF	C. D. Weiswall	
G-AZTD	PA-32 Cherokee Six 300D	Presshouse Publications Ltd/Enstone	
G-AZTF	Cessna F.177RG	H. H. Elder	
G-AZTK	Cessna F.172F	C. O. Simpson	
G-AZTO	PA-34-200 Seneca II	Bulldog Aviation Ltd	
G-AZTR	SNCAN Stampe SV-4C	P. G. Palumbo/Booker	
G-AZTS	Cessna F.172L	C. E. Stringer	
G-AZTV	Stolp SA.500 Starlet	G. R. Rowland	
G-AZTW	Cessna F.177RG	R. M. Clarke/Leicester	
G-AZUK	BAC One-Eleven 476FM	Dawson Trading Ltd/Southend	
G-AZUM	Cessna F.172L	Fowlmere Fliers	
G-AZUP	Cameron O-65 balloon	R. S. Bailey & A. B. Simpson	
G-AZUT	M.S.893A Rallye Commodore 180	Rallye Flying Group	
G-AZUV	Cameron O-65 balloon ★	British Balloon Museum	
G-AZUY	Cessna E.310L	Euromarine Group Ltd	
G-AZUZ	Cessna FRA.150L	D. J. Parker/Netherthorpe	
G-AZVA	MBB Bo 209 Monsun 150FF	J. Nivison	
G-AZVB	MBB Bo 209 Monsun 150FF	P. C. Logsdon/Dunkeswell	
G-AZVE	AA-5 Traveler	G-AZVE Flying Group/Rochester	
G-AZVF	M.S.894A Rallye Minerva	P. D. Lloyd	
G-AZVG	AA-5 Traveler	Grumair Flying Group	
G-AZVH	M.S.894A Rallye Minerva	Bristol Cars Ltd/White Waltham	
G-AZVI	M.S.892A Rallye Commodore	Shobdon Flying Group	
G-AZVJ	PA-34-200 Seneca II	Skyfotos Ltd/Lydd	
G-AZVL	Jodel D.119	Forest Flying Group/Stapleford	
G-AZVM	Hughes 369HS	Diagnostic Reagents Ltd	
G-AZVP	Cessna F.177RG	Cardinal Flyers Ltd	
G-AZWB	PA-28 Cherokee 140	Skyscraper Ltd	
G-AZWD	PA-28 Cherokee 140	BM Aviation (Winchester)	
G-AZWE	PA-28 Cherokee 140	P. M. Tucker & H. Sanai	
G-AZWF	SAN Jodel DR.1050	G-AZWF Jodel Syndicate	
G-AZWS	PA-28R Cherokee Arrow 180	J. E. Shepherd & C. A. Douglas	
G-AZWT	Westland Lysander IIIA (V9441)	Strathallan Aircraft Collection	
G-AZWW	PA-23 Aztec 250E	Clacton Aero Club (1988) Ltd	
G-AZWY	PA-24 Comanche 260	Keymer Son & Co Ltd/Biggin Hill	
G-AZXA	Beech 95-C55 Baron	F.R. Aviation Ltd/Bournemouth	
G-AZXB	Cameron O-65 balloon	R. J. Mitchener & P. F.Smart	
G-AZXC	Cessna F.150L	S. Redfearn/Netherthorpe	
G-AZXD	Cessna F.172L	Birdlake Ltd/Wellesbourne	
G-AZYA	GY-80 Horizon 160	T. Poole & ptnrs/Sywell	
G-AZYB	Bell 47H-1 ★	International Helicopter Museum/ Weston-s-Mare	
G-AZYD	M.S.893A Rallye Commodore	Buckminster Gliding Club Ltd/Saltby	
G-AZYF	PA-28 Cherokee 180	J. C. Glynn/E. Midlands	
G-AZYM	Cessna E.310Q	Kingswinford Engineering Co Ltd	
G-AZYS	CP.301C-1 Emeraude	F. P. L. Clauson	
G-AZYU	PA-23 Aztec 250E	L. J. Martin/Biggin Hill	
G-AZYV	Burns O-77 balloon	B. F. G. Ribbans Contrary Mary	
G-AZYY	Slingsby T.61A Falke	J. A. Towers	
G-AZYZ	WA.51A Pacific	Yankee Zulu Ltd/Biggin Hill	
G-AZZG	Cessna 188 Agwagon	N. C. Kensington	
G-AZZH	Practavia Pilot Sprite 115	K. G. Stewart	
G-AZZK	Cessna 414	D. O. McIntyre	
G-AZZO	PA-28 Cherokee 140	R. J. Hind/Elstree	
G-AZZP	Cessna F.172H	M. Bell & P. W. J. Gove	
G-AZZR	Cessna F.150L	R. J. Doughton	
G-AZZS	PA-34-200 Seneca II	Robin Cook Aviation/Shoreham	
G-AZZT	PA-28 Cherokee 180 ★	Ground instruction airframe/Cranfield	
G-AZZV	Cessna F.172L	D. M. Charrington	
G-AZZW	Fournier RF-5	R. G. Trute	
G-AZZX	Cessna FRA.150L	J. E. Uprichard & ptnrs/Newtownards	

Notes	Reg.	Type	Owner or Operator
	G-AZZZ	D.H.82A Tiger Moth	S. W. McKay
	G-BAAD	Evans Super VP-1	R. A. Burn
	G-BAAF	Manning-Flanders MF1 (replica)	Aviation Film Services Ltd/Booker
	G-BAAI	M.S.893A Rallye Commodore	R. D. Taylor/Thruxton
	G-BAAK	Cessna 207	B. W. Wells
	G-BAAL	Cessna 172A	Rochester Aviation Ltd
	G-BAAP	PA-28R Cherokee Arrow 200	F. T. Cole
	G-BAAT	Cessna 182P Skylane	A. H. Hunt/St Just
	G-BAAU	Enstrom F-28C-UK	M. Upton
	G-BAAW	Jodel D.119	K. J. Cockrill/Ipswich
	G-BAAX	Cameron O-84 balloon	The New Holker Estates Co Ltd *Holker Hall*
	G-BAAZ	PA-28R Cherokee Arrow 200D	A. W. Rix/Guernsey
	G-BABB	Cessna F.150L	Seawing Flying Club Ltd/Southend
	G-BABC	Cessna F.150L	Fordaire Aviation Ltd
	G-BABD	Cessna FRA.150L	C. J. Hopewell
	G-BABE	Taylor JT.2 Titch	P. D. G. Grist/Sibson
	G-BABG	PA-28 Cherokee 180	Mendip Flying Group/Bristol
	G-BABK	PA-34-200 Seneca II	D. F. J. Flashman/Biggin Hill
	G-BABY	Taylor JT.2 Titch	R. E. Finlay
	G-BACB	PA-34-200 Seneca II	London Flight Centre (Stansted) Ltd
	G-BACC	Cessna FRA.150L	C. M. & J. H. Cooper/Cranfield
	G-BACE	Fournier RF-5	R. W. K. Stead/Perranporth
	G-BACH	Enstrom F-28A	M. & P. Food Products Ltd
	G-BACJ	Jodel D.120	Wearside Flying Association/Newcastle
	G-BACL	Jodel D.150	M. L. Sargeant/Biggin Hill
	G-BACN	Cessna FRA.150L	Air Service Training Ltd/Perth
	G-BACO	Cessna FRA.150L	W. R. Burgess & ptnrs/Sibson
	G-BACP	Cessna FRA.150L	B. A. Mills
	G-BADC	Luton Beta B.2A	H. M. Mackenzie
	G-BADH	Slingsby T.61A Falke	Falke Flying Group
	G-BADI	PA-23 Aztec 250D	W. London Aero Services Ltd/ White Waltham
	G-BADJ	PA-E23 Aztec 250E	Bell Aviation
	G-BADL	PA-34-200 Seneca II	K. Smith & M. Corbett
	G-BADM	D.62B Condor	M. Harris & J. Taylor
	G-BADO	PA-32 Cherokee Six 300E	M. A. S. Talbot
	G-BADU	Cameron O-56 balloon	J. Philp *Dream Machine*
	G-BADV	Brochet MB-50	P. A. Cairns/Dunkeswell
	G-BADW	Pitts S-2A Special	R. E. Mitchell/Coventry
	G-BADZ	Pitts S-2A Special	A. F. D. Kingdon
	G-BAEB	Robin DR.400/160	P. D. W. King
	G-BAEC	Robin HR.100/210	Robin Travel & Designways (Interior Design) Ltd
	G-BAED	PA-23 Aztec 250C	K. G. Manktelow & N. Brewitt
	G-BAEE	Jodel DR.1050/M1	R. Little
	G-BAEM	Robin DR.400/125	M. A. Webb/Booker
	G-BAEN	Robin DR.400/180	European Soaring Club Ltd
	G-BAEP	Cessna FRA.150L (modified)	A. M. Lynn
	G-BAER	Cosmic Wind	R. S. Voice/Redhill
	G-BAET	Piper J-3C-65 Cub	C. J. Rees
	G-BAEU	Cessna F.150L	Skyviews & General Ltd
	G-BAEV	Cessna FRA.150L	N. J. Wiszowaty/Blackbushe
	G-BAEW	Cessna F.172M	Northamptonshire School of Flying Ltd/ Sywell
	G-BAEY	Cessna F.172M	R. Fursman/Southampton
	G-BAEZ	Cessna FRA.150L	Donair Flying Club Ltd/E. Midlands
	G-BAFA	AA-5 Traveler	C. F. Mackley/Stapleford
	G-BAFD	MBB Bo 105D	Bond Helicopters Ltd/Aberdeen
	G-BAFG	D.H.82A Tiger Moth	J. E. & P. J. Shaw
	G-BAFH	Evans VP-1	C. M. Gibson
	G-BAFI	Cessna F.177RG	Gloucestershire Flying Club
	G-BAFL	Cessna 182P	Farm Aviation Services Ltd
	G-BAFM	AT-16 Harvard IIB (FS728)	N. G. R. Moffat
	G-BAFP	Robin DR.400/160	A. S. Langdale & J. Bevis-Lawson/ Shoreham
	G-BAFS	PA-18 Super Cub 150	G-BAFS Group/Sandown
	G-BAFT	PA-18 Super Cub 150	T. J. Wilkinson
	G-BAFU	PA-28 Cherokee 140	R. C. Saunders/Gamston
	G-BAFV	PA-18 Super Cub 95	T. F. & S. J. Thorpe
	G-BAFW	PA-28 Cherokee 140	P. H. Marlow
	G-BAFX	Robin DR.400/140	Nicholas Advertising Ltd
	G-BAGB	SIAI-Marchetti SF.260	British Midland Airways Ltd/E. Midlands

Reg.	Type	Owner or Operator	Notes
G-BAGC	Robin DR.400/140	Aeroquest Aviation	
G-BAGF	Jodel D.92 Bebe	E. Evans	
G-BAGG	PA-32 Cherokee Six 300E	Hornair Ltd	
G-BAGI	Cameron O-31 balloon	Red Section Balloon Group	
G-BAGL	SA.341G Gazelle Srs 1	Autokraft Ltd	
G-BAGN	Cessna F.177RG	R. W. J. Andrews	
G-BAGO	Cessna 421B	Jadealto (Sales & Marketing) Ltd	
G-BAGR	Robin DR.400/140	F. C. Aris & J. D. Last/Mona	
G-BAGS	Robin DR.400/180 2+2	Headcorn Flying School Ltd	
G-BAGT	Helio H.295 Courier	B. J. C. Woodall Ltd	
G-BAGV	Cessna U.206F	Scottish Parachute Club/Strathallan	
G-BAGX	PA-28 Cherokee 140	Klingair Ltd/Conington	
G-BAGY	Cameron O-84 balloon	P. G. Dunnington *Beatrice*	
G-BAHD	Cessna 182P Skylane	G. G. Ferriman	
G-BAHE	PA-28 Cherokee 140	A. H. Evans & A. O. Jones/Sleap	
G-BAHF	PA-28 Cherokee 140	S. J. Green/Halfpenny Green	
G-BAHG	PA-24 Comanche 260	Friendly Aviation (Jersey) Ltd	
G-BAHH	Wallis WA-121	K. H. Wallis	
G-BAHI	Cessna F.150H	A. G. Brindle/Blackpool	
G-BAHJ	PA-24 Comanche 250	K. Cooper	
G-BAHL	Robin DR.400/160	M. A. Newman/Thruxton	
G-BAHN	Beech 95-58TC Baron	Remoteassist Ltd	
G-BAHO	Beech C.23 Sundowner	T. Durham	
G-BAHP	Volmer VJ.22 Sportsman	Seaplane Group	
G-BAHS	PA-28R Cherokee Arrow 200-II	A. A. Wild & ptnrs	
G-BAHX	Cessna 182P	PP Dupost Group	
G-BAHZ	PA-28R Cherokee Arrow 200-II	J. H. Reynolds	
G-BAIA	PA-32 Cherokee Six 300E	J. Barham	
G-BAIB	Enstrom F-28A	Farmax Helicopters	
G-BAIH	PA-28R Cherokee Arrow 200-II	G. J. Williamson	
G-BAII	Cessna FRA.150L	Air Service Training Ltd/Perth	
G-BAIK	Cessna F.150L	Wickenby Aviation Ltd	
G-BAIL	Cessna FR.172J	G. Greenall	
G-BAIM	Cessna 310Q	(*Instructional airframe*)/Perth	
G-BAIN	Cessna FRA.150L	Air Service Training Ltd/Perth	
G-BAIP	Cessna F.150L	G. & S. A. Jones	
G-BAIR	Thunder Ax7-77 balloon	P. A. & Mrs M. Hutchins	
G-BAIS	Cessna F.177RG	A. J. Everex & T. W. Goodall	
G-BAIW	Cessna F.172M	Humber Aviation Ltd	
G-BAIX	Cessna F.172M	R. A. Nichols/Elstree	
G-BAIY	Cameron O-65 balloon	Budget Rent A Car (UK) Ltd	
G-BAIZ	Slingsby T.61A Falke	Falke Syndicate	
G-BAJA	Cessna F.177RG	Don Ward Productions Ltd/Biggin Hill	
G-BAJB	Cessna F.177RG	G. J. Banfield	
G-BAJC	Evans VP-1	R. A. Hazelton	
G-BAJE	Cessna 177 Cardinal	N. C. Butcher	
G-BAJN	AA-5 Traveler	Janacrew Flying Group	
G-BAJO	AA-5 Traveler	J. R. Howard/Blackpool	
G-BAJR	PA-28 Cherokee 180	Chosen Few Flying Group/Newtownards	
G-BAJY	Robin DR.400/180	F. Birch & K. J. Pike/Sturgate	
G-BAJZ	Robin DR.400/125	Rochester Aviation Ltd	
G-BAKD	PA-34-200 Seneca II	Andrews Professional Colour Laboratories/ Elstree	
G-BAKH	PA-28 Cherokee 140	Marnham Investments Ltd	
G-BAKJ	PA-30 Twin Comanche 160B	M. F. Fisher & W. R. Lawes/Biggin Hill	
G-BAKK	Cessna 172H ★	*Parachute jump trainer*/Coventry	
G-BAKL	F.27 Friendship Mk 200	Air UK Ltd/Norwich	
G-BAKM	Robin DR.400/140	MKS Syndicate	
G-BAKN	SNCAN Stampe SV-4C	M. Holloway	
G-BAKR	Jodel D.117	A. B. Bailey/White Waltham	
G-BAKS	AB-206B JetRanger 2	Dollar Air Services Ltd/Coventry	
G-BAKV	PA-18 Super Cub 150	Pounds Marine Shipping Ltd/Goodwood	
G-BAKW	B.121 Pup 2	Oakley Motor Units Ltd & J. P. Baudrier	
G-BAKY	Slingsby T.61C Falke	G. A. Schulz & A. Jones/Leicester	
G-BALF	Robin DR.400/140	C. G. Gray	
G-BALG	Robin DR.400/180	R. Jones	
G-BALH	Robin DR.400/140B	J. D. Copsey	
G-BALI	Robin DR.400 2+2	Robin Flying Group	
G-BALJ	Robin DR.400/180	D. A. Bett & D. de Lacey-Rowe	
G-BALK	SNCAN Stampe SV-4C	L. J. Rice	
G-BALN	Cessna T.310Q	O'Brien Properties Ltd/Shoreham	
G-BALT	Enstrom F-28A	Codnor Pet-Aquatics	
G-BALX	D.H.82A Tiger Moth (N6848)	Aviation Heritage Ltd	

Notes	Reg.	Type	Owner or Operator
	G-BALY	Practavia Pilot Sprite 150	A. L. Young
	G-BALZ	Bell 212	B.E.A.S. Ltd/Redhill
	G-BAMB	Slingsby T.61C Falke	D. C. Mayle
	G-BAMC	Cessna F.150L	Barry Aviation Ltd
	G-BAME	Volmer VJ-22 Sportsman	A. McLeod
	G-BAMF	MBB Bo 105D	Bond Helicopters Ltd/Bourn
	G-BAMJ	Cessna 182P	A. E. Kedros
	G-BAMK	Cameron D-96 airship	D. W. Liddiard
	G-BAML	Bell 206B JetRanger 2	Heliscott Ltd
	G-BAMM	PA-28 Cherokee 235	T. A. Astell/Shoreham
	G-BAMR	PA-16 Clipper	H. Royce
	G-BAMS	Robin DR.400/160	G-BAMS Ltd/Headcorn
	G-BAMU	Robin DR.400/160	The Alternative Flying Group
	G-BAMV	Robin DR.400/180	K. Jones & E. A. Anderson/Booker
	G-BAMY	PA-28R Cherokee Arrow 200-II	G-BAMY Group/Birmingham
	G-BANA	Robin DR.221	G. T. Pryor
	G-BANB	Robin DR.400/180	Time Electronics Ltd/Biggin Hill
	G-BANC	GY-201 Minicab	J. T. S. Lewis & J. E. Williams
	G-BAND	Cameron O-84 balloon	Mid-Bucks Farmers Balloon Group *Clover*
	G-BANE	Cessna FRA.150L	Spectrum Flying Group/Newtownards
	G-BANF	Luton LA-4A Minor	W. J. McCollum
	G-BANG	Cameron O-84 balloon	R. F. Harrower
	G-BANK	PA-34-200 Seneca II	Cleveland Flying School Ltd/Teesside
	G-BANU	Wassmer Jodel D.120	C. E. McKinney
	G-BANV	Phoenix Currie Wot	K. Knight
	G-BANW	CP.1330 Super Emeraude	P. S. Milner
	G-BANX	Cessna F.172M	J. F. Davis/Badminton
	G-BAOB	Cessna F.172M	V. B. Cheesewright & ptnrs/Earls Colne
	G-BAOG	M.S.880B Rallye Club	G. W. Simpson
	G-BAOH	M.S.880B Rallye Club	W. E. Taylor & Son Ltd
	G-BAOJ	M.S.880B Rallye Club	BAOJ Ltd
	G-BAOM	M.S.880B Rallye Club	D. H. Tonkin
	G-BAOP	Cessna FRA.150L	M. K. Field
	G-BAOS	Cessna F.172M	F. W. Ellis & ptnrs
	G-BAOU	AA-5 Traveler	C. J. Earle & I. S. Hacon
	G-BAOV	AA-5A Cheetah	A. Kerridge
	G-BAOY	Cameron S-31 balloon	Shell-Mex BP Ltd *New Potato*
	G-BAPA	Fournier RF-5B Sperber	Nuthampstead G-BAPA Group
	G-BAPB	D.H.C.1 Chipmunk 22	R. C. P. Brookhouse/Redhill
	G-BAPC	Luton LA-4A Minor ★	Midland Aircraft Preservation Soc
	G-BAPF	V.814 Viscount	British World Airlines Ltd/Southend
	G-BAPI	Cessna FRA.150L	Industrial Supplies (Peterborough) Ltd/Sibson
	G-BAPJ	Cessna FRA.150L	M. D. Page/Manston
	G-BAPK	Cessna F.150L	Andrewsfield Flying Club Ltd
	G-BAPL	PA-23 Turbo Aztec 250E	Donington Aviation Ltd/E. Midlands
	G-BAPM	Fuji FA.200-160	R. P. Munday/Biggin Hill
	G-BAPP	Evans VP-1	R. J. Humphries
	G-BAPR	Jodel D.11	R. G. Marshall
	G-BAPS	Campbell Cougar ★	International Helicopter Museum/Weston-s-Mare
	G-BAPV	Robin DR.400/160	J. D. & M. Millne
	G-BAPW	PA-28R Cherokee Arrow 180	I. W. Lindsey & P. S. Ferren/Elstree
	G-BAPX	Robin DR.400/160	M. A. Musselwhite
	G-BAPY	Robin HR.100/210	Gloria Baby Aviation Ltd
	G-BARB	PA-34-200 Seneca II	S. Wood
	G-BARC	Cessna FR.172J	Severn Valley Aviation Group
	G-BARD	Cessna 337C	D. W. Horton
	G-BARF	Jodel D.112 Club	J. J. Penney
	G-BARG	Cessna E.310Q	Sally Marine Ltd
	G-BARH	Beech C.23 Sundowner	G. A. Davitt
	G-BARJ	Bell 212	Autair International Ltd/Panshanger
	G-BARN	Taylor JT.2 Titch	R. G. W. Newton
	G-BARP	Bell 206B JetRanger 2	S.W. Electricity Board/Bristol
	G-BARS	D.H.C.1 Chipmunk 22	M. R. Keen/Liverpool
	G-BARV	Cessna 310Q	Old England Watches Ltd/Elstree
	G-BARZ	Scheibe SF.28A Tandem Falke	K. Kiely
	G-BASB	Enstrom F-28A	GTS Engineering (Coventry) Ltd
	G-BASG	AA-5 Traveler	ASG Aviation Group/Glenrothes
	G-BASH	AA-5 Traveler	J. J. Woodhouse
	G-BASJ	PA-28 Cherokee 180	W. Brown
	G-BASL	PA-28 Cherokee 140	Air Navigation & Trading Ltd/Blackpool
	G-BASM	PA-34-200 Seneca II	Poplar Aviation Group/Ipswich

Reg.	Type	Owner or Operator	Notes
G-BASN	Beech C.23 Sundowner	M. F. Fisher	
G-BASO	Lake LA-4 Amphibian	R. J. Willies	
G-BASP	B.121 Pup 1	B. J. Coutts/Sywell	
G-BASX	PA-34-200 Seneca II	J. W. Anstee & Anstee & Ware Ltd	
G-BATC	MBB Bo 105D	Bond Helicopters Ltd/Swansea	
G-BATJ	Jodel D.119	E. G. Waite/Shobdon	
G-BATM	PA-32 Cherokee Six 300E	Patgrove Ltd/Bolney	
G-BATN	PA-23 Aztec 250E	Marshall of Cambridge Ltd	
G-BATR	PA-34-200 Seneca II	Aerohire Ltd/Halfpenny Green	
G-BATT	Hughes 269C	Victoria Helicopters	
G-BATV	PA-28 Cherokee 180D	J. N. Rudsdale	
G-BATW	PA-28 Cherokee 140	Tango Whiskey Flying Partnership	
G-BATX	PA-23 Aztec 250E	Tayside Aviation Ltd/Dundee	
G-BAUA	PA-23 Aztec 250D	David Parr & Associates Ltd/Shobdon	
G-BAUC	PA-25 Pawnee 235	Southdown Gliding Club Ltd	
G-BAUE	Cessna 310Q	A. J. Dyer/Elstree	
G-BAUH	Jodel D.112	G. A. & D. Shepherd	
G-BAUI	PA-23 Aztec 250D	SFT Aviation Ltd/Bournemouth	
G-BAUJ	PA-23 Aztec 250E	S. J. & C. J. Westley/Cranfield	
G-BAUK	Hughes 269C	Curtis Engineering (Frome) Ltd	
G-BAUN	Bell 206B Jet Ranger	Bristow Helicopters Ltd	
G-BAUR	F.27 Friendship Mk 200	Air UK Ltd *Robert Louis Stevenson*/ Norwich	
G-BAUV	Cessna F.150L	Skyviews & General Ltd	
G-BAUW	PA-23 Aztec 250E	R. E. Myson	
G-BAUY	Cessna FRA.150L	The PMM Group/Glenrothes	
G-BAUZ	SNCAN NC.854S	W. A. Ashley & D. Horne	
G-BAVB	Cessna F.172M	T. J. Nokes & T. V. Phillips	
G-BAVC	Cessna F.150L	P. C. & J. P. Gulliver	
G-BAVH	D.H.C.1 Chipmunk 22	Portsmouth Naval Gliding Club/ Lee-on-Solent	
G-BAVL	PA-23 Aztec 250E	S. P. & A. V. Chillott	
G-BAVO	Boeing Stearman N2S (26)	V. A. Holliday & T. E. W. Terrell	
G-BAVR	AA-5 Traveler	E. R. Pyatt	
G-BAVS	AA-5 Traveler	V. J. Peake/Headcorn	
G-BAVU	Cameron A-105 balloon	J. D. Michaelis	
G-BAVZ	PA-23 Aztec 250E	Ravenair/Manchester	
G-BAWB	PA-23 Aztec 250C	Emberden Ltd/Biggin Hill	
G-BAWG	PA-28R Cherokee Arrow 200-II	Solent Air Ltd	
G-BAWI	Enstrom F-28A-UK	M. & P. Food Products Ltd	
G-BAWK	PA-28 Cherokee 140	Newcastle-upon-Tyne Aero Club Ltd	
G-BAWN	PA-30 Twin Comanche 160C	R. A. & J. M. Nunn	
G-BAWR	Robin HR.100/210	T. Taylor	
G-BAWU	PA-30 Twin Comanche 160B	CCH Aviation Ltd	
G-BAWW	Thunder Ax7-77 balloon	M. L. C. Hutchins *Taurus*/Holland	
G-BAXD	BN-2A Mk III Trislander	Aurigny Air Services/Guernsey	
G-BAXE	Hughes 269A	Reethorpe Engineering Ltd	
G-BAXF	Cameron O-77 balloon	R. D. Sargeant & M. F. Lasson	
G-BAXH	Cessna 310Q	D. A. Williamson	
G-BAXJ	PA-32 Cherokee Six 300B	UK Parachute Services/Ipswich	
G-BAXK	Thunder Ax7-77 balloon	A. R. Snook	
G-BAXP	PA-23 Aztec 250E	Ashcombe Ltd	
G-BAXS	Bell 47G-5	LRC Leisure Ltd	
G-BAXT	PA-28R Cherokee Arrow 200-II	P. R. Phealon/Old Sarum	
G-BAXU	Cessna F.150L	W. Lancs Aero Club Ltd/Woodvale	
G-BAXY	Cessna F.172M	A. Rashid	
G-BAXZ	PA-28 Cherokee 140	H. Martin & D. Norris/Halton	
G-BAYL	Nord 1203/III Norecrin	D. M. Fincham	
G-BAYO	Cessna 150L	Cheshire Air Training School (Merseyside) Ltd/Liverpool	
G-BAYP	Cessna 150L	Three Counties Aero Engineering Ltd/ Lasham	
G-BAYR	Robin HR.100/210	L. A. Christie/Stapleford	
G-BAYV	SNCAN 1101 Noralpha (3) ★	Booker Aircraft Museum	
G-BAYZ	Bellanca 7GCBC Citabria	Cambridge University Gliding Trust Ltd/ Gransdon	
G-BAZC	Robin DR.400/160	Southern Sailplanes	
G-BAZJ	HPR-7 Herald 209 ★	Guernsey Airport Fire Services	
G-BAZM	Jodel D.11	Bingley Flying Group/Leeds	
G-BAZS	Cessna F.150L	Sherburn Aero Club Ltd	
G-BAZT	Cessna F.172M	M. Fraser/Exeter	
G-BAZU	PA-28R Cherokee Arrow 200	S. C. Simmons/White Waltham	

Notes	Reg.	Type	Owner or Operator
	G-BBAE	L.1011-385 TriStar 100	Caledonian Airways *Loch Earn*/Gatwick
	G-BBAF	L.1011-385 TriStar 100	Caledonian Airways *Loch Fyne*/Gatwick
	G-BBAH	L.1011-385 TriStar 100	Caledonian Airways *Loch Avon*/Gatwick
	G-BBAI	L.1011-385 TriStar 1	Caledonian Airways *Loch Inver*/Gatwick
	G-BBAJ	L.1011-385 TriStar 100	Caledonian Airways *Loch Rannoch*/Gatwick
	G-BBAK	M.S.894A Rallye Minerva	R. B. Hemsworth & C. L. Hill/Exeter
	G-BBAW	Robin HR.100/210	J. R. Williams
	G-BBAX	Robin DR.400/140	S. R. Young
	G-BBAY	Robin DR.400/140	Rothwell Group
	G-BBAZ	Hiller UH-12E	Copley Farms Ltd
	G-BBBC	Cessna F.150L	W. J. Greenfield
	G-BBBI	AA-5 Traveler	C. S. Jenks
	G-BBBK	PA-28 Cherokee 140	Bencray Ltd/Blackpool
	G-BBBM	Bell 206B JetRanger 2	Express Newspapers PLC
	G-BBBN	PA-28 Cherokee 180	Estuary Aviation Ltd
	G-BBBO	SIPA 903	J. S. Hemmings & C. R. Steer
	G-BBBW	FRED Srs 2	C. Briggs
	G-BBBX	Cessna E310L	Atlantic Air Transport Ltd/Coventry
	G-BBBY	PA-28 Cherokee 140	J. L. Yourell/Luton
	G-BBCA	Bell 206B JetRanger 2	E. Wootton
	G-BBCC	PA-23 Aztec 250D	Northamptonshire School of Flying Ltd/Sywell
	G-BBCD	Beech 95-B55 Baron	L. M. Tulloch
	G-BBCH	Robin DR.400/2+2	Headcorn Flying School Ltd
	G-BBCI	Cessna 150H	L. Jayasekara
	G-BBCN	Robin HR.100/210	K. T. G. Atkins/Teesside
	G-BBCP	Thunder Ax6-56 balloon	J. M. Robinson *Jack Frost*
	G-BBCS	Robin DR.400/140	A. R. G. Besler
	G-BBCW	PA-23 Aztec 250E	JDT Holdings Ltd/Sturgate
	G-BBCY	Luton LA-4A Minor	Shoestring Flying Group/Shoreham
	G-BBCZ	AA-5 Traveler	Languedoc Aviation Ltd/France
	G-BBDB	PA-28 Cherokee 180	T. D. Strange/Newtownards
	G-BBDC	PA-28 Cherokee 140	A. Dunk
	G-BBDD	PA-28 Cherokee 140	Midland Air Training School
	G-BBDE	PA-28R Cherokee Arrow 200-II	R. L. Coleman & A. E. Stevens
	G-BBDG	Concorde 100 ★	British Aerospace PLC/Filton
	G-BBDH	Cessna F.172M	P. S. C. & B. J. Comina
	G-BBDJ	Thunder Ax6-56 balloon	S. W. D. & H. B. Ashby *Jack Tar*
	G-BBDK	V.808C Viscount Freightmaster	British World Airlines Ltd *Viscount Linley*/Southend
	G-BBDL	AA-5 Traveler	D. G. Hopkins & W. Woods/Coventry
	G-BBDM	AA-5 Traveler	D. J. & P. L. Hazell
	G-BBDN	Taylor JT.1 Monoplane	T. Barnes
	G-BBDO	PA-23 Turbo Aztec 250E	Anstee & Ware Ltd/Bristol
	G-BBDP	Robin DR.400/160	Robin Lance Aviation Associates Ltd
	G-BBDT	Cessna 150H	U. K. Mercer & J. K. Sibbald
	G-BBDV	SIPA S.903	W. McAndrew
	G-BBEA	Luton LA-4A Minor	G. C. Bishop
	G-BBEB	PA-28R Cherokee Arrow 200-II	R. D. Rippingale/Thruxton
	G-BBEC	PA-28 Cherokee 180	C. F. Bishop/Clacton
	G-BBED	M.S.894A Rallye Minerva 220	Vista Products
	G-BBEF	PA-28 Cherokee 140	Air Navigation & Trading Ltd/Blackpool
	G-BBEI	PA-31 Turbo Navajo	BKS Surveys Ltd/Exeter
	G-BBEL	PA-28R Cherokee Arrow 180	G. R. Cole & A. Grimshaw/Ronaldsway
	G-BBEN	Bellanca 7GCBC Citabria	C. A. G. Schofield
	G-BBEO	Cessna FRA.150L	R. H. Ford
	G-BBEV	PA-28 Cherokee 140	Comed Aviation Ltd/Blackpool
	G-BBEX	Cessna 185A Skywagon	Westward Airways (Lands End) Ltd
	G-BBEY	PA-23 Aztec 250E	M. Hall
	G-BBFC	AA-1B Trainer	I. J. Hiatt
	G-BBFD	PA-28R Cherokee Arrow 200-II	CR Aviation Ltd
	G-BBFS	Van Den Bemden gas balloon	A. J. F. Smith *Le Tomate*
	G-BBFV	PA-32 Cherokee Six 260	C. J. Janson
	G-BBGB	PA-E23 Aztec 250E	Ravenair/Manchester
	G-BBGC	M.S.893E Rallye 180GT	Mark Thorpe & ptnrs
	G-BBGE	PA-23 Aztec 250D	B. Jones
	G-BBGH	AA-5 Traveler	L. W. Mitchell & D. Abbiss
	G-BBGI	Fuji FA.200-160	D. T. C. Pollock
	G-BBGJ	Cessna 180	B. W. Wells & Burbage Farms Ltd
	G-BBGL	Baby Great Lakes	F. Ball
	G-BBGR	Cameron O-65 balloon	M. L. & L. P. Willoughby
	G-BBGX	Cessna 182P Skylane	WOC Hire Ltd

Reg.	Type	Owner or Operator	Notes
G-BBGZ	CHABA 42 balloon	G. Laslett & ptnrs	
G-BBHC	Enstrom F-28A	Blades Helicopters Ltd/Goodwood	
G-BBHD	Enstrom F-28A	R. E. Harvey	
G-BBHF	PA-23 Aztec 250E	Bevan Lynch Aviation Ltd/Birmingham	
G-BBHG	Cessna E310Q	G. P. Williams	
G-BBHI	Cessna 177RG	T. G. W. Bunce	
G-BBHJ	Piper J-3C-65 Cub	R. V. Miller & J. Stanbridge	
G-BBHK	AT-16 Harvard IIB (FH153)	Bob Warner Aviation/Exeter	
G-BBHL	Sikorsky S-61N Mk II	Bristow Helicopters Ltd *Glamis*	
G-BBHM	Sikorsky S-61N	Bristow Helicopters Ltd	
G-BBHX	M.S.893E Rallye Commodore	JKP Aviation	
G-BBHY	PA-28 Cherokee 180	Air Operations Ltd/Guernsey	
G-BBIA	PA-28R Cherokee Arrow 200-II	A. G. (Commodities) Ltd/Stapleford	
G-BBID	PA-28 Cherokee 140	M. & J. M. McCormac	
G-BBIF	PA-23 Aztec 250E	Accolade Flying Club/Shoreham	
G-BBIH	Enstrom F-28A-UK	Pyramid Precision Engineering Ltd	
G-BBII	Fiat G-46-3B (14)	V. S. E. Norman	
G-BBIL	PA-28 Cherokee 140	India Lima Flying Group	
G-BBIN	Enstrom F-28A	Southern Air Ltd/Shoreham	
G-BBIO	Robin HR.100/210	R. A. King/Headcorn	
G-BBIT	Hughes 269B	Contract Development & Projects (Leeds) Ltd (*stored*)	
G-BBIV	Hughes 269C	A. Harvey	
G-BBIX	PA-28 Cherokee 140	Sterling Contract Hire Ltd	
G-BBJB	Thunder Ax7-77 balloon	St Crispin Balloon Group *Dick Darby*	
G-BBJI	Isaacs Spitfire (RN218)	A. N. R. Houghton & ptnrs	
G-BBJU	Robin DR.400/140	J. C. Lister	
G-BBJV	Cessna F.177RG	Pilot Magazine/Biggin Hill	
G-BBJX	Cessna F.150L	Yorkshire Flying Services Ltd/Leeds	
G-BBJY	Cessna F.172M	J. Luccketti/Barton	
G-BBJZ	Cessna F.172M	Burks, Green & ptnrs	
G-BBKA	Cessna F.150L	R. Hall & L. W. Scattergood	
G-BBKB	Cessna F.150L	Justgold Ltd/Blackpool	
G-BBKC	Cessna F.172M	W. F. Hall	
G-BBKE	Cessna F.150L	Wickenby Aviation Ltd	
G-BBKF	Cessna FRA.150L	Compton Abbas Airfield Ltd	
G-BBKG	Cessna FR.172J	H. J. Edwards & Son	
G-BBKI	Cessna F.172M	C. W. & S.A . Burman	
G-BBKL	CP.301A Emeraude	P. J. Griggs	
G-BBKR	Scheibe SF.24A Motorspatz	P. I. Morgans	
G-BBKU	Cessna FRA.150L	Penguin Group	
G-BBKX	PA-28 Cherokee 180	RAE Flying Club Ltd/Farnborough	
G-BBKY	Cessna F.150L	Howells Group PLC	
G-BBKZ	Cessna 172M	Exeter Flying Club Ltd	
G-BBLA	PA-28 Cherokee 140	Woodgate Aviation Co Ltd/Woodvale	
G-BBLE	Hiller UH-12E	Agricopters Ltd/Chilbolton	
G-BBLH	Piper J-3C-65 Cub	M. J. Dunkerley & P. Greenyer/Biggin Hill	
G-BBLL	Cameron O-84 balloon	University of East Anglia Hot-Air Ballooning Club *Boadicea*	
G-BBLM	SOCATA Rallye 100S	M. & J. Grafton	
G-BBLP	PA-23 Aztec 250D	Donington Aviation Ltd/E. Midlands	
G-BBLS	AA-5 Traveler	D. A. Reid & G. Graham/Prestwick	
G-BBLU	PA-34-200 Seneca II	F. Tranter/Manchester	
G-BBMB	Robin DR.400/180	J. T. M. Ball/Biggin Hill	
G-BBME	BAC One-Eleven 401AK	Maersk Air/British Airways (G-AZMI)/Birmingham	
G-BBMG	BAC One-Eleven 408EF	Maersk Air/British Airways (G-AWEJ)/Birmingham	
G-BBMH	EAA. Sports Biplane Model P.1	K. Dawson	
G-BBMJ	PA-23 Aztec 250E	Microlight Aircraft	
G-BBMN	D.H.C.1 Chipmunk 22	R. Steiner/Panshanger	
G-BBMO	D.H.C.1 Chipmunk 22	Holland Aerobatics Ltd	
G-BBMR	D.H.C.1 Chipmunk T.10 (WB763) ★	Southall Technical College	
G-BBMT	D.H.C.1 Chipmunk 22	V. F. J. Falconer & W. A. Lee/Dunstable	
G-BBMV	D.H.C.1 Chipmunk 22 (WG348)	P. J. Morgan (Aviation) Ltd	
G-BBMW	D.H.C.1 Chipmunk 22 (WK628)	Mike Whisky Group/Shoreham	
G-BBMX	D.H.C.1 Chipmunk 22	A. L. Brown & P. S. Murchison	
G-BBMZ	D.H.C.1 Chipmunk 22	Wycombe Gliding School Syndicate/Booker	
G-BBNA	D.H.C.1 Chipmunk 22 (Lycoming)	Coventry Gliding Club Ltd/Husbands Bosworth	

Notes	Reg.	Type	Owner or Operator
	G-BBNC	D.H.C.1 Chipmunk T.10 (WP790) ★	Mosquito Aircraft Museum
	G-BBND	D.H.C.1 Chipmunk 22 (WD286)	A. J. Organ/Bourn
	G-BBNG	Bell 206B JetRanger 2	Helicopter Crop Spraying Ltd
	G-BBNH	PA-34-200 Seneca II	Lawrence Goodwin Machine Tools Ltd/ Coventry
	G-BBNI	PA-34-200 Seneca II	Channel Aviation Holdings Ltd
	G-BBNJ	Cessna F.150L	Sherburn Aero Club Ltd
	G-BBNN	PA-23 Aztec 250D	Woodgate Executive Air Charter Ltd
	G-BBNO	PA-23 Aztec 250E	Falcon Flying Services/Biggin Hill
	G-BBNT	PA-31-350 Navajo Chieftain	Northern Executive Aviation Ltd/ Manchester
	G-BBNV	Fuji FA.200-160	G. C. Thomas/Kidlington
	G-BBNX	Cessna FRA.150L	General Airline Ltd
	G-BBNZ	Cessna F.172M	R. J. Nunn
	G-BBOA	Cessna F.172M	J. W. J. Adkins/Southend
	G-BBOC	Cameron O-77 balloon	J. A. B. Gray
	G-BBOD	Thunder O-45 balloon	B. R. & M. Boyle
	G-BBOE	Robin HR.200/100	Aberdeen Flying Group
	G-BBOH	Pitts S-1S Special	Venom Jet Promotions Ltd/Bournemouth
	G-BBOJ	PA-23 Aztec 250E ★	Instructional airframe/Cranfield
	G-BBOL	PA-18 Super Cub 150	Lakes Gliding Club Ltd
	G-BBOO	Thunder Ax6-56 balloon	K. Meehan Tigerjack
	G-BBOX	Thunder Ax7-77 balloon	R. C. Weyda Rocinante
	G-BBPK	Evans VP-1	G. D. E. Macdonald
	G-BBPM	Enstrom F-28A	D. Newman
	G-BBPN	Enstrom F-28A	Selecting Ltd
	G-BBPO	Enstrom F-28A	Southern Air Ltd/Shoreham
	G-BBPS	Jodel D.117	A. Appleby/Redhill
	G-BBPU	Boeing 747-136	British Airways Virginia Water
	G-BBPW	Robin HR.100/210	D. H. Smith
	G-BBPX	PA-34-200 Seneca II	Richel Investments Ltd/Guernsey
	G-BBPY	PA-28 Cherokee 180	Sunsaver Ltd
	G-BBRA	PA-23 Aztec 250D	Directair Leasing Ltd
	G-BBRB	D.H.82A Tiger Moth (DF198)	R. Barham/Biggin Hill
	G-BBRC	Fuji FA.200-180	BBRC Ltd
	G-BBRH	Bell 47G-5A	Helicopter Supplies & Engineering Ltd
	G-BBRI	Bell 47G-5A	Alan Mann Helicopters Ltd/Fairoaks
	G-BBRJ	PA-23 Aztec 250E	Duellist Enterprises Ltd
	G-BBRN	Procter Kittiwake (XW784)	J. A. Rees/Haverfordwest
	G-BBRV	D.H.C.1 Chipmunk 22	Liverpool Flying School Ltd
	G-BBRX	SIAI-Marchetti S.205-18F	A. L. Cogswell & R. C. West
	G-BBRZ	AA-5 Traveler	C. P. Osbourne
	G-BBSA	AA-5 Traveler	K. Lynn
	G-BBSB	Beech C23 Sundowner	Sundowner Group/Manchester
	G-BBSC	Beech B24R Sierra	Beechcombers Flying Group
	G-BBSM	PA-32 Cherokee Six 300E	Wardle/Smith Group
	G-BBSS	D.H.C.1A Chipmunk 22	Coventry Gliding Club Ltd/ Husbands Bosworth
	G-BBSU	Cessna 421B	Hoe (Office Equipment Ltd)/Elstree
	G-BBSW	Pietenpol Air Camper	J. K. S. Wills
	G-BBTB	Cessna FRA.150L	C. M. Vlieland-Boddy/Compton Abbas
	G-BBTG	Cessna F.172M	D. H. Laws
	G-BBTH	Cessna F.172M	S. Gilmore/Newtownards
	G-BBTJ	PA-23 Aztec 250E	Geonex Ltd
	G-BBTK	Cessna FRA.150L	Air Service Training Ltd/Perth
	G-BBTL	PA-23 Aztec 250C	Air Navigation & Trading Co Ltd/Blackpool
	G-BBTS	Beech V35B Bonanza	P. S. Bubbear & J. M. Glanville
	G-BBTU	ST-10 Diplomate	Wreck stored/Coventry
	G-BBTX	Beech C23 Sundowner	K. Harding/Blackbushe
	G-BBTY	Beech C23 Sundowner	A. W. Roderick & W. Price
	G-BBTZ	Cessna F.150L	Marnham Investments Ltd
	G-BBUD	Sikorsky S-61N Mk II	British International Helicopters
	G-BBUE	AA-5 Traveler	Hebog (Mon) Cyfyngedig
	G-BBUF	AA-5 Traveler	W. McLaren
	G-BBUG	PA-16 Clipper	J. Dolan
	G-BBUJ	Cessna 421B	Continental Services PLC
	G-BBUL	Mitchell-Procter Kittiwake 1	R. Bull
	G-BBUT	Western O-65 balloon	G. F. Turnbull
	G-BBUU	Piper J-3C-65 Cub	O. J. J. Rogers
	G-BBVA	Sikorsky S-61N Mk II	Bristow Helicopters Ltd Vega
	G-BBVF	SA Twin Pioneer III ★	Museum of Flight/E. Fortune
	G-BBVG	PA-23 Aztec 250C ★	(stored)/Little Staughton

Reg.	Type	Owner or Operator	Notes
G-BBVI	Enstrom F-28A ★	Ground trainer/Kidlington	
G-BBVJ	Beech B24R Sierra	S. K. T. & C. M. Neofytou	
G-BBVO	Isaacs Fury II (S1579)	C. M. Barnes & D. A. Wirdnam	
G-BBVP	Westland-Bell 47G-3B1	CKS Air Ltd/Southend	
G-BBWN	D.H.C.1 Chipmunk 22 (WZ876)	D. C. Budd	
G-BBXB	Cessna FRA.150L	M. L. Swain (stored)/Bourn	
G-BBXG	PA-34-200 Seneca II	SFC (Air Taxis) Ltd/Stapleford	
G-BBXH	Cessna FR.172F	D. Ridley	
G-BBXK	PA-34-200 Seneca	Poyston Aviation	
G-BBXL	Cessna E310Q	Chatsworth Studios Ltd/Newcastle	
G-BBXO	Enstrom F-28A	Repetek Ltd	
G-BBXS	Piper J-3C-65 Cub	M. J. Butler (G-ALMA)/Langham	
G-BBXU	Beech B24R Sierra	B. M. Russell/Coventry	
G-BBXW	PA-28-151 Warrior	Shropshire Aero Club Ltd	
G-BBXX	PA-31-350 Navajo Chieftain	Natural Environment Research Council	
G-BBXY	Bellanca 7GCBC Citabria	J. Turner/Shoreham	
G-BBXZ	Evans VP-1	D. W. Smart	
G-BBYB	PA-18 Super Cub 95	Tiger Club (1990) Ltd/Headcorn	
G-BBYE	Cessna 195	S. H. C. Whitfield	
G-BBYH	Cessna 182P	Croftmarsh Ltd	
G-BBYK	PA-23 Aztec 250E	Kraken Air/Cardiff	
G-BBYL	Cameron O-77 balloon	Buckingham Balloon Club Jammy	
G-BBYM	H.P.137 Jetstream 200	British Aerospace PLC (G-AYWR)/Warton	
G-BBYO	BN-2A Mk.III Trislander	Aurigny Air Services (G-BBWR)/Guernsey	
G-BBYP	PA-28 Cherokee 140	R. A. Wakefield	
G-BBYS	Cessna 182P Skylane	I. M. Jones	
G-BBZF	PA-28 Cherokee 140	J. A. Havers & M. G. West/Elstree	
G-BBZH	PA-28R Cherokee Arrow 200-II	Zulu Hotel Club	
G-BBZI	PA-31-310 Turbo Navajo	Air Care (South West) Ltd	
G-BBZJ	PA-34-200 Seneca II	Sentry Courier Ltd/Blackbushe	
G-BBZN	Fuji FA.200-180	J. Westwood & P. D. Wedd	
G-BBZO	Fuji FA.200-160	G-BBZO Group	
G-BBZS	Enstrom F-28A	Southern Air Ltd/Shoreham	
G-BBZV	PA-28R Cherokee Arrow 200-II	Unicol Engineering/Kidlington	
G-BCAC	M.S.894A Rallye Minerva 220	R. S. Rogers/Cardiff	
G-BCAH	D.H.C.1 Chipmunk 22 (WG316)	V. B. Wheele/Shoreham	
G-BCAN	Thunder Ax7-77 balloon	Wessex Hot-Air Team	
G-BCAP	Cameron O-56 balloon	S. R. Seager	
G-BCAR	Thunder Ax7-77 balloon ★	British Balloon Museum/Newbury	
G-BCAT	PA-31-310 Turbo Navajo	Hubbardair Ltd	
G-BCAZ	PA-12 Super Cruiser	A. D. Williams	
G-BCBD	Bede BD-5B	Brockmore-Bede Aircraft (UK) Ltd/ Shobdon	
G-BCBG	PA-23 Aztec 250E	M. J. L. Batt/Booker	
G-BCBH	Fairchild 24R-46A Argus III	Ebork Ltd	
G-BCBJ	PA-25 Pawnee 235	Deeside Gliding Club (Aberdeenshire) Ltd	
G-BCBK	Cessna 421B	Brown Pestell Ltd	
G-BCBL	Fairchild 24R-46A Argus III (HB751)	F. J. Cox	
G-BCBM	PA-23 Aztec 250C	S. Lightbrown & M. Kavanagh	
G-BCBR	AJEP/Wittman W.8 Tailwind	C. W. N. Huke & M. J. A. Trudgill	
G-BCBW	Cessna 182P	Teesside Aero Club Ltd	
G-BCBX	Cessna F.150L	J. Kelly/Newtownards	
G-BCBY	Cessna F.150L	Scottish Airways Flyers (Prestwick) Ltd	
G-BCBZ	Cessna 337C	J. J. Zwetsloot	
G-BCCB	Robin HR.200/100	M. J. Ellis	
G-BCCC	Cessna F.150L	Fleeting Moments Ltd	
G-BCCD	Cessna F.172M	Austin Aviation Ltd	
G-BCCE	PA-23 Aztec 250E	Falcon Flying Services/Biggin Hill	
G-BCCF	PA-28 Cherokee 180	J. T. Friskney Ltd/Skegness	
G-BCCG	Thunder Ax7-65 balloon	N. H. Ponsford	
G-BCCJ	AA-5 Traveler	T. Needham/Manchester	
G-BCCK	AA-5 Traveler	Prospect Air Ltd/Barton	
G-BCCR	CP.301A Emeraude (modified)	J. H. & C. J. Waterman	
G-BCCU	BN-2A Mk.III-1 Trislander	Cormack (Aircraft Services) Ltd	
G-BCCX	D.H.C.1 Chipmunk 22 (Lycoming)	RAFGSA/Dishforth	
G-BCCY	Robin HR.200/100	Bristol Strut Flying Group	
G-BCDA	Boeing 727-46		
G-BCDB	PA-34-200 Seneca II	A. & G. Aviation Ltd/Bournemouth	
G-BCDC	PA-18 Super Cub 95	Cotswold Aero Club Ltd/Staverton	
G-BCDJ	PA-28 Cherokee 140	C. Wren/Southend	
G-BCDK	Partenavia P.68B	Truman Aviation Ltd/Tollerton	

Notes	Reg.	Type	Owner or Operator
	G-BCDL	Cameron O-42 balloon	D. P. & Mrs B. O. Turner *Chums*
	G-BCDN	F.27 Friendship Mk 200	Air UK/Norwich
	G-BCDR	Thunder Ax7-77 balloon	W. G. Johnston & ptnrs Obelix
	G-BCDY	Cessna FRA.150L	Air Service Training Ltd/Perth
	G-BCEA	Sikorsky S-61N Mk II	British International Helicopters
	G-BCEB	Sikorsky S-61N Mk II	British International Helicopters/Penzance
	G-BCEC	Cessna F.172M	United Propedent Ltd/Manchester
	G-BCEE	AA-5 Traveler	Echo Echo Ltd/Bournemouth
	G-BCEF	AA-5 Traveler	Forest Aviation Ltd/Guernsey
	G-BCEN	BN-2A Islander	Atlantic Air Transport Ltd/Coventry
	G-BCEO	AA-5 Traveler	N. F. Lyons
	G-BCEP	AA-5 Traveler	P. Curley & A. J. Radford
	G-BCER	GY-201 Minicab	D. Beaumont/Sherburn
	G-BCEU	Cameron O-42 balloon	Entertainment Services Ltd *Harlequin*
	G-BCEX	PA-23 Aztec 250E	Weekes Bros (Welling) Ltd/Biggin Hill
	G-BCEY	D.H.C.1 Chipmunk 22	Gopher Flying Group
	G-BCEZ	Cameron O-84 balloon	Balloon Collection
	G-BCFC	Cameron O-65 balloon	B. H. Mead *Candy Twist*
	G-BCFD	West balloon ★	British Balloon Museum *Hellfire*/Newbury
	G-BCFF	Fuji FA-200-160	G. W. Brown & M. R. Gibbons
	G-BCFO	PA-18 Super Cub 150	Portsmouth Naval Gliding Club/Lee-on-Solent
	G-BCFR	Cessna FRA.150L	Rentair Ltd
	G-BCFW	SAAB 91D Safir	D. R. Williams
	G-BCFY	Luton LA-4A Minor	G. Capes
	G-BCGB	Bensen B.8	A. Melody
	G-BCGC	D.H.C.1 Chipmunk 22 (WP903)	Culdrose Gliding Club
	G-BCGG	Jodel DR.250 Srs 160	C. G. Gray (G-ATZL)
	G-BCGH	SNCAN NC.854S	Nord Flying Group
	G-BCGI	PA-28 Cherokee 140	A. Dodd/Redhill
	G-BCGJ	PA-28 Cherokee 140	J. Miller & J. L. Hunter/Edinburgh
	G-BCGL	Jodel D.112	C. L. Betts & ptnrs/Shoreham
	G-BCGM	Jodel D.120	D. N. K. & M. A. Symon
	G-BCGN	PA-28 Cherokee 140	Oxford Flyers Ltd/Kidlington
	G-BCGS	PA-28R Cherokee Arrow 200	Arrow Aviation Group
	G-BCGT	PA-28 Cherokee 140	T. D. Bugg
	G-BCGW	Jodel D.11	G. H. & M. D. Chittenden
	G-BCGX	Bede BD-5A/B	R. Hodgson
	G-BCHK	Cessna F.172H	E. C. & A. K. Shimmin
	G-BCHL	D.H.C.1 Chipmunk 22A (WP788)	Shropshire Soaring Ltd/Sleap
	G-BCHM	SA.341G Gazelle 1	Westland Helicopters Ltd/Yeovil
	G-BCHP	CP.1310-C3 Super Emeraude	R. F. Sothcott (G-JOSI)
	G-BCHT	Schleicher ASK.16	Dunstable K16 Group
	G-BCHV	D.H.C.1 Chipmunk 22	N. F. Charles/Sywell
	G-BCHX	SF.23A Sperling	*(stored)*/Rufforth
	G-BCID	PA-34-200 Seneca II	C. J. Freeman/Headcorn
	G-BCIE	PA-28-151 Warrior	Scottish Airways Flyers (Prestwick) Ltd
	G-BCIF	PA-28 Cherokee 140	Fryer-Robins Aviation Ltd/E. Midlands
	G-BCIH	D.H.C.1 Chipmunk 22 (WD363)	J. M. Hosey/Stansted
	G-BCIJ	AA-5 Traveler	I. J. Boyd & D. J. McCooke
	G-BCIK	AA-5 Traveler	Trent Aviation Ltd
	G-BCIN	Thunder Ax7-77 balloon	P. G & R. A. Vale
	G-BCIO	PA-39 Twin Comanche 160 C/R	F. Duckworth
	G-BCIR	PA-28-151 Warrior	P. J. Brennan
	G-BCIT	CIT/A1 Srs 1	Cranfield Institute of Technology
	G-BCJF	Beagle B.206 Srs 1	A. A. Mattacks & G. H. Nolan
	G-BCJH	Mooney M.20F	P. B. Bossard
	G-BCJM	PA-28 Cherokee 140	Top Cat Aviation Ltd
	G-BCJN	PA-28 Cherokee 140	A. J. Steed/Goodwood
	G-BCJO	PA-28R Cherokee Arrow 200	Tomcat Aviation/Norwich
	G-BCJP	PA-28 Cherokee 140	K. E. Tolliday & ptnrs
	G-BCJS	PA-23 Aztec 250C ★	*derelict*/Aldergrove
	G-BCKN	D.H.C.1A Chipmunk 22	RAFGSA/Cranwell
	G-BCKO	PA-23 Aztec 250E	Geonex UK Ltd
	G-BCKP	Luton LA-5A Major	D. & W. H. Gough
	G-BCKS	Fuji FA.200-180	J. T. Hicks/Goodwood
	G-BCKT	Fuji FA.200-180	Littlewick Green Service Station Ltd/Booker
	G-BCKU	Cessna FRA.150L	Air Service Training Ltd/Perth
	G-BCKV	Cessna FRA.150L	Air Service Training Ltd/Perth
	G-BCLC	Sikorsky S-61N	Bristow Helicopters/HM Coastguard
	G-BCLD	Sikorsky S-61N	Bristow Helicopters Ltd
	G-BCLI	AA-5 Traveler	Albemotive Ltd

Reg.	Type	Owner or Operator	Notes
G-BCLJ	AA-5 Traveler	E. A. A. A. Wiltens	
G-BCLL	PA-28 Cherokee 180	K. J. Scamp	
G-BCLS	Cessna 170B	Teesside Flight Centre Ltd	
G-BCLT	M.S.894A Rallye Minerva 220	S. Clough	
G-BCLU	Jodel D.117	N. A. Wallace	
G-BCLW	AA-1B Trainer	E. J. McMillan	
G-BCMD	PA-18 Super Cub 95	J. G. Brooks/Dunkeswell	
G-BCMJ	SA.102.5 Cavalier (tailwheel)	R. G. Sykes/Shoreham	
G-BCMT	Isaacs Fury II	M. H. Turner	
G-BCNC	GY.201 Minicab	J. R. Wraight	
G-BCNP	Cameron O-77 balloon	M. L. J. Ritchie	
G-BCNR	Thunder Ax7-77A balloon	S. J. Miliken & ptnrs	
G-BCNT	Partenavia P.68B	Welsh Airways Ltd	
G-BCNX	Piper J-3C-65 Cub	K. J. Lord/Ipswich	
G-BCNZ	Fuji FA.200-160	J. Bruton & A. Lincoln/Manchester	
G-BCOB	Piper J-3C-65 Cub	R. W. & Mrs J. W. Marjoram	
G-BCOF	H.S.748 Srs 2B	British Aerospace PLC/Woodford	
G-BCOG	Jodel D.112	C. Hughes & W. K. Rose/Kidlington	
G-BCOI	D.H.C.1 Chipmunk 22	D. S. McGregor & A. T. Letham	
G-BCOJ	Cameron O-56 balloon	T. J. Knott & M. J. Webber	
G-BCOL	Cessna F.172M	A. H. Creaser	
G-BCOM	Piper J-3C-65 Cub	Dougal Flying Group/Shoreham	
G-BCOO	D.H.C.1 Chipmunk 22	T. G. Fielding & M. S. Morton/Blackpool	
G-BCOP	PA-28R Cherokee Arrow 200-II	E. A. Saunders/Halfpenny Green	
G-BCOR	SOCATA Rallye 100ST	W. E. Taylor & Son Ltd/Exeter	
G-BCOU	D.H.C.1 Chipmunk 22 (WK522)	P. J. Loweth	
G-BCOX	Bede BD-5A	H. J. Cox	
G-BCOY	D.H.C.1 Chipmunk 22 (Lycoming)	Coventry Gliding Club Ltd/Husbands Bosworth	
G-BCPB	Howes radio-controlled model free balloon	R. B. & Mrs C. Howes *Posbee 1*	
G-BCPD	GY-201 Minicab	A. H. K. Denniss/Halfpenny Green	
G-BCPE	Cessna F.150M	Smallfry Leasing Ltd	
G-BCPF	PA-23 Aztec 250D	Chapman Commercials Ltd	
G-BCPG	PA-28R Cherokee Arrow 200-II	Roses Flying Group/Liverpool	
G-BCPH	Piper J-3C-65 Cub (329934)	M. J. Janaway	
G-BCPJ	Piper J-3C-65 Cub	Piper Cub Group	
G-BCPK	Cessna F.172M	J. G. Bell	
G-BCPN	AA-5 Traveler	B.W. Agricultural Equipments Ltd	
G-BCPO	Partenavia P.68B	H. Russell	
G-BCPU	D.H.C.1 Chipmunk T.10	P. Waller/Booker	
G-BCPX	Szep HFC.125	A. Szep/Netherthorpe	
G-BCRB	Cessna F.172M	D. Nelligan/Biggin Hill	
G-BCRE	Cameron O-77 balloon	A. R. Langton	
G-BCRH	Alaparma Baldo B.75	A. L. Scadding/(*stored*)	
G-BCRI	Cameron O-65 balloon	V. J. Thorne *Joseph*	
G-BCRJ	Taylor JT.1 Monoplane	S. Wolstenholme	
G-BCRK	SA.102.5 Cavalier	R. Simpson	
G-BCRL	PA-28-151 Warrior	F. N. Garland/Biggin Hill	
G-BCRN	Cessna FRA.150L	Air Service Training Ltd/Perth	
G-BCRP	PA-E23 Aztec 250E	County Garage (Cheltenham) Ltd	
G-BCRR	AA-5B Tiger	Capulet Flying Group/Elstree	
G-BCRT	Cessna F.150M	Fordaire Aviation Ltd	
G-BCRX	D.H.C.1 Chipmunk 22 (WD292)	Tuplin Ltd/Denham	
G-BCSA	D.H.C.1 Chipmunk 22	RAFGSA/Kinloss	
G-BCSB	D.H.C.1 Chipmunk 22 (Lycoming)	RAFGSA/Cosford	
G-BCSL	D.H.C.1 Chipmunk 22	Jalawain Ltd/Barton	
G-BCSM	Bellanca 8GCBC Scout	B. T. Spreckley/Southampton	
G-BCST	M.S.893A Rallye Commodore 180	P. J. Wilcox/Cranfield	
G-BCSX	Thunder Ax7-77 balloon	C. Wolstenholm	
G-BCSY	Taylor JT.2 Titch	T. Hartwell & D. Wilkinson ·	
G-BCTA	PA-28-151 Warrior	T. G. Aviation Ltd/Manston	
G-BCTF	PA-28-151 Warrior	Premier Plane Leasing Co Ltd	
G-BCTI	Schleicher ASK.16	Tango India Syndicate/Cranfield	
G-BCTJ	Cessna 310Q	TJ Flying Group	
G-BCTK	Cessna FR.172J	G-BCTK Group	
G-BCTT	Evans VP-1	B. J. Boughton	
G-BCTU	Cessna FRA.150M	J. H. Fisher & N. D. Hall	
G-BCUB	Piper J-3C-65 Cub	A. L. Brown & G. Attwell/Bourn	
G-BCUF	Cessna F.172M	D. J. Parkinson	
G-BCUH	Cessna F.150M	M. G. Montgomerie	
G-BCUI	Cessna F.172M	Hillhouse Estates Ltd	
G-BCUJ	Cessna F.150M	Sandtoft Air Services (1985) Ltd	

Notes	Reg.	Type	Owner or Operator
	G-BCUL	SOCATA Rallye 100ST	C. A. Ussher & Fountain Estates Ltd
	G-BCUW	Cessna F.177RG	S. J. Westley
	G-BCUY	Cessna FRA.150M	S. R. Cameron
	G-BCVA	Cameron O-65 balloon	J. C. Bass & ptnrs Crepe Suzette
	G-BCVB	PA-17 Vagabond	A. T. Nowak/Popham
	G-BCVC	SOCATA Rallye 100ST	J. L. & T. A. Hodges
	G-BCVE	Evans VP-2	D. Masterson & D. B. Winstanley
	G-BCVF	Practavia Pilot Sprite	D. G. Hammersley
	G-BCVG	Cessna FRA.150L	Air Service Training Ltd/Perth
	G-BCVH	Cessna FRA.150L	Yorkshire Light Aircraft Ltd/Leeds
	G-BCVI	Cessna FR.172J	Cumbria Aero Club/Carlisle
	G-BCVJ	Cessna F.172M	Rothland Ltd
	G-BCVW	GY-80 Horizon 180	P. M. A. Parrett/Dunkeswell
	G-BCVY	PA-34-200T Seneca II	C.S.E. Aviation Ltd/Kidlington
	G-BCWB	Cessna 182P	G. McCabe
	G-BCWH	Practavia Pilot Sprite	R. Tasker/Blackpool
	G-BCWK	Alpavia Fournier RF-3	T. J. Hartwell & D. R. Wilkinson
	G-BCWL	Westland Lysander III (V9281)	Wessex Aviation & Transport Ltd
	G-BCWR	BN-2A-21 Islander	Pilatus BN Ltd/Bembridge
	G-BCXB	SOCATA Rallye 100ST	A. Smails
	G-BCXE	Robin DR.400/2+2	C. J. Freeman
	G-BCXJ	Piper J-3C-65 Cub (413048)	W. F. Stockdale/Compton Abbas
	G-BCXN	D.H.C.1 Chipmunk 22 (WP800)	G. M. Turner/Duxford
	G-BCYH	DAW Privateer Mk. 2	D. B. Limbert
	G-BCYJ	D.H.C.1 Chipmunk 22 (WG307)	R. A. L. Falconer
	G-BCYK	Avro CF.100 Mk 4 Canuck (18393) ★	Imperial War Museum/Duxford
	G-BCYM	D.H.C.1 Chipmunk 22	C. R. R. Eagleton/Headcorn
	G-BCYR	Cessna F.172M	Donne Enterprises
	G-BCZH	D.H.C.1 Chipmunk 22 (WK622)	A. C. Byrne/Norwich
	G-BCZI	Thunder Ax7-77 balloon	R. G. Griffin & R. Blackwell
	G-BCZM	Cessna F.172M	Cornwall Flying Club Ltd/Bodmin
	G-BCZN	Cessna F.150M	Mona Aviation Ltd
	G-BCZO	Cameron O-77 balloon	W. O. T. Holmes Leo
	G-BDAB	SA.102.5 Cavalier	A. H. Brown
	G-BDAC	Cameron O-77 balloon	D. Fowler & J. Goody Chocolate Ripple
	G-BDAD	Taylor JT.1 Monoplane	G-BDAD Group
	G-BDAG	Taylor JT.1 Monoplane	R. S. Basinger
	G-BDAH	Evans VP-1	A. M. Carter
	G-BDAI	Cessna FRA.150M	A. Sharma
	G-BDAK	R. Commander 112A	C. Boydon
	G-BDAL	R. 500S Shrike Commander	Quantel Ltd
	G-BDAM	AT-16 Harvard IIB (FE992)	N. A. Lees & E. C. English
	G-BDAO	SIPA S.91	A. L. Rose
	G-BDAP	AJEP Tailwind	J. Whiting
	G-BDAR	Evans VP-1	R. B. Valler
	G-BDAX	PA-23 Aztec 250C	P. G. Lawrence
	G-BDAY	Thunder Ax5-42A balloon	T. M. Donnelly Meconium
	G-BDBD	Wittman W.8 Tailwind	A. J. Chaplin
	G-BDBF	FRED Srs 2	I. D. Worthington
	G-BDBH	Bellanca 7GCBC Citabria	Inkpen Gliding Club Ltd/Thruxton
	G-BDBI	Cameron O-77 balloon	C. A. Butter & J. J. Cook
	G-BDBJ	Cessna 182P	H. C. Wilson
	G-BDBL	D.H.C.1 Chipmunk 22 (WK621)	R. J. Fox
	G-BDBP	D.H.C.1 Chipmunk 22 (WP843)	Glidegold Ltd/Booker
	G-BDBU	Cessna F.150M	Andrewsfield Flying Club Ltd
	G-BDBV	Jodel D.11A	Seething Jodel Group
	G-BDBZ	W.S.55 Whirlwind Srs 2 ★	Ground instruction airframe/Kidlington
	G-BDCB	D.H.C.1 Chipmunk 22 (WP835)	R. F. Tolhurst
	G-BDCC	D.H.C.1 Chipmunk 22 (Lycoming)	Coventry Gliding Club Ltd/ Husbands Bosworth
	G-BDCD	Piper J-3C-85 Cub (480133)	Suzanne C. Brooks/Slinfold
	G-BDCE	Cessna F.172H	A. T. Booth & G. Owens
	G-BDCI	CP.301A Emeraude	D. L. Sentance
	G-BDCK	AA-5 Traveler	Northfield Garage Ltd
	G-BDCL	AA-5 Traveler	J. Crowe
	G-BDCM	Cessna F.177RG	P. R. Gunnel/Gamston
	G-BDCO	B.121 Pup 1	K. R. Knapp
	G-BDCS	Cessna 421B	British Aerospace PLC/Warton
	G-BDCU	Cameron O-77 balloon	H. P. Carlton
	G-BDDD	D.H.C.1 Chipmunk 22	RAE Aero Club Ltd/Farnborough
	G-BDDF	Jodel D.120	Sywell Skyriders Flying Group

Reg.	Type	Owner or Operator	Notes
G-BDDG	Jodel D.112	Wandering Imp Group	
G-BDDS	PA-25 Pawnee 235	Vale of Neath Gliding Club	
G-BDDT	PA-25 Pawnee 235	Boston Aviation Services	
G-BDDX	Whittaker MW.2B Excalibur ★	Cornwall Aero Park/Helston	
G-BDDZ	CP.301A Emeraude	V. W. Smith & E. C. Mort	
G-BDEC	SOCATA Rallye 100ST	L. J. R. C. Bolingbroke	
G-BDEF	PA-34-200T Seneca II	Haylock Son & Hunter	
G-BDEH	Jodel D.120A	EH Flying Group/Bristol	
G-BDEI	Jodel D.9 Bebe	G. M. Roberts	
G-BDET	D.H.C.1 Chipmunk 22	D. Algra	
G-BDEU	D.H.C.1 Chipmunk 22 (WP808)	A. Taylor	
G-BDEV	Taylor JT.1 Monoplane	D. A. Bass	
G-BDEW	Cessna FRA.150M	C. M. Vlieland-Boddy/Compton Abbas	
G-BDEX	Cessna FRA.150M	C. M. Vlieland-Boddy/Compton Abbas	
G-BDEY	Piper J-3C-65 Cub	Ducksworth Flying Club	
G-BDEZ	Piper J-3C-65 Cub	R. J. K. Spurrell	
G-BDFB	Currie Wot	J. Jennings	
G-BDFC	R. Commander 112A	R. Fletcher	
G-BDFG	Cameron O-65 balloon	N. A. Robertson *Golly II*	
G-BDFH	Auster AOP.9 (XR240)	R. O. Holden/Booker	
G-BDFI	Cessna F.150M	Willowair Flying Club Ltd/Southend	
G-BDFJ	Cessna F.150M	T. J. Lynn/Sibson	
G-BDFM	Caudron C.270 Luciole	G. V. Gower	
G-BDFR	Fuji FA.200-160	A. Wright	
G-BDFS	Fuji FA.200-160	B. Sharbati & B. Lawrence	
G-BDFU	Dragonfly MPA Mk 1 ★	Museum of Flight/E. Fortune	
G-BDFW	R. Commander 112A	M. & D. A. Doubleday	
G-BDFX	Auster 5 (TW517)	Bee Flight Flying Group	
G-BDFY	AA-5 Traveler	Grumman Group	
G-BDFZ	Cessna F.150M	Skyviews & General Ltd	
G-BDGA	Bushby-Long Midget Mustang	J. R. Owen	
G-BDGB	GY-20 Minicab	D. G. Burden	
G-BDGH	Thunder Ax7-77 balloon	R. J. Mitchener & P. F. Smart	
G-BDGM	PA-28-151 Warrior	B. Whiting	
G-BDGN	AA-5B Tiger	R. Stone	
G-BDGO	Thunder Ax7-77 balloon	International Distillers & Vintners Ltd	
G-BDGP	Cameron V-65 balloon	A. Mayers & V. Lawton	
G-BDGY	PA-28 Cherokee 140	R. E. Woolridge/Staverton	
G-BDHJ	Pazmany PL.1	C. T. Millner	
G-BDHK	Piper J-3C-65 Cub (329417)	A. Liddiard	
G-BDHL	PA-23 Aztec 250E	North West Air Charter Ltd	
G-BDIC	D.H.C.1 Chipmunk 22 (WD388)	Woodvale Aviation Co Ltd	
G-BDIE	R. Commander 112A	T. D. Saveker	
G-BDIG	Cessna 182P	R. J. & J. M. Z. Keel	
G-BDIH	Jodel D.117	N. D. H. Stokes	
G-BDIJ	Sikorsky S-61N	Bristow Helicopters Ltd	
G-BDIM	D.H.C.1 Chipmunk 22	Historic Flying Ltd/Cambridge	
G-BDIX	D.H.106 Comet 4C ★	Museum of Flight/E. Fortune	
G-BDJB	Taylor JT.1 Monoplane	J. F. Barber	
G-BDJC	AJEP W.8 Tailwind	J. H. Medforth	
G-BDJD	Jodel D.112	Drem Sport Aviation Group	
G-BDJF	Bensen B.8MV	R. P. White	
G-BDJG	Luton LA-4A Minor	A. W. Anderson & A. J. Short	
G-BDJN	Robin HR.200/100	Haimoss Ltd/Old Sarum	
G-BDJP	Piper J-3C-90 Cub	J. M. Pothecary (*stored*)/Shoreham	
G-BDJR	SNCAN NC.858	R. F. M. Marson & P. M. Harmer	
G-BDKB	SOCATA Rallye 150ST	N. C. Anderson	
G-BDKC	Cessna A185F	Bridge of Tilt Co Ltd	
G-BDKD	Enstrom F-28A	TR Bitz	
G-BDKH	CP.301A Emeraude	P. N. Marshall	
G-BDKI	Sikorsky S-61N	British International Helicopters	
G-BDKJ	K. & S. SA.102.5 Cavalier	B. D. Battman	
G-BDKK	Bede BD-5B	A. W. Odell (*stored*)/Headcorn	
G-BDKM	SIPA 903	S. W. Markham	
G-BDKU	Taylor JT.1 Monoplane	C. M. Harding & J. Ball	
G-BDKV	PA-28R Cherokee Arrow 200-II	Bravo Juliet Whisky Flying Ltd	
G-BDKW	R. Commander 112A	R. W. Denny/Ipswich	
G-BDLO	AA-5A Cheetah	S. & J. Dolan/Denham	
G-BDLR	AA-5B Tiger	MAGEC Aviation Ltd/Luton	
G-BDLS	AA-1B Trainer	Lima Sierra Partnership	
G-BDLT	R. Commander 112A	D. L. Churchward	
G-BDLY	SA.102.5 Cavalier	P. R. Stevens/Southampton	

Notes	Reg.	Type	Owner or Operator
	G-BDMB	Robin HR.100/210	R. J. Hitchman & Son
	G-BDMM	Jodel D.11	P. N. Marshall
	G-BDMO	Thunder Ax7-77A ballon	G. C. Elson
	G-BDMS	Piper J-3C-65 Cub	A. T. H. Martin
	G-BDMW	Jodel DR.100	R. O. F. Harper
	G-BDNC	Taylor JT.1 Monoplane	G. A. Stanley
	G-BDNG	Taylor JT.1 Monoplane	J. M. Fforde
	G-BDNO	Taylor JT.1 Monoplane	D. A. Healey
	G-BDNP	BN-2A Islander ★	*Ground parachute trainer*/Headcorn
	G-BDNR	Cessna FRA.150M	Cheshire Air Training School Ltd/Liverpool
	G-BDNT	Jodel D.92	R. F. Morton
	G-BDNU	Cessna F.172M	C. H. P. Bell
	G-BDNW	AA-1B Trainer	P. R. Huntley
	G-BDNX	AA-1B Trainer	R. M. North
	G-BDNZ	Cameron O-77 balloon	I. L. McHale
	G-BDOC	Sikorsky S-61N Mk II	Bristow Helicopters Ltd
	G-BDOD	Cessna F.150M	M. C. Latham
	G-BDOE	Cessna FR.172J	Rocket Partnership
	G-BDOF	Cameron O-56 balloon	The New Holker Estates Co Ltd
	G-BDOG	SA Bulldog Srs 200/2100	D. C. Bonsall/Netherthorpe
	G-BDOL	Piper J-3C-65 Cub	U. E. Allman & M. C. Jordan/Shoreham
	G-BDON	Thunder Ax7-77A balloon	J. R. Henderson & ptnrs
	G-BDOR	Thunder Ax6-56A balloon	M. S. Drinkwater & G. Fitzpatrick
	G-BDOT	BN-2A Mk.III-2 Trislander	Cormack (Aircraft Services) Ltd
	G-BDOW	Cessna FRA.150M	TT & Co
	G-BDPA	PA-28-151 Warrior	G-BDPA Flying Group/Staverton
	G-BDPF	Cessna F.172M	Semloh Aviation Services/Andrewsfield
	G-BDPK	Cameron O-56 balloon	Rango Balloon & Kite Co
	G-BDPV	Boeing 747-136	British Airways *Blea Water*
	G-BDRB	AA-5B Tiger	Dorset Air Ltd
	G-BDRC	V.724 Viscount ★	Fire School/Manston
	G-BDRD	Cessna FRA.150M	Air Service Training Ltd/Perth
	G-BDRF	Taylor JT.1 Monoplane	B. R. Ratcliffe
	G-BDRG	Taylor JT.2 Titch	D. R. Gray
	G-BDRJ	D.H.C.1 Chipmunk 22 (WP857)	J. C. Schooling
	G-BDRK	Cameron O-65 balloon	D. L. Smith *Smirk*
	G-BDRL	Stitts SA-3A Playboy	W. McNally & J. L. Clarke
	G-BDSA	FRED Srs 2	W. D. M. Turtle
	G-BDSB	PA-28-181 Archer II	Testair Ltd/Blackbushe
	G-BDSE	Cameron O-77 balloon	British Airways *Concorde*
	G-BDSF	Cameron O-56 balloon	A. R. Greensides & B. H. Osbourne
	G-BDSH	PA-28 Cherokee 140	P. M. Ireland
	G-BDSK	Cameron O-65 balloon	Southern Balloon Group *Carousel II*
	G-BDSL	Cessna F.150M	Cleveland Flying School Ltd/Teesside
	G-BDSM	Slingsby T.31B Cadet III	J. A. L. Parton
	G-BDSO	Cameron O-31 balloon	Budget Rent-a-Car *Baby Budget*
	G-BDTB	Evans VP-1	A. M. Witt
	G-BDTL	Evans VP-1	A. K. Lang
	G-BDTN	BN-2A Mk III-2 Trislander	Aurigny Air Services Ltd/Guernsey
	G-BDTU	Omega III gas balloon	G. F. Turnbull
	G-BDTV	Mooney M.20F	S. Redfearn
	G-BDTW	Cassutt Racer	B. E. Smith & C. S. Thompson/Redhill
	G-BDTX	Cessna F.150M	A. A. & R. N. Croxford/Southend
	G-BDUI	Cameron V-56 balloon	D. C. Johnson
	G-BDUJ	PA-31-310 Turbo Navajo	Club Air (Europe) Ltd
	G-BDUL	Evans VP-1	J. T. Taylor
	G-BDUM	Cessna F.150M	SFG Ltd/Shipdham
	G-BDUN	PA-34-200T Seneca II	Air Medical Ltd
	G-BDUO	Cessna F.150M	Sandown Aero Club
	G-BDUX	Slingsby T.31B Cadet III	J. C. Anderson/Cranfield
	G-BDUY	Robin DR.400/140B	J. M. Dean & A. L. Jubb
	G-BDUZ	Cameron V-56 balloon	Zebedee Balloon Service
	G-BDVA	PA-17 Vagabond	I. M. Callier
	G-BDVB	PA-15 (PA-17) Vagabond	B. P. Gardner
	G-BDVC	PA-17 Vagabond	A. R. Caveen
	G-BDVG	Thunder Ax6-56A balloon	R. F. Pollard *Argonaut*
	G-BDVS	F.27 Friendship Mk 200	Air UK *Eric Gandar Dower*/Norwich
	G-BDVU	Mooney M.20F	Digital Duplication Ltd/Stapleford
	G-BDWA	SOCATA Rallye 150ST	J. Thompson-Wilson/Newtownards
	G-BDWE	Flaglor Scooter	D. W. Evernden
	G-BDWG	BN-2A Islander	Wilsons Transport Ltd
	G-BDWH	SOCATA Rallye 150ST	M. A. Jones
	G-BDWJ	SE-5A (replica) (F8010)	S. M. Smith/Booker

Reg.	Type	Owner or Operator	Notes
G-BDWK	Beech 95-58 Baron	Cammac Coal Ltd	
G-BDWL	PA-25 Pawnee 235	Peterborough & Spalding Gliding Club	
G-BDWM	Mustang scale replica (FB226)	D. C. Bonsall	
G-BDWO	Howes Ax6 balloon	R. B. & C. Howes *Griffin*	
G-BDWP	PA-32R Cherokee Lance 300	W. M. Brown & B. J. Wood/Birmingham	
G-BDWV	BN-2A Mk III-2 Trislander	Aurigny Air Services Ltd/Guernsey	
G-BDWX	Jodel D.120A	J. P. Lassey	
G-BDWY	PA-28 Cherokee 140	Comed Aviation Ltd/Blackpool	
G-BDXA	Boeing 747-236B	British Airways *City of Peterborough*	
G-BDXB	Boeing 747-236B	British Airways *City of Liverpool*	
G-BDXC	Boeing 747-236B	British Airways *City of Manchester*	
G-BDXD	Boeing 747-236B	British Airways *City of Plymouth*	
G-BDXE	Boeing 747-236B	British Airways *City of Glasgow*	
G-BDXF	Boeing 747-236B	British Airways *City of York*	
G-BDXG	Boeing 747-236B	British Airways *City of Oxford*	
G-BDXH	Boeing 747-236B	British Airways *City of Elgin*	
G-BDXI	Boeing 747-236B	British Airways *City of Cambridge*	
G-BDXJ	Boeing 747-236B	British Airways *City of Birmingham*	
G-BDXK	Boeing 747-236B	British Airways *City of Canterbury*	
G-BDXL	Boeing 747-236B	British Airways *City of Winchester*	
G-BDXM	Boeing 747-236B (SCD)	British Airways *City of Derby*	
G-BDXN	Boeing 747-236B (SCD)	British Airways *City of Stoke-on-Trent*	
G-BDXO	Boeing 747-236B	British Airways *City of Bath*	
G-BDXP	Boeing 747-236B (SCD)	British Airways *City of Salisbury*	
G-BDXX	SNCAN NC.858S	J. R. Rowell & J. E. Hobbs/Sandown	
G-BDYD	R. Commander 114	L. A. & A. A. Buckley	
G-BDYF	Cessna 421C	Simco 408 Ltd	
G-BDYG	P.56 Provost T.1 (WV493) ★	Museum of Flight/E. Fortune	
G-BDYH	Cameron V-56 balloon	B. J. Godding	
G-BDYM	Skysales S-31 balloon	Miss A. I. Smith & M. J. Moore *Cheeky Devil*	
G-BDZA	Scheibe SF.25E Super Falke	Norfolk Gliding Club Ltd/Tibenham	
G-BDZB	Cameron S-31 balloon	Kenning Motor Group Ltd *Kenning*	
G-BDZD	Cessna F.172M	Three Counties Aero Engineering Ltd/Lasham	
G-BDZS	Scheibe SF.25E Super Falke	S. Sagar	
G-BDZU	Cessna 421C	E. E. Smith Contracts Ltd	
G-BDZX	PA-28-151 Warrior	Catalina Seaplanes Ltd	
G-BDZY	Luton LA-4A Minor	P. J. Dalby	
G-BEAB	Jodel DR.1051	C. Fitton	
G-BEAC	PA-28 Cherokee 140	G. D. Bowd	
G-BEAD	WG.13 Lynx ★	*Instructional airframe*/Middle Wallop	
G-BEAG	PA-34-200T Seneca II	C.S.E. Aviation Ltd/Kidlington	
G-BEAH	J/2 Arrow	W. J. & Mrs M. D. Horler	
G-BEAK	L-1011-385 TriStar 50	British Airways *Carmarthen Bay*	
G-BEAL	L-1011-385 TriStar 50	Caledonian Airways Ltd *Loch Moy*	
G-BEAM	L-1011-385 TriStar 50	British Airways *Swansea Bay*	
G-BEBC	W.S.55 Whirlwind 3 (XP355) ★	Norwich Aviation Museum	
G-BEBE	AA-5A Cheetah	Bills Aviation Ltd	
G-BEBF	Auster AOP.9	M. D. N. & Mrs A. C. Fisher	
G-BEBG	WSK-PZL SDZ-45A Ogar	The Ogar Syndicate	
G-BEBI	Cessna F.172M	Calder Equipment Ltd/Hatfield	
G-BEBL	Douglas DC-10-30	British Airways *Forest of Dean*/Gatwick	
G-BEBM	Douglas DC-10-30	British Airways *Sherwood Forest*/Gatwick	
G-BEBN	Cessna 177B	A. J. Franchi & Franchi Aviation Ltd	
G-BEBO	Turner TSW-2 Wot	The Turner Special Flying Group	
G-BEBR	GY-201 Minicab	A. S. Jones & D. R. Upton	
G-BEBS	Andreasson BA-4B	N. J. W. Reid	
G-BEBT	Andreasson BA-4B	A. Horsfall	
G-BEBU	R. Commander 112A	M. Rowland & J. K. Woodford	
G-BEBZ	PA-28-151 Warrior	Goodwood Terrena Ltd/Goodwood	
G-BECA	SOCATA Rallye 100ST	Bredon Flying Group	
G-BECB	SOCATA Rallye 100ST	A. J. Trible	
G-BECC	SOCATA Rallye 150ST	Golf Charlie Group/Booker	
G-BECD	SOCATA Rallye 150ST	G-BECD Flying Group	
G-BECF	Scheibe SF.25A Falke	D. A. Wilson & ptnrs	
G-BECJ	Partenavia P.68B	Covex PLC	
G-BECK	Cameron V-56 balloon	D. W. & P. Allum	
G-BECN	Piper J-3C-65 Cub (480480)	R. C. Partridge & M. Oliver	
G-BECT	C.A.S.A.1.131 Jungmann	Shoreham 131 Group	
G-BECW	C.A.S.A.1.131 Jungmann	N. C. Jensen/Redhill	
G-BECZ	CAARP CAP.10B	Aerobatic Associates Ltd	

Notes	Reg.	Type	Owner or Operator
	G-BEDA	C.A.S.A.1.131 Jungmann	M. G. Kates & D. J. Berry
	G-BEDB	Nord 1203 Norecrin (5)	B. F. G. Lister (stored)/Chirk
	G-BEDD	Jodel D.117A	A. T. Croy/Kirkwall
	G-BEDF	Boeing B-17G-105-VE (124485)	B-17 Preservation Ltd/Duxford
	G-BEDG	R. Commander 112A	L. E. Blackburn
	G-BEDI	Sikorsky S-61N	British International Helicopters
	G-BEDJ	Piper J-3C-65 Cub (44-80594)	R. Earl
	G-BEDK	Hiller UH-12E	Agricopters Ltd/Chilbolton
	G-BEDL	Cessna T.337D	T. J. Brammer & R. Masterman
	G-BEDP	BN-2A Mk.III-2 Trislander	Cormack (Aircraft Services) Ltd
	G-BEDV	V.668 Varsity T.1 (WJ945) ★	D. S. Selway/Duxford
	G-BEDZ	BN-2A Islander	Loganair Ltd/Glasgow
	G-BEEE	Thunder Ax6-56A balloon	I. R. M. Jacobs Avia
	G-BEEG	BN-2A Islander	Howells Group PLC/Manchester
	G-BEEH	Cameron V-56 balloon	B. & N. V. Moreton
	G-BEEI	Cameron N-77 balloon	P. S. & G. G. Rankin
	G-BEEJ	Cameron O-77 balloon	DAL (Builders Merchants) Ltd Dal's Pal
	G-BEEP	Thunder Ax5-42 balloon	B. C. Faithfull/Holland
	G-BEER	Isaacs Fury II (K2075)	Baycol Aviation
	G-BEEU	PA-28 Cherokee 140E	Touch & Go Ltd
	G-BEEW	Taylor JT.1 Monoplane	K. Wigglesworth/Breighton
	G-BEFA	PA-28-151 Warrior	Firmbeam Ltd/Booker
	G-BEFC	AA-5B Tiger	Portway Aviation/Shobdon
	G-BEFF	PA-28 Cherokee 140	C. Haymes & S. Besoby
	G-BEFR	Fokker Dr.1/(replica) (425/17)	R. A. Bowes & P. A. Crawford
	G-BEFV	Evans VP-2	D. A. Cotton
	G-BEGA	Westland-Bell 47G-3B1	Flight 47 Ltd
	G-BEGG	Scheibe SF.25E Super Falke	G-BEGG Flying Group
	G-BEGV	PA-23 Aztec 250F	Flamex Ltd
	G-BEHH	PA-32R Cherokee Lance 300	SMK Engineering Ltd/Leeds
	G-BEHS	PA-25 Pawnee 260C	Winchester Trust Ltd
	G-BEHU	PA-34-200T Seneca II	ANT Aviation/Cambridge
	G-BEHV	Cessna F.172N	J. Easson/Edinburgh
	G-BEHW	Cessna F.150M	W. Lancashire Aero Club Ltd/Woodvale
	G-BEHX	Evans VP-2	G. S. Adams
	G-BEIA	Cessna FRA.150M	Air Service Training Ltd/Perth
	G-BEIB	Cessna F.172N	Sheltons of Wollaston (Garages) Ltd
	G-BEIC	Sikorsky S-61N	British International Helicopters/Aberdeen
	G-BEIF	Cameron O-65 balloon	C. Vening
	G-BEIG	Cessna F.150M	Herefordshire Aero Club Ltd/Shobdon
	G-BEII	PA-25 Pawnee 235D	Burn Gliding Club Ltd
	G-BEIL	SOCATA Rallye 150T	The Rallye Flying Group
	G-BEIP	PA-28-181 Archer II	C. Royale
	G-BEIS	Evans VP-1	P. J. Hunt
	G-BEJA	Thunder Ax6-56A balloon	P. A. Hutchins Jackson
	G-BEJB	Thunder Ax6-56A balloon	International Distillers & Vinters Ltd
	G-BEJD	H.S.748 Srs 1	Emerald Airways Ltd/Liverpool
	G-BEJE	H.S.748 Srs 1	Emerald Airways Ltd/Liverpool
	G-BEJK	Cameron S-31 balloon	Rango Balloon & Kite Co
	G-BEJL	Sikorsky S-61N	British International Helicopters
	G-BEJM	BAC One-Eleven 423ET	Ford Motor Co Ltd/Stansted
	G-BEJP	D.H.C.6 Twin Otter 310	Loganair Ltd/Glasgow
	G-BEJV	PA-34-200T Seneca II	C.S.E. Aviation Ltd/Kidlington
	G-BEKL	Bede BD-4E	H. B. Carter
	G-BEKM	Evans VP-1	G. J. McDill/Glenrothes
	G-BEKN	Cessna FRA.150M	RFC (Bourn) Ltd
	G-BEKO	Cessna F.182Q	Tyler International
	G-BEKR	Rand KR-2	A. N. Purchase
	G-BELF	BN-2A Islander	Activity Aviation Ltd
	G-BELP	PA-28-151 Warrior	Devon School of Flying/Dunkeswell
	G-BELR	PA-28 Cherokee 140	H. M. Clarke
	G-BELT	Cessna F.150J	Yorkshire Light Aircraft Ltd (G-AWUV)/ Leeds
	G-BELX	Cameron V-56 balloon	V. & A. M. Dyer
	G-BEMB	Cessna F.172M	Stocklaunch Ltd
	G-BEMD	Beech 95-B55 Baron	A. G. Perkins
	G-BEMM	Slingsby T.31B Motor Cadet	M. N. Martin
	G-BEMU	Thunder Ax5-42 balloon	I. J. Liddiard & A. Merritt
	G-BEMW	PA-28-181 Archer II	J. A. Pothecary
	G-BEMY	Cessna FRA.150M	A. C. Roles
	G-BEND	Cameron V-56 balloon	Dante Balloon Group Le Billet
	G-BENJ	R. Commander 112B	R. C. Wilcox/Blackbushe
	G-BENK	Cessna F.172M	Graham Churchill Plant Ltd

Reg.	Type	Owner or Operator	Notes
G-BENN	Cameron V-56 balloon	S. H. Budd	
G-BENT	Cameron N-77 balloon	N. Tasker	
G-BEOD	Cessna 180	Avionics Research Ltd/Cranfield	
G-BEOE	Cessna FRA.150M	W. J. Henderson	
G-BEOH	PA-28R-201T Turbo Arrow III	G-BEOH Group	
G-BEOI	PA-18 Super Cub 150	Southdown Gliding Club Ltd	
G-BEOK	Cessna F.150M	Stardial Ltd/Southend	
G-BEOO	Sikorsky S-61N Mk. II	British International Helicopters	
G-BEOX	L-414 Hudson IV (A16-199) ★	RAF Museum/Hendon	
G-BEOY	Cessna FRA.150L	R. W. Denny	
G-BEOZ	A.W.650 Argosy 101 ★	Aeropark/E. Midlands	
G-BEPB	Pereira Osprey II	J. J. & A. J. C. Zwetsloot/Bourn	
G-BEPC	SNCAN Stampe SV-4C	Andy Foan Aviation Services Ltd	
G-BEPE	SC.5 Belfast	HeavyLift Cargo Airlines Ltd (G-ASKE) (*withdrawn*)/Southend	
G-BEPF	SNCAN Stampe SV-4A	L. J. Rice	
G-BEPH	BN-2A Mk III-2 Trislander	Aurigny Air Services Ltd/Guernsey	
G-BEPI	BN-2A Mk III-2 Trislander	Aurigny Air Services Ltd/Guernsey	
G-BEPO	Cameron N-77 balloon	G. Camplin & V. Aitken	
G-BEPS	SC.5 Belfast	HeavyLift Cargo Airlines Ltd/Stansted	
G-BEPV	Fokker S.11-1 Instructor	L. C. MacKnight	
G-BEPY	R. Commander 112B	Abdex Hose & Couplings Ltd	
G-BEPZ	Cameron D-96 hot-air airship	M. E. White	
G-BERA	SOCATA Rallye 150ST	Air Touring Services Ltd/Biggin Hill	
G-BERC	SOCATA Rallye 150ST	Severn Valley Aero Group	
G-BERD	Thunder Ax6-56A balloon	P. M. Gaines	
G-BERI	R. Commander 114	K. B. Harper/Blackbushe	
G-BERN	Saffrey S-330 balloon	B. Martin *Beeze*	
G-BERT	Cameron V-56 balloon	Southern Balloon Group *Bert*	
G-BERW	R. Commander 114	Malvern Holdings Ltd	
G-BERY	AA-1B Trainer	R. H. J. Levi	
G-BESO	BN-2A Islander	Isles of Scilly Skybus Ltd/St Just	
G-BETD	Robin HR.200/100	R. A. Parsons/Bourn	
G-BETE	Rollason B.2A Beta	T. M. Jones/Tatenhill	
G-BETF	Cameron 'Champion' SS balloon	British Balloon Museum/Newbury	
G-BETG	Cessna 180K Skywagon	T. P. A. Norman	
G-BETI	Pitts S-1D Special	P. Metcalfe/Teesside	
G-BETL	PA-25 Pawnee 235D	Boston Aviation Services	
G-BETM	PA-25 Pawnee 235D	Yorkshire Gliding Club (Pty) Ltd	
G-BETO	M.S.885 Super Rallye	BETO Group	
G-BETP	Cameron O-65 balloon	J. R. Rix & Sons Ltd	
G-BETT	PA-34-200 Seneca II	Andrews Professional Colour Laboratories Ltd/Headcorn	
G-BETV	HS.125 Srs 600B	Rolls-Royce PLC/Filton	
G-BEUA	PA-18 Super Cub 150	London Gliding Club (Pty) Ltd/Dunstable	
G-BEUD	Robin HR.100/285R	E. A. & L. M. C. Payton/Cranfield	
G-BEUI	Piper J-3C-65 Cub	M. J. Whatley	
G-BEUK	Fuji FA.200-160	BM Aviation	
G-BEUL	Beech 95-58 Baron	Foyle Flyers Ltd/Eglinton	
G-BEUM	Taylor JT.1 Monoplane	M. T. Taylor	
G-BEUN	Cassutt Racer IIIm	R. S. Voice/Redhill	
G-BEUP	Robin DR.400/180	A. V. Pound & Co Ltd	
G-BEUR	Cessna F.172M	M. E. Moore/Compton Abbas	
G-BEUS	AIA Stampe SV-4C	G-BEUS Flying Group	
G-BEUU	PA-18 Super Cub 95	F. Sharples/Sandown	
G-BEUV	Thunder Ax6-56A balloon	Silhouette Balloon Group	
G-BEUX	Cessna F.172N	Ladel Ltd	
G-BEUY	Cameron N-31 balloon	M. W. A. Shemilt	
G-BEVA	SOCATA Rallye 150ST	The Rallye Group	
G-BEVB	SOCATA Rallye 150ST	N. R. Haines	
G-BEVC	SOCATA Rallye 150ST	B. W. Walpole	
G-BEVG	PA-34-200T-2 Seneca	Aranair Ltd/Bournemouth	
G-BEVI	Thunder Ax7-77A balloon	The Painted Clouds Balloon Co Ltd	
G-BEVO	Sportavia-Pützer RF-5	T. Barlow	
G-BEVP	Evans VP-2	G. Moscrop & R. C. Crowley	
G-BEVS	Taylor JT.1 Monoplane	D. Hunter	
G-BEVT	BN-2A Mk III-2 Trislander	Aurigny Air Services Ltd/Guernsey	
G-BEVW	SOCATA Rallye 150ST	P. C. Goodwin	
G-BEWJ	Westland-Bell 47G-3B1	Ropeleyville Ltd	
G-BEWM	Sikorsky S-61N Mk II	British International Helicopters	
G-BEWN	D.H.82A Tiger Moth	H. D. Labouchere	
G-BEWO	Zlin Z.326 Trener Master	Nimrod Group Ltd/Staverton	

Notes	Reg.	Type	Owner or Operator
	G-BEWR	Cessna F.172N	Cheshire Air Training School (Merseyside) Ltd/Liverpool
	G-BEWX	PA-28R-201 Arrow III	A. Vickers
	G-BEWY	Bell 206B JetRanger	Dollar Air Services Ltd (G-CULL)
	G-BEXK	PA-25 Pawnee 235D	Howard Avis (Aviation) Ltd
	G-BEXN	AA-1C Lynx	Lynx Flying Group
	G-BEXO	PA-23 Apache 160	Man-Air
	G-BEXR	Mudry/CAARP CAP-10B	Man-Air
	G-BEXS	Cessna F.150M	Firecrest Aviation Ltd
	G-BEXW	PA-28-181 Archer II	Barmoor Aviation
	G-BEXX	Cameron V-56 balloon	K. A. Schlussler
	G-BEXZ	Cameron N-56 balloon	D. C. Eager & G. C. Clark
	G-BEYA	Enstrom 280C Shark	Aspleys Antiques Ltd
	G-BEYB	Fairey Flycatcher (replica) (S1287)	John S. Fairey/Duxford
	G-BEYD	HPR-7 Herald 401	*Stored*/Southend
	G-BEYF	HPR-7 Herald 401	Channel Express (Air Services) Ltd/ Bournemouth
	G-BEYK	HPR-7 Herald 401	Nordic Oil Services Ltd/Aberdeen
	G-BEYL	PA-28 Cherokee 180	B. G. & G. Airlines Ltd/Jersey
	G-BEYO	PA-28 Cherokee 140	E. Dyer
	G-BEYT	PA-28 Cherokee 140	H. Foulds
	G-BEYV	Cessna T.210M	Forth Engineering Ltd
	G-BEYW	Taylor JT.1 Monoplane	R. A. Abrahams/Barton
	G-BEYZ	Jodel DR.1051/M1	M. J. McCarthy & S. Aarons/Biggin Hill
	G-BEZA	Zlin Z.226T Trener	L. Bezak
	G-BEZC	AA-5 Traveler	P. N. & S. E. Field
	G-BEZE	Rutan Vari-Eze	H. C. Mackinnon
	G-BEZF	AA-5 Traveler	G. A. Randall/Exeter
	G-BEZG	AA-5 Traveler	M. D. R. Harling
	G-BEZH	AA-5 Traveler	L. & S. M. Sims
	G-BEZI	AA-5 Traveler	BEZI Flying Group/Cranfield
	G-BEZJ	MBB Bo 105D	Bond Helicopters Ltd/Bourn
	G-BEZK	Cessna F.172H	Zulu Kilo Flying Group
	G-BEZL	PA-31-310 Turbo Navajo C	London Flight Centre (Stansted) Ltd
	G-BEZM	Cessna F.182Q	Ashcombe Ltd (G-WALK)
	G-BEZO	Cessna F.172M	Staverton Flying Services Ltd
	G-BEZP	PA-32 Cherokee Six 300D	Falcon Styles Ltd/Booker
	G-BEZR	Cessna F.172M	Kirmington Aviation Ltd
	G-BEZS	Cessna FR.172J	B. A. Wallace
	G-BEZV	Cessna F.172M	Insch Flying Group/Aberdeen
	G-BEZY	Rutan Vari-Eze	R. J. Jones
	G-BEZZ	Jodel D.112	G-BEZZ Jodel Group
	G-BFAA	GY-80 Horizon 160	Mary Poppins Ltd
	G-BFAB	Cameron N-56 balloon	Phonogram Ltd *Phonogram*
	G-BFAC	Cessna F.177RG	J. J. Baumhardt/Southend
	G-BFAF	Aeronca 7BCM (7797)	D. C. W. Harper/Finmere
	G-BFAH	Phoenix Currie Wot	R. W. Clarke
	G-BFAI	R. Commander 114	D. S. Innes/Guernsey
	G-BFAK	M.S.892A Rallye Commodore 150	P. G. Wells & J. D. Hensby
	G-BFAM	PA-31P Pressurised Navajo	CMH Management Services
	G-BFAN	H.S.125 Srs 600F	British Aerospace (G-AZHS)/Hatfield
	G-BFAO	PA-20 Pacer 135	J. Day & ptnrs/Goodwood
	G-BFAP	SIAI-Marchetti S.205-20R	A. O. Broin
	G-BFAS	Evans VP-1	A. I. Sutherland
	G-BFAW	D.H.C.1 Chipmunk 22	R. V. Bowles
	G-BFAX	D.H.C.1 Chipmunk 22 (WG422)	B. Earl/Biggin Hill
	G-BFBA	Jodel DR.100A	Woodside Flying Group
	G-BFBB	PA-23 Aztec 250E	Alpha-Air
	G-BFBD	Partenavia P.68B	B. Swindell
	G-BFBE	Robin HR.200/100	D. V. Pell & J. Dyson
	G-BFBF	PA-28 Cherokee 140	Marnham Investments Ltd
	G-BFBM	Saffery S.330 balloon	B. Martin *Beeze II*
	G-BFBR	PA-28-161 Warrior II	Lowery Holdings Ltd/Fairoaks
	G-BFBU	Partenavia P.68B	P. Savage
	G-BFBY	Piper J-3C-65 Cub	L. W. Usherwood
	G-BFCT	Cessna TU.206F	Cecil Aviation Ltd/Cambridge
	G-BFCZ	Sopwith Camel (B7270) ★	Brooklands Museum Trust Ltd/Weybridge
	G-BFDC	D.H.C.1 Chipmunk 22	N. F. O'Neill/Newtownards
	G-BFDE	Sopwith Tabloid (replica) (168) ★	RAF Museum Storage & Restoration Centre/Cardington
	G-BFDF	SOCATA Rallye 235E	J. H. Atkinson/Skegness
	G-BFDG	PA-28R-201T Turbo-Arrow III	Southern Union Trading Ltd

Reg.	Type	Owner or Operator	Notes
G-BFDI	PA-28-181 Archer II	Truman Aviation Ltd/Tollerton	
G-BFDK	PA-28-161 Warrior II	C.S.E. Aviation Ltd/Kidlington	
G-BFDL	Piper J-3C-65 Cub (454537)	P. B. Rice & A. White	
G-BFDM	Jodel D.120	Worcestershire Gliding Ltd	
G-BFDN	PA-31-350 Navajo Chieftain	Genoex Ltd	
G-BFDO	PA-28R-201T Turbo Arrow III	M. I. & D. G. Goss	
G-BFDZ	Taylor JT.1 Monoplane	L. J. Greenhough	
G-BFEB	Jodel D.150	S. Russell	
G-BFEC	PA-23 Aztec 250F	P. V. Naylor-Leyland	
G-BFEE	Beech 95-E55 Baron	Interair (Aviation) Ltd/Bournemouth	
G-BFEF	Agusta-Bell 47G-3B1	R. J. Chilton	
G-BFEH	Jodel D.117A	C. V. & S. J. Philpott	
G-BFEI	Westland-Bell 47G-3B1	Trent Air Services Ltd/Cranfield	
G-BFEK	Cessna F.152	Staverton Flying Services Ltd	
G-BFER	Bell 212	Bristow Helicopters Ltd	
G-BFEV	PA-25 Pawnee 235	Hammond Aerial Spraying Ltd	
G-BFEW	PA-25 Pawnee 235	B. Walker & Co (Dursley) Ltd	
G-BFEY	PA-25 Pawnee 235	Howard Avis Aviation Ltd	
G-BFFC	Cessna F.152-II	Yorkshire Flying Services Ltd/Leeds	
G-BFFE	Cessna F.152-II	J. Easson	
G-BFFG	Beech 95-B55 Baron	V. Westley	
G-BFFJ	Sikorsky S-61N Mk II	British International Helicopters	
G-BFFK	Sikorsky S-61N Mk II	British International Helicopters	
G-BFFP	PA-18 Super Cub 150 (modified)	Booker Gliding Club Ltd	
G-BFFT	Cameron V-56 balloon	R. I. M. Kerr & D. C. Boxall	
G-BFFW	Cessna F.152	Tayside Aviation Ltd/Dundee	
G-BFFY	Cessna F.150M	Northside Aviation Ltd/Liverpool	
G-BFFZ	Cessna FR.172 Hawk XP	Bravo Aviation Ltd	
G-BFGD	Cessna F.172N-II	J. T. Armstrong	
G-BFGF	Cessna F.177RG	Keelex 121 Ltd	
G-BFGG	Cessna FRA.150M	Far North Flight Training Ltd/Wick	
G-BFGH	Cessna F.337G	T. Perkins/Sherburn	
G-BFGK	Jodel D.117	B. F. J. Hope	
G-BFGL	Cessna FA.152	Yorkshire Flying Services Ltd/Leeds	
G-BFGO	Fuji FA.200-160	Butane Buzzard Aviation Corporation Ltd	
G-BFGS	M.S.893E Rallye 180GT	K. M. & H. Bowen	
G-BFGW	Cessna F.150H	C. E. Stringer	
G-BFGX	Cessna FRA.150M	Air Service Training Ltd/Perth	
G-BFGZ	Cessna FRA.150M	Air Service Training Ltd/Perth	
G-BFHH	D.H.82A Tiger Moth	P. Harrison & M. J. Gambrell/Redhill	
G-BFHI	Piper J-3C-65 Cub	J. McD. Robinson/Bann Foot	
G-BFHP	Champion 7GCAA Citabria	T. A. Holding	
G-BFHR	Jodel DR.220/2+2	T. W. Greaves	
G-BFHT	Cessna F.152-II	Westward Airways (Lands End) Ltd	
G-BFHU	Cessna F.152-II	Deltair Ltd/Chester	
G-BFHV	Cessna F.152-II	Falcon Flying Services/Biggin Hill	
G-BFHX	Evans VP-1	P. Johnson	
G-BFIB	PA-31 Turbo Navajo	Mann Aviation Ltd/Fairoaks	
G-BFID	Taylor JT.2 Titch Mk III	G. Hunter	
G-BFIE	Cessna FRA.150M	B. J. Parker	
G-BFIG	Cessna FR.172K XPII	Tenair Ltd	
G-BFIJ	AA-5A Cheetah	J. H. Wise/Redhill	
G-BFIN	AA-5A Cheetah	G-BFIN Group	
G-BFIP	Wallbro Monoplane 1909 replica	K. H. Wallis/Swanton Morley	
G-BFIR	Avro 652A Anson 21 (WD413)	G. M. K. Fraser (*stored*)/Arbroath	
G-BFIT	Thunder Ax6-56Z balloon	J. A. G. Tyson	
G-BFIU	Cessna FR.172K XP	B. M. Jobling	
G-BFIV	Cessna F.177RG	Kingfishair Ltd/Blackbushe	
G-BFIX	Thunder Ax7-77A balloon	R. Owen	
G-BFJA	AA-5B Tiger	European Flyers (Blackbushe Airport) Ltd	
G-BFJH	SA.102-5 Cavalier	B. F. J. Hope	
G-BFJI	Robin HR.100/250	Financial Services Training Ltd	
G-BFJJ	Evans VP-1	M. J. Collins	
G-BFJK	PA-23 Aztec 250F	R. Marsden & P. E. T. Price	
G-BFJN	Westland-Bell 47G-3B1	Howden Helicopters	
G-BFJR	Cessna F.337G	Mannix Aviation/E. Midlands	
G-BFJV	Cessna F.172H	Southport & Merseyside Aero Club Ltd	
G-BFJW	AB-206B JetRanger	European Aviation Ltd	
G-BFJZ	Robin DR.400/140B	Rochester Aviation Ltd	
G-BFKA	Cessna F.172N	D. J. A. Seagram	
G-BFKB	Cessna F.172N	R. E. Speigel	
G-BFKC	Rand KR-2	L. H. S. Stephens & I. S. Hewitt	

Notes	Reg.	Type	Owner or Operator
	G-BFKD	R. Commander 114B	M. D. Faiers
	G-BFKF	Cessna FA.152	Klingair Ltd/Conington
	G-BFKG	Cessna F.152	Luton Flight Training Ltd
	G-BFKH	Cessna F.152	T. G. Aviation Ltd/Manston
	G-BFKL	Cameron N-56 balloon	Merrythought Toys Ltd *Merrythought*
	G-BFKY	PA-34-200 Seneca II	S.L.H. Construction Ltd/Biggin Hill
	G-BFLH	PA-34-200T Seneca II	C.S.E. Aviation Ltd/Kidlington
	G-BFLI	PA-28R-201T Turbo Arrow III	J. K. Chudzicki
	G-BFLL	H.S.748 Srs 2A	Euroair Transport Ltd
	G-BFLM	Cessna 150M	Cornwall Flying Club Ltd/Bodmin
	G-BFLN	Cessna 150M	Sherburn Aero Club Ltd
	G-BFLP	Amethyst Ax6 balloon	K. J. Hendry *Amethyst*
	G-BFLU	Cessna F.152	Inverness Flying Services Ltd
	G-BFLV	Cessna F.172N	Cheshire Air Training School (Merseyside) Ltd/Liverpool
	G-BFLX	AA-5A Cheetah	Abraxas Aviation Ltd/Denham
	G-BFLZ	Beech 95-A55 Baron	K. A. Clarke
	G-BFME	Cameron V-56 balloon	Warwick Balloons
	G-BFMF	Cassutt Racer Mk IIIM	P. H. Lewis
	G-BFMG	PA-28-161 Warrior II	Bailey Aviation Ltd
	G-BFMH	Cessna 177B	Span Aviation Ltd/Newcastle
	G-BFMK	Cessna F.152	RAF Halton Aeroplane Club Ltd
	G-BFMM	PA-28-181 Archer II	Bristol & Wessex Aeroplane Club Ltd
	G-BFMR	PA-20 Pacer 125	J. E. Cummings
	G-BFMX	Cessna F.172N	P. Wilkinson
	G-BFMY	Sikorsky S-61N	Bristow Helicopters Ltd
	G-BFMZ	Payne Ax6 balloon	G. F. Payne
	G-BFNC	AS.350B Ecureuil	Dollar Air Services Ltd/Coventry
	G-BFNG	Jodel D.112	E. N. & L. K. Simmons
	G-BFNI	PA-28-161 Warrior II	P. Elliott/Biggin Hill
	G-BFNJ	PA-28-161 Warrior II	C.S.E. Aviation Ltd/Kidlington
	G-BFNK	PA-28-161 Warrior II	C.S.E. Aviation Ltd/Kidlington
	G-BFNM	Globe GC.1 Swift	Nottingham Flying Group/Tatenhill
	G-BFNU	BN-2B Islander	Isle of Scilly Sky Bus Ltd/St Just
	G-BFOD	Cessna F.182Q	G. N. Clarke
	G-BFOE	Cessna F.152	London Aviation Ltd/Elstree
	G-BFOF	Cessna F.152	Staverton Flying School Ltd
	G-BFOG	Cessna 150M	W. J. Pinches & M. D. Bayliss
	G-BFOJ	AA-1 Yankee	A. J. Morton/Bournemouth
	G-BFOP	Jodel D.120	R. J. Wesley & G. D. Western/Ipswich
	G-BFOS	Thunder Ax6-56A balloon	N. T. Petty
	G-BFOU	Taylor JT.1 Monoplane	G. Bee
	G-BFOV	Cessna F.172N	D. J. Walker
	G-BFOZ	Thunder Ax6-56 balloon	R. L. Harbord
	G-BFPA	Scheibe SF.25B Super Falke	Yorkshire Gliding Club (Pty) Ltd/ Sutton Bank
	G-BFPB	AA-5B Tiger	Guernsey Aero Club
	G-BFPH	Cessna F.172K	J. M. Reid
	G-BFPL	Fokker D.VII (replica) (4253/18)	A. E. Hutton/North Weald
	G-BFPM	Cessna F.172M	N. R. Havercroft
	G-BFPO	R. Commander 112B	J. G. Hale Ltd
	G-BFPP	Bell 47J-2	J. F. Kelly
	G-BFPS	PA-25 Pawnee 235D	Kent Gliding Club Ltd/Challock
	G-BFPZ	Cessna F.177RG	A. B. van Eeckhoudt/Belgium
	G-BFRA	R. Commander 114	Sabre Engines Ltd/Bournemouth
	G-BFRD	Bowers Fly-Baby 1A	F. R. Donaldson
	G-BFRF	Taylor JT.1 Monoplane	E. R. Bailey
	G-BFRI	Sikorsky S-61N	Bristow Helicopters Ltd *Braerich*
	G-BFRL	Cessna F.152	M. K. Barnes & G. N. Olsen
	G-BFRM	Cessna 550 Citation II	Marshall of Cambridge (Engineering) Ltd
	G-BFRO	Cessna F.150M	Skyviews & General Ltd/Carlisle
	G-BFRR	Cessna FRA.150M	Airtime Aviation Services/Bournemouth
	G-BFRS	Cessna F.172N	Poplar Toys Ltd
	G-BFRV	Cessna FA.152	Turnhouse Flying Club
	G-BFRX	PA-25 Pawnee 260	Yorkshire Gliding Club (Pty) Ltd/ Sutton Bank
	G-BFRY	PA-25 Pawnee 260	B. Walker & Co (Dursley) Ltd
	G-BFSA	Cessna F.182Q	Clark Masts Ltd/Sandown
	G-BFSB	Cessna F.152	Tatenhill Aviation
	G-BFSC	PA-25 Pawnee 235D	Farm Aviation Services Ltd/Enstone
	G-BFSD	PA-25 Pawnee 235D	Deeside Gliding Club Ltd/Aboyne
	G-BFSK	PA-23 Apache 160 ★	Oxford Air Training School/Kidlington

Reg.	Type	Owner or Operator	Notes
G-BFSP	H.S.125 Srs 700B	Raytheon Corporate Jets Inc (G-PRMC)	
G-BFSR	Cessna F.150J	Air Fenland Ltd	
G-BFSS	Cessna FR.172G	Minerva Services	
G-BFSY	PA-181 Archer II	Downland Aviation	
G-BFTC	PA-28R-201T Turbo Arrow III	D. Hughes/Sherburn	
G-BFTF	AA-5B Tiger	F. C. Burrow Ltd/Leeds	
G-BFTG	AA-5B Tiger	D. Hepburn & G. R. Montgomery	
G-BFTH	Cessna F.172N	J. Birkett	
G-BFTT	Cessna 421C	P&B Metal Components Ltd/Manston	
G-BFTX	Cessna F.172N	E. Kent Flying Group	
G-BFTY	Cameron V-77 balloon	Regal Motors (Bilston) Ltd *Regal Motors*	
G-BFTZ	MS.880B Rallye Club	R. & B. Legge Ltd	
G-BFUB	PA-32RT-300 Lance II	Jolida Holdings Ltd	
G-BFUD	Scheibe SF.25E Super Falke	S. H. Hart	
G-BFUG	Cameron N-77 balloon	Headland Services Ltd	
G-BFUZ	Cameron V-77 balloon	Skysales Ltd	
G-BFVF	PA-38-112 Tomahawk	Ipswich School of Flying Ltd	
G-BFVG	PA-28-181 Archer II	G-BFVG Flying Group/Blackpool	
G-BFVH	D.H.2 Replica (5894)	Wessex Aviation & Transport Ltd	
G-BFVI	H.S.125 Srs 700B	Bristow Helicopters Ltd	
G-BFVM	Westland-Bell 47G-3B1	K. R. Dossett	
G-BFVO	Partenavia P.68B	Airmark Aviation Services Ltd	
G-BFVP	PA-23 Aztec 250F	Litton Aviation Services Ltd	
G-BFVS	AA-5B Tiger	S. W. Biroth & T. Chapman/Denham	
G-BFVU	Cessna 150L	Thruxton Flight Centre Ltd	
G-BFWB	PA-28-161 Warrior II	C.S.E. Aviation Ltd/Kidlington	
G-BFWD	Currie Wot	F. R. Donaldson	
G-BFWE	PA-23 Aztec 250E	Air Navigation & Trading Co Ltd/Blackpool	
G-BFWK	PA-28-161 Warrior II	Woodgate Air Services (IoM) Ltd	
G-BFWL	Cessna F.150L	N. C. Caple	
G-BFWW	Robin HR.100/210	Willingair Ltd	
G-BFXD	PA-28-161 Warrior II	C.S.E. Aviation Ltd/Kidlington	
G-BFXE	PA-28-161 Warrior II	C.S.E. Aviation Ltd/Kidlington	
G-BFXF	Andreasson BA.4B	A. Brown/Sherburn	
G-BFXH	Cessna F.152	M. Entwistle	
G-BFXI	Cessna F.172M	Thanet Electronics/Manston	
G-BFXK	PA-28 Cherokee 140	G. S. & Mrs M. T. Pritchard/Southend	
G-BFXL	Albatross D.5A (D5397/17)	F.A.A. Museum/Yeovilton	
G-BFXR	Jodel D.112	G. Barthorpe	
G-BFXS	R. Commander 114	Keats Printing Ltd	
G-BFXW	AA-5B Tiger	Crosswind Aviation Ltd/Leeds	
G-BFXX	AA-5B Tiger	M. J. Porter	
G-BFYA	MBB Bo 105DB	Mennak Ltd	
G-BFYB	PA-28-161 Warrior II	C.S.E. Aviation Ltd/Kidlington	
G-BFYC	PA-32RT-300 Lance II	A. A. Barnes	
G-BFYE	Robin HR.100/285 ★	*stored*/Sywell	
G-BFYI	Westland-Bell 47G-3B1	B. Walker & Co (Dursley) Ltd	
G-BFYK	Cameron V-77 balloon	D. M. Williams	
G-BFYL	Evans VP-2	A. G. Wilford	
G-BFYM	PA-28-161 Warrior II	C.S.E. Aviation Ltd/Kidlington	
G-BFYN	Cessna FA.152	Tayside Aviation Ltd/Dundee	
G-BFYO	Spad XIII (replica) (3398) ★	F.A.A. Museum/Yeovilton	
G-BFYP	Bensen B.7	A. J. Philpotts	
G-BFZB	Piper J-3C-85 Cub	Zebedee Flying Group/Shoreham	
G-BFZD	Cessna FR.182RG	R. B. Lewis & Co/Sleap	
G-BFZG	PA-28-161 Warrior II	C.S.E. Aviation Ltd/Kidlington	
G-BFZH	PA-28R Cherokee Arrow 200	K. E. Miles	
G-BFZL	V.836 Viscount	British World Airlines Ltd/Southend	
G-BFZM	R. Commander 112TC	Rolls-Royce Ltd/Filton	
G-BFZN	Cessna FA.152	Falcon Flying Services/Biggin Hill	
G-BFZO	AA-5A Cheetah	Heald Air Ltd/Manchester	
G-BFZT	Cessna FA.152	Zulu Tango Ltd/Guernsey	
G-BFZU	Cessna FA.152	R. T. Love	
G-BFZV	Cessna F.172M	R. Thomas	
G-BGAA	Cessna 152 II	PJC Leasing Ltd	
G-BGAB	Cessna F.152 II	TG Aviation Ltd/Manston	
G-BGAD	Cessna F.152 II	J. G. Bell	
G-BGAE	Cessna F.152 II	Klingair Ltd/Conington	
G-BGAF	Cessna FA.152	Suffolk Aero Club Ltd/Ipswich	
G-BGAG	Cessna F.172N	Aerohire Ltd/Halfpenny Green	
G-BGAJ	Cessna F.182Q II	Ground Airport Services/Guernsey	
G-BGAK	Cessna F.182Q II	Safari World Services Ltd	

Notes	Reg.	Type	Owner or Operator
	G-BGAX	PA-28 Cherokee 140	Devon School of Flying/Dunkeswell
	G-BGAY	Cameron O-77 balloon	S. W. C. & P. C. A. Hall
	G-BGAZ	Cameron V-77 balloon	Cameron Balloons Ltd *Silicon Chip*
	G-BGBA	Robin R.2100A	D. Faulkner/Redhill
	G-BGBC	L.1011-385 TriStar 200	British Airways *St Andrews Bay*
	G-BGBE	Jodel DR.1050	J. A. & B. Mawby
	G-BGBF	D.31A Turbulent	S. P. Wakeham
	G-BGBG	PA-28-181 Archer II	Harlow Printing Ltd/Newcastle
	G-BGBI	Cessna F.150L	Bugby Flying Group
	G-BGBK	PA-38-112 Tomahawk	F. Marshall & R. C. Priest/Netherthorpe
	G-BGBN	PA-38-112 Tomahawk	Leavesden Flight Centre Ltd
	G-BGBP	Cessna F.152	Stapleford Flying Club Ltd
	G-BGBR	Cessna F.172N	Falcon Flying Services/Biggin Hill
	G-BGBU	Auster AOP.9 (XN435)	P. Neilson
	G-BGBW	PA-38-112 Tomahawk	Truman Aviation Ltd/Tollerton
	G-BGBX	PA-38-112 Tomahawk	Ipswich School of Flying Ltd
	G-BGBY	PA-38-112 Tomahawk	Ravenair/Manchester
	G-BGBZ	R. Commander 114	R. S. Fenwick/Biggin Hill
	G-BGCG	Douglas C-47A	*on rebuild*
	G-BGCL	AA-5A Cheetah	AIG Air Services Ltd
	G-BGCM	AA-5A Cheetah	Deltaflight Ltd
	G-BGCO	PA-44-180 Seminole	J. R. Henderson
	G-BGCX	Taylor JT.1 Monoplane	G. M. R. Walters
	G-BGCY	Taylor JT.1 Monoplane	M. T. Taylor
	G-BGDA	Boeing 737-236	British Airways Manchester *River Tamar*
	G-BGDB	Boeing 737-236	GB Airways Ltd *Mons Valeta*
	G-BGDC	Boeing 737-236	British Airways *River Humber*
	G-BGDD	Boeing 737-236	British Airways *River Tees*
	G-BGDE	Boeing 737-236	British Airways Birmingham *River Avon*
	G-BGDF	Boeing 737-236	British Airways Manchester *River Thames*
	G-BGDG	Boeing 737-236	British Airways Manchester *River Medway*
	G-BGDH	Boeing 737-236	British Airways Manchester *River Clyde*
	G-BGDI	Boeing 737-236	British Airways Manchester *River Ouse*
	G-BGDJ	Boeing 737-236	British Airways Manchester *River Trent*
	G-BGDK	Boeing 737-236	British Airways Manchester *River Mersey*
	G-BGDL	Boeing 737-236	British Airways Manchester *River Don*
	G-BGDN	Boeing 737-236	British Airways Manchester *River Tyne*
	G-BGDO	Boeing 737-236	GB Airways Ltd *Mons Chaambi*
	G-BGDP	Boeing 737-236	British Airways *River Taff*
	G-BGDR	Boeing 737-236	British Airways *River Bann*
	G-BGDS	Boeing 737-236	GB Airways Ltd *Mons Calpe*
	G-BGDT	Boeing 737-236	British Airways Manchester *River Forth*
	G-BGDU	Boeing 737-236	GB Airways Ltd *Mons Abyla*
	G-BGEA	Cessna F.150M	Agricultural & General Aviation Ltd
	G-BGED	Cessna U.206F	Chapman Aviation Ltd
	G-BGEE	Evans VP-1	B. Murphy
	G-BGEF	Jodel D.112	G. G. Johnson & S. J. Davies
	G-BGEH	Monnet Sonerai II	P. C. Dowbor-Musnicki
	G-BGEI	Baby Great Lakes	I. D. Trask
	G-BGEK	PA-38-112 Tomahawk	Ravenair/Manchester
	G-BGEL	PA-38-112 Tomahawk	Ravenair/Manchester
	G-BGEM	Partenavia P.68B	Meridian Air Services Ltd/Staverton
	G-BGEP	Cameron D-38 balloon	Cameron Balloons Ltd/Italy
	G-BGEW	SNCAN NC.854S	Tavair Ltd
	G-BGEX	Brookland Mosquito 2	R. T. Gough
	G-BGFC	Evans VP-2	S. W. C. Hollins
	G-BGFF	FRED Srs 2	F. Bolton
	G-BGFG	AA-5A Cheetah	Fletcher Aviation Ltd/Biggin Hill
	G-BGFH	Cessna F.182Q	Sunseeker Leisure PLC
	G-BGFI	AA-5A Cheetah	I. J. Hay & A. Nayyar/Biggin Hill
	G-BGFJ	Jodel D.9 Bebe	M. D. Mold
	G-BGFK	Evans VP-1	I. N. M. Cameron
	G-BGFT	PA-34-200T Seneca II	C.S.E. Aviation Ltd/Kidlington
	G-BGFX	Cessna F.152	Falcon Flying Services/Biggin Hill
	G-BGGA	Bellanca 7GCBC Citabria	L. A. King
	G-BGGB	Bellanca 7GCBC Citabria	M. D. Cowburn
	G-BGGC	Bellanca 7GCBC Citabria	R. P. Ashfield & J. P. Stone
	G-BGGD	Bellanca 8GCBC Scout	Bristol & Gloucestershire Gliding Club/Nympsfield
	G-BGGE	PA-38-112 Tomahawk	Truman Aviation Ltd/Tollerton
	G-BGGF	PA-38-112 Tomahawk	Truman Aviation Ltd/Tollerton
	G-BGGG	PA-38-112 Tomahawk	Teesside Flight Centre Ltd
	G-BGGI	PA-38-112 Tomahawk	Truman Aviation Ltd/Tollerton

Reg.	Type	Owner or Operator	Notes
G-BGGL	PA-38-112 Tomahawk	Grunwick Processing Laboratories Ltd/ Elstree	
G-BGGM	PA-38-112 Tomahawk	Grunwick Processing Laboratories Ltd/ Elstree	
G-BGGN	PA-38-112 Tomahawk	Domeastral Ltd/Elstree	
G-BGGO	Cessna F.152	E. Midlands Flying School Ltd	
G-BGGP	Cessna F.152	E. Midlands Flying School Ltd	
G-BGGU	Wallis WA-116R-R	K. H. Wallis	
G-BGGV	Wallis WA-120 Srs 2	K. H. Wallis	
G-BGGW	Wallis WA-112	K. H. Wallis	
G-BGGY	AB-206B Jet Ranger ★	*Instructional airframe*/Cranfield	
G-BGHE	Convair L-13A	J. M. Davis/Wichita	
G-BGHF	Westland WG.30 ★	International Helicopter Museum/ Weston-s-Mare	
G-BGHI	Cessna F.152	Taxon Ltd/Shoreham	
G-BGHM	Robin R.1180T	H. Price	
G-BGHP	Beech 76 Duchess	B. Houghton/Liverpool	
G-BGHS	Cameron N-31 balloon	W. R. Teasdale	
G-BGHT	Falconar F-12	C. R. Coates	
G-BGHU	NA T-6G Texan (115042)	C. E. Bellhouse	
G-BGHV	Cameron V-77 balloon	E. Davies	
G-BGHW	Thunder Ax8-90 balloon	Edinburgh University Balloon Group	
G-BGHY	Taylor JT.1 Monoplane	R. A. Hand	
G-BGHZ	FRED Srs 2	A. Smith	
G-BGIB	Cessna 152 II	Mona Aviation Ltd	
G-BGIC	Cessna 172N	T. R. Sinclair	
G-BGID	Westland-Bell 47G-3B1	M. J. Cuttell	
G-BGIG	PA-38-112 Tomahawk	Scotia Safari Ltd/Prestwick	
G-BGII	PA-32 Cherokee Six 300E	D. L. P. Milligan	
G-BGIO	Bensen B.8M	C. G. Johns	
G-BGIP	Colt 56A balloon	J. G. N. Perfect	
G-BGIU	Cessna F.172H	MG Services	
G-BGIV	Bell 47G-5	Abraxas Aviation Ltd	
G-BGIX	H.295 Super Courier	C. M. Lee/Andrewsfield	
G-BGIY	Cessna F.172N	Glasgow 172 Group	
G-BGIZ	Cessna F.152	Creaton Aviation Services Ltd	
G-BGJE	Boeing 737-236	British Airways *River Wear*/Gatwick	
G-BGJF	Boeing 737-236	British Airways *River Axe*/Gatwick	
G-BGJG	Boeing 737-236	British Airways *River Arun*/Gatwick	
G-BGJH	Boeing 737-236	British Airways *River Lyne*/Gatwick	
G-BGJI	Boeing 737-236	British Airways *River Wey*/Gatwick	
G-BGJJ	Boeing 737-236	British Airways *River Swale*/Gatwick	
G-BGJK	Boeing 737-236	British Airways *River Cherwell*/Gatwick	
G-BGJM	Boeing 737-236	British Airways *River Ribble*/Gatwick	
G-BGJU	Cameron V-65 Balloon	J. A Folkes	
G-BGJW	GA-7 Cougar	P. M. G. Day	
G-BGKC	SOCATA Rallye 110ST	J. H. Cranmer & T. A. Timms	
G-BGKD	SOCATA Rallye 110ST	W. G. Dunn & A. G. Cameron	
G-BGKE	BAC One-Eleven 539GL	Defence Research Agency/Thurleigh	
G-BGKJ	MBB Bo 105C	Bond Helicopters Ltd	
G-BGKO	GY-20 Minicab	R. B. Webber	
G-BGKS	PA-28-161 Warrior II	Marnham Investments Ltd	
G-BGKT	Auster AOP.9 (XN441)	K. H. Wallis	
G-BGKU	PA-28R-201 Arrow III	Caplane Ltd	
G-BGKV	PA-28R-201 Arrow III	R. Haverson & R. G. Watson	
G-BGKY	PA-38-112 Tomahawk	Prospect Air Ltd	
G-BGKZ	J/5F Aiglet Trainer	J. K. Cook	
G-BGLA	PA-38-112 Tomahawk	Norwich School of Flying	
G-BGLB	Bede BD-5B	W. Sawney	
G-BGLF	Evans VP-1 Srs 2	Fenland Strut Flying Group	
G-BGLG	Cessna 152	Skyviews & General Ltd/Bourn	
G-BGLI	Cessna 152	Luton Flying Club (*stored*)	
G-BGLK	Monnet Sonerai II	N. M. Smorthit	
G-BGLN	Cessna FA.152	Bournemouth Flying Club	
G-BGLO	Cessna F.172N	A. H. Slaughter/Southend	
G-BGLS	Oldfield Super Baby Lakes	J. F. Dowe	
G-BGLW	PA-34-200 Seneca	Stapleford Flying Club Ltd	
G-BGLX	Cameron N-56 balloon	Sara A. G. Williams	
G-BGLZ	Stits SA-3A Playboy	B. G. Ell	
G-BGMA	D.31 Turbulent	G. C. Masterton	
G-BGME	SIPA S.903	M. Emery & C. A. Suckling (G-BCML)/ Redhill	
G-BGMJ	GY-201 Minicab	S. L. Wakefield & ptnrs	

Notes	Reg.	Type	Owner or Operator
	G-BGMP	Cessna F.172G	D. Rowe
	G-BGMR	GY-201 Minicab	T. J. D. Hodge & ptnrs
	G-BGMS	Taylor JT.2 Titch	M. A. J. Spice
	G-BGMT	MS.894E Rallye 235GT	J. Murray
	G-BGMU	Westland-Bell 47G-3B1	V. L. J. & V. English
	G-BGMV	Scheibe SF.25B Falke	Mendip Falke Flying Group
	G-BGNB	Short SD3-30 Variant 100	Gill Aviation Ltd/Newcastle
	G-BGND	Cessna F.172N	Stansted Fluid Power (Products) Ltd
	G-BGNG	Short SD3-30	Gill Aviation Ltd/Newcastle
	G-BGNR	Cessna F.172N	Accolade Flying Club/Shoreham
	G-BGNT	Cessna F.152	Klingair Ltd/Conington
	G-BGNV	GA-7 Cougar	E. C. & C. E. E. Craven Walker
	G-BGNZ	Cessna FRA.150L	G. P. Grant-Suttie
	G-BGOD	Colt 77A balloon	C. Allen & M. D. Steuer
	G-BGOG	PA-28-161 Warrior II	W. D. Moore
	G-BGOI	Cameron O-56 balloon	S. H. Budd
	G-BGOL	PA-28R-201T Turbo Arrow III	Clark Aviation Services Ltd
	G-BGOM	PA-31-310 Turbo Navajo	Oxford Aero Charter Ltd/Kidlington
	G-BGON	GA-7 Cougar	BLS Aviation Ltd/Elstree
	G-BGOO	Colt 56 SS balloon	British Gas Corporation
	G-BGOP	Dassault Falcon 20F	Nissan (UK) Ltd/Heathrow
	G-BGOR	AT-6D Harvard III (14863)	M. L. Sargeant
	G-BGOX	PA-31-350 Navajo Chieftain	Woodgate Executive Air Charter Ltd
	G-BGPA	Cessna 182Q	Guildcroft Enterprises Ltd
	G-BGPB	CCF T-6J Texan (20385)	Aircraft Restorations Ltd/Duxford
	G-BGPD	Piper J-3C-65 Cub	P. D. Whiteman
	G-BGPH	AA-5B Tiger	A. J. Dales
	G-BGPI	Plumb BGP-1	B. G. Plumb
	G-BGPJ	PA-28-161 Warrior II	W. Lancs Warrior Co Ltd
	G-BGPK	AA-5B Tiger	G. A. Platon/Bournemouth
	G-BGPL	PA-28-161 Warrior II	T. G. Aviation Ltd/Manston
	G-BGPM	Evans VP-2	M. G. Reilly
	G-BGPN	PA-18 Super Cub 150	Clacton Aero Club (1988) Ltd
	G-BGPU	PA-28 Cherokee 140	Air Navigation & Trading Ltd/Blackpool
	G-BGPZ	M.S.890A Rallye Commodore	Popham Flying Group
	G-BGRC	PA-28 Cherokee 140	Arrow Air Centre Ltd/Shipdham
	G-BGRD	Beech 200 Super King Air	Flightline Ltd (G-IPRA)/Southend
	G-BGRE	Beech A200 Super King Air	Martin-Baker (Engineering) Ltd/Chalgrove
	G-BGRG	Beech 76 Duchess	Motionscope Ltd/Blackpool
	G-BGRH	Robin DR.400/22	Rochester Aviation Ltd
	G-BGRI	Jodel DR.1051	B. Gunn & K. L. Burnett
	G-BGRK	PA-38-112 Tomahawk	Goodwood Terrena Ltd
	G-BGRL	PA-38-112 Tomahawk	Goodwood Terrena Ltd
	G-BGRM	PA-38-112 Tomahawk	Goodwood Terrena Ltd
	G-BGRN	PA-38-112 Tomahawk	Goodwood Terrena Ltd
	G-BGRO	Cessna F.172M	Northfield Garage Ltd/Prestwick
	G-BGRR	PA-38-112 Tomahawk	Prospect Air Ltd
	G-BGRS	Thunder Ax7-77Z balloon	P. M. Gaines & P. B. Fountain
	G-BGRT	Steen Skybolt	R. C. Nichols & ptnrs/Stapleford
	G-BGRX	PA-38-112 Tomahawk	Leavesden Flight Centre Ltd
	G-BGSA	M.S.892E Rallye 150GT	D. H. Tonkin
	G-BGSG	PA-44-180 Seminole	D. J. McSorley
	G-BGSH	PA-38-112 Tomahawk	Scotia Safari Ltd/Prestwick
	G-BGSI	PA-38-112 Tomahawk	Ravenair/Manchester
	G-BGSJ	Piper J-3C-65 Cub	W. J. Higgins/Dunkeswell
	G-BGST	Thunder Ax7-65 balloon	J. L. Bond
	G-BGSV	Cessna F.172N	Southwell Air Services Ltd
	G-BGSW	Beech F33 Debonair	Marketprior Ltd/Swansea
	G-BGSX	Cessna F.152	London Aviation Ltd/Elstree
	G-BGSY	GA-7 Cougar	Van Allen Ltd/Guernsey
	G-BGTB	SOCATA TB.10 Tobago ★	D. Pope (stored)
	G-BGTC	Auster AOP.9 (XP282)	P. T. Bolton/Tollerton
	G-BGTF	PA-44-180 Seminole	New Guarantee Trust Properties Ltd
	G-BGTG	PA-23 Aztec 250F	R. J. Howard/Sherburn
	G-BGTI	Piper J-3C-65 Cub	A. P. Broad
	G-BGTJ	PA-28 Cherokee 180	Serendipity Aviation/Staverton
	G-BGTK	Cessna FR.182RG	R. J. Howard
	G-BGTP	Robin HR.100/210	J. C. Parker
	G-BGTR	PA-28 Cherokee 140	Liverpool Flying School Ltd
	G-BGTT	Cessna 310R	Aviation Beauport Ltd/Jersey
	G-BGTU	BAC One-Eleven 409AY	Turbo Union Ltd/Filton
	G-BGTX	Jodel D.117	Madley Flying Group/Shobdon
	G-BGUA	PA-38-112 Tomahawk	Rhodair Maintenance Ltd/Cardiff

Reg.	Type	Owner or Operator	Notes
G-BGUB	PA-32 Cherokee Six 300E	R. Howton	
G-BGUY	Cameron V-56 balloon	J. L. Guy	
G-BGVB	Robin DR.315	Victor Bravo Group	
G-BGVE	CP.1310-C3 Super Emeraude	Victor Echo Group	
G-BGVH	Beech 76 Duchess	Velco Marketing	
G-BGVK	PA-28-161 Warrior II	D. S. Wells	
G-BGVN	PA-28RT-201 Arrow IV	H. S. Davies	
G-BGVR	Thunder Ax6-56Z balloon	A. N. G. Howie	
G-BGVS	Cessna F.172M	P. D. A. Aviation Ltd/Tollerton	
G-BGVT	Cessna R.182RG	D. C. Massey	
G-BGVU	PA-28 Cherokee 180	P. E. Toleman	
G-BGVV	AA-5A Cheetah	A. H. McVicar	
G-BGVW	AA-5A Cheetah	Air (BH) Associates Ltd/Biggin Hill	
G-BGVY	AA-5B Tiger	Porter Bell Ltd/Goodwood	
G-BGVZ	PA-28-181 Archer II	MS 124 Ltd	
G-BGWA	GA-7 Cougar	Lough Erne Aviation Ltd	
G-BGWC	Robin DR.400/180	E. F. Braddon & D. C. Shepherd/Rochester	
G-BGWH	PA-18 Super Cub 150	Clacton Aero Club (1988) Ltd	
G-BGWI	Cameron V-65 balloon	Army Balloon Club/Germany	
G-BGWJ	Sikorsky S-61N	British Executive Air Services Ltd	
G-BGWK	Sikorsky S-61N	Bristow Helicopters Ltd	
G-BGWM	PA-28-181 Archer II	Thames Valley Flying Club Ltd	
G-BGWN	PA-38-112 Tomahawk	Teesside Flight Centre Ltd	
G-BGWO	Jodel D.112	K. McBride	
G-BGWS	Enstrom 280C Shark	Parish Developments Ltd	
G-BGWU	PA-38-112 Tomahawk	Barmoor Aviation	
G-BGWV	Aeronca 7AC Champion	RFC Flying Group/Popham	
G-BGWW	PA-23 Turbo Aztec 250E	L. B. Pegg	
G-BGWY	Thunder Ax6-56Z balloon	J. G. O'Connel	
G-BGWZ	Eclipse Super Eagle ★	F.A.A. Museum/Yeovilton	
G-BGXA	Piper J-3C-65 Cub (32947)	K. Nicholls	
G-BGXB	PA-38-112 Tomahawk	Sightest Ltd/Biggin Hill	
G-BGXC	SOCATA TB.10 Tobago	N. N. Tullah/Cranfield	
G-BGXD	SOCATA TB.10 Tobago	Selles Dispensing Chemists Ltd	
G-BGXJ	Partenavia P.68B	Cecil Aviation Ltd/Cambridge	
G-BGXK	Cessna 310R	Air Service Training Ltd/Perth	
G-BGXL	Bensen B.8MV	B. P. Triefus	
G-BGXN	PA-38-112 Tomahawk	Panshanger School of Flying Ltd	
G-BGXO	PA-38-112 Tomahawk	Goodwood Terrena Ltd	
G-BGXP	Westland-Bell 47G-3B1	Ace Motor Salvage (Norfolk)	
G-BGXR	Robin HR.200/100	J. P. Kistner & E. G. Cleobury	
G-BGXS	PA-28-236 Dakota	Bawtry Road Service Station Ltd	
G-BGXT	SOCATA TB.10 Tobago	D. A. H. Morris	
G-BGXZ	Cessna FA.152	Falcon Flying Services/Biggin Hill	
G-BGYG	PA-28-161 Warrior II	C.S.E. Aviation Ltd/Kidlington	
G-BGYH	PA-28-161 Warrior II	C.S.E. Aviation Ltd/Kidlington	
G-BGYN	PA-18 Super Cub 150	A. G. Walker	
G-BGYR	H.S.125 Srs 600B	British Aerospace PLC/Warton	
G-BGYV	EMB-110P1 Bandeirante	AirCam Ltd	
G-BGZF	PA-38-112 Tomahawk	Cambrian Flying Club/Swansea	
G-BGZJ	PA-38-112 Tomahawk	W. R. C. M. Foyle	
G-BGZK	Westland-Bell 47G-3B1	I. M. Harvey	
G-BGZL	Eiri PIK-20E	G-BGZL Flying Group/Enstone	
G-BGZN	WMB.2 Windtracker balloon	S. R. Woolfries	
G-BGZO	M.S.880B Rallye Club	G-BGZO Flying Group	
G-BGZW	PA-38-112 Tomahawk	Ravenair/Manchester	
G-BGZY	Jodel D.120	M. Hale	
G-BGZZ	Thunder Ax6-56 balloon	J. M. Robinson	
G-BHAA	Cessna 152	Herefordshire Aero Club Ltd/Shobdon	
G-BHAC	Cessna A.152	Herefordshire Aero Club Ltd/Shobdon	
G-BHAD	Cessna A.152	Shropshire Aero Club Ltd/Sleap	
G-BHAF	PA-38-112 Tomahawk	Notelevel Ltd	
G-BHAI	Cessna F.152	P. P. D. Howard-Johnston/Edinburgh	
G-BHAJ	Robin DR.400/160	Rowantask Ltd	
G-BHAL	Rango Saffery S.200 SS	A. M. Lindsay *Anneky Panky*	
G-BHAM	Thunder Ax6-56 balloon	D. Sampson	
G-BHAR	Westland-Bell 47G-3B1	E. A. L. Sturmer	
G-BHAT	Thunder Ax7-77 balloon	C. P. Witter Ltd *Witter*	
G-BHAV	Cessna F.152	Iceni Leasing	
G-BHAW	Cessna F.172N	A. J. Osmond/Biggin Hill	
G-BHAX	Enstrom F-28C-UK-2	PVS (Barnsley) Ltd	

Notes	Reg.	Type	Owner or Operator
	G-BHAY	PA-28RT-201 Arrow IV	Alpha Yankee Group/Newcastle
	G-BHBA	Campbell Cricket	S. M. Irwin
	G-BHBB	Colt 77A balloon	S. D. Bellew
	G-BHBE	Westland-Bell 47G-3B1 (Soloy)	T. R. Smith (Agricultural Machinery) Ltd
	G-BHBF	Sikorsky S-76A	Bristow Helicopters Ltd
	G-BHBG	PA-32R Cherokee Lance 300	R. W. F. Warner
	G-BHBI	Mooney M.20J	M. Smith
	G-BHBL	L.1011-385 TriStar 200	British Airways *Largs Bay*
	G-BHBM	L.1011-385 TriStar 200	British Airways *Poole Bay*
	G-BHBN	L.1011-385 TriStar 200	British Airways *Bideford Bay*
	G-BHBO	L.1011-385 TriStar 200	British Airways *St Magnus Bay*
	G-BHBR	L.1011-385 TriStar 200	British Airways *Bude Bay*
	G-BHBS	PA-28RT-201T Turbo Arrow IV	B. C. Oates/Barton
	G-BHBT	Marquart MA.5 Charger	R. G. & C. J. Maidment/Shoreham
	G-BHBZ	Partenavia P.68B	Philip Hamer & Co
	G-BHCC	Cessna 172M	Langtry Flying Group Ltd
	G-BHCE	Jodel D.112	D. M. Parsons
	G-BHCM	Cessna F.172H	The English Connection Ltd/Panshanger
	G-BHCP	Cessna F.152	Sherburn Aero Club Ltd
	G-BHCT	PA-23 Aztec 250F	Falcon Flying Services (G-OLBC)/ Biggin Hill
	G-BHCW	PA-22 Tri-Pacer 150	B. Brooks
	G-BHCX	Cessna F.152	A. S. Bamrah/Biggin Hill
	G-BHCZ	PA-38-112 Tomahawk	J. E. Abbott
	G-BHDD	V.668 Varsity T.1 (WL626) ★	Aeropark/E. Midlands
	G-BHDE	SOCATA TB.10 Tobago	A. A. Dooley/Popham
	G-BHDH	Douglas DC-10-30	Caledonian Airways Ltd *Loch Terridon*
	G-BHDI	Douglas DC-10-30	British Airways *Forest of Ae*/Gatwick
	G-BHDJ	Douglas DC-10-30	British Airways *Glengap Forest*/Gatwick
	G-BHDK	Boeing B-29A-BN (461748) ★	Imperial War Museum/Duxford
	G-BHDM	Cessna F.152 II	Tayside Aviation Ltd/Dundee
	G-BHDP	Cessna F.182Q II	P. S. Blackledge
	G-BHDR	Cessna F.152 II	Tayside Aviation Ltd/Dundee
	G-BHDS	Cessna F.152 II	Tayside Aviation Ltd/Dundee
	G-BHDT	SOCATA TB.10 Tobago	R. D. Hill
	G-BHDU	Cessna F.152 II	Falcon Flying Services/Biggin Hill
	G-BHDV	Cameron V-77 balloon	P. Glydon
	G-BHDW	Cessna F.152	Tayside Aviation Ltd/Dundee
	G-BHDX	Cessna F.172N	Skyhawk Group
	G-BHDZ	Cessna F.172N	J. B. Roberts
	G-BHEC	Cessna F.152	W. R. C. M. Foyle
	G-BHED	Cessna FA.152	TG Aviation Ltd/Manston
	G-BHEG	Jodel D.150	P. R. Underhill
	G-BHEH	Cessna 310G	K. Ebbrell
	G-BHEK	CP.1315-C3 Super Emeraude	D. B. Winstanley/Barton
	G-BHEL	Jodel D.117	J. F. Dowe
	G-BHEM	Bensen B.8M	A. M. Sands
	G-BHEN	Cessna FA.152	Leicestershire Aero Club Ltd
	G-BHEO	Cessna FR.182RG	J. G. Hogg
	G-BHER	SOCATA TB.10 Tobago	Vale Aviation Ltd
	G-BHET	SOCATA TB.10 Tobago	Claude Hooper Ltd
	G-BHEU	Thunder Ax7-65 balloon	J. E. R. Govett
	G-BHEV	PA-28R Cherokee Arrow 200	E. & G. H. Kelk
	G-BHEX	Colt 56A balloon	A. S. Dear & ptnrs *Super Wasp*
	G-BHEZ	Jodel D.150	D. R. Elpick/O. Warden
	G-BHFC	Cessna F.152	TG Aviation Ltd/Manston
	G-BHFE	PA-44-180 Seminole	Grunwick Ltd/Elstree
	G-BHFF	Jodel D.112	P. J. Swain
	G-BHFG	SNCAN Stampe SV-4C (45)	Stormswift Ltd
	G-BHFH	PA-34-200T Seneca II	Hendefern Ltd/Goodwood
	G-BHFI	Cessna F.152	BAe (Warton) Flying Group/Blackpool
	G-BHFJ	PA-28RT-201T Turbo Arrow IV	T. L. P. Delaney
	G-BHFK	PA-28-151 Warrior	Ilkeston Car Sales Ltd
	G-BHFM	Murphy S.200 balloon	M. Murphy
	G-BHFR	Eiri PIK-20E-1	J. MacWilliam & T. Dalrymple-Smith
	G-BHFS	Robin DR.400/180	D. S. Chandler
	G-BHGA	PA-31-310 Turbo Navajo	Heltor Ltd
	G-BHGC	PA-18 Super Cub 150	Portsmouth Naval Gliding Club/ Lee-on-Solent
	G-BHGF	Cameron V-56 balloon	P. Smallward
	G-BHGJ	Jodel D.120	Q. M. B. Oswell
	G-BHGK	Sikorsky S-76A	Bond Helicopters Ltd
	G-BHGM	Beech 76 Duchess	Visual Phantom Ltd

Reg.	Type	Owner or Operator	Notes
G-BHGO	PA-32 Cherokee Six 260	A. J. Crisp	
G-BHGP	SOCATA TB.10 Tobago	C. Flanagan	
G-BHGX	Colt 56B balloon	M. N. Dixon	
G-BHGY	PA-28R Cherokee Arrow 200	V. Humphries/Gamston	
G-BHHB	Cameron V-77 balloon	R. Powell	
G-BHHE	Jodel DR.1051/M1	P. Bridges	
G-BHHG	Cessna F.152	Northamptonshire School of Flying Ltd/ Sywell	
G-BHHH	Thunder Ax7-65 balloon	C. A. Hendley (Essex) Ltd	
G-BHHK	Cameron N-77 balloon	I. S. Bridge	
G-BHHN	Cameron V-77 balloon	Itchen Valley Balloon Group	
G-BHHU	Short SD3-30	Gill Aviation Ltd/Newcastle	
G-BHHX	Jodel D.112	D. I. Walker	
G-BHHZ	Rotorway Scorpion 133	L. W. & O. Usherwood	
G-BHIB	Cessna F.182Q	J. Blackburn & J. J. Feeney/Elstree	
G-BHIC	Cessna F.182Q	General Building Services Ltd/Leeds	
G-BHIG	Colt 31A balloon	P. A. Lindstrand	
G-BHIH	Cessna F.172N	K. R. Gough & W. J. Baker	
G-BHII	Cameron V-77 balloon	R. V. Brown	
G-BHIJ	Eiri PIK-20E-1	I. W. Paterson	
G-BHIK	Adam RA-14 Loisirs	L. Lewis	
G-BHIN	Cessna F.152	P. Skinner/Netherthorpe	
G-BHIR	PA-28R Cherokee Arrow 200	Factorcore Ltd/Barton	
G-BHIS	Thunder Ax7-65 balloon	Hedgehoppers Balloon Group	
G-BHIT	SOCATA TB.9 Tampico	Air Touring Services Ltd/Biggin Hill	
G-BHIY	Cessna F.150K	Westfield Flying Group	
G-BHJA	Cessna A.152	Cornwall Flying Club Ltd/Bodmin	
G-BHJB	Cessna A.152	Sky Pro Ltd	
G-BHJF	SOCATA TB.10 Tobago	D. G. Dedman/Leavesden	
G-BHJI	Mooney M.20J	S. F. Lister	
G-BHJK	Maule M5-235C Lunar Rocket	P. F. Hall & R. L. Sambell/Coventry	
G-BHJN	Fournier RF-4D	RF-4 Flying Group	
G-BHJO	PA-28-161 Warrior II	Inverness Flying Services Ltd	
G-BHJS	Partenavia P.68B	Richard Nass Cars Ltd/Norwich	
G-BHJU	Robin DR.400/2+2	T. J. Harlow	
G-BHJZ	EMB-110P2 Bandeirante	Streamline Aviation/E. Midlands	
G-BHKA	Evans VP-1	M. L. Perry	
G-BHKH	Cameron O-65 balloon	D. G. Body	
G-BHKJ	Cessna 421C	Crosslee PLC	
G-BHKR	Colt 12A balloon ★	British Balloon Museum	
G-BHKT	Jodel D.112	M. L. & P. J. Moore	
G-BHKV	AA-5A Cheetah	Alouette Flying Club Ltd/Biggin Hill	
G-BHKY	Cessna 310R II	Air Service Training Ltd/Perth	
G-BHLE	Robin DR.400/180	L. H. Mayall	
G-BHLH	Robin DR.400/180	W. A. Clark	
G-BHLJ	Saffery-Rigg S.200 balloon	I. A. Rigg	
G-BHLK	GA-7 Cougar	Autair Ltd	
G-BHLT	D.H.82A Tiger Moth	P. J. & A. J. Borsberry	
G-BHLU	Fournier RF-3	M. C. Roper	
G-BHLW	Cessna 120	R. T. Meston	
G-BHLX	AA-5B Tiger	Tiger Aviation (Jersey) Ltd	
G-BHLY	Sikorsky S-76A	Bristow Helicopters Ltd	
G-BHMA	SIPA 903	H. J. Taggart	
G-BHMC	M.S.880B Rallye Club	The G-BHMC Group	
G-BHME	WMB.2 Windtracker balloon	I. R. Bell & ptnrs	
G-BHMG	Cessna FA.152	R. D. Smith	
G-BHMI	Cessna F.172N	W. Lancs Aero Club Ltd (G-WADE)/ Woodvale	
G-BHMJ	Avenger T.200-2112 balloon	R. Light *Lord Anthony 1*	
G-BHMK	Avenger T.200-2112 balloon	P. Kinder *Lord Anthony 2*	
G-BHMM	Avenger T.200-2112 balloon	M. Murphy *Lord Anthony 4*	
G-BHMO	PA-20M Cerpa Special (Pacer)	A. B. Holloway & ptnrs	
G-BHMR	Stinson 108-3	D. G. French/Sandown	
G-BHMT	Evans VP-1	P. E. J. Sturgeon	
G-BHMU	Colt 21A balloon	J. R. Parkington & Co Ltd	
G-BHMW	F.27 Friendship Mk 200	Air UK *Sir John Hall*/Norwich	
G-BHMX	F.27 Friendship Mk 200	Air UK *Fred Truman*/Norwich	
G-BHMY	F.27 Friendship Mk 200	Air UK/Norwich	
G-BHMZ	F.27 Friendship Mk 200	Air UK *R. J. Mitchell*/Norwich	
G-BHNA	Cessna F.152	Sheffield Aero Club Ltd/Netherthorpe	
G-BHNC	Cameron O-65 balloon	D. & C. Bareford	
G-BHND	Cameron N-65 balloon	S. M. Wellband	
G-BHNL	Jodel D.112	G. van der Gaag	

Notes	Reg.	Type	Owner or Operator
	G-BHNM	PA-44-180 Seminole	Standby One Flight Services Ltd
	G-BHNO	PA-28-181 Archer II	Davison Plant Hire Co/Compton Abbas
	G-BHNP	Eiri PIK-20E-1	J. T. Morgan
	G-BHNU	Cessna F.172N	B. Swindell Ltd/Barton
	G-BHNV	Westland-Bell 47G-3B1	Leyline Helicopters Ltd
	G-BHNX	Jodel D.117	R. V. Rendall
	G-BHOA	Robin DR.400/160	M. J. Ferguson
	G-BHOF	Sikorsky S-61N	Bristow Helicopters Ltd
	G-BHOG	Sikorsky S-61N	Bristow Helicopters Ltd
	G-BHOH	Sikorsky S-61N	Bristow Helicopters Ltd
	G-BHOL	Jodel DR.1050	D. G. Hart
	G-BHOM	PA-18 Super Cub 95	C. H. A. Bott
	G-BHOO	Thunder Ax7-65 balloon	D. Livesey & J. M. Purves *Scraps*
	G-BHOP	Thunder Ax3 balloon	B. Meeson
	G-BHOR	PA-28-161 Warrior II	Oscar Romeo Flying Group/Biggin Hill
	G-BHOT	Cameron V-65 balloon	Dante Balloon Group
	G-BHOU	Cameron V-65 balloon	F. W. Barnes
	G-BHOW	Beech 95-58PA Baron	Anglo-African Machinery Ltd/Coventry
	G-BHOZ	SOCATA TB.9 Tampico	M. Brown
	G-BHPJ	Eagle Microlite	G. Breen/Enstone
	G-BHPK	Piper J-3C-65 Cub (236800)	L-4 Group
	G-BHPL	C.A.S.A. 1.131E Jungmann	M. G. Jeffries
	G-BHPM	PA-18 Super Cub 95	P. I. Morgans
	G-BHPN	Colt 14A balloon	Lindstrand Balloons Ltd
	G-BHPO	Colt 14A balloon	C. J. Boxall
	G-BHPS	Jodel D.120A	J. P. Leigh
	G-BHPT	Piper J-3C-65 Cub	D. I. Cooke
	G-BHPX	Cessna 152	J. A. Pothecary/Shoreham
	G-BHPY	Cessna 152	A. T. Hooper & T. E. Evans/Wellesbourne
	G-BHPZ	Cessna 172N	O'Brian Properties Ltd/Redhill
	G-BHRA	R. Commander 114A	P. A. Warner
	G-BHRB	Cessna F.152	Lancashire Aero Club/Barton
	G-BHRC	PA-28-161 Warrior II	Sherwood Flying Club Ltd/Tollerton
	G-BHRD	D.H.C.1 Chipmunk 22 (WP977)	A. J. Dunstan & P. R. Joshua/Kidlington
	G-BHRH	Cessna FA.150K	Merlin Flying Club Ltd/Hucknall
	G-BHRI	Saffery S.200 balloon	N. J. & H. L. Dunnington
	G-BHRM	Cessna F.152	Aerohire Ltd/Halfpenny Green
	G-BHRN	Cessna F.152	J. Easson/Edinburgh
	G-BHRO	R. Commander 112A	John Raymond Transport Ltd/Cardiff
	G-BHRP	PA-44-180 Seminole	E. Midlands Flying School Ltd
	G-BHRR	CP.301A Emeraude	T. W. Offen
	G-BHRW	Jodel DR.221	Dauphin Flying Group
	G-BHRY	Colt 56A balloon	A. S. Davidson
	G-BHSA	Cessna 152	Skyviews & General Ltd/Sherburn
	G-BHSB	Cessna 172N	Saunders Caravans Ltd
	G-BHSD	Scheibe SF.25E Super Falke	Lasham Gliding Soc Ltd
	G-BHSE	R. Commander 114	604 Sqdn Flying Group Ltd
	G-BHSL	C.A.S.A. 1.131 Jungmann	Cotswold Flying Group
	G-BHSN	Cameron N-56 balloon	I. Bentley
	G-BHSP	Thunder Ax7-77Z balloon	Out-Of-The-Blue
	G-BHSS	Pitts S-1C Special	Bottoms Up Syndicate
	G-BHST	Hughes 369D	Acme Jewellery Ltd
	G-BHSV	H.S.125 Srs 700B	Shell Aircraft Ltd/Heathrow
	G-BHSW	H.S.125 Srs 700B	Shell Aircraft Ltd/Heathrow
	G-BHSY	Jodel DR.1050	S. R. Orwin & T. R. Allebone
	G-BHTA	PA-28-236 Dakota	Dakota Ltd
	G-BHTC	Jodel DR.1050/M1	G. Clark
	G-BHTD	Cessna T.188C AgHusky	ADS (Aerial) Ltd/Southend
	G-BHTG	Thunder Ax6-56 balloon	F. R. & Mrs S. H. MacDonald
	G-BHTH	NA T-6G Texan (2807)	J. J. Woodhouse
	G-BHTR	Bell 206B JetRanger 3	Huktra (UK) Ltd
	G-BHTT	Cessna 500 Citation	Specialised Management Ltd
	G-BHUB	Douglas C-47A (315509) ★	Imperial War Museum/Duxford
	G-BHUE	Jodel DR.1050	M. J. Harris
	G-BHUG	Cessna 172N	Air Group 6/Gamston
	G-BHUI	Cessna 152	Cheshire Air Training School Ltd
	G-BHUJ	Cessna 172N	Three Counties Aero Engineering Ltd/Lasham
	G-BHUM	D.H.82A Tiger Moth	S. G. Towers
	G-BHUO	Evans VP-2	D. A. Wood
	G-BHUP	Cessna F.152	Stapleford Flying Club Ltd
	G-BHUR	Thunder Ax3 balloon	B. F. G. Ribbans
	G-BHUU	PA-25 Pawnee 235	Pawnee Aviation/Boston

Reg.	Type	Owner or Operator	Notes
G-BHVB	PA-28-161 Warrior II	Bobbington Air Training School Ltd/ Halfpenny Green	
G-BHVC	Cessna 172RG Cutlass	I. B. Willis/Panshanger	
G-BHVE	Saffery S.330 balloon	P. M. Randles	
G-BHVF	Jodel D.150A	Wessex Flying Group	
G-BHVN	Cessna 152	Three Counties Aero Engineering Ltd/ Lasham	
G-BHVP	Cessna 182Q	Air Tows/Lasham	
G-BHVR	Cessna 172N	Three Counties Aero Engineering Ltd/ Lasham	
G-BHVV	Piper J-3C-65 Cub	W. A. N. Jenkins	
G-BHVZ	Cessna 180	R. Moore/Blackpool	
G-BHWA	Cessna F.152	Wickenby Aviation Ltd	
G-BHWB	Cessna F.152	Wickenby Aviation Ltd	
G-BHWG	Mahatma S.200SR balloon	H. W. Gandy *Spectrum*	
G-BHWH	Weedhopper JC-24A	G. A. Clephane	
G-BHWK	M.S.880B Rallye Club	Arrow Flying Group	
G-BHWS	Cessna F.152	Turnhouse Flying Club	
G-BHWY	PA-28R Cherokee Arrow 200-II	W. B. Risdale/Sandown	
G-BHWZ	PA-28-181 Archer II	I. R. McCue	
G-BHXA	SA Bulldog Srs 120/1210	SAYF Aviation Ltd	
G-BHXB	SA Bulldog Srs 120/1210	SAYF Aviation Ltd	
G-BHXD	Jodel D.120	P. H. C. Hall	
G-BHXK	PA-28 Cherokee 140	GXK Flying Group	
G-BHXL	Evans VP-2	R. S. Wharton	
G-BHXS	Jodel D.120	I. R. Willis	
G-BHXT	Thunder Ax6-56Z balloon	Ocean Traffic Services Ltd	
G-BHXU	AB-206B JetRanger 3	Castle Air Charters Ltd	
G-BHXV	AB-206B JetRanger 3	Dollar Air Services Ltd (G-OWJM)	
G-BHXY	Piper J-3C-65 Cub (44-79609)	Grasshopper Flyers	
G-BHYA	Cessna R.182RG II	Stainless Steel Profile Cutters Ltd	
G-BHYC	Cessna 172RG Cutlass	Richard Nash Cars Ltd	
G-BHYD	Cessna R.172K XP II	Sylmar Aviation Services Ltd	
G-BHYE	PA-34-200T Seneca II	C.S.E. Aviation Ltd/Kidlington	
G-BHYF	PA-34-200T Seneca II	C.S.E. Aviation Ltd/Kidlington	
G-BHYG	PA-34-200T Seneca II	C.S.E. Aviation Ltd/Kidlington	
G-BHYI	SNCAN Stampe SV-4A	P. A. Irwin	
G-BHYN	Evans VP-2	D. Cromie	
G-BHYO	Cameron N-77 balloon	C. Sisson	
G-BHYP	Cessna F.172M	D. C. W. Sanders/Biggin Hill	
G-BHYR	Cessna F.172M	Alumvale Ltd/Stapleford	
G-BHYV	Evans VP-1	L. Chiappi/Blackpool	
G-BHYX	Cessna 152 II	Stapleford Flying Club Ltd	
G-BHZE	PA-28-181 Archer II	Northfield Garage Ltd	
G-BHZF	Evans VP-2	W. J. Evans	
G-BHZH	Cessna F.152	1013 Ltd/Guernsey	
G-BHZK	AA-5B Tiger	N. K. Margolis/Elstree	
G-BHZM	Jodel DR.1050	G. H. Wylde/Manchester	
G-BHZO	AA-5A Cheetah	Scotia Safari Ltd/Prestwick	
G-BHZR	SA Bulldog Srs 120/1210	SAYF Aviation Ltd	
G-BHZS	SA Bulldog Srs 120/1210	SAYF Aviation Ltd	
G-BHZT	SA Bulldog Srs 120/1210	SAYF Aviation Ltd	
G-BHZU	Piper J-3C-65 Cub	J. K. Tomkinson	
G-BHZV	Jodel D.120A	J. G. Munro/Perth	
G-BHZX	Thunder Ax7-65A balloon	R. J. & H. M. Beattie	
G-BIAB	SOCATA TB.9 Tampico	H. W. A. Thirlway	
G-BIAC	SOCATA Rallye 235E	Anpal Finance Ltd & Aerial Facilities Ltd/ Biggin Hill	
G-BIAH	Jodel D.112	D. Mitchell	
G-BIAI	WMB.2 Windtracker balloon	I. Chadwick	
G-BIAK	SOCATA TB.10 Tobago	Real Life Ltd	
G-BIAL	Rango NA.8 balloon	A. M. Lindsay	
G-BIAO	Evans VP-2	P. J. Hall	
G-BIAP	PA-16 Clipper	P. J. Bish & M. J. Mothershaw/ White Waltham	
G-BIAR	Rigg Skyliner II balloon	I. A. Rigg	
G-BIAU	Sopwith Pup (replica) (N6452)	F.A.A. Museum/Yeovilton	
G-BIAX	Taylor JT.2 Titch	G. F. Rowley	
G-BIAY	AA-5 Traveler	M. D. Dupay & ptnrs	
G-BIBA	SOCATA TB.9 Tampico	TB Aviation Ltd	
G-BIBB	Mooney M.20C	J. R. Gardiner	
G-BIBC	Cessna 310R	Air Service Training Ltd/Perth	

Notes	Reg.	Type	Owner or Operator
	G-BIBD	Rotec Rally 2B	A. Clarke
	G-BIBG	Sikorsky S-76A	Bristow Helicopters Ltd
	G-BIBJ	Enstrom 280C-UK-2 Shark	Tindon Ltd/Little Snoring
	G-BIBK	Taylor JT.2 Titch	J. G. McTaggart
	G-BIBN	Cessna FA.150K	P. H. Lewis
	G-BIBO	Cameron V-65 balloon	I. Harris
	G-BIBP	AA-5A Cheetah	Scotia Safari Ltd/Prestwick
	G-BIBS	Cameron P-20 balloon	Cameron Balloons Ltd
	G-BIBT	AA-5B Tiger	Fergusons (Blyth) Ltd/Newcastle
	G-BIBU	Morris Ax7-77 balloon	K. Morris
	G-BIBW	Cessna F.172N	Deltair Ltd/Chester
	G-BIBX	WMB.2 Windtracker balloon	I. A. Rigg
	G-BIBY	Beech F33A Bonanza	Baythorne Ltd/Fairoaks
	G-BIBZ	Thunder Ax3 balloon	F. W. Barnes/Nairobi
	G-BICC	Vulture Tx3 balloon	C. P. Clitheroe
	G-BICD	Auster 5	R. T. Parsons
	G-BICE	AT-6C Harvard IIA (41-33275)	C. M. L. Edwards/Ipswich
	G-BICG	Cessna F.152	Falcon Flying Services/Biggin Hill
	G-BICJ	Monnet Sonerai II	D. J. Marks
	G-BICM	Colt 56A balloon	Avon Advertiser Balloon Club
	G-BICN	F.8L Falco	R. J. Barber
	G-BICP	Robin DR.360	Bravo India Flying Group/Woodvale
	G-BICR	Jodel D.120A	Beehive Flying Group/White Waltham
	G-BICS	Robin R.2100A	G-BICS Group/Sibson
	G-BICT	Evans VP-1	A. S. Coombe & D. L. Tribe
	G-BICU	Cameron V-56 balloon	K. C. Tanner
	G-BICW	PA-28-161 Warrior II	D. Gellhorn
	G-BICX	Maule M5-235C Lunar Rocket	A. T. Jeans & J. F. Clarkson/Old Sarum
	G-BICY	PA-23 Apache 160	A. M. Lynn/Sibson
	G-BIDD	Evans VP-1	W. Thomas
	G-BIDE	CP.301A Emeraude	D. Elliott
	G-BIDF	Cessna F.172P	E. Alexander
	G-BIDG	Jodel D.150A	D. R. Gray/Barton
	G-BIDH	Cessna 152 II	Cumbria Aero Club (G-DONA)/Carlisle
	G-BIDI	PA-28R-201 Arrow III	LBE Contract Tooling Ltd
	G-BIDJ	PA-18A Super Cub 150	AB Plant (Bristol) Ltd
	G-BIDK	PA-18 Super Cub 150	Scottish Gliding Union Ltd
	G-BIDM	Cessna F.172H	(stored)
	G-BIDO	CP.301A Emeraude	A. R. Plumb
	G-BIDP	PA-28-181 Archer II	Sky Aviation Ltd
	G-BIDU	Cameron V-77 balloon	E. Eleazor
	G-BIDV	Colt 14A balloon	International Distillers & Vintners (House Trade) Ltd
	G-BIDW	Sopwith 1½ Strutter (replica) (A8226) ★	RAF Museum/Hendon
	G-BIDX	Jodel D.112	H. N. Nuttall & R. P. Walley
	G-BIEC	AB-206A JetRanger 2	Autair Helicopters Ltd
	G-BIEF	Cameron V-77 balloon	D. S. Bush
	G-BIEJ	Sikorsky S-76A	Bristow Helicopters Ltd
	G-BIEN	Jodel D.120A	R. J. Baker
	G-BIEO	Jodel D.112	Clipgate Flyers
	G-BIES	Maule M5-235C Lunar Rocket	William Proctor Farms
	G-BIET	Cameron O-77 balloon	G. M. Westley
	G-BIEY	PA-28-151 Warrior	J. A. Pothecary/Shoreham
	G-BIFA	Cessna 310R-II	D. S. Milne
	G-BIFB	PA-28 Cherokee 150	N. A. Ayub
	G-BIFH	Short SD3-30	Gill Aviation Ltd/Newcastle
	G-BIFK	Short SD3-30	Gill Aviation Ltd/Newcastle
	G-BIFN	Bensen B.8M	B. Gunn
	G-BIFO	Evans VP-1	R. Broadhead
	G-BIFP	Colt 56C balloon	J. Philp
	G-BIFY	Cessna F.150L	Jureen Aviation
	G-BIFZ	Partenavia P.68C	ALY Aviation Ltd/Henstridge
	G-BIGD	Cameron V-77 balloon	D. L. Clark *Frog*
	G-BIGF	Thunder Ax7-77 balloon	M. D. Stever & C. A. Allen
	G-BIGH	Piper J-3C-65 Cub	W. McNally
	G-BIGJ	Cessna F.172M	Clacton Aero Club (1988) Ltd
	G-BIGK	Taylorcraft BC-12D	H. L. M. & G. R. Williams
	G-BIGL	Cameron O-65 balloon	P. L. Mossman
	G-BIGM	Avenger T.200-2112 balloon	M. Murphy
	G-BIGP	Bensen B.8M	R. H. S. Cooper
	G-BIGR	Avenger T.200-2112 balloon	R. Light
	G-BIGX	Bensen B.8M	P. R. Moore & M. B. Stone

Reg.	Type	Owner or Operator	Notes
G-BIGY	Cameron V-65 balloon	Dante Balloon Group	
G-BIGZ	Scheibe SF.25B Falke	G-BIGZ Syndicate	
G-BIHD	Robin DR.400/160	Alexander Howden Group Sports & Social Club/Biggin Hill	
G-BIHE	Cessna FA.152	Inverness Flying Services Ltd	
G-BIHF	SE-5A (replica) (F943)	K. J. Garrett *Lady Di*/Booker	
G-BIHG	PA-28 Cherokee 140	T. M. Plewman	
G-BIHI	Cessna 172M	J. H. Ashley-Rogers	
G-BIHN	Skyship 500 airship	Airship Industries Ltd/Cardington	
G-BIHP	Van Den Bemden gas balloon	J. J. Harris	
G-BIHT	PA-17 Vagabond	G. H. Cork	
G-BIHU	Saffery S.200 balloon	B. L. King	
G-BIHW	Aeronca A65TAC Defender	T. J. Ingrouille	
G-BIHY	Isaacs Fury	P. C. Butler	
G-BIIA	Fournier RF-3	T. M. W. Webster	
G-BIIB	Cessna F.172M	Civil Service Flying Club (Biggin Hill) Ltd	
G-BIID	PA-18 Super Cub 95	875 (Westhill) Squadron ATC/Aberdeen	
G-BIIE	Cessna F.172P	Shoreham Flight Simulation Ltd/ Bournemouth	
G-BIIF	Fournier RF-4D	J. A. Bridges & J. A. Taylor (G-BVET)/ Biggin Hill	
G-BIIG	Thunder Ax-6-56Z balloon	Chiltern Flyers Ltd	
G-BIIJ	Cessna F.152	Leicestershire Aero Club Ltd	
G-BIIK	M.S.883 Rallye 115	Chiltern Flyers Ltd	
G-BIIL	Thunder Ax6-56 balloon	G. W. Reader	
G-BIIT	PA-28-161 Warrior II	Tayside Aviation Ltd/Dundee	
G-BIIV	PA-28-181 Archer II	Stratton Motor Co Ltd	
G-BIIX	Rango NA.12 balloon	Rango Kite Co	
G-BIIZ	Great Lakes 2T-1A Sport Trainer	J. R. Lindsay/Booker	
G-BIJB	PA-18 Super Cub 150	Essex Gliding Club/North Weald	
G-BIJD	Bo 208C Junior	C. G. Stone	
G-BIJE	Piper J-3C-65 Cub	R. L. Hayward & A. G. Scott	
G-BIJS	Luton LA-4A Minor	I. J. Smith	
G-BIJT	AA-5A Cheetah	Mid-Sussex Timber Co Ltd	
G-BIJU	CP.301A Emeraude	Eastern Taildraggers Flying Group (G-BHTX)	
G-BIJV	Cessna F.152 II	Falcon Flying Services/Biggin Hill	
G-BIJW	Cessna F.152 II	Falcon Flying Services/Biggin Hill	
G-BIJX	Cessna F.152 II	Civil Service Flying Club (Biggin Hill) Ltd	
G-BIKA	Boeing 757-236	British Airways *Dover Castle*	
G-BIKB	Boeing 757-236	British Airways *Windsor Castle*	
G-BIKC	Boeing 757-236	British Airways *Edinburgh Castle*	
G-BIKD	Boeing 757-236	British Airways *Caernafon Castle*	
G-BIKE	PA-28R Cherokee Arrow 200	R. V. Webb Ltd/Elstree	
G-BIKF	Boeing 757-236	British Airways *Carrickfergus Castle*	
G-BIKG	Boeing 757-236	British Airways *Stirling Castle*	
G-BIKH	Boeing 757-236	British Airways *Richmond Castle*	
G-BIKI	Boeing 757-236	British Airways *Tintagel Castle*	
G-BIKJ	Boeing 757-236	British Airways *Conwy Castle*	
G-BIKK	Boeing 757-236	British Airways *Eilean Donan Castle*	
G-BIKL	Boeing 757-236	British Airways *Nottingham Castle*	
G-BIKM	Boeing 757-236	British Airways *Glamis Castle*	
G-BIKN	Boeing 757-236	British Airways *Bodiam Castle*	
G-BIKO	Boeing 757-236	British Airways *Harlech Castle*	
G-BIKP	Boeing 757-236	British Airways *Enniskillen Castle*	
G-BIKR	Boeing 757-236	British Airways *Bamburgh Castle*	
G-BIKS	Boeing 757-236	British Airways *Corfe Castle*	
G-BIKT	Boeing 757-236	British Airways *Carisbrooke Castle*	
G-BIKU	Boeing 757-236	British Airways *Inveraray Castle*	
G-BIKV	Boeing 757-236	British Airways *Raglan Castle*	
G-BIKW	Boeing 757-236	British Airways *Belvoir Castle*	
G-BIKX	Boeing 757-236	British Airways *Warwick Castle*	
G-BIKY	Boeing 757-236	British Airways *Leeds Castle*	
G-BIKZ	Boeing 757-236	British Airways *Kenilworth Castle*	
G-BILA	Daletol DM.165L Viking	R. Lamplough (*stored*)	
G-BILB	WMB.2 Windtracker balloon	B. L. King	
G-BILE	Scruggs BL.2B balloon	P. D. Ridout	
G-BILF	Practavia Sprite 125	G. Harfield	
G-BILG	Scruggs BL.2B balloon	P. D. Ridout	
G-BILI	Piper J-3C-65 Cub (454467)	G-BILI Flying Group	
G-BILJ	Cessna FA.152	Shoreham Flight Simulation Ltd/ Bournemouth	
G-BILK	Cessna FA.152	Exeter Flying Club Ltd	

Notes	Reg.	Type	Owner or Operator
	G-BILL	PA-25 Pawnee 235	Pawnee Aviation
	G-BILR	Cessna 152	Skyviews & General Ltd
	G-BILS	Cessna 152	Skyviews & General Ltd
	G-BILU	Cessna 172RG	Full Sutton Flying Centre Ltd
	G-BILZ	Taylor JT.1 Monoplane	A. Petherbridge
	G-BIMK	Tiger T.200 Srs 1 balloon	M. K. Baron
	G-BIMM	PA-18 Super Cub 150	Clacton Aero Club (1988) Ltd
	G-BIMN	Steen Skybolt	C. R. Williamson
	G-BIMO	SNCAN Stampe SV-4C	R. A. Roberts
	G-BIMT	Cessna FA.152	Staverton Flying Services Ltd
	G-BIMU	Sikorsky S-61N	Bristow Helicopters Ltd
	G-BIMX	Rutan Vari-Eze	D. G. Crew/Biggin Hill
	G-BIMZ	Beech 76 Duchess	Barrein Engineers Ltd/Lulsgate
	G-BINF	Saffery S.200 balloon	T. Lewis
	G-BING	Cessna F.172P	J. E. M. Patrick
	G-BINI	Scruggs BL.2C balloon	S. R. Woolfries
	G-BINL	Scruggs BL.2B balloon	P. D. Ridout
	G-BINM	Scruggs BL.2B balloon	P. D. Ridout
	G-BINO	Evans VP-1	A. M. S. Liggat
	G-BINR	Unicorn UE.1A balloon	Unicorn Group
	G-BINS	Unicorn UE.2A balloon	Unicorn Group
	G-BINT	Unicorn UE.1A balloon	Unicorn Group
	G-BINU	Saffery S.200 balloon	T. Lewis
	G-BINX	Scruggs BL.2B balloon	P. D. Ridout
	G-BINY	Oriental balloon	J. L. Morton
	G-BIOB	Cessna F.172P	Aerofilms Ltd/Elstree
	G-BIOC	Cessna F.150L	Seawing Flying Club/Southend
	G-BIOE	Short SD3-30 Variant 100	Gill Aviation Ltd/Newcastle
	G-BIOI	Jodel DR.1051/M	H. F. Hambling
	G-BIOJ	R. Commander 112TCA	A. T. Dalby
	G-BIOK	Cessna F.152	Tayside Aviation Ltd/Dundee
	G-BIOM	Cessna F.152	Falcon Flying Services/Biggin Hill
	G-BION	Cameron V-77 balloon	Flying Doctors Balloon Syndicate
	G-BIOR	M.S.880B Rallye Club	Aircraft Dept. Royal Aircraft Establishment/ Farnborough
	G-BIOU	Jodel D.117A	M. S. Printing & Graphics Machinery Ltd/ Booker
	G-BIOW	Slingsby T.67A	A. B. Slinger/Sherburn
	G-BIPA	AA-5B Tiger	J. Campbell/Walney Island
	G-BIPH	Scruggs BL.2B balloon	C. M. Dewsnap
	G-BIPI	Everett Blackbird Mk 1	R. Spall
	G-BIPJ	PA-36-375 Brave	G. B. Pearce/Shoreham
	G-BIPN	Fournier RF-3	S. N. Lawrence
	G-BIPO	Mudry/CAARP CAP.20LS-200	D. C. MacDonald
	G-BIPS	SOCATA Rallye 100ST	McAully Flying Group/Little Snoring
	G-BIPT	Jodel D.112	C. R. Davies
	G-BIPV	AA-5B Tiger	Solent Flight
	G-BIPW	Avenger T.200-2112 balloon	B. L. King
	G-BIPY	Bensen B.8	W. J. Pope
	G-BIRD	Pitts S-1C Special	Pitts Artists Flying Group
	G-BIRE	Colt 56 Bottle SS balloon	K. R. Gafney
	G-BIRH	PA-18 Super Cub 135 (R-163)	I. R. F. Hammond/Lee-on-Solent
	G-BIRI	C.A.S.A. 1.131E Jungmann	M. G. & J. R. Jeffries
	G-BIRK	Avenger T.200-2112 balloon	D. Harland
	G-BIRL	Avenger T.200-2112 balloon	R. Light
	G-BIRM	Avenger T.200-2112 balloon	P. Higgins
	G-BIRP	Arena Mk 17 Skyship balloon	A. S. Viel
	G-BIRS	Cessna 182P	John E. Birks & Associates Ltd (G-BBBS)
	G-BIRT	Robin R.1180TD	W. D'A. Hall/Booker
	G-BIRW	M.S.505 Criquet (F+IS) ★	Museum of Flight/E. Fortune
	G-BIRY	Cameron V-77 balloon	J. J. Winter
	G-BIRZ	Zenair CH.250	A. W. F. Richards
	G-BISB	Cessna F.152 II	Sheffield Aero Club Ltd/Netherthorpe
	G-BISG	FRED Srs 3	R. A. Coombe
	G-BISH	Cameron O-42 balloon	Zebedee Balloon Service
	G-BISJ	Cessna 340A	Billair
	G-BISK	R. Commander 112B ★	P. A. Warner
	G-BISL	Scruggs BL.2B balloon	P. D. Ridout
	G-BISM	Scruggs BL.2B balloon	P. D. Ridout
	G-BISS	Scruggs BL.2C balloon	P. D. Ridout
	G-BIST	Scruggs BL.2C balloon	P. D. Ridout
	G-BISV	Cameron O-65 balloon	Hylyne Rabbits Ltd
	G-BISW	Cameron O-65 balloon	Rango Balloon & Kite Co

Reg.	Type	Owner or Operator	Notes
G-BISX	Colt 56A balloon	J. R. Gore	
G-BISZ	Sikorsky S-76A	Bristow Helicopters Ltd	
G-BITA	PA-18 Super Cub 150	J. & S. A. S. McCullough	
G-BITE	SOCATA TB.10 Tobago	M. A. Smith & R. J. Bristow/Fairoaks	
G-BITF	Cessna F.152	Tayside Aviation Ltd/Dundee	
G-BITH	Cessna F.152	Tayside Aviation Ltd/Dundee	
G-BITK	FRED Srs 2	D. J. Wood	
G-BITM	Cessna F.172P	D. G. Crabtree/Barton	
G-BITO	Jodel D.112D	A. Dunbar/Barton	
G-BITR	Sikorsky S-76A	Bristow Helicopters Ltd	
G-BITS	Drayton B-56 balloon	M. J. Betts	
G-BITW	Short SD3-30 Variant 100	Streamline Aviation (SW) Ltd (G-EASI)/ Exeter	
G-BITY	FD.31T balloon	A. J. Bell	
G-BIUL	Cameron 60 SS balloon	D. C. Patrick-Brown	
G-BIUM	Cessna F.152	Sheffield Aero Club Ltd/Netherthorpe	
G-BIUP	SNCAN NC.854S	C. M. Mogg	
G-BIUU	PA-23 Aztec 250D ★	G. Cormack/Glasgow	
G-BIUV	H.S.748 Srs 2A	Emerald Airways Ltd (G-AYYH)/Liverpool	
G-BIUW	PA-28-161 Warrior II	D. R. Staley	
G-BIUY	PA-28-181 Archer II	W. S. Robertson	
G-BIVA	Robin R.2112	Cotswold Aero Club Ltd/Staverton	
G-BIVB	Jodel D.112	D. H. Anderson	
G-BIVC	Jodel D.112	M. J. Barmby/Cardiff	
G-BIVK	Bensen B.8	J. G. Toy	
G-BIVL	Bensen B.8	R. Gardiner	
G-BIVT	Saffery S.80 balloon	L. F. Guyot	
G-BIVV	AA-5A Cheetah	W. Dass	
G-BIVY	Cessna 172N	Goodwood Aircraft Management Services Ltd	
G-BIVZ	D.31A Turbulent	The Tiger Club (1990) Ltd/Headcorn	
G-BIWB	Scruggs RS.5000 balloon	P. D. Ridout	
G-BIWC	Scruggs RS.5000 balloon	P. D. Ridout	
G-BIWD	Scruggs RS.5000 balloon	D. Eaves	
G-BIWF	Warren balloon	P. D. Ridout	
G-BIWG	Zelenski Mk 2 balloon	P. D. Ridout	
G-BIWJ	Unicorn UE.1A balloon	B. L. King	
G-BIWK	Cameron V-65 balloon	I. R. Williams & R. G. Bickerdicke	
G-BIWL	PA-32-301 Saratoga	Harwoods of Essex Ltd	
G-BIWN	Jodel D.112	C. R. Coates	
G-BIWP	Mooney M.20J	J. K. McWhinney	
G-BIWR	Mooney M.20F	A. C. Brink	
G-BIWU	Cameron V-65 balloon	J. T. Whicker & J. W. Unwin	
G-BIWW	AA-5 Traveler	B&K Aviation/Cranfield	
G-BIWX	AT-16 Harvard IV (FT239)	A. E. Hutton/North Weald	
G-BIWY	Westland WG.30 ★	*Instructional airframe*/Sherborne	
G-BIXA	SOCATA TB.9 Tampico	Lord de Saumarez	
G-BIXB	SOCATA TB.9 Tampico	Kitchen Bros/Little Snoring	
G-BIXH	Cessna F.152	Cambridge Aero Club Ltd	
G-BIXI	Cessna 172RG Cutlass	J. F. P. Lewis/Sandown	
G-BIXL	P-51D Mustang (472216)	R. Lamplough/North Weald	
G-BIXN	Boeing Stearman A.75N1	I. L. Craig-Wood & ptnrs	
G-BIXR	Cameron A-140 balloon	Skysales Ltd	
G-BIXS	Avenger T.200-2112 balloon	M. Stuart	
G-BIXV	Bell 212	Bristow Helicopters Ltd	
G-BIXW	Colt 56B balloon	N. A. P. Bates	
G-BIXX	Pearson Srs 2 balloon	D. Pearson	
G-BIXZ	Grob G-109	V. J. R. Day	
G-BIYG	Short SD3-30	Gill Aviation Ltd/Newcastle	
G-BIYH	Short SD3-30	Gill Aviation Ltd/Newcastle	
G-BIYI	Cameron V-65 balloon	Sarnia Balloon Group	
G-BIYJ	PA-18 Super Cub 95	S. Russell	
G-BIYK	Isaacs Fury	R. S. Martin/Dunkeswell	
G-BIYM	PA-32R-301 Saratoga SP	Pinta Investments Ltd	
G-BIYO	PA-31-310 Turbo Navajo	Island Aviation & Travel Ltd	
G-BIYP	PA-20 Pacer 135	R. J. Whitcombe	
G-BIYR	PA-18 Super Cub 135	Delta Foxtrot Flying Group/Dunkeswell	
G-BIYT	Colt 17A balloon	A. F. Selby	
G-BIYU	Fokker S.11.1 Instructor (E-15)	H. R. Smallwood & A. J. Lee/Denham	
G-BIYW	Jodel D.112	Pollard/Balaam/Bye Flying Group	
G-BIYX	PA-28 Cherokee 140	A. Gowlett/Blackpool	
G-BIYY	PA-18 Super Cub 95	A. E. & W. J. Taylor/Ingoldmells	
G-BIZF	Cessna F.172P	R. S. Bentley/Bourn	

Notes	Reg.	Type	Owner or Operator
	G-BIZG	Cessna F.152	M. A. Judge
	G-BIZI	Robin DR.400/120	Headcorn Flying School Ltd
	G-BIZK	Nord 3202	A. I. Milne/Swanton Morley
	G-BIZM	Nord 3202	Magnificent Obsessions Ltd
	G-BIZN	Slingsby T.67A	G. A. Gee
	G-BIZO	PA-28R Cherokee Arrow 200	Bowlish Roofing Supplies Ltd
	G-BIZR	SOCATA TB.9 Tampico	R. M. Shears (G-BSEC)
	G-BIZT	Bensen B.8M	J. Ferguson
	G-BIZU	Thunder Ax6-56Z balloon	M. J. Loades
	G-BIZV	PA-18 Super Cub 95 (18-2001)	S. J. Pugh & R. L. Wademan
	G-BIZW	Champion 7GCBC Citabria	G. Read & Sons
	G-BIZY	Jodel D.112	Wayland Tunley & Associates
	G-BJAD	FRED Srs 2	C. Allison
	G-BJAE	Lavadoux Starck AS.80	D. J. & S. A. E. Phillips/Coventry
	G-BJAF	Piper J-3C-65 Cub	J. M. Mooney
	G-BJAG	PA-28-181 Archer II	K. F. Hudson & D. J. Casson/Sherburn
	G-BJAJ	AA-5B Tiger	A. H. McVicar/Prestwick
	G-BJAL	C.A.S.A. 1.131E Jungmann	W. J. Perrins & E. A. C. Elliott
	G-BJAN	SA.102-5 Cavalier	J. Powlesland
	G-BJAO	Bensen B.8M	A. Gault
	G-BJAP	D.H.82A Tiger Moth	J. A. Pothecary
	G-BJAR	Unicorn UE.3A balloon	Unicorn Group
	G-BJAS	Rango NA.9 balloon	A. Lindsay
	G-BJAV	GY-80 Horizon 160	A. J. Martlew
	G-BJAW	Cameron V-65 balloon	G. W. McCarthy
	G-BJAX	Pilatus P2-05 (U-108)	Memorex Telex (UK) Ltd
	G-BJAY	Piper J-3C-65 Cub	K. L. Clarke/Ingoldmells
	G-BJBI	Cessna 414A	Borfin Ltd/Manchester
	G-BJBK	PA-18 Super Cub 95	M. S. Bird/Old Sarum
	G-BJBM	Monnet Sonerai II	J. Pickrell/Southend
	G-BJBO	Jodel DR.250/160	Wiltshire Flying Group
	G-BJBV	PA-28-161 Warrior II	C.S.E. Aviation Ltd/Kidlington
	G-BJBW	PA-28-161 Warrior II	C.S.E. Aviation Ltd/Kidlington
	G-BJBX	PA-28-161 Warrior II	C.S.E. Aviation Ltd/Kidlington
	G-BJBY	PA-28-161 Warrior II	C.S.E. Aviation Ltd/Kidlington
	G-BJBZ	Rotorway Executive 133	P. J. D. Kerr
	G-BJCA	PA-28-161 Warrior II	D. M. & J. E. Smith
	G-BJCD	Bede BD-5BH	Brockmoor-Bede Aircraft (UK) Ltd
	G-BJCF	CP.1310-C3 Super Emeraude	K. M. Hodson & C. G. H. Gurney
	G-BJCI	PA-18 Super Cub 150 (modified)	The Borders (Milfield) Aero-Tour Club Ltd
	G-BJCW	PA-32R-301 Saratoga SP	G. R. Patrick & Co Ltd
	G-BJDE	Cessna F.172M	H. P. K. Ferdinand/Denham
	G-BJDF	M.S.880B Rallye 100T	W. R. Savin & ptnrs
	G-BJDI	Cessna FR.182RG	Sunningdale Aviation Services Ltd
	G-BJDK	European E.14 balloon	Aeroprint Tours
	G-BJDO	AA-5A Cheetah	J. R. Nutter & ptnrs
	G-BJDT	SOCATA TB.9 Tampico	E. H. J. Moody/Blackbushe
	G-BJDW	Cessna F.172M	J. Rae/Ipswich
	G-BJEI	PA-18 Super Cub 95	H. J. Cox
	G-BJEL	SNCAN NC.854	N. F. & S. G. Hunter
	G-BJEN	Scruggs RS.5000 balloon	N. J. Richardson
	G-BJEO	PA-34-220T Seneca III	D. W. Clark Land Drainage Ltd (G-TOMF)
	G-BJEV	Aeronca 11AC Chief (897)	R. F. Willcox
	G-BJEX	Bo 208C Junior	G. D. H. Crawford/Thruxton
	G-BJFB	Mk 1A balloon	Aeroprint Tours
	G-BJFC	European E.8 balloon	P. D. Ridout
	G-BJFE	PA-18 Super Cub 95	J. H. Allistone
	G-BJFI	Bell 47G-2A1	Helicopter Supplies & Engineering Ltd/ Bournemouth
	G-BJFL	Sikorsky S-76A	Bristow Helicopters Ltd
	G-BJFM	Jodel D.120	J. V. George & P. A. Smith/Popham
	G-BJGD	Mk IV balloon	Windsor Balloon Group
	G-BJGE	Thunder Ax3 balloon	K. A. Williams
	G-BJGF	Mk 1 balloon	D. & D. Eaves
	G-BJGG	Mk 2 balloon	D. & D. Eaves
	G-BJGK	Cameron V-77 balloon	P. A. Harridge & T. J. Orchard
	G-BJGL	Cremer balloon	G. Lowther
	G-BJGM	Unicorn UE.1A balloon	D. Eaves & P. D. Ridout
	G-BJGO	Cessna 172N	R. M. Hunt
	G-BJGX	Sikorsky S-76A	Bristow Helicopters Ltd
	G-BJGY	Cessna F.172P	Lucca Wines Ltd
	G-BJHA	Cremer balloon	G. Cape

Reg.	Type	Owner or Operator	Notes
G-BJHB	Mooney M.20J	Zitair Flying Club Ltd/Redhill	
G-BJHK	EAA Acro Sport	D. Calabritto	
G-BJHP	Osprey 1C balloon	N. J. Richardson	
G-BJHT	Thunder Ax7-65 balloon	A. H. & L. Symonds	
G-BJHV	Voisin Replica ★	Brooklands Museum of Aviation/Weybridge	
G-BJHW	Osprey 1C balloon	N. J. Richardson	
G-BJIA	Allport balloon	D. J. Allport	
G-BJIB	D.31 Turbulent	N. H. Lemon	
G-BJIC	Dodo 1A balloon	P. D. Ridout	
G-BJID	Osprey 1B balloon	P. D. Ridout	
G-BJIF	Bensen B.8M	H. Redwin	
G-BJIG	Slingsby T.67A	Acebell G-BJIG Syndicate/Redhill	
G-BJIR	Cessna 550 Citation II	Gator Aviation Ltd	
G-BJIV	PA-18 Super Cub 180	Yorkshire Gliding Club (Pty) Ltd/ Sutton Bank	
G-BJJE	Dodo Mk 3 balloon	D. Eaves	
G-BJJN	Cessna F.172M	Ospreystar Ltd (stored)/Stapleford	
G-BJKB	SA.365C-3 Dauphin 2	Bond Helicopters Ltd	
G-BJKF	SOCATA TB.9 Tampico	Manor Promotion Services Ltd/Booker	
G-BJKW	Wills Aera II	J. K. S. Wills	
G-BJKY	Cessna F.152	Air Charter & Travel Ltd/Ronaldsway	
G-BJLB	SNCAN NC.854S	M. J. Barnaby	
G-BJLC	Monnet Sonerai IIL	P. J. Robins & R. King/Sywell	
G-BJLE	Osprey 1B balloon	I. Chadwick	
G-BJLF	Unicorn UE.1C balloon	I. Chadwick	
G-BJLG	Unicorn UE.1B balloon	I. Chadwick	
G-BJLH	PA-18 Super Cub 95 (44)	D. S. Kirkham	
G-BJLK	Short SD3-30 Variant 100	Streamline Aviation (SW) Ltd/Exeter	
G-BJLO	PA-31-310 Turbo Navajo	Linco (Holdings) Ltd	
G-BJLX	Cremer balloon	P. W. May	
G-BJLY	Cremer balloon	P. Cannon	
G-BJMG	European E.26C balloon	D. Eaves & A. P. Chown	
G-BJMI	European E.84 balloon	D. Eaves	
G-BJMJ	Bensen B.8M	J. I. Hewlett	
G-BJML	Cessna 120	D. F. Lawlor/Inverness	
G-BJMO	Taylor JT.1 Monoplane	R. C. Mark	
G-BJMR	Cessna 310R	J. McL. Robinson/Sherburn	
G-BJMW	Thunder Ax8-105 balloon	G. M. Westley	
G-BJMX	Jarre JR.3 balloon	P. D. Ridout	
G-BJMZ	European EA.8A balloon	P. D. Ridout	
G-BJNA	Arena Mk 117P balloon	P. D. Ridout	
G-BJND	Osprey Mk 1E balloon	A. Billington & D. Whitmore	
G-BJNF	Cessna F.152	Exeter Flying Club Ltd	
G-BJNG	Slingsby T.67A	Dophin Property (Management) Ltd	
G-BJNN	PA-38-112 Tomahawk	Scotia Safari Ltd/Prestwick	
G-BJNP	Rango NA.32 balloon	N. H. Ponsford	
G-BJNX	Cameron O-65 balloon	B. J. Petteford	
G-BJNY	Aeronca 11CC Super Chief	P. I. & D. M. Morgans	
G-BJNZ	PA-23 Aztec 250F	Leavesden Flight Centre Ltd (G-FANZ)	
G-BJOA	PA-28-181 Archer II	Channel Islands Aero Holdings (Jersey) Ltd	
G-BJOB	Jodel D.140C	T. W. M. Beck & M. J. Smith	
G-BJOE	Jodel D.120A	Forth Flying Group	
G-BJOP	BN-2B Islander	Loganair Ltd/Glasgow	
G-BJOT	Jodel D.117	E. Davies	
G-BJOV	Cessna F.150K	W. H. Webb & P. F. N. Burrow	
G-BJOZ	Scheibe SF.25B Falke	P. W. Hextall	
G-BJPI	Bede BD-5G	M. D. McQueen	
G-BJPV	Haigh balloon	M. J. Haigh	
G-BJRA	Osprey Mk 4B balloon	E. Osborn	
G-BJRB	European E.254 balloon	D. Eaves	
G-BJRC	European E.84R balloon	D. Eaves	
G-BJRD	European E.84R balloon	D. Eaves	
G-BJRG	Osprey Mk 4B balloon	A. E. de Gruchy	
G-BJRH	Rango NA.36 balloon	N. H. Ponsford	
G-BJRP	Cremer balloon	M. D. Williams	
G-BJRV	Cremer balloon	M. D. Williams	
G-BJRW	Cessna U.206G	A. I. Walgate & Son Ltd	
G-BJRY	PA-28-151 Warrior	A. M. R. Dudley	
G-BJRZ	Partenavia P.68C	Air Kilroe Ltd (G-OAKP)/Manchester	
G-BJSA	BN-2A Islander	Foxair/Glasgow	
G-BJSC	Osprey Mk 4D balloon	N. J. Richardson	
G-BJSD	Osprey Mk 4D balloon	N. J. Richardson	

Notes	Reg.	Type	Owner or Operator
	G-BJSF	Osprey Mk 4B balloon	N. J. Richardson
	G-BJSG	V.S.361 Spitfire LF.IXE (ML417)	Patina Ltd/Duxford
	G-BJSI	Osprey Mk 1E balloon	N. J. Richardson
	G-BJSP	Guido 1A Srs 61 balloon	G. A. Newsome
	G-BJSS	Allport balloon	D. J. Allport
	G-BJST	CCF Harvard 4 (MM53795)	V. Norman & M. Lawrence *(stored)*
	G-BJSU	Bensen B.8M	J. D. Newlyn
	G-BJSV	PA-28-161 Warrior II	R. Gilbert & J. Cole
	G-BJSW	Thunder Ax7-65 balloon	Sandicliffe Garage Ltd
	G-BJSX	Unicorn UE-1C balloon	N. J. Richardson
	G-BJSZ	Piper J-3C-65 Cub	H. Gilbert
	G-BJTB	Cessna A.150M	Clacton Aero Club (1988) Ltd
	G-BJTK	Taylor JT.1 Monoplane	E. N. Simmons
	G-BJTO	Piper J-3C-65 Cub	K. R. Nunn
	G-BJTP	PA-18 Super Cub 95 (115302)	J. T. Parkins
	G-BJTV	M.S.880B Rallye Club	E. C. Hender
	G-BJTW	European E.107 balloon	C. J. Brealey
	G-BJTY	Osprey Mk 4B balloon	A. E. de Gruchy
	G-BJUB	BVS Special 01 balloon	P. G. Wild
	G-BJUC	Robinson R-22	The Helicentre/Blackpool
	G-BJUD	Robin DR.400/180R	Lasham Gliding Soc Ltd
	G-BJUG	SOCATA TB.9 Tampico	CB Helicopters
	G-BJUI	Osprey Mk 4B balloon	B. A. de Gruchy
	G-BJUK	Short SD3-30	Shorts Aircraft Leasing Ltd (G-OCAS)
	G-BJUR	PA-38-112 Tomahawk	Truman Aviation Ltd/Tollerton
	G-BJUS	PA-38-112 Tomahawk	Panshanger School of Flying
	G-BJUV	Cameron V-20 balloon	Cameron Balloons Ltd
	G-BJUY	Colt Ax-77 balloon	Lindstrand Balloons Ltd
	G-BJVC	Evans VP-2	J. J. Morrissey
	G-BJVF	Thunder Ax3 balloon	A. G. R. Calder/California
	G-BJVH	Cessna F.182Q	R. J. de Courcy Cuming/ Wellesbourne
	G-BJVJ	Cessna F.152	Cambridge Aero Club Ltd
	G-BJVK	Grob G-109	B. Kimberley/Enstone
	G-BJVM	Cessna 172N	I. C. MacLennan
	G-BJVS	CP.1310-C3 Super Emeraude	A. E. Futter/Norwich
	G-BJVT	Cessna F.152	Cambridge Aero Club Ltd
	G-BJVU	Thunder Ax6-56 balloon	G. V. Beckwith
	G-BJVV	Robin R.1180	Medway Flying Group Ltd/Rochester
	G-BJVX	Sikorsky S-76A	Bristow Helicopters Ltd
	G-BJWC	Saro Skeeter AOP.12 (XK 482)★	Wilkie Museum Collection/Blackpool
	G-BJWH	Cessna F.152	Biggin Hill School of Flying
	G-BJWI	Cessna F.172P	Agricultural & General Aviation Ltd/ Bournemouth
	G-BJWJ	Cameron V-65 balloon	R. G. Turnbull & S. G. Forse
	G-BJWO	BN-2A-8 Islander	Peterborough Parachute Centre Ltd (G-BAXC)/Sibson
	G-BJWT	Wittman W.10 Tailwind	J. F. Bakewell & R. A. Shelley
	G-BJWV	Colt 17A balloon	D. T. Meyes
	G-BJWW	Cessna F.172N	Air Charter & Travel Ltd/Blackpool
	G-BJWX	PA-18 Super Cub 95	Acebell JWX Syndicate
	G-BJWY	S-55 Whirlwind HAR.21 (WV198)	Wilkie Museum Collection/Blackpool
	G-BJWZ	PA-18 Super Cub 95	G. V. Harfield/Thruxton
	G-BJXA	Slingsby T.67A	Comed Aviation Ltd/Blackpool
	G-BJXB	Slingsby T.67A	A. K. Halvorsen/Barton
	G-BJXK	Fournier RF-5	G-BJXK Syndicate/Cardiff
	G-BJXP	Colt 56B balloon	C. J. Travis
	G-BJXR	Auster AOP.9 (XR267)	Cotswold Aircraft Restoration Group
	G-BJXU	Thunder Ax7-77 balloon	S. M. Vardey
	G-BJXX	PA-23 Aztec 250E	V. Bojovic
	G-BJXZ	Cessna 172N	T. M. Jones
	G-BJYD	Cessna F.152 II	Cleveland Flying School Ltd/Teesside
	G-BJYF	Colt 56A balloon	Hot Air Balloon Co Ltd
	G-BJYG	PA-28-161 Warrior II	Browns of Stoke Ltd
	G-BJYK	Jodel D.120A	T. Fox & D. A. Thorpe
	G-BJYN	PA-38-112 Tomahawk	Panshanger School of Flying Ltd (G-BJTE)
	G-BJYA	Cameron N-65 balloon	A. D. Pinner
	G-BJYB	Evans VP-2	J. A. McLeod
	G-BJYC	Thunder Ax7-65Z balloon	Greenpeace (UK) Ltd/S. Africa
	G-BJZF	D.H.82A Tiger Moth	R. Blast
	G-BJZL	Cameron V-65 balloon	S. L. G. Williams
	G-BJZN	Slingsby T.67A	D. M. Upfield
	G-BJZR	Colt 42A balloon	Selfish Balloon Group

Reg.	Type	Owner or Operator	Notes
G-BJZT	Cessna FA.152	E. Blanche/Biggin Hill	
G-BJZX	Grob G.109	Oxfordshire Sport Flying Ltd/Enstone	
G-BJZY	Bensen B.8MV	D. E. & M. A. Cooke	
G-BKAC	Cessna F.150L	Seawing Flying Club Ltd/Southend	
G-BKAE	Jodel D.120	M. P. Wakem	
G-BKAF	FRED Srs 2	L. G. Millen	
G-BKAM	Slingsby T.67M Firefly	A. J. Daley	
G-BKAN	Cessna 340A	Arrows Aviation Co Ltd/Manchester	
G-BKAO	Jodel D.112	R. Broadhead	
G-BKAR	PA-38-112 Tomahawk	D. A. Williams	
G-BKAS	PA-38-112 Tomahawk	K. J. Scott	
G-BKAY	R. Commander 114	The Rockwell Group	
G-BKAZ	Cessna 152	Skyviews & General Ltd	
G-BKBD	Thunder Ax3 balloon	G. A. McCarthy	
G-BKBF	M.S.894A Rallye Minerva 220	M. S. Wright	
G-BKBH	H.S.125 Srs 600B	Westminster Aviation Ltd (G-BDJE)	
G-BKBK	SNCAN Stampe SV-4A	Freshname No77 Ltd	
G-BKBN	SOCATA TB.10 Tobago	RFA Flying Club Ltd	
G-BKBO	Colt 17A balloon	J. Armstrong & ptnrs	
G-BKBP	Bellanca 7GCBC Scout	H. G. Jefferies & Son/Little Gransden	
G-BKBR	Cameron Chateau 84 SS balloon	Forbes Europe Ltd/France	
G-BKBS	Bensen B.8MV	Construction & Site Administration Ltd	
G-BKBV	SOCATA TB.10 Tobago	R. M. Messenger	
G-BKBW	SOCATA TB.10 Tobago	Merlin Aviation	
G-BKCB	PA-28R Cherokee Arrow 200	Bristol & Wessex Aeroplane Club Ltd	
G-BKCC	PA-28 Cherokee 180	Cowie Aviation Ltd/Staverton	
G-BKCE	Cessna F.172P II	Holmes Rentals	
G-BKCF	Rutan LongEz	I. C. Fallows	
G-BKCH	Thompson Cassutt	S. C. Thompson/Redhill	
G-BKCI	Brügger MB.2 Colibri	E. R. Newall	
G-BKCJ	Oldfield Baby Great Lakes	S. V. Roberts/Sleap	
G-BKCK	CCF Harvard IV (P5865)	E. T. Webster & A. Haig-Thomas/ North Weald	
G-BKCL	PA-30 Twin Comanche 160C	Yorkair Ltd/Leeds	
G-BKCN	Currie Wot	S. E. Tomlinson	
G-BKCR	SOCATA TB.9 Tampico	Surrey & Kent Flying Club (1982) Ltd/ Biggin Hill	
G-BKCT	Cameron V-77 balloon	Quality Products General Engineering (Wickwat) Ltd	
G-BKCV	EAA Acro Sport II	M. J. Clark	
G-BKCW	Jodel D.120A	A. Greene & G. Kerr/Dundee	
G-BKCX	Mudry CAARP CAP.10	Mahon & Associates/Booker	
G-BKCY	PA-38-112 Tomahawk II	Wellesbourne Aviation Ltd	
G-BKCZ	Jodel D.120A	M. R. Baker/Shoreham	
G-BKDC	Monnet Sonerai II	K. J. Towell	
G-BKDD	Bell 206B JetRanger	Dollar Air Services Ltd/Coventry	
G-BKDH	Robin DR.400/120	Wiltshire Aeroplane Club/Old Sarum	
G-BKDI	Robin DR.400/120	Cotswold Aero Club Ltd/Staverton	
G-BKDJ	Robin DR.400/120	Wiltshire Aeroplane Club/Old Sarum	
G-BKDK	Thunder Ax7-77Z balloon	A. J. Byrne	
G-BKDP	FRED Srs 3	M. Whittaker	
G-BKDR	Pitts S.1S Special	N. A. Bloom	
G-BKDT	SE-5A (replica) (F943) ★	Yorkshire Air Museum/Elvington	
G-BKDX	Jodel DR.1050	T. G. Collins	
G-BKEK	PA-32 Cherokee Six 300	S. W. Turley	
G-BKEM	SOCATA TB.9 Tampico	C. J. Burt/Biggin Hill	
G-BKEP	Cessna F.172M	R. Green/Glasgow	
G-BKER	SE-5A (replica) (F5447)	N. K. Geddes	
G-BKET	PA-18 Super Cub 95	H. M. Mackenzie	
G-BKEU	Taylor JT.1 Monoplane	R. J. Whybrow & J. M. Springham	
G-BKEV	Cessna F.172M	One Zero One Three Ltd	
G-BKEW	Bell 206B JetRanger 3	N. R. Foster	
G-BKEX	Rich Prototype glider	D. B. Rich	
G-BKEY	FRED Srs 3	G. S. Taylor	
G-BKEZ	PA-18 Super Cub 95	G. V. Harfield	
G-BKFA	Monnet Sonerai IIL	R. F. Bridge	
G-BKFC	Cessna F.152 II	Sulby Aerial Surveys Ltd	
G-BKFG	Thunder Ax3 balloon	P. Ray	
G-BKFI	Evans VP-1	F. A. R. de Lavergne	
G-BKFK	Isaacs Fury II	G. C. Jones	
G-BKFM	QAC Quickie	R. Scroby	
G-BKFP	Bell 214ST	Bristow Helicopters Ltd	

Notes	Reg.	Type	Owner or Operator
	G-BKFR	CP.301C Emeraude	C. R. Beard
	G-BKFW	P.56 Provost T.1 (XF597)	Slymar Aviation & Services Ltd
	G-BKFZ	PA-28R Cherokee Arrow 200	Shacklewell Flying Group/Leicester
	G-BKGA	M.S.892E Rallye 150GT	BJJ Aviation
	G-BKGB	Jodel D.120	R. W. Greenwood
	G-BKGC	Maule M.6-235	Stol-Air Ltd/Sibson
	G-BKGL	Beech 18 (1164)	The Aircraft Restoration Co/Duxford
	G-BKGM	Beech D.18S (HB275)	A. E. Hutton/North Weald
	G-BKGR	Cameron O-65 balloon	K. Kidner & L. E. More
	G-BKGT	SOCATA Rallye 110ST	Long Marston Flying Group
	G-BKGW	Cessna F.152-II	Leicestershire Aero Club Ltd
	G-BKHA	W.S.55 Whirlwind HAR.10 (XJ763)	C. J. Evans
	G-BKHC	W.S.55 Whirlwind HAR.10 (XP328)	Flight C Helicopters Ltd
	G-BKHD	Oldfield Baby Great Lakes	P. J. Tanulak
	G-BKHG	Piper J-3C-65 Cub (479766)	K. G. Wakefield
	G-BKHL	Thunder Ax9-140 balloon	R. Carr/France
	G-BKHR	Luton LA-4 Minor	C. B. Buscombe & R. Goldsworthy
	G-BKHT	BAe 146-100	Fortis Aviation Group Ltd
	G-BKHW	Stoddard-Hamilton Glasair SH.2RG	N. Clayton
	G-BKHY	Taylor JT.1 Monoplane	M. C. Holmes & A. Shuttleworth
	G-BKHZ	Cessna F.172P	Warwickshire Flying Training Centre Ltd
	G-BKIA	SOCATA TB.10 Tobago	D. H. Barton/Redhill
	G-BKIB	SOCATA TB.9 Tampico	A. J. Baggerley & F. D. J. Simmons/ Goodwood
	G-BKIC	Cameron V-77 balloon	C. A. Butler
	G-BKIE	Short SD3-30 Variant 100	BAC Group Ltd (G-SLUG/G-METP/ G-METO)
	G-BKIF	Fournier RF-6B	G. G. Milton
	G-BKII	Cessna F.172M	M. S. Knight/Goodwood
	G-BKIJ	Cessna F.172M	V. Speck
	G-BKIK	Cameron DG-10 airship	Airspace Outdoor Advertising Ltd
	G-BKIM	Unicorn UE.5A balloon	I. Chadwick & K. H. Turner
	G-BKIN	Alon A.2A Aircoupe	P. A. Williams & M. Quinn/Blackbushe
	G-BKIR	Jodel D.117	R. Shaw & D. M. Hardaker/Sherburn
	G-BKIS	SOCATA TB.10 Tobago	Ospreystar Ltd
	G-BKIT	SOCATA TB.9 Tampico	Kit Aviation Club/Southend
	G-BKIU	Colt 17A balloon	Robert Pooley Ltd
	G-BKIV	Colt 21A balloon	Colt Balloons Ltd
	G-BKIX	Cameron V-31 balloon	G. Stevens
	G-BKIY	Thunder Ax3 balloon	A. Hornak
	G-BKIZ	Cameron V-31 balloon	A. P. S. Cox
	G-BKJB	PA-18 Super Cub 135	Cormack (Aircraft Services) Ltd/Glasgow
	G-BKJD	Bell 214ST	Bristow Helicopters Ltd
	G-BKJE	Cessna 172N	The G-BKJE Group
	G-BKJF	M.S.880B Rallye 100T	Nova Flying Group
	G-BKJG	BN-2B-21 Islander	Pilatus BN Ltd/Bembridge
	G-BKJR	Hughes 269C	March Helicopters Ltd/Sywell
	G-BKJS	Jodel D.120A	S. Walmsley
	G-BKJT	Cameron O-65 balloon	K. A. Ward
	G-BKJW	PA-23 Aztec 250E	Alan Williams Entertainments Ltd
	G-BKKN	Cessna 182R	R A. Marven/Elstree
	G-BKKO	Cessna 182R	B. & G. Jebson Ltd/Crosland Moor
	G-BKKR	Rand KR-2	D. Beale & S. P. Gardner
	G-BKKZ	Pitts S-1D Special	G. C. Masterton
	G-BKLC	Cameron V-56 balloon	M. A. & J. R. H. Ashworth
	G-BKLJ	Westland Scout AH.1 ★	Wilkie Museum Collection/Blackpool
	G-BKLM	Thunder Ax9-140 balloon	Aerial Promotions Balloon Club
	G-BKLO	Cessna F.172M	Stapleford Flying Club Ltd
	G-BKLP	Cessna F.172N	Pagodaplan Ltd
	G-BKLT	SA.341G Gazelle 1	J. L. Laborde
	G-BKMA	Mooney M.20J Srs 201	Foxtrot Whisky Aviation
	G-BKMB	Mooney M.20J Srs 201	W. A. Cook & ptnrs/Sherburn
	G-BKMD	SC.7 Skyvan Srs 3	Army Parachute Association/Netheravon
	G-BKMG	Handley Page O/400 (replica)	Paralyser Group
	G-BKMI	V.S.359 Spitfire HF.VIIIc (MT928)	Aerial Museum (North Weald) Ltd
	G-BKMK	PA-38-112 Tomahawk	D. J. Campbell/Glasgow
	G-BKMM	Cessna 180K	M. J. Kirk
	G-BKMN	BAe 146-100	British Aerospace PLC (G-ODAN)
	G-BKMR	Thunder Ax3 balloon	B. F. G. Ribbans
	G-BKMT	PA-32R-301 Saratoga SP	Severn Valley Aviation Group
	G-BKMX	Short SD3-60	Manx Airlines Ltd/Ronaldsway
	G-BKNA	Cessna 421	Launchapart Ltd

Reg.	Type	Owner or Operator	Notes
G-BKNB	Cameron V-42 balloon	D. N. Close	
G-BKND	Colt 56A balloon	Flying Colours Balloon Group	
G-BKNI	GY-80 Horizon 160D	A. Hartigan & ptnrs/Fenland	
G-BKNO	Monnet Sonerai IIL	M. D. Hughes	
G-BKNY	Bensen B.8MPV	D. A. C. MacCormack	
G-BKNZ	CP.301A Emeraude	D. F. Micklethwait	
G-BKOA	SOCATA M.S.893E Rallye 180GT	P. J. Clegg	
G-BKOB	Z.326 Trener Master	W. G. V. Hall	
G-BKOR	Barnes 77 balloon	Robert Pooley Ltd	
G-BKOT	Wassmer WA.81 Piranha	R. Skingley & B. N. Rolfe	
G-BKOU	P.84 Jet Provost T.3 (XN637)	A. S. Topen/Cranfield	
G-BKOV	Jodel DR.220A	Merlin Flying Club Ltd/Hucknall	
G-BKOW	Colt 77A balloon	Hot Air Balloon Co Ltd	
G-BKPA	Hoffman H-36 Dimona	A. Mayhew	
G-BKPB	Aerosport Scamp	E. D. Burke	
G-BKPC	Cessna A.185F	Black Knights Parachute Centre	
G-BKPD	Viking Dragonfly	E. P. Browne & G. J. Sargent	
G-BKPE	Jodel DR.250/160	J. S. & J. D. Lewer	
G-BKPG	Luscombe Rattler Strike	Luscombe Aircraft Ltd	
G-BKPK	John McHugh Gyrocopter	J. C. McHugh	
G-BKPM	Schempp-Hirth HS.5 Nimbus 2	J. L. Rolls	
G-BKPN	Cameron N-77 balloon	R. H. Sanderson	
G-BKPS	AA-5B Tiger	Earthline Ltd	
G-BKPT	M.H.1521M Broussard (192)	R. M. Johnston	
G-BKPV	Stevex 250.1	A. F. Stevens	
G-BKPW	Boeing 767-204	Britannia Airways Ltd *The Earl Mountbatten of Burma*/Luton	
G-BKPX	Jodel D.120A	N. H. Martin	
G-BKPY	SAAB 91B/2 Safir (56321)★	Newark Air Museum Ltd	
G-BKPZ	Pitts S-1T Special	P. R. Rutterford/Redhill	
G-BKRA	NA T-6G Texan (51-15227)	Pulsegrove Ltd/Shoreham	
G-BKRB	Cessna 172N	Saunders Caravans Ltd	
G-BKRF	PA-18 Super Cub 95	K. M. Bishop	
G-BKRG	Beechcraft C-45G	Aces High Ltd/North Weald	
G-BKRH	Brügger MB.2 Colibri	M. R. Benwell	
G-BKRI	Cameron V-77 balloon	J. R. Lowe & R. J. Fuller	
G-BKRJ	Colt 105A balloon	Owners Abroad Group PLC	
G-BKRK	SNCAN Stampe SV-4C	J. M. Alexander & ptnrs/Aberdeen	
G-BKRL	Chichester-Miles Leopard	Chichester-Miles Consultants Ltd	
G-BKRN	Beechcraft D.18S ★	A. S. Topen/Cranfield	
G-BKRR	Cameron N-56 balloon	S. L. G. Williams	
G-BKRS	Cameron V-56 balloon	D. N. & L. J. Close	
G-BKRU	Ensign Crossley Racer	M. Crossley	
G-BKRV	Hovey Beta Bird	A. V. Francis	
G-BKRW	Cameron O-160 balloon	Bondbaste Ltd	
G-BKRX	Cameron O-160 balloon	Bondbaste Ltd	
G-BKRZ	Dragon 77 balloon	J. R. Barber	
G-BKSC	Saro Skeeter AOP.12 (XN351)	R. A. L. Falconer	
G-BKSD	Colt 56A balloon	M. J. & G. C. Casson	
G-BKSE	QAC Quickie Q.2	M. D. Burns	
G-BKSH	Colt 21A balloon	J. Bartholomew & D. L. Smith	
G-BKSP	Schleicher ASK.14	J. H. Bryson	
G-BKSS	Jodel D.150	D. H. Wilson-Spratt/Ronaldsway	
G-BKST	Rutan Vari-Eze	R. Towle	
G-BKSX	SNCAN Stampe SV-4C	C. A. Bailey & J. A. Carr	
G-BKSZ	Cessna P.210N	Blessvale Ltd	
G-BKTA	PA-18 Super Cub 95	K. E. Chapman/Southend	
G-BKTH	CCF Hawker Sea Hurricane IB (Z7015)	Shuttleworth Collection/Duxford	
G-BKTM	PZL SZD-45A Ogar	Ogar Syndicate	
G-BKTR	Cameron V-77 balloon	R. W. Keron	
G-BKTU	Colt 56A balloon	E. Ten Houten	
G-BKTV	Cessna F.152	London Flight Centre Ltd/Stansted	
G-BKTY	SOCATA TB.10 Tobago	B. M. & G. M. McClelland	
G-BKTZ	Slingsby T.67M Firefly	E. Hopper (G-SFTV)	
G-BKUE	SOCATA TB.9 Tampico	W. J. Moore/Kirkbride	
G-BKUJ	Thunder Ax6-56 balloon	R. J. Bent	
G-BKUR	CP.301A Emeraude	R. Wells & H. V. Hunter	
G-BKUS	Bensen B.8M	G. F. Gardener	
G-BKUU	Thunder Ax7-77-1 balloon	D. A. Kozuba-Kozubska	
G-BKUY	BAe Jetstream 3102	British Aerospace PLC/Hatfield	
G-BKVA	SOCATA Rallye 180T	Buckminster Gliding Club Syndicate	
G-BKVB	SOCATA Rallye 110ST	Martin Ltd/Biggin Hill	

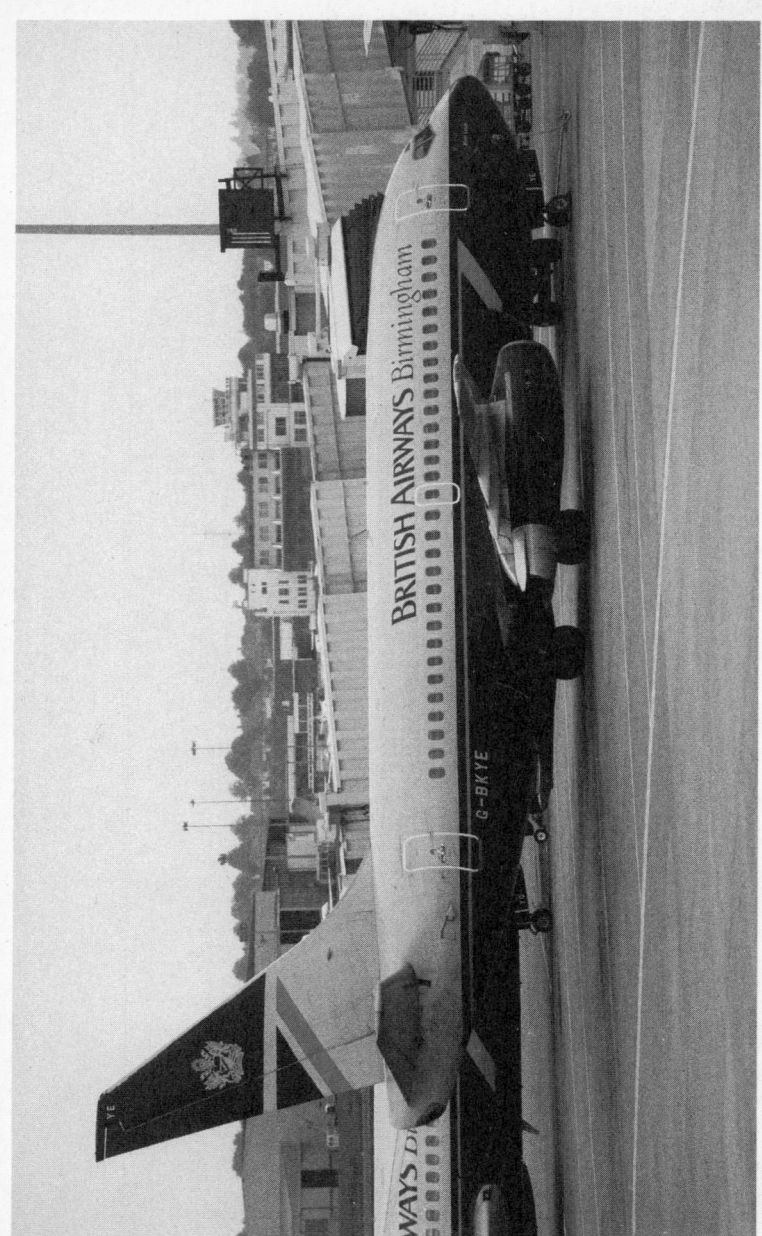

G-BKYE, Boeing 737-236 of British Airways Birmingham. AJW

Reg.	Type	Owner or Operator	Notes
G-BKVC	SOCATA TB.9 Tampico	Air Touring Services Ltd/Biggin Hill	
G-BKVE	Rutan Vari-Eze	R. M. Smith (G-EZLT)	
G-BKVF	FRED Srs 3	D. Coging	
G-BKVG	Scheibe SF.25E Super Falke	G-BKVG Ltd	
G-BKVK	Auster AOP.9 (WZ662)	J. D. Butcher	
G-BKVL	Robin DR.400/160	The Cotswold Aero Club Ltd/Staverton	
G-BKVM	PA-18 Super Cub 150	D. G. Caffrey	
G-BKVN	PA-23 Aztec 250F	B. A. Eastwell/Shoreham	
G-BKVO	Pietenpol Air Camper	B. P. Waites	
G-BKVP	Pitts S-1D Special	P. J. Leggo	
G-BKVR	PA-28 Cherokee 140	D. P. Alexander	
G-BKVS	Bensen B.8M	K. Stephenson	
G-BKVT	PA-23 Aztec 250E	Express Bond Ltd (G-HARV)	
G-BKVV	Beech 95-B55 Baron	L. McG. Tulloch	
G-BKVW	Airtour 56 balloon	L. D. & H. Vaughan	
G-BKVX	Airtour 56 balloon	E. G. Woolnough	
G-BKVY	Airtour 31 balloon	M. Davies	
G-BKVZ	Boeing 767-204	Britannia Airways Ltd *Sir Winston Churchill*	
G-BKWB	EMB-110P2 Bandeirante	Knight Air Ltd (G-CHEV)/Leeds	
G-BKWD	Taylor JT.2 Titch	E. Shouler	
G-BKWE	Colt 17A balloon	Hot-Air Balloon Co Ltd	
G-BKWG	PZL-104 Wilga 35A	M. A. Johnston/Tayside	
G-BKWI	Pitts S-2A	R. A. Seeley/Denham	
G-BKWP	Thunder Ax7-77 balloon	G. V. Beckwith	
G-BKWR	Cameron V-65 balloon	K. J. Foster	
G-BKWW	Cameron O-77 balloon	A. M. Marten	
G-BKWY	Cessna F.152	Cambridge Aero Club	
G-BKXA	Robin R.2100	G. J. Anderson & ptnrs	
G-BKXD	SA.365N Dauphin 2	Bond Helicopters Ltd	
G-BKXE	SA.365N Dauphin 2	Bond Helicopters Ltd	
G-BKXF	PA-28R Cherokee Arrow 200	P. L. Brunton	
G-BKXG	Cessna T.303	Wilton Construction Ltd	
G-BKXL	Cameron 70 Bottle SS balloon	Cameron Balloons Ltd/Canada	
G-BKXM	Colt 17A balloon	R. G. Turnbull	
G-BKXN	ICA IS-28M2A	A. D. Pearce	
G-BKXO	Rutan LongEz	P. J. Wareham	
G-BKXP	Auster AOP.6	B. J. & W. J. Ellis	
G-BKXR	D.31A Turbulent	M. B. Hill	
G-BKXS	Colt 56A balloon	Zebedee Balloon Service	
G-BKXT	Cameron D-50 airship	Cameron Balloons Ltd/USA	
G-BKXX	Cameron V-65 balloon	J. D. Pilkington	
G-BKYA	Boeing 737-236	British Airways Birmingham *River Derwent*	
G-BKYB	Boeing 737-236	British Airways Birmingham *River Stour*	
G-BKYC	Boeing 737-236	British Airways Birmingham *River Wye*	
G-BKYD	Boeing 737-236	British Airways Birmingham *River Conwy*	
G-BKYE	Boeing 737-236	British Airways Birmingham *River Lagan*	
G-BKYF	Boeing 737-236	British Airways Birmingham *River Spey*	
G-BKYG	Boeing 737-236	British Airways Birmingham *River Exe*	
G-BKYH	Boeing 737-236	British Airways Birmingham *River Dart*	
G-BKYI	Boeing 737-236	British Airways *River Waveney*	
G-BKYJ	Boeing 737-236	British Airways Birmingham *River Neath*	
G-BKYK	Boeing 737-236	British Airways *River Foyle*	
G-BKYL	Boeing 737-236	British Airways Birmingham *River Isis*	
G-BKYM	Boeing 737-236	British Airways Birmingham *River Cam*	
G-BKYN	Boeing 737-236	British Airways Birmingham *River Ayr*	
G-BKYO	Boeing 737-236	British Airways Birmingham *River Kennet*	
G-BKYP	Boeing 737-236	British Airways Manchester *River Ystwyth*	
G-BKZB	Cameron V-77 balloon	A. J. Montgomery	
G-BKZE	AS.332L Super Puma	British International Helicopters/Aberdeen	
G-BKZF	Cameron V-56 balloon	G. M. Hobster	
G-BKZG	AS.332L Super Puma	British International Helicopters/Aberdeen	
G-BKZH	AS.332L Super Puma	British International Helicopters/Aberdeen	
G-BKZI	Bell 206L JetRanger 2	Western Air Trading Ltd/Thruxton	
G-BKZJ	Bensen B.8MV	J. C. Birdsall	
G-BKZR	Short SD3-60 Variant 100	Lynrise Aircraft Financing Ltd (G-OAEX/ G-SALU)	
G-BKZT	FRED Srs 2	M. G. Rusby	
G-BKZV	Bede BD-4A	A. L. Bergamasco/Headcorn	
G-BKZY	Cameron N-77 balloon	W. Counties Automobile Co Ltd	
G-BLAA	Fournier RF-5	A. D. Wren/Southend	
G-BLAC	Cessna FA.152	Ofteneasy Ltd	
G-BLAD	Thunder Ax7-77-1 balloon	P. J. Bish	

Notes	Reg.	Type	Owner or Operator
	G-BLAF	Stolp SA.900 V-Star	P. R. Skeels
	G-BLAG	Pitts S-1D Special	R. G. Gee & E. H. Williams
	G-BLAH	Thunder Ax7-77-1 balloon	T. Donnelly
	G-BLAI	Monnet Sonerai IIL	T. Simpson
	G-BLAM	Jodel DR.360	B. F. Baldock
	G-BLAT	Jodel D.150	D. J. Dulborough & A. J. Court
	G-BLAW	PA-28-181 Archer II	Luton Flight Training Ltd
	G-BLAX	Cessna FA.152	Shoreham Flight Simulation Ltd/ Bournemouth
	G-BLAY	Robin HR.100/200B	B. A. Mills
	G-BLCA	Bell 206B JetRanger 3	R.M.H. Stainless Ltd
	G-BLCC	Thunder Ax7-77Z balloon	P. Hassell Ltd
	G-BLCF	EAA Acro Sport 2	M. J. Watkins & ptnrs
	G-BLCG	SOCATA TB.10 Tobago	Charlie Golf Flying Group (G-BHES)/ Shoreham
	G-BLCH	Colt 56D balloon	Balloon Flights Club Ltd
	G-BLCI	EAA Acro Sport	M. R. Holden
	G-BLCK	V.S.361 Spitfire F.IX (TE566)	Historic Aircraft Collection Ltd
	G-BLCM	SOCATA TB.9 Tampico	Repclif Aviation Ltd/Liverpool
	G-BLCT	Jodel DR.220 2+2	H. W. Jemmett
	G-BLCU	Scheibe SF.25B Falke	Falke Syndicate
	G-BLCV	Hoffman H-36 Dimona	Charlie Victor Motor Glider Group
	G-BLCW	Evans VP-1	K. D. Pearce
	G-BLCY	Thunder Ax7-65Z balloon	Thunder Balloons Ltd
	G-BLDB	Taylor JT.1 Monoplane	C. J. Bush
	G-BLDC	K&S Jungster 1	A. W. Brown
	G-BLDD	WAG-Aero CUBy AcroTrainer	C. A. Laycock
	G-BLDG	PA-25 Pawnee 260C	Ouse Gliding Club Ltd/Rufforth
	G-BLDH	BAC One-Eleven 475EZ	World Oil & Gas Resources Ltd
	G-BLDK	Robinson R-22	J. A. Boardman/Barton
	G-BLDL	Cameron 56 Truck SS balloon	Cameron Balloons Ltd
	G-BLDN	Rand KR-2	G. R. Burgess
	G-BLDP	Slingsby T.67M Firefly	Sherburn Aero Club Ltd
	G-BLEB	Colt 69A balloon	I. R. M. Jacobs
	G-BLEJ	PA-28-161 Warrior II	Eglinton Flying Club Ltd
	G-BLEL	Price Ax7-77-245 balloon	T. S. Price
	G-BLEP	Cameron V-65 balloon	D. Chapman
	G-BLES	Stolp SA.750 Acroduster Too	T. W. Harris
	G-BLET	Thunder Ax7-77-1 balloon	Servatruc Ltd
	G-BLEW	Cessna F.182Q	GT Aviation
	G-BLEY	SA.365N Dauphin 2	Bond Helicopters Ltd
	G-BLEZ	SA.365N Dauphin 2	Bond Helicopters Ltd
	G-BLFE	Cameron Sphinx SS balloon	Forbes Europe Inc
	G-BLFF	Cessna F.172M	Air Advertising UK Ltd
	G-BLFI	PA-28-181 Archer II	Leavesden Flight Centre Ltd
	G-BLFJ	F.27 Friendship Mk 100	Air UK Ltd (G-OMAN/G-SPUD)/Norwich
	G-BLFT	P.56 Provost T.1 (WV686)	B. W. H. Parkhouse
	G-BLFW	AA-5 Traveler	Grumman Club
	G-BLFY	Cameron V-77 balloon	A. N. F. Pertwee
	G-BLFZ	PA-31-310 Turbo Navajo C	Bravair Ltd/Leavesden
	G-BLGB	Short SD3-60	Loganair Ltd/Glasgow
	G-BLGH	Robin DR.300/180R	Booker Gliding Club Ltd
	G-BLGM	Cessna 425	M. J. L. Batt
	G-BLGO	Bensen B.8M	F. Vernon
	G-BLGR	Bell 47G-4A	Lowland Advertising Ltd
	G-BLGS	SOCATA Rallye 180T	Lasham Gliding Society Ltd
	G-BLGT	PA-18 Super Cub 95	T. A. Reed/Dunkeswell
	G-BLGV	Bell 206B JetRanger	Part Reward Ltd
	G-BLGW	F.27 Friendship Mk 200	Air UK Ltd *Louis Marchesi*/Norwich
	G-BLGX	Thunder Ax7-65 balloon	Harper & Co (Glasgow) Ltd
	G-BLHA	Thunder Ax10-160 balloon	Thunder Balloons Ltd
	G-BLHB	Thunder Ax10-160 balloon	Thunder Balloons Ltd
	G-BLHF	Nott-Cameron ULD-2 balloon	J. R. P. Nott
	G-BLHH	Jodel DR.315	G. G. Milton
	G-BLHI	Colt 17A balloon	J. A. Folkes
	G-BLHJ	Cessna F.172P	J. Eassen/Edinburgh
	G-BLHK	Colt 105A balloon	Hale Hot-Air Balloon Club
	G-BLHM	PA-18 Super Cub 95	B. N. C. Mogg
	G-BLHN	Robin HR.100/285	H. M. Bouquiere/Biggin Hill
	G-BLHR	GA-7 Cougar	Fotex Aviation Ltd
	G-BLHS	Bellanca 7ECA Citabria	J. W. Platten & E. J. Timmins
	G-BLHW	Varga 2150A Kachina	D. M. Jagger
	G-BLID	D.H.112 Venom FB.50 (J-1605) ★	P. G. Vallance Ltd/Charlwood

Reg.	Type	Owner or Operator	Notes
G-BLIE	D.H.112 Venom FB.50	R. J. Everett	
G-BLIG	Cameron V-65 balloon	W. Davison	
G-BLIH	PA-18 Super Cub 135	I. R. F. Hammond	
G-BLIK	Wallis WA-116/F/S	K. H. Wallis	
G-BLIP	Cameron N-77 balloon	L. A. Beardall & G. R. Hunt	
G-BLIT	Thorp T-18 CW	K. B. Hallam	
G-BLIW	P.56 Provost T.51 (177)	Pulsegrove Ltd (stored)/Shoreham	
G-BLIX	Saro Skeeter Mk 12 (XL809)	A. P. Nowicki	
G-BLIY	M.S.892A Rallye Commodore	A. J. Brasher & K. R. Haynes	
G-BLJD	Glaser-Dirks DG.400	G. G. Hearne & M. I. Gee	
G-BLJE	AB-206B JetRanger	Rees Aviation/Birmingham	
G-BLJF	Cameron O-65 balloon	C. E. C. Dupernex & M. D. Mitchell	
G-BLJH	Cameron N-77 balloon	Phillair	
G-BLJI	Colt 105A balloon	Tempowish Ltd	
G-BLJJ	Cessna 305 Bird Dog	P. Dawe	
G-BLJM	Beech 95-B55 Baron	Elstree Aircraft Hire Ltd	
G-BLJN	Nott-Cameron ULD-1 balloon	J. R. P. Nott	
G-BLJO	Cessna F.152	Redhill School of Flying Ltd	
G-BLJP	Cessna F.150L	C. R. & S. Hardiman	
G-BLKA	D.H.112 Venom FB.54 (WR410)	A. S. Topen/Cranfield	
G-BLKF	Thunder Ax10-160 balloon	Thunder Balloons Ltd	
G-BLKG	Thunder Ax10-160 balloon	Thunder Balloons Ltd	
G-BLKH	Thunder Ax10-160 balloon	Thunder Balloons Ltd	
G-BLKI	Thunder Ax10-160 balloon	Thunder Balloons Ltd	
G-BLKJ	Thunder Ax7-65 balloon	D. T. Watkins	
G-BLKK	Evans VP-1	R. W. Burrows	
G-BLKL	D.31 Turbulent	D. L. Ripley	
G-BLKM	Jodel DR.1051	T. C. Humphreys	
G-BLKP	BAe Jetstream 3102	British Aerospace PLC/Warton	
G-BLKU	Colt 56 Flame SS balloon	Hot-Air Balloon Co Ltd	
G-BLKY	Beech 95-58 Baron	Kebbell Holdings Ltd/Leavesden	
G-BLKZ	Pilatus P2-05	Autokraft Ltd	
G-BLLA	Bensen B.8M	K. T. Donaghey	
G-BLLB	Bensen B.8M	D. H. Moss	
G-BLLD	Cameron O-77 balloon	I. O. Gracie	
G-BLLH	Jodel DR.220A 2+2	D. R. Scott-Longhurst & V. D. Stotter	
G-BLLM	PA-23 Aztec 250E	C. & M. Thomas (G-BBNM)/Cardiff	
G-BLLN	PA-18 Super Cub 95	A. L. Hall-Carpenter	
G-BLLO	PA-18 Super Cub 95	D. G. & M. G. Margetts	
G-BLLP	Slingsby T.67B	Cleveland Flying School Ltd/Teesside	
G-BLLR	Slingsby T.67B	Trent Air Services Ltd/Cranfield	
G-BLLS	Slingsby T.67B	Chikka Ltd	
G-BLLT	AA-5B Tiger	Alpha Welding & Engineering Ltd	
G-BLLV	Slingsby T.67B	R. L. Brinklow	
G-BLLW	Colt 56B balloon	J. C. Stupples	
G-BLLZ	Rutan LongEz	R. S. Stoddart-Stones	
G-BLMA	Zlin 326 Trener Master	G. P. Northcott/Shoreham	
G-BLMC	Avro 698 Vulcan B.2A (XM575) ★	Aeropark/E. Midlands	
G-BLME	Robinson R-22	Skyline Helicopters Ltd	
G-BLMG	Grob G.109B	Mike Golf Syndicate	
G-BLMI	PA-18 Super Cub 95	B. J. Borsberry	
G-BLMN	Rutan LongEz	G-BLMN Flying Group	
G-BLMP	PA-17 Vagabond	M. Austin/Popham	
G-BLMR	PA-18 Super Cub 150	South Midlands Commercial Aviation School Ltd	
G-BLMT	PA-18 Super Cub 135	I. S. Runnalls	
G-BLMV	Jodel DR.1051	S. Windsor	
G-BLMW	T.66 Nipper 3	S. L. Millar	
G-BLMX	Cessna FR.172H	C. J. W. Littler/Felthorpe	
G-BLMZ	Colt 105A balloon	M. J. Hutchins	
G-BLNB	V.802 Viscount	British World Airlines Ltd (G-AOHV)/Southend	
G-BLNJ	BN-2B-26 Islander	Loganair Ltd/Glasgow	
G-BLNO	FRED Srs 3	L. W. Smith	
G-BLNW	BN-2B-27 Islander	Loganair Ltd/Glasgow	
G-BLOA	V.806 Viscount Freightmaster II	withdrawn/Southend	
G-BLOB	Colt 31A balloon	Jacques W. Soukup Ltd	
G-BLOE	PA-31-350 Navajo Chieftain	PW Cleaning Services Ltd (G-NITE)	
G-BLOK	Colt 77A balloon	D. L. Clark Spritsa	
G-BLOL	SNCAN Stampe SV-4A	Skysport Engineering Ltd (G-AXRP)	
G-BLOR	PA-30 Twin Comanche 160	J. A. Burton	
G-BLOS	Cessna 185A (also flown with floats)	E. Brun	

Notes	Reg.	Type	Owner or Operator
	G-BLOT	Colt Ax6-56B balloon	H. J. Anderson
	G-BLOU	Rand KR-2	D. G. Cole
	G-BLOV	Colt Ax5-42 Srs 1 balloon	Thunder & Colt Ltd
	G-BLPA	Piper J-3C-65 Cub	G. A. Card
	G-BLPB	Turner TSW Hot Two Wot	J. R. Woolford
	G-BLPE	PA-18 Super Cub 95	A. Haig-Thomas
	G-BLPF	Cessna FR.172G	W. A. F. Cuninghame
	G-BLPG	J/1N Alpha (16693)	Q. J. Ball (G-AZIH)
	G-BLPH	Cessna FRA.150L	New Aerobat Group/Shoreham
	G-BLPI	Slingsby T.67B	Keepcase Ltd
	G-BLPK	Cameron V-65 balloon	A. J. & C. P. Nicholls
	G-BLPM	AS.332L Super Puma	Bristow Helicopters Ltd
	G-BLPP	Cameron V-77 balloon	L. P. Purfield
	G-BLPV	Short SD3-60 Variant 100	—
	G-BLRC	PA-18 Super Cub 135	A. J. McBurnie
	G-BLRD	MBB Bo.209 Monsun 150FV	M. D. Ward
	G-BLRF	Slingsby T.67C	Bristow Helicopters Ltd/Redhill
	G-BLRG	Slingsby T.67B	R. L. Brinklow
	G-BLRH	Rutan LongEz	G. L. Thompson
	G-BLRJ	Jodel DR.1051	M. P. Hallam
	G-BLRL	CP.301C-1 Emeraude	B. C. Davis
	G-BLRM	Glaser-Dirks DG.400	D. J. Barke
	G-BLRN	D.H.104 Dove 8 (WB531)	C.W. Simpson/Exeter
	G-BLRP	FMA IA.58A Pucará	R. J. H. Butterfield
	G-BLRW	Cameron 77 Elephant SS balloon	Forbes Europe Inc/France
	G-BLRX	SOCATA TB.9 Tampico	Wiselock Ltd/Elstree
	G-BLRY	AS.332L Super Puma	Bristow Helicopters Ltd
	G-BLSC	Consolidated PBY-5A Catalina	J. P. Warren Wilson/Duxford
	G-BLSD	D.H.112 Venom FB.55 (J-1758)	Aces High Ltd/North Weald
	G-BLSF	AA-5A Cheetah	J. P. E. Walsh (G-BGCK)
	G-BLSH	Cameron V-77 balloon	C. N. Luffingham
	G-BLSJ	Thunder Ax8-90 balloon	Thunder & Colt Ltd
	G-BLSK	Colt 77A balloon	Solarmoor Ltd
	G-BLSM	H.S.125 Srs 700B	Dravidian Air Services Ltd/Heathrow
	G-BLSN	Colt AS-56 airship	D. K. Fish
	G-BLSO	Colt AS-42 airship	Huntair Ltd/Germany
	G-BLST	Cessna 421C	Cecil Aviation Ltd/Cambridge
	G-BLSU	Cameron A-210 balloon	Skysales Ltd
	G-BLSX	Cameron O-105 balloon	B. J. Petteford
	G-BLTA	Thunder Ax7-77A	K. A. Schlussler
	G-BLTC	D.31 Turbulent	G. P. Smith & A. W. Burton
	G-BLTF	Robinson R-22A	Brian Seedle Helicopters/Blackpool
	G-BLTG	WAR Sea Fury (WJ237)	A. N. R. Houghton & D. H. Nourish
	G-BLTK	R. Commander 112TC	B. Rogalewski/Denham
	G-BLTM	Robin HR.200/100	B. D. Balcanquall
	G-BLTN	Thunder Ax7-65 balloon	J. A. Liddle
	G-BLTO	Short SD3-60 Variant 100	Lynrise Aircraft Financing Ltd
	G-BLTP	H.S.125 Srs 700B	Dravidian Air Services Ltd/Heathrow
	G-BLTR	Scheibe SF.25B Falke	V. Mallon/Germany
	G-BLTS	Rutan LongEz	R. W. Cutler
	G-BLTT	Slingsby T.67B	S. E. Marples
	G-BLTU	Slingsby T.67B	The Neiderhein Powered Flying Club/ Germany
	G-BLTV	Slingsby T.67B	R. L. Brinklow
	G-BLTW	Slingsby T.67B	R. L. Brinklow
	G-BLTZ	SOCATA TB.10 Tobago	Martin Ltd/Biggin Hill
	G-BLUA	Robinson R-22	J. R. Budgen
	G-BLUE	Colting Ax7-77A balloon	R. H. Etherington
	G-BLUI	Thunder Ax7-65 balloon	S. Johnson
	G-BLUJ	Cameron V-56 balloon	J. N. W. West
	G-BLUK	Bond Sky Dancer	J. Owen
	G-BLUL	Jodel DR.1051/M1	J. Owen
	G-BLUM	SA.365N Dauphin 2	Bond Helicopters Ltd
	G-BLUO	SA.365N Dauphin 2	Bond Helicopters Ltd
	G-BLUP	SA.365N Dauphin 2	Bond Helicopters Ltd
	G-BLUV	Grob G.109B	Go-Grob Ltd
	G-BLUX	Slingsby T.67M	Slingsby Aviation Ltd/Kirkbymoorside
	G-BLUY	Colt 69A balloon	The Balloon Goes Up Ltd
	G-BLUZ	D.H.82B Queen Bee (LF858)	B. Bayes
	G-BLVA	Airtour AH-56 balloon	Airtour Balloon Co Ltd
	G-BLVB	Airtour AH-56 balloon	T. C. Hinton
	G-BLVC	Airtour AH-31 balloon	Airtour Balloon Co Ltd
	G-BLVI	Slingsby T.67M	Slingsby Aviation Ltd/Kirkbymoorside

Reg.	Type	Owner or Operator	Notes
G-BLVK	CAARP CAP-10B	E. K. Coventry/Earls Colne	
G-BLVL	PA-28-161 Warrior II	C.S.E. Aviation Ltd/Kidlington	
G-BLVN	Cameron N-77 balloon	Servo & Electronic Sales Ltd	
G-BLVS	Cessna 150M	W. Lancs Aero Club Ltd/Woodvale	
G-BLVW	Cessna F.172H	R. & D. Holloway Ltd	
G-BLWB	Thunder Ax6-56 balloon	J. R. Tonkin/Norwich	
G-BLWD	PA-34-200T Seneca	C.S.E. Aviation Ltd/Kidlington	
G-BLWE	Colt 90A balloon	Huntair Ltd/Germany	
G-BLWF	Robin HR.100/210	K. J. Weston	
G-BLWH	Fournier RF-6B-100	Gloster Aero Club Ltd/Staverton	
G-BLWM	Bristol M.1C (replica) (C4994) ★	RAF Museum/Hendon	
G-BLWP	PA-38-112 Tomahawk	A. Dodd/Booker	
G-BLWT	Evans VP-1	C. J. Bellworthy	
G-BLWV	Cessna F.152	Redhill Flying Club	
G-BLWW	Taylor Mini Imp Model C	M. K. Field	
G-BLWX	Cameron N-56 balloon	W. Evans	
G-BLWY	Robin 2161D	A. Spencer & D. A. Rolfe	
G-BLXA	SOCATA TB.20 Trinidad	Shropshire Aero Club Ltd	
G-BLXF	Cameron V-77 balloon	G. McFarland	
G-BLXG	Colt 21A balloon	E. J. A. Macholc	
G-BLXH	Fournier RF-3	A. Rawicz-Szczerbo	
G-BLXI	CP.1310-C3 Super Emeraude	DRA Bedford Flying Club	
G-BLXO	Jodel D.150	P. R. Powell	
G-BLXP	PA-28R Cherokee Arrow 200	A. M. Bailey & T. A. Shears	
G-BLXR	AS.332L Super Puma	Bristow Helicopters Ltd	
G-BLXS	AS.332L Super Puma	Bristow Helicopters Ltd	
G-BLXT	RAF SE-5A (B4863) ★	Museum of Army Flying/Middle Wallop	
G-BLXX	PA-23 Aztec 250F	Falcon Flying Service (G-PIED)/Biggin Hill	
G-BLXY	Cameron V-65 balloon	Gone With The Wind Ltd/Tanzania	
G-BLYC	PA-38-112 Tomahawk	Liverpool Flying School Ltd	
G-BLYD	SOCATA TB.20 Trinidad	Gourmet Trotters	
G-BLYE	SOCATA TB.10 Tobago	G. Hatton	
G-BLYK	PA-34-220T Seneca III	P. G. Somers	
G-BLYP	Robin 3000/120	Lydd Air Training Centre Ltd	
G-BLYR	Airtour AH-77B balloon	Airtour Balloon Co Ltd	
G-BLYT	Airtour AH-77 balloon	I. J. & B. A. Taylor	
G-BLYY	PA-28-181 Archer II	A. C. Clarke	
G-BLZA	Scheibe SF.25B Falke	P. Downes & D. Gardner	
G-BLZB	Cameron N-65 balloon	D. Bareford	
G-BLZD	Robin R.1180T	Berkshire Aviation Services Ltd	
G-BLZE	Cessna F.152	Flairhire Ltd (G-CSSC)/Redhill	
G-BLZF	Thunder Ax7-77 balloon	H. M. Savage	
G-BLZH	Cessna F.152	Blackbushe School of Flying Ltd	
G-BLZM	Rutan LongEz	Zulu Mike Group	
G-BLZN	Bell 206B JetRanger	Helicopter Services	
G-BLZP	Cessna F.152	E. Midlands Flying School Ltd	
G-BLZR	Cameron A-140 balloon	Clipper Worldwide Trading/Venezuela	
G-BLZS	Cameron O-77 balloon	M. M. Cobbold	
G-BLZT	Short SD3-60	Jersey European Airways Ltd	
G-BMAB	Douglas DC-9-15	British Midland Airways Ltd The Great Mogul Diamond/E. Midlands	
G-BMAC	Douglas DC-9-15	British Midland Airways Ltd The Eugenie Diamond/E. Midlands	
G-BMAD	Cameron V-77 balloon	F. J. J. Fielder	
G-BMAF	Cessna 180F	P. Channon	
G-BMAG	Douglas DC-9-15	British Midland Airways Ltd The Nassak Diamond/E. Midlands	
G-BMAH	Douglas DC-9-14	British Midland Airways Ltd The Florentine Diamond/E. Midlands	
G-BMAI	Douglas DC-9-14	British Midland Airways Ltd The Star of Este Diamond/E. Midlands	
G-BMAK	Douglas DC-9-30	British Midland Airways Ltd The Stewart Diamond/E. Midlands	
G-BMAL	Sikorsky S-76A	Bond Helicopters Ltd	
G-BMAM	Douglas DC-9-30	British Midland Airways Ltd The Cullinan Diamond/E. Midlands	
G-BMAO	Taylor JT.1 Monoplane	V. A. Wordsworth	
G-BMAR	Short SD3-60	Loganair Ltd (G-BLCR)/Glasgow	
G-BMAV	AS.350B Ecureuil	Southern Trust Co Ltd/Jersey	
G-BMAX	FRED Srs 2	D. A. Arkley	
G-BMAY	PA-18 Super Cub 135	R. W. Davies	
G-BMBB	Cessna F.150L	Dacebow Aviation	

Notes	Reg.	Type	Owner or Operator
	G-BMBC	PA-31-350 Navajo Chieftain	Air Navigation & Trading Ltd/Blackpool
	G-BMBE	PA-46-310P Malibu	Barfax Distributing Co Ltd & Glasdon Group Ltd/Blackpool
	G-BMBJ	Schempp-Hirth Janus CM	RAF Germany Gliding Assoc
	G-BMBS	Colt 105A balloon	H. G. Davies
	G-BMBT	Thunder Ax8-90 balloon	Capital Balloon Club Ltd
	G-BMBW	Bensen B.8MR	M. Vahdat
	G-BMBZ	Scheibe SF.25E Super Falke	Buckminster Super Falke Syndicate
	G-BMCC	Thunder Ax7-77 balloon	H. N. Harben Ltd
	G-BMCD	Cameron V-65 balloon	M. C. Drye
	G-BMCG	Grob G.109B	Lagerholm Finnimport Ltd/Booker
	G-BMCI	Cessna F.172H	A. B. Davis/Edinburgh
	G-BMCJ	PA-31-350 Navajo Chieftain	Chelsea Land (Finance) Ltd
	G-BMCK	Cameron O-77 balloon	D. L. Smith
	G-BMCN	Cessna F.152	Lincoln Aero Club Ltd/Sturgate
	G-BMCO	Colomban MC.15 Cri-Cri	G. P. Clarke/Enstone
	G-BMCS	PA-22 Tri-Pacer 135	C. J. Weaver
	G-BMCV	Cessna F.152	Leicestershire Aero Club Ltd
	G-BMCW	AS.332L Super Puma	Bristow Helicopters Ltd
	G-BMCX	AS.332L Super Puma	Bristow Helicopters Ltd
	G-BMDB	SE-5A (replica) (F235)	D. Biggs
	G-BMDC	PA-32-301 Saratoga	MacLaren Aviation/Newcastle
	G-BMDD	Slingsby T.29	A. R. Worters
	G-BMDE	Pientenpol Air Camper	U. Schumacher
	G-BMDF	Boeing 737-2E7	Capita Ltd
	G-BMDJ	Price Ax7-77S balloon	D. A. Kozuba-Kozubska
	G-BMDK	PA-34-220T Seneca III	A1 Air Ltd
	G-BMDO	ARV Super 2	R. Lloyd
	G-BMDP	Partenavia P.64B Oscar 200	D. Foey
	G-BMDS	Jodel D.120	J. V. Thompson
	G-BMDV	Bell 47G-5	Trent Air Services Ltd/Cranfield
	G-BMDW	Dangerous Sports Club/Colt Hoppalong 1 balloon	D. A. C. Kirke
	G-BMDY	GA-7 Cougar	P. J. Bristow
	G-BMEA	PA-18 Super Cub 95	C. L. Towell
	G-BMEB	Rotorway Scorpion 145	I. M. Bartlett
	G-BMEE	Cameron O-105 balloon	A. G. R. Calder/Los Angeles
	G-BMEG	SOCATA TB.10 Tobago	G. H. N. & R. V. Chamberlain
	G-BMEH	Jodel Special Super Mascaret	W. Coupar Ltd
	G-BMEJ	PA-28R Cherokee Arrow 200	London Flight Centre (Stansted) Ltd
	G-BMEK	Mooney M.20K	Atlantic Film Investments Ltd/USA
	G-BMET	Taylor JT.1 Monoplane	M. K. A. Blyth
	G-BMEU	Isaacs Fury II	A. W. Austin
	G-BMEV	PA-32RT-300T Turbo Lance II	Danton Aviation Ltd
	G-BMEX	Cessna A.150K	S. G. Eldred & N. A. M. Brain
	G-BMFD	PA-23 Aztec 250F	Rangemile Ltd (G-BGYY)/Coventry
	G-BMFG	Dornier Do.27A-4 (3460)	R. F. Warner
	G-BMFI	PZL SZD-45A Ogar	Marrix Ltd/Redhill
	G-BMFL	Rand KR-2	E. W. B. Comber & M. F. Leusby
	G-BMFN	QAC Quickie Tri-Q.200	A. H. Hartog
	G-BMFP	PA-28-161 Warrior II	Bravo-Mike-Fox-Papa Group
	G-BMFT	H.S.748 Srs 2A	Euroair Transport Ltd
	G-BMFU	Cameron N-90 balloon	J. J. Rudoni
	G-BMFW	Hughes 369E	Ford Helicopters Ltd
	G-BMFY	Grob G.109B	P. J. Shearer
	G-BMFZ	Cessna F.152	Cornwall Flying Club Ltd
	G-BMGB	PA-28R Cherokee Arrow 200	Malmesbury Specialist Cars
	G-BMGC	Fairey Swordfish Mk II (W5856)	F.A.A. Museum/Yeovilton
	G-BMGG	Cessna 152	Falcon Flying Services/Biggin Hill
	G-BMGR	Grob G.109B	M. Clarke & D. S. Hawes
	G-BMGT	Cessna 310R	Air Service Training Ltd/Perth
	G-BMGV	Robinson R-22	D. L. Weldon
	G-BMGY	Lake LA-4-200 Buccaneer	M. A. Ashmole (G-BWKS/G-BDDI)
	G-BMHA	Rutan LongEz	S. F. Elvins
	G-BMHC	Cessna U.206G	Clacton Aero Club (1988) Ltd
	G-BMHJ	Thunder Ax7-65 balloon	M. G. Robinson
	G-BMHK	Cameron V-77 balloon	E. Evans & J. Wilkinson
	G-BMHL	Wittman W.8 Tailwind	T. G. Hoult
	G-BMHR	Grob G.109B	HRN Aviation Ltd
	G-BMHS	Cessna F.172M	Tango X-Ray Flying Group
	G-BMHT	PA-28RT-201T Turbo Arrow IV	Relay Services Ltd
	G-BMHX	Short SD3-60	Loganair Ltd/Glasgow
	G-BMHZ	PA-28RT-201T Turbo Arrow IV	M. A. Grayburn

Reg.	Type	Owner or Operator	Notes
G-BMIA	Thunder Ax8-90 balloon	A. G. R. Calder/Los Angeles	
G-BMID	Jodel D.120	M. J. Ireland	
G-BMIF	AS.350B Ecureuil	Colt Car Co Ltd/Staverton	
G-BMIG	Cessna 172N	J. R. Nicholls/Conington	
G-BMIM	Rutan LongEz	R. M. Smith	
G-BMIO	Stoddard-Hamilton Glasair RG	A. H. Carrington	
G-BMIP	Jodel D.112	M. T. Kinch	
G-BMIR	Westland Wasp HAS.1 (XT788)	R. Windley	
G-BMIS	Monnet Sonerai II	B. A. Bower/Thruxton	
G-BMIV	PA-28R-201T Turbo Arrow III	Maurice Mason Ltd	
G-BMIW	PA-28-181 Archer II	Oldbus Ltd	
G-BMIY	Oldfield Baby Great Lakes	J. B. Scott (G-NOME)	
G-BMJA	PA-32R-301 Saratoga SP	J. A. Varndell	
G-BMJB	Cessna 152	Bobbington Air Training School Ltd/ Halfpenny Green	
G-BMJC	Cessna 152	Cambridge Aero Club Ltd	
G-BMJD	Cessna 152	Donair Flying Club Ltd/E. Midlands	
G-BMJG	PA-28R Cherokee Arrow 200	D. J. D. Ritchie & ptnrs/Elstree	
G-BMJL	R. Commander 114	H. Snelson	
G-BMJM	Evans VP-1	C. A. Macleod	
G-BMJN	Cameron O-65 balloon	E. J. A. Machole	
G-BMJO	PA-34-220T Seneca III	B. Walker & Co (Dursley) Ltd & John Ward (Holdings) Ltd	
G-BMJR	Cessna T.337H	John Roberts Services Ltd (G-NOVA)	
G-BMJS	Thunder Ax7-77 balloon	Foulger Transport Ltd	
G-BMJT	Beech 76 Duchess	Mike Osborne Properties Ltd	
G-BMJW	NA AT-6D Harvard III (EZ259)	J. Woods	
G-BMJX	Wallis WA-116X	K. H. Wallis	
G-BMJY	Yakolev C18M	R. Lamplough/North Weald	
G-BMJZ	Cameron N-90 balloon	Bristol University Hot Air Ballooning Soc	
G-BMKB	PA-18 Super Cub 135	Cubair Ltd/Redhill	
G-BMKC	Piper J-3C-65 Cub (329854)	R. J. H. Springall	
G-BMKD	Beech C90A King Air	A. E. Bristow	
G-BMKF	Jodel DR.221	L. Gilbert	
G-BMKG	PA-38-112 Tomahawk	R. J. Hickson	
G-BMKH	Colt 105A balloon	Scotia Balloons Ltd	
G-BMKI	Colt 21A balloon	Thunder & Colt Ltd	
G-BMKJ	Cameron V-77 balloon	R. C. Thursby	
G-BMKK	PA-28R Cherokee Arrow 200	J. H. Hutchinson	
G-BMKP	Cameron V-77 balloon	Jacques W. Soukup Enterprises Ltd	
G-BMKR	PA-28-161 Warrior II	Field Flying Group (G-BGKR)/Goodwood	
G-BMKV	Thunder Ax7-77 balloon	A. Hornak & M. J. Nadel	
G-BMKW	Cameron V-77 balloon	A. C. Garnett	
G-BMKX	Cameron 77 Elephant SS balloon	Cameron Balloons Ltd	
G-BMKY	Cameron O-65 balloon	K. M. Taylor & A. R. Rich	
G-BMLB	Jodel D.120A	W. O. Brown	
G-BMLC	Short SD3-60 Variant 100	Loganair Ltd/Glasgow	
G-BMLJ	Cameron N-77 balloon	C. J. Dunkley	
G-BMLK	Grob G.109B	Brams Syndicate	
G-BMLL	Grob G.109B	A. H. R. Stansfield	
G-BMLS	PA-28R-201 Arrow III	M. C. Thomas & D. G. Bean	
G-BMLT	Pietenpol Air Camper	W. E. R. Jenkins	
G-BMLU	Colt 90A balloon	Danish Catering Services Ltd	
G-BMLV	Robinson R-22A	Skyline Helicopters Ltd/Booker	
G-BMLW	Cameron V-65 balloon	M. L. & L. P. Willoughby	
G-BMLX	Cessna F.150L	Cinque Ports Flying Club Ltd/Lydd	
G-BMLZ	Cessna 421C	Hadagain Investments Ltd (G-OTAD/ G-BEVL)	
G-BMMC	Cessna T310Q	Cooper Clegg Ltd	
G-BMMD	Rand KR-2	E. J. Lloyd	
G-BMMF	FRED Srs 2	J. M. Jones	
G-BMMG	Thunder Ax 7-77 balloon	G. V. Beckwith	
G-BMMI	Pazmany PL.4	M. K. Field	
G-BMMJ	Siren PIK-30	J. R. Greig	
G-BMMK	Cessna 182P	M. S. Knight/Goodwood	
G-BMML	PA-38-112 Tomahawk	Cumbernauld Aviation Ltd	
G-BMMM	Cessna 152	Luton Flight Training Ltd	
G-BMMN	Thunder Ax8-105 balloon	R. C. Weyda	
G-BMMP	Grob G.109B	E. W. Reynolds	
G-BMMR	Dornier Do.228-200	Suckling Airways Ltd/Cambridge	
G-BMMU	Thunder Ax8-105 balloon	C. J. P. Trinder	
G-BMMV	ICA-Brasov IS-28M2A	T. Cust	
G-BMMW	Thunder Ax7-77 balloon	P. A. Georges	

Notes	Reg.	Type	Owner or Operator
	G-BMMX	ICA-Brasov IS-28M2A	G-BMMX Syndicate
	G-BMMY	Thunder Ax7-77 balloon	D. A. Lawson
	G-BMNF	Beech B200 Super King Air	Bernard Matthews PLC/Norwich
	G-BMNL	PA-28R Cherokee Arrow 200	I. H. Nettleton
	G-BMNP	PA-38-112 Tomahawk	APB Leasing Ltd/Welshpool
	G-BMNT	PA-34-220T Seneca III	P. R. & M. R. Parr
	G-BMNV	SNCAN Stampe SV-4D	Wessex Aviation & Transport Ltd
	G-BMNW	PA-31-350 Navajo Chieftain	Crosswind Consultants
	G-BMNX	Colt 56A balloon	J. H. Dryden
	G-BMNZ	Cessna U206F	Macpara Ltd/Shobdon
	G-BMOE	PA-28R Cherokee Arrow 200	B. J. Mason/Shoreham
	G-BMOF	Cessna U206G	Integrated Hydraulics Ltd
	G-BMOG	Thunder Ax7-77A balloon	P. J. Burn
	G-BMOH	Cameron N-77 balloon	P. J. Marshall & M. A. Clarke
	G-BMOI	Partenavia P.68B	Simmette Ltd
	G-BMOJ	Cameron V-56 balloon	S. R. Bridge
	G-BMOK	ARV Super 2	P. E. Barker
	G-BMOL	PA-23 Aztec 250D	LDL Enterprises (G-BBSR)/Elstree
	G-BMOM	ICA-Brasov IS-28M2A	Brasov Flying Group
	G-BMOO	FRED Srs 2	N. Purllant
	G-BMOP	PA-28R-201T Turbo Arrow III	B. Thatcher
	G-BMOT	Bensen B.8M	R. S. W. Jones
	G-BMOV	Cameron O-105 balloon	C. Gillott
	G-BMOX	Hovey Beta Bird	A. K. Jones
	G-BMPA	G.159 Gulfstream 1	—
	G-BMPC	PA-28-181 Archer II	C. J. & R. J. Barnes
	G-BMPD	Cameron V-65 balloon	D. E. & J. M. Hartland
	G-BMPL	OA.7 Optica	Lovaux Ltd/Bournemouth
	G-BMPP	Cameron N-77 balloon	Sarnia Balloon Group
	G-BMPR	PA-28R-201 Arrow III	AH Flight Services Ltd
	G-BMPS	Strojnik S-2A	G. J. Green
	G-BMPY	D.H.82A Tiger Moth	S. M. F. Eisenstein
	G-BMRA	Boeing 757-236	British Airways *Beaumaris Castle*
	G-BMRB	Boeing 757-236	British Airways *Colchester Castle*
	G-BMRC	Boeing 757-236	British Airways *Rochester Castle*
	G-BMRD	Boeing 757-236	British Airways *Bothwell Castle*
	G-BMRE	Boeing 757-236	British Airways *Killyleagh Castle*
	G-BMRF	Boeing 757-236	British Airways *Hever Castle*
	G-BMRG	Boeing 757-236	British Airways *Caerphilly Castle*
	G-BMRH	Boeing 757-236	British Airways *Norwich Castle*
	G-BMRI	Boeing 757-236	British Airways *Tonbridge Castle*
	G-BMRJ	Boeing 757-236	British Airways *Loch Tummel*
	G-BMRK	Boeing 757-236	British Airways
	G-BMRL	Boeing 757-236	British Airways
	G-BMRM	Boeing 757-236	British Airways
	G-BMSA	Stinson HW.75 Voyager	M. A. Thomas (G-BCUM)/Barton
	G-BMSB	V.S.509 Spitfire IX (MJ627)	M. S. Bayliss (G-ASOZ)
	G-BMSC	Evans VP-2	E. J. Bedser
	G-BMSD	PA-28-181 Archer II	European Flyers (Blackbushe Airport) Ltd
	G-BMSE	Valentin Taifun 17E	A. J. Nurse
	G-BMSF	PA-38-112 Tomahawk	N. Bradley/Leeds
	G-BMSG	SAAB 32A Lansen ★	Aces High Ltd/Cranfield
	G-BMSI	Cameron N-105 balloon	Direction Air Conditioning Ltd
	G-BMSK	Hoffman H-36 Dimona	J. P. Kovacs
	G-BMSL	FRED Srs 3	A. C. Coombe
	G-BMSR	G.159 Gulfstream 1	—
	G-BMST	Cameron N-31 balloon	Hot Air Balloon Co Ltd
	G-BMSU	Cessna 152	G-BMSU Group
	G-BMSX	PA-30 Twin Comanche 160	N. Scott & G. McNeil
	G-BMSY	Cameron A-140 balloon	GT Flying Clubs Ltd
	G-BMSZ	Cessna 152	Falcon Flying Services/Biggin Hill
	G-BMTA	Cessna 152	Turnhouse Flying Club
	G-BMTB	Cessna 152	J. A. Pothecary/Shoreham
	G-BMTJ	Cessna 152	Creaton Aviation Services Ltd
	G-BMTL	Cessna 152	Agricultural & General Aviation/Bournemouth
	G-BMTN	Cameron O-77 balloon	Industrial Services (MH) Ltd
	G-BMTO	PA-38-112 Tomahawk	Falcon Flying Services/Biggin Hill
	G-BMTP	PA-38-112 Tomahawk	R. A. Wakefield
	G-BMTR	PA-28-161 Warrior II	London Flight Centre (Stansted) Ltd
	G-BMTS	Cessna 172N	Luton Flight Training Ltd
	G-BMTU	Pitts S-1E Special	O. R. Howe
	G-BMTW	PA-31-350 Navajo Chieftain	Air Northwest Ltd

Reg.	Type	Owner or Operator	Notes
G-BMTX	Cameron V-77 balloon	J. A. Langley	
G-BMTY	Colt 77A balloon	L. D. Ormerod	
G-BMUD	Cessna 182P	J. P. Edwards	
G-BMUG	Rutan LongEz	P. Richardson & J. Shanley	
G-BMUH	Bensen B.8MR	A. Shuttleworth	
G-BMUI	Brügger MB.2 Colibri	D. Adlington	
G-BMUJ	Colt Drachenfisch balloon	Air 2 Air Ltd	
G-BMUK	Colt UFO balloon	Air 2 Air Ltd	
G-BMUL	Colt Kindermond balloon	Air 2 Air Ltd	
G-BMUN	Cameron 78 Harley SS balloon	Forbes Europe Inc/France	
G-BMUO	Cessna A.152	Redhill Flying Club	
G-BMUR	Cameron gas airship	Cameron Balloons Ltd	
G-BMUT	PA-34-200T Seneca II	G. G. Long	
G-BMUU	Thunder Ax7-77 balloon	G. Anorewartha	
G-BMUZ	PA-28-161 Warrior II	Newcastle-upon-Tyne Aero Club Ltd	
G-BMVA	Schiebe SF.25B Falke	C. A. Simmonds	
G-BMVB	Cessna 152	Lancashire Aero Club/Barton	
G-BMVE	PA-28RT-201 Arrow IV	F. E. Gooding/Biggin Hill	
G-BMVG	QAC Quickie Q.1	P. M. Wright	
G-BMVI	Cameron O-105 balloon	Heart of England Balloons	
G-BMVJ	Cessna 172N	G & B Aviation Ltd/Coventry	
G-BMVK	PA-38-112 Tomahawk	Airways Aero Associations Ltd/Booker	
G-BMVL	PA-38-112 Tomahawk	Airways Aero Associations Ltd/Booker	
G-BMVM	PA-38-112 Tomahawk	Airways Aero Associations Ltd/Booker	
G-BMVO	Cameron O-77 balloon	Warners Motors (Leasing) Ltd	
G-BMVS	Cameron 77 SS balloon	Shellrise Ltd/Miami	
G-BMVT	Thunder Ax7-77A balloon	M. L. & L. P. Willoughby	
G-BMVU	Monnet Moni	F. S. Beckett	
G-BMVV	Rutan Vari-Viggen	G. B. Roberts	
G-BMVW	Cameron O-65 balloon	S. P. Richards	
G-BMVX	M.S.733 Alcyon Srs 1	J. D. Read	
G-BMWA	Hughes 269C	R. Taylor	
G-BMWE	ARV Super 2	N. R. F. McNally	
G-BMWF	ARV Super 2	J. McBeth	
G-BMWG	ARV Super 2	Falstaff Finance Ltd/Sandown	
G-BMWJ	ARV Super 2	Mid-West Aero Engines Ltd	
G-BMWM	ARV Super 2	R. Scroby	
G-BMWN	Cameron 80 SS Temple balloon	Forbes Europe Inc/France	
G-BMWP	PA-34-200T Seneca II	R. H. Steward & G. .P. Gregg	
G-BMWR	R. Commander 112A	M. & J. Edwards	
G-BMWU	Cameron N-42 balloon	The Hot Air Balloon Co Ltd	
G-BMWV	Putzer Elster B	E. A. J. Hibberd	
G-BMWX	Robinson R-22B	A. Ruggieri & D. Clifton	
G-BMXA	Cessna 152	Chamberlain Leasing	
G-BMXB	Cessna 152	Semloch Aviation Services/Andrewsfield	
G-BMXC	Cessna 152	Vectair Aviation Ltd	
G-BMXD	F.27 Friendship Mk 500	Air UK Ltd *Victor Hugo*/Norwich	
G-BMXH	Robinson R-22HP	R. H. Ryan	
G-BMXJ	Cessna F.150L	Arrow Aircraft Group	
G-BMXL	PA-38-112 Tomahawk	Airways Aero Associations Ltd/Booker	
G-BMXX	Cessna 152	Aerohire Ltd/Halfpenny Green	
G-BMXY	Scheibe SF.25B Falke	Marrix Ltd	
G-BMYA	Colt 56A balloon	Flying Pictures (Balloons) Ltd	
G-BMYC	SOCATA TB.10 Tobago	E. A. Grady	
G-BMYD	Beech A36 Bonanza	Seabeam Partners Ltd	
G-BMYE	BAe 146-200	British Aerospace PLC (G-WAUS/ G-WISC)/ Hatfield	
G-BMYF	Bensen B.8M	T. H. G. Russell	
G-BMYG	Cessna F.152	Rolim Ltd/Aberdeen	
G-BMYI	AA-5 Traveler	W. C. & S. C. Westran	
G-BMYJ	Cameron V-65 balloon	S. M. Antony & R. J. Christopher	
G-BMYN	Colt 77A balloon	J. D. Shapland & ptnrs	
G-BMYP	Fairey Gannet AEW.3 (XL502)	R. King	
G-BMYR	Robinson R-22	Ranger Helicopters Ltd/Manchester	
G-BMYS	Thunder Ax7-77Z balloon	J. E. Weidema	
G-BMYU	Jodel D.120	I. A. Marsh/Elstree	
G-BMYV	Bensen B.8M	R. G. Cotman	
G-BMYW	Hughes 269C	C. H. Tomkins Ltd	
G-BMZA	Air Command 503 Commander	R. W. Husband	
G-BMZB	Cameron N-77 balloon	D. C. Eager	
G-BMZC	Cessna 421C	Gilchrist Enterprises	
G-BMZD	Beech C90 King Air	Colt Transport Ltd	
G-BMZE	SOCATA TB.9 Tampico	Air Touring Services Ltd/Biggin Hill	

Notes	Reg.	Type	Owner or Operator
	G-BMZF	Mikoyan Gurevich MiG-15 (1420) ★	F.A.A. Museum/Yeovilton
	G-BMZG	QAC Quickie Q.2	T. D. Edmunds
	G-BMZH	Cameron A-140 balloon	The Balloon Stable Ltd
	G-BMZJ	Colt 400A balloon	Thunder & Colt Ltd
	G-BMZN	Everett gyroplane	R. J. Brown
	G-BMZP	Everett gyroplane	B. C. Norris
	G-BMZS	Everett gyroplane	C. W. Cload
	G-BMZV	Cessna 172P	Shoreham Flight Simulation/Bournemouth
	G-BMZW	Bensen B.8	P. D. Widdicombe
	G-BMZX	Wolf W-II Boredom Fighter (146-11042)	A. R. Meakin & S. W. Watkins
	G-BMZZ	Stephens Akro Z	P. G. Kynsey & J. Harper/Redhill
	G-BNAB	GA-7 Cougar	Chalrey Ltd (G-BGYP)
	G-BNAD	Rand KR-2	P. J. Brookman
	G-BNAG	Colt 105A balloon	R. W. Batcholer
	G-BNAH	Colt Paper Bag SS balloon	Thrustell Ltd
	G-BNAI	Wolf W-II Boredom Fighter (146-11083)	P. J. D. Gronow
	G-BNAJ	Cessna 152	G. Duncan
	G-BNAL	F.27 Friendship Mk 600	Air UK Ltd/Norwich
	G-BNAN	Cameron V-65 balloon	A. M. Lindsay
	G-BNAO	Colt AS-105 airship	Heather Flight Ltd
	G-BNAP	Colt 240A balloon	Heather Flight Ltd
	G-BNAR	Taylor JT.1 Monoplane	C. J. Smith
	G-BNAU	Cameron V-65 balloon	J. Buckle
	G-BNAW	Cameron V-65 balloon	A. Walker
	G-BNAY	Grob G.109B	Total Support Inc (UK) Ltd
	G-BNBJ	AS.355F-1 Twin Squirrel	Coln Helicopters Ltd
	G-BNBL	Thunder Ax7-77 balloon	J. R. Henderson
	G-BNBM	Colt 90A balloon	Huntair Ltd
	G-BNBR	Cameron N-90 balloon	Airbourne Promotions Ltd
	G-BNBU	Bensen B.8MV	R. Retallick
	G-BNBV	Thunder Ax7-77 balloon	J. M. Robinson
	G-BNBW	Thunder Ax7-77 balloon	I. S. & S. W. Watthews
	G-BNBY	Beech 95-B55A Baron	C. Wright (G-AXXR)
	G-BNBZ	LET L-200D Morava	C. A. Suckling/Redhill
	G-BNCA	Lightning F.2A ★	P. Hoar/Cranfield
	G-BNCB	Cameron V-77 balloon	Tyred & Battered Balloon Group
	G-BNCC	Thunder Ax7-77 balloon	C. J. Burnhope
	G-BNCG	QAC Quickie Q.2	T. F. Francis
	G-BNCH	Cameron V-77 balloon	Royal Engineers Balloon Club
	G-BNCJ	Cameron V-77 balloon	I. S. Bridge
	G-BNCK	Cameron V-77 balloon	G. Randall/Germany
	G-BNCL	WG.13 Lynx HAS.2 (XX469) ★	Wilkie Museum Collection/Blackpool
	G-BNCM	Cameron N-77 balloon	S. & A. Stone Ltd
	G-BNCN	Glaser-Dirks DG.400	M. C. Costin
	G-BNCO	PA-38-112 Tomahawk	Cambrian Flying Club/Swansea
	G-BNCR	PA-28-161 Warrior II	Airways Aero Associations Ltd/Booker
	G-BNCS	Cessna 180	C. Elwell Transport Ltd
	G-BNCU	Thunder Ax7-77 balloon	J. A. Lister
	G-BNCV	Bensen B.8	L. W. Cload
	G-BNCW	Boeing 767-204	Britannia Airways Ltd/Luton
	G-BNCX	Hunter T.7	Lovaux Ltd (stored)/Bournemouth
	G-BNCY	F.27 Friendship Mk 500	Air UK Ltd Lillie Langtry/Norwich
	G-BNCZ	Rutan LongEz	R. M. Bainbridge/Sherburn
	G-BNDG	Wallis WA-201/R Srs1	K. H. Wallis
	G-BNDH	Colt 21A balloon	Hot-Air Balloon Co Ltd
	G-BNDN	Cameron V-77 balloon	J. A. Smith
	G-BNDO	Cessna 152 II	V. B. Cheesewright
	G-BNDP	Brügger MB.2 Colibri	D. A. Peet
	G-BNDR	SOCATA TB.10 Tobago	A. N. Reardon
	G-BNDS	PA-31-350 Navajo Chieftain	Solomon Investment Co Ltd
	G-BNDT	Brügger MB.2 Colibri	T. C. Bayes
	G-BNDV	Cameron N-77 balloon	R. E. Jones
	G-BNDW	D.H.82A Tiger Moth	N. D. Welch
	G-BNDY	Cessna 425-1	Standard Aviation Ltd/Newcastle
	G-BNED	PA-22 Tri-Pacer 135	P. Storey
	G-BNEE	PA-28R-201 Arrow III	Britannic Management (Aviation) Ltd
	G-BNEF	PA-31-310 Turbo Navajo B	Seraph Aviation/Shoreham
	G-BNEI	PA-34-200T Seneca II	A. Bucknole
	G-BNEJ	PA-38-112 Tomahawk	V. C. & S. G. Swindell

Reg.	Type	Owner or Operator	Notes
G-BNEK	PA-38-112 Tomahawk	Pool Aviation Ltd/Welshpool	
G-BNEL	PA-28-161 Warrior II	J. A. Pothecary/Shoreham	
G-BNEN	PA-34-200T Seneca II	Warwickshire Aerocentre Ltd	
G-BNEO	Cameron V-77 balloon	J. G. O'Connell	
G-BNEP	PA-34-220T Seneca III	Handhorn Ltd/Blackpool	
G-BNER	PA-34-200T Seneca II	R. I. Sharpe	
G-BNES	Cameron V-77 balloon	G. Wells	
G-BNET	Cameron O-84 balloon	J. Bennett & Son (Insurance Brokers) Ltd	
G-BNEU	Colt 105A balloon	I. Lilja	
G-BNEV	Viking Dragonfly	N. W. Eyre	
G-BNEX	Cameron O-120 balloon	The Balloon Club Ltd	
G-BNFG	Cameron O-77 balloon	Capital Balloon Club Ltd	
G-BNFI	Cessna 150J	M. Jackson	
G-BNFK	Cameron 89 Egg SS balloon	Forbes Europe Inc/France	
G-BNFL	WHE Airbuggy	Roger Savage (Photography) (G-AXXN)	
G-BNFM	Colt 21A balloon	M. E. Dworksi	
G-BNFN	Cameron N-105 balloon	Air 2 Air Ltd	
G-BNFO	Cameron V-77 balloon	D. C. Patrick-Brown	
G-BNFP	Cameron O-84 balloon	A. J. & E. J. Clarke	
G-BNFR	Cessna 152 II	London Flight Centre (Stansted) Ltd	
G-BNFS	Cessna 152 II	London Flight Centre (Stansted) Ltd	
G-BNFU	Colt 105A balloon	Basemore Ltd	
G-BNFV	Robin DR.400/120	P. D. W. King	
G-BNFW	H.S.125 Srs 700B	British Aerospace PLC	
G-BNFY	Cameron N-77 balloon	The New Holker Estates Co Ltd	
G-BNGC	Robinson R-22	T. J. Clark	
G-BNGD	Cessna 152	AV Aviation Ltd	
G-BNGE	Auster AOP.6 (TW536)	R. W. W. Eastman	
G-BNGJ	Cameron V-77 balloon	Latham Timber Centres (Holdings) Ltd	
G-BNGN	Cameron V-77 balloon	A. R. & L. J. McGregor	
G-BNGO	Thunder Ax7-77 balloon	J. S. Finlan	
G-BNGP	Colt 77A balloon	Headland Services Ltd	
G-BNGR	PA-38-112 Tomahawk	Teesside Flight Centre Ltd	
G-BNGS	PA-38-112 Tomahawk	Frontline Aviation Ltd/Teesside	
G-BNGT	PA-28-181 Archer II	Berry Air/Edinburgh	
G-BNGV	ARV Super 2	A. S. Faiers	
G-BNGW	ARV Super 2	Southern Gas Turbines Ltd	
G-BNGX	ARV Super 2	Southern Gas Turbines Ltd	
G-BNGY	ARV Super 2	N. R. F. McNally (G-BMWL)	
G-BNHB	ARV Super 2	Super Two Group	
G-BNHC	ARV Super 2	M. J. Snelling	
G-BNHD	ARV Super 2	Aviation (Scotland) Ltd	
G-BNHE	ARV Super 2	Aviation (Scotland) Ltd	
G-BNHF	Cameron N-31 balloon	P. G. Dunnington	
G-BNHG	PA-38-112 Tomahawk	D. A. Whitmore	
G-BNHH	Thunder Ax7-77 balloon	Gee-Tee Signs Ltd	
G-BNHI	Cameron V-77 balloon	Phillair	
G-BNHJ	Cessna 152	DLM (Flying School) Ltd	
G-BNHK	Cessna 152	Osprey Flying Club/Cranfield	
G-BNHL	Colt 90 Beer Glass SS balloon	G. V. Beckwith	
G-BNHN	Colt Aerial Bottle SS balloon	The Balloon Stable Ltd	
G-BNHO	Thunder Ax7-77 balloon	M. J. Forster	
G-BNHP	Saffrey S.330 balloon	N. H. Ponsford Alpha II	
G-BNHR	Cameron V-77 balloon	P. C. Waterhouse	
G-BNHT	Fournier RF-3	C. W. N. Huke & A-L. N. M. Cox	
G-BNHV	Thunder Ax10-180 balloon	Thunder & Colt Ltd	
G-BNIB	Cameron A-105 balloon	A. G. E. Faulkner	
G-BNID	Cessna 152	Mercia Aircraft Leasing & Sales Ltd/Coventry	
G-BNIE	Cameron O-160 balloon	Bristol Balloons	
G-BNIF	Cameron O-56 balloon	D. V. Fowler	
G-BNII	Cameron N-90 balloon	Continu-Forms Holdings PLC	
G-BNIJ	SOCATA TB.10 Tobago	Alandi Investments Ltd	
G-BNIK	Robin HR.200/120	W. C. Smeaton/Popham	
G-BNIM	PA-38-112 Tomahawk	F. R. H. Parker	
G-BNIN	Cameron V-77 balloon	Cloud Nine Balloon Group	
G-BNIO	Luscombe 8A Silvaire	G. G. Pugh	
G-BNIP	Luscombe 8A Silvaire	D. R. C. Hunter & S. Maric	
G-BNIU	Cameron O-77 balloon	Nottingham Hot Air Balloon Club & Mitchell Air Power Ltd	
G-BNIV	Cessna 152	Aerohire Ltd/Halfpenny Green	
G-BNIW	Boeing Stearman PT-17	Lintally Ltd/E. Midlands	
G-BNIX	EMB-110P1 Bandeirante	Aeroservices (E. Midlands) Ltd	

Notes	Reg.	Type	Owner or Operator
	G-BNJA	WAG-Aero Wag-a-Bond	R. R. Hadley
	G-BNJB	Cessna 152	Klingair Ltd/Conington
	G-BNJC	Cessna 152	Stapleford Flying Club Ltd
	G-BNJD	Cessna 152	J. A Pothecary/Shoreham
	G-BNJE	Cessna A.152	Seawing Flying Club Ltd/Southend
	G-BNJF	PA-32RT-300 Lance II	Biggles Aviation Ltd
	G-BNJG	Cameron O-77 balloon	A. M. Figiel
	G-BNJH	Cessna 152	Turnhouse Flying Club
	G-BNJJ	Cessna 152	Merrett Aviation Ltd
	G-BNJK	Macavia BAe 748 Turbine Tanker	Macavia International Ltd
	G-BNJL	Bensen B.8	T. G. Ogilvie
	G-BNJM	PA-28-161 Warrior II	Teesside Flight Centre Ltd
	G-BNJO	QAC Quickie Q.2	J. D. McKay
	G-BNJR	PA-28RT-201T Turbo Arrow IV	Intelligent Micro Software Ltd
	G-BNJT	PA-28-161 Warrior II	Airways Aero Associations Ltd/Booker
	G-BNJU	Cameron 80 Bust SS balloon	Forbes Europe Inc/France
	G-BNJX	Cameron N-90 balloon	Mars UK Ltd
	G-BNKC	Cessna 152	Herefordshire Aero Club Ltd/Shobdon
	G-BNKD	Cessna 172N	Bristol Flying Centre Ltd
	G-BNKE	Cessna 172N	Top Cat Aviation Ltd
	G-BNKF	Colt AS-56 airship	Formtrack Ltd
	G-BNKG	Alexander Todd Steen Skybolt	Cavendish Aviation Ltd (G-RATS/G-RHFI)
	G-BNKH	PA-38-112 Tomahawk	Goodwood Terrena Ltd
	G-BNKI	Cessna 152	RAF Halton Aeroplane Club Ltd
	G-BNKL	Beech 95-58PA Baron	E. L. Klinge/Fairoaks
	G-BNKP	Cessna 152	Clacton Aero Club (1988) Ltd
	G-BNKR	Cessna 152	Marnham Investments Ltd
	G-BNKS	Cessna 152	Shropshire Aero Club Ltd/Shobdon
	G-BNKT	Cameron O-77 balloon	British Airways PLC
	G-BNKV	Cessna 152	I. C. Adams & Vectair Aviation Ltd
	G-BNKW	PA-38-112 Tomahawk	D. M. MacLean
	G-BNKX	Robinson R-22	Weller Helicopters
	G-BNKZ	Hughes 369HS	Reeds Motor Co/Sywell
	G-BNLA	Boeing 747-436	British Airways City of London
	G-BNLB	Boeing 747-436	British Airways City of Edinburgh
	G-BNLC	Boeing 747-436	British Airways City of Cardiff
	G-BNLD	Boeing 747-436	British Airways City of Belfast
	G-BNLE	Boeing 747-436	British Airways City of Newcastle
	G-BNLF	Boeing 747-436	British Airways City of Leeds
	G-BNLG	Boeing 747-436	British Airways City of Southampton
	G-BNLH	Boeing 747-436	British Airways City of Westminster
	G-BNLI	Boeing 747-436	British Airways City of Sheffield
	G-BNLJ	Boeing 747-436	British Airways City of Nottingham
	G-BNLK	Boeing 747-436	British Airways City of Bristol
	G-BNLL	Boeing 747-436	British Airways City of Leicester
	G-BNLM	Boeing 747-436	British Airways City of Durham
	G-BNLN	Boeing 747-436	British Airways City of Portsmouth
	G-BNLO	Boeing 747-436	British Airways City of Dundee
	G-BNLP	Boeing 747-436	British Airways City of Aberdeen
	G-BNLR	Boeing 747-436	British Airways City of Hull
	G-BNLS	Boeing 747-436	British Airways City of Chester
	G-BNLT	Boeing 747-436	British Airways City of Lincoln
	G-BNLU	Boeing 747-436	British Airways City of Bangor
	G-BNLV	Boeing 747-436	British Airways City of Exeter
	G-BNLW	Boeing 747-436	British Airways City of Norwich
	G-BNLX	Boeing 747-436	British Airways City of Worcester
	G-BNLY	Boeing 747-436	British Airways City of Swansea
	G-BNLZ	Boeing 747-436	British Asia Airways City of Perth
	G-BNMA	Cameron O-77 balloon	Flying Colours Balloon Group
	G-BNMB	PA-28-151 Warrior	Angelchain Ltd/Manchester
	G-BNMC	Cessna 152	M. L. Jones
	G-BNMD	Cessna 152	T. M. Jones
	G-BNME	Cessna 152	L. V. Atkinson
	G-BNMF	Cessna 152	Aerohire Ltd
	G-BNMG	Cameron V-77 balloon	Windsor Life Assurance Co Ltd
	G-BNMH	Pietenpol Air Camper	N. M. Hitchman
	G-BNMI	Colt Flying Fantasy SS balloon	Air 2 Air Ltd
	G-BNMK	Dornier Do.27A-1	G. Machie
	G-BNML	Rand KR-2	R. J. Smyth
	G-BNMN	PA-28R-201 Arrow III	T. W. Pullin
	G-BNMO	Cessna TR.182RG	G-BNMO Flying Group
	G-BNMP	Cessna R.182RG	P. M. Breton
	G-BNMX	Thunder Ax7-77 balloon	S. A. D. Beard

Reg.	Type	Owner or Operator	Notes
G-BNNA	Stolp SA.300 Starduster Too	D. F. Simpson	
G-BNNB	PA-34-200 Seneca II	Shoreham Flight Simulation/Bournemouth	
G-BNNC	Cameron N-77 balloon	T. M. McCoy/Barrow	
G-BNNE	Cameron N-77 balloon	The Balloon Stable Ltd	
G-BNNF	SA.315B Alouette III Lama	Dollar Air Services Ltd/Coventry	
G-BNNG	Cessna T.337D	Somet Ltd (G-COLD)	
G-BNNI	Boeing 727-276	Arkia Leasing Ltd	
G-BNNJ	Boeing 737-3Q8	British Airways	
G-BNNK	Boeing 737-4Q8	British Airways	
G-BNNL	Boeing 737-4Q8	British Airways	
G-BNNO	PA-28-161 Warrior II	W. Lancs Aero Club Ltd/Woodvale	
G-BNNR	Cessna 152	Sussex Flying Club Ltd/Shoreham	
G-BNNS	PA-28-161 Warrior II	A. Pucher & G. Cataldo	
G-BNNT	PA-28-151 Warrior	S. T. Gilbert & D. J. Kirkwood	
G-BNNU	PA-38-112 Tomahawk	APB Leasing Ltd/Welshpool	
G-BNNX	PA-28R-201T Turbo Arrow III	P. J. Lague	
G-BNNY	PA-28-161 Warrior II	Falcon Flying Services/Biggin Hill	
G-BNNZ	PA-28-161 Warrior II	D. Heater/Fairoaks	
G-BNOA	PA-38-112 Tomahawk	I. A. Qureshi	
G-BNOB	Wittman W.8 Tailwind	M. Robson-Robinson	
G-BNOE	PA-28-161 Warrior II	BAe Flying College/Prestwick	
G-BNOF	PA-28-161 Warrior II	BAe Flying College/Prestwick	
G-BNOG	PA-28-161 Warrior II	BAe Flying College/Prestwick	
G-BNOH	PA-28-161 Warrior II	BAe Flying College/Prestwick	
G-BNOI	PA-28-161 Warrior II	BAe Flying College/Prestwick	
G-BNOJ	PA-28-161 Warrior II	BAe Flying College/Prestwick	
G-BNOK	PA-28-161 Warrior II	BAe Flying College/Prestwick	
G-BNOL	PA-28-161 Warrior II	BAe Flying College/Prestwick	
G-BNOM	PA-28-161 Warrior II	BAe Flying College/Prestwick	
G-BNON	PA-28-161 Warrior II	BAe Flying College/Prestwick	
G-BNOO	PA-28-161 Warrior II	BAe Flying College/Prestwick	
G-BNOP	PA-28-161 Warrior II	BAe Flying College/Prestwick	
G-BNOR	PA-28-161 Warrior II	BAe Flying College/Prestwick	
G-BNOS	PA-28-161 Warrior II	BAe Flying College/Prestwick	
G-BNOT	PA-28-161 Warrior II	BAe Flying College/Prestwick	
G-BNOU	PA-28-161 Warrior II	BAe Flying College/Prestwick	
G-BNOV	PA-28-161 Warrior II	BAe Flying College/Prestwick	
G-BNOW	PA-28-161 Warrior II	BAe Flying College/Prestwick	
G-BNOX	Cessna R.182	J. Lloyd	
G-BNOY	Colt 90A balloon	Huntair Ltd	
G-BNOZ	Cessna 152	Pool Aviation Ltd/Welshpool	
G-BNPD	PA-23 Aztec 250E	County Garage (Cheltenham) Ltd/ Staverton	
G-BNPE	Cameron N-77 balloon	Kent Garden Centres Ltd	
G-BNPF	Slingsby T.31M	S. Luck & ptnrs	
G-BNPH	P.66 Pembroke C.1 (WV740)	R. J. F. Parker/Denham	
G-BNPI	Colt 21A balloon	Airship & Balloon Co Ltd	
G-BNPK	Cameron DP-70 airship	Cameron Balloons Ltd	
G-BNPL	PA-38-112 Tomahawk	Tomahawk Aviation Ltd/Leavesden	
G-BNPM	PA-38-112 Tomahawk	Papa Mike Aviation Ltd/Leavesden	
G-BNPN	PA-28-181 Archer II	Sherani Aviation/Elstree	
G-BNPO	PA-28-181 Archer II	Leavesden Flight Centre Ltd	
G-BNPT	PA-38-112 Tomahawk II	Cumbernauld Aviation Ltd	
G-BNPV	Bowers Fly-Baby 1A	J. G. Day	
G-BNPY	Cessna 152	Doncaster Aero Club Ltd	
G-BNPZ	Cessna 152	Bristol Flying Centre Ltd	
G-BNRA	SOCATA TB.10 Tobago	W. R. M. Beesley	
G-BNRC	AB-206A JetRanger	M. & P. Food Products Ltd	
G-BNRD	AB-206A JetRanger	Eclipse (UK) Ltd	
G-BNRE	AB-206A JetRanger	Tindon Ltd/Little Snoring	
G-BNRF	PA-28-181 Archer II	G-Air Ltd/Goodwood	
G-BNRG	PA-28-161 Warrior II	RAF Brize Norton Flying Club Ltd	
G-BNRH	Beech 95-E55 Baron	Nairn Flying Services Ltd/Inverness	
G-BNRI	Cessna U.206G	Target Technology Ltd	
G-BNRK	Cessna 152	Redhill Flying Club	
G-BNRL	Cessna 152	J. R. Nicholls/Sibson	
G-BNRP	PA-28-181 Archer II	Atomchoice Ltd/Goodwood	
G-BNRR	Cessna 172P	Skyhawk Group	
G-BNRU	Cameron V-77 balloon	M. A. Mueller	
G-BNRW	Colt 69A balloon	Callers Pegasus Travel Service Ltd	
G-BNRX	PA-34-200T Seneca II	Futurama Signs Ltd	
G-BNRY	Cessna 182Q	Reefly Ltd	
G-BNRZ	Robinson R-22B	W. Jordan Millers Ltd	

Notes	Reg.	Type	Owner or Operator
	G-BNSG	PA-28R-201 Arrow III	Armada Aviation Ltd/Redhill
	G-BNSI	Cessna 152	Airtime Aviation Services/Bournemouth
	G-BNSL	PA-38-112 Tomahawk II	M. H. Kleiser
	G-BNSM	Cessna 152	Cornwall Flying Club Ltd/Bodmin
	G-BNSN	Cessna 152	M. K. Barnes & G. N. Olson/Bristol
	G-BNSO	Slingsby T.67M Mk II	Trent Air Services Ltd/Cranfield
	G-BNSP	Slingsby T.67M Mk II	Trent Air Services Ltd/Cranfield
	G-BNSR	Slingsby T.67M Mk II	Trent Air Services Ltd/Cranfield
	G-BNSS	Cessna 150M	Languedoc Aviation Ltd/France
	G-BNST	Cessna 172N	E. J. H. Morgan
	G-BNSU	Cessna 152	Channel Aviation Ltd/Bourn
	G-BNSV	Cessna 152	Channel Aviation Ltd/Bourn
	G-BNSW	Cessna 152	One Zero One Three Ltd
	G-BNSY	PA-28-161 Warrior II	Carill Aviation Ltd/Southampton
	G-BNSZ	PA-28-161 Warrior II	Carill Aviation Ltd/Southampton
	G-BNTC	PA-28RT-201T Turbo Arrow IV	M. Gardiner
	G-BNTD	PA-28-161 Warrior II	S. S. Copsey/Ipswich
	G-BNTE	FFA AS.202/18A4 Bravo	BAe Flying College Ltd/Prestwick
	G-BNTF	FFA AS.202/18A4 Bravo	BAe Flying College Ltd/Prestwick
	G-BNTH	FFA AS.202/18A4 Bravo	BAe Flying College Ltd/Prestwick
	G-BNTI	FFA AS.202/18A4 Bravo	BAe Flying College Ltd/Prestwick
	G-BNTJ	FFA AS.202/18A4 Bravo	BAe Flying College Ltd/Prestwick
	G-BNTK	FFA AS.202/18A4 Bravo	BAe Flying College Ltd/Prestwick
	G-BNTL	FFA AS.202/18A4 Bravo	BAe Flying College Ltd/Prestwick
	G-BNTM	FFA AS.202/18A4 Bravo	BAe Flying College Ltd/Prestwick
	G-BNTN	FFA AS.202/18A4 Bravo	BAe Flying College Ltd/Prestwick
	G-BNTO	FFA AS.202/18A4 Bravo	BAe Flying College Ltd/Prestwick
	G-BNTP	Cessna 172N	M. Bond & P. Smith
	G-BNTS	PA-28RT-201T Turbo Arrow IV	Nasaire Ltd/Liverpool
	G-BNTT	Beech 76 Duchess	L. & J. Donne
	G-BNTW	Cameron V-77 balloon	I. R. Comley
	G-BNTX	Short SD3-30 Variant 100	Shorts Aircraft Leasing Ltd (G-BKDN)
	G-BNTY	Short SD3-30 Variant 100	Shorts Aircraft Leasing Ltd (G-BKDO)
	G-BNTZ	Cameron N-77 balloon	Balloon Team
	G-BNUC	Cameron O-77 balloon	T. J. Bucknall
	G-BNUG	Cameron O-105 balloon	Thunder & Colt Ltd
	G-BNUH	Cameron O-105 balloon	Thunder & Colt Ltd
	G-BNUI	Rutan Vari-Eze	T. N. F. Skead
	G-BNUL	Cessna 152	Osprey Air Services Ltd
	G-BNUN	Beech 95-58PA Baron	British Midland Airways Ltd/E. Midlands
	G-BNUO	Beech 76 Duchess	B. & W. Aircraft Ltd
	G-BNUR	Cessna 172E	A. P. Howells
	G-BNUS	Cessna 152	Stapleford Flying Club Ltd
	G-BNUT	Cessna 152 Turbo	Stapleford Flying Club Ltd
	G-BNUU	PA-44-180T Turbo Seminole	TEL (IoM) Ltd/Ronaldsway
	G-BNUV	PA-23 Aztec 250F	L. J. Martin
	G-BNUX	Hoffmann H-36 Dimona	K. H. Abel
	G-BNUY	PA-38-112 Tomahawk II	AT Aviation Ltd/Cardiff
	G-BNUZ	Robinson R-22B	J. C. Reid
	G-BNVB	AA-5A Cheetah	W. J. Siertsema & A. M. Glazer
	G-BNVD	PA-38-112 Tomahawk	Channel Aviation Ltd
	G-BNVE	PA-28-181 Archer II	Steve Parrish Racing
	G-BNVG	ARV Super 2	Aviation (Scotland) Ltd
	G-BNVH	ARV Super 2	Aviation (Scotland) Ltd
	G-BNVI	ARV Super 2	Adrianair Ltd
	G-BNVJ	ARV Super 2	Aviation (Scotland) Ltd
	G-BNVT	PA-28R-201T Turbo Arrow III	Victor Tango Group
	G-BNVZ	Beech 95-B55 Baron	C. A. Breeze/Barton
	G-BNWA	Boeing 767-336ER	British Airways *City of Brussels*
	G-BNWB	Boeing 767-336ER	British Airways *City of Paris*
	G-BNWC	Boeing 767-336ER	British Airways *City of Frankfurt*
	G-BNWD	Boeing 767-336ER	British Airways *City of Copenhagen*
	G-BNWE	Boeing 767-336ER	British Airways *City of Lisbon*
	G-BNWF	Boeing 767-336	British Airways *City of Milan*
	G-BNWG	Boeing 767-336	British Airways *City of Strasbourg*
	G-BNWH	Boeing 767-336	British Airways *City of Rome*
	G-BNWI	Boeing 767-336	British Airways *City of Madrid*
	G-BNWJ	Boeing 767-336ER	British Airways *City of Athens*
	G-BNWK	Boeing 767-336ER	British Airways *City of Amsterdam*
	G-BNWL	Boeing 767-336ER	British Airways *City of Luxembourg*
	G-BNWM	Boeing 767-336ER	British Airways *City of Toulouse*
	G-BNWN	Boeing 767-336ER	British Airways *William Wordsworth*
	G-BNWO	Boeing 767-336ER	British Airways *Sir William Shakespeare*

Reg.	Type	Owner or Operator	Notes
G-BNWP	Boeing 767-336ER	British Airways *City of Dublin*	
G-BNWR	Boeing 767-336ER	British Airways *City of Hamburg*	
G-BNWS	Boeing 767-336ER	British Airways *City of Oporto*	
G-BNWT	Boeing 767-336ER	British Airways *City of Cork*	
G-BNWU	Boeing 767-336ER	British Airways *Robert Burns*	
G-BNWV	Boeing 767-336ER	British Airways *City of Bonn*	
G-BNWW	Boeing 767-336ER	British Airways *City of Bordeaux*	
G-BNWX	Boeing 767-336ER	British Airways	
G-BNWY	Boeing 767-336ER	British Airways	
G-BNWZ	Boeing 767-336ER	British Airways	
G-BNXA	BN-2A Islander	Atlantic Air Transport Ltd/Coventry	
G-BNXC	Cessna 152	Sir W. G. Armstrong-Whitworth Flying Group/Coventry	
G-BNXD	Cessna 172N	Airtime Aviation Services/Bournemouth	
G-BNXE	PA-28-161 Warrior II	Rugby Autobody Repairs	
G-BNXI	Robin DR.400/180R	London Gliding Club Ltd/Dunstable	
G-BNXK	Nott-Cameron ULD-3 balloon	J. R. P. Nott	
G-BNXL	Glaser-Dirks DG.400	A. J. Chappell & D. A. Triplett	
G-BNXM	PA-18 Super Cub 95	G-BNXM Group	
G-BNXO	Colt 21A balloon	Thunder & Colt Ltd	
G-BNXR	Cameron O-84 balloon	J. A. & N. J. Ballard Gray	
G-BNXS	Cessna 404	Turnbull Associates	
G-BNXT	PA-28-161 Warrior II	Falcon Flying Services/Biggin Hill	
G-BNXU	PA-28-161 Warrior II	Friendly Warrior Group	
G-BNXV	PA-38-112 Tomahawk	Falcon Flying Services/Biggin Hill	
G-BNXX	SOCATA TB.20 Trinidad	D. M. Carr	
G-BNXZ	Thunder Ax7-77 balloon	Hale Hot Air Balloon Group	
G-BNYA	Short SD3-30 Variant 100	Shorts Bros PLC (G-BKSU)/Belfast City	
G-BNYB	PA-28-201T Turbo Dakota	Blackpool Air Centre	
G-BNYD	Bell 206B JetRanger	Sterling Helicopters Ltd	
G-BNYJ	Cessna 421B	Charles Robertson (Developments) Ltd	
G-BNYK	PA-38-112 Tomahawk	APB Leasing Ltd/Welshpool	
G-BNYL	Cessna 152	APB Leasing Ltd/Welshpool	
G-BNYM	Cessna 172N	N. B. Lindley	
G-BNYN	Cessna 152	Redhill Flying Club	
G-BNYO	Beech 76 Duchess	Skyhawk Ltd	
G-BNYP	PA-28-181 Archer II	R. D. Cooper/Cranfield	
G-BNYS	Boeing 767-204	Britannia Airways Ltd/Luton	
G-BNYU	Faithfull Ax7-61A balloon	M. L. Faithfull	
G-BNYV	PA-38-112 Tomahawk	Channel Aviation Ltd	
G-BNYX	Denney Aerocraft Kitfox	R. W. Husband	
G-BNYZ	SNCAN Stampe SV-4E	Tapestry Colour Ltd	
G-BNZB	PA-28-161 Warrior II	Falcon Flying Services/Biggin Hill	
G-BNZC	D.H.C.1 Chipmunk 22 (671)	Memorex Telex (UK) Ltd (G-ROYS)/ White Waltham	
G-BNZG	PA-28RT-201T Turbo Arrow IV	Trinity Garage (Gainsborough) Ltd	
G-BNZJ	Colt 21A balloon	Willowbest Ltd	
G-BNZK	Thunder Ax7-77 balloon	P. M. Davies & D. R .Groves	
G-BNZL	Rotorway Scorpion 133	J. R. Wraight	
G-BNZM	Cessna T.210N	Stansted Fluid Power (Products) Ltd	
G-BNZO	Rotorway Executive	M. G. Wiltshire	
G-BNZR	FRED Srs 2	R. M. Waugh	
G-BNZS	Mooney M.20K	D. G. Millington	
G-BNZV	PA-25 Pawnee 235	Northumbria Soaring Co Ltd	
G-BNZX	PA-34-200T Seneca II	Chaseside Holdings Ltd	
G-BNZZ	PA-28-161 Warrior II	J. P. Alexander/Denham	
G-BOAA	Concorde 102	British Airways (G-N94AA)	
G-BOAB	Concorde 102	British Airways (G-N94AB)	
G-BOAC	Concorde 102	British Airways (G-N81AC)	
G-BOAD	Concorde 102	British Airways (G-N94AD)	
G-BOAE	Concorde 102	British Airways (G-N94AE)	
G-BOAF	Concorde 102	British Airways (G-N94AF/G-BFKX)	
G-BOAG	Concorde 102	British Airways (G-BFKW)	
G-BOAH	PA-28-161 Warrior II	Denham School of Flying Ltd	
G-BOAI	Cessna 152	G. Duncan	
G-BOAK	PA-22 Tri-Pacer 150	A. M. Noble	
G-BOAL	Cameron V-65 balloon	A. M. Lindsay	
G-BOAM	Robinson R-22B	Bristow Helicopters Ltd/Redhill	
G-BOAN	PA-30 Twin Comanche 160B	R. L. C. Appleton	
G-BOAO	Thunder Ax7-77 balloon	D. V. Fowler	
G-BOAS	Air Command 503 Commander	R. Robinson	
G-BOAU	Cameron V-77 balloon	G. T. Barstow	

Notes	Reg.	Type	Owner or Operator
	G-BOAY	D.H.C.7-110 Dash Seven	—
	G-BOBA	PA-28R-201 Arrow III	GNJ Engineering Ltd
	G-BOBB	Cameron O-120 balloon	J. M. Albury
	G-BOBC	BN-2T Islander	Rhine Army Parachute Association (G-BJYZ)
	G-BOBD	Cameron O-160 balloon	A. C. K. Rawson & J. J. Rudoni
	G-BOBF	Brügger MB.2 Colibri	R. Bennett
	G-BOBG	Jodel D.150	C. A. Laycock
	G-BOBH	Airtour AH-77 balloon	J. & K. Francis
	G-BOBJ	PA-38-112 Tomahawk	Air Touring Services Ltd/Biggin Hill
	G-BOBK	PA-38-112 Tomahawk	Air Touring Services Ltd/Biggin Hill
	G-BOBL	PA-38-112 Tomahawk	Salcombe Crane Hire Ltd
	G-BOBN	Cessna 310R	Edinburgh Air Charter Ltd
	G-BOBR	Cameron N-77 balloon	C. Bradley
	G-BOBS	Quickie Q.2	M. A. Hales
	G-BOBT	Stolp SA.300 Starduster Too	A. M. Bailey & T. A. Shears
	G-BOBU	Colt 90A balloon	Thunder & Colt Ltd
	G-BOBV	Cessna F.150M	Sky Pro Ltd
	G-BOBX	G.159 Gulfstream 1 ★	Airport Fire Section/Birmingham
	G-BOBY	Monnet Sonerai II	R. G. Hallam (stored)/Sleap
	G-BOBZ	PA-28-181 Archer II	Trustcomms International Ltd
	G-BOCB	H.S.125 Srs 1B/522	MAGEC Aviation Ltd (G-OMCA/ G-DJMJ/G-AWUF)/Luton
	G-BOCC	PA-38-112 Tomahawk	Goodwood Terrena Ltd
	G-BOCD	Grob G.115	Landlink PLC
	G-BOCF	Colt 77A balloon	P. S. J. Mason
	G-BOCG	PA-34-200T Seneca II	Airways Flight Training (Exeter) Ltd
	G-BOCH	PA-32 Cherokee Six 300	Basic Vale Ltd
	G-BOCI	Cessna 140A	D. Nieman
	G-BOCK	Sopwith Triplane (replica) (N6290)	Shuttleworth Collection/O. Warden
	G-BOCL	Slingsby T.67C	C.S.E. Aviation Ltd/Kidlington
	G-BOCM	Slingsby T.67C	C.S.E. Aviation Ltd/Kidlington
	G-BOCN	Robinson R-22B	J. Bignall
	G-BOCP	PA-34-220T Seneca III	BAe Flying College Ltd/Prestwick
	G-BOCR	PA-34-220T Seneca III	BAe Flying College Ltd/Prestwick
	G-BOCS	PA-34-220T Seneca III	BAe Flying College Ltd/Prestwick
	G-BOCT	PA-34-220T Seneca III	BAe Flying College Ltd/Prestwick
	G-BOCU	PA-34-220T Seneca III	BAe Flying College Ltd/Prestwick
	G-BOCV	PA-34-220T Seneca III	BAe Flying College Ltd/Prestwick
	G-BOCW	PA-34-220T Seneca III	BAe Flying College Ltd/Prestwick
	G-BOCX	PA-34-220T Seneca III	BAe Flying College Ltd/Prestwick
	G-BOCY	PA-34-220T Seneca III	BAe Flying College Ltd/Prestwick
	G-BODA	PA-28-161 Warrior II	C.S.E. Aviation Ltd/Kidlington
	G-BODB	PA-28-161 Warrior II	C.S.E. Aviation Ltd/Kidlington
	G-BODC	PA-28-161 Warrior II	C.S.E. Aviation Ltd/Kidlington
	G-BODD	PA-28-161 Warrior II	C.S.E. Aviation Ltd/Kidlington
	G-BODE	PA-28-161 Warrior II	C.S.E. Aviation Ltd/Kidlington
	G-BODF	PA-28-161 Warrior II	C.S.E. Aviation Ltd/Kidlington
	G-BODG	Slingsby T.31 Motor Cadet III	H. P. Vox
	G-BODH	Slingsby T.31 Motor Cadet III	H. P. Vox
	G-BODI	Stoddard-Hamilton Glasair III	Jackson Barr Ltd
	G-BODK	Rotorway Scorpion 133	J. Brannigan
	G-BODL	Steen Skybolt	R. R. & C. B. K. Cuthbert
	G-BODM	PA-28 Cherokee 180	Bristol & Wessex Aeroplane Club Ltd
	G-BODN	PA-28R-201 Arrow III	N. M. G. Pearson/Bristol
	G-BODO	Cessna 152	A. R. Sarson
	G-BODP	PA-38-112 Tomahawk	N. C. Gray
	G-BODR	PA-28-161 Warrior II	Airways Aero Associations Ltd/Booker
	G-BODS	PA-38-112 Tomahawk	Ipswich School of Flying Ltd
	G-BODT	Jodel D.18	L. D. McPhillips
	G-BODU	Scheibe SF.25C	Monica English Memorial Trust
	G-BODW	Bell 206B JetRanger	Wood Hall Helicopters Ltd
	G-BODX	Beech 76 Duchess	Uphill Aviation Ltd
	G-BODY	Cessna 310R	Atlantic Air Transport Ltd/Coventry
	G-BODZ	Robinson R-22B	Langley Construction Ltd
	G-BOEC	PA-38-112 Tomahawk	R. A. Wakefield
	G-BOED	Cameron Opera House SS balloon	Cameron Balloons Ltd/Australia
	G-BOEE	PA-28-181 Archer II	T. B. Parmenter
	G-BOEH	Jodel DR.340	Piper Flyers Group
	G-BOEK	Cameron V-77 balloon	A. J. E. Jones
	G-BOEM	Aerotek-Pitts S-2A	Walsh Bros (Tunneling) Ltd

Reg.	Type	Owner or Operator	Notes
G-BOEN	Cessna 172M	G-BOEN Group	
G-BOER	PA-28-161 Warrior II	M. & W. Fraser-Urquhart	
G-BOES	Cessna FA.152	J. R. Nicholls (G-FLIP)	
G-BOET	PA-28RT-201 Arrow IV	B. C. Chambers (G-IBEC)	
G-BOEW	Robinson R-22B	Bristow Helicopters Ltd/Redhill	
G-BOEX	Robinson R-22B	Bristow Helicopters Ltd/Redhill	
G-BOEY	Robinson R-22B	Bristow Helicopters Ltd/Redhill	
G-BOEZ	Robinson R-22B	Bristow Helicopters Ltd/Redhill	
G-BOFA	Robinson R-22	Panair Ltd	
G-BOFC	Beech 76 Duchess	Wickenby Aviation Ltd	
G-BOFD	Cessna U.206G	D. M. Penny	
G-BOFE	PA-34-200T Seneca II	E. C. English	
G-BOFF	Cameron N-77 balloon	Systems-80 Double Glazing Ltd & N. M. Gabriel	
G-BOFL	Cessna 152	Coventry (Civil) Aviation Ltd	
G-BOFM	Cessna 152	Coventry (Civil) Aviation Ltd	
G-BOFO	Ultimate Aircraft 10-200	M. Werdmuller	
G-BOFW	Cessna A.150M	Three Counties Aero Engineering Ltd/ Lasham	
G-BOFX	Cessna A.150M	Shropshire Aero Club Ltd/Sleap	
G-BOFY	PA-28 Cherokee 140	Bristol & Wessex Aeroplane Club Ltd	
G-BOFZ	PA-28-161 Warrior II	R. W. Harris	
G-BOGB	Hawker Tempest II replica	D. L. Riley	
G-BOGC	Cessna 152	Skyviews & General Ltd/Leeds	
G-BOGG	Cessna 152	J. S. & S. Peplow	
G-BOGI	Robin DR.400/180	Shepair Ltd	
G-BOGK	ARV Super 2	D. R. Trouse	
G-BOGL	Thunder Ax7-77 balloon	Thunder & Colt Ltd	
G-BOGM	PA-28RT-201T Turbo Arrow IV	RJP Aviation	
G-BOGO	PA-32R-301T Saratoga SP	G. W. Dimmer	
G-BOGP	Cameron V-77 balloon	The Wealden Balloon Group	
G-BOGR	Colt 180A balloon	The Balloon Club of Great Britain Ltd	
G-BOGT	Colt 77A balloon	The Hot Air Balloon Co Ltd	
G-BOGV	Air Command 532 Elite	G. M. Hobman	
G-BOGW	Air Command 532 Elite	K. Ashford	
G-BOGY	Cameron V-77 balloon	Dante Balloon Group	
G-BOHA	PA-28-161 Warrior II	London Flight Centre (Stansted) Ltd	
G-BOHD	Colt 77A balloon	D. B. Court	
G-BOHF	Thunder Ax8-84 balloon	Slater Hogg & Howison Ltd	
G-BOHG	Air Command 532 Elite	T. E. McDonald	
G-BOHH	Cessna 172N	J. S. Baxter	
G-BOHI	Cessna 152	Clacton Aero Club (1988) Ltd	
G-BOHJ	Cessna 152	F. E. P. Holmes	
G-BOHL	Cameron A-120 balloon	J. M. Holmes	
G-BOHM	PA-28 Cherokee 180	M. J. Anthony & B. Keogh	
G-BOHN	PA-38-112 Tomahawk	AT Aviation Ltd/Cardiff	
G-BOHO	PA-28-161 Warrior II	Egressus Flying Club	
G-BOHR	PA-28-151 Warrior	L. T. Evans	
G-BOHS	PA-38-112 Tomahawk	Falcon Flying Services/Biggin Hill	
G-BOHT	PA-38-112 Tomahawk	Falcon Flying Services/Biggin Hill	
G-BOHU	PA-38-112 Tomahawk	Ambrit Ltd & Peter Smith Photography	
G-BOHV	Wittman W.8 Tailwind	R. A. Povall	
G-BOHW	Van's RV-4	R. W. H. Cole	
G-BOHX	PA-44-180 Seminole	K. D. & D. C. Horton	
G-BOIA	Cessna 180K	R. E. Styles & ptnrs	
G-BOIB	Wittman W.10 Tailwind	P. H. Lewis	
G-BOIC	PA-28R-201T Turbo Arrow III	M. J. Pearson	
G-BOID	Bellanca 7ECA Citabria	T. M. Cammidge	
G-BOIG	PA-28-161 Warrior II	D. Vallence-Pell/Jersey	
G-BOIH	Pitts S-1E Special	S. L. Goldspink	
G-BOII	Cessna 172N	Trevair Group/Bournemouth	
G-BOIJ	Thunder Ax7-77 balloon	R. A. Hughes	
G-BOIK	Air Command 503 Commander	D. W. Smith	
G-BOIL	Cessna 152	Upperstack Ltd	
G-BOIM	Cessna 150M	E. Alexander	
G-BOIN	Bellanca 7ECA Citabria	J. R. Dobson	
G-BOIO	Cessna 152	AV Aviation Ltd	
G-BOIP	Cessna 152	Stapleford Flying Club Ltd	
G-BOIR	Cessna 152	Shropshire Aero Club Ltd/Sleap	
G-BOIS	PA-31 Turbo Navajo	Air Care (South West) Ltd (G-AYNB)	
G-BOIT	SOCATA TB.10 Tobago	CB Helicopters	
G-BOIU	SOCATA TB.10 Tobago	R & B Aviation Ltd	
G-BOIV	Cessna 150M	Andrewsfield Pension Scheme	

Notes	Reg.	Type	Owner or Operator
	G-BOIW	Cessna 152	London Flight Centre (Stansted) Ltd
	G-BOIX	Cessna 172N	JR Flying Ltd
	G-BOIY	Cessna 172N	London Flight Centre (Stansted) Ltd
	G-BOIZ	PA-34-200T Seneca II	Northumbria Aviation Ltd
	G-BOJB	Cameron V-77 balloon	K. L. Heron & R. M. Trotter
	G-BOJD	Cameron V-77 balloon	L. H. Ellis
	G-BOJF	Air Command 532 Elite	P. J. Davies
	G-BOJH	PA-28R Cherokee Arrow 200	P. S. Kirby
	G-BOJI	PA-28RT-201 Arrow IV	Market Penetration Services (UK) Ltd
	G-BOJJ	BAe 146-300	British Aerospace PLC/Hatfield
	G-BOJK	PA-34-220T Seneca III	Redhill Flying Club (G-BRUF)
	G-BOJL	M.S.885 Super Rallye	J. A. Rees
	G-BOJM	PA-28-181 Archer II	H. Skelton
	G-BOJO	Colt 120A balloon	M. G. Ferguson
	G-BOJR	Cessna 172P	Exeter Flying Club Ltd
	G-BOJS	Cessna 172P	J. D. Beckett/Exeter
	G-BOJU	Cameron N-77 balloon	M. A. Scholes
	G-BOJW	PA-28-161 Warrior II	Piper Warrior G-BOJW Flying Group
	G-BOJX	PA-28-181 Archer II	Southern Air Ltd/Shoreham
	G-BOJY	PA-28-161 Warrior II	Southern Air Ltd/Shoreham
	G-BOJZ	PA-28-161 Warrior II	Southern Air Ltd/Shoreham
	G-BOKA	PA-28-201T Turbo Dakota	CBG Aviation Ltd/Biggin Hill
	G-BOKB	PA-28-161 Warrior II	Southern Air Ltd/Shoreham
	G-BOKE	PA-34-200T Seneca II	Gwent Plant Sales
	G-BOKF	Air Command 532 Elite	D. Beevers
	G-BOKG	Slingsby T.31 Motor Cadet III	A. M. Witt
	G-BOKH	Whittaker MW.7	M. W. J. Whittaker
	G-BOKI	Whittaker MW.7	R. K. Willcox
	G-BOKJ	Whittaker MW.7	M. N. Gauntlett
	G-BOKK	PA-28-161 Warrior II	C. J. Freeman/Headcorn
	G-BOKL	PA-28-161 Warrior II	BAe Flying College Ltd/Prestwick
	G-BOKM	PA-28-161 Warrior II	BAe Flying College Ltd/Prestwick
	G-BOKN	PA-28-161 Warrior II	BAe Flying College Ltd/Prestwick
	G-BOKO	PA-28-161 Warrior II	BAe Flying College Ltd/Prestwick
	G-BOKP	PA-28-161 Warrior II	BAe Flying College Ltd/Prestwick
	G-BOKR	PA-28-161 Warrior II	BAe Flying College Ltd/Prestwick
	G-BOKS	PA-28-161 Warrior II	BAe Flying College Ltd/Prestwick
	G-BOKT	PA-28-161 Warrior II	BAe Flying College Ltd/Prestwick
	G-BOKU	PA-28-161 Warrior II	BAe Flying College Ltd/Prestwick
	G-BOKW	Bo 208C Junior	R. A. Farrington (G-BITT)
	G-BOKX	PA-28-161 Warrior II	W. P. J. Jackson
	G-BOKY	Cessna 152	London Flight Centre (Stansted) Ltd
	G-BOLB	Taylorcraft BC-12-65	G-BOLB Flying Group
	G-BOLC	Fournier RF-6B-100	W. H. Hendy
	G-BOLD	PA-38-112 Tomahawk	B. R. Pearson & B. F. Fraser-Smith/Eaglescott
	G-BOLE	PA-38-112 Tomahawk	M. W. Kibble & E. A. Minard
	G-BOLF	PA-38-112 Tomahawk	Teesside Flight Centre Ltd
	G-BOLG	Bellanca 7KCAB Citabria	B. R. Pearson/Eaglescott
	G-BOLI	Cessna 172P	Boli Flying Club
	G-BOLJ	GA-7 Cougar	N. M. Morris
	G-BOLL	Lake LA-4 Skimmer	S. D. Foster
	G-BOLN	Colt 21A balloon	Airship & Balloon Co Ltd
	G-BOLO	Bell 206B JetRanger	Hargreaves Construction Co Ltd/Shoreham
	G-BOLP	Colt 21A balloon	Airship & Balloon Co Ltd
	G-BOLR	Colt 21A balloon	Airship & Balloon Co Ltd
	G-BOLS	FRED Srs 2	I. F. Vaughan
	G-BOLT	R. Commander 114	R. D. Rooke/Elstree
	G-BOLU	Robin R.3000/120	Classair
	G-BOLV	Cessna 152	Falcon Flying Services/Biggin Hill
	G-BOLW	Cessna 152	Seawing Flying Club Ltd/Southend
	G-BOLX	Cessna 172N	London Flight Centre (Stansted) Ltd
	G-BOLY	Cessna 172N	London Flight Centre (Headcorn) Ltd
	G-BOLZ	Rand KR-2	B. Normington
	G-BOMB	Cussutt Racer	P. P. Chapman/Biggin Hill
	G-BOML	Hispano HA.1112MIL (—)	Classic Aviation Ltd/Duxford
	G-BOMN	Cessna 150F	D. G. Williams & B. L. Wratten
	G-BOMO	PA-38-112 Tomahawk	Naiad Air Services
	G-BOMP	PA-28-181 Archer II	Falcon Flying Services/Biggin Hill
	G-BOMS	Cessna 172N	Aerohire Ltd/Halfpenny Green
	G-BOMT	Cessna 172N	Herefordshire Aero Club Ltd/Shobdon
	G-BOMU	PA-28-181 Archer II	RJ Aviation/Blackbushe

Reg.	Type	Owner or Operator	Notes
G-BOMY	PA-28-161 Warrior II	Carill Aviation Ltd/Southampton	
G-BOMZ	PA-38-112 Tomahawk	BOMZ Aviation/White Waltham	
G-BONC	PA-28RT-201 Arrow IV	Modern Air	
G-BOND	Sikorsky S-76A	Manchester Helicopter Centre/Barton	
G-BONE	Pilatus P2-06 (U-142)	D. C. R. Writer	
G-BONG	Enstrom F-28A	A. Lloyd-Mears	
G-BONK	Colt 180A balloon	Wye Valley Aviation Ltd	
G-BONO	Cessna 172N	M. Rowe/Sywell	
G-BONP	CFM Streak Shadow	CFM Metal-Fax Ltd	
G-BONR	Cessna 172N	Atlaslocal Ltd/Biggin Hill	
G-BONS	Cessna 172N	BONS Group/Leavesden	
G-BONT	Slingsby T.67M Mk II	Slingsby Aviation Ltd/Kirkbymoorside	
G-BONU	Slingsby T.67B	R. L. Brinklow	
G-BONV	Colt 17A balloon	Bryant Group PLC	
G-BONW	Cessna 152	Lincoln Aero Club Ltd/Sturgate	
G-BONY	Denney Aerocraft Kitfox	M. J. Walker	
G-BONZ	Beech V35B Bonanza	P. M. Coulten	
G-BOOB	Cameron N-65 balloon	I. J. Sadler	
G-BOOC	PA-18 Super Cub 150	R. R. & S. A. Marriott	
G-BOOD	Slingsby T.31M Motor Tutor	G. F. M. Garner	
G-BOOE	GA-7 Cougar	G. L. Cailes	
G-BOOF	PA-28-181 Archer II	Golf Boof Group	
G-BOOG	PA-28RT-201T Turbo Arrow IV	A. W. D. Perkins & J. C. Walton	
G-BOOH	Jodel D.112	M. J. Hayman	
G-BOOI	Cessna 152	Stapleford Flying Club Ltd	
G-BOOJ	Air Command 532 Elite	G. Snook	
G-BOOL	Cessna 172N	AVA Flyers/Biggin Hill	
G-BOOM	Hunter T.7	R. C. McCarthy	
G-BOON	PA-32RT-300 Lance II	G-BOON Ltd/Luton	
G-BOOO	Brügger MB .2 Colibri	D. G. Cole	
G-BOOP	Cameron N-90 balloon	The Hot Air Balloon Co Ltd (G-BOMX)	
G-BOOS	Colt 240A balloon	Thunder & Colt Ltd	
G-BOOT	Colt 240A balloon	Thunder & Colt Ltd	
G-BOOU	Cameron N-77 balloon	Aqualisa Products Ltd	
G-BOOV	AS.355F-2 Twin Squirrel	Merseyside Police Authority	
G-BOOW	Aerosport Scamp	Walavia	
G-BOOX	Rutan LongEz	I. R. Thomas & I. R. Wilde	
G-BOOZ	Cameron N-77 balloon	J. E. F. Kettlety	
G-BOPA	PA-28-181 Archer II	J. E. Strutt (London) Ltd	
G-BOPB	Boeing 767-204ER	Britannia Airways Ltd *Captain Sir Ross Smith*/Luton	
G-BOPC	PA-28-161 Warrior II	Channel Aviation Ltd	
G-BOPD	Bede BD-4	S. T. Dauncey	
G-BOPG	Cessna 182Q	J. Tomkins	
G-BOPH	Cessna TR.182RG	E. A. L. Sturmer	
G-BOPL	PA-28-161 Warrior II	Cambrian Flying Club/Swansea	
G-BOPN	FLS Aerospace OA.7 Optica	FLS Aerospace (Lovaux) Ltd/Bournemouth	
G-BOPP	FLS Aerospace OA.7 Optica	FLS Aerospace (Lovaux) Ltd/Bournemouth	
G-BOPR	FLS Aerospace OA.7 Optica	FLS Aerospace (Lovaux) Ltd/Bournemouth	
G-BOPT	Grob G.115	Lancashire Aero Club/Barton	
G-BOPU	Grob G.115	Lancashire Aero Club/Barton	
G-BOPV	PA-34-200T Seneca II	Tewin Aviation	
G-BOPW	Cessna A.152	Northamptonshire School of Flying Ltd/ Sywell	
G-BOPX	Cessna A.152	Aerohire Ltd/Halfpenny Green	
G-BOPZ	Cameron DP-70 airship	The Hot Air Balloon Co Ltd (G-BOMW)	
G-BORA	Colt 77A balloon	Cala Homes (Southern) Ltd	
G-BORB	Cameron V-77 balloon	M. H. Wolff	
G-BORC	Colt 180A balloon	Airship & Balloon Co Ltd	
G-BORD	Thunder Ax7-77 balloon	D. D. Owen	
G-BORE	Colt 77A balloon	Little Secret Hot-Air Balloon Group	
G-BORG	Campbell Cricket	N. G. Bailey	
G-BORH	PA-34-200T Seneca II	C. Dugard Ltd & SCA Ltd	
G-BORI	Cessna 152	Staryear Ltd	
G-BORJ	Cessna 152	APB Leasing Ltd/Welshpool	
G-BORK	PA-28-161 Warrior II	J. A. Hilton/Coventry	
G-BORL	PA-28-161 Warrior II	D. C. Harry	
G-BORM	H.S.748 Srs 2B	*(stored)*/Exeter	
G-BORN	Cameron N-77 balloon	I. Chadwick	
G-BORO	Cessna 152	APB Leasing Ltd/Welshpool	
G-BORR	Thunder Ax8-90 balloon	W. J. Harris	
G-BORS	PA-28-181 Archer II	Modern Air/Fowlmere	
G-BORT	Colt 77A balloon	Y.-J. Joslyn/Germany	

Notes	Reg.	Type	Owner or Operator
	G-BORV	Bell 206B JetRanger 2	P. V. Doman
	G-BORW	Cessna 172P	Briter Aviation Ltd/Coventry
	G-BORY	Cessna 150L	Swansea Aviation Ltd
	G-BOSA	Boeing 737-204ADV	Santa Fe Aviation Leasing Ltd (G-BAZI)
	G-BOSB	Thunder Ax7-77 balloon	M. Gallagher
	G-BOSC	Cessna U.206G	A. J. Buczkowski/Cranfield
	G-BOSD	PA-34-200T Seneca II	Barnes Olson Aeroleasing Ltd
	G-BOSE	PA-28-181 Archer II	G. Fleck
	G-BOSF	Colt 69A balloon	Airship & Balloon Co Ltd
	G-BOSG	Colt 17A balloon	Airship & Balloon Co Ltd
	G-BOSH	Thunder Ax8-84 balloon	Ace Balloons (Bath) Ltd
	G-BOSJ	Nord 3400	A. I. Milne
	G-BOSM	Jodel DR.253B	J. Cantellow
	G-BOSO	Cessna A.152	Redhill Flying Club
	G-BOSP	PA-28-151 Warrior	M. E. Williams/Andrewsfield
	G-BOSR	PA-28 Cherokee 140	R. D. Cornish
	G-BOSU	PA-28 Cherokee 140	Memorex Telex (UK) Ltd
	G-BOSV	Cameron V-77 balloon	K. H. Greenaway
	G-BOTB	Cessna 152	Stapleford Flying Club Ltd
	G-BOTD	Cameron O-105 balloon	P. J. Beglan
	G-BOTE	Thunder Ax8-90 balloon	D. Grimshaw
	G-BOTF	PA-28-151 Warrior	G-BOTF Group/Southend
	G-BOTG	Cessna 152	Donington Aviation Ltd/E. Midlands
	G-BOTH	Cessna 182Q	G-BOTH Group
	G-BOTI	PA-28-151 Warrior	Tango India Flying Group/Biggin Hill
	G-BOTK	Cameron O-105 balloon	F. R. & V. L. Higgins
	G-BOTM	Bell 206B JetRanger 3	Spiritbusy Ltd
	G-BOTN	PA-28-161 Warrior II	W. Lancashire Aero Club Ltd/Woodvale
	G-BOTO	Bellanca 7ECA Citabria	G-BOTO Group
	G-BOTP	Cessna 150J	R. E. Thorne
	G-BOTS	Hughes 269C	Horizon Helicopters
	G-BOTT	Rand KR-2	M. D. Ott & M. R. Hutchins
	G-BOTU	Piper J-3C-65 Cub	T. L. Giles
	G-BOTV	PA-32RT-300 Lance II	Robin Lance Aviation Association Ltd
	G-BOTW	Cameron V-77 balloon	D. N. Malcolm
	G-BOTY	Cessna 150J	T. J. C. Darby & G. Webster
	G-BOTZ	Bensen B.80R	C. Jones
	G-BOUD	PA-38-112 Tomahawk	K. & C. J. Powell/Southend
	G-BOUE	Cessna 172N	E. Alexander
	G-BOUF	Cessna 172N	Amber Valley Aviation
	G-BOUJ	Cessna 150M	J. B. Mills
	G-BOUK	PA-34-200T Seneca II	Airtime (Hampshire) Ltd
	G-BOUL	PA-34-200T Seneca II	C.S.E. Aviation Ltd/Kidlington
	G-BOUM	PA-34-200T Seneca II	C.S.E. Aviation Ltd/Kidlington
	G-BOUN	Rand KR-2	W. J. Allan
	G-BOUP	PA-28-161 Warrior II	C.S.E. Aviation Ltd/Kidlington
	G-BOUR	PA-28-161 Warrior II	C.S.E. Aviation Ltd/Kidlington
	G-BOUS	PA-28RT-201 Arrow IV	Hamilton Compass Aviation Ltd
	G-BOUT	Colomban MC.12 Cri-Cri	C. K. Farley
	G-BOUV	Bensen B.8R	P. Wilkinson
	G-BOUZ	Cessna 150G	G. Webster & T. J. C. Darby
	G-BOVB	PA-15 Vagabond	Oscar Flying Group/Shoreham
	G-BOVC	Everett gyroplane	J. W. Highton
	G-BOVG	Cessna F.172H	The G-BOVG Group
	G-BOVH	PA-28-161 Warrior II	R. W. Tebby
	G-BOVK	PA-28-161 Warrior II	Hamilton Compass Aviation Ltd
	G-BOVP	Air Command 532 Elite	C. K. Park
	G-BOVR	Robinson R-22	P. J. Homan
	G-BOVS	Cessna 150M	V. B. Cheesewright
	G-BOVT	Cessna 150M	R. G. Moss
	G-BOVU	Stoddard-Hamilton Glasair III	W. N. Blair-Hickman
	G-BOVV	Cameron V-77 balloon	J. P. Clifford
	G-BOVW	Colt 69A balloon	V. Hyland
	G-BOVX	Hughes 269C	McIntyre Aviation Ltd/Staverton
	G-BOWA	Thunder Ax8-90 balloon	T. C. Hinton
	G-BOWB	Cameron V-77 balloon	R. C. Stone
	G-BOWC	Cessna 150J	M. R. Wilson & C. J. Moore
	G-BOWD	Cessna F.337G	Badgehurst Ltd (G-BLSB)
	G-BOWE	PA-34-200T Seneca II	C.S.E. Aviation Ltd/Kidlington
	G-BOWK	Cameron N-90 balloon	S. R. Bridge
	G-BOWL	Cameron V-77 balloon	Matrix Computers Ltd
	G-BOWM	Cameron V-56 balloon	C. G. Caldecott & G. Pitt
	G-BOWN	PA-12 Super Cruiser	F. E. P. Holmes/Andrewsfield

Reg.	Type	Owner or Operator	Notes
G-BOWO	Cessna R.182	D. P. Bennett	
G-BOWP	Jodel D.120A	A. G. Gedney & ptnrs/Sibson	
G-BOWS	Cessna 150M	Semloh Aviation Services/Andrewsfield	
G-BOWT	Stolp SA.300 Starduster Too	F. E. P. Holmes/Andrewsfield	
G-BOWU	Cameron O-84 balloon	St Elmos Fire Syndicate	
G-BOWV	Cameron V-65 balloon	C. P. R. & S. J. Baxter	
G-BOWY	PA-28RT-201T Turbo Arrow IV	Overview Europe Ltd	
G-BOWZ	Bensen B.80V	W. M. Day	
G-BOXA	PA-28-161 Warrior II	CI Aero Holdings Ltd	
G-BOXB	PA-28-161 Warrior II	CI Aero Holdings Ltd	
G-BOXC	PA-28-161 Warrior II	CI Aero Holdings Ltd	
G-BOXG	Cameron O-77 balloon	J. Reeves	
G-BOXH	Pitts S-1S Special	S. Fenwick	
G-BOXJ	Piper J-3C-65 Cub	J. L. Quick & A. J. P. Jackson/Biggin Hill	
G-BOXK	Slingsby T.67C	Slingsby Aviation Ltd/Kirkbymoorside	
G-BOXN	Robinson R-22B	Conguess Aviation Ltd	
G-BOXR	GA-7 Cougar	Campbell Air Services Ltd/Booker	
G-BOXS	Hughes 269C	Ford Helicopters Ltd	
G-BOXT	Hughes 269C	Elite Helicopters Ltd	
G-BOXU	AA-5B Tiger	J. J. Woodhouse	
G-BOXV	Pitts S-1S Special	G. R. Clark	
G-BOXW	Cassutt Racer Srs IIIM	D. I. Johnson	
G-BOXX	Robinson R-22B	J. D. Forbes-Nixon & G. E. Mendham	
G-BOXZ	PA-28-181 Archer II	Sheffield Aero Club Ltd/Netherthorpe	
G-BOYB	Cessna A.152	Northamptonshire School of Flying Ltd/Sywell	
G-BOYC	Robinson R-22B	Northern Helicopters (Leeds) Ltd	
G-BOYF	Sikorsky S-76B	Darley Steel Management Co Ltd	
G-BOYH	PA-28-151 Warrior	Superpause Ltd/Booker	
G-BOYI	PA-28-161 Warrior II	Rankart Ltd/Kidlington	
G-BOYK	Montgomerie-Bensen B.8	H. P. Latham	
G-BOYL	Cessna 152	Sandtoft Air Services (1985) Ltd	
G-BOYM	Cameron O-84 balloon	Frontline Distribution Ltd	
G-BOYO	Cameron V-20 balloon	J. M. Willard	
G-BOYP	Cessna 172N	Guildtons Ltd	
G-BOYR	Cessna F.337G	Bournewood Aviation	
G-BOYS	Cameron N-77 balloon	The Independent Balloon Co Ltd	
G-BOYT	PA-38-112 Tomahawk	APB Leasing Ltd/Welshpool	
G-BOYU	Cessna A.150L	Flightwheel Group	
G-BOYV	PA-28R-201T Turbo Arrow III	P. R. Goldsworthy	
G-BOYX	Robinson R-22B	R. Towle	
G-BOYY	Cameron A-105 balloon	Hoyers (UK) Ltd	
G-BOYZ	Laser Z.200	M. G. Jefferies	
G-BOZI	PA-28-161 Warrior II	Klingair Ltd/Conington	
G-BOZK	AS.332L Super Puma	British International Helicopters	
G-BOZM	PA-38-112 Tomahawk	S. J. Green	
G-BOZN	Cameron N-77 balloon	Calarel Developments Ltd	
G-BOZO	AA-5B Tiger	Becketts Honda Car Centre Ltd	
G-BOZP	Beech 76 Duchess	Millhouse Developments Ltd	
G-BOZR	Cessna 152	Interair (Aviation) Ltd/Bournemouth	
G-BOZS	Pitts S-1C Special	R. J. & M. B. Trickey	
G-BOZT	PA-28-181 Archer II	Andrews Aviation Ltd	
G-BOZU	Sparrow Hawk Mk II	R. V. Phillimore	
G-BOZV	CEA DR.340 Major	EH Group	
G-BOZW	Benson B.8M	M. E. Wills	
G-BOZX	Robinson R-22B	Rentatruck (Self Drive) Ltd	
G-BOZY	Cameron RTW-120 balloon	G. C. Ludlow	
G-BOZZ	AA-5B Tiger	Solent Tiger Group/Southampton	
G-BPAA	Acro Advanced	Acro Engines & Airframes Ltd	
G-BPAB	Cessna 150M	R. C. W. Wheeler & ptnrs/Earls Colne	
G-BPAC	PA-28-161 Warror II	G. G. Pratt	
G-BPAE	Cameron V-77 balloon	C. Dunseath	
G-BPAF	PA-28-161 Warrior II	Hendafern Ltd	
G-BPAG	Bellanca 8KCAB Decathlon	P. Hartley	
G-BPAH	Colt 69A balloon	International Distillers & Vintners Ltd	
G-BPAI	Bell 47F-2A1	LRC Leisure Ltd	
G-BPAJ	D.H.82A Tiger Moth	P. A. Jackson (G-AOIX)	
G-BPAL	D.H.C.1 Chipmunk 22 (WG350)	D. F. Ranger (G-BCYE)	
G-BPAM	Jodel D.150A	A. J. Symes-Bullen	
G-BPAO	Air Command 503 Commander	D. J. Sagar	
G-BPAS	SOCATA TB.20 Trinidad	South East Aviation Ltd	
G-BPAU	PA-28-161 Warrior II	Lapwing Flying Group Ltd/Denham	

Notes	Reg.	Type	Owner or Operator
	G-BPAV	FRED Srs 2	P. A. Valentine
	G-BPAW	Cessna 150M	Magnificent Obsessions Ltd
	G-BPAX	Cessna 150M	Barry Aviation Ltd
	G-BPAY	PA-28-181 Archer II	C. Rees
	G-BPBA	Benson B.8	M. E. Green
	G-BPBB	Evans VP-2	J. S. & J. D. Penny
	G-BPBG	Cessna 152	Atlantic Air Transport Ltd/Coventry
	G-BPBI	Cessna 152	B. W. Wells & Burbage Farms Ltd
	G-BPBJ	Cessna 152	A. Windley/Tattershall
	G-BPBK	Cessna 152	B. W. Wells & Burbage Farms Ltd
	G-BPBM	PA-28-161 Warrior II	Sandtoft Air Services (1985) Ltd
	G-BPBO	PA-28RT-201T Turbo Arrow IV	Arrow Associates/Bournemouth
	G-BPBP	Brügger MB.2 Colibri	E. H. Booker
	G-BPBR	PA-38-112 Tomahawk	AT Aviation Ltd/Cardiff
	G-BPBU	Cameron V-77 balloon	G-BPBU Skymaid Balloon
	G-BPBV	Cameron V-77 balloon	W. E. & L. A. Newman
	G-BPBW	Cameron O-105 balloon	R. J. Mansfield
	G-BPBY	Cameron V-77 balloon	T. J. & K. A. Brewster (G-BPCS)
	G-BPBZ	Thunder Ax7-77 balloon	Wye Valley Aviation Ltd
	G-BPCA	BN-2B Islander	Loganair Ltd (G-BLNX)/Glasgow
	G-BPCE	Stolp SA.300 Starduster Too	R. E. Todd
	G-BPCF	Piper J-3C-65 Cub	A. J. Cook
	G-BPCG	Colt AS-80 airship	Willowbest Ltd
	G-BPCI	Cessna R.172K	B. E. Simpson
	G-BPCK	PA-28-161 Warrior II	C. R. Hughes & B. E. Simpson
	G-BPCL	SA Bulldog Srs 120/128	Isohigh Ltd/Denham
	G-BPCM	Rotorway Executive	Normans (Burton-on-Trent) Ltd
	G-BPCN	Cameron A-160 balloon	Golf Centres Balloons Ltd
	G-BPCR	Mooney M.20K	T. & R. Harris
	G-BPCV	Montgomerie-Bensen B.8MR	J. Fisher
	G-BPCX	PA-28-236 Dakota	Offshore Marine Consultants Ltd
	G-BPCY	PA-34-200T Seneca	Compton Abbas Airfield Ltd
	G-BPDA	H.S.748 Srs 2A	Emerald Airways Ltd (G-GLAS)/Liverpool
	G-BPDD	Colt 240A balloon	Heather Flight Ltd
	G-BPDE	Colt 56A balloon	J. W. Weidema
	G-BPDF	Cameron V-77 balloon	The Ballooning Business Ltd
	G-BPDG	Cameron V-77 balloon	A. & M. A. Dunning
	G-BPDJ	Chris Tena Mini Coupe	Air Time Acquisition Ltd
	G-BPDK	Sorrell SNS-7 Hyperbipe	A. J. Cable/Barton
	G-BPDM	C.A.S.A. 1.131E Jungmann (E3B-369)	Spanish Acquisition/Shoreham
	G-BPDN	PA-28R-201 Arrow III	J. M. C. Crompton
	G-BPDS	PA-28-161 Warrior II	Hendafern Ltd
	G-BPDT	PA-28-161 Warrior II	Hendafern Ltd
	G-BPDU	PA-28-161 Warrior II	Hendafern Ltd
	G-BPDV	Pitts S-1S Special	J. Vize
	G-BPDY	Westland-Bell 47G-3B1	Howden Helicopters/Spaldington
	G-BPEA	Boeing 757-236ER	Caledonian Airways Ltd *Loch of the Clans*
	G-BPEB	Boeing 757-236ER	Caledonian Airways Ltd *Loch Lomond*
	G-BPEC	Boeing 757-236ER	Caledonian Airways Ltd *Loch Katrine*
	G-BPED	Boeing 757-236ER	British Airways *Blair Castle*
	G-BPEE	Boeing 757-236ER	Caledonian Airways Ltd *Loch Tay*
	G-BPEF	Boeing 757-236ER	Caledonian Airways Ltd *Loch Fainnach* (G-BOHC)
	G-BPEH	Boeing 757-236ER	Caledonian Airways Ltd *Loch Hourn* (G-BNSE)
	G-BPEI	Boeing 757-236ER	British Airways
	G-BPEJ	Boeing 757-236	British Airways
	G-BPEK	Boeing 757-236	British Airways
	G-BPEL	PA-28-151 Warrior	R. W. Harris & A. J. Jahanfar
	G-BPEM	Cessna 150K	G. P. Robinson & R. G. Lindsey
	G-BPEO	Cessna 152	R. W. Harris & A. J. Jahanfar
	G-BPER	PA-38-112 Tomahawk	E. Midlands Flying School Ltd
	G-BPES	PA-38-112 Tomahawk	Sherwood Flying Club Ltd/Tollerton
	G-BPEW	Robinson R-22B	Trade Photographic Services Ltd
	G-BPEZ	Colt 77A balloon	A. Stace
	G-BPFA	Knight GK-2 Swallow	G. Knight & D. G. Pridham
	G-BPFB	Colt 77A balloon	S. Ingram
	G-BPFC	Mooney M.20C	J. E. Thomas
	G-BPFD	Jodel D.112	K. Manley
	G-BPFE	Lightning T.5 (XS452)	Ruanil Investments Ltd/Cranfield
	G-BPFF	Cameron DP-70 airship	Cameron Balloons Ltd
	G-BPFG	SOCATA TB.20 Trinidad	F. T. Arnold

Reg.	Type	Owner or Operator	Notes
G-BPFH	PA-28-161 Warrior II	M. H. Kleiser	
G-BPFI	PA-28-181 Archer II	R. N. Dixon-Smith & B. M. Chilvers	
G-BPFJ	Cameron 90 Can SS balloon	The Hot-Air Balloon Co Ltd	
G-BPFK	Bensen B.8MR	J. W. Birkett	
G-BPFL	Davis DA-2	C. A. Lightfoot	
G-BPFM	Aeronca 7AC Champion	Foxtrot Mike Group	
G-BPFR	Short SD3-60 Variant 100	Shorts Aircraft Financing Ltd	
G-BPFV	Boeing 767-204ER	Britannia Airways Ltd/Luton	
G-BPFX	Colt 21A balloon	The Hot-Air Balloon Co Ltd	
G-BPFY	Consolidated PBY-6A Catalina	D. W. Arnold/Biggin Hill	
G-BPFZ	Cessna 152	M. Entwistle	
G-BPGA	Mooney M.20J	Medallionair Ltd	
G-BPGB	Cessna 150J	Magnificent Obsessions Ltd	
G-BPGC	Air Command 532 Elite	E. C. E. Brown	
G-BPGD	Cameron V-65 balloon	Gone With The Wind Ltd	
G-BPGE	Cessna U.206C	The Scottish Parachute Club	
G-BPGF	Thunder Ax7-77 balloon	Mill Bros Ltd	
G-BPGH	EAA Acro Sport 2	G. M. Bradley & R. R. Harris	
G-BPGJ	Colt 31A balloon	Thunder & Colt Ltd	
G-BPGK	Aeronca 7AC Champion	T. M. Williams	
G-BPGL	PA-28 Cherokee 180	C. N. Ellerbrook	
G-BPGM	Cessna 152	Westward Airways (Land's End) Ltd	
G-BPGN	Cameron 90 Tractor SS balloon	Cameron Balloons Ltd	
G-BPGU	PA-28-181 Archer II	G. Underwood	
G-BPGV	Robinson R-22B	Featureford Ltd	
G-BPGX	SOCATA TB.9 Tampico	CB Helicopters	
G-BPGY	Cessna 150H	Three Counties Aero Engineering Ltd/ Lasham	
G-BPGZ	Cessna 150G	D. F. & B. L. Sperring	
G-BPHB	PA-28-161 Warrior II	Channel Islands Aero Holdings (Jersey) Ltd	
G-BPHD	Cameron N-42 balloon	P. J. Marshall & M. A. Clarke	
G-BPHE	PA-28-161 Warrior II	Pool Aviation Ltd/Welshpool	
G-BPHF	AB-206A JetRanger	RCR Aviation Ltd/Southampton	
G-BPHG	Robin DR.400/180	K. J. & M. B. White/Redhill	
G-BPHH	Cameron V-77 balloon	C. J. Madigan	
G-BPHJ	Cameron V-77 balloon	C. W. Brown	
G-BPHK	Whittaker MW.7	R. V. Hogg	
G-BPHL	PA-28-161 Warrior II	Teesside Flight Centre Ltd	
G-BPHM	Beech A36 Bonanza	A. P. Vonk	
G-BPHO	Taylorcraft BC-12D	J. Roberts	
G-BPHP	Taylorcraft BC-12-65	D. C. Stephens	
G-BPHR	D.H.82A Tiger Moth (A17-48)	N. Parry	
G-BPHT	Cessna 152	A. E. Kedros	
G-BPHU	Thunder Ax7-77 balloon	R. P. Waite	
G-BPHW	Cessna 140	J. A. Pothecary	
G-BPHX	Cessna 140	Ark Ltd	
G-BPHZ	M.S.505 Criquet (TA+RC)	The Aircraft Restoration Co/Duxford	
G-BPID	PA-28-161 Warrior II	P. M. Ireland	
G-BPIE	Bell 206B JetRanger	BLS Aviation Ltd/Elstree	
G-BPIF	Bensen-Parsons 2 seat	N. J. Stoneham	
G-BPIH	Rand KR-2	J. R. Rowley	
G-BPII	Denney Aerocraft Kitfox	J. K. Cross	
G-BPIJ	Brantly B.2B	R. B. Payne	
G-BPIK	PA-38-112 Tomahawk	Cumbernauld Aviation Ltd	
G-BPIL	Cessna 310B	A. L. Brown & R. A. Parsons	
G-BPIM	Cameron N-77 balloon	Thermalite Ltd	
G-BPIN	Glaser-Dirks DG.400	M. P. Seth-Smith & J. N. Stevenson	
G-BPIO	Cessna F.152 II	S. Harcourt	
G-BPIP	Slingsby T.31 Motor Cadet III	J. H. Beard	
G-BPIR	Scheibe SF.25E Super Falke	Coventry Gliding Club Ltd	
G-BPIU	PA-28-161 Warrior II	I. R. Jones & P. C. Rowlands	
G-BPIV	B.149 Bolingbroke Mk IVT (Z5722)	The Aircraft Restoration Co/Duxford	
G-BPIY	Cessna 152	Rentair Ltd	
G-BPIZ	AA-5B Tiger	D. A. Horsley	
G-BPJA	Beech 95-58 Baron	Morse Computers Ltd	
G-BPJB	Schweizer 269C	Elborne Holdings Ltd	
G-BPJC	Robinson R-22B	Getin Helicopters Ltd	
G-BPJD	SOCATA Rallye 110ST	C. G. Wheeler	
G-BPJE	Cameron A-105 balloon	J. S. Eckersley	
G-BPJF	PA-38-112 Tomahawk	Air Yorkshire Ltd	
G-BPJG	PA-18 Super Cub 150	Trent Valley Aerotowing Ltd	
G-BPJH	PA-18 Super Cub 95	P. J. Heron	

Notes	Reg.	Type	Owner or Operator
	G-BPJK	Colt 77A balloon	Akal Ltd
	G-BPJL	Cessna 152	London Flight Centre (Headcorn) Ltd
	G-BPJN	Jodel D.18	J. A. Nugent
	G-BPJO	PA-28-161 Cadet	C.S.E. Aviation Ltd/Kidlington
	G-BPJP	PA-28-161 Cadet	C.S.E. Aviation Ltd/Kidlington
	G-BPJR	PA-28-161 Cadet	C.S.E. Aviation Ltd/Kidlington
	G-BPJS	PA-28-161 Cadet	C.S.E. Aviation Ltd/Kidlington
	G-BPJU	PA-28-161 Cadet	C.S.E. Aviation Ltd/Kidlington
	G-BPJV	Taylorcraft F-21	TC Flying Group
	G-BPJW	Cessna A.150K	City Air Charter (London) Ltd/Cranfield
	G-BPJZ	Cameron O-160 balloon	M. L. Gabb
	G-BPKF	Grob G.115	Tayside Aviation Ltd/Dundee
	G-BPKH	Robinson R-22B	Findon Air Services
	G-BPKI	EAA Acro Sport 1	D. T. Kaberry
	G-BPKJ	Colt AS-80 Mk II airship	Thunder & Co Ltd
	G-BPKK	Denney Aerocraft Kitfox	L. A. James
	G-BPKL	Mooney M.20J	Astraflight Ltd
	G-BPKM	PA-28-161 Warrior II	M. J. Greasby
	G-BPKN	Colt AS-80 Mk II airship	C. Turnbull
	G-BPKO	Cessna 140	I. R. March
	G-BPKR	PA-28-151 Warrior	R. R. Harris
	G-BPLE	Cameron A-160 balloon	Balloons & Airships International Ltd
	G-BPLF	Cameron V-77 balloon	C. L. Luffingham
	G-BPLG	Morane-Saulnier M.S.317	R. A. Anderson
	G-BPLH	Jodel DR.1051	M. N. King
	G-BPLI	Colt 77A balloon	Yanin International Ltd
	G-BPLJ	Colt 90A balloon	Thunder & Colt Ltd
	G-BPLM	AIA Stampe SV-4C	C. J. Jesson/Redhill
	G-BPLU	Thunder Ax10-160 balloon	Subsearch Ltd
	G-BPLV	Cameron V-77 balloon	Jessops (Tailors) Ltd
	G-BPLY	Pitts S-2B Special	M. Mountstephen
	G-BPLZ	Hughes 369HS	S. G. Good
	G-BPMB	Maule M5-235C Lunar Rocket	A. P. Le Coyte & A. D. Massey
	G-BPMC	Air Command 503 Commander	M. A. Cheshire
	G-BPMD	Boeing Stearman A.75L-3 (320)	M. G. Saunders/White Waltham
	G-BPME	Cessna 152	London Flight Centre (Headcorn) Ltd
	G-BPMF	PA-28-151 Warrior	L. & A. Hill
	G-BPMG	Bensen B.8MR	P. Doherty
	G-BPMH	Schempp-Hirth Nimbus 3DM	Southern Sailplanes
	G-BPMI	Colt 56A balloon	Thunder & Colt Ltd
	G-BPMJ	Colt 56A balloon	Thunder & Colt Ltd
	G-BPML	Cessna 172M	J. Birnie/Sandown
	G-BPMM	Champion 7ECA Citabria	D. M. Griffiths
	G-BPMN	Aerocar Super Coot Model A	P. M. Napp
	G-BPMO	Cessna 150M	S. L. Mills
	G-BPMP	Douglas C-47A-50-DL (224211)	Atlantic Air Transport Ltd/Coventry
	G-BPMR	PA-28-161 Warrior II	McIntyre Aviation/Staverton
	G-BPMU	Nord 3202B	D. Fenwick (G-BIZJ)
	G-BPMV	PA-28-161 Warrior II	J. W. E. P. Donald
	G-BPMW	QAC Quickie Q.2	C. W. Tattersall (G-OICI/G-OGKN)
	G-BPMX	ARV Super 2	G-BPMX Flying Group
	G-BPMY	Cameron A-120 balloon	British School of Ballooning
	G-BPNA	Cessna 150L	C. M. Vlieland-Boddy/Compton Abbas
	G-BPNC	Rotorway Executive	S. J. Hanson
	G-BPNF	Robinson R-22B	K. N. Tolley
	G-BPNG	Bell 206B JetRanger 2	Tindon Ltd (G-ORTC)
	G-BPNI	Robinson R-22B	Arrowbury Ltd
	G-BPNL	QAC Quickie Q.2	J. Catley
	G-BPNN	Montgomerie-Bensen B.8MR	M. E. Vahdat
	G-BPNO	Zlin Z.326 Trener Master	J. A. S. Bailey & S. T. Logan
	G-BPNT	BAe 146-300	Palmair Flightline/Bournemouth
	G-BPNU	Thunder Ax7-77 balloon	J. Fenton
	G-BPNZ	Boeing 737-4Q8	British Airways
	G-BPOA	Gloster Meteor T.7 (WF877)	Aces High Ltd/North Weald
	G-BPOB	Sopwith Camel F.1 (replica) (B2458)	Bianchi Aviation Film Services Ltd/ Booker
	G-BPOD	Stolp SA.300 Starduster Too	P. Howard & R. Boswell
	G-BPOE	Colt 77A balloon	Albatross Aviation Ltd
	G-BPOL	Pietenpol Air Camper	G. W. Postance
	G-BPOM	PA-28-161 Warrior II	McIntyre Aviation/Staverton
	G-BPON	PA-34-200T Seneca II	London Flight Centre Air Charter Ltd
	G-BPOO	Montgomerie-Bensen B.8MR	M. E. Vahdat
	G-BPOR	Bell 206B JetRanger 2	Thetford Compactors Finance Ltd

Reg.	Type	Owner or Operator	Notes
G-BPOS	Cessna 150M	Lanx Engineering Ltd	
G-BPOT	PA-28-181 Archer II	Cumbernauld Aviation Ltd	
G-BPOU	Luscombe 8A Silvaire	E. T. Wicks	
G-BPOV	Cameron 90 Magazine SS balloon	Forbes Europe Inc/France	
G-BPOX	Enstrom 280C Shark	J. Evans	
G-BPOY	Enstrom F-28A	M. & P. Food Products Ltd	
G-BPOZ	Enstrom F-28A	M. & P. Food Products Ltd	
G-BPPA	Cameron O-65 balloon	Rix Petroleum Ltd	
G-BPPB	PA-34-220T Seneca III	A. Smith	
G-BPPD	PA-38-112 Tomahawk	AT Aviation Ltd/Cardiff	
G-BPPE	PA-38-112 Tomahawk	Norwich School of Flying	
G-BPPF	PA-38-112 Tomahawk	R. D. Preston/Wellesbourne	
G-BPPG	PA-38-112 Tomahawk	AT Aviation Ltd/Cardiff	
G-BPPI	Colt 180A balloon	A. G. E. Faulkner	
G-BPPJ	Cameron A-180 Balloon	H. R. Evans	
G-BPPK	PA-28-151 Warrior	Balgold Ltd	
G-BPPL	Enstrom F-28A	M. & P. Food Products Ltd	
G-BPPM	Beech B200 Super King Air	Gama Aviation Ltd/Fairoaks	
G-BPPN	Cessna F.182Q	Hunt Norris Ltd	
G-BPPO	Luscombe 8A Silvaire	C. C. Lovell	
G-BPPP	Cameron V-77 balloon	Sarnia Balloon Group	
G-BPPR	Air Command 532 Elite	T. D. Inch	
G-BPPS	Mudry CAARP CAP.21	J. M. & E. M. Wicks/Earls Colne	
G-BPPU	Air Command 532 Elite	J. Hough	
G-BPPW	Schweizer 269C	K. W. Harding	
G-BPPY	Hughes 269B	R. W. Carr & C. F. Collier	
G-BPPZ	Taylorcraft BC-12D	Zulu Warriors Flying Group	
G-BPRA	Aeronca 11AC Chief	K. Handley	
G-BPRC	Cameron Elephant SS balloon	Cameron Balloons Ltd	
G-BPRD	Pitts S-1C Special	S. M. Trickey	
G-BPRJ	AS.355F-1 Twin Squirrel	G. Greenall	
G-BPRL	AS.355F-1 Twin Squirrel	Yorkshire Helicopters/Leeds	
G-BPRM	Cessna F.172L	A. J. Moseley (G-AZKG)	
G-BPRN	PA-28-161 Warrior II	Air Navigation & Trading Co Ltd/Blackpool	
G-BPRO	Cessna A.150K	Armphase Ltd	
G-BPRP	Cessna 150E	P. G. Powter/Shoreham	
G-BPRR	Rand KR-2	M. W. Albery	
G-BPRS	Air Command 532 Elite	B. K. Snoxall	
G-BPRT	Piel CP.328	N. Reddish	
G-BPRV	PA-28-161 Warrior II	AT Aviation Ltd/Cardiff	
G-BPRX	Aeronca 11AC Chief	R. D. Ward & J. M. Taylor	
G-BPRY	PA-28-161 Warrior II	B. McIntyre	
G-BPRZ	Robinson R-22A	Bristol Rotary Training Ltd	
G-BPSA	Luscombe 8A Silvaire	K. P. Gorman/Staverton	
G-BPSB	Air Command 532 Elite	D. K. Duckworth	
G-BPSE	NA AT-6D Harvard (483009)	Aces High Ltd/North Weald	
G-BPSH	Cameron V-77 balloon	P. G. Hossack	
G-BPSI	Thunder Ax10-160 balloon	Airborne Adventures Ltd	
G-BPSJ	Thunder Ax6-56 balloon	Capricorn Balloons Ltd	
G-BPSK	Montgomerie-Bensen B.8M	R. J. Mann	
G-BPSL	Cessna 177	I. P. Burnett & ptnrs/White Waltham	
G-BPSO	Cameron N-90 balloon	L. A. Sadler & K. J. Holt	
G-BPSP	Cameron 90 Ship SS balloon	Forbes Europe Inc/France	
G-BPSR	Cameron V-77 balloon	K. J. A. Maxwell	
G-BPSS	Cameron A-120 balloon	J. P. Clifford	
G-BPSV	Cessna F.406 Caravan II	Directflight Ltd/Norwich	
G-BPSY	Grob G.115	Soaring (Oxford) Ltd	
G-BPSZ	Cameron N-180 balloon	The Balloon Club Ltd	
G-BPTA	Stinson 108-2	D. N. H. Martin/Booker	
G-BPTB	Boeing Stearman A.75N1 (442)	Aero Vintage Ltd	
G-BPTC	Taylorcraft BC-12D	J. R. Surbey	
G-BPTD	Cameron V-77 balloon	J. Lippett	
G-BPTE	PA-28-181 Archer II	London Flight Centre (Stansted) Ltd	
G-BPTF	Cessna 152	London Flight Centre (Stansted) Ltd	
G-BPTG	R. Commander 112TC	G. J. Deadman	
G-BPTH	Air Command 532 Elite	R. Wheeler	
G-BPTI	SOCATA TB.20 Trinidad	Lyndon Scaffolding Hire Ltd/Birmingham	
G-BPTL	Cessna 172N	Cleveland Flying School Ltd/Teesside	
G-BPTM	Pitts S-1T Special	RPM Aviation Ltd	
G-BPTO	Zenith CH.200-AA	B. Philips	
G-BPTP	Robinson R-22	Sarahs Lakeland Fudge	
G-BPTS	C.A.S.A 1.131E Jungmann	Aerobatic Displays Ltd/Booker	
G-BPTT	Robin DR.400/120	The Cotswold Aero Club Ltd/Staverton	

Notes	Reg.	Type	Owner or Operator
	G-BPTU	Cessna 152	Flyteam Aviation Ltd
	G-BPTV	Bensen B.8	L. Chiappi
	G-BPTW	Cameron A-160 balloon	Newbury Ballooning Co Ltd
	G-BPTX	Cameron O-120 balloon	R. W. Keron
	G-BPTZ	Robinson R-22B	J. Lucketti
	G-BPUA	EAA P-2 Biplane	G. H. Cork
	G-BPUB	Cameron V-31 balloon	M. T. Evans
	G-BPUC	QAC Quickie Q.200	R. Wells
	G-BPUD	Ryan PT-22 (I-492)	R. I. Warman
	G-BPUE	Air Command 532 Elite	R. A. Fazackerley
	G-BPUF	Thunder Ax6-56Z balloon	R. C. & M. A. Trimble (G-BHRL)
	G-BPUG	Air Command 532 Elite	T. A. Holmes
	G-BPUH	Cameron A-180 balloon	Golf Centres Balloons Ltd
	G-BPUI	Air Command 532 Elite	M. A. Turner
	G-BPUJ	Cameron N-90 balloon	Touch Panel Products Ltd
	G-BPUL	PA-18 Super Cub 150	Crissair Ltd
	G-BPUM	Cessna R.182RG	R. H. Stradling
	G-BPUP	Whittaker MW-7	J. H. Beard
	G-BPUR	Piper J-3L-65 Cub	J3 Group
	G-BPUS	Rans S.9	P. M. Shipman
	G-BPUU	Cessna 140	A. R. Lansdown/Swansea
	G-BPUW	Colt 90A balloon	Huntair Ltd
	G-BPUX	Cessna 150J	H. H. Goodman
	G-BPUY	Cessna 150K	M. Hewison/Luton
	G-BPVA	Cessna 172F	J. E. Stevens
	G-BPVC	Cameron V-77 balloon	A. R. Noble
	G-BPVE	Bleriot 1909 replica	Bianchi Aviation Film Services Ltd/Booker
	G-BPVH	Cub Aircraft J-3C-65 Prospector	D. E. Cooper-Maguire
	G-BPVI	PA-32R-301 Saratoga SP	J. D. Macpherson
	G-BPVJ	Cessna 152	D. C. & V. R. Fieldhouse
	G-BPVK	Varga 2150A Kachina	H. W. Hall
	G-BPVM	Cameron V-77 balloon	Royal Engineers Balloon Club
	G-BPVN	PA-32R-301T Turbo Saratoga SP	Hero Aviation/Stapleford
	G-BPVO	Cassutt Racer IIIM	Lanx Engineering Ltd
	G-BPVT	Thunder Ax7-65 balloon	Anglia Balloon School Ltd
	G-BPVU	Thunder Ax7-77 balloon	J. C. K. Robinson
	G-BPVW	C.A.S.A. 1.131E Jungmann	S. A. W. Becker/Goodwood
	G-BPVX	Cassutt Racer IIIM	A. A. A. White/Manchester
	G-BPVY	Cessna 172D	R. P. Crosier
	G-BPVZ	Luscombe 8E Silvaire	W. E. Gillham & P. Ryman
	G-BPWA	PA-28-161 Warrior II	Mid America UK Ltd
	G-BPWC	Cameron V-77 balloon	H. B. Roberts
	G-BPWD	Cessna 120	Peregrine Flying Group
	G-BPWE	PA-28-161 Warrior II	AT Aviation Ltd/Cardiff
	G-BPWF	PA-28 Cherokee 140 ★	(static display)/1244 Sqdn ATC/Swindon
	G-BPWG	Cessna 150M	G. & S. A. Jones
	G-BPWI	Bell 206B JetRanger 2	RCR Aviation Ltd/Thruxton
	G-BPWK	Sportavia Fournier RF-5B	S. L. Reed
	G-BPWM	Cessna 150L	J. P. Walter
	G-BPWN	Cessna 150L	Premier Plane Leasing Co Ltd
	G-BPWP	Rutan LongEz	J. F. O'Hara & A. J. Voyle
	G-BPWR	Cessna R.172K	A. M. Skelton
	G-BPWS	Cessna 172P	Holmes Rentals
	G-BPWT	Cameron DG-19 airship	Airspace Outdoor Advertising Ltd
	G-BPWV	Colt 56A balloon	W. D. Young
	G-BPWW	Piaggio FWP.149D	I. H. Leach-Allen
	G-BPWX	Montgomerie Bensen B.8MR	M. S. Lloyd
	G-BPWY	Isaacs Fury II	R. J. Knights
	G-BPWZ	PA-28-161 Warrior II	Hamilton Compass Aviation Ltd
	G-BPXA	PA-28-181 Archer II	Cherokee Flying Group/Netherthorpe
	G-BPXB	Glaser-Dirks DG.400	G. S. Griffiths
	G-BPXE	Enstrom 280C Shark	P. Lancaster
	G-BPXF	Cameron V-65 balloon	D. Pascall
	G-BPXG	Colt 42A balloon	Cooper Group Ltd
	G-BPXH	Colt 17A balloon	Gone With The Wind Ltd
	G-BPXJ	PA-28RT-201T Turbo Arrow IV	K. M. Hollamby/Biggin Hill
	G-BPXX	PA-34-200T Seneca II	Hockstar Ltd
	G-BPXY	Aeronca 11AC Chief	S. Hawksworth
	G-BPXZ	Cameron V-77 balloon	British School of Ballooning
	G-BPYA	Rotorway Executive	Orchard Engineering Co Ltd
	G-BPYB	Air Command 532 Elite	P. J. Houtman
	G-BPYC	Cessna 310R	Air Service Training Ltd/Perth
	G-BPYH	Robinson R-22B	Status Investments Ltd

Reg.	Type	Owner or Operator	Notes
G-BPYI	Cameron O-77 balloon	MacLeod Garage Ltd	
G-BPYJ	Wittman W.8 Tailwind	J. Dixon	
G-BPYK	Thunder Ax7-77 balloon	A. R. Swinnerton	
G-BPYL	Hughes 369D	Aly Aviation Ltd/Henstridge	
G-BPYN	Piper J-3C-65 Cub	The Aquila Group/White Waltham	
G-BPYO	PA-28-181 Archer II	Premier Flight Services Ltd	
G-BPYP	Cameron O-105 balloon	C. N. Marshall	
G-BPYR	PA-31-310 Turbo Navajo	Multi Ltd (G-ECMA)	
G-BPYS	Cameron O-77 balloon	D. J. Goldsmith	
G-BPYT	Cameron V-77 balloon	M. W. Talbot	
G-BPYV	Cameron V-77 balloon	M. E. Weston	
G-BPYW	Air Command 532 Elite	W. V. Tatters	
G-BPYX	Robinson R-22B	Glentworth Scottish Farms Ltd	
G-BPYY	Cameron A-180 balloon	G. D. Fitzpatrick	
G-BPYZ	Thunder Ax7-77 balloon	J. E. Astall	
G-BPZA	Luscombe 8A Silvaire	T. P. W. Hyde	
G-BPZB	Cessna 120	C. & M. A. Grime	
G-BPZC	Luscombe 8A Silvaire	C. C. & J. M. Lovell	
G-BPZD	SNCAN NC.858S	G. Richards	
G-BPZE	Luscombe 8E Silvaire	WFG Luscombe Associates	
G-BPZF	PA-46-310P Malibu	Jenrick Engineering Services Ltd	
G-BPZG	PA-28R-201T Turbo Arrow III	Salborne Farms Ltd	
G-BPZI	Christen Eagle II	S. D. Quigley	
G-BPZK	Cameron O-120 balloon	D. L. Smith	
G-BPZM	PA-28RT-201 Arrow IV	J. H. Kimber (G-ROYW/G-CRTI)	
G-BPZO	Cameron N-90 balloon	Seaward PLC	
G-BPZP	Robin DR.400/180R	Tatenhill Aviation	
G-BPZS	Colt 105A balloon	The Balloon Club of GB Ltd	
G-BPZT	Cameron N-90 balloon	Peter Lane Transport Ltd	
G-BPZU	Scheibe SF.25C Falke	G-BPZU Group	
G-BPZW	SOCATA TB.20 Trinidad	Air Touring Services Ltd/Biggin Hill	
G-BPZX	Cessna 152	Woodward & Co (Sheffield) Ltd	
G-BPZY	Pitts S-1C Special	J. S. Mitchell	
G-BPZZ	Thunder Ax8-105 balloon	Breachwood Motors Ltd	
G-BRAA	Pitts S-1C Special	C. Davidson	
G-BRAB	BAe 146-300	British World Airlines Ltd/Stansted	
G-BRAE	Colt 69A balloon	Jentime Ltd	
G-BRAF	V.S.394 Spitfire FR.XVIII (SM969)	D. W. Arnold/Biggin Hill	
G-BRAJ	Cameron V-77 balloon	H. R. Evans	
G-BRAK	Cessna 172N	C. Docketty	
G-BRAL	G.159 Gulfstream 1	Ford Motor Co Ltd/Stansted	
G-BRAM	Mikoyan MiG-21PF (503)	Universal Aviation Group	
G-BRAP	Thermal Aircraft 104	Thermal Aircraft	
G-BRAR	Aeronca 7AC Champion	C. D. Ward	
G-BRAV	PA-23 Aztec 250E	Hartfield Aviation Ltd (G-BBCM)	
G-BRAW	Pitts S-1 Special	P. G. Bond & P. B. Hunter	
G-BRAX	Payne Knight Twister 85B	R. Earl	
G-BRBA	PA-28-161 Warrior II	Hendafern Ltd	
G-BRBB	PA-28-161 Warrior II	D. P. Hughes	
G-BRBC	NA T-6G Texan	A. P. Murphy	
G-BRBD	PA-28-151 Warrior	B. E. Simpson & C. R. Hughes	
G-BRBE	PA-28-161 Warrior II	Solo Services Ltd/Shoreham	
G-BRBF	Cessna 152	Cumbria Aero Club/Carlisle	
G-BRBG	PA-28 Cherokee 180	Anderson MacArthur & Co	
G-BRBH	Cessna 150H	P. J. Webb/Elstree	
G-BRBI	Cessna 172N	D. T. Searchfield/Blackbushe	
G-BRBJ	Cessna 172M	L. C. MacKnight/Elstree	
G-BRBK	Robin DR.400/180	R. Kemp	
G-BRBL	Robin DR.400/180	Crown Export Services	
G-BRBM	Robin DR.400/180	R. W. Davies/Headcorn	
G-BRBN	Pitts S-1S Special	D. R. Evans	
G-BRBO	Cameron V-77 balloon	Matrix Computers Ltd	
G-BRBP	Cessna 152	Staverton Flying Services Ltd	
G-BRBR	Cameron V-77 balloon	1066 Balloon Group	
G-BRBS	Bensen B.8M	J. Simpson	
G-BRBT	Trotter Ax3-20 balloon	R. M. Trotter	
G-BRBU	Colt 17A balloon	Airship & Balloon Co Ltd	
G-BRBV	Piper J-4A Cub Coupé	J. Schonburg	
G-BRBW	PA-28 Cherokee 140	Cherokee Cruiser Aircraft Group	
G-BRBX	PA-28-181 Archer II	M. J. Ireland	
G-BRBY	Robinson R-22B	Arden Consultancy Ltd	
G-BRBZ	Beech 400 Beechjet	Bass PLC	

Notes	Reg.	Type	Owner or Operator
	G-BRCA	Jodel D.112	D. I. Walker & W. H. Sherlock
	G-BRCC	Cessna 152	Falcon Flying Services/Biggin Hill
	G-BRCD	Cessna A.152	D. E. Simmons/Shoreham
	G-BRCE	Pitts S-1C Special	R. O. Rogers
	G-BRCF	Montgomerie-Bensen B.8MR	J. S. Walton
	G-BRCG	Grob G.109	Oxfordshire Sportflying Ltd/Enstone
	G-BRCI	Pitts S-1 Special	R. N. Crosland
	G-BRCJ	Cameron NS-20 balloon	Cameron Balloons Ltd
	G-BRCM	Cessna 172L	S. G. E. Plessis & D. C. C. Handley
	G-BRCO	Cameron NS-20 balloon	M. Davies
	G-BRCP	Enstrom F-28F	Southern Air Ltd/Shoreham
	G-BRCR	Cameron V-77 balloon	E. E. Clark
	G-BRCT	Denney Aerocraft Kitfox	Wessex Aviation & Transport Ltd
	G-BRCV	Aeronca 7AC Champion	A. P. Wellings/Sandown
	G-BRCW	Aeronca 11AC Chief	R. B. McComish
	G-BRDB	Zenair CH.701 STOL	D. L. Bowtell
	G-BRDC	Thunder Ax7-77 balloon	N. J. Morley & D. M. Levene
	G-BRDD	Avions Mudry CAP.10B	R. D. Dickson/Gamston
	G-BRDE	Thunder Ax7-77 balloon	C. C. Brash
	G-BRDF	PA-28-161 Warrior II	White Waltham Airfield Ltd
	G-BRDG	PA-28-161 Warrior II	White Waltham Airfield Ltd
	G-BRDJ	Luscombe 8A Silvaire	C. C. & J. M. Lovell
	G-BRDL	Bell 206B JetRanger	Clyde Helicopters Ltd
	G-BRDM	PA-28-161 Warrior II	White Waltham Airfield Ltd
	G-BRDN	M.S.880B Rallye Club	C. R. Owen
	G-BRDO	Cessna 177B	Cardinal Group
	G-BRDP	Colt Jumbo SS balloon	Airship & Balloon Co Ltd
	G-BRDS	Colt Flying Coke Can SS balloon	Thunder & Colt Ltd
	G-BRDT	Cameron DP-70 airship	M. M. Cobbold
	G-BRDU	Cameron DG-14 airship	Cameron Balloons Ltd
	G-BRDV	Viking Wood Products Spitfire Prototype replica (K5054)	C. Du Cros
	G-BRDW	PA-24 Comanche 180	I. P. Gibson/Switzerland
	G-BREA	Bensen B.8MR	R. Firth
	G-BREB	Piper J-3C-65 Cub	C. L. H. Parr & I. Watts
	G-BREE	Whittaker MW.7	R. H. Y. Farrer
	G-BREH	Cameron V-65 balloon	P. A. & N. J. Foot
	G-BREK	Piper J-3C-65 Cub	C. L. H. Parr & I. Watts
	G-BREL	Cameron O-77 balloon	A. J. Moore & D. J. Green
	G-BREM	Air Command 532 Elite	Modern Air
	G-BREP	PA-28RT-201 Arrow IV	P. G. McQuaid
	G-BRER	Aeronca 7AC Champion	D. & S. M. Jerwood
	G-BREU	Montgomerie-Bensen B.8	M. A. Hayward
	G-BREX	Cameron O-84 balloon	Ovolo Ltd
	G-BREY	Taylorcraft BC-12D	BREY Group
	G-BRFA	PA-31-350 Navajo Chieftain	Sunseeker Leisure PLC (G-BREW)
	G-BRFB	Rutan LongEz	R. A. Gardiner
	G-BRFC	P.57 Sea Prince T.1 (WP321)	Rural Naval Air Service/Bourn
	G-BRFE	Cameron V-77 balloon	N. J. Appleton
	G-BRFF	Colt 90A balloon	Amber Valley Aviation
	G-BRFH	Colt 90A balloon	Polydron UK Ltd
	G-BRFI	Aeronca 7DC Champion	I. J. Boyd & D. J. McCooke
	G-BRFJ	Aeronca 11AC Chief	C. M. G. Ellis
	G-BRFK	Colt Flying Drinks Can SS balloon	Thunder & Colt Ltd
	G-BRFL	PA-38-112 Tomahawk	Technology & Marketing Ltd
	G-BRFM	PA-28-161 Warrior II	G. C. J. Moffatt & Co Ltd
	G-BRFN	PA-38-112 Tomahawk	Technology & Marketing Ltd
	G-BRFO	Cameron V-77 balloon	Hedge Hoppers Balloon Group
	G-BRFP	Schweizer 269C	Daedalus Aviation Ltd
	G-BRFR	Cameron N-105 balloon	Flying Pictures (Balloons) Ltd
	G-BRFS	Cameron N-90 balloon	Flying Pictures (Balloons) Ltd
	G-BRFU	Fouga CM.170 Magister (MT-11)	P. F. A. Hoar/Cranfield
	G-BRFW	Montgomerie-Bensen B.8 Two Seat	J. M. Montgomerie
	G-BRFX	Pazmany PL.4A	D. E. Hills
	G-BRGD	Cameron O-84 balloon	J. R. H. & M. A. Ashworth
	G-BRGE	Cameron N-90 balloon	Oakfield Farm Products Ltd
	G-BRGF	Luscombe 8E Silvaire	M. H. Wood
	G-BRGG	Luscombe 8A Silvaire	M. P. & V. H. Weatherby
	G-BRGI	PA-28 Cherokee 180	Golf India Aviation Ltd
	G-BRGN	BAe Jetstream 3102	British Aerospace PLC (G-BLHC)/Prestwick
	G-BRGO	Air Command 532 Elite	D. A. Wood

Reg.	Type	Owner or Operator	Notes
G-BRGP	Colt Flying Stork SS balloon	Thunder & Colt Ltd	
G-BRGT	PA-32 Cherokee Six 260	M. J. Smith & P. Cowley	
G-BRGW	GY-201 Minicab	R. G. White	
G-BRGX	Rotorway Executive	D. W. J. Lee	
G-BRHA	PA-32RT-300 Lance II	M. J. Sparshatt (Holdings) Ltd	
G-BRHB	Boeing Stearman B.75N1	D. Calabritto	
G-BRHC	Cameron V-77 balloon	Golf Centres Balloons Ltd	
G-BRHE	Piper J-3C-65 Cub	S. M. Kearney	
G-BRHG	Colt 90A balloon	Bath University Students Union	
G-BRHJ	PA-34-200T Seneca II	Draycott Seneca Group	
G-BRHL	Montgomerie-Bensen B.8M	K. Simpkins	
G-BRHM	Bensen B.8M	P. M. Crook	
G-BRHN	Robinson R-22B	Barhale Surveying Ltd	
G-BRHO	PA-34-200 Seneca	D. A. Lewis/Luton	
G-BRHP	Aeronca O-58B Grasshopper (31923)	J. G. Townsend	
G-BRHR	PA-38-112 Tomahawk	Hamilton Compass Aviation Ltd	
G-BRHS	PA-38-112 Tomahawk	Hamilton Compass Aviation Ltd	
G-BRHT	PA-38-112 Tomahawk	Hamilton Compass Aviation Ltd	
G-BRHU	Montgomerie-Bensen B.8MR	G. L. & S. R. Moon	
G-BRHW	D.H.82A Tiger Moth	P. J. & A. J. Borsberry	
G-BRHX	Luscombe 8E Silvaire	J. Lakin	
G-BRHY	Luscombe 8E Silvaire	D. Lofts & A. R. W. Taylor	
G-BRHZ	Stephens Akro Astro 235	N. M. Bloom & ptnrs	
G-BRIA	Cessna 310L	R. C. Pugsley	
G-BRIB	Cameron N-77 balloon	D. Stitt	
G-BRIE	Cameron N-77 balloon	Vokins Estates Ltd	
G-BRIF	Boeing 767-204ER	Britannia Airways Ltd *Horatio Nelson*	
G-BRIG	Boeing 767-204ER	Britannia Airways Ltd	
G-BRIH	Taylorcraft BC-12D	G. J. Taylor	
G-BRII	Zenair CH.600 Zodiac	A. C. Bowdrey	
G-BRIJ	Taylorcraft F-19	M. Beamand & K. E. Ballington	
G-BRIK	T.66 Nipper 3	C. W. R. Piper	
G-BRIL	Piper J-5A Cub Cruiser	R. J. Baron & P. L. Jobes	
G-BRIM	Cameron O-160 balloon	Golf Centres Balloons Ltd	
G-BRIN	SOCATA TB.20 Trinidad	Booth Plant & Equipment Ltd	
G-BRIO	Turner Super T-40A	D. McIntyre	
G-BRIR	Cameron V-56 balloon	Century Factors Ltd	
G-BRIS	Steen Skybolt	Eriskay Atlantic Ltd	
G-BRIV	SOCATA TB.9 Tampico	CB Group Ltd/Biggin Hill	
G-BRIW	Hughes 269C	March Helicopters Ltd	
G-BRIY	Taylorcraft DF-65 (42-58678)	J. A. Rollason/North Weald	
G-BRIZ	D.31 Turbulent	M. C. Hunt	
G-BRJA	Luscombe 8A Silvaire	C. W. Thirtle	
G-BRJB	Zenair CH.600 Zodiac	E. G. Brown	
G-BRJC	Cessna 120	One Twenty Group	
G-BRJI	Boeing 757-236	Rednall Ltd	
G-BRJK	Luscombe 8A Silvaire	C. J. L. Peat	
G-BRJL	PA-15 Vagabond	D. D. Saint	
G-BRJM	Cameron A-210 balloon	R. S. Hunjan	
G-BRJN	Pitts S-1C Special	G-BRJN Group	
G-BRJR	PA-38-112 Tomahawk	Chester Aviation Ltd	
G-BRJT	Cessna 150H	Technology & Marketing Ltd	
G-BRJU	PA-28-151 Warrior	C.S.E. Aviation Ltd/Kidlington	
G-BRJV	PA-28-161 Cadet	Newcastle-upon-Tyne Aero Club Ltd	
G-BRJW	Bellanca 7GCBC Citabria	H. W. Weston/Staverton	
G-BRJX	Rand KR-2	J. M. Mortimer	
G-BRJY	Rand KR-2	A. J. Wilkinson & R. P. H. Hancock	
G-BRKA	Luscombe 8F Silvaire	C. H. J. Andrews	
G-BRKC	J/1 Autocrat	J. W. Conlon	
G-BRKD	Piaggio FWP.149D	Operation Ability Ltd	
G-BRKE	Hawker Sea Hurricane XIIA (BW853)	AJD Engineering Ltd	
G-BRKH	PA-28-236 Dakota	P. A. Wright	
G-BRKJ	Stoddard-Hamilton Glasair III	R. F. E. Simard	
G-BRKL	Cameron H-34 balloon	Cameron Balloons Ltd	
G-BRKN	Robinson R-22 Mariner	P. M. Webber/Greece	
G-BRKO	Oldfield Baby Great Lakes	C. Wren	
G-BRKP	Colt 31A balloon	Bavarian Balloon Co Ltd	
G-BRKR	Cessna 182R	A. R. D. Brooker	
G-BRKS	Air Command 532 Elite	G. Sandercock	
G-BRKW	Cameron V-77 balloon	T. J. Parker	
G-BRKX	Air Command 532 Elite	K. Davis	

Notes	Reg.	Type	Owner or Operator
	G-BRKY	Viking Dragonfly Mk II	G. D. Price
	G-BRKZ	Air Command 532 Elite	S. C. West
	G-BRLB	Air Command 532 Elite	D. Wilson
	G-BRLC	Thunder Ax7-77 balloon	Fuji Photo Film (UK) Ltd
	G-BRLE	PA-28-181 Archer II	Charles Clowes (Estates) Co Ltd
	G-BRLF	Campbell Cricket	D. Wood
	G-BRLG	PA-28RT-201T Turbo Arrow IV	Specialist Welding & Metallurgical Services Ltd
	G-BRLH	Air Command 532 Elite	Childs Garages (Sherborne) Ltd
	G-BRLI	Piper J-5A Cub Cruiser	A. E. Poulson
	G-BRLJ	Evans VP-2	R. L. Jones
	G-BRLK	Air Command 532 Elite	G. L. Hunt
	G-BRLL	Cameron A-105 balloon	Adventure Flights Ltd
	G-BRLM	BAe 146-100	British Aerospace PLC
	G-BRLO	PA-38-112 Tomahawk	Scotia Safari Ltd/Prestwick
	G-BRLP	PA-38-112 Tomahawk	Lightstrong Ltd
	G-BRLR	Cessna 150G	D. C. Maxwell
	G-BRLS	Thunder Ax7-77 balloon	E. C. Meek
	G-BRLT	Colt 77A balloon	D. Bareford
	G-BRLU	Cameron H-24 balloon	Airspace Outdoor Advertising Ltd
	G-BRLV	CCF Harvard IV (93542)	B. C. Abela
	G-BRLW	Cessna 150M	Visionkind Ltd
	G-BRLX	Cameron N-77 balloon	National Power
	G-BRLY	BAe ATP	British Airways
	G-BRMA	W.S.51 Dragonfly HR.5 (WG718) ★	International Helicopter Museum/ Weston-s-Mare
	G-BRMB	B.192 Belvedere HC.1 (XG452) ★	International Helicopter Museum/ Weston-s-Mare
	G-BRMD	Cameron O-160 balloon	Ballooning Endeavours Ltd
	G-BRME	PA-28-181 Archer II	S. Edgar
	G-BRMF	Bell 206B JetRanger 3	Heliwork Services Ltd/Thruxton
	G-BRMG	V.S.384 Seafire XVII (SX336)	P. J. Woods
	G-BRMH	Bell 206B JetRanger 2	RCR Aviation Ltd (G-BBUX)
	G-BRMI	Cameron V-65 balloon	M. Davies
	G-BRMJ	PA-38-112 Tomahawk	P. H. Rogers/Coventry
	G-BRML	PA-38-112 Tomahawk	P. H. Rogers/Coventry
	G-BRMM	Air Command 532 Elite	R. de Serville
	G-BRMN	Thunder Ax7-77 balloon	G. Restell & R. Higham
	G-BRMS	PA-28RT-201 Arrow IV	Fleetbridge Ltd
	G-BRMT	Cameron V-31 balloon	R. M. Trotter & K. L. Heron
	G-BRMU	Cameron V-77 balloon	K. J. & G. R. Ibbotson
	G-BRMV	Cameron O-77 balloon	P. D. Griffiths
	G-BRMW	Whittaker MW.7	M. R. Grunwell
	G-BRMY	Short SD3-60	Short Bros PLC/Belfast City
	G-BRNC	Cessna 150M	P. & B. Investment Holdings (Grimsby) Ltd
	G-BRND	Cessna 152	A. C. Roles
	G-BRNE	Cessna 152	Aerohire Ltd/Halfpenny Green
	G-BRNJ	PA-38-112 Tomahawk	S. Eddison
	G-BRNK	Cessna 152	Sheffield Aero Club Ltd/Netherthorpe
	G-BRNM	Chichester-Miles Leopard	Chichester-Miles Consultants Ltd
	G-BRNN	Cessna 152	Sheffield Aero Club Ltd/Netherthorpe
	G-BRNP	Rotorway Executive	C. A. Laycock
	G-BRNR	Schweizer 269C	C.S.E. Aviation Ltd/Kidlington
	G-BRNS	Avid Flyer	Ladel Ltd
	G-BRNT	Robin DR.400/180	M. J. Cowham
	G-BRNU	Robin DR.400/180	Pranconic Ltd
	G-BRNV	PA-28-181 Archer II	Valley Flying Co Ltd
	G-BRNW	Cameron V-77 balloon	N. Robertson & G. Smith
	G-BRNX	PA-22 Tri-Pacer 150	R. S. Tomlinson & B. Yager
	G-BRNY	Thunder Ax6-56A balloon	P. A. Clent
	G-BRNZ	PA-32 Cherokee Six 300B	IML Aviation Ltd
	G-BROB	Cameron V-77 balloon	R. W. Richardson
	G-BROE	Cameron N-65 balloon	R. H. Sanderson
	G-BROF	Air Command 532 Elite	M. J. Hoskins
	G-BROG	Cameron V-65 balloon	R. Kunert
	G-BROH	Cameron O-90 balloon	A. & W. Derbyshire
	G-BROI	CFM Streak Shadow Srs SA	G. W. Rowbotham
	G-BROJ	Colt 31A balloon	Airship & Balloon Co Ltd
	G-BROL	Colt AS-80 Mk II airship	Wellfarrow Ltd
	G-BROM	ICA IS-282MA	Kent Motor Gliding & Soaring Centre
	G-BROO	Luscombe 8A Silvaire	Bedwell Hey Flying Group
	G-BROP	Van's RV-4	K. E. Armstrong
	G-BROR	Piper J-3C-65 Cub	White Hart Flying Group

Reg.	Type	Owner or Operator	Notes
G-BROV	Colt 105A balloon	Thunder & Colt Ltd	
G-BROX	Robinson R-22B	D. J. Gilmour & Ten Tenths Ltd	
G-BROY	Cameron V-77 balloon	Zebedee Balloon Service	
G-BROZ	PA-18 Super Cub 150	P. G. Kynsey	
G-BRPE	Cessna 120	C. Briggs	
G-BRPF	Cessna 120	D. Sharp	
G-BRPG	Cessna 120	I. C. Lomax	
G-BRPH	Cessna 120	T. W. Greaves	
G-BRPI	Pitts S-1C Special	J. C. Lister	
G-BRPJ	Cameron N-90 balloon	Paul Johnson Cars Ltd	
G-BRPK	PA-28 Cherokee 140	Niederrhein Powered Flying Club/Holland	
G-BRPL	PA-28 Cherokee 140	Comed Aviation Ltd/Blackpool	
G-BRPM	T.66 Nipper 3	T. C. Horner	
G-BRPO	Enstrom 280C	R. Moffett	
G-BRPP	Brookland Hornet	D. E. Cox	
G-BRPR	Aeronca O-58B Grasshopper (31952)	N. Davis	
G-BRPS	Cessna 177B	N. W. Beresford	
G-BRPT	Rans S.10 Sakota	P. A. Aston	
G-BRPU	Beech 76 Duchess	Hamilton Compass Aviation	
G-BRPV	Cessna 152	Coventry (Civil) Aviation Ltd	
G-BRPX	Taylorcraft BC-12D	M. J. Brett	
G-BRPY	PA-15 Vagabond	J. P. Esson	
G-BRPZ	Luscombe 8A Silvaire	S. L. & J. P. Waring	
G-BRRA	V.S.361 Spitfire LF.IX	Historic Aircraft Collection Ltd	
G-BRRB	Luscombe 8E Silvaire	C. G. Ferguson & D. W. Gladwin	
G-BRRD	Scheibe SF.25B Falke	K. E. Ballington	
G-BRRE	Colt 77A balloon	P. Patel	
G-BRRF	Cameron O-77 balloon	Mid-Bucks Farmers Balloon Group	
G-BRRG	Glaser-Dirks DG.500M	A. W. White	
G-BRRJ	PA-28RT-201T Turbo Arrow IV	M. & E. Machinery Ltd	
G-BRRK	Cessna 182Q	Clacton Aviation	
G-BRRL	PA-18 Super Cub 95	T. J. McRae	
G-BRRM	PA-28-161 Cadet	R. H. Sellier	
G-BRRN	PA-28-161 Warrior II	C. J. & L. M. Worsley	
G-BRRO	Cameron N-77 balloon	Newbury Building Soc	
G-BRRP	Pitts S-1S Special	P. R. Underhill & J. E. Sweetman	
G-BRRR	Cameron V-77 balloon	L. M. Heal & A. P. Wilcox	
G-BRRS	Pitts S-1C Special	R. C. Atkinson	
G-BRRT	C.A.S.A. 1-131E Jungmann	R. A. L. Hubbard/Syerston	
G-BRRU	Colt 90A balloon	Thunder & Colt Ltd	
G-BRRW	Cameron O-77 balloon	D. V. Fowler	
G-BRRY	Robinson R-22B	Bristow Helicopters Ltd/Redhill	
G-BRRZ	Robinson R-22B	Heligroup Syndicate	
G-BRSA	Cameron N-56 balloon	C. Wilkinson	
G-BRSC	Rans S.10 Sakota	M. A. C. Stephenson	
G-BRSD	Cameron V-77 balloon	T. J. Porter & J. E. Kelly	
G-BRSE	PA-28-161 Warrior II	Air Service Training Ltd/Perth	
G-BRSF	V.S.361 Spitfire HF.IXc (RR232)	Sussex Spraying Services Ltd	
G-BRSG	PA-28-161 Cadet	Denham School of Flying Ltd	
G-BRSH	C.A.S.A. 1-131E Jungmann (E3B-540)	J. D. Haslam	
G-BRSI	PA-28-161 Cadet	Denham School of Flying Ltd	
G-BRSJ	PA-38-112 Tomahawk	Pool Aviation Ltd/Welshpool	
G-BRSK	Boeing Stearman N2S-3 (180)	Wymondham Engineering	
G-BRSL	Cameron N-56 balloon	S. Budd	
G-BRSN	Rand-Robinson KR-2	K. W. Darby	
G-BRSO	CFM Streak Shadow Srs SA	D. J. Smith	
G-BRSP	Air Command 532 Elite	D. R. G. Griffith	
G-BRSW	Luscombe 8A Silvaire	J. Regan	
G-BRSX	PA-15 Vagabond	C. Milne-Fowler	
G-BRSY	Hatz CB-1	G. A. Barrett & Son	
G-BRSZ	MEM RSZ-05/1 balloon	Zebedee Balloon Service	
G-BRTA	PA-38-112 Tomahawk	R. A. Wakefield	
G-BRTB	Bell 206B JetRanger 2	Harris Technology Ltd	
G-BRTC	Cessna 150G	Thorpe Air Ltd/Goodwood	
G-BRTD	Cessna 152 II	152 Group/Goodwood	
G-BRTH	Cameron A-180 balloon	The Ballooning Business Ltd	
G-BRTJ	Cessna 150F	P. M. Evans	
G-BRTK	Boeing Stearman E.75 (217786)	Eastern Stearman Ltd/North Walsham	
G-BRTL	Hughes 369E	P. C. Shann Management & Research Ltd	
G-BRTM	PA-28-161 Warrior II	Air Service Training Ltd/Perth	
G-BRTN	Beech 95-B58 Baron	Colneway Ltd	

Notes	Reg.	Type	Owner or Operator
	G-BRTO	Cessna 152	Monument Trust Co Ltd
	G-BRTP	Cessna 152	Anglia Aviation Ltd
	G-BRTR	Colt GA-42 airship	Thunder & Colt Ltd
	G-BRTT	Schweizer 269C	Fairthorpe Ltd/Denham
	G-BRTV	Cameron O-77 balloon	C. Vening
	G-BRTW	Glaser-Dirks DG.400	I. J. Carruthers
	G-BRTX	PA-28-151 Warrior	T. Gracey
	G-BRTZ	Slingsby T.31 Motor Cadet III	M. N. Martin
	G-BRUA	Cessna 152	C. M. Vlieland-Boddy/Compton Abbas
	G-BRUB	PA-28-161 Warrior II	Flytrek Ltd/Bournemouth
	G-BRUD	PA-28-181 Archer II	Wilkins & Wilkins Special Auctions Ltd
	G-BRUE	Cameron V-77 balloon	B. J. Newman & P. L. Harrison
	G-BRUG	Luscombe 8E Silvaire	P. A. Cain & N. W. Barratt
	G-BRUH	Colt 105A balloon	D. C. Chipping
	G-BRUI	PA-44-180 Seminole	Bath Stone Co Ltd
	G-BRUJ	Boeing Stearman A.75N1	Early Birds Ltd/Staverton
	G-BRUM	Cessna A.152	Aerohire Ltd/Halfpenny Green
	G-BRUN	Cessna 120	O. C. Brun (G-BRDH)
	G-BRUO	Taylor JT.1 Monoplane	G. Verity
	G-BRUR	Grob G.115	Risestat Ltd
	G-BRUS	Cessna 140	M. J. Fogarty
	G-BRUT	Thunder Ax8-90 balloon	Moet & Chandon (London) Ltd
	G-BRUU	EAA Biplane Model P.1	M. J. Fogarty
	G-BRUV	Cameron V-77 balloon	T. W. & R. F. Benbrook
	G-BRUX	PA-44-180 Seminole	Hambrair Ltd/Tollerton
	G-BRUZ	Raven Europe FS-57A balloon	R. H. Etherington
	G-BRVB	Stolp SA.300 Starduster Too	C. J. R. Flint & S. C. Lever
	G-BRVC	Cameron N-180 balloon	The Apollo Balloon Co Ltd
	G-BRVE	Beech D.17S	Intrepid Aviation Co/North Weald
	G-BRVF	Colt 77A balloon	Airborne Adventures Ltd
	G-BRVG	NA SNJ-7 Texan (27)	Intrepid Aviation Co/North Weald
	G-BRVH	Smyth Model S Sidewinder	I. S. Bellamy
	G-BRVI	Robinson R-22B	Burnell Helicopters Ltd
	G-BRVJ	Slingsby T.31 Motor Cadet III	B. Outhwaite
	G-BRVK	Cameron A-210 Balloon	The Balloon Club Ltd
	G-BRVL	Pitts S-1C Special	I. Duncan
	G-BRVN	Thunder Ax7-77 balloon	J. T. Hughes Ltd
	G-BRVO	AS.350B Ecureuil	Radstrong Ltd/Booker
	G-BRVR	Barnett J4B-2	Ilkeston Contractors
	G-BRVS	Barnett J4B-2	Ilkeston Contractors
	G-BRVT	Pitts S-2B Special	C. J. & M. D. Green
	G-BRVU	Colt 77A balloon	D. J. Harber
	G-BRVV	Colt 56B balloon	S. J. Hollingsworth
	G-BRVX	Cameron A-210 balloon	Bath Hot Air Balloon Club Ltd
	G-BRVY	Thunder Ax8-90 balloon	G. E. Morris
	G-BRVZ	Jodel D.117	J.G. Patton
	G-BRWA	Aeronca 7AC Champion	D. D. Smith & J. R. Edwards
	G-BRWB	NA T-6G Texan (51-14526)	Aircraft Restorations Ltd/Duxford
	G-BRWC	Cessna 152	T. Hayselden (Doncaster) Ltd
	G-BRWD	Robinson R22B	Odanrose Ltd
	G-BRWF	Thunder Ax7-77	D. J. Greaves
	G-BRWH	Cameron N-77	D. J. Usher
	G-BRWO	PA-28 Cherokee 140	ML Associates
	G-BRWP	CFM Streak Shadow Srs SA	A. D. Stewart
	G-BRWR	Aeronca 11AC Chief	O. T. Taylor
	G-BRWT	Scheibe SF.25C Falke	Soaring Ahead Ltd & Booker Gliding Club Ltd
	G-BRWU	Luton LA-4A Minor	R. B. Webber & P. K. Pike
	G-BRWV	Brügger MB.2 Colibri	S. J. McCollum
	G-BRWX	Cessna 172P	D. A. Abels
	G-BRWY	Cameron H-34 balloon	Cameron Balloons Ltd
	G-BRWZ	Cameron 90 Macaw SS balloon	Forbes Europe Inc/France
	G-BRXA	Cameron O-120 balloon	Gone With The Wind Ltd
	G-BRXB	Thunder Ax7-77 balloon	H. Peel
	G-BRXC	PA-28-161 Warrior II	Air Service Training Ltd/Perth
	G-BRXD	PA-28-181 Archer II	Gosky Aviation Ltd
	G-BRXE	Taylorcraft BC-12D	W. J. Durrad
	G-BRXF	Aeronca 11AC Chief	A. B. Newman
	G-BRXG	Aeronca 7AC Champion	X-Ray Golf Flying Group
	G-BRXH	Cessna 120	J. N. Pittock & A. P. Fox
	G-BRXK	Soko P-2 Kraguj	Cavok Ltd
	G-BRXL	Aeronca 11AC Chief (42-78044)	R. L. Jones
	G-BRXN	Montgomerie-Bensen B.8MR	J. C. Aitken

Reg.	Type	Owner or Operator	Notes
G-BRXO	PA-34-200T Seneca II	Aviation Services Ltd	
G-BRXP	SNCAN Stampe SV-4C (modified)	P. G. Kavanagh & D. T. Kaberry	
G-BRXS	Howard Special T Minus	H. C. Cox	
G-BRXV	Robinson R-22B	Pearce Enterprise Ltd	
G-BRXW	PA-24 Comanche 260	The Oak Group	
G-BRXX	Colt 180A balloon	J. P. Clifford	
G-BRXY	Pietenpol Air Camper	A. E. Morris	
G-BRYA	D.H.C.7-110 Dash Seven	Brymon Airways Ltd/British Airways Aberdeenshire	
G-BRYB	D.H.C.7-110 Dash Seven	Brymon Airways Ltd/British Airways Shetland Islands	
G-BRYC	D.H.C.7-110 Dash Seven	Brymon Airways Ltd/British Airways Devon	
G-BRYD	D.H.C.7-110 Dash Seven	Brymon Airways Ltd/British Airways Cornwall	
G-BRYE	D.H.C.7-102 Dash Seven	Brymon Airways Ltd/British Airways Channel Islands	
G-BRYG	D.H.C.8-102A Dash Eight	Brymon Airways Ltd/British Airways Lothian	
G-BRYH	D.H.C.8-102A Dash Eight	Brymon Airways Ltd/British Airways Lanarkshire	
G-BRYI	D.H.C.8-311 Dash Eight	Brymon Airways Ltd/British Airways Northumberland	
G-BRYJ	D.H.C.8-311 Dash Eight	Brymon Airways Ltd/British Airways Somerset	
G-BRYK	D.H.C.8-311 Dash Eight	Brymon Airways Ltd/British Airways Gloucestershire	
G-BRYM	D.H.C.8-311 Dash Eight	Brymon Airways Ltd/British Airways Wiltshire	
G-BRYN	SOCATA TB.20 Trinidad	Jones & Bradbourn (Guernsey) Ltd	
G-BRZA	Cameron O-77 balloon	L. & R. J. Mold	
G-BRZB	Cameron A-105 balloon	Headland Services Ltd	
G-BRZC	Cameron N-90 balloon	Flying Pictures (Balloons) Ltd	
G-BRZD	Hapi Cygnet SF-2A	L. G. Millen	
G-BRZE	Thunder Ax7-77 balloon	G. V. Beckwith	
G-BRZG	Enstrom F-28A	Chart Planes Inland Ltd	
G-BRZI	Cameron N-180 balloon	Pegasus Balloon Co Ltd	
G-BRZK	Stinson 108-2	F. H. Wheeler & G. P. A. Elborough	
G-BRZL	Pitts S-1D Special	R. T. Cardwell/Elstree	
G-BRZO	Jodel D.18	J. D. Anson	
G-BRZP	PA-28-161 Warrior II	Air Service Training Ltd/Perth	
G-BRZS	Cessna 172P	YP Flying Group/Blackpool	
G-BRZT	Cameron V-77 balloon	B. Drawbridge	
G-BRZU	Colt Flying Cheese SS balloon	Willow Best Ltd	
G-BRZV	Colt Flying Apple SS balloon	Thrust Drive Ltd	
G-BRZW	Rans S.10 Sakota	D. L. Davies	
G-BRZX	Pitts S-1S Special	G-BRZX Group	
G-BRZZ	CFM Streak Shadow	P. R. Oakes	
G-BSAB	PA-46-350P Malibu Mirage	D. O. Hooper	
G-BSAI	Stoddard-Hamilton Glasair III	K. J. & P. J. Whitehead	
G-BSAJ	C.A.S.A. 1-131E Jungmann	P. G. Kynsey/Redhill	
G-BSAK	Colt 21A balloon	Airship & Balloon Co Ltd	
G-BSAR	Air Command 532 Elite	S. A. Ryder	
G-BSAS	Cameron V-65 balloon	J. R. Barber	
G-BSAT	PA-28-181 Archer II	A1 Aircraft Ltd/Biggin Hill	
G-BSAV	Thunder Ax7-77 balloon	E. A. Evans & ptnrs	
G-BSAW	PA-28-161 Warrior II	Carill Aviation Ltd/Southampton	
G-BSAX	Piper J-3C-65 Cub	Crop Aviation (UK) Ltd	
G-BSAZ	Denney Aerocraft Kitfox	D. J. Richardson	
G-BSBA	PA-28-161 Warrior II	P. A. Lancaster/White Waltham	
G-BSBB	CCF Harvard IV	Pulsegrove Ltd/Thruxton	
G-BSBD	NA T-6G Texan	Pulsegrove Ltd/Thruxton	
G-BSBF	CCF Harvard IV	Pulsegrove Ltd/Thruxton	
G-BSBG	CCF Harvard IV (20310)	Flying Services	
G-BSBH	Short SD3-30★	Ulster Aviation Soc Museum *(stored)*	
G-BSBI	Cameron O-77 balloon	Calibre Motor Co Ltd	
G-BSBK	Colt 105A balloon	Zebra Ballooning Ltd	
G-BSBM	Cameron N-77 balloon	Nuclear Electric	
G-BSBN	Thunder Ax7-77 balloon	B. Pawson	
G-BSBP	Jodel D.18	R. T. Pratt	
G-BSBR	Cameron V-77 balloon	B. Bromiley	
G-BSBT	Piper J-3C-65 Cub	M. B. & L. J. Proudfoot	

Notes	Reg.	Type	Owner or Operator
	G-BSBU	Firefly 8B	A. R. Peart
	G-BSBV	Rans S.10 Sakota	Sportair UK Ltd
	G-BSBW	Bell 206B JetRanger 3	Leeds Central Helicopters
	G-BSBX	Montgomerie-Bensen B.8MR	B. Ibbott
	G-BSBY	Cessna 150L	Languedoc Aviation/France
	G-BSBZ	Cessna 150M	DTG Aviation
	G-BSCA	Cameron N-90 balloon	P. J. Marshall & M. A. Clarke
	G-BSCB	Air Command 532 Elite	P. H. Smith
	G-BSCC	Colt 105A balloon	A. F. Selby
	G-BSCD	Hughes 269C	McIntyre Aviation Ltd
	G-BSCE	Robinson R-22B	Alpha Helicopters
	G-BSCF	Thunder Ax7-77 balloon	V. P. Gardiner
	G-BSCG	Denney Aerocraft Kitfox	A. C. & T. G. Pinkstone
	G-BSCH	Denney Aerocraft Kitfox	Baldoon Leisure Flying Co Ltd
	G-BSCI	Colt 77A balloon	J. L. & S. Wrigglesworth
	G-BSCK	Cameron H-24 balloon	J. D. Shapland
	G-BSCL	Robinson R-22B	Ketton Holdings Ltd
	G-BSCM	Denney Aerocraft Kitfox	M. J. Wells
	G-BSCN	SOCATA TB.20 Trinidad	T. & G. Engineering Co Ltd & P. W. Huntley
	G-BSCO	Thunder Ax7-77 balloon	F. J. Whalley
	G-BSCP	Cessna 152	Moray Flying Club (1990) Ltd/Kinloss
	G-BSCR	Cessna 172M	London Link Flying Club Ltd
	G-BSCS	PA-28-181 Archer II	Wing Task Ltd
	G-BSCV	PA-28-161 Warrior II	Southwood Flying Group/Southend
	G-BSCW	Taylorcraft BC-65	S. Leach
	G-BSCX	Thunder Ax8-105 balloon	Balloon Flights Club Ltd
	G-BSCY	PA-28-151 Warrior	Cinque Ports Flying Club Ltd/Lydd
	G-BSCZ	Cessna 152	London Flight Centre (Stansted) Ltd
	G-BSDA	Taylorcraft BC-12D	D. G. Edwards
	G-BSDB	Pitts S-1C Special	M. K. Whitaker
	G-BSDC	—	—
	G-BSDD	Denney Aerocraft Kitfox	J. Windmill
	G-BSDF	Cameron N-105 balloon	G. V. Beckwith
	G-BSDG	Robin DR.400/180	B. Hodge
	G-BSDH	Robin DR.400/180	R. L. Brucciani
	G-BSDI	Corben Junior Ace Model E	J. Pearson/Eaglescott
	G-BSDJ	Piper J-4E Cub Coupé	J. Pearson/Eaglescott
	G-BSDL	SOCATA TB.10 Tobago	Delta Lima Group
	G-BSDN	PA-34-200T Seneca II	Belso Aviation Ltd
	G-BSDO	Cessna 152	J. Vickers
	G-BSDP	Cessna 152	P. F. W. Edgar
	G-BSDS	Boeing Stearman E.75 (118)	E. Hopper
	G-BSDU	Bell 206B JetRanger 3	RJS Aviation Ltd
	G-BSDV	Colt 31A balloon	Airship & Balloon Co Ltd
	G-BSDW	Cessna 182P	Kerygma Trust
	G-BSDX	Cameron V-77 balloon	D. K. Fish
	G-BSDY	Beech 58 Baron	Astra Aviation Ltd
	G-BSEA	Thunder Ax7-77 balloon	R. Titterton
	G-BSED	PA-22 Tri-Pacer 160 (modified)	M. Henderson
	G-BSEE	Rans S.9	P. M. Semler
	G-BSEF	PA-28 Cherokee 180	Prestwick Pilots Group
	G-BSEG	Ken Brock KB-2	H. A. Bancroft-Wilson
	G-BSEI	Cameron N-90 balloon	Flying Pictures (Balloons) Ltd
	G-BSEJ	Cessna 150M	Hollyclass Ltd
	G-BSEK	Robinson R-22	Skyline Helicopters Ltd
	G-BSEL	Slingsby T.61G Super Falke	RAFGSA/Hullavington
	G-BSEM	Cameron 90 Four-Pack SS balloon	Flying Pictures (Balloons) Ltd
	G-BSEN	Colt 31A balloon	Thunder & Colt Ltd
	G-BSEP	Cessna 172	B. Myers & C. H. Moore/Doncaster
	G-BSER	PA-28 Cherokee 160	Yorkair Ltd/Leeds
	G-BSES	Denney Aerocraft Kitfox	M. Albert-Brecht & J. J. M. Donnelly
	G-BSET	B.206 Srs 1 Basset	Beagle Basset Ltd/Shoreham
	G-BSEU	PA-28-181 Archer II	Euro Aviation 91 Ltd
	G-BSEV	Cameron O-77 balloon	UK Transplant Co-ordinators Assoc
	G-BSEW	Sikorsky S-76A	Bond Helicopters Ltd
	G-BSEX	Cameron A-180 balloon	Heart of England Balloons
	G-BSEY	Beech A36 Bonanza	K. Phillips Ltd
	G-BSEZ	Air Command 532 Elite	D. S. Robinson
	G-BSFA	Aero Designs Pulsar	S. A. Gill
	G-BSFB	C.A.S.A. 1.131E Jungmann 2000 (S5-B06)	J. A. Sykes
	G-BSFD	Piper J-3C-65 Cub	E. C. English

Reg.	Type	Owner or Operator	Notes
G-BSFE	PA-38-112 Tomahawk II	D. J. Campbell	
G-BSFF	Robin DR.400/180R	Lasham Gliding Soc Ltd	
G-BSFJ	Thunder Ax8-105 balloon	Airborne Adventures Ltd	
G-BSFK	PA-28-161 Warrior II	Air Service Training Ltd/Perth	
G-BSFN	SE.313B Alouette II	M & P Food Products Ltd	
G-BSFO	Cameron 60 House SS balloon	Clipsal UK Ltd	
G-BSFP	Cessna 152	J. R. Nicholls	
G-BSFR	Cessna 152	Galair Ltd	
G-BSFS	SE.313B Alouette II	M & P Food Products Ltd	
G-BSFV	Woods Woody Pusher	B. Brown	
G-BSFW	PA-15 Vagabond	J. R. Kimberley	
G-BSFX	Denney Aerocraft Kitfox	D. A. McFadyean	
G-BSFY	Denney Aerocraft Kitfox	J. R. Howard	
G-BSGB	Gaertner Ax4 Skyranger balloon	B. Gaertner	
G-BSGC	PA-18 Super Cub 95	G. Churchill	
G-BSGD	PA-28 Cherokee 180	R. J. Cleverley	
G-BSGF	Robinson R-22B	Garingdell Aviation Ltd	
G-BSGG	Denney Aerocraft Kitfox	C. G. Richardson	
G-BSGH	Airtour AH-56B balloon	G. Luck	
G-BSGJ	Monnet Sonerai 2	A. N. Burrows	
G-BSGK	PA-34-200T Seneca II	J. A. Burrett & P. A. Greenhalgh	
G-BSGL	PA-28-161 Warrior II	Keywest Air Charter Ltd/Liverpool	
G-BSGM	Cameron V-77 balloon	5th Regiment Royal Artillery	
G-BSGN	PA-28-151 Warrior	J. R. Whetlor & M. Gipps/Denham	
G-BSGP	Cameron N-65 balloon	Mid Sussex Flying School	
G-BSGR	Boeing Stearman E.75	A. G. Dunkerley	
G-BSGS	Rans S.10 Sakota	M. R. Parr	
G-BSGT	Cessna T.210N	B. J. Sharpe/Booker	
G-BSGV	Rotorway Executive	D. T. Price	
G-BSGY	Thunder Ax7-77 balloon	Thunder & Colt Ltd	
G-BSHA	PA-34-200T Seneca II	Warrior Aircraft Sales & Leasing Ltd	
G-BSHB	Colt 69A balloon	Airship & Balloon Co Ltd	
G-BSHC	Colt 69A balloon	Airship & Balloon Co Ltd	
G-BSHD	Colt 69A balloon	Airship & Balloon Co Ltd	
G-BSHE	Cessna 152	J. A. Pothecary/Shoreham	
G-BSHH	Luscombe 8E Silvaire	Golf Centres Balloons Ltd	
G-BSHI	Luscombe 8F Silvaire	W. H. J. Knowles	
G-BSHK	Denney Aerocraft Kitfox	A. E. Cree & G. J. Cuzzocrea	
G-BSHM	Slingsby T.31 Motor Cadet III	R. R. Hadley	
G-BSHN	Cessna 152	C. Walsh	
G-BSHO	Cameron V-77 balloon	T. P. Barlass & D. J. Duckworth	
G-BSHP	PA-28-161 Warrior II	Air Service Training Ltd/Perth	
G-BSHR	Cessna F.172N	H. Rothwell (G-BFGE)/Blackpool	
G-BSHS	Colt 105A balloon	Prescott Hot Air Balloon Ltd	
G-BSHT	Cameron V-77 balloon	ECM Construction Ltd	
G-BSHV	PA-18 Super Cub 135	Fen Tigers Flying Group	
G-BSHW	Hawker Tempest II	D. N. H. Martin	
G-BSHX	Enstrom F-28A	Stephenson Aviation Ltd	
G-BSHY	EAA Acro Sport 1	A. W. Hughes & R. J. Hodder	
G-BSHZ	Enstrom F-28F	Heliway Aviation	
G-BSIB	PA-28-161 Warrior II	Bobbington Air Training School Ltd	
G-BSIC	Cameron V-77 balloon	P. D. Worthy	
G-BSIF	Denney Aerocraft Kitfox	R. M. Kimbell & M. H. Wylde	
G-BSIG	Colt 21A balloon	E. C. & A. J. Moore	
G-BSIH	Rutan LongEz	W. S. Allen	
G-BSII	PA-34-200T Seneca II	N. H. N. Gardner	
G-BSIJ	Cameron V-77 balloon	A. S. Jones	
G-BSIK	Denney Aerocraft Kitfox	I. A. Davies & B. Barr	
G-BSIL	Colt 120A balloon	A. Bolger	
G-BSIM	PA-28-181 Archer II	E. Midlands Aircraft Hire Ltd	
G-BSIN	Robinson R-22B	H. P. Knapp & A. H. Feast	
G-BSIO	Cameron 80 Shed SS balloon	Furness Building Soc	
G-BSIP	Cameron V-77 balloon	R. S. Ham	
G-BSIR	Cessna 340	Airmaster Aviation Ltd/Cardiff	
G-BSIT	Robinson R-22B	P. R. Earp	
G-BSIU	Colt 90A balloon	Thunder & Colt Ltd	
G-BSIY	Schleicher ASK.14	H. F. Lamprey	
G-BSIZ	PA-28-181 Archer II	Firmdale Ltd	
G-BSJA	Cameron N-77 balloon	N. Sanders (G-SPAR)	
G-BSJB	Bensen B.8	J. W. Limbrick	
G-BSJC	Bell 206B JetRanger 3	JETC Helicopters	
G-BSJU	Cessna 150M	A. C. Williamson	
G-BSJV	Cessna 172N	Local Basic Ltd	

Notes	Reg.	Type	Owner or Operator
	G-BSJW	Everett Srs 2 gyroplane	A. R. Willis
	G-BSJX	PA-28-161 Warrior II	Border Air Training Ltd/Ronaldsway
	G-BSJY	Murphy Renegade II	J. Hatswell
	G-BSJZ	Cessna 150J	M. Tye
	G-BSKA	Cessna 150M	K. J. Farrance
	G-BSKB	—	
	G-BSKC	PA-38-112 Tomahawk	Bath Stone Co Ltd
	G-BSKD	Cameron V-77 balloon	M. J. Gunston
	G-BSKG	Maule MX-7-180	Beeches Auto Services
	G-BSKH	Cessna 421C	Bristol & Mendip Estates Ltd
	G-BSKI	Thunder Ax8-90 balloon	G-BSKI Balloon Group
	G-BSKJ	Mooney M.20J	M. C. Wroe
	G-BSKK	PA-38-112 Tomahawk	Falcon Flying Services/Biggin Hill
	G-BSKL	PA-38-112 Tomahawk	Falcon Flying Services/Biggin Hill
	G-BSKN	Grob G.109B	C. S. Faber
	G-BSKO	Maule MXT-7-180	G. B. Esslemont
	G-BSKP	V.S.379 Spitfire F.XIV	Historic Aircraft Collection Ltd
	G-BSKR	Rand Robinson KR-2	D. K. Lawry
	G-BSKT	Maule MX-7-180	D. D. Smith
	G-BSKU	Cameron O-84 balloon	Alfred Bagnall & Sons (West) Ltd
	G-BSKV	PA-28-181 Archer II	BAe Flying College Ltd/Prestwick
	G-BSKW	PA-28-181 Archer II	BAe Flying College Ltd/Prestwick
	G-BSKX	PA-28-181 Archer II	BAe Flying College Ltd/Prestwick
	G-BSLA	Robin DR.400/180	A. B. McCoig/Biggin Hill
	G-BSLC	Robinson R-22B	Modern Air/Fowlmere
	G-BSLD	PA-28RT-201 Arrow IV	E. D. Gawronek
	G-BSLE	PA-28-161 Warrior II	Air Service Training Ltd/Perth
	G-BSLF	Robinson R-22B	Arian Helicopters Ltd
	G-BSLG	Cameron A-180 balloon	West Country Balloons
	G-BSLH	C.A.S.A. 1-131E Jungmann 2000	P. Warden
	G-BSLI	Cameron V-77 balloon	J. D. C. & F. E. Bevan
	G-BSLJ	Denney Aerocraft Kitfox	A. F. Reid
	G-BSLK	PA-28-161 Warrior II	R. A. Rose
	G-BSLM	PA-28 Cherokee 160	L. A. Maynard & C. L. Melhuish
	G-BSLN	Thunder Ax10-180 balloon	Albatross Aviation Ltd
	G-BSLO	Cameron A-180 balloon	Adventure Balloon Co Ltd
	G-BSLT	PA-28-161 Warrior II	Warrior Aircraft Sales & Leasing Ltd
	G-BSLU	PA-28 Cherokee 140	D. J. Budden
	G-BSLW	Bellanca 7ECA Citabria	J. A. Killerby
	G-BSLX	WAR Focke-Wulf Fw.190 (4+)	E. Sussex Aviation/Shoreham
	G-BSLY	Colt AS-80 GD airship	Huntair Ltd
	G-BSMB	Cessna U.206E	Army Parachute Association/Netheravon
	G-BSMD	Nord 1101 Noralpha	W. R. M. Beesley
	G-BSME	Bo 208C Junior	D. J. Hampson
	G-BSMF	Avro 652A Anson C.19 (TX183)	G. M. K. Fraser
	G-BSMG	Montgomerie-Bensen B.8M	A. C. Timperley
	G-BSMH	Colt 240A balloon	Formtrack Ltd
	G-BSMJ	—	—
	G-BSMK	Cameron O-84 balloon	J. C. Reavley
	G-BSML	Schweizer 269C	Nunkeeling Ltd
	G-BSMM	Colt 31A balloon	D. V. Fowler
	G-BSMN	CFM Streak Shadow	K. Daniels
	G-BSMO	Denney Aerocraft Kitfox	G-BSMO Group
	G-BSMP	PA-34-220T Seneca III	Gabriel Enterprises Ltd
	G-BSMS	Cameron V-77 balloon	Sade Balloon Group
	G-BSMT	Rans S.10 Sakota	N. Woodworth
	G-BSMU	Rans S.6	W. D. Walker (G-MWJE)
	G-BSMV	PA-17 Vagabond (modified)	A. Cheriton
	G-BSMX	Bensen B.8MR	J. S. E. McGregor
	G-BSMZ	PA-28-161 Warrior II	Air Service Training Ltd/Perth
	G-BSND	Air Command 532 Elite	K. Brogan & W. B. Lumb
	G-BSNE	Luscombe 8A Silvaire	Aerolite Luscombe Group
	G-BSNF	Piper J-3C-65 Cub	D. A. Hammant
	G-BSNG	Cessna 172N	A. J. & P. C. MacDonald
	G-BSNI	Bensen B.8V	B. D. Gibbs
	G-BSNJ	Cameron N-90 balloon	D. P. H. Smith
	G-BSNL	Bensen B.8MR	A. C. Breane
	G-BSNN	Rans S.10 Sakota	S. Adams
	G-BSNO	Denney Aerocraft Kitfox	A. G. V. McClintock
	G-BSNP	PA-28-201T Turbo Arrow III	V. Dowd/Stapleford
	G-BSNR	BAe 146-300A	Trident Aviation Leasing Services Ltd
	G-BSNS	BAe 146-300A	Crossair
	G-BSNT	Luscombe 8A Silvaire	B. J. Robe

Reg.	Type	Owner or Operator	Notes
G-BSNU	Colt 105A balloon	Sun Life Assurance Soc PLC	
G-BSNV	Boeing 737-4Q8	British Airways	
G-BSNW	Boeing 737-4Q8	British Airways	
G-BSNX	PA-28-181 Archer II	Newtonair Ltd	
G-BSNY	Bensen B.8M	A. S. Deakin	
G-BSNZ	Cameron O-105 balloon	Aire Valley Balloons	
G-BSOE	Luscombe 8A Silvaire	S. B. Marsden	
G-BSOF	Colt 25A Mk II balloon	Thunder & Colt Ltd	
G-BSOG	Cessna 172M	B. Chapman & A. R. Budden	
G-BSOI	AS.332L Super Puma	British International Helicopters	
G-BSOJ	Thunder Ax7-77 balloon	P. J. S. & S. Hughes	
G-BSOK	PA-28-161 Warrior II	C. Wyn-Jones	
G-BSOM	Glaser-Dirks DG.400	G-BSOM Group	
G-BSON	Green S.25	J. J. Green	
G-BSOO	Cessna 172F	Double Oscar Flying Group	
G-BSOR	CFM Streak Shadow Srs SA	J. P. Sorenson	
G-BSOT	PA-38-112 Tomahawk II	D. J. Campbell/Glasgow	
G-BSOU	PA-38-112 Tomahawk II	D. J. Campbell/Glasgow	
G-BSOV	PA-38-112 Tomahawk II	C. R. Welden	
G-BSOW	PA-32R Cherokee Lance 300	Halsmith (Aircraft Sales) Ltd	
G-BSOX	Luscombe 8A Silvaire	D. Gill	
G-BSOY	PA-34-220T Seneca III	BAe Flying College Ltd/Prestwick	
G-BSOZ	PA-28-161 Warrior II	Moray Flying Club Ltd/Kinloss	
G-BSPA	QAC Quickie Q.2	M. Ward	
G-BSPB	Thunder Ax8-84 balloon	Nigs Pertwee Ltd	
G-BSPC	Jodel D.140C	B. E. Cotton/Headcorn	
G-BSPE	Cessna F.172P	A. M. J. Clark	
G-BSPF	Cessna T.303	G-BSPF Crusader Group	
G-BSPG	PA-34-200T Seneca II	C. M. Vlieland-Boddy/Compton Abbas	
G-BSPI	PA-28-161 Warrior II	Snapfleet Ltd/Wellesbourne	
G-BSPJ	Bensen B.8	P. Soanes	
G-BSPK	Cessna 195A	Walavia	
G-BSPL	CFM Streak Shadow Srs SA	MEL (Aviation Oxygen) Ltd	
G-BSPM	PA-28-161 Warrior II	White Waltham Airfield Ltd	
G-BSPN	PA-28R-201T Turbo Arrow III	R. G. & W. Allison	
G-BSPW	Light Aero Avid Flyer C	M. J. Sewell	
G-BSPX	Lancair 320	C. H. Skelt	
G-BSPY	BN-2A Islander	Aerohire Ltd (G-AXYM)/Halfpenny Green	
G-BSPZ	PA-28-161 Warrior II	Air Service Training Ltd/Perth	
G-BSRC	Cessna 150M	R. W. Boote	
G-BSRD	Cameron N-105 balloon	J. R. Joiner	
G-BSRH	Pitts S-1C Special	J. R. Groom/Biggin Hill	
G-BSRI	Lancair 235	G. Lewis	
G-BSRJ	Colt AA-1050 balloon	Thunder & Colt Ltd	
G-BSRK	ARV Super 2	Orion Aviation (Chester) Ltd	
G-BSRL	Everett Srs 2 gyroplane	R. F. E. Burley	
G-BSRP	Rotorway Executive	J. P. Dennison	
G-BSRR	Cessna 182Q	Comet Aviation Ltd	
G-BSRT	Denney Aerocraft Kitfox	L. A. James	
G-BSRU	BAe 146-200	British Aerospace PLC (G-OSKI)	
G-BSRV	BAe 146-200	British Aerospace PLC (G-OSUN)	
G-BSRX	CFM Streak Shadow	R. G. M-J. Proost & F-J. Luckhurst	
G-BSRY	Cessna F.406 Caravan II	Directflight Ltd/Norwich	
G-BSRZ	Air Command 532 Elite 2-seat	A. S. G. Crabb	
G-BSSA	Luscombe 8E Silvaire	Punters Promotions Ltd/Denham	
G-BSSB	Cessna 150L	D. T. A. Rees	
G-BSSC	PA-28-161 Warrior II	Air Service Training Ltd/Perth	
G-BSSE	PA-28 Cherokee 140	Comed Aviation Ltd/Blackpool	
G-BSSF	Denney Aerocraft Kitfox	D. M. Orrock	
G-BSSI	Rans S.6 Coyote II	D. A. Farnworth (G-MWJA)	
G-BSSJ	FRED Srs 2	R. F. Jopling	
G-BSSK	QAC Quickie Q.2	D. G. Greatrex	
G-BSSN	Air Command 532 Elite 2-seat	R. C. Bettany	
G-BSSO	Cameron O-90 balloon	J. N. H. Purvis	
G-BSSP	Robin DR.400/180R	Soaring (Oxford) Ltd	
G-BSSR	PA-28-151 Warrior	G. Webster & R. J. Sixsmith	
G-BSST	Concorde 002★	F.A.A. Museum/Yeovilton	
G-BSSV	CFM Streak Shadow	R. W. Payne	
G-BSSW	PA-28-161 Warrior II	MJ Leasing/Cardiff	
G-BSSX	PA-28-161 Warrior II	Airpart Supply Ltd/Booker	
G-BSSY	Polikarpov Po-2W	Sussex Spraying Services Ltd	
G-BSSZ	Thunder Ax8-90 balloon	Capital Balloon Club Ltd	
G-BSTC	Aeronca 11AC Chief	B. Bridgman & N. J. Mortimore	

Notes	Reg.	Type	Owner or Operator
	G-BSTE	AS.355F-2 Twin Squirrel	Hygrade Foods Ltd
	G-BSTH	PA-25 Pawnee 235	Scottish Gliding Union Ltd
	G-BSTI	Piper J-3C-65 Cub	I. Fraser & G. L. Nunn
	G-BSTJ	D.H.82A Tiger Moth	C. A. Parker
	G-BSTK	Thunder Ax8-90 balloon	M. Williams
	G-BSTL	Rand Robinson KR-2	T. M. Scale
	G-BSTM	Cessna 172L	G-BSTM Group/Cambridge
	G-BSTO	Cessna 152	Plymouth School of Flying Ltd
	G-BSTP	Cessna 152	FR Aviation Ltd/Bournemouth
	G-BSTR	AA-5 Traveler	James Allan (Aviation & Engineering) Ltd
	G-BSTS	Schleicher ASW.20L	T. I. Gardiner
	G-BSTT	Rans S.6 Coyote II	M. W. Holmes
	G-BSTU	Cessna P.210N	Boomselect Ltd
	G-BSTV	PA-32 Cherokee Six 300	J. V. Hudson
	G-BSTY	Thunder Ax8-90 balloon	J. W. Cato
	G-BSTZ	PA-28 Cherokee 140	Air Navigation & Trading Co Ltd/Blackpool
	G-BSUA	Rans S.6 Coyote II	P. S. Dopson & A. J. Todd
	G-BSUB	Colt 77A balloon	R. R. J. Wilson & M. P. Hill
	G-BSUD	Luscombe 8A Silvaire	I. G. Harrison
	G-BSUE	Cessna U.206G	R. A. Robinson
	G-BSUF	PA-32RT-300 Lance II	HPS Aviation
	G-BSUH	Cessna 140	Classic Cessna Group
	G-BSUI	Robinson R-22B	C. T. Norman
	G-BSUJ	Brügger MB.2 Colibri	M. A. Farrelly
	G-BSUK	Colt 77A balloon	K. J. Foster
	G-BSUL	BAe 125 Srs 800B	Raytheon Corporate Jets Inc
	G-BSUM	Scheibe SF.27MB	M Syndicate
	G-BSUO	Scheibe SF.25C Falke	British Gliding Association Ltd
	G-BSUR	Rotorway Executive 90	Coaching for Results Ltd
	G-BSUS	Taylor JT.1 Monoplane	R. Parker
	G-BSUT	Rans S.6 Coyote II	P. J. Clegg
	G-BSUU	Colt 180A balloon	J. P. Clifford
	G-BSUV	Cameron O-77 balloon	R. Moss
	G-BSUW	PA-34-200T Seneca II	Berry Air
	G-BSUX	Carlson Sparrow II	J. Stephenson
	G-BSUZ	Denney Aerocraft Kitfox	E. T. Wicks
	G-BSVA	Christen A.1 Husky	Deeside Husky Group/Aberdeen
	G-BSVB	PA-28-181 Archer II	Redhill Flying Club
	G-BSVC	Cameron A-120 balloon	First Class Ballooning Ltd
	G-BSVE	Binder CP.301S Smaragd	Smaragd Flying Group
	G-BSVF	PA-28-161 Warrior II	Airways Aero Associations Ltd/Booker
	G-BSVG	PA-28-161 Warrior II	Airways Aero Associations Ltd/Booker
	G-BSVH	Piper J-3C-65 Cub	A. R. Meakin
	G-BSVI	PA-16 Clipper	Robhurst Flying Group
	G-BSVJ	—	—
	G-BSVK	Denney Aerocraft Kitfox Mk 2	C. M. Looney
	G-BSVM	PA-28-161 Warrior II	Falcon Flying Services/Biggin Hill
	G-BSVN	Thorp T-18	J. H. Kirkham
	G-BSVO	Sikorsky S-61N	Bristow Helicopters Ltd
	G-BSVP	PA-23 Aztec 250	Time Electronics Ltd/Biggin Hill
	G-BSVR	Schweizer 269C	Nunkeeling Ltd
	G-BSVS	Robin DR.400/100	J. MacDonald
	G-BSVU	Stemme S.10	Sonic Aviation Ltd
	G-BSVV	PA-38-112 Tomahawk	A. J. & C. C. Leicester
	G-BSVW	PA-38-112 Tomahawk	Falcon Flying Services/Biggin Hill
	G-BSVX	PA-38-112 Tomahawk	Smallfry (Leasing) Ltd
	G-BSVY	PA-38-112 Tomahawk	Smallfry (Leasing) Ltd
	G-BSVZ	Pietenpol Air Camper	A. F. Cashin
	G-BSWA	Luscombe 8A Silvaire	J. W. Street
	G-BSWB	Rans S.10 Sakota	F. A. Hewitt
	G-BSWC	Boeing Stearman E.75 (112)	R. J. & N. R. Lancaster
	G-BSWF	PA-16 Clipper	T. M. Storey
	G-BSWG	PA-17 Vagabond	J. P. Taylor
	G-BSWH	Cessna 152	Swansea Aviation Ltd
	G-BSWI	Rans S.10 Sakota	A. Gault
	G-BSWJ	Cameron O-77 balloon	T. Charlwood
	G-BSWK	Robinson R-22B	Clarity Aviation Ltd
	G-BSWM	Slingsby T.61F	L. J. McKelvie
	G-BSWR	BN-2B-26 Islander	Police Authority for Northern Ireland
	G-BSWS	BN-2B-26 Islander	Pilatus BN Ltd/Bembridge
	G-BSWV	Cameron N-77 balloon	Leicester Mercury Ltd
	G-BSWW	Cameron O-105 balloon	R. B. & R. A. Naylor
	G-BSWX	Cameron V-90 balloon	Cameron Balloons Ltd

Reg.	Type	Owner or Operator	Notes
G-BSWY	Cameron N-77 balloon	Nottingham Hot Air Balloon Club	
G-BSXA	PA-28-161 Warrior II	Hillvine Ltd	
G-BSXB	PA-28-161 Warrior II	Hillvine Ltd	
G-BSXC	PA-28-161 Warrior II	L. T. Halpin/Booker	
G-BSXD	Soko P-2 Kraguj (30146)	C. J. Pearce	
G-BSXE	Bell 206B JetRanger	Sterling Helicopters Ltd	
G-BSXF	Cameron A-180 balloon	Gone With The Wind Ltd	
G-BSXH	Pitts S-1 Special	A. Howard	
G-BSXI	Mooney M.20E	Halsmith (Aircraft Sales) Ltd	
G-BSXM	Cameron V-77 balloon	C. A. Oxby	
G-BSXN	Robinson R-22B	J. G. Gray	
G-BSXP	Air Command 532 Elite	B. J. West	
G-BSXR	Air Command 532 Elite	T. Wing	
G-BSXS	PA-28-181 Archer II	Pipe-Air Ltd	
G-BSXT	Piper J-5A Cub Cruiser	M. G. & K. J. Thompson	
G-BSXW	PA-28-161 Warrior II	Ryland Aviation Ltd/Wellesbourne	
G-BSXX	Whittaker MW.7	H. J. Stanley	
G-BSXY	Oldfield Baby Great Lakes	B. Freeman-Jones (G-JENY)	
G-BSYA	Jodel D.18	S. Harrison	
G-BSYB	Cameron N-120 balloon	Cameron Balloons Ltd	
G-BSYC	PA-32R-300 Lance	Arrow Aviation	
G-BSYD	Cameron A-180 balloon	A. A. Brown	
G-BSYE	Cessna 140	P. E. Villiers	
G-BSYF	Luscombe 8A Silvaire	M. K. Whitaker	
G-BSYG	PA-12 Super Cruiser	M. K. Whitaker	
G-BSYH	Luscombe 8A Silvaire	N. R. Osborne	
G-BSYI	AS.355F-1 Twin Squirrel	Lynton Aviation Ltd/Denham	
G-BSYJ	Cameron N-77 balloon	Chubb Fire Ltd	
G-BSYK	PA-38-112 Tomahawk	Joyset Ltd	
G-BSYL	PA-38-112 Tomahawk	Joyset Ltd	
G-BSYM	PA-38-112 Tomahawk	Joyset Ltd	
G-BSYO	Piper J-3C-65 Cub	C. R. Reynolds & J. D. Fuller	
G-BSYP	Bensen B.8M	C. R. Gordon	
G-BSYT	BAe 146-300A	Trident Aviation Leasing Services Ltd	
G-BSYU	Robin DR.400/180	P. A. Desoutter	
G-BSYV	Cessna 150M	R. D. & S. R. Spencer	
G-BSYW	Cessna 150M	J. A. F. Waller	
G-BSYX	Cessna 152	J. Cunliffe	
G-BSYY	PA-28-161 Warrior II	Air Service Training Ltd/Perth	
G-BSYZ	PA-28-161 Warrior II	Air Service Training Ltd/Perth	
G-BSZB	Stolp SA.300 Starduster Too	Cambrian Flying Club/Swansea	
G-BSZC	Beech C-45H	A. A. Hodgson	
G-BSZD	Robin DR.400/180	Trantshore Ltd	
G-BSZF	Jodel DR.250/160	J. B. Randle	
G-BSZG	Stolp SA.100 Starduster	S. W. Watkins	
G-BSZH	Thunder Ax7-77 balloon	M. S. Drinkwater	
G-BSZI	Cessna 152	Eglinton Flying Club Ltd	
G-BSZJ	PA-28-181 Archer II	R. D. Fuller	
G-BSZL	Colt 77A balloon	Airship & Balloon Co Ltd	
G-BSZM	Bensen B.8	J. H. H. Turner	
G-BSZN	Bucker Bu133D-1 Jungmeister	V. Lindsay	
G-BSZO	Cessna 152	A. T. Hooper & T. E. Evans/Wellesbourne	
G-BSZS	Robinson R-22B	South West Helicopters Ltd	
G-BSZT	PA-28-161 Warrior II	Lynair Aviation & Franchi Aviation Ltd	
G-BSZU	Cessna 150F	L. A. Maynard	
G-BSZV	Cessna 150F	Midair Aviation Ltd/Bournemouth	
G-BSZW	Cessna 152	Midair Aviation Ltd/Bournemouth	
G-BSZY	Cameron A-180 balloon	Wickers World Hot Air Balloon Co	
G-BTAA	EMB-110P1 Bandeirante	Knight Air Ltd (G-BHJY)/Leeds	
G-BTAB	BAe 125 Srs 800B	Abbey Investments Co Ltd (G-BOOA)	
G-BTAD	Macair Merlin	A. T. & M. R. Dowie	
G-BTAF	PA-28-181 Archer II	Enpar (North) Ltd	
G-BTAG	Cameron O-77 balloon	H. Phethean & R. A. Shapland	
G-BTAH	Bensen B.8A	T. B. Johnson	
G-BTAI	BAe Jetstream 3109	Jetstream Aircraft Ltd/Prestwick	
G-BTAJ	PA-34-200T Seneca II	Ravenair Aircraft Engineering Ltd/ Manchester	
G-BTAK	EAA Acro Sport 2	P. G. Harrison	
G-BTAL	Cessna F.152	Thanet Flying Club/Manston	
G-BTAM	PA-28-181 Archer II	RJH Air Services Ltd/Fowlmere	
G-BTAN	Thunder Ax7-65Z balloon	P. M. Gaines	
G-BTAO	Cameron A-180 balloon	R. M. Bishop & D. C. La Beaume	

Notes	Reg.	Type	Owner or Operator
	G-BTAP	PA-38-112 Tomahawk	I. J. McGarrigle
	G-BTAR	PA-38-112 Tomahawk	Rhodair Maintenance Ltd/Cardiff
	G-BTAS	PA-38-112 Tomahawk	Rhodair Maintenance Ltd/Cardiff
	G-BTAT	Denny Aerocraft Kitfox	Fast Ford Centre Ltd
	G-BTAU	Thunder Ax7-77 balloon	Thunder & Colt Ltd
	G-BTAV	Colt 105A balloon	D. C. Chipping
	G-BTAW	PA-28-161 Warrior II	Enpar (North) Ltd
	G-BTAX	PA-31-350 Navajo Chieftain	Jet West Ltd/Exeter
	G-BTAY	—	
	G-BTAZ	Evans VP-2	G. S. Poulter
	G-BTBA	Robinson R-22B	Forestdale Hotels Ltd
	G-BTBB	Thunder Ax8-105 balloon	Scotia Balloons Ltd
	G-BTBC	PA-28-161 Warrior II	M. J. L. MacDonald
	G-BTBE	—	
	G-BTBF	Super Koala	E. A. Taylor (G-MWOZ)
	G-BTBG	Denny Aerocraft Kitfox	J. Catley
	G-BTBH	Ryan ST3KR (854)	Ryan Group
	G-BTBI	WAR P-47 Thunderbolt (replica) (85)	J. Berry/Manchester
	G-BTBJ	Cessna 195B	P. G. Palumbo
	G-BTBL	Montgomerie-Bensen B.8MR	R. de H. Dobree-Carey
	G-BTBN	Denney Aerocraft Kitfox	Avon Valley Flying Group
	G-BTBO	Cameron N-77 balloon	Cameron Balloons Ltd
	G-BTBP	Cameron N-90 balloon	Gone With The Wind Ltd
	G-BTBR	Cameron DP-80 airship	Cameron Balloons Ltd
	G-BTBS	Cameron N-180 balloon	G. Scaife & B. Smith
	G-BTBT	PA-32R-301 Saratoga SP	B. Taylor
	G-BTBU	PA-18 Super Cub 150	Acebell Aviation Ltd & H. J. Rose
	G-BTBV	Cessna 140	A. Brinkley
	G-BTBW	Cessna 120	P. B. Cox
	G-BTBX	Piper J-3C-65 Cub	Henlow Taildraggers
	G-BTBY	PA-17 Vagabond	M. M. Wallis
	G-BTCA	PA-32R-300 Lance	P. Taylor
	G-BTCB	Air Command 582 Sport	G. Scurrah
	G-BTCC	Grumman F6F-5 Hellcat (19)	Patina Ltd/Duxford
	G-BTCD	P-51D-25-NA Mustang (463221)	Patina Ltd/Duxford
	G-BTCE	Cessna 152	S. T. Gilbert
	G-BTCF	CFM Streak Shadow	P. Crossman
	G-BTCH	Luscombe 8E Silvaire	P. Eastwood
	G-BTCI	PA-17 Vagabond	C. F. Kennedy
	G-BTCJ	Luscombe 8C Silvaire	C. C. & J. M. Lovell
	G-BTCK	Cameron A-210 balloon	Golf Centres Balloons Ltd
	G-BTCL	Cameron A-210 balloon	Exeter Balloons
	G-BTCM	Cameron N-90 balloon	S. C. & G. C. Jones
	G-BTCN	Cameron A-300 balloon	Cameron Balloons Ltd
	G-BTCO	FRED Srs 2	I. P. Manley
	G-BTCR	Rans S.10 Sakota	S. H. Barr
	G-BTCS	Colt 90A balloon	D. N. Belton
	G-BTCT	AS.332L Super Puma	Bristow Helicopters Ltd
	G-BTCU	WSK PZL Antonov An-2T (77)	Wessex Aviation & Transport Ltd
	G-BTCW	Cameron A-180 balloon	Bristol Balloons
	G-BTCX	Hunter F.4	Gray Tuplin Ltd
	G-BTCY	Hunter F.4	Gray Tuplin Ltd
	G-BTCZ	Cameron 84 Chateau SS balloon	Forbes Europe Inc/France
	G-BTDA	Slingsby T.61G	RAFGSA/Bicester
	G-BTDC	Denney Aerocraft Kitfox	D. Collinson
	G-BTDD	CFM Streak Shadow	S. J. Evans
	G-BTDE	Cessna C-165	G. S. Moss
	G-BTDF	Luscombe 8A Silvaire	M. Stow
	G-BTDG	Colt 105A balloon	Thunder & Colt Ltd
	G-BTDH	P.56 Provost T.1 (WV666)	Pulsegrove Ltd/Shoreham
	G-BTDI	Robinson R-22B	Fibernet Ltd
	G-BTDK	Cessna 421C	RK Carbon Fibre Ltd/Manchester
	G-BTDN	Denney Aerocraft Kitfox	L. A. James
	G-BTDP	TBM-3R Avenger (53319)	A. Haig-Thomas/North Weald
	G-BTDR	Aero Designs Pulsar	R. M. Hughes
	G-BTDS	Colt 77A balloon	C. P. Witter Ltd
	G-BTDT	C.A.S.A. 1-131E Jungmann	T. A. Reed
	G-BTDV	PA-28-161 Warrior II	R. E. Thorne
	G-BTDW	Cessna 152 II	J. A. Blenkharn/Carlisle
	G-BTDX	PA-18 Super Cub 150	Cubair Ltd/Redhill
	G-BTDY	PA-18 Super Cub 150	Rodger Aircraft Ltd
	G-BTDZ	C.A.S.A. 1-131E Jungmann 2000	R. J. Pickin

Reg.	Type	Owner or Operator	Notes
G-BTEA	Cameron N-105 balloon	Southern Balloon Group	
G-BTEE	Cameron O-120 balloon	W. H. & J. P. Morgan	
G-BTEF	Pitts S-1 Special	Northwest Aerobatics	
G-BTEH	Colt 77A balloon	Thunder & Colt Ltd	
G-BTEI	Everett Srs 3 gyroplane	J. W. Highton	
G-BTEK	SOCATA TB.20 Trinidad	D. F. Fagan/Booker	
G-BTEL	CFM Streak Shadow	J. E. Eatwell	
G-BTEN	Thunder Ax7-77 balloon	E. Reichart/Germany	
G-BTEO	Cameron V-90 balloon	Cameron Balloons Ltd	
G-BTEP	Cameron DP-80 airship	Cameron Balloons Ltd	
G-BTER	Cessna 150J	Universal Air Services Ltd/Sywell	
G-BTES	Cessna 150H	M. Entwistle	
G-BTET	Piper J-3C-65 Cub	W. F. Crozier	
G-BTEU	SA.365N-2 Dauphin	Bond Helicopters Ltd	
G-BTEV	PA-38-112 Tomahawk	T. R. Blockley & J. Mingay/Cardiff	
G-BTEW	Cessna 120	D. J. Carter/Little Snoring	
G-BTEX	PA-28 Cherokee 140	McAully Flying Group Ltd/Little Snoring	
G-BTFA	Denney Aerocraft Kitfox	K. R. Peek	
G-BTFB	Cameron DG-14 airship	Cameron Balloons Ltd	
G-BTFC	Cessna F.152 II	Tayside Aviation Ltd	
G-BTFD	Colt AS-105 airshiip Mk II	Media Fantasy Aviation UK Ltd	
G-BTFE	Bensen-Parsons 2-seat gyroplane	I. Brewster	
G-BTFF	Cessna T.310R II	Rajmech Ltd	
G-BTFG	Boeing Stearman A.75N1 (441)	S. J. Ellis	
G-BTFJ	PA-15 Vagabond	Eastbach Aircraft Preservation	
G-BTFK	Taylorcraft BC-12D	J. J. Penney	
G-BTFL	Aeronca 11AC Chief	BTFL Group	
G-BTFM	Cameron O-105 balloon	Edinburgh University Hot Air Balloon Club	
G-BTFN	Beech F33C Bonanza	Robert Hinton Design & Creative Communications Ltd	
G-BTFO	PA-28-161 Warrior II	Flyfar Ltd	
G-BTFP	PA-38-112 Tomahawk	Teesside Flight Centre Ltd	
G-BTFR	Colt AS-105 airship	Heather Flight Ltd	
G-BTFS	Cessna A.150M	Birmingham Airport Flying Group	
G-BTFT	Beech 58 Baron	Roseberry Management Ltd	
G-BTFU	Cameron N-90 balloon	J. J. Rudoni & A. C. K. Rawson	
G-BTFV	Whittaker MW.7	S. J. Luck	
G-BTFW	Montgomerie-Bensen B.8MR	A. Mansfield	
G-BTFX	Bell 206B JetRanger 2	J. Selwyn Smith (Shepley) Ltd	
G-BTFY	Bell 206B JetRanger 2	Northern Helicopters (Leeds) Ltd	
G-BTFZ	Cameron A-120 balloon	A. G. E. Faulkner	
G-BTGA	Boeing Stearman A.751N1	J. C. Lister	
G-BTGC	PA-38-112 Tomahawk	R. E. Wooldridge & T. Hayselden (Doncaster) Ltd	
G-BTGD	Rand-Robinson KR-2	D. W. Mullin	
G-BTGG	Rans S.10 Sakota	A. R. Cameron	
G-BTGH	Cessna 152	R. S. Trayhurn & P. D. Myson	
G-BTGI	Rearwin 175 Skyranger	A. H. Hunt/St Just	
G-BTGJ	Smith DSA-1 Miniplane	G. J. Knowles	
G-BTGK	PA-28-161 Warrior II	S. Dorrington	
G-BTGL	Light Aero Avid Flyer	A. J. Maxwell	
G-BTGM	Aeronca 7AC Champion	J. Zemlik	
G-BTGN	Cessna 310R	Air Service Training Ltd/Perth	
G-BTGO	PA-28 Cherokee 140	Hadleyridge Ltd	
G-BTGP	Cessna 150M	Billins Air Service Ltd	
G-BTGR	Cessna 152 II	A. J. Gomes	
G-BTGS	Stolp SA.300 Starduster Too	T. G. Solomon (G-AYMA)/Shoreham	
G-BTGT	CFM Streak Shadow	M. P. Allinson (G-MWPY)	
G-BTGU	PA-34-220T Seneca III	Carill Aviation Ltd	
G-BTGV	PA-34-200T Seneca II	Hollowbrook Flying Group	
G-BTGW	Cessna 152 II	Stapleford Flying Club Ltd	
G-BTGX	Cessna 152 II	Stapleford Flying Club Ltd	
G-BTGY	PA-28-161 Warrior II	Stapleford Flying Club Ltd	
G-BTGZ	PA-28-181 Archer II	Allzones Travel Ltd/Biggin Hill	
G-BTHA	Cessna 182P	N. J. Douglas	
G-BTHB	Bell 212	Autair Helicopters Ltd	
G-BTHC	Bell 212	Autair Helicopters Ltd	
G-BTHD	Yakolev Yak-3U	Patina Ltd/Duxford	
G-BTHE	Cessna 150L	Humberside Police Flying Club	
G-BTHF	Cameron V-90 balloon	N. J. & S. J. Langley	
G-BTHH	Jodel DR.100A	H. R. Leefe	
G-BTHI	Robinson R-22B	A. M. Green	
G-BTHJ	Evans VP-2	C. J. Moseley	

Notes	Reg.	Type	Owner or Operator
	G-BTHK	Thunder Ax7-77 balloon	Krauss Maffei (UK) Ltd
	G-BTHM	Thunder Ax8-105 balloon	Anglia Balloons
	G-BTHN	Murphy Renegade 912	F. A. Purvis
	G-BTHP	Thorp T.211	Arrow Air Sales/Shipdham
	G-BTHR	SOCATA TB.10 Tobago	Eclipse (Rother) Ltd
	G-BTHT	BAe 146-300	Compagnie Air Jet
	G-BTHU	Light Aero Avid Flyer	M. Morris
	G-BTHV	MBB Bo 105DBS/4	Bond Helicopers Ltd
	G-BTHW	Beech F33C Bonanza	Robin Lance Aviation Associates Ltd
	G-BTHX	Colt 105A balloon	R. Ollier
	G-BTHY	Bell 206B JetRanger 3	J. W. Sandle
	G-BTHZ	Cameron V-56 balloon	C. N. Marshall
	G-BTIB	Dassault Falcon 900B	Glaxo Holdings Ltd
	G-BTIC	PA-22 Tri-Pacer 150	T. Richards & G. C. Winters
	G-BTID	PA-28-161 Warrior II	P. G. Lawrence
	G-BTIE	SOCATA TB.10 Tobago	Rotaters Ltd/Machester
	G-BTIF	Denney Aerocraft Kitfox	C. R. Thompson
	G-BTIG	Montgomerie-Bensen B.8MR	D. Beevers
	G-BTIH	PA-28-151 Warrior	MPM Aviation
	G-BTII	AA-5B Tiger	B. D. Greenwood
	G-BTIJ	Luscombe 8E Silvaire	C. P. Wadlow
	G-BTIK	Cessna 152	B. R. Pearson/Eaglescott
	G-BTIL	PA-38-112 Tomahawk	B. R. Pearson/Eaglescott
	G-BTIM	PA-28-161 Cadet	Mid-Sussex Timber Co Ltd
	G-BTIN	Cessna 150C	Cormack (Aircraft Services) Ltd
	G-BTIO	SNCAN Stampe SV-4C	L. J. & A. A. Rice
	G-BTIP	Denney Aerocraft Kitfox Mk 3	P. A. Hardy
	G-BTIR	Denney Aerocraft Kitfox Mk 2	Bluetit Group
	G-BTIS	AS.355F-1 Twin Squirrel	Walsh Aviation (G-TALI)
	G-BTIU	M.S.892A Rallye Commodore 150	W. H. Cole
	G-BTIV	PA-28-161 Warrior II	Warrior Group/Eaglescott
	G-BTIW	Jodel DR.1050/M1	P. A. Hardy
	G-BTIX	Cameron V-77 balloon	S. A. Simington
	G-BTIZ	Cameron A-105 balloon	A. G. E. Faulkner
	G-BTJA	Luscombe 8E Silvaire	M. W. & L. M. Rudkin
	G-BTJB	Luscombe 8E Silvaire	M. Loxton
	G-BTJC	Luscombe 8F Silvaire	S. C. & M. Goddard
	G-BTJD	Thunder Ax8-90 balloon	T. C. Restell
	G-BTJE	Hiller UH-12E4	T. J. Clark
	G-BTJF	Thunder Ax10-180 balloon	Airborne Adventures Ltd
	G-BTJG	BAe 146-300A	Crossair
	G-BTJH	Cameron O-77 balloon	H. Stringer
	G-BTJI	Beech F33C Bonanza	Neil Brown Engineering Ltd
	G-BTJJ	PA-38-112 Tomahawk	Deltair Ltd
	G-BTJK	PA-38-112 Tomahawk	Network Enterprise International Ltd
	G-BTJL	PA-38-112 Tomahawk	S. & B. Ebrahimi-Ashtiany
	G-BTJN	Montgomerie-Bensen B.8MR	A. Hamilton
	G-BTJO	Thunder Ax9-140 balloon	Abbey Plant Co Ltd
	G-BTJS	Montgomerie-Bensen B.8MR	T. C. & P. K. Jackson
	G-BTJU	Cameron V-90 balloon	C. W. Jones (Flooring) Ltd
	G-BTJV	PZL SZD-50-3 Puchacz	Kent Gliding Club Ltd
	G-BTJX	Rans S.10 Sakota	M. Goacher
	G-BTJZ	Taylorcraft BC-12D-1	K. E. Ballington
	G-BTKA	Piper J-5A Cub Cruiser	S. J. Rudkin
	G-BTKB	Renegade Spirit 912	G. S. Blundell
	G-BTKD	Denney Aerocraft Kitfox	J. F. White
	G-BTKE	Colt 90A balloon	N. C. Lindsay
	G-BTKG	Light Aero Avid Flyer	P. R. Snowden
	G-BTKH	Colt GA-42 airship	Thunder & Colt Ltd
	G-BTKI	NA T-6G Texan	P. S. & S. M. Warner
	G-BTKJ	G.44 Widgeon	B. J. Snoxall
	G-BTKL	MBB Bo 105DB-4	Veritair Ltd/Cardiff
	G-BTKN	Cameron O-120 balloon	The Ballooning Business Ltd
	G-BTKO	Cameron A-180 balloon	Balloon Flights International Ltd
	G-BTKP	CFM Streak Shadow	K. S. Woodward
	G-BTKS	Rans S.10 Sakota	J. R. I. Rolfe & ptnrs
	G-BTKT	PA-28-161 Warrior II	C. R. Herbert
	G-BTKU	Cameron A-105 balloon	Champagne Flights International Ltd
	G-BTKV	PA-22 Tri-Pacer 160	M. Hanna
	G-BTKW	Cameron O-105 balloon	P. Spellward
	G-BTKX	PA-28-181 Archer II	Goldhawk Aviation
	G-BTKY	PA-28-181 Archer II	Primark Enterprises Ltd
	G-BTKZ	Cameron V-77 balloon	S. P. Richards

Reg.	Type	Owner or Operator	Notes
G-BTLA	Sikorsky S-76B	Falcon of Friendship Ltd	
G-BTLB	Wassmer WA.52 Europa	M. D. O'Brien/Shoreham	
G-BTLC	SA.365N2 Dauphin 2	Bond Helicopters Ltd	
G-BTLE	PA-31-350 Navajo Chieftain	Orient Aviation Ltd	
G-BTLF	Enstrom 280	M. A. Crook	
G-BTLG	PA-28R Cherokee Arrow 200	A. P. Reilly	
G-BTLI	Scheibe SF.25B Falke	S. F. Duerden/Germany	
G-BTLL	Pilatus P3-05 (A-806)	D. L. Masters/Biggin Hill	
G-BTLM	PA-22 Tri-Pacer 160	F & H (Aircraft) Ltd	
G-BTLP	AA-1C Lynx	Partlease Ltd	
G-BTLY	BN-2B-26 Islander	Pilatus BN Ltd/Bembridge	
G-BTMA	Cessna 172N	Cheshire Air Training School (Merseyside) Ltd	
G-BTMB	Colt 120A balloon	Picksteed Ltd	
G-BTMC	Colt 120A balloon	Picksteed Ltd	
G-BTMF	Taylorcraft BC-12D	C. M. Churchill/Cambridge	
G-BTMH	Colt 90A balloon	Douwe Egberts UK Ltd	
G-BTMJ	Maule MX-7-180	C. M. McGill	
G-BTMK	Cessna R.172K XP	Strand Coachworks	
G-BTML	Cameron 90 Rupert Bear SS balloon	Flying Pictures (Balloons) Ltd	
G-BTMM	Cameron N-105 balloon	M. F. Glue	
G-BTMN	Thunder Ax9-120 S2 balloon	Canterbury Balloons	
G-BTMO	Colt 69A balloon	Thunder & Colt Ltd	
G-BTMP	Everett Srs 2 gyroplane	D. G. Hill	
G-BTMR	Cessna 172M	Cumbria Aero Club/Carlisle	
G-BTMS	Light Aero Avid Flyer	M. J. Schyns	
G-BTMT	Denney Aerocraft Kitfox	Skulk Flying Group	
G-BTMV	Everett Srs 2 gyroplane	L. Armes	
G-BTMW	Zenair CH.701 STOL	L. Lewis	
G-BTMX	Denney Aerocraft Kitfox Mk 3	M. E. F. Reynolds	
G-BTMY	Cameron 80 Train SS balloon	Cameron Balloons Ltd	
G-BTMZ	PA-38-112 Tomahawk	T. Drew	
G-BTNA	Robinson R-22B	MG Group Ltd	
G-BTNB	Robinson R-22B	Davron Aviation	
G-BTNC	AS.365N-2 Dauphin 2	Bond Helicopters Ltd	
G-BTND	PA-38-112 Tomahawk	S. Edmunds	
G-BTNE	PA-28-161 Warrior II	A. T. Hooper & T. E. Evans/Wellesbourne	
G-BTNH	PA-28-161 Warrior II	C. R. Herbert	
G-BTNJ	Cameron V-90 balloon	P. L. Harrison & B. J. Newman	
G-BTNL	Thunder Ax10-180 balloon	Airships Ltd	
G-BTNN	Colt 21A balloon	Thunder & Colt Ltd	
G-BTNO	Aeronca 7AC Champion	November Oscar Group/Netherthorpe	
G-BTNP	Light Aero Avid Flyer Commuter	N. Evans	
G-BTNR	Denney Aerocraft Kitfox Mk 3	J. W. G. Ellis	
G-BTNS	PZL-104 Wilga 80	R. W. Husband	
G-BTNT	PA-28-151 Warrior	Britannia Airways Ltd/Luton	
G-BTNU	BAe 146-300	British Aerospace PLC (G-BSLS)	
G-BTNV	PA-28-161 Warrior II	D. K. Oakeley & A. M. Dawson	
G-BTNW	Rans S.6-ESA Coyote II	G. N. J. King & K. J. Dixon	
G-BTNX	Colt 105A balloon	Thunder & Colt Ltd	
G-BTNY	Fairchild M-62A	C. L. H. Parr	
G-BTNZ	AS.332L-1 Super Puma	British International Helicopters	
G-BTOA	Mong Sport MS-2	R. Wheeler	
G-BTOC	Robinson R-22B	T. Kressner	
G-BTOD	PA-38-112 Tomahawk	V. F. & J. A. Shirley	
G-BTOG	D.H.82A Tiger Moth	P. T. Szluha	
G-BTOH	Cameron A-105 balloon	R. E. Jones	
G-BTOI	Cameron N-77 balloon	The Nestle Co Ltd	
G-BTOJ	Mooney M.10 Cadet	D. W. Vernon	
G-BTOL	Denney Aerocraft Kitfox Mk 3	C. R. Phillips	
G-BTON	PA-28 Cherokee 140	W. A. & K. C. Ryan	
G-BTOO	Pitts S-1C Special	G. H. Matthews	
G-BTOP	Cameron V-77 balloon	J. J. Winter	
G-BTOR	Lancair 320	R. W. Fairless	
G-BTOS	Cessna 140	G. N. Smith	
G-BTOT	PA-15 Vagabond	D. Harker	
G-BTOU	Cameron O-120 balloon	First Class Ballooning Ltd	
G-BTOW	SOCATA Rallye 180GT	Cambridge University Gliding Trust Ltd	
G-BTOZ	Thunder Ax9-120 S2 balloon	H. G. Davies	
G-BTPA	BAe ATP	British Airways *Strathallan*/Glasgow	
G-BTPB	Cameron N-105 balloon	Test Valley Balloon Group	
G-BTPC	BAe ATP	British Airways *Strathblane*/Glasgow	

Notes	Reg.	Type	Owner or Operator
	G-BTPD	BAe ATP	British Airways *Strathconan*/Glasgow
	G-BTPE	BAe ATP	British Airways *Strathdon*/Glasgow
	G-BTPF	BAe ATP	British Airways *Strathearn*/Glasgow
	G-BTPG	BAe ATP	British Airways *Strathfillan*/Glasgow
	G-BTPH	BAe ATP	British Airways *Strathhaver*/Glasgow
	G-BTPJ	BAe ATP	British Airways *Strathpeffer*/Glasgow
	G-BTPK	BAe ATP	British Airways *Strathrannoch*/Glasgow
	G-BTPL	BAe ATP	British Airways *Strathspey*/Glasgow
	G-BTPM	BAe ATP	British Airways *Strathrory*/Glasgow
	G-BTPN	BAe ATP	British Airways *Strathbrora*/Glasgow
	G-BTPO	BAe ATP	British Airways *Strathclyde*/Glasgow
	G-BTPP	—	—
	G-BTPR	—	—
	G-BTPS	—	—
	G-BTPT	Cameron N-77 balloon	Derbyshire Building Soc
	G-BTPV	Colt 90A balloon	Airship & Balloon Co Ltd
	G-BTPX	Thunder Ax8-90 balloon	J. L. Guy
	G-BTPZ	Isaacs Fury II	M. A. Farrelly
	G-BTRA	Denney Aerocraft Kitfox Mk 3	T. P. Spurge
	G-BTRB	Colt Mickey Mouse SS balloon	Wellfarrow Ltd
	G-BTRC	Light Aero Avid Speedwing	B. Williams
	G-BTRE	Cessna F.172H	Hero Aviation/Stapleford
	G-BTRF	Aero Designs Pulsar	C. Smith
	G-BTRG	Aeronca 65C Super Chief	H. J. Cox
	G-BTRH	Aeronca 7AC Champion	D. W. Leach
	G-BTRI	Aeronca 11CC Super Chief	H. J. Cox
	G-BTRJ	Boeing Stearman B.75N1 (390)	G. L. Carpenter
	G-BTRK	PA-28-161 Warrior II	C. R. Herbert
	G-BTRL	Cameron N-105 balloon	J. Lippett
	G-BTRN	Thunder Ax9-120 S2 balloon	Solar Communications Ltd
	G-BTRO	Thunder Ax8-90 balloon	Capital Balloon Club Ltd
	G-BTRP	Hughes 369E	Southern Air Ltd/Shoreham
	G-BTRR	Thunder Ax7-77 balloon	S. M. Roberts
	G-BTRS	PA-28-161 Warrior II	Tyberry Aviation
	G-BTRT	PA-28R Cherokee Arrow 200-II	C. E. Yates
	G-BTRU	Robin DR.400/180	R. & M. Engineering Ltd
	G-BTRV	Boeing Stearman B.75N1	J. M. & R. J. Knights
	G-BTRW	Slingsby T.61F Venture T.2	B. Kerby & G. Grainer
	G-BTRX	Cameron V-77 balloon	R. P. Jones & N. P.Hemsley
	G-BTRY	PA-28-161 Warrior II	Air Service Training Ltd/Perth
	G-BTRZ	Jodel D.18	R. M. Johnson & R. Collin
	G-BTSA	Cessna 150K	M. E. Bartlett
	G-BTSB	Corben Baby Ace D	J. J. Naughton
	G-BTSC	Evans VP-2	B. P. Irish
	G-BTSD	Midget Mustang	R. Fitzpatrick
	G-BTSE	—	—
	G-BTSI	BAe 125-1000	Shell Aircraft Ltd/Heathrow
	G-BTSJ	PA-28-161 Warrior II	Plymouth School of Flying Ltd
	G-BTSK	Beech F33C Bonanza	J. A. Hart/White Waltham
	G-BTSL	Cameron Glass SS balloon	M. R. Humphrey & J. R .Clifton
	G-BTSM	Cessna 180A	C. Couston
	G-BTSN	Cessna 150G	N. A. Bilton/Norwich
	G-BTSO	Cessna 150M	M. L. Brenner
	G-BTSP	Piper J-3C-65 Cub	D. J. Bone & D. Jones
	G-BTSR	Aeronca 11AC Chief	R. W. Sage
	G-BTSS	Colt Flying Shopping Trolley SS balloon	Jentime Ltd
	G-BTST	Bensen B.9	V. Scott
	G-BTSU	Bensen B.8MR	B. T. Goggin
	G-BTSV	Denney Aerocraft Kitfox Mk 3	D. J. Sharland
	G-BTSW	Colt AS-80 Mk II airship	Huntair Ltd
	G-BTSX	Thunder Ax7-77 balloon	C. Moris-Gallimore
	G-BTSY	EE Lightning F.6 (XR724)	Lightning Association
	G-BTSZ	Cessna 177A	W. B. Pope
	G-BTTA	Hawker Sea Fury FB.10 (115)	Classic Aviation Ltd/Duxford
	G-BTTB	Cameron V-90 balloon	Royal Engineers Balloon Club
	G-BTTD	Montgomerie-Bensen B.8MR	K. J. Parker
	G-BTTE	Cessna 150L	I. J. Lawson
	G-BTTH	Beech F33C Bonanza	N. K. Mere/Germany
	G-BTTI	Thunder Ax8-90 balloon	Capital Balloon Club Ltd
	G-BTTJ	Thunder Ax9-120 S2 balloon	G. D. & L. Fitzpatrick
	G-BTTK	Thunder Ax8-105 balloon	Tempowish Ltd
	G-BTTL	Cameron V-90 balloon	A. J. Baird

Reg.	Type	Owner or Operator	Notes
G-BTTN	V.S.349 Spitfire Vb (BL628)	Aerofab Restorations	
G-BTTO	BAe ATP	Trident Aviation Leasing & Services Ltd	
G-BTTP	BAe 146-300	Air UK Ltd/Stansted	
G-BTTR	Aerotek Pitts S-2A Special	Ebork Ltd	
G-BTTS	Colt 77A balloon	Rutland Balloon Club	
G-BTTU	Cameron V-90 balloon	Heather Flight Ltd	
G-BTTW	Thunder Ax7-77 balloon	Thunder & Colt Ltd	
G-BTTY	Denney Aerocraft Kitfox Mk 2	K. J. Fleming	
G-BTTZ	Slingsby T.61F Venture T.2	I. R. F. Hammond	
G-BTUA	Slingsby T.61F Venture T.2	M. W. Olliver	
G-BTUB	Yakolev C.11	M. G. & J. R. Jefferies	
G-BTUC	EMB-312 Tucano	Short Bros PLC/Belfast City	
G-BTUD	CFM Image	D. G. Cook (G-MWPV)	
G-BTUE	BAe ATP	Trident Aviation Leasing Services Ltd	
G-BTUG	SOCATA Rallye 180T	Lasham Gliding Soc	
G-BTUH	Cameron N-65 balloon	B. J. Godding	
G-BTUJ	Thunder Ax9-120 balloon	R. T. Revel	
G-BTUK	Aerotek Pitts S-2A Special	Wickenby Aviation Ltd	
G-BTUL	Aerotek Pitts S-2A Special	C. & S. Aviation	
G-BTUM	Piper J-3C-65 Cub	Bar-Belle Aviation/North Weald	
G-BTUN	Colt Flying Drinks Can SS balloon	BIAS UK Ltd	
G-BTUR	PA-18 Super Cub 95 (modified)	D. C. Long/Glasgow	
G-BTUS	Whittaker MW.7	J. F. Bakewell	
G-BTUT	PA-34-200T Seneca II	A. G. Norman-Thorpe	
G-BTUU	Cameron O-120 balloon	Henley-on-Thames Air Balloons	
G-BTUV	Aeronca A65TAC Defender	J. T. Ingrouille	
G-BTUW	PA-28-151 Warrior	J. Robinson	
G-BTUX	AS.365N-2 Dauphin 2	Bond Helicopters Ltd/Aberdeen	
G-BTUY	BAe 146-300	British Aerospace PLC	
G-BTUZ	American General AG-5B Tiger	The Cabair Group Ltd/Elstree	
G-BTVA	Thunder Ax7-77 balloon	C. E. Wood	
G-BTVB	Everett Srs 3 gyroplane	J. Pumford	
G-BTVC	Denney Aerocraft Kitfox Mk 2	P. Mitchell	
G-BTVE	Hawker Demon	H. M. Davies	
G-BTVF	Rotorway Executive 90	E. P. Sadler	
G-BTVG	Cessna 140	V. C. Gover	
G-BTVH	Colt 77A balloon	D. N. & L. J. Close (G-ZADT/G-ZBCA)	
G-BTVN	BN-2B-26 Islander	Pilatus BN Ltd/Bembridge	
G-BTVP	Currie Wot	B. V. Mayo & V. Panteli	
G-BTVR	PA-28 Cherokee 140	West of Scotland Flying Club Ltd	
G-BTVS	AS.355F-1 Twin Squirrel	BLS Aviation Ltd (G-STVE/G-TOFF/ G-BKJX)	
G-BTVU	Robinson R-22B	Sloane Helicopters Ltd/Sywell	
G-BTVV	Cessna F.337G	Taylor Aircraft Services	
G-BTVW	Cessna 152	A. T. Hooper & T. E. Evans/Wellesbourne	
G-BTVX	Cessna 152	A. T. Hooper & T. E. Evans/Wellesbourne	
G-BTWB	Denney Aerocraft Kitfox Mk 3	J. E. Tootell (G-BTTM)	
G-BTWC	Slingsby T.61F Venture T.2	RAFGSA/Bicester	
G-BTWD	Slingsby T.61F Venture T.2	York Gliding Centre	
G-BTWE	Slingsby T.61F Venture T.2	RAFGSA/Bicester	
G-BTWF	D.H.C.1 Chipmunk 22	J. A. & V. G. Sims	
G-BTWG	Thunder Ax10-160 S2 balloon	W. O. T. Holmes & R. J. Barr	
G-BTWH	Thunder Ax7-77 balloon	Jim Barker Motor Factor	
G-BTWI	EAA Acro Sport 1	Detail Offers Ltd	
G-BTWJ	Cameron V-77 balloon	F. W. Barnes	
G-BTWK	Colt 210A balloon	Airship & Balloon Co Ltd	
G-BTWL	WAG-Aero Acro Sport Trainer	D. H. Tonkin	
G-BTWM	Cameron V-77 balloon	D. I. Gray-Fisk	
G-BTWN	Maule MXT-7-180	C. T. Rolls	
G-BTWO	—	—	
G-BTWP	Robinson R-22B	Sloane Helicopters Ltd/Sywell	
G-BTWR	Bell P-63A-7-BE Kingcobra	Patina Ltd/Duxford	
G-BTWS	Thunder Ax7-77 balloon	Bavarian Balloon Co Ltd	
G-BTWU	PA-22 Tri-Pacer 135	G. A. Bentley	
G-BTWV	Cameron O-90 balloon	Bodkin House Hotel	
G-BTWW	AB-206B JetRanger 2	Dollar Air Services Ltd/Coventry	
G-BTWX	SOCATA TB.9 Tampico	Air Touring Services Ltd/Biggin Hill	
G-BTWY	Aero Designs Pulsar	J. J. Pridal & A. K. Pirie	
G-BTWZ	Rans S.10 Sakota	D. G. Hey	
G-BTXB	Colt 77A balloon	Shellgas South West Area	
G-BTXC	Team Minimax	M. H. D. Soltau (G-MWFC)	
G-BTXD	Rans S.6-ESA Coyote II	M. Isterling	
G-BTXF	Cameron V-90 balloon	Gone With The Wind Ltd	

Notes	Reg.	Type	Owner or Operator
	G-BTXH	Colt AS-56 airship	Huntair Ltd
	G-BTXI	Noorduyn AT-16 Harvard IIB	Patina Ltd/Duxford
	G-BTXK	Thunder Ax7-65 balloon	E. J. Jacobs
	G-BTXM	Colt 21A balloon	Airship & Balloon Co Ltd
	G-BTXP	Cameron RX-100 balloon	Cameron Balloons Ltd
	G-BTXR	Cassutt Racer	J. Cull/Popham
	G-BTXS	Cameron O-120 balloon	Southern Balloon Group
	G-BTXT	Maule MXT-7-180	R. G. Humphries
	G-BTXU	Cameron A-210 balloon	P. J. D. Kerr & A. J. Street
	G-BTXV	Cameron A-210 balloon	The Ballooning Business Ltd
	G-BTXW	Cameron V-77 balloon	P. C. Waterhouse
	G-BTXX	Bellanca 8KCAB Decathlon	Sherwood Flying Club Ltd
	G-BTXZ	Zenair CH.250	B. F. Arnall
	G-BTYC	Cessna 150L	JJ Aviation
	G-BTYD	Cameron N-90 balloon	S. J. Colin
	G-BTYE	Cameron A-180 balloon	Fight Flight
	G-BTYF	Thunder Ax10-180 S2 balloon	Champagne Flights International Ltd
	G-BTYH	Pottier P.80S	R. Pickett
	G-BTYI	PA-28-181 Archer II	T. E. Westley
	G-BTYJ	Schleicher ASH.25	T. I. Gardiner
	G-BTYK	Cessna 310R	R. J. Lane & D. R. C. Knight
	G-BTYT	Cessna 152	M. J. Green
	G-BTYW	Cessna 120	P. J. Singleton & C. J. Archer
	G-BTYX	Cessna 140	G-BTYX Group
	G-BTYY	Curtiss Robin C-2	R. R. L. Windus
	G-BTYZ	Colt 210A balloon	T. M. Donnelly
	G-BTZA	Beech F33A Bonanza	G-BTZA Group/Edinburgh
	G-BTZB	Yakovlev Yak-50	Patina Ltd/Duxford
	G-BTZD	Yakovlev Yak-1	Historic Aircraft Collection Ltd
	G-BTZE	LET Yakovlev C.11	Bianchi Aviation Film Services Ltd/Booker
	G-BTZL	Oldfield Baby Lakes	J. M. Roach
	G-BTZO	SOCATA TB.20 Trinidad	C.S.E. Aviation Ltd/Kidlington
	G-BTZP	SOCATA TB.9 Tampico	Newcastle upon Tyne Aero Club Ltd
	G-BTZR	Colt 77B balloon	P. J. Fell
	G-BTZS	Colt 77B balloon	Thunder & Colt Ltd
	G-BTZU	Cameron Concept SS balloon	Gone With The Wind Ltd
	G-BTZV	Cameron V-77 balloon	A. W. Sumner
	G-BTZW	Piper J-3C-65 Cub	D. A. Woodhams
	G-BTZX	Piper J-3C-65 Cub	D. A. Woodhams & J. T. Coulthard
	G-BTZY	Colt 56A balloon	T. M. Donnelly
	G-BTZZ	CFM Streak Shadow	D. R. Stennett
	G-BUAA	Corben Bay Ace D	B. F. Hill
	G-BUAB	Aeronca 11AC Chief	J. Reed
	G-BUAC	Slingsby T.31 Motor Cadet III	D. A. Wilson
	G-BUAD	Colt AS-105 Mk II airship	Thunder & Colt Ltd
	G-BUAE	Thunder Ax8-105 S2 balloon	T. M. Donnelly
	G-BUAF	Cameron N-77 balloon	S. J. Colin
	G-BUAG	Jodel D.18	A. L. Silcox
	G-BUAI	Everett Srs 3 gyroplane	P. Stanlake
	G-BUAJ	Cameron N-90 balloon	J. R. & S. J. Huggins
	G-BUAK	Thunder Ax8-105 S2 balloon	G. D. & L. Fitzpatrick
	G-BUAM	Cameron V-77 balloon	Broadland Balloons Ltd
	G-BUAN	Cessna 172N	Bell Aviation
	G-BUAO	Luscombe 8A Silvaire	G. H. Matthews
	G-BUAR	V.S.358 Seafire LF.IIIc (PP972)	Wizzard Investments Ltd
	G-BUAT	Thunder Ax9-120 balloon	J. Fenton
	G-BUAU	Cameron A-180 balloon	GT Flying Club Ltd
	G-BUAV	Cameron O-105 balloon	K. D. Johnson
	G-BUAW	Pitts S-1C Special	E. J. Hedges
	G-BUAX	Rans S.10 Sakota	J. W. Topham
	G-BUAY	Cameron A-210 balloon	Ballooning World Ltd
	G-BUBA	PA-18 Super Cub 150	B. Jackson
	G-BUBB	Light Aero Avid Flyer	D. Hookins
	G-BUBC	QAC Quickie Tri-Q.200	D. J. Clarke
	G-BUBF	BN-2B-26 Islander	Pilatus BN Ltd/Bembridge
	G-BUBG	BN-2B-26 Islander	Pilatus BN Ltd/Bembridge
	G-BUBH	BN-2B-26 Islander	Pilatus BN Ltd/Bembridge
	G-BUBJ	BN-2B-26 Islander	Pilatus BN Ltd/Bembridge
	G-BUBK	BN-2B-26 Islander	Pilatus BN Ltd/Bembridge
	G-BUBL	Thunder Ax8-105 balloon	Moet & Chandon (London) Ltd
	G-BUBM	BN-2B-26 Islander	Pilatus BN Ltd/Bembridge
	G-BUBN	BN-2B-26 Islander	Pilatus BN Ltd/Bembridge

Reg.	Type	Owner or Operator	Notes
G-BUBO	BN-2B-26 Islander	Pilatus BN Ltd/Bembridge	
G-BUBP	BN-2B-26 Islander	Pilatus BN Ltd/Bembridge	
G-BUBR	Cameron A-250 balloon	Bath Hot-Air Balloon Club	
G-BUBS	—	—	
G-BUBT	Stoddard-Hamilton Glasair IIRGS	M. D. Evans	
G-BUBU	PA-34-220T Seneca III	Brinor (Holdings) Ltd/Ipswich	
G-BUBW	Robinson R-22B	Forth Helicopters	
G-BUBX	Cameron O-120 balloon	Balloons International	
G-BUBY	Thunder Ax8-105 S2 balloon	T. M. Donnelly	
G-BUCA	Cessna A.150K	A. Bucknole	
G-BUCB	Cameron H-34 balloon	Flying Pictures (Balloons) Ltd	
G-BUCC	C.A.S.A. 1.131E Jungmann (BU+EM)	E. J. F. McEntee (G-BUEM)	
G-BUCG	Schleicher ASW.20L (modified)	W. B. Andrews	
G-BUCH	Stinson V-77 Reliant	Rare Aeroplane Soc	
G-BUCI	Auster AOP.9 (XP242)	Historic Aircraft Flight Reserve Collection/ Middle Wallop	
G-BUCJ	D.H.C.2 Beaver 1 (XP772)	Historic Aircraft Flight Reserve Collection/ Middle Wallop	
G-BUCK	C.A.S.A. 1.131E Jungmann (BU+CK)	Jungmann Flying Group/White Waltham	
G-BUCL	Robinson R-22B	Crispian Motor Co Ltd	
G-BUCM	Hawker Sea Fury FB.11 (VX653)	Patina Ltd/Duxford	
G-BUCO	Pietenpol Air Camper	A. James	
G-BUCP	BAe 125 Srs 800B	CIBC Finance Ltd	
G-BUCS	Cessna 150F	A. Bucknole	
G-BUCT	Cessna 150L	A. Bucknole	
G-BUDA	Slingsby T.61F Venture T.2	RAF Germany Gliding Association	
G-BUDB	Slingsby T.61F Venture T.2	RAF Germany Gliding Association	
G-BUDC	Slingsby T.61F Venture T.2	D. Collinson	
G-BUDD	Team Minimax Z	M. A. J. Hutt (G-MWZM)	
G-BUDE	PA-22 Tri-Pacer 135 (tailwheel)	B. A. Bower/Thruxton	
G-BUDF	Rand-Robinson KR-2	J. B. McNab	
G-BUDH	Light Aero Avid Flyer	D. Cowen	
G-BUDI	Aero Designs Pulsar	R. W. L. Oliver	
G-BUDK	Thunder Ax7-77 balloon	C. J. Warriner	
G-BUDL	Auster 3	M. Pocock	
G-BUDM	Colt Flying Hand SS balloon	BIAS (UK) Ltd	
G-BUDN	Cameron 30 Shoe SS balloon	Converse Europe Ltd	
G-BUDO	PZL-110 Koliber 150	P. C. Dimond	
G-BUDR	Denney Aerocraft Kitfox Mk 3	N. J. Wills	
G-BUDS	Rand-Robinson KR-2	D. W. Munday	
G-BUDT	Slingsby T.61F Venture T.2	G-BUDT Group	
G-BUDU	Cameron V-77 balloon	T. M. G. Amery	
G-BUDV	Cameron A-210 balloon	Bridges Van Hire Ltd	
G-BUDW	Brügger MB.2 Colibri	J. M. Hoblyn	
G-BUDX	Boeing 757-236	Ambassador Airlines Ltd	
G-BUDY	Colt 17A balloon	Bondbaste Ltd	
G-BUDZ	Boeing 757-236	Ambassador Airlines Ltd	
G-BUEA	Aérospatiale ATR-42-300	CityFlyer Express Ltd/British Airways	
G-BUEB	Aérospatiale ATR-42-300	CityFlyer Express Ltd/British Airways	
G-BUEC	Van's RV-6	D. W. Richardson & R. D. Harper	
G-BUED	Slingsby T.61F Venture T.2	SE Kent Civil Service Flying Club	
G-BUEE	Cameron A-210 balloon	Bristol Balloons	
G-BUEF	Cessna 152	Three Counties Aero Engineering Ltd/ Lasham	
G-BUEG	Cessna 152	Three Counties Aero Engineering Ltd/ Lasham	
G-BUEI	Thunder Ax8-105 balloon	Anglia Balloons	
G-BUEJ	Colt 77B balloon	P. M. Taylor	
G-BUEK	Slingsby T.61F Venture T.2	P. B. Duhig & W. Retzler	
G-BUEL	Colt Bottle II SS balloon	Jentime Ltd	
G-BUEN	VPM M.14 Scout	A. T. Wortley	
G-BUEO	Maule MX-7-180	K. & S. C. Knight	
G-BUEP	Maule MX-7-180	Continental Services PLC	
G-BUER	Robinson R-22B	Sloane Helicopters Ltd/Sywell	
G-BUES	Cameron N-77 balloon	Bath City Council-Parks Section	
G-BUET	Colt Flying Drinks Can SS balloon	Flying Pictures (Balloons) Ltd	
G-BUEU	Colt 21A balloon	Flying Pictures (Balloons) Ltd	
G-BUEV	Cameron O-77 balloon	Council for Positively Belfast	
G-BUEW	Rans S.6 Coyote II	D. J. O'Gorman (G-MWYF)	
G-BUEX	Schweizer 269C	Vic Lamb Aviation Ltd (G-HFLR)	
G-BUEZ	Hunter F.6A (XF375)	Old Flying Machine Co Ltd/Duxford	

Notes	Reg.	Type	Owner or Operator
	G-BUFA	Cameron R-77 balloon	Noble Adventures Ltd
	G-BUFC	Cameron R-77 balloon	Noble Adventures Ltd
	G-BUFE	Cameron R-77 balloon	Noble Adventures Ltd
	G-BUFG	Slingsby T.61F Venture T.2	P. K. J. Spencer & R. I. Davidson
	G-BUFH	PA-28-161 Warrior II	A. Tootell
	G-BUFI	BAe 146-100	British Aerospace PLC
	G-BUFJ	Cameron V-90 balloon	Whitebread Hop Farm
	G-BUFK	Cassutt Racer IIIM	D. I. H. Johnstone & W. T. Barnard
	G-BUFL	BAe Jetstream 3102	British Aerospace PLC
	G-BUFN	Slingsby T.61F Venture T.2	BUFN Group
	G-BUFO	Cameron 70 UFO SS balloon	Airship & Balloon Co Ltd
	G-BUFP	Slingsby T.61F Venture T.2	Venture Group
	G-BUFR	Slingsby T.61F Venture T.2	R. F. Warren & P. A. Hazell
	G-BUFT	Cameron O-120 balloon	Prime Time Balloons Ltd
	G-BUFU	Colt 105A balloon	Basemore Ltd
	G-BUFV	Light Aero Avid Flyer	S. C. Ord
	G-BUFX	Cameron N-90 balloon	Kerridge Computer Co Ltd
	G-BUFY	PA-28-161 Warrior II	GT Aviation
	G-BUGB	Stolp SA.750 Acroduster Too	D. Burnham
	G-BUGC	Jurca MJ.5 Sirocco	A. Burani (G-BWDJ)
	G-BUGD	Cameron V-77 balloon	Cameron Balloons Ltd
	G-BUGE	Bellanca 7GCAA Cltabria	Welsh Dragon Aviation Ltd
	G-BUGF	Cameron A-210 balloon	Adventure Ballooning
	G-BUGG	Cessna 150F	A. Passfield
	G-BUGH	Rans S.10 Sakota	D. T. Smith
	G-BUGI	Evans VP-2	R. G. Boyes
	G-BUGJ	Robin DR.400/180	Alfred Graham Ltd
	G-BUGL	Slnigsby T.61F Venture T.2	VMG Group
	G-BUGM	CFM Streak Shadow	W. J. de Gier
	G-BUGN	Colt 210A balloon	Balloon Club of GB Ltd
	G-BUGO	Colt 56B balloon	D. W. & P. Allum
	G-BUGP	Cameron V-77 balloon	G. J. & R. Plant
	G-BUGS	Cameron V-77 balloon	A Load of Hot Air
	G-BUGT	Slingsby T.61F Venture T.2	J. F. R. Jones
	G-BUGV	Slingsby T.61F Venture T.2	K. E. Ballington
	G-BUGW	Slingsby T.61F Venture T.2	F. W. Cater & Son Ltd
	G-BUGX	M.S.880B Rallye Club	The Rallye Group
	G-BUGY	Cameron V-65 balloon	Dante Balloon Group
	G-BUGZ	Slingsby T.61F Venture T.2	Dishforth Flying Club
	G-BUHA	Slingsby T.61F Venture T.2	A. W. Swales
	G-BUHB	BAe 146-300	TAS Airways SpA (G-BSYS)
	G-BUHC	BAe 146-300	British Aerospace Defence Ltd (G-BTMI)
	G-BUHH	—	—
	G-BUHI	Boeing 737-	
	G-BUHJ	Boeing 737-4Q8	British Airways
	G-BUHK	Boeing 737-4Q8	British Airways
	G-BUHL	Boeing 737-4S3	British Airways
	G-BUHM	Cameron V-77 balloon	L. A. Watts
	G-BUHN	Cameron N-90 balloon	Cameron Balloons Ltd
	G-BUHO	Cessna 140	D. F. Cumberlidge
	G-BUHP	Flyair 1100	R. White
	G-BUHR	Slingsby T.61F Venture T.2	Lleweni Parc Ltd
	G-BUHS	Stoddard-Hamilton Glasair SH-TD-1	S. J. Marsh
	G-BUHT	Cameron A-210 balloon	British School of Ballooning
	G-BUHU	Cameron N-105 balloon	Flying Pictures (Balloons) Ltd
	G-BUHW	BAe 146-300	British Aerospace PLC
	G-BUHX	Robinson R-22B	Rotaflite Helicopter Sales
	G-BUHY	Cameron A-210 balloon	Adventure Balloon Co Ltd
	G-BUHZ	Cessna 120	C. P. & C. J. Wilkes
	G-BUIA	Colt 77B balloon	R. A. Riley
	G-BUIB	MBB Bo 105DBS/4	Bond Helicopters Ltd (G-BDYZ)
	G-BUIC	Denney Aerocraft Kitfox Mk 2	C. R. Northrop & B. M. Chilvers
	G-BUIE	Cameron N-90 balloon	Flying Pictures (Balloons) Ltd
	G-BUIF	PA-28-161 Warior II	Newcastle upon Tyne Aero Club Ltd
	G-BUIG	Campbell Cricket	T. A. Holmes
	G-BUIH	Slingsby T.61F Venture T.2	Yorkshire Gliding Club (Pty) Ltd
	G-BUII	Cameron A-210 balloon	Aire Valley Balloons
	G-BUIJ	PA-28-161 Warrior II	Tradecliff Ltd
	G-BUIK	PA-28-161 Warrior II	I. H. Webb
	G-BUIL	CFM Streak Shadow	P. N. Bevan & L. M. Poor
	G-BUIN	Thunder Ax7-77 balloon	Free Flight Aerostat Group
	G-BUIP	Denney Aerocraft Kitfox Mk 2	Avcomm Developments Ltd

Reg.	Type	Owner or Operator	Notes
G-BUIR	Light Aero Avid Speedwing Mk 4	K. N. Pollard	
G-BUIU	Cameron V-90 balloon	Prescott Hot Air Balloons Ltd	
G-BUIW	Robinson R-22B	Findon Air Services/Shoreham	
G-BUIX	BAe 125-1000B	Raytheon Corporate Jets Inc	
G-BUIY	BAe 125 Srs 800B	Raytheon Corporate Jets Inc	
G-BUIZ	Cameron N-90 balloon	Airship & Balloon Co Ltd	
G-BUJA	Slingsby T.61F Venture T.2	RAFGSA/Bicester	
G-BUJB	Slingsby T.61F Venture T.2	Falke Syndicate	
G-BUJC	Partenavia P.68C	J. W. Bate	
G-BUJE	Cessna 177B	FG93 Group	
G-BUJG	AS.350B-2 Ecureuil	R. J. & E. M. Frost (G-HEAR)	
G-BUJH	Colt 77B balloon	A. D. Watt & ptnrs	
G-BUJI	Slingsby T.61F Venture T.2	R. A. Kilvington	
G-BUJJ	Light Aero Avid Flyer	A. C. Debrett	
G-BUJK	Montgomerie-Bensen B.8MR	J. M. Montgomerie	
G-BUJL	Aero Designs Pulsar	J. J. Lynch	
G-BUJM	Cessna 120	De Cadenet Engineering Ltd/Shipdham	
G-BUJN	Cessna 172N	De Cadenet Engineering Ltd/Shipdham	
G-BUJO	PA-28-161 Warrior II	De Cadenet Engineering Ltd/Shipdham	
G-BUJP	PA-28-161 Warrior II	De Cadenet Engineering Ltd/Shipdham	
G-BUJR	Cameron A-180 balloon	W. I. Hooker & C. Parker	
G-BUJS	Colt 17A balloon	Thunder & Colt Ltd	
G-BUJT	BAe Jetstream 3100	British Aerospace PLC/Prestwick	
G-BUJU	Cessna 150H	S. J. N. Robbie	
G-BUJV	Light Aero Avid Speedwing Mk 4	D. N. Anderson	
G-BUJW	Thunder Ax8-90 balloon	R. T. Fagan	
G-BUJX	Slingsby T.61F Venture T.2	R. J. Chichester-Constable	
G-BUJY	D.H.82A Tiger Moth	Aero Vintage Ltd	
G-BUJZ	Rotorway Executive 90	T. W. Aisthorpe & R. J. D. Crick	
G-BUKA	Fairchild SA227AC Metro III	Air Corbière Ltd/Coventry	
G-BUKB	Rans S.10 Sakota	M. K. Blatch & M. P. Lee	
G-BUKC	Cameron A-180 balloon	Cloud Nine Balloon Co	
G-BUKE	Boeing Stearman A.75N1	R. G. Rance (G-BRIP)	
G-BUKF	Denney Aerocraft Kitfox Mk 4	M. R. Crosland	
G-BUKG	Robinson R-22B	Streamline Aviation Ltd	
G-BUKH	D.31 Turbulent	J. S. Smith	
G-BUKI	Thunder Ax7-77 balloon	Adventure Aloft	
G-BUKJ	BAe ATP	Trident Aviation Leasing Services Ltd	
G-BUKK	Bucker Bu133 Jungmeister (U-80)	E. J. F. McEntee/White Waltham	
G-BUKL	Brantly B.2B	Helihire Ltd	
G-BUKN	PA-15 Vagabond	M. R. Masters	
G-BUKO	Cessna 120	N. G. Abbott	
G-BUKP	Denney Aerocraft Kitfox Mk 2	T. D. Reid	
G-BUKR	M.S.880B Rallye Club 100T	G-BUKR Flying Group	
G-BUKS	Colt 77B balloon	R. & M. Bairstow	
G-BUKT	Luscombe 8A Silvaire	R. C. Steel	
G-BUKU	Luscombe 8E Silvaire	F. G. Miskelly	
G-BUKX	PA-28-161 Warrior II	Creswick Air Ltd	
G-BUKY	CCF Harvard IVM	P. R. Monk & A. C. Savage	
G-BUKZ	Evans VP-2	P. R. Farnell	
G-BULA	Cameron 77 Raindrop SS balloon	Cameron Balloons Ltd	
G-BULB	Thunder Ax7-77 balloon	Shiltons of Rothbury	
G-BULC	Light Aero Avid Flyer Mk 4	A. G. Batchelor	
G-BULD	Cameron N-105 balloon	S. D. Baker	
G-BULE	Price TPB.2 balloon	A. G. R. Calder	
G-BULF	Colt 77A balloon	M. V. Farrant	
G-BULG	Van's RV-4	J. R. Ware	
G-BULH	Cessna 172N	B. R. Gaunt	
G-BULJ	CFM Steak Shadow	C. C. Brown	
G-BULK	Thunder Ax9-120 S2 balloon	Rapidflame Ltd	
G-BULL	SA Bulldog 120/128	J. D. Richardson	
G-BULM	Aero Designs Pulsar	W. R. Davis-Smith	
G-BULN	Colt 210A balloon	H. G. Davies	
G-BULO	Luscombe 8A Silvaire	G-BULO Flying Group/Andrewsfield	
G-BULP	Thunder Ax9-120 S2 balloon	Regency Balloons Ltd	
G-BULR	PA-28 Cherokee 140	Fordaire Aviation Ltd	
G-BULS	Cameron A-210 balloon	Airship & Balloon Co Ltd	
G-BULT	Campbell Cricket	A. T. Pocklington	
G-BULU	Short S.312 Tucano T.1 (ZF485)	Short Bros PLC/Belfast City	
G-BULW	Rans S.10 Sakota	V. G. Gale	
G-BULX	Robinson R-22B	Sloane Helicopters Ltd/Sywell	
G-BULY	Light Aero Avid Flyer	M. O. Breen	
G-BULZ	Denney Aerocraft Kitfox Mk 2	D. J. Dumolo & C. R. Barnes	

Notes	Reg.	Type	Owner or Operator
	G-BUMP	PA-28-181 Archer II	M. Dunlop
	G-BUNB	Slingsby T.61F Venture T.2	RAFGSA Cranwell Gliding Club
	G-BUNC	PZL-104 Wilga 35	Paravia Group
	G-BUND	PA-28RT-201T Turbo Arrow IV	W. S. Stanley
	G-BUNE	Colt Flying Drinks Can SS balloon	Pepsi Cola Overseas Ltd
	G-BUNF	Colt Flying Drinks Can SS balloon	Pepsi Cola Overseas Ltd
	G-BUNG	Cameron N-77 balloon	T. S. King
	G-BUNH	PA-28RT-201T Turbo Arrow IV	A. Tootell
	G-BUNI	Cameron 90 Bunny SS balloon	Virgin Airship & Balloon Co Ltd
	G-BUNJ	Squarecraft SA.102-5 Cavalier	J. A. Smith
	G-BUNM	Denney Aerocraft Kitfox Mk 3	P. J. Carter
	G-BUNN	Whittaker MW.6-S Fatboy Flyer	M. R. Grunwell
	G-BUNO	Lancair 320	J. Softley
	G-BUNR	PA-34-200T Seneca II	A. C. Gradidge
	G-BUNS	Cessna F.150K	R. W. H. Cole
	G-BUNT	AIA Stampe SV-4C	J. F. Graham (G-AYCK)
	G-BUNV	Thunder Ax7-77 balloon	P. J. Waller
	G-BUNX	Cameron V-77 balloon	J. H. Bailey
	G-BUNZ	Thunder Ax10-180 S2 balloon	T. M. Donnelly
	G-BUOA	Whittaker MW.6-S Fatboy Flyer	D. A. Izod
	G-BUOB	CFM Streak Shadow	A. M. Simmons
	G-BUOC	Cameron A-210 balloon	G. N. & K. A. Connolly
	G-BUOD	SE-5A (replica)	M. D. Waldron
	G-BUOE	Cameron V-90 balloon	Dusters & Co
	G-BUOF	D.62B Condor	K. Jones
	G-BUOG	Colt 90A balloon	Magicteam Management Ltd
	G-BUOH	Jet Hawk Ducted Fan Trainer	C. Herbert
	G-BUOI	PA-20 Pacer	A. Phillips
	G-BUOJ	Cessna 172N	Skytronics Ltd
	G-BUOK	Rans S.6-ESA Coyote II	M. Morris
	G-BUOL	Denney Aerocraft Kitfox Mk 3	J. G. D. Barbour
	G-BUON	Light Aero Avid Aerobat	I. A. J. Lappin
	G-BUOO	QAC Quickie Tri-Q.200	D. E. Johnson
	G-BUOP	Skycycle D.2 airship	G. E. Dorrington
	G-BUOR	C.A.S.A. 1.131E Jungmann 2000	M. J. Aherne
	G-BUOS	V.S.394 Spitfire FR.XVIII	A. J. Reynard & Park Avenue Investments Ltd
	G-BUOT	Colt 77A balloon	Thunder & Colt Ltd
	G-BUOU	Colt 90A balloon	Thunder & Colt Ltd
	G-BUOW	Aero Designs Pulsar XP	M. P. Allinson
	G-BUOX	Cameron V-77 balloon	R. M. Pursey & C. M. Richardson
	G-BUOY	SA.315B Alouette III	Dollar Air Services Ltd/Coventry
	G-BUOZ	Thunder Ax10-180 balloon	Ashleader Ltd
	G-BUPA	Rutan LongEz	M. D. Faiers
	G-BUPB	Stolp SA.300 Starduster Too	Summit Aviation Ltd/Shoreham
	G-BUPC	Rollason Beta B.2	C. A. Rolph
	G-BUPF	Bensen B.8R	G. M. Hobman
	G-BUPG	Cessna 180K	T. P. A. Norman
	G-BUPH	Colt 25A balloon	Wellfarrow Ltd
	G-BUPI	Cameron V-77 balloon	S. A. Masey (G-BOUC)
	G-BUPJ	Fournier RF-4D	M. R. Shelton
	G-BUPM	VPM M.16 Tandem Trainer	A. T. Wortley
	G-BUPN	PA-46-350P Malibu	K. Fletcher/Coventry
	G-BUPO	Zlin Z.526F	P. J. Behr & F. Mendelssohn/France
	G-BUPP	Cameron V-42 balloon	J. A. Hibberd
	G-BUPR	Jodel D.18	R. W. Burrows
	G-BUPS	Aérospatiale ATR-42-300	—
	G-BUPT	Cameron O-105 balloon	Chiltern Balloons
	G-BUPU	Thunder Ax7-77 balloon	R. C. Barkworth & D. G. Maguire
	G-BUPV	Great Lakes 2T-1A	R. J. Fray
	G-BUPW	Denney Aerocraft Kitfox Mk 3	D. Sweet
	G-BURA	Thunder Ax8-105 S2 balloon	Airship Shop Ltd
	G-BURB	Denney Aerocraft Kitfox Mk 3	G. J. Langston
	G-BURC		—
	G-BURD	Cessna F.172N	Bobbington Air Training School Ltd
	G-BURE	Jodel D.9	L. J. Kingsford
	G-BURF	Rand KR-2	P. J. H. Moorhouse & B. L. Hewart
	G-BURG	Colt 77A balloon	S. J. Humphreys
	G-BURH	Cessna 150E	BURH Flying Group
	G-BURI	Enstrom F-28C	F. B. Holben
	G-BURK	Luscombe 8A Silvaire	M. Stow
	G-BURL	Colt 105A balloon	Scotia Balloons Ltd
	G-BURM	EE Canberra TT.18	A. R. Mitchell

Reg.	Type	Owner or Operator	Notes
G-BURN	Cameron O-120 balloon	I. Bentley	
G-BURO	PZL-104 Wilga 80	S. F. Elvins	
G-BURP	Rotorway Executive 90	A. G. A. Edwards	
G-BURR	Auster AOP.9	R. P. D. Folkes	
G-BURS	Sikorsky S-76A	Lynton Aviation Ltd (G-OHTL)	
G-BURT	PA-28-161 Warrior II	I. P. Stockwell	
G-BURV	BAe 125 Srs 800B	Raytheon Corporate Jets Inc	
G-BURW	Light Aero Avid Speedwing	A. Charlton	
G-BURY	Cessna 152	M. L. Grunnill	
G-BURZ	Hawker Nimrod	Historic Aircraft Collection Ltd	
G-BUSB	Airbus A.320-111	British Airways	
G-BUSC	Airbus A.320-111	British Airways	
G-BUSD	Airbus A.320-111	British Airways	
G-BUSE	Airbus A.320-111	British Airways *Isles of Scilly*	
G-BUSF	Airbus A.320-111	British Airways	
G-BUSG	Airbus A.320-211	British Airways *Isle of Wight*	
G-BUSH	Airbus A.320-211	British Airways *Isle of Jura*	
G-BUSI	Airbus A.320-211	British Airways *Isle of Anglesey*	
G-BUSJ	Airbus A.320-211	British Airways *Island of Sark*	
G-BUSK	Airbus A.320-211	British Airways *Island of Guernsey*	
G-BUSN	Rotorway Executive 90	B. Seymour	
G-BUSP	Cameron Cart SS balloon	Cameron Balloons Ltd	
G-BUSR	Aero Designs Pulsar	S. S. Bateman & R. A. Watts	
G-BUSS	Cameron 90 Bus SS balloon	A. G. E. Faulkner	
G-BUST	Lancair IV	C. C. Butt	
G-BUSU	Colt 42A balloon	Thunder & Colt Ltd	
G-BUSV	Colt 105A balloon	Thunder & Colt Ltd	
G-BUSW	R. Commander 114	K. Costello	
G-BUSY	Thunder Ax6-56A balloon	M. S. Drinkwater	
G-BUSZ	Light Aero Avid Speedwing Mk 4	G. N. S. Farrant	
G-BUTA	C.A.S.A. 1.131E Jungmann 2000	K. D. Dunkerley	
G-BUTB	CFM Streak Shadow	F. A. H. Ashmead	
G-BUTC	Cyclone AX3/582	Cyclone Hovercraft Ltd (G-MYHO)	
G-BUTD	Van's RV-6	N. Reddish	
G-BUTE	Anderson EA-1 Kingfisher	T. C. Crawford (G-BRCK)	
G-BUTF	Aeronca 11AC Chief	N. J. Mortimore	
G-BUTG	Zenair CH.601HD	J. M. Scott	
G-BUTH	CEA DR.220 2+2	E. J. Horsfall	
G-BUTI	Firefly 7-15 balloon	P. J. McK. Hutton	
G-BUTJ	Cameron O-77 balloon	A. J. A. Bubb	
G-BUTK	Murphy Rebel	D. Webb	
G-BUTL	PA-24 Comanche 250	D. Buttle (G-ARLB)/Blackbushe	
G-BUTM	Rans S.6-116 Coyote II	M. Rudd	
G-BUTN	MBB Bo 105DBS/4	Bond Helicopters Ltd (G-AZTI)	
G-BUTO	Pitts S-1 Special	J. A. Alexander	
G-BUTP	Bede BD-5G	Heather Flight Ltd	
G-BUTT	Cessna FA.150K	C. R. Guggenheim (G-AXSJ)	
G-BUTU	OA.7 Optica Srs 300	FLS Aerospace (Lovaux) Ltd/Bournemouth	
G-BUTV	OA.7 Optica Srs 300	FLS Aerospace (Lovaux) Ltd/Bournemouth	
G-BUTX	C.A.S.A. 1.133C Jungmeister	A. J. E. Smith & D. T. Kaberry	
G-BUTY	Brügger MB.2 Colibri	R. M. Lawday	
G-BUTZ	PA-28 Cherokee 180C	A. J. & J. M. Davis (G-DARL)	
G-BUUA	Slingsby T.67M Mk II	Hunting Aircraft Ltd/Topcliffe	
G-BUUB	Slingsby T.67M Mk II	Hunting Aircraft Ltd/Topcliffe	
G-BUUC	Slingsby T.67M Mk II	Hunting Aircraft Ltd/Topcliffe	
G-BUUD	Slingsby T.67M Mk II	Hunting Aircraft Ltd/Topcliffe	
G-BUUE	Slingsby T.67M Mk II	Hunting Aircraft Ltd/Topcliffe	
G-BUUF	Slingsby T.67M Mk II	Hunting Aircraft Ltd/Topcliffe	
G-BUUG	Slingsby T.67M Mk II	Hunting Aircraft Ltd/Topcliffe	
G-BUUH	Slingsby T.67M Mk II	Hunting Aircraft Ltd/Topcliffe	
G-BUUI	Slingsby T.67M Mk II	Hunting Aircraft Ltd/Topcliffe	
G-BUUJ	Slingsby T.67M Mk II	Hunting Aircraft Ltd/Topcliffe	
G-BUUK	Slingsby T.67M Mk II	Hunting Aircraft Ltd/Topcliffe	
G-BUUL	Slingsby T.67M Mk II	Hunting Aircraft Ltd/Topcliffe	
G-BUUM	PA-28RT-201 Arrow IV	Bluebird Flying Group	
G-BUUN	Lindstrand LBL-105A balloon	Flying Pictures (Balloons) Ltd	
G-BUUO	Cameron N-90 balloon	Bryan Bros Ltd	
G-BUUP	BAe ATP	British Aerospace PLC	
G-BUUR	BAe ATP	Manx Airlines Ltd/Ronaldsway	
G-BUUS	Skyraider	Sycamore Aviation Ltd	
G-BUUT	Interavia 70TA	Aero Vintage Ltd	
G-BUUU	Cameron 77 Bottle SS balloon	United Distillers UK Ltd	
G-BUUV	Lindstrand LBL-77A balloon	Virgin Airship & Balloon Co Ltd	

Notes	Reg.	Type	Owner or Operator
	G-BUUW	BAe 125 Srs 800A	Raytheon Corporate Jets Inc
	G-BUUX	PA-28 Cherokee 180D	Aero Group 78/Netherthorpe
	G-BUVA	PA-22 Tri-Pacer 135	Mid-West Aviation Ltd
	G-BUVB	Colt 77A balloon	T. L. Regan
	G-BUVE	Colt 77B balloon	R. J. Anley
	G-BUVF	D.H.C.2 Beaver 1	DSG (Guernsey) Ltd
	G-BUVG	Cameron N-56 balloon	Cameron Balloons Ltd
	G-BUVH	Cameron Dragon SS balloon	Cameron Balloons Ltd
	G-BUVI	Colt 210A balloon	R. J. Hunjan
	G-BUVK	Cameron A-210 balloon	British School of Ballooning
	G-BUVL	Fisher Super Koala	A. D. Malcolm
	G-BUVM	CEA DR.250/160	G. G. Milton
	G-BUVN	C.A.S.A. 1.131E Jungmann	DSG (Guernsey) Ltd
	G-BUVO	Cessna F.182P	Flightline Ltd (G-WTFA)/Southend
	G-BUVP	C.A.S.A. 1.131E Jungmann	DSG (Guernsey) Ltd
	G-BUVR	Christen A.1 Husky	STOL Aviation Ltd
	G-BUVS	Colt 77A balloon	Supergas Ltd
	G-BUVT	Colt 77A balloon	Supergas Ltd
	G-BUVW	Cameron N-90 balloon	Bristol Balloon Fiestas Ltd
	G-BUVX	CFM Streak Shadow	G. K. R. Linney
	G-BUVZ	Thunder Ax10-180 S2 balloon	Travellin' Light Ballooning
	G-BUWA	V.S.349 Spitfire Vc (AR614)	Classic Aviation Ltd/Duxford
	G-BUWE	SE-5A (replica)	D. Biggs
	G-BUWF	Cameron N-105 balloon	R. E. Jones
	G-BUWG	Falcon XP	G. C. Elson
	G-BUWH	Parsons 2-seat gyroplane	R. V. Brunskill
	G-BUWI	Lindstrand LBL-77A balloon	Capital Balloon Club Ltd
	G-BUWJ	Pitts S-1C Special	J. R. Marshall
	G-BUWK	Rans S.6-116 Coyote II	R. Warriner
	G-BUWL	Piper J-4A Cub Coupé	V. F. Kemp
	G-BUWM	BAe ATP	Jetstream Aircraft Ltd/Prestwick
	G-BUWN	Lindstrand LBL-180A balloon	Lindstrand Balloons Ltd
	G-BUWO	Lindstrand LBL-240A balloon	Lindstrand Balloons Ltd
	G-BUWP	BAe ATP	British Airways
	G-BUWR	CFM Streak Shadow	T. Harvey
	G-BUWS	Denney Aerocraft Kitfox Mk 2	J. E. Brewis
	G-BUWT	Rand-Robinson KR-2	C. M. Coombe
	G-BUWU	Cameron V-77 balloon	M. J. Newman
	G-BUWV	CFM Streak Shadow	J. Morris
	G-BUWW	Cameron O-105 balloon	M. D. Hammond
	G-BUWX	BAe 125-1000B	Raytheon Corporate Jets Inc
	G-BUWY	Cameron V-77 balloon	C. Dunseath
	G-BUWZ	Robin HR.200-120B	Ambrion Aviation Engineering/Leavesden
	G-BUXA	Colt 210A balloon	R. S. Hunjan
	G-BUXB	Sikorsky S-76A	Air Hanson Aircraft Sales Ltd
	G-BUXC	CFM Streak Shadow	J. Hosier
	G-BUXD	Maule MXT-7-160	A. R. Binnington
	G-BUXE	Cameron A-250 balloon	B. J. Petteford
	G-BUXF	Cameron A-180 balloon	Gone With The Wind Ltd
	G-BUXG	Glaser-Dirks DG.400	J. J. Mason
	G-BUXI	Steen Skybolt	M. Frankland
	G-BUXJ	Slingsby T.61F Venture T.2	Glaser-Dirks UK/Rufforth
	G-BUXK	Pietenpol Air Camper	G. R. G. Smith
	G-BUXL	Taylor JT.1 Monoplane	M. W. Elliott
	G-BUXM	QAC Quickie Q.2	A. J. Ross & D. Ramwell
	G-BUXN	Beech C23 Sundowner	S. A. J. Emmerton
	G-BUXO	Pober P-9 Pixie	T. Moore
	G-BUXP	Falcon XPS	J. C. & B. E. Greenslade
	G-BUXR	Cameron A-250 balloon	Celebration Balloon Flights
	G-BUXS	MBB Bo 105DBS/4	Bond Helicopters Ltd
	G-BUXT	Dornier Do.228-202K	Suckling Airways Ltd/Cambridge
	G-BUXU	Beech D.17S	S. J. Ellis
	G-BUXV	PA-22 Tri-Pacer 160	S. J. Ellis
	G-BUXW	Thunder Ax8-90 S2 balloon	C. W. Brown
	G-BUXX	PA-17 Vagabond	R. H. Hunt
	G-BUXY	PA-25 Pawnee 235	Bath, Wilts & North Dorset Gliding Club Ltd
	G-BUXZ	—	—
	G-BUYA	Lindstrand LBL-77A balloon	Lindstrand Balloons Ltd
	G-BUYB	Aero Designs Pulsar	A. P. Fenn
	G-BUYC	Cameron 80 Concept balloon	P. J. Dorward
	G-BUYD	Thunder Ax8-90 balloon	Anglia Balloons
	G-BUYE	Aeronca 7AC Champion	R. Mazey
	G-BUYF	Falcon XP	J. C. Greenslade

Reg.	Type	Owner or Operator	Notes
G-BUYG	Thunder Ax8-90 Gin Bottle SS balloon	United Distillers PLC	
G-BUYH	Cameron A-210 balloon	Newbury Ballooning Co & Land Securities Properties Ltd	
G-BUYI	Thunder Ax7-77 balloon	Chelmsford Management Ltd	
G-BUYJ	Lindstrand LBL-105A balloon	N. R. Mason	
G-BUYK	Denney Aerocraft Kitfox Mk 4	R. D. L. Mayes	
G-BUYL	RAF 2000 gyroplane	M. H. J. Goldring	
G-BUYM	Thunder Ax8-105 balloon	Scotair Balloons	
G-BUYN	Cameron O-84 balloon	Gone With The Wind Ltd	
G-BUYO	Colt 77A balloon	J. Deans	
G-BUYP	Lindstrand LBL Salami SS balloon	Lindstrand Balloons Ltd	
G-BUYR	Mooney M.20C	S. J. Ellis	
G-BUYS	Robin DR.400/180	F. A. Spear	
G-BUYT	Ken Brock KB-2	J. E. Harris	
G-BUYU	Bowers Fly-Baby 1A	J. A. Nugent	
G-BUYW	BAe ATP	British Aerospace PLC	
G-BUYY	PA-28 Cherokee 180	Global Trading Aviation Services Ltd	
G-BUZA	Denney Aerocraft Kitfox Mk 3	R. Hill	
G-BUZB	Aero Designs Pulsar XP	M. J. Whatley	
G-BUZC	Everett Srs 3A gyroplane	M. P. L'Hermette	
G-BUZD	AS.332L Super Puma	Brintel Leasing Ltd	
G-BUZE	Light Aero Avid Speedwing	N. L. E. & R. A. Dupee	
G-BUZF	Colt 77B balloon	Thunder & Colt Ltd	
G-BUZG	Zenair CH.601HD	N. C. White	
G-BUZH	Aero Designs Star-Lite SL-1	R. J. W. Wood	
G-BUZI	AS.355F-1 Twin Squirrel	B. C. Seedle Helicopters/Blackpool	
G-BUZJ	Lindstrand LBL-105A balloon	Flying Pictures (Balloons) Ltd	
G-BUZK	Cameron V-77 balloon	J. T. Wilkinson & E. Evans	
G-BUZL	VPM M.16 Tandem Trainer	Roger Savage (Photography)	
G-BUZM	Light Aero Avid Flyer Mk 3	R. McLuckie & O. G. Jones	
G-BUZN	Cessna 172H	H. Jones	
G-BUZO	Pietenpol Air Camper	D. A. Jones	
G-BUZR	Lindstrand LBL-77A balloon	Lindstrand Balloons Ltd	
G-BUZS	Colt Flying Pig SS balloon	Banco Bilbao Vizcaya	
G-BUZT	Kölb Twinstar Mk 3	A. C. Goadby	
G-BUZU	V.S.379 Spitfire FR.XIV (NH799)	Patina Ltd/Duxford	
G-BUZV	Ken Brock KB-2	K. Hughes	
G-BUZX	BAe 125 Srs 800B	Raytheon Corporate Jets Inc	
G-BUZY	Cameron A-250 balloon	P. J. D. Kerr	
G-BUZZ	AB-206B JetRanger	Crest Fame Ltd	
G-BVAA	Light Aero Avid Aerobat Mk 4	R. W. Brown	
G-BVAB	Zenair CH.601HDS	A. R. Bender	
G-BVAC	Zenair CH.601HD	A. G. Cozens	
G-BVAF	Piper J-3C-65 Cub	R. W. L. Breckell	
G-BVAG	Lindstrand LBL-90A balloon	T. Moult & ptnrs	
G-BVAH	Denney Aerocraft Kitfox Mk 3	V. A. Hutchinson	
G-BVAI	PZL-110 Koliber 150	Pektron Ltd	
G-BVAJ	Rotorway Executive 90	Rotorbuild Helicopters Ltd	
G-BVAK	Slingsby T.67M-260	Slingsby Aviation Ltd/Kirkbymoorside	
G-BVAL	Slingsby T.67M-260	Slingsby Aviation Ltd/Kirkbymoorside	
G-BVAM	Evans VP-1	R. F. Selby	
G-BVAN	M.S.892E Rallye 150	C. J. Freeman & A. G. E. Camisa	
G-BVAO	Colt 25A balloon	J. M. Fraser	
G-BVAP	Thunder Ax10-180 S2 balloon	British School of Ballooning	
G-BVAR	Lindstrand LBL-105A balloon	Lindstrand Balloons Ltd	
G-BVAS	BAe 125 Srs 800B	Raytheon Corporate Jets Inc	
G-BVAT	Murphy Renegade 912	B. J. Towers	
G-BVAU	Cameron A-210 balloon	Broadland Balloons Ltd	
G-BVAW	Staaken Z-1 Flitzer (D-692)	D. J. Evans & L. R. Williams	
G-BVAX	Colt 77A balloon	Vax Appliances Ltd	
G-BVAY	Rutan Vari-Eze	D. A. Young	
G-BVAZ	Montgomerie-Bensen B.8MR	R. Patrick	
G-BVBA	Colt 69A balloon	Thunder & Colt Ltd	
G-BVBB	Lindstrand LBL-120A balloon	Lindstrand Balloons Ltd	
G-BVBC	Cessna 172K	C. C. Bruce	
G-BVBD	Sikorsky S-52-3	J. Windmill	
G-BVBE	P.84 Jet Provost T.3A	R. E. Todd	
G-BVBF	PA-28-151 Warrior	R. K. Spence	
G-BVBG	PA-32R Cherokee Lance 300	R. K. Spence	
G-BVBH	BAe 125 Srs 800B	Raytheon Corporate Jets Inc	
G-BVBI	D.H.114 Heron 2	Gloster Aviation Services Ltd/Staverton	

Notes	Reg.	Type	Owner or Operator
	G-BVBJ	Colt Flying Jar 1 SS balloon	Flying Pictures (Balloons) Ltd
	G-BVBK	Colt Flying Jar 2 SS balloon	Flying Pictures (Balloons) Ltd
	G-BVBL	PA-38-112 Tomahawk	Aerohire Ltd/Halfpenny Green
	G-BVBM	Lindstrand LBL-180A balloon	A. M. Rocliffe & S. R. Wong
	G-BVBN	Cameron A-210 balloon	Heart of England Balloons
	G-BVBO	Sikorsky S-52-3	Ilkeston Contractors
	G-BVBP	Avro 683 Lancaster X	Aces High Ltd/North Weald
	G-BVBR	Light Aero Avid Speedwing	H. R. Rowley
	G-BVBS	Cameron N-77 balloon	Marley Building Materials Ltd
	G-BVBT	D.H.C.1 Chipmunk T.10 (WK511)	T. J. Manna
	G-BVBU	Cameron V-77 balloon	Cameron Balloons Ltd
	G-BVBV	Light Aero Avid Flyer	D. A. Jarvis
	G-BVBW	Lindstrand LBL-120A balloon	Lindstrand Balloons Ltd
	G-BVBX	Cameron N-90M balloon	Virgin Airship & Balloon Co Ltd
	G-BVBY	Boeing 737-436	British Airways (G-DOCY)
	G-BVBZ	Boeing 737-436	British Airways (G-DOCZ)
	G-BVCA	Cameron N-105 balloon	Fying Pictures (Balloons) Ltd
	G-BVCB	Rans S.10 Sakota	M. D. T. Barley
	G-BVCC	Monett Sonerai 2LT	J. Eggleston
	G-BVCD	BAe 146-200	British Aerospace PLC
	G-BVCE	BAe 146-300	British Aerospace PLC
	G-BVCF	Lindstrand Flying M SS balloon	International Balloons Ltd
	G-BVCG	Van's RV-6	G. J. Newby & E. M. Farquharson
	G-BVCI	Robinson R-22B	Ocean Shields Ltd
	G-BVCJ	Agusta A.109A-II	Castle Air Charters Ltd (G-CLRL/G-EJCB)
	G-BVCK	Lindstrand LBL-105A balloon	International Balloons Ltd
	G-BVCL	Rans S.6-116 Coyote II	W. E. Willets
	G-BVCM	—	
	G-BVCN	Colt 56A balloon	N. R. Mason
	G-BVCO	FRED Srs 2	I. W. Bremner
	G-BVCP	Metisse	C. W. R. Piper
	G-BVCS	Aeronca 7BCN Champion	M. R. Masters
	G-BVCT	Denney Aerocraft Kitfox Mk 4	A. F. Reid
	G-BVCV	Fairchild PT-19A	R. J. Fox
	G-BVCW	Sikorsky S-76A	British International Helicopters
	G-BVCX	Sikorsky S-76A	British International Helicopters
	G-BVCY	Cameron H-24 balloon	Bryant Group PLC
	G-BVCZ	Colt 240A balloon	Schemedraw Ltd
	G-BVDA	Lindstrand LBL-240A balloon	International Balloons Ltd
	G-BVDB	Thunder Ax7-77 balloon	M. J. Smith
	G-BVDC	Van's RV-3	D. Calabritto
	G-BVDD	Colt 69A balloon	R. M. Cambidge & D. R. Groves
	G-BVDE	Taylor JT.1 Monoplane	C. R. J. Norman
	G-BVDF	Cameron 115 Doll SS balloon	Cameron Balloons Ltd
	G-BVDG	VPM M.15	T. B. Johnson
	G-BVDH	PA-28RT-201 Arrow IV	F. B. Miles
	G-BVDI	Van's RV-4	B. F. Hill
	G-BVDJ	Campbell Cricket (replica)	S. Jennings
	G-BVDK	BAe Jetstream 3100	Jetstream Aircraft Ltd/Prestwick
	G-BVDL	BAe 125-1000B	Raytheon Corporate Jets Inc
	G-BVDM	Cameron C-60 balloon	G. W. G. C. Sudlow
	G-BVDN	PA-34-220T Seneca III	Cormack (Aircraft Services) Ltd (G-IGHA/G-IPUT)
	G-BVDO	Lindstrand LBL-105A balloon	J. Burlinson
	G-BVDP	Sequoia F.8L Falco	T. G. Painter
	G-BVDR	Cameron O-77 balloon	T. Duggan
	G-BVDS	Lindstrand LBL-69A balloon	I. Ollerenshaw
	G-BVDT	CFM Streak Shadow	H. J. Bennet
	G-BVDU	Cameron N-77 balloon	Cameron Balloons Ltd
	G-BVDV	Cameron A-120 balloon	Cameron Balloons Ltd
	G-BVDW	Thunder Ax8-90 balloon	R. P. Jones
	G-BVDX	Cameron V-90 balloon	Cameron Balloons Ltd
	G-BVDY	Cameron 60 Concept balloon	K. A. & G. N. Connolly
	G-BVDZ	Taylorcraft BC-12D	P. N. W. England
	G-BVEA	Mosler Motors N.3 Pup	N. Lynch (G-MWEA)
	G-BVEB	PA-32R-301 Saratoga SP	Central Sales Contracting Ltd
	G-BVEC	Aérospatiale ATR-42-300	CityFlyer Express Ltd/British Airways
	G-BVED	Aérospatiale ATR-42-300	CityFlyer Express Ltd/British Airways
	G-BVEE	—	
	G-BVEF	—	
	G-BVEG	P.84 Jet Provost T.3A	Magnificent Obsessions Ltd
	G-BVEH	Jodel D.112	D. J. Rees
	G-BVEI	Colt 90A balloon	Thunder & Colt Ltd

Reg.	Type	Owner or Operator	Notes
G-BVEJ	Cameron V-90 balloon	J. D. A. Snields & A. R. Craze	
G-BVEK	Cameron 80 Concept balloon	J. G. Andrews	
G-BVEL	Evans VP-1 Srs 2	M. J. & S. J. Quinn	
G-BVEM	Lindstrand LBL-77A balloon	Lindstrand Balloons Ltd	
G-BVEN	Cameron 80 Concept balloon	Aire Valley Balloons	
G-BVEO	BAe ATP	Jetstream Aircraft Ltd	
G-BVEP	Luscombe 8A Silvaire	Mid-West Aviation Ltd	
G-BVER	D.H.C.2 Beaver 1 (XV268)	A. F. Allan (G-BTDM)	
G-BVES	Cessna 340A	Welsh Dragon Aviation Ltd/Cardiff	
G-BVEU	Cameron O-105 balloon	H. C. Wright	
G-BVEV	PA-34-200 Seneca	Executive Aviation Services	
G-BVEW	Lindstrand LBL-150A balloon	N. D. Hicks	
G-BVEX	Lindstrand LBL-105A balloon	Lindstrand Balloons Ltd	
G-BVEY	Denney Aerocraft Kitfox Mk 4	Penny Hydraulics Ltd	
G-BVEZ	P.84 Jet Provost T.3A	Magnificent Obsessions Ltd	
G-BVFA	Rans S.10 Sakota	D. Parkinson & D. Allam	
G-BVFB	Cameron N-31 balloon	Bath City Council	
G-BVFC	BAe 125 Srs 800B	Tiphook PLC (G-TPHK/G-FDSL)	
G-BVFD	PA-38-112 Tomahawk	Network Enterprises International Ltd	
G-BVFE	BAe 125 Srs 800B	Raytheon Corporate Jets Inc	
G-BVFF	Cameron V-77 balloon	R. G. Barry	
G-BVFG	BN-2T Turbine Islander	Pilatus BN Ltd/Bembridge	
G-BVFH	BN-2T Turbine Islander	Pilatus BN Ltd/Bembridge	
G-BVFI	BN-2T Turbine Islander	Pilatus BN Ltd/Bembridge	
G-BVFJ	BN-2T Turbine Islander	Pilatus BN Ltd/Bembridge	
G-BVFK	BN-2T Turbine Islander	Pilatus BN Ltd/Bembridge	
G-BVFL	Lindstrand LBL-21A balloon	M. J. Green	
G-BVFM	Rans S.6-ESA Coyote II	P. G. Walton	
G-BVFN	Pitts S-1 Special	I. McKenzie	
G-BVFO	Light Aero Avid Speedwing	P. Chisman	
G-BVFP	Cameron V-90 balloon	C. Duppa-Miller	
G-BVFR	CFM Streak Shadow	M. G. B. Stebbing	
G-BVFS	Slingsby T.31M	V. M. Crabb	
G-BVFT	Maule M5-235C	J. Schunsel	
G-BVFU	Cameron 105 Sphere SS balloon	Lascar Investments Ltd	
G-BVFW	Nanchang CJ-6A	Elmair Ltd	
G-BVFX	Nanchang CJ-6A	Elmair Ltd	
G-BVFY	Colt 210A balloon	Scotair Balloons	
G-BVFZ	—		
G-BVGA	Bell 206B JetRanger	Findon Air Services/Shoreham	
G-BVGB	Thunder Ax8-105 S2 balloon	Flying Pictures (Balloons) Ltd	
G-BVGC	Cessna 411A	Taylor Aircraft Services Ltd (G-AVEK)	
G-BVGD	Aerotechnik L-13 SEH Vivat	Oxfordshire Sport Flying Ltd/Enstone	
G-BVGE	W.S.55 Whirlwind HAR.10	Austen Associates Partnership	
G-BVGF	Shaw Europa	A. Graham & G. G. Beal	
G-BVGG	Lindstrand LBL-69A balloon	Lindstrand Balloons Ltd	
G-BVGH	Hunter T.7 (XL573)	B. J. Pover	
G-BVGI	Pereira Osprey II	B. Weare	
G-BVGJ	Cameron C-80 balloon	D. T. Watkins	
G-BVGK	Lindstrand LBL Flying Newspaper SS balloon	International Balloons Ltd	
G-BVGL	Sikorsky S-76A	Bond Helicopters Ltd	
G-BVGM	Sikorsky S-76A	Bond Helicopters Ltd	
G-BVGO	Denney Aerocraft Kitfox Mk 4-1200	Willow Motors	
G-BVGP	Bücker Bul33C Jungmeister	R. H. Reeves	
G-BVGR	RAF BE-2e	Aero Vintage Ltd	
G-BVGS	Robinson R-22B	Innkeepers Ltd	
G-BVGT	Auster J/1 (modified)	L. A. Groves	
G-BVGU	Cameron N-90 balloon	Cameron Balloons Ltd	
G-BVGV	Colt 21A balloon	Thunder & Colt Ltd	
G-BVGW	Luscombe 8A Silvaire	L. A. Groves	
G-BVGX	Thunder Ax8-90 S2 balloon	G-BVGX Group	
G-BVGY	Luscombe 8E Silvaire	T. Groves	
G-BVGZ	Fokker Dr.1 (replica)	Museum of Army Flying/Middle Wallop	
G-BVHA	Boeing 737-436	British Airways	
G-BVHB	Boeing 737-436	British Airways	
G-BVHC	Grob G.115D-2	Airwork Ltd	
G-BVHD	Grob G.115D-2	Airwork Ltd	
G-BVHE	Grob G.115D-2	Airwork Ltd	
G-BVHF	Grob G.115D-2	Airwork Ltd	
G-BVHG	Grob G.115D-2	Airwork Ltd	
G-BVHH	Cameron D-96 airship	Sport Promotion SRL/Italy	

Notes	Reg.	Type	Owner or Operator
	G-BVHI	Rans S.10 Sakota	P. D. Rowley
	G-BVHJ	Cameron A-180 balloon	Southern Flight Company Ltd
	G-BVHK	Cameron V-77 balloon	G. Rich
	G-BVHL	Nicollier HN.700 Menestrel	I. H. R. Walker
	G-BVHM	PA-38-112 Tomahawk	A. J. Gomes (G-DCAN)
	G-BVHN	Lindstrand LBL G144 balloon	Lindstrand Balloons Ltd
	G-BVHO	Cameron V-90 balloon	R. S. Mohr
	G-BVHP	Colt 42A balloon	Huntair Ltd
	G-BVHR	Cameron V-90 balloon	D. C. Boxall
	G-BVHS	Murphy Rebel	J. Brown & ptnrs
	G-BVHT	Light Aero Avid Speedwing Mk 4	R. S. Holt
	G-BVHU	Colt Flying Bottle SS balloon	BIAS International Ltd
	G-BVHV	Cameron N-105 balloon	Flying Pictures (Balloons) Ltd
	G-BVHW	BAe 125 Srs 800B	Raytheon Corporate Jets Inc (G-GJCB)
	G-BVHX	BN-2T-4R Turbine Islander	Pilatus BN Ltd/Bembridge
	G-BVHY	BN-2T-4R Turbine Islander	Pilatus BN Ltd/Bembridge
	G-BVHZ	BN-2T-4R Turbine Islander	Pilatus BN Ltd/Bembridge
	G-BVIA	Rand KR-2	K. Atkinson
	G-BVIB	Bell 206L-3 LongRanger 3	Alan Mann Helicopters Ltd
	G-BVIC	EE Canberra B.6 (XH568)	F. M. Gill
	G-BVID	Lindstrand Lozenge SS balloon	Lindstrand Balloons Ltd
	G-BVIE	PA-18 Super Cub 95 (modified)	R. W. Sage (G-CLIK)
	G-BVIF	Montgomerie-Bensen B.8MR	R. M. Mann
	G-BVIG	Cameron A-250 balloon	Balloon Flights International Ltd
	G-BVIH	PA-28-161 Warrior II	Ocean Developments Ltd (G-GFCE/ G-BNJP)
	G-BVII	Cameron N-90 balloon	Cameron Balloons Ltd
	G-BVIJ	Cameron O-90 balloon	Cameron Balloons Ltd
	G-BVIK	Maule MXT-7-180	Aeromarine Ltd
	G-BVIL	Maule MXT-7-180	Aeromarine Ltd
	G-BVIM	—	—
	G-BVIN	Rans S.6-ESA Coyote II	K. J. Vincent
	G-BVIO	—	—
	G-BVIP	—	—
	G-BVIR	—	—
	G-BVIS	—	—
	G-BVIT	—	—
	G-BVIU	—	—
	G-BVIV	Light Aero Avid Aerobat	J. & V. Hobday
	G-BVIW	—	—
	G-BVIX	—	—
	G-BVIY	—	—
	G-BVIZ	Shaw Europa	T. J. Punter & P. G. Jeffers
	G-BVJA	—	—
	G-BVJB	—	—
	G-BVJC	—	—
	G-BVJD	—	—
	G-BVJE	—	—
	G-BVJF	—	—
	G-BVJG	—	—
	G-BVJH	—	—
	G-BVJI	—	—
	G-BVJJ	—	—
	G-BVJK	—	—
	G-BVJL	—	—
	G-BVJM	—	—
	G-BVJN	—	—
	G-BVKE	Team Minimax 88	A. M. Pepper
	G-BVMA	Beech 200 Super King Air	Manhattan Air Ltd (G-VLPC)/Bournemouth
	G-BVMM	Robin HR.200/100	M. G. Owne
	G-BVMX	Short SD3-60 Variant 100	CityFlyer Express Ltd/British Airways (G-BPFS/G-REGN/G-OCIA)
	G-BVMY	Short SD3-60 Variant 100	CityFlyer Express Ltd/British Airways (G-OEEC/G-BPKY)
	G-BVMZ	Robin HR.100/210	Chiltern Handbags (London) Ltd
	G-BVNM	Boeing 737-4S3	British Airways (G-BPKA)
	G-BVNN	Boeing 737-4S3	British Airways (G-BPKB)
	G-BVNO	Boeing 737-4S3	British Airways (G-BPKE)
	G-BVPI	Evans VP-1	C. M. Gibson
	G-BVPM	Evans VP-2 Coupé	P. Marigold
	G-BVRS	Beech B90 King Air	Cook Aviation Services Ltd (G-KJET/ G-AXFE)

Out-of-Sequence Registrations

Notes	Reg.	Type	Owner or Operator
	G-BWAC	Waco YKS-7	J. R. D. Bygraves
	G-BWEF	SNCAN Stampe SV-4C	Acebell BWEF Syndicate (G-BOVL)/ Redhill
	G-BWAS	PA-31-350 Navajo Chieftain	BWOC Ltd/Bristol
	G-BWAY	Beech A36 Bonanza	Vuewood Ltd
	G-BWBW	Cameron A-180 balloon	Ballooning World Ltd
	G-BWCI	Light Aero Avid Flyer	R. A. Kilvington
	G-BWDT	PA-34-220T Seneca II	A. J. Wickenden (G-BKHS)
	G-BWEC	Cassutt-Colson Variant	N. R. Thomason & M. P. J. Hill
	G-BWFJ	Evans VP-1	G. F. Kennedy
	G-BWHY	Robinson R-22	R. E. Benke
	G-BWJB	Thunder Ax8-105 balloon	Justerini & Brooks Ltd *Whiskey J. & B.*
	G-BWKK	Auster AOP.9 (XP279)	R. W. Fairless & D. R. White
	G-BWLY	Rotorway Executive 90	P. W. & I. P. Bewley
	G-BWMA	Colt 105A balloon	Bristol & West Motor Auction Ltd
	G-BWMB	Jodel D.119	K. Jarman & KM Services Ltd
	G-BWMR	Robinson R-22B	Bowmur Haulage Co Ltd
	G-BWOC	PA-31-350 Navajo Chieftain	BWOC Ltd
	G-BWSI	K&S SA.102.5 Cavalier	B. W. Shaw
	G-BWTX	PA-42-720 Cheyenne III	Broome & Wellington (Aviation) Ltd
	G-BWVE	Bell 206B JetRanger	Willow Vale Electronics Ltd (G-BOSX)
	G-BWWJ	Hughes 269C	Dave Nieman Models Ltd (G-BMYZ)
	G-BWWW	BAe Jetstream 3102	British Aerospace PLC/Dunsfold
	G-BXAX	Cameron N-77 balloon	Flying Pictures Ltd
	G-BXPS	PA-23 Aztec 250C	N. H. Bailey (G-AYLY)
	G-BXVI	V.S.361 Spitfire F.XVI (RW386)	D. Arnold
	G-BYAA	Boeing 767-204ER	Britannia Airways Ltd
	G-BYAB	Boeing 767-204ER	Britannia Airways Ltd
	G-BYAC	Boeing 757-204ER	Britannia Airways Ltd
	G-BYAD	Boeing 757-204ER	Britannia Airways Ltd
	G-BYAE	Boeing 757-204ER	Britannia Airways Ltd
	G-BYAF	Boeing 757-204	Britannia Airways Ltd
	G-BYAG	Boeing 757-204	Britannia Airways Ltd
	G-BYAH	Boeing 757-204	Britannia Airways Ltd
	G-BYAI	Boeing 757-204	Britannia Airways Ltd
	G-BYAJ	Boeing 757-204ER	Britannia Airways Ltd
	G-BYAK	Boeing 757-28AER	Britannia Airways Ltd
	G-BYAL	Boeing 757-28AER	Britannia Airways Ltd
	G-BYAM	Boeing 757-2T7	Britannia Airways Ltd (G-DRJC)
	G-BYAN	Boeing 757-204	Britannia Airways Ltd
	G-BYAO	Boeing 757-204	Britannia Airways Ltd
	G-BYAP	Boeing 757-204	Britannia Airways Ltd
	G-BYAR	Boeing 757-204	Britannia Airways Ltd
	G-BYAS	Boeing 757-204	Britannia Airways Ltd
	G-BYAT	Boeing 757-204	Britannia Airways Ltd
	G-BYAU	Boeing 757-204	Britannia Airways Ltd
	G-BYEE	Mooney M.20K	Axe & Status Ltd
	G-BYIJ	C.A.S.A. 1-131E Jungmann 2000	K. B. Palmer
	G-BYLL	F.8L Falco	N. J. Langrick/Sherburn
	G-BYLS	Bede BD-4	G. H. Bayliss
	G-BYNG	Cessna T.303	J. M. E. Byng (G-PTWB)
	G-BYRE	Rans S.10 Sakota	R. J. & M. B. Trickey
	G-BYRN	PA-31-350 Navajo Chieftain	Byrne Group PLC (G-YLAN)
	G-BYSE	AB-206B JetRanger 2	Bewise Ltd (G-BFND)
	G-BYSL	Cameron O-56 balloon	Charles of the Ritz Ltd
	G-BYTE	Robinson R-22B	Datel Electronics Ltd
	G-BZBH	Thunder Ax6-65 balloon	R. B. & G. Clarke
	G-BZKK	Cameron V-56 balloon	P. J. Green & C. Bosley *Gemini II*
	G-BZZZ	Enstrom F-28C-UK	Chartec Ltd (G-BBBZ)
	G-CAFZ	PA-31-350 Navajo Chieftain	London Flight Centre (Stansted) Ltd (G-BPPT)
	G-CALL	PA-23 Aztec 250F	Woodgate Aviation Ltd/Ronaldsway
	G-CALV	PA-39 Twin Comanche 160 C/R	Rhoburt Ltd (G-AZFO)
	G-CAMM	Hawker Cygnet (replica)	D. M. Cashmore
	G-CAPT	Taylor JT.2 Titch	V. W. B. Davies (G-BTJM)
	G-CARS	Pitts S-2A Special (replica) ★	Toyota Ltd

Reg.	Type	Owner or Operator	Notes
G-CAXF	Cameron O-77 balloon	R. D. & S. J. Sarjeant	
G-CAYN	Dornier Do.228-201	Cayenne Ltd (G-MLNR)	
G-CBEA	BAe Jetstream 3102-01	Maersk Air/Birmingham	
G-CBIL	Cessna 182K	K. A. Clarke/Newcastle	
G-CBJB	Sikorsky S-76A	Bond Helicopters Ltd	
G-CBKT	Cameron O-77 balloon	Caledonian Airways Ltd	
G-CBOR	Cessna F.172N	P. Seville	
G-CCAR	Cameron N-77 balloon	The Colt Car Co Ltd	
G-CCAT	AA-5A Cheetah	BLS Aviation Ltd (G-OAJH/G-KILT/ G-BJFA)/Elstree	
G-CCCC	Cessna 172H	K. E. Wilson	
G-CCCP	Yakovlev Yak-52	R. J. N. Howarth	
G-CCDI	Cameron N-77 balloon	Charles Church Developments PLC	
G-CCOL	AA-5A Cheetah	Lowlog Ltd (G-BIVU)	
G-CCON	Beech F33C Bonanza	P. J. Withinshaw	
G-CCOZ	Monnet Sonerai II	P. R. Cozens	
G-CCUB	Piper J-3C-65 Cub	Cormack (Aircraft Services) Ltd	
G-CDBS	MBB Bo 105DBS	Bond Helicopters Ltd/Aberdeen	
G-CDEE	Pitts S-2B Special	G. C. Dodds & R. W. Davies	
G-CDET	Culver LCA Cadet	H. B. Fox/Booker	
G-CDGA	Taylor JT.1 Monoplane	R. M. Larimore	
G-CDGL	Saffery S.330 balloon	C. J. Dodd & G. J. Luckett Penny	
G-CDON	PA-28-161 Warrior II	East Midlands Flying Club PLC	
G-CDRU	C.A.S.A. 1-131E Jungmann	P. Cunniff/White Waltham	
G-CEAS	HPR-7 Herald 214	Channel Express (Air Services) Ltd (G-BEBB)/Bournemouth	
G-CEGA	PA-34-200T Seneca II	Hendefern Ltd	
G-CEJA	Cameron V-77 balloon	N. L. Jaques (G-BTOF)	
G-CELL	PA-32R-301 Saratoga SP	CEL Electronics Ltd	
G-CERT	Mooney M.20K	Fairline Boats PLC/Conington	
G-CEXP	HPR-7 Herald 209	Channel Express (Air Services) Ltd (G-BFRJ)/Bournemouth	
G-CEXS	L.188C Electra	Channel Express (Air Services) Ltd/ Bournemouth	
G-CFBI	Colt 56A balloon	G. A. Fisher	
G-CFLT	AS.355F-1 Twin Squirrel	Osten Airfinance Ltd (G-BNBI)	
G-CFLY	Cessna 172F	I. Hughes & B. T. Williams	
G-CGCG	Robinson R-22B	J .M. Henderson	
G-CGHM	PA-28 Cherokee 140	M. J. Flynn	
G-CGOD	Cameron N-77 balloon	Abbey Plant Co Ltd	
G-CHAA	Cameron O-90 balloon	Cloudhoppers Ltd	
G-CHAL	Robinson R-22B	Cabair Helicopters Ltd/Elstree	
G-CHAM	Cameron 90 Pot SS balloon	Nestlé UK Ltd	
G-CHAR	Grob G.109B	RAFGSA/Bicester	
G-CHAS	PA-28-181 Archer II	C. H. Elliott	
G-CHEM	PA-34-200T Seneca II	ML Associates	
G-CHIK	Cessna F.152	Stapleford Flying Club Ltd (G-BHAZ)	
G-CHIL	Robinson R-22HP	Skyline Helicopters Ltd	
G-CHIP	PA-28-181 Archer II	C. M. Hough/Fairoaks	
G-CHIS	Robinson R-22B	Bradmore Helicopter Leasing	
G-CHLT	Stemme S.10	F. C. Y. Cheung/Hong Kong	
G-CHMP	Bellanca 7ECA Citabria	J. T. Parkins	
G-CHOK	Cameron V-77 balloon	K. W. Overton	
G-CHOP	Westland-Bell 47G-3B1	Wessex Air Contracts Ltd	
G-CHRP	Colt Flying Book SS balloon	Chronicle Communications Ltd	
G-CHRR	Colt Flying Book SS balloon	Chronicle Communications Ltd	
G-CHSR	BAe 146-200	British Aerospace PLC/Warton	
G-CHTA	AA-5A Cheetah	Rapid Spin Ltd (G-BFRC)/Biggin Hill	
G-CHTT	Varga 2150A Kachina	C.H.T. Trace	
G-CHUB	Colt N-51 balloon	Chubb Fire Security Ltd	
G-CHUK	Cameron O-77 balloon	Converse Europe Ltd	
G-CHYL	Robinson R-22B	L. M. Dresher	
G-CIAS	BN-2B-21 Islander	Channel Island Air Search Ltd (G-BKJM)	
G-CICI	Cameron R-15 balloon	Ballooning Endeavours Ltd	
G-CIII	Oldfield Baby Lakes	G. Cooper	
G-CIPI	AJEP Wittman W.8 Tailwind	M. H. D. Soltau (G-AYDU)	
G-CITY	PA-31-350 Navajo Chieftain	Woodgate Aviation Ltd/Ronaldsway	
G-CIVA	Boeing 747-436	British Airways City of St. Davids	
G-CIVB	Boeing 747-436	British Airways City of Lichfield	
G-CIVC	Boeing 747-436	British Airways City of St. Andrews	
G-CIVD	Boeing 747-436	British Airways	
G-CIVE	Boeing 747-436	British Airways	
G-CIVF	Boeing 747-436	British Airways	

Notes	Reg.	Type	Owner or Operator
	G-CIVG	Boeing 747-436	British Airways
	G-CJBC	PA-28 Cherokee 180	J. B. Cave/Halfpenny Green
	G-CJCI	Pilatus P2-06 (CC+43)	Pilatus P2 Flying Group
	G-CJET	Learjet 35A	Sure-Wings Ltd (G-SEBE/G-ZIPS/ G-ZONE)/Heathrow
	G-CJIM	Taylor JT.1 Monoplane	J. Crawford
	G-CJUD	Denney Aerocraft Kitfox	C. W. Judge
	G-CKEN	Wombat autogyro	K. H. Durran
	G-CLAC	PA-28-161 Warrior II	Clacton Light Aviation Co
	G-CLAS	Short SD3-60 Variant 100	Bon Accord Airways Ltd (G-BLED)/ Aberdeen
	G-CLEA	PA-28-161 Warrior II	Creative Logistics Enterprises & Aviation Ltd & R. J. Harrison
	G-CLEM	Bo 208A2 Junior	A. W. Webster (G-ASWE)
	G-CLIC	Cameron N-105 balloon	Matrix Computer Maintenance Ltd
	G-CLIK	PA-18 Super Cub 95	R. Wheeler
	G-CLIV	PA-28R-201T Turbo Arrow III	T. J. Caton
	G-CLOS	PA-34-200 Seneca II	Greenclose Aviation Services Ltd/ Bournemouth
	G-CLUB	Cessna FRA.150M	J. J. Woodhouse
	G-CLUE	PA-34-200T Seneca II	Bristol Office Machines Ltd
	G-CLUX	Cessna F.172N	J. & K. Aviation/Liverpool
	G-CLYV	Robinson R-22B	C. A. Ecroyd
	G-CMDR	R. Commander 114	J. D. Hallahan & G. C. Bishop
	G-CMGC	PA-25 Pawnee 235	Tatenhill Aviation (G-BFEX)
	G-CNIS	Partenavia P.68B	Dollar Air Services Ltd (G-BJOF/G-PAUL)/ Coventry
	G-COCO	Cessna F.172M	P. C. Sheard & R. C. Larder
	G-COES	McD Douglas MD-83	Airtours International Aviation Ltd
	G-COIN	Bell 206B JetRanger 2	C. Sarno
	G-COKE	Cameron O-65 balloon	M. C. Bradley
	G-COLA	Beech F33C Bonanza	John Bradley & Barry Ltd and J. A. Kelman (G-BUAZ)
	G-COLL	Enstrom 280C-UK-2 Shark	John Pearson (Motors) 1924 Ltd
	G-COLR	Colt 69A balloon	British School of Ballooning
	G-COMB	PA-30 Twin Comanche 160B	J. T. Bateson (G-AVBL)/Ronaldsway
	G-COMM	PA-23 Aztec 250C	M. G. Wild (G-AZMG)
	G-COMP	Cameron N-90 balloon	Computacenter Ltd
	G-CONB	Robin DR.400/180	Winchcombe Farm (G-BUPX)
	G-CONC	Cameron N-90 balloon	British Airways
	G-COOK	Cameron N-77 balloon	IAZ (International) Ltd
	G-COOP	Cameron N-31 balloon	Aire Valley Balloons
	G-COPS	Piper J-3C-65 Cub	R. W. Sproat & C. E. Simpson
	G-COPY	AA-5A Cheetah	Emberden Ltd (G-BIEU)/Biggin Hill
	G-CORC	Bell 206B JetRanger 2	Air Corcoran Ltd (G-CJHI/G-BBFB)
	G-CORD	Slingsby T.66 Nipper 3	B. A. Wright (G-AVTB)
	G-CORK	Air Command 532 Elite	D. N. B. McCorquodale
	G-COSY	Lindstrand LBL-56A balloon	Eastern Electricity PLC
	G-COTT	Cameron 60 Cottage SS balloon	Nottingham Hot-Air Balloon Club
	G-COUP	Ercoupe 415C	S. M. Gerrard
	G-COWE	Beech C90A King Air	Cowie Aviation Ltd/Newcastle
	G-COWS	ARV Super 2	T. C. Harrold (G-BONB)
	G-COYS	Colt 42A balloon	Thunder & Colt Ltd
	G-COZI	Rutan Cozy III	D. G. Machin
	G-CPCD	CEA DR.221	P. G. Bumpus & R. Thwaites
	G-CPCH	PA-28-151 Warrior	P. C. Hancock (G-BRGJ)
	G-CPEL	Boeing 757-236	British Airways (G-BRJE) *Walmer Castle*
	G-CPFC	Cessna F.152	Falcon Flying Services/Biggin Hill
	G-CPLI	Robinson R-22B	Thurston Helicopters (Engineering) Ltd
	G-CPTM	PA-28-151 Warrior	T. J. Mackay & C. M. Pollett (G-BTOE)
	G-CPTS	AB-206B JetRanger 2	A. R. B. Aspinall
	G-CRAK	Cameron N-77 balloon	Mobile Windscreens Ltd
	G-CRAN	Robin R.1180T	D. S. Watson
	G-CRAY	Robinson R-22B	W. H. Grimshaw
	G-CRES	Denney Aerocraft Kitfox	R. J. Cresswell
	G-CRIC	Colomban MC.15 Cri-Cri	A. B. Cameron
	G-CRIL	R. Commander 112B	Rockwell Aviation Group/Cardiff
	G-CRIS	Taylor JT.1 Monoplane	C. R. Steer
	G-CRML	Cessna 414A	Fairport Ltd
	G-CROL	Maule MXT-7-180	Aeromarine Ltd
	G-CRUS	Cessna T.303	B. A. Groves
	G-CRUZ	Cessna T.303	Bank Farm Ltd
	G-CRZY	Thunder Ax8-105 balloon	R. Carr (G-BDLP)/France

Reg.	Type	Owner or Operator	Notes
G-CSBM	Cessna F.150M	Galaxy Enterprises Ltd	
G-CSCS	Cessna F.172N	Conegate Ltd	
G-CSFC	Cessna 150L	Shropshire Aero Club Ltd	
G-CSFT	PA-23 Aztec 250D	Islerealm Ltd (G-AYKU)	
G-CSNA	Cessna 421C	Zulu Airlines Ltd	
G-CSVS	Boeing 757-236	Airtours International Airways Ltd (G-IEAC)	
G-CSZB	V.807B Viscount	British World Airlines Ltd (G-AOXU)/ Aberdeen	
G-CTCL	SOCATA TB.10 Tobago	Merryfield Leasing Ltd (G-BSIV)	
G-CTIX	V.S.509 Spitfire T.IX (PT462)	S. B. Church	
G-CTKL	CCF Harvard IV (54137)	G. J. & S. P. Keegan	
G-CTOY	Denney Aerocraft Kitfox Mk 3	G. S. Cass	
G-CTRN	Enstrom F-28C-UK	Manchester Helicopter Centre/Barton	
G-CTRX	H.P.137 Jetstream 200	Centrax Ltd (G-BCWW/G-AXUN)/Exeter	
G-CTWW	PA-34-200T Seneca II	Control Techniques Drives Ltd (G-ROYZ/G-GALE)	
G-CUBB	PA-18 Super Cub 180	G. J. Busby/Booker	
G-CUBI	PA-18 Super Cub 135 (51-15673)	T. Watson	
G-CUBJ	PA-18 Super Cub 150	A. K. Leasing (Jersey) Ltd	
G-CUGA	GA-7 Cougar	Teesside Flight Centre Ltd	
G-CURE	Colt 77A balloon	Flying Pictures (Balloons) Ltd	
G-CWAG	F. 8L Falco	C. C. Wagner	
G-CWOT	Currie Wot	D. A. Lord	
G-CXCX	Cameron N-90 balloon	Cathay Pacific Airways (London) Ltd	
G-CYGI	HAPI Cygnet SF-2A	B. Brown	
G-CYLS	Cessna T.303	Gledhill Water Storage Ltd & M. F. Joseph (G-BKXI)/Blackpool	
G-CYMA	GA-7 Cougar	Cyma Petroleum Ltd (G-BKOM)/Elstree	
G-CZAR	Cessna 560 Citation V	Aviation Beauport Ltd/Jersey	
G-DAAH	PA-28RT-201T Turbo Arrow IV	R. Peplow	
G-DAAL	Avro 748 Srs 1A	Emerald Airways Ltd (G-BEKG/G-VAJK)/ Liverpool	
G-DAAM	Robinson R-22B	A. A. Macaskill	
G-DACA	P.57 Sea Prince T.1 ★	P. G. Vallance Ltd/Charlwood	
G-DACC	Cessna 401B	Niglon Ltd (G-AYOU)/Birmingham	
G-DADS	Hughes 369HS	B. Wronski	
G-DAFL	Thunder Ax8-90 balloon	Thunder & Colt Ltd	
G-DAFT	AS.355F-2 Twin Squirrel	Powersense Ltd (G-BNNN)/Hayes	
G-DAFY	Beech 58 Baron	Ortac Air Ltd/Guernsey	
G-DAJB	Boeing 757-2T7	Monarch Airlines Ltd/Luton	
G-DAJC	Boeing 767-31KER	Airtours International Airways Ltd	
G-DAKS	Dakota 3 (TS423)	Aces High Ltd/North Weald	
G-DAND	SOCATA TB.10 Tobago	Whitemoor Engineering Co Ltd	
G-DANI	Cessna 500 Citation	Assigntravel Ltd (G-BFAR)	
G-DANN	Stampe et Renard SV-4B	I. M. White	
G-DANS	AS.355F-2 Twin Squirrel	GB Dee Knitwear Ltd (G-BTNM)	
G-DAPH	Cessna 180K	M. R. L. Astor	
G-DARA	PA-34-220T Seneca III	P. Hartley	
G-DARE	PA-34-200T Seneca II	Diamond Airways Ltd (G-WOTS/G-SEVL)	
G-DARR	Cessna 421C	Venuetime Ltd (G-BNEZ)	
G-DASH	R. Commander 112A	Josef D. J. Jons & Co Ltd (G-BDAJ)	
G-DASI	Short SD3-60	Air UK Ltd (G-BKKW)/Norwich	
G-DASU	Cameron V-77 balloon	D. & L. S. Litchfield	
G-DAVE	Jodel D.112	D. A. Porter/Sturgate	
G-DBAF	BAC One-Eleven 201AC	British Air Ferries Ltd (G-ASJG)/Stansted	
G-DBAL	H.S.125 Srs 3B	Osprey Aviation Ltd (G-BSAA)	
G-DBAR	Beech 200 Super King Air	Brown & Root (UK) Ltd	
G-DCAC	McD Douglas MD-83	Airtours International Aviation Ltd	
G-DCCH	MBB Bo 105D	Devon & Cornwall Police Authority	
G-DCCI	BAe 125-1000B	Consolidated Contractors International (UK) Ltd (G-BUPL)	
G-DCEA	PA-34-200T Seneca II	M. J. Greasby	
G-DCIO	Douglas DC-10-30	British Airways *Epping Forest*/Gatwick	
G-DCKK	Cessna F.172N	A. R. Mead/Clacton	
G-DCSW	PA-32R-301 Saratoga SP	A. W. Kendrick	
G-DCXL	Jodel D.140C	P. Underhill	
G-DDAY	PA-28R-201T Turbo Arrow III	W. Haynes (G-BPDO)	
G-DDCD	D.H.104 Dove 8	C. Daniel (G-ARUM)/Biggin Hill	
G-DDMV	NA T-6G Texan (41)	E. A. Morgan	
G-DEBB	Beech 35-B33 Debonair	Spitfire Aviation Ltd/Bournemouth	
G-DEJL	Robinson R-22B	D. E. J. Lomas	

Notes	Reg.	Type	Owner or Operator
	G-DELB	Robinson R-22B	Hields Aviation
	G-DELI	Thunder Ax7-77 balloon	Heather Flight Ltd
	G-DELL	Robinson R-22B	Delta Helicopters Ltd/Luton
	G-DELS	Robin DR.400/180	W. D. Nightingale
	G-DELT	Robinson R-22B	Mortec Services
	G-DEMH	Cessna F.172M (modified)	M. Hammond (G-BFLO)
	G-DENS	Binder CP.301S Smaragd	W. St G. V. Stoney
	G-DENW	PA-44-180 Seminole	D. A. Woodhams
	G-DERV	Cameron Truck SS balloon	J. M. Percival
	G-DESI	Aero Designs Pulsar XP	D. F. Gaughan
	G-DESS	Mooney M.20J	W. E. Newnes
	G-DEVS	PA-28 Cherokee 180	180 Group (G-BGVJ)
	G-DEXP	ARV Super 2	J. P. Jenkins
	G-DEXY	Beech E90 King Air	Tornado Ltd
	G-DFLT	Cessna F.406 Caravan II	Direct Flight Ltd/Norwich
	G-DFLY	PA-38-112 Tomahawk	I. R. March & N. W. Woodward
	G-DFVA	Cessna R.172K	R. A. Plowright
	G-DGDG	Glaser-Dirks DG.400/17	DG400 Flying Group/Lasham
	G-DGLD	HPR-7 Herald 214	Channel Express Group (Air Services) Ltd (G-BAVX)/Bournemouth
	G-DGWW	Rand-Robinson KR-2	W. Wilson
	G-DHCB	D.H.C.2 Beaver 1	Sealife Ltd (G-BTDL)
	G-DHCI	D.H.C.1 Chipmunk 22	Felthorpe Flying Group Ltd (G-BBSE)
	G-DHSW	Boeing 737-3Y0	Monarch Airlines Ltd/EuroBerlin
	G-DHTM	D.H.82A Tiger Moth replica	E. G. Waite-Roberts
	G-DHVV	D.H.115 Vampire T.55	Lindsay Wood Promotions Ltd
	G-DHWW	D.H.115 Vampire T.55	Lindsay Wood Promotions Ltd
	G-DHXX	D.H.100 Vampire FB.6	Lindsay Wood Promotions Ltd
	G-DHZZ	D.H.115 Vampire T.55 (U-1230)	Lindsay Wood Promotions Ltd
	G-DIAL	Cameron N-90 balloon	Datacentre Ltd
	G-DIAT	PA-28 Cherokee 140	RAF Benevolent Fund's IAT/Bristol & Wessex Aeroplane Club (G-BCGK)/Lulsgate
	G-DICK	Thunder Ax6-56Z balloon	R. D. Sargeant
	G-DIME	R. Commander 114	Badminton Horse Boxes Ltd
	G-DINA	AA-5B Tiger	MRM of Fenton
	G-DING	Colt 77A balloon	G. J. Bell
	G-DINT	B.156 Beaufighter 1F	T. E. Moore
	G-DIPI	Cameron Tub SS balloon	Airship & Balloon Co Ltd
	G-DIPS	Taylor JT.1 Monoplane	B. J. Halls
	G-DIRE	Robinson R-22B	Techspan Aviation Ltd
	G-DIRK	Glaser-Dirks DG.400	D. M. Chalmers
	G-DIRT	Thunder Ax7-77Z balloon	R. J. Ngbaronye
	G-DISC	Cessna U.206A	C. M. J. Parton (G-BGWR)
	G-DISK	PA-24 Comanche 250	M. A. McLoughlin (G-APZG)/Booker
	G-DISO	Jodel D.150	P. F. Craven & J. H. Shearer
	G-DIVA	Cessna R.172K XPII	R. A. Plowright & J. A. Kaye/Biggin Hill
	G-DIWY	PA-32 Cherokee Six 300	Industrial Foam Systems Ltd
	G-DIZO	Jodel D.120A	D. Aldersea (G-EMKM)
	G-DIZY	PA-28R-201T Turbo Arrow III	Medway Arrow Group
	G-DJEM	AS.350B Ecureuil	Maynard & Harris Plastics Ltd (G-ZBAC/G-SEBI/G-BMCU)
	G-DJHB	Beech A23-19 Musketeer	M. J. Wells (G-AZZE)
	G-DJIM	MHCA-I	J. Crawford
	G-DJJA	PA-28-181 Archer II	P. Lawrence
	G-DJLW	H.S.125 Srs 3B/RA	Lindsay Wood Promotions Ltd (G-AVVB)
	G-DJNH	Denney Aerocraft Kitfox	D. J. N. Hall
	G-DKDP	Grob G.109	D. W. & J. E. Page
	G-DKGF	Viking Dragonfly	K. G. Fathers
	G-DLDL	Robinson R-22B	D. A. Lawson
	G-DLOM	SOCATA TB.20 Trinidad	J. N. A. Adderley/Guernsey
	G-DLTA	Slingsby T.67M Firefly	Firefly Aerial Promotions Ltd (G-SFTX)
	G-DLTI	Robinson R-22B	D. L. Taylor
	G-DMCS	PA-28R Cherokee Arrow 200-II	D. L. Johns & F. K. Parker (G-CPAC)
	G-DNCS	PA-28R-201T Turbo Arrow III	BRT Arrow Ltd/Barton
	G-DNLB	MBB Bo 105DBS/4	Bond Helicopters Ltd (G-BCDH/G-BTBD/G-BUDP)
	G-DNLD	Cameron 97 Donald SS balloon	The Walt Disney Co Ltd
	G-DNVT	G.1159C Gulfstream IV	Shell Aircraft Ltd/Heathrow
	G-DOCA	Boeing 737-436	British Airways *River Ballindery*
	G-DOCB	Boeing 737-436	British Airways *River Bush*
	G-DOCC	Boeing 737-436	British Airways *Rver Affric*
	G-DOCD	Boeing 737-436	British Airways *River Aire*

Reg.	Type	Owner or Operator	Notes
G-DOCE	Boeing 737-436	British Airways *River Alness*	
G-DOCF	Boeing 737-436	British Airways *River Beauly*	
G-DOCG	Boeing 737-436	British Airways *River Blackwater*	
G-DOCH	Boeing 737-436	British Airways *River Brue*	
G-DOCI	Boeing 737-436	British Airways *River Carron*	
G-DOCJ	Boeing 737-436	British Airways *River Glass*	
G-DOCK	Boeing 737-436	British Airways *River Lochay*	
G-DOCL	Boeing 737-436	British Airways *River Lune*	
G-DOCM	Boeing 737-436	British Airways *River Meon*	
G-DOCN	Boeing 737-436	British Airways *River Ottery*	
G-DOCO	Boeing 737-436	British Airways *River Parett*	
G-DOCP	Boeing 737-436	British Airways *River Swift*	
G-DOCR	Boeing 737-436	British Airways *River Tavy*	
G-DOCS	Boeing 737-436	British Airways *River Teifi*	
G-DOCT	Boeing 737-436	British Airways *River Tene*	
G-DOCU	Boeing 737-436	British Airways *River Teviot*	
G-DOCV	Boeing 737-436	British Airways *River Thurso*	
G-DOCW	Boeing 737-436	British Airways *River Till*	
G-DOCX	Boeing 737-436	British Airways *River Tirry*	
G-DODD	Cessna F.172P-II	K. Watts/Elstree	
G-DODS	PA-46-310P Malibu	HPM Investments Ltd	
G-DOFY	Bell 206B JetRanger 3	Cinnamond Ltd	
G-DOGS	Cessna R.182RG	P. Bennett & J. R. Shawe	
G-DONS	PA-28RT-201T Turbo Arrow IV	D. J. Murphy	
G-DOOR	M.S.893E Rallye 180GT	Lynair Flying Group	
G-DOOZ	AS.355F-2 Twin Squirrel	Lynton Aviation Ltd (G-BNSX)	
G-DORB	Bell 206B JetRanger 3	Dorb Crest Homes Ltd	
G-DORK	EMB-110P1 Bandeirante	Union Discount Equipment Finance Ltd	
G-DOVE	Cessna 182Q	P. J. Contracting	
G-DOWN	Colt 31A	M. Williams	
G-DPPS	AS.355N Twin Squirrel	Dyfed-Powys Police Authority	
G-DRAC	Cameron Dracula Skull SS balloon	Shiplake Investments Ltd	
G-DRAG	Cessna 152 (tailwheel)	L. M. Maynard & D. C. Scouller (G-REME/G-BRNF)	
G-DRAI	Robinson R-22B	Aerial Images Ltd	
G-DRAW	Colt 77A balloon	Readers Digest Association Ltd	
G-DRAY	Taylor JT.1 Monoplane	L. J. Dray	
G-DRGN	Cameron N-105 balloon	W. I. Hooker & C. Parker	
G-DRNT	Sikorsky S-76A	Bond Helicopters Ltd/Aberdeen	
G-DROP	Cessna U.206C	I. A. Louttit (G-UKNO/G-BAMN)/ Dunkeswell	
G-DRSV	CEA DR.315 (modified)	R. S. Voice	
G-DRYI	Cameron N-77 balloon	J. Barbour & Sons Ltd	
G-DRZF	CEA DR.360	C. A. Parker/Sywell	
G-DSGN	Robinson R-22B	Synter Aviation Ltd	
G-DTCP	PA-32R Cherokee Lance 300	Campbell Aviation Ltd (G-TEEM)	
G-DTOO	PA-38-112 Tomahawk	A. Todd	
G-DUCH	Beech 76 Duchess	C. D. Weiswall	
G-DUDS	C.A.S.A. 1-131E Jungmann 2000	D. H. Pattison	
G-DUET	Wood Duet	C. Wood	
G-DUGY	Emstrom 280C-UK-2 Shark	Pool Helicopter Services UK Ltd (G-BEEL)	
G-DUNN	Zenair CH.250	A. Dunn	
G-DURO	Shaw Europa	R. Swinden	
G-DURX	Thunder 77A balloon	V. Trimble	
G-DUST	Stolp SA.300 Starduster Too	J. V. George	
G-DUVL	Cessna F.172N	A. J. Simpson/Denham	
G-DVON	D.H.104 Devon C.2 (VP955)	C. L. Thatcher	
G-DWIA	Chilton D.W.1A	D. Elliott	
G-DWIB	Chilton D.W.1B	J. Jennings	
G-DXRG	Cameron 105 Agfa SS balloon	Cameron Balloons Ltd	
G-DYNE	Cessna 414	Commair Aviation Ltd/E. Midlands	
G-DYOU	PA-38-112 Tomahawk	Airways Aero Associations Ltd/Booker	
G-EAGL	Cessna 421C	Moseley Group (PSV) Ltd/E. Midlands	
G-EBJI	Hawker Cygnet (replica)	C. J. Essex	
G-ECAV	Beech 200 Super King Air	GEC Avionics Ltd/Rochester	
G-ECBH	Cessna F.150K	Air Fenland Ltd	
G-ECGC	Cessna F.172N-II	Leicestershire Aero Club Ltd	
G-ECGO	Bo208C Junior	M. F. R. B. Collett	
G-ECHO	Enstrom 280C-UK-2 Shark	ALP Electrical (Maidenhead) Ltd (G-LONS/ G-BDIB)/White Waltham	
G-ECJM	PA-28R-201T Turbo Arrow III	Regishire Ltd (G-FESL/G-BNRN)	

Notes	Reg.	Type	Owner or Operator
	G-ECKE	Avro 504K (replica)	N. Wright & C. M. Kettlewell
	G-ECKO	Colt 180A balloon	T. M. Donnelly
	G-ECOS	AS.355F-1 Twin Squirrel	Golden Harvest Ltd (G-DOLR/G-BPVB)
	G-ECOX	Grega GN.1 Air Camper	H. C. Cox
	G-EDDI	Robinson R-22B	Serve Offer Ltd
	G-EDEN	SOCATA TB.10 Tobago	N. G. Pistol & ptnrs
	G-EDGE	Jodel D.150	A. D. Edge
	G-EDIT	Beech B95 TravelAir	Warrior Aircraft Sales & Leasing (G-AXUX)
	G-EDNA	PA-38-112 Tomahawk	Ravenair Trading Ltd/Manchester
	G-EDOT	Cessna T.337D	A. Brinkley (G-BJIY)
	G-EDRY	Cessna T.303	Pat Eddery Ltd
	G-EEEE	Slingsby T.31 Motor Glider	R. F. Selby
	G-EEGL	Christen Eagle II	A. J. Wilson
	G-EENY	GA-7 Cougar	BLS Aviation Ltd/Elstree
	G-EEUP	SNCAN Stampe SV-4C	A. M. Wajih
	G-EEVS	Agusta A.109A-II	Norbrook Laboratories Ltd (G-OTSL)
	G-EEZE	Rutan LongEz	A. J. Nurse
	G-EFRY	Light Aero Avid Aerobat	J. J. Donely
	G-EFSM	Slingsby T.67M-260	Slingsby Aviation Ltd (G-BPLK)
	G-EFTE	Bolkow Bo 207	N. J. Heaton
	G-EGAP	Sequoia F.8L Falco	E. G. A. Prance
	G-EGEE	Cessna 310Q	R. Carr & A. Szymanski (G-AZVY)
	G-EGEL	Christen Eagle II	D. J. Daly
	G-EGGS	Robin DR.400/180	R. Foot
	G-EGJA	SOCATA TB.20 Trinidad	D. A. Williamson/Alderney
	G-EGLD	PA-28-161 Cadet	J. Appleton
	G-EGLE	Christen Eagle II	R. L. Mitcham & ptnrs
	G-EGLT	Cessna 310R	Tilling Associates Ltd (G-BHTV)
	G-EGUL	Christen Eagle II	P. N. Davis (G-FRYS)
	G-EHAP	Sportavia-Pützer RF.7	R. G. Boyes
	G-EHBJ	C.A.S.A. 1-131E Jungmann 2000	Mangreen Holdings Ltd
	G-EHIL	Westland-Agusta EH.101	Westland Helicopters Ltd/Yeovil
	G-EHMM	Robin DR.400/180R	Booker Gliding Club Ltd
	G-EIIR	Cameron N-77 balloon	D. V. Howard
	G-EIST	Robinson R-22B	European Executive Ltd
	G-EITE	Luscombe 8A Silvaire	D. L. Eite
	G-EIWT	Cessna FR.182RG	P. P. D. Howard-Johnston/Edinburgh
	G-EJGO	Z.226HE Trener	N. J. Radford
	G-ELBC	PA-34-200 Seneca II	Stapleford Flying Club Ltd (G-BANS)
	G-ELDG	Douglas DC-9-32	British Midland Airways Ltd *The Orloff Diamond*/E. Midlands
	G-ELDH	Douglas DC-9-32	British Midland Airways Ltd *The Hastings Diamond*/E. Midlands
	G-ELDI	Douglas DC-9-32	British Midland Airways Ltd *The Regent Diamond*/E. Midlands
	G-ELEC	Westland WG.30 Srs 200	Westland Helicopters Ltd (G-BKNV)/Yeovil
	G-ELFI	Robinson R-22B	Tiger Helicopters
	G-ELIZ	Denney Aerocraft Kitfox	A. J. Ellis
	G-ELMH	NA AT-6D Harvard III	M. Hammond
	G-ELRA	BAe 125-1000	British Aerospace PLC
	G-EMAK	PA-28R-201 Arrow III	D. & G. Rathbone
	G-EMAU	AS.355N Twin Squirrel	McAlpine Helicopters Ltd/Kidlington
	G-EMAZ	PA-28-181 Archer II	E. J. Stanley
	G-EMER	PA-34-200 Seneca II	Haimoss Ltd
	G-EMMA	Cessna F.182Q	Watkiss Group Aviation
	G-EMMS	PA-38-112 Tomahawk	Ravenair Trading Ltd/Manchester
	G-EMMY	Rutan Vari-Eze	M. J. Tooze
	G-EMSY	D.H.82A Tiger Moth	B. E. Micklewright (G-ASPZ)
	G-ENCE	Partenavia P.68B	P. Davies(G-OROY/G-BFSU)
	G-ENIE	Tipsy T.66 Nipper 3	I. D. Daniels
	G-ENII	Cessna F.172M	J. Howley
	G-ENNA	PA-28-161 Warrior II	A. J. Wood
	G-ENNY	Cameron V-77 balloon	B. G. Jones
	G-ENOA	Cessna F.172F	M. K. Acors (G-ASZW)
	G-ENRY	Cameron N-105 balloon	Numatic International Ltd
	G-ENSI	Beech F33A Bonanza	Special Analysis & Simulation Technology Ltd
	G-ENTT	Cessna F.152 II	Aeroleasing Assets (G-BHHI)/Coventry
	G-ENTW	Cessna F.152 II	M. Entwistle (G-BFLK)
	G-ENUS	Cameron N-90 balloon	The Hot-Air Balloon Co Ltd
	G-EOFF	Taylor JT.2 Titch	G. H. Wylde
	G-EORG	PA-38-112 Tomahawk	Airways Aero Association/Booker
	G-EPDI	Cameron N-77 balloon	R. Moss

Reg.	Type	Owner or Operator	Notes
G-ERCO	Ercoupe 415D	J. H. Stanton	
G-ERIC	R. Commander 112TC	P. P. Patterson/Newcastle	
G-ERIK	Cameron N-77 balloon	Cultural Resource Management Ltd	
G-ERIN	BAe ATP	Manx Airlines Ltd (G-BMYK)/Ronaldsway	
G-ERIX	Boeing Stearman A75N-1	P. P. Stanitzeck/Munich	
G-ERMO	ARV Super 2	P. R. Booth (G-BMWK)	
G-ERMS	Thunder Ax3 balloon	B. R. & M. Boyle	
G-ERNI	PA-28-181 Archer II	E. L. Collins (G-OSSY)	
G-EROS	Cameron H-34 balloon	Evening Standard Co Ltd	
G-ERRY	AA-5B Tiger	P. D. Cullen (G-BFMJ)	
G-ESSX	PA-28-161 Warrior II	Courtenay Enterprises (G-BHYY)/ Biggin Hill	
G-ESTE	AA-5A Cheetah	Biblio International Ltd (G-GHNC)	
G-ETBY	PA-32 Cherokee Six 260	Yarnhaven Ltd (G-AWCY)	
G-ETCD	Colt 77A balloon	Philips Electronics Ltd	
G-ETDA	PA-28-161 Warrior II	T. Griffiths	
G-ETDB	PA-38-112 Tomahawk	R. A. Wakefield	
G-ETDC	Cessna 172P	Osprey Air Services Ltd	
G-ETFT	Colt Financial Times SS balloon	Financial Times Ltd (G-BSGZ)	
G-ETIN	Robinson R-22B	Getin Helicopters Ltd	
G-EURA	Agusta-Bell 47J-2	E. W. Schnedlitz (G-ASNV)	
G-EVAN	Taylor JT.2 Titch	E. Evans	
G-EVER	Robinson R-22B	Everards Brewery Ltd	
G-EVNT	Lindstrand LBL-180A balloon	Redmalt Ltd	
G-EWAN	Prostar PT-2C	C. G. Shaw	
G-EWEL	Sikorsky S-76A	Ratners Group PLC	
G-EWFN	SOCATA TB-20 Trinidad	Trinidair Ltd (G-BRTY)	
G-EWIZ	Pitts S-2E Special	R. H. Jago	
G-EXEC	PA-34-200 Seneca	J. P. Edwards	
G-EXEX	Cessna 404	Atlantic Air Transport Ltd/Coventry	
G-EXIT	M.S.893E Rallye 180GT	G-Exit Ltd/Rochester	
G-EXLR	BAe 125-1000B	Raytheon Corporate Jets Inc	
G-EXOR	Robinson R-22B	Ex-Or Ltd (G-CMCM)	
G-EXPR	Colt 90A balloon	B. M. Howard	
G-EXTR	Extra EA.260	D. M. Britten	
G-EYAS	Denney Aerocraft Kitfox Mk 2	E. J. Young	
G-EYCO	Robin DR.400/180	L. M. Gould	
G-EYES	Cessna 402C	Air Corbière Ltd (G-BLCE)/Coventry	
G-EYRE	Bell 206L-1 LongRanger	Hideroute Ltd (G-STVI)	
G-EZEE	Rutan Vari-Eze	D. & M. Schwier	
G-EZIO	EMB-120RT Brasilia	—	
G-EZOS	Rutan Vari-Eze	O. Smith/Teesside	
G-FABB	Cameron V-77 balloon	V. P. F. Haines	
G-FABM	Beech 95-B55 Baron	F. B. Miles (G-JOND/G-BMVC)	
G-FABS	Thunder Ax9-120 S2 balloon	Fabulous Flights Balloon Co	
G-FAGN	Robinson R-22B	C. R. Weldon	
G-FAIR	SOCATA TB.10 Tobago	Sally Marine Ltd/Guernsey	
G-FALC	Aeromere F.8L Falco	P. W. Hunter (G-AROT)/Elstree	
G-FAMY	Maule M5-180C	Land Reclamation (Southern) Ltd	
G-FANC	Fairchild 24R-46 Argus III	J. I. Hyslop	
G-FANG	AA-5A Cheetah	Church & Co	
G-FANL	Cessna FR.172K XP-II	J. Woodhouse & Co/Staverton	
G-FANN	H.S.125 Srs 600B	Osprey Aviation Ltd (G-BARR)	
G-FARM	SOCATA Rallye 235GT	Bristol Cars Ltd	
G-FARO	Aero Designs Star-Lite SL.1	M. K. Faro	
G-FARR	Jodel D.150	G. H. Farr	
G-FAST	Cessna 337G	Seillans Land Investigations Ltd	
G-FAYE	Cessna F.150M	Cheshire Air Training School Ltd/Liverpool	
G-FBIX	D.H.100 Vampire FB.9 (WL505)	D. G. Jones	
G-FBMB	Canadair CL.600-2B16 Challenger	Challenger Aviation Ltd	
G-FBMW	Cameron N-90 balloon	Bayrische Motorenwerke	
G-FBWH	PA-28R Cherokee Arrow 180	F. A. Short	
G-FCHJ	Cessna 340A	P. L. & M. J. E. Builder (G-BJLS)	
G-FCSP	Robin DR.400/180	FCS Photochemicals	
G-FDAV	SA.341G Gazelle 1	Federal Aviation Ltd (G-RIFA/G-ORGE/G-BBHU)	
G-FDGM	Beech B60 Duke	Parissi Air Ltd/Perth	
G-FEBE	Cessna 340A	R. H. Everett	
G-FELT	Cameron N-77 balloon	Allan Industries Ltd	
G-FENI	Robinson R-22B	I. Fenwick	
G-FFBR	Thunder Ax8-105 balloon	Fuji Photo Film (UK) Ltd	

Notes	Reg.	Type	Owner or Operator
	G-FFEN	Cessna F.150M	Suffolk Aero Club Ltd/Ipswich
	G-FFLT	H.S.125 Srs 600B	Albion Aviation Management Ltd
	G-FFOR	Cessna 310R	Air Service Training Ltd (G-BMGF)/Perth
	G-FFRA	Dassault Falcon 20DC	FR Aviation Ltd/Bournemouth
	G-FFRB	Dassault Falcon 20DC	FR Aviation Ltd/Bournemouth
	G-FFRI	AS.355F-1 Twin Squirrel	Ford Farm Racing G-GLOW/G-PAPA/G-CNET/G-MCAH)
	G-FFTI	SOCATA TB.20 Trinidad	Blicqair Ltd
	G-FFTN	Bell 206B JetRanger	Kensington Aviation Ltd
	G-FFWD	Cessna 310R	Keef & Co Ltd (G-TVKE/G-EURO)
	G-FGID	FG-1D Corsair (88297)	Patina Ltd/Duxford
	G-FHAS	Scheibe SF.25E Super Falke	Burn Gliding Club Ltd
	G-FIAT	PA-28 Cherokee 140	RAF Benevolent Fund's IAT/ Bristol & Wessex Aeroplane Club (G-BBYW)/Lulsgate
	G-FIFI	SOCATA TB.20 Trinidad	D. J. & M. Gower (G-BMWS)
	G-FIGA	Cessna 152	Aerohire Ltd/Halfpenny Green
	G-FIGB	Cessna 152	Aerohire Ltd/Halfpenny Green
	G-FIJR	L.188PF Electra	Hunting Cargo Airlines Ltd
	G-FIJV	L.188CF Electra	Hunting Cargo Airlines Ltd
	G-FILE	PA-34-200T Seneca	S. D. Cole
	G-FILO	Robin DR.400/180	F. Friedenberg
	G-FINA	Cessna F.150L	D. Norris (G-BIFT)
	G-FIND	Cessna F.406 Caravan II	Air Corbière Ltd/Coventry
	G-FINN	Cameron 90 Reindeer SS balloon	Forbes Europe Inc/France
	G-FINS	AB-206B JetRanger 2	Brian Seedle Helicopters (G-FSCL)
	G-FISH	Cessna 310R-II	Bostonair Ltd/Humberside
	G-FISK	Pazmany PL-4A	K. S. Woodard
	G-FISS	Robinson R-22B	B. G. & D. Bushell
	G-FIST	Fieseler Fi.156C Storch	Aero Vintage Ltd
	G-FIZU	L.188C Electra	Hunting Cargo Airlines Ltd/E. Midlands
	G-FIZZ	PA-28-161 Warrior II	Arrow Air Centre Ltd/Shipdham
	G-FJMS	Partenavia P.68B	F. J. M. Sanders (G-SVHA)
	G-FKKM	PA-28RT-201T Turbo Arrow IV	D. J. Kaye
	G-FLAG	Colt 77A balloon	Thunder & Colt Ltd
	G-FLAK	Beech 95-E55 Baron	J. K. Horne
	G-FLCA	Fleet Model 80 Canuck	E. C. Taylor
	G-FLCO	Sequoia F.8L Falco	J. B. Mowforth
	G-FLEA	SOCATA TB.10 Tobago	Fleair Trading Co/Biggin Hill
	G-FLEN	PA-28-161 Warrior II	Winchfield Enterprises Ltd
	G-FLII	GA-7 Cougar	BLS Aviation Ltd (G-GRAC)/Elstree
	G-FLIK	Pitts S.1S Special	R. P. Millinship
	G-FLPI	R. Commander 112A	L. Freeman & Son/Newcastle
	G-FLSI	FLS Aerospace Sprint 160	FLS Aerospace (Lovaux) Ltd/Bournemouth
	G-FLTI	Beech F90 King Air	Flightline Ltd/Southend
	G-FLTY	EMB-110P1 Bandeirante	Flightline Ltd (G-ZUSS/G-REGA)/ Southend
	G-FLTZ	Beech 58 Baron	Stesco Ltd (G-PSVS)
	G-FLUF	Lindstrand Bunny SS balloon	Lindstrand Balloons Ltd
	G-FLUG	Gyroflug SC.01B-160 Speed Canard	ITPS Ltd/Cranfield
	G-FLUT	Stits SA.6B Flut-R-Bug	B. J. Towers
	G-FLYA	Mooney M.20J	Flya Aviation Ltd
	G-FLYI	PA-34-200 Seneca	BLS Aviation Ltd (G-BHVO)/Elstree
	G-FLYR	AB-206B JetRanger 2	Kwik Fit Euro Ltd (G-BAKT)
	G-FLYV	Slingsby T.67M-200	Firefly Aerial Promotions Ltd
	G-FMAL	AB-206A JetRanger	Catto Helicopters (G-RIAN/G-BHSG)
	G-FMAM	PA-28-151 Warrior	Essex Radio PLC (G-BBXV)/Southend
	G-FMUS	Robinson R-22	Brendan McNamee Ltd (G-BJBT)
	G-FNLD	Cessna 172N	Papa Hotel Flying Group
	G-FNLY	Cessna F.172M	London Aviation Ltd (G-WACX/G-BAEX)/ Biggin Hill
	G-FOEL	PA-31-350 Navajo Chieftain	Oxaero (G-BBXR)/Kidlington
	G-FOGG	Cameron N-90 balloon	J. P. E. Money-Kyrle
	G-FOLD	Light Aero Avid Speedwing	S. R. Winder
	G-FOLY	Aerotek Pitts S-2A Modified	A. A. Laing
	G-FOOD	Beech B200 Super King Air	Specbridge Ltd/Gamston
	G-FOPP	Lancair 320	Airsport (UK) Ltd
	G-FORC	SNCAN Stampe SV-4C	G. Pullan
	G-FORD	SNCAN Stampe SV-4B	P. Meeson & R. A. J. Spurrell/ White Waltham
	G-FOTO	PA-E23 Aztec 250F	Aerofilms Ltd (G-BJDH/G-BDXV)/ Leavesden

Reg.	Type	Owner or Operator	Notes
G-FOWL	Colt 90A balloon	Chesterfield Cold Storage Ltd	
G-FOXA	PA-28-161 Cadet	Leicestershire Aero Club Ltd	
G-FOXC	Denney Aerocraft Kitfox	Junipa Sales (Aviation) Ltd	
G-FOXD	Denney Aerocraft Kitfox	M. Hanley	
G-FOXE	Denney Aerocraft Kitfox	K. M. Pinkard	
G-FOXG	Denney Aerocraft Kitfox	Kitfox Group	
G-FOXI	Denney Aerocraft Kitfox	B. Johns	
G-FOXM	Bell 206B JetRanger 2	Tyringham Charter & Group Services (G-STAK/G-BNIS)	
G-FOXS	Denney Aerocraft Kitfox	S. P. Watkins & C. C. Rea	
G-FOXX	Denney Aerocraft Kitfox	R. O. F. Harper	
G-FOXZ	Denney Aerocraft Kitfox	M. Smalley & ptnrs	
G-FPCL	GA-7 Cougar	Eurowide Ltd	
G-FRAA	Dassault Falcon 20F	FR Aviation Ltd/Bournemouth	
G-FRAB	Dassault Falcon 20F	FR Aviation Ltd/Bournemouth	
G-FRAC	Dassault Falcon 20F	FR Aviation Ltd/Bournemouth	
G-FRAD	Dassault Falcon 20E	FR Aviation Ltd (G-BCYF)/Bournemouth	
G-FRAE	Dassault Falcon 20E	FR Aviation Ltd/Bournemouth	
G-FRAF	Dassault Falcon 20E	FR Aviation Ltd/Bournemouth	
G-FRAG	PA-32 Cherokee Six 300E	G-FRAG Group	
G-FRAH	Dassault Falcon 20DC	FR Aviation Ltd/Bournemouth	
G-FRAI	Dassault Falcon 20E	FR Aviation Ltd/Bournemouth	
G-FRAJ	Dassault Falcon 20E	FR Aviation Ltd/Bournemouth	
G-FRAK	Dassault Falcon 20DC	FR Aviation Ltd/Bournemouth	
G-FRAL	Dassault Falcon 20DC	FR Aviation Ltd/Bournemouth	
G-FRAM	Dassault Falcon 20DC	FR Aviation Ltd/Bournemouth	
G-FRAN	Piper J-3C-90 Cub (480321)	Essex L-4 Group (G-BIXY)	
G-FRAO	Dassault Falcon 20DC	FR Aviation Ltd/Bournemouth	
G-FRAP	Dassault Falcon 20DC	FR Aviation Ltd/Bournemouth	
G-FRAR	Dassault Falcon 20DC	FR Aviation Ltd/Bournemouth	
G-FRAS	Dassault Falcon 20C	FR Aviation Ltd/Bournemouth	
G-FRAT	Dassault Falcon 20C	FR Aviation Ltd/Bournemouth	
G-FRAU	Dassault Falcon 20C	FR Aviation Ltd/Bournemouth	
G-FRAW	Dassault Falcon 20ECM	FR Aviation Ltd/Bournemouth	
G-FRAX	Cessna 441	FR Aviation Ltd (G-BMTZ)/Bournemouth	
G-FRAY	Cassutt IIIM (modified)	C. I. Fray	
G-FRAZ	Cessna 441	FR Aviation Ltd/Bournemouth	
G-FRCE	H.S. Gnat T.1	Butane Buzzard Aviation Corporation Ltd	
G-FREE	Pitts S-2A Special	Pegasus Flying Group/Fairoaks	
G-FRJB	Britten Sheriff SA-1 ★	Aeropark/E. Midlands	
G-FRST	PA-44-180T Turbo Seminole	WAM (GB) Ltd	
G-FSDC	Enstrom 280C-UK Shark	The Pixel Image Factory PLC (G-BKTG)	
G-FSDG	AB-206B JetRanger	Flair (Soft Drinks) Ltd (G-ROOT/G-JETR)	
G-FSDH	Hughes 269A	West Country Aviation Ltd	
G-FSDT	Hughes 269A	S. G. Oliphant-Hope/Shoreham	
G-FSII	Gregory Free Spirit Mk II	M. J. Gregory & R. P. Hallam	
G-FSIX	EE Lightning F.6	Downderry Construction Group Ltd	
G-FSPL	PA-32R Cherokee Lance 300	J. D. L. Richardson & Goodridge (UK) Ltd	
G-FTAX	Cessna 421C	Hadagain Investments Ltd (G-BFFM)	
G-FTFT	Colt Financial Times SS balloon	Financial Times Ltd	
G-FTIL	Robin DR.400/180R	C. C. Blakey	
G-FTIM	Robin DR.400/100	P. D. W. King/Kidlington	
G-FTIN	Robin DR.400/100	G. D. Clark & M. J. D. Theobold	
G-FTWO	AS.355F-2 Twin Squirrel	McAlpine Helicopters Ltd (G-OJOR/ G-BMUS)/Hayes	
G-FUEL	Robin DR.400/180	R. Darch/Compton Abbas	
G-FUGA	Fouga CM.170R Magister	Royalair Services Ltd (G-BSCT)	
G-FUJI	Fuji FA.200-180	R. Gizzi	
G-FULL	PA-28R Cherokee Arrow 200-II	Arrow Flight Services Ltd (G-HWAY/G-JULI)/Shoreham	
G-FUND	Thunder Ax7-65Z balloon	Soft Sell Ltd	
G-FUZY	Cameron N-77 balloon	Allan Industries Ltd	
G-FUZZ	PA-18 Super Cub 95	G. W. Cline	
G-FWPW	PA-28-236 Dakota	P. A. & F. C. Winters	
G-FWRP	Cessna 421C	Aerienne Ltd/Southampton	
G-FXII	V.S.366 Spitfire F.XII (EN224)	P. R. Arnold	
G-FXIV	V.S.379 Spitfire FR.XIV (MV370)	R. Lamplough	
G-FZZI	Cameron H-34 balloon	Airship & Balloon Co Ltd	
G-FZZY	Colt 69A balloon	Hot-Air Balloon Co Ltd	
G-FZZZ	Colt 56A balloon	Hot-Air Balloon Co Ltd	
G-GABD	GA-7 Cougar	Scotia Safari Ltd/Prestwick	
G-GACA	P.57 Sea Prince T.1 ★	P. G. Vallance Ltd/Charlwood	

Notes	Reg.	Type	Owner or Operator
	G-GAGA	AA-5B Tiger	S. Spier (G-BGPG)
	G-GAJB	AA-5B Tiger	G. A. J. Bowles (G-BHZN)
	G-GALA	PA-28 Cherokee 180E	E. Alexander (G-AYAP)
	G-GAMA	Beech 95-58 Baron	Gama Aviation Ltd (G-BBSD)/Fairoaks
	G-GAME	Cessna T.303	JJB Sports Ltd
	G-GANE	Sequoia F.8L Falco	S. J. Gane
	G-GANJ	Fournier RF-6B-100	Soaring Equipment Ltd/Coventry
	G-GASC	Hughes 369HS	Crewhall Ltd (G-WELD/G-FROG)
	G-GASP	PA-28-181 Archer II	G-GASP Flying Group
	G-GASS	Thunder Ax7-77 balloon	Travel Gas (Midlands) Ltd
	G-GAUL	Cessna 550 Citation II	Chauffair Leasing Ltd
	G-GAWA	Cessna 140	R. A. Page (G-BRSM)/Coventry
	G-GAYL	Learjet 35A	Northern Executive Aviation Ltd (G-ZING)/ Manchester
	G-GAZA	SA.341G Gazelle 1	Stratton Motor Co (Norfolk) Ltd (G-RALE/ G-SFTG)
	G-GAZI	SA.341G Gazelle 1	Stratton Motor Co (Norfolk) Ltd & UCC International Group Ltd (G-BKLU)
	G-GAZZ	SA.341G Gazelle 1	Stratton Motor Co (Norfolk) Ltd & UCC International Group Ltd
	G-GBAO	Robin R.1180TD	J. Kay-Movat
	G-GBLR	Cessna F.150L	Blue Max Flying Group
	G-GBSL	Beech 76 Duchess	R. M. Jones (G-BGVG)
	G-GBUE	Robin DR.400/120A	G. Higgins & ptnrs (G-BPXD)
	G-GCAA	PA-28R Cherokee Arrow 200	Southern Air Ltd/Shoreham
	G-GCAB	PA-30 Twin Comanche 180	Southern Air Ltd/Shoreham
	G-GCAT	PA-28 Cherokee 140B	F. C. Odie (G-BFRH)
	G-GCCL	Beech 76 Duchess	Multirun Ltd
	G-GCJL	BAe Jetstream 4100	British Aerospace PLC/Prestwick
	G-GCKI	Mooney M.20K	A. L. Burton & A. J. Daly
	G-GCNZ	Cessna 150M	Firecrest Aviation Ltd/Leavesden
	G-GDAM	PA-18 Super Cub 135	A. D. Martin
	G-GDAY	Robinson R-22B	K. Shaw/Norwich
	G-GDOG	PA-28R Cherokee Arrow 200-II	E. J. Percival (G-BDXW)
	G-GEAR	Cessna FR.182Q	Deeperton Ltd
	G-GEDS	AS.350B Ecureuil	GAMA Aviation Ltd (G-HMAN/G-SKIM/ G-BIVP)
	G-GEEE	Hughes 369HS	B. P. Stein (G-BDOY)
	G-GEEP	Robin R.1180T	Organic Concentrates Ltd/Booker
	G-GEES	Cameron N-77 balloon	Mark Jarvis Ltd *Mark Jarvis*
	G-GEEZ	Cameron N-77 balloon	Charnwood Forest Turf Accountants Ltd
	G-GEMS	Thunder Ax8-90 S2 balloon	Alexander The Jewellers Ltd (G-BUNP)
	G-GEOF	Pereira Osprey 2	G. Crossley
	G-GEUP	Cameron N-77 balloon	D. P. & B. O. Turner
	G-GFAB	Cameron N-105 balloon	The Andrew Brownsword Collection Ltd
	G-GFCA	PA-28-161 Cadet	Swallow Aviation Ltd/Staverton
	G-GFCB	PA-28-161 Cadet	S. F. Tebby & Sons
	G-GFCC	PA-28-161 Cadet	Swallow Aviation Ltd/Staverton
	G-GFCD	PA-34-220T Seneca III	BWOC Ltd (G-KIDS)/Staverton
	G-GFCF	PA-28-161 Cadet	Swallow Aviation Ltd (G-RHBH)/Staverton
	G-GFKY	Zenair CH.250	B. F. Arnall
	G-GFLY	Cessna F.150L	W. Lancs Aero Club Ltd/Woodvale
	G-GFRY	Bell 206L-3 LongRanger	Turbine Helicopters Ltd
	G-GGGG	Thunder Ax7-77A balloon	T. A. Gilmour
	G-GGLE	PA-22 Colt 108 (tailwheel)	J. R. Coulthurst
	G-GGOW	Colt 77A balloon	City of Glasgow District Council
	G-GHCL	Bell 206B JetRanger 2	Grampian Helicopter Charter Ltd (G-SHVV)
	G-GHIA	Cameron N-120 balloon	Bristol Street Motors (Cheltenham) Ltd
	G-GHIN	Thunder Ax7-77 balloon	G. M. Ghinn
	G-GHRW	PA-28RT-201 Arrow IV	Leavesden Flight Centre Ltd (G-ONAB/ G-BHAK)
	G-GIGI	M.S.893A Rallye Commodore	P. J. C. Phillips (G-AYVX)
	G-GILY	Robinson R-22B	Reynard Racing Cars Ltd
	G-GIRO	Schweizer 269C	D. E. McDowell
	G-GJCB	BAe 125 Srs 800B	J. C. Bamford Excavators Ltd
	G-GJCD	Robinson R-22B	A. G. Forshaw
	G-GJKK	Mooney M.20K	Davey & Shaw
	G-GLAM	BAe Jetstream 3102	British Aerospace PLC (G-IBLX)
	G-GLAW	Cameron N-90 balloon	George Law Ltd
	G-GLED	Cessna 150M	Firecrest Aviation Ltd/Leavesden
	G-GLOS	H.P.137 Jetstream 200	Ashcombe Ltd (G-BCGU/G-AXRI)
	G-GLUE	Cameron N-65 balloon	L. J. M. Muir & G. D. Hallett
	G-GMAX	SNCAN Stampe SV-4C	Glidegold Ltd (G-BXNW)

Reg.	Type	Owner or Operator	Notes
G-GMJM	McD Douglas MD-83	Airtours International Aviation Ltd	
G-GMPA	AS.355F-2 Twin Squirrel	Greater Manchester Police Authority (G-BPOI)	
G-GMSI	SOCATA TB.9 Tampico	ML Associates	
G-GNAT	H.S. Gnat T.1 (XS101)	Ruanil Investments Ltd/Cranfield	
G-GNSY	HPR-7 Herald 209	Channel Express (Air Services) Ltd (G-BFRK)/Bournemouth	
G-GNTA	SAAB SF.340A	Business Air Ltd/Aberdeen	
G-GNTB	SAAB SF.340A	Business Air Ltd/Aberdeen	
G-GNTC	SAAB SF.340A	Business Air Ltd/Aberdeen	
G-GNTD	SAAB SF.340A	Business Air Ltd/Aberdeen	
G-GNTE	SAAB SF.340A	Business Air Ltd/Aberdeen	
G-GNTF	—	—	
G-GOBP	Bell 206B JetRanger 2	Clyde Helicopters Ltd (G-BOUY)	
G-GOBT	Colt 77A balloon	British Telecom PLC	
G-GOCC	AA-5A Cheetah	Lowlog Ltd (G-BPIX)	
G-GOCX	Cameron N-90 balloon	Cathay Pacific Airways Ltd	
G-GOGO	Hughes 369D	A. W. Alloys Ltd	
G-GOLD	Thunder Ax6-56A balloon	Joseph Terry & Sons Ltd	
G-GOLF	SOCATA TB.10 Tobago	E. H. Scamell & ptnrs	
G-GOMM	PA-32R Cherokee Lance 300	A. Kazaz/Leicester	
G-GONE	D.H.112 Venom FB.50	J. E. Davies	
G-GOOS	Cessna F.182Q	P. J. Clegg	
G-GORE	CFM Streak Shadow	D. N. & E. M. Gore	
G-GOSS	Jodel DR.221	D. Folens	
G-GOZO	Cessna R.182	Transmatic Fyllan Ltd (G-BJZO)/Cranfield	
G-GPMW	PA-28RT-201T Turbo Arrow IV	M. Worrall & ptnrs	
G-GPST	Phillips ST.1 Speedtwin	P. J. C. Phillips	
G-GRAM	PA-31-350 Navajo Chieftain	Newquay Air Ltd (G-BRHF)	
G-GRAY	Cessna 172N	Truman Aviation Ltd/Tollerton	
G-GREG	Jodel DR.220 2+2	J. T. Wilson	
G-GREN	Cessna T.310R	D. Hughes & P. Appleyard/Leeds	
G-GRID	AS.355F-1 Twin Squirrel	National Grid Co PLC	
G-GRIF	R. Commander 112TCA	M. J. Chilton (G-BHXC)	
G-GROW	Cameron N-77 balloon	Derbyshire Building Society	
G-GSFC	Robinson R-22B	Weller Helicopters Ltd	
G-GSML	Enstrom 280C-UK	Guardwell Security Management Ltd (G-BNNV)	
G-GTAX	PA-31-350 Navajo Chieftain	Hadagain Investments Ltd (G-OIAS)	
G-GTHM	PA-38-112 Tomahawk	Truman Aviation Ltd/Tollerton	
G-GTPL	Mooney M.20K	W. R. Emberton/Sywell	
G-GUCK	Beech C23 Sundowner 180	G-GUCK Group (G-BPYG)	
G-GUNN	Cessna F.172H	J. G. Gunn (G-AWGC)	
G-GUNS	Cameron V-77 balloon	Royal School of Artillery Hot Air Balloon Club	
G-GURL	Cameron A-210 balloon	Hot Airlines Ltd	
G-GUYI	PA-28-181 Archer II	B. Butler	
G-GUYS	PA-34-200T Seneca	H. Jowett & Co Ltd (G-BMWT)	
G-GWEN	Cessna F.172M	R. E. Youngsworth (G-GBLP)	
G-GWHH	AS.355F Twin Squirrel	Wimpey Homes Holdings Ltd (G-BKUL)	
G-GWIL	AS.350B Ecureuil	Talan Ltd	
G-GWIT	Cameron O-84 balloon	M. A. Campbell	
G-GWIZ	Colt Clown SS balloon	Oxford Promotions (UK) Ltd	
G-GWYN	Cessna F.172M	Gwyn Aviation	
G-GYAV	Cessna 172N	Southport & Merseyside Aero Club (1979) Ltd	
G-GYMM	PA-28R Cherokee Arrow 200	D. J. Warner & J. B. A. Ainsworth (G-AYWW)	
G-GYRO	Campbell Cricket	N. A. Pitcher & A. L. Howell	
G-GZDO	Cessna 172N	Cambridge Hall Aviation	
G-HAEC	CAC-18 Mustang 23 (472917)	Classic Aviation Ltd/Duxford	
G-HAGT	Airbus A.320-212	Excalibur Airways Ltd/E. Midlands	
G-HAIG	Rutan LongEz	P. N. Haigh	
G-HAJJ	Glaser-Dirks DG.400	P. W. Endean	
G-HALC	PA-28R Cherokee Arrow 200	Halcyon Aviation Ltd	
G-HALL	PA-22 Tri-Pacer 160	F. P. Hall (G-ARAH)	
G-HALO	Elisport CH-7 Angel	Taylor Woolhouse Ltd	
G-HALP	SOCATA TB.10 Tobago	D. Halpera (G-BITD)/Elstree	
G-HAMA	Beech 200 Super King Air	Gama Aviation Ltd/Fairoaks	
G-HAMI	Fuji FA.200-180	Hamilton Rentals (UK) Ltd (G-OISF/ G-BAPT)	
G-HAMP	Bellanca 7ACA Champ	R. J. Grimstead	
G-HANS	Robin DR.400 2+2	Headcorn Flying School Ltd	

Notes	Reg.	Type	Owner or Operator
	G-HAPR	B.171 Sycamore HR.14 (XG547) ★	International Helicopter Museum/Weston-s-Mare
	G-HARE	Cameron N-77 balloon	M. A. Pratt & N. I. Cakebread
	G-HARF	G.1159C Gulfstream 4	Fayair (Jersey) Ltd
	G-HARH	Sikorsky S-76B	Fayair (Jersey) 1984 Ltd
	G-HART	Cessna 152	Atlantic Air Transport Ltd/Coventry
	G-HARY	Alon A-2 Aircoupe	Northumbria Horse Riding Holidays (G-ATWP)
	G-HASL	AA-5A Cheetah	D.B.G. Ltd (G-BGSL)/(stored)
	G-HATZ	Hatz CB-1	J. Pearson
	G-HAUL	Westland WG.30 Srs 300★	International Helicopter Museum/Weston-super-Mare
	G-HAZE	Thunder Ax8-90 balloon	T. G. Church
	G-HBAC	AS.355F-1 Twin Squirrel	BAC Ltd (G-HJET)
	G-HBUG	Cameron N-90 balloon	Thorn EMI Computeraid (G-BRCN)
	G-HCRP	McD Douglas MD-83	Airtours International Aviation Ltd
	G-HCSL	PA-34-220T Seneca III	Hollowbrook Computer Services Ltd
	G-HCTL	PA-31-350 Navajo Chieftain	Field Aircraft Services (Heathrow) Ltd (G-BGOY)
	G-HDBA	H.S.748 Srs 2B	Trident Aviation Leasing Services Ltd
	G-HDBB	H.S.748 Srs 2B	Trident Aviation Leasing Services Ltd
	G-HDBD	H.S.748 Srs 2B	British Aerospace PLC/Woodford
	G-HDEW	PA-32R-301 Saratoga SP	Lord Howard de Walden (G-BRGZ)
	G-HDOG	Colt Flying Hot Dog SS balloon	Longbreak Ltd
	G-HEAD	Colt 56 Flying Head SS balloon	Lindstrand Balloons Ltd
	G-HELE	Bell 206B JetRanger 3	B. E. E. Smith (G-OJFR)
	G-HELI	Saro Skeeter Mk 12 (XM556) ★	International Helicopter Museum/Weston-s-Mare
	G-HELN	PA-18 Super Cub 95	J. J. Anziani (G-BKDG)/Booker
	G-HELP	Colt 17A balloon	Airship & Balloon Co Ltd
	G-HELV	D.H.115 Vampire T.55 (U-1215)	Hunter Wing Ltd
	G-HELX	Cameron N-31 balloon	Hot-Air Balloon Co Ltd
	G-HEMS	SA.365N Dauphin 2	Express Newspapers PLC
	G-HENS	Cameron N-65 balloon	Horrells Dairies Ltd
	G-HENY	Cameron V-77 balloon	R. S. D'Alton
	G-HERA	Robinson R-22B	J. Malcolm
	G-HERB	PA-28R-201 Arrow III	D. I. Weidner
	G-HERO	PA-32RT-300 Lance II	R. P. Thomas & C. Moore (G-BOGN)
	G-HERS	Jodel D.18	A. Usherwood
	G-HEVY	Boeing 707-324C	HeavyLift Cargo Airlines Ltd/Stansted
	G-HEWI	Piper J-3C-90 Cub	Denham Grasshopper Group (G-BLEN)
	G-HEWS	Hughes 369D ★	Spares use/Sywell
	G-HEYY	Cameron 77 Bear SS balloon	Hot-Air Balloon Co Ltd George
	G-HFBM	Curtiss Robin C-2	Colin Crabbe Holdings Ltd
	G-HFCA	Cessna A.150L	Horizon Flying Club Ltd/Ipswich
	G-HFCB	Cessna F.150L	Horizon Flying Club Ltd (G-AZVR)/Ipswich
	G-HFCI	Cessna F.150L	Horizon Flying Club Ltd/Ipswich
	G-HFCL	Cessna F.152	Horizon Flying Club Ltd (G-BGLR)/Ipswich
	G-HFCT	Cessna F.152	Stapleford Flying Club Ltd
	G-HFIX	V.S.361 Spitfire HF.IXe (MJ730)	D. W. Pennell (G-BLAS)
	G-HFLA	Schweizer 269C	Sterling Helicopters Ltd/Norwich
	G-HFTG	PA-23 Aztec 250E	Clacton Aero Club (1988) Ltd (G-BSOB/G-BCJR)
	G-HGAS	Cameron V-77 balloon	Handygas Ltd
	G-HGPI	SOCATA TB.20 Trinidad	M. J. Jackson/Bournemouth
	G-HHUN	Hunter F.4 (XE677)	Hunter Wing Ltd/Bournemouth
	G-HIEL	Robinson R-22B	Hields Aviation
	G-HIER	Bell 206B JetRanger 3	Rentatruck Self Drive Ltd (G-BRFD)
	G-HIHI	PA-32R-301 Saratoga SP	Longslow Dairy Ltd
	G-HILS	Cessna F.172H	Lowdon Aviation Group (G-AWCH)
	G-HILT	SOCATA TB.10 Tobago	P. J. Morrison
	G-HINT	Cameron N-90 balloon	Hinton Garage Bath Ltd
	G-HIPO	Robinson R-22B	Hippo Helicopters Ltd (G-BTGB)
	G-HIRE	GA-7 Cougar	London Aerial Tours Ltd (G-BGSZ)/Biggin Hill
	G-HISS	Aerotek Pitts S-2A Special	S. Byers (G-BLVU)
	G-HIVA	Cessna 337A	High Voltage Applications Ltd (G-BAES)
	G-HIVE	Cessna F.150M	M. P. Lynn (G-BCXT)/Sibson
	G-HJCB	BAe 125-1000B	J. C. Bamford Excavators Ltd (G-BUUY)
	G-HJSS	AIA Stampe SV-4C (modified)	H. J. Smith (G-AZNF)
	G-HLEN	AS.350B Ecureuil	N. Edmonds (G-LOLY)
	G-HLFT	SC.5 Belfast 2	HeavyLift Cargo Airlines Ltd/Stansted
	G-HLIX	Cameron 80 Oil Can SS balloon	Hot-Air Balloon Co Ltd

Reg.	Type	Owner or Operator	Notes
G-HMBB	MBB BK-117B-1C	McAlpine Helicopters Ltd	
G-HMES	PA-28-161 Warrior II	Cleveland Flying School Ltd/Teesside	
G-HMJB	PA-34-220T Seneca III	M. Gavaghan	
G-HMMM	Cameron N-65 balloon	S. Moss	
G-HMPH	Bell 206B JetRanger 2	Mightycraft Ltd (G-BBUY)	
G-HMPT	AB-206B JetRanger 2	Kensington Aviation Ltd	
G-HNRY	Cessna 650 Citation VI	Quantel Ltd/Biggin Hill	
G-HNTR	Hunter T.7 (XL572) ★	Hunter Wing Ltd/Bournemouth	
G-HOBO	Denney Aerocraft Kitfox Mk 4	W. M. Hodgkins & C. A. Boswell	
G-HOCK	PA-28 Cherokee 180	Arabact Ltd (G-AVSH)	
G-HOFM	Cameron N-56 balloon	Hot-Air Balloon Co Ltd	
G-HOHO	Colt Santa Claus SS balloon	Oxford Promotions (UK) Ltd	
G-HOLY	ST.10 Diplomate	Sussex Spraying Services Ltd/Shoreham	
G-HOME	Colt 77A balloon	Anglia Balloon School *Tardis*	
G-HONK	Cameron O-105 balloon	T. F. W. Dixon & Son Ltd	
G-HOOV	Cameron N-56 balloon	H. R. Evans	
G-HOPE	Beech F33A Bonanza	Hurn Aviation Ltd	
G-HOPI	Cameron N-42 balloon	Cameron Balloons Ltd	
G-HOPS	Thunder Ax8-90 balloon	A. C. & B. Munn	
G-HORN	Cameron V-77 balloon	Travel Gas (Midlands) Ltd	
G-HORS	Cameron Horse SS balloon	Cameron Balloons Ltd	
G-HOST	Cameron N-77 balloon	D. Grimshaw	
G-HOTI	Colt 77A balloon	R. Ollier	
G-HOTT	Cameron O-120 balloon	D. L. Smith	
G-HOTZ	Colt 77B balloon	C. J. & S. M. Davies	
G-HOUS	Colt 31A balloon	Anglia Balloons Ltd	
G-HOWE	Thunder Ax7-77 balloon	M. F. Howe	
G-HPAA	BN-2B-26 Islander	Hampshire Police Authority (Air Support Unit) (G-BSWP)	
G-HPLC	Sikorsky S-76B	Air Hanson Ltd/Blackbushe	
G-HRAY	AB-206B JetRanger 3	Hecray Co Ltd (G-VANG/G-BIZA)	
G-HRHI	B.206 Srs 1 Basset (XS770)	Universal Salvage (Holdings) Ltd	
G-HRIO	Robin HR.100/120	D. Peters	
G-HRIS	Cessna P210N	Birmingham Aviation Ltd	
G-HRLK	SAAB 91D/2 Safir	Sylmar Aviation & Services Ltd (G-BRZY)	
G-HRLM	Brügger MB.2 Colibri	R. A. Harris	
G-HROI	R. Commander 112A	H. R. Oldland	
G-HRON	D.H.114 Heron 2 (XR442)	M. E. R. Coghlan (G-AORH)	
G-HRVD	CCF Harvard IV	M. Slater (G-BSBC)	
G-HRZN	Colt 77A balloon	A. J. Spindler	
G-HSDW	Bell 206B JetRanger	Winfield Shoe Co Ltd	
G-HSHS	Colt 105A balloon	H. & S. Aviation Ltd	
G-HSOO	Hughes 369HE	Helisport Ltd (G-BFYJ)	
G-HTAX	PA-31-350 Navajo Chieftain	Hadagain Investments Ltd	
G-HTPS	SA. 341G Gazelle 1	ITPS Ltd (G-BRNI)	
G-HTRF	Robinson R-22B	Ellmar Plant Hire Ltd	
G-HUBB	Partenavia P.68B	G-HUBB Ltd	
G-HUCH	Cameron 80 Carrots SS balloon	Airship & Balloon Co Ltd (G-BYPS)	
G-HUEY	Bell UH-1H	Butane Buzzard Aviation Corporation Ltd	
G-HUFF	Cessna 182P	A. E. G. Cousins	
G-HULL	Cessna F.150M	A. D. McLeod	
G-HUMF	Robinson R-22B	R. A. Wright	
G-HUNY	Cessna F.150G	T. J. Lynn (G-AVGL)	
G-HURI	CCF Hawker Hurricane XIIA (Z7381)	Patina Ltd/Duxford	
G-HURN	Robinson R-22B	Yorkshire Helicopter Centre Ltd	
G-HURR	Hawker Hurricane XIIB (BE417)	Autokraft Ltd	
G-HURY	Hawker Hurricane IV (KZ321)	Patina Ltd/Duxford	
G-HUTT	Denney Aerocraft Kitfox	B. W. Davies	
G-HVDM	V.S.361 Spitfire F.IX (H-25)	DSG (Guernsey) Ltd/Holland	
G-HVRD	PA-31-350 Navajo Chieftain	London Flight Centre Air Charter Ltd (G-BEZU)	
G-HVRS	Robinson R-22B	Northern Helicopters (Leeds) Ltd	
G-HWBK	Agusta A.109A	Camlet Helicopters Ltd	
G-HWKN	PA-31P Pressurised Navajo	Valk Air Ltd/Shoreham	
G-HWKR	Colt 90A balloon	P. A. Henderson	
G-HYGA	BAe 125 Srs 800B	M. S. Healey	
G-HYLT	PA-32R-301 Saratoga SP	Pump & Plant Services	
G-IAMP	Cameron H-34 balloon	Air 2 Air Ltd	
G-IBED	Robinson R-22A	P. D. Spinks (G-BMHN)	
G-IBET	Cameron 70 Can SS balloon	M. R. Humphrey & J. R. Clifton	
G-IBFW	PA-28R-201 Arrow III	Speedway Car & Van Hire Ltd	

Notes	Reg.	Type	Owner or Operator
	G-IBTX	Boeing 737-2M8	GB Airways Ltd (G-BTEB) *Pico Ruivo*/Gatwick
	G-ICCL	Robinson R-22B	Cicely Ltd (G-ORZZ)
	G-ICES	Thunder Ax6-56 balloon	British Balloon Museum & Library Ltd
	G-ICEY	Lindstrand LBL-77A balloon	Iceland Frozen Foods PLC
	G-ICKY	Lindstrand LBL-77A balloon	R. R. Green & ptnrs
	G-ICSG	AS.355F-1 Twin Squirrel	Industrial Control Services PLC (G-PAMI/G-BUSA)
	G-IDDI	Cameron N-77 balloon	Allen & Harris Ltd
	G-IDDY	D.H.C.1 Super Chipmunk	P. G. Kavanagh & D. T. Kaberry (G-BBMS)
	G-IDEA	AA-5A Cheetah	Lowlog Ltd (G-BGNO)
	G-IDJB	Cessna 150L	R. J. Browne
	G-IDUP	Enstrom 280C Shark	Stephenson Marine Ltd (G-BRZF)
	G-IDWR	Hughes 369HS	Ryburn Air Ltd (G-AXEJ)
	G-IECL	H.S.125 Srs 700B	Inflite Executive Charter Ltd/Stansted
	G-IEPF	Robinson R-22B	V. T. Nash
	G-IEYE	Robin DR. 400/180	J. S. Haslam
	G-IFIT	PA-31-350 Navajo Chieftain	Dart Group PLC (G-NABI/G-MARG)/Bournemouth
	G-IFLI	AA-5A Cheetah	ABC Aviation Ltd
	G-IFLP	PA-34-200T Seneca II	Golf-Sala Ltd
	G-IFOX	Robinson R-22B	Munn & Chapman Ltd
	G-IFTB	Beech 200C Super King Air	Interflight (Learjet) Ltd
	G-IGEL	Cameron N-90 balloon	Computacenter Ltd
	G-IGLA	Colt 240A balloon	P. J. Stapley
	G-IGLE	Cameron V-90 balloon	A. A. Laing
	G-IHSA	Robinson R-22B	R. J. Everett
	G-IHSB	Robinson R-22B	Polar Save Aviation Ltd
	G-IIAC	Aeronca 11AC Chief	Bailey Aviation Ltd (G-BTPY)
	G-IIAN	Aero Designs Pulsar	I. G. Harrison
	G-IIBD	PA-44-180T Seminole	H. S. Davies
	G-IIIG	Boeing Stearman A.75N1	Aerosuperbatics Ltd (G-BSDR)/Rendcomb
	G-IIII	Aerotek Pitts S-2B Special	B. K. Lecomber
	G-IIIL	Pitts S-1T Special	Skylark Aerobatics
	G-IIIR	Pitts S-1 Special	R. O. Rogers
	G-IIIT	Aerotek Pitts S-2A Special	Aerobatic Displays Ltd
	G-IIIX	Pitts S-1S Special	L. C. Seeger (G-LBAT/G-UCCI/G-BIYN)
	G-IINA	AS.350B-2 Ecureuil	Endeavour Aviation Ltd
	G-IIRB	Bell 206B JetRanger 3	Robard Consultants Ltd
	G-IIRG	Stoddard-Hamilton Glasair IIRGS	D. S. Watson
	G-IITI	Extra EA.300	Aerobatic Displays Ltd/Booker
	G-IIXX	Parsons 2-seat gyroplane	J. K. Padden
	G-IJAC	Light Aero Avid Speedwing Mk 4	I. J. A. Charlton
	G-IJOE	PA-28RT-201T Turbo Arrow IV	R. P. Wilson
	G-IJRC	Robinson R-22B	J. R. Clark Ltd (G-BTJP)
	G-IJYS	BAe Jetstream 3102	Jackie Stewart (G-BTZT)
	G-IKBP	PA-28-161 Warrior II	Hendafern Ltd/Shoreham
	G-IKIS	Cessna 210M	A. C. Davison
	G-ILES	Cameron O-90 balloon	G. N. Lantos
	G-ILLE	Boeing Stearman A.75L3 (379)	J. Griffin
	G-ILLS	H.S.125 Srs 3B	S. Gill (G-AVRF)/Luton
	G-ILLY	PA-28-181 Archer II	A. G. & K. M. Spiers
	G-ILSE	Corby CJ-1 Starlet	S. Stride
	G-ILTS	PA-32 Cherokee Six 300	Comed Aviation Ltd (G-CVOK)/Blackpool
	G-ILYS	Robinson R-22B	BJ Aviation/Welshpool
	G-IMAG	Colt 77A balloon	Flying Pictures (Balloons) Ltd
	G-IMBY	Pietenpol Air Camper	P. F. Bockh
	G-IMLI	Cessna 310Q	P. D. Carne (G-AZYK)
	G-IMPW	PA-32R-301 Saratoga SP	C. M. Juggins
	G-IMPX	R. Commander 112B	T. L. & S. Hull
	G-IMPY	Light Aero Avid Flyer C	T. R. C. Griffin
	G-INAV	Aviation Composites Mercury	Europa Aviation Ltd
	G-INCA	Glaser-Dirks DG.400	H. W. Ober
	G-INCH	Montgomerie-Bensen B.8MR	I. H. C. Branson (G-BRES)
	G-INDC	Cessna T.303	Howarth Timber (Aircharters) Ltd
	G-INGA	Thunder Ax8-84 balloon	M. L. J. Ritchie
	G-INGB	Robinson R-22B	N. J. Montford
	G-INNY	SE-5A (replica) (F5459)	R. M. Ordish/Old Sarum
	G-INOW	Monnet Moni	T. W. Clark
	G-INTC	Robinson R-22B	Intec Project Engineering Ltd
	G-IOOI	Robin DR.400/160	Freshname No 77 Ltd
	G-IOSI	Jodel DR.1051	A. Burbidge & R. Slater

Reg.	Type	Owner or Operator	Notes
G-IPEC	SIAI-Marchetti S.205-18F	P. M. Wright (G-AVEG)	
G-IPSI	Grob G.109B	G-IPSI Ltd (G-BMLO)	
G-IPSY	Rutan Vari-Eze	R. A. Fairclough/Biggin Hill	
G-IRIS	AA-5B Tiger	E. I. Bett (G-BIXU)	
G-IRLS	Cessna FR.172J	R. C. Chapman	
G-IRLY	Colt 90A balloon	S. A. Burnett & L. P. Purfield	
G-IRPC	Cessna 182Q	R. P. Carminke (G-BSKM)	
G-ISCA	PA-28RT-201 Arrow IV	D. J. & P. Pay	
G-ISEB	Agusta A.109A-II	Air Hanson Aircraft Sales Ltd (G-IADT/ G-HCBA)/Blackbushe	
G-ISEE	BAe 146-200	British Aerospace PLC	
G-ISEH	Cessna 182R	SEH (Holdings) Ltd (G-BIWS)/Ipswich	
G-ISIS	D.H.82A Tiger Moth	D. R. & M. Wood (G-AODR)	
G-ISLE	Short SD3-60	Manx Airlines Ltd (G-BLEG)/Ronaldsway	
G-ISMO	Robinson R-22B	LGH Aviation Ltd/Bournemouth	
G-ISTT	Thunder Ax8-84 balloon	RAF Halton Hot Air Balloon Club	
G-ITPS	Pilatus PC-6/B2-H2 Turbo Porter	ITPS Ltd/Cranfield	
G-ITTU	PA-23 Aztec 250E	D. Byrne & M. Cummings (G-BCSW)	
G-IVAC	Airtour AH-77B balloon	D. A. Haward/Germany	
G-IVAN	Shaw TwinEze	I. Shaw	
G-IVAR	Yakovlev Yak-50	I. G. Anderson	
G-IVIV	Robinson R-44 Astro	Sloane Helicopters Ltd/Sywell	
G-IVOR	Aeronca 11AC Chief	South Western Aeronca Group/Plymouth	
G-IWON	Cameron V-90 balloon	D. P. P. Jenkinson (G-BTCV)	
G-IZEL	SA.341G Gazelle 1	Fairview Securities (Investments) Ltd (G-BBHW)	
G-IZMO	Thunder Ax8-90 balloon	Landrell Fabric Engineering Ltd	
G-JACT	Partenavia P.68C	JCT 600 Ltd (G-NVIA)/Leeds	
G-JAKE	D.H.C.1 Chipmunk 22	J. M. W. Henstock (G-BBMY) Netherthorpe	
G-JANA	PA-28-181 Archer II	Croaker Aviation/Stapleford	
G-JANB	Colt Flying Bottle SS balloon	Justerini & Brooks Ltd	
G-JANN	PA-34-220T Seneca III	J. A. Powell	
G-JANS	Cessna FR.172J	I. G. Aizlewood/Luton	
G-JANT	PA-28-181 Archer II	Janair Aviation Ltd	
G-JARA	Robinson R-22B	J. A. R. Allwright	
G-JASE	PA-28-161 Warrior II	J. T. Matthews	
G-JASP	PA-23 Turbo Aztec 250E	Landsurcon (Air Survey) Ltd/Staverton	
G-JAYI	J/1 Autocrat	Bravo Aviation Ltd	
G-JAZZ	AA-5A Cheetah	Jazz Club	
G-JBDH	Robin DR.400/180	D. Hoolahan/Biggin Hill	
G-JBET	Beech F33A Bonanza	J. Bett/Glasgow	
G-JBJB	Colt 69A balloon	Justerini & Brooks Ltd	
G-JBPR	Wittman W.10 Tailwind	P. A. Rose & J. P. Broadhurst	
G-JBWI	Robinson R-22B	N. J. Wagstaff Leasing	
G-JCAS	PA-28-181 Archer II	Charlie Alpha Ltd	
G-JCJC	Colt Flying Jeans SS balloon	J. C. Balloon Co Ltd	
G-JCUB	PA-18 Super Cub 135	Piper Cub Consortium Ltd/Jersey	
G-JDEE	SOCATA TB.20 Trinidad	Melville Associates Ltd (G-BKLA)	
G-JDHI	Enstrom F-28C-UK	B. J. W. Carter (G-BCOT)	
G-JDIX	Mooney M.20B	J. E. Dixon (G-ARTB)	
G-JDLI	Jodel D.150	K. F. & R. Richardson	
G-JDTI	Cessna 421C	Eastfield Air Ltd/Sturgate	
G-JEAA	F.27 Friendship Mk 500F	Jersey European Airways Ltd	
G-JEAB	F.27 Friendship Mk 500F	Jersey European Airways Ltd	
G-JEAD	F.27 Friendship Mk 500	Jersey European Airways Ltd	
G-JEAE	F.27 Friendship Mk 500	Jersey European Airways Ltd	
G-JEAF	F.27 Friendship Mk 500	Jersey European Airways Ltd	
G-JEAG	F.27 Friendship Mk 500	Jersey European Airways Ltd	
G-JEAH	F.27 Friendship Mk 500	Jersey European Airways Ltd	
G-JEAI	F.27 Friendship Mk 500	Jersey European Airways Ltd	
G-JEAJ	BAe 146-200	Jersey European Airways Ltd (G-OLCA)	
G-JEAK	BAe 146-200	Jersey European Airways Ltd (G-OLCB)	
G-JEAL	BAe 146-300	Jersey European Airways Ltd (G-BTXN)	
G-JEAM	BAe 146-300	Jersey European Airways Ltd (G-BTJT)	
G-JEAN	Cessna 500 Citation	Foster Associates Ltd	
G-JEET	Cessna FA.152	Luton Flight Training (G-BHMF)	
G-JEFF	PA-38-112 Tomahawk	R. J. Alford	
G-JENA	Mooney M.20K	P. Leverkuehn/Biggin Hill	
G-JENI	Cessna R.182	R. A. Bentley	
G-JENN	AA-5B Tiger	BLS Aviation Ltd/Elstree	
G-JENS	SOCATA Rallye 100ST	Palmer Pastoral Co Ltd (G-BDEG)	
G-JERS	Robinson R-22B	Ravenheat Manufacturing Ltd	

Notes	Reg.	Type	Owner or Operator
	G-JETA	Cessna 550 Citation II	IDS Aircraft Ltd/Heathrow
	G-JETC	Cessna 550 Citation II	Colt Car Co Ltd/Staverton
	G-JETH	Hawker Sea Hawk FGA.6 (XE489) ★	P. G. Vallance Ltd/Charlwood
	G-JETI	BAe 125 Srs 800B	Alkharafi Aviation Ltd
	G-JETJ	Cessna 550 Citation II	North West Property Management Ltd (G-EJET/G-DJBE)
	G-JETM	Gloster Meteor T.7 (VZ638) ★	P. G. Vallance Ltd/Charlwood
	G-JETN	Learjet 35A	Heathrow Jet Charter Ltd (G-JJSG)
	G-JETP	P.84 Jet Provost T.52A (T.4)	Shadow Valley Investments Ltd
	G-JETX	Bell 206B JetRanger	Tripgate Ltd
	G-JFWI	Cessna F.172N	Staryear Ltd
	G-JGAL	Beech E90 King Air	Vaux (Aviation) Ltd/Newcastle
	G-JGMN	C.A.S.A. 1.131E Jungmann 2000	P. D. Scandrett/Staverton
	G-JHAS	Schweizer 269C	Albany Helicopters Ltd
	G-JHEW	Robinson R-22B	Burbage Farms Ltd
	G-JHSX	BAe 125 Srs 800A	Raytheon Corporate Jets Inc
	G-JIII	Stolp SA.300 Starduster Too	VT10 Co
	G-JILL	R. Commander 112TCA	J. J. J. C. Herbaux
	G-JIMS	Cessna 340A-II	Cox-Johnston Management Services Ltd (G-PETE)/Dundee
	G-JJAN	PA-28-181 Archer II	Redhill Flying Club
	G-JLEE	AB-206B JetRanger 3	Lee Aviation Ltd (G-JOKE/G-CSKY G-TALY)
	G-JLHS	Beech A36 Bonanza	I. G. Meredith
	G-JLMW	Cameron V-77 balloon	The Apollo Balloon Co Ltd
	G-JLRW	Beech 76 Duchess	Moorfield Developments Ltd/Elstree
	G-JMAC	BAe Jetstream 4100	British Aerospace PLC (G-JAMD/G-JXLI)
	G-JMAT	Schweizer 269C	John Matchett Ltd
	G-JMDI	Schweizer 269C	Lind of Norwich Ltd (G-FLAT)
	G-JMTS	Robin DR.400/180	J. R. Whiting
	G-JMTT	PA-28R-201T Turbo Arrow III	E. W. Passmore (G-BMHM)
	G-JNNB	Colt 90A balloon	Justerini & Brooks Ltd
	G-JODL	Jodel DR.1050/M	M. D. Mold
	G-JODY	Bell 206B JetRanger 3	Maztest Motors Ltd
	G-JOEY	BN-2A Mk III-2 Trislander	Aurigny Air Services (G-BDGG)/Guernsey
	G-JOIN	Cameron V-65 balloon	Derbyshire Building Society
	G-JOJO	Cameron A-210 balloon	Worcester Balloons
	G-JOLY	Cessna 120	J. D. Tarrant/Bristol
	G-JONE	Cessna 172M	A. Pierce
	G-JONH	Robinson R-22B	J. McW. Henderson
	G-JONI	Cessna FA.152	Luton Flight Training Ltd (G-BFTU)
	G-JONO	Colt 77A balloon	The Sandcliffe Motor Group
	G-JONZ	Cessna 172P	Truman Aviation Ltd/Tollerton
	G-JOON	Cessna 182D	Taylor Aircraft Services Ltd/Sywell
	G-JOSH	Cameron N-105 balloon	GT Flying Clubs Ltd
	G-JOYC	Beech F33A Bonanza	Dunmhor Transport Ltd
	G-JOYT	PA-28-181 Archer II	S. W. Taylor (G-BOVO)/Redhill
	G-JSCL	Rans S.10 Sakota	D. L. Davies
	G-JSMC	McD Douglas MD-83	Airtours International Aviation Ltd
	G-JSON	Cameron N-105 balloon	J. Bennett & Son (Insurance Brokers) Ltd
	G-JSSD	SA. Jetstream 3001	British Aerospace (G-AXJZ) Ltd/Prestwick
	G-JTCA	PA-23 Aztec 250E	J. D. Tighe (G-BBCU)/Sturgate
	G-JTWO	Piper J-2 Cub	A. T. Hooper & C. C. Silk (G-BPZR)
	G-JTYE	Aeronca 7AC Champion	J. Tye
	G-JUDE	CEA DR.400/180	R. G. Carrell
	G-JUDI	AT-6D Harvard III (FX301)	A. A. Hodgson
	G-JUDY	AA-5A Cheetah	Brandon Aviation/Biggin Hill
	G-JUIN	Cessna 303	M. J. Newman/Denham
	G-JUNG	C.A.S.A. 1.131E Jungmann 1000	K. H. Wilson
	G-JURE	SOCATA TB.10 Tobago	J. & C. A. Ure
	G-JURG	R. Commander 114A	Jurgair Ltd
	G-JVJA	Partenavia P.68C	Twinflite Aviation Ltd (G-BMEI)
	G-JVMD	Cessna 172N	Brandon Aviation (G-BNTV)
	G-JVMR	Partenavia P.68B	Sonardyne Ltd (G-JCTI/G-OJOE)/ Blackbushe
	G-JWBB	Jodel DR.1050	J. E. Worthy & B. F. Baldock (G-LAKI)
	G-JWDG	AA-5A Cheetah	JWDG Aviation (G-OCML/G-JAVA)
	G-JWDS	Cessna F.150G	London Aerial Tours Ltd (G-AVNB)
	G-JWFT	Robinson R-22B	Tukair Aircraft Charter
	G-JWIV	Jodel DR.1051	R. A. Bragger
	G-KAFE	Cameron N-65 balloon	Hot-Air Balloon Co Ltd
	G-KAIR	PA-28-181 Archer II	Academy Lithoplates Ltd/Aldergrove

Reg.	Type	Owner or Operator	Notes
G-KARI	Fuji FA.200-160	I. Mansfield & F. M. Fiore (G-BBRE)	
G-KART	PA-28-161 Warrior II	Newcastle-upon-Tyne Aero Club Ltd	
G-KARY	Fuji FA.200-180AO	C. J. Zetter (G-BEYP)	
G-KATE	Westland WG.30 Srs 100	*(stored)*/Penzance	
G-KATH	Cessna P.210N	S. P. Woods	
G-KATS	PA-28 Cherokee 140	Ipswich School of Flying Ltd (G-BIRC)	
G-KATT	Cessna 152	Aerohire Ltd (G-BMTK)/Halfpenny Green	
G-KAWA	Denney Aerocraft Kitfox	T. W. Maton	
G-KBKB	Thunder Ax8-90 S2 balloon	G. Boulden	
G-KBPI	PA-28-161 Warrior II	Hendafern Ltd (G-BFSZ)/Shoreham	
G-KCIG	Sportavia RF-5B	Exeter Sperber Syndicate	
G-KDET	PA-28-161 Cadet	Rapidspin Ltd/Biggin Hill	
G-KDFF	Scheibe SF.25E Super Falke	M. Lee & K. Dudley	
G-KDIX	Jodel D.9 Bebe	D. J. Wells	
G-KEAA	Beech 65-70 Queen Air	D. Cockburn (G-REXP/G-AYPC)	
G-KEAB	Beech 65-B80 Queen Air ★	*Instructional airframe* (G-BSSL/ G-BFEP)/Shoreham	
G-KEAC	Beech 65-A80 Queen Air	D. Cockburn (G-REXY/G-AVNG)	
G-KEEN	Stolp SA.300 Starduster Too	Holland Aerobatics Ltd	
G-KEMC	Grob G.109	Eye-Fly	
G-KENB	Air Command 503 Commander	K. Brogden	
G-KENI	Rotorway Executive	P. J. Clegg	
G-KENM	Luscombe 8A Silvaire	B. N. Stevens	
G-KENN	Robinson R-22B	Echo Helicopters	
G-KERY	PA-28 Cherokee 180	Hollingworth & Co (Midlands) Ltd (G-ATWO)	
G-KEST	Steen Skybolt	S. Thursfield & K. E. Eld	
G-KEVN	Robinson R-22B	K. P. Gallen (G-BONX)	
G-KEYB	Cameron O-84 balloon	B. P. Key	
G-KEYS	PA-23 Aztec 250F	T. M. Tuke & W. T. McCarter	
G-KEYY	Cameron N-77 balloon	Business Design Group Ltd (G-BORZ)	
G-KFIT	Beech F90 King Air	Kwik Fit Euro Ltd (G-BHUS)/Edinburgh	
G-KFOX	Denney Aerocraft Kitfox	C. H. T. Trace	
G-KFZI	KFZ-1 Tigerfalck	L. R. Williams	
G-KHRE	M.S.893E Rallye 150SV	B. Proctor/Dunkeswell	
G-KILY	Robinson R-22A	Julians Supermarket Ltd	
G-KIMB	Robin DR.340/140	R. M. Kimbell	
G-KINE	AA-5A Cheetah	Walsh Aviation	
G-KINK	Cessna 340	Hulbert of Dudley (Holdings) Ltd (G-PLEV)	
G-KIRK	Piper J-3C-65 Cub	M. J. Kirk	
G-KISS	Rand KR-2	E. A. Rooney	
G-KITE	PA-28-181 Archer II	World Business Publications Ltd/Elstree	
G-KITF	Denney Aerocraft Kitfox	Junipa Sales (Aviation) Ltd	
G-KITI	Pitts S-2E Special	P. A. Grant	
G-KITY	Denney Aerocraft Kitfox	Kitfox KFM Group	
G-KIWI	Cessna 404 Titan	Aviation Beauport Ltd (G-BHNI)	
G-KKDL	SOCATA TB.20 Trinidad	Egerton Hospital Equipment Ltd (G-BSHU)	
G-KKES	SOCATA TB.20 Trinidad	Kestrel Aviation International Ltd/ Biggin Hill	
G-KKJV	Zlin Z.37A-2	Free Enterprise Games	
G-KLAY	Enstrom 280C Shark	I. G. Shrigley (G-BGZD)	
G-KLIK	Air Command 532 Elite	Roger Savage (Photography)	
G-KMAM	Airbus A.320-212	Excalibur Airways Ltd/E. Midlands	
G-KNAP	PA-28-161 Warrior II	Newland Aeroleasing Ltd (G-BIUX)	
G-KNDY	Bell 206B JetRanger 3	ASP Helicopter Co Ltd	
G-KNIT	Robinson R-22B	BHM Knitwear Ltd	
G-KNOB	Lindstrand LBL-180A balloon	Wye Valley Aviation Ltd	
G-KNOW	PA-32 Cherokee Six 300	P. H. Knowland	
G-KODA	Cameron O-77 balloon	United Photofinishers Ltd	
G-KOLB	Kölb Twinstar Mk 3	P. A. Akines	
G-KOLI	PZL-110 Koliber 150	T. D. A. George & F. H. Buckland	
G-KOOL	D.H.104 Devon C.2 ★	E. Surrey Technical College/nr Redhill	
G-KORN	Cameron 70 Brentzen SS balloon	Cameron Balloons Ltd	
G-KOTA	PA-28-236 Dakota	JF Packaging	
G-KRII	Rand KR-2	M. R. Cleveley	
G-KRIS	Maule M5-235C Lunar Rocket	M. G. Pickering	
G-KSVB	PA-24 Comanche 260	C. M. Gill (G-ENIU/G-AVJU)	
G-KTEE	Cameron V-77 balloon	D. C. & N. P. Bull	
G-KUKU	Pfalzkuku (BS676)	A. D. Lawrence	
G-KUTU	Quickie Q.2	R. Nash & J. Parkinson	
G-KWAX	Cessna 182E Skylane	A. R. Carrillo & J. E. Brewis	
G-KWIK	Partenavia P.68B	Travelair UK Ltd	
G-KWKI	QAC Quickie Q.200	B. M. Jackson	

Notes	Reg.	Type	Owner or Operator
	G-LACA	PA-28-161 Warrior II	Light Planes (Lancashire) Ltd/Barton
	G-LACB	PA-28-161 Warrior II	Light Planes (Lancashire) Ltd/Barton
	G-LACR	Denney Aerocraft Kitfox	C. M. Rose
	G-LADE	PA-32 Cherokee Six 300E	A. G. & D. Webb
	G-LADN	PA-28-161 Warrior II	A. J. Diplock (G-BOLK)/Biggin Hill
	G-LADS	R. Commander 114	D. F. Soul
	G-LAGR	Cameron N-90 balloon	Bass & Tennent Sales Ltd
	G-LAIN	Robinson R-22B	R&R Developments Ltd
	G-LAIR	Stoddard-Hamilton Glasair IIS	D. L. Swallow
	G-LAKC	Cessna 404 Titan II	– (G-BKTW/G-WTVE)
	G-LAKD	Cessna 404 Titan II	– (G-BKWA/G-BELV)
	G-LAKE	Lake LA-250 Renegade	Stanford Ltd
	G-LAKH	BAe Jetstream 3102	– (G-BUFM)
	G-LAMS	Cessna F.152	Rentair Ltd
	G-LANC	Avro 683 Lancaster X (KB889) ★	Imperial War Museum/Duxford
	G-LAND	Robinson R-22B	Heli-Point Hire
	G-LANE	Cessna F.172N	G. C. Bantin
	G-LANG	Denney Aerocraft Kitfox	J. W. Lang
	G-LAPN	Light Aero Avid Aerobat	R. M. & A. P. Shorter
	G-LARA	Robin DR.400/180	K. D. & C. A. Brackwell
	G-LARE	PA-39 Twin Comanche C/R	J. R. W. Keates/Biggin Hill
	G-LARK	Helton Lark 95	J. Fox
	G-LASR	Stoddard-Hamilton Glasair II	P. Taylor
	G-LASS	Rutan Vari-Eze	S. Roberts
	G-LAXO	Agusta A.109C	Glaxo Holdings Ltd
	G-LAZR	Cameron O-77 balloon	Laser Civil Engineering Ltd
	G-LBCS	Colt 31A balloon	Airship & Balloon Co Ltd
	G-LBLI	Lindstrand LBL-105A balloon	Lindstrand Balloons Ltd
	G-LBLZ	Lindstrand LBL-105A balloon	Lindstrand Balloons Ltd
	G-LBMM	PA-28-161 Warrior II	S. C. May
	G-LBRC	PA-28RT-201 Arrow IV	D. J. V. Morgan & J. C. Lloyd
	G-LCIO	Colt 240A balloon	Star Micronics UK Ltd
	G-LCGL	CLA.7 Swift (replica)	J. M. Greenland
	G-LCOK	Colt 69A balloon	Hot-Air Balloon Co Ltd (G-BLWI)
	G-LCRC	Boeing 757-23A	Airtours International Airways Ltd (G-IEAB)
	G-LDYS	Colt 56A balloon	A. Green
	G-LEAM	PA-28-236 Dakota	South Yorkshire Caravans Ltd (G-BHLS)
	G-LEAP	BN-2T Islander	Army Parachute Association (G-BLND)/ Netheravon
	G-LEAR	Learjet 35A	Northern Executive Aviation Ltd/ Manchester
	G-LEAU	Cameron N-31 balloon	P. L. Mossman
	G-LECA	AS.355F-1 Twin Squirrel	S. W. Electricity Board (G-BNBK)/Bristol
	G-LEDN	Short SD3-30 Variant 100	Streamline Aviation (SW) Ltd (G-BIOF)/ Exeter
	G-LEED	Denney Aerocraft Kitfox Mk 2	G. T. Leedham
	G-LEES	Glaser-Dirks DG.400	T. B. Sargeant & C. A. Marren
	G-LEEZ	Bell 206L-1 LongRanger 2	RJS Aviation Ltd (G-BPCT)/Halfpenny Green
	G-LEGO	Cameron O-77 balloon	C. H. Pearce Construction PLC
	G-LEGS	Short SD3-60	Manx Airlines Ltd (G-BLEF)/Ronaldsway
	G-LEIC	Cessna FA.152	Leicestershire Aero Club Ltd
	G-LEND	Cameron N-77 balloon	Southern Flight Co Ltd
	G-LENN	Cameron V-56 balloon	Anglia Balloon School Ltd
	G-LENS	Thunder Ax7-77Z balloon	Big Yellow Balloon Group
	G-LEON	PA-31-350 Navajo Chieftain	Ryland Aviation Ltd
	G-LEOS	Robin DR.400/120	P. G. Newens
	G-LEPF	Fairchild 24R-46A Argus III	J. M. Greenland
	G-LEPI	Colt 160A balloon	Thunder & Colt Ltd
	G-LEVI	Aeronca 7AC Champion	L. Perry & J. P. A. Pumphrey
	G-LEXI	Cameron N-77 balloon	Sedgemoor 500 Balloon Group
	G-LEZE	Rutan LongEz	K. G. M. Loyal & ptnrs
	G-LFIX	V.S.509 Spitfire T.IX (ML407)	C. S. Grace
	G-LFSA	PA-38-112 Tomahawk	Liverpool Flying School Ltd (G-BSFC)
	G-LFSI	PA-28 Cherokee 140	M. R. Keen (G-AYKV)/Liverpool
	G-LGIO	Colt 240A balloon	Thunder & Colt Ltd
	G-LIAN	Robinson R-22B	Cotwell Air Services
	G-LIBB	Cameron V-77 balloon	B. G. Glibbery
	G-LIBS	Hughes 369HS	G. Hinckley
	G-LICK	Cessna 172N	Dacebow Aviation (G-BNTR)
	G-LIDA	Hoffmann HK-36R Super Dimona	W. D. Inglis
	G-LIDE	PA-31-350 Navajo Chieftain	Woodgate Executive Air Charter Ltd
	G-LIFE	Thunder Ax6-56Z balloon	M. J. & J. Evans

Reg.	Type	Owner or Operator	Notes
G-LIGG	Cessna F.182Q	Hi-Travel Ltd (G-THAM)	
G-LILI	Cessna 425	Ortac Air Ltd (G-YOTT/G-NORC)	
G-LIMA	R. Commander 114	Tricolore Ltd/Biggin Hill	
G-LINC	Hughes 369HS	March Helicopters Ltd/Sywell	
G-LIOA	Lockheed 10A Electra ★ (NC5171N)	Science Museum/Wroughton	
G-LION	PA-18 Super Cub 135 (542457 R-167)	A. W. Kennedy	
G-LIOT	Cameron O-77 balloon	D. Eliot	
G-LIPE	Robinson R-22B	Sloane Helicopters Ltd & Westleigh Construction Ltd (G-BTXJ)	
G-LIPP	BN-2T Turbine Islander	Rhine Army Parachute Association (G-BKJG)	
G-LISA	Steen Skybolt	T. C. Humphreys	
G-LITE	R. Commander 112A	J. Males	
G-LITZ	Pitts S-1 Special	J. A. Hughes	
G-LIZA	Cessna 340A	M. D. Joy (G-BMDM)	
G-LIZI	PA-28 Cherokee 160	R. J. Walker & J. R. Lawson (G-ARRP)	
G-LIZY	Westland Lysander III (V9673) ★	G. A. Warner/Duxford	
G-LIZZ	PA-E23 Aztec 250E	Michael Orr Ltd (G-BBWM)/Guernsey	
G-LJET	Learjet 35A	Tiger Aviation Ltd/Gatwick	
G-LNYS	Cessna 177RG	G. R. E. & G. Evans (G-BDCM)	
G-LOAF	Schempp-Hirth Janus CM	G. W. Kirton & K. J. Sleigh-Ives	
G-LOAN	Cameron N-77 balloon	Newbury Building Soc	
G-LOCH	Piper J-3C-90 Cub	J. M. Greenland	
G-LOFA	L.188CF Electra	Air Atlantique Ltd/Coventry	
G-LOFB	L.188CF Electra	Air Atlantique Ltd/Coventry	
G-LOGA	BAe ATP	Loganair Ltd/Glasgow	
G-LOGB	BAe ATP	Loganair Ltd/Glasgow	
G-LOGC	BAe ATP	Loganair Ltd (G-OLCC)/Glasgow	
G-LOGD	BAe ATP	Loganair Ltd (G-OLCD)/Glasgow	
G-LOGE	BAe ATP	Loganair Ltd (G-BMYL)/Glasgow	
G-LOGF	BAe ATP	Loganair Ltd/Glasgow	
G-LOGG	BAe ATP	Loganair Ltd/Glasgow	
G-LOGH	BAe ATP	Loganair Ltd/Glasgow	
G-LOGJ	BAe Jetstream 4102	Loganair Ltd/Glasgow	
G-LOGK	BAe Jetstream 4102	Loganair Ltd/Glasgow	
G-LOGL	BAe Jetstream 4102	Loganair Ltd/Glasgow	
G-LOGP	BAe Jetstream 3102	Loganair Ltd (G-BPZJ)/Glasgow	
G-LOGR	BAe Jetstream 3102	Loganair Ltd (G-BRGR)/Glasgow	
G-LOGS	Robinson R-22B	M. Chantler & ptnrs	
G-LOGU	BAe Jetstream 3102	Loganair Ltd (G-BRGL)/Glasgow	
G-LOGV	BAe Jetstream 3102	Loganair Ltd (G-BSZK)/Glasgow	
G-LOLL	Cameron V-77 balloon	Gone With The Wind Ltd	
G-LONG	Bell 206L LongRanger	Walsh Aviation	
G-LOOP	Pitts S-1C Special	B. G. Salter	
G-LOOT	EMB-110P1 Bandeirante	Tech Air (Cambridge) Ltd (G-BNOC)	
G-LORD	PA-34-200T Seneca II	Aerohire Ltd/Halfpenny Green	
G-LORI	H.S.125 Srs 403B	Re-Enforce Trading Co Ltd (G-AYOJ)	
G-LORT	Light Aero Avid Speedwing 4	G. E. Laucht	
G-LORY	Thunder Ax4-31Z balloon	A. J. Moore	
G-LOSM	Gloster Meteor NF.11 (WM167)	Hunter Wing Ltd/Bournemouth	
G-LOSS	Cameron N-77 balloon	D. K. Fish	
G-LOTI	Bleriot XI (replica) ★	Brooklands Museum Trust Ltd	
G-LOUI	Extra EA.300	L. C. A. Knapp (G-OHER)	
G-LOVX	Cessna 441 Conquest	Hustlepon Ltd/(G-BLCJ)	
G-LOWA	Colt 77A balloon	K. D. Pierce	
G-LOWE	Monnet Sonerai II	J. L. Kinch	
G-LOYA	Cessna FR.172J	T. R. Scorer (G-BLVT)	
G-LOYD	SA.341G Gazelle 1	Appollo Manufacturing (Derby) Ltd (G-SFTC)	
G-LRII	Bell 206L LongRanger	Carroll Aircraft Operational Services Ltd	
G-LSFI	AA-5A Cheetah	D. P. Williams (G-BGSK)	
G-LSHI	Colt 77A balloon	Lambert Smith Hampton Ltd	
G-LSLH	Schweizer 269C	Homewood Park (Helicopters) Ltd	
G-LSMI	Cessna F.152	M. Entwistle	
G-LTEC	H.S.125 Srs 700B	La Teq Aviation Ltd (G-BHSU)	
G-LTEK	Bell 206B JetRanger 2	La Teq Aviation Ltd (G-BMIB)	
G-LTNG	EE Lightning T.5 (XS451)	Lightning Flying Club	
G-LUAR	SOCATA TB.10 Tobago	CB Air Ltd	
G-LUBE	Cameron N-77 balloon	A. C. K. Rawson	
G-LUCA	Thunder Ax7-77Z balloon	R. De-Leyser	
G-LUCE	Cameron A-210 balloon	Aerial Promotions Ltd	
G-LUCK	Cessna F.150M	S. J. Tolhurst	

Notes	Reg.	Type	Owner or Operator
	G-LUED	Aero Designs Pulsar	R. & H. D. Blamires
	G-LUFT	Pützer Elster C	Bath Stone Co Ltd (G-BOPY)
	G-LUGG	Colt 21A balloon	Zebedee Balloon Service
	G-LUKE	Rutan LongEz	S. G. Busby
	G-LULU	Grob G.109	A. P. Bowden
	G-LUNA	PA-32RT-300T Turbo Lance II	E. Cliffe/Norwich
	G-LUSC	Luscombe 8E Silvaire	M. Fowler
	G-LUSI	Luscombe 8E Silvaire	R. J. Walker & J. Wrayton/O. Sarum
	G-LUST	Luscombe 8E Silvaire	M. Griffiths
	G-LUXE	BAe 146-300	British Aerospace PLC (G-SSSH)/Hatfield
	G-LYND	PA-25 Pawnee 235	Lleweni Parc Ltd (G-BSFZ/G-ASFZ)
	G-LYNX	Westland WG.13 Lynx	Westland Helicopters Ltd/Yeovil
	G-LYTE	Thunder Ax7-77 balloon	G. M. Bulmer
	G-MAAC	Advanced Airship Corporation ANR-1	Advanced Airship Corporation Ltd
	G-MABI	Cessna F.150L	Shobdon Aircraft Maintenance (G-BGOJ)
	G-MACH	SIAI-Marchetti SF.260	Cheyne Motors Ltd/Popham
	G-MACK	PA-28R Cherokee Arrow 200-II	Haimoss Ltd
	G-MADD	Robinson R-22B	Great Excitement Ltd (G-MEAT)
	G-MAFE	Dornier Do.228-202K	FR Aviation Ltd (G-OALF/G-MLDO)/ Bournemouth
	G-MAFF	BN-2T Islander	FR Aviation Ltd (G-BJEO)/Bournemouth
	G-MAFI	Dornier Do.228-200	FR Aviation Ltd/Bournemouth
	G-MAGG	Pitts S-1SE Special	C. A. Boardman
	G-MAGY	AS.350B Ecureuil	Quantel Ltd (G-BIYC)
	G-MAIR	PA-34-200T Seneca II	Barnes Olson Aeroleasing Ltd
	G-MAJS	Airbus A.300-605R	Monarch Airlines Ltd/Luton
	G-MALA	PA-28-181 Archer II	Firfax Systems Ltd (G-BIIU)
	G-MALC	AA-5 Traveler	B. P. Hogan (G-BCPM)
	G-MALK	Cessna F.172N	J. Easson/Edinburgh
	G-MALL	PA-32R-301 Saratoga SP	Mala Services Ltd (G-ITDA)
	G-MALS	Mooney M.20K-231	G-MALS Group/White Waltham
	G-MALT	Colt Flying Hop SS balloon	P. J. Stapley
	G-MAMO	Cameron V-77 balloon	The Marble Mosaic Co Ltd
	G-MAND	PA-28-161 Warrior II	M & D Aviation (G-BRKT)
	G-MANI	Cameron V-90 balloon	M. P. G. Papworth
	G-MANN	SA.341G Gazelle 1	First City Air PLC (G-BKLW)
	G-MANX	FRED Srs 2	S. Styles
	G-MAPR	Beech A36 Bonanza	Openair Ltd
	G-MARC	AS.350B Ecureuil	Gabriel Enterprises Ltd (G-BKHU)
	G-MARE	Schweizer 269C	The Earl of Caledon
	G-MARR	Cessna 421C	Levenmere Ltd (G-JTIE/G-RBBE)
	G-MASA	Air & Space 18A gyroplane	M. A. Schumann (G-MELI)
	G-MASC	Jodel D.150A	K. F. & R. Richardson
	G-MASH	Westland-Bell 47G-4A	Defence Products Ltd (G-AXKU)
	G-MATE	Moravan Zlin Z.50LS	V. S. E. Norman
	G-MATI	Stolp SA.300 Starduster Too	M. R. Clark & J. McM. Rosser/Newcastle
	G-MATP	BAe ATP/Jetstream 61	British Aerospace PLC/Prestwick
	G-MATS	Colt GA-42 airship	Lindstrand Balloons Ltd
	G-MATT	Robin R.2160	Sierra Flying Group (G-BKRC)/Newcastle
	G-MATZ	PA-28 Cherokee 140	Midland Air Training School (G-BASI)
	G-MAUD	BAe ATP	Manx Airlines Ltd (G-BMYM)/Ronaldsway
	G-MAUK	Colt 77A balloon	B. Meeson
	G-MAVI	Robinson R-22B	Yorkshire Helicopter Centre Ltd/Doncaster
	G-MAWL	Maule M4-210C Rocket	D. Group
	G-MAXI	PA-34-200T Seneca II	G. C. Rogers
	G-MAXW	Short SD3-60 Variant 100	Lynrise Aircraft Financing Ltd (G-BLPY)
	G-MAYO	PA-28-161 Warrior II	Jermyk Engineering/Fairoaks
	G-MCAR	PA-32 Cherokee Six 300D	Miller Aerial Spraying Ltd (G-LADA/ G-AYWK)/Wickenby
	G-MCKE	Boeing 757-28A	Monarch Airlines Ltd/Luton
	G-MCMS	Aero Designs Pulsar	M. C. Manning
	G-MCOX	Fuji FA.200-180AO	W. Surrey Engineering (Shepperton) Ltd
	G-MCPI	Bell 206B JetRanger 3	D. A. C. Pipe (G-ONTB)
	G-MDAC	PA-28-181 Archer II	B. R. McKay/Bournemouth
	G-MDKD	Robinson R-22B	D. K. Duckworth
	G-MDTV	Cameron N-105 balloon	Ideas Factory
	G-MEAH	PA-28R Cherokee Arrow 200-II	E. J. Meah (G-BSNM)
	G-MEAN	Agusta A.109A	Castle Air Charters Ltd (G-BRYL/G-ROPE/ G-OAMH)
	G-MEBC	Cessna 310-1	P. H. Johnson (G-ROGA/G-ASVV)
	G-MEGA	PA-28R-201T Turbo Arrow III	Travelworth Ltd

Reg.	Type	Owner or Operator	Notes
G-MELD	AA-5A Cheetah	Fletcher Aviation Ltd (G-BHCB)/Blackbushe	
G-MELT	Cessna F.172H	Vectair Aviation Ltd (G-AWTI)	
G-MELV	SOCATA Rallye 235E	Wallis & Sons Ltd (G-BIND)	
G-MEME	PA-28R-201 Arrow III	Henry J. Clare Ltd	
G-MEOW	CFM Streak Shadow	S. D. Hicks	
G-MERC	Colt 56A balloon	A. F. & C. D. Selby	
G-MERG	Mooney M.20J	Danyderwen Consultants Co Ltd	
G-MERI	PA-28-181 Archer II	Scotia Safari Ltd/Glasgow	
G-MERL	PA-28RT-201 Arrow IV	M. Giles	
G-MERV	PA-28-161 Warrior II	M. N. Choules	
G-META	Bell 222	The Metropolitan Police/Lippitts Hill	
G-METB	Bell 222	The Metropolitan Police/Lippitts Hill	
G-METC	Bell 222	The Metropolitan Police (G-JAMC)/ Lippitts Hill	
G-METD	AS.355N Twin Squirrel	The Metropolitan Police (G-BUJF)/ Lippitts Hill	
G-METE	Gloster Meteor F.8	Air Support Aviation Systems Ltd	
G-METO	AS.355N Twin Squirrel	McAlpine Helicopters Ltd (G-BUJF)/ Kidlington	
G-METR	Cessna 414A	Hunting Aircraft Ltd/Biggin Hill	
G-MEUP	Cameron A-120 balloon	N. J. Tovey	
G-MFHL	Robinson R-22B	MFH Ltd	
G-MFLI	Cameron V-90 balloon	J. M. Percival	
G-MFMF	Bell 206B JetRanger 3	S.W. Electricity Board (G-BJNJ)/Bristol	
G-MFMM	Scheibe SF.25C Falke	S. Lancs Falke Syndicate	
G-MHBD	Cameron O-105 balloon	K. Hull	
G-MHCA	Enstrom F-28C-UK	Trimcares Ltd (G-SHWW/G-SMUJ/G-BHTF)	
G-MHIH	H.S. 125 Srs 700B	Queens Moat Houses PLC (G-BKAA)	
G-MICH	Robinson R-22B	A. P. Codling (G-BNKY)	
G-MICK	Cessna F.172N	G-MICK Flying Group	
G-MICY	Everett Srs 1 gyroplane	D. M. Hughes	
G-MIDG	Midget Mustang	C. E. Bellhouse	
G-MIFF	Robin DR.400/180	G. E. Bickerton	
G-MIKE	Brookland Hornet	M. H. J. Goldring	
G-MIKY	Cameron 90 Mickey SS balloon	The Walt Disney Co Ltd	
G-MILE	Cameron N-77 balloon	Miles Air Ltd	
G-MIMA	BAe 146-200	Manx Airlines Ltd (G-CNMF)	
G-MIND	Cessna 404	Atlantic Air Transport Ltd (G-SKKC/G-OHUB)	
G-MINI	Currie Wot	D. Collinson	
G-MINS	Nicollier HN.700 Menestrel II	B. J. Little	
G-MINT	Pitts S-1S Special	T. G. Sanderson/Tollerton	
G-MINX	Bell 47G-4A	R. F. Warner (G-FOOR)	
G-MISS	Taylor JT.2 Titch	A. Brennan	
G-MIST	Cessna T.210K	J. Summers (G-AYGM)	
G-MITS	Cameron N-77 balloon	Colt Car Co Ltd	
G-MITZ	Cameron N-77 balloon	Colt Car Co Ltd	
G-MKAK	Colt 77A balloon	Airship & Balloon Co Ltd	
G-MKIX	V.S.361 Spitfire F.IX (NH238)	D. W. Arnold	
G-MKVB	V.S.349 Spitfire LF.VB (BM597)	Historic Aircraft Collection Ltd	
G-MKVI	D.H. Vampire FB.6 (VZ304)	T. C. Topen (G-DHYY)/Cranfield	
G-MKXI	V.S.365 Spitfire PR.XI (PL965)	C. P. B. Horsley	
G-MLAS	Cessna 182E	*Parachute jump trainer*/St Merryn	
G-MLFF	PA-23 Aztec 250E	Brands Hatch Circuit Ltd (G-WEBB/ G-BJBU)	
G-MLGL	Colt 21A balloon	Colt Balloons Ltd	
G-MLWI	Thunder Ax7-77 balloon	M. L. & L. P. Willoughby	
G-MOAC	Beech F33A Bonanza	Chalkfarm Productions Ltd	
G-MOAK	Schempp-Hirth Nimbus 3DM	P. W. Lever	
G-MOAT	Beech 200 Super King Air	Thurston Aviation (Stansted) Ltd	
G-MOBI	AS.355F-1 Twin Squirrel	M. J. O'Brien (G-MUFF/G-CORR)	
G-MOET	Partenavia P.68B	R. Pritchard & Phlight Avia Ltd (G-HPVC)	
G-MOFF	Cameron O-77 balloon	D. M. Moffat	
G-MOGG	Cessna F.172N	I. Grimshaw (G-BHDY)	
G-MOGI	AA-5A Cheetah	TL Aviation Ltd (G-BFMU)	
G-MOGY	Robinson R-22B	Hireheli Ltd	
G-MOHR	Cameron 105 Sarotti balloon	Cameron Balloons Ltd	
G-MOLE	Taylor JT.2 Titch	S. R. Mowle	
G-MOLL	PA-32-301T Turbo Saratoga	K. Morrissey	
G-MOLY	PA-23 Apache 160	R. R. & M. T. Thorogood (G-APFV)/St Just	
G-MONB	Boeing 757-2T7ER	Monarch Airlines Ltd/Luton	
G-MONC	Boeing 757-2T7	Monarch Airlines Ltd/Luton	
G-MOND	Boeing 757-2T7	Monarch Airlines Ltd/Luton	

Notes	Reg.	Type	Owner or Operator
	G-MONE	Boeing 757-2T7ER	Monarch Airlines Ltd/Luton
	G-MONF	Boeing 737-3Y0	Monarch Airlines Ltd/EuroBerlin
	G-MONG	Boeing 737-3Y0	Monarch Airlines Ltd/EuroBerlin
	G-MONH	Boeing 737-3Y0	Monarch Airlines Ltd/EuroBerlin
	G-MONI	Monnet Moni	B. S. Carpenter/Booker
	G-MONJ	Boeing 757-2T7ER	Monarch Airlines Ltd/Luton
	G-MONK	Boeing 757-2T7ER	Monarch Airlines Ltd/Luton
	G-MONP	Boeing 737-33A	Monarch Airlines Ltd/EuroBerlin
	G-MONR	Airbus A.300-605R	Monarch Airlines Ltd/Luton
	G-MONS	Airbus A.300-605R	Monarch Airlines Ltd/Luton
	G-MONV	Boeing 737-33A	Monarch Airlines Ltd/Luton
	G-MONW	Airbus A.320-212	Monarch Airlines Ltd/Luton
	G-MONX	Airbus A.320-212	Monarch Airlines Ltd/Luton
	G-MONY	Airbus A.320-212	Monarch Airlines Ltd/Canada 3000 (C-GVNY)
	G-MONZ	Airbus A.320.212	Monarch Airlines Ltd/Luton
	G-MOON	Mooney M.20K	M. A. Eccles
	G-MOOR	SOCATA TB.10 Tobago	G. A. Moore (G-MILK)
	G-MOOS	P.56 Provost T.1 (XF690)	T. J. Hanna (G-BGKA)
	G-MOTH	D.H.82A Tiger Moth (K2567)	M. C. Russell/Duxford
	G-MOTO	PA-24 Comanche 160	C. C. Letchford & A. J. Redknapp (G-EDHE/G-ASFH)
	G-MOTT	Light Aero Avid Speedwing	J. B. Ott
	G-MOUL	Maule M6-235	B. C. Abela
	G-MOUR	H.S. Gnat T.1 (XR991)	D. J. Gilmour
	G-MOUS	Cameron 90 Mickey SS balloon	The Walt Disney Co Ltd
	G-MOVE	PA-60-601P Aerostar	Peeters Karel NV
	G-MOVI	PA-32R-301 Saratoga SP	Rentair (G-MARI)
	G-MOZZ	Avions Mudry CAP.10B	M. B. Smith/Booker
	G-MPBH	Cessna FA.152	Metropolitan Police Flying Club (G-FLIC/G-BILV)
	G-MPCD	Airbus A.320-212	Monarch Airlines Ltd/Luton
	G-MPCU	Cessna 402B	Atlantic Air Transport Ltd/Coventry
	G-MPWH	Rotorway Executive	Neric Ltd
	G-MPWI	Robin HR.100/210	Propwash Investments Ltd/Cardiff
	G-MPWT	PA-34-220T Seneca III	Neric Ltd
	G-MRCI	Sequoia F.8L Falco	M. R. Clark
	G-MRKT	Lindstrand LBL-90A balloon	Marketplace Public Relations (London) Ltd
	G-MRPP	PA-34-220T Seneca III	P. E. Pearce
	G-MRSL	Robin DR.400/180	I. A. S. Laidlaw (G-BUAP)
	G-MRSN	Robinson R-22B	Sloane Helicopters Ltd/Sywell
	G-MRST	PA-28RT-201 Arrow IV	Winchfield Enterprises Ltd
	G-MRTC	Cessna 550 Citation II	Terry Coleman (UK) Ltd (G-SSOZ)
	G-MRTY	Cameron N-77 balloon	R. A. & P. G. Vale
	G-MSAL	MS.733 Alcyon	D. R. C. Bell/Booker
	G-MSDJ	AS.350B-1 Ecureuil	Denis Ferranti Hoverknights Ltd (G-BPOH)
	G-MSFC	PA-38-112 Tomahawk	Sherwood Flying Club Ltd/Tollerton
	G-MSFY	H.S.125 Srs 700B	Mohamed Said Fakhry/Heathrow
	G-MTLE	Cessna 501 Citation	Talan Ltd (G-GENE)
	G-MUIL	Cessna 172M	Aqualink Ltd
	G-MUIR	Cameron V-65 balloon	L. C. M. Muir
	G-MULL	Douglas DC-10-30	British Airways *New Forest*/Gatwick
	G-MUMS	PA-28-161 Warrior II	A. J. Wood
	G-MUNI	Mooney M.20J	Sequoia Aviation Ltd
	G-MUSO	Rutan LongEz	M. Moran
	G-MUST	CA-18 Mustang 22	Fairoaks Aviation Services Ltd
	G-MUTE	Colt 31A balloon	Redmalt Ltd
	G-MXVI	V.S.361 Spitfire LF.XVIe (TE184)	Myrick Aviation Services Ltd
	G-NAAT	H.S. Gnat T.1 (XM697)	Hunter Wing Ltd/Bournemouth
	G-NABS	Robinson R-22B	Arian Helicopters Ltd
	G-NACA	Norman NAC.2 Freelance 180	Aeronortec Ltd
	G-NACI	Norman NAC.1 Srs 100	I. J. Blackwood
	G-NACL	Norman NAC.6 Fieldmaster	EPA Aircraft Co Ltd (G-BNEG)
	G-NACM	Norman NAC.6 Fieldmaster	EPA Aircraft Co Ltd
	G-NACN	Norman NAC.6 Fieldmaster	EPA Aircraft Co Ltd
	G-NACO	Norman NAC.6 Fieldmaster	EPA Aircraft Co Ltd
	G-NACP	Norman NAC.6 Fieldmaster	EPA Aircraft Co Ltd
	G-NAIL	Cessna 340A	Parelarch Ltd (G-DEXI)
	G-NASA	Lockheed T-33A-5-LO (91007)	A. S. Topen (G-TJET)/Cranfield
	G-NASH	AA-5A Cheetah	F. P. Lund
	G-NATT	R. Commander 114A	Northgleam Ltd
	G-NATX	Cameron O-65 balloon	A. Faulkner

Reg.	Type	Owner or Operator	Notes
G-NATY	H. S. Gnat T.1 (XR537)	F. C. Hackett-Jones	
G-NAVO	PA-31-325 Navajo C/R	Shoprite Aviation Ltd	
G-NAZO	PA-31-310 Navajo B	Pathway Holdings Ltd (G-AZIM)	
G-NBDD	Robin DR.400/180	J. N. Binks	
G-NBSI	Cameron N-77 balloon	Nottingham Hot-Air Balloon Club	
G-NCUB	Piper J-3C-65 Cub	N. Thomson (G-BGXV)/Norwich	
G-NDGC	Grob G.109	C. H. Appleyard	
G-NDNI	NDN-1 Firecracker	Norman Marsh Aircraft Ltd	
G-NDOL	Shaw Europa	G. K. Brunwin	
G-NDRW	Colt AS-80 Mk II airship	Huntair Ltd	
G-NEAL	PA-32 Cherokee Six 260	VSD Group (G-BFPY)	
G-NEEL	Rotorway Executive 90	P. N. Haigh	
G-NEGS	Thunder Ax7-77 balloon	R. Holden	
G-NEIL	Thunder Ax3 balloon	Islington Motors (Trowbridge) Ltd	
G-NEPB	Cameron N-77 balloon	The Post Office	
G-NERI	PA-28-181 Archer II	Moulin Ltd (G-BMKO)	
G-NEVS	Aero Designs Pulsar XP	N. Warrener	
G-NEWR	PA-31-350 Navajo Chieftain	Eastern Air Executive Ltd/Sturgate	
G-NEWS	Bell 206B JetRanger 3	Peter Press Ltd	
G-NEWT	Beech 35 Bonanza	D. W. Mickleburgh (G-APVW)	
G-NGBI	AA-5B Tiger	G-NGBI Group (G-JAKK/G-BHWI)/ Southend	
G-NGRM	Spezio DAL.1	C. D. O'Malley	
G-NHRH	PA-28 Cherokee 140	H. Dodd	
G-NHVH	Maule M5-235C Lunar Rocket	Commercial Go-Karts Ltd/Exeter	
G-NICH	Robinson R-22B	Panair Ltd	
G-NICK	PA-18 Super Cub 95	J. G. O'Donnell & I. Woolacott	
G-NICO	Robinson R-22B	H. J. Pessall	
G-NIGE	Luscombe 8E Silvaire	Pullmerit Ltd (G-BSHG)	
G-NIGS	Thunder Ax7-65 balloon	A. N. F. Pertwee	
G-NIKE	PA-28-181 Archer II	Key Properties Ltd/White Waltham	
G-NIKI	Robinson R-22B	N. M. Leatherhead	
G-NINA	PA-28-161 Warrior II	Bailey Aviation Ltd (G-BEUC)	
G-NINE	Murphy Renegade 912	R. F. Bond	
G-NIOS	PA-32R-301 Saratoga SP	Metafin Holdings Ltd	
G-NISR	R. Commander 690A	Z. I. Bilbeisi	
G-NITA	PA-28 Cherokee 180	Dove Naish & Ptnrs (G-AVVG)	
G-NIUK	Douglas DC-10-30	British Airways *Cairn Edward Forest*/ Gatwick	
G-NJAG	Cessna 207	G. H. Nolan Ltd	
G-NJML	PA-34-220T Seneca III	Oxford Management Ltd	
G-NJSH	Robinson R-22B	T. F. Hawes	
G-NLEE	Cessna 182Q	J. S. Lee (G-TLTD)	
G-NNAC	PA-18 Super Cub 135	P. A. Wilde	
G-NOBI	Spezio Sport HES-1	M. R. Clark	
G-NODE	AA-5B Tiger	Curd & Green Ltd/Elstree	
G-NODY	American General AG-5B Tiger	Curd & Green Ltd	
G-NOIR	Bell 222	Arlington Securities Ltd (G-OJLC/G-OSEB/ G-BNDA)	
G-NONI	AA-5 Traveler	E. B. Landsler (G-BBDA)	
G-NORD	SNCAN NC.854	W. J. McCollum	
G-NOTA	McD Douglas MD-520N Notar	Prodrive Ltd	
G-NOTR	McD MD-520N NOTAR	Air Hanson	
G-NOTT	Nott ULD-2 balloon	J. R. P. Nott	
G-NOVO	Colt AS-56 airship	Thunder & Colt Ltd	
G-NPNP	Cameron N-105 balloon	Air 2 Air Ltd (G-BURX)	
G-NPWR	Cameron RX-100 balloon	Nuclear Electric PLC	
G-NRDC	NDN-6 Fieldmaster	EPA Aircraft Co Ltd	
G-NROY	PA-32RT-300 Lance II	Roys Motor Co (G-LYNN/G-BGNY)	
G-NSGI	Cessna 421C	Northern Scaffold Group PLC	
G-NSTG	Cessna F.150F	N. S. T. Griffin (G-ATNI)/Blackpool	
G-NTBI	Bell 206B JetRanger 3	E. Midlands Helicopters Ltd	
G-NTEE	Robinson R-44	Springfield Helicopters Ltd	
G-NTOO	SA.365N-2 Dauphin 2	Bond Helicopters Ltd	
G-NTWO	SA.365N-2 Dauphin 2	Bond Helicopters Ltd	
G-NUIG	Beech C90-1 King Air	Universal Salvage (Holdings) Ltd (G-BKIP)	
G-NUTZ	AS.355F-1 Twin Squirrel	Cotfast Ltd (G-BLRI)	
G-NWNW	Cameron V-90 balloon	Royal Mail	
G-NWPA	AS.355F-1 Twin Squirrel	McAlpine Helicopters Ltd (G-NAAS/ G-BPRG)	
G-NWPR	Cameron N-77 balloon	Post Office N.W. Postal Board	
G-NYTE	Cessna F.337G	Photoair (G-BATH)	

169

Notes	Reg.	Type	Owner or Operator
	G-NZGL	Cameron O-105 balloon	P. G. & P. M. Vale
	G-NZSS	Boeing Stearman N2S-5 (343251)	Ace Aviation Ltd
	G-OAAA	PA-28-161 Warrior II	Anglo American Airmotive Ltd/ Bournemouth
	G-OAAC	Airtour AH-77B balloon	Army Air Corps
	G-OAAL	PA-38-112 Tomahawk	Cumbernauld Aviation Ltd
	G-OAAS	Short SD3-60 Variant 100	Aurigny Air Services Ltd (G-BLIL)/Guernsey
	G-OABC	Colt 69A balloon	P. A. C. Stuart-Kregor
	G-OABG	Hughes 369E	A. B. Gee of Ripley Ltd
	G-OACE	Valentin Taifun 17E	J. E. Dallison
	G-OADY	Beech 76 Duchess	Citation Leasing Ltd
	G-OAFC	Airtour 56AH balloon	P. J. Donnellan & L. A. Watts
	G-OAFT	Cessna 152	L. E. Steynor (G-BNKM)
	G-OAFY	SA.341G Gazelle 1	First City Air Ltd (G-SFTH/G-BLAP)
	G-OAHC	Beech F33C Bonanza	Clacton Aero Club (1988) Ltd (G-BTTF)
	G-OAHF	Boeing 757-27B	Britannia Airways Ltd/Luton
	G-OAKC	PA-31-350 Navajo Chieftain	Air Kilroe Ltd (G-WSSC)/Manchester
	G-OAKI	BAe Jetstream 3102	Air Kilroe Ltd/Manchester
	G-OAKJ	BAe Jetstream 3200	Air Kilroe Ltd (G-BOTJ)/Manchester
	G-OAKK	BAe Jetstream 3100	Air Kilroe Ltd (G-BSIW)/Manchester
	G-OAKL	Beech 200 Super King Air	Air Kilroe Ltd (G-BJZG)/Manchester
	G-OALD	SOCATA TB.20 Trinidad	Thorne Aviation
	G-OALS	Colt Football SS balloon	Polecroft Ltd
	G-OAMG	Bell 206B JetRanger 3	Alan Mann Helicopters Ltd/Fairoaks
	G-OAMP	Cessna F.172RG	Ampy Automation Digilog Ltd (G-AYPF)
	G-OAMY	Cessna 152	Warwickshire Flying Training Centre Ltd/ Birmingham
	G-OANC	PA-28-161 Warrior II	Woodvale Aviation Co Ltd (G-BFAD)
	G-OANI	PA-28-161 Warrior II	J. A. Caliva
	G-OAPR	Brantly B.2B	Helicopter International Magazine/ Weston-s-Mare
	G-OAPW	Glaser-Dirks DG.400	S. W. Brown & D. T. S. Walsh
	G-OART	PA-23 Aztec 250D	Levenmere Ltd (G-AXKD)
	G-OARV	ARV Super 2	P. R. Snowden
	G-OASH	Robinson R-22B	J. C. Lane
	G-OATP	BAe ATP	Manx Airlines Ltd (G-BZWW)/*King Godred Crovan 1079-1095*/Ronaldsway
	G-OATS	PA-38-112 Tomahawk	Truman Aviation Ltd/Tollerton
	G-OATV	Cameron V-77 balloon	W. G. Andrews
	G-OAUS	Sikorsky S-76A	Darley Stud Management Co Ltd
	G-OAVX	Beech 200 Super King Air	ATS Vulcan Ltd (G-IBCA/G-BMCA)
	G-OBAA	Beech B200 Super King Air	BAA PLC
	G-OBAL	Mooney M.20J	Britannia Airways Ltd/Luton
	G-OBAN	Jodel D.140B	Total Logistic Concepts Ltd (G-ATSU)
	G-OBAT	Cessna F.152	M. & M. Entwistle (G-OENT)
	G-OBBC	Colt 90A balloon	R. A. & M. A. Riley
	G-OBEA	BAe Jetstream 3102-01	Maersk Air/Birmingham
	G-OBED	PA-34-200T Seneca II	V. J. Holden/Newcastle
	G-OBEL	Cessna 500 Citation	Gator Aviation Ltd (G-BOGA)
	G-OBEN	Cessna 152	Astra Associates (G-NALI/G-BHVM)
	G-OBEY	PA-23 Aztec 250C	Creaton Aircraft Services (G-BAAJ)
	G-OBHD	Short SD3-60 Variant 100	Jersey European Airways Ltd (G-BNDK)
	G-OBHX	Cessna F.172H	BHX Flying Group (G-AWMU)
	G-OBIL	Robinson R-22B	Pentech
	G-OBLC	Beech 76 Duchess	Tatenhill Aviation
	G-OBLK	Short SD3-60 Variant 100	Jersey European Airways Ltd (G-BNDI)
	G-OBLT	BAe 125 Srs 800B	P. Thomas
	G-OBMC	Boeing 737-33A	British Midland Airways Ltd/E. Midlands
	G-OBMD	Boeing 737-33A	British Midland Airways Ltd/E. Midlands
	G-OBMF	Boeing 737-4Y0	British Midland Airways Ltd/E. Midlands
	G-OBMG	Boeing 737-4Y0	British Midland Airways Ltd/E. Midlands
	G-OBMH	Boeing 737-33A	British Midland Airways Ltd/E. Midlands
	G-OBMJ	Boeing 737-33A	British Midland Airways Ltd/E. Midlands
	G-OBMK	Boeing 737-4S3	British Midland Airways Ltd/E. Midlands
	G-OBML	Boeing 737-3Q8	British Midland Airways Ltd (G-KKUH)/ E. Midlands
	G-OBMM	Boeing 737-4Y0	British Midland Airways Ltd/E. Midlands
	G-OBMN	Boeing 737-46B	British Midland Airways Ltd (G-BOPJ)/ E. Midlands
	G-OBMO	Boeing 737-4Q8	British Midland Airways Ltd/E. Midlands
	G-OBMP	Boeing 737-3Y0	British Midland Airways Ltd/E. Midlands
	G-OBMS	Cessna F.172N	D. Beverley & W. F. van Schoten

Reg.	Type	Owner or Operator	Notes
G-OBMW	AA-5 Traveler	Fretcourt Ltd (G-BDFV)	
G-OBMX	Boeing 737-59D	British Midland Airways Ltd/E. Midlands	
G-OBMY	Boeing 737-59D	British Midland Airways Ltd/E. Midlands	
G-OBMZ	Boeing 737-53A	British Midland Airways Ltd/E. Midlands	
G-OBOH	Short SD3-60	Jersey European Airways (G-BNDJ)	
G-OBRY	Cameron N-180 balloon	Bryant Group PLC	
G-OBSF	AA-5A Cheetah	Lowlog Ltd (G-ODSF/G-BEUW)	
G-OBSV	Partenavia P.68B Observer	Porton Holdings Ltd	
G-OBUD	Colt 69A balloon	Hot-Air Balloon Co Ltd	
G-OBUY	Colt 69A balloon	Airship & Balloon Co Ltd	
G-OBWA	BAC One-Eleven 518FG	British World Airlines Ltd (G-BDAT/ G-AYOR)/Stansted	
G-OBWB	BAC One-Eleven 518FG	British World Airlines Ltd (G-BDAS/ G-AXMH)/Stansted	
G-OBWC	BAC One-Eleven 520FN	British World Airlines Ltd (G-BEKA)/ Stansted	
G-OBWD	BAC One-Eleven 518FG	British World Airlines Ltd (G-BDAE/ G-AXMI) *City of Bucharest*/Stansted	
G-OBWE	BAC One-Eleven 531FS	British World Airlines Ltd (G-BJYM)/ Stansted	
G-OBWF	BAC One-Eleven 509EW	British World Airlines Ltd (G-AXYD)/ Stansted	
G-OBWG	BAC One-Eleven 509EW	British World Airlines Ltd (G-AWWX)/ Stansted	
G-OBWH	BAC One-Eleven 515FB	British World Airlines Ltd (G-BJYL/ G-AZPE)/Stansted	
G-OCAA	H.S. 125 Srs 700B	MAGEC Aviation Ltd (G-BHLF)/Luton	
G-OCAD	Sequoia F.8L Falco	Falco Flying Group	
G-OCAR	Colt 77A balloon	Ridgeway Balloon Group	
G-OCAT	Eiri PIK-20E	W. A. D. Thorp/Doncaster	
G-OCBA	H.S.125 Srs 3B	FLS Aerospace Ltd (G-MRFB/G-AZVS)	
G-OCBB	Bell 206B JetRanger 2	CG Group Ltd (G-BASE)	
G-OCBC	Cameron A-120 balloon	Corporate Balloon Co	
G-OCCA	PA-32R-301 Saratoga SP	CC Aviation Ltd (G-BRIX)/Elstree	
G-OCCC	BAe 125 Srs 800B	Raytheon Corporate Jets Inc	
G-OCCI	BAe 125 Srs 800B	Consolidated Contractors International (UK) Ltd	
G-OCDB	Cessna 550 Citation II	Paycourt Ltd (G-ELOT)	
G-OCDS	Aviamilano F.8L Falco II	P. J. Collins (G-VEGL)	
G-OCFR	Learjet 35A	Chauffair (CI) Ltd (G-VIPS/G-SOVN/ G-PJET)	
G-OCGJ	Robinson R-22B	Pyramid Aviation Ltd/Halfpenny Green	
G-OCJK	Schweizer 269C	Bradford Independent Helicopters	
G-OCJR	SA.341G Gazelle 1	Reeds Motor Co (G-BRGS)	
G-OCJS	Cameron V-90 balloon	C. J. Sandell	
G-OCND	Cameron O-77 balloon	D. P. H. Smith & Dalby	
G-OCNW	BAC One-Eleven 201AC	British Air Ferries (G-ASJH)/Stansted	
G-OCPC	Cessna FA.152	Westward Airways (Lands End) Ltd/St Just	
G-OCPI	Cessna 500 Citation	Cooling Power Industries Ltd (G-OXEC)	
G-OCPL	AA-5A Cheetah	BLS Aviation Ltd (G-RCPW/G-BERM)	
G-OCPS	Colt 120A balloon	CPS Fuels Ltd	
G-OCRI	Colomban MC.15 Cri-Cri	M. J. J. Dunning	
G-OCTA	BN-2A Mk III-2 Trislander	Aurigny Air Services Ltd (G-BCXW)	
G-OCTI	PA-32 Cherokee Six 260	J. K. Sharkey (G-BGZX)/Elstree	
G-OCTU	PA-28-161 Cadet	J. P. Alexander	
G-OCUB	Piper J-3C-90 Cub	C. A. Foss & P. A. Brook/Shoreham	
G-OCWC	AA-5A Cheetah	Garrick Aviation (G-WULL)	
G-OCWT	AS.350B-2 Ecureuil	Carter Wind Turbines (Aviation) Ltd	
G-ODAD	Colt 77A balloon	K. Meehan	
G-ODAM	AA-5A Cheetah	Stop & Go Ltd (G-FOUX)	
G-ODAY	Cameron N-56 balloon	C. O. Day (Estate Agents)	
G-ODDY	Lindstrand LBL-105A balloon	V. Hyland	
G-ODEL	Falconar F-11-3	G. F. Brummell	
G-ODEN	PA-28-161 Cadet	J. Appleton	
G-ODER	Cameron O-77 balloon	W. H. Morgan	
G-ODHL	Cameron N-77 balloon	DHL International (UK) Ltd	
G-ODIG	Bell 206B JetRanger 2	Caledon Coal Co Ltd (G-NEEP)	
G-ODIL	Bell 206B JetRanger	Yorkshire Helicopter Centre Ltd	
G-ODIN	Avion Mudry CAP.10B	S. J. Wood	
G-ODIR	PA-23 Aztec 250D	Metstar Ltd (G-AZGB)	
G-ODIS	Cameron Cabin SS balloon	Cameron Balloons Ltd	
G-ODIY	Colt 69A balloon	Flying Pictures (Balloons) Ltd	
G-ODJH	Mooney M.20C	D. J. Hockings (G-BMLH)/Biggin Hill	

Notes	Reg.	Type	Owner or Operator
	G-ODJP	Robinson R-22	R. E. Todd
	G-ODLY	Cessna 310J	R. J. Huband (G-TUBY/G-ASZZ)
	G-ODMC	AS.350B-1 Ecureuil	D. M. Coombs (G-PBVF)
	G-ODNP	Cessna 310R	Bostonair Ltd/Humberside
	G-OEAC	Mooney M.20J	Trifik Services Ltd
	G-OEBA	Robin DR.400/140B	EB Aviation (G-JMHB)
	G-OECH	AA-5A Cheetah	G. W. Plowman & Sons Ltd (G-BKBE)
	G-OEDB	PA-38-112 Tomahawk	Air Delta Bravo Ltd (G-BGGJ)/Elstree
	G-OEDP	Cameron N-77 balloon	M. J. Betts
	G-OEGG	Cameron 65 Egg SS balloon	Airship & Balloon Co Ltd
	G-OEMH	Westland-Bell 47G-4A	East Midlands Helicopters (G-AXKK)
	G-OEXC	Airbus A.320-212	Excalibur Airways Ltd/E. Midlands
	G-OEYE	Rans S.10 Sakota	P. Thompson
	G-OFBJ	Thunder Ax7-77 balloon	N. D. Hicks
	G-OFCM	Cessna F172L	F. C. M Aviation Ltd (G-AZUN)/Guernsey
	G-OFER	PA-18 Super Cub 150	M. S. W. Meagher
	G-OFHJ	Cessna 441	Tilling Associates Ltd (G-HSON)
	G-OFHL	AS.350B Ecureuil	Ford Helicopters Ltd (G-BLSP)
	G-OFIT	SOCATA TB.10 Tobago	G. S.M. Brain (G-BRIU)
	G-OFIZ	Cameron 80 Can SS balloon	Airship & Balloon Co Ltd
	G-OFJC	Eiri PIK-20E	M. J. Aldridge
	G-OFJS	Robinson R-22B	F. J. Saunders (G-BNXJ)
	G-OFLG	SOCATA TB.10 Tobago	Studley Pool Management Ltd (G-JMWT)
	G-OFLI	Colt 105A balloon	Airship & Balloon Co Ltd
	G-OFLT	EMB-110P1 Bandeirante	Flightline Ltd (G-MOBL/G-BGCS)/ Southend
	G-OFLY	Cessna 210L	A. P. Mothew/Stapleford
	G-OFOR	Thunder Ax3 balloon	A. Walker
	G-OFOX	Denney Aerocraft Kitfox	P. R. Skeels
	G-OFRB	Everett gyroplane	Roger Savage (Photography)
	G-OFRH	Cessna 421C	Aquila Aviation Ltd (G-NORX)
	G-OFRT	L.188C Electra	Channel Express (Air Services) Ltd/ Bournemouth
	G-OFRY	Cessna 152	Monument Trust Co Ltd (G-BPHS)
	G-OFTI	PA-28 Cherokee 140	E. Alexander (G-BRKU)
	G-OGAR	PZL SZD-45A Ogar	N. C. Grayson
	G-OGAS	Westland WG.30 Srs 100	*(stored)* (G-BKNW)/Penzance
	G-OGAT	Beech 200 Super King Air	Branderman Ltd
	G-OGCA	PA-28-161 Warrior II	Eurojet Aviation Ltd
	G-OGCI	Short SD3-60 Variant 100	Short Bros PLC (G-BNBD)/Belfast City
	G-OGEM	PA-28-181 Archer II	GEM Rewinds Ltd
	G-OGET	PA-39 Twin Comanche 160 C/R	P. G. Kitchingman (G-AYXY)
	G-OGGS	Thunder Ax8-84 balloon	G. Gamble & Sons (Quorn) Ltd
	G-OGIL	Short SD3-30 ★	N.E. Aircraft Museum (G-BITV)/Usworth
	G-OGJS	Puffer Cozy	G. J. Stamper
	G-OGOA	AS.350B Ecureuil	Lomas Helicopters Ltd (G-PLMD/G-NIAL)
	G-OGOB	Schweizer 269C	Lomas Helicopters (Training) Ltd (G-GLEE/ G-BRUW)
	G-OGOC	Robinson R-22B	M. Horn & Rainbow Wholesale Suppliers Ltd (G-HODG)
	G-OGOS	Everett gyroplane	R. Abercrombie
	G-OGTS	Air Command 532 Elite	GTS Engineering (Coventry) Ltd
	G-OHCA	SC.5 Belfast (XR363)	HeavyLift Cargo Airlines Ltd/Southend
	G-OHEA	H.S.125 Srs 3B/RA	B. L. Schroder (G-AVRG)
	G-OHHL	Robinson R-22B	Hillar Helicopters Ltd
	G-OHMS	AS.355F-1 Twin Squirrel	S.W. Electricity PLC
	G-OHOG	PA-28 Cherokee 140	C. R. Guggenheim (G-AVFY)
	G-OHOP	PA-31 Turbo Navajo	Rhumbline Aviation Ltd (G-BEYY)
	G-OHOT	V.813 Viscount	British World Airlines Ltd (G-BMAT/ G-AZLT)/Southend
	G-OIAN	M.S.880B Rallye Club	Ian Richard Transport Services Ltd
	G-OIBC	Bell 47G-4A	IBC Executive Travel Ltd (G-FORE)
	G-OIBO	R. Commander 114	South Coast Computers Ltd (G-BLVZ)
	G-OIBO	PA-28 Cherokee 180	D. P. Tinsley (G-AVAZ)
	G-OICE	Cessna 525 Citationjet	Iceland Frozen Foods PLC
	G-OICV	Robinson R-22B	ICV Ltd (G-BPWH)
	G-OIDW	Cessna F.150GF	I. D. Wakeling
	G-OIEA	PA-31P Pressurised Navajo	Skyrock Aviation Ltd/Cyprus
	G-OIFM	Cameron 90 Dude SS balloon	Air 2 Air Ltd
	G-OIGS	Enstrom F-28C	I. R. Gowrie-Smith (G-BGSN)
	G-OIII	BAe 146-300	British Aerospace PLC
	G-OILX	AS.355F-1 Twin Squirrel	Firstearl Ltd (G-RMGN/G-BMCY)
	G-OIMC	Cessna 152	E. Midlands Flying School Ltd

Reg.	Type	Owner or Operator	Notes
G-OING	AA-5A Cheetah ★	Abraxas Aviation Ltd (G-BFPD)/Denham	
G-OINK	Piper J-3C-65 Cub	A. R. Harding (G-BILD/G-KERK)	
G-OIOI	EH Industries EH.101	Westland Helicopters Ltd/Yeovil	
G-OISO	Cessna FRA.150L	Les Oiseaux	
G-OITN	AS.355F-1 Twin Squirrel	Independent Television News Ltd	
G-OJAC	Mooney M.20J	Hornet Engineering Ltd	
G-OJAE	Hughes 269C	Draycott Ltd	
G-OJAV	BN-2A Mk III-2 Trislander	Willow Air Ltd (G-BDOS)/Southend	
G-OJAY	EMB-110PI Bandeirante	—	
G-OJBM	Cameron N-90 balloon	JMB Communications Ltd	
G-OJCB	AB-206B JetRanger 2	Yorkshire Helicopter Centre Ltd	
G-OJCM	Rotorway Executive 90	J. C. Mead & N. Rogers	
G-OJCW	PA-32RT-300 Lance II	M. J. Metham/Blackbushe	
G-OJDC	Thunder Ax7-77 balloon	J. Crosby	
G-OJET	BAe 146-100	British Aerospace PLC (G-BRJS/G-OBAF/ G-SCHH)	
G-OJIM	PA-28R-201T Turbo Arrow III	Motomecca Spares Ltd	
G-OJJB	Mooney M.20K	Jeff Brown (Aviation Services)	
G-OJMR	Airbus A.300-605R	Monarch Airlines Ltd/Luton	
G-OJON	Taylor JT.2 Titch	J. H. Fell	
G-OJSY	Short SD3-60	Business Air Ltd (G-BKKT)/Aberdeen	
G-OJVH	Cessna F.150H	Yorkshire Light Aircraft Ltd (G-AWJZ)/ Leeds	
G-OJVI	Robinson R-22B	JV Investments Ltd (G-OJVJ)	
G-OJWS	PA-28-161 Warrior II	Metacomco PLC	
G-OKAG	PA-28R Cherokee Arrow 180	N. F. & B. R. Green/Stapleford	
G-OKAT	AS.350B Ecureuil	Tom Walkinshaw Racing Ltd (G-BGIM)	
G-OKAY	Pitts S-1E Special	J. S. Mortimore & R. J. Allan	
G-OKBT	Colt 25A Mk II balloon	British Telecommunications PLC	
G-OKCC	Cameron N-90 balloon	D. J. Head	
G-OKED	Cessna 150L	Midair Aviation Ltd	
G-OKEN	PA-28R-201T Turbo Arrow III	K. Hassall	
G-OKEY	Robinson R-22B	Key Properties Ltd	
G-OKIS	Tri Kis	B. W. Davies	
G-OKIT	Rotorway Executive	P. T. Waldron	
G-OKPW	Tri Kis	K. P. Wordsworth	
G-OKYA	Cameron V-77 balloon	Army Balloon Club	
G-OKYM	PA-28 Cherokee 140	D. Hotham (G-AVLS)	
G-OLAF	Beech C90 King Air	Westair Flying Services Ltd (G-BFVX)/ Blackpool	
G-OLAH	Short SD3-60 Variant 100	Gill Aviation Ltd (G-BPCO/G-RMSS/ G-BKKU)	
G-OLAU	Robinson R-22B	MPW Aviation Ltd	
G-OLDE	Cessna 421C	Richard Nash Cars Ltd (G-BBSV)	
G-OLDN	Bell 206L LongRanger	Gulfstream Air Services (UK) Ltd (G-TBCA/G-BFAL)	
G-OLDY	Luton LA-5 Major	M. P. & A. P. Sargent	
G-OLEE	Cessna F.152	Aerohire Ltd/Halfpenny Green	
G-OLFC	PA-38-112 Tomahawk	T. F. L. Hayes (G-BGZG)	
G-OLFT	R. Commander 114	B. C. Richens (G-WJMN)/Redhill	
G-OLIZ	Robinson R-22B	P & I Data Services Ltd	
G-OLLE	Cameron O-84 balloon	N. A. Robertson	
G-OLLI	Cameron O-31 SS balloon	N. A. Robertson	
G-OLLY	PA-31-350 Navajo Chieftain	Barnes Olsen Aeroleasing Ltd (G-BCES)	
G-OLMA	Partenavia P.68B	C. M. Evans (G-BGBT)	
G-OLRT	Robinson R-22B	J. W. Benbom	
G-OLSC	Cessna 182A	Factultra (G-ATNU)	
G-OLVR	FRED Srs 2	A. R. Oliver	
G-OMAC	Cessna FR.172E	R. Knox & R. Conway	
G-OMAF	Dornier Do.228-200	FR Aviation Ltd/Bournemouth	
G-OMAR	PA-34-220T Seneca III	Redhill Flying Club	
G-OMAT	PA-28 Cherokee 140	Midland Air Training School (G-JIMY/ G-AYUG)/Coventry	
G-OMAX	Brantly B.2B	P. D. Benmax (G-AVJN)	
G-OMDH	Hughes 369E	Stilgate Ltd/Booker	
G-OMEC	AB-206B JetRanger 3	Kallas Ltd (G-OBLD)	
G-OMED	AA-5B Tiger	Caslon Ltd (G-BERL)/Elstree	
G-OMGA	H.S.125 Srs 600B/2	MAGEC Aviation Ltd (G-BSHL/G-BBMD)/ Luton	
G-OMGB	H.S.125 Srs 600B	MAGEC Aviation Ltd (G-BKBM/G-BCCL)/ Luton	
G-OMGC	H.S.125 Srs 600B	MAGEC Aviation Ltd (G-BKCD/G-BDOA)	
G-OMGE	BAe 125 Srs 800B	GEC Marconi Ltd (G-BTMG)/Luton	

Notes	Reg.	Type	Owner or Operator
	G-OMHC	PA-28RT-201 Arrow IV	M. H. Cundley/Redhill
	G-OMIG	Aero-Vodochody MiG-15UTI (6247)	G. P. Hinkley/Shoreham
	G-OMJB	Bell 206B JetRanger	Martin Brundle (Overseas) Ltd
	G-OMJT	Rutan LongEz	M. J. Timmons
	G-OMKF	Aero Designs Pulsar	M. K. Faro
	G-OMMC	Mooney M.20J	A. D. Russell/Bourn
	G-OMMM	Colt 90A balloon	3M Health Care Ltd
	G-OMNI	PA-28R Cherokee Arrow 200D	R. J. Fray
	G-OMOG	AA-5A Cheetah	Popham Flight (G-BHWR)
	G-OMRB	Cameron V-77 balloon	M. R. Bayne
	G-OMRG	Hoffmann H-36 Dimona	M. R. Grimwood (G-BLHG)
	G-ONAF	Naval Aircraft Factory N3N-1	P. M. H. Threadway
	G-ONAV	PA-31-310 Turbo Navajo C	Panther Aviation Ltd (G-IGAR)
	G-ONCL	Colt 77A balloon	N. C. Lindsay
	G-ONEA	Beech 200 Super King Air	Northern Executive Aviation Ltd/ Manchester
	G-ONEX	Beech 200 Super King Air	Northern Executive Aviation Ltd (G-VRES)/Manchester
	G-ONHH	Forney F-1A Aircoupe	H. Dodd (G-ARHA)
	G-ONKA	Aeronca K	L. D. Chapman
	G-ONOR	Cessna 425	G. Dolan (G-BKSA)
	G-ONOW	Bell 206A JetRanger 2	Mega Yield Ltd (G-AYMX)
	G-ONPI	Thunder Ax10-160 balloon	Ballooning World Ltd
	G-ONZO	Cameron N-77 balloon	J. A. Kershaw
	G-OOAA	Airbus A.320-231	Air 2000 Ltd/Manchester
	G-OOAB	Airbus A.320-231	Air 2000 Ltd/Manchester
	G-OOAC	Airbus A.320-231	Air 2000 Ltd/Manchester
	G-OOAD	Airbus A.320-231	Air 2000 Ltd/Manchester
	G-OODE	SNCAN Stampe SV-4C (G)	The Biplane Co Ltd (G-AZNN)
	G-OODI	Pitts S-1D Special	I. R. B. Frank (G-BBBU)
	G-OODW	PA-28-181 Archer II	Goodwood Terrena Ltd
	G-OOFI	Cameron N-77 balloon	I. Fishwick
	G-OOGA	GA-7 Cougar	Denham School of Flying Ltd
	G-OOJB	Cessna 421C	Ferron Trading Ltd (G-BKSO)
	G-OOLE	Cessna 172M	P. S. Eccersley (G-BOSI)
	G-OOLI	Robinson R-22B	Wyatt Air Partnership (G-DMCD)
	G-OONE	Mooney M.20J	N. Skipworth/Booker
	G-OONI	Thunder Ax7-77 balloon	Fivedata Ltd
	G-OONS	AB-206B JetRanger 3	Central Sales Contracting Ltd
	G-OONY	PA-28-161 Warrior II	D. A. Field & P. B. Jenkins
	G-OOOA	Boeing 757-28AER	Air 2000/Canada 3000 (C-FOOA)
	G-OOOB	Boeing 757-28AER	Air 2000/Canada 3000 (C-FOOB)
	G-OOOC	Boeing 757-28AER	Air 2000/Canada 3000
	G-OOOD	Boeing 757-28AER	Air 2000/Canada 3000 (C-FXOD)
	G-OOOG	Boeing 757-23AER	Air 2000/Canada 3000 (C-FOOG)
	G-OOOH	Boeing 757-23AER	Air 2000 Ltd/Manchester
	G-OOOI	Boeing 757-23AER	Air 2000 Ltd/Manchester
	G-OOOJ	Boeing 757-23AER	Air 2000 Ltd/Manchester
	G-OOOM	Boeing 757-225ER	Air 2000 Ltd/Manchester
	G-OOOO	Mooney M.20J	Michael Jackson Motors Ltd
	G-OOOS	Boeing 757-236	Air 2000 Ltd (G-BRJD)/Manchester
	G-OOOT	Boeing 757-236ER	Air 2000 Ltd (G-BRJJ)/Manchester
	G-OOOU	Boeing 757-2Y0ER	Air 2000 Ltd/Manchester
	G-OOOV	Boeing 757-225	Air 2000 Ltd/Manchester
	G-OOOW	Boeing 757-225	Air 2000 Ltd/Manchester
	G-OOOX	Boeing 757-2Y0	Air 2000 Ltd/Manchester
	G-OOSE	Rutan Vari-Eze	J. A. Towers
	G-OOUT	Colt Flying Shuttlecock SS balloon	Shiplake Investments Ltd
	G-OOXP	Aero Designs Pulsar XP	T. D. Baker
	G-OPAC	Robinson R-22B	Crest Engineering Ltd
	G-OPAG	PA-34-200 Seneca II	A. H. Lavender (G-BNGB)
	G-OPAL	Robinson R-22B	Pebblestar Ltd
	G-OPAM	Cessna F.152	PJC Leasing Ltd (G-BFZS)/Stapleford
	G-OPAT	Beech 76 Duchess	Ray Holt (Land Drainage) Ltd/(G-BHAO)
	G-OPBH	Aero Designs Pulsar	P. B. Hutchinson
	G-OPDS	Denney Aerocraft Kitfox Mk 4	P. D. Sparling
	G-OPED	Partenavia P.68B	Pedley Woodwork Ltd/(G-BFKP)
	G-OPFC	BAe 125-1000	Raytheon Corporate Jets PLC
	G-OPFI	V.806 Viscount	British World Airlines Ltd (G-AOYP)/ Southend
	G-OPIB	EE Lightning F.6	Downderry Construction Group Ltd
	G-OPIK	Eiri PIK-20E	A. J. McWilliam

Reg.	Type	Owner or Operator	Notes
G-OPIT	CFM Streak Shadow Srs SA	L. W. Opit & W. M. Kilner	
G-OPIX	Cessna 180K	Steve Bicknell Productions Ltd	
G-OPJC	Cessna 152	PJC Leasing Ltd/Stapleford	
G-OPJD	PA-28RT-201T Turbo Arrow IV	M. P. Hughes	
G-OPJK	Shaw Europa	P. J. Kember	
G-OPKF	Cameron 90 Bowler SS balloon	Flying Pictures (Balloons) Ltd	
G-OPLC	D.H.104 Dove 8	W. G. T. Pritchard & I. Darcy-Bean (G-BLRB)	
G-OPMT	Lindstrand LBL-105A balloon	Virgin Airship & Balloon Co Ltd	
G-OPOL	H.S.125 Srs F3B/RA	Launchroy Ltd (G-BXPU/G-IBIS/G-AXPU)/Luton	
G-OPOP	Enstrom 280C-UK-2 Shark	Crewhall Ltd (G-OFED)	
G-OPPL	AA-5A Cheetah	London School of Flying Ltd (G-BGNN)/Elstree	
G-OPPP	EMB-110P1 Bandeirante	Streamline Aviation/E. Midlands	
G-OPPS	Mudry CAP.231	Bianchi Aviation Film Services Ltd/Booker	
G-OPRA	PA-31 Turbo Navajo	Ryland Aviation Ltd (G-VICK/G-AWED)	
G-OPSF	PA-38-112 Tomahawk	Neric Ltd (G-BGZI)/Pahshanger	
G-OPST	Cessna 182R	Lota Ltd/Shoreham	
G-OPUP	B.121 Pup 2	P. W. Hunter (G-AXEU)	
G-OPWK	AA-5A Cheetah	A. H. McVicar (G-OAEL)/Prestwick	
G-OPWS	Mooney M.20K	A. C. Clarke	
G-ORAF	CFM Streak Shadow	G. A. & S. M. Taylor	
G-ORAY	Cessna F.182Q II	S. E. Ward & Sons (Engineers) Ltd (G-BHDN)	
G-ORBY	Sukhoi Su-26MX	R. N. Goode/White Waltham	
G-ORCL	Cessna 421C	Oracle Corporation UK Ltd	
G-ORDN	PA-31R Cherokee Arrow 200-II	M. T. Coppen (G-BAJT)	
G-ORDO	PA-30 Twin Comanche B	A. C. & A. M. Gordon	
G-ORED	BN-2T Islander	The Red Devils (G-BJYW)/Farnborough	
G-OREG	BN-2A Mk III-1 Trislander	Industrial Marketing Group Ltd (G-OAVW/G-AZLJ)	
G-OREX	Short SD3-60 Variant 100	— (G-BMHY)	
G-OREY	Cameron O-90 balloon	P. McCallum	
G-ORFC	Jurca MJ.5 Sirocco	D. J. Phillips	
G-ORFE	Cameron 76 Golf SS balloon	Balloon-A-Drome Ltd	
G-ORFH	Aérospatiale ATR-42-300	Gill Air Ltd/Newcastle	
G-ORIX	ARV K1 Super 2	P. M. Harrison (G-BUXH)	
G-ORJB	Cessna 500 Citation	L'Equipe Air Ltd (G-OKSP)	
G-ORJS	Bell 206L-3 LongRanger	Carr Aviation	
G-ORJW	Laverda F.8L Falco Srs 4	W. R. M. Sutton	
G-ORMB	Robinson R-22B	R. M. Bailey	
G-OROB	Robinson R-22B	Corniche Helicopters (G-TBFC)	
G-OROD	PA-18 Super Cub 150	R. J. O. Walker	
G-ORON	Cameron 77A balloon	A. M. Rocliffe	
G-OROZ	AS.350B-2 Ecureuil	Flightpaths Ltd	
G-ORPR	Cameron O-77 balloon	Outright PR Ltd	
G-ORSP	Beech A36 Bonanza	Select Plant Hire Co Ltd	
G-ORTM	Glaser-Dirks DG.400	I. Godfrey	
G-ORVB	McCulloch J-2	R. V. Bowles (G-BLGI/G-BKKL)	
G-OSAB	Enstrom 280FX	Goadby Air Services Ltd	
G-OSAL	Cessna 421C	Cityshare Ltd	
G-OSAS	BAe 146-200	British Aerospace PLC	
G-OSCB	Colt 90A balloon	J. Willis	
G-OSCC	PA-32 Cherokee Six 300	Plant Aviation Ltd (G-BGFD)/Elstree	
G-OSDI	Beech 95-58 Baron	K. L. Hawes (G-BHFY)	
G-OSEA	BN-2B-26 Islander	W. T. Johnson & Sons (Huddersfield) Ltd (G-BKOL)	
G-OSEE	Robinson R-22B	J. P. Dennison	
G-OSFC	Cessna F.152	Stapleford Flying Club Ltd (G-BIVJ)	
G-OSFT	PA-31-310 Turbo Navajo C	SFT Aviation Ltd (G-MDAS/G-BCJZ)/Bournemouth	
G-OSHC	Hughes 269C	Neil Brown Engineering Ltd	
G-OSHD	Hughes 269B	The Hughes Helicopter Co Ltd	
G-OSIX	PA-32 Cherokee Six 260	Strata Surveys Ltd (G-AZMO)	
G-OSKY	Cessna 172M	D. D. Stone	
G-OSLO	Schwiezer 269C	Metham Aviation Ltd	
G-OSNB	Cessna 550 Citation II	Scottish & Newcastle Breweries PLC (G-JFRS)	
G-OSND	Cessna FRA.150M	Barmoor Aviation (G-BDOU)	
G-OSOO	Hughes 369E	Malcolm Wilson (Motorsport) Ltd	
G-OSPS	PA-18 Super Cub 95	J. W. Macleod	
G-OSST	Colt 77A balloon	British Airways PLC	

Notes	Reg.	Type	Owner or Operator
	G-OSTC	AA-5A Cheetah	C. B. Dew
	G-OSVO	Cameron 30 Hopper Servo SS balloon	Servo & Electronic Sales Ltd
	G-OTAL	ARV Super 2	Cyclone Hovercraft Ltd (G-BNGZ)
	G-OTAM	Cessna 172M	T. W. Woods
	G-OTBY	PA-32 Cherokee Six 300	GOTBY Ltd
	G-OTCH	CFM Streak Shadow	H. E. Gotch
	G-OTEL	Thunder Ax8-90 balloon	Stakis Hotels & Inns Ltd
	G-OTHE	Enstrom 280C-UK Shark	The Engineering Co Ltd (G-OPJT/G-BKCO)
	G-OTIM	Bensen B.8MV	T. J. Deane
	G-OTNT	Cameron Cider Bottle SS balloon	A. J. Round
	G-OTOE	Aeronca 7AC Champion	J. M. Gale (G-BRWW)
	G-OTOW	Cessna 175BX	G-OTOW Flying Group (G-AROC)
	G-OTRG	Cessna TR.182RG	A. Hopper
	G-OTSB	BN-2A Mk III-2 Trislander	Aurigny Air Services Ltd (G-BDTO)
	G-OTSW	Pitts S-1E Special	R. A. Bowes (G-BLHE)
	G-OTTO	Cameron 82 Katalog SS balloon	Cameron Balloons Ltd
	G-OTUG	PA-18 Super Cub 150	B. Walker & Co (Dursley) Ltd
	G-OTVS	BN-2T Islander	Headcorn Parachute Club Ltd (G-BPBN/G-BCMY)
	G-OTWO	Rutan Defiant	D. G. Foreman
	G-OTYJ	PA-28-161 Cadet	Holmes Rentals (G-OLSF)
	G-OUAE	Cameron 90 Wimmi Airbus SS balloon	PPP Ltd
	G-OULD	Gould Mk I balloon	C. A. Gould
	G-OURO	Shaw Europa	D. Dufton
	G-OUSA	Colt 105A balloon	Continental Airlines Inc
	G-OUVI	Cameron O-105 balloon	Bristol University Hot Air Ballooning Soc
	G-OVAA	Colt Jumbo SS balloon	Airship & Balloon Co Ltd
	G-OVAN	SC.7 Skyvan 3 Variant 100	Peterborough Parachute Centre (G-AYZA)/Sibson
	G-OVAX	Colt AS-80 Mk II airship	Vax Appliances Ltd
	G-OVFM	Cessna 120	Industrial Foam Systems Ltd
	G-OVFR	Cessna F.172N	Chikka Ltd
	G-OVID	Light Aero Avid Flyer	M. Stow
	G-OVMC	Cessna F.152 II	Staverton Flying Services Ltd
	G-OVNE	Cessna 401A	M. A. Billings/Ipswich
	G-OVNR	Robinson R-22B	R. A. Kingston & R. Ballard
	G-OVVB	Beech A36 Bonanza	Videovision Broadcast (1988 IoM) Ltd
	G-OWAC	Cessna F.152	Barnes Olson Aeroleasing Ltd (G-BHEB)
	G-OWAR	Cessna F.152	Falcon Flying Services (G-BHEA)
	G-OWAR	PA-28-161 Warrior II	Bickertons Aerodromes Ltd
	G-OWBC	Thunder Ax10-180 S2 balloon	Thunder & Colt Ltd
	G-OWEL	Colt 105A balloon	Autohaus of Aylesbury Ltd
	G-OWEN	K & S Jungster	R. C. Owen
	G-OWGC	Slingsby T.61F Venture T.2	Wolds Gliding Club Ltd
	G-OWIN	BN-2A-8 Islander	UK Parachute Services Ltd (G-AYXE)
	G-OWIZ	Luscombe 8A Silvaire	J. Wilson & J. V. George
	G-OWLC	PA-31 Turbo Navajo	Top Nosh Ltd (G-AYFZ)
	G-OWVA	PA-28 Cherokee 140	Woodvale Aviation Co Ltd
	G-OWWF	Colt 2500A balloon	Virgin Atlantic Airways Ltd
	G-OWYN	Aviamilano F.14 Nibbio	J. R. Wynn
	G-OXLI	BAe Jetstream 4100	British Aerospace PLC/Prestwick
	G-OXRG	Colt Film Can SS balloon	Flying Pictures (Balloons) Ltd
	G-OXTC	PA-23 Aztec 250D	Falcon Flying Services (G-AZOD)/Biggin Hill
	G-OXVI	V.S.361 Spitfire LF.XVIe (TD248)	BAC Aviation Ltd
	G-OYAK	Yakovlev C-11 (27)	E. K. Coventry
	G-OZBA	Airbus A.320-212	Monarch Airlines Ltd/Luton
	G-OZBB	Airbus A.320-212	Monarch Airlines Ltd/Luton
	G-OZLN	Zlin Z.242L	I. E. Humphries
	G-OZOI	Cessna R.182	Velcourt (East) Ltd (G-ROBK)
	G-OZUP	Colt 77A balloon	Yanin International Ltd
	G-PACE	Robin R.1180T	Millicron Instruments Ltd/Coventry
	G-PACL	Robinson R-22B	D. K. Griffiths
	G-PADI	Cameron V-77 balloon	T. R. Duffell
	G-PALS	Enstrom 280C-UK-2 Shark	Sonus Wholesale Audio Products
	G-PAMS	PA-60 Aerostar 601P	E. G. Rigby (G-GAIR)
	G-PAPU	Beech 58PA Baron	ADL Aviation Ltd (G-NIPU)
	G-PARA	Cessna 207	Paraski/Swansea
	G-PARI	Cessna 172RG Cutlass	Applied Signs Ltd
	G-PARR	Cameron 90 Bottle SS balloon	Airship & Balloon Co Ltd

Reg.	Type	Owner or Operator	Notes
G-PART	Partenavia P.68B	Dollar Air Services Ltd/Coventry	
G-PASA	MBB Bo 105D	Medical Aviation Services Ltd (G-BGWP)/ Shoreham	
G-PASB	MBB Bo 105D	Bond Helicopters Ltd (G-BDMC)	
G-PASC	MBB Bo 105DBS/4	Police Aviation Services Ltd (G-BNPS)	
G-PASD	MBB Bo 105DBS/4	Police Aviation Services Ltd (G-BNRS)	
G-PASE	AS.355F-1 Twin Squirrel	Police Aviation Services Ltd	
G-PASF	AS.355F-1 Twin Squirrel	Police Aviation Services Ltd (G-SCHU)	
G-PASG	MBB Bo 105DBS/4	Medical Aviation Services Ltd (G-MHSL)	
G-PASU	BN-2T Turbine Islander	Medical Aviation Services Ltd (G-BJYY)	
G-PASV	BN-2B-21 Islander	Medical Aviation Services Ltd (G-BKJH)	
G-PASX	MBB Bo 105DBS/4	Police Aviation Services Ltd	
G-PASY	BN-2A-26 Islander	Medical Aviation Services Ltd (G-BPCB/ G-BEXA/G-MALI/G-DIVE)/Shoreham	
G-PATY	Colt Flying Sausage balloon	Colt Balloons Ltd	
G-PAWL	PA-28 Cherokee 140	M. Y. Choudhury (G-AWEU)	
G-PAWS	AA-5A Cheetah	M. Entwistle	
G-PAXX	PA-20 Pacer 135	D. W. & M. R. Grace	
G-PAZY	Pazmany PL.4A	A. Louth (G-BLAJ)	
G-PBBT	Cameron N-56 balloon	Test Valley Balloon Club	
G-PBHF	Robinson R-22B	Broughton-Hall Security Fencing	
G-PBWH	BAe 125 Srs 800B	Lynton Aviation Ltd	
G-PCUB	PA-18 Super Cub 135	M. J. Wilson/Redhill	
G-PDHJ	Cessna T.182R	P. G. Vallance Ltd	
G-PDOC	PA-44-180 Seminole	Medicare (G-PVAF)	
G-PDON	WMB.2 Windtracker balloon	P. Donnellan	
G-PDSI	Cessna 172N	Dan-Air Flying Club/Lasham	
G-PEAL	Aerotek Pitts S-2A	Plymouth Executive Aviation Ltd	
G-PEAT	Cessna 421B	Forest City Export Ltd (G-BBIJ)/Manchester	
G-PEEL	BAe ATP	Manx Airlines Ltd/Ronaldsway	
G-PEGG	Colt 90A balloon	Michael Pegg Partnership Ltd	
G-PEGI	PA-34-200T Seneca II	Tayflite Ltd	
G-PEKT	SOCATA TB.20 Trinidad	Premier Plane Leasing Co Ltd	
G-PELE	Cameron 80 Pele SS balloon	Cameron Balloons Ltd	
G-PELI	Pelican Club GS	Pelican Aircraft Ltd	
G-PENN	AA-5B Tiger	Compair	
G-PENY	Sopwith LC-1T Triplane (5492)	J. S. Penny	
G-PERL	Robinson R-22B	R. Fawcett	
G-PERR	Cameron 60 Bottle SS balloon ★	British Balloon Museum	
G-PERS	Colt Soapbox SS balloon	G. V. Beckwith	
G-PEST	Hawker Tempest II	Autokraft Ltd	
G-PETR	PA-28 Cherokee 140	E. W. Keeble (G-BCJL)/Ipswich	
G-PFAA	EAA Biplane Model P	E. W. B. Comber	
G-PFAB	Colomban MC.15 Cri-Cri	P. Fabish	
G-PFAC	FRED Srs 2	G. R. Yates	
G-PFAD	Wittman W.8 Tailwind	M. R. Stamp	
G-PFAF	FRED Srs 2	M. S. Perkins	
G-PFAG	Evans VP-1	P. A. Evans	
G-PFAH	Evans VP-1	J. A. Scott	
G-PFAI	Clutton EC.2 Easy Too	G. W. Cartledge	
G-PFAL	FRED Srs 2	J. McD. Robinson/Bann Foot	
G-PFAO	Evans VP-1	P. W. Price	
G-PFAP	Currie Wot/SE-5A (C1904)	J. H. Seed	
G-PFAR	Isaacs Fury II (K2059)	C. J. Repik	
G-PFAT	Monnet Sonerai II	H. B. Carter	
G-PFAU	Rand KR-2	D. E. Peace	
G-PFAW	Evans VP-1	R. F. Shingler	
G-PFAY	EAA Biplane	A. K. Lang & A. L. Young	
G-PHIL	Brookland Hornet	A. J. Philpotts	
G-PHON	Cameron Phone SS balloon	Redmalt Ltd (G-BTEY)	
G-PHSI	Colt 90A balloon	P. H. Strickland & Simpson (Piccadilly) Ltd	
G-PHTG	SOCATA TB.10 Tobago	G. G. L. Thomas	
G-PIAF	Thunder Ax7-65 balloon	Ballooning Adventures Ltd	
G-PICS	Cessna 182F	D. A. Cresswell (G-ASHO)	
G-PICT	Colt 180A balloon	Scotia Balloons	
G-PIEL	CP.301A Emeraude	P. R. Thorne (G-BARY)	
G-PIES	Thunder Ax7-77Z balloon	Pork Farms Ltd	
G-PIET	Pietenpol Air Camper	N. D. Marshall	
G-PIGS	SOCATA Rallye 150ST	Boonhill Flying Group (G-BDWB)	
G-PIKE	Robinson R-22 Mariner	M. D. Cook	
G-PIKK	PA-28 Cherokee 140	L. P. & I. Keegan (G-AVLA)	
G-PILE	Rotorway Executive 90	J. B. Russell	
G-PINE	Thunder Ax8-90 balloon	J. A. Pine	

177

Notes	Reg.	Type	Owner or Operator
	G-PINT	Cameron 65 Barrel SS balloon	D. K. Fish
	G-PINX	Lindstrand Pink Panther SS balloon	Virgin Airship & Balloon Co Ltd
	G-PIPE	Cameron N-56 Pipe SS balloon	Carreras Rothmans Ltd
	G-PIPS	Van's RV-4	C. J. Marsh
	G-PITS	Pitts S-2AE Special	D. Rolfe
	G-PITZ	Pitts S-2A Special	A. K. Halvorsen
	G-PIXS	Cessna 336	D. A. Cresswell
	G-PJCB	Agusta A.109A-II	J. C. Bamford Excavators Ltd
	G-PJMD	Hughes 369D	Dodici Ltd (G-BMJV)
	G-PJRT	BAe Jetstream 4100	British Aerospace PLC/Prestwick
	G-PKBD	Douglas DC-9-32	British Midland Airways Ltd *The Jubilee Diamond*/E. Midlands
	G-PKBE	Douglas DC-9-32	British Midland Airways Ltd *The Excelsior Diamond*/E. Midlands
	G-PKBM	Douglas DC-9-32	British Midland Airways Ltd *The Tiffany Diamond*/E. Midlands
	G-PKPK	Schweizer 269C	Lift Off Services Ltd
	G-PLAN	Cessna F.150L	Howells Group PLC
	G-PLAS	GA-7 Cougar	London Aviation Ltd (G-BGHL)/Biggin Hill
	G-PLAX	AS.355F-1 Twin Squirrel	Dollar Air Services Ltd (G-BPMT)
	G-PLAY	Robin R.2100A	Cotswold Aero Club Ltd/Staverton
	G-PLEE	Cessna 182Q	W. J. & M. Barnes
	G-PLIV	Pazmany PL.4	B. P. North
	G-PLMA	AS.350B Ecureuil	PLM Helicopters Ltd (G-BMMA)
	G-PLMB	AS.350B Ecureuil	PLM Helicopters Ltd (G-BMMB)
	G-PLMC	AS.350B Ecureuil	PLM Helicopters Ltd (G-BKUM)
	G-PLMF	AS.350B-1 Ecureuil	PLM Helicopters Ltd
	G-PLMG	AS.350B-2 Ecureuil	PLM Helicopters Ltd
	G-PLOW	Hughes 269B	Sulby Aerial Surveys Ltd (G-AVUM)
	G-PLUG	Colt 105A balloon	Eastern Electricity PLC
	G-PLUS	PA-34-200T Seneca II	C. G. Strasser/Jersey
	G-PLYD	SOCATA TB.20 Trinidad	Crocker Air Services/Biggin Hill
	G-PMAM	Cameron V-65 balloon	P. A. Meecham
	G-PNAV	PA-31P Pressurised Navajo	Airtime Aviation Services
	G-POAH	Sikorsky S-76B	P&O Aviation Ltd
	G-POLY	Cameron N-77 balloon	Empty Wallets Balloon Group
	G-POND	Oldfield Baby Lakes	C. R. Weldon
	G-PONY	Colt 31A balloon	Ace Balloons (Bath) Ltd
	G-POOH	Piper J-3C-65 Cub	P. & H. Robinson
	G-POOL	ARV Super 2	Falstaff Finance Ltd (G-BNHA)
	G-POPA	Beech A36 Bonanza	R. G. Jones
	G-POPE	Eiri PIK-20E-1	C. J. Hadley
	G-POPI	SOCATA TB.10 Tobago	Rocol Aviation Ltd (G-BKEN)
	G-POPP	Colt 105A balloon	Flying Pictures (Balloons) Ltd
	G-POPS	PA-34-220T Seneca III	Continental Aero & Marine Ltd
	G-PORK	AA-5B Tiger	J. W. & B. A. Flint (G-BFHS)
	G-PORT	Bell 206B JetRanger 3	C. Clark
	G-POSH	Colt 56A balloon	Columna Ltd (G-BMPT)
	G-POSN	BAe 125 Srs 800B	P&O Containers (Assets) Ltd
	G-POST	EMB-110P1 Bandeirante	Eagle European/Exeter
	G-POTS	Cessna FA.150K	L. J. Potts (G-AYUY)
	G-POWL	Cessna 182R	Glasdon Group Ltd/Blackpool
	G-POZO	SOCATA TB-20 Trinidad	Eurorent SRL
	G-PPLH	Robinson R-22B	Henderson Financial Management Ltd
	G-PPLI	Pazmany PL.1	G. Anderson
	G-PPPE	Colt 77A balloon	Thunder & Colt Ltd
	G-PPPP	Denney Aerocraft Kitfox	W. J. Dale
	G-PRAG	Brügger MB.2 Colibri	D. Frankland & ptnrs
	G-PRIM	PA-38-112 Tomahawk	Braddock Ltd
	G-PRIT	Cameron N-90 balloon	J. M. Albury
	G-PRNT	Cameron V-90 balloon	GS Print (West Midlands) Ltd
	G-PROP	AA-5A Cheetah	Photonic Science Ld (G-BHKU)
	G-PROV	P.84 Jet Provost T.52A (T.4)	Bushfire Investments Ltd
	G-PRTT	Cameron N-31 balloon	J. M. Albury
	G-PRUE	Cameron O-84 balloon	Lalondes Residential Ltd
	G-PRXI	V.S.365 Spitfire PR.XI (PL983)	D. W. Arnold/Biggin Hill
	G-PSCI	Bell 206B JetRanger 3	Abbeyflight Ltd (G-BOKD)
	G-PTER	Beech C90 King Air	Moseley Group (PSV) Ltd (G-BIEE)
	G-PTRE	SOCATA TB.20 Trinidad	Solving Systems Ltd (G-BNKU)
	G-PTWO	Pilatus P2-05 (U-110)	C. M. Lee
	G-PUBS	Colt 56 Glass SS balloon	The Balloonatics
	G-PUDD	Robinson R-22B	Riggarna UK Ltd

Reg.	Type	Owner or Operator	Notes
G-PUFF	Thunder Ax7-77A balloon	Intervarsity Balloon Club *Puffin II*	
G-PULS	Aero Designs Pulsar	M. J. McBride	
G-PUMA	AS.332L Super Puma	Bond Helicopters Ltd	
G-PUMB	AS.332L Super Puma	Bond Helicopters Ltd	
G-PUMD	AS.332L Super Puma	Bond Helicopters Ltd	
G-PUME	AS.332L Super Puma	Bond Helicopters Ltd	
G-PUMG	AS.332L Super Puma	Bond Helicopters Ltd	
G-PUMH	AS.332L Super Puma	Bond Helicopters Ltd	
G-PUMI	AS.332L Super Puma	Bond Helicopters Ltd	
G-PUMJ	AS.332L Super Puma	Bond Helicopters Ltd (G-BLZJ)	
G-PUMK	AS.332L Super Puma	Bond Helicopters Ltd	
G-PUML	AS.332L Super Puma	Bond Helicopters Ltd	
G-PUNK	Thunder Ax8-105 balloon	G. E. Harris	
G-PUPP	B.121 Pup 2	P. A. Teichman (G-BASD)/Elstree	
G-PURE	Cameron 70 Can SS balloon	The Hot-Air Balloon Co Ltd	
G-PURR	AA-5A Cheetah	D. T. Smith (G-BJDN)	
G-PURS	Rotorway Executive	J. E. Houseman	
G-PUSH	Rutan LongEz	E. G. Peterson	
G-PUSI	Cessna T.303	W. R. Swinburn Ltd	
G-PUSS	Cameron N-77 balloon	Bristol Balloons	
G-PYLN	Cameron Pylon SS balloon	Air 2 Air Ltd (G-BUSO)	
G-PYRO	Cameron N-65 balloon	N. A. Mitchell	
G-RAAD	Mooney M.20L	As-Al Ltd	
G-RAAR	BAe 125 Srs 800B	Osprey Executive Aviation Ltd/Southend	
G-RACA	P.57 Sea Prince T.1 ★	Stratford Aircraft Collection/Long Marston	
G-RACH	Robinson R-22B	TWS Helicopters Ltd	
G-RACO	PA-28R Cherokee Arrow 200-II	Graco Group Ltd	
G-RAEM	Rutan LongEz	G. F. H. Singleton	
G-RAFA	Grob G.115	RAF College Flying Club Ltd/Cranwell	
G-RAFB	Grob G.115	RAF College Flying Club Ltd/Cranwell	
G-RAFC	Robin R.2112	S. J. Cropley	
G-RAFE	Thunder Ax7-77 balloon	N. A. & J. K. Fishlock	
G-RAFF	Learjet 35A	Graff Aviation Ltd/Heathrow	
G-RAFG	Slingsby T.67C	S. J. Donkin	
G-RAFI	P.84 Jet Provost T.4	R. M. Muir	
G-RAFT	Rutan LongEz	H. C. Mackinnon	
G-RAFW	Mooney M.20E	S. L. Monksfield (G-ATHW)	
G-RAHL	Beech 400A Beechjet	Air Hanson Aircraft Sales Ltd	
G-RAID	AD-4NA Skyraider (126922)	Patina Ltd/Duxford	
G-RAIL	Colt 105A balloon	Ballooning World Ltd	
G-RAIN	Maule M5-235C Lunar Rocket	D. S. McKay & J. A. Rayment/Hinton-in-the-Hedges	
G-RALI	Hughes 369HS	Kallas Ltd (G-BLKO)	
G-RAMI	Bell 206B JetRanger 3	R. & M. International Helicopters Ltd	
G-RAMM	Hughes 369HM	Richard Mulloch Homes Ltd	
G-RAMP	Piper J-3C-65 Cub	K. N. Whittall	
G-RAMS	PA-32R-301 Saratoga SP	Air Tobago Ltd/Netherthorpe	
G-RAND	Rand KR-2	R. L. Wharmby	
G-RANS	Rans S.10 Sakota	J. D. Weller	
G-RANZ	Rans S.10 Sakota	B. A. Phillips	
G-RAPE	Colt 300A balloon	Adventure Balloon Co Ltd	
G-RAPH	Cameron O-77 balloon	P. H. Jenkins	
G-RAPP	Cameron H-34 balloon	Cameron Balloons Ltd	
G-RARE	Thunder Ax5-42 SS balloon	International Distillers & Vintners Ltd	
G-RASC	Evans VP-2	R. A. Codling	
G-RATE	AA-5A Cheetah	Blackbushe School of Flying Ltd (G-BIFF)	
G-RAVI	Colt 300A balloon	R. S. Hunjan	
G-RAVL	H.P.137 Jetstream Srs 200	Cranfield Institute of Technology (G-AWVK)	
G-RAYA	Denney Aerocraft Kitfox Mk 4	A. K. Ray	
G-RAYS	Zenair CH.250	B. O. & F. A. Smith	
G-RBOS	Colt AS-105 airship ★	Science Museum/Wroughton	
G-RBOW	Thunder Ax-7-65 balloon	P. G. & S. D. Viney	
G-RBUT	Hughes 369HS	R. C. Button	
G-RCDI	H.S.125 Srs 700B	Aravco Ltd (G-BJDJ)/Heathrow	
G-RCED	R. Commander 114	Echo Delta Ltd	
G-RCMC	Murphy Renegade 912	B. D. Godden	
G-RCMF	Cameron V-77 balloon	Mouldform Ltd	
G-RDCI	R. Commander 112A	A. C. Hendriksen (G-BFWG)	
G-RDON	WMB.2 Windtracker balloon	P. J. Donnellan (G-BICH)	
G-REAP	Pitts S-1S Special	R. Dixon	
G-REAT	GA-7 Cougar	Denham School of Flying Ltd	
G-REBE	Bensen B.8MR	Chartersteps Ltd	

Notes	Reg.	Type	Owner or Operator
	G-REBI	Colt 90A balloon	Capricorn Balloons Ltd (G-BOYD)
	G-REBL	Hughes 269B	M. I. Edwards
	G-RECK	PA-28 Cherokee 140B	R. J. Grantham & D. Boatswain (G-AXJW)
	G-RECO	Jurca MJ-5L Sirocco	J. D. Tseliki
	G-REDB	Cessna 310Q	Copythorne Motor Co Ltd (G-BBIC)
	G-REEK	AA-5A Cheetah	J. R. & S. Nutter
	G-REEN	Cessna 340	E. & M. Green (G-AZYR)/Guernsey
	G-REES	Jodel D.140C	W. H. Greenwood
	G-REFI	Enstrom 280C-UK	B. Murphy
	G-REGS	Thunder Ax7-77 balloon	M. E. Gregory
	G-REID	Rotorway Scorpion 133	G. F. Burridge & S. B. Evans
	G-REIS	PA-28R-201T Turbo Arrow III	G. Webster & J. D. Caudwell
	G-RENE	Murphy Renegade 912	J. A. Cutherton
	G-RENO	SOCATA TB.10 Tobago	Lamond Ltd
	G-RENT	Robinson R-22B	Rentatruck Self Drive Ltd
	G-REPM	PA-38-112 Tomahawk	Nultree Ltd
	G-REST	Beech P35 Bonanza	C. R. Taylor (G-ASFJ)
	G-RETA	C.A.S.A. 1.131 Jungmann	J. S. Allison (G-BGZC)/Denham
	G-REVS	Bell 206B JetRanger	Helispeed Ltd (G-AWOL)
	G-REXS	PA-28-181 Archer II	Channel Islands Aero Holdings (Jersey) Ltd
	G-REZE	Rutan Vari-Eze	S. D. Brown & S. P. Evans
	G-RFAB	Cessna 182R	La Patron Holdings Ltd (G-BIXT)
	G-RFIL	Colt 77A balloon	The Aerial Display Co Ltd
	G-RFSB	Sportavia RF-5B	S. W. Brown
	G-RGUS	Fairchild 24R-46A Argus 3 (44-83184)	R. C. Handcraff
	G-RHCN	Cessna FR.182RG	R. H. C. Neville
	G-RHHT	PA-32RT-300 Lance II	R. W. Struth & ptnrs
	G-RHYS	Rotorway Executive 90	B. Williams
	G-RICC	AS.350B-2 Ecureuil	McAlpine Helicopters Ltd & Gabriel Enterprises Ltd (G-BTXA)
	G-RICH	Cessna F.152	Ford Equipment Hire
	G-RICK	Beech 95-B55 Baron	James Jack (Invergordon) Ltd (G-BAAG)
	G-RIDE	Stephens Akro	R. Mitchell/Coventry
	G-RIDS	Lancair 235	R. Y. Kendal
	G-RIFB	Hughes 269C	R. F. Rhodes & J. C. McHugh
	G-RIGB	Thunder Ax7-77 balloon	Antrum & Andrews Ltd
	G-RIGS	PA-60 Aerostar 601P	Techno Engineering
	G-RILL	Cessna 421C	Channel Aviation Holdings Ltd (G-BGZM)
	G-RILY	Monnet Sonerai II	R. Wheeler
	G-RIND	Cessna 335	ATA Grinding Processes/Leavesden
	G-RINO	Thunder Ax7-77 balloon	D. J. Head
	G-RINT	CFM Streak Shadow	D. Grint
	G-RISE	Cameron V-77 balloon	D. L. Smith
	G-RIST	Cessna 310R-II	Air Service Training Ltd (G-DATS)/Perth
	G-RIZE	Cameron O-90 balloon	S. F. Burden/Netherlands
	G-RIZI	Cameron N-90 balloon	R. Wiles
	G-RJAH	Boeing Stearman A.75N1	R. J. Horne
	G-RJER	McD Douglas MD-83	Airtours International Aviation Ltd
	G-RJMI	AA-5A Cheetah	Garrick Aviation
	G-RJMS	PA-28R-201 Arrow III	M. G. Hill
	G-RJWW	Maule M5-235C Lunar Rocket	Paw Flying Services Ltd (G-BRWG)
	G-RLFI	Cessna FA.152	Tayside Aviation Ltd (G-DFTS)/Dundee
	G-RLMC	Cessna 421C	R. D. Lygo
	G-RMCT	Short SD3-60 Variant 100	Streamline Aviation (G-BLPU)
	G-RMGW	Denney Aerocraft Kitfox Mk 3	G. H. Gilmour-White
	G-RNAS	D.H.104 Sea Devon C.20 (XK896)	D. W. Hermiston-Hooper/Staverton
	G-RNIE	Cameron 70 Ball SS balloon	Airship & Balloon Co Ltd
	G-RNLI	V.S.236 Walrus 1	R. E. Melton
	G-RNRM	Cessna A.185F	RN & R. Marines Sport Parachute Association/Dunkeswell
	G-ROAR	Cessna 401	Aviation (Scotland) Ltd (G-BZFL/G-AWSF)
	G-ROBB	Grob G.109B	A. P. Mayne
	G-ROBI	Grob G.109B	A. W. McGarrigle/Cardiff
	G-ROBN	Robin R.1180T	J. G. Beaumont
	G-ROBO	Robinson R-22B	Cabair Air Taxis Ltd/Elstree
	G-ROBY	Colt 17A balloon	Airship & Balloon Co Ltd
	G-ROCH	Cessna T.303	R. S. Bentley
	G-ROCK	Thunder Ax7-77 balloon	The Long Rake Spar Co Ltd
	G-ROCR	Schweizer 269C	W. Murphy
	G-RODD	Cessna 310R II	R. J. Herbert Engineering Ltd (G-TEDD/G-MADI)
	G-RODI	Isaacs Fury (K3731)	M. R. Baker/Shoreham

Reg.	Type	Owner or Operator	Notes
G-RODS	A-Bell 206B JetRanger 2	Crook & Son (G-NOEL/G-BCWN)	
G-ROGG	Robinson R-22B	Catto Helicopters	
G-ROGY	Cameron 60 Concept balloon	A. A. Laing	
G-ROLA	PA-34-200T Seneca	Highsteeple Ltd	
G-ROLF	PA-32R-301 Saratoga SP	P. F. Larkins	
G-ROLL	Pitts S-2A Special	Aerial & Aerobatic Services	
G-ROLO	Robinson R-22B	London Aviation Ltd/Elstree	
G-ROMA	Hughes 369S	Helicopters (Northern) Ltd (G-ROPI/ G-ONPP)/Blackpool	
G-RONC	Aeronca 11AC Chief	S. F. Bancroft (G-BULV)/Redhill	
G-RONG	PA-28R Cherokee Arrow 200-II	W. R. Griffiths	
G-RONI	Cameron V-77 balloon	R. E. Simpson	
G-RONS	Robin DR.400/180	R. & K. Baker	
G-RONT	Enstrom F-28A	R. Thomas (G-BDAW)	
G-RONW	FRED Srs 2	K. Atkinson	
G-ROOK	Cessna F.172P	Crop Aviation (UK) Ltd	
G-ROPA	Shaw Europa	R. G. Gray	
G-RORI	Folland Gnat T.1	R. C. McCarthy	
G-RORO	Cessna 337B	C. Keane (G-AVIX)	
G-RORY	Piaggio FW P.149D	R. McCarthy (G-TOWN)/Booker	
G-ROSE	Evans VP-1	W. K. Rose	
G-ROSI	Thunder Ax7-77 balloon	Scotia Balloons Ltd	
G-ROSS	Practavia Pilot Sprite	F. M. T. Ross	
G-ROSY	Robinson R-22B	Aquaprint Ltd	
G-ROTI	Luscombe 8A Silvaire	A. L. Chapman & ptnrs	
G-ROTO	Rotorway Executive 90	S. R. Porter	
G-ROTR	Brantly B.2B	GP Services	
G-ROTS	CFM Streak Shadow Srs SA	P. White	
G-ROUP	Cessna F.172M	Stapleford Flying Club Ltd (G-BDPH)	
G-ROUS	PA-34-200T Seneca II	C.S.E. Aviation Ltd/Kidlington	
G-ROUT	Robinson R-22B	Hooley Bridge Helicopter Services	
G-ROVE	PA-18 Super Cub 135	Cormack (Aircraft Services) Ltd/Glasgow	
G-ROWL	AA-5B Tiger	Aviation Simulation/Biggin Hill	
G-ROWN	Beech 200 Super King Air	Chauffair Ltd (G-BHLC)	
G-ROWS	PA-28-151 Warrior	Mustarrow Ltd	
G-ROZY	Cameron R.36 balloon	Jacques W. Soukup Ltd	
G-RPEZ	Rutan LongEz	B. A. Fairston & D. Richardson	
G-RRRR	Privateer Motor Glider	R. F. Selby	
G-RRSG	Thunder Ax7-77 balloon	M. T. Stevens	
G-RRTM	Sikorsky S-70C	Rolls-Royce PLC/Filton	
G-RSSF	Denney Aerocraft Kitfox Mk 2	R. W. Somerville	
G-RSWW	Robinson R-22B	Woodstock Enterprises	
G-RUBB	AA-5B Tiger	R. Bessant	
G-RUBI	Thunder Ax7-77 balloon	Warren & Johnson	
G-RUBY	PA-28RT-201T Turbo Arrow IV	Arrow Aircraft Group (G-BROU)	
G-RUDD	Cameron V-65 balloon	N. A. Apsey	
G-RUDI	QAC Quickie Q.2	R. Brandenberger	
G-RUGB	Cameron 89 Egg SS balloon	The Hot-Air Balloon Co Ltd	
G-RUIA	Cessna F.172M	F. Daly	
G-RUMN	AA-1A Trainer	G. J. Richardson	
G-RUMP	Robinson R-22B	I. P. Crane	
G-RUNT	Cassutt Racer IIIM	S. B. Jones	
G-RUSO	Robinson R-22B	N. P. Graham	
G-RUSS	Cessna 172N	Leisure Lease/Southend	
G-RVEE	Van's RV-6	J. C. A. Wheeler	
G-RVVI	Van's RV-6	J. E. Alsford & J. N. Parr	
G-RWHC	Cameron A-180 balloon	Hourds Ltd	
G-RWIN	Rearwin 175	G. Kay	
G-RWSS	Denney Aerocraft Kitfox	R. W. Somerville	
G-RWWW	W.S.55 Whirlwind HCC.12 (XR486)	R. Windley	
G-RZZB	Robinson R-22B	Heli-Link Ltd	
G-SAAB	R. Commander 112TC	R. R. White (G-BEFS)	
G-SAAM	Cessna T.182R	Hopstop Ltd (G-TAGL)/Elstree	
G-SABA	PA-28R-201T Turbo Arrow III	R. J. Everett (G-BFEN)	
G-SABR	NA F-86A Sabre (8178)	Golden Apple Operations Ltd/Bournemouth	
G-SACB	Cessna F.152 II	Westward Airways (Land's End) Ltd (G-BFRB)/St Just	
G-SACD	Cessna F.172H	Northbrook College of Design & Technology (G-AVCD)/Shoreham	
G-SACE	Cessna F.150L	Arrow Aircraft Group (G-AZLK)	
G-SACF	Cessna 152 II	T. M. & M. L. Jones	
G-SACI	PA-28-161 Warrior II	PJC (Leasing) Ltd	

Notes	Reg.	Type	Owner or Operator
	G-SACO	PA-28-161 Warrior II	The Barn Gallery
	G-SACR	PA-28-161 Cadet	Sherburn Aero Club Ltd
	G-SACS	PA-28-161 Cadet	Sherburn Aero Club Ltd
	G-SACT	PA-28-161 Cadet	Sherburn Aero Club Ltd
	G-SACU	PA-28-161 Cadet	Sherburn Aero Club Ltd
	G-SACZ	PA-28-161 Warrior II	B. A. Groves
	G-SADE	Cessna F.150L	Bath Stone Co Ltd (G-AZJW)
	G-SAFE	Cameron N-77 balloon	P. J. Waller
	G-SAGA	Grob G.109B	G-GROB Ltd/Booker
	G-SAGE	Luscombe 8A Silvaire	S. J. Sage (G-AKTL)
	G-SAHI	Trago Mills SAH-1	Lovaux Ltd/Bournemouth
	G-SAIR	Cessna 421C	Air Support Aviation Services Ltd
	G-SALA	PA-32 Cherokee Six 300E	Stonebold Ltd
	G-SALI	Cessna 421C	Vak Aero Enterprises Ltd
	G-SALL	Cessna F.150L (Tailwheel)	Accolade Flying Club/Shoreham
	G-SAMG	Grob G.109B	RAFGSA/Bicester
	G-SAMM	Cessna 340A	M. R. Cross
	G-SAMS	M.S.880B Rallye Club	K. Lewis
	G-SAMZ	Cessna 150D	N. E. Sames (G-ASSO)
	G-SANB	Beech E90 King Air	ITPS Ltd (G-BGNU)/Cranfield
	G-SAND	Schweizer 269C	Aerocroft Ltd
	G-SARA	PA-28-181 Archer II	L. C. MacKnight
	G-SARH	PA-28-161 Warrior II	Bath Stone Co Ltd
	G-SARO	Saro Skeeter Mk 12 (XL812)	F. F. Chamberlain
	G-SASU	AS.355F-1 Twin Squirrel	Gulf & UK Industrial Consultants Ltd (G-BSSM/G-BMTC/G-BKUK)
	G-SATI	Cameron 105 Sphere SS balloon	Cameron Balloons Ltd
	G-SATL	Cameron 105 Sphere SS balloon	Cameron Balloons Ltd
	G-SAUF	Colt 90A balloon	K. H. Medau
	G-SAVE	PA-31-350 Navajo Chieftain	Osten Airfinance Ltd
	G-SAVS	Murphy Rebel	D. M. & E. Savage
	G-SBAC	Short SD3-60 Variant 100	BAC Leasing Ltd/Gill Aviation (G-BLEE)
	G-SBAS	Beech B200 Super King Air	Bond Helicopters Ltd (G-BJJV)/Aberdeen
	G-SBLT	Steen Skybolt	M. A. McCallum & H. Lees
	G-SBUS	BN-2A Islander	Isles of Scilly Skybus Ltd (G-BMMH)/St Just
	G-SCAN	Vinten-Wallis WA-116/100	K. H. Wallis
	G-SCAT	Cessna F.150F	Cheshire Air Training School (Merseyside) Ltd (G-ATRN)/Liverpool
	G-SCCC	BAe 125-1000B	Consolidated Contractors International (UK) Ltd
	G-SCFO	Cameron O-77 balloon	M. K. Grigson
	G-SCPL	PA-28 Cherokee 140	Hillvine Ltd (G-BPVL)/Staverton
	G-SCSR	Airbus A.320-212	Excalibur Airways Ltd/E. Midlands
	G-SCTT	HPR-7 Herald 210	Channel Express (Air Services) Ltd (G-ASPJ)/Bournemouth
	G-SCUB	PA-18 Super Cub 135 (542447)	N. D. Needham Farms
	G-SDEV	D.H.104 Sea Devon C.20 (XK895)	P. C. Gill & W. Gentle
	G-SDLW	Cameron O-105 balloon	P. J. Smart
	G-SEAB	Republic RC-3 Seabee	B. A. Farries
	G-SEAH	Hawker Sea Hawk FB.3	Jet Heritage Ltd/Bournemouth
	G-SEAI	Cessna U.206G	Seaplane Safaris (Scotland) Ltd
	G-SEAT	Colt 42 balloon	Airship & Balloon Co Ltd
	G-SEED	Piper J-3C-65 Cub	J. H. Seed
	G-SEEK	Cessna T.210N	Melrose Pigs Ltd
	G-SEGA	Cameron 90 Sonic SS balloon	Virgin Airship & Balloon Co Ltd
	G-SEGO	Robinson R-22B	G. Seago
	G-SEJW	PA-28-161 Warrior II	Truman Aviation Ltd/Tollerton
	G-SELL	Robin DR.400/180	L. S. Thorne
	G-SEND	Colt 90A balloon	Redmalt Ltd
	G-SEPT	Cameron N-105 balloon	Deproco UK Ltd
	G-SERA	Enstrom F-28A-UK	W. R. Pitcher (G-BAHU)
	G-SERL	SOCATA TB.10 Tobago	R. J. & G. Searle (G-LANA)/Rochester
	G-SETA	AS.355F-1 Twin Squirrel	McAlpine Helicopters Ltd (G-NEAS/ G-CMMM/G-BNBJ)
	G-SEVA	SE-5A (replica) (F141)	I. D. Gregory
	G-SEVE	Cessna 172N	S. Patterson
	G-SEWL	PA-28-151 Warrior	A. R. Sewell & Sons/Andrewsfield
	G-SEXI	Cessna 172M	Trade Orders Ltd
	G-SEXY	AA-1 Yankee	H. Morris (G-AYLM)
	G-SFHR	PA-23 Aztec 250F	Nett Supply Co Ltd (G-BHSO)
	G-SFOX	Rotorway Executive 90	Magpie Computer Services Ltd (G-BUAH)
	G-SFPA	Cessna F.406	Scottish Fisheries Protection Agency
	G-SFPB	Cessna F.406	Scottish Fisheries Protection Agency

Reg.	Type	Owner or Operator	Notes
G-SFRY	Thunder Ax7-77 balloon	R. J. Fry	
G-SFTZ	Slingsby T.67M Firefly	Mega Yield Ltd	
G-SGAS	Colt 77A balloon	Avongas Ltd	
G-SHAA	Enstrom 280-UK	Manchester Helicopter Centre/Barton	
G-SHAW	PA-30 Twin Comanche 160B	PTC Ltd	
G-SHCC	AB-206B JetRanger 2	Yorkshire Helicopter Centre Ltd	
G-SHEA	BAe 125 Srs 800B	Shell Aircraft Ltd (G-BUWC)/Heathrow	
G-SHEB	BAe 125 Srs 800B	Raytheon Corporate Jets Inc (G-BUWD)	
G-SHED	PA-28-181 Archer II	S. V. Smeeth (G-BRAU)	
G-SHEL	Cameron O-56 balloon	The Shell Company of Hong Kong Ltd	
G-SHFL	Cameron N-77 balloon	M. C. Bradley/Hong Kong	
G-SHGG	Enstrom 280C Shark	Haversham Helicopters Ltd	
G-SHIM	CFM Streak Shadow	E. S. Shimmin	
G-SHIP	PA-23 Aztec 250F ★	Midland Air Museum/Coventry	
G-SHIV	GA-7 Cougar	Westley Aviation Services	
G-SHKK	Hughes 269A	Starline Helicopters Ltd	
G-SHNN	Enstrom 280C	CJ Services	
G-SHOO	Hughes TH-55A	Starline Helicopters Ltd	
G-SHOP	H.S. 125 Srs F400B	GB Dee Knitwear Ltd (G-BTUF)/Coventry	
G-SHOT	Cameron V-77 balloon	E. C. Moore	
G-SHOW	M.S.733 Alycon	Vintage Aircraft Team/Cranfield	
G-SHPP	Hughes TH-55A	R. P. Bateman & A. C. Braithwaite	
G-SHRL	Jodel D.18	K. Fern	
G-SHRR	AB-206B JetRanger 2	Woodhey Helicopters (G-FSDA/G-AWJW)	
G-SHUG	PA-28R-201T Turbo Arrow III	N. E. Rennie	
G-SHUU	Enstrom 280C-UK-2 Shark	D. Ellis (G-OMCP/G-KENY/G-BJFG)	
G-SHZZ	Bell 206B JetRanger 3	Corporate Enterprises Ltd (G-BNUW)	
G-SIAN	Cameron V-77 balloon	S. M. Jones	
G-SIGN	PA-39 Twin Comanche 160 C/R	Comanche Travel Ltd/Elstree	
G-SIIB	Pitts S-2B Special	M. Davies (G-BUVY)	
G-SING	Beech B60 Duke	Sasha Fashions International Ltd/ Leavesden	
G-SION	PA-38-112 Tomahawk II	Bath Stone Co Ltd	
G-SIPA	SIPA 903	T. J. McRae (G-BGBM)	
G-SITE	AS.355F-1 Twin Squirrel	Bridge Street Nominees Ltd (G-BPHC)	
G-SIXC	Douglas DC-6A	Atlantic Air Transport Ltd/Coventry	
G-SIXX	Colt 77A balloon	G. E. Harris & S. C. Kinsey	
G-SIZE	Lindstrand LBL-310A balloon	Adventure Balloon Co Ltd	
G-SIZL	Bell 206B JetRanger 3	P. G. Osborn (G-BOSW)	
G-SJAB	PA-39 Twin Comanche 160 C/R	Foyle Flyers Ltd	
G-SJGM	Cessna 182R	Crystal Air Ltd	
G-SJMC	Boeing 767-31KER	Airtours International Airways Ltd	
G-SKAN	Cessna F.172M	R. Mitchell & J. D. Walton (G-BFKT)	
G-SKIL	Cameron N-77 balloon	Windermere Balloon Co	
G-SKIP	Cameron N-77 balloon	Skipton Building Soc	
G-SKKA	PA-31 Turbo Navajo	J. J. Baumhardt (G-FOAL/G-RMAE/ G-BAEG)	
G-SKKB	PA-31 Turbo Navajo	Bulldog Aviation Ltd/(G-BBDS)/Earls Colne	
G-SKSA	Airship Industries SKS.500	Airship Industries Ltd/Cardington	
G-SKSG	Airship Industries SKS.600/03	Interport Marine Agencies Ltd	
G-SKYD	Pitts S-2B Special	Skydancer Aviation Ltd	
G-SKYE	Cessna TU.206G	RAF Sport Parachute Association	
G-SKYH	Cessna 172N	Elgor Hire Purchase & Credit Ltd/ Southend	
G-SKYI	Air Command 532 Elite	P. J. Troy-Davies	
G-SKYM	Cessna F.337E	Bencray Ltd (G-AYHW) (stored)/Blackpool	
G-SKYP	Cameron A-120 balloon	PSH Skypower Ltd	
G-SKYR	Cameron A-180 balloon	PSH Skypower Ltd	
G-SKYS	Cameron O-84 balloon	J. R. Christopher	
G-SLAC	Cameron N-77 balloon	The Scottish Life Assurance Co	
G-SLCI	Thunder Ax8-90 balloon	S. L. Cuhat	
G-SLEA	Mudry/CAARP CAP.10B	P. D. Southerington/Sturgate	
G-SLII	Cameron O-90 balloon	R. B. & A. M. Harris	
G-SLIM	Colt 56A balloon	Hot-Air Balloon Co Ltd	
G-SLYN	PA-28-161 Warrior II	G. E. Layton	
G-SMAF	Sikorsky S-76A	Fayair (Jersey) 1984 Ltd	
G-SMAX	Cameron O-105 balloon	Cameron Balloons Ltd	
G-SMIG	Cameron O-65 balloon	Hong Kong Balloon & Airship Club	
G-SMIT	Messerschmitt Bf.109G-6	Fairoaks Aviation Services Ltd	
G-SMJJ	Cessna 414A	Gull Air Ltd/Guernsey	
G-SMTC	Colt Flying Hut SS balloon	Shiplake Investments Ltd	
G-SMTH	PA-28 Cherokee 140	D. M. Banner (G-AYJS)	
G-SNAP	Cameron V-77 balloon	P. A. George	

Notes	Reg.	Type	Owner or Operator
	G-SNAX	Colt 69A balloon	Derwent Valley Foods Ltd
	G-SNDY	Piper J-3C-65 Cub	R. R. K. Mayall
	G-SNOW	Cameron V-77 balloon	M. J. Snow
	G-SOAR	Eiri PIK-20E	F. W. Fay
	G-SOAS	PA-60 Aerostar 601P	Kenilgate Ltd
	G-SOFA	Cameron N-65 balloon	GT Flying Club Ltd
	G-SOFI	PA-60 Aerostar 601P	Allzones Travel Ltd/Biggin Hill
		(Machen Superstar II)	
	G-SOFT	Thunder Ax7-77 balloon	A. J. Brown
	G-SOLA	Aero Designs Star-Lite SL.1	P. Clifton & A. Clarke
	G-SOLD	Robinson R-22A	Travel Management Ltd
	G-SOLO	Pitts S-2S Special	Landitfast Ltd
	G-SONA	SOCATA TB.10 Tobago	J. Greenwood (G-BIBI)
	G-SONY	Aero Commander 200D	General Airline Ltd (G-BGPS)
	G-SOOC	Hughes 369HS	Colour Library Books (G-BRRX)
	G-SOOE	Hughes 369E	Feabrex Steel Fabrication Ltd
	G-SOOM	Glaser-Dirks DG.500M	Glaser-Dirks UK
	G-SOOS	Colt 21A balloon	P. J. Stapley
	G-SOOT	PA-28 Cherokee 180	Thornton Browne Ltd (G-AVNM)/Exeter
	G-SORT	Cameron N-90 balloon	The Post Office
	G-SOUL	Cessna 310R	Atlantic Air Transport Ltd/Coventry
	G-SPAM	Light Aero Avid Aerobat	C. M. Hicks
	G-SPEY	AB-206B JetRanger 3	Castle Air Charters Ltd (G-BIGO)
	G-SPIN	Pitts S-2A Special	R. P. Grace & P. L. Goldberg
	G-SPIT	V.S.379 Spitfire FR.XIV (MV293)	Patina Ltd (G-BGHB)/Duxford
	G-SPOL	MBB Bo 105CBS/4	Clyde Helicopters Ltd
	G-SSBS	Colting Ax77 balloon	K. J. & M. E. Gregory
	G-SSFT	PA-28-161 Warrior II	SFT Aviation Ltd (G-BHIL)/Bournemouth
	G-SSKY	BN-2B-26 Islander	Isles of Scilly Skybus Ltd (G-BSWT)
	G-SSRS	Cessna 172N	Romair
	G-SSSC	Sikorsky S-76C	Bond Helicopters Ltd/Aberdeen
	G-SSSD	Sikorsky S-76C	Bond Helicopters Ltd/Aberdeen
	G-SSSE	Sikorsky S-76C	Bond Helicopters Ltd
	G-SSWV	Sportavia Fournier RF-5B	J. L. Collins & J. A. Melville
	G-STAG	Cameron O-65 balloon	The New Holker Estates Co Ltd
	G-STAN	F.27 Friendship Mk.200	Air UK Jimmy Saville OBE/Norwich
	G-STAT	Cessna U.206F	SMK Engineers Ltd
	G-STAV	Cameron O-84 balloon	Nestle UK Ltd
	G-STEF	Hughes 369HS	D. J. L. Wood (G-BKTK)
	G-STEN	Stemme S.10	W. A. H. Kahn
	G-STEP	Schweizer 269C	Wood Hall Helicopters Ltd
	G-STEV	Jodel DR.221	S. W. Talbot/Long Marston
	G-STMI	Robinson R-22B	Image Computer Systems Ltd
	G-STMP	SNCAN Stampe SV-4A	W. R. Partridge
	G-STOX	Bell 206B JetRanger 2	Tickstop Ltd (G-BNIR)
	G-STOY	Robinson R-22B	Tickstop Ltd
	G-STRK	CFM Streak Shadow Srs SA	M. E. Dodd
	G-STST	Bell 206B JetRanger 3	Petrochemical Supplies Ltd
	G-STUA	Aerotek Pitts S-2A Special	Aero-Balance Aviation/White Waltham
		(modified)	
	G-STVN	HPR-7 Herald 210	Channel Express (Air Services) Ltd
			/Bournemouth
	G-STWO	ARV Super 2	Aviation (Scotland) Ltd
	G-STYL	Pitts S-1S Special	A. Stanford
	G-SUEE	Airbus A.320-231	Airtours International Airways Ltd
			(G-IEAG)
	G-SUIT	Cessna 210N	Edinburgh Air Centre Ltd
	G-SUKI	PA-38-112 Tomahawk	Bath Stone Co Ltd (G-BPNV)
	G-SULL	PA-32R-301 Saratoga SP	B. R. Chaplin
	G-SULY	Monnet Moni	M. J. Sullivan
	G-SUMT	Robinson R-22B	Frankham Bros Ltd (G-BUKD)
	G-SUPA	PA-18 Super Cub 150	Crop Aviation (UK) Ltd
	G-SURG	PA-30 Twin Comanche 160B	A. R. Taylor (G-VIST/G-AVHZ)
	G-SUSI	Cameron V-77 balloon	H. S. & C. J. Dryden
	G-SUSY	P-51D-25-NA Mustang (472773)	P. J. Morgan
	G-SUZI	Beech 95-B55 Baron	Bebecar (UK) Ltd (G-BAXR)
	G-SUZN	PA-28-161 Warrior II	Bath Stone Co Ltd
	G-SUZY	Taylor JT.1 Monoplane	D. I. Law
	G-SVIV	SNCAN Stampe SV-4C	A. J. Clarry & S. F. Bancroft
	G-SVJM	AS.355F-1 Twin Squirrel	UB Air Ltd & Jensen & Nicholson Ltd
			(G-BOPS)
	G-SVSS	Beech C90A King Air	Terry Coleman (UK) Ltd (G-OAKZ)
	G-SWEB	Cameron N-90 balloon	Air 2 Air Ltd

Reg.	Type	Owner or Operator	Notes
G-SWET	Cessna 500 Citation	Michael Car Centres Ltd	
G-SWFT	Beech 200 Super King Air	Airswift Ltd (G-SIBE/G-MCEO/G-BILY)	
G-SWIF	V.S.541 Swift F.7	Jet Heritage Ltd/Bournemouth	
G-SWIM	Taylor Coot Amphibian (modified)	R. J. Hopkins	
G-SWIS	D.H.100 Vampire F.6 (J-1149)	Hunter Wing Ltd/Bournemouth	
G-SWIV	Lindstrand LBL-240A balloon	Airborne Adventures Ltd	
G-SWOT	Currie Super Wot (C3011)	J. D. Haslam	
G-SWPR	Cameron N-56 balloon	A. Brown	
G-SYFW	Focke-Wulf Fw.190 replica (2+1)	M. R. Parr	
G-TACK	Grob G.109B	Oval (275) Ltd/Bristol	
G-TAFF	C.A.S.A. 1.131 Jungmann	A. Horsfall (G-BFNE)	
G-TAFI	Bücker Bu133 Jungmeister	A. J. E. Smith	
G-TAFY	Piper J-3F-65 Cub	C. P. Goodley	
G-TAGS	PA-28-161 Warrior II	Air Service Training Ltd/Perth	
G-TAIL	Cessna 150J	Routair Aviation Services Ltd/Southend	
G-TAIR	PA-34-200T Seneca II	Wessex Mouldings Ltd	
G-TAMY	Cessna 421B	Malcolm Enamellers (Midlands) Ltd	
G-TAPE	PA-23 Aztec 250D	D. J. Hare (G-AWVW)	
G-TART	PA-28-236 Dakota	Withercourt Ltd	
G-TASK	Cessna 404	Bravo Aviation Ltd	
G-TATE	Cameron A-180 balloon	Freetime (UK) Ltd	
G-TATT	GY-20 Minicab	L. Tattershall	
G-TAXI	PA-23 Aztec 250E	Yorkair Ltd/Leeds	
G-TAYI	Grob G.115	Tayside Aviation Ltd (G-DODO)/Dundee	
G-TAYS	Cessna F.152	Tayside Aviation Ltd (G-LFCA)/Dundee	
G-TBAC	Short SD3-60 Variant 100	BAC Leasing Ltd/Gill Aviation (G-BMNK)	
G-TBAG	Murphy Renegade II	M. R. Tetley	
G-TBIO	SOCATA TB.10 Tobago	R. A. Perrot	
G-TBIX	MDH Hughes 369E	Weetabix Ltd/Sywell	
G-TBXX	SOCATA TB.20 Trinidad	D. A. Phillips & Co	
G-TBZO	SOCATA TB.20 Trinidad	D. L. Clarke & M. J. M. Hopper/Shoreham	
G-TCAN	Colt 69A balloon	Thunder & Colt Ltd	
G-TCAR	Robin HR.100/210	Gibad Aviation Ltd	
G-TCMP	Robinson R-22B	M. S. Wilford	
G-TCSL	R. Commander 112A	Trans-Channel Services Ltd	
G-TCTC	PA-28RT-201 Arrow IV	Terry Coleman (UK) Ltd	
G-TCUB	Piper J-3C-65 Cub	C. Kirk	
G-TDFS	IMCO Callair A.9	Dollarhigh Ltd (G-AVZA)	
G-TEAC	AT-6C Harvard IIA (889696)	E. C. English/North Weald	
G-TEAL	Thurston TSC-1A1 Teal	K. Heeley	
G-TECC	Aeronca 7AC Champion	T. E. C. Cushing/Little Snoring	
G-TECH	R. Commander 114	P. A. Reed (G-BEDH)/Denham	
G-TECK	Cameron V-77 balloon	G. M. N. Spencer	
G-TEDF	Cameron N-90 balloon	Fort Vale Engineering Ltd	
G-TEDS	SOCATA TB.10 Tobago	E. W. Lyon (G-BHCO)	
G-TEDY	Evans VP-1	C. J. D. Edwards (G-BHGN)	
G-TEFC	PA-28 Cherokee 140	A. R. Knight	
G-TEFH	Cessna 500 Citation	Birmingham Aviation Ltd (G-BCII)	
G-TELL	Cessna 421C	Holding & Barnes Ltd	
G-TELY	Agusta A.109A-II	Castle Air Charters Ltd	
G-TEMP	PA-28 Cherokee 180	BEV Piper Group (G-AYBK)/Andrewsfield	
G-TEMT	Hawker Tempest II	Autokraft Ltd	
G-TENT	J/1N Alpha	R. Callaway-Lewis (G-AKJU)	
G-TERY	PA-28-181 Archer II	T. Barlow (G-BOXZ)/Barton	
G-TESS	Quickie Q.2	D. Evans	
G-TEST	PA-34-200 Seneca	Stapleford Flying Club Ltd (G-BLCD)	
G-TEWS	PA-28 Cherokee 140	M. J. & M. J. Tew (G-KEAN/G-AWTM)	
G-TFCI	Cessna FA.152	Tayside Aviation Ltd/Dundee	
G-TFOX	Denney Aerocraft Kitfox Mk 2	F. A. Roberts	
G-TFRB	Air Command 532 Elite	F. R. Blennerhassett	
G-TFUN	Valentin Taifun 17E	NW Taifun Group	
G-TGAS	Cameron O-160 balloon	G. A. Fisher	
G-TGER	AA-5B Tiger	A. Wuensche (G-BFZP)	
G-THCL	Cessna 550 Citation II	Tower House Consultants Ltd	
G-THEA	Boeing Stearman E.75	L. M. Walton	
G-THLS	MBB Bo 105DBS/4	Bond Helicopters Ltd (G-BCXO)	
G-THOM	Thunder Ax6-56 balloon	T. H. Wilson	
G-THOR	Thunder Ax8-105 balloon	N. C. Faithfull/Holland	
G-THOS	Thunder Ax7-77 balloon	M. J. Wilson-Whittaker & S. Walkin	
G-THSL	PA-28R-201 Arrow III	G. Fearnley/Southend	
G-THUR	Beech 200 Super King Air	Flightline Ltd/Southend	
G-TIBC	Cameron A-180 balloon	Aerial Promotions Ltd	

Notes	Reg.	Type	Owner or Operator
	G-TICK	Cameron V-77 balloon	T. J. Tickler
	G-TIDS	Jodel D.150	J. B. Dovey/Ipswich
	G-TIGA	D.H.82A Tiger Moth	D. E. Leatherland (G-AOEG)
	G-TIGB	AS.332L Super Puma	Bristow Helicopters Ltd (G-BJXC)
	G-TIGC	AS.332L Super Puma	Bristow Helicopters Ltd (G-BJYH)
	G-TIGE	AS.332L Super Puma	Bristow Helicopters Ltd (G-BJYJ)
	G-TIGF	AS.332L Super Puma	Bristow Helicopters Ltd
	G-TIGG	AS.332L Super Puma	Bristow Helicopters Ltd
	G-TIGI	AS.332L Super Puma	Bristow Helicopters Ltd
	G-TIGK	AS.332L Super Puma	Bristow Helicopters Ltd
	G-TIGL	AS.332L Super Puma	Bristow Helicopters Ltd
	G-TIGM	AS.332L Super Puma	Bristow Helicopters Ltd
	G-TIGO	AS.332L Super Puma	Bristow Helicopters Ltd
	G-TIGP	AS.332L Super Puma	Bristow Helicopters Ltd
	G-TIGR	AS.332L Super Puma	Bristow Helicopters Ltd
	G-TIGS	AS.332L Super Puma	Bristow Helicopters Ltd
	G-TIGT	AS.332L Super Puma	Bristow Helicopters Ltd
	G-TIGU	AS.332L Super Puma	Bristow Helicopters Ltd
	G-TIGV	AS.332L Super Puma	Bristow Helicopters Ltd
	G-TIGW	AS.332L Super Puma	Bristow Helicopters Ltd
	G-TIGZ	AS.332L Super Puma	British International Helicopters
	G-TIII	Aerotek Pitts S-2A	Aerobatic Displays Ltd (G-BGSE)/Booker
	G-TILE	Robinson R-22B	S. Lee
	G-TILL	Robinson R-22B	G. Till
	G-TILT	Bell 206B JetRanger 3	Aviation Metals Ltd (G-BRJO)
	G-TIMB	Rutan Vari-Eze	T. M. Bailey (G-BKXJ)
	G-TIME	Ted Smith Aerostar 601P	Business Aircraft Rental Service Ltd
	G-TIMJ	Rand KR-2	N. Seaton
	G-TIMK	PA-28-181 Archer II	T. Baker
	G-TIMM	Folland Gnat T.1 (XM693)	T. J. Manna/Leavesden
	G-TIMP	Aeronca 7BCM Champion	T. E. Phillips
	G-TIMS	Falconar F-12A	T. Sheridan
	G-TIMW	PA-28 Cherokee 140C	W. H. Sanders (G-AXSH)
	G-TINA	SOCATA TB.10 Tobago	A. Lister
	G-TINS	Cameron N-90 balloon	Bass & Tennent Sales Ltd
	G-TJAY	PA-22 Tri-Pacer 135	T. M. Justice
	G-TJHI	Cessna 500 Citation	Trustair Ltd (G-CCCL/G-BEIZ)/Blackpool
	G-TKIS	Tri Kis	T. J. Bone
	G-TKPZ	Cessna 310R	Auxili-Air Aviation Ltd (G-BRAH)/Humberside
	G-TLOL	Cessna 421C	Littlewoods Organisation Ltd/Liverpool
	G-TMKI	P.56 Provost T.1	T. J. Manna/Leavesden
	G-TMMC	AS.355F-1 Twin Squirrel	The Colt Car Co Ltd (G-JLCO)
	G-TNTA	BAe 146-200QT	TNT Express Worldwide Ltd
	G-TNTB	BAe 146-200QT	TNT Express Worldwide Ltd
	G-TNTE	BAe 146-300QT	TNT Express Worldwide Ltd (G-BRPW)
	G-TNTG	BAe 146-300QT	TNT European Airlines Ltd (G-BSUY)
	G-TNTK	BAe 146-300QT	TNT European Airlines Ltd (G-BSXL)
	G-TNTL	BAe 146-300QT	TNT European Airlines Ltd (G-BSGI)
	G-TNTM	BAe 146-300QT	TNT European Airlines Ltd (G-BSLZ)
	G-TNTN	Thunder Ax6-56 balloon	D. P. & A. Dickinson
	G-TNTO	BAe 146-200QT	TNT Express Worldwide Ltd (G-BPBS)
	G-TNTP	BAe 146-200QT	TNT Express Worldwide Ltd (G-BOMI)
	G-TOAD	Jodel D.140B	Mothballs Ltd
	G-TOAK	SOCATA TB.20 Trinidad	Self Adhesive Fixings Ltd
	G-TOBA	SOCATA TB.10 Tobago	E. Downing
	G-TOBE	PA-28R Cherokee Arrow 200	J. Bradley & Barry Ltd (G-BNRO)
	G-TOBI	Cessna F.172K	G. Hall (G-AYVB)
	G-TODD	ICA IS-28M2A	C. I. Roberts & C. D. King
	G-TOFT	Colt 90A balloon	C. S. Perceval
	G-TOMI	H.S.125 Srs 600B	Falcon Jet Centre Ltd(G-BBEP/G-BJOY)/Heathrow
	G-TOMS	PA-38-112 Tomahawk	R. J. Alford
	G-TOMY	Mitsubishi Mu.300 Diamond	Lynton Aviation Ltd
	G-TONE	Pazmany PL.4	J. A. Walmsley
	G-TONI	Cessna 421C	M. Scott
	G-TONW	McD Douglas MD-83	Airtours International Aviation Ltd
	G-TOOL	Thunder Ax8-105 balloon	W. J. Honey
	G-TOPS	AS.355F-1 Twin Squirrel	ICS Worldwide Couriers Ltd (G-BPRH)
	G-TORE	P.84 Jet Provost T.3A (XM405)	Butane Buzzard Aviation Corpn Ltd
	G-TOTO	Cessna F.177RG	C. R. & J. Cox (G-OADE/G-AZKH)
	G-TOUR	Robin R.2112	Barnes Martin Ltd
	G-TOWS	PA-25 Pawnee 260	Blackpool & Fylde Gliding Club Ltd

Reg.	Type	Owner or Operator	Notes
G-TOYS	Enstrom 280C-UK-2 Shark	B. Murphy (G-BISE)	
G-TRAN	Beech 76 Duchess	Transair (UK) Ltd (G-NIFR)/Fairoaks	
G-TRAV	Cameron A-210 balloon	Bakers World Travel Ltd	
G-TREE	Bell 206B JetRanger 3	LGH Aviation Ltd	
G-TREK	Jodel D.18	R. H. Mole	
G-TREN	Boeing 737-4S3	British Airways (G-BRKG)	
G-TRIC	D.H.C.1 Chipmunk 22A	D. M. Barnett (G-AOSZ)	
G-TRIK	Bell 206B JetRanger 2	Annabelle Casion Ltd (G-BMWY)	
G-TRIM	Monnet Moni	J. E. Bennell	
G-TRIN	SOCATA TB.20 Trinidad	Isnet Ltd	
G-TRIO	Cessna 172M	Biggin Hill School of Flying (G-BNXY)	
G-TRIP	PA-32R-301 Saratoga SP	C. P. Lockyer (G-HOSK)	
G-TRIX	V.S.509 Spitfire T.IX (PV202)	R. A. Roberts	
G-TROP	Cessna 310R	R. A. D. Wilson & D. J. Morris	
G-TRUC	Cassutt Speed One	J. A. H. Chadwick	
G-TRUK	Stoddard-Hamilton Glasair RG	Compustar Ltd	
G-TRUX	Colt 77A balloon	Highway Truck Rental Ltd	
G-TSAM	BAe 125 Srs 800B	British Aerospace PLC/Hatfield	
G-TSFT	PA-28-161 Warrior II	SFT Aviation Ltd (G-BLDJ)/Bournemouth	
G-TSGJ	PA-28-181 Archer II	Golf Juliet Flying Club	
G-TSIX	AT-6C Harvard IIA	D. Taylor/E. Midlands	
G-TSMI	R. Commander 114	W. P. J. Davison	
G-TTAM	Taylor JT.2 Titch	C. H. Morris	
G-TTEL	PA-E23 Aztec 250D	Target Technology Electronics Ltd (G-BBXE)	
G-TTHC	Robinson R-22B	Paul Hopper Entertainments Ltd	
G-TTPT	McD Douglas MD-83	Airtours International Aviation Ltd	
G-TTWO	Colt 56A balloon	P. N. Tilney	
G-TUBS	Beech 65-80 Queen Air	A. H. Bowers (G-ASKM)/Staverton	
G-TUDR	Cameron V-77 balloon	Jacques W. Soukup Ltd	
G-TUGG	PA-18 Super Cub 150	Ulster Gliding Club Ltd	
G-TUKE	Robin DR.400/160	Tukair/Headcorn	
G-TURB	D.31 Turbulent	A. Ryan-Fecitt	
G-TURK	Cameron 80 Sultan SS balloon	Forbes Europe Inc/France	
G-TURN	Steen Skybolt	M. Hammond	
G-TVIJ	CCF Harvard IV (T-6J) (28521)	R. W. Davies (G-BSBE)	
G-TVMM	Cessna 310Q	TVMM Aviation Ltd (G-CETA/G-BBIM)	
G-TVPA	AS.355F-1 Twin Squirrel	Thames Valley Police Authority (G-BPRI)	
G-TVSI	Campbell Cricket	W. H. Beevers (G-AYHH)	
G-TVTV	Cameron 90 TV SS balloon	Cameron Balloons Ltd	
G-TWEL	PA-28-181 Archer II	Universal Salvage (Holdings) Ltd	
G-TWEY	Colt 69A balloon	British Telecom Thameswey	
G-TWIN	PA-44-180 Seminole	Leavesden Flight Centre Ltd	
G-TWIZ	R. Commander 114	B. C. Cox & K. E. Kirkland	
G-TYGA	AA-5B Tiger	Hovemere Ltd (G-BHNZ)/Biggin Hill	
G-TYRE	Cessna F.172M	Staverton Flying Services Ltd	
G-UBBE	Cameron Clown SS balloon	Cameron Balloons Ltd	
G-UDAY	Robinson R-22B	Oakover Holdings Ltd	
G-UEST	Bell 206B JetRanger 2	Leisure & Retail Consultants Ltd (G-ROYB/ G-BLWU)	
G-UFLY	Cessna F.150H	Westair Flying Services Ltd (G-AVVY)/ Blackpool	
G-UIDA	Aero Designs Star-Lite SL.1	I. J. Widger (G-BRKK)	
G-UIDE	Jodel D.120	S. T. Gilbert/Popham	
G-UIET	BAe ATP	Manx Airlines Ltd/Ronaldsway	
G-UILD	Grob G.109B	Runnymede Consultants Ltd	
G-UKAC	BAe 146-300	Air UK Ltd/Stansted	
G-UKAG	BAe 146-300	Air UK Ltd/Stansted	
G-UKFA	Fokker 100	Air UK Ltd/Stansted	
G-UKFB	Fokker 100	Air UK Ltd/Stansted	
G-UKFC	Fokker 100	Air UK Ltd/Stansted	
G-UKFD	Fokker 100	Air UK Ltd/Stansted	
G-UKFE	Fokker 100	Air UK Ltd/Stansted	
G-UKFF	Fokker 100	Air UK Ltd/Stansted	
G-UKFG	Fokker 100	Air UK Ltd/Stansted	
G-UKFH	Fokker 100	Air UK Ltd/Stansted	
G-UKFI	Fokker 100	Air UK Ltd/Stansted	
G-UKHP	BAe 146-300	Air UK Ltd/Stansted	
G-UKID	BAe 146-300	Air UK Ltd/Stansted	
G-UKJF	BAe 146-100	Air UK Ltd/Stansted	
G-UKLA	Boeing 737-4Y0	Air UK Leisure Ltd St Andrew/Stansted	
G-UKLB	Boeing 737-4Y0	Air UK Leisure Ltd St Bernard/Stansted	

Notes	Reg.	Type	Owner or Operator
	G-UKLC	Boeing 737-42C	Air UK Leisure Ltd *St Christopher*/Stansted
	G-UKLD	Boeing 737-42C	Air UK Leisure Ltd *St David*/Stansted
	G-UKLE	Boeing 737-4Y0	Air UK Leisure Ltd *St Emilion*/Stansted
	G-UKLF	Boeing 737-42C	Air UK Leisure Ltd *St Francis*/Stansted
	G-UKLG	Boeing 737-42C	Air UK Leisure Ltd *St George*/Stansted
	G-UKLH	Boeing 767-39HER	Leisure International Airways Ltd *Caribbean Star*
	G-UKLI	Boeing 767-39HER	Leisure International Airways Ltd *Atlantic Star*
	G-UKLM	Sikorsky S-76B	KLM ERA Helicopters BV/Schiphol
	G-UKLN	BAe 146-200	Air UK Ltd (G-BNKJ)/Stansted
	G-UKPC	BAe 146-100	British Aerospace PLC (G-BKXZ)
	G-UKRB	Colt 105A balloon	Airship & Balloon Co Ltd
	G-UKRC	BAe 146-300	Air UK Ltd (G-BSMR)/Stansted
	G-UKRH	BAe 146-200	Air UK Ltd (G-BRNG)/Stansted
	G-UKSC	BAe 146-300	Air UK Ltd/Stansted
	G-ULIA	Cameron V-77 balloon	J. & R. Bayly
	G-ULPS	Everett Srs 1 gyroplane	The Aziz Corporation Ltd (G-BMNY)
	G-UMBO	Thunder Ax7-77A balloon	Airship & Balloon Co Ltd
	G-UMMI	PA-31-310 Turbo Navajo	Everts Balloon Co Ltd (G-BGSO)
	G-UNDY	Cessna 340	Morris Cohen (Underwear) Ltd (G-BBNR)
	G-UNIK	AB-206B JetRanger 2	First City Air PLC (G-TPPH/G-BCYP)
	G-UNIP	Cameron Oil Container SS balloon	Flying Pictures (Balloons) Ltd
	G-UNIT	Partenavia P.68B	Phlight Avia Ltd & Rhodair Aircraft Maintenance Ltd (G-BCNT)
	G-UPCC	Robinson R-22B	Deltair Ltd (G-MUSS)
	G-UPDN	Cameron V-65 balloon	R. J. O. Evans
	G-UPHL	Cameron 80 Concept SS balloon	Uphil Motor Co Ltd
	G-UPMW	Robinson R-22B	M. Wood Haulage
	G-UPPP	Colt 77A balloon	M. Williams
	G-UPPY	Cameron DP-80 balloon	Jacques W. Soukup Enterprises Ltd
	G-UPUP	Cameron V-77 balloon	S. F. Burden
	G-UROP	Beech 95-B55 Baron	Pooler International Ltd
	G-URRR	Air Command 582 Sport	L. Armes
	G-USAM	Cameron Uncle Sam SS balloon	Jacques W. Soukup Enterprises Ltd
	G-USGB	Colt 105A balloon	Thunder & Colt Ltd
	G-USIL	Thunder Ax7-77 balloon	Capital Balloon Club Ltd
	G-USMC	Cameron 90 Chestie SS balloon	Jacques W. Soukup Enterprises Ltd
	G-USSR	Cameron 90 Doll SS balloon	Jacques W. Soukup Enterprises Ltd
	G-USSY	PA-28-181 Archer II	Western Air Training Ltd/Thruxton
	G-USTI	Cameron H-34 balloon	Allen & Harris Ltd
	G-USTV	Messerschmitt Bf.109G-2 (6)	Imperial War Museum/Duxford
	G-USTY	FRED Srs 2	K. Jones
	G-UTSI	Rand KR-2	K. B. Gutridge
	G-UTSY	PA-28R-201 Arrow III	D. G. Perry/Stapleford
	G-UTZY	SA.341G Gazelle 1	Da Vinci Aviation Ltd (G-BKLV)
	G-UZEL	SA.341G Gazelle 1	Kepak Ltd (G-BRNH)
	G-UZLE	Colt 77A balloon	Flying Pictures (Balloons) Ltd
	G-VAEL	Airbus A.340-311	Virgin Atlantic Airways Ltd
	G-VAGA	PA-15 Vagabond	G. L. Carpenter
	G-VAJT	M.S.894E Rallye 220GT	R. W. B. Rolfe
	G-VANS	Van's RV-4	T. R. Grief
	G-VANZ	Van's RV-6A	S. J. Baxter
	G-VARG	Varga 2150A Kachina	J. Hannibal/Halfpenny Green
	G-VAUN	Cessna 340	H. E. Peacock
	G-VBUS	Airbus A.340-311	Virgin Atlantic Airways Ltd *Lady in Red*
	G-VCJH	Robinson R-22B	Great Northern Helicopters Ltd
	G-VCSI	Rotorway Executive	Qual-Rect Ltd
	G-VDIR	Cessna T.310R	Van Diemen International Racing Ltd
	G-VELA	SIAI-Marchetti S.205-22R	D. P. & P. A. Dawson
	G-VENI	D.H.112 Venom FB.50 (WE402)	Source Premium & Promotional Consultants Ltd/Cranfield
	G-VERT	Bell 222	Arlington Securities PLC (G-JLBZ/G-BNDB)
	G-VFAB	Boeing 747-4Q8	Virgin Atlantic Airways Ltd
	G-VFLY	Airbus A.340-311	Virgin Atlantic Airways Ltd
	G-VGIN	Boeing 747-243B	Virgin Atlantic Airways Ltd *Scarlet Lady*/Gatwick
	G-VHFA	PA-23 Aztec 250	Hartfield Aviation Ltd (G-BZFE/G-AZFE)
	G-VIBA	Cameron DP-80 airship	Jacques W. Soukup Enterprises Ltd
	G-VICC	PA-28-161 Warrior II	Design Publications Ltd (G-JFHL)
	G-VICM	Beech F33C Bonanza	Charles W. Michie Ltd

Reg.	Type	Owner or Operator	Notes
G-VIDI	D.H.112 Venom FB.50	Source Premium & Promotional Consultants Ltd/Cranfield	
G-VIEW	Vinten-Wallis WA-116/100	K. H. Wallis	
G-VIKE	Bellanca 1730A Viking	Peter Dolan & Co Ltd	
G-VIKY	Cameron A-120 balloon	D. W. Pennell	
G-VIPI	BAe 125 Srs 800B	Yeates of Leicester Ltd	
G-VIPP	PA-31-350 Navajo Chieftain	Magenta Ltd (G-OGRV/G-BMPX)	
G-VIRG	Boeing 747-287B	Virgin Atlantic Airways Ltd *Maiden Voyager*/Gatwick	
G-VISA	Cessna A.152	K. W. Felton	
G-VITE	Robin R.1180T	G-VITE Flying Group	
G-VIVA	Thunder Ax7-65 balloon	N. Duppa-Miller	
G-VIXN	D.H.110 Sea Vixen FAW.2 (XS587) ★	P. G. Vallance Ltd/Charlwood	
G-VIZZ	Sportavia RS.180 Sportsman	Exeter Fournier Group	
G-VJAI	GA-7 Cougar	UB Air Ltd (G-OCAB/G-BICF)/Elstree	
G-VJCB	Agusta A.109A-II	J. C. Bamford Excavators Ltd (G-BOUA)	
G-VJCT	Partenavia P.68C	Gough Kneale Group	
G-VJET	Avro 698 Vulcan B.2 (XL426) ★	Vulcan Restoration Trust/Southend	
G-VJFK	Boeing 747-238B	Virgin Atlantic Airways Ltd *Boston Belle*/Gatwick	
G-VJIM	Colt 77 Jumbo Jim SS balloon	Airship & Balloon Co Ltd	
G-VLAD	Yakovlev Yak-50	W. J. J. Kamper	
G-VLAX	Boeing 747-238B	Virgin Atlantic Airways Ltd *California Girl*/Gatwick	
G-VMAX	Mooney M.20K	Glidegold Ltd	
G-VMDE	Cessna P.210N	Royton Express Deliveries (Welwyn) Ltd	
G-VMIA	Boeing 747-123	Virgin Atlantic Airways Ltd (G-HIHO) *The Spirit of Sir Freddie*	
G-VMJM	SOCATA TB.10 Tobago	J. H. Michaels (G-BTOK)	
G-VNOM	D.H.112 Venom FB.50	A. Topen/Cranfield	
G-VODA	Cameron N-77 balloon	Racal Telecom PLC	
G-VOID	PA-28RT-201 Arrow IV	Newbus Aviation Ltd	
G-VOLT	Cameron N-77 balloon	National Power	
G-VOYG	Boeing 747-283B	Virgin Atlantic Airways Ltd (G-BMGS) *Shady Lady*	
G-VPII	Evans VP-2	V. D. J. Hitchings (G-EDIF)	
G-VPSJ	Shaw Europa	J. D. Bean	
G-VRVI	Cameron O-90 balloon	Cooling Services Ltd	
G-VSBC	Beech B200 Super King Air	Vickers Shipbuilding & Engineering Ltd	
G-VSKY	Airbus A.340-311	Virgin Atlantic Airways Ltd	
G-VSOP	Cameron 60 Bottle SS balloon	J. R. Parkington & Co Ltd	
G-VTAX	PA-31-350 Navajo Chieftain	Jet West Ltd/Exeter	
G-VTII	D.H.115 Vampire T.11 (WZ507)	J. Turnbull & ptnrs/Cranfield	
G-VTOL	H.S. Harrier T.52 ★	Brooklands Museum of Aviation/Weybridge	
G-VULC	Avro 698 Vulcan B.2A (XM655) ★	Radarmoor Ltd/Wellesbourne	
G-VVBK	PA-34-200T Seneca II	Computaplane Ltd (G-BSBS/G-BDRI)	
G-VVIP	Cessna 421C	Capital Trading Aviation Ltd (G-BMWB)	
G-VYGR	Colt 120A balloon	Voyager Balloons	
G-WAAC	Cameron N-56 balloon	Newbury Ballooning Co Ltd	
G-WACA	Cessna F.152	Wycombe Air Centre Ltd	
G-WACB	Cessna F.152	Wycombe Air Centre Ltd	
G-WACC	Cessna F.152	Wycombe Air Centre Ltd	
G-WACE	Cessna F.152	Wycombe Air Centre Ltd	
G-WACF	Cessna 152	Wycombe Air Centre Ltd	
G-WACG	Cessna F.152	Wycombe Air Centre Ltd	
G-WACH	Cessna FA.152	Wycombe Air Centre Ltd	
G-WACI	Beech 76 Duchess	Wycombe Air Centre Ltd	
G-WACJ	Beech 76 Duchess	Wycombe Air Centre Ltd	
G-WACK	Short SD3-60 Variant 100	Loganair Ltd (G-BMAJ)/Glasgow	
G-WACL	Cessna F.172N	Wycombe Air Centre Ltd (G-BHGG)	
G-WACO	Waco UPF-7	RGV (Aircraft Services) & Co/Staverton	
G-WACP	PA-28 Cherokee 180	RAF Halton Aeroplane Club Ltd	
G-WACR	PA-28 Cherokee 180	Wycombe Air Centre Ltd (G-BCZF)	
G-WACS	Cessna F.152	RAF Halton Aeroplane Club Ltd	
G-WACT	Cessna F.152-II	Plymouth School of Flying Ltd (G-BFKT)	
G-WACU	Cessna FA.152	Hartmann Ltd (G-BJZU)/Booker	
G-WACW	Cessna 172P	Wycombe Air Centre Ltd	
G-WACY	Cessna F.172P	Wycombe Air Centre Ltd	
G-WACZ	Cessna F.172M	Wycombe Air Centre Ltd (G-BCUK)	
G-WAFT	BAe Jetstream 4100	Manx Airlines Ltd	

Notes	Reg.	Type	Owner or Operator
	G-WAGI	Robinson R-22B	J. Wagstaff
	G-WAIR	PA-32-301 Saratoga	Ware Aviation Ltd
	G-WAIT	Cameron V-77 balloon	G. & D. A. Waite
	G-WALS	Cessna A.152	Redhill Flying Club
	G-WALT	Cameron Flying Castle SS balloon	Cameron Balloons Ltd
	G-WAND	BAe Jetstream 4100	Manx Airlines Ltd
	G-WARD	Taylor JT.1 Monoplane	A. Nelson
	G-WARE	PA-28-161 Warrior II	W. J. Ware
	G-WARI	PA-28-161 Warrior II	Abraxas Aviation Ltd
	G-WARK	Schweizer 269C	Warwickshire Constabulary
	G-WARR	PA-28-161 Warrior II	T. J. & G. M. Laundy
	G-WASH	Noble 1250 balloon	Noble Adventures Ltd
	G-WASP	Brantly B.2B	W. C. Evans & M. L. Morris (G-ASXE)
	G-WATH	Colt 77A balloon	Ballooning Adventures Ltd
	G-WATS	PA-34-220T Seneca III	Aerohire Ltd (G-BOVJ)/Halfpenny Green
	G-WATT	Cameron Cooling Tower SS balloon	National Power
	G-WATZ	PA-28-151 Warrior	Air Nova/Liverpool
	G-WAVE	Grob G.109B	M. L. Murdoch/Cranfield
	G-WAWL	BAe Jetstream 4102	Manx Airlines Ltd
	G-WAWR	BAe Jetstream 4102	Manx Airlines Ltd
	G-WAYR	BAe Jetstream 4102	Manx Airlines Ltd
	G-WBAT	Wombat gyroplane	C. D. Julian (G-BSID)
	G-WBMG	Cameron N Ele-90 balloon	WBMG Environmental Communications (G-BUYV)
	G-WBPR	BAe 125 Srs 800B	Trusthouse Forte PLC/Heathrow
	G-WBTS	Falconair F-11	W. C. Brown (G-BDPL)
	G-WCAT	Colt Flying Mitt SS balloon	Interline Develoments Ltd
	G-WCEI	M.S.894E Rallye 220GT	R. A. L. Lucas (G-BAOC)
	G-WDEB	Thunder Ax-7-77 balloon	W. de Bock
	G-WEEZ	Mooney M.20J	Weyland Ltd
	G-WELA	SA.341G Gazelle 1	Weller Helicopters Ltd (G-SFTD/G-RIFC)
	G-WELI	Cameron N-77 balloon	M. A. Shannon
	G-WELL	Beech E90 King Air	CEGA Aviation Ltd/Goodwood
	G-WELS	Cameron N-65 balloon	K. J. VIckery
	G-WEND	PA-28RT-201 Arrow IV	Chingford Magnetic Signs
	G-WENT	BAe Jetstream 3102	British Aerospace PLC (G-IBLW)
	G-WERY	SOCATA TB.20 Trinidad	Wery Flying Group/Sherburn
	G-WEST	Agusta A.109A	Westland Helicopters Ltd/Yeovil
	G-WESX	CFM Streak Shadow	Wessex Aviation Ltd
	G-WETI	Cameron N-31 balloon	C. A. Butter & J. J. T. Cooke
	G-WFFW	PA-28-161 Warrior II	D. F. F. Williams
	G-WGAL	Bell 206B JetRanger 3	Watkiss Group Aviation Ltd (G-OICS)
	G-WGCS	PA-18 Super Cub 95	S. C. Thompson
	G-WGSC	Pilatus PC-6/B2-H4 Turbo Porter	D. M. Penny
	G-WHAT	Colt 77A balloon	Thunder & Colt Ltd
	G-WHFO	Colt 10 Bottle SS balloon	Airship & Balloon Co Ltd (G-BUCN)
	G-WHIM	Colt 77A balloon	D. L. Morgan
	G-WHIR	Montgomerie-Bensen B.8MR	A. P. Barden (G-BROT)
	G-WHIZ	Pitts S-1 Special	K. M. McLeod
	G-WHIZ†	V.701 Viscount ★	Saltwell Park (G-AMOE)/Gateshead
	G-WHOW	Thunder Ax7-65 balloon	Thunder & Colt Ltd
	G-WHRL	Schweizer 269C	Aviation Metals Ltd
	G-WICK	Partenavia P.68B	J. C. Taylor (G-BGFZ)
	G-WIEN	Rans S.10 Sakota	C. B. Sloots
	G-WILD	Pitts S-1T Special	S. W. Knox
	G-WILI	PA-32R-301 Saratoga SP	Minster Enterprises Ltd
	G-WILY	Rutan LongEz	G. V. Waters
	G-WIMP	Colt 56A balloon	C. Wolstenholme *Wimp*
	G-WINE	Thunder Ax7-77Z balloon	R. Brooker
	G-WINK	AA-5B Tiger	B. St J. Cooke
	G-WINS	PA-32 Cherokee Six 300	Cheyenne Ltd
	G-WIRE	AS.355F-1 Twin Squirrel	National Grid Co PLC (G-CEGB/G-BLJL)
	G-WIRL	Robinson R-22B	C. A. Rosenberg
	G-WISH	Lindstrand LBL Cake SS balloon	Oxford Promotions (UK) Ltd
	G-WIZD	Lindstrand 180A balloon	T. H. Wilson
	G-WIZO	PA-34-220T Seneca III	Extrajet Ltd
	G-WIZZ	AB-206B JetRanger 2	Lateq Aviation Ltd
	G-WLLY	Bell 206A JetRanger	J. W. F. Ashworth (G-RODY/G-ROGR/ G-AXMM)
	G-WMCC	BAe Jetstream 3102	Maersk Air (G-TALL)/Birmingham
	G-WMPA	AS.355F-2 Twin Squirrel	W. Midlands Police Authority/Birmingham

Reg.	Type	Owner or Operator	Notes
G-WMTM	AA-5B Tiger	T. & W. E. Menham/Biggin Hill	
G-WOLF	PA-28 Cherokee 140	N. B. Savage	
G-WOOD	Beech 95-B55A Baron	T. D. Broadhurst (G-AYID)	
G-WOOL	Colt 77A balloon	A. P. Woolhouse	
G-WORK	Thunder Ax10-180 S2 balloon	T. J. Bucknall	
G-WOSP	Bell 206B JetRanger 3	Lakeside Helicopters Ltd	
G-WOTG	BN-2T Islander	RAF Sport Parachute Association (G-BJYT)	
G-WOZA	PA-32RT-300 Lance II	O. C. Kruppa (G-BYBB)/Germany	
G-WRCF	Beech 200 Super King Air	W. R. C. M. Foyle/Luton	
G-WREN	Pitts S-2A Special	Northamptonshire School of Flying Ltd/ Sywell	
G-WRFM	Enstrom 280C-UK Shark	Skywalker Enterprises (G-CTSI/G-BKIO)/ Shoreham	
G-WRIT	Thunder Ax7-77A balloon	J. Edge	
G-WRLD	Cameron R-15 gas balloon	Cameron Balloons Ltd	
G-WRMN	Glaser-Dirks DG.400	W. R. McNair	
G-WSEC	Enstrom F-28C	M. J. Easy (G-BONF)	
G-WSFT	PA-23 Aztec 250F	SFT Aviation Ltd (G-BTHS)/Bournemouth	
G-WSKY	Enstrom 280C-UK-2 Shark	GTS Engineering (Coventry) Ltd (G-BEEK)	
G-WTBC	Partenavia P.68C	Wild Touch Aviazione Ltd (G-SITU/G-NEWU/ G-BHJX)	
G-WULF	WAR Focke-Wulf Fw.190 (08)	P. C. Logsdon	
G-WWII	V.S. 379 Spitfire XIV (SM832)	Patina Ltd/Duxford	
G-WYCH	Cameron 90 Witch SS balloon	Jacques W. Soukup Enterprises Ltd	
G-WYLX	Cessna 550 Citation II	Citation Lesaing Ltd (G-JETD)	
G-WYMP	Cessna F.150J	L. Scattergood & R. Hall (G-BAGW)	
G-WYNN	Rand KR-2	W. Thomas	
G-WYNS	Aero Designs Pulsar XP	G. Griffith	
G-WYNT	Cameron N-56 balloon	Jacques W. Soukup Enterprises Ltd	
G-WYPA	MBB Bo 105DBS/4	W. Yorkshire Police Authority	
G-WYTE	Bell 47G-2A-1	Howden Helicopters/Spaldington	
G-WYZZ	Air Command 532 Elite	C. H. Gem (G-BPAK)	
G-WZZZ	Colt AS-56 airship	Hot-Air Balloon Co Ltd	
G-XALP	Schweizer 269C	R. F. Jones	
G-XANT	Cameron N-105 balloon	Flying Pictures (Balloons) Ltd	
G-XCUB	PA-18 Super Cub 150	M. C. Barraclough	
G-XGBE	Cessna 340A	G. B. Express Ltd (G-MAGS)	
G-XIIX	Robinson R-22B	G. Clarke	
G-XLXL	Robin DR.400/160	Reinsurance Flying Group (G-BAUD)	
G-XPOL	AS.355F-1 Twin Squirrel	Aeromega Ltd (G-BPRF)	
G-XPXP	Aero Designs Pulsar XP	B. J. Edwards	
G-XRAY	Rand KR-2	R. S. Smith	
G-XRMC	BAe 125 Srs 800B	RMC Group Services Ltd	
G-XSFT	PA-23 Aztec 250F	SFT Aviation Ltd (G-CPPC/G-BGBH)/ Bournemouth	
G-XSKY	Cameron N-77 balloon	Ballooning World Ltd	
G-XTRA	Extra EA.230	Firebird Aerobatics Ltd/Booker	
G-XVIA	V.S.361 Spitfire LF.XVIe (RW382)	Historic Flying Ltd	
G-XVIE	V.S.361 Spitfire LF.XVIe	Historic Flying Ltd	
G-XXII	AB-206B JetRanger 2	Defence Products Ltd (G-GGCC/G-BEHG)	
G-XXIV	AB-206B JetRanger 3	Hampton Printing (Bristol) Ltd	
G-XXVI	Sukhoi Su-26M	A. N. Onn & T. R. G. Barnaby	
G-YAKS	Yakovlev Yak-52	Two Bees Associates Ltd	
G-YANK	PA-28-181 Archer II	E. T. Savidge	
G-YAWW	PA-28R-201T Turbo Arrow III	Barton Aviation Ltd	
G-YBAA	Cessna FR.172J	H. Norman	
G-YEOM	PA-31-350 Navajo Chieftain	Foster Yeoman Ltd/Exeter	
G-YEWS	Rotorway Executive	D. G. Pollard	
G-YIII	Cessna F.150L	Skyviews & General Ltd/Sherburn	
G-YJBM	Airbus A.320-231	Airtours International Airways Ltd (G-IEAF)	
G-YKSZ	Yakovlev Yak-52	Aerobuild Ltd	
G-YMYM	Lindstrand LBL Ice Cream SS balloon	Lindstrand Balloons Ltd	
G-YNOT	D.62B Condor	T. Littlefair (G-AYFH)	
G-YOGI	Robin DR.400/140B	R. M. & A. M. Gosling (G-BDME)	
G-YORK	Cessna F.172M	P. J. Smith	
G-YPSY	Andreasson BA-4B	C. Briggs	
G-YRAT	VPM M.16 Tandem Trainer	A. J. Unwin	
G-YRIL	Luscombe 8E Silvaire	C. Potter	
G-YROI	Air Command Commander 532	W. B. Lumb	
G-YROS	Bensen B.80-D	C. Tuxworth	

Notes	Reg.	Type	Owner or Operator
	G-YROY	Montgomerie-Bensen B.8MR	R. D. Armishaw
	G-YSFT	PA-23 Aztec 250F	SFT Aviation Ltd (G-BEJT)/Bournemouth
	G-YSKY	PA-31-350 Navajo Chieftain	Clacton Aero Club (1988) Ltd
	G-YTWO	Cessna F.172M	Sherburn Aero Club Ltd
	G-YUCS	PA-32R-301 Saratoga SP	Eastman Securities Ltd (G-BSOL)
	G-YUGO	H.S.125 Srs 1B/R-522	RCR Aviation Ltd (G-ATWH)
	G-YULL	PA-28 Cherokee 180E	Lansdowne Chemical Co (G-BEAJ)/ Kidlington
	G-YUMM	Cameron N-90 balloon	Wunderbar Ltd
	G-YUPI	Cameron N-90 balloon	H. C. Wright
	G-YURO	Shaw Europa	Europa Aviation Ltd
	G-YVET	Cameron V-90 balloon	K. J. Foster
	G-ZACH	Robin DR.400/100	G. de Botton (G-FTIO)
	G-ZAIR	Zenair CH 601HD	C. B. Shaw
	G-ZAND	Robinson R-22B	Sloane Helicopters Ltd/Sywell
	G-ZAPC	Short SD3-30 Variant 100	Titan Airways Ltd (G-RNMO/G-BFZW)/ Stansted
	G-ZAPD	Short SD3-60 Variant 100	Titan Airways Ltd (G-OLGW/G-BOFK)/ Stansted
	G-ZAPF	Short SD3-60 Variant 100	Titan Airways Ltd (G-OLTN/G-BOFH)/ Stansted
	G-ZAPG	Short SD3-60 Variant 100	Titan Airways Ltd (G-CPTL/G-BOFI)/ Stansted
	G-ZARA	Nord 3400	D. E. Bain & ptnrs
	G-ZARI	AA-5B Tiger	C. A. Ringrose (G-BHVY)
	G-ZAZA	PA-18 Super Cub 95	Airbourne Taxi Services Ltd
	G-ZBRA	Thunder Ax10-160 balloon	Zebra Ballooning Ltd
	G-ZEBO	Thunder Ax8-105 S2 balloon	E. Herndon
	G-ZEBR	Colt 210A balloon	Zebra Ballooning Ltd
	G-ZELL	SA.341G Gazelle 1	Sarpendon Ltd
	G-ZEPI	Colt GA-42 gas airship	Lindstrand Balloons Ltd (G-ISPY/G-BPRB)
	G-ZEPY	Colt GA-42 gas airship	Thunder & Colt Ltd (G-BSCU)
	G-ZERO	AA-5B Tiger	Snowadem Ltd/Luton
	G-ZFDB	AS.355F-1 Twin Squirrel	Haydon-Baillie Naval & Aircraft Museum (G-BLEV)/Southampton
	G-ZIGG	Robinson R-22B	Uriah Woodhead & Son Ltd
	G-ZIGI	Robin DR.400/180	J. Nivison
	G-ZIPI	Robin DR.400/180	Stahl Engineering Co Ltd/Headcorn
	G-ZIPP	Cessna E.310Q	Zipp Aviation Ltd (G-BAYU)
	G-ZIPY	Wittman W.8 Tailwind	M. J. Butler
	G-ZLIN	Z.526 Trener Master	R. P. Hallam
	G-ZSFT	PA-23 Aztec 250	SFT Aviation Ltd (G-SALT/G-BGTH)/ Bournemouth
	G-ZSOL	Zlin Z.50L	A. J. E. Ditheridge
	G-ZULU	PA-28-161 Warrior II	Denham School of Flying Ltd
	G-ZUMP	Cameron N-77 balloon	Allen & Harris Ltd
	G-ZUMY	Task Silouette	P. J. Wells
	G-ZZIP	Mooney M.20J	D. A. H. Dixon

G-BYAD, Boeing 767-204ER. AJW

G-UKFA, Fokker 100. *AJW*

G-LOGE, BAe ATP/Jetstream 61. *AJW*

Toy Balloons

Notes	Reg.	Type	Owner or Operator
	G-FYAN	Williams	M. D. Williams
	G-FYAO	Williams	M. D. Williams
	G-FYAU	Williams MK 2	M. D. Williams
	G-FYAV	Osprey Mk 4E2	C. D. Egan & C. Stiles
	G-FYAZ	Osprey Mk 4D2	M. A. Roblett
	G-FYBP	European E.84PW	D. Eaves
	G-FYBR	Osprey Mk 4G2	A. J. Pugh
	G-FYBU	Portswood Mk XVI	M. A. Roblett
	G-FYBX	Portswood Mk XVI	I. Chadwick
	G-FYCC	Osprey Mk 4G2	A. Russell
	G-FYCL	Osprey Mk 4G	P. J. Rogers
	G-FYCV	Osprey Mk 4D	M. Thomson
	G-FYCZ	Osprey Mk 4D2	P. Middleton
	G-FYDC	European EDH-1	D. Eaves & H. Goddard
	G-FYDF	Osprey Mk 4D	K. A. Jones
	G-FYDI	Williams Westwind Two	M. D. Williams
	G-FYDN	European 8C	P. D. Ridout
	G-FYDO	Osprey Mk 4D	N. L. Scallan
	G-FYDP	Williams Westwind Three	M. D. Williams
	G-FYDS	Osprey Mk 4D	N. L. Scallan
	G-FYDW	Osprey Mk 4B	R. A. Balfre
	G-FYEB	Rango Rega	N. H. Ponsford
	G-FYEI	Portswood Mk XVI	A. Russell
	G-FYEJ	Rango NA.24	N. H. Ponsford
	G-FYEK	Unicorn UE.1C	D. & D. Eaves
	G-FYEL	European E.84Z	D. Eaves
	G-FYEO	Eagle Mk 1	M. E. Scallon
	G-FYEV	Osprey Mk 1C	M. E. Scallen
	G-FYEZ	Firefly Mk 1	M. E. & N. L. Scallan
	G-FYFA	European E.84LD	D. Goddard & D. Eaves
	G-FYFG	European E.84DE	D. Eaves
	G-FYFH	European E.84DS	D. Eaves
	G-FYFI	European E.84DS	M. Stelling
	G-FYFJ	Williams Westland 2	M. D. Williams
	G-FYFN	Osprey Saturn 2	J. & M. Woods
	G-FYFT	Rango NA-32BC	Rango Kite & Balloon Co
	G-FYFV	Saffrey Grand Edinburgh	I. G. & G. M. McIntosh
	G-FYFW	Rango NA-55	Rango Kite & Balloon Co
	G-FYFY	Rango NA-55RC	A. M. Lindsay
	G-FYGA	Rango NA-50RC	Rango Kite & Balloon Co
	G-FYGB	Rango NA-105RC	Rango Kite & Balloon Co
	G-FYGC	Rango NA-42B	L. J. Wardle
	G-FYGH	Busby Buz B.20W	D. P. Busby
	G-FYGI	Rango NA-55RC	Advertair Ltd
	G-FYGJ	Airspeed 300	N. Wells
	G-FYGK	Rango NA-42POC	Rango Balloon & Kite Co
	G-FYGL	Glowball	J. J. Noble

Reg.	Type	Notes	Reg.	Type	Notes
G-MBAA	Hiway Skytrike Mk 2		G-MBFF	Southern Aerosports Scorpion	
G-MBAB	Hovey Whing-Ding II				
G-MBAD	Weedhopper JC-24A		G-MBFK	Hiway Demon	
G-MBAF	R. J. Swift 3		G-MBFM	Hiway Hang Glider	
G-MBAL	Hiway Demon		G-MBFU	Ultrasports Tripacer	
G-MBAM	Skycraft Scout 2		G-MBFX	Hiway Skytrike 250	
G-MBAN	American Aerolights Eagle		G-MBFY	Mirage II	
G-MBAR	Skycraft Scout		G-MBFZ	M. S. S. Goldwing	
G-MBAS	Typhoon Tripacer 250		G-MBGA	Solar Wings Typhoon	
G-MBAU	Hiway Skytrike		G-MBGB	American Aerolights Eagle	
G-MBAW	Pterodactyl Ptraveller		G-MBGF	Twamley Trike	
G-MBAZ	Rotec Rally 2B		G-MBGJ	Hiway Skytrike Mk 2	
G-MBBB	Skycraft Scout 2		G-MBGK	Electra Flyer Eagle	
G-MBBG	Weedhopper JC-24B		G-MBGP	Solar Wings Typhoon Skytrike	
G-MBBJ	Hiway Demon Trike				
G-MBBM	Eipper Quicksilver MX		G-MBGS	Rotec Rally 2B	
G-MBBN	Eagle Microlight		G-MBGV	Skyhook Cutlass	
G-MBBT	Ultrasports Tripacer 330		G-MBGW	Hiway Skytrike	
G-MBBU	Southdown Savage		G-MBGX	Southdown Lightning	
G-MBBW	Flexiform Hilander		G-MBGY	Hiway Demon Skytrike	
G-MBBX	Chargus Skytrike		G-MBHA	Trident Trike	
G-MBBY	Flexiform Sealander		G-MBHC	Chargus Lightning T.250	
G-MBBZ	Volmer Jensen VJ-24W		G-MBHE	American Aerolights Eagle	
G-MBCA	Chargus Cyclone T.250		G-MBHH	Flexiform Sealander Skytrike	
G-MBCD	La Mouette Atlas				
G-MBCE	American Aerolights Eagle		G-MBHJ	Hornet Skyhook Cutlass	
G-MBCF	Pterodactyl Ptraveler		G-MBHK	Flexiform Skytrike	
G-MBCG	Ultrasports Tripacer T.250		G-MBHP	American Aerolights Eagle II	
G-MBCI	Hiway Skytrike				
G-MBCJ	Mainair Sports Tri-Flyer		G-MBHT	Chargus T.250	
G-MBCK	Eipper Quicksilver MX		G-MBHW	American Aerolights Eagle	
G-MBCL	Hiway Demon Triflyer		G-MBHX	Pterodactyl Ptraveler	
G-MBCM	Hiway Demon 175		G-MBHZ	Pterodactyl Ptraveller	
G-MBCO	Flexiform Sealander Buggy		G-MBIA	Flexiform Sealander Skytrike	
G-MBCR	Ultraflight Mirage		G-MBIC	Maxair Hummer	
G-MBCU	American Aerolights Eagle		G-MBIO	American Aerolights Eagle Z Drive	
G-MBCX	Airwave Nimrod 165				
G-MBCZ	Chargus Skytrike 160		G-MBIT	Hiway Demon Skytrike	
G-MBDD	Skyhook Skytrike		G-MBIU	Hiway Super Scorpion	
G-MBDE	Flexiform Skytrike		G-MBIV	Flexiform Skytrike	
G-MBDF	Rotec Rally 2B		G-MBIW	Hiway Demon Tri-Flyer Skytrike	
G-MBDG	Eurowing Goldwing				
G-MBDH	Hiway Demon Triflyer		G-MBIY	Ultra Sports	
G-MBDI	Flexiform Sealander		G-MBIZ	Mainair Tri-Flyer	
G-MBDJ	Flexiform Sealander Triflyer		G-MBJA	Eurowing Goldwing	
			G-MBJD	American Aerolights Eagle	
G-MBDM	Southdown Sigma Trike		G-MBJE	Airwave Nimrod	
G-MBDR	U.A.S. Stormbuggy		G-MBJF	Hiway Skytrike Mk II	
G-MBDU	Chargus Titan 38		G-MBJG	Airwave Nimrod	
G-MBDW	Ultrasports Tripacer Skytrike A		G-MBJI	Southern Aerosports Scorpion	
G-MBDX	Electraflyer Eagle		G-MBJK	American Aerolights Eagle	
G-MBDZ	Eipper Quicksilver MX		G-MBJL	Airwave Nimrod	
G-MBEA	Hornet Nimrod		G-MBJM	Striplin Lone Ranger	
G-MBED	Chargus Titan 38		G-MBJN	Electraflyer Eagle	
G-MBEE	Hiway Super Scorpion Skytrike 160		G-MBJO	Birdman Cherokee	
			G-MBJP	Hiway Skytrike	
G-MBEG	Eipper Quicksilver MX		G-MBJR	American Aerolights Eagle	
G-MBEJ	Electraflyer Eagle		G-MBJS	Mainair Tri-Flyer	
G-MBEN	Eipper Quicksilver MX		G-MBJT	Hiway Skytrike II	
G-MBEP	American Aerolights Eagle		G-MBJU	American Eagle 215B	
G-MBES	Skyhook Cutlass		G-MBJZ	Eurowing Catto CP.16	
G-MBET	MEA Mistral Trainer		G-MBKA	Mistral Trainer	
G-MBEU	Hiway Demon T.250		G-MBKC	Southdown Lightning	
G-MBEV	Chargus Titan 38		G-MBKG	Batchelor-Hunt Skytrike	
G-MBFA	Hiway Skytrike 250		G-MBKH	Southdown Skytrike	
G-MBFE	American Aerolights Eagle		G-MBKS	Hiway Skytrike 160	

Reg.	Type	Notes	Reg.	Type	Notes
G-MBKT	Mitchell Wing B.10		G-MBPW	Weedhopper	
G-MBKU	Hiway Demon Skytrike		G-MBPX	Eurowing Goldwing	
G-MBKV	Eurowing Goldwing		G-MBPY	Ultrasports Tripacer 330	
G-MBKW	Pterodactyl Ptraveller		G-MBPZ	Flexiform Striker	
G-MBKY	American Aerolight Eagle		G-MBRB	Electraflyer Eagle 1	
G-MBKZ	Hiway Skytrike		G-MBRD	American Aerolights Eagle	
G-MBLA	Flexiform Skytrike		G-MBRE	Wheeler Scout	
G-MBLB	Eipper Quicksilver MX		G-MBRF	Weedhopper 460C	
G-MBLD	Flexiform Striker		G-MBRH	Ultraflight Mirage Mk II	
G-MBLF	Hiway Demon 195 Tri		G-MBRM	Hiway Demon	
	Pacer		G-MBRO	Hiway Skytrike 160	
G-MBLH	Flexwing Tri-Flyer 330		G-MBRS	American Aerolights Eagle	
G-MBLJ	Eipper Quicksilver MX		G-MBRV	Eurowing Goldwing	
G-MBLK	Southdown Puma		G-MBRZ	Hiway Vulcan 250	
G-MBLM	Hiway Skytrike		G-MBSA	Ultraflight Mirage II	
G-MBLN	Pterodactyl Ptraveller		G-MBSC	Ultraflight Mirage II	
G-MBLO	Sealander Skytrike		G-MBSD	Southdown Puma DS	
G-MBLR	Ultrasports Tripacer		G-MBSF	Ultraflight Mirage II	
G-MBLS	MEA Mistral		G-MBSG	Ultraflight Mirage II	
G-MBLU	Southdown Lightning L.195		G-MBSN	American Aerolights Eagle	
G-MBLV	Ultrasports Hybrid		G-MBSR	Southdown Puma DS	
G-MBLY	Flexiform Sealander Trike		G-MBSS	Ultrasports Puma 2	
G-MBLZ	Southern Aerosports		G-MBST	Mainair Gemini Sprint	
	Scorpion		G-MBSX	Ultraflight Mirage II	
G-MBME	American Aerolights Eagle		G-MBTA	UAS Storm Buggy 5 Mk 2	
	Z Drive		G-MBTB	Davies Tri-Flyer S	
G-MBMG	Rotec Rally 2B		G-MBTC	Weedhopper	
G-MBMJ	Mainair Tri-Flyer		G-MBTE	Hiway Demon	
G-MBMO	Hiway Skytrike 160		G-MBTF	Mainair Tri-Flyer Skytrike	
G-MBMR	Ultrasports Tripacer		G-MBTG	Mainair Gemini	
	Typhoon		G-MBTH	Whittaker MW.4	
G-MBMS	Hornet		G-MBTI	Hovey Whing Ding	
G-MBMT	Mainair Tri-Flyer		G-MBTJ	Solar Wings Microlight	
G-MBMU	Eurowing Goldwing		G-MBTO	Mainair Tri-Flyer 250	
G-MBMW	Solar Wings Typhoon		G-MBTS	Hovey WD-II Whing-Ding	
G-MBMZ	Sealander Tripacer		G-MBTW	Raven Vector 600	
G-MBNA	American Aerolights Eagle		G-MBTZ	Huntair Pathfinder	
G-MBNF	American Aerolights Eagle		G-MBUA	Hiway Demon	
G-MBNG	Hiway Demon Skytrike		G-MBUB	Horne Sigma Skytrike	
G-MBNH	Southern Airsports		G-MBUC	Huntair Pathfinder	
	Scorpion		G-MBUD	Wheeler Scout Mk III	
G-MBNJ	Eipper Quicksilver MX		G-MBUE	MBA Tiger Cub 440	
G-MBNK	American Aerolights Eagle		G-MBUH	Hiway Skytrike	
G-MBNN	Southern Microlight		G-MBUI	Wheeler Scout Mk I	
	Gazelle P.160N		G-MBUK	Mainair 330 Tri Pacer	
G-MBNT	American Aerolights Eagle		G-MBUL	American Aerolights Eagle	
G-MBNY	Steer Terror Fledge II		G-MBUO	Southern Aerosports	
G-MBNZ	Hiway Skytrike Demon			Scorpion	
G-MBOA	Flexiform Hilander		G-MBUP	Hiway Skytrike	
G-MBOD	American Aerolights Eagle		G-MBUT	UAS Storm Buggy	
G-MBOE	Solar Wing Typhoon Trike		G-MBUZ	Wheeler Scout Mk II	
G-MBOF	Pakes Jackdaw		G-MBVA	Volmer Jensen VJ-23E	
G-MBOH	Microlight Engineering		G-MBVC	American Aerolights Eagle	
	Mistral		G-MBVH	Mainair Triflyer Striker	
G-MBOK	Dunstable Microlight		G-MBVJ	Skyhook Trike	
G-MBOM	Hiway Hilander		G-MBVK	Ultraflight Mirage II	
G-MBON	Eurowing Goldwing		G-MBVL	Southern Aerosports	
	Canard			Scorpion	
G-MBOR	Chotia 460B Weedhopper		G-MBVP	Mainair Triflyer 330 Striker	
G-MBOT	Hiway 250 Skytrike		G-MBVR	Rotec Rally 2B	
G-MBOU	Wheeler Scout		G-MBVS	Hiway Skytrike	
G-MBOV	Southdown Lightning Trike		G-MBVU	Flexiform Sealander	
G-MBOX	American Aerolights Eagle			Triflyer	
G-MBPA	Weedhopper Srs 2		G-MBVV	Hiway Skytrike	
G-MBPC	American Aerolights Eagle		G-MBVW	Skyhook TR.2	
G-MBPD	American Aerolights Eagle		G-MBVY	Eipper Quicksilver MX	
G-MBPG	Hunt Skytrike		G-MBWA	American Aerolights Eagle	
G-MBPJ	Moto-Delta		G-MBWB	Hiway Skytrike	
G-MBPM	Eurowing Goldwing		G-MBWD	Rotec Rally 2B	
G-MBPN	American Aerolights Eagle		G-MBWE	American Aerolights Eagle	
G-MBPO	Volnik Arrow		G-MBWF	Mainair Triflyer Striker	
G-MBPS	Gryphon Willpower		G-MBWG	Huntair Pathfinder	
G-MBPU	Hiway Demon		G-MBWH	Designability Duet I	

Reg.	Type	Notes	Reg.	Type	Notes
G-MBWL	Huntair Pathfinder		G-MJAV	Hiway Demon Skytrike	
G-MBWO	Hiway Demon Skytrike			244cc	
G-MBWP	Ultrasports Trike		G-MJAZ	Aerodyne Vector 610	
G-MBWT	Huntair Pathfinder		G-MJBF	Southdown Puma 330	
G-MBWU	Hiway Demon Skytrike		G-MJBH	American Aerolights Eagle	
G-MBWW	Southern Aerosports		G-MJBI	Eipper Quicksilver MX	
	Scorpion		G-MJBK	Swallow AeroPlane	
G-MBWX	Southern Aerosports			Swallow B	
	Scorpion		G-MJBL	American Aerolights Eagle	
G-MBWY	American Aerolights Eagle		G-MJBN	American Aerolights Eagle	
G-MBXB	Southdown Sailwings		G-MJBS	Ultralight Stormbuggy	
	Puma		G-MJBT	Eipper Quicksilver MX	
G-MBXE	Hiway Skytrike		G-MJBV	American Aerolights Eagle	
G-MBXF	Hiway Skytrike		G-MJBX	Pterodactyl Ptraveller	
G-MBXI	Hiway Skytrike		G-MJBZ	Huntair Pathfinder	
G-MBXJ	Hiway Demon Skytrike		G-MJCA	Skyhook Sabre	
G-MBXK	Ultrasports Puma		G-MJCB	Hornet 330	
G-MBXO	Sheffield Trident		G-MJCC	Ultrasports Puma	
G-MBXP	Hornet Skytrike		G-MJCD	Sigma Tetley Skytrike	
G-MBXR	Hiway Skytrike 150		G-MJCE	Ultrasports Tripacer	
G-MBXT	Eipper Quicksilver MX2		G-MJCF	Maxair Hummer	
G-MBXW	Hiway Skytrike		G-MJCG	S.M.C. Flyer Mk 1	
G-MBXX	Ultraflight Mirage II		G-MJCI	Kruchek Firefly 440	
G-MBYD	American Aerolights Eagle		G-MJCJ	Hiway Spectrum	
G-MBYH	Maxair Hummer		G-MJCK	Southern Aerosports	
G-MBYI	Ultraflight Lazair			Scorpion	
G-MBYJ	Hiway Super Scorpion IIC		G-MJCN	S.M.C. Flyer Mk 1	
G-MBYK	Huntair Pathfinder Mk 1		G-MJCU	Tarjani	
G-MBYL	Huntair Pathfinder 330		G-MJCW	Hiway Super Scorpion	
G-MBYM	Eipper Quicksilver MX		G-MJCY	Eurowing Goldwing	
G-MBYO	American Aerolights Eagle		G-MJCZ	Southern Aerosports	
G-MBYR	American Aerolights Eagle			Scorpion 2	
G-MBYS	Ultraflight Mirage II		G-MJDA	Hornet Trike Executive	
G-MBYT	Ultraflight Mirage II		G-MJDB	Birdman Cherokee	
G-MBYU	American Aerolights Eagle		G-MJDE	Huntair Pathfinder	
G-MBYX	American Aerolights Eagle		G-MJDG	Hornet Supertrike	
G-MBYY	Southern Aerosports		G-MJDH	Huntair Pathfinder	
	Scorpion		G-MJDI	Southern Flyer Mk 1	
G-MBZA	Ultrasports Tripacer 330		G-MJDJ	Hiway Skytrike Demon	
G-MBZB	Hiway Skytrike		G-MJDK	American Aerolights Eagle	
G-MBZF	American Aerolights Eagle		G-MJDO	Southdown Puma 440	
G-MBZG	Twinflight Scorpion 2 seat		G-MJDP	Eurowing Goldwing	
G-MBZH	Eurowing Goldwing		G-MJDR	Hiway Demon Skytrike	
G-MBZK	Ultrasports Tripacer 250		G-MJDU	Eipper Quicksilver MX2	
G-MBZL	Weedhopper		G-MJDW	Eipper Quicksilver MX	
G-MBZM	UAS Storm Buggy		G-MJDY	Ultrasports Solarwings	
G-MBZN	Ultrasports Puma		G-MJEC	Ultrasports Puma	
G-MBZO	Mainair Triflyer 330		G-MJEE	Mainair Triflyer Trike	
G-MBZP	Skyhook TR2		G-MJEF	Gryphon 180	
G-MBZU	Skyhook Sabre C		G-MJEG	Eurowing Goldwing	
G-MBZV	American Aerolights Eagle		G-MJEH	Rotec Rally 2B	
G-MBZZ	Southern Aerosports		G-MJEJ	American Aerolights Eagle	
	Scorpion		G-MJEL	GMD-01 Trike	
G-MGAG	Aviasud Mistral		G-MJEO	American Aerolights Eagle	
G-MGOD	Medway Raven		G-MJEP	Pterodactyl Ptraveller	
G-MGOM	Medway Hybred 44XLR		G-MJER	Flexiform Striker	
G-MGOO	Renegade Spirit UK Ltd		G-MJET	Stratos Prototype 3 Axis 1	
G-MGRW	Cyclone AX3/503		G-MJEX	Eipper Quicksilver MX	
G-MGUY	CFM Shadow Srs BD		G-MJEY	Southdown Lightning	
G-MGWH	Thruster T.300		G-MJFB	Flexiform Striker	
G-MJAA	Ultrasports Tripacer		G-MJFD	Ultrasports Tripacer	
G-MJAB	Ultrasports Skytrike		G-MJFF	Huntair Pathfinder	
G-MJAD	Eipper Quicksilver MX		G-MJFH	Eipper Quicksilver MX	
G-MJAE	American Aerolights Eagle		G-MJFI	Flexiform Striker	
G-MJAF	Ultrasports Puma 440		G-MJFJ	Hiway Skytrike 250	
G-MJAG	Skyhook TR1		G-MJFK	Flexiform Skytrike Dual	
G-MJAH	American Aerolights Eagle		G-MJFL	Mainair Tri-Flyer 440	
G-MJAI	American Aerolights Eagle		G-MJFM	Huntair Pathfinder	
G-MJAJ	Eurowing Goldwing		G-MJFO	Eipper Quicksilver MX	
G-MJAL	Wheeler Scout 3		G-MJFP	American Aerolights Eagle	
G-MJAM	Eipper Quicksilver MX		G-MJFS	American Aerolights Eagle	
G-MJAN	Hiway Skytrike		G-MJFV	Ultrasports Tripacer	
G-MJAP	Hiway 160		G-MJFX	Skyhook TR-1	

Reg.	Type	Notes	Reg.	Type	Notes
G-MJGC	Hornet		G-MJKU	Hiway Demon 175	
G-MJGE	Eipper Quicksilver MX		G-MJKV	Hornet	
G-MJGG	Skyhook TR-1		G-MJKX	Ultralight Skyrider	
G-MJGI	Eipper Quicksilver MX			Phantom	
G-MJGM	Hiway Demon 195 Skytrike		G-MJKY	Hiway Skytrike	
G-MJGN	Greenslade Monotrike		G-MJLA	Ultrasports Puma 2	
G-MJGO	Barnes Avon Skytrike		G-MJLB	Ultrasports Puma 2	
G-MJGT	Skyhook Cutlass Trike		G-MJLD	Wheeler Scout Mk III	
G-MJGV	Eipper Quicksilver MX2		G-MJLF	Southern Microlight Trike	
G-MJGW	Solar Wings Trike		G-MJLH	American Aerolights	
G-MJGX	Ultrasports Puma 250			Eagle 2	
G-MJHA	Hiway Skytrike 250 Mk II		G-MJLI	Hiway Demon Skytrike	
G-MJHC	Ultrasports Tripacer 330		G-MJLJ	Flexiform Sealander	
G-MJHE	Hiway Demon Skytrike		G-MJLL	Hiway Demon Skytrike	
G-MJHF	Skyhook Sailwing Trike		G-MJLM	Mainair Triflyer 250	
G-MJHK	Hiway Demon 195		G-MJLR	Skyhook SK-1	
G-MJHM	Ultrasports Trike		G-MJLS	Rotec Rally 2B	
G-MJHN	American Aerolights Eagle		G-MJLT	American Aerolights Eagle	
G-MJHO	Shilling Bumble Bee Srs 1		G-MJLU	Skyhook	
G-MJHP	American Aerolights Eagle		G-MJLY	American Aerolights Eagle	
G-MJHR	Southdown Lightning		G-MJMA	Hiway Demon	
G-MJHU	Eipper Quicksilver MX		G-MJMB	Weedhopper	
G-MJHV	Hiway Demon 250		G-MJME	Ultrasports Tripacer Mega II	
G-MJHW	Ultrasports Puma 1		G-MJMM	Chargus Vortex	
G-MJHX	Eipper Quicksilver MX		G-MJMP	Eipper Quicksilver MX	
G-MJHZ	Southdown Sailwings		G-MJMR	Solar Wings Typhoon	
G-MJIA	Flexiform Striker		G-MJMS	Hiway Skytrike	
G-MJIB	Hornet 250		G-MJMT	Hiway Demon Skytrike	
G-MJIC	Ultrasports Puma 330		G-MJMW	Eipper Quicksilver MX2	
G-MJID	Southdown Sailwings		G-MJMX	Ultrasports Tripacer	
	Puma DS		G-MJNB	Hiway Skytrike	
G-MJIE	Hornet 330		G-MJNE	Hornet Supreme Dual Trike	
G-MJIF	Mainair Triflyer		G-MJNH	Skyhook Cutlass Trike	
G-MJIG	Hiway Demon Skytrike		G-MJNK	Hiway Skytrike	
G-MJIJ	Ultrasports Tripacer 250		G-MJNL	American Aerolights Eagle	
G-MJIK	Southdown Sailwings		G-MJNM	American Aerolights	
	Lightning			Double Eagle	
G-MJIL	Bremner Mitchell B.10		G-MJNN	Ultraflight Mirage II	
G-MJIN	Hiway Skytrike		G-MJNO	American Aerolights	
G-MJIO	American Aerolights Eagle			Double Eagle	
G-MJIR	Eipper Quicksilver MX		G-MJNP	American Aerolights Eagle	
G-MJIS	American Aerolights Eagle		G-MJNR	Ultralight Solar Buggy	
G-MJIU	Eipper Quicksilver MX		G-MJNS	Swallow AeroPlane	
G-MJIV	Pterodactyl Ptraveller			Swallow B	
G-MJIY	Flexiform Voyage		G-MJNT	Hiway Skytrike	
G-MJIZ	Southdown Lightning		G-MJNU	Skyhook Cutlass	
G-MJJA	Huntair Pathfinder		G-MJNV	Eipper Quicksilver MX	
G-MJJB	Eipper Quicksilver MX		G-MJNY	Skyhook Sabre Trike	
G-MJJF	Sealey		G-MJOA	Chargus T.250 Vortex	
G-MJJJ	Moyes Knight		G-MJOC	Huntair Pathfinder	
G-MJJK	Eipper Quicksilver MX2		G-MJOD	Rotec Rally 2B	
G-MJJL	Solar Wings Storm		G-MJOE	Eurowing Goldwing	
G-MJJM	Birdman Cherokee Mk 1		G-MJOG	American Aerolights Eagle	
G-MJJN	Ultrasports Puma		G-MJOI	Hiway Demon	
G-MJJO	Flexiform Skytrike Dual		G-MJOJ	Flexiform Skytrike	
G-MJJS	Swallow AeroPlane		G-MJOK	Mainair Triflyer 250	
	Swallow B		G-MJOL	Skyhook Cutlass	
G-MJJV	Wheeler Scout		G-MJOM	Southdown Puma 40F	
G-MJJX	Hiway Skytrike		G-MJOO	Southdown Puma 40F	
G-MJJY	Tirith Firefly		G-MJOR	Solair Phoenix	
G-MJKA	Skyhook Sabre Trike		G-MJOS	Southdown Lightning 170	
G-MJKB	Striplin Skyranger		G-MJOU	Hiway Demon 175	
G-MJKC	Mainair Triflyer 330 Striker		G-MJOV	Solar Wings Typhoon	
G-MJKE	Mainair Triflyer 330		G-MJOW	Eipper Quicksilver MX	
G-MJKF	Hiway Demon		G-MJPA	Rotec Rally 2B	
G-MJKG	John Ivor Skytrike		G-MJPC	American Aerolights	
G-MJKH	Eipper Quicksilver MX II			Double Eagle	
G-MJKI	Eipper Quicksilver MX		G-MJPD	Hiway Demon Skytrike	
G-MJKJ	Eipper Quicksilver MX		G-MJPE	Hiway Demon Skytrike	
G-MJKO	Goldmarque 250 Skytrike		G-MJPG	American Aerolights Eagle	
G-MJKP	Hiway Super Scorpion			430R	
G-MJKR	Rotec Rally 2B		G-MJPI	Flexiform Striker	
G-MJKS	Mainair Triflyer		G-MJPK	Hiway Vulcan	
			G-MJPO	Eurowing Goldwing	

Reg.	Type	Notes	Reg.	Type	Notes
G-MJPS	American Aerolights Eagle 430R		G-MJVM	Dragon 150	
			G-MJVN	Ultrasports Puma 440	
G-MJPT	Dragon		G-MJVP	Eipper Quicksilver MX II	
G-MJPU	Solar Wings Typhoon		G-MJVR	Flexiform Striker	
G-MJPV	Eipper Quicksilver MX		G-MJVT	Eipper Quicksilver MX	
G-MJRA	Hiway Demon		G-MJVU	Eipper Quicksilver MX II	
G-MJRE	Hiway Demon		G-MJVV	Hornet Supreme Dual	
G-MJRG	Ultrasports Puma		G-MJVW	Airwave Nimrod	
G-MJRH	Hiway Skytrike		G-MJVX	Skyrider Phantom	
G-MJRI	American Aerolights Eagle		G-MJVY	Dragon Srs 150	
G-MJRK	Flexiform Striker		G-MJVZ	Hiway Demon Tripacer	
G-MJRL	Eurowing Goldwing		G-MJWB	Eurowing Goldwing	
G-MJRN	Flexiform Striker		G-MJWD	Solar Wings Typhoon XL	
G-MJRO	Eurowing Goldwing		G-MJWF	Tiger Cub 440	
G-MJRP	Mainair Triflyer 330		G-MJWG	MBA Tiger Cub	
G-MJRR	Striplin Skyranger Srs 1		G-MJWI	Flexiform Striker	
G-MJRS	Eurowing Goldwing		G-MJWJ	MBA Tiger Cub 440	
G-MJRT	Southdown Lightning DS		G-MJWK	Huntair Pathfinder	
G-MJRU	MBA Tiger Cub 440		G-MJWN	Flexiform Striker	
G-MJRX	Ultrasports Puma II		G-MJWO	Hiway Skytrike	
G-MJSA	Mainair 2-Seat Trike		G-MJWR	MBA Tiger Cub 440	
G-MJSE	Skyrider Airsports Phantom		G-MJWS	Eurowing Goldwing	
G-MJSF	Skyrider Airsports Phantom		G-MJWU	Maxair Hummer TX	
G-MJSL	Dragon 200		G-MJWV	Southdown Puma MS	
G-MJSO	Hiway Skytrike		G-MJWW	MBA Super Tiger Cub 440	
G-MJSP	MBA Super Tiger Cub 440		G-MJWX	Flexiform Striker	
G-MJSS	American Aerolights Eagle		G-MJWY	Flexiform Striker	
G-MJST	Pterodactyl Ptraveler		G-MJWZ	Ultrasports Panther XL	
G-MJSV	MBA Tiger Cub		G-MJXA	Flexiform Striker	
G-MJSY	Eurowing Goldwing		G-MJXB	Eurowing Goldwing	
G-MJSZ	DH Wasp		G-MJXD	MBA Tiger Cub 440	
G-MJTC	Solar Wings Typhoon		G-MJXE	Hiway Demon	
G-MJTD	Gardner T-M Scout		G-MJXF	MBA Tiger Cub 440	
G-MJTE	Skyrider Airsports Phantom		G-MJXJ	MBA Tiger Cub 440	
G-MJTF	Gryphon Wing		G-MJXM	Hiway Skytrike	
G-MJTH	S.M.D. Gazelle		G-MJXR	Huntair Pathfinder II	
G-MJTI	Huntair Pathfinder II		G-MJXS	Huntair Pathfinder II	
G-MJTL	Aerostructure Pipistrelle 2B		G-MJXT	Phoenix Falcon 1	
G-MJTM	Aerostructure Pipistrelle 2B		G-MJXV	Flexiform Striker	
G-MJTN	Eipper Quicksilver MX		G-MJXX	Flexiform Striker Dual	
G-MJTO	Jordan Duet Srs 1		G-MJXY	Hiway Demon Skytrike	
G-MJTP	Flexiform Striker		G-MJXZ	Hiway Demon	
G-MJTR	Southdown Puma DS Mk 1		G-MJYA	Huntair Pathfinder	
G-MJTW	Eurowing Trike		G-MJYC	Ultrasports Panther XL Dual 440	
G-MJTX	Skyrider Phantom				
G-MJTY	Huntair Pathfinder		G-MJYD	MBA Tiger Cub 440	
G-MJTZ	Skyrider Airsports Phantom		G-MJYF	Mainair Gemini Flash	
G-MJUB	MBA Tiger Cub 440		G-MJYG	Skyhook Orion Canard	
G-MJUC	MBA Tiger Cub 440		G-MJYI	Mainair Triflyer	
G-MJUE	Southdown Lightning II		G-MJYM	Southdown Puma Sprint	
G-MJUH	MBA Tiger Cub 440		G-MJYP	Mainair Triflyer 440	
G-MJUI	Flexiform Striker		G-MJYR	Catto CP.16	
G-MJUJ	Eipper Quicksilver Mk II		G-MJYS	Southdown Puma Sprint	
G-MJUK	Eipper Quicksilver MX II		G-MJYT	Southdown Puma Sprint	
G-MJUL	Southdown Puma Sprint		G-MJYV	Mainair Triflyer 2 Seat	
G-MJUM	Flexiform Striker		G-MJYW	Wasp Gryphon III	
G-MJUO	Eipper Quicksilver MX II		G-MJYX	Mainair Triflyer	
G-MJUP	Weedhopper B		G-MJYY	Hiway Demon	
G-MJUR	Skyrider Airsports Phantom		G-MJZA	MBA Tiger Cub	
G-MJUS	MBA Tiger Cub 440		G-MJZB	Flexiform Striker Dual	
G-MJUT	Eurowing Goldwing		G-MJZC	MBA Tiger Cub 440	
G-MJUU	Eurowing Goldwing		G-MJZD	Mainair Gemini Flash	
G-MJUW	MBA Tiger Cub 440		G-MJZF	La Mouette Atlas 16	
G-MJUX	Skyrider Airsports Phantom		G-MJZG	Mainair Triflyer 440	
G-MJUY	Eurowing Goldwing		G-MJZH	Southdown Lightning 195	
G-MJUZ	Dragon Srs 150		G-MJZJ	Hiway Cutlass Skytrike	
G-MJVA	Skyrider Airsports Phantom		G-MJZK	Southdown Puma Sprint 440	
G-MJVC	Hiway Skytrike				
G-MJVE	Hybred Skytrike		G-MJZL	Eipper Quicksilver MX II	
G-MJVF	CFM Shadow		G-MJZO	Flexiform Striker	
G-MJVG	Hiway Skytrike		G-MJZP	MBA Tiger Cub 440	
G-MJVJ	Flexiform Striker Dual		G-MJZT	Flexiform Striker	
G-MJVL	Flexiform Striker		G-MJZU	Flexiform Striker	

Reg.	Type	Notes	Reg.	Type	Notes
G-MJZW	Eipper Quicksilver MX II		G-MMDZ	Flexiform Dual Strike	
G-MJZX	Maxair Hummer TX		G-MMEB	Hiway Super Scorpion	
G-MMAC	Dragon Srs 150		G-MMEE	American Aerolights Eagle	
G-MMAE	Dragon Srs 150		G-MMEF	Hiway Super Scorpion	
G-MMAG	MBA Tiger Cub 440		G-MMEG	Eipper Quicksilver MX	
G-MMAH	Eipper Quicksilver MX II		G-MMEI	Hiway Demon	
G-MMAI	Dragon Srs 150		G-MMEJ	Flexiform Striker	
G-MMAJ	Mainair Tri-Flyer 440		G-MMEK	Solar Wings Typhoon XL2	
G-MMAK	MBA Tiger Cub 440		G-MMEL	Solar Wings Typhoon XL2	
G-MMAL	Flexiform Striker Dual		G-MMEN	Solar Wings Typhoon XL2	
G-MMAM	MBA Tiger Cub 440		G-MMEP	MBA Tiger Cub 440	
G-MMAN	Flexiform Striker		G-MMES	Southdown Puma Sprint	
G-MMAO	Southdown Puma Sprint		G-MMET	Skyhook Sabre TR-1 Mk II	
G-MMAP	Hummer TX		G-MMEU	MBS Tiger Cub 440	
G-MMAR	Southdown Puma Sprint		G-MMEW	MBA Tiger Cub 440	
G-MMAS	Southdown Sprint		G-MMEX	Solar Wings Sprint	
G-MMAT	Southdown Puma Sprint		G-MMEY	MBA Tiger Cub 440	
G-MMAU	Flexiform Rapier		G-MMEZ	Southdown Puma Sprint	
G-MMAW	Mainair Rapier		G-MMFB	Flexiform Striker	
G-MMAX	Flexiform Striker		G-MMFC	Flexiform Striker	
G-MMAZ	Southdown Puma Sprint		G-MMFD	Flexiform Striker	
G-MMBA	Hiway Super Scorpion		G-MMFE	Flexiform Striker	
G-MMBB	American Aerolights Eagle		G-MMFG	Flexiform Striker	
G-MMBD	Spectrum 330		G-MMFI	Flexiform Striker	
G-MMBE	MBA Tiger Cub 440		G-MMFJ	Flexiform Striker	
G-MMBF	American Aerolights Eagle		G-MMFK	Flexiform Striker	
G-MMBH	MBA Super Tiger Cub 440		G-MMFL	Flexiform Striker	
G-MMBJ	Solar Wings Typhoon		G-MMFM	Piranha Srs 200	
G-MMBK	American Aerolights Eagle		G-MMFN	MBA Tiger Cub 440	
G-MMBL	Southdown Puma		G-MMFS	MBA Tiger Cub 440	
G-MMBN	Eurowing Goldwing		G-MMFT	MBA Tiger Cub 440	
G-MMBS	Flexiform Striker		G-MMFV	Tri-Flyer 440	
G-MMBT	MBA Tiger Cub 440		G-MMFX	MBA Tiger Cub 440	
G-MMBU	Eipper Quicksilver MX II		G-MMFY	Flexiform Dual Striker	
G-MMBV	Huntair Pathfinder		G-MMFZ	AES Sky Ranger	
G-MMBW	MBA Tiger Cub 440		G-MMGA	Bass Gosling	
G-MMBX	MBA Tiger Cub 440		G-MMGB	Southdown Puma Sprint	
G-MMBZ	Solar Wings Typhoon P		G-MMGC	Southdown Puma Sprint	
G-MMCD	Southdown Lightning DS		G-MMGD	Southdown Puma Sprint	
G-MMCE	MBA Tiger Cub 440		G-MMGE	Hiway Super Scorpion	
G-MMCF	Solar Wings Panther 330		G-MMGF	MBA Tiger Cub 440	
G-MMCG	Eipper Quicksilver MX I		G-MMGL	MBA Tiger Cub 440	
G-MMCI	Southdown Puma Sprint		G-MMGN	Southdown Puma Sprint	
G-MMCJ	Flexiform Striker		G-MMGO	MBA Tiger Cub 440	
G-MMCM	Southdown Puma Sprint		G-MMGP	Southdown Puma Sprint	
G-MMCN	Solar Wings Storm		G-MMGS	Solar Wings Panther Dual	
G-MMCO	Southdown Sprint		G-MMGT	Solar Wings Typhoon	
G-MMCR	Eipper Quicksilver MX		G-MMGU	Flexiform Sealander	
G-MMCS	Southdown Puma Sprint		G-MMGX	Southdown Puma	
G-MMCV	Solar Wings Typhoon III		G-MMGY	Dean Piranha 1000	
G-MMCW	Southdown Puma Sprint		G-MMHA	Skyhook TR-1 Pixie	
G-MMCX	MBA Super Tiger Cub 440		G-MMHB	Skyhook TR-1 Pixie	
G-MMCY	Flexiform Striker		G-MMHD	Hiway Demon 175	
G-MMCZ	Flexiform Striker		G-MMHE	Southdown Puma Sprint	
G-MMDB	La Mouette Atlas		G-MMHF	Southdown Puma Sprint	
G-MMDC	Eipper Quicksilver MXII		G-MMHJ	Flexiform Hilander	
G-MMDD	Huntair Pathfinder		G-MMHK	Hiway Super Scorpion	
G-MMDE	Solar Wings Typhoon		G-MMHL	Hiway Super Scorpion	
G-MMDF	Southdown Lightning II		G-MMHM	Goldmarque Gyr	
G-MMDH	Manta Fledge 2B		G-MMHN	MBA Tiger Cub 440	
G-MMDJ	Solar Wings Typhoon		G-MMHP	Hiway Demon	
G-MMDK	Flexiform Striker		G-MMHR	Southdown Puma Sprint	
G-MMDN	Flexiform Striker		G-MMHS	SMD Viper	
G-MMDO	Southdown Sprint		G-MMHT	Flexiform Viper	
G-MMDP	Southdown Sprint		G-MMHX	Hornet Invader 440	
G-MMDR	Huntair Pathfinder II		G-MMHY	Hornet Invader 440	
G-MMDS	Ultrasports Panther XLS		G-MMHZ	Solar Wings Typhoon XL	
G-MMDT	Flexiform Striker		G-MMIB	MEA Mistral	
G-MMDU	MBA Tiger Cub 440		G-MMIC	Luscombe Vitality	
G-MMDV	Ultrasports Panther		G-MMID	Flexiform Dual Striker	
G-MMDW	Pterodactyl Pfledgling		G-MMIE	MBA Tiger Cub 440	
G-MMDX	Solar Wings Typhoon		G-MMIF	Wasp Gryphon	
G-MMDY	Southdown Puma Sprint		G-MMIH	MBA Tiger Cub 440	

Reg.	Type	Notes	Reg.	Type	Notes
G-MMII	Southdown Puma Sprint 440		G-MMMG	Eipper Quicksilver MXL	
			G-MMMH	Hadland Willow	
G-MMIJ	Ultrasports Tripacer		G-MMMI	Southdown Lightning	
G-MMIL	Eipper Quicksilver MX II		G-MMMJ	Southdown Sprint	
G-MMIM	MBA Tiger Cub 440		G-MMMK	Hornet Invader	
G-MMIO	Huntair Pathfinder II		G-MMML	Dragon 150	
G-MMIR	Mainair Tri-Flyer 440		G-MMMN	Ultrasports Panther Dual 440	
G-MMIS	Hiway Demon				
G-MMIV	Southdown Puma Sprint		G-MMMP	Flexiform Dual Striker	
G-MMIW	Southdown Puma Sprint		G-MMMR	Flexiform Striker	
G-MMIX	MBA Tiger Cub 440		G-MMMS	MBA Tiger Cub 440	
G-MMIY	Eurowing Goldwing		G-MMMT	Hornet Sigma	
G-MMIZ	Southdown Lightning II		G-MMMU	Skyhook Cutlass CD	
G-MMJC	Southdown Sprint		G-MMMV	Skyhook Cutlass Dual	
G-MMJD	Southdown Puma Sprint		G-MMMW	Flexiform Striker	
G-MMJE	Southdown Puma Sprint		G-MMMX	Hornet Nimrod	
G-MMJF	Ultrasports Panther Dual 440		G-MMNA	Eipper Quicksilver MX II	
			G-MMNB	Eipper Quicksilver MX	
G-MMJG	Mainair Tri-Flyer 440		G-MMNC	Eipper Quicksilver MX	
G-MMJJ	Solar Wings Typhoon		G-MMND	Eipper Quicksilver MX II-Q2	
G-MMJK	Hiway Demon		G-MMNE	Eipper Quicksilver MX II	
G-MMJL	Flexiform 1+1 Sealander		G-MMNF	Hornet	
G-MMJM	Southdown Puma Sprint		G-MMNG	Solar Wings Typhoon XL	
G-MMJN	Eipper Quicksilver MX II		G-MMNN	Buzzard	
G-MMJO	MBA Tiger Cub 440		G-MMNP	Ultrasports Panther 250	
G-MMJS	MBA Tiger Cub		G-MMNS	Mitchell U-2 Super Wing	
G-MMJT	Southdown Puma Sprint		G-MMNT	Flexiform Striker	
G-MMJU	Hiway Demon		G-MMNU	Ultrasports Panther	
G-MMJV	MBA Tiger Cub 440		G-MMNW	Mainair Tri-Flyer 330	
G-MMJW	Southdown Puma Sprint		G-MMNX	Solar Wings Panther XL	
G-MMJX	Teman Mono-Fly		G-MMOB	Southdown Sprint	
G-MMJY	MBA Tiger Cub 440		G-MMOD	MBA Tiger Cub 440	
G-MMJZ	Skyhook Pixie		G-MMOF	MBA Tiger Cub 440	
G-MMKA	Ultrasports Panther Dual		G-MMOG	Huntair Pathfinder	
G-MMKB	Ultralight Flight Mirage II		G-MMOH	Solar Wings Typhoon XL	
G-MMKC	Southdown Puma Sprint		G-MMOI	MBA Tiger Cub 440	
G-MMKD	Southdown Puma Sprint		G-MMOK	Solar Wings Panther XL	
G-MMKE	Birdman Chinook WT-11		G-MMOL	Skycraft Scout R3	
G-MMKF	Ultrasports Panther Dual 440		G-MMOO	Southdown Storm	
			G-MMOW	Mainair Gemini Flash	
G-MMKG	Solar Wings Typhoon XL		G-MMOX	Mainair Gemini Flash	
G-MMKH	Solar Wings Typhoon XL		G-MMOY	Mainair Gemini Sprint	
G-MMKI	Ultrasports Panther 330		G-MMPE	Eurowing Goldwing	
G-MMKJ	Ultrasports Panther 330		G-MMPG	Southdown Puma	
G-MMKK	Mainair Flash		G-MMPH	Southdown Puma Sprint	
G-MMKL	Mainair Flash		G-MMPI	Pterodactyl Ptraveller	
G-MMKM	Flexiform Dual Striker		G-MMPJ	Mainair Tri-Flyer 440	
G-MMKO	Southdown Puma Sprint		G-MMPL	Flexiform Dual Striker	
G-MMKP	MBA Tiger Cub 440		G-MMPN	Chargus T250	
G-MMKR	Southdown Lightning DS		G-MMPO	Mainair Gemini Flash	
G-MMKS	Southdown Lightning 195		G-MMPT	SMD Gazelle	
G-MMKT	MBA Tiger Cub 440		G-MMPU	Ultrasports Tripacer 250	
G-MMKU	Southdown Puma Sprint		G-MMPW	Airwave Nimrod	
G-MMKV	Southdown Puma Sprint		G-MMPX	Ultrasports Panther Dual 440	
G-MMKW	Solar Wings Storm				
G-MMKY	Jordan Duet		G-MMPZ	Teman Mono-Fly	
G-MMKZ	Ultrasports Puma 440		G-MMRA	Mainair Tri-Flyer 250	
G-MMLB	MBA Tiger Cub 440		G-MMRC	Southdown Lightning	
G-MMLD	Solar Wings Typhoon S		G-MMRD	Skyhook Cutlass CD	
G-MMLE	Eurowing Goldwing SP		G-MMRF	MBA Tiger Cub 440	
G-MMLF	MBA Tiger Cub 440		G-MMRH	Hiway Demon	
G-MMLG	Solar Wings Typhoon XL		G-MMRJ	Solar Wings Panther XL	
G-MMLH	Hiway Demon		G-MMRK	Ultrasports Panther XL	
G-MMLI	Solar Wings Typhoon S		G-MMRL	Solar Wings Panther XL	
G-MMLK	MBA Tiger Cub 440		G-MMRN	Southdown Puma Sprint	
G-MMLM	MBA Tiger Cub 440		G-MMRO	Mainair Gemini 440	
G-MMLN	Skyhook Pixie		G-MMRP	Mainair Gemini	
G-MMLO	Skyhook Pixie		G-MMRT	Southdown Puma Sprint	
G-MMLP	Southdown Sprint		G-MMRU	Tirith Firebird FB-2	
G-MMLV	Southdown Puma 330		G-MMRV	MBA Tiger Cub 440	
G-MMLX	Ultrasports Panther		G-MMRW	Flexiform Dual Striker	
G-MMMB	Mainair Tri-Flyer		G-MMRX	Willmot J.W.1	
G-MMMD	Flexiform Dual Striker		G-MMRY	Chargus T.250	

Reg.	Type	Notes
G-MMRZ	Ultrasports Panther Dual 440	
G-MMSA	Ultrasports Panther XL	
G-MMSC	Mainair Gemini	
G-MMSE	Eipper Quicksilver MX	
G-MMSG	Solar Wings Panther XL	
G-MMSH	Solar Wings Panther XL	
G-MMSM	Mainair Gemini Flash	
G-MMSN	Mainair Gemini	
G-MMSO	Mainair Tri-Flyer 440	
G-MMSP	Mainair Gemini Flash	
G-MMSR	MBA Tiger Cub 440	
G-MMSS	Solar Wings Panther 330	
G-MMST	Southdown Puma Sprint	
G-MMSV	Southdown Puma Sprint	
G-MMSW	MBA Tiger Cub 440	
G-MMSZ	Medway Half Pint	
G-MMTA	Ultrasports Panther XL	
G-MMTC	Ultrasports Panther Dual	
G-MMTD	Mainair Tri-Flyer 330	
G-MMTG	Mainair Gemini	
G-MMTH	Southdown Puma Sprint	
G-MMTI	Southdown Puma Sprint	
G-MMTJ	Southdown Puma Sprint	
G-MMTK	Medway Hybred	
G-MMTL	Mainair Gemini	
G-MMTM	Mainair Tri-Flyer 440	
G-MMTO	Mainair Tri-Flyer	
G-MMTR	Ultrasports Panther	
G-MMTS	Solar Wings Panther XL	
G-MMTT	Solar Wings Panther XL	
G-MMTV	American Aerolights Eagle	
G-MMTX	Mainair Gemini 440	
G-MMTY	Fisher FP.202U	
G-MMTZ	Eurowing Goldwing	
G-MMUA	Southdown Puma Sprint	
G-MMUC	Mainair Gemini 440	
G-MMUE	Mainair Gemini Flash	
G-MMUG	Mainair Tri-Flyer	
G-MMUH	Mainair Tri-Flyer	
G-MMUJ	Southdown Puma Sprint 440	
G-MMUK	Mainair Tri-Flyer	
G-MMUL	Ward Elf E.47	
G-MMUM	MBA Tiger Cub 440	
G-MMUN	Ultrasports Panther Dual XL	
G-MMUO	Mainair Gemini Flash	
G-MMUP	Airwave Nimrod 140	
G-MMUS	Mainair Gemini	
G-MMUU	ParaPlane PM-1	
G-MMUV	Southdown Puma Sprint	
G-MMUW	Mainair Gemini Flash	
G-MMUX	Mainair Gemini	
G-MMVA	Southdown Puma Sprint	
G-MMVC	Ultrasports Panther XL	
G-MMVG	MBA Tiger Cub 440	
G-MMVH	Southdown Raven	
G-MMVI	Southdown Puma Sprint	
G-MMVJ	Southdown Puma Sprint	
G-MMVL	Ultrasports Panther XL-S	
G-MMVM	Whiteley Orion 1	
G-MMVN	Solar Wings Typhoon	
G-MMVO	Southdown Puma Sprint	
G-MMVP	Mainair Gemini Flash	
G-MMVR	Hiway Skytrike 1	
G-MMVS	Skyhook Pixie	
G-MMVW	Skyhook Pixie	
G-MMVX	Southdown Puma Sprint	
G-MMVY	American Aerolights Eagle	
G-MMVZ	Southdown Puma Sprint	
G-MMWA	Mainair Gemini Flash	
G-MMWB	Huntair Pathfinder II	
G-MMWC	Eipper Quicksilver MXII	
G-MMWF	Hiway Skytrike 250	
G-MMWG	Greenslade Mono-Trike	
G-MMWH	Southdown Puma Sprint 440	
G-MMWI	Southdown Lightning	
G-MMWJ	Pterodactyl Ptraveler	
G-MMWK	Hiway Demon	
G-MMWL	Eurowing Goldwing	
G-MMWN	Ultrasports Tripacer	
G-MMWO	Ultrasports Panther XL	
G-MMWP	American Aerolights Eagle	
G-MMWS	Mainair Tri-Flyer	
G-MMWT	CFM Shadow	
G-MMWX	Southdown Puma Sprint	
G-MMWY	Skyhook Pixie	
G-MMWZ	Southdown Puma Sprint	
G-MMXC	Mainair Gemini Flash	
G-MMXD	Mainair Gemini Flash	
G-MMXE	Mainair Gemini Flash	
G-MMXG	Mainair Gemini Flash	
G-MMXH	Mainair Gemini Flash	
G-MMXI	Horizon Prototype	
G-MMXJ	Mainair Gemini Flash	
G-MMXK	Mainair Gemini Flash	
G-MMXL	Mainair Gemini Flash	
G-MMXM	Mainair Gemini Flash	
G-MMXN	Southdown Puma Sprint	
G-MMXO	Southdown Puma Sprint	
G-MMXP	Southdown Puma Sprint	
G-MMXR	Southdown Puma DS	
G-MMXT	Mainair Gemini Flash	
G-MMXU	Mainair Gemini Flash	
G-MMXV	Mainair Gemini Flash	
G-MMXW	Mainair Gemini	
G-MMXX	Mainair Gemini	
G-MMXZ	Eipper Quicksilver MXII	
G-MMYA	Solar Wings Pegasus XL	
G-MMYB	Solar Wings Pegasus XL	
G-MMYD	CFM Shadow Srs B	
G-MMYF	Southdown Puma Sprint	
G-MMYI	Southdown Puma Sprint	
G-MMYJ	Southdown Puma Sprint	
G-MMYK	Southdown Puma Sprint	
G-MMYL	Cyclone 70	
G-MMYN	Ultrasports Panther XL	
G-MMYO	Southdown Puma Sprint	
G-MMYR	Eipper Quicksilver MXII	
G-MMYS	Southdown Puma Sprint	
G-MMYT	Southdown Puma Sprint	
G-MMYU	Southdown Puma Sprint	
G-MMYV	Webb Trike	
G-MMYY	Southdown Puma Sprint	
G-MMYZ	Southdown Puma Sprint	
G-MMZA	Mainair Gemini Flash	
G-MMZB	Mainair Gemini Flash	
G-MMZC	Mainair Gemini Flash	
G-MMZE	Mainair Gemini Flash	
G-MMZF	Mainair Gemini Flash	
G-MMZG	Ultrasports Panther XL-S	
G-MMZH	Ultrasports Tripacer	
G-MMZI	Medway 130SX	
G-MMZJ	Mainair Gemini Flash	
G-MMZK	Mainair Gemini Flash	
G-MMZL	Mainair Gemini Flash	
G-MMZM	Mainair Gemini Flash	
G-MMZN	Mainair Gemini Flash	
G-MMZO	Microflight Spectrum	
G-MMZP	Ultrasports Panther XL	
G-MMZR	Southdown Puea Sprint	
G-MMZS	Eipper Quicksilver MX1	
G-MMZU	Southdown Puma DS	
G-MMZV	Mainair Gemini Flash	
G-MMZW	Southdown Puma Sprint	

Reg.	Type	Notes	Reg.	Type	Notes
G-MMZX	Southdown Puma Sprint		G-MNDG	Southdown Puma Sprint	
G-MMZY	Ultrasports Tripacer 330		G-MNDH	Hiway Skytrike	
G-MMZZ	Maxair Hummer		G-MNDI	MBA Tiger Cub 440	
G-MNAA	Striplin Sky Ranger		G-MNDM	Mainair Gemini Flash	
G-MNAD	Mainair Gemini Flash		G-MNDO	Mainair Flash	
G-MNAE	Mainair Gemini Flash		G-MNDP	Southdown Puma Sprint	
G-MNAF	Solar Wings Panther XL		G-MNDU	Midland Sirocco 377GB	
G-MNAG	Hiway Skytrike 1		G-MNDV	Midland Sirocco 377GB	
G-MNAH	Solar Wings Panther XL		G-MNDW	Midland Sirocco 377GB	
G-MNAI	Ultrasports Panther XL-S		G-MNDY	Southdown Puma Sprint	
G-MNAJ	Solar Wings Panther XL-S		G-MNDZ	Southdown Puma Sprint	
G-MNAK	Solar Wings Panther XL-S		G-MNEF	Mainair Gemini Flash	
G-MNAL	MBA Tiger Cub 440		G-MNEG	Mainair Gemini Flash	
G-MNAM	Solar Wings Panther XL-S		G-MNEH	Mainair Gemini Flash	
G-MNAN	Solar Wings Panther XL-S		G-MNEI	Medway Hybred 440	
G-MNAO	Solar Wings Panther XL-S		G-MNEK	Medway Half Pint	
G-MNAR	Solar Wings Panther XL-S		G-MNEL	Medway Half Pint	
G-MNAT	Solar Wings Pegasus XL-R		G-MNEM	Solar Wings Pegasus Dual	
G-MNAU	Solar Wings Pegasus XL-R		G-MNEN	Southdown Puma Sprint	
G-MNAV	Southdown Puma Sprint		G-MNEO	Southdown Raven	
G-MNAW	Solar Wings Pegasus XL-R		G-MNEP	Aerostructure Pipstrelle	
G-MNAX	Solar Wings Pegasus XL-R			P.2B	
G-MNAY	Ultrasports Panther XL-S		G-MNER	CFM Shadow Srs B	
G-MNAZ	Solar Wings Pegasus XL-R		G-MNET	Mainair Gemini Flash	
G-MNBA	Solar Wings Pegasus XL-R		G-MNEV	Mainair Gemini Flash	
G-MNBB	Solar Wings Pegasus XL-R		G-MNEW	Mainair Tri-Flyer	
G-MNBC	Solar Wings Pegasus XL-R		G-MNEX	Mainair Gemini Flash	
G-MNBD	Mainair Gemini Flash		G-MNEY	Mainair Gemini Flash	
G-MNBE	Southdown Puma Sprint		G-MNEZ	Skyhook TR1 Mk 2	
G-MNBF	Mainair Gemini Flash		G-MNFA	Solar Wings Typhoon	
G-MNBG	Mainair Gemini Flash		G-MNFB	Southdown Puma Sprint	
G-MNBH	Southdown Puma Sprint		G-MNFC	Midland Ultralights Sirocco	
G-MNBI	Ultrasports Panther XL			377GB	
G-MNBJ	Skyhook Pixie		G-MNFE	Mainair Gemini Flash	
G-MNBK	Hiway Skytrike		G-MNFF	Mainair Gemini Flash	
G-MNBL	American Aerolights Z		G-MNFG	Southdown Puma Sprint	
	Eagle		G-MNFH	Mainair Gemini Flash	
G-MNBM	Southdown Puma Sprint		G-MNFI	Medway Half Pint	
G-MNBN	Mainair Gemini Flash		G-MNFJ	Mainair Gemini Flash	
G-MNBP	Mainair Gemini Flash		G-MNFK	Mainair Gemini Flash	
G-MNBR	Mainair Gemini Flash		G-MNFL	AMF Chevron	
G-MNBS	Mainair Gemini Flash		G-MNFM	Mainair Gemini Flash	
G-MNBT	Mainair Gemini Flash		G-MNFN	Mainair Gemini Flash	
G-MNBU	Mainair Gemini Flash		G-MNFP	Mainair Gemini Flash	
G-MNBV	Mainair Gemini Flash		G-MNFR	Wright Tri-Flyer	
G-MNBW	Mainair Gemini Flash		G-MNFT	Mainair Gemini Flash	
G-MNBY	Mainair Gemini		G-MNFV	Ultrasports Trike	
G-MNCA	Hiway Demon 175		G-MNFW	Medway Hybred 44XL	
G-MNCB	Mainair Gemini Flash		G-MNFX	Southdown Puma Sprint	
G-MNCD	Harmsworth Trike		G-MNFY	Hornet 250	
G-MNCF	Mainair Gemini Flash		G-MNFZ	Southdown Puma Sprint	
G-MNCG	Mainair Gemini Flash		G-MNGA	Aerial Arts Chaser 110SX	
G-MNCH	Lancashire Micro Trike 330		G-MNGB	Mainair Gemini Flash	
G-MNCI	Southdown Puma Sprint		G-MNGD	Quest Air Services	
G-MNCJ	Mainair Gemini Flash		G-MNGF	Solar Wings Pegasus	
G-MNCK	Southdown Puma Sprint		G-MNGG	Solar Wings Pegasus XL-R	
G-MNCL	Southdown Puma Sprint		G-MNGH	Skyhook Pixie	
G-MNCM	CFM Shadow Srs B		G-MNGJ	Skyhook Zipper	
G-MNCO	Eipper Quicksilver MXII		G-MNGK	Mainair Gemini Flash	
G-MNCP	Southdown Puma Sprint		G-MNGL	Mainair Gemini Flash	
G-MNCR	Flexiform Striker		G-MNGM	Mainair Gemini Flash	
G-MNCS	Skyrider Airsports Phantom		G-MNGN	Mainair Gemini Flash	
G-MNCU	Medway Hybred		G-MNGO	Solar Wings Storm	
G-MNCV	Medway Typhoon XL		G-MNGR	Southdown Puma Sprint	
G-MNCW	Hornet Dual Trainer		G-MNGS	Southdown Puma 330	
G-MNCX	Mainair Gemini Flash		G-MNGT	Mainair Gemini Flash	
G-MNCZ	Solar Wings Pegasus XL		G-MNGU	Mainair Gemini Flash	
G-MNDA	Thruster TST		G-MNGW	Mainair Gemini Flash	
G-MNDB	Southdown Puma Sprint		G-MNGX	Southdown Puma Sprint	
G-MNDC	Mainair Gemini Flash		G-MNGY	Hiway Skytrike 160	
G-MNDD	Mainair Scorcher Solo		G-MNGZ	Mainair Gemini Flash	
G-MNDE	Medway Half Pint		G-MNHB	Solar Wings Pegasus XL-R	
G-MNDF	Mainair Gemini Flash		G-MNHC	Solar Wings Pegasus XL-R	

Reg.	Type	Notes	Reg.	Type	Notes
G-MNHD	Solar Wings Pegasus XL-R			Photon	
G-MNHE	Solar Wings Pegasus XL-R		G-MNKD	Solar Wings Pegasus	
G-MNHF	Solar Wings Pegasus XL-R			Photon	
G-MNHH	Solar Wings Panther XL-S		G-MNKE	Solar Wings Pegasus	
G-MNHI	Solar Wings Pegasus XL-R			Photon	
G-MNHJ	Solar Wings Pegasus XL-R		G-MNKG	Solar Wings Pegasus	
G-MNHK	Solar Wings Pegasus XL-R			Photon	
G-MNHL	Solar Wings Pegasus XL-R		G-MNKH	Solar Wings Pegasus	
G-MNHM	Solar Wings Pegasus XL-R			Photon	
G-MNHN	Solar Wings Pegasus XL-R		G-MNKI	Solar Wings Pegasus	
G-MNHP	Solar Wings Pegasus XL-R			Photon	
G-MNHR	Solar Wings Pegasus XL-R		G-MNKJ	Solar Wings Pegasus	
G-MNHS	Solar Wings Pegasus XL-R			Photon	
G-MNHT	Solar Wings Pegasus XL-R		G-MNKK	Solar Wings Pegasus	
G-MNHU	Solar Wings Pegasus XL-R			Photon	
G-MNHV	Solar Wings Pegasus XL-R		G-MNKL	Mainair Gemini Flash	
G-MNHX	Solar Wings Typhoon S4		G-MNKM	MBA Tiger Cub 440	
G-MNHZ	Mainair Gemini Flash		G-MNKN	Skycraft Scout Mk III	
G-MNIA	Mainair Gemini Flash		G-MNKO	Solar Wings Pegasus Flash	
G-MNIB	American Aerolights Eagle		G-MNKP	Solar Wings Pegasus Flash	
	215B		G-MNKR	Solar Wings Pegasus Flash	
G-MNID	Mainair Gemini Flash		G-MNKS	Solar Wings Pegasus Flash	
G-MNIE	Mainair Gemini Flash		G-MNKT	Solar Wings Typhoon S4	
G-MNIF	Mainair Gemini Flash		G-MNKU	Southdown Puma Sprint	
G-MNIG	Mainair Gemini Flash		G-MNKV	Solar Wings Pegasus Flash	
G-MNIH	Mainair Gemini Flash		G-MNKW	Solar Wings Pegasus Flash	
G-MNII	Mainair Gemini Flash		G-MNKX	Solar Wings Pegasus Flash	
G-MNIL	Southdown Puma Sprint		G-MNKY	Southdown Raven	
G-MNIM	Maxair Hummer		G-MNKZ	Southdown Raven	
G-MNIN	Designability Duet		G-MNLB	Southdown Raven X	
G-MNIO	Mainair Gemini Flash		G-MNLC	Southdown Raven	
G-MNIP	Mainair Gemini Flash		G-MNLE	Southdown Raven X	
G-MNIR	Skyhook Pixie 130		G-MNLH	Romain Cobra Biplane	
G-MNIS	CFM Shadow Srs B		G-MNLI	Mainair Gemini Flash	
G-MNIT	Aerial Arts 130SX		G-MNLK	Southdown Raven	
G-MNIU	Solar Wings Pegasus		G-MNLL	Southdown Raven	
	Photon		G-MNLM	Southdown Raven	
G-MNIV	Solar Wings Typhoon		G-MNLN	Southdown Raven	
G-MNIW	Airwave Nimrod 165		G-MNLO	Southdown Raven	
G-MNIX	Mainair Gemini Flash		G-MNLP	Southdown Raven	
G-MNIY	Skyhook Pixie Zipper		G-MNLS	Southdown Raven	
G-MNIZ	Mainair Gemini Flash		G-MNLT	Southdown Raven	
G-MNJA	Southdown Lightning		G-MNLU	Southdown Raven	
G-MNJB	Southdown Raven		G-MNLV	Southdown Raven	
G-MNJC	MBA Tiger Cub 440		G-MNLW	Medway Halt Pint	
G-MNJD	Southdown Puma Sprint		G-MNLX	Mainair Gemini Flash	
G-MNJE	Southdown Puma Sprint		G-MNLY	Mainair Gemini Flash	
G-MNJF	Dragon 150		G-MNLZ	Southdown Raven	
G-MNJG	Mainair Tri-Flyer		G-MNMA	Solar Wings Pegasus Flash	
G-MNJH	Solar Wings Pegasus Flash		G-MNMB	Solar Wings Pegasus Flash	
G-MNJI	Solar Wings Pegasus Flash		G-MNMC	Southdown Puma MS	
G-MNJJ	Solar Wings Pegasus Flash		G-MNMD	Southdown Raven	
G-MNJK	Solar Wings Pegasus Flash		G-MNME	Hiway Skytrike	
G-MNJL	Solar Wings Pegasus Flash		G-MNMF	Maxair Hummer TX	
G-MNJM	Solar Wings Pegasus Flash		G-MNMG	Mainair Gemini Flash	
G-MNJN	Solar Wings Pegasus Flash		G-MNMH	Mainair Gemini Flash	
G-MNJO	Solar Wings Pegasus Flash		G-MNMI	Mainair Gemini Flash	
G-MNJP	Solar Wings Pegasus Flash		G-MNMJ	Mainair Gemini Flash	
G-MNJR	Solar Wings Pegasus Flash		G-MNMK	Solar Wings Pegasus XL-R	
G-MNJS	Southdown Puma Sprint		G-MNML	Southdown Puma Sprint	
G-MNJT	Southdown Raven		G-MNMM	Aerotech MW.5 Sorcerer	
G-MNJU	Mainair Gemini Flash		G-MNMN	Medway Hybred 44XLR	
G-MNJV	Medway Half Pint		G-MNMO	Mainair Gemini Flash	
G-MNJW	Mitchell Wing B10		G-MNMR	Solar Wings Typhoon 180	
G-MNJX	Medway Hybred 44XL		G-MNMS	Wheeler Scout	
G-MNJY	Medway Half Pint		G-MNMT	Southdown Raven	
G-MNJZ	Aerial Arts Alpha 130SX		G-MNMU	Southdown Raven	
G-MNKA	Solar Wings Pegasus		G-MNMV	Mainair Gemini Flash	
	Photon		G-MNMW	Aerotech MW.6 Merlin	
G-MNKB	Solar Wings Pegasus		G-MNMY	Cyclone 70	
	Photon		G-MNNA	Southdown Raven	
G-MNKC	Solar Wings Pegasus		G-MNNB	Southdown Raven	
			G-MNNC	Southdown Raven	

Reg.	Type	Notes	Reg.	Type	Notes
G-MNND	Solar Wings Pegasus Flash		G-MNSW	Southdown Raven X	
G-MNNE	Mainair Gemini Flash		G-MNSX	Southdown Raven X	
G-MNNF	Mainair Gemini Flash		G-MNSY	Southdown Raven X	
G-MNNG	Solar Wings Photon		G-MNTB	Solar Wings Typhoon S4	
G-MNNI	Mainair Gemini Flash		G-MNTC	Southdown Raven X	
G-MNNJ	Mainair Gemini Flash		G-MNTD	Aerial Arts Chaser 110SX	
G-MNNK	Mainair Gemini Flash		G-MNTE	Southdown Raven X	
G-MNNL	Mainair Gemini Flash		G-MNTF	Southdown Raven X	
G-MNNM	Mainair Scorcher Solo		G-MNTG	Southdown Raven X	
G-MNNN	Southdown Raven		G-MNTH	Mainair Gemini Flash	
G-MNNO	Southdown Raven		G-MNTI	Mainair Gemini Flash	
G-MNNP	Mainair Gemini Flash		G-MNTK	CFM Shadow Srs B	
G-MNNR	Mainair Gemini Flash		G-MNTL	Arbee Wasp Gryphon	
G-MNNS	Eurowing Goldwing		G-MNTM	Southdown Raven X	
G-MNNT	Medway Hybred 44XLR		G-MNTN	Southdown Raven X	
G-MNNU	Mainair Gemini Flash		G-MNTO	Southdown Raven X	
G-MNNV	Mainair Gemini Flash		G-MNTP	CFM Shadow Srs B	
G-MNNY	Solar Wings Pegasus Flash		G-MNTS	Mainair Gemini Flash II	
G-MNNZ	Solar Wings Pegasus Flash		G-MNTT	Medway Half Pint	
G-MNPA	Solar Wings Pegasus Flash		G-MNTU	Mainair Gemini Flash II	
G-MNPB	Solar Wings Pegasus Flash		G-MNTV	Mainair Gemini Flash II	
G-MNPC	Mainair Gemini Flash		G-MNTW	Mainair Gemini Flash II	
G-MNPD	Midland Ultralights 130SX		G-MNTX	Mainair Gemini Flash II	
G-MNPF	Mainair Gemini Flash		G-MNTY	Southdown Raven X	
G-MNPG	Mainair Gemini Flash		G-MNTZ	Mainair Gemini Flash II	
G-MNPH	Flexiform Dual Striker		G-MNUA	Mainair Gemini Flash II	
G-MNPI	Southdown Pipistrelle 2C		G-MNUB	Mainair Gemini Flash II	
G-MNPL	Ultrasports Panther 330		G-MNUC	Solar Wings Pegasus Flash II	
G-MNPP	Romain Cobra Biplane				
G-MNPR	Hiway Demon 175		G-MNUD	Solar Wings Pegasus Flash II	
G-MNPV	Mainair Scorcher Solo				
G-MNPW	AMF Chevron		G-MNUE	Solar Wings Pegasus Flash II	
G-MNPX	Mainair Gemini Flash				
G-MNPY	Mainair Scorcher Solo		G-MNUF	Mainair Gemini Flash II	
G-MNPZ	Mainair Scorcher Solo		G-MNUG	Mainair Gemini Flash II	
G-MNRA	CFM Shadow Srs B		G-MNUH	Southdown Raven X	
G-MNRD	Ultraflight Lazair		G-MNUI	Skyhook Cutlass Dual	
G-MNRE	Mainair Scorcher Solo		G-MNUJ	Solar Wings Pegasus Photon	
G-MNRF	Mainair Scorcher Solo				
G-MNRG	Mainair Scorcher Solo		G-MNUK	Midland Ultralights SX130	
G-MNRI	Hornet Dual Trainer		G-MNUL	Midland Ultralights SX130	
G-MNRJ	Hornet Dual Trainer		G-MNUM	Southdown Puma Sprint	
G-MNRK	Hornet Dual Trainer		G-MNUO	Mainair Gemini Flash II	
G-MNRL	Hornet Dual Trainer		G-MNUP	Mainair Gemini Flash II	
G-MNRM	Hornet Dual Trainer		G-MNUR	Mainair Gemini Flash II	
G-MNRN	Hornet Dual Trainer		G-MNUS	Mainair Gemini Flash II	
G-MNRP	Southdown Raven		G-MNUT	Southdown Raven X	
G-MNRR	Southdown Raven X		G-MNUU	Southdown Raven X	
G-MNRS	Southdown Raven X		G-MNUV	Southdown Raven X	
G-MNRT	Midland Ultralights Sirocco		G-MNUW	Southdown Raven X	
G-MNRW	Mainair Gemini Flash II		G-MNUX	Solar Wings Pegasus XL-R	
G-MNRX	Mainair Gemini Flash II		G-MNUY	Mainair Gemini Flash II	
G-MNRY	Mainair Gemini Flash		G-MNUZ	Solar Wings Pegasus XL-R	
G-MNRZ	Mainair Scorcher Solo		G-MNVA	Solar Wings Pegasus XL-R	
G-MNSA	Mainair Gemini Flash		G-MNVB	Solar Wings Pegasus XL-R	
G-MNSB	Southdown Puma Sprint		G-MNVC	Solar Wings Pegasus XL-R	
G-MNSD	Solar Wings Typhoon		G-MNVE	Solar Wings Pegasus XL-R	
G-MNSE	Mainair Gemini Flash		G-MNVF	Solar Wings Pegasus Flash II	
G-MNSF	Hornet Dual Trainer				
G-MNSH	Solar Wings Pegasus Flash II		G-MNVG	Solar Wings Pegasus Flash II	
G-MNSI	Mainair Gemini Flash		G-MNVH	Solar Wings Pegasus Flash II	
G-MNSJ	Mainair Gemini Flash				
G-MNSK	Hiway Skytrike		G-MNVI	CFM Shadow Srs B	
G-MNSL	Southdown Raven X		G-MNVJ	CFM Shadow Srs B	
G-MNSM	Hornet Demon		G-MNVK	CFM Shadow Srs B	
G-MNSN	Solar Wings Pegasus Flash II		G-MNVL	Medway Half Pint	
			G-MNVM	Southdown Raven X	
G-MNSP	Aerial Arts 130SX		G-MNVN	Southdown Raven X	
G-MNSR	Mainair Gemini Flash		G-MNVO	Hovey Whing-Ding II	
G-MNSS	American Aerolights Eagle		G-MNVP	Southdown Raven X	
G-MNST	Vector 600		G-MNVR	Mainair Gemini Flash II	
G-MNSV	CFM Shadown Srs B		G-MNVS	Mainair Gemini Flash II	

MICROLIGHTS

Reg.	Type	Notes	Reg.	Type	Notes
G-MNVT	Mainair Gemini Flash II		G-MNYV	Solar Wings Pegasus XL-R	
G-MNVU	Mainair Gemini Flash II		G-MNYW	Solar Wings Pegasus XL-R	
G-MNVV	Mainair Gemini Flash II		G-MNYX	Solar Wings Pegasus XL-R	
G-MNVW	Mainair Gemini Flash II		G-MNYZ	Solar Wings Pegasus Flash	
G-MNVY	Solar Wings Pegasus Photon		G-MNZA	Solar Wings Pegasus Flash II	
G-MNVZ	Solar Wings Pegasus Photon		G-MNZB	Mainair Gemini Flash II	
G-MNWA	Southdown Raven X		G-MNZC	Mainair Gemini Flash II	
G-MNWB	Thruster TST		G-MNZD	Mainair Gemini Flash II	
G-MNWC	Mainair Gemini Flash II		G-MNZE	Mainair Gemini Flash II	
G-MNWD	Mainair Gemini Flash		G-MNZF	Mainair Gemini Flash II	
G-MNWF	Southdown Raven X		G-MNZG	Aerial Arts 110SX	
G-MNWG	Southdown Raven X		G-MNZI	Prone Power Typhoon 2	
G-MNWH	Aerial Arts 130SX		G-MNZJ	CFM Shadow Srs BD	
G-MNWI	Mainair Gemini Flash II		G-MNZK	Solar Wings Pegasus XL-R	
G-MNWJ	Mainair Gemini Flash II		G-MNZL	Solar Wings Pegasus XL-R	
G-MNWK	CFM Shadow Srs B		G-MNZM	Solar Wings Pegasus XL-R	
G-MNWL	Aerial Arts 130SX		G-MNZN	Solar Wings Pegasus Flash II	
G-MNWN	Mainair Gemini Flash II		G-MNZO	Solar Wings Pegasus Flash II	
G-MNWO	Mainair Gemini Flash II				
G-MNWP	Solar Wings Pegasus Flash II		G-MNZP	CFM Shadow Srs B	
G-MNWR	Medway Hybred 44LR		G-MNZR	CFM Shadow Srs BD	
G-MNWT	Southdown Raven		G-MNZS	Aerial Arts 130SX	
G-MNWU	Solar Wings Pegasus Flash II		G-MNZU	Eurowing Goldwing	
			G-MNZV	Southdown Raven X	
G-MNWV	Solar Wings Pegasus Flash II		G-MNZW	Southdown Raven X	
			G-MNZX	Southdown Raven X	
G-MNWW	Solar Wings Pegasus XL-R		G-MNZY	Striker Tri-Flyer 330	
G-MNWX	Solar Wings Pegasus XL-R		G-MNZZ	CFM Shadow Srs B	
G-MNWY	CFM Shadown Srs B		G-MTAA	Solar Wings Pegasus XL-R	
G-MNWZ	Mainair Gemini Flash II		G-MTAB	Mainair Gemini Flash II	
G-MNXA	Southdown Raven X		G-MTAC	Mainair Gemini Flash II	
G-MNXB	Solar Wings Photon		G-MTAD	Mainair Gemini Skyflash	
G-MNXC	Aerial Arts 110SX		G-MTAE	Mainair Gemini Flash II	
G-MNXD	Southdown Raven		G-MTAF	Mainair Gemini Flash II	
G-MNXE	Southdown Raven X		G-MTAG	Mainair Gemini Flash II	
G-MNXF	Southdown Raven		G-MTAH	Mainair Gemini Flash II	
G-MNXG	Southdown Raven X		G-MTAI	Solar Wings Pegasus XL-R	
G-MNXI	Southdown Raven X		G-MTAJ	Solar Wings Pegasus XL-R	
G-MNXJ	Medway Half Pint		G-MTAK	Solar Wings Pegasus XL-R	
G-MNXM	Medway Hybred 44XLR		G-MTAL	Solar Wings Photon	
G-MNXN	Medway Hybred 44XLR		G-MTAM	Solar Wings Pegasus Flash	
G-MNXO	Medway Hybred 44XLR		G-MTAO	Solar Wings Pegasus XL-R	
G-MNXP	Solar Wings Pegasus Flash II		G-MTAP	Southdown Raven X	
			G-MTAR	Mainair Gemini Flash II	
G-MNXR	Mainair Gemini Flash II		G-MTAS	Whittaker MW.5 Sorcerer	
G-MNXS	Mainair Gemini Flash II		G-MTAT	Solar Wings Pegasus XL-R	
G-MNXT	Mainair Gemini Flash II		G-MTAV	Solar Wings Pegasus XL-R	
G-MNXU	Mainair Gemini Flash II		G-MTAW	Solar Wings Pegasus XL-R	
G-MNXX	CFM Shadow Srs BD		G-MTAX	Solar Wings Pegasus XL-R	
G-MNXY	Whittaker MW.5 Sorcerer		G-MTAY	Solar Wings Pegasus XL-R	
G-MNXZ	Whittaker MW.5 Sorcerer		G-MTAZ	Solar Wings Pegasus XL-R	
G-MNYA	Solar Wings Pegasus Flash II		G-MTBA	Solar Wings Pegasus XL-R	
			G-MTBB	Southdown Raven X	
G-MNYB	Solar Wings Pegasus XL-R		G-MTBC	Mainair Gemini Flash II	
G-MNYC	Solar Wings Pegasus XL-R		G-MTBD	Mainair Gemini Flash II	
G-MNYD	Aerial Arts 110SX Chaser		G-MTBE	CFM Shadow Srs BD	
G-MNYE	Aerial Arts 110SX Chaser		G-MTBF	Mirage Mk II	
G-MNYF	Aerial Arts 110SX Chaser		G-MTBG	Mainair Gemini Flash II	
G-MNYG	Southdown Raven		G-MTBH	Mainair Gemini Flash II	
G-MNYH	Southdown Puma Sprint		G-MTBI	Mainair Gemini Flash II	
G-MNYI	Southdown Raven X		G-MTBJ	Mainair Gemini Flash II	
G-MNYJ	Mainair Gemini Flash II		G-MTBK	Southdown Raven X	
G-MNYK	Mainair Gemini Flash II		G-MTBL	Solar Wings Pegasus XL-R	
G-MNYL	Southdown Raven X		G-MTBM	Airwave Nimrod	
G-MNYM	Southdown Raven X		G-MTBN	Southdown Raven X	
G-MNYO	Southdown Raven X		G-MTBO	Southdown Raven X	
G-MNYP	Southdown Raven X		G-MTBP	Aerotech MW.5 Sorcerer	
G-MNYS	Southdown Raven X		G-MTBR	Aerotech MW.5 Sorcerer	
G-MNYT	Solar Wings Pegasus XL-R		G-MTBS	Aerotech MW.5 Sorcerer	
G-MNYU	Solar Wings Pegasus XL-R		G-MTBT	Aerotech MW.5 Sorcerer	
			G-MTBU	Solar Wings Pegasus XL-R	

Reg.	Type	Notes	Reg.	Type	Notes
G-MTBV	Solar Wings Pegasus XL-R		G-MTEX	Solar Wings Pegasus XL-R	
G-MTBW	Mainair Gemini Flash II		G-MTEY	Mainair Gemini Flash II	
G-MTBX	Mainair Gemini Flash II		G-MTEZ	Ultraflight Lazair IIIE	
G-MTBY	Mainair Gemini Flash II		G-MTFA	Solar Wings Pegasus XL-R	
G-MTBZ	Southdown Raven X		G-MTFB	Solar Wings Pegasus XL-R	
G-MTCA	CFM Shadow Srs B		G-MTFC	Medway Hybred 44XLR	
G-MTCB	Snowbird Mk III		G-MTFE	Solar Wings Pegasus XL-R	
G-MTCC	Mainair Gemini Flash II		G-MTFF	Mainair Gemini Flash II	
G-MTCD	Southdown Raven X		G-MTFG	AMF Chevvron 232	
G-MTCE	Mainair Gemini Flash II		G-MTFH	Aerotech MW.5B Sorcerer	
G-MTCG	Solar Wings Pegasus XL-R		G-MTFI	Mainair Gemini Flash II	
G-MTCH	Solar Wings Pegasus XL-R		G-MTFJ	Mainair Gemini Flash II	
G-MTCJ	Aerial Arts Avenger		G-MTFL	AMF Lazair IIIE	
G-MTCK	Solar Wings Pegasus Flash		G-MTFM	Solar Wings Pegasus XL-R	
G-MTCL	Southdown Raven X		G-MTFN	Aerotech MW.5 Sorcerer	
G-MTCM	Southdown Raven X		G-MTFO	Solar Wings Pegasus XL-R	
G-MTCN	Solar Wings Pegasus XL-R		G-MTFP	Solar Wings Pegasus XL-R	
G-MTCO	Solar Wings Pegasus XL-R		G-MTFR	Solar Wings Pegasus XL-R	
G-MTCP	Aerial Arts Chaser 110SX		G-MTFS	Solar Wings Pegasus XL-R	
G-MTCR	Solar Wings Pegasus XL-R		G-MTFT	Solar Wings Pegasus XL-R	
G-MTCT	CFM Shadow Srs BD		G-MTFU	CFM Shadow Series BD	
G-MTCU	Mainair Gemini Flash II.		G-MTFX	Mainair Gemini Flash	
G-MTCV	Microflight Spectrum		G-MTFY	CFM Shadow Srs BD	
G-MTCW	Mainair Gemini Flash		G-MTFZ	CFM Shadow Srs BD	
G-MTCX	Solar Wings Pegasus XL-R		G-MTGA	Mainair Gemini Flash	
G-MTCZ	Ultrasports Tripacer 250		G-MTGB	Thruster TST Mk 1	
G-MTDA	Hornet Dual Trainer		G-MTGC	Thruster TST Mk 1	
G-MTDB	Owen Pola Mk 1		G-MTGD	Thruster TST Mk 1	
G-MTDC	Owen Pola Mk 1		G-MTGE	Thruster TST Mk 1	
G-MTDD	Aerial Arts Chaser 110SX		G-MTGF	Thruster TST Mk 1	
G-MTDE	American Aerolights 110SX		G-MTGH	Mainair Gemini Flash IIA	
			G-MTGI	Solar Wings Pegasus XL-R	
G-MTDF	Mainair Gemini Flash II		G-MTGJ	Solar Wings Pegasus XL-R	
G-MTDG	Solar Wings Pegasus XL-R		G-MTGK	Solar Wings Pegasus XL-R	
G-MTDH	Solar Wings Pegasus XL-R		G-MTGL	Solar Wings Pegasus XL-R	
G-MTDI	Solar Wings Pegasus XL-R		G-MTGM	Solar Wings Pegasus XL-R	
G-MTDJ	Medway Hybred 44XL		G-MTGO	Mainair Gemini Flash	
G-MTDK	Aerotech MW.5 Sorcerer		G-MTGP	Thruster TST Mk 1	
G-MTDL	Solar Wings Pegasus XL-R		G-MTGR	Thruster TST Mk 1	
G-MTDM	Mainair Gemini Flash II		G-MTGS	Thruster TST Mk 1	
G-MTDN	Ultraflight Lazair IIIE		G-MTGT	Thruster TST Mk 1	
G-MTDO	Eipper Quicksilver MXII		G-MTGU	Thruster TST Mk 1	
G-MTDP	Solar Wings Pegasus XL-R		G-MTGV	CFM Shadow Srs BD	
G-MTDR	Mainair Gemini Flash II		G-MTGX	Hornet Dual Trainer	
G-MTDS	Solar Wings Photon		G-MTGY	Southdown Lightning	
G-MTDT	Solar Wings Pegasus XL-R		G-MTHB	Aerotech MW.5B Sorcerer	
G-MTDU	CFM Shadow Srs BD		G-MTHC	Raven X	
G-MTDV	Solar Wings Pegasus XL-R		G-MTHD	Hiway Demon 195	
G-MTDW	Mainair Gemini Flash II		G-MTHF	Solar Wings Pegasus XL-R	
G-MTDX	CFM Shadow Srs BD		G-MTHG	Solar Wings Pegasus XL-R	
G-MTDY	Mainair Gemini Flash II		G-MTHH	Solar Wings Pegasus XL-R	
G-MTDZ	Eipper Quicksilver MXII		G-MTHI	Solar Wings Pegasus XL-R	
G-MTEA	Solar Wings Pegasus XL-R		G-MTHJ	Solar Wings Pegasus XL-R	
G-MTEB	Solar Wings Pegasus XL-R		G-MTHK	Solar Wings Pegasus XL-R	
G-MTEC	Solar Wings Pegasus XL-R		G-MTHL	Solar Wings Pegasus XL-R	
G-MTED	Solar Wings Pegasus XL-R		G-MTHM	Solar Wings Pegasus XL-R	
G-MTEE	Solar Wings Pegasus XL-R		G-MTHN	Solar Wings Pegasus XL-R	
G-MTEF	Solar Wings Pegasus XL-R		G-MTHO	Solar Wings Pegasus XL-R	
G-MTEG	Mainair Gemini Flash II		G-MTHP	Solar Wings Pegasus XL-R	
G-MTEH	Mainair Gemini Flash II		G-MTHS	CFM Shadow Srs BD	
G-MTEJ	Mainair Gemini Flash II		G-MTHT	CFM Shadow Srs BD	
G-MTEK	Mainair Gemini Flash II		G-MTHU	Hornet Dual Trainer	
G-MTEL	Mainair Gemini Flash II		G-MTHV	CFM Shadow Srs BD	
G-MTEM	Mainair Gemini Flash II		G-MTHW	Mainair Gemini Flash II	
G-MTEN	Mainair Gemini Flash II		G-MTHX	Mainair Gemini Flash IIA	
G-MTEO	Midland Ultralight Sirocco 337		G-MTHY	Mainair Gemini Flash IIA	
			G-MTHZ	Mainair Gemini Flash IIA	
G-MTER	Solar Wings Pegasus XL-R		G-MTIA	Mainair Gemini Flash IIA	
G-MTES	Solar Wings Pegasus XL-R		G-MTIB	Mainair Gemini Flash IIA	
G-MTET	Solar Wings Pegasus XL-R		G-MTIC	Mainair Gemini Flash IIA	
G-MTEU	Solar Wings Pegasus XL-R		G-MTID	Southdown Raven X	
G-MTEV	Solar Wings Pegasus XL-R		G-MTIE	Solar Wings Pegasus XL-R	
G-MTEW	Solar Wings Pegasus XL-R		G-MTIF	Solar Wings Pegasus XL-R	

Reg.	Type	Notes	Reg.	Type	Notes
G-MTIG	Solar Wings Pegasus XL-R		G-MTLL	Mainair Gemini Flash IIA	
G-MTIH	Solar Wings Pegasus XL-R		G-MTLM	Thruster TST Mk 1	
G-MTII	Solar Wings Pegasus XL-R		G-MTLN	Thruster TST Mk 1	
G-MTIJ	Solar Wings Pegasus XL-R		G-MTLO	Thruster TST Mk 1	
G-MTIK	Southdown Raven X		G-MTLP	Thruster TST Mk 1	
G-MTIL	Mainair Gemini Flash IIA		G-MTLR	Thruster TST Mk 1	
G-MTIM	Mainair Gemini Flash IIA		G-MTLS	Solar Wings Pegasus XL-R	
G-MTIN	Mainair Gemini Flash IIA		G-MTLT	Solar Wings Pegasus XL-R	
G-MTIO	Solar Wings Pegasus XL-R		G-MTLU	Solar Wings Pegasus XL-R	
G-MTIP	Solar Wings Pegasus XL-R		G-MTLV	Solar Wings Pegasus XL-R	
G-MTIR	Solar Wings Pegasus XL-R		G-MTLW	Solar Wings Pegasus XL-R	
G-MTIS	Solar Wings Pegasus XL-R		G-MTLX	Medway Hybred 44XLR	
G-MTIT	Solar Wings Pegasus XL-R		G-MTLY	Solar Wings Pegasus XL-R	
G-MTIU	Solar Wings Pegasus XL-R		G-MTLZ	Whittaker MW.5 Sorceror	
G-MTIV	Solar Wings Pegasus XL-R		G-MTMA	Mainair Gemini Flash IIA	
G-MTIW	Solar Wings Pegasus XL-R		G-MTMB	Mainair Gemini Flash IIA	
G-MTIX	Solar Wings Pegasus XL-R		G-MTMC	Mainair Gemini Flash IIA	
G-MTIY	Solar Wings Pegasus XL-R		G-MTMD	Whittaker MW.6 Merlin	
G-MTIZ	Solar Wings Pegasus XL-R		G-MTME	Solar Wings Pegasus XL-R	
G-MTJA	Mainair Gemini Flash IIA		G-MTMF	Solar Wings Pegasus XL-R	
G-MTJB	Mainair Gemini Flash IIA		G-MTMG	Solar Wings Pegasus XL-R	
G-MTJC	Mainair Gemini Flash IIA		G-MTMH	Solar Wings Pegasus XL-R	
G-MTJD	Mainair Gemini Flash IIA		G-MTMI	Solar Wings Pegasus XL-R	
G-MTJE	Mainair Gemini Flash IIA		G-MTMJ	Maxair Hummer	
G-MTJF	Mainair Gemini Flash IIA		G-MTMK	Raven X	
G-MTJG	Medway Hybred 44XLR		G-MTML	Mainair Gemini Flash IIA	
G-MTJH	Solar Wings Pegasus Flash		G-MTMM	CFM Shadow Srs BD	
G-MTJI	Raven X		G-MTMO	Raven X	
G-MTJK	Mainair Gemini Flash IIA		G-MTMP	Hornet Dual Trainer/Raven	
G-MTJL	Mainair Gemini Flash IIA		G-MTMR	Hornet Dual Trainer/Raven	
G-MTJM	Mainair Gemini Flash IIA		G-MTMT	Mainair Gemini Flash IIA	
G-MTJN	Midland Ultralights Sirocco 377GB		G-MTMU	Mainair Gemini Flash IIA	
			G-MTMV	Mainair Gemini Flash IIA	
G-MTJP	Medway Hybred 44XLR		G-MTMW	Mainair Gemini Flash IIA	
G-MTJR	Solar Wings Pegasus XL-R		G-MTMX	CFM Shadow Srs BD	
G-MTJS	Solar Wings Pegasus XL-Q		G-MTMY	CFM Shadow Srs BD	
G-MTJT	Mainair Gemini Flash IIA		G-MTMZ	CFM Shadow Srs BD	
G-MTJV	Mainair Gemini Flash IIA		G-MTNB	Raven X	
G-MTJW	Mainair Gemini Flash IIA		G-MTNC	Mainair Gemini Flash IIA	
G-MTJX	Hornet Dual Trainer		G-MTND	Medway Hybred 44XLR	
G-MTJY	Mainair Gemini Flash IIA		G-MTNE	Medway Hybred 44XLR	
G-MTJZ	Mainair Gemini Flash IIA		G-MTNF	Medway Hybred 44XLR	
G-MTKA	Thruster TST Mk 1		G-MTNG	Mainair Gemini Flash IIA	
G-MTKB	Thruster TST Mk 1		G-MTNH	Mainair Gemini Flash IIA	
G-MTKD	Thruster TST Mk 1		G-MTNI	Mainair Gemini Flash IIA	
G-MTKE	Thruster TST Mk 1		G-MTNJ	Mainair Gemini Flash IIA	
G-MTKG	Solar Wings Pegasus XL-R		G-MTNK	Weedhopper JC-24B	
G-MTKH	Solar Wings Pegasus XL-R		G-MTNL	Mainair Gemini Flash IIA	
G-MTKI	Solar Wings Pegasus XL-R		G-MTNM	Mainair Gemini Flash IIA	
G-MTKJ	Solar Wings Pegasus XL-R		G-MTNO	Solar Wings Pegasus XL-Q	
G-MTKK	Solar Wings Pegasus XL-R		G-MTNP	Solar Wings Pegasus XL-Q	
G-MTKM	Gardner T-M Scout S.2		G-MTNR	Thruster TST Mk 1	
G-MTKN	Mainair Gemini Flash IIA		G-MTNS	Thruster TST Mk 1	
G-MTKO	Mainair Gemini Flash IIA		G-MTNT	Thruster TST Mk 1	
G-MTKP	Solar Wings Pegasus XL-R		G-MTNU	Thruster TST Mk 1	
G-MTKR	CFM Shadow Srs BD		G-MTNV	Thruster TST Mk 1	
G-MTKS	CFM Shadow Srs BD		G-MTNW	Thruster TST Mk 1	
G-MTKU	CFM Shadow Srs BD		G-MTNX	Mainair Gemini Flash II	
G-MTKV	Mainair Gemini Flash		G-MTNY	Mainair Gemini Flash IIA	
G-MTKW	Mainair Gemini Flash IIA		G-MTNZ	Solar Wings Pegasus XL-Q	
G-MTKX	Mainair Gemini Flash IIA		G-MTOA	Solar Wings Pegasus XL-R	
G-MTKY	Mainair Gemini Flash IIA		G-MTOB	Solar Wings Pegasus XL-R	
G-MTKZ	Mainair Gemini Flash IIA		G-MTOC	Solar Wings Pegasus XL-R	
G-MTLA	Mainair Gemini Flash IIA		G-MTOD	Solar Wings Pegasus XL-R	
G-MTLB	Mainair Gemini Flash IIA		G-MTOE	Solar Wings Pegasus XL-R	
G-MTLC	Mainair Gemini Flash IIA		G-MTOF	Solar Wings Pegasus XL-R	
G-MTLD	Mainair Gemini Flash IIA		G-MTOG	Solar Wings Pegasus XL-R	
G-MTLE	See main Register		G-MTOH	Solar Wings Pegasus XL-R	
G-MTLG	Solar Wings Pegasus XL-R		G-MTOI	Solar Wings Pegasus XL-R	
G-MTLH	Solar Wings Pegasus XL-R		G-MTOJ	Solar Wings Pegasus XL-R	
G-MTLI	Solar Wings Pegasus XL-R		G-MTOK	Solar Wings Pegasus XL-R	
G-MTLJ	Solar Wings Pegasus XL-R		G-MTOL	Solar Wings Pegasus XL-R	
G-MTLK	Raven X		G-MTOM	Solar Wings Pegasus XL-R	

Reg.	Type	Notes	Reg.	Type	Notes
G-MTON	Solar Wings Pegasus XL-R		G-MTSL	Thruster TST Mk 1	
G-MTOO	Solar Wings Pegasus XL-R		G-MTSM	Thruster TST Mk 1	
G-MTOP	Solar Wings Pegasus XL-R		G-MTSN	Solar Wings Pegasus XL-R	
G-MTOR	Solar Wings Pegasus XL-R		G-MTSO	Solar Wings Pegasus XL-R	
G-MTOS	Solar Wings Pegasus XL-R		G-MTSP	Solar Wings Pegasus XL-R	
G-MTOT	Solar Wings Pegasus XL-R		G-MTSR	Solar Wings Pegasus XL-R	
G-MTOU	Solar Wings Pegasus XL-R		G-MTSS	Solar Wings Pegasus XL-R	
G-MTOV	Solar Wings Pegasus XL-R		G-MTST	Thruster TST Mk 1	
G-MTOW	Solar Wings Pegasus XL-R		G-MTSU	Solar Wings Pegasus XL-R	
G-MTOX	Solar Wings Pegasus XL-R		G-MTSV	Solar Wings Pegasus XL-R	
G-MTOY	Solar Wings Pegasus XL-R		G-MTSX	Solar Wings Pegasus XL-R	
G-MTOZ	Solar Wings Pegasus XL-R		G-MTSY	Solar Wings Pegasus XL-R	
G-MTPA	Mainair Gemini Flash IIA		G-MTSZ	Solar Wings Pegasus XL-R	
G-MTPB	Mainair Gemini Flash IIA		G-MTTA	Solar Wings Pegasus XL-R	
G-MTPC	Raven X		G-MTTB	Solar Wings Pegasus XL-R	
G-MTPE	Solar Wings Pegasus XL-R		G-MTTC	Solar Wings Pegasus XL-R	
G-MTPF	Solar Wings Pegasus XL-R		G-MTTD	Solar Wings Pegasus XL-R	
G-MTPG	Solar Wings Pegasus XL-R		G-MTTE	Solar Wings Pegasus XL-R	
G-MTPH	Solar Wings Pegasus XL-R		G-MTTF	Aerotech MW.6 Merlin	
G-MTPI	Solar Wings Pegasus XL-R		G-MTTG	Excalibur TriPacer 250	
G-MTPJ	Solar Wings Pegasus XL-R		G-MTTH	CFM Shadow Srs BD	
G-MTPK	Solar Wings Pegasus XL-R		G-MTTI	Mainair Gemini Flash IIA	
G-MTPL	Solar Wings Pegasus XL-R		G-MTTK	Southdown Lightning DS	
G-MTPM	Solar Wings Pegasus XL-R		G-MTTL	Hiway Sky-Trike	
G-MTPN	Solar Wings Pegasus XL-Q		G-MTTM	Mainair Gemini Flash IIA	
G-MTPO	Solar Wings Pegasus XL-Q		G-MTTN	Ultralight Flight Phantom	
G-MTPP	Solar Wings Pegasus XL-R		G-MTTO	Mainair Gemini Flash IIA	
G-MTPR	Solar Wings Pegasus XL-R		G-MTTP	Mainair Gemini Flash IIA	
G-MTPS	Solar Wings Pegasus XL-Q		G-MTTR	Mainair Gemini Flash IIA	
G-MTPT	Thruster TST Mk Mk 1		G-MTTS	Mainair Gemini Flash IIA	
G-MTPU	Thruster TST Mk 1		G-MTTU	Solar Wings Pegasus XL-R	
G-MTPV	Thruster TST Mk 1		G-MTTW	Mainair Gemini Flash IIA	
G-MTPW	Thruster TST Mk 1		G-MTTX	Solar Wings Pegasus XL-Q	
G-MTPX	Thruster TST Mk 1		G-MTTY	Solar Wings Pegasus XL-Q	
G-MTPY	Thruster TST Mk 1		G-MTTZ	Solar Wings Pegasus XL-Q	
G-MTPZ	Solar Wings Pegasus XL-R		G-MTUA	Solar Wings Pegasus XL-R	
G-MTRA	Mainair Gemini Flash IIA		G-MTUB	Thruster TST Mk 1	
G-MTRB	Mainair Gemini Flash IIA		G-MTUC	Thruster TST Mk 1	
G-MTRC	Midlands Ultralights Sirocco 377GB		G-MTUD	Thruster TST Mk 1	
			G-MTUE	Thruster TST Mk 1	
G-MTRD	Midlands Ultralights Sirocco 377GB		G-MTUF	Thruster TST Mk 1	
			G-MTUG	Thruster TST Mk 1	
G-MTRE	Whittaker MW.6 Merlin		G-MTUH	Solar Wings Pegasus XL-R	
G-MTRF	Mainair Gemini Flash IIA		G-MTUI	Solar Wings Pegasus XL-R	
G-MTRG	Mainair Gemini Flash IIA		G-MTUJ	Solar Wings Pegasus XL-R	
G-MTRH	Hiway Demon		G-MTUK	Solar Wings Pegasus XL-R	
G-MTRJ	AMF Chevvron 232		G-MTUL	Solar Wings Pegasus XL-R	
G-MTRK	Hornet Dual Trainer		G-MTUN	Solar Wings Pegasus XL-Q	
G-MTRL	Hornet Dual Trainer		G-MTUO	Solar Wings Pegasus XL-Q	
G-MTRM	Solar Wings Pegasus XL-R		G-MTUP	Solar Wings Pegasus XL-Q	
G-MTRN	Solar Wings Pegasus XL-R		G-MTUR	Solar Wings Pegasus XL-Q	
G-MTRO	Solar Wings Pegasus XL-R		G-MTUS	Solar Wings Pegasus XL-Q	
G-MTRP	Solar Wings Pegasus XL-R		G-MTUT	Solar Wings Pegasus XL-Q	
G-MTRR	Solar Wings Pegasus XL-R		G-MTUU	Mainair Gemini Flash IIA	
G-MTRS	Solar Wings Pegasus XL-R		G-MTUV	Mainair Gemini Flash IIA	
G-MTRT	Raven X		G-MTUX	Medway Hybred 44XLR	
G-MTRU	Solar Wings Pegasus XL-Q		G-MTUY	Solar Wings Pegasus XL-Q	
G-MTRV	Solar Wings Pegasus XL-Q		G-MTUZ	Hornet Dual Trainer	
G-MTRW	Raven X		G-MTVA	Solar Wings Pegasus XL-R	
G-MTRX	Whittaker MW.5 Sorceror		G-MTVB	Solar Wings Pegasus XL-R	
G-MTRY	Noble Hardman Snowbird IV		G-MTVC	Solar Wings Pegasus XL-R	
G-MTRZ	Mainair Gemini Flash IIA		G-MTVE	Solar Wings Pegasus XL-R	
G-MTSA	Mainair Gemini Flash IIA		G-MTVF	Solar Wings Pegasus XL-R	
G-MTSB	Mainair Gemini Flash IIA		G-MTVG	Mainair Gemini Flash IIA	
G-MTSC	Mainair Gemini Flash IIA		G-MTVH	Mainair Gemini Flash IIA	
G-MTSD	Raven X		G-MTVI	Mainair Gemini Flash IIA	
G-MTSE	Flexiform Striker		G-MTVJ	Mainair Gemini Flash IIA	
G-MTSF	Aerial Arts Chaser 110SX		G-MTVK	Solar Wings Pegasus XL-R	
G-MTSG	CFM Shadow Srs BD		G-MTVL	Solar Wings Pegasus XL-R	
G-MTSH	Thruster TST Mk 1		G-MTVM	Solar Wings Pegasus XL-R	
G-MTSI	Thruster TST Mk 1		G-MTVN	Solar Wings Pegasus XL-R	
G-MTSJ	Thruster TST Mk 1		G-MTVO	Solar Wings Pegasus XL-R	
G-MTSK	Thruster TST Mk 1		G-MTVP	Thruster TST Mk 1	

Reg.	Type	Notes	Reg.	Type	Notes
G-MTVR	Thruster TST Mk 1		G-MTZB	Thruster TST Mk 1	
G-MTVS	Thruster TST Mk 1		G-MTZC	Thruster TST Mk 1	
G-MTVT	Thruster TST Mk 1		G-MTZD	Thruster TST Mk 1	
G-MTVV	Thruster TST Mk 1		G-MTZE	Thruster TST Mk 1	
G-MTVX	Solar Wings Pegasus XL-Q		G-MTZF	Thruster TST Mk 1	
G-MTVY	Solar Wings Pegasus XL-Q		G-MTZG	Mainair Gemini Flash IIA	
G-MTVZ	Powerchute Raider		G-MTZH	Mainair Gemini Flash IIA	
G-MTWA	Solar Wings Pegasus XL-R		G-MTZI	Solar Wings Pegasus XL-R	
G-MTWB	Solar Wings Pegasus XL-R		G-MTZJ	Solar Wings Pegasus XL-R	
G-MTWD	Solar Wings Pegasus XL-R		G-MTZK	Solar Wings Pegasus XL-R	
G-MTWE	Solar Wings Pegasus XL-R		G-MTZL	Mainair Gemini Flash IIA	
G-MTWF	Mainair Gemini Flash IIA		G-MTZM	Mainair Gemini Flash IIA	
G-MTWG	Mainair Gemini Flash IIA		G-MTZN	Mainair Gemini Flash IIA	
G-MTWH	CFM Shadow Srs BD		G-MTZO	Mainair Gemini Flash IIA	
G-MTWK	CFM Shadow Srs BD		G-MTZP	Solar Wings Pegasus XL-Q	
G-MTWL	CFM Shadow Srs BD		G-MTZR	Solar Wings Pegasus XL-Q	
G-MTWM	CFM Shadow Srs BD		G-MTZS	Solar Wings Pegasus XL-Q	
G-MTWN	CFM Shadow Srs BD		G-MTZT	Solar Wings Pegasus XL-Q	
G-MTWO	Weedhopper JC-24B		G-MTZU	Solar Wings Pegasus XL-Q	
G-MTWP	CFM Shadow Srs BD		G-MTZV	Mainair Gemini Flash IIA	
G-MTWR	Mainair Gemini Flash IIA		G-MTZW	Mainair Gemini Flash IIA	
G-MTWS	Mainair Gemini Flash IIA		G-MTZX	Mainair Gemini Flash IIA	
G-MTWW	Solar Wings Typhoon		G-MTZY	Mainair Gemini Flash IIA	
G-MTWX	Mainair Gemini Flash IIA		G-MTZZ	Mainair Gemini Flash IIA	
G-MTWY	Thruster TST Mk 1		G-MVAA	Mainair Gemini Flash IIA	
G-MTWZ	Thruster TST Mk 1		G-MVAB	Mainair Gemini Flash IIA	
G-MTXA	Thruster TST Mk 1		G-MVAC	CFM Shadow Srs BD	
G-MTXB	Thruster TST Mk 1		G-MVAD	Mainair Gemini Flash IIA	
G-MTXC	Thruster TST Mk 1		G-MVAF	Southdown Puma Sprint	
G-MTXD	Thruster TST Mk 1		G-MVAG	Thruster TST Mk 1	
G-MTXE	Hornet Dual Trainer		G-MVAH	Thruster TST Mk 1	
G-MTXG	Solar Wings Pegasus XL-Q		G-MVAI	Thruster TST Mk 1	
G-MTXH	Solar Wings Pegasus XL-Q		G-MVAJ	Thruster TST Mk 1	
G-MTXI	Solar Wings Pegasus XL-Q		G-MVAK	Thruster TST Mk 1	
G-MTXJ	Solar Wings Pegasus XL-Q		G-MVAL	Thruster TST Mk 1	
G-MTXK	Solar Wings Pegasus XL-Q		G-MVAM	CFM Shadow Srs BD	
G-MTXL	Noble Hardman Snowbird Mk IV		G-MVAN	CFM Shadow Srs BD	
G-MTXM	Mainair Gemini Flash IIA		G-MVAO	Mainair Gemini Flash IIA	
G-MTXO	Whittaker MW.6		G-MVAP	Mainair Gemini Flash IIA	
G-MTXP	Mainair Gemini Flash IIA		G-MVAR	Solar Wings Pegasus XL-R	
G-MTXR	CFM Shadow Srs BD		G-MVAS	Solar Wings Pegasus XL-R	
G-MTXS	Mainair Gemini Flash IIA		G-MVAT	Solar Wings Pegasus XL-R	
G-MTXT	MBA Tiger Cub 440		G-MVAU	Solar Wings Pegasus XL-R	
G-MTXU	Noble Hardman Snowbird Mk IV		G-MVAV	Solar Wings Pegasus XL-R	
			G-MVAW	Solar Wings Pegasus XL-Q	
G-MTXW	Noble Hardman Snowbird Mk IV		G-MVAX	Solar Wings Pegasus XL-Q	
			G-MVAY	Solar Wings Pegasus XL-Q	
G-MTXY	Hornet Dual Trainer		G-MVAZ	Solar Wings Pegasus XL-Q	
G-MTXZ	Mainair Gemini Flash IIA		G-MVBA	Solar Wings Pegasus XL-Q	
G-MTYA	Solar Wings Pegasus XL-Q		G-MVBB	CFM Shadow Srs BD	
G-MTYC	Solar Wings Pegasus XL-Q		G-MVBC	Aerial Arts Tri-Flyer 130SX	
G-MTYD	Solar Wings Pegasus XL-Q		G-MVBD	Mainair Gemini Flash IIA	
G-MTYE	Solar Wings Pegasus XL-Q		G-MVBE	Mainair Scorcher	
G-MTYF	Solar Wings Pegasus XL-Q		G-MVBF	Mainair Gemini Flash IIA	
G-MTYG	Solar Wings Pegasus XL-Q		G-MVBG	Mainair Gemini Flash IIA	
G-MTYH	Solar Wings Pegasus XL-Q		G-MVBH	Mainair Gemini Flash IIA	
G-MTYI	Solar Wings Pegasus XL-Q		G-MVBI	Mainair Gemini Flash IIA	
G-MTYK	Solar Wings Pegasus XL-Q		G-MVBJ	Solar Wings Pegasus XL-R	
G-MTYL	Solar Wings Pegasus XL-Q		G-MVBK	Mainair Gemini Flash IIA	
G-MTYM	Solar Wings Pegasus XL-Q		G-MVBL	Mainair Gemini Flash IIA	
G-MTYN	Solar Wings Pegasus XL-Q		G-MVBM	Mainair Gemini Flash IIA	
G-MTYO	Solar Wings Pegasus XL-Q		G-MVBN	Mainair Gemini Flash IIA	
G-MTYP	Solar Wings Pegasus XL-Q		G-MVBO	Mainair Gemini Flash IIA	
G-MTYR	Solar Wings Pegasus XL-Q		G-MVBP	Thruster TST Mk 1	
G-MTYS	Solar Wings Pegasus XL-Q		G-MVBR	Thruster TST Mk 1	
G-MTYT	Solar Wings Pegasus XL-Q		G-MVBS	Thruster TST Mk 1	
G-MTYU	Solar Wings Pegasus XL-Q		G-MVBT	Thruster TST Mk 1	
G-MTYV	Raven X		G-MVBU	Thruster TST Mk 1	
G-MTYW	Raven X		G-MVBY	Solar Wings Pegasus XL-R	
G-MTYX	Raven X		G-MVBZ	Solar Wings Pegasus XL-R	
G-MTYY	Solar Wings Pegasus XL-R		G-MVCA	Solar Wings Pegasus XL-R	
G-MTZA	Thruster TST Mk 1		G-MVCB	Solar Wings Pegasus XL-R	
			G-MVCC	CFM Shadow Srs BD	

Reg.	Type	Notes	Reg.	Type	Notes
G-MVCD	Medway Hybred 44XLR		G-MVFE	Solar Wings Pegasus XL-Q	
G-MVCE	Mainair Gemini Flash IIA		G-MVFF	Solar Wings Pegasus XL-Q	
G-MVCF	Mainair Gemini Flash IIA		G-MVFG	Solar Wings Pegasus XL-Q	
G-MVCH	Noble Hardman Snowbird		G-MVFH	CFM Shadow Srs BD	
	Mk IV		G-MVFJ	Thruster TST Mk 1	
G-MVCI	Noble Hardman Snowbird		G-MVFK	Thruster TST Mk 1	
	Mk IV		G-MVFL	Thruster TST Mk 1	
G-MVCJ	Noble Hardman Snowbird		G-MVFM	Thruster TST Mk 1	
	Mk IV		G-MVFN	Thruster TST Mk 1	
G-MVCL	Solar Wings Pegasus XL-Q		G-MVFO	Thruster TST Mk 1	
G-MVCM	Solar Wings Pegasus XL-Q		G-MVFP	Solar Wings Pegasus XL-R	
G-MVCN	Solar Wings Pegasus XL-Q		G-MVFR	Solar Wings Pegasus XL-R	
G-MVCO	Solar Wings Pegasus XL-Q		G-MVFS	Solar Wings Pegasus XL-R	
G-MVCP	Solar Wings Pegasus XL-Q		G-MVFT	Solar Wings Pegasus XL-R	
G-MVCR	Solar Wings Pegasus XL-Q		G-MVFU	Solar Wings Pegasus XL-R	
G-MVCS	Solar Wings Pegasus XL-Q		G-MVFV	Solar Wings Pegasus XL-R	
G-MVCT	Solar Wings Pegasus XL-Q		G-MVFW	Solar Wings Pegasus XL-R	
G-MVCV	Solar Wings Pegasus XL-Q		G-MVFX	Solar Wings Pegasus XL-R	
G-MVCW	CFM Shadow Srs BD		G-MVFY	Solar Wings Pegasus XL-R	
G-MVCY	Mainair Gemini Flash IIA		G-MVFZ	Solar Wings Pegasus XL-R	
G-MVCZ	Mainair Gemini Flash IIA		G-MVGA	Aerial Arts Chaser S	
G-MVDA	Mainair Gemini Flash IIA		G-MVGB	Medway Hybred 44XLR	
G-MVDB	Medway Hybred 44XLR		G-MVGC	AMF Chevvron 232	
G-MVDC	Medway Hybred 44XLR		G-MVGD	AMF Chevvron 232	
G-MVDD	Thruster TST Mk 1		G-MVGE	AMF Chevvron 232	
G-MVDE	Thruster TST Mk 1		G-MVGF	Aerial Arts Chaser S	
G-MVDF	Thruster TST Mk 1		G-MVGG	Aerial Arts Chaser S	
G-MVDG	Thruster TST Mk 1		G-MVGH	Aerial Arts Chaser S	
G-MVDH	Thruster TST Mk 1		G-MVGI	Aerial Arts Chaser S	
G-MVDI	Thruster TST Mk 1		G-MVGJ	Aerial Arts Chaser S	
G-MVDJ	Medway Hybred 44XLR		G-MVGK	Aerial Arts Chaser S	
G-MVDK	Aerial Arts Chaser S		G-MVGL	Medway Hybred 44XLR	
G-MVDL	Aerial Arts Chaser S		G-MVGM	Mainair Gemini Flash IIA	
G-MVDM	Aerial Arts Chaser S		G-MVGN	Solar Wings Pegasus XL-R	
G-MVDN	Aerial Arts Chaser S		G-MVGO	Solar Wings Pegasus XL-R	
G-MVDO	Aerial Arts Chaser S		G-MVGR	Solar Wings Pegasus XL-R	
G-MVDP	Aerial Arts Chaser S		G-MVGS	Solar Wings Pegasus XL-R	
G-MVDR	Aerial Arts Chaser S		G-MVGT	Solar Wings Pegasus XL-Q	
G-MVDS	Hiway Skytrike		G-MVGU	Solar Wings Pegasus XL-Q	
G-MVDT	Mainair Gemini Flash IIA		G-MVGV	Solar Wings Pegasus XL-Q	
G-MVDU	Solar Wings Pegasus XL-R		G-MVGW	Solar Wings Pegasus XL-Q	
G-MVDV	Solar Wings Pegasus XL-R		G-MVGX	Solar Wings Pegasus XL-Q	
G-MVDW	Solar Wings Pegasus XL-R		G-MVGY	Medway Hybred 44XL	
G-MVDX	Solar Wings Pegasus XL-R		G-MVGZ	Ultraflight Lazair IIIE	
G-MVDY	Solar Wings Pegasus XL-R		G-MVHA	Aerial Arts Chaser S	
G-MVDZ	Solar Wings Pegasus XL-R		G-MVHB	Powerchute Raider	
G-MVEA	Solar Wings Pegasus XL-R		G-MVHC	Powerchute Raider	
G-MVEB	Solar Wings Pegasus XL-R		G-MVHD	CFM Shadow Srs BD	
G-MVEC	Solar Wings Pegasus XL-R		G-MVHE	Mainair Gemini Flash IIA	
G-MVED	Solar Wings Pegasus XL-R		G-MVHF	Mainair Gemini Flash IIA	
G-MVEE	Medway Hybred 44XLR		G-MVHG	Mainair Gemini Flash IIA	
G-MVEF	Solar Wings Pegasus XL-R		G-MVHH	Mainair Gemini Flash IIA	
G-MVEG	Solar Wings Pegasus XL-R		G-MVHI	Thruster TST Mk 1	
G-MVEH	Mainair Gemini Flash IIA		G-MVHJ	Thruster TST Mk 1	
G-MVEI	CFM Shadow Srs BD		G-MVHK	Thruster TST Mk 1	
G-MVEJ	Mainair Gemini Flash IIA		G-MVHL	Thruster TST Mk 1	
G-MVEK	Mainair Gemini Flash IIA		G-MVHM	Whittaker MW.5 Sorcerer	
G-MVEL	Mainair Gemini Flash IIA		G-MVHN	Aerial Arts Chaser S	
G-MVEN	CFM Shadow Srs BD		G-MVHO	Solar Wings Pegasus XL-Q	
G-MVEO	Mainair Gemini Flash IIA		G-MVHP	Solar Wings Pegasus XL-Q	
G-MVEP	Mainair Gemini Flash IIA		G-MVHR	Solar Wings Pegasus XL-Q	
G-MVER	Mainair Gemini Flash IIA		G-MVHS	Solar Wings Pegasus XL-Q	
G-MVES	Mainair Gemini Flash IIA		G-MVHT	Solar Wings Pegasus XL-Q	
G-MVET	Mainir Gemini Flash IIA		G-MVHU	Solar Wings Pegasus XL-Q	
G-MVEV	Mainair Gemini Flash IIA		G-MVHV	Solar Wings Pegasus XL-Q	
G-MVEW	Mainair Gemini Flash IIA		G-MVHW	Solar Wings Pegasus XL-Q	
G-MVEX	Solar Wings Pegasus XL-Q		G-MVHX	Solar Wings Pegasus XL-Q	
G-MVEY	Solar Wings Pegasus XL-Q		G-MVHY	Solar Wings Pegasus XL-Q	
G-MVEZ	Solar Wings Pegasus XL-Q		G-MVHZ	Hornet Dual Trainer	
G-MVFA	Solar Wings Pegasus XL-Q		G-MVIA	Solar Wings Pegasus XL-R	
G-MVFB	Solar Wings Pegasus XL-Q		G-MVIB	Mainair Gemini Flash IIA	
G-MVFC	Solar Wings Pegasus XL-Q		G-MVIC	Mainair Gemini Flash IIA	
G-MVFD	Solar Wings Pegasus XL-Q		G-MVID	Aerial Arts Chaser S	

Reg.	Type	Notes	Reg.	Type	Notes
G-MVIE	Aerial Arts Chaser S		G-MVLE	Aerial Arts Chaser S	
G-MVIF	Medway Hybred 44XLR		G-MVLF	Aerial Arts Chaser S	
G-MVIG	CFM Shadow Srs B		G-MVLG	Aerial Arts Chaser S	
G-MVIH	Mainair Gemini Flash IIA		G-MVLH	Aerial Arts Chaser S	
G-MVIL	Noble Hardman Snowbird Mk IV		G-MVLJ	CFM Shadow Srs B	
			G-MVLL	Mainair Gemini Flash IIA	
G-MVIM	Noble Hardman Snowbird Mk IV		G-MVLM	Solar Wings Pegasus Bandit	
G-MVIN	Noble Hardman Snowbird Mk IV		G-MVLP	CFM Shadow Srs BD	
			G-MVLR	Mainair Gemini Flash IIA	
G-MVIO	Noble Hardman Snowbird Mk IV		G-MVLS	Aerial Arts Chaser S	
			G-MVLT	Aerial Arts Chaser S	
G-MVIP	AMF Chevvron 232		G-MVLU	Aerial Arts Chaser S	
G-MVIR	Thruster TST Mk 1		G-MVLW	Aerial Arts Chaser S	
G-MVIS	Thruster TST Mk 1		G-MVLX	Solar Wings Pegasus XL-Q	
G-MVIU	Thruster TST Mk 1		G-MVLY	Solar Wings Pegasus XL-Q	
G-MVIV	Thruster TST Mk 1		G-MVLZ	Solar Wings Pegasus XL-Q	
G-MVIW	Thruster TST Mk 1		G-MVMA	Solar Wings Pegasus XL-Q	
G-MVIX	Mainair Gemini Flash IIA		G-MVMB	Solar Wings Pegasus XL-Q	
G-MVIY	Mainair Gemini Flash IIA		G-MVMC	Solar Wings Pegasus XL-Q	
G-MVIZ	Mainair Gemini Flash IIA		G-MVMD	Powerchute Raider	
G-MVJA	Mainair Gemini Flash IIA		G-MVME	Thruster TST Mk 1	
G-MVJB	Mainair Gemini Flash IIA		G-MVMG	Thruster TST Mk 1	
G-MVJC	Mainair Gemini Flash IIA		G-MVMI	Thruster TST Mk 1	
G-MVJD	Solar Wings Pegasus XL-R		G-MVMK	Medway Hybred 44XLR	
G-MVJE	Mainair Gemini Flash IIA		G-MVML	Aerial Arts Chaser S	
G-MVJF	Aerial Arts Chaser S		G-MVMM	Aerial Arts Chaser S	
G-MVJG	Aerial Arts Chaser S		G-MVMN	Mainair Gemini Flash IIA	
G-MVJH	Aerial Arts Chaser S		G-MVMO	Mainair Gemini Flash IIA	
G-MVJI	Aerial Arts Chaser S		G-MVMP	Eipper Quicksilver MXII	
G-MVJJ	Aerial Arts Chaser S		G-MVMR	Mainair Gemini Flash IIA	
G-MVJK	Aerial Arts Chaser S		G-MVMT	Mainair Gemini Flash IIA	
G-MVJL	Mainair Gemini Flash IIA		G-MVMU	Mainair Gemini Flash IIA	
G-MVJM	Microflight Spectrum		G-MVMV	Aerotech MW.5 (K) Sorcerer	
G-MVJN	Solar Wings Pegasus XL-Q				
G-MVJO	Solar Wings Pegasus XL-Q		G-MVMW	Mainair Gemini Flash IIA	
G-MVJP	Solar Wings Pegasus XL-Q		G-MVMX	Mainair Gemini Flash IIA	
G-MVJR	Solar Wings Pegasus XL-Q		G-MVMY	Mainair Gemini Flash IIA	
G-MVJS	Solar Wings Pegasus XL-Q		G-MVMZ	Mainair Gemini Flash IIA	
G-MVJT	Solar Wings Pegasus XL-Q		G-MVNA	Powerchute Raider	
G-MVJU	Solar Wings Pegasus XL-Q		G-MVNB	Powerchute Raider	
G-MVJV	Solar Wings Pegasus XL-Q		G-MVNC	Powerchute Raider	
G-MVJW	Solar Wings Pegasus XL-Q		G-MVND	Powerchute Raider	
G-MVJX	Solar Wings Pegasus XL-Q		G-MVNF	Powerchute Raider	
G-MVJZ	Birdman Cherokee		G-MVNI	Powerchute Raider	
G-MVKA	Medway Hybred 44XLR		G-MVNJ	Powerchute Raider	
G-MVKB	Medway Hybred 44XLR		G-MVNK	Powerchute Raider	
G-MVKC	Mainair Gemini Flash IIA		G-MVNL	Powerchute Raider	
G-MVKE	Solar Wings Pegasus XL-R		G-MVNM	Mainair Gemini Flash IIA	
G-MVKF	Solar Wings Pegasus XL-R		G-MVNN	Whittaker MW.5 (K) Sorcerer	
G-MVKG	Solar Wings Pegasus XL-R				
G-MVKH	Solar Wings Pegasus XL-R		G-MVNO	Aerotech MW.5 (K) Sorcerer	
G-MVKI	Solar Wings Pegasus XL-R				
G-MVKJ	Solar Wings Pegasus XL-R		G-MVNP	Aerotech MW.5 (K) Sorcerer	
G-MVKK	Solar Wings Pegasus XL-R				
G-MVKL	Solar Wings Pegasus XL-R		G-MVNR	Aerotech MW.5 (K) Sorcerer	
G-MVKM	Solar Wings Pegasus XL-R				
G-MVKN	Solar Wings Pegasus XL-Q		G-MVNS	Aerotech MW.5 (K) Sorcerer	
G-MVKO	Solar Wings Pegasus XL-Q				
G-MVKP	Solar Wings Pegasus XL-Q		G-MVNT	Whittaker MW.5 (K) Sorcerer	
G-MVKR	Solar Wings Pegasus XL-Q				
G-MVKS	Solar Wings Pegasus XL-Q		G-MVNU	Aerotech MW.5 Sorcerer	
G-MVKT	Solar Wings Pegasus XL-Q		G-MVNV	Aerotech MW.5 Sorcerer	
G-MVKU	Solar Wings Pegasus XL-Q		G-MVNW	Mainair Gemini Flash IIA	
G-MVKV	Solar Wings Pegasus XL-Q		G-MVNX	Mainair Gemini Flash IIA	
G-MVKW	Solar Wings Pegasus XL-Q		G-MVNY	Mainair Gemini Flash IIA	
G-MVKX	Solar Wings Pegasus XL-Q		G-MVNZ	Mainair Gemini Flash IIA	
G-MVKY	Aerial Arts Chaser S		G-MVOA	Aerial Arts Alligator	
G-MVKZ	Aerial Arts Chaser S		G-MVOB	Mainair Gemini Flash IIA	
G-MVLA	Aerial Arts Chaser S		G-MVOD	Aerial Arts Chaser 110SX	
G-MVLB	Aerial Arts Chaser S		G-MVOE	Solar Wings Pegasus XL-R	
G-MVLC	Aerial Arts Chaser S		G-MVOF	Mainair Gemini Flash IIA	
G-MVLD	Aerial Arts Chaser S				

Reg.	Type	Notes	Reg.	Type	Notes
G-MVOG	Huntair Pathfinder Mk 1		G-MVSD	Solar Wings Pegasus XL-Q	
G-MVOH	CFM Shadow Srs B		G-MVSE	Solar Wings Pegasus XL-Q	
G-MVOI	Noble Hardman Snowbird Mk IV		G-MVSG	Aerial Arts Chaser S	
			G-MVSI	Medway Hybred 44XLR	
G-MVOJ	Noble Hardman Snowbird Mk IV		G-MVSJ	Aviasud Mistral 532	
			G-MVSK	Aerial Arts Chaser S	
G-MVOK	Noble Hardman Snowbird Mk IV		G-MVSL	Aerial Arts Chaser S	
			G-MVSM	Midland Ultralights Sirocco	
G-MVOL	Noble Hardman Snowbird Mk IV		G-MVSN	Mainair Gemini Flash IIA	
G-MVON	Mainair Gemini Flash IIA		G-MVSO	Mainair Gemini Flash IIA	
G-MVOO	AMF Chevvron 232		G-MVSP	Mainair Gemini Flash IIA	
G-MVOP	Aerial Arts Chaser S		G-MVSR	Medway Hybred 44XLR	
G-MVOR	Mainair Gemini Flash IIA		G-MVSS	Hornet RS-ZA	
G-MVOS	Southdown Raven		G-MVST	Mainair Gemini Flash IIA	
G-MVOT	Thruster TST Mk 1		G-MVSU	Microflight Spectrum	
G-MVOU	Thruster TST Mk 1		G-MVSV	Mainair Gemini Flash IIA	
G-MVOV	Thruster TST Mk 1		G-MVSW	Solar Wings Pegasus XL-Q	
G-MVOW	Thruster TST Mk 1		G-MVSX	Solar Wings Pegasus XL-Q	
G-MVOX	Thruster TST Mk 1		G-MVSY	Solar Wings Pegasus XL-Q	
G-MVOY	Thruster TST Mk 1		G-MVSZ	Solar Wings Pegasus XL-Q	
G-MVOZ	Mainair Gemini Flash IIA		G-MVTA	Solar Wings Pegasus XL-Q	
G-MVPA	Mainair Gemini Flash IIA		G-MVTC	Mainair Gemini Flash IIA	
G-MVPB	Mainair Gemini Flash IIA		G-MVTD	Whittaker MW.6 Merlin	
G-MVPC	Mainair Gemini Flash IIA		G-MVTE	Whittaker MW.6 Merlin	
G-MVPD	Mainair Gemini Flash IIA		G-MVTF	Aerial Arts Chaser S	
G-MVPE	Mainair Gemini Flash IIA		G-MVTG	Solar Wings Pegasus XL-Q	
G-MVPF	Medway Hybred 44XLR		G-MVTI	Solar Wings Pegasus XL-Q	
G-MVPG	Medway Hybred 44XLR		G-MVTJ	Solar Wings Pegasus XL-Q	
G-MVPH	Whittaker MW.6 Merlin		G-MVTK	Solar Wings Pegasus XL-Q	
G-MVPI	Mainair Gemini Flash IIA		G-MVTL	Aerial Arts Chaser S	
G-MVPJ	Rans S.5		G-MVTM	Aerial Arts Chaser S	
G-MVPK	CFM Shadow Srs B		G-MVUA	Mainair Gemini Flash IIA	
G-MVPL	Medway Hybred 44XLR		G-MVUB	Thruster T.300	
G-MVPM	Whittaker MW.6 Merlin		G-MVUC	Medway Hybred 44XLR	
G-MVPN	Whittaker MW.6 Merlin		G-MVUD	Medway Hybred 44XLR	
G-MVPO	Mainair Gemini Flash IIA		G-MVUE	Solar Wings Pegasus XL-Q	
G-MVPR	Solar Wings Pegasus XL-Q		G-MVUF	Solar Wings Pegasus XL-Q	
G-MVPS	Solar Wings Pegasus XL-Q		G-MVUG	Solar Wings Pegasus XL-Q	
G-MVPT	Solar Wings Pegasus XL-Q		G-MVUH	Solar Wings Pegasus XL-Q	
G-MVPU	Solar Wings Pegasus XL-Q		G-MVUI	Solar Wings Pegasus XL-Q	
G-MVPV	Solar Wings Pegasus XL-Q		G-MVUJ	Solar Wings Pegasus XL-Q	
G-MVPW	Solar Wings Pegasus XL-R		G-MVUK	Solar Wings Pegasus XL-Q	
G-MVPX	Solar Wings Pegasus XL-Q		G-MVUL	Solar Wings Pegasus XL-Q	
G-MVPY	Solar Wings Pegasus XL-Q		G-MVUM	Solar Wings Pegasus XL-Q	
G-MVPZ	Rans S.5		G-MVUN	Solar Wings Pegasus XL-Q	
G-MVRA	Mainair Gemini Flash IIA		G-MVUO	AMF Chevvron 232	
G-MVRB	Mainair Gemini Flash IIA		G-MVUP	Aviasud Mistral	
G-MVRC	Mainair Gemini Flash IIA		G-MVUR	Hornet ZA	
G-MVRD	Mainair Gemini Flash IIA		G-MVUS	Aerial Arts Chaser S	
G-MVRE	CFM Shadow Srs BD		G-MVUT	Aerial Arts Chaser S	
G-MVRF	Rotec Rally 2B		G-MVUU	Hornet R-ZA	
G-MVRG	Aerial Arts Chaser S		G-MVVF	Medway Hybred 44XLR	
G-MVRH	Solar Wings Pegasus XL-Q		G-MVVG	Medway Hybred 44XLR	
G-MVRI	Solar Wings Pegasus XL-Q		G-MVVH	Medway Hybred 44XLR	
G-MVRJ	Solar Wings Pegasus XL-Q		G-MVVI	Medway Hybred 44XLR	
G-MVRK	Solar Wings Pegasus XL-Q		G-MVVJ	Medway Hybred 44XLR	
G-MVRL	Aerial Arts Chaser S		G-MVVK	Solar Wings Pegasus XL-R	
G-MVRM	Mainair Gemini Flash IIA		G-MVVM	Solar Wings Pegasus XL-R	
G-MVRN	Rans S.4 Coyote		G-MVVN	Solar Wings Pegasus XL-Q	
G-MVRO	CFM Shadow Srs BD		G-MVVP	Solar Wings Pegasus XL-Q	
G-MVRP	CFM Shadow Srs BD		G-MVVR	Medway Hybred 44XLR	
G-MVRR	CFM Shadow Srs BD		G-MVVS	Southdown Puma Sprint	
G-MVRT	CFM Shadow Srs BD		G-MVVT	CFM Shadow Srs BD	
G-MVRU	Solar Wings Pegasus XL-Q		G-MVVU	Aerial Arts Chaser S	
G-MVRV	Powerchute Kestrel		G-MVVV	AMF Chevvron 232	
G-MVRW	Solar Wings Pegasus XL-Q		G-MVVW	Aerial Arts Chaser S	
G-MVRX	Solar Wings Pegasus XL-Q		G-MVVZ	Powerchute Raider	
G-MVRY	Medway Hybred 44XLR		G-MVWA	Powerchute Raider	
G-MVRZ	Medway Hybred 44XLR		G-MVWB	Powerchute Raider	
G-MVSA	Solar Wings Pegasus XL-Q		G-MVWD	Powerchute Raider	
G-MVSB	Solar Wings Pegasus XL-Q		G-MVWE	Powerchute Raider	
G-MVSC	Solar Wings Pegasus XL-Q		G-MVWF	Powerchute Raider	
			G-MVWH	Powerchute Raider	

Reg.	Type	Notes	Reg.	Type	Notes
G-MVWI	Powerchute Raider		G-MVZF	Thruster T.300	
G-MVWJ	Powerchute Raider		G-MVZG	Thruster T.300	
G-MVWK	Powerchute Raider		G-MVZH	Thruster T.300	
G-MVWL	Powerchute Raider		G-MVZI	Thruster T.300	
G-MVWM	Powerchute Raider		G-MVZJ	Solar Wings Pegasus XL-Q	
G-MVWN	Thruster T.300		G-MVZK	Challenger II	
G-MVWO	Thruster T.300		G-MVZL	Solar Wings Pegasus XL-Q	
G-MVWP	Thruster T.300		G-MVZM	Aerial Arts Chaser S	
G-MVWR	Thruster T.300		G-MVZN	Aerial Arts Chaser S	
G-MVWS	Thruster T.300		G-MVZO	Medway Hybred 44XLR	
G-MVWU	Medway Hybred 44XLR		G-MVZP	Renegade Spirit UK	
G-MVWV	Medway Hybred 44XLR		G-MVZR	Aviasud Mistral	
G-MVWW	Aviasud Mistral 532		G-MVZS	Mainair Gemini Flash IIA	
G-MVWX	Microflight Spectrum		G-MVZT	Solar Wings Pegasus XL-Q	
G-MVWZ	Aviasud Mistral		G-MVZU	Solar Wings Pegasus XL-Q	
G-MVXA	Whittaker MW.6 Merlin		G-MVZV	Solar Wings Pegasus XL-Q	
G-MVXB	Mainair Gemini Flash IIA		G-MVZW	Hornet R-ZA	
G-MVXC	Mainair Gemini Flash IIA		G-MVZX	Renegade Spirit UK	
G-MVXD	Medway Hybred 44XLR		G-MVZY	Aerial Arts Chaser S	
G-MVXE	Medway Hybred 44XLR		G-MVZZ	AMF Chevvron 232	
G-MVXF	Weedhopper JC-31A		G-MWAA	Medway Hybred 44XLR	
G-MVXG	Aerial Arts Chaser S		G-MWAB	Mainair Gemini Flash IIA	
G-MVXH	Microflight Spectrum		G-MWAC	Solar Wings Pegasus XL-Q	
G-MVXI	Medway Hybred 44XLR		G-MWAD	Solar Wings Pegasus XL-Q	
G-MVXJ	Medway Hybred 44XLR		G-MWAE	CFM Shadow Srs BD	
G-MVXK	Medway Hybred 44XLR		G-MWAF	Solar Wings Pegasus XL-R	
G-MVXL	Thruster TST Mk 1		G-MWAG	Solar Wings Pegasus XL-R	
G-MVXM	Medway Hybred 44XLR		G-MWAH	Hornet RS-ZA	
G-MVXN	Aviasud Mistral		G-MWAI	Solar Wings Pegasus XL-R	
G-MVXO	Aerial Arts Chaser S		G-MWAJ	Renegade Spirit UK	
G-MVXP	Aerial Arts Chaser S		G-MWAL	Solar Wings Pegasus XL-Q	
G-MVXR	Mainair Gemini Flash IIA		G-MWAM	Thruster T.300	
G-MVXS	Mainair Gemini Flash IIA		G-MWAN	Thruster T.300	
G-MVXT	Mainair Gemini Flash IIA		G-MWAO	Thruster T.300	
G-MVXU	Aviasud Mistral		G-MWAP	Thruster T.300	
G-MVXV	Aviasud Mistral		G-MWAR	Thruster T.300	
G-MVXW	Rans S.4 Coyote		G-MWAS	Thruster T.300	
G-MVXX	AMF Chevvron 232		G-MWAT	Solar Wings Pegasus XL-Q	
G-MVXY	AMF Paracat 1-24		G-MWAU	Mainair Gemini Flash IIA	
G-MVXZ	Minimax		G-MWAV	Solar Wings Pegasus XL-R	
G-MVYA	Aerial Arts Chaser S		G-MWAW	Whittaker MW.6 Merlin	
G-MVYB	Solar Wings Pegasus XL-Q		G-MWBH	Hornet RS-ZA	
G-MVYC	Solar Wings Pegasus XL-Q		G-MWBI	Medway Hybred 44XLR	
G-MVYD	Solar Wings Pegasus XL-Q		G-MWBJ	Medway Sprint	
G-MVYE	Thruster TST Mk 1		G-MWBK	Solar Wings Pegasus XL-Q	
G-MVYG	Hornet R-ZA		G-MWBL	Solar Wings Pegasus XL-Q	
G-MVYH	Hornet R-ZA		G-MWBM	Hornet RS-ZA	
G-MVYI	Hornet R-ZA		G-MWBN	Hornet RS-ZA	
G-MVYJ	Hornet R-ZA		G-MWBO	Rans S.4	
G-MVYK	Hornet R-ZA		G-MWBP	Hornet RS-ZA	
G-MVYM	Hornet R-ZA		G-MWBR	Hornet RS-ZA	
G-MVYN	Hornet R-ZA		G-MWBS	Hornet RS-ZA	
G-MVYO	Hornet R-ZA		G-MWBU	Hornet RS-ZA	
G-MVYP	Medway Hybred 44XLR		G-MWBV	Hornet RS-ZA	
G-MVYR	Medway Hybred 44XLR		G-MWBW	Hornet RS-ZA	
G-MVYS	Mainair Gemini Flash IIA		G-MWBX	Hornet RS-ZA	
G-MVYT	Noble Hardman Snowbird Mk IV		G-MWBY	Hornet RS-ZA	
G-MVYU	Noble Hardman Snowbird Mk IV		G-MWBZ	Hornet RS-ZA	
G-MVYV	Noble Hardman Snowbird Mk IV		G-MWCA	Hornet RS-ZA	
			G-MWCB	Solar Wings Pegasus XL-Q	
G-MVYW	Noble Hardman Snowbird Mk IV		G-MWCC	Solar Wings Pegasus XL-R	
			G-MWCE	Mainair Gemini Flash IIA	
G-MVYX	Noble Hardman Snowbird Mk IV		G-MWCF	Solar Wings Pegasus XL-R	
			G-MWCG	Microflight Spectrum	
G-MVYY	Aerial Arts Chaser S508		G-MWCH	Rans S.6	
G-MVYZ	CFM Shadow Srs BD		G-MWCI	Powerchute Kestrel	
G-MVZA	Thruster T.300		G-MWCJ	Powerchute Kestrel	
G-MVZB	Thruster T.300		G-MWCK	Powerchute Kestrel	
G-MVZC	Thruster T.300		G-MWCL	Powerchute Kestrel	
G-MVZD	Thruster T.300		G-MWCM	Powerchute Kestrel	
			G-MWCN	Powerchute Kestrel	
G-MVZE	Thruster T.300		G-MWCO	Powerchute Kestrel	
			G-MWCP	Powerchute Kestrel	

Reg.	Type	Notes	Reg.	Type	Notes
G-MWCR	Southdown Puma Sprint		G-MWGI	Whittaker MW.5 (K) Sorcerer	
G-MWCS	Powerchute Kestrel		G-MWGJ	Whittaker MW.5 (K) Sorcerer	
G-MWCU	Solar Wings Pegasus XL-R				
G-MWCV	Solar Wings Pegasus XL-Q		G-MWGK	Whittaker MW.5 (K) Sorcerer	
G-MWCW	Mainair Gemini Flash IIA				
G-MWCX	Medway Hybred 44XLR		G-MWGL	Solar Wings Pegasus XL-Q	
G-MWCY	Medway Hybred 44XLR		G-MWGM	Solar Wings Pegasus XL-Q	
G-MWCZ	Medway Hybred 44XLR		G-MWGN	Rans S.4	
G-MWDA	Jakeway Powered Parachute		G-MWGO	Aerial Arts Chaser 110SX	
			G-MWGR	Solar Wings Pegasus XL-Q	
G-MWDB	CFM Shadow Srs BD		G-MWGT	Powerchute Kestrel	
G-MWDC	Solar Wings Pegasus XL-R		G-MWGU	Powerchute Kestrel	
G-MWDD	Solar Wings Pegasus XL-Q		G-MWGV	Powerchute Kestrel	
G-MWDE	Hornet RS-ZA		G-MWGW	Powerchute Kestrel	
G-MWDF	Hornet RS-ZA		G-MWGY	Powerchute Kestrel	
G-MWDG	Hornet RS-ZA		G-MWGZ	Powerchute Kestrel	
G-MWDH	Hornet RS-ZA		G-MWHC	Solar Wings Pegasus XL-Q	
G-MWDI	Hornet RS-ZA		G-MWHD	Microflight Spectrum	
G-MWDJ	Mainair Gemini Flash IIA		G-MWHE	Microflight Spectrum	
G-MWDK	Solar Wings Pegasus XL-R		G-MWHF	Solar Wings Pegasus XL-Q	
G-MWDL	Solar Wings Pegasus XL-R		G-MWHG	Solar Wings Pegasus XL-Q	
G-MWDM	Renegade Spirit UK		G-MWHH	Team Minimax	
G-MWDN	CFM Shadow Srs BD		G-MWHI	Mainair Gemini Flash IIA	
G-MWDO	Spencer Cub		G-MWHJ	Solar Wings Pegasus XL-Q	
G-MWDP	Thruster TST Mk 1		G-MWHK	Renegade Spirit UK	
G-MWDS	Thruster T.300		G-MWHL	Solar Wings Pegasus XL-Q	
G-MWDZ	Eipper Quicksilver MXL II		G-MWHM	Whittaker MW.6 Merlin	
G-MWEE	Solar Wings Pegasus XL-Q		G-MWHO	Mainair Gemini Flash IIA	
G-MWEF	Solar Wings Pegasus XL-Q		G-MWHP	Rans S.6	
G-MWEG	Solar Wings Pegasus XL-Q		G-MWHR	Mainair Gemini Flash IIA	
G-MWEH	Solar Wings Pegasus XL-Q		G-MWHS	AMF Chevvron 232	
G-MWEI	Mainair Gemini Flash IIA		G-MWHT	Solar Wings Pegasus Quasar	
G-MWEK	Whittaker MW.5 Sorcerer				
G-MWEL	Mainair Gemini Flash IIA		G-MWHU	Solar Wings Pegasus Quasar	
G-MWEM	Medway Hybred 44XLR				
G-MWEN	CFM Shadow Srs BD		G-MWHV	Solar Wings Pegasus Quasar	
G-MWEO	Whittaker MW.5 Sorcerer				
G-MWEP	Rans S.4		G-MWHW	Solar Wings Pegasus XL-Q	
G-MWER	Solar Wings Pegasus XL-Q		G-MWHX	Solar Wings Pegasus XL-Q	
G-MWES	Rans S.4		G-MWHY	Mainair Gemini Flash IIA	
G-MWET	Hornet RS-ZA		G-MWHZ	Trion J-1	
G-MWEU	Hornet RS-ZA		G-MWIA	Mainair Gemini Flash IIA	
G-MWEV	Hornet RS-ZA		G-MWIB	Aviasud Mistral	
G-MWEY	Hornet RS-ZA		G-MWIC	Whittaker MW.5 Sorcerer	
G-MWEZ	CFM Shadow Srs CD		G-MWID	Solar Wings Pegasus XL-Q	
G-MWFA	Solar Wings Pegasus XL-R		G-MWIE	Solar Wings Pegasus XL-Q	
G-MWFB	CFM Shadow Srs BD		G-MWIF	Rans S.6	
G-MWFD	Team Minimax		G-MWIG	Mainair Gemini Flash IIA	
G-MWFE	Robin 330/Lightning 195		G-MWIH	Mainair Gemini Flash IIA	
G-MWFF	Rans S.4		G-MWII	Medway Hybred 44XLR	
G-MWFG	Powerchute Kestrel		G-MWIJ	Medway Hybred 44XLR	
G-MWFH	Powerchute Kestrel		G-MWIK	Medway Hybred 44XLR	
G-MWFI	Powerchute Kestrel		G-MWIL	Medway Hybred 44XLR	
G-MWFK	Powerchute Kestrel		G-MWIM	Solar Wings Pegasus Quasar	
G-MWFL	Powerchute Kestrel				
G-MWFN	Powerchute Kestrel		G-MWIN	Mainair Gemini Flash IIA	
G-MWFO	Solar Wings Pegasus XL-R		G-MWIO	Rans S.4	
G-MWFP	Solar Wings Pegasus XL-R		G-MWIP	Whittaker MW.6 Merlin	
G-MWFS	Solar Wings Pegasus XL-Q		G-MWIR	Solar Wings Pegasus XL-Q	
G-MWFT	MBA Tiger Cub 440		G-MWIS	Solar Wings Pegasus XL-Q	
G-MWFU	Quad City Challenger II UK		G-MWIT	Solar Wings Pegasus XL-Q	
G-MWFV	Quad City Challenger II UK		G-MWIU	Solar Wings Pegasus XL-Q	
G-MWFW	Rans S.4		G-MWIV	Mainair Gemini Flash IIA	
G-MWFX	Quad City Challenger II UK		G-MWIW	Solar Wings Pegasus Quasar	
G-MWFY	Quad City Challenger II UK				
G-MWFZ	Quad City Challenger II UK		G-MWIX	Solar Wings Pegasus Quasar	
G-MWGA	Rans S.5				
G-MWGB	Medway Hybred 44XLR		G-MWIY	Solar Wings Pegasus Quasar	
G-MWGC	Medway Hybred 44XLR				
G-MWGD	Medway Hybred 44XLR		G-MWIZ	CFM Shadow Srs BD	
G-MWGE	Medway Hybred 44XLR		G-MWJD	Solar Wings Pegasus Quasar	
G-MWGF	Renegade Spirit UK				
G-MWGG	Mainair Gemini Flash IIA				

Reg.	Type	Notes	Reg.	Type	Notes
G-MWJF	CFM Shadow Srs BD			Quasar	
G-MWJG	Solar Wings Pegasus XL-R		G-MWMJ	Solar Wings Pegasus	
G-MWJH	Solar Wings Pegasus			Quasar	
	Quasar		G-MWMK	Solar Wings Pegasus	
G-MWJI	Solar Wings Pegasus			Quasar	
	Quasar		G-MWML	Solar Wings Pegasus	
G-MWJJ	Solar Wings Pegasus			Quasar	
	Quasar		G-MWMM	Mainair Gemini Flash IIA	
G-MWJK	Solar Wings Pegasus		G-MWMN	Solar Wings Pegasus XL-Q	
	Quasar		G-MWMO	Solar Wings Pegasus XL-Q	
G-MWJL	AMF Chevvron 232		G-MWMP	Solar Wings Pegasus XL-Q	
G-MWJM	AMF Chevvron 232		G-MWMR	Solar Wings Pegasus XL-R	
G-MWJN	Solar Wings Pegasus XL-Q		G-MWMS	Mainair Gemini Flash	
G-MWJO	Solar Wings Pegasus XL-Q		G-MWMT	Mainair Gemini Flash IIA	
G-MWJP	Medway Hybred 44XLR		G-MWMU	CFM Shadow Srs CD	
G-MWJR	Medway Hybred 44XLR		G-MWMV	Solar Wings Pegasus XL-R	
G-MWJS	Solar Wings Pegasus		G-MWMW	Renegade Spirit UK	
	Quasar		G-MWMX	Mainair Gemini Flash IIA	
G-MWJT	Solar Wings Pegasus		G-MWMY	Mainair Gemini Flash IIA	
	Quasar		G-MWMZ	Solar Wings Pegasus XL-Q	
G-MWJU	Solar Wings Pegasus		G-MWNA	Solar Wings Pegasus XL-Q	
	Quasar		G-MWNB	Solar Wings Pegasus XL-Q	
G-MWJV	Solar Wings Pegasus		G-MWNC	Solar Wings Pegasus XL-Q	
	Quasar		G-MWND	Tiger Cub Developments	
G-MWJW	Whittaker MW.5 Sorcerer			RL.5A	
G-MWJX	Medway Puma Sprint		G-MWNE	Mainair Gemini Flash IIA	
G-MWJY	Mainair Gemini Flash IIA		G-MWNF	Renegade Spirit UK	
G-MWJZ	CFM Shadow Srs CD		G-MWNG	Solar Wings Pegasus XL-Q	
G-MWKA	Renegade Spirit UK		G-MWNH	Powerchute Mk III	
G-MWKE	Hornet R-ZA		G-MWNK	Solar Wings Pegasus	
G-MWKO	Solar Wings Pegasus XL-Q			Quasar	
G-MWKP	Solar Wings Pegasus XL-Q		G-MWNL	Solar Wings Pegasus	
G-MWKW	Microflight Spectrum			Quasar	
G-MWKX	Microflight Spectrum		G-MWNM	Solar Wings Pegasus	
G-MWKY	Solar Wings Pegasus XL-Q			Quasar	
G-MWKZ	Solar Wings Pegasus XL-Q		G-MWNN	Solar Wings Pegasus	
G-MWLA	Rans S.4			Quasar	
G-MWLB	Medway Hybred 44XLR		G-MWNO	AMF Chevvron 232	
G-MWLC	Medway Hybred 44XLR		G-MWNP	AMF Chevvron 232	
G-MWLD	CFM Shadow Srs BD		G-MWNR	Renegade Spirit UK	
G-MWLE	Solar Wings Pegasus XL-R		G-MWNS	Mainair Gemini Flash IIA	
G-MWLF	Solar Wings Pegasus XL-R		G-MWNT	Mainair Gemini Flash IIA	
G-MWLG	Solar Wings Pegasus XL-R		G-MWNU	Mainair Gemini Flash IIA	
G-MWLH	Solar Wings Pegasus XL-R		G-MWNV	Powerchute Kestrel	
G-MWLI	Solar Wings Pegasus		G-MWNW	Powerchute Kestrel	
	Quasar		G-MWNX	Powerchute Kestrel	
G-MWLJ	Solar Wings Pegasus		G-MWNY	Powerchute Kestrel	
	Quasar		G-MWNZ	Powerchute Kestrel	
G-MWLK	Solar Wings Pegasus		G-MWOA	Powerchute Kestrel	
	Quasar		G-MWOB	Powerchute Kestrel	
G-MWLL	Solar Wings Pegasus XL-Q		G-MWOC	Powerchute Kestrel	
G-MWLM	Solar Wings Pegasus XL-Q		G-MWOD	Powerchute Kestrel	
G-MWLN	Whittaker MW.6-S Fatboy		G-MWOE	Powerchute Kestrel	
	Flyer		G-MWOF	Microflight Spectrum	
G-MWLO	Whittaker MW.6 Merlin		G-MWOH	Solar Wings Pegasus XL-R	
G-MWLP	Mainair Gemini Flash IIA		G-MWOI	Solar Wings Pegasus XL-R	
G-MWLR	Mainair Gemini Flash IIA		G-MWOJ	Mainair Gemini Flash IIA	
G-MWLS	Medway Hybred 44XLR		G-MWOK	Mainair Gemini Flash IIA	
G-MWLT	Mainair Gemini Flash IIA		G-MWOL	Mainair Gemini Flash IIA	
G-MWLU	Solar Wings Pegasus XL-R		G-MWOM	Solar Wings Pegasus	
G-MWLW	Team Minimax			Quasar TC	
G-MWLX	Mainair Gemini Flash IIA		G-MWON	CFM Shadow Srs CD	
G-MWLY	Rans S.4		G-MWOO	Renegade Spirit UK	
G-MWLZ	Rans S.4		G-MWOP	Solar Wings Pegasus	
G-MWMA	Powerchute Kestrel			Quasar	
G-MWMB	Powerchute Kestrel		G-MWOR	Solar Wings Pegasus XL-Q	
G-MWMC	Powerchute Kestrel		G-MWOS	Cosmos Chronos	
G-MWMD	Powerchute Kestrel		G-MWOT	Icarus Covert Insertion &	
G-MWME	Powerchute Kestrel			Recovery Vehicle	
G-MWMF	Powerchute Kestrel		G-MWOU	Medway Hybred 44XLR	
G-MWMG	Powerchute Kestrel		G-MWOV	Whittaker MW.6 Merlin	
G-MWMH	Powerchute Kestrel		G-MWOW	CFM Shadow Srs B	
G-MWMI	Solar Wings Pegasus		G-MWOX	Solar Wings Pegasus XL-Q	

Reg.	Type	Notes
G-MWOY	Solar Wings Pegasus XL-Q	
G-MWPA	Mainair Gemini Flash IIA	
G-MWPB	Mainair Gemini Flash IIA	
G-MWPC	Mainair Gemini Flash IIA	
G-MWPD	Mainair Gemini Flash IIA	
G-MWPE	Solar Wings Pegasus XL-Q	
G-MWPF	Mainair Gemini Flash IIA	
G-MWPG	Microflight Spectrum	
G-MWPH	Microflight Spectrum	
G-MWPI	Microflight Spectrum	
G-MWPJ	Solar Wings Pegasus XL-Q	
G-MWPK	Solar Wings Pegasus XL-Q	
G-MWPL	MBA Tiger Cub 440	
G-MWPM	Medway Flaven	
G-MWPN	CFM Shadow Srs CD	
G-MWPO	Mainair Gemini Flash IIA	
G-MWPP	CFM Streak Shadow (G-BTEM)	
G-MWPR	Whittaker MW.6 Merlin	
G-MWPS	Renegade Spirit UK	
G-MWPT	Hunt Avon Trike	
G-MWPU	Solar Wings Pegasus Quasar TC	
G-MWPX	Solar Wings Pegasus XL-R	
G-MWPZ	Renegade Spirit UK	
G-MWRA	Mainair Gemini Flash IIA	
G-MWRB	Mainair Gemini Flash IIA	
G-MWRC	Mainair Gemini Flash IIA	
G-MWRD	Mainair Gemini Flash IIA	
G-MWRE	Mainair Gemini Flash IIA	
G-MWRF	Mainair Gemini Flash IIA	
G-MWRG	Mainair Gemini Flash IIA	
G-MWRH	Mainair Gemini Flash IIA	
G-MWRI	Mainair Gemini Flash IIA	
G-MWRJ	Mainair Gemini Flash IIA	
G-MWRK	Rans S.6	
G-MWRL	CFM Shadow Srs CD	
G-MWRM	Medway Hybred 44XLR	
G-MWRN	Solar Wings Pegasus XL-R	
G-MWRO	Solar Wings Pegasus XL-R	
G-MWRP	Solar Wings Pegasus XL-R	
G-MWRR	Mainair Gemini Flash IIA	
G-MWRS	Ultravia Super Pelican	
G-MWRT	Solar Wings Pegasus XL-R	
G-MWRU	Solar Wings Pegasus XL-R	
G-MWRV	Solar Wings Pegasus XL-R	
G-MWRW	Solar Wings Pegasus XL-Q	
G-MWRX	Solar Wings Pegasus XL-Q	
G-MWRY	CFM Shadow Srs CD	
G-MWRZ	AMF Chevvron 232	
G-MWSA	Team Minimax	
G-MWSB	Mainair Gemini Flash IIA	
G-MWSC	Rans S.6-ESD Coyote II	
G-MWSD	Solar Wings Pegasus XL-Q	
G-MWSE	Solar Wings Pegasus XL-R	
G-MWSF	Solar Wings Pegasus XL-R	
G-MWSG	Solar Wings Pegasus XL-R	
G-MWSH	Solar Wings Pegasus Quasar TC	
G-MWSI	Solar Wings Pegasus Quasar TC	
G-MWSJ	Solar Wings Pegasus XL-Q	
G-MWSK	Solar Wings Pegasus XL-Q	
G-MWSL	Mainair Gemini Flash IIA	
G-MWSM	Mainair Gemini Flash IIA	
G-MWSN	Solar Wings Pegasus Quasar TC	
G-MWSO	Solar Wings Pegasus XL-R	
G-MWSP	Solar Wings Pegasus XL-R	
G-MWSR	Solar Wings Pegasus XL-R	
G-MWSS	Medway Hybred 44XLR	
G-MWST	Medway Hybred 44XLR	
G-MWSU	Medway Hybred 44XLR	
G-MWSV	Solar Wings Pegasus Quasar TC	
G-MWSW	Whittaker MW.6 Merlin	
G-MWSX	Whittaker MW.5 Sorcerer	
G-MWSY	Whittaker MW.5 Sorcerer	
G-MWSZ	CFM Shadow Srs CD	
G-MWTA	Solar Wings Pegasus XL-Q	
G-MWTB	Solar Wings Pegasus XL-Q	
G-MWTC	Solar Wings Pegasus XL-Q	
G-MWTD	Spectrum	
G-MWTE	Spectrum	
G-MWTF	Mainair Gemini	
G-MWTG	Mainair Gemini Flash IIA	
G-MWTH	Mainair Gemini Flash IIA	
G-MWTI	Solar Wings Pegasus XL-Q	
G-MWTJ	CFM Shadow Srs CD	
G-MWTK	Solar Wings Pegasus XL-R	
G-MWTL	Solar Wings Pegasus XL-R	
G-MWTM	Solar Wings Pegasus XL-R	
G-MWTN	CFM Shadow Srs CD	
G-MWTO	Mainair Gemini Flash IIA	
G-MWTP	CFM Shadow Srs CD	
G-MWTR	Mainair Gemini Flash IIA	
G-MWTS	Whittaker MW.6-S Fatboy Flyer	
G-MWTT	Rans S.6-ESD Coyote II	
G-MWTU	Solar Wings Pegasus XL-R	
G-MWTX	Medway Hybred 44XLR	
G-MWTY	Mainair Gemini Flash IIA	
G-MWTZ	Mainair Gemini Flash IIA	
G-MWUA	CFM Shadow Srs CD	
G-MWUB	Solar Wings Pegasus XL-R	
G-MWUC	Solar Wings Pegasus XL-R	
G-MWUD	Solar Wings Pegasus XL-R	
G-MWUF	Solar Wings Pegasus XL-R	
G-MWUG	Solar Wings Pegasus XL-R	
G-MWUH	Renegade Spirit UK	
G-MWUI	AMF Chevvron 232C	
G-MWUJ	Medway Hybred 44XLR	
G-MWUK	Rans S.6-ESD Coyote II	
G-MWUL	Rans S.6-ESD Coyote II	
G-MWUM	Rans S.6-ESD Coyote II	
G-MWUN	Rans S.6-ESD Coyote II	
G-MWUO	Solar Wings Pegasus XL-Q	
G-MWUP	Solar Wings Pegasus XL-R	
G-MWUR	Solar Wings Pegasus XL-R	
G-MWUT	Solar Wings Pegasus XL-R	
G-MWUU	Solar Wings Pegasus XL-R	
G-MWUV	Solar Wings Pegasus XL-R	
G-MWUW	Solar Wings Pegasus XL-R	
G-MWUX	Solar Wings Pegasus XL-Q	
G-MWUY	Solar Wings Pegasus XL-Q	
G-MWUZ	Solar Wings Pegasus XL-Q	
G-MWVA	Solar Wings Pegasus XL-Q	
G-MWVB	Solar Wings Pegasus XL-R	
G-MWVE	Solar Wings Pegasus XL-R	
G-MWVF	Solar Wings Pegasus XL-R	
G-MWVG	CFM Shadow Srs CD	
G-MWVH	CFM Shadow Srs CD	
G-MWVI	Whittaker MW.6 Merlin	
G-MWVJ	Mainair Mercury	
G-MWVK	Mainair Mercury	
G-MWVL	Rans S.6-ESD Coyote II	
G-MWVM	Solar Wings Pegasus Quasar II	
G-MWVN	Mainair Gemini Flash IIA	
G-MWVO	Mainair Gemini Flash IIA	
G-MWVP	Renegade Spirit UK	
G-MWVS	Mainair Gemini Flash IIA	
G-MWVT	Mainair Gemini Flash IIA	
G-MWVU	Medway Hybred 44XLR	
G-MWVV	Solar Wings Pegasus XL-Q	
G-MWVW	Mainair Gemini Flash IIA	

MICROLIGHTS

Reg.	Type	Notes	Reg.	Type	Notes
G-MWVX	Quad City Challenger II UK		G-MWYS	—	
G-MWVY	Mainair Gemini Flash IIA		G-WMYT	Mainair Gemini Flash IIA	
G-MWVZ	Mainair Gemini Flash IIA		G-MWYU	Solar Wings Pegasus XL-Q	
G-MWWA	Solar Wings Pegasus Quasar II		G-WMYV	Mainair Gemini Flash IIA	
			G-MWYX	Mainair Gemini Flash IIA	
G-MWWB	Mainair Gemini Flash IIA		G-MWYY	Mainair Gemini Flash IIA	
G-MWWC	Mainair Gemini Flash IIA		G-MWYZ	Solar Wings Pegasus XL-Q	
G-MWWD	Mainair Gemini Flash IIA		G-WMZA	Mainair Mercury	
G-MWWE	Team Minimax		G-MWZB	AMF Chevvron 2-32C	
G-MWWF	Kolb Twinstar Mk 3		G-MWZC	Mainair Gemini Flash IIA	
G-MWWG	Solar Wings Pegasus XL-Q		G-WMZD	Solar Wings Pegasus Quasar IITC	
G-MWWH	Solar Wings Pegasus XL-Q				
G-MWWI	Mainair Gemini Flash IIA		G-MWZE	Solar Wings Pegasus Quasar IITC	
G-MWWJ	Mainair Gemini Flash IIA				
G-MWWK	Mainair Gemini Flash IIA		G-MWZF	Solar Wings Pegasus Quasar IITC	
G-MWWL	Rans S.6-ESD Coyote II				
G-MWWM	Kolb Twinstar Mk 2		G-MWZG	Mainair Gemini Flash IIA	
G-MWWN	Mainair Gemini Flash IIA		G-MWZH	Solar Wings Pegasus XL-R	
G-MWWO	Solar Wings Pegasus XL-R		G-MWZI	Solar Wings Pegasus XL-R	
G-MWWP	Rans S.4		G-MWZJ	Solar Wings Pegasus XL-R	
G-MWVR	Mainair Gemini Flash IIA		G-MWZK	Solar Wings Pegasus XL-R	
G-MWWR	Spectrum		G-MWZL	Mainair Gemini Flash IIA	
G-MWWS	Thruster T.300		G-MWZN	Mainair Gemini Flash IIA	
G-MWWT	Thruster Super T.300		G-MWZO	Solar Wings Pegasus Quasar IITC	
G-MWWU	Air Creation Fun 18 GTBI				
G-MWWV	Solar Wings Pegasus XL-Q		G-MWZP	Solar Wings Pegasus Quasar IITC	
G-MWWW	Whittaker MW.6-S Fatboy Flyer				
			G-MWZR	Solar Wings Pegasus Quasar IITC	
G-MWWX	Spectrum				
G-MWWY	Spectrum		G-MWZT	Solar Wings Pegasus XL-R	
G-MWWZ	Cyclone Chaser S		G-MWZU	Solar Wings Pegasus XL-R	
G-MWXA	Mainair Gemini Flash IIA		G-MWZV	Solar Wings Pegasus XL-R	
G-MWXB	Mainair Gemini Flash IIA		G-MWZW	Solar Wings Pegasus XL-R	
G-MWXC	Mainair Gemini Flash IIA		G-MWZX	Solar Wings Pegasus XL-R	
G-MWXD	Mainair Gemini Flash IIA		G-MWZY	Solar Wings Pegasus XL-R	
G-MWXE	Flexiform Skytrike		G-MWZZ	Solar Wings Pegasus XL-R	
G-MWXF	Mainair Mercury		G-MYAA	CFM Shadow Srs CD	
G-MWXG	Solar Wings Pegasus Quasar IITC		G-MYAB	Solar Wings Pegasus XL-R	
			G-MYAC	Solar Wings Pegasus XL-Q	
G-MWXH	Solar Wings Pegasus Quasar IITC		G-MYAD	Solar Wings Pegasus XL-Q	
			G-MYAE	Solar Wings Pegasus XL-Q	
G-MWXI	Solar Wings Pegasus Quasar IITC		G-MYAF	Solar Wings Pegasus XL-Q	
			G-MYAG	Quad City Challenger II	
G-MWXJ	Mainair Mercury		G-MYAH	Whittaker MW.5 Sorcerer	
G-MWXK	Mainair Mercury		G-MYAI	Mainair Mercury	
G-MWXL	Mainair Gemini Flash IIA		G-MYAJ	Rans S.6-ESD Coyote II	
G-MWXN	Mainair Gemini Flash IIA		G-MYAK	Solar Wings Pegasus Quasar IITC	
G-MWXO	Mainair Gemini Flash IIA				
G-MWXP	Solar Wings Pegasus XL-Q		G-MYAL	Rotec Rally 2B	
G-MWXR	Solar Wings Pegasus XL-Q		G-MYAM	Renegade Spirit UK	
G-MWXS	Mainair Gemini Flash IIA		G-MYAN	Whittaker MW.5 (K) Sorcerer	
G-MWXU	Mainair Gemini Flash IIA				
G-MWXV	Mainair Gemini Flash IIA		G-MYAO	Mainair Gemini Flash IIA	
G-MWXW	Cyclone Chaser S		G-MYAP	Thruster T.300	
G-MWXX	Cyclone Chaser S 447		G-MYAR	Thruster T.300	
G-MWXY	Cyclone Chaser S 447		G-MYAS	Mainair Gemini Flash IIA	
G-MWXZ	Cyclone Chaser S 508		G-MYAT	Team Minimax	
G-MWYA	Mainair Gemini Flash IIA		G-MYAU	Mainair Gemini Flash IIA	
G-MWYB	Solar Wings Pegasus XL-Q		G-MYAV	Mainair Mercury	
G-MWYC	Solar Wings Pegasus XL-Q		G-MYAW	Team Minimax	
G-MWYD	CFM Shadow Srs C		G-MYAX	Mainair Gemini Flash IIA	
G-MWYE	Rans S.6-ESD Coyote II		G-MYAY	Spectrum	
G-MWYF	Rans S.6		G-MYAZ	Renegade Spirit UK	
G-MWYG	Mainair Gemini Flash IIA		G-MYBA	Rans S.6-ESD Coyote II	
G-MWYH	Mainair Gemini Flash IIA		G-MYBB	Drifter	
G-MWYI	Solar Wings Pegasus Quasar II		G-MYBC	CFM Shadow Srs CD	
			G-MYBD	Solar Wings Pegasus Quaser IITC	
G-MWYJ	Solar Wings Pegasus Quasar IITC				
			G-MYBE	Solar Wings Pegasus Quaser IITC	
G-MWYK	Mainair Gemini Flash IIA				
G-MWYL	Mainair Gemini Flash IIA		G-MYBF	Solar Wings Pegasus XL-Q	
G-MWYM	Cyclone Chaser S 1000		G-MYBG	Solar Wings Pegasus XL-Q	
G-MWYN	Rans S.6-ESD Coyote II		G-MYBH	Quicksilver GT500	

Reg.	Type	Notes	Reg.	Type	Notes
G-MYBI	Rans S.6-ESD Coyote II		G-MYEC	SolarWings Pegasus XL-Q	
G-MYBJ	Mainair Gemini Flash IIA		G-MYED	SolarWings Pegasus XL-R	
G-MYBK	Solar Wings Pegasus Quasar IITC		G-MYEE	Thruster TST Mk 1	
			G-MYEF	–	
G-MYBL	CFM Shadow Srs C		G-MYEG	SolarWings Pegasus XL-R	
G-MYBM	Team Minimax		G-MYEH	SolarWings Pegasus XL-R	
G-MYBN	Hiway Demon 175		G-MYEI	Cyclone Chaser S447	
G-MYBO	SolarWings Pegasus XL-R		G-MYEJ	Cyclone Chaser S447	
G-MYBP	SolarWings Pegasus XL-R		G-MYEK	Solar Wings Pegasus Quasar IITC	
G-MYBR	SolarWings Pegasus XL-Q				
G-MYBS	SolarWings Pegasus XL-Q		G-MYEL	Solar Wings Pegasus Quasar IITC	
G-MYBT	SolarWings Pegasus Quasar IITC		G-MYEM	Solar Wings Pegasus Quasar IITC	
G-MYBU	Cyclone Chaser S447		G-MYEN	Solar Wings Pegasus Quasar IITC	
G-MYBV	SolarWings Pegasus XL-Q				
G-MYBW	SolarWings Pegasus XL-Q		G-MYEO	Solar Wings Pegasus Quasar IITC	
G-MYBX	SolarWings Pegasus XL-Q		G-MYEP	CFM Shadow Srs CD	
G-MYBY	SolarWings Pegasus XL-Q		G-MYER	Cyclone AX3/503	
G-MYBZ	SolarWings Pegasus XL-Q		G-MYES	Rans S.6-ESD Coyote II	
G-MYCA	Whittaker MW.6 Merlin		G-MYET	Whittaker MW.6 Merlin	
G-MYCB	Cyclone Chaser S 447		G-MYEU	Mainair Gemini Flash IIA	
G-MYCC	Renegade Spirit UK		G-MYEV	Whittaker MW.6 Merlin	
G-MYCD	CFM Shadow Srs CD		G-MYEW	Powerchute Kestrel	
G-MYCE	Solar Wings Pegasus Quasar IITC		G-MYEX	Powerchute Kestrel	
			G-MYEY	Powerchute Kestrel	
G-MYCF	Solar Wings Pegasus Quasar IITC		G-MYEZ	Powerchute Kestrel	
			G-MYFC	Powerchute Kestrel	
G-MYCG	Solar Wings Pegasus Quasar IITC		G-MYFD	Powerchute Kestrel	
			G-MYFE	Rans S.6-ESD Coyote II	
G-MYCH	SolarWings Pegasus XL-R		G-MYFF	–	
G-MYCJ	Mainair Mercury		G-MYFG	Hunt Avon Skytrike	
G-MYCK	Mainair Gemini Flash IIA		G-MYFH	Quad City Challenger II	
G-MYCL	Mainair Mercury		G-MYFI	Cyclone AX3/503	
G-MYCM	CFM Shadow Srs CD		G-MYFJ	Solar Wings Pegasus Quasar IITC	
G-MYCN	Mainair Mercury				
G-MYCO	Whittaker MW.6 Merlin		G-MYFK	Solar Wings Pegasus Quasar IITC	
G-MYCP	Whittaker MW.6 Merlin				
G-MYCR	Mainair Gemini Flash IIA		G-MYFL	Solar Wings Pegasus Quasar IITC	
G-MYCS	Mainair Gemini Flash IIA				
G-MYCT	Team Minimax		G-MYFM	Renegade Spirit UK	
G-MYCU	Whittaker MW.6 Merlin		G-MYFN	Rans S.5	
G-MYCV	Mainair Mercury		G-MYFO	Cyclone Chaser S	
G-MYCW	Powerchute Kestrel		G-MYFP	Mainair Gemini Flash IIA	
G-MYCX	Powerchute Kestrel		G-MYFR	Mainair Gemini Flash IIA	
G-MYCY	Powerchute Kestrel		G-MYFS	SolarWings Pegasus XL-R	
G-MYCZ	Powerchute Kestrel		G-MYFT	Mainair Scorcher	
G-MYDA	Powerchute Kestrel		G-MYFU	Mainair Gemini Flash IIA	
G-MYDB	Powerchute Kestrel		G-MYFV	Cyclone AX3/503	
G-MYDC	Mainair Mercury		G-MYFW	Cyclone AX3/503	
G-MYDD	CFM Shadow Srs CD		G-MYFX	Solar Wings Pegasus XL-Q	
G-MYDE	CFM Shadow Srs CD		G-MYFY	Cyclone AX3/503	
G-MYDF	Team Minimax		G-MYFZ	Cyclone AX3/503	
G-MYDG	SolarWings Pegasus XL-R		G-MYGA	SolarWings Pegasus XL-R	
G-MYDI	SolarWings Pegasus XL-R		G-MYGB	SolarWings Pegasus XL-R	
G-MYDJ	SolarWings Pegasus XL-R		G-MYGC	SolarWings Pegasus XL-R	
G-MYDK	Rans S.6-ESD Coyote II		G-MYGD	Cyclone AX3/503	
G-MYDL	Whittaker MW.5 (K) Sorcerer		G-MYGE	Whittaker MW.6 Merlin	
			G-MYGF	Team Minimax	
G-MYDM	Whittaker MW.6-S Fatboy Flyer		G-MYGG	Mainair Mercury	
			G-MYGH	Rans S.6-ESD Coyote II	
G-MYDN	Quad City Challenger II		G-MYGI	Cyclone Chaser S447	
G-MYDO	Rans S.5		G-MYGJ	Mainair Mercury	
G-MYDP	Kolb Twinstar Mk 3		G-MYGK	Cyclone Chaser S508	
G-MYDR	Thruster T.300		G-MYGL	Team Minimax	
G-MYDS	Quad City Challenger II		G-MYGM	Quad City Challenger II	
G-MYDT	Thruster T.300		G-MYGN	AMF Chevvron 240	
G-MYDU	Thruster T.300		G-MYGO	CFM Shadow Srs CD	
G-MYDV	Thruster T.300		G-MYGP	Rans S.6-ESD Coyote II	
G-MYDW	Whittaker MW.6 Merlin		G-MYGR	Rans S.6-ESD Coyote II	
G-MYDX	Rans S.6-ESD Coyote II		G-MYGS	Whittaker MW.5 (K)	
G-MYDZ	Mignet HM.1000 Balerit				
G-MYEA	SolarWings Pegasus XL-Q				
G-MYEB	SolarWings Pegasus XL-Q				

Reg.	Type	Notes	Reg.	Type	Notes
	Sorcerer			Quasar IITC	
G-MYGT	Solar Wings Pegasus XL-R		G-MYJL	Rans S.6-ESD Coyote II	
G-MYGU	Solar Wings Pegasus XL-R		G-MYJM	Mainair Gemini Flash IIA	
G-MYGV	Solar Wings Pegasus XL-R		G-MYJN	Mainair Mercury	
G-MYGW	Solar Wings Pegasus XL-Q		G-MYJO	Cyclone Chaser S 508	
G-MYGX	Solar Wings Pegasus XL-Q		G-MYJP	Renegade Spirit UK	
G-MYGY	Solar Wings Pegasus XL-Q		G-MYJR	Mainair Mercury	
G-MYGZ	Mainair Gemini Flash IIA		G-MYJS	Solar Wings Pegasus	
G-MYHA	Solar Wings Pegasus XL-R			Quasar IITC	
G-MYHB	Solar Wings Pegasus XL-R		G-MYJT	Solar Wings Pegasus	
G-MYHC	Solar Wings Pegasus XL-R			Quasar IITC	
G-MYHD	Solar Wings Pegasus XL-R		G-MYJU	Solar Wings Pegasus	
G-MYHE	Solar Wings Pegasus XL-R			Quasar IITC	
G-MYHF	Mainair Gemini Flash IIA		G-MYJW	Cyclone Chaser S 508	
G-MYHG	Cyclone AX/503		G-MYJX	Whittaker MW.8	
G-MYHH	Cyclone AX/503		G-MYJY	Rans S.6-ESD Coyote II	
G-MYHI	Rans S.6-ESD Coyote II		G-MYJZ	Whittaker MW.5D Sorcerer	
G-MYHJ	Cyclone AX3/503		G-MYKA	Cyclone AX3/503	
G-MYHK	Rans S.6-ESD Coyote II		G-MYKB	Kölb Twinstar Mk 3	
G-MYHL	Mainair Gemini Flash IIA		G-MYKC	Mainair Gemini Flash IIA	
G-MYHM	Cyclone AX3/503		G-MYKD	Cyclone Chaser S 447	
G-MYHN	Mainair Gemini Flash IIA		G-MYKE	CFM Shadow Srs BD	
G-MYHP	Rans S.6-ESD Coyote II		G-MYKF	Cyclone AX3/503	
G-MYHR	Cyclone AX3/503		G-MYKG	Mainair Gemini Flash IIA	
G-MYHS	Powerchute Kestrel		G-MYKH	Mainair Gemini Flash IIA	
G-MYHT	Powerchute Kestrel		G-MYKI	Mainair Mercury	
G-MYHU	Powerchute Kestrel		G-MYKJ	Team Minimax	
G-MYHV	Powerchute Kestrel		G-MYKK	—	
G-MYHW	Powerchute Kestrel		G-MYKL	Medway Raven	
G-MYHY	Powerchute Kestrel		G-MYKM	Medway Raven	
G-MYHX	Mainair Gemini Flash IIA		G-MYKN	Rans S.6-ESD Coyote II	
G-MYHZ	Powerchute Kestrel		G-MYKO	Whittaker MW.6-S Fat Boy	
G-MYIA	Quad City Challenger II			Flyer	
G-MYIB	Powerchute Kestrel		G-MYKP	Solar Wings Pegasus	
G-MYIC	Powerchute Kestrel			Quasar IITC	
G-MYID	Powerchute Kestrel		G-MYKR	Solar Wings Pegasus	
G-MYIE	Whittaker MW.6 Merlin			Quasar IITC	
G-MYIF	CFM Shadow Srs CD		G-MYKS	Solar Wings Pegasus	
G-MYIG	Renegade Spirit			Quasar IITC	
G-MYIH	Mainair Gemini Flash IIA		G-MYKT	Cyclone AX3/503	
G-MYII	Team Minimax		G-MYKU	Medway Raven	
G-MYIJ	Cyclone AX3/503		G-MYKV	Mainair Gemini Flash IIA	
G-MYIK	Kolb Twinstar Mk 3		G-MYKW	Mainair Mercury	
G-MYIL	Cyclone Chaser S 508		G-MYKX	Mainair Mercury	
G-MYIM	Solar Wings Pegasus		G-MYKY	Mainair Mercury	
	Quasar IITC		G-MYKZ	Team Minimax (G-BVAV)	
G-MYIN	Solar Wings Pegasus		G-MYLA	Rans S.6-ESD Coyote II	
	Quasar IITC		G-MYLB	Team Minimax	
G-MYIO	Solar Wings Pegasus		G-MYLC	Solar Wings Pegasus	
	Quasar IITC			Quantum 15	
G-MYIP	CFM Shadow Srs CD		G-MYLD	Rans S.6-ESD Coyote II	
G-MYIR	Rans S.6-ESD Coyote II		G-MYLE	Solar Wings Pegasus	
G-MYIS	Rans S.6-ESD Coyote II			Quantum 15	
G-MYIT	Cyclone Chaser S 508		G-MYLF	Rans S.6-ESD Coyote II	
G-MYIU	Cyclone AX3/503		G-MYLG	Mainair Gemini Flash IIA	
G-MYIV	Mainair Gemini Flash IIA		G-MYLH	Solar Wings Pegasus	
G-MYIW	Mainair Mercury			Quantum 15	
G-MYIX	Quad City Challenger II		G-MYLI	Solar Wings Pegasus	
G-MYIY	Mainair Gemini Flash IIA			Quantum 15	
G-MYIZ	Team Minimax 2		G-MYLJ	Cyclone Chaser S 447	
G-MYJA	—		G-MYLK	Solar Wings Pegasus	
G-MYJB	Mainair Gemini Flash IIA			Quantum 15	
G-MYJC	Mainair Gemini Flash IIA		G-MYLL	Solar Wings Pegasus	
G-MYJD	Rans S.6-ESD Coyote II			Quantum 15	
G-MYJE	CFM Shadow Srs CD		G-MYLN	Kölb Twinstar Mk 3	
G-MYJF	Thruster T.300		G-MYLO	Rans S.6-ESD Coyote II	
G-MYJG	Thruster Super T.300		G-MYLP	Kölb Twinstar Mk 3	
G-MYJH	Thruster Super T.300			(G-BVCR)	
G-MYJI	Solar Wings Pegasus		G-MYLR	Mainair Gemini Flash IIA	
	Quasar IITC		G-MYLS	Mainair Mercury	
G-MYJJ	Solar Wings Pegasus		G-MYLT	Mainair Starlet	
	Quasar IITC		G-MYLU	Experience/Hunt Wing	
G-MYJK	Solar Wings Pegasus		G-MYLV	CFM Shadow Srs CD	

Reg.	Type	Notes	Reg.	Type	Notes
G-MYLW	Rans S.6-ESD Coyote II		G-MYNZ	Solar Wings Pegasus	
G-MYLX	Medway Raven			Quantum 15	
G-MYLY	Medway Raven		G-MYOA	Rans S.6-ESD Coyote II	
G-MYLZ	Solar Wings Pegasus		G-MYOB	Mainair Mercury	
	Quantum 15		G-MYOC	—	
G-MYMA	Cuby II		G-MYOD	Solar Wings Pegasus	
G-MYMB	Solar Wings Pegasus			Quasar IITC	
	Quantum 15		G-MYOE	Solar Wings Pegasus	
G-MYMC	Solar Wings Pegasus			Quantum 15	
	Quantum 15		G-MYOF	Mainair Mercury	
G-MYMD	Solar Wings Pegasus		G-MYOG	Kölb Twinstar Mk 3	
	Quantum 15		G-MYOH	CFM Shadow Srs CD	
G-MYME	Cyclone AX3/503		G-MYOI	—	
G-MYMF	Cyclone AX3/503		G-MYOJ	—	
G-MYMG	Team Minimax		G-MYOK	—	
G-MYMH	Rans S.6-ESD Coyote II		G-MYOL	—	
G-MYMI	Kölb Twinstar Mk 3		G-MYOM	—	
G-MYMJ	Medway Raven		G-MYON	CFM Shadow Srs CD	
G-MYMK	Mainair Gemini Flash IIA		G-MYOO	Kölb Twinstar Mk 3	
G-MYML	Mainair Mercury		G-MYPG	Solar Wings Pegasus XL-Q	
G-MYMM	Ultraflight Fun 18S		G-MYRK	Renegade Spirit UK	
G-MYMN	Whittaker MW.6 Merlin		G-MYSL	Aviasud Mistral	
G-MYMO	Mainair Gemini Flash IIA		G-MYSP	Rans S.6-ESD Coyote II	
G-MYMP	Rans S.6-ESD Coyote II		G-MYST	Aviasud Mistral	
	(G-CHAZ)		G-MYTH	CFM Shadow Srs BD	
G-MYMR	Rans S.6-ESD Coyote II		G-MYWZ	Thruster TST Mk 1	
G-MYMS	Rans S.6-ESD Coyote II		G-MZAH	Rans S.6-ESD Coyote II	
G-MYMT	Mainair Mercury		G-MZCP	Solar Wings Pegasus XL-Q	
G-MYMU	Kölb Twinstar Mk 3		G-MZDP	AMF Chevvron 232	
G-MYMV	Mainair Gemini Flash IIA		G-MZIP	Renegade Spirit UK	
G-MYMW	Cyclone AX3/503		G-MZIZ	Renegade Spirit UK	
G-MYMX	Solar Wings Pegasus			(G-MWGP)	
	Quantum 15		G-MZMA	Solar Wings Pegasus	
G-MYMY	Cyclone Chaser S 508			Quasar IITC	
G-MYMZ	Cyclone AX3/503		G-MZOO	Renegade Spirit UK	
G-MYNA	CFM Shadow Srs BD		G-MZPJ	Team Minimax	
G-MYNB	Solar Wings Pegasus		G-MZRS	CFM Shadow Srs CD	
	Quantum 15		G-MZZZ	Whittaker MW.6-S Fatboy	
G-MYNC	Mainair Mercury			Flyer	
G-MYND	Mainair Gemini Flash IIA				
G-MYNE	Rans S.6-ESD Coyote II				
G-MYNF	Mainair Mercury				
G-MYNG	CFM Streak Shadow SA-M				
G-MYNH	Rans S.6-ESD Coyote II				
G-MYNI	Team Minimax				
G-MYNJ	Mainair Mercury				
G-MYNK	Solar Wings Pegasus				
	Quantum 15				
G-MYNL	Solar Wings Pegasus				
	Quantum 15				
G-MYNM	Solar Wings Pegasus				
	Quantum 15				
G-MYNN	Solar Wings Pegasus				
	Quantum 15				
G-MYNO	Solar Wings Pegasus				
	Quantum 15				
G-MYNP	Solar Wings Pegasus				
	Quantum 15				
G-MYNR	Solar Wings Pegasus				
	Quantum 15				
G-MYNS	Solar Wings Pegasus				
	Quantum 15				
G-MYNT	Solar Wings Pegasus				
	Quantum 15				
G-MYNU	Solar Wings Pegasus				
	Quasar IITC				
G-MYNV	Solar Wings Pegasus				
	Quantum 15				
G-MYNW	Cyclone Chaser S 447				
G-MYNX	CFM Streak Shadow Srs S-AI				
G-MYNY	Kölb Twinstar Mk 3				

Military to Civil Cross-Reference

Serial carried	Civil identity	Serial carried	Civil identity
3 (Luftwaffe)	G-BAYV	34037 (USAAF)	N9115Z
5 (Croatian AF)	G-BEDB	53319 (319/RB USN)	G-BTDP
19 (USN)	G-BTCC	54137 (69 USN)	G-CTKL
23 (USAAC)	N49272	56321 (U-AB RNorAF)	G-BKPY
26 (US)	G-BAVO	86711 (USN)	N4845V
27 (USN)	G-BRVG	88297 (29 USN)	G-FGID
27 (CIS)	G-OYAK	88439 (USN)	N55JP
41 (BA USN)	G-DDMV	91007 (USAF)	G-NASA
44 (K-33 USAAF)	G-BJLH	93542 (LTA-542 USAF)	G-BRLV
45 (Aeronavale)	G-BHFG	115042 (TA-042 USAF)	G-BGHU
75	G-AFDX	115302 (TP USAAF)	G-BJTP
77 (Soviet AF)	G-BTCU	121714	NX700HL
85 (USAAF)	G-BTBI	124485 (DF-A USAAF)	G-BEDF
112 (USAAC)	G-BSWC	126922 (JS/937 USN)	G-RAID
115 (RNeth Navy)	G-BTTA	151632 (USAAF)	NL9494Z
118 (USAAC)	G-BSDS	18-2001 (USAAF)	G-BIZV
120 (Fr AF)	G-AZGC	217786 (USAAF)	G-BRTK
152/17	G-ATJM	224211 (M2-Z USAF)	G-BPMP
157 (Fr AF)	G-AVEB	226671 (MX-X USAAF)	N47DD
168	G-BFDE	231983 (USAAF)	F-BDRS
177 (Irish AC)	G-BLIW	236800 (A-44 USAAF)	G-BHPK
180 (USN)	G-BRSK	314887 (USAAF)	G-AJPI
192 (Fr AF)	G-BKPT	315509 (USAAF)	G-BHUB
208 (USN)	N75664	329417 (USAAF)	G-BDHK
320 (USAAC)	G-BPMD	329601 (D-44 USAAF)	G-AXHR
361 (USN)	G-ELAN	329854 (R-44 USAAF)	G-BMKC
379 (USAAC)	G-ILLE	329934 (B-72 USAAF)	G-BCPH
385 (RCAF)	G-BGPB	330485 (C-44 USAAF)	G-AJES
390 (USAAC)	G-BTRJ	343251 (USAAC)	G-NZSS
422-15	G-AVJO	40-1766	N50755
425/17	G-BEFR	413048 (E-39 USAAF)	G-BCXJ
441 (USN)	G-BTFG	413573 (B6-K USAF)	N6526D
442 (USN)	G-BPTB	430823	N1042B
503 (Hungarian AF)	G-BRAM	454467 (J-44 USAAF)	G-BILI
671 (RCAF)	G-BNZC	454537 (J-04 USAAF)	G-BFDL
854 (USAAC)	G-BTBH	461748	G-BHDK
855 (USAAC)	N56421	463221 (G4-S USAAF)	G-BTCD
897 (USN)	G-BJEV	472216 (AJ-L USAAF)	G-BIXL
1164 (USAAC)	G-BKGL	472773 (AJ-C USAF)	G-SUSY
1411 (US Coast Guard)	N444M	472917 (AJ-A USAF)	G-HAEC
1420 (Polish AF)	G-BMZF	479766 (D-63 USAAF)	G-BKHG
2345	G-ATVP	474008 (VF-R USAF)	N51RR
2807 (VE-103 USN)	G-BHTH	480015 (USAAF)	G-AKIB
3066	G-AETA	480133 (B-44 USAAF)	G-BDCD
3398 (FrAF)	G-BFYO	480321 (H-44 USAAF)	G-FRAN
3460	G-BMFG	480480 (E-44 USAAF)	G-BECN
4253/18	G-BFPL	483009 (USAF)	G-BPSE
5492	G-PENY	41-33275 (CE USAAC)	G-BICE
5894	G-BFVH	42-58678 (IY USAAC)	G-BRIY
6247 (Polish AF)	G-OMIG	42-78044 (USAAC)	G-BRXL
7198/18	G-AANJ	44-30861	N9089Z
7797 (USAAF)	G-BFAF	44-79609 (PR USAAF)	G-BHXY
8178 (FU-178 USAF)	G-SABR	44-80594 (USAAF)	G-BEDJ
8449M	G-ASWJ	44-83184	G-RGUS
14863 (USAAF)	G-BGOR	45-49192	N47DD
16693 (693 RCAF)	G-BLPG	511371 (VF-S USAAF)	NL1051S
18393 (RCAF)	G-BCYK	542447	G-SCUB
20310 (310 RCAF)	G-BSBG	542457	G-LION
20385 (385 RCAF)	G-BGPB	542474 (R-184)	G-PCUB
28521 (TA-521 USAF)	G-TVIJ	51-14526 (USAF)	G-BRWB
30146 (Yugoslav Army)	G-BSXD	51-15227 (USN)	G-BKRA
31923 (USAAC)	G-BRHP	51-15673 (USAF)	G-CUBI
31952 (USAAC)	G-BRPR	54-21261 (USAF)	N33VC
32947 (F-44 USAAF)	G-BEXA	607327 (09-L USAAF)	G-ARAO

Serial carried	Civil identity	Serial carried	Civil identity
889696 (688 USN)	G-TEAC	N6848	G-BALX
A16-199 (SF-R RAAF)	G-BEOX	N6965 (FL-J)	G-AJTW
A17-48 (RAAF)	G-BPHR	N6985	G-AHMN
A-806 (Swiss AF)	G-BTLL	N9191	G-ALND
A8226	G-BIDW	N9389	G-ANJA
B1807	G-EAVX	P5865 (LE-W)	G-BKCK
B2458	G-BPOB	P6382	G-AJRS
B4863 (G)	G-BLXT	R-163 (RNethAF)	G-BIRH
B6291	G-ASOP	R-167 (RNethAF)	G-LION
B6401	G-AWYY	R1914	G-AHUJ
B7270	G-BFCZ	R4907	G-ANCS
C1904 (Z)	G-PFAP	R5086	G-APIH
C3011 (S)	G-SWOT	S1287	G-BEYB
C4994	G-BLWM	S1579	G-BBVO
D5397/17	G-BFXL	T5424	G-AJOA
D7889	G-AANM	T5493	G-ANEF
D8084	G-ACAA	T5672	G-ALRI
D8096 (D)	G-AEPH	T5854	G-ANKK
E-15 (RNethAF)	G-BIYU	T5879	G-AXBW
E3B-369 (781-32 Span AF)	G-BPDM	T6099	G-AOGR
E3B-540 (781-25 Span AF)	G-BRSH	T6313	G-AHVU
E449	G-EBJE	T6818 (44)	G-ANKT
EM-01 (Spanish AF)	G-AAOR	T6991	G-ANOR
F141 (G)	G-SEVA	T7230	G-AFVE
F235 (B)	G-BMDB	T7281	G-ARTL
F904	G-EBIA	T7404 (04)	G-ANMV
F938	G-EBIC	T7909	G-ANON
F943	G-BIHF	T9707	G-AKKR
F943	G-BKDT	T9738	G-AKAT
F5447 (N)	G-BKER	U-80 (Swiss AF)	G-BUKK
F5459 (Y)	G-INNY	U-0247 (Class B identity)	G-AGOY
F8010	G-BDWJ	U-108 (Swiss AF)	G-BJAX
F8614	G-AWAU	U-110 (Swiss AF)	G-PTWO
G-48-1 (Class B)	G-ALSX	U-142 (Swiss AF)	G-BONE
H-25 (RNethAF)	G-HVDM	U-1215 (215)	G-HELV
H2311	G-ABAA	U-1230 (Swiss AF)	G-DHZZ
H5199	G-ADEV	V1075	G-AKPF
— (I-492 USAAC)	G-BPUD	V3388	G-AHTW
J-1149 (Swiss AF)	G-SWIS	V9281 (RU-M)	G-BCWL
J-1605 (Swiss AF)	G-BLID	V9441 (AR-A)	G-AZWT
J-1758 (Swiss AF)	G-BLSD	V9673 (MA-J)	G-LIZY
J7326	G-EBQP	W5856 (A2A)	G-BMGC
J9941 (57)	G-ABMR	Z5722 (WM-Z)	G-BPIV
K1786	G-AFTA	Z7015	G-BKTH
K2050	G-ASCM	Z7197	G-AKZN
K2059	G-PFAR	Z7381 (XR-T)	G-HURI
K2075	G-BEER	AP507 (KX-P)	G-ACWP
K2567	G-MOTH	AR213 (PR-D)	G-AIST
K2568	G-APMM	AR501 (NN-D)	G-AWII
K2572	G-AOZH	AR614	G-BUWA
K3215	G-AHSA	BB807	G-ADWO
K3731	G-RODI	BE417 (AE-K)	G-HURR
K4235	G-AHMJ	BL628	G-BTTN
K5054	G-BRDV	BM597 (PR-O)	G-MKVB
K5414 (XV)	G-AENP	BS676 (K-U)	G-KUKU
L2301	G-AIZG	BW853	G-BRKE
MM53795 (SC-52 ItAF)	G-BJST	DE208	G-AGYU
N1854	G-AIBE	DE623	G-ANFI
N2308 (HP-B)	G-AMRK	DE970	G-AOBJ
N4877 (VX-F)	G-AMDA	DE992	G-AXXV
N5182	G-APUP	DF128 (RCO-U)	G-AOJJ
N5195	G-ABOX	DF155	G-ANFV
N6181	G-EBKY	DF198	G-BBRB
N6290	G-BOCK	DG590	G-ADMW
N6452	G-BIAU	DK431	G-ASTL
N6466	G-ANKZ	DR613	G-AFJB
N6532	G-ANTS	EM720	G-AXAN
N6847	G-APAL	EM903	G-APBI

Serial carried	Civil identity	Serial carried	Civil identity
EN224	G-FXII	TE566 (DU-A)	G-BLCK
EZ259	G-BMJW	TJ569	G-AKOW
FB226 (MT-A)	G-BDWM	TJ672	G-ANIJ
FE992	G-BDAM	TS423	G-DAKS
FH153	G-BBHK	TS798	G-AGNV
FR870 (GA-S)	N1009N	TW384	G-ANHZ
FS728	G-BAFM	TW439	G-ANRP
FT239	G-BIWX	TW467 (ROD-F)	G-ANIE
FT391	G-AZBN	TW511	G-APAF
FX301 (FD-NQ)	G-JUDI	TW517	G-BDFX
HB275	G-BKGM	TW536 (TS-V)	G-BNGE
HB751	G-BCBL	TW591	G-ARIH
HM580	G-ACUU	TW641	G-ATDN
KB889 (NA-I)	G-LANC	TX183	G-BSMF
KL161 (VO-B)	N88972	VF516	G-ASMZ
KZ321	G-HURY	VF526	G-ARXU
LB294	G-AHWJ	VF548	G-ASEG
LB312	G-AHXE	VL348	G-AVVO
LB375	G-AHGW	VL349	G-AWSA
LF858	G-BLUZ	VM360	G-APHV
LZ766	G-ALCK	VP955	G-DVON
MD497	G-ANLW	VR192	G-APIT
MH434	G-ASJV	VR249 (FA-EY)	G-APIY
MJ627	G-BMSB	VR259	G-APJB
MJ730 (GN-?)	G-HFIX	VS356	G-AOLU
ML407 (OU-V)	G-LFIX	VS610 (K-L)	G-AOKL
ML417 (2I-T)	G-BJSG	VS623	G-AOKZ
MP425	G-AITB	VX118	G-ASNB
MT-11 (RBelgAF)	G-BRFU	VX147	G-AVIL
MT438	G-AREI	VX653	G-BUCM
MT928 (ZX-M)	G-BKMI	VX926	G-ASKJ
MV293 (OI-C)	G-SPIT	VZ304 (A-T)	G-MKVI
MV370 (EB-Q)	G-FXIV	VZ638	G-JETM
NH238 (D-A)	G-MKIX	VZ728	G-AGOS
NH799	G-BUZU	WA576	G-ALSS
NJ695	G-AJXV	WA577	G-ALST
NJ703	G-AKPI	WB531	G-BLRN
NJ719	G-ANFU	WB585 (RCU-X)	G-AOSY
NM181	G-AZGZ	WB588 (D)	G-AOTD
NP181	G-AOAR	WB660	G-ARMB
NP184	G-ANYP	WB702	G-AOFE
NP303	G-ANZJ	WB703	G-ARMC
NX611 (YF-C)	G-ASXX	WB763	G-BBMR
NZ5648	NX55JP	WD286 (J)	G-BBND
PL965	G-MKVI	WD292	G-BCRX
PL983	G-PRXI	WD305	G-ARGG
PP972 (6M-D)	G-BUAR	WD363 (5)	G-BCIH
PT462	G-CTIX	WD379 (K)	G-APLO
PV202 (VZ-M)	G-TRIX	WD388	G-BDIC
RG333	G-AIEK	WD413	G-BFIR
RG333	G-AKEZ	WE402	G-VENI
RH377	G-ALAH	WE569	G-ASAJ
RL962	G-AHED	WF877	G-BPOA
RM221	G-ANXR	WG307	G-BCYJ
RN218 (N)	G-BBJI	WG316	G-BCAH
RR232	G-BRSF	WG348	G-BBMV
RR299 (HT-E)	G-ASKH	WG350	G-BPAL
RT486	G-AJGJ	WG422 (16)	G-BFAX
RT520	G-ALYB	WG472	G-AOTY
RW382 (NG-C)	G-XVIA	WG718	G-BRMA
RW386	G-BXVI	WJ237 (113/O)	G-BLTG
SM832	G-WWII	WJ358	G-ARYD
SM969 (D-A)	G-BRAF	WJ945	G-BEDV
SX336	G-BRMG	WK511 (RN)	G-BVBT
TA634 (8K-K)	G-AWJV	WK522	G-BCOU
TA719	G-ASKC	WK611	G-ARWB
TD248 (D)	G-OXVI	WK621	G-BDBL
TE184	G-MXVI	WK622	G-BCZH

Serial carried	Civil identity	Serial carried	Civil identity
WK628	G-BBMW	XM655	G-VULC
WL505	G-FBIX	XM685 (513/PO)	G-AYZJ
WL626	G-BHDD	XM693	G-TIMM
WM167	G-LOSM	XM697	G-NAAT
WP321 (750/CU)	G-BRFC	XN351	G-BKSC
WP788	G-BCHL	XN435	G-BGBU
WP790	G-BBNC	XN437	G-AXWA
WP800 (2)	G-BCXN	XN441	G-BGKT
WP808	G-BDEU	XN461	G-BVBE
WP835	G-BDCB	XN637	G-BKOU
WP843 (F)	G-BDBP	XP279	G-BWKK
WP857 (24)	G-BDRJ	XP282	G-BGTC
WP903	G-BCGC	XP328	G-BKHC
WP971	G-ATHD	XP355	G-BEBC
WP977	G-BHRD	XR240	G-BDFH
WR410 (N)	G-BLKA	XR241	G-AXRR
WT933	G-ALSW	XR267	G-BJXR
WV198	G-BJWY	XR363	G-OHCA
WV493 (A-P)	G-BDYG	XR442	G-HRON
WV666 (O-D)	G-BTDH	XR486	G-RWWW
WV686	G-BLFT	XR537	G-NATY
WV740	G-BNPH	XR724	G-BTSY
WV783	G-ALSP	XR944	G-ATTB
WZ507	G-VTII	XR991	G-MOUR
WZ662	G-BKVK	XS101	G-GNAT
WZ711	G-AVHT	XS451	G-LTNG
WZ876	G-BBWN	XS452 (BT)	G-BPFE
XE489	G-JETH	XS587 (252/V)	G-VIXN
XE677	G-HHUN	XS770	G-HRHI
XF375	G-BUEZ	XT788 (442)	G-BMIR
XF597 (AH)	G-BKFW	XV268	G-BVER
XF690	G-MOOS	XW635	G-AWSW
XF785	G-ALBN	XW784	G-BBRN
XF836 (J-G)	G-AWRY	XX469	G-BNCL
XF877 (JX)	G-AWVF	ZF485	G-BULU
XG452	G-BRMB	2+1 (Luftwaffe)	G-SYFW
XG496	G-ANDX	4+ (Luftwaffe)	G-BSLX
XG547	G-HAPR	6+ (Luftwaffe)	G-USTV
XH568	G-BVIC	08+ (Luftwaffe)	G-WULF
XJ389	G-AJJP	14+ (Luftwaffe)	G-BBII
XJ763	G-BKHA	F+IS (Luftwaffe)	G-BIRW
XK416	G-AYUA	BU+CK (Luftwaffe)	G-BUCK
XK417	G-AVXY	BU+EM (Luftwaffe)	G-BUCC
XK482	G-BJWC	CC+43 (Luftwaffe)	G-CJCI
XK895 (19/CU)	G-SDEV	LG+01 (Luftwaffe)	G-AYSJ
XK896	G-RNAS	NJ+C11 (Luftwaffe)	G-ATBG
XK940	G-AYXT	RF+16 (Luftwaffe)	G-PTWO
XL426	G-VJET	S5-B06 (Luftwaffe)	G-BSFB
XL502	G-BMYP	TA+RC (Luftwaffe)	G-BPHZ
XL572	G-HNTR	6J+PR	G-AWHB
XL573	G-BVGH	7A+WN (Luftwaffe)	G-AZMH
XL809	G-BLIX	97+04 (Luftwaffe)	G-APVF
XL812	G-SARO	⓪ (Russian AF)	G-KYAK
XM405 (42)	G-TORE	— (Luftwaffe)	G-BOML
XM553	G-AWSV	— (HL-6⁷/₈ USAAF)	G-AKAZ
XM556	G-HELI	146-11042 (7)	G-BMZX
XM575	G-BLMC	146-11083 (5)	G-BNAI

G-BNPV, Bowers Flybaby 1A. *AJW*

G-CEXS, L.188C Electra. *AJW*

G-JEAL, BAe146-300. *AJW*

Overseas Airliner Registrations

(Aircraft included in this section are those most likely to be seen at UK and major European airports on scheduled or charter services.)

Reg.	Type	Owner or Operator	Notes

A6 (United Arab Emirates)

Reg.	Type	Owner or Operator	Notes
A6-EKA	Airbus A.310-304	Emirate Airlines	
A6-EKB	Airbus A.310-304	Emirate Airlines	
A6-EKC	Airbus A.300-605R	Emirate Airlines	
A6-EKD	Airbus A.300-605R	Emirate Airlines	
A6-EKE	Airbus A.300-605R	Emirate Airlines	
A6-EKF	Airbus A.300-605R	Emirate Airlines	
A6-EKG	Airbus A.310-308	Emirate Airlines	
A6-EKH	Airbus A.310-308	Emirate Airlines	
A6-EKI	Airbus A.310-308	Emirate Airlines	
A6-EKJ	Airbus A.310-308	Emirate Airlines	
A6-EKK	Airbus A.310-308	Emirate Airlines	
A6-EKL	Airbus A.310-308	Emirate Airlines	
A6-EKM	Airbus A.300-605R	Emirate Airlines	

A40 (Oman)

Reg.	Type	Owner or Operator	Notes
A40-GF	Boeing 767-3P6ER (601)	Gulf Air	
A40-GG	Boeing 767-3P6ER (602)	Gulf Air	
A40-GH	Boeing 767-3P6ER (603)	Gulf Air	
A40-GI	Boeing 767-3P6ER (604)	Gulf Air	
A40-GJ	Boeing 767-3P6ER (605)	Gulf Air	
A40-GK	Boeing 767-3P6ER (606)	Gulf Air	
A40-GL	Boeing 767-3P6ER (607)	Gulf Air	
A40-GM	Boeing 767-3P6ER (608)	Gulf Air	
A40-GN	Boeing 767-3P6ER (609)	Gulf Air	
A40-GO	Boeing 767-3P6ER (610)	Gulf Air	
A40-GP	Boeing 767-3P6ER (611)	Gulf Air	
A40-GR	Boeing 767-3P6ER (612)	Gulf Air	
A40-GS	Boeing 767-3P6ER (613)	Gulf Air	
A40-GT	Boeing 767-3P6ER (614)	Gulf Air	
A40-GU	Boeing 767-3P6ER (615)	Gulf Air	
A40-GV	Boeing 767-3P6ER (616)	Gulf Air	
A40-GW	Boeing 767-3P6ER (617)	Gulf Air	
A40-GX	Boeing 767-3P6ER (618)	Gulf Air	
A40-GY	Boeing 767-3P6ER	Gulf Air	
A40-GZ	Boeing 767-3P6ER	Gulf Air	
A40-SO	Boeing 747SP-27	Oman Royal Flight	
A40-SP	Boeing 747SP-27	Oman Government	
A40-TA	L-1011-385 TriStar 200 (105)	Gulf Air	
A40-TB	L-1011-385 TriStar 200 (106)	Gulf Air	
A40-TT	L-1011-385 TriStar 200 (107)	Gulf Air	
A40-TV	L-1011-385 TriStar 200 (108)	Gulf Air	
A40-TW	L-1011-385 TriStar 200 (101)	Gulf Air	
A40-TX	L-1011-385 TriStar 200 (102)	Gulf Air	
A40-TY	L-1011-385 TriStar 200 (103)	Gulf Air	
A40-TZ	L-1011-385 TriStar 200 (104)	Gulf Air	

AP (Pakistan)

Reg.	Type	Owner or Operator	Notes
AP-AXA	Boeing 707-340C	Pakistan International Airlines	
AP-AXG	Boeing 707-340C	Pakistan International Airlines	
AP-AYV	Boeing 747-282B	Pakistan International Airlines	
AP-AYW	Boeing 747-282B	Pakistan International Airlines	
AP-AZW	Boeing 707-351B	Pakistan International Airlines	
AP-BAK	Boeing 747-240B (SCD)	Pakistan International Airlines	
AP-BAT	Boeing 747-240B (SCD)	Pakistan International Airlines	
AP-BBK	Boeing 707-323C	Pakistan International Airlines	
AP-BCL	Boeing 747-217B	Pakistan International Airlines	
AP-BCM	Boeing 747-217B	Pakistan International Airlines	
AP-BCN	Boeing 747-217B	Pakistan International Airlines	
AP-BCO	Boeing 747-217B	Pakistan International Airlines	

B (China/Taiwan)

Reg.	Type	Owner or Operator
B-160	Boeing 747-209F (SCD)	China Airlines
B-161	Boeing 747-409	China Airlines
B-162	Boeing 747-409	China Airlines
B-163	Boeing 747-409	China Airlines
B-164	Boeing 747-409	China Airlines
B-1862	Boeing 747SP-09	China Airlines
B-1864	Boeing 747-209B (SCD)	China Airlines
B-1866	Boeing 747-209B	China Airlines
B-1880	Boeing 747SP-09	China Airlines
B-1886	Boeing 747-209B	China Airlines
B-1888	Boeing 747-209B	China Airlines
B-1894	Boeing 747-209F (SCD)	China Airlines
B-2414	Boeing 707-3J6C	Air China
B-2420	Boeing 707-3J6C	Air China
B-2438	Boeing 747SP-J6	Air China
B-2442	Boeing 747SP-J6	Air China
B-2443	Boeing 747-4J6	Air China
B-2445	Boeing 747-4J6	Air China
B-2446	Boeing 747-2J6B (SCD)	Air China
B-2447	Boeing 747-4J6	Air China
B-2448	Boeing 747-2J6B (SCD)	Air China
B-2450	Boeing 747-2J6B (SCD)	Air China
B-2452	Boeing 747SP-J6	Air China
B-2454	Boeing 747SP-27	Air China
B-2456	Boeing 747-4J6 (SCD)	Air China
B-2458	Boeing 747-4J6 (SCD)	Air China
B-2460	Boeing 747-4J6 (SCD)	Air China
B-2462	Boeing 747-2J6F (SCD)	Air China
B-2464	Boeing 747-4J6	Air China
B-2466	Boeing 747-4J6	Air China
B-16401	Boeing 747-45E	EVA Airways
B-16402	Boeing 747-45E	EVA Airways
B-16461	Boeing 747-45E (SCD)	EVA Airways
B-16462	Boeing 747-45E (SCD)	EVA Airways
B-16463	Boeing 747-45E (SCD)	EVA Airways
B-16465	Boeing 747-45E (SCD)	EVA Airways
B-16601	Boeing 767-3T7ER	EVA Airways
B-16602	Boeing 767-3T7ER	EVA Airways
B-16603	Boeing 767-35EER	EVA Airways
B-16605	Boeing 767-35EER	EVA Airways
B-16688	Boeing 767-3S1ER	EVA Airways

Note: China Airlines also operates N4508H and N4522V, both Boeing 747SP-09s.
EVA Airways operates Boeing 747-45Es which retain the US registrations
N403EV and N405EV.

C5 (Gambia)

Note: Air Gambia operates two Boeing 707s registered HR-AMV and HR-AMW.

C9 (Mozambique)

Reg.	Type	Owner or Operator
C9-BAE	Ilyushin IL-62M	Linhas Aéreas de Mocambique (LAM) *Mozambique*
C9-	Boeing 767-2B1ER	LAM

Note: LAM also operates Boeing 767-2B1ER EI-CEM on lease.

C-F and C-G (Canada)

Reg.	Type	Owner or Operator
C-FBCA	Boeing 747-475 (884)	Canadian Airlines International *Grant McConachie*
C-FBEF	Boeing 767-233ER (617)	Air Canada
C-FBEG	Boeing 767-233ER (618)	Air Canada
C-FBEM	Boeing 767-233ER (619)	Air Canada
C-FCAB	Boeing 767-375ER (631)	Canadian Airlines International
C-FCAE	Boeing 767-375ER (632)	Canadian Airlines International
C-FCAF	Boeing 767-375ER (633)	Canadian Airlines International

Reg.	Type	Owner or Operator
C-FCAG	Boeing 767-375ER (634)	Canadian Airlines International
C-FCAJ	Boeing 767-375ER (635)	Canadian Airlines International
C-FCAU	Boeing 767-375ER (636)	Canadian Airlines International
C-FCRA	Boeing 747-475 (882)	Canadian Airlines International
		T. Russ Baker
C-FDJC	Boeing 747-1D1 (411)	—
C-FIWW	Douglas DC-8-55F	ACS of Canada
C-FNXA	Boeing 747-230B	—
C-FOCA	Boeing 767-375ER (640)	Canadian Airlines International
C-FOOA	Boeing 757-28A	Canada 3000/Air 2000 (G-OOOA)
C-FOOB	Boeing 757-28A	Canada 3000/Air 2000 (G-OOOB)
C-FOOE	Boeing 757-28A	Canada 3000 Airlines
C-FOOG	Boeing 757-23A	Canada 3000/Air 2000 (G-GOOG)
C-FPCA	Boeing 767-375ER (637)	Canadian Airlines International
C-FTCA	Boeing 767-375ER (638)	Canadian Airlines International
C-FTNA	L.1011-385 TriStar 150 (501)	Air Transat
C-FTNB	L.1011-385 TriStar 150 (549)	Air Transat
C-FTNC	L.1011-385 TriStar 150 (503)	Air Transat
C-FTNH	L.1011-385 TriStar 150	Air Transat
C-FTNI	L.1011-385 TriStar 100	Royal Airlines
C-FTNK	L.1011-385 TriStar 100	Royal Airlines
C-FTOC	Boeing 747-133 (303)	Air Canada
C-FTOD	Boeing 747-133 (304)	Air Canada
C-FTOE	Boeing 747-133 (305)	Air Canada
C-FXCA	Boeing 767-375ER (639)	Canadian Airlines International
C-FXOD	Boeing 757-28A	Canada 3000/Air 2000 (G-OOOD)
C-FXOF	Boeing 757-28A	Canada 3000 Airlines
C-FXOK	Boeing 757-23A	Canada 3000 Airlines
C-FXOO	Boeing 757-28A	Canada 3000 Airlines
C-GAGA	Boeing 747-233B (SCD) (306)	Air Canada
C-GAGB	Boeing 747-233B (SCD) (307)	Air Canada
C-GAGC	Boeing 747-238B (SCD) (308)	Air Canada
C-GAGL	Boeing 747-433 (SCD) (341)	Air Canada
C-GAGM	Boeing 747-433 (SCD) (342)	Air Canada
C-GAGN	Boeing 747-433 (SCD) (343)	Air Canada
C-GAUY	Boeing 767-233ER (609)	Air Canada
C-GAVA	Boeing 767-233ER (610)	Air Canada
C-GAVC	Boeing 767-233ER (611)	Air Canada
C-GAVF	Boeing 767-233ER (612)	Air Canada
C-GCPC	Douglas DC-10-30 (901)	Canadian Airlines International
C-GCPD	Douglas DC-10-30 (902)	Canadian Airlines International
C-GCPE	Douglas DC-10-30ER (903)	Canadian Airlines International
C-GCPF	Douglas DC-10-30ER (904)	Canadian Airlines International
C-GCPG	Douglas DC-10-30ER (905)	Canadian Airlines International
C-GCPH	Douglas DC-10-30ER (906)	Canadian Airlines International
C-GCPI	Douglas DC-10-30ER (907)	Canadian Airlines International
C-GCPJ	Douglas DC-10-30 (908)	Canadian Airlines International
C-GDSP	Boeing 767-233ER (613)	Air Canada
C-GDSS	Boeing 767-233ER (614)	Air Canada
C-GDSU	Boeing 767-233ER (615)	Air Canada
C-GDSY	Boeing 767-233ER (616)	Air Canada
C-GLCA	Boeing 767-375ER (641)	Canadian Airlines International
C-GMWW	Boeing 747-475 (881)	Canadian Airlines International
		Maxwell W. Ward
C-GNXA	Boeing 747-230B	—
C-GNXH	Boeing 747-129 (SCD) (413)	—
C-GTSE	Boeing 757-23A	Air Transat
C-GTSF	Boeing 757-23A	Air Transat
C-GTSJ	Boeing 757-28A	Air Transat
C-GTSN	Boeing 757-28A	Air Transat
C-GTSZ	L.1011-385 TriStar 100 (548)	Air Transat

Note: Airline fleet number carried on aircraft is shown in parenthesis.

CN (Morocco)

CN-CCH	Boeing 727-2B6	Royal Air Maroc *Marrakech*
CN-CCW	Boeing 727-2B6	Royal Air Maroc *Agadir*
CN-RGA	Boeing 747-428	Royal Air Maroc
CN-RMB	Boeing 707-351C	Royal Air Maroc *Tangier*
CN-RMC	Boeing 707-351C	Royal Air Maroc *Casablanca*
CN-RME	Boeing 747-2B6B (SCD)	Royal Air Maroc
CN-RMF	Boeing 737-4B6	Royal Air Maroc

Notes	Reg.	Type	Owner or Operator
	CN-RMG	Boeing 737-4B6	Royal Air Maroc
	CN-RMI	Boeing 737-2B6	Royal Air Maroc *El Ayounne*
	CN-RMJ	Boeing 737-2B6	Royal Air Maroc *Oujda*
	CN-RMK	Boeing 737-2B6	Royal Air Maroc *Smara*
	CN-RML	Boeing 737-2B6	Royal Air Maroc
	CN-RMM	Boeing 737-2B6C	Royal Air Maroc
	CN-RMN	Boeing 737-2B6C	Royal Air Maroc
	CN-RMO	Boeing 727-2B6	Royal Air Maroc
	CN-RMP	Boeing 727-2B6	Royal Air Maroc
	CN-RMQ	Boeing 727-2B6	Royal Air Maroc
	CN-RMR	Boeing 727-2B6	Royal Air Maroc
	CN-RMS	Boeing 747SP-44	Royal Air Maroc
	CN-RMT	Boeing 757-2B6	Royal Air Maroc
	CN-RMU	Boeing 737-53A	Royal Air Maroc
	CN-RMV	Boeing 737-5B6	Royal Air Maroc
	CN-RMW	Boeing 737-5B6	Royal Air Maroc
	CN-RMX	Boeing 737-4B6	Royal Air Maroc
	CN-RMY	Boeing 737-5B6	Royal Air Maroc
	CN-RMZ	Boeing 757-2B6	Royal Air Maroc
	CN-RNA	Boeing 737-4B6	Royal Air Maroc
	CN-RNB	Boeing 737-5B6	Royal Air Maroc
	CN-RNC	Boeing 737-4B6	Royal Air Maroc
	CN-RND	Boeing 737-4B6	Royal Air Maroc

CS (Portugal)

Reg.	Type	Owner or Operator
CS-TEA	L.1011-385 TriStar 500	TAP — Air Portugal *Luis de Camoes*
CS-TEB	L.1011-385 TriStar 500	TAP — Air Portugal *Infante D. Henrique*
CS-TEC	L.1011-385 TriStar 500	TAP — Air Portugal *Gago Coutinho*
CS-TED	L.1011-385 TriStar 500	TAP — Air Portugal *Bartolomeu de Gusmao*
CS-TEE	L.1011-385 TriStar 500	TAP — Air Portugal *St Antonio de Lisboa*
CS-TEF	L.1011-385 TriStar 500	TAP — Air Portugal *Fernando Pessoa*
CS-TEG	L.1011-385 TriStar 500	TAP — Air Portugal *Eca de Queiroz*
CS-TEH	Airbus A.310-304	TAP — Air Portugal *Bartolomeu Dias*
CS-TEI	Airbus A.310-304	TAP — Air Portugal *Fernao de Magalhaes*
CS-TEJ	Airbus A.310-304	TAP — Air Portugal *Pedro Nunes*
CS-TEK	Boeing 737-282	TAP — Air Portugal *Ponta Delgada*
CS-TEM	Boeing 737-282	TAP — Air Portugal *Setubal*
CS-TEN	Boeing 737-282	TAP — Air Portugal *Braga*
CS-TEO	Boeing 737-282	TAP — Air Portugal *Evora*
CS-TEP	Boeing 737-282	TAP — Air Portugal *Porto*
CS-TEQ	Boeing 737-282C	TAP — Air Portugal *Vila Real*
CS-TER	Boeing 737-230	TAP — Air Portugal *Aveiro*
CS-TES	Boeing 737-230	TAP — Air Portugal *Viana do Castelo*
CS-TEV	Boeing 737-230	TAP — Air Portugal
CS-TEW	Airbus A.310-304	TAP — Air Portugal *Vasco da Gama*
CS-TEX	Airbus A.310-304	TAP — Air Portugal *Joao XXI*
CS-TIA	Boeing 737-382	TAP — Air Portugal *Madeira*
CS-TIB	Boeing 737-382	TAP — Air Portugal *Acores*
CS-TIC	Boeing 737-382	TAP — Air Portugal *Algarve*
CS-TID	Boeing 737-382	TAP — Air Portugal *Alto Minho*
CS-TIE	Boeing 737-382	TAP — Air Portugal *Costa Azul*
CS-TIF	Boeing 737-3K9	TAP — Air Portugal
CS-TIG	Boeing 737-3K9	TAP — Air Portugal
CS-TIH	Boeing 737-3K9	TAP — Air Portugal
CS-TII	Boeing 737-382	TAP — Air Portugal
CS-TIJ	Boeing 737-382	TAP — Air Portugal
CS-TIK	Boeing 737-382	TAP — Air Portugal *Costa do Estoril*
CS-TIL	Boeing 737-382	TAP — Air Portugal *Lisboa*
CS-TIM	Boeing 737-3Q8	TAP — Air Portugal
CS-TKA	Boeing 727-2J4RE	Air Columbus *Cristovao Colombo*
CS-TKB	Boeing 727-2J4RE	Air Columbus *Joao Concalves Zarco*
CS-TKC	Boeing 737-33A	Air Columbus *Santa Maria*
CS-TKD	Boeing 737-33A	Air Columbus *Caravela Nino*
CS-TNA	Airbus A.320-211	TAP — Air Portugal *Grao Vasco*
CS-TNB	Airbus A.320-211	TAP — Air Portugal *Gil Vicente*
CS-TNC	Airbus A.320-211	TAP — Air Portugal *Pero da Covilha*
CS-TND	Airbus A.320-211	TAP — Air Portugal *Garcia de Orta*
CS-TNE	Airbus A.320-211	TAP — Air Portugal
CS-TNF	Airbus A.320-211	TAP — Air Portugal
CS-TPA	Fokker 100	Portugalia *Albatroz*
CS-TPB	Fokker 100	Portugalia *Pelicano*

Reg.	Type	Owner or Operator	Notes
CS-TPC	Fokker 100	Portugalia	
CS-TPD	Fokker 100	Portugalia *Condor*	
CS-TPE	Fokker 100	Portugalia *Gaviao*	

CU (Cuba)

CU-T1208	Ilyushin IL-62M	Cubana *Capt Wifredo Perez*	
CU-T1209	Ilyushin IL-62M	Cubana	
CU-T1215	Ilyushin IL-62M	Cubana	
CU-T1216	Ilyushin IL-62M	Cubana	
CU-T1217	Ilyushin IL-62M	Cubana	
CU-T1218	Ilyushin IL-62M	Cubana	
CU-T1225	Ilyushin IL-62M	Cubana	
CU-T1226	Ilyushin IL-62M	Cubana	
CU-T1252	Ilyushin IL-62M	Cubana	
CU-T1259	Ilyushin IL-62M	Cubana	
CU-T1280	Ilyushin IL-62M	Cubana	
CU-T1282	Ilyushin IL-62M	Cubana	
CU-T1283	Ilyushin IL-62M	Cubana	

D2 (Angola)

D2-TOK	Boeing 707-324C	Angola Air Charter	
D2-TOL	Boeing 707-347C	Angola Air Charter	
D2-TON	Boeing 707-324C	Angola Air Charter	

D (Germany)

D-AASL	Boeing 737-3M8	Saarland Airlines	
D-ABAB	Boeing 737-4K5	Air Berlin	
D-ABAC	Boeing 737-4Y0	Air Berlin	
D-ABAD	Boeing 737-4Y0	Air Berlin	
D-ABAE	Boeing 737-46J	Air Berlin	
D-ABAF	Boeing 737-4Y0	Air Berlin	
D-ABAG	Boeing 737-46J	Air Berlin	
D-ABEA	Boeing 737-330	Lufthansa *Saarbrücken*	
D-ABEB	Boeing 737-330	Lufthansa *Xanten*	
D-ABEC	Boeing 737-330	Lufthansa Express *Karlsruhe*	
D-ABED	Boeing 737-330	Lufthansa Express *Hagen*	
D-ABEE	Boeing 737-330	Lufthansa Express *Ulm*	
D-ABEF	Boeing 737-330	Lufthansa Express *Weiden i.d. Opf*	
D-ABEH	Boeing 737-330	Lufthansa Express *Bad Kissingen*	
D-ABEI	Boeing 737-330	Lufthansa Express *Bamberg*	
D-ABEK	Boeing 737-330	Lufthansa Express *Wuppertal*	
D-ABEL	Boeing 737-330	Lufthansa Express *Pforzheim*	
D-ABEM	Boeing 737-330	Lufthansa Express *Eberswalde*	
D-ABEN	Boeing 737-330	Lufthansa Express	
D-ABEO	Boeing 737-330	Lufthansa Express	
D-ABEP	Boeing 737-330	Lufthansa Express	
D-ABER	Boeing 737-330	Lufthansa Express *Merseburg*	
D-ABES	Boeing 737-330	Lufthansa Express *Koethen/Anhalt*	
D-ABFA	Boeing 737-230	Lufthansa *Regensburg*	
D-ABFB	Boeing 737-230	Lufthansa *Flensburg*	
D-ABFC	Boeing 737-230	Lufthansa *Würzburg*	
D-ABFF	Boeing 737-230	Lufthansa *Gelsenkirchen*	
D-ABFP	Boeing 737-230	Lufthansa *Offenbach*	
D-ABFR	Boeing 737-230	Lufthansa *Solingen*	
D-ABFS	Boeing 737-230	Lufthansa *Oldenburg*	
D-ABFU	Boeing 737-230	Lufthansa *Mülheim a.d.Ruhr*	
D-ABFW	Boeing 737-230	Lufthansa *Wolfsburg*	
D-ABFX	Boeing 737-230	Lufthansa *Tübingen*	
D-ABFY	Boeing 737-230	Lufthansa *Göttingen*	
D-ABFZ	Boeing 737-230	Lufthansa *Wilhelmshaven*	
D-ABGE	Boeing 737-230F	German Cargo	
D-ABHA	Boeing 737-230	Lufthansa *Koblenz*	
D-ABHB	Boeing 737-230	Lufthansa *Goslar*	
D-ABHC	Boeing 737-230	Lufthansa *Friedrichshafen*	
D-ABHE	Boeing 737-230F	German Cargo	
D-ABHF	Boeing 737-230	Lufthansa *Heilbronn*	
D-ABHH	Boeing 737-230	Lufthansa *Marburg*	
D-ABHL	Boeing 737-230	Lufthansa *Worms*	
D-ABHM	Boeing 737-230	Lufthansa *Landshut*	

Notes	Reg.	Type	Owner or Operator
	D-ABHN	Boeing 737-230	Lufthansa *Trier*
	D-ABHR	Boeing 737-230	Lufthansa *Darmstadt*
	D-ABHU	Boeing 737-230	Lufthansa *Konstanz*
	D-ABIA	Boeing 737-530	Lufthansa *Greifswald*
	D-ABIB	Boeing 737-530	Lufthansa *Esslingen*
	D-ABIC	Boeing 737-530	Lufthansa *Krefeld*
	D-ABID	Boeing 737-530	Lufthansa *Aachen*
	D-ABIE	Boeing 737-530	Lufthansa *Hildesheim*
	D-ABIF	Boeing 737-530	Lufthansa *Landau*
	D-ABIH	Boeing 737-530	Lufthansa *Bruchsal*
	D-ABII	Boeing 737-530	Lufthansa *Lörrach*
	D-ABIK	Boeing 737-530	Lufthansa *Rastatt*
	D-ABIL	Boeing 737-530	Lufthansa *Memmingen*
	D-ABIM	Boeing 737-530	Lufthansa *Salzgitter*
	D-ABIN	Boeing 737-530	Lufthansa *Langenhagen*
	D-ABIO	Boeing 737-530	Lufthansa Express *Wesel*
	D-ABIP	Boeing 737-530	Lufthansa Express *Oberhausen*
	D-ABIR	Boeing 737-530	Lufthansa *Anklam*
	D-ABIS	Boeing 737-530	Lufthansa Express *Rendsburg*
	D-ABIT	Boeing 737-530	Lufthansa *Neumünster*
	D-ABIU	Boeing 737-530	Lufthansa *Limburg a.d. Lahn*
	D-ABIW	Boeing 737-530	Lufthansa *Bad Nauheim*
	D-ABIX	Boeing 737-530	Lufthansa *Bamberg*
	D-ABIY	Boeing 737-530	Lufthansa *Lingen*
	D-ABIZ	Boeing 737-530	Lufthansa *Kirchheim unter Teck*
	D-ABJA	Boeing 737-530	Lufthansa *Bad Segeberg*
	D-ABJB	Boeing 737-530	Lufthansa *Rheine*
	D-ABJC	Boeing 737-530	Lufthansa *Erding*
	D-ABJD	Boeing 737-530	Lufthansa *Freising*
	D-ABJE	Boeing 737-530	Lufthansa *Ingelheim am Rhein*
	D-ABJF	Boeing 737-530	Lufthansa *Aalen*
	D-ABJH	Boeing 737-530	Lufthansa *Heppenheim an der Bergstr*
	D-ABJI	Boeing 737-530	Lufthansa
	D-ABKA	Boeing 737-430	Lufthansa Express *Heide*
	D-ABKB	Boeing 737-430	Lufthansa Express *Tegernsee*
	D-ABKC	Boeing 737-430	Lufthansa Express *Straubing*
	D-ABKD	Boeing 737-430	Lufthansa Express *Helmstedt*
	D-ABKF	Boeing 737-430	Lufthansa Express *Hameln*
	D-ABKK	Boeing 737-430	Lufthansa Express *Weimar*
	D-ABMA	Boeing 737-230	Lufthansa *Idar-Oberstein*
	D-ABMB	Boeing 737-230	Lufthansa *Ingolstadt*
	D-ABMC	Boeing 737-230	Lufthansa *Norderstedt*
	D-ABMD	Boeing 737-230	Lufthansa *Paderborn*
	D-ABME	Boeing 737-230	Lufthansa *Schweinfurt*
	D-ABMF	Boeing 737-230	Lufthansa *Verden*
	D-ABNA	Boeing 757-230	Condor Flugdienst
	D-ABNB	Boeing 757-230	Condor Flugdienst
	D-ABNC	Boeing 757-230	Condor Flugdienst
	D-ABND	Boeing 757-230	Condor Flugdienst
	D-ABNE	Boeing 757-230	Condor Flugdienst
	D-ABNF	Boeing 757-230	Condor Flugdienst
	D-ABNH	Boeing 757-230	Condor Flugdienst
	D-ABNI	Boeing 757-230	Condor Flugdienst
	D-ABNK	Boeing 757-230	Condor Flugdienst
	D-ABNL	Boeing 757-230	Condor Flugdienst
	D-ABNM	Boeing 757-230	Condor Flugdienst
	D-ABNN	Boeing 757-230	Condor Flugdienst
	D-ABNO	Boeing 757-230	Condor Flugdienst
	D-APNP	Boeing 757-230	Condor Flugdienst
	D-ABNR	Boeing 757-230	Condor Flugdienst
	D-ABNS	Boeing 757-230	Condor Flugdienst
	D-ABNT	Boeing 757-230	Condor Flugdienst
	D-ABNX	Boeing 757-27B	Condor Flugdienst
	D-ABOA	Boeing 757-230	Condor Flugdienst
	D-ABOB	Boeing 757-230	Condor Flugdienst
	D-ABOC	Boeing 757-230	Condor Flugdienst
	D-ABOE	Boeing 757-230	Condor Flugdienst
	D-ABOF	Boeing 757-230	Condor Flugdienst
	D-ABOH	Boeing 757-230	Condor Flugdienst
	D-ABTA	Boeing 747-430 (SCD)	Lufthansa *Sachsen*
	D-ABTB	Boeing 747-430 (SCD)	Lufthansa *Brandenburg*
	D-ABTC	Boeing 747-430 (SCD)	Lufthansa *Mecklenburg-Verpommern*
	D-ABTD	Boeing 747-430 (SCD)	Lufthansa/Condor Flugdienst *Hamburg*

Reg.	Type	Owner or Operator	Notes
D-ABTE	Boeing 747-430 (SCD)	Lufthansa *Sachsen-Anhalt*	
D-ABTF	Boeing 747-430 (SCD)	Lufthansa *Thüringen*	
D-ABTH	Boeing 747-430 (SCD)	Lufthansa *Duisburg*	
D-ABUA	Boeing 767-330ER	Condor Flugdienst	
D-ABUB	Boeing 767-330ER	Condor Flugdienst	
D-ABUC	Boeing 767-330ER	Condor Flugdienst	
D-ABUD	Boeing 767-330ER	Condor Flugdienst	
D-ABUE	Boeing 767-330ER	Condor Flugdienst	
D-ABUF	Boeing 767-330ER	Condor Flugdienst	
D-ABUH	Boeing 767-330ER	Condor Flugdienst	
D-ABUI	Boeing 767-330ER	Condor Flugdienst	
D-ABUX	Boeing 767-330ER	Condor Flugdienst	
D-ABUY	Boeing 767-330ER	Condor Flugdienst	
D-ABUZ	Boeing 767-330ER	Condor Flugdienst	
D-ABVA	Boeing 747-430	Lufthansa *Berlin*	
D-ABVB	Boeing 747-430	Lufthansa *Bonn*	
D-ABVC	Boeing 747-430	Lufthansa *Baden-Württemberg*	
D-ABVD	Boeing 747-430	Lufthansa *Bochum*	
D-ABVE	Boeing 747-430	Lufthansa *Potsdam*	
D-ABVF	Boeing 747-430	Lufthansa *Frankfurt am Main*	
D-ABVH	Boeing 747-430	Lufthansa *Düsseldorf*	
D-ABVK	Boeing 747-430	Lufthansa *Hannover*	
D-ABVL	Boeing 747-430	Lufthansa *Muenchen*	
D-ABVN	Boeing 747-430	Lufthansa *Dortmund*	
D-ABWA	Boeing 737-330	Condor Flugdienst *Claus Gillmann*	
D-ABWB	Boeing 737-330	Condor Flugdienst	
D-ABWC	Boeing 737-330QC	Lufthansa	
D-ABWD	Boeing 737-330QC	Lufthansa	
D-ABWE	Boeing 737-330QC	Lufthansa	
D-ABWF	Boeing 737-330	Lufthansa	
D-ABWH	Boeing 737-330	Condor Flugdienst	
D-ABXA	Boeing 737-330QC	Lufthansa *Giessen*	
D-ABXB	Boeing 737-330QC	Lufthansa *Passau*	
D-ABXC	Boeing 737-330QC	Lufthansa *Delmenhorst*	
D-ABXD	Boeing 737-330QC	Lufthansa *Siegen*	
D-ABXE	Boeing 737-330	Lufthansa *Hamm*	
D-ABXF	Boeing 737-330	Lufthansa *Minden*	
D-ABXH	Boeing 737-330	Lufthansa *Cuxhaven*	
D-ABXI	Boeing 737-330	Lufthansa *Berchtesgaden*	
D-ABXK	Boeing 737-330	Lufthansa *Ludwigsburg*	
D-ABXL	Boeing 737-330	Lufthansa *Neuss*	
D-ABXM	Boeing 737-330	Lufthansa *Herford*	
D-ABXN	Boeing 737-330	Lufthansa *Böblingen*	
D-ABXO	Boeing 737-330	Lufthansa *Schwäbisch-Gmünd*	
D-ABXP	Boeing 737-330	Lufthansa *Fulda*	
D-ABXR	Boeing 737-330	Lufthansa *Celle*	
D-ABXS	Boeing 737-330	Lufthansa *Sindelfingen*	
D-ABXT	Boeing 737-330	Lufthansa *Reutlingen*	
D-ABXU	Boeing 737-330	Lufthansa *Seeheim-Jugenheim*	
D-ABXW	Boeing 737-330	Lufthansa *Hanau*	
D-ABXX	Boeing 737-330	Lufthansa *Bad Homburg v.d. Höhe*	
D-ABXY	Boeing 737-330	Lufthansa *Hof*	
D-ABXZ	Boeing 737-330	Lufthansa *Bad Mergentheim*	
D-ABYJ	Boeing 747-230B (SCD)	Lufthansa *Hessen*	
D-ABYK	Boeing 747-230B (SCD)	Lufthansa *Rheinland-Pfalz*	
D-ABYL	Boeing 747-230B (SCD)	Lufthansa *Saarland*	
D-ABYM	Boeing 747-230B (SCD)	Lufthansa *Schleswig-Holstein*	
D-ABYO	Boeing 747-230F (SCD)	Lufthansa *America*	
D-ABYP	Boeing 747-230B	Lufthansa *Niedersachen*	
D-ABYQ	Boeing 747-230B	Lufthansa *Bremen*	
D-ABYR	Boeing 747-230B (SCD)	Lufthansa *Nordrhein-Westfalen*	
D-ABYS	Boeing 747-230B (SCD)	Lufthansa *Bayern*	
D-ABYT	Boeing 747-230F (SCD)	Lufthansa Cargo	
D-ABYU	Boeing 747-230F (SCD)	Lufthansa *Asia*	
D-ABYW	Boeing 747-230F (SCD)	German Cargo	
D-ABYX	Boeing 747-230B (SCD)	Lufthansa *Köln*	
D-ABYY	Boeing 747-230F (SCD)	German Cargo	
D-ABZA	Boeing 747-230F (SCD)	Lufthansa *Düsseldorf*	
D-ABZB	Boeing 747-230F (SCD)	Lufthansa *Europa*	
D-ABZC	Boeing 747-230F (SCD)	Lufthansa Cargo	
D-ABZD	Boeing 747-230B	Lufthansa *Kiel*	
D-ABZE	Boeing 747-230B (SCD)	Lufthansa *Stuttgart*	
D-ABZF	Boeing 747-230F (SCD)	Lufthansa *Africa*	

Notes	Reg.	Type	Owner or Operator
	D-ABZH	Boeing 747-230B	Lufthansa *Bonn*
	D-ABZI	Boeing 747-230F (SCD)	Lufthansa *Australia*
	D-ACFA	BAe 146-200	Conti-Flug
	D-ACLA	Canadair Regional Jet 100ER	Lufthansa CityLine
	D-ACLB	Canadair Regional Jet 100ER	Lufthansa CityLine
	D-ACLC	Canadair Regional Jet 100ER	Lufthansa CityLine
	D-ACLD	Canadair Regional Jet 100ER	Lufthansa CityLine
	D-ACLE	Canadair Regional Jet 100ER	Lufthansa CityLine
	D-ACLF	Canadair Regional Jet 100ER	Lufthansa CityLine
	D-ACLG	Canadair Regional Jet 100ER	Lufthansa CityLine
	D-ACLH	Canadair Regional Jet 100ER	Lufthansa CityLine
	D-ACLI	Canadair Regional Jet 100ER	Lufthansa CityLine
	D-ACLJ	Canadair Regional Jet 100ER	Lufthansa CityLine
	D-ACLK	Canadair Regional Jet 100ER	Lufthansa CityLine
	D-ACLL	Canadair Regional Jet 100ER	Lufthansa CityLine
	D-ACLM	Canadair Regional Jet 100ER	Lufthansa CityLine
	D-AC	Canadair Regional Jet 100ER	Lufthansa CityLine
	D-AC	Canadair Regional Jet 100ER	Lufthansa CityLine
	D-ACVK	S.E.210 Caravelle 10R	Aero Lloyd *Otto Trump* (stored)
	D-ADBA	Boeing 737-3L9	Deutsche BA
	D-ADBB	Boeing 737-3L9	Deutsche BA
	D-ADBC	Boeing 737-3L9	Deutsche BA
	D-ADBD	Boeing 737-3L9	Deutsche BA
	D-ADBE	Boeing 737-3L9	Deutsche BA
	D-ADBF	Boeing 737-3L9	Deutsche BA
	D-ADBG	Boeing 737-3L9	Deutsche BA
	D-ADBO	Douglas DC-10-30	Lufthansa
	D-ADCO	Douglas DC-10-30	Lufthansa
	D-ADDO	Douglas DC-10-30	Lufthansa *Duisburg*
	D-ADEP	F.27 Friendship Mk 600	Ratioflug
	D-ADFO	Douglas DC-10-30	Lufthansa
	D-ADHO	Douglas DC-10-30	Lufthansa
	D-ADJO	Douglas DC-10-30	Lufthansa *Essen*
	D-ADKO	Douglas DC-10-30	Lufthansa
	D-ADLO	Douglas DC-10-30	Lufthansa *Nürnberg*
	D-ADPO	Douglas DC-10-30	Condor Flugdienst
	D-ADQO	Douglas DC-10-30	Condor Flugdienst
	D-ADSO	Douglas DC-10-30	Condor Flugdienst
	D-ADUA	Douglas DC-8-73AF	German Cargo
	D-ADUC	Douglas DC-8-73AF	German Cargo
	D-ADUE	Douglas DC-8-73AF	German Cargo
	D-ADUI	Douglas DC-8-73AF	German Cargo
	D-ADUO	Douglas DC-8-73AF	German Cargo
	D-AELC	F.27 Friendship Mk 600	WDL
	D-AELD	F.27 Friendship Mk 600	WDL
	D-AELE	F.27 Friendship Mk 600	WDL
	D-AELF	F.27 Friendship Mk 600	WDL
	D-AELG	F.27 Friendship Mk 600	WDL
	D-AERB	McD Douglas MD-11	LTU
	D-AERE	L.1011-385 TriStar 1	LTU
	D-AERL	L.1011-385 TriStar 500	LTU
	D-AERM	L.1011-385 TriStar 1	LTU
	D-AERN	L.1011-385 TriStar 200	LTU
	D-AERP	L.1011-385 TriStar 1	LTU
	D-AERT	L.1011-385 TriStar 500	LTU
	D-AERU	L.1011-385 TriStar 100	LTU
	D-AERV	L.1011-385 TriStar 500	LTU
	D-AERW	McD Douglas MD-11	LTU
	D-AERX	McD Douglas MD-11	LTU
	D-AERY	L.1011-385 TriStar 1	LTU
	D-AERZ	McD Douglas MD-11	LTU
	D-AEWG	Aérospatiale ATR-72-212	Eurowings
	D-AEWH	Aérospatiale ATR-72-212	Eurowings
	D-	Aérospatiale ATR-72-212	Eurowings
	D-	Aérospatiale ATR-72-212	Eurowings
	D-	Aérospatiale ATR-72-212	Eurowings
	D-	Aérospatiale ATR-72-212	Eurowings
	D-	Aérospatiale ATR-72-212	Eurowings
	D-	Aérospatiale ATR-72-212	Eurowings
	D-AFFD	Fokker 50	Lufthansa CityLine
	D-AFFE	Fokker 50	Lufthansa CityLine
	D-AFFF	Fokker 50	Lufthansa CityLine
	D-AFFG	Fokker 50	Lufthansa CityLine
	D-AFFH	Fokker 50	Lufthansa CityLine

Reg.	Type	Owner or Operator	Notes
D-AFFI	Fokker 50	Lufthansa CityLine	
D-AFFJ	Fokker 50	Lufthansa CityLine	
D-AFFK	Fokker 50	Lufthansa CityLine	
D-AFFL	Fokker 50	Lufthansa CityLine	
D-AFKH	Fokker 50	Lufthansa CityLine	
D-AFKI	Fokker 50	Lufthansa CityLine	
D-AFKJ	Fokker 50	Lufthansa CityLine	
D-AFKK	Fokker 50	Lufthansa CityLine	
D-AFKL	Fokker 50	Lufthansa CityLine	
D-AFKM	Fokker 50	Lufthansa CityLine	
D-AFKN	Fokker 50	Lufthansa CityLine	
D-AFKO	Fokker 50	Lufthansa CityLine	
D-AFKP	Fokker 50	Lufthansa CityLine	
D-AFKT	Fokker 50	Lufthansa CityLine	
D-AFKU	Fokker 50	Lufthansa CityLine	
D-AFKV	Fokker 50	Lufthansa CityLine	
D-AFKW	Fokker 50	Lufthansa CityLine	
D-AFKX	Fokker 50	Lufthansa CityLine	
D-AFKY	Fokker 50	Lufthansa CityLine	
D-AFKZ	Fokker 50	Lufthansa CityLine	
D-AGEA	Boeing 737-35B	Germania	
D-AGEB	Boeing 737-35B	Germania	
D-AGEC	Boeing 737-35B	Germania/Condor Flugdienst	
D-AGED	Boeing 737-35B	Germania/Condor Flugdienst	
D-AGEE	Boeing 737-35B	Germania	
D-AGEF	Boeing 737-35B	Germania	
D-AGEG	Boeing 737-35B	Germania	
D-AGEH	Boeing 737-3L9	Germania	
D-AGEI	Boeing 737-3L9	Germania	
D-AGEJ	Boeing 737-3L9	Germania	
D-AGWB	McD Douglas MD-83	Aero Lloyd	
D-AGWC	McD Douglas MD-83	Aero Lloyd	
D-AHLA	Airbus A.310-304	Hapag-Lloyd	
D-AHLB	Airbus A.310-304	Hapag-Lloyd	
D-AHLC	Airbus A.310-308	Hapag-Lloyd	
D-AHLD	Boeing 737-5K5	Hapag-Lloyd	
D-AHLE	Boeing 737-5K5	Hapag-Lloyd	
D-AHLF	Boeing 737-5K5	Hapag-Lloyd	
D-AHLI	Boeing 737-5K5	Hapag-Lloyd	
D-AHLJ	Boeing 737-4K5	Hapag-Lloyd	
D-AHLK	Boeing 737-4K5	Hapag-Lloyd	
D-AHLL	Boeing 737-4K5	Hapag-Lloyd	
D-AHLM	Boeing 737-4K5	Hapag-Lloyd	
D-AHLN	Boeing 737-5K5	Hapag-Lloyd	
D-AHLO	Boeing 737-4K5	Hapag-Lloyd	
D-AHLP	Boeing 737-4K5	Hapag-Lloyd	
D-AHLQ	Boeing 737-4K5	Hapag-Lloyd	
D-AHLR	Boeing 737-4K5	Hapag-Lloyd	
D-AHLS	Boeing 737-4K5	Hapag-Lloyd	
D-AHLV	Airbus A.310-204	Hapag-Lloyd	
D-AHLW	Airbus A.310-204	Hapag-Lloyd	
D-AHLX	Airbus A.310-204	Hapag-Lloyd	
D-AHLZ	Airbus A.310-204	Hapag-Lloyd	
D-AIAH	Airbus A.300-603	Lufthansa *Lindau/Bodensee*	
D-AIAI	Airbus A.300-603	Lufthansa *Erbach/Odenwald*	
D-AIAK	Airbus A.300-603	Lufthansa *Kronberg/Taunus*	
D-AIAL	Airbus A.300-603	Lufthansa *Stade*	
D-AIAM	Airbus A.300-603	Lufthansa *Rosenheim*	
D-AIAN	Airbus A.300-603	Lufthansa Express *Nördlingen*	
D-AIAP	Airbus A.300-603	Lufthansa Express *Donauwörth*	
D-AIAR	Airbus A.300-603	Lufthansa *Bingen am Rhein*	
D-AIAS	Airbus A.300-603	Lufthansa *Monchengladbach*	
D-AIAT	Airbus A.300-603	Lufthansa Express *Bottrop*	
D-AIAU	Airbus A.300-603	Lufthansa Express *Bocholt*	
D-AIBA	Airbus A.340-211	Lufthansa *Neurnberg*	
D-AIBC	Airbus A.340-211	Lufthansa *Leverkusen*	
D-AIBD	Airbus A.340-211	Lufthansa	
D-AIBE	Airbus A.340-211	Lufthansa	
D-AIBF	Airbus A.340-211	Lufthansa	
D-AIBH	Airbus A.340-211	Lufthansa	
D-AICA	Airbus A.310-203	Lufthansa *Neustadt an der Weinstrasse*	
D-AICB	Airbus A.310-203	Lufthansa *Garmisch-Partenkirchen*	
D-AICC	Airbus A.310-203	Lufthansa *Kaiserslautern*	
D-AICD	Airbus A.310-203	Lufthansa *Detmold*	

Notes	Reg.	Type	Owner or Operator
	D-AICF	Airbus A.310-203	Lufthansa *Rüdesheim am Rhein*
	D-AICH	Airbus A.310-203	Lufthansa *Lüneburg*
	D-AICK	Airbus A.310-203	Lufthansa *Westerland/Sylt*
	D-AICL	Airbus A.310-203	Lufthansa *Rothenburg ob der Tauber*
	D-AICM	Airbus A.310-203	Lufthansa
	D-AICN	Airbus A.310-203	Lufthansa *Lübeck*
	D-AICP	Airbus A.310-203	Lufthansa *Bremerhaven*
	D-AICR	Airbus A.310-203	Lufthansa Express *Freudenstadt*
	D-AICS	Airbus A.310-203	Lufthansa Express *Recklinghausen/ Schwarzwald*
	D-AIDA	Airbus A.310-304	Lufthansa
	D-AIDB	Airbus A.310-304	Lufthansa *Fürth*
	D-AIDC	Airbus A.310-304	Lufthansa
	D-AIDD	Airbus A.310-304	Lufthansa *Emden*
	D-AIDE	Airbus A.310-304	Lufthansa *Speyer*
	D-AIDF	Airbus A.310-304	Lufthansa *Aschaffenburg*
	D-AIDH	Airbus A.310-304	Lufthansa *Wetzlar*
	D-AIDI	Airbus A.310-304	Lufthansa *Fellbach*
	D-AIDK	Airbus A.310-304	Lufthansa *Donaueschingen*
	D-AIDL	Airbus A.310-304	Lufthansa *Obersdorf*
	D-AIDM	Airbus A.310-304	Lufthansa *Chemnitz*
	D-AIDN	Airbus A.310-304	Lufthansa *Gütersloh*
	D-AIGA	Airbus A.340-311	Lufthansa
	D-AIGB	Airbus A.340-311	Lufthansa
	D-AIGC	Airbus A.340-311	Lufthansa
	D-AIGD	Airbus A.340-311	Lufthansa
	D-AIGF	Airbus A.340-311	Lufthansa
	D-AIGH	Airbus A.340-311	Lufthansa
	D-AIGI	Airbus A.340-311	Lufthansa
	D-AIGK	Airbus A.340-311	Lufthansa
	D-AIPA	Airbus A.320-211	Lufthansa *Buxtehude*
	D-AIPB	Airbus A.320-211	Lufthansa *Heidelberg*
	D-AIPC	Airbus A.320-211	Lufthansa *Mannheim*
	D-AIPD	Airbus A.320-211	Lufthansa *Freiburg*
	D-AIPE	Airbus A.320-211	Lufthansa *Kassel*
	D-AIPF	Airbus A.320-211	Lufthansa *Leipzig*
	D-AIPH	Airbus A.320-211	Lufthansa *Münster*
	D-AIPK	Airbus A.320-211	Lufthansa *Wiesbaden*
	D-AIPL	Airbus A.320-211	Lufthansa *Ludwigshafen am Rhein*
	D-AIPM	Airbus A.320-211	Lufthansa *Troisdorf*
	D-AIPP	Airbus A.320-211	Lufthansa *Starnberg*
	D-AIPR	Airbus A.320-211	Lufthansa *Kaufbeuren*
	D-AIPS	Airbus A.320-211	Lufthansa *Augsburg*
	D-AIPT	Airbus A.320-211	Lufthansa *Cottbus*
	D-AIPU	Airbus A.320-211	Lufthansa *Dresden*
	D-AIPW	Airbus A.320-211	Lufthansa *Schwerin*
	D-AIPX	Airbus A.320-211	Lufthansa *Mannheim*
	D-AIPY	Airbus A.320-211	Lufthansa *Magdeburg*
	D-AIPZ	Airbus A.320-211	Lufthansa *Erfurt*
	D-AIQA	Airbus A.320-211	Lufthansa *Mainz*
	D-AIQB	Airbus A.320-211	Lufthansa *Bielefeld*
	D-AIQC	Airbus A.320-211	Lufthansa *Zwickau*
	D-AIQD	Airbus A.320-211	Lufthansa *Jena*
	D-AIQE	Airbus A.320-211	Lufthansa *Gera*
	D-AIQF	Airbus A.320-211	Lufthansa *Halle a.d. Saale*
	D-AIQH	Airbus A.320-211	Lufthansa *Dessau*
	D-AIQK	Airbus A.320-211	Lufthansa *Rostock*
	D-AIQL	Airbus A.320-211	Lufthansa *Sralsund*
	D-AIQM	Airbus A.320-211	Lufthansa *Nordenham*
	D-AIQN	Airbus A.320-211	Lufthansa
	D-AIQP	Airbus A.320-211	Lufthansa
	D-AIQR	Airbus A.320-211	Lufthansa
	D-AIQS	Airbus A.320-211	Lufthansa
	D-AIRA	Airbus A.321-131	Lufthansa
	D-AIRB	Airbus A.321-131	Lufthansa
	D-AIRC	Airbus A.321-131	Lufthansa
	D-AIRD	Airbus A.321-131	Lufthansa
	D-AIRE	Airbus A.321-131	Lufthansa
	D-AIRF	Airbus A.321-131	Lufthansa
	D-AIRH	Airbus A.321-131	Lufthansa
	D-AIRK	Airbus A.321-131	Lufthansa
	D-AIRL	Airbus A.321-131	Lufthansa
	D-AIRM	Airbus A.321-131	Lufthansa

Reg.	Type	Owner or Operator	Notes
D-AIRN	Airbus A.321-131	Lufthansa	
D-AIRO	Airbus A.321-131	Lufthansa	
D-AIRP	Airbus A.321-131	Lufthansa	
D-AISY	F.27 Friendship Mk 600	Ratioflug	
D-AJET	BAe 146-200	Conti-Flug	
D-ALLB	Douglas DC-9-32	Aero Lloyd	
D-ALLC	Douglas DC-9-32	Aero Lloyd	
D-ALLD	McD Douglas MD-83	Aero Lloyd	
D-ALLE	McD Douglas MD-83	Aero Lloyd	
D-ALLF	McD Douglas MD-83	Aero Lloyd	
D-ALLG	McD Douglas MD-87	Aero Lloyd	
D-ALLH	McD Douglas MD-87	Aero Lloyd	
D-ALLI	McD Douglas MD-87	Aero Lloyd	
D-ALLJ	McD Douglas MD-87	Aero Lloyd	
D-ALLK	McD Douglas MD-83	Aero Lloyd	
D-ALLL	McD Douglas MD-83	Aero Lloyd	
D-ALLM	McD Douglas MD-83	Aero Lloyd	
D-ALLN	McD Douglas MD-83	Aero Lloyd	
D-ALLO	McD Douglas MD-83	Aero Lloyd	
D-ALLP	McD Douglas MD-83	Aero Lloyd *Kassel*	
D-ALLQ	McD Douglas MD-83	Aero Lloyd	
D-ALLR	McD Douglas MD-83	Aero Lloyd	
D-AMUK	Boeing 757-225	LTU-Sud	
D-AMUL	Boeing 757-236	LTU-Sud	
D-AMUM	Boeing 757-2G5ER	LTU-Sud	
D-AMUN	Boeing 767-3G5ER	LTU-Sud	
D-AMUP	Boeing 767-33AER	LTU-Sud	
D-AMUR	Boeing 767-3G5ER	LTU-Sud	
D-AMUS	Boeing 767-3G5ER	LTU-Sud	
D-AMUU	Boeing 757-225	LTU-Sud	
D-AMUV	Boeing 757-2G5ER	LTU-Sud	
D-AMUW	Boeing 757-2G5ER	LTU-Sud	
D-AMUX	Boeing 757-2G5ER	LTU-Sud	
D-AMUY	Boeing 757-2G5ER	LTU-Sud	
D-AMUZ	Boeing 757-2G5ER	LTU-Sud	
D-ANFA	Aérospatiale ATR-72-202	Eurowings	
D-ANFB	Aérospatiale ATR-72-202	Eurowings	
D-ANFC	Aérospatiale ATR-72-202	Eurowings	
D-ANFD	Aérospatiale ATR-72-202	Eurowings	
D-ANFE	Aérospatiale ATR-72-202	Eurowings	
D-ANFF	Aérospatiale ATR-72-202	Eurowings	
D-ANTJ	BAe 146-200QT	Eurowings/TNT Express Europe	
D-APOL	Airbus A.310-304	Middle East Airlines	
D-BAAA	Aérospatiale ATR-42-300	Eurowings	
D-BACH	D.H.C. 8-314 Dash Eight	Interot Airways	
D-BAGB	D.H.C.8 Dash Eight	Interot Airways	
D-BAKA	F.27 Friendship Mk 100	WDL	
D-BAKI	F.27 Friendship Mk 100	WDL	
D-BAKO	F.27 Friendship Mk 100	WDL	
D-BAKU	F.27 Friendship Mk 200	WDL	
D-BBBB	Aérospatiale ATR-42-300	Eurowings	
D-BCCC	Aérospatiale ATR-42-300	Eurowings	
D-BCRM	Aérospatiale ATR-42-300	Eurowings	
D-BCRN	Aérospatiale ATR-42-300	Eurowings	
D-BCRO	Aérospatiale ATR-42-300QC	Eurowings	
D-BCRP	Aérospatiale ATR-42-300QC	Eurowings	
D-BCRQ	Aérospatiale ATR-42-300	Eurowings	
D-BCRR	Aérospatiale ATR-42-300	Eurowings	
D-BCRS	Aérospatiale ATR-42-300	Eurowings	
D-BCRT	Aérospatiale ATR-42-300	Eurowings	
D-BDDD	Aérospatiale ATR-42-300	Eurowings	
D-BEEE	Aérospatiale ATR-42-300	Eurowings	
D-BELT	D.H.C.8-311 Dash Eight	Contactair/Lufthansa CityLine	
D-BERT	D.H.C.8-103 Dash Eight	Contactair/Lufthansa CityLine	
D-BEST	D.H.C.8-103 Dash Eight	Contactair/Lufthansa CityLine	
D-BEYT	D.H.C.8-311 Dash Eight	Contactair/Lufthansa CityLine	
D-BFFF	Aérospatiale ATR-42-300	Eurowings	
D-BGGG	Aérospatiale ATR-42-300	Eurowings	
D-BHHH	Aérospatiale ATR-42-300	Eurowings	
D-BIER	D.H.C.8-103 Dash Eight	Interot Airways	
D-BIII	Aérospatiale ATR-42-300	Eurowings	
D-BIRT	D.H.C.8-103 Dash Eight	Interot Airways	
D-BJJJ	Aérospatiale ATR-42-300	Eurowings	

Notes	Reg.	Type	Owner or Operator
	D-BKIM	D.H.C.8-311 Dash Eight	Contactair/Lufthansa CityLine
	D-BKIR	D.H.C.8-311 Dash Eight	Contactair/Lufthansa CityLine
	D-BKIS	D.H.C.8-311 Dash Eight	Contactair/Lufthansa CityLine
	D-B	D.H.C.8-311 Dash Eight	Contactair/Lufthansa CityLine
	D-BOBA	D.H.C.8-311 Dash Eight	Hamburg Airlines
	D-BOBL	D.H.C.8-102 Dash Eight	Hamburg Airlines
	D-BOBO	D.H.C.8-102 Dash Eight	Hamburg Airlines
	D-BOBU	D.H.C.8-311 Dash Eight	Hamburg Airlines
	D-BOBY	D.H.C.8-102 Dash Eight	Hamburg Airlines
	D-CABE	Swearingen SA227AC Metro III	Saxonia Airlines
	D-CALK	Dornier Do.228-202K	Ratioflug/Suckling Airways
	D-CDIA	SAAB SF.340A	Deutsche BA
	D-CDIB	SAAB SF.340A	Deutsche BA
	D-CDIC	SAAB SF.340A	Deutsche BA
	D-CDID	SAAB SF.340A	Deutsche BA
	D-CDIE	SAAB SF.340A	Deutsche BA
	D-CDIF	SAAB SF.340A	Deutsche BA
	D-CDIG	SAAB SF.340A	Deutsche BA
	D-CDIH	SAAB SF.340A	Deutsche BA
	D-CDIJ	SAAB SF.340A	Deutsche BA
	D-CDIZ	Dornier Do.228-201	Deutsche BA
	D-CIRB	Beech 1900C-1	Interot Airways
	D-CISA	Beech 1900C	Interot Airways
	D-CMIC	Dornier Do.228-202K	Ratioflug
	D-CONA	BAe Jetstream 3102	Contactair
	D-CONU	BAe Jetstream 3102	Contactair

Note: Lufthansa is to remove all Express and CityLine titles in 1994.

EC (Spain)

EC-BIG	Douglas DC-9-32	Iberia *Villa de Madrid*
EC-BIH	Douglas DC-9-32	Aviaco
EC-BIJ	Douglas DC-9-32	Iberia *Santa Cruz de Tenerife*
EC-BIK	Douglas DC-9-32	Aviaco *Castillo de Guanapay*
EC-BIM	Douglas DC-9-32	Iberia *Ciudad de Santander*
EC-BIN	Douglas DC-9-32	Iberia *Palma de Mallorca*
EC-BIO	Douglas DC-9-32	Aviaco
EC-BIP	Douglas DC-9-32	Aviaco *Castillo de Monteagudo*
EC-BIR	Douglas DC-9-32	Iberia *Ciudad de Valencia*
EC-BIS	Douglas DC-9-32	Iberia *Ciudad de Alicante*
EC-BIT	Douglas DC-9-32	Iberia
EC-BPG	Douglas DC-9-32	Iberia *Ciudad de Vigo*
EC-BPH	Douglas DC-9-32	Iberia *Ciudad de Gerona*
EC-BQT	Douglas DC-9-32	Iberia *Ciudad de Murcia*
EC-BQU	Douglas DC-9-32	Iberia *Ciudad de La Coruna*
EC-BQV	Douglas DC-9-32	Iberia *Ciudad de Ibiza*
EC-BQX	Douglas DC-9-32	Iberia *Ciudad de Valladolid*
EC-BQY	Douglas DC-9-32	Aviaco
EC-BQZ	Douglas DC-9-32	Iberia *Ciudad de Sta Cruz de La Palma*
EC-BRQ	Boeing 747-256B	Iberia *Calderon de la Barca*
EC-BYE	Douglas DC-9-32	Aviaco
EC-BYF	Douglas DC-9-32	Aviaco *Hernan Cortes*
EC-BYI	Douglas DC-9-32	Aviaco *Pedro de Valdivia*
EC-BYJ	Douglas DC-9-32	Aviaco
EC-CAI	Boeing 727-256	Iberia *Castilla la Nueva*
EC-CAJ	Boeing 727-256	Iberia *Cataluna*
EC-CBA	Boeing 727-256	Iberia *Vascongadas*
EC-CBD	Boeing 727-256	Iberia *Murcia*
EC-CBF	Boeing 727-256	Iberia *Gran Canaria*
EC-CBG	Boeing 727-256	Iberia *Extremadura*
EC-CBH	Boeing 727-256	Iberia *Galicia*
EC-CBI	Boeing 727-256	Iberia *Asturias*
EC-CBJ	Boeing 727-256	Iberia *Andalucia*
EC-CBO	Douglas DC-10-30	Iberia *Costa del Sol*
EC-CBP	Douglas DC-10-30	Iberia *Costa Dorada*
EC-CEZ	Douglas DC-10-30	Iberia *Costa del Azahar*
EC-CFA	Boeing 727-256	Iberia *Jerez Xeres Sherry*
EC-CFB	Boeing 727-256	Iberia *Rioja*
EC-CFC	Boeing 727-256	Iberia *Tarragona*
EC-CFD	Boeing 727-256	Iberia *Montilla-Moriles*
EC-CFE	Boeing 727-256	Iberia *Penedes*
EC-CFF	Boeing 727-256	Iberia *Valdepenas*

Reg.	Type	Owner or Operator	Notes
EC-CFG	Boeing 727-256	Iberia *La Mancha*	
EC-CFH	Boeing 727-256	Iberia *Priorato*	
EC-CFI	Boeing 727-256	Iberia *Carinena*	
EC-CFK	Boeing 727-256	Iberia *Ribeiro*	
EC-CGN	Douglas DC-9-32	Aviaco *Martin Alonso Pinzon*	
EC-CGO	Douglas DC-9-32	Aviaco *Pedro Alonso Nino*	
EC-CGP	Douglas DC-9-32	Aviaco *Juan Sebastian Elcano*	
EC-CGQ	Douglas DC-9-32	Aviaco *Alonso de Ojeda*	
EC-CGR	Douglas DC-9-32	Aviaco *Francisco de Orellana*	
EC-CID	Boeing 727-256	Iberia *Malaga*	
EC-CIE	Boeing 727-256	Iberia *Esparragosa*	
EC-CLB	Douglas DC-10-30	Iberia *Costa Blanca*	
EC-CLD	Douglas DC-9-32	Aviaco *Hernando de Soto*	
EC-CLE	Douglas DC-9-32	Aviaco *Juan Ponce de Leon*	
EC-CSJ	Douglas DC-10-30	Iberia *Costa de la Luz*	
EC-CSK	Douglas DC-10-30	Iberia *Cornisa Cantabrica*	
EC-CTR	Douglas DC-9-34CF	Iberia *Hernan Cortes*	
EC-CTS	Douglas DC-9-34CF	Aviaco *Francisco de Pizarro*	
EC-CTT	Douglas DC-9-34CF	Iberia *Pedro de Valladolid*	
EC-CTU	Douglas DC-9-34CF	Aviaco *Pedro de Alvarado*	
EC-DCC	Boeing 727-256	Iberia *Albarino*	
EC-DCD	Boeing 727-256	Iberia *Chacoli-Txakoli*	
EC-DCE	Boeing 727-256	Iberia *Mentrida*	
EC-DDV	Boeing 727-256	Iberia *Acueducto de Segovia*	
EC-DDX	Boeing 727-256	Iberia *Monasterio de Poblet*	
EC-DDY	Boeing 727-256	Iberia *Cuevas de Altamira*	
EC-DDZ	Boeing 727-256	Iberia *Murallas de Avila*	
EC-DEA	Douglas DC-10-30	Iberia *Rias Gallegas*	
EC-DGB	Douglas DC-9-34	Iberia *Castillo de Javier*	
EC-DGC	Douglas DC-9-34	Aviaco *Castillo de Sotomayor*	
EC-DGD	Douglas DC-9-34	Aviaco *Castillo de Arcos*	
EC-DGE	Douglas DC-9-34	Aviaco *Castillo de Bellver*	
EC-DHZ	Douglas DC-10-30	Iberia *Costas Canarias*	
EC-DIA	Boeing 747-256B	Iberia *Tirso de Molina*	
EC-DIB	Boeing 747-256B	Iberia *Cervantes*	
EC-DLC	Boeing 747-256B (SCD)	Iberia *Francisco de Quevedo*	
EC-DLD	Boeing 747-256B (SCD)	Iberia *Lupe de Vega*	
EC-DLE	Airbus A.300B4-120	Iberia *Donana*	
EC-DLF	Airbus A.300B4-120	Iberia *Canadas del Teide*	
EC-DLG	Airbus A.300B4-120	Iberia *Las Tablas de Daimiel*	
EC-DLH	Airbus A.300B4-120	Iberia *Aigues Tortes*	
EC-DNP	Boeing 747-256B	Iberia *Juan Ramon Jimenez*	
EC-DNQ	Airbus A.300B4-120	Iberia *Islas Cies*	
EC-DNR	Airbus A.300B4-120	Iberia *Ordesa*	
EC-EEK	Boeing 747-256B (SCD)	Iberia *Garcia Lorca*	
EC-EFX	Boeing 757-2G5	LTE International Airways *Bluebird I*	
EC-EGH	Boeing 757-2G5	LTE International Airways *Bluebird II*	
EC-EIG	McD Douglas MD-83	Spanair *Sunlight*	
EC-EJU	McD Douglas MD-83	Spanair *Sunbird*	
EC-ELM	Douglas DC-8-62F	Cargosur	
EC-ELT	BAe 146-200QT	Pan Air Lineas Aéreas/TNT	
EC-ELY	Boeing 737-3K9	Viva Air	
EC-EMD	Douglas DC-8-62F	Cargosur	
EC-EMX	Douglas DC-8-62F	Cargosur	
EC-ENQ	Boeing 757-2G5	LTE International Airways *Bluebird III*	
EC-EON	Airbus A.300B4-203	Iberia *Penalara*	
EC-EOO	Airbus A.300B4-203	Iberia *Covadouga*	
EC-EOZ	McD Douglas MD-83	Spanair *Sunbeam*	
EC-EPA	BAe 146-200QT	Pan Air Lineas Aéreas/TNT	
EC-EPL	McD Douglas MD-83	Spanair *Sunseeker*	
EC-ESJ	McD Douglas MD-83	Spanair *Sunflower*	
EC-ETB	Boeing 737-4Y0	Futura International Airways	
EC-EUC	McD Douglas MD-87	Iberia *Ciudad de Burgos*	
EC-EUD	McD Douglas MD-87	Iberia *Ciudad de Toledo*	
EC-EUE	McD Douglas MD-87	Iberia *Ciudad de Sevilla*	
EC-EUL	McD Douglas MD-87	Iberia *Ciudad de Cadiz*	
EC-EVB	McD Douglas MD-87	Iberia *Arrecife de Lanzarote*	
EC-EVE	Boeing 737-4Y0	Futura International Airways	
EC-EXF	McD Douglas MD-87	Iberia *Ciudad de Pamplona*	
EC-EXG	McD Douglas MD-87	Iberia *Ciudad de Almeria*	
EC-EXM	McD Douglas MD-87	Iberia *Ciudad de Zaragoza*	
EC-EXN	McD Douglas MD-87	Iberia *Ciudad de Badajoz*	
EC-EXR	McD Douglas MD-87	Iberia *Ciudad de Oviedo*	

Notes	Reg.	Type	Owner or Operator
	EC-EXT	McD Douglas MD-87	Iberia *Ciudad de Albacete*
	EC-EXY	Boeing 737-4Y0	Futura International Airways
	EC-EYB	McD Douglas MD-87	Iberia *Ciudad de Onis*
	EC-EYX	McD Douglas MD-87	Iberia *Ciudad de Caceres*
	EC-EYY	McD Douglas MD-87	Iberia *Ciudad de Barcelona*
	EC-EYZ	McD Douglas MD-87	Iberia *Ciudad de Las Palmas*
	EC-EZA	McD Douglas MD-87	Iberia *Ciudad de Segovia*
	EC-EZS	McD Douglas MD-87	Iberia *Ciudad de Mahon*
	EC-FAS	Airbus A.320-211	Iberia *Sierra de Cazorla*
	EC-FBP	Boeing 737-4Y0	Futura International Airways
	EC-FBQ	Airbus A.320-211	Iberia *Montseny*
	EC-FBR	Airbus A.320-211	Iberia *Sierra de Segura*
	EC-FBS	Airbus A.320-211	Iberia *Timanfaya*
	EC-FCB	Airbus A.320-211	Iberia *Montana de Covadonga*
	EC-FCU	Boeing 767-3Y0ER	Spanair *Baleares*
	EC-FDA	Airbus A.320-211	Iberia *Lagunas de Ruidera*
	EC-FDB	Airbus A.320-211	Iberia *Lago de Sanabria*
	EC-FEE	Boeing 757-236	Air Europa
	EC-FEF	Boeing 757-236	Air Europa
	EC-FEO	Airbus A.320-211	Iberia *Delta del Ebro*
	EC-FER	Boeing 737-3Q8	Viva Air
	EC-FET	Boeing 737-3Q8	Viva Air
	EC-FEY	McD Douglas MD-87	Iberia *Ciudad de Jaen*
	EC-FEZ	McD Douglas MD-87	Iberia *Ciudad de Malaga*
	EC-FFA	McD Douglas MD-87	Iberia *Ciudad de Avila*
	EC-FFC	Boeing 737-3Q8	Viva Air
	EC-FFH	McD Douglas MD-87	Iberia *Ciudad de Logrono*
	EC-FFI	McD Douglas MD-87	Iberia *Ciudad de Cuenca*
	EC-FFK	Boeing 757-236	Air Europa
	EC-FFN	Boeing 737-36E	Viva Air
	EC-FFY	BAe 146-300	Pan Air Lineas Aéreas/TNT
	EC-FGH	Airbus A.320-211	Iberia *Caldera de Taburiente*
	EC-FGM	McD Douglas MD-88	Aviaco *Torre de Hércules*
	EC-FGR	Airbus A.320-211	Iberia *Dehesa de Moncayo*
	EC-FGU	Airbus A.320-211	Iberia *Sierra Espuna*
	EC-FGV	Airbus A.320-211	Iberia *Monfrague*
	EC-FHA	Boeing 767-3Y0ER	Spanair *Canarias*
	EC-FHD	McD Douglas MD-87	Iberia *Ciudad de Leon*
	EC-FHG	McD Douglas MD-88	Aviaco *La Almudiana*
	EC-FHK	McD Douglas MD-87	Iberia *Ciudad de Tarragona*
	EC-FHR	Boeing 737-36E	Viva Air
	EC-FIA	Airbus A.320-211	Iberia *Isla de la Cartuja*
	EC-FIC	Airbus A.320-211	Iberia *Sierra de Grazalema*
	EC-FIG	McD Douglas MD-88	Aviaco *Penon de Ifach*
	EC-FIH	McD Douglas MD-88	Aviaco *Albaicin*
	EC-FIX	McD Douglas MD-83	Centennial Airlines
	EC-FJE	McD Douglas MD-88	Aviaco *Gibralfaro*
	EC-FJQ	McD Douglas MD-82	Spanair
	EC-FJR	Boeing 737-3Y0	Air Europa
	EC-FJZ	Boeing 737-3Y0	Air Europa
	EC-FKC	Boeing 737-3L9	Air Europa
	EC-FKD	Airbus A.320-211	Iberia *Monte Alhoya*
	EC-FKH	Airbus A.320-211	Iberia *Canon del Rio Lobos*
	EC-FKI	Boeing 737-375	Air Europa
	EC-FKJ	Boeing 737-3Y0	Air Europa
	EC-FKS	Boeing 737-3L9	Air Europa
	EC-FLD	Boeing 737-4Y0	Futura International Airways
	EC-FLF	Boeing 737-36E	Viva Air
	EC-FLG	Boeing 737-36E	Viva Air
	EC-FLK	McD Douglas MD-88	Aviaco *Palacio de la Magdalena*
	EC-FLN ·	McD Douglas MD-88	Aviaco *Puerta de Tierra*
	EC-FLP	Airbus A.320-211	Iberia *Torcal de Antequera*
	EC-FLQ	Airbus A.320-211	Iberia *Dunas de Liencres*
	EC-FML	Airbus A.320-211	Iberia *Hayedo de Tejera Negra*
	EC-FMN	Airbus A.320-211	Iberia *Cadi Moixeroi*
	EC-FMP	Boeing 737-33A	Viva Air
	EC-FND	McD Douglas MD-88	Aviaco
	EC-FNI	Airbus A.310-324	Oasis International Airlines
	EC-FNO	McD Douglas MD-88	Aviaco *Playa de la Concha*
	EC-FNR	Airbus A.320-211	Iberia *Monte el Valle*
	EC-FOF	McD Douglas MD-88	Aviaco *La Giralda*
	EC-FOG	McD Douglas MD-88	Aviaco *Puerta de Alcala*
	EC-FOZ	McD Douglas MD-88	Aviaco *Montjuic*

Reg.	Type	Owner or Operator	Notes
EC-FPD	McD Douglas MD-88	Aviaco *Lagos de Coradonga*	
EC-FPJ	McD Douglas MD-88	Aviaco	
EC-FQB	Boeing 737-3Y0	Air Europa	
EC-FQP	Boeing 737-348	Futura International Airways	
EC-FQY	Airbus A.320-211	Iberia	
EC-FSC	Boeing 737-348	Futura International Airways	
EC-FSY	McD Douglas MD-83	Spanair *Sunrise*	
EC-FSZ	McD Douglas MD-83	Centennial Airlines	
EC-FTL	Boeing 757-236	Air Europe	
EC-FTR	Boeing 757-256	Iberia	
EC-FTS	McD Douglas MD-83	Spanair	
EC-FTT	McD Douglas MD-83	Spanair *Sunray*	
EC-FTU	McD Douglas MD-83	Spanair	
EC-	Airbus A.321-111	Iberia	
EC-	Airbus A.321-111	Iberia	
EC-	Airbus A.321-111	Iberia	
EC-	Airbus A.321-111	Iberia	
EC-	Airbus A.321-111	Iberia	
EC-	Airbus A.321-111	Iberia	
EC-	Airbus A.321-111	Iberia	
EC-	Airbus A.321-111	Iberia	
EC-	Airbus A.321-111	Iberia	
EC-	Boeing 757-256	Iberia	
EC-	Boeing 757-256	Iberia	
EC-	Boeing 757-256	Iberia	
EC-	Boeing 757-256	Iberia	
EC-	Boeing 757-256	Iberia	
EC-	Boeing 757-256	Iberia	
EC-	Boeing 757-256	Iberia	
EC-	Boeing 757-256	Iberia	

EI (Republic of Ireland)

Including complete current Irish Civil Register

EI-ABI	D.H.84 Dragon	Aer Lingus *Iolar* (EI-AFK)	
EI-ADV	PA-12 Super Cruiser	R. E. Levis	
EI-AFE	Piper J3C-65 Cub	O. Bruton	
EI-AFF	B.A. Swallow 2 ★	J. McCarthy	
EI-AFN	B.A. Swallow 2 ★	J. McCarthy	
EI-AGB	Miles M.38 Messenger 4 ★	J. McLoughlin	
EI-AGD	Taylorcraft Plus D ★	H. Wolf	
EI-AGJ	J/1 Autocrat	W. G. Rafter	
EI-AHA	D.H.82A Tiger Moth ★	J. H. Maher	
EI-AHI	D.H.82A Tiger Moth	High Fidelity Flyers	
EI-AHR	D.H.C.1 Chipmunk 22 ★	C. Lane	
EI-AKM	Piper J-3C-65 Cub	Setanta Flying Group	
EI-ALH	Taylorcraft Plus D	N. Reilly	
EI-ALP	Avro 643 Cadet	J. C. O'Loughlin	
EI-ALU	Avro 631 Cadet	M. P. Cahill (*stored*)	
EI-AMK	J/1 Autocrat	Irish Aero Club	
EI-AND	Cessna 175A	M. A. Cooke	
EI-ANT	Champion 7ECA Citabria	S. Donohoe	
EI-ANY	PA-18 Super Cub 95	Bogavia Group	
EI-AOB	PA-28 Cherokee 140	J. Survival & ptnrs	
EI-AOK	Cessna F.172G	R. J. Cloughley & N. J. Simpson	
EI-AOP	D.H.82A Tiger Moth ★	Institute of Technology/Dublin	
EI-AOS	Cessna 310B	Joyce Aviation Ltd	
EI-APF	Cessna F.150F	L. O. Kennedy	
EI-APS	Schleicher ASK.14	SLG Group	
EI-ARH	Currie Wot/S.E.5 Replica	L. Garrison	
EI-ARM	Currie Wot/S.E.5 Replica	L. Garrison	
EI-ARW	Jodel D.R.1050	P. Walsh & P. Ryan	
EI-ASD	Boeing 737-248C	Aer Lingus	
EI-ASE	Boeing 737-248C	Aer Lingus	
EI-ASG	Boeing 737-248 ★	*Instructional airframe*/Dublin	
EI-ASH	Boeing 737-248	Aer Lingus *St Eugene*	
EI-ASI	Boeing 747-148	Aer Lingus *St Patrick*	
EI-ASJ	Boeing 747-148	Aer Lingus *St Colmcille*	
EI-AST	Cessna F.150H	Liberty Flying Group	
EI-ATJ	B.121 Pup 1	Wexford Aero Club	
EI-ATK	PA-28 Cherokee 140	Mayo Flying Club Ltd	
EI-ATS	M.S.880B Rallye Club	ATS Group	

Notes	Reg.	Type	Owner or Operator
	EI-AUC	Cessna FA.150K Aerobat	Kestrel Flying Group
	EI-AUE	M.S.880B Rallye Club	Kilkenny Flying Club Ltd
	EI-AUG	M.S.894 Rallye Minerva 220	K. O'Leary
	EI-AUJ	M.S.880B Rallye Club	Ormond Flying Club Ltd
	EI-AUM	J/1 Autocrat	J. G. Rafter
	EI-AUO	Cessna FA.150K Aerobat	Kerry Aero Club
	EI-AUS	J/5F Aiglet Trainer	T. Stephens & T. Lennon
	EI-AUT	Forney F-1A Aircoupe	Joyce Aviation Ltd
	EI-AUV	PA-23 Aztec 250C	Shannon Executive Aviation
	EI-AUY	Morane-Saulnier M.S.502	G. Warner/Duxford
	EI-AVB	Aeronca 7AC Champion	P. Ryan
	EI-AVC	Cessna F.337F	337 Flying Group
	EI-AVM	Cessna F.150L	P. Kearney
	EI-AWE	Cessna F.150M	Third Flight Group
	EI-AWH	Cessna 210J	Cork Flying Club Ltd
	EI-AWP	D.H.82A Tiger Moth	O. Bruton
	EI-AWR	Malmo MFI-9 Junior	M. R. Nesbitt & S. Duignan
	EI-AWU	M.S.880B Rallye Club	Longford Aviation Ltd
	EI-AWW	Cessna 414	Shannon Executive Aviation Ltd
	EI-AYA	M.S.880B Rallye Club	D. Bothwell & ptnrs
	EI-AYB	GY-80 Horizon 180	Westwing Flying Group
	EI-AYD	AA-5 Traveler	P. Howick & ptnrs
	EI-AYF	Cessna FRA.150L	Garda Flying Club
	EI-AYI	M.S.880B Rallye Club	J. McNamara
	EI-AYK	Cessna F.172M	S. T. Scully
	EI-AYN	BN-2A Islander	Aer Arann *Inis-Mór*
	EI-AYO	Douglas DC-3A ★	Science Museum, Wroughton
	EI-AYR	Schleicher ASK-16	Kilkenny Airport Ltd
	EI-AYS	PA-22 Colt 108	M. Skelly & R. Hall
	EI-AYV	M.S.892A Rallye Commodore 150	P. Murtagh
	EI-AYY	Evans VP-1	M. Donoghue
	EI-BAF	Thunder Ax6-56 balloon	W. G. Woollett
	EI-BAJ	SNCAN Stampe SV-4C	Dublin Tiger Group
	EI-BAO	Cessna F.172G	Garda Flying Club
	EI-BAR	Thunder Ax8-105 balloon	J. Burke & V. Hourihane
	EI-BAS	Cessna F.172M	Falcon Aviation Ltd
	EI-BAT	Cessna F.150M	Donegal Aero Club Ltd
	EI-BAV	PA-22 Colt 108	J. Davy
	EI-BBC	PA-28 Cherokee 180C	Piper Aero Club Ltd
	EI-BBD	Evans VP-1	Volksplane Group
	EI-BBE	Champion 7FC Tri-Traveler (tailwheel)	P. Forde & D. Connaire
	EI-BBG	M.S.880B Rallye Club	Weston Ltd
	EI-BBI	M.S.892 Rallye Commodore	Kilkenny Airport Ltd
	EI-BBJ	M.S.880B Rallye Club	Weston Ltd
	EI-BBM	Cameron O-65 balloon	Dublin Ballooning Club
	EI-BBN	Cessna F.150M	Sligo N.W. Aero Club
	EI-BBO	M.S.893E Rallye 180GT	J. G. Lacey & ptnrs
	EI-BBV	Piper J-3C-65 Cub	F. Cronin
	EI-BCE	BN-2A-26 Islander	Aer Arann
	EI-BCF	Bensen B.8M	T. A. Brennan
	EI-BCH	M.S.892A Rallye Commodore 150	The Condor Group
	EI-BCJ	F.8L Falco 1 Srs 3	D. Kelly
	EI-BCK	Cessna F.172K	H. Caulfield
	EI-BCL	Cessna 182P	Iona National Airways
	EI-BCM	Piper J-3C-65 Cub	Kilmoon Flying Group
	EI-BCN	Piper J-3C-65 Cub	Snowflake Flying Group
	EI-BCO	Piper J-3C-65 Cub	J. Molloy
	EI-BCP	D.628 Condor	A. Delaney
	EI-BCR	Boeing 737-281	Aer Lingus *St Oliver Plunkett*
	EI-BCS	M.S.880B Rallye Club	Organic Fruit & Vegetables of Ireland Ltd
	EI-BCU	M.S.880B Rallye Club	Weston Ltd
	EI-BCW	M.S.880B Rallye Club	Kilkenny Flying Club
	EI-BCY	Beech 200 Super King Air (232)	Minister of Defence
	EI-BDH	M.S.880B Rallye Club	Munster Wings Ltd
	EI-BDK	M.S.880B Rallye Club	Limerick Flying Club Ltd
	EI-BDL	Evans VP-2	M. Blake
	EI-BDM	PA-23 Aztec 250D ★	Industrial Training School
	EI-BDP	Cessna 182P	S. Bruton
	EI-BDR	PA-28 Cherokee 180	Cherokee Group
	EI-BDY	Boeing 737-2E1	Aer Lingus Teo *St Brigid*
	EI-BEA	M.S.880B Rallye 100ST	Weston Ltd

Reg.	Type	Owner or Operator	Notes
EI-BED	Boeing 747-130	Aer Linte Eireann Teo *St Kieran*	
EI-BEN	Piper J-3C-65 Cub	J. J. Sullivan	
EI-BEO	Cessna 310Q	Iona National Airways	
EI-BEP	M.S.892A Rallye Commodore 150	H. Lynch & J. O'Leary	
EI-BEY	Naval N3N-3 ★	Huntley & Huntley Ltd	
EI-BFF	Beech A.23 Musketeer	E. Hopkins	
EI-BFH	Bell 212	Irish Helicopters Ltd	
EI-BFI	M.S.880B Rallye 100ST	J. O'Neill	
EI-BFJ	Beech A.200 Super King Air (234)	Minister of Defence	
EI-BFM	M.S.893E Rallye 235GT	FM Group	
EI-BFO	Piper J-3C-90 Cub	D. Gordon	
EI-BFP	M.S.800B Rallye 100ST	Weston Ltd	
EI-BFR	M.S.880B Rallye 100ST	J. Power	
EI-BFV	M.S.880B Rallye 100T	Ormond Flying Club	
EI-BGA	SOCATA Rallye 100ST	J. J. Frew	
EI-BGB	M.S.880B Rallye Club	Limerick Flying Club	
EI-BGD	M.S.880B Rallye Club	N. Kavanagh	
EI-BGG	M.S.892E Rallye 150GT	M. J. Hanlon	
EI-BGH	Cessna F.172N	Iona National Airways	
EI-BGJ	Cessna F.152	Hibernian Flying Club	
EI-BGO	Canadair CL-44D-4J ★	Irish Airports Authority/Dublin	
EI-BGT	Colt 77A balloon	K. Haugh	
EI-BGU	M.S.880B Rallye Club	M. F. Neary	
EI-BHB	M.S.887 Rallye 125	Hotel Bravo Flying Club	
EI-BHC	Cessna F.177RG	P. V. Maguire	
EI-BHF	M.S.892A Rallye Commodore 150	B. Mullen	
EI-BHI	Bell 206B JetRanger 2	J. Mansfield	
EI-BHK	M.S.880B Rallye Club	J. Lawlor & B. Lyons	
EI-BHL	Beech E90 King Air	Stewart Singlam Fabrics Ltd	
EI-BHM	Cessna 337E	Positively Belfast	
EI-BHN	M.S.893A Rallye Commodore 180	T. Garvan	
EI-BHO	Sikorsky S-61N	Irish Helicopters Ltd	
EI-BHP	M.S.893A Rallye Commodore 180	Spanish Point Flying Club	
EI-BHT	Beech 77 Skipper	Waterford Aero Club	
EI-BHV	Champion 7EC Traveler	Condor Group	
EI-BHW	Cessna F.150F	R. Sharpe	
EI-BHY	SOCATA Rallye 150ST	D. Killian	
EI-BIB	Cessna F.152	Galway Flying Club	
EI-BIC	Cessna F.172N	Oriel Flying Group Ltd	
EI-BID	PA-18 Super Cub 95	D. MacCarthy	
EI-BIF	SOCATA Rallye 235E	Empire Enterprises Ltd	
EI-BIG	Zlin 526	P. von Lonkhuyzen	
EI-BIJ	AB-206B JetRanger 2	Celtic Helicopters Ltd	
EI-BIK	PA-18 Super Cub 180	Dublin Gliding Club	
EI-BIM	M.S.880B Rallye Club	D. Millar	
EI-BIO	Piper J-3C-65 Cub	Monasterevin Flying Club	
EI-BIR	Cessna F.172M	B. Harrison & ptnrs	
EI-BIS	Robin R.1180TD	Robin Aiglon Group	
EI-BIT	M.S.887 Rallye 125	Spanish Point Flying Club	
EI-BIU	Robin R.2112A	Wicklow Flying Group	
EI-BIV	Bellanca 8KCAB Citabria	Aerocrats Flying Group	
EI-BIW	M.S.880B Rallye Club	E. J. Barr	
EI-BJA	Cessna FRA.150L	Blackwater Flying Group	
EI-BJC	Aeronca 7AC Champion	B. Lyons	
EI-BJG	Robin R.1180	N. Hanley	
EI-BJJ	Aeronca 15AC Sedan	A. A. Alderdice & S. H. Boyd	
EI-BJK	M.S.880B Rallye 110ST	Jordan Larkin Flying Group	
EI-BJM	Cessna A.152	Leinster Aero Club	
EI-BJO	Cessna R.172K	P. Hogan & G. Ryder	
EI-BJS	AA-5B Tiger	P. Morrisey	
EI-BJT	PA-38-112 Tomahawk	O. Bruton	
EI-BJW	D.H.104 Dove 6 ★	Waterford Museum	
EI-BKC	Aeronca 115AC Sedan	J. Lynch	
EI-BKD	Mooney M.20J	Limerick Warehousing Ltd	
EI-BKF	Cessna F.172H	M. & M. C. Veale	
EI-BKK	Taylor JT.1 Monoplane	Waterford Aero Club	
EI-BKM	Zenith CH.200	D. van de Braam	
EI-BKN	M.S.880B Rallye 100ST	Weston Ltd	
EI-BKS	Eipper Quicksilver	Irish Microlight Ltd	
EI-BKT	AB-206B JetRanger 3	Irish Helicopters Ltd	
EI-BKU	M.S.892A Rallye Commodore 150	Limerick Flying Club	
EI-BLB	SNCAN Stampe SV-4C	J. E. Hutchinson & R. A. Stafford	
EI-BLD	Bolkow Bo 105C	Irish Helicopters Ltd	

Notes	Reg.	Type	Owner or Operator
	EI-BLE	Eipper Microlight	R. P. St George-Smith
	EI-BLG	AB-206B JetRanger 3	Monarch Property Services Ltd
	EI-BLN	Eipper Quicksilver MX	O. J. Conway & B. Daffy
	EI-BLO	Catto CP.16	R. W. Hall
	EI-BLR	PA-34-200T Seneca II	R. Paris
	EI-BLU	Evans VP-1	S. Pallister
	EI-BLW	PA-23 Aztec 250C	— (stored)
	EI-BLY	Sikorsky S-61N	Irish Helicopters Ltd
	EI-BMA	M.S.880B Rallye Club	W. Rankin & M. Kelleher
	EI-BMB	M.S.880B Rallye 100T	Clyde Court Development Ltd
	EI-BMC	Hiway Demon Skytrike	S. Pallister
	EI-BMF	Laverda F.8L Falco	M. Slazenger & H. McCann
	EI-BMH	M.S.880B Rallye Club	N. J. Bracken
	EI-BMI	SOCATA TB.9 Tampico	Weston Ltd
	EI-BMJ	M.S.880B Rallye 100T	Weston Ltd
	EI-BML	PA-23 Aztec 250	Bruton Aircraft Engineering Ltd
	EI-BMM	Cessna F.152 II	E. Hopkins
	EI-BMN	Cessna F.152 II	Iona National Airways Ltd
	EI-BMO	Robin R.2160	L. Gavin & ptnrs
	EI-BMS	Cessna F.177RG	A. M. Smyth
	EI-BMU	Monnet Sonerai II	P. Forde & D. Connaire
	EI-BMV	AA-5 Traveler	E. Tierney & K. Harold
	EI-BMW	Vulcan Air Trike	L. Maddock
	EI-BNA	Douglas DC-8-63CF	Aer Turas Teo
	EI-BNB	Lake LA-4-200 Buccaneer	L. McNamara & M. Ledwith
	EI-BNC	Cessna F.152	Iona National Airlines
	EI-BND	Conroy CL-44-0	Buffalo Airways
	EI-BNF	Goldwing Canard	T. Morelli
	EI-BNG	M.S.892A Rallye Commodore 150	Shannon Executive Aviation
	EI-BNH	Hiway Skytrike	M. Martin
	EI-BNJ	Evans VP-2	G. A. Cashman
	EI-BNK	Cessna U.206F	Irish Parachute Club Ltd
	EI-BNL	Rand KR-2	K. Hayes
	EI-BNP	Rotorway 133	R. L. Renfroe
	EI-BNT	Cvjetkovic CA-65	B. Tobin & P. G. Ryan
	EI-BNU	M.S.880B Rallye Club	P. A. Doyle
	EI-BOA	Pterodactyl Ptraveller	A. Murphy
	EI-BOE	SOCATA TB.10 Tobago	P. Byron & ptnrs
	EI-BOH	Eipper Quicksilver	J. Leech
	EI-BOM	Boeing 737-2T4	Air Tara Ltd (leased to Delta A/L)
	EI-BON	Boeing 737-2T4	Air Tara Ltd (leased to Delta A/L)
	EI-BOO	PA-23 Aztec 250C	K. A. O'Connor
	EI-BOR	Bell 222	Westair Ltd
	EI-BOV	Rand KR-2	G. O'Hara & G. Callan
	EI-BOX	Duet	K. Riccius
	EI-BPB	PA-28R Cherokee Arrow 200	Rathcoole Flying Club
	EI-BPE	Viking Dragonfly	G. Bracken
	EI-BPJ	Cessna 182A	Falcon Parachute Club Ltd
	EI-BPL	Cessna F.172K	Phoenix Flying
	EI-BPO	Puma Skytrike	A. Morelli
	EI-BPP	Quicksilver MX	J. A. Smith
	EI-BPS	PA-30 Twin Comanche 160	Group Air
	EI-BPT	Skyhook Sabre	T. McGrath
	EI-BPU	Hiway Demon	A. Channing
	EI-BRH	Mainair Gemini Flash	F. Warren & T. McGrath
	EI-BRK	Flexiform Trike	L. Maddock
	EI-BRO	Cessna F.152	Iona National Airways
	EI-BRS	Cessna P.172D	D. & M. Hillery
	EI-BRT	Flexwing M17727	M. J. McCrystal
	EI-BRU	Evans VP-1	R. Smith & T. Coughlan
	EI-BRV	Hiway Demon	M. Garvey & C. Tully
	EI-BRW	Ultralight Deltabird	A. & E. Aerosports
	EI-BRX	Cessna FRA.150L	Trim Flying Club Ltd
	EI-BSB	Jodel D.112	W. Kennedy
	EI-BSC	Cessna F.172N	S. Phelan
	EI-BSE	Enstrom F-28A	Clark Aviation
	EI-BSF	H.S.748 Srs 1 ★	S.E. Aviation Museum/Waterford
	EI-BSG	Bensen B.80	J. Todd
	EI-BSK	SOCATA TB.9 Tampico	Weston Ltd
	EI-BSL	PA-34-220T Seneca	E. L. Symons
	EI-BSN	Cameron O-65 balloon	W. Woollett
	EI-BSO	PA-28 Cherokee 140B	D. Rooney
	EI-BSQ	Thundercolt Ax6-56Z balloon	D. Hooper

Reg.	Type	Owner or Operator	Notes
EI-BST	Bell 206B JetRanger	Celtic Helicopters Ltd	
EI-BSU	Champion 7KCAB	R. Bentley	
EI-BSV	SOCATA TB.20 Trinidad	J. Condron	
EI-BSW	Solar Wings Pegasus XL-R	E. Fitzgerald	
EI-BSX	Piper J-3C-65 Cub	J. & T. O'Dwyer	
EI-BTN	L.1101-385 TriStar 1	Air Tara Ltd (leased to Air America)	
EI-BTS	Boeing 747-283B (SCD)	Air Tara Ltd (leased to Philippine A/L)	
EI-BTU	McD Douglas MD-83	Irish Aerospace Ltd	
EI-BTV	McD Douglas MD-83	Irish Aerospace Ltd	
EI-BTX	McD Douglas MD-82	Air Tara Ltd (leased to AeroMexico)	
EI-BTY	McD Douglas MD-82	Air Tara Ltd	
EI-BUA	Cessna 172M	Skyhawks Flying Club	
EI-BUC	Jodel D.9 Bebe	L. Maddock	
EI-BUF	Cessna 210N	210 Group	
EI-BUG	SOCATA ST.10 Diplomate	J. Cooke	
EI-BUH	Lake LA.4-200 Buccaneer	Derg Aviation (Group) Ltd	
EI-BUJ	M.S.892A Rallye Commodore 150	T. Cunniffe	
EI-BUL	MW-5 Sorcerer	J. Conlon	
EI-BUM	Cessna 404	Iona National Airways Ltd	
EI-BUN	Beech 76 Duchess	The 172 Flying Group Ltd	
EI-BUO	Aero Composites Sea Hawker	C. Lavery & C. Donaldson	
EI-BUR	PA-38-112 Tomahawk	Leoni Aviation Ltd	
EI-BUS	PA-38-112 Tomahawk	Leoni Aviation Ltd	
EI-BUT	M.S.893A Commodore 180	T. Keating	
EI-BUU	Solar Wings Pegasus XL-R	R. L. T. Hudson	
EI-BUV	Cessna 172RG	J. J. Spollen	
EI-BUW	Noble Hardman Snowbird IIIA	T.I.F.C. & I.S. Ltd	
EI-BUX	Agusta A.109A	Orring Ltd	
EI-BUZ	Robinson R-22	Leoni Aviation Ltd	
EI-BVB	Whittaker MW.6 Merlin	R. England	
EI-BVC	Cameron N-65 balloon	E. Shepherd	
EI-BVE	Jodel D.9 Bebe	J. Greene	
EI-BVF	Cessna F.172N	First Phantom Group	
EI-BVJ	AMF Chevvron 232	W. T. King & S. G. Dunne	
EI-BVK	PA-38-112 Tomahawk	Pegasus Flying Group Ltd	
EI-BVN	Bell 206B Jet Ranger 3	Helicopter Hire (Ireland) Ltd	
EI-BVQ	Cameron Can SS balloon	T. McCormack	
EI-BVS	Cessna 172RG	P. Bruno	
EI-BVT	Evans VP-2	J. J. Sullivan	
EI-BVU	Cessna 152	Iona National Airways Ltd	
EI-BVW	Cessna 152	Iona National Airways Ltd	
EI-BVX	EMB-110P1 Bandeirante	Iona National Airways Ltd	
EI-BVY	Zenith 200AA-RW	J. Matthews & ptnrs	
EI-BVZ	Scheibe SF.25B Falke	D. Lamb & ptnrs	
EI-BWD	McD Douglas MD-83	Air Tara Ltd (leased to BWIA)	
EI-BWF	Boeing 747-283B	Air Tara Ltd (leased to Philippine A/L)	
EI-BWH	Partenavia P.68C	K. Buckley	
EI-BWT	BAC One-Eleven 414ED	Air Tara Ltd	
EI-BXA	Boeing 737-448	Aer Lingus Teo St Conleth	
EI-BXB	Boeing 737-448	Aer Lingus Teo St Gall	
EI-BXC	Boeing 737-448	Aer Lingus Teo St Brendan	
EI-BXD	Boeing 737-448	Aer Lingus Teo St Colman	
EI-BXI	Boeing 737-448	Aer Lingus Teo St Finnian	
EI-BXK	Boeing 737-448	Aer Lingus Teo St Caimin	
EI-BXL	Polaris F1B-OK350	M. McKeon	
EI-BXM	Boeing 737-2T4	Air Tara Ltd	
EI-BXN	Boeing 737-448	Aer Lingus Teo	
EI-BXO	Fouga CM.170 Magister	G. W. Connolly	
EI-BXP	PA-23 Aztec 250E	Aer Arann Inis Oirr	
EI-BXS	Aérospatiale ATR-42-300	GPA Group	
EI-BXT	D.62B Condor	J. Sweeney	
EI-BXU	PA-28-161 Warrior II	W. T. King	
EI-BXX	AB-206B JetRanger	Leoni Aviation Ltd	
EI-BXZ	Flexiwing	R. England	
EI-BYA	Thruster TST Mk 1	E. Fagan	
EI-BYC	Bensen B.8MR	C. Kirwan	
EI-BYD	Cessna 150J	Kestrel Flying Group	
EI-BYE	PA-31-350 Navajo Chieftain	EI-Air Exports Ltd	
EI-BYF	Cessna 150M	Twentieth Air Training Group	
EI-BYG	SOCATA TB.9 Tampico	Weston Ltd	
EI-BYH	Cessna 340A	Claddagh Air Carriers	
EI-BYI	Colt 77A balloon	J. Keena	
EI-BYJ	Bell 206B JetRanger	Celtic Helicopters Ltd	

Notes	Reg.	Type	Owner or Operator
	EI-BYK	PA-23 Aztec 250E	M. F. Hilary
	EI-BYL	Zenith CH.250	A. Corcoran & J. Martin
	EI-BYN	Cessna 550 Citation II	Stickbury Enterprises Ltd
	EI-BYO	Aérospatiale ATR-42-300	GPA Group (leased to Brit Air)
	EI-BYP	Cameron balloon	Airship & Balloon Services Ltd
	EI-BYS	Robinson R-22B	G. V. Maloney
	EI-BYV	Hughes 369D	Irish Helicopters Ltd
	EI-BYX	Champion 7GCAA	P. J. Gallagher
	EI-BYY	Piper J-3C-85 Cub	A. J. Haines
	EI-BYZ	PA-44-180 Seminole	European College of Aeronautics
	EI-BZA	Boeing 747-283B	Air Tara Ltd (leased to Philippine A/L)
	EI-BZB	Airbus A.300C4	GPA Finance (leased to Philippine A/L)
	EI-BZE	Boeing 737-3Y0	GPA Group Ltd (leased to Philippine A/L)
	EI-BZF	Boeing 737-3Y0	GPA Group Ltd (leased to Philippine A/L)
	EI-BZH	Boeing 737-3Y0	GPA Group Ltd (leased to Philippine A/L)
	EI-BZI	Boeing 737-3Y0	GPA Group Ltd (leased to Philippine A/L)
	EI-BZJ	Boeing 737-3Y0	GPA Group Ltd (leased to Philippine A/L)
	EI-BZK	Boeing 737-3Y0	GPA Group Ltd (leased to Philippine A/L)
	EI-BZL	Boeing 737-3Y0	GPA Group Ltd (leased to Philippine A/L)
	EI-BZM	Boeing 737-3Y0	GPA Group Ltd (leased to Philippine A/L)
	EI-BZN	Boeing 737-3Y0	GPA Group Ltd (leased to Philippine A/L)
	EI-BZZ	Douglas DC-9-15	GPA Finance Ltd (stored)
	EI-CAA	Cessna FR.172J	A. Ross
	EI-CAB	Grob G.115	European College of Aeronautics
	EI-CAC	Grob G.115	European College of Aeronautics
	EI-CAD	Grob G.115	European College of Aeronautics
	EI-CAE	Grob B.115	European College of Aeronautics
	EI-CAF	Bell 206B JetRanger 2	Irish Helicopters Ltd
	EI-CAG	PA-31 Navajo	Leoni Aviation Ltd
	EI-CAH	G.1159C Gulfstream 4	Ardesir Ltd
	EI-CAJ	O'Leary Biplane	J. O. Leary
	EI-CAK	Douglas DC-8-63AF	Aer Turas Teo
	EI-CAL	Boeing 767-3Y0ER	Aer Lingus Teo
	EI-CAM	Boeing 767-3Y0ER	Aer Lingus Teo
	EI-CAN	Aerotech MW.5 Sorcerer	J. Conlon
	EI-CAO	Cameron O-84 balloon	K. Haugh
	EI-CAP	Cessna R.182RG	Skyline Flight Management Ltd
	EI-CAU	AMF Chevvron 232	H. Sydner
	EI-CAW	Bell 206B JetRanger	Celtic Helicopters Ltd
	EI-CAX	Cessna P.210N	N. Dunne
	EI-CAY	Mooney M.20C	Ranger Flights Ltd
	EI-CBB	Douglas DC-9-15	GPA Finance Ltd (stored)
	EI-CBC	Aérospatiale ATR-72	Air Tara Ltd
	EI-CBD	Aérospatiale ATR-72	Air Tara Ltd
	EI-CBE	McD Douglas MD-83	Irish Aerospace Ltd
	EI-CBF	Aérospatiale ATR-42-300	Air Tara Ltd (leased to Trans World Express)
	EI-CBG	Douglas DC-9-51	GPA Finance Ltd (leased to Hawaiian)
	EI-CBH	Douglas DC-9-51	GPA Finance Ltd (leased to Hawaiian)
	EI-CBI	Douglas DC-9-51	Air Tara Ltd (leased to Hawaiian)
	EI-CBJ	D.H.C. 8-102 Dash Eight	GPA Group Ltd (leaesd in Alaska)
	EI-CBK	Aérospatiale ATR-42-300	Air Tara Ltd
	EI-CBO	McD Douglas MD-83	Air Tara Ltd
	EI-CBP	Boeing 737-3Y0	Air Tara Ltd (leased to LAM)
	EI-CBQ	Boeing 737-3Y0	Air Tara Ltd (leased to LAM)
	EI-CBR	McD Douglas MD-83	Irish Aerospace (leased to Avianca)
	EI-CBS	McD Douglas MD-83	Irish Aerospace (leased to Avianca)
	EI-CBU	McD Douglas MD-87	Air Tara Ltd (leased to AeroMexico)
	EI-CBY	McD Douglas MD-83	Air Tara Ltd (leased to Avianca)
	EI-CBZ	McD Douglas MD-83	Air Tara Ltd (leased to Avianca)
	EI-CCA	Beech 19A Musketeer	P. F. McCooke
	EI-CCB	PA-44-180 Seminole	S. Bruton
	EI-CCC	McD Douglas MD-83	Irish Aerospace Ltd (leased to Avianca)
	EI-CCD	Grob G.115A	European College of Aeronautics
	EI-CCE	McD Douglas MD-83	Irish Aerospace Ltd (leased to Avianca)
	EI-CCF	Aeronca 11AC Chief	O. Bruton
	EI-CCH	Piper J-3C-65 Cub	M. Slattery
	EI-CCJ	Cessna 152	Irish Aero Club
	EI-CCK	Cessna 152	Irish Aero Club
	EI-CCM	Cessna 152	Irish Aero Club
	EI-CCN	Grob G.115A	European College of Aeronautics
	EI-CCO	PA-44-180 Seminole	S. Bruton
	EI-CCQ	Slingsby T.31F Motor Cadet	Kerry Aero Club Ltd
	EI-CCR	Gulfstream 690D	Earl of Granard

Reg.	Type	Owner or Operator	Notes
EI-CCT	Robinson R-22B	Air Investments Ltd	
EI-CCU	BAC One-Eleven 531FS	Ryanair Ltd	
EI-CCV	Cessna R.172K-XP	Kerry Aero Club	
EI-CCW	BAC One-Eleven 509EW	Ryanair Ltd	
EI-CCX	BAC One-Eleven 531FS	Ryanair Ltd	
EI-CCY	AA-1B Trainer	N. & C. Whisler	
EI-CCZ	Cessna F.150L	Comprehensive Enterprises Ltd	
EI-CDA	Boeing 737-548	Aer Lingus Teo *St Columba*	
EI-CDB	Boeing 737-548	Aer Lingus Teo *St Albert*	
EI-CDC	Boeing 737-548	Aer Lingus Teo *St Munchin*	
EI-CDD	Boeing 737-548	Aer Lingus Teo *St Macartan*	
EI-CDF	Boeing 737-548	Aer Lingus Teo *St Cronan*	
EI-CDG	Boeing 737-548	Aer Lingus Teo *St Moling*	
EI-CDH	Boeing 737-548	Aer Lingus Teo *St Ronan*	
EI-CDI	McD Douglas MD-11	GPA Group *(leased to Garuda)*	
EI-CDJ	McD Douglas MD-11	GPA Group *(leased to Garuda)*	
EI-CDK	McD Douglas MD-11	GPA Group *(leased to Garuda)*	
EI-CDL	McD Douglas MD-11	GPA Group *(leased to Garuda)*	
EI-CDM	McD Douglas MD-11	GPA Group *(leased to Garuda)*	
EI-CDN	McD Douglas MD-11	GPA Group *(leased to Garuda)*	
EI-CDO	BAC One-Eleven 518FG	Ryanair Ltd	
EI-CDP	Cessna 182L	O. Bruton	
EI-CDQ	SA.300 Starduster Too	J. Keane	
EI-CDR	—	—	
EI-CDS	Boeing 737-548	Aer Lingus Teo *St Malachy*	
EI-CDT	Boeing 737-548	Aer Lingus Teo *St Declan*	
EI-CDU	Cessna 150F	Blue Heron Aircraft Services Ltd	
EI-CDV	Cessna 150F	Blue Heron Aircraft Services Ltd	
EI-CDW	Robinson R-22B	J. Martyn	
EI-CDX	Cessna 210K	Falcon Aviation Ltd	
EI-CDY	McD Douglas MD-83	Irish Aerospace Ltd *(leased to Avianca)*	
EI-CDZ	Luscombe 8A Silvaire	S. Bruton	
EI-CEB	Airbus A.300B4	GPA Finance Ltd	
EI-CEC	PA-31-350 Navajo Chieftain	M. Knopek	
EI-CED	D.H.C.8-311 Dash Eight	GPA Finance Ltd	
EI-CEF	Robinson R-22HP	Santail Ltd	
EI-CEG	M.S.893A Rallye 180GT	M. Farrelly	
EI-CEH	McD Douglas MD-83	Irish Aerospace Ltd	
EI-CEJ	Robinson R-22B	Helifly Ltd	
EI-CEK	McD Douglas MD-83	Irish Aerospace Ltd	
EI-CEL	Rans S.6 Coyote	D. O'Gorman	
EI-CEM	Boeing 767-2B1ER	GPA Group *(leased to LAM)*	
EI-CEN	Thruster T.300	J. Conlon	
EI-CEO	Boeing 747-259B (SCD)	GPA Group *(leased to Avianca)*	
EI-CEP	McD Douglas MD-83	Irish Aerospace Ltd	
EI-CEQ	McD Douglas MD-83	Irish Aerospace Ltd *(leased to Avianca)*	
EI-CER	McD Douglas MD-83	Irish Aerospace Ltd *(leased to Avianca)*	
EI-CES	Taylorcraft BC-65	N. O'Brien	
EI-CET	L.188CF Electra	Hunting Cargo Airlines (Ireland) Ltd	
EI-CEX	Lake LA-4-200	Derg Developments Ltd	
EI-CEY	Boeing 757-2Y0	GPA Group *(leased to Avianca)*	
EI-CEZ	Boeing 757-2Y0	GPA Group *(leased to Avianca)*	
EI-CFA	SAAB SF.340B	Aer Lingus Commuter *St Eithne*	
EI-CFB	SAAB SF.340B	Aer Lingus Commuter *St Aoife*	
EI-CFC	SAAB SF.340B	Aer Lingus Commuter *St Finbarr*	
EI-CFD	SAAB SF.340B	Aer Lingus Commuter *St Senan*	
EI-CFE	Robinson R-22B	Windsor Motors Ltd	
EI-CFF	PA-12 Super Cruiser	J. O'Dwyer & J. Molloy	
EI-CFG	CP.301B Emeraude	Southlink Ltd	
EI-CFH	PA-12 Super Cruiser	G. Treacy	
EI-CFI	PA-34-200T Seneca II	Mockfield Construction	
EI-CFK	Varga 2150A Kachina	W. M. Patterson	
EI-CFL	Airbus A.300B4	Air Tara Ltd	
EI-CFM	Cessna 172P	M. P. Cahill	
EI-CFN	Cessna 172P	M. P. Cahill	
EI-CFO	Piper J-3C-65 Cub	S. Bruton	
EI-CFP	Cessna 172P	S. Bruton	
EI-CFR	Boeing 767-375ER	GPA Group Ltd *(leased to China)*	
EI-CFV	M.S.880B Rallye Club	Kilkenny Flying Club	
EI-CFX	Robinson R-22B	Glenwood Transport	
EI-CFY	Cessna 172N	Transatlantic Ferry Services Ltd	
EI-CFZ	McD Douglas MD-83	Irish Aerospace Ltd	
EI-CGA	McD Douglas MD-83	GPA Group Ltd *(leased in US)*	

Notes	Reg.	Type	Owner or Operator
	EI-CGB	Team Minimax	M. Garvey
	EI-CGC	Stinson 108-3	S. Bruton
	EI-CGD	Cessna 172M	Hibernian Flying Club Ltd
	EI-CGE	Hiway Demon	T. E. Carr
	EI-CGF	Luton LA-5 Major	F. Doyle & J. Duggan
	EI-CGG	Ercoupe 415C	Irish Ercoupe Group
	EI-CGH	Cessna 210N	J. J. Spollen
	EI-CGI	McD Douglas MD-83	Irish Aerospace Ltd
			(leased to Trans Alsace)
	EI-CGJ	Solar Wings Pegasus XL-R	P. Heraty
	EI-CGK	Robinson R-22B	Rathcoole Flying Club Ltd
	EI-CGL	Solar Wings Pegasus XL-R	Microflight Ltd
	EI-CGM	Solar Wings Pegasus XL-R	Microflight Ltd
	EI-CGN	Solar Wings Pegasus XL-R	M. Ffrench
	EI-CGO	Douglas DC-8-63AF	Aer Turas Teo
	EI-CGP	PA-28 Cherokee 140C	M. Goss
	EI-CGQ	AS.350B Ecureuil	Caulstown Air Ltd
	EI-CGR	McD Douglas MD-83	Irish Aerospace Ltd
	EI-CGS	McD Douglas MD-83	Irish Aerospace Ltd
	EI-CGT	Cessna 152 II	Eitleann Property Ltd
	EI-CGU	Robinson R-22HP	K. A. O'Connor
	EI-CGV	Piper J-5A Cub Cruiser	J5 Group
	EI-CGW	Powerchute Kestrel	C. Kiernan
	EI-CGX	Cessna 340A	Meckfield Construction Ltd
	EI-CGZ	Boeing 737-2L9	Air Tara Ltd
	EI-CHC	Boeing 737-2L9	Air Tara Ltd
	EI-CHD	Boeing 737-317	Air Tara Ltd (leased to Morris Air)
	EI-CHE	Boeing 737-33A	GPA Group (leased to Morris Air)
	EI-CHF	PA-44-180 Seminole	—
	EI-CHH	Boeing 737-317	GPA Group (leased to Markair)
	EI-CHI	Mooney M.20C	—
	EI-CHJ	Cessna FR.172K	O. Bruton
	EI-CHK	Piper J-3C-65 Cub	N. Higgins
	EI-CHL	Bell 206L-3 Long Ranger 3	Celtic Helicopters Ltd
	EI-CHM	Cessna 150M	K. A. O'Connor
	EI-CHN	M.S.880B Rallye Club	P. & O. Furlong
	EI-CHO	L.188F Electra	Iona National Airways/Channel Express
	EI-CHP	D.H.C.8-103 Dash Eight	GPA Jetprop (leased USAir Express)
	EI-CHQ	Boeing 737-317	GPA Group Ltd (leased to Markair)
	EI-CHR	CFM Shadow Srs B0	N. Irwin
	EI-CHS	Cessna 172M	Kerry Aero Club Ltd
	EI-CHT	Solar Wings Pegasus XL-R	G. W. Maher
	EI-CHV	Agusta A.109A	Celtic Helicopters Ltd
	EI-CHW	L.188CF Electra	Hunting Cargo Airlines (Ireland) Ltd
	EI-CHX	L.188CF Electra	Hunting Cargo Airlines (Ireland) Ltd
	EI-CHY	—	
	EI-CHZ	L.188CF Electra	Hunting Cargo Airlines (Ireland) Ltd
	EI-CIA	M.S.880B Rallye Club	M. Maher
	EI-CIF	PA-28 Cherokee 180C	E. Tierney & K. A. Harold
	EI-CIG	PA-18 Super Cub 150	K. A. O'Connor
	EI-CIH	Ercoupe 415CD	J. G. Lacey
	EI-CII	—	
	EI-CIJ	Cessna 340A	Airlink Airways Ltd
	EI-CIK	Mooney M.20C	A. & P. Aviation Ltd
	EI-CIL	Hughes 269C	Mayo Helicopters Ltd
	EI-CIM	Light Aero Avid Speedwing Mk IV	P. Swan
	EI-CIN	Cessna 150K	W. T. King
	EI-CIO	Bell 206L-3 LongRanger	Sean Quinn Properties Ltd
	EI-CIP	Solar Wings Pegasus Quasar IIITC	B. Van Duykeren
	EI-CIQ	Aérospatiale ATR-42-300	GPA Finance Ltd
	EI-CIR	Cessna 550 Citation II	Air Group Finance Ltd
	EI-CIS	D.H.C.6-311A Dash Eight	GPA Propjet Ltd
	EI-CIT	D.H.C.8-311 Dash Eight	GPA Finance Ltd
	EI-CIU	—	
	EI-CIV	PA-28 Cherokee 140	G. Cashman & E. Callanan
	EI-CIW	—	
	EI-CIX	Boeing 737-4Y0	GPA Finance Ltd (leased to Markair)
	EI-CIY	Boeing 767-330ER	Air Europe SpA
	EI-CIZ	Steen Skybolt	J. Keane
	EI-CJA	Boeing 767-35HER	Air Europe SpA (I-AEJD not taken up)
	EI-CJB	—	
	EI-CJC	Boeing 737-204	Ryanair Ltd

Reg.	Type	Owner or Operator	Notes
EI-CJD	Boeing 737-204	Ryanair Ltd	
EI-CJE	Boeing 737-204	Ryanair Ltd	
EI-CJF	Boeing 737-204	Ryanair Ltd	
EI-CJG	Boeing 737-204	Ryanair Ltd	
EI-CJH	Boeing 737-204	Ryanair Ltd	
EI-CJI	Boeing 737-	Ryanair Ltd	
EI-CJJ	Boeing 737-	Ryanair Ltd	
EI-	Airbus A.330-300	Aer Lingus Teo	
EI-	Airbus A.330-300	Aer Lingus Teo	
EI-	Airbus A.330-300	Aer Lingus Teo	
EI-CTY	BAe 146-200	CityJet	
EI-CUB	Piper J-3C-65 Cub	Galway Flying Club	
EI-DMI	PA-31-325 Turbo Navajo C	Dawn Meats	
EI-EDR	PA-28R Cherokee Arrow 200	Victor Mike Flying Group Ltd	
EI-EEC	PA-23 Aztec 250	Westair Ltd	
EI-EIO	PA-34-200T Seneca II	M. Casey & ptnrs	
EI-ETC	Aeronca 15AC Sedan	H. Moreau	
EI-EXP	Short SD3-30 Variant 100	EI Air Exports	
EI-FKA	Fokker 50	Aer Lingus Commuter *St Fintan*	
EI-FKB	Fokker 50	Aer Lingus Commuter *St Fergal*	
EI-FKC	Fokker 50	Aer Lingus Commuter *St Fidelma*	
EI-FKD	Fokker 50	Aer Lingus Commuter *St Flannan*	
EI-FKE	Fokker 50	Aer Lingus Commuter *St Pappin*	
EI-FKF	Fokker 50	Aer Lingus Commuter *St Ultan*	
EI-FKG	—	Aer Lingus Commuter	
EI-FKH	—	Aer Lingus Commuter	
EI-FLY	SOCATA TB.9 Tampico	Hotel Bravo Flying Group Ltd	
EI-GFC	SOCATA TB.9 Tampico	Galway Flying Club Ltd	
EI-JET	BAe 146-200	CityJet	
EI-JTC	PA-31-350 Navajo Chieftain	T. Brennan	
EI-JWM	Robinson R-22B	Jair Aviation Co Ltd	
EI-LMG	Bell 206L-3 LongRanger	Ven Air	
EI-SNN	Cessna 650 Citation III	Westair Aviation Ltd	
EI-TCK	Cessna 421A	T. C. Killeen	
EI-TKI	Robinson R-22B	Hydraulic Services Ltd	
EI-TLA	Douglas DC-8-71F	TransLift Airways Ltd	
EI-TLB	Douglas DC-8-71F	TransLift Airways Ltd	
EI-TLC	Douglas DC-8-71	TransLift Airways Ltd	
EI-TLE	Airbus A.320-231	TransLift Airways Ltd	
EI-WCC	Robinson R-22B	Westair Aviation Ltd	
EI-XMA	Robinson R-22B	Leoni Aviation Ltd	
EI-XMC	Robinson R-22B	McAuliffe Photographic Laboratories	

EK (Armenia)

The following are operated by Armenian Airlines with the registrations prefixed by EK.

65044	Tu-134A
65822	Tu-134A
65831	Tu-134A
65848	Tu-134A-3
65975	Tu-134A
76724	IL-76TD
85162	Tu-154B
85166	Tu-154B
85196	Tu-154B
85200	Tu-154B
85403	Tu-154B-2
85411	Tu-154B-2
85442	Tu-154B-2
85536	Tu-154B-2
86118	IL-86

EL (Liberia)

EL-AJO	Douglas DC-8-55F	Liberia World Airlines
EL-AJQ	Douglas DC-8-54F	Liberia World Airlines
EL-AJT	Boeing 707-344B	Liberia World Airlines
EL-JNS	Boeing 707-323C	Skyair Cargo
EL-ZGS	Boeing 707-309C	Jet Cargo Liberia

EP (Iran)

Reg.	Type	Owner or Operator
EP-IAA	Boeing 747SP-86	Iran Air *Kurdistan*
EP-IAB	Boeing 747SP-86	Iran Air
EP-IAC	Boeing 747SP-86	Iran Air *Fars*
EP-IAD	Boeing 747SP-86	Iran Air *Rushdie*
EP-IAG	Boeing 747-286B (SCD)	Iran Air *Azarabadegan*
EP-IAH	Boeing 747-286B (SCD)	Iran Air *Khuzestan*
EP-IAM	Boeing 747-186B	Iran Air
EP-ICA	Boeing 747-2J9F	Iran Air
EP-ICC	Boeing 747-2J9F	Iran Air

ER (Moldova)

The following are operated by Air Moldova with the registrations prefixed by ER.

65036	Tu-134A
65050	Tu-134A
65051	Tu-134A
65071	Tu-134A-3
65072	Tu-134A-3
65094	Tu-134A-3
65140	Tu-134A-3
65707	Tu-134A-3
65741	Tu-134A
65791	Tu-134A-3
65897	Tu-134A
85044	Tu-154
85324	Tu-154B-2
85332	Tu-154B-2
85384	Tu-154B-2
85405	Tu-154B-2
85442	Tu-154B-2
85565	Tu-154B-2

ES (Estonia)

Reg.	Type	Owner or Operator
ES-AAE	Tupolev Tu-134A	Estonian Air
ES-AAF	Tupolev Tu-134A-3	Estonian Air
ES-AAG	Tupolev Tu-134A	Estonian Air
ES-AAH	Tupolev Tu-134A	Estonian Air
ES-AAI	Tupolev Tu-134A	Estonian Air
ES-AAK	Tupolev Tu-134A	Estonian Air
ES-AAL	Tupolev Tu-134A	Estonian Air
ES-AAM	Tupolev Tu-134A	Estonian Air
ES-AAN	Tupolev Tu-134A	Estonian Air
ES-AAO	Tupolev Tu-134A	Estonian Air
ES-AAP	Tupolev Tu-134A	Estonian Air
ES-LTP	Tupolev Tu-154M	Estonian Air

ET (Ethiopia)

Reg.	Type	Owner or Operator
ET-AIE	Boeing 767-260ER	Ethiopian Airlines
ET-AIF	Boeing 767-260ER	Ethiopian Airlines
ET-AIV	Boeing 707-327C	Ethiopian Airlines
ET-AIZ	Boeing 767-260ER	Ethiopian Airlines
ET-AJS	Boeing 757-260PF	Ethiopian Airlines
ET-AJX	Boeing 757-260ER	Ethiopian Airlines
ET-AKC	Boeing 757-260ER	Ethiopian Airlines
ET-AKE	Boeing 757-260ER	Ethiopian Airlines
ET-AKF	Boeing 757-260ER	Ethiopian Airlines

EW (Belarus)

The following are operated by Belavia with the registrations prefixed by EW.

65049	Tu-134A
65082	Tu-134A
65085	Tu-134A
65106	Tu-134A
65108	Tu-134A
65133	Tu-134A-3

Reg.	Type	Owner or Operator	Notes
65145	Tu-134A		
65149	Tu-134A		
65565	Tu-134A-1		
65623	Tu-134A		
65664	Tu-134A		
65676	Tu-134A		
65706	Tu-134A		
65731	Tu-134A		
65754	Tu-134A		
65769	Tu-134A-3		
65772	Tu-134A		
65803	Tu-134A		
65821	Tu-134A		
65832	Tu-134A		
65861	Tu-134A		
65892	Tu-134A		
65957	Tu-134A		
65974	Tu-134A		
76837	IL-76TD		
85059	Tu-154B		
85260	Tu-154B-1		
85331	Tu-154B-2		
85339	Tu-154B-2		
85352	Tu-154B-2		
85372	Tu-154B-2		
85411	Tu-154B-2		
85419	Tu-154B-2		
85465	Tu-154B-2		
85509	Tu-154B-2		
85538	Tu-154B-2		
85545	Tu-154B-2		
85580	Tu-154B-2		
85581	Tu-154B-2		
85582	Tu-154B-2		
85583	Tu-154B-2		
85591	Tu-154B-2		
85593	Tu-154B-2		
85703	Tu-154M		
85706	Tu-154M		

EY (Tajikistan)

The following are operated by Tajik Air with the registrations prefixed by EY.

65127	Tu-134B	
85281	Tu-154B-1	
85511	Tu-154B-2	
85691	Tu-154M	
85717	Tu-154M	
N149UA	Boeing 747SP-21	

EZ (Turkmenistan)

Turkmenistan Airlines operates the following with the registrations prefixed by EZ.

A001	Boeing 737-341	
F421	IL-76TD	
F422	IL-76TD	
85250	Tu-154B-1	
85345	Tu-154B	
85394	Tu-154B-2	
85492	Tu-154B-2	
85507	Tu-154B-2	
85532	Tu-154B-2	
85549	Tu-154B-2	
85560	Tu-154B-2	

F (France)

F-BGNR	V.708 Viscount ★	Air Service Training Ltd/Perth	
F-BJEN	S.E.210 Caravelle 10B	Europe Aero Service (stored)	
F-BMKS	S.E.210 Caravelle 10B	Air Toulouse International	
F-BPJV	Boeing 727-214	Air Charter	

Notes	Reg.	Type	Owner or Operator
	F-BPPA	Aero Spacelines Super Guppy-201	Airbus Industrie *Airbus Skylink 2*
	F-BPUA	F.27 Friendship Mk 500	Air France
	F-BPUB	F.27 Friendship Mk 500	Air France
	F-BPUC	F.27 Friendship Mk 500	Air France
	F-BPUD	F.27 Friendship Mk 500	Air France
	F-BPUE	F.27 Friendship Mk 500	Air France
	F-BPUF	F.27 Friendship Mk 500	Air France
	F-BPUG	F.27 Friendship Mk 500	Air France
	F-BPUH	F.27 Friendship Mk 500	Air France
	F-BPUI	F.27 Friendship Mk 500	Air France
	F-BPUJ	F.27 Friendship Mk 500	Air France
	F-BPUK	F.27 Friendship Mk 500	Air France
	F-BPUL	F.27 Friendship Mk 500	Air France
	F-BPVA	Boeing 747-128	Air France
	F-BPVB	Boeing 747-128	Air France
	F-BPVD	Boeing 747-128	Air France
	F-BPVE	Boeing 747-128	Air France/Corsair International
	F-BPVF	Boeing 747-128	Air France
	F-BPVG	Boeing 747-128	Air France
	F-BPVH	Boeing 747-128	Air France
	F-BPVJ	Boeing 747-128	Air France
	F-BPVK	Boeing 747-128	Air France
	F-BPVL	Boeing 747-128	Air France
	F-BPVM	Boeing 747-128	Air France
	F-BPVN	Boeing 747-128	Air France
	F-BPVP	Boeing 747-128	Air France
	F-BPVR	Boeing 747-228F (SCD)	Air France
	F-BPVS	Boeing 747-228B (SCD)	Air France
	F-BPVT	Boeing 747-228B (SCD)	Air France
	F-BPVU	Boeing 747-228B (SCD)	Air France
	F-BPVV	Boeing 747-228F (SCD)	Air France
	F-BPVX	Boeing 747-228B (SCD)	Air France
	F-BPVY	Boeing 747-228B	Air France
	F-BPVZ	Boeing 747-228F (SCD)	Air France
	F-BSUM	F.27 Friendship Mk 500	Air France
	F-BSUN	F.27 Friendship Mk 500	Air France
	F-BSUO	F.27 Friendship Mk 500	Air France
	F-BTDB	Douglas DC-10-30	Union de Transports Aériens (UTA)
	F-BTDC	Douglas DC-10-30	Union de Transports Aériens (UTA)
	F-BTDD	Douglas DC-10-30	AOM French Airlines
	F-BTDE	Douglas DC-10-30	Union de Transports Aériens (UTA)
	F-BTDG	Boeing 747-3B3 (SCD)	Air France
	F-BTDH	Boeing 747-3B3 (SCD)	Air France
	F-BTGV	Aero Spacelines Super Guppy-201	Airbus Industrie *Airbus Skylink 1*
	F-BTSC	Concorde 101	Air France
	F-BTSD	Concorde 101	Air France
	F-BTTA	Mercure 100	Air Inter
	F-BTTB	Mercure 100	Air Inter
	F-BTTD	Mercure 100	Air Inter
	F-BTTE	Mercure 100	Air Inter
	F-BTTF	Mercure 100	Air Inter
	F-BTTG	Mercure 100	Air Inter
	F-BTTH	Mercure 100	Air Inter
	F-BTTI	Mercure 100	Air Inter
	F-BTTJ	Mercure 100	Air Inter
	F-BUAF	Airbus A.300B2	Air Inter
	F-BUAG	Airbus A.300B2	Air Inter
	F-BUAH	Airbus A.300B2	Air Inter
	F-BUAI	Airbus A.300B2	Air Inter
	F-BUAJ	Airbus A.300B2	Air Inter
	F-BUAK	Airbus A.300B2	Air Inter
	F-BUAL	Airbus A.300B4	Air Inter
	F-BUAN	Airbus A.300B2	Air Inter
	F-BUAO	Airbus A.300B2	Air Inter
	F-BUAP	Airbus A.300B2	Air Inter
	F-BUAQ	Airbus A.300B4	Air Inter
	F-BUAR	Airbus A.300B4	Air Inter
	F-BUTI	F.28 Fellowship 1000	T.A.T. European
	F-BVFA	Concorde 101	Air France
	F-BVFB	Concorde 101	Air France
	F-BVFC	Concorde 101	Air France
	F-BVFF	Concorde 101	Air France
	F-BVGA	Airbus A.300B2	Air France

Reg.	Type	Owner or Operator	Notes
F-BVGB	Airbus A.300B2	Air France	
F-BVGC	Airbus A.300B2	Air France	
F-BVGD	Airbus A.300B2	Air Inter	
F-BVGE	Airbus A.300B2	Air Inter	
F-BVGF	Airbus A.300B2	Air Inter	
F-BVGG	Airbus A.300B4	Air France	
F-BVGH	Airbus A.300B4	Air France	
F-BVGI	Airbus A.300B4	Air Charter	
F-BVGJ	Airbus A.300B4	Air France	
F-BVGL	Airbus A.300B4	Air France	
F-BVGM	Airbus A.300B4	Air France	
F-BVGN	Airbus A.300B4	Air France	
F-BVGO	Airbus A.300B4	Air France	
F-BVGQ	Airbus A.300B4	Air France	
F-BVGT	Airbus A.300B4	Air Charter	
F-BVJL	Beech 99A	T.A.T. European	
F-BYAB	F.27 Friendship Mk 600	Air Jet	
F-GATS	EMB-110P2 Bandeirante	Compagnie Air Littoral *Hérault*	
F-GBBR	F.28 Fellowship 1000	T.A.T. European/Air France	
F-GBBS	F.28 Fellowship 1000	T.A.T. European/Air France	
F-GBBT	F.28 Fellowship 1000	T.A.T. European/Air France	
F-GBBX	F.28 Fellowship 1000	T.A.T. European	
F-GBEA	Airbus A.300B2	Air Inter	
F-GBEB	Airbus A.300B2	Air Inter	
F-GBEC	Airbus A.300B2	Air France	
F-GBEK	Nord 262A	Compagnie Air Littoral	
F-GBGA	EMB-110P2 Bandeirante	Aigle Azur	
F-GBLE	EMB-110P2 Bandeirante	Air Atlantique	
F-GBME	EMB-110P2 Bandeirante	Air Atlantique	
F-GBOX	Boeing 747-2B3F (SCD)	Air France Cargo	
F-GBRM	EMB-110P2 Bandeirante	Air Atlantique	
F-GBRQ	FH.227B Friendship	T.A.T. European	
F-GBRU	F.27J Friendship	T.A.T. European	
F-GBRV	F.27J Friendship	ACE Transvalair	
F-GBYA	Boeing 737-228	Air France	
F-GBYB	Boeing 737-228	Air France	
F-GBYC	Boeing 737-228	Air France	
F-GBYD	Boeing 737-228	Air France	
F-GBYE	Boeing 737-228	Air France	
F-GBYF	Boeing 737-228	Air France	
F-GBYG	Boeing 737-228	Air France	
F-GBYH	Boeing 737-228	Air France	
F-GBYI	Boeing 737-228	Air France	
F-GBYJ	Boeing 737-228	Air France	
F-GBYK	Boeing 737-228	Air France	
F-GBYL	Boeing 737-228	Air France	
F-GBYM	Boeing 737-228	Air France	
F-GBYN	Boeing 737-228	Air France	
F-GBYO	Boeing 737-228	Air France	
F-GBYP	Boeing 737-228	Air France	
F-GBYQ	Boeing 737-228	Air France	
F-GCBA	Boeing 747-228B	Air France	
F-GCBB	Boeing 747-228B (SCD)	Air France/SABENA	
F-GCBD	Boeing 747-228B (SCD)	Air France	
F-GCBE	Boeing 747-228F (SCD)	Air France	
F-GCBF	Boeing 474-228B (SCD)	Air France	
F-GCBG	Boeing 747-228B (SCD)	Air France	
F-GCBH	Boeing 747-228B (SCD)	Air France	
F-GCBI	Boeing 747-228B (SCD)	Air France	
F-GCBJ	Boeing 747-228B (SCD)	Air France	
F-GCBK	Boeing 747-228F (SCD)	Air France	
F-GCBL	Boeing 747-228F (SCD)	Air France	
F-GCBM	Boeing 747-228F	Air France Cargo	
F-GCDA	Boeing 727-228	Euralair International	
F-GCDB	Boeing 727-228	Euralair International/Air Charter	
F-GCDD	Boeing 727-228	Air Charter	
F-GCDE	Boeing 727-228	Air Charter	
F-GCFC	FH.227B Friendship	T.A.T. European	
F-GCGQ	Boeing 727-227	EAS Europe Airlines	
F-GCJL	Boeing 737-222	Euralair International/Air Charter	
F-GCJO	FH.227B Friendship	ACE Transvalair	
F-GCJV	F.27 Friendship Mk 400	Air Jet	

Notes	Reg.	Type	Owner or Operator
	F-GCLA	EMB-110P1 Bandeirante	Aigle Azur
	F-GCLL	Boeing 737-222	Euralair International
	F-GCLM	FH.227B Friendship	ACE Transvalair
	F-GCLO	FH.227B Friendship	ACE Transvalair
	F-GCMV	Boeing 727-2X3	Air Charter
	F-GCMX	Boeing 727-2X3	Air Charter
	F-GCPT	FH.227B Friendship	T.A.T. European
	F-GCPU	FH.227B Friendship	T.A.T. European
	F-GCPX	FH.227B Friendship	T.A.T. European
	F-GCPY	FH.227B Friendship	T.A.T. European
	F-GCSL	Boeing 737-222	Euralair International/Air Charter
	F-GDAQ	L.100-30 Hercules	Jet Fret
	F-GDFC	F.28 Fellowship 4000	T.A.T. European/Air France
	F-GDFD	F.28 Fellowship 4000	T.A.T. European/Air France
	F-GDJK	Douglas DC-10-30	Air Martinique
	F-GDMR	Swearingen SA.226TC Metro II	Compagnie Air Littoral
	F-GDPP	Douglas DC-3C	France DC-3/L'Envolée Air Inter
	F-GDRM	Douglas DC-8-73	Aire D'Evasions
	F-GDSG	UTA Super Guppy	Airbus Industrie *Airbus Skylink 3*
	F-GDSK	F.28 Fellowship 4000	T.A.T. European/Air France
	F-GDUS	F.28 Fellowship 2000	T.A.T. European
	F-GDUT	F.28 Fellowship 2000	T.A.T. European/Air France
	F-GDUU	F.28 Fellowship 2000	T.A.T. European/British Airways
	F-GDUV	F.28 Fellowship 2000	T.A.T. European/British Airways
	F-GDUY	F.28 Fellowship 4000	T.A.T. European/Air France
	F-GDUZ	F.28 Fellowship 4000	T.A.T. European/Air France
	F-GDXL	Aérospatiale ATR-42-300	Brit Air
	F-GEAI	UTA Super Guppy	Airbus Industrie *Airbus Skylink 4*
	F-GECK	F.28 Fellowship 1000	T.A.T. European/Air France
	F-GEGD	Aérospatiale ATR-42-300	Compagnie Air Littoral
	F-GEGE	Aérospatiale ATR-42-300	Compagnie Air Littoral
	F-GEGF	Aérospatiale ATR-42-300	Compagnie Air Littoral
	F-GELG	SAAB SF.340A	Brit Air/Air France
	F-GELP	S.E.210 Caravelle	Air Toulouse International
	F-GEMA	Airbus A.310-203	Air France
	F-GEMB	Airbus A.310-203	Air France
	F-GEMC	Airbus A.310-203	Air France
	F-GEMD	Airbus A.310-203	Air France
	F-GEME	Airbus A.310-203	Air France
	F-GEMF	Airbus A.310-203	Air France
	F-GEMG	Airbus A.310-203	Air France
	F-GEMN	Airbus A.310-304	Air France
	F-GEMO	Airbus A.310-304	Air France
	F-GEMP	Airbus A.310-304	Air France
	F-GEMQ	Airbus A.310-304	Air France
	F-GEOM	Douglas DC-3C	—
	F-GEPC	S.E. 210 Caravelle 10B3	—
	F-GEQJ	Aérospatiale ATR-42-300	T.A.T. European/Cimber Air
	F-GETB	Boeing 747-3B3 (SCD)	Air France
	F-GEXA	Boeing 747-4B3	Air France
	F-GEXB	Boeing 747-4B3	Air France
	F-GEXI	Boeing 737-2L9	Air Charter/EAS Europe Airlines
	F-GEXJ	Boeing 737-2Q8	Air Charter/EAS Europe Airlines
	F-GEXZ	F.27J Friendship	Stellair (*stored*)
	F-GFBA	S.E.210 Caravelle 10B	EAS Europe Airlines (*stored*)
	F-GFBZ	SAAB SF.340A	Brit Air
	F-GFEN	EMB-120 Brasilia	Compagnie Air Littoral
	F-GFEO	EMB-120 Brasilia	Compagnie Air Littoral
	F-GFEP	EMB-120 Brasilia	Compagnie Air Littoral
	F-GFEQ	EMB-120 Brasilia	Compagnie Air Littoral
	F-GFER	EMB-120 Brasilia	Compagnie Air Littoral
	F-GFES	Aérospatiale ATR-42-300	Compagnie Air Littoral
	F-GFIN	EMB-120 Brasilia	Compagnie Air Littoral
	F-GFJE	Aérospatiale ATR-42-300	Brit Air/Air France
	F-GFJH	Aérospatiale ATR-42-300	Brit Air/Air France
	F-GFJP	Aérospatiale ATR-42-300	Brit Air/Air France
	F-GFJS	F.27 Friendship Mk 600	Air Jet
	F-GFKA	Airbus A.320-111	Air France *Ville de Paris*
	F-GFKB	Airbus A.320-111	Air France *Ville de Rome*
	F-GFKD	Airbus A.320-111	Air France
	F-GFKE	Airbus A.320-111	Air France
	F-GFKF	Airbus A.320-111	Air France *Ville de Madrid*
	F-GFKG	Airbus A.320-111	Air France *Ville d'Amsterdam*

Reg.	Type	Owner or Operator	Notes
F-GFKH	Airbus A.320-211	Air France *Ville de Bruxelles*	
F-GFKI	Airbus A.320-211	Air France *Ville de Lisbonne*	
F-GFKJ	Airbus A.320-211	Air France *Ville de Copenhagen*	
F-GFKK	Airbus A.320-211	Air France *Ville d'Athenes*	
F-GFKL	Airbus A.320-211	Air France *Ville de Dublin*	
F-GFKM	Airbus A.320-211	Air France *Ville de Luxembourg*	
F-GFKN	Airbus A.320-211	Air France	
F-GFKO	Airbus A.320-211	Air France	
F-GFKP	Airbus A.320-211	Air France *Ville de Nice*	
F-GFKQ	Airbus A.320-111	Air France *Ville de Berlin*	
F-GFKR	Airbus A.320-211	Air France	
F-GFKS	Airbus A.320-211	Air France	
F-GFKT	Airbus A.320-211	Air France	
F-GFKU	Airbus A.320-211	Air France	
F-GFKV	Airbus A.320-211	Air France *Ville de Bordeaux*	
F-GFKX	Airbus A.320-211	Air France	
F-GFKY	Airbus A.320-211	Air France *Ville de Toulouse*	
F-GFKZ	Airbus A.320-211	Air France *Ville de Turin*	
F-GFLV	Boeing 737-2K5	Air France/Air Charter	
F-GFLX	Boeing 737-2K5	Air France/Air Charter	
F-GFPR	Swearingen SA226AT Merlin IVA	Regional Airlines	
F-GFUA	Boeing 737-33A	Air France	
F-GFUB	Boeing 737-33A	Air France	
F-GFUC	Boeing 737-33A	Air Charter	
F-GFUD	Boeing 737-33A	Air France	
F-GFUG	Boeing 737-4B3	Corsair International	
F-GFUH	Boeing 737-4B3	Corsair International	
F-GFUJ	Boeing 737-33A	Air France	
F-GFVI	Boeing 737-230C	L'Aeropostale	
F-GFVK	Boeing 737-242C	L'Aeropostale	
F-GFYL	Boeing 737-2A9C	Euralair International/Air Charter	
F-GFYN	Aérospatiale ATR-42-300	Compagnie Air Littoral	
F-GFZB	McD Douglas MD-83	Air Liberte	
F-GGBV	SAAB SF.340A	Aigle Azur	
F-GGEA	Airbus A.320-111	Air Inter	
F-GGEB	Airbus A.320-111	Air Inter	
F-GGEC	Airbus A.320-111	Air Inter	
F-GGEE	Airbus A.320-111	Air Inter	
F-GGEF	Airbus A.320-111	Air Inter	
F-GGEG	Airbus A.320-111	Air Inter	
F-GGFI	Boeing 737-210C	T.A.T. European	
F-GGFJ	Boeing 737-248C	T.A.T. European	
F-GGGR	Boeing 727-2H3	EAS Europe Airlines	
F-GGKD	S.E.210 Caravelle 10B	Air Service Nantes	
F-GGLK	Aérospatiale ATR-42-300	T.A.T. European	
F-GGLR	Aérospatiale ATR-42-300	Brit Air	
F-GGMA	McD Douglas MD-83	AOM French Airlines	
F-GGMB	McD Douglas MD-83	AOM French Airlines	
F-GGMC	McD Douglas MD-83	AOM French Airlines	
F-GGMD	McD Douglas MD-83	AOM French Airlines	
F-GGME	McD Douglas MD-83	AOM French Airlines	
F-GGML	Boeing 737-53A	Euralair International/Air France	
F-GGMX	Douglas DC-10-30	AOM French Airlines	
F-GGMY	Douglas DC-10-30	AOM French Airlines	
F-GGMZ	Douglas DC-10-30	AOM French Airlines	
F-GGPA	Boeing 737-242C	T.A.T. European	
F-GGPB	Boeing 737-204C	T.A.T. European	
F-GGPC	Boeing 737-204C	T.A.T. European	
F-GGVP	Boeing 737-2K2C	L'Aeropostale	
F-GGVQ	Boeing 737-2K2C	L'Aeropostale	
F-GHDB	SAAB SF.340A	Brit Air/Air France	
F-GHEB	McD Douglas MD-83	Air Liberte	
F-GHEC	McD Douglas MD-83	Air Liberte	
F-GHED	McD Douglas MD-83	Air Liberte	
F-GHEF	Airbus A.300-622R	Air Liberte	
F-GHEG	Airbus A.300-622R	Air Liberte	
F-GHEI	McD Douglas MD-83	Air Liberte	
F-GHEJ	Airbus A.310-324	Air Liberte	
F-GHEK	McD Douglas MD-83	Air Liberte	
F-GHEX	EMB-120RT Brasilia	Alsavia/T.A.T. European	
F-GHEY	EMB-120RT Brasilia	Alsavia/T.A.T. European	
F-GHGD	Boeing 767-27EER	Air France/Balkan	
F-GHGE	Boeing 767-27EER	Air France/Balkan *Preslav*	

Notes	Reg.	Type	Owner or Operator
	F-GHGF	Boeing 767-3Q8ER	Air France
	F-GHGG	Boeing 767-3Q8ER	Air France
	F-GHGH	Boeing 767-37EER	Air France
	F-GHGI	Boeing 767-328ER	Air France
	F-GHGJ	Boeing 767-328ER	Air France
	F-GHGK	Boeing 767-328ER	Air France
	F-GHGR	Swearingen SA226AT Merlin IVA	Regional Airlines
	F-GHHO	McD Douglas MD-83	Trans Alsace
	F-GHHP	McD Douglas MD-83	Air Liberte
	F-GHIA	EMB-120RT Brasilia	Compagnie Air Littoral
	F-GHIB	EMB-120RT Brasilia	Compagnie Air Littoral
	F-GHJE	Aérospatiale ATR-42-300	Brit Air
	F-GHLA	Swearingen SA226AT Merlin IVA	Regional Airlines
	F-GHME	Aérospatiale ATR-42-300	Brit Air
	F-GHMI	SAAB SF.340A	Brit Air/Air France
	F-GHMJ	SAAB SF.340A	Brit Air
	F-GHMK	SAAB SF.340A	Brit Air
	F-GHMU	S.E.210 Caravelle 10B3	Air Toulouse International
	F-GHOI	Douglas DC-10-30	—
	F-GHOL	Boeing 737-53C	Euralair International/Air Inter
	F-GHPI	Aérospatiale ATR-42-300	Brit Air
	F-GHPK	Aérospatiale ATR-42-300	Brit Air
	F-GHPS	Aérospatiale ATR-42-300	Brit Air
	F-GHPU	Aérospatiale ATR-72-101	Brit Air
	F-GHPV	Aérospatiale ATR-72-101	Brit Air
	F-GHPX	Aérospatiale ATR-42-300	Brit Air
	F-GHPY	Aérospatiale ATR-72-102	Brit Air
	F-GHPZ	Aérospatiale ATR-42-300	Brit Air
	F-GHQA	Airbus A.320-211	Air Inter
	F-GHQB	Airbus A.320-211	Air Inter
	F-GHQC	Airbus A.320-211	Air Inter
	F-GHQD	Airbus A.320-211	Air Inter
	F-GHQE	Airbus A.320-211	Air Inter
	F-GHQF	Airbus A.320-211	Air Inter
	F-GHQG	Airbus A.320-211	Air Inter
	F-GHQH	Airbus A.320-211	Air Inter
	F-GHQI	Airbus A.320-211	Air Inter
	F-GHQJ	Airbus A.320-211	Air Inter
	F-GHQK	Airbus A.320-211	Air Inter
	F-GHQL	Airbus A.320-211	Air Inter
	F-GHQM	Airbus A.320-211	Air Inter
	F-GHQO	Airbus A.320-211	Air Inter
	F-GHQP	Airbus A.320-211	Air Inter
	F-GHQQ	Airbus A.320-211	Air Inter
	F-GHQR	Airbus A.320-211	Air Inter
	F-GHRC	F.27 Friendship Mk 600	Air Jet
	F-GHUL	Boeing 737-53C	Euralair International/Air France
	F-GHVA	Swearingen SA227AC Metro III	Regional Airlines
	F-GHVC	Swearingen SA227AC Metro III	Regional Airlines
	F-GHVD	Swearingen SA227AC Metro III	Regional Airlines
	F-GHVG	Swearingen SA227AC Metro III	Regional Airlines
	F-GHVM	Boeing 737-33A	Air France
	F-GHVN	Boeing 737-33A	Air France
	F-GHVO	Boeing 737-33A	Air France
	F-GHVS	SAAB SF.340B	Regional Airlines
	F-GHVT	SAAB SF.340B	Regional Airlines
	F-GHVU	SAAB SF.340B	Regional Airlines
	F-GHXK	Boeing 737-2A1	EAS Europe Airlines
	F-GHXL	Boeing 737-2S3	EAS Europe Airlines
	F-GHXM	Boeing 737-53A	EAS Europe Airlines/Air Charter
	F-GIAH	F.28 Fellowship 1000	T.A.T. European
	F-GIAI	F.28 Fellowship 1000	T.A.T. European/Palair Macedonia
	F-GIAJ	F.28 Fellowship 1000	T.A.T. European
	F-GIDK	Douglas DC-3C	Air Dakota
	F-GIGO	Aérospatiale ATR-72-201	Compagnie Air Littoral
	F-GIGU	Aérospatiale ATR-72-202	Compagnie Air Littoral
	F-GIIA	Aérospatialé ATR-42-300	Air Atlantique
	F-GIJS	Airbus A.300B4	Air Inter
	F-GIJT	Airbus A.300B4	Air Inter
	F-GIJU	Airbus A.300B4	Air Inter
	F-GILN	Swearingen SA227AC Metro III	Regional Airlines
	F-GIMH	F.28 Fellowship 1000	T.A.T. European
	F-GIMJ	Boeing 747-121	Corsair International

Reg.	Type	Owner or Operator	Notes
F-GINL	Boeing 737-53C	Euralair International/Air France	
F-GIOA	Fokker 100	T.A.T. European	
F-GIOB	Fokker 100	T.A.T. European	
F-GIOC	Fokker 100	T.A.T. European	
F-GIOD	Fokker 100	T.A.T. European/British Airways	
F-GIOE	Fokker 100	T.A.T. European	
F-GIOF	Fokker 100	T.A.T. European/British Airways	
F-GIOG	Fokker 100	T.A.T. European	
F-GIOH	Fokker 100	T.A.T. European	
F-GIOI	Fokker 100	T.A.T. European	
F-GIOJ	Fokker 100	T.A.T. European/British Airways	
F-GIOK	Fokker 100	T.A.T. European	
F-GIOV	Fokker 100	T.A.T. European/BerLine	
F-GIOX	Fokker 100	T.A.T. European/BerLine	
F-GIRC	Aérospatiale ATR-42-300	T.A.T. European	
F-GISA	Boeing 747-428 (SCD)	Air France	
F-GISB	Boeing 747-428 (SCD)	Air France	
F-GISC	Boeing 747-428 (SCD)	Air France	
F-GISD	Boeing 747-428 (SCD)	Air France	
F-GISE	Boeing 747-428 (SCD)	Air France	
F-GITA	Boeing 747-428	Air France	
F-GITB	Boeing 747-428	Air France	
F-GITC	Boeing 747-428	Air France	
F-GITD	Boeing 747-428	Air France	
F-GITE	Boeing 747-428	Air France	
F-GITF	Boeing 747-428	Air France	
F-GITH	Boeing 747-428	Air France	
F-GIUA	Boeing 747-428F (SCD)	Air France	
F-GIUB	Boeing 747-428F (SCD)	Air France	
F-GIXA	Boeing 737-2K2C	L'Aeropostale	
F-GIXB	Boeing 737-33AQC	L'Aeropostale	
F-GIXC	Boeing 737-38BQC	L'Aeropostale	
F-GIXD	Boeing 737-33AQC	L'Aeropostale	
F-GIXE	Boeing 737-3B3QC	L'Aeropostale	
F-GIXF	Boeing 737-3B3QC	L'Aeropostale	
F-GIXG	Boeing 737-3B3QC	L'Aeropostale	
F-GIXH	Boeing 737-3B3QC	L'Aeropostale	
F-GJAK	EMB-120RT Brasilia	Compagnie Air Littoral	
F-GJAO	Fokker 100	Air Littoral	
F-GJDL	Boeing 737-210C	Air Charter/Euralair International	
F-GJDM	S.E.210 Caravelle 10B	STAIR	
F-GJEG	Beech 1900-1	T.A.T. European	
F-GJNA	Boeing 737-528	Air France	
F-GJNB	Boeing 737-528	Air France	
F-GJNC	Boeing 737-528	Air France	
F-GJND	Boeing 737-528	Air France	
F-GJNE	Boeing 737-528	Air France	
F-GJNF	Boeing 737-528	Air France	
F-GJNG	Boeing 737-528	Air France	
F-GJNH	Boeing 737-528	Air France	
F-GJNI	Boeing 737-528	Air France	
F-GJNJ	Boeing 737-528	Air France	
F-GJNK	Boeing 737-528	Air France	
F-GJNM	Boeing 737-528	Air France	
F-GJVA	Airbus A.320-211	Air Inter	
F-GJVB	Airbus A.320-211	Air Inter	
F-GJVC	Airbus A.320-211	Air Inter	
F-GJVD	Airbus A.320-211	Air Inter	
F-GJVE	Airbus A.320-211	Air Inter	
F-GJVF	Airbus A.320-211	Air Inter	
F-GJVG	Airbus A.320-211	Air Inter	
F-GJVZ	Airbus A.320-211	Air Inter	
F-GKJC	F.27 Friendship Mk 600	Air Jet	
F-GKLJ	Boeing 747-121	Corsair International	
F-GKLX	Fokker 100	Air Littoral	
F-GKLY	Fokker 100	Air Littoral	
F-GKMY	Douglas DC-10-30	AOM French Airlines	
F-GKNA	Aérospatiale ATR-42-300	T.A.T. European	
F-GKNB	Aérospatiale ATR-42-300	T.A.T. European	
F-GKNC	Aérospatiale ATR-42-300	T.A.T. European	
F-GKND	Aérospatiale ATR-42-300	T.A.T. European	
F-GKNE	Aérospatiale ATR-42-300	T.A.T. European	
F-GKNF	Aérospatiale ATR-42-300	T.A.T. European	

F

Notes	Reg.	Type	Owner or Operator
	F-GKNH	Aérospatiale ATR-42-300	T.A.T. European
	F-GKOA	Aérospatiale ATR-72-202	T.A.T. European
	F-GKOB	Aérospatiale ATR-72-202	T.A.T. European
	F-GKOC	Aérospatiale ATR-72-202	T.A.T. European
	F-GKOD	Aérospatiale ATR-72-202	T.A.T. European
	F-GKOE	Aérospatiale ATR-72-202	T.A.T. European
	F-GKOF	Aérospatiale ATR-72-202	T.A.T. European
	F-GKOG	Aérospatiale ATR-72-202	T.A.T. European
	F-GKOH	Aérospatiale ATR-72-202	T.A.T. European
	F-GKOI	Aérospatiale ATR-72-202	T.A.T. European
	F-GKOJ	Aérospatiale ATR-72-202	T.A.T. European
	F-GKOK	Aérospatiale ATR-72-202	T.A.T. European
	F-GKOL	Aérospatiale ATR-72-202	T.A.T. European
	F-GKOM	Aérospatiale ATR-72-202	T.A.T. European
	F-GKON	Aérospatiale ATR-72-202	T.A.T. European
	F-GKPC	Aérospatiale ATR-72-102	Compagnie Corse Mediterranee
	F-GKPD	Aérospatiale ATR-72-102	Compagnie Corse Mediterranee
	F-GKPE	Aérospatiale ATR-72-102	Compagnie Corse Mediterranee
	F-GKPF	Aérospatiale ATR-72-102	Compagnie Corse Mediterranee
	F-GKPH	Aérospatiale ATR-72-102	Compagnie Corse Mediterranee
	F-GKST	Beech 1900-1	Proteus Air System
	F-GKTA	Boeing 737-3M8	EAS Europe Airlines
	F-GKTB	Boeing 737-3M8	EAS Europe Airlines
	F-GKTD	Airbus A.310-304	Sudan Airways
	F-GKTK	Boeing 737-248C	L'Aéropostale
	F-GKXA	Airbus A.320-211	Air France Ville de Nantes
	F-GLMX	Douglas DC-10-30	AOM French Airlines
	F-GLNA	Boeing 747-206B	Corsair International
	F-GLNI	BAe 146-200	Air Jet
	F-GLXF	Boeing 737-219	SNEAS
	F-GLXG	Boeing 737-2M8	EAS Europe Airlines
	F-GLXH	Boeing 737-2D6	Air Toulouse International
	F-GLZA	Airbus A.340-311	Air France
	F-GLZB	Airbus A.340.311	Air France
	F-GLZC	Airbus A.340-311	Air France
	F-GLZD	Airbus A.340-211	Air France
	F-GLZE	Airbus A.340-211	Air France
	F-GLZF	Airbus A.340-211	Air France
	F-GLZG	Airbus A.340-211	Air France
	F-GMCD	McD Douglas MD-83	Trans Alsace
	F-GMDA	Airbus A.330-301	Air Inter
	F-GMDB	Airbus A.330-301	Air Inter
	F-GMDC	Airbus A.330-301	Air Inter
	F-GMDD	Airbus A.330-301	Air Inter
	F-GMJD	Boeing 737-2K5	Aigle Azur
	F-GMPG	Fokker 100	T.A.T. European
	F-GMPP	McD Douglas MD-83	Trans Alsace
	F-GMVH	BAe Jetstream 3206	Regional Airlines
	F-GMVI	BAe Jetstream 3206	Regional Airlines
	F-GMVJ	BAe Jetstream 3206	Regional Airlines
	F-GMVK	BAe Jetstream 3206	Regional Airlines
	F-GMVL	BAe Jetstream 3206	Regional Airlines
	F-GMVM	BAe Jetstream 3206	Regional Airlines
	F-GMVV	SAAB SF.340B	Regional Airlines
	F-GMVX	SAAB SF.340B	Regional Airlines
	F-GMZA	Airbus A.321-111	Air Inter
	F-GMZB	Airbus A.321-111	Air Inter
	F-GNEM	Douglas DC-10-30	AOM French Airlines
	F-GNFS	Boeing 737-4Y0	Trans Alsace
	F-GNIA	Airbus A.340-211	Air France
	F-GNIB	Airbus A.340-211	Air France
	F-GNIC	Airbus A.340-211	Air France
	F-GNID	Airbus A.340-311	Air France
	F-GNIE	Airbus A.340-311	Air France
	F-GNME	Canadair Regional Jet 100ER	Air Littoral/Air France
	F-GNMN	Canadair Regional Jet 100ER	Air Littoral/Air France
	F-GPAN	Boeing 747-2B3F (SCD)	Air France
	F-ODJG	Boeing 747-2Q2B	Air Gabon
	F-ODLX	Douglas DC-10-30	AOM French Airlines Diamant
	F-ODLY	Douglas DC-10-30	AOM French Airlines Turquoise
	F-ODLZ	Douglas DC-10-30	AOM French Airlines Saphir
	F-ODSV	Airbus A.310-304	Alyemda
	F-ODVD	Airbus A.310-304	—

Reg.	Type	Owner or Operator	Notes
F-ODVE	Airbus A.310-304	—	
F-ODVF	Airbus A.310-304	Royal Jordanian *Princess Raiyah*	
F-ODVG	Airbus A.310-304	Royal Jordanian *Prince Faisal*	
F-ODVH	Airbus A.310-304	Royal Jordanian *Prince Hamzeh*	
F-ODVI	Airbus A.310-304	Royal Jordanian *Princess Haya*	
F-OGQN	Airbus A.310-304	Sudan Airways	
F-OGQQ	Airbus A.310-308	Aeroflot *Tchaikovski*	
F-OGQR	Airbus A.310-308	Aeroflot *Rachmaninov*	
F-OGQS	Airbus A.310-308	Aeroflot *Glinka*	
F-OGQT	Airbus A.310-308	Aeroflot *Muossorgksi*	
F-OGQU	Airbus A.310-308	Aeroflot *Skriabin*	
F-OGQY	Airbus A.310-324	Uzbekistan Airways	
F-OGQZ	Airbus A.310-324	Uzbekistan Airways	
F-OGYA	Airbus A.320-211	Royal Jordanian *Cairo*	
F-OGYB	Airbus A.320-211	Royal Jordanian *Baghdad*	

Note: UTA also operates one DC-10-30 registered N54649. Air France also operates the Airbus A.340s OO-SCD, OO-SCE, OO-SCF, OO-SCG and OO-SCH on lease from Sabena.

HA (Hungary)

HA-LBI	Tupolev Tu-134A-3	Malev	
HA-LBK	Tupolev Tu-134A-3	Malev	
HA-LBN	Tupolev Tu-134A-3	Malev	
HA-LBO	Tupolev Tu-134A-3	Malev	
HA-LBP	Tupolev Tu-134A-3	Malev	
HA-LBR	Tupolev Tu-134A-3	Malev	
HA-LCA	Tupolev Tu-154B-2	Malev Cargo	
HA-LCB	Tupolev Tu-154B-2	Malev	
HA-LCE	Tupolev Tu-154B-2	Malev	
HA-LCG	Tupolev Tu-154B-2	Malev	
HA-LCH	Tupolev Tu-154B-2	Malev	
HA-LCM	Tupolev Tu-154B-2	Malev	
HA-LCN	Tupolev Tu-154B-2	Malev	
HA-LCO	Tupolev Tu-154B-2	Malev	
HA-LCP	Tupolev Tu-154B-2	Malev	
HA-LCR	Tupolev Tu-154B-2	Malev	
HA-LCU	Tupolev Tu-154B-2	Malev	
HA-LCV	Tupolev Tu-154B-2	Malev	
HA-LEA	Boeing 737-2QB	Malev	
HA-LEB	Boeing 737-2M8	Malev	
HA-LEC	Boeing 737-2T5	Malev	
HA-LED	Boeing 737-3Y0	Malev	
HA-LEF	Boeing 737-3Y0	Malev	
HA-LEG	Boeing 737-3Y0	Malev *Szent Istvan-Sanctus Stephanus*	
HA-LHA	Boeing 767-27GER	Malev	
HA-LHB	Boeing 767-27GER	Malev	

HB (Switzerland)

HB-AHB	SAAB SF.340A	Crossair	
HB-AHC	SAAB SF.340A	Crossair	
HB-AHD	SAAB SF.340A	Crossair	
HB-AHO	SAAB SF.340A	Crossair	
HB-AHR	SAAB SF.340A	Crossair	
HB-AHS	SAAB SF.340A	Crossair	
HB-AHT	SAAB SF.340A	Crossair	
HB-AKA	SAAB SF.340B	Crossair	
HB-AKB	SAAB SF.340B	Crossair	
HB-AKC	SAAB SF.340B	Crossair	
HB-AKD	SAAB SF.340B	Crossair	
HB-AKE	SAAB SF.340B	Crossair	
HB-AKF	SAAB SF.340B	Crossair	
HB-AKG	SAAB SF.340B	Crossair	
HB-AKH	SAAB SF.340B	Crossair	
HB-AKI	SAAB SF.340B	Crossair	
HB-AKK	SAAB SF.340B	Crossair	
HB-AKL	SAAB SF.340B	Crossair	
HB-AKM	SAAB SF.340B	Crossair	
HB-AKN	SAAB SF.340B	Crossair	
HB-AKO	SAAB SF.340B	Crossair	

Notes	Reg.	Type	Owner or Operator
	HB-AKP	SAAB SF.340B	Crossair
	HB-IAN	Fokker 50	Crossair
	HB-IAO	Fokker 50	Crossair
	HB-IAP	Fokker 50	Crossair
	HB-IAR	Fokker 50	Crossair
	HB-IAS	Fokker 50	Crossair
	HB-IBF	Douglas DC-8-63	ASA Air Starline
	HB-ICJ	S.E. 210 Caravelle 10B3	Aero Jet
	HB-IGC	Boeing 747-357 (SCD)	Swissair *Bern*
	HB-IGD	Boeing 747-357 (SCD)	Swissair *Basel*
	HB-IGE	Boeing 747-357	Swissair *Genève*
	HB-IGF	Boeing 747-357	Swissair *Zürich*
	HB-IGG	Boeing 747-357 (SCD)	Swissair *Ticino*
	HB-IIA	Boeing 737-3M8	TEA Basle *City of Akureyri*
	HB-IIB	Boeing 737-3M8	TEA Basle *Isle of Avalon*
	HB-IIC	Boeing 737-3M8	TEA Basle *Emmental*
	HB-IID	Boeing 737-3Y0	TEA Basle
	HB-IKK	McD Douglas MD-82	Meridiana
	HB-IKL	McD Douglas MD-82	Meridiana
	HB-INA	McD Douglas MD-81	Swissair *Höri*
	HB-INB	McD Douglas MD-82	Balair CTA
	HB-INC	McD Douglas MD-81	Swissair *Lugano*
	HB-IND	McD Douglas MD-81	Swissair *Bachenbülach*
	HB-INE	McD Douglas MD-81	Swissair *Rümlang*
	HB-INF	McD Douglas MD-81	Swissair *Steinmaur*
	HB-ING	McD Douglas MD-81	Swissair *Winkel*
	HB-INH	McD Douglas MD-81	Swissair *Winterthur*
	HB-INI	McD Douglas MD-81	Swissair *Kloten*
	HB-INK	McD Douglas MD-81	Swissair *Opfikon*
	HB-INL	McD Douglas MD-81	Swissair *Embrach*
	HB-INM	McD Douglas MD-81	Swissair *Lausanne*
	HB-INN	McD Douglas MD-81	Swissair *Bülach*
	HB-INO	McD Douglas MD-81	Swissair *Bellinzona*
	HB-INP	McD Douglas MD-81	Swissair *Oberglatt*
	HB-INR	McD Douglas MD-82	Balair CTA/Swissair
	HB-INS	McD Douglas MD-81	Swissair *Meyrin*
	HB-INT	McD Douglas MD-81	Swissair *Grand-Saconnex*
	HB-INU	McD Douglas MD-81	Swissair *Vernier*
	HB-INV	McD Douglas MD-81	Swissair *Dubendorf*
	HB-INW	McD Douglas MD-82	Balair CTA
	HB-INX	McD Douglas MD-81	Swissair *Wallisellen*
	HB-INY	McD Douglas MD-81	Swissair *Bassersdorf*
	HB-INZ	McD Douglas MD-81	Swissair *Regensdorf*
	HB-IPA	Airbus A.310-221	Swissair *Aargau*
	HB-IPB	Airbus A.310-221	Swissair *Neuchatel*
	HB-IPC	Airbus A.310-221	Swissair *Schwyz*
	HB-IPD	Airbus A.310-221	Swissair *Solothurn*
	HB-IPE	Airbus A.310-221	Swissair *Basel-Land*
	HB-IPF	Airbus A.310-322	Swissair *Glarus*
	HB-IPG	Airbus A.310-322	Swissair *Zug*
	HB-IPH	Airbus A.310-322	Swissair *Appenzell i. Rh*
	HB-IPI	Airbus A.310-322	Swissair *Luzern*
	HB-IPK	Airbus A.310-322	Balair CTA
	HB-IPL	Airbus A.310-325	Balair CTA
	HB-IPM	Airbus A.310-325	Balair CTA
	HB-IPN	Airbus A.310-325	Balair CTA
	HB-ISB	Douglas DC-3C	Classic Air
	HB-ISC	Douglas DC-3C	Classic Air
	HB-ISG	F.27 Friendship Mk 200	Sunshine Aviation (*stored*)
	HB-ISH	F.27 Friendship Mk 200	Sunshine Aviation *Locarno* (*stored*)
	HB-ISX	McD Douglas MD-81	Swissair *Binningen*
	HB-ISZ	McD Douglas MD-83	Balair CTA
	HB-IUA	McD Douglas MD-87	Balair CTA
	HB-IUB	McD Douglas MD-87	Balair CTA
	HB-IUC	McD Douglas MD-87	Balair CTA
	HB-IUD	McD Douglas MD-87	Balair CTA
	HB-IUG	McD Douglas MD-81	Swissair *Illnau-Effretikon*
	HB-IUH	McD Douglas MD-81	Swissair *Wangen-Brüttisellen*
	HB-IVA	Fokker 100	Swissair *Aarau*
	HB-IVB	Fokker 100	Swissair *Biel/Bienne*
	HB-IVC	Fokker 100	Swissair *Chur*
	HB-IVD	Fokker 100	Swissair *Dietlikon*
	HB-IVE	Fokker 100	Swissair *Baden*

Reg.	Type	Owner or Operator	Notes
HB-IVF	Fokker 100	Swissair *Sion*	
HB-IVG	Fokker 100	Swissair *Genthod*	
HB-IVH	Fokker 100	Swissair *Stadel*	
HB-IVI	Fokker 100	Swissair *Bellevue*	
HB-IVK	Fokker 100	Swissair *Hochfelden*	
HB-IWA	McD Douglas MD-11	Swissair *Obwalden*	
HB-IWB	McD Douglas MD-11	Swissair *Graubünden*	
HB-IWC	McD Douglas MD-11	Swissair *Schaffhausen*	
HB-IWD	McD Douglas MD-11	Swissair *Thurgau*	
HB-IWE	McD Douglas MD-11	Swissair *Nidwalden*	
HB-IWF	McD Douglas MD-11	Swissair *Vaud*	
HB-IWG	McD Douglas MD-11	Swissair *Valais/Wallis*	
HB-IWH	McD Douglas MD-11	Swissair *St Gallen*	
HB-IWI	McD Douglas MD-11	Swissair *Uri*	
HB-IWK	McD Douglas MD-11	Swissair *Fribourg*	
HB-IWL	McD Douglas MD-11	Swissair *Appenzell a.Rh*	
HB-IWM	McD Douglas MD-11	Swissair *Jura*	
HB-IWN	McD Douglas MD-11	Swissair	
HB-IXB	BAe 146-200A	Business Air (*To become G- *)	
HB-IXF	Avro RJ85	Crossair	
HB-IXG	Avro RJ85	Crossair	
HB-IXH	Avro RJ85	Crossair	
HB-IXK	Avro RJ85	Crossair	
HB-	BAe 146-300	Crossair (G-BSNS)	
HB-	BAe 146-300	Crossair (G-BTJG)	
HB-IXZ	BAe 146-300	Crossair	
HB-IZA	SAAB 2000	Crossair	
HB-IZB	SAAB 2000	Crossair	
HB-IZC	SAAB 2000	Crossair	
HB-IZD	SAAB 2000	Crossair	
HB-IZE	SAAB 2000	Crossair	
HB-IZF	SAAB 2000	Crossair	
HB-IZG	SAAB 2000	Crossair	
HB-IZH	SAAB 2000	Crossair	

HK (Colombia)

Note: Avianca operates a Boeing 747-259B (SCD) registered EI-CEO.

HL (Korea)

HL7315	Douglas DC-10-30	Korean Air	
HL7316	Douglas DC-10-30	Korean Air	
HL7317	Douglas DC-10-30	Korean Air	
HL7371	McD Douglas MD-11	Korean Air	
HL7372	McD Douglas MD-11	Korean Air	
HL7373	McD Douglas MD-11	Korean Air	
HL7374	McD Douglas MD-11	Korean Air	
HL7375	McD Douglas MD-11	Korean Air	
HL7441	Boeing 747-230F	Korean Air Cargo	
HL7443	Boeing 747-2B5B	Korean Air	
HL7451	Boeing 747-2B5F (SCD)	Korean Air Cargo	
HL7452	Boeing 747-2B5F (SCD)	Korean Air Cargo	
HL7453	Boeing 747-212B	Korean Air	
HL7454	Boeing 747-2B5B (SCD)	Korean Air Cargo	
HL7458	Boeing 747-2B5F (SCD)	Korean Air Cargo	
HL7459	Boeing 747-2B5F (SCD)	Korean Air Cargo	
HL7463	Boeing 747-2B5B	Korean Air	
HL7464	Boeing 747-2B5B	Korean Air	
HL7468	Boeing 747-3B5	Korean Air	
HL7469	Boeing 747-3B5	Korean Air	
HL7470	Boeing 747-3B5 (SCD)	Korean Air	
HL7471	Boeing 747-273C	Korean Air Cargo	
HL7474	Boeing 747-2S4F (SCD)	Korean Air Cargo	
HL7475	Boeing 747-2B5F (SCD)	Korean Air Cargo	
HL7476	Boeing 747-2B5F (SCD)	Korean Air Cargo	
HL7477	Boeing 747-4B5	Korean Air	
HL7478	Boeing 747-4B5	Korean Air	
HL7479	Boeing 747-4B5	Korean Air	
HL7480	Boeing 747-4B5 (SCD)	Korean Air	
HL7481	Boeing 747-4B5	Korean Air	

Notes	Reg.	Type	Owner or Operator
	HL7482	Boeing 747-4B5 (SCD)	Korean Air
	HL7483	Boeing 747-4B5	Korean Air
	HL7484	Boeing 747-4B5	Korean Air
	HL7485	Boeing 747-4B5	Korean Air
	HL7486	Boeing 747-4B5	Korean Air
	HL7487	Boeing 747-4B5	Korean Air
	HL7488	Boeing 747-4B5	Korean Air
	HL7490	Boeing 747-4B5	Korean Air

HR (Honduras)

HR-AMC	L.1011 TriStar	Air Ops Sweden
HR-AME	Boeing 707-351C	Impala Air Cargo
HR-AMV	Boeing 707-321B	Air Gambia
HR-AMW	Boeing 707-323B	Air Gambia

HS (Thailand)

HS-TGA	Boeing 747-2D7B	Thai Airways International *Visuthakasatriya*
HS-TGB	Boeing 747-2D7B	Thai Airways International *Sirisobhakya*
HS-TGC	Boeing 747-2D7B	Thai Airways International *Dararasmi*
HS-TGD	Boeing 747-3D7	Thai Airways International *Suchada*
HS-TGE	Boeing 747-3D7	Thai Airways International *Chutamat*
HS-TGF	Boeing 747-2D7B	Thai Airways International *Phimara*
HS-TGG	Boeing 747-2D7B	Thai Airways International *Sriwanna*
HS-TGH	Boeing 747-4D7	Thai Airways International *Chaiprakarn*
HS-TGJ	Boeing 747-4D7	Thai Airways International *Hariphunchai*
HS-TGK	Boeing 747-4D7	Thai Airways International *Alongkorn*
HS-TGL	Boeing 747-4D7	Thai Airways International
HS-TGM	Boeing 747-4D7	Thai Airways International
HS-TGN	Boeing 747-4D7	Thai Airways International
HS-TGO	Boeing 747-4D7	Thai Airways International *Bowonrangsi*
HS-TGP	Boeing 747-4D7	Thai Airways International
HS-TGS	Boeing 747-2D7B	Thai Airways International *Chainarai*
HS-TMA	Douglas DC-10-30ER	Thai Airways International *Kwanmuang*
HS-TMB	Douglas DC-10-30ER	Thai Airways International *Thepalai*
HS-TMC	Douglas DC-10-30ER	Thai Airways International *Sri Ubon*
HS-TMD	McD Douglas MD-11	Thai Airways International *Phra Nakhon*
HS-TME	McD Douglas MD-11	Thai Airways International
HS-TMF	McD Douglas MD-11	Thai Airways International
HS-TMG	McD Douglas MD-11	Thai Airways International

HZ (Saudi Arabia)

HZ-AHA	L.1011-385 TriStar 200	Saudia — Saudi Arabian Airlines
HZ-AHB	L.1011-385 TriStar 200	Saudia — Saudi Arabian Airlines
HZ-AHC	L.1011-385 TriStar 200	Saudia — Saudi Arabian Airlines
HZ-AHD	L.1011-385 TriStar 200	Saudia — Saudi Arabian Airlines
HZ-AHE	L.1011-385 TriStar 200	Saudia — Saudi Arabian Airlines
HZ-AHF	L.1011-385 TriStar 200	Saudia — Saudi Arabian Airlines
HZ-AHG	L.1011-385 TriStar 200	Saudia — Saudi Arabian Airlines
HZ-AHH	L.1011-385 TriStar 200	Saudia — Saudi Arabian Airlines
HZ-AHI	L.1011-385 TriStar 200	Saudia — Saudi Arabian Airlines
HZ-AHJ	L.1011-385 TriStar 200	Saudia — Saudi Arabian Airlines
HZ-AHL	L.1011-385 TriStar 200	Saudia — Saudi Arabian Airlines
HZ-AHM	L.1011-385 TriStar 200	Saudia — Saudi Arabian Airlines
HZ-AHN	L.1011-385 TriStar 200	Saudia — Saudi Arabian Airlines
HZ-AHO	L.1011-385 TriStar 200	Saudia — Saudi Arabian Airlines
HZ-AHP	L.1011-385 TriStar 200	Saudia — Saudi Arabian Airlines
HZ-AHQ	L.1011-385 TriStar 200	Saudia — Saudi Arabian Airlines
HZ-AHR	L.1011-385 TriStar 200	Saudia — Saudi Arabian Airlines
HZ-AIA	Boeing 747-168B	Saudia — Saudi Arabian Airlines
HZ-AIB	Boeing 747-168B	Saudia — Saudi Arabian Airlines
HZ-AIC	Boeing 747-168B	Saudia — Saudi Arabian Airlines
HZ-AID	Boeing 747-168B	Saudia — Saudi Arabian Airlines
HZ-AIE	Boeing 747-168B	Saudia — Saudi Arabian Airlines
HZ-AIF	Boeing 747SP-68	Saudia — Saudi Arabian Airlines
HZ-AIG	Boeing 747-168B	Saudia — Saudi Arabian Airlines
HZ-AIH	Boeing 747-168B	Saudia — Saudi Arabian Airlines
HZ-AII	Boeing 747-168B	Saudia — Saudi Arabian Airlines
HZ-AIJ	Boeing 747SP-68	Saudi Royal Flight
HZ-AIK	Boeing 747-368	Saudia — Saudi Arabian Airlines

Reg.	Type	Owner or Operator	Notes
HZ-AIL	Boeing 747-368	Saudia — Saudi Arabian Airlines	
HZ-AIM	Boeing 747-368	Saudia — Saudi Arabian Airlines	
HZ-AIN	Boeing 747-368	Saudia — Saudi Arabian Airlines	
HZ-AIO	Boeing 747-368	Saudia — Saudi Arabian Airlines	
HZ-AIP	Boeing 747-368	Saudia — Saudi Arabian Airlines	
HZ-AIQ	Boeing 747-368	Saudia — Saudi Arabian Airlines	
HZ-AIR	Boeing 747-368	Saudia — Saudi Arabian Airlines	
HZ-AIS	Boeing 747-368	Saudia — Saudi Arabian Airlines	
HZ-AIT	Boeing 747-368	Saudia — Saudi Arabian Airlines	
HZ-AIU	Boeing 747-268F (SCD)	Saudia — Saudi Arabian Airlines	
HZ-AJA	Airbus A.300-620	Saudia — Saudi Arabian Airlines	
HZ-AJB	Airbus A.300-620	Saudia — Saudi Arabian Airlines	
HZ-AJC	Airbus A.300-620	Saudia — Saudi Arabian Airlines	
HZ-AJD	Airbus A.300-620	Saudia — Saudi Arabian Airlines	
HZ-AJE	Airbus A.300-620	Saudia — Saudi Arabian Airlines	
HZ-AJF	Airbus A.300-620	Saudia — Saudi Arabian Airlines	
HZ-AJG	Airbus A.300-620	Saudia — Saudi Arabian Airlines	
HZ-AJH	Airbus A.300-620	Saudia — Saudi Arabian Airlines	
HZ-AJI	Airbus A.300-620	Saudia — Saudi Arabian Airlines	
HZ-AJJ	Airbus A.300-620	Saudia — Saudi Arabian Airlines	
HZ-AJK	Airbus A.300-620	Saudia — Saudi Arabian Airlines	

Note: Saudia also operates other aircraft on lease.

I (Italy)

Reg.	Type	Owner or Operator
I-AEJD	Boeing 767-35HER	Air Europe SpA (S7-AAQ)
I-AEJE	Boeing 767-35HER	Air Europe SpA (S7-AAV)
I-ATSC	BAe 146-300	TAS Airways
I-ATSD	BAe 146-300	TAS Airways
I-BUSB	Airbus A.300B4	Alitalia *Tiziano*
I-BUSC	Airbus A.300B4	Alitalia *Botticelli*
I-BUSD	Airbus A.300B4	Alitalia *Caravaggio*
I-BUSF	Airbus A.300B4	Alitalia *Tintoretto*
I-BUSG	Airbus A.300B4	Alitalia *Canaletto*
I-BUSH	Airbus A.300B4	Alitalia *Mantegna*
I-BUSJ	Airbus A.300B4	Alitalia *Tiepolo*
I-BUSL	Airbus A.300B4	Alitalia *Pinturicchio*
I-BUSM	Airbus A.300B2	Alitalia *Raffaello*
I-BUSN	Airbus A.300B2	Alitalia *Giotto*
I-BUSP	Airbus A.300B4	Alitalia *Masaccio*
I-BUSQ	Airbus A.300B4	Alitalia *Michelangelo*
I-BUSR	Airbus A.300B4	Alitalia *Cimabue*
I-BUST	Airbus A.300B4	Alitalia *Piero della Francesca*
I-DACM	McD Douglas MD-82	Aero Trasporti Italiani (ATI) *La Spezia*
I-DACN	McD Douglas MD-82	ATI *Rieti*
I-DACP	McD Douglas MD-82	ATI *Padova*
I-DACQ	McD Douglas MD-82	Alitalia *Taranto*
I-DACR	McD Douglas MD-82	Alitalia *Carrara*
I-DACS	McD Douglas MD-82	Alitalia *Maratea*
I-DACT	McD Douglas MD-82	Alitalia *Valtellina*
I-DACU	McD Douglas MD-82	ATI *Brindisi*
I-DACV	McD Douglas MD-82	ATI *Riccione*
I-DACW	McD Douglas MD-82	Alitalia *Vieste*
I-DACX	McD Douglas MD-82	Alitalia *Piacenza*
I-DACY	McD Douglas MD-82	Alitalia *Novara*
I-DACZ	McD Douglas MD-82	Alitalia *Castelfidardo*
I-DAND	McD Douglas MD-82	ATI *Trani*
I-DANF	McD Douglas MD-82	ATI *Vicenza*
I-DANG	McD Douglas MD-82	ATI *Benevento*
I-DANH	McD Douglas MD-82	ATI *Messina*
I-DANL	McD Douglas MD-82	ATI *Cosenza*
I-DANM	McD Douglas MD-82	Alitalia *Vicenza*
I-DANP	McD Douglas MD-82	Alitalia *Fabriano*
I-DANQ	McD Douglas MD-82	ATI *Lecce*
I-DANR	McD Douglas MD-82	ATI *Matera*
I-DANU	McD Douglas MD-82	ATI *Trapani*
I-DANV	McD Douglas MD-82	Alitalia *Forte dei Marmi*
I-DANW	McD Douglas MD-82	Alitalia
I-DATA	McD Douglas MD-82	Alitalia
I-DATE	McD Douglas MD-82	Alitalia

OVERSEAS AIRLINERS

Notes	Reg.	Type	Owner or Operator
	I-DATI	McD Douglas MD-82	ATI
	I-DATO	McD Douglas MD-82	Alitalia *Reggio Emilia*
	I-DAVA	McD Douglas MD-82	ATI *Cuneo*
	I-DAVB	McD Douglas MD-82	Alitalia *Ferrara*
	I-DAVC	McD Douglas MD-82	ATI *Lucca*
	I-DAVD	McD Douglas MD-82	ATI *Mantova*
	I-DAVF	McD Douglas MD-82	ATI *Oristano*
	I-DAVG	McD Douglas MD-82	ATI *Pesaro*
	I-DAVH	McD Douglas MD-82	ATI *Salerno*
	I-DAVI	McD Douglas MD-82	Alitalia *Assisi*
	I-DAVJ	McD Douglas MD-82	Alitalia *Parma*
	I-DAVK	McD Douglas MD-82	Alitalia *Pompei*
	I-DAVL	McD Douglas MD-82	ATI *Reggio Calabria*
	I-DAVM	McD Douglas MD-82	Alitalia *Caserta*
	I-DAVN	McD Douglas MD-82	ATI *Volterra*
	I-DAVP	McD Douglas MD-82	ATI *Gorizia*
	I-DAVR	McD Douglas MD-82	ATI *Pisa*
	I-DAVS	McD Douglas MD-82	ATI *Catania*
	I-DAVT	McD Douglas MD-82	ATI *Como*
	I-DAVU	McD Douglas MD-82	ATI *Udine*
	I-DAVV	McD Douglas MD-82	ATI *Pavia*
	I-DAVW	McD Douglas MD-82	ATI *Camerino*
	I-DAVX	McD Douglas MD-82	ATI *Asti*
	I-DAVZ	McD Douglas MD-82	ATI *Brescia*
	I-DAWA	McD Douglas MD-82	Alitalia *Roma*
	I-DAWB	McD Douglas MD-82	Alitalia *Cagliari*
	I-DAWC	McD Douglas MD-82	Alitalia *Campobasso*
	I-DAWD	McD Douglas MD-82	Alitalia *Catanzaro*
	I-DAWE	McD Douglas MD-82	Alitalia *Milano*
	I-DAWF	McD Douglas MD-82	Alitalia *Firenze*
	I-DAWG	McD Douglas MD-82	Alitalia *L'Aquila*
	I-DAWH	McD Douglas MD-82	Alitalia *Palermo*
	I-DAWI	McD Douglas MD-82	Alitalia *Ancona*
	I-DAWJ	McD Douglas MD-82	Alitalia *Genova*
	I-DAWL	McD Douglas MD-82	Alitalia *Perugia*
	I-DAWM	McD Douglas MD-82	Alitalia *Potenza*
	I-DAWO	McD Douglas MD-82	Alitalia *Bari*
	I-DAWP	McD Douglas MD-82	Alitalia *Torino*
	I-DAWQ	McD Douglas MD-82	Alitalia *Trieste*
	I-DAWR	McD Douglas MD-82	Alitalia *Venezia*
	I-DAWS	McD Douglas MD-82	Alitalia *Aosta*
	I-DAWT	McD Douglas MD-82	ATI *Napoli*
	I-DAWU	McD Douglas MD-82	Alitalia *Bologna*
	I-DAWV	McD Douglas MD-82	ATI *Trento*
	I-DAWW	McD Douglas MD-82	ATI *Riace*
	I-DAWY	McD Douglas MD-82	ATI *Agrigento*
	I-DAWZ	McD Douglas MD-82	ATI *Avellino*
	I-DEMC	Boeing 747-243B (SCD)	Alitalia *Taormina*
	I-DEMD	Boeing 747-243B (SCD)	Alitalia *Cortina d'Ampezzo*
	I-DEMF	Boeing 747-243B (SCD)	Alitalia *Portofino*
	I-DEMG	Boeing 747-243B	Alitalia *Cervinia*
	I-DEML	Boeing 747-243B	Alitalia *Sorrento*
	I-DEMN	Boeing 747-243B	Alitalia *Portocervo*
	I-DEMP	Boeing 747-243B	Alitalia *Capri*
	I-DEMR	Boeing 747-243F (SCD)	Alitalia *Stresa*
	I-DEMS	Boeing 747-243B	Alitalia *Monte Argentario*
	I-DEMT	Boeing 747-243B (SCD)	Alitalia *Monte Catini*
	I-DEMV	Boeing 747-243B	Alitalia *Sestriere*
	I-DEMW	Boeing 747-243B (SCD)	Alitalia *Spoleto*
	I-DEMX	Boeing 747-230F (SCD)	Alitalia *Ciclop*
	I-DEMY	Boeing 747-230B	Alitalia *Asolo*
	I-DIBA	Douglas DC-9-32	Alitalia *Isola di Capri*
	I-DIBE	Douglas DC-9-32	Alitalia *Isola di Murano*
	I-DIBI	Douglas DC-9-32	Alitalia *Isola del Giglio*
	I-DIBL	Douglas DC-9-32	Alitalia *Isola d'Ischia*
	I-DIBM	Douglas DC-9-32	Alitalia *Isola di Panarea*
	I-DIBP	Douglas DC-9-32	Alitalia *Isola di Lipari*
	I-DIBU	Douglas DC-9-32	Alitalia *Isola di Pantelleria*
	I-DIKM	Douglas DC-9-32	Alitalia *Positano*
	I-DIKP	Douglas DC-9-32	Alitalia *Isola di Marettimo*
	I-DIKR	Douglas DC-9-32	Alitalia *Piemonte*
	I-DIZE	Douglas DC-9-32	Alitalia *Isola della Meloria*
	I-DUPA	McD Douglas MD-11C	Alitalia *Teatro alla Scala*

OVERSEAS AIRLINERS

Reg.	Type	Owner or Operator	Notes
I-DUPB	McD Douglas MD-11	Alitalia *Valle dei Templi*	
I-DUPE	McD Douglas MD-11C	Alitalia *Arena di Verona*	
I-DUPI	McD Douglas MD-11C	Alitalia *Fontana di Trevi*	
I-DUPO	McD Douglas MD-11C	Alitalia *Canal Grande*	
I-DUPU	McD Douglas MD-11C	Alitalia *Ponte Vecchio*	
I-FLRV	BAe 146-200	Meridiana	
I-FLRW	BAe 146-200	Meridiana	
I-FLRX	BAe 146-200	Meridiana	
I-FLYY	Douglas DC-9-51	Eurofly	
I-FLYZ	Douglas DC-9-51	Eurofly	
I-JETA	Boeing 737-229	Fortune Aviation	
I-LAUD	Boeing 767-31AER	Lauda Air SpA *Enzo Ferrari*	
I-RIFB	Douglas DC-9-32	Alitalia *Abruzzo*	
I-RIFC	Douglas DC-9-32	Alitalia *Isola di Lampedusa*	
I-RIFD	Douglas DC-9-32	Alitalia *Isola di Montecristo*	
I-RIFE	Douglas DC-9-32	Alitalia *Erice*	
I-RIFG	Douglas DC-9-32	Alitalia *Isola di Nisida*	
I-RIFH	Douglas DC-9-32	Alitalia *Isola di Ponza*	
I-RIFJ	Douglas DC-9-32	Alitalia *Isola della Capraia*	
I-RIFL	Douglas DC-9-32	Alitalia *Molise*	
I-RIFM	Douglas DC-9-32	ATI *Marche*	
I-RIFP	Douglas DC-9-32	Alitalia/Eurofly	
I-RIFS	Douglas DC-9-32	Alitalia *Isola di Filicudi*	
I-RIFT	Douglas DC-9-32	Alitalia *Friuli Venezia Giulia*	
I-RIFU	Douglas DC-9-32	ATI *Valle d'Aosta*	
I-RIFV	Douglas DC-9-32	ATI *Lazio*	
I-RIFW	Douglas DC-9-32	ATI *Lombardia*	
I-RIFY	Douglas DC-9-32	Alitalia *Puglia*	
I-RIFZ	Douglas DC-9-32	Alitalia *Toscana*	
I-RIZA	Douglas DC-9-32	Alitalia *Isola di Palmarola*	
I-RIZJ	Douglas DC-9-32	Alitalia *Umbria*	
I-RIZL	Douglas DC-9-32	Alitalia *Romagna*	
I-RIZN	Douglas DC-9-32	ATI *Calabria*	
I-RIZX	Douglas DC-9-32	Alitalia *Isola di Procida*	
I-SMEA	Douglas DC-9-51	Meridiana	
I-SMEE	Douglas DC-9-51	Meridiana	
I-SMEI	Douglas DC-9-51	Meridiana	
I-SMEJ	Douglas DC-9-51	Meridiana	
I-SMEO	Douglas DC-9-51	Meridiana	
I-SMEP	McD Douglas MD-82	Meridiana	
I-SMER	McD Douglas MD-82	Meridiana/TEA Italia	
I-SMES	McD Douglas MD-82QT	Meridiana	
I-SMET	McD Douglas MD-82	Meridiana	
I-SMEU	Douglas DC-9-51	Meridiana	
I-SMEV	McD Douglas MD-82	Meridiana	
I-TEAA	Boeing 737-3M8	TEA Italia	
I-TEAE	Boeing 737-3M8	TEA Italia	
I-TEAI	Boeing 737-3M8	TEA Italia	
I-TIAN	Douglas DC-9-15RC	Fortune Aviation	
I-TIAR	Douglas DC-9-15RC	Fortune Aviation	
I-TNTC	BAe146-200QT	Mistral Air/TNT	

Note: Meridiana also uses three MD-82s which retain the registrations HB-IKK, HB-IKL and PH-SEZ. Air Europe SpA operates two Boeing 767s registered S7-AAQ and S7-AAV due to be registered I-AEJD and I-AEJE.

JA (Japan)

JA8071	Boeing 747-446	Japan Airlines	
JA8072	Boeing 747-446	Japan Airlines	
JA8073	Boeing 747-446	Japan Airlines	
JA8074	Boeing 747-446	Japan Airlines	
JA8075	Boeing 747-446	Japan Airlines	
JA8076	Boeing 747-446	Japan Airlines	
JA8077	Boeing 747-446	Japan Airlines	
JA8078	Boeing 747-446	Japan Airlines	
JA8079	Boeing 747-446	Japan Airlines	

Notes	Reg.	Type	Owner or Operator
	JA8080	Boeing 747-446	Japan Airlines
	JA8081	Boeing 747-446	Japan Airlines
	JA8082	Boeing 747-446	Japan Airlines
	JA8085	Boeing 747-446	Japan Airlines
	JA8086	Boeing 747-446	Japan Airlines
	JA8087	Boeing 747-446	Japan Airlines
	JA8088	Boeing 747-446	Japan Airlines
	JA8089	Boeing 747-446	Japan Airlines
	JA8094	Boeing 747-481	All Nippon Airways
	JA8095	Boeing 747-481	All Nippon Airways
	JA8096	Boeing 747-481	All Nippon Airways
	JA8097	Boeing 747-481	All Nippon Airways
	JA8098	Boeing 747-481	All Nippon Airways
	JA8104	Boeing 747-246B	Japan Airlines
	JA8105	Boeing 747-246B	Japan Airlines
	JA8106	Boeing 747-246B	Japan Airlines
	JA8108	Boeing 747-246B	Japan Airlines
	JA8110	Boeing 747-246B	Japan Airlines
	JA8111	Boeing 747-246B	Japan Airlines
	JA8113	Boeing 747-246B	Japan Airlines
	JA8114	Boeing 747-246B	Japan Airlines
	JA8115	Boeing 747-146A	Japan Airlines
	JA8116	Boeing 747-146A	Japan Airlines
	JA8122	Boeing 747-246B	Japan Airlines
	JA8123	Boeing 747-246F (SCD)	Japan Airlines
	JA8125	Boeing 747-246B	Japan Airlines
	JA8130	Boeing 747-246B	Japan Airlines
	JA8131	Boeing 747-246B	Japan Airlines
	JA8132	Boeing 747-246F	Japan Airlines
	JA8140	Boeing 747-246B	Japan Airlines
	JA8141	Boeing 747-246B	Japan Airlines
	JA8144	Boeing 747-246F (SCD)	Japan Airlines
	JA8149	Boeing 747-246B	Japan Airlines
	JA8150	Boeing 747-246B	Japan Airlines
	JA8151	Boeing 747-246F (SCD)	Japan Airlines
	JA8154	Boeing 747-246B	Japan Airlines
	JA8160	Boeing 747-221F (SCD)	Japan Airlines/JUST
	JA8161	Boeing 747-246B	Japan Airlines
	JA8162	Boeing 747-246B	Japan Airlines
	JA8163	Boeing 747-346	Japan Airlines
	JA8165	Boeing 747-221F (SCD)	Japan Airlines
	JA8166	Boeing 747-346	Japan Airlines
	JA8169	Boeing 747-246B	Japan Airlines
	JA8171	Boeing 747-246F (SCD)	Japan Airlines
	JA8173	Boeing 747-346	Japan Airlines
	JA8174	Boeing 747-281B	All Nippon Airways
	JA8175	Boeing 747-281B	All Nippon Airways
	JA8177	Boeing 747-346	Japan Airlines
	JA8178	Boeing 747-346	Japan Airlines
	JA8179	Boeing 747-346	Japan Airlines
	JA8180	Boeing 747-246F (SCD)	Japan Airlines
	JA8181	Boeing 747-281B	All Nippon Airways
	JA8182	Boeing 747-281B	All Nippon Airways
	JA8185	Boeing 747-346	Japan Airlines
	JA8190	Boeing 747-281B	All Nippon Airways
	JA8192	Boeing 747-2D3B	All Nippon Airways
	JA8193	Boeing 747-212F (SCD)	Japan Airlines
	JA8535	Douglas DC-10-40	Japan Airlines
	JA8538	Douglas DC-10-40	Japan Airlines
	JA8541	Douglas DC-10-40	Japan Airlines
	JA8542	Douglas DC-10-40	Japan Airlines
	JA8543	Douglas DC-10-40	Japan Airlines
	JA8545	Douglas DC-10-40	Japan Airlines
	JA8547	Douglas DC-10-40	Japan Airlines
	JA8901	Boeing 747-446	Japan Airlines
	JA8902	Boeing 747-446	Japan Airlines
	JA8906	Boeing 747-446	Japan Airlines
	JA8909	Boeing 747-446	Japan Airlines
	JA8910	Boeing 747-446	Japan Airlines
	JA8911	Boeing 747-446	Japan Airlines
	JA8912	Boeing 747-446	Japan Airlines
	JA8913	Boeing 747-446	Japan Airlines
	JA8914	Boeing 747-446	Japan Airlines

Reg.	Type	Owner or Operator	Notes
JA8915	Boeing 747-446	Japan Airlines	
JA8916	Boeing 747-446	Japan Airlines	
JA8917	Boeing 747-446	Japan Airlines	
JA8918	Boeing 747-446	Japan Airlines	
JA8919	Boeing 747-446	Japan Airlines	
JA8958	Boeing 747-481	All Nippon Airways	
JA8962	Boeing 747-481	All Nippon Airways	
JA8965	Boeing 747-481	All Nippon Airways	

Note: Japan Airlines also operates a Boeing 747-246F which retains its US registration N211JL and two 747-346s N212JL and N213JL.

JY (Jordan)

JY-AGA	L.1011-385 TriStar 500	Royal Jordanian *Amman*	
JY-AGB	L.1011-385 TriStar 500	Royal Jordanian *Princess Alia*	
JY-AGC	L.1011-385 TriStar 500	Royal Jordanian *Princess Zein*	
JY-AGD	L.1011-385 TriStar 500	Royal Jordanian *Prince Ali*	
JY-AGE	L.1011-385 TriStar 500	Royal Jordanian *Princess Aysha*	
JY-AJK	Boeing 707-384C	Royal Jordanian *City of Jerash*	
JY-AJL	Boeing 707-324C	Royal Jordanian	
JY-AJM	Boeing 707-365C	Royal Jordanian Cargo	
JY-HKJ	L.1011-385 TriStar 500	Jordan Government	

Note: Royal Jordanian also operates four A.310-304s registered F-ODVF, F-ODVG, F-ODVH and F-ODVI. The marks JY-CAF, JY-CAG, JY-CAH and JY-CAI respectively have been reserved for them. Similarly two A.320-211s retain the registrations F-OGYA and F-OGYB.

LN (Norway)

LN-AKA	F.27 Friendship Mk 200	—	
LN-AKC	F.27 Friendship Mk 200	—	
LN-AKD	F.27 Friendship Mk 200	—	
LN-BRA	Boeing 737-405	Braathens SAFE *Eirik Blodoeks*	
LN-BRB	Boeing 737-405	Braathens SAFE *Inge Bardson*	
LN-BRC	Boeing 737-505	Braathens SAFE	
LN-BRD	Boeing 737-505	Braathens SAFE	
LN-BRE	Boeing 737-405	Braathens SAFE	
LN-BRF	Boeing 737-505	Braathens SAFE	
LN-BRG	Boeing 737-505	Braathens SAFE	
LN-BRH	Boeing 737-505	Braathens SAFE	
LN-BRI	Boeing 737-405	Braathens SAFE	
LN-BRJ	Boeing 737-505	Braathens SAFE	
LN-BRK	Boeing 737-505	Braathens SAFE	
LN-BRL	Boeing 737-405	Braathens SAFE	
LN-BRM	Boeing 737-505	Braathens SAFE	
LN-BRN	Boeing 737-505	Braathens SAFE	
LN-BRO	Boeing 737-505	Braathens SAFE	
LN-BRP	Boeing 737-405	Braathens SAFE *Harald Hardrade*	
LN-BRQ	Boeing 737-405	Braathens SAFE	
LN-BRR	Boeing 737-505	Braathens SAFE	
LN-BRS	Boeing 737-505	Braathens SAFE	
LN-BRT	Boeing 737-505	Braathens SAFE	
LN-BRU	Boeing 737-505	Braathens SAFE	
LN-BRV	Boeing 737-505	Braathens SAFE	
LN-BRX	Boeing 737-505	Braathens SAFE	
LN-FOG	L-188AF Electra	Fred Olsen Airtransport/DHL	
LN-FOH	L-188AF Electra	Fred Olsen Airtransport/DHL	
LN-FOI	L-188CF Electra	Fred Olsen Airtransport	
LN-FOL	L-188AF Electra	Fred Olsen Airtransport/DHL	
LN-KOC	EMB-120RT Brasilia	Wideroe Norskair	
LN-KOD	EMB-120RT Brasilia	Wideroe Norskair	
LN-KOE	EMB-120RT Brasilia	Wideroe Norskair	
LN-RCB	Boeing 767-383ER	S.A.S.	
LN-RCD	Boeing 767-383ER	S.A.S. *Gyda Viking*	
LN-RCE	Boeing 767-383ER	S.A.S. *Aase Viking*	
LN-RCG	Boeing 767-383ER	S.A.S. *Yrsa Viking*	
LN-RLA	Douglas DC-9-41	S.A.S. *Are Viking*	
LN-RLE	McD Douglas MD-82	S.A.S. *Vegard Viking*	
LN-RLF	McD Douglas MD-82	S.A.S. *Finn Viking*	
LN-RLH	Douglas DC-9-41	S.A.S. *Einar Viking*	

LN/LV/LX/LY

Notes	Reg.	Type	Owner or Operator
	LN-RLN	Douglas DC-9-41	S.A.S. *Halldor Viking*
	LN-RLP	Douglas DC-9-41	S.A.S. *Froste Viking*
	LN-RLR	McD Douglas MD-82	S.A.S. *Kettil Viking*
	LN-RLS	Douglas DC-9-41	S.A.S. *Asmund Viking*
	LN-RLT	Douglas DC-9-41	S.A.S. *Audun Viking*
	LN-RLX	Douglas DC-9-41	S.A.S. *Sote Viking*
	LN-RLZ	Douglas DC-9-41	S.A.S. *Bodvar Viking*
	LN-RMA	McD Douglas MD-81	S.A.S. *Hasting Viking*
	LN-RMD	McD Douglas MD-82	Scanair *Fenge Viking*
	LN-RMF	McD Douglas MD-83	S.A.S. *Piff Viking*
	LN-RMG	McD Douglas MD-87	S.A.S. *Snorre Viking*
	LN-RMH	McD Douglas MD-87	S.A.S. *Solmund Viking*
	LN-RMJ	McD Douglas MD-81	S.A.S. *Rand Viking*
	LN-RMK	McD Douglas MD-87	S.A.S. *Ragnhild Viking*
	LN-RML	McD Douglas MD-81	S.A.S. *Aud Viking*
	LN-RMM	McD Douglas MD-81	S.A.S. *Blenda Viking*
	LN-RMN	McD Douglas MD-82	S.A.S. *Ivar Viking*
	LN-RMO	McD Douglas MD-81	S.A.S. *Bergljot Viking*
	LN-RMP	McD Douglas MD-87	S.A.S. *Reidun Viking*
	LN-RMR	McD Douglas MD-81	S.A.S. *Olav Viking*
	LN-RMS	McD Douglas MD-81	S.A.S. *Nial Viking*
	LN-RMT	McD Douglas MD-81	S.A.S. *Jarl Viking*
	LN-RMU	McD Douglas MD-87	S.A.S. *Grim Viking*
	LN-RNB	Fokker 50	S.A.S. Commuter *Bardufoss*
	LN-RNC	Fokker 50	S.A.S. Commuter *Evenes*
	LN-RND	Fokker 50	S.A.S. Commuter *Lakselv*
	LN-RNE	Fokker 50	S.A.S. Commuter *Alta*
	LN-RNF	Fokker 50	S.A.S. Commuter *Kirkenes*
	LN-RNG	Fokker 50	S.A.S. Commuter *Bodö*
	LN-RNH	Fokker 50	S.A.S. Commuter *Trondheim*
	LN-WND	Douglas DC-3C	Dakota Norway

Note: Braathens also operates the Boeing 737-205s N73TH and N891FS (ex-LN-SUK and -SUJ respectively).

LV (Argentina)

	LV-MLO	Boeing 747-287B	Aerolineas Argentinas
	LV-MLP	Boeing 747-287B	Aerolineas Argentinas
	LV-MLR	Boeing 747-287B	Aerolineas Argentinas
	LV-OEP	Boeing 747-287B	Aerolineas Argentinas
	LV-OOZ	Boeing 747-287B	Aerolineas Argentinas
	LV-OPA	Boeing 747-287B	Aerolineas Argentinas

LX (Luxembourg)

	LX-ACV	Boeing 747-271C (SCD)	Cargolux *City of Echternach*
	LX-BCV	Boeing 747-271C (SCD)	Cargolux
	LX-DCV	Boeing 747-228F (SCD)	Cargolux/El Al
	LX-ECV	Boeing 747-271C (SCD)	Cargolux *City of Luxembourg*
	LX-FCV	Boeing 747-4R7F (SCD)	Cargolux
	LX-GCV	Boeing 747-4R7F (SCD)	Cargolux
	LX-LGB	Fokker 50	Luxair
	LX-LGC	Fokker 50	Luxair *Prince Guillaume*
	LX-LGD	Fokker 50	Luxair *Prince Felix*
	LX-LGE	Fokker 50	Luxair *Prince Louis*
	LX-LGF	Boeing 737-4C9	Luxair *Chateau de Vianden*
	LX-LGG	Boeing 737-4C9	Luxair *Chateau de Bourscheid*
	LX-LGK	EMB-120RT Brasilia	Luxair
	LX-LGL	EMB-120RT Brasilia	Luxair
	LX-LGM	EMB-120RT Brasilia	Luxair
	LX-LGO	Boeing 737-5C9	Luxair
	LX-LGP	Boeing 737-5C9	Luxair
	LX-LGX	Boeing 747SP-44	Luxair
	LX-SKS	EMB-110P1 Bandeirante	Sky Service
	LX-ZCV	Boeing 747-2D3B (SCD)	Cargolux

LY (Lithuania)

	LY-AAM	Yakovlev Yak-42	Lithuanian Airlines
	LY-AAN	Yakovlev Yak-42	Lithuanian Airlines

Reg.	Type	Owner or Operator	Notes
LY-AAO	Yakovlev Yak-42	Lithuanian Airlines	
LY-AAP	Yakovlev Yak-42	Lithuanian Airlines	
LY-AAQ	Yakovlev Yak-42	Lithuanian Airlines	
LY-AAR	Yakovlev Yak-42	Lithuanian Airlines	
LY-AAS	Yakovlev Yak-42	Lithuanian Airlines	
LY-AAT	Yakovlev Yak-42	Lithuanian Airlines	
LY-AAU	Yakovlev Yak-42	Lithuanian Airlines	
LY-AAV	Yakovlev Yak-42	Lithuanian Airlines	
LY-AAW	Yakovlev Yak-42	Lithuanian Airlines	
LY-AAX	Yakovlev Yak-42	Lithuanian Airlines	
LY-ABA	Tupolev Tu-134A	Lithuanian Airlines	
LY-ABB	Tupolev Tu-134A	Lithuanian Airlines	
LY-ABC	Tupolev Tu-134A	Lithuanian Airlines	
LY-ABD	Tupolev Tu-134A	Lithuanian Airlines	
LY-ABE	Tupolev Tu-134A	Lithuanian Airlines	
LY-ABF	Tupolev Tu-134A	Lithuanian Airlines	
LY-ABG	Tupolev Tu-134A-3	Lithuanian Airlines	
LY-ABH	Tupolev Tu-134A	Lithuanian Airlines	
LY-ABI	Tupolev Tu-134A	Lithuanian Airlines	
LY-GPA	Boeing 737-2Q8	Lithuanian Airlines	

LZ (Bulgaria)

LZ-ABA	Airbus A.320-231	Balkan Bulgarian Airlines *Vitosha*	
LZ-ABB	Airbus A.320-231	Balkan Bulgarian Airlines *Rila*	
LZ-ABC	Airbus A.320-231	Balkan Bulgarian Airlines *Rhodope*	
LZ-ABD	Airbus A.320-231	Balkan Bulgarian Airlines *Pirin*	
LZ-BAC	Antonov An-12	Balkan Bulgarian Airlines	
LZ-BAE	Antonov An-12	Balkan Bulgarian Airlines	
LZ-BAF	Antonov An-12	Balkan Bulgarian Airlines	
LZ-BEH	Ilyushin IL-18V	Balkan Bulgarian Airlines	
LZ-BEI	Ilyushin IL-18V	Balkan Bulgarian Airlines	
LZ-BEU	Ilyushin IL-18V	Balkan Bulgarian Airlines	
LZ-BOA	Boeing 737-53A	Balkan Bulgarian Airlines *City of Sofia*	
LZ-BOB	Boeing 737-53A	Balkan Bulgarian Airlines *City of Plovdiv*	
LZ-BOC	Boeing 737-53A	Balkan Bulgarian Airlines	
LZ-	Boeing 767-300ER	Balkan Bulgarian Airlines	
LZ-	Boeing 767-300ER	Balkan Bulgarian Airlines	
LZ-BTA	Tupolev Tu-154B	Balkan Bulgarian Airlines	
LZ-BTC	Tupolev Tu-154B	Balkan Bulgarian Airlines	
LZ-BTE	Tupolev Tu-154B	Balkan Bulgarian Airlines	
LZ-BTF	Tupolev Tu-154B	Balkan Bulgarian Airlines	
LZ-BTG	Tupolev Tu-154B	Balkan Bulgarian Airlines	
LZ-BTH	Tupolev Tu-154M	Balkan Bulgarian Airlines	
LZ-BTI	Tupolev Tu-154M	Balkan Bulgarian Airlines	
LZ-BTJ	Tupolev Tu-154B-1	Palair Macedonian	
LZ-BTK	Tupolev Tu-154B	Balkan Bulgarian Airlines	
LZ-BTL	Tupolev Tu-154B	Balkan Bulgarian Airlines	
LZ-BTM	Tupolev Tu-154B	Balkan Bulgarian Airlines	
LZ-BTN	Tupolev Tu-154M	Balkan Bulgarian Airlines	
LZ-BTO	Tupolev Tu-154B-1	Balkan Bulgarian Airlines	
LZ-BTP	Tupolev Tu-154B-1	Balkan Bulgarian Airlines	
LZ-BTQ	Tupolev Tu-154M	Balkan Bulgarian Airlines	
LZ-BTR	Tupolev Tu-154B-2	Balkan Bulgarian Airlines	
LZ-BTS	Tupolev Tu-154B-2	Balkan Bulgarian Airlines	
LZ-BTT	Tupolev Tu-154B-2	Balkan Bulgarian Airlines	
LZ-BTU	Tupolev Tu-154B-2	Palair Macedonian	
LZ-BTV	Tupolev Tu-154B-2	Balkan Bulgarian Airlines	
LZ-BTW	Tupolev Tu-154M	Balkan Bulgarian Airlines	
LZ-BTX	Tupolev Tu-154M	Balkan Bulgarian Airlines	
LZ-BTY	Tupolev Tu-154M	Balkan Bulgarian Airlines	
LZ-BTZ	Tupolev Tu-154M	Balkan Bulgarian Airlines	
LZ-MIG	Tupolev Tu-154M	Varna International Airways (VIA)	
LZ-MIK	Tupolev Tu-154M	Varna International Airways (VIA)	
LZ-MIL	Tupolev Tu-154M	Varna International Airways (VIA)	
LZ-MIR	Tupolev Tu-154M	Varna International Airways (VIA)	
LZ-MIS	Tupolev Tu-154M	Varna International Airways (VIA)	
LZ-MIV	Tupolev Tu-154M	Varna International Airways (VIA)	
LZ-MNA	Tupolev Tu-154M	Macedonia Air Services/Air Kona	
LZ-PVA	Boeing 707-330C	Global Air	
LZ-PVB	Boeing 707-331B	Global Air	
LZ-TUG	Tupolev Tu-134A-3	Balkan Bulgarian Airlines	
LZ-TUK	Tupolev Tu-134A	Balkan Bulgarian Airlines	

Notes	Reg.	Type	Owner or Operator
	LZ-TUM	Tupolev Tu-134A-3	Balkan Bulgarian Airlines
	LZ-TUP	Tupolev Tu-134A	Balkan Bulgarian Airlines
	LZ-TUS	Tupolev Tu-134A	Balkan Bulgarian Airlines
	LZ-TUT	Tupulev Tu-134A-3	Balkan Bulgarian Airlines
	LZ-TUU	Tupolev Tu-134A-3	Balkan Bulgarian Airlines
	LZ-TUV	Tupolev Tu-134A-3	Balkan Bulgarian Airlines
	LZ-TUZ	Tupolev Tu-134A-3	Balkan Bulgarian Airlines

Note: Balkan also operates two Boeing 767-27EERs F-GHGD and F-GHGE on lease from Air France.

N (USA)

	N14AZ	Boeing 707-336C	Seagreen Air Transport
	N21AZ	Boeing 707-351C	Seagreen Air Transport
	N25UA	Douglas DC-8-61F	American International Airways
	N73TH	Boeing 737-205	Braathens SAFE *Magnus Erlingsson*
	N105WA	Douglas DC-10-30CF	World Airways/Federal Express
	N106WA	Douglas DC-10-30CF	World Airways/Federal Express
	N107WA	Douglas DC-10-30CF	World Airways/Federal Express
	N108WA	Douglas DC-10-30CF	World Airways/Federal Express
	N112WA	Douglas DC-10-30CF	World Airways/Federal Express
	N114FE	Boeing 727-24C	Federal Express
	N115FE	Boeing 727-116C	Federal Express
	N116KB	Boeing 747-312	Singapore Airlines
	N117AA	Douglas DC-10-10ER	American Airlines
	N117FE	Boeing 727-25C	Federal Express
	N117KC	Boeing 747-312	Singapore Airlines
	N119KE	Boeing 747-312	Singapore Airlines
	N120KF	Boeing 747-312	Singapore Airlines
	N121KG	Boeing 747-312	Singapore Airlines
	N122KH	Boeing 747-312	Singapore Airlines
	N123KJ	Boeing 747-312	Singapore Airlines
	N124KK	Boeing 747-312	Singapore Airlines
	N125AA	Douglas DC-10-10ER	American Airlines
	N125KL	Boeing 747-312	Singapore Airlines
	N133JC	Douglas DC-10-40	Northwest Airlines
	N133TW	Boeing 747-156	Trans World Airlines
	N134TW	Boeing 747-156	Trans World Airlines
	N137AA	Douglas DC-10-30	American Airlines
	N138AA	Douglas DC-10-30	American Airlines (*stored*)
	N140AA	Douglas DC-10-30	American Airlines (*stored*)
	N140UA	Boeing 747SP-21	United Airlines
	N141AA	Douglas DC-10-30	American Airlines
	N141UA	Boeing 747SP-21	United Airlines
	N141US	Douglas DC-10-40	Northwest Airlines
	N142AA	Douglas DC-10-30	American Airlines
	N142UA	Boeing 747SP-21	United Airlines
	N143AA	Douglas DC-10-30	American Airlines
	N143FE	Boeing 727-21C	Federal Express
	N143UA	Boeing 747SP-21	United Airlines
	N144AA	Douglas DC-10-30	American Airlines
	N144FE	Boeing 727-21C	Federal Express
	N144JC	Douglas DC-10-40	Northwest Airlines
	N144UA	Boeing 747SP-21	United Airlines
	N145UA	Boeing 747SP-21	United Airlines
	N145US	Douglas DC-10-40	Northwest Airlines
	N146UA	Boeing 747SP-21	United Airlines
	N146US	Douglas DC-10-40	Northwest Airlines
	N147UA	Boeing 747SP-21	United Airlines
	N147US	Douglas DC-10-40	Northwest Airlines
	N148UA	Boeing 747SP-21	United Airlines
	N148US	Douglas DC-10-40	Northwest Airlines
	N149UA	Boeing 747SP-21	Tajik Air
	N149US	Douglas DC-10-40	Northwest Airlines
	N150US	Douglas DC-10-40	Northwest Airlines
	N151UA	Boeing 747-222B	United Airlines
	N151US	Douglas DC-10-40	Northwest Airlines
	N152UA	Boeing 747-222B	United Airlines
	N152US	Douglas DC-10-40	Northwest Airlines
	N153UA	Boeing 747-123	United Airlines
	N153US	Douglas DC-10-40	Northwest Airlines
	N154US	Douglas DC-10-40	Northwest Airlines

Reg.	Type	Owner or Operator	Notes
N155UA	Boeing 747-123	United Airlines	
N155US	Douglas DC-10-40	Northwest Airlines	
N156UA	Boeing 747-123	United Airlines	
N156US	Douglas DC-10-40	Northwest Airlines	
N157UA	Boeing 747-123	United Airlines	
N157US	Douglas DC-10-40	Northwest Airlines	
N158UA	Boeing 747-238B	United Airlines	
N158US	Douglas DC-10-40	Northwest Airlines	
N159UA	Boeing 747-238B	United Airlines	
N159US	Douglas DC-10-40	Northwest Airlines	
N160UA	Boeing 747-238B	United Airlines	
N160US	Douglas DC-10-40	Northwest Airlines	
N161UA	Boeing 747-238B	United Airlines	
N161US	Douglas DC-10-40	Northwest Airlines	
N162US	Douglas DC-10-40	Northwest Airlines	
N163AA	Douglas DC-10-30	American Airlines	
N163UA	Boeing 747-238B	United Airlines	
N164AA	Douglas DC-10-30	American Airlines	
N164UA	Boeing 747-238B	United Airlines	
N165UA	Boeing 747-238B	United Airlines	
N166AA	Douglas DC-10-10ER	American Airlines	
N171DN	Boeing 767-332ER	Delta Air Lines	
N171UA	Boeing 747-422	United Airlines *Spirit of Seattle II*	
N172DN	Boeing 767-332ER	Delta Air Lines	
N172UA	Boeing 747-422	United Airlines	
N173DN	Boeing 767-332ER	Delta Air Lines	
N173UA	Boeing 747-422	United Airlines	
N174DN	Boeing 767-332ER	Delta Air Lines	
N174UA	Boeing 747-422	United Airlines	
N175DN	Boeing 767-332ER	Delta Air Lines	
N175UA	Boeing 747-422	United Airlines	
N176DN	Boeing 767-332ER	Delta Air Lines	
N176UA	Boeing 747-422	United Airlines	
N177DN	Boeing 767-332ER	Delta Air Lines	
N177UA	Boeing 747-422	United Airlines	
N178DN	Boeing 767-332ER	Delta Air Lines	
N178UA	Boeing 747-422	United Airlines	
N179DN	Boeing 767-332ER	Delta Air Lines	
N179UA	Boeing 747-422	United Airlines	
N180DN	Boeing 767-332ER	Delta Air Lines	
N180UA	Boeing 747-422	United Airlines	
N181DN	Boeing 767-332ER	Delta Air Lines	
N181UA	Boeing 747-422	United Airlines	
N182DN	Boeing 767-332ER	Delta Air Lines	
N182UA	Boeing 747-422	United Airlines	
N183DN	Boeing 767-332ER	Delta Air Lines	
N183UA	Boeing 747-422	United Airlines	
N184DN	Boeing 767-332ER	Delta Air Lines	
N184UA	Boeing 747-422	United Airlines	
N185AT	L-1011 TriStar 50	American Trans Air	
N185UA	Boeing 747-422	United Airlines	
N186AT	Boeing 747-422	American Trans Air	
N186UA	Boeing 747-422	United Airlines	
N187AT	L.1011 TriStar 50	American Trans Air	
N187UA	Boeing 747-422	United Airlines	
N188AT	L.1011 TriStar 50	American Trans Air	
N188UA	Boeing 747-422	United Airlines	
N189AT	L.1011 TriStar 50	American Trans Air	
N189UA	Boeing 747-422	United Airlines	
N190AT	L.1011 TriStar 50	American Trans Air	
N190UA	Boeing 747-422	United Airlines	
N191AT	L.1011 TriStar 50	American Trans Air	
N191UA	Boeing 747-422	United Airlines	
N192AT	L.1011 TriStar 50	American Trans Air	
N192UA	Boeing 747-422	United Airlines	
N193AT	L.1011 TriStar 50	American Trans Air	
N193UA	Boeing 747-422	United Airlines	
N194UA	Boeing 747-422	United Airlines	
N195AT	L.1011 TriStar 150	American Trans Air	
N195UA	Boeing 747-422	United Airlines	
N202AE	Boeing 747-2B4B (SCD)	Middle East Airlines	
N202PH	Boeing 747-121	Tower Air	
N203AE	Boeing 747-2B4B (SCD)	Middle East Airlines	

Notes	Reg.	Type	Owner or Operator
	N204AE	Boeing 747-2B4B (SCD)	Middle East Airlines
	N207AE	Boeing 747-211B	Philippine Airlines
	N208AE	Boeing 747-211B	Philippine Airlines
	N211JL	Boeing 747-246F	Japan Airlines
	N211NW	Douglas DC-10-30	Northwest Airlines
	N212JL	Boeing 747-346	Japan Airlines
	N213JL	Boeing 747-346	Japan Airlines
	N220NW	Douglas DC-10-30	Northwest Airlines
	N221NW	Douglas DC-10-30	Northwest Airlines
	N223NW	Douglas DC-10-30	Northwest Airlines
	N224NW	Douglas DC-10-30	Northwest Airlines
	N225NW	Douglas DC-10-30	Northwest Airlines
	N226NW	Douglas DC-10-30	Northwest Airlines
	N227NW	Douglas DC-10-30	Northwest Airlines
	N271WA	McD Douglas MD-11	World Airways
	N272WA	McD Douglas MD-11	World Airways
	N273WA	McD Douglas MD-11	World Airways
	N280WA	McD Douglas MD-11	World Airways
	N301FE	Douglas DC-10-30AF	Federal Express
	N302FE	Douglas DC-10-30AF	Federal Express
	N303EA	L.1011 TriStar 1	Rich International Airways
	N303FE	Douglas DC-10-30AF	Federal Express
	N303TW	Boeing 747-257B	—
	N304FE	Douglas DC-10-30AF	Federal Express
	N304TW	Boeing 747-257B	—
	N305FE	Douglas DC-10-30AF	Federal Express *John David*
	N305TW	Boeing 747-284B	Trans World Airlines
	N306FE	Douglas DC-10-30AF	Federal Express *John Peter Jr*
	N307FE	Douglas DC-10-30AF	Federal Express *Erin Lee*
	N308FE	Douglas DC-10-30AF	Federal Express *Ann*
	N309FE	Douglas DC-10-30AF	Federal Express *Stacey*
	N310FE	Douglas DC-10-30AF	Federal Express *John Shelby*
	N311FE	Douglas DC-10-30AF	Federal Express *Abe*
	N312AA	Boeing 767-223ER	American Airlines
	N312FE	Douglas DC-10-30AF	Federal Express *Angela*
	N313AA	Boeing 767-223ER	American Airlines
	N313EA	L.1011 TriStar 1	Rich International Airways
	N313FE	Douglas DC-10-30AF	Federal Express *Brandon Parks*
	N314FE	Douglas DC-10-30AF	Federal Express *Caitlin-Ann*
	N315AA	Boeing 767-223ER	American Airlines
	N315FE	Douglas DC-10-30AF	Federal Express *Kevin*
	N316AA	Boeing 767-223ER	American Airlines
	N316FE	Douglas DC-10-30AF	Federal Express *Brandon*
	N317AA	Boeing 767-223ER	American Airlines
	N319AA	Boeing 767-223ER	American Airlines
	N319EA	L.1011 TriStar 1	Rich International Airways
	N320AA	Boeing 767-223ER	American Airlines
	N320FE	Douglas DC-10-30CF	Federal Express
	N321AA	Boeing 767-223ER	American Airlines
	N321FE	Douglas DC-10-30CF	Federal Express
	N322AA	Boeing 767-223ER	American Airlines
	N322FE	Douglas DC-10-30CF	Federal Express *King Frank*
	N323AA	Boeing 767-223ER	American Airlines
	N324AA	Boeing 767-223ER	American Airlines
	N325AA	Boeing 767-223ER	American Airlines
	N327AA	Boeing 767-223ER	American Airlines
	N328AA	Boeing 767-223ER	American Airlines
	N329AA	Boeing 767-223ER	American Airlines
	N330AA	Boeing 767-223ER	American Airlines
	N332AA	Boeing 767-223ER	American Airlines
	N334AA	Boeing 767-223ER	American Airlines
	N335AA	Boeing 767-223ER	American Airlines
	N336AA	Boeing 767-223ER	American Airlines
	N338AA	Boeing 767-223ER	American Airlines
	N339AA	Boeing 767-223ER	American Airlines
	N341HA	L.188F Electra	Channel Express (Air Services) Ltd
	N343HA	L.188AF Electra	Channel Express (Air Services) Ltd
	N345HC	Douglas DC-10-30ER	Finnair
	N345JW	Douglas DC-8-63AF	Arrow Air
	N351AA	Boeing 767-323ER	American Airlines
	N352AA	Boeing 767-323ER	American Airlines
	N353AA	Boeing 767-323ER	American Airlines
	N354AA	Boeing 767-323ER	American Airlines

Reg.	Type	Owner or Operator	Notes
N355AA	Boeing 767-323ER	American Airlines	
N356Q	L.188F Electra	Hunting Cargo Airlines Ltd	
N357AA	Boeing 767-323ER	American Airlines	
N358AA	Boeing 767-323ER	American Airlines	
N359AA	Boeing 767-323ER	American Airlines	
N360AA	Boeing 767-323ER	American Airlines	
N361AA	Boeing 767-323ER	American Airlines	
N362AA	Boeing 767-323ER	American Airlines	
N363AA	Boeing 767-323ER	American Airlines	
N366AA	Boeing 767-323ER	American Airlines	
N368AA	Boeing 767-323ER	American Airlines	
N369AA	Boeing 767-323ER	American Airlines	
N370AA	Boeing 767-323ER	American Airlines	
N371AA	Boeing 767-323ER	American Airlines	
N372AA	Boeing 767-323ER	American Airlines	
N373AA	Boeing 767-323ER	American Airlines	
N374AA	Boeing 767-323ER	American Airlines	
N376AN	Boeing 767-323ER	American Airlines	
N377AN	Boeing 767-323ER	American Airlines	
N378AN	Boeing 767-323ER	American Airlines	
N379AA	Boeing 767-323ER	American Airlines	
N380AN	Boeing 767-323ER	American Airlines	
N381AN	Boeing 767-323ER	American Airlines	
N382AN	Boeing 767-323ER	American Airlines	
N383AN	Boeing 767-323ER	American Airlines	
N384AA	Boeing 767-323ER	American Airlines	
N385AM	Boeing 767-323ER	American Airlines	
N386AA	Boeing 767-323ER	American Airlines	
N387AM	Boeing 767-323ER	American Airlines	
N403EV	Boeing 747-45E	EVA Airways	
N405EV	Boeing 747-45E	EVA Airways	
N417DG	Douglas DC-10-30	Aeromexico *Ciudad de Mexico*	
N441J	Douglas DC-8-63CF	Arrow Air	
N470EV	Boeing 747-273C	Evergreen International Airlines	
N471EV	Boeing 747-273C	Evergreen International Airlines	
N472EV	Boeing 747-131	Evergreen International Airlines	
N473EV	Boeing 747-121F (SCD)	Evergreen International Airlines	
N474EV	Boeing 747-121	Evergreen International Airlines	
N475EV	Boeing 747-121F (SCD)	Evergreen International Airlines	
N477EV	Boeing 747SR-46 (SCD)	Evergreen International Airlines	
N478EV	Boeing 747SR-46 (SCD)	Evergreen International Airlines	
N479EV	Boeing 747-132 (SCD)	Evergreen International Airlines	
N480EV	Boeing 747-121 (SCD)	Evergreen International Airlines	
N481EV	Boeing 747-132 (SCD)	Evergreen International Airlines	
N482EV	Boeing 747-212B (SCD)	Evergreen International Airlines/Saudia	
N485EV	Boeing 747-212B (SCD)	Evergreen International Airlines	
N522SJ	L-100-20 Hercules	Southern Air Transport	
N601FE	McD Douglas MD-11F	Federal Express *Christy*	
N601US	Boeing 747-151	Northwest Airlines	
N602AA	Boeing 747SP-31	American Airlines	
N602FE	McDouglas MD-11F	Federal Express *Malcolm Baldrige*	
N602FF	Boeing 747-124	Tower Air	
N602UA	Boeing 767-222ER	United Airlines	
N602US	Boeing 747-151	Northwest Airlines	
N603FE	McD Douglas MD-11F	Federal Express *Elizabeth*	
N603FF	Boeing 747-130	Tower Air *Suzie*	
N603US	Boeing 747-151	Northwest Airlines	
N604FE	McD Douglas MD-11F	Federal Express *Hollis*	
N604FF	Boeing 747-121	Tower Air	
N604US	Boeing 747-151	Northwest Airlines	
N605FE	McD Douglas MD-11F	Federal Express *April Star*	
N605FF	Boeing 747-136	Tower Air	
N605UA	Boeing 767-222ER	United Airlines	
N605US	Boeing 747-151	Northwest Airlines (*stored*)	
N606FE	McD Douglas MD-11F	Federal Express *Louis III*	
N606FF	Boeing 747-136	Tower Air	
N606UA	Boeing 767-222ER	United Airlines *City of Chicago*	
N606US	Boeing 747-151	Northwest Airlines	
N607FE	McD Douglas MD-11F	Federal Express *Dana Elena*	
N607PE	Boeing 747-238B (022)	Continental Airlines *(to become N50022)*	
N607UA	Boeing 767-222ER	United Airlines *City of Denver*	
N607US	Boeing 747-151	Northwest Airlines	
N608FE	McD Douglas MD-11F	Federal Express *Scott*	

Notes	Reg.	Type	Owner or Operator
	N608FF	Boeing 747-131	Tower Air
	N608UA	Boeing 767-222ER	United Airlines
	N608US	Boeing 747-151	Northwest Airlines
	N609FE	McD Douglas MD-11F	Federal Express
	N609FF	Boeing 747-121	Tower Air
	N609UA	Boeing 767-222ER	United Airlines
	N609US	Boeing 747-151	Northwest Airlines (stored)
	N610FE	McD Douglas MD-11F	Federal Express
	N610FF	Boeing 747-282B	Tower Air
	N610UA	Boeing 767-222ER	United Airlines
	N610US	Boeing 747-151	Northwest Airlines
	N611FF	Boeing 747-282B	Tower Air
	N611FE	McD Douglas MD-11F	Federal Express
	N611UA	Boeing 767-222ER	United Airlines
	N611US	Boeing 747-251B	Northwest Airlines
	N612FE	McD Douglas MD-11F	Federal Express
	N612US	Boeing 747-251B	Northwest Airlines
	N613US	Boeing 747-251B	Northwest Airlines
	N614FE	McD Douglas MD-11F	Federal Express
	N614US	Boeing 747-251B	Northwest Airlines
	N615US	Boeing 747-251B	Northwest Airlines
	N616US	Boeing 747-251F (SCD)	Northwest Airlines
	N617US	Boeing 747-251F (SCD)	Northwest Airlines
	N618US	Boeing 747-251F (SCD)	Northwest Airlines
	N619US	Boeing 747-251F (SCD)	Northwest Airlines
	N620FE	Boeing 747-133	Federal Express
	N620US	Boeing 747-135	Northwest Airlines (stored)
	N621US	Boeing 747-135	Northwest Airlines
	N622US	Boeing 747-251B	Northwest Airlines
	N623US	Boeing 747-251B	Northwest Airlines
	N624US	Boeing 747-251B	Northwest Airlines
	N625US	Boeing 747-251B	Northwest Airlines
	N626US	Boeing 747-251B	Northwest Airlines
	N627US	Boeing 747-251B	Northwest Airlines
	N628US	Boeing 747-251B	Northwest Airlines
	N629US	Boeing 747-251F (SCD)	Northwest Airlines
	N630SJ	Boeing 747-124	Polar Air Cargo
	N630US	Boeing 747-2J9F	Northwest Airlines
	N631FE	Boeing 747-249F (SCD)	Federal Express
	N631US	Boeing 747-251B	Northwest Airlines
	N632US	Boeing 747-251B	Northwest Airlines
	N633US	Boeing 747-227B	Northwest Airlines
	N634US	Boeing 747-227B	Northwest Airlines
	N635US	Boeing 747-227B	Northwest Airlines
	N636FE	Boeing 747-245F (SCD)	Federal Express
	N636US	Boeing 747-251B	Northwest Airlines
	N637US	Boeing 747-251B	Northwest Airlines
	N638FE	Boeing 747-245F (SCD)	Federal Express
	N638US	Boeing 747-251B	Northwest Airlines
	N639US	Boeing 747-251F (SCD)	Northwest Airlines
	N640FE	Boeing 747-245F (SCD)	Federal Express
	N640US	Boeing 747-251F (SCD)	Northwest Airlines
	N641FE	Boeing 747-245F (SCD)	Federal Express
	N641UA	Boeing 767-322ER	United Airlines
	N642UA	Boeing 767-322ER	United Airlines
	N643UA	Boeing 767-322ER	United Airlines
	N644UA	Boeing 767-322ER	United Airlines
	N645UA	Boeing 767-322ER	United Airlines
	N645US	Boeing 767-201ER	USAir Pride of Piedmont
	N646UA	Boeing 767-322ER	United Airlines
	N646US	Boeing 767-201ER	USAir City of London
	N647UA	Boeing 767-322ER	United Airlines
	N647US	Boeing 767-201ER	USAir City of Charlotte
	N648UA	Boeing 767-322ER	United Airlines
	N648US	Boeing 767-201ER	USAir City of Tampa
	N649UA	Boeing 767-322ER	United Airlines
	N649US	Boeing 767-201ER	USAir City of Los Angeles
	N650UA	Boeing 767-322ER	United Airlines
	N650US	Boeing 767-201ER	USAir Pride of Baltimore
	N651UA	Boeing 767-322ER	United Airlines
	N651US	Boeing 767-2B7ER	USAir
	N652UA	Boeing 767-322ER	United Airlines
	N652US	Boeing 767-2B7ER	USAir

Reg.	Type	Owner or Operator	Notes
N653UA	Boeing 767-322ER	United Airlines	
N653US	Boeing 767-2B7ER	USAir	
N654UA	Boeing 767-322ER	United Airlines	
N654US	Boeing 767-2B7ER	USAir/British Airways	
N655UA	Boeing 767-322ER	United Airlines	
N655US	Boeing 767-2B7ER	USAir/British Airways	
N656UA	Boeing 767-322ER	United Airlines	
N657UA	Boeing 767-322ER	United Airlines	
N658UA	Boeing 767-322ER	United Airlines	
N659UA	Boeing 767-322ER	United Airlines	
N660UA	Boeing 767-322ER	United Airlines	
N661AV	Douglas DC-8-63AF	Arrow Air	
N661UA	Boeing 767-322ER	United Airlines	
N661US	Boeing 747-451	Northwest Airlines	
N662UA	Boeing 767-322ER	United Airlines	
N662US	Boeing 747-451	Northwest Airlines	
N663UA	Boeing 767-322ER	United Airlines	
N663US	Boeing 747-451	Northwest Airlines	
N664UA	Boeing 767-322ER	United Airlines	
N664US	Boeing 747-451	Northwest Airlines	
N665UA	Boeing 767-322ER	United Airlines	
N665US	Boeing 747-451	Northwest Airlines	
N666UA	Boeing 767-322ER	United Airlines	
N666US	Boeing 747-451	Northwest Airlines	
N667UA	Boeing 767-322ER	United Airlines	
N667US	Boeing 747-451	Northwest Airlines	
N668UA	Boeing 767-322ER	United Airlines	
N668US	Boeing 747-451	Northwest Airlines	
N669UA	Boeing 767-322ER	United Airlines	
N669US	Boeing 747-451	Northwest Airlines	
N670UA	Boeing 767-322ER	United Airlines	
N670US	Boeing 747-451	Northwest Airlines	
N671UA	Boeing 767-322ER	United Airlines	
N671UP	Boeing 747-123F (SCD)	United Parcel Service	
N671US	Boeing 747-451	Northwest Airlines	
N672UP	Boeing 747-123F (SCD)	United Parcel Service	
N672US	Boeing 747-451	Northwest Airlines	
N673UP	Boeing 747-123F (SCD)	United Parcel Service	
N674UP	Boeing 747-123F (SCD)	United Parcel Service	
N675UP	Boeing 747-123F (SCD)	United Parcel Service	
N676UP	Boeing 747-123F (SCD)	United Parcel Service	
N677UP	Boeing 747-123F (SCD)	United Parcel Service	
N681UP	Boeing 747-121F (SCD)	United Parcel Service	
N682UP	Boeing 747-121F (SCD)	United Parcel Service	
N683UP	Boeing 747-121F (SCD)	United Parcel Service	
N701CK	Boeing 747-146F (SCD)	American International Airways	
N702CK	Boeing 747-146F (SCD)	American International Airways	
N703CK	Boeing 747-146F (SCD)	American International Airways	
N704CK	Boeing 747-146F (SCD)	American Internatioanl Airways	
N724DA	L.1011-385 TriStar 200	Delta Air Lines	
N735SJ	Boeing 747-121	Polar Air Cargo	
N736DY	L.1011-385 TriStar 250	Delta Air Lines	
N737D	L.1011-385 TriStar 250	Delta Air Lines	
N740DA	L.1011-385 TriStar 250	Delta Air Lines	
N741DA	L.1011-385 TriStar 250	Delta Air Lines	
N741PR	Boeing 747-2F6B	Philippine Airlines	
N741SJ	Boeing 747-121	Polar Air Cargo	
N742PR	Boeing 747-2F6B	Philippine Airlines	
N743PR	Boeing 747-2F6B	Philippine Airlines	
N744PR	Boeing 747-2F6B	Philippine Airlines	
N750AT	Boeing 757-212ER	American Trans Air	
N751AT	Boeing 757-212ER	American Trans Air	
N751DA	L-1011-385 TriStar 500	Delta Air Lines	
N752AT	Boeing 757-212ER	American Trans Air	
N752DA	L-1011-385 TriStar 500	Delta Air Lines	
N753DA	L-1011-385 TriStar 500	Delta Air Lines	
N754AT	Boeing 757-2Q8	American Trans Air	
N754DL	L.1011-385 TriStar 500	Delta Air Lines	
N755AT	Boeing 757-2Q8	American Trans Air	
N755DL	L.1011-385 TriStar 500	Delta Air Lines	
N756DR	L.1011-385 TriStar 500	Delta Air Lines	
N757AT	Boeing 757-212ER	American Trans Air	
N759DA	L.1011-385 TriStar 500	Delta Air Lines	

Notes	Reg.	Type	Owner or Operator
	N760DH	L.1011-385 TriStar 500	Delta Air Lines
	N761DA	L.1011-385 TriStar 500	Delta Air Lines
	N762BE	L.1011-385 TriStar 50	Hawaiian Air *Waikiki*
	N762DA	L.1011-385 TriStar 500	Delta Air Lines
	N763DL	L.1011-385 TriStar 500	Delta Air Lines
	N764BE	L.1011-385 TriStar 50	Hawaiian Air *Wahwaii*
	N764DA	L.1011-385 TriStar 500	Delta Air Lines
	N765BE	L.1011-385 TriStar 50	Hawaiian Air *Kauai*
	N765DA	L.1011-385 TriStar 500	Delta Air Lines
	N766BE	L.1011-385 TriStar 50	Hawaiian Air *Oahu*
	N766DA	L.1011-385 TriStar 500	Delta Air Lines
	N767DA	L.1011-385 TriStar 500	Delta Air Lines
	N768DL	L.1011-385 TriStar 500	Delta Air Lines
	N769DL	L.1011-385 TriStar 500	Delta Air Lines
	N772CA	Douglas DC-8-62	Rich International Airways
	N784AL	Douglas DC-8-63CF	Arrow Air
	N791AL	Douglas DC-8-62AF	Arrow Air
	N791FT	Douglas DC-8-73AF	Emery Worldwide
	N792FT	Douglas DC-8-73AF	Emery Worldwide
	N795FT	Douglas DC-8-73AF	Emery Worldwide
	N796AL	Douglas DC-8-63AF	Emery Worldwide
	N796FT	Douglas DC-8-73AF	Emery Worldwide
	N797AL	Douglas DC-8-63AF	Emery Worldwide
	N798AL	Douglas DC-8-62CF	Arrow Air
	N799AL	Douglas DC-8-62CF	Arrow Air
	N801CK	Douglas DC-8-55F	American International Airways
	N801DE	McD Douglas MD-11	Delta Air Lines
	N801PA	Airbus A.310-222	Delta Air Lines
	N801UP	Douglas DC-8-73AF	United Parcel Service
	N802BN	Douglas DC-8-62AF	Arrow Air
	N802DE	McD Douglas MD-11	Delta Air Lines
	N802PA	Airbus A.310-222	Delta Air Lines
	N802UP	Douglas DC-8-73AF	United Parcel Service
	N803DE	McD Douglas MD-11	Delta Air Lines
	N803PA	Airbus A.310-222	Delta Air Lines
	N803UP	Douglas DC-8-63AF	United Parcel Service
	N804DE	McD Douglas MD-11	Delta Air Lines
	N804PA	Airbus A.310-222	Delta Air Lines
	N804UP	Douglas DC-8-51	United Parcel Service
	N805CK	Douglas DC-8-51F	American International Airways
	N805DE	McD Douglas MD-11	Delta Air Lines
	N805PA	Airbus A.310-222	Delta Air Lines
	N805UP	Douglas DC-8-73CF	United Parcel Service
	N806DE	McD Douglas MD-11	Delta Air Lines
	N806PA	Airbus A.310-222	Delta Air Lines
	N806UP	Douglas DC-8-73AF	United Parcel Service
	N807CK	Douglas DC-8-55F	American International Airways
	N807DE	McD Douglas MD-11	Delta Air Lines
	N807PA	Airbus A.310-222	Delta Air Lines
	N807UP	Douglas DC-8-73AF	United Parcel Service
	N808CK	Douglas DC-8-55F	American International Airways
	N808DE	McD Douglas MD-11	Delta Air Lines
	N808UP	Douglas DC-8-73AF	United Parcel Service
	N809CK	Douglas DC-8-73AF	American International Airways
	N809DE	McD Douglas MD-11	Delta Air Lines
	N809UP	Douglas DC-8-73AF	United Parcel Service
	N810CK	Douglas DC-8-52F	American International Airways
	N810DE	McD Douglas MD-11	Delta Air Lines
	N810UP	Douglas DC-8-71AF	United Parcel Service
	N811CK	Douglas DC-8-63AF	American International Airways
	N811DE	McD Douglas MD-11	Delta Air Lines
	N811PA	Airbus A.310-324	Delta Air Lines
	N811UP	Douglas DC-8-73AF	United Parcel Service
	N812CK	Douglas DC-8-61AF	American International Airways
	N812DE	McD Douglas MD-11	Delta Air Lines
	N812PA	Airbus A.310-324	Delta Air Lines
	N812UP	Douglas DC-8-73AF	United Parcel Service
	N813CK	Douglas DC-8-61AF	American International Airways
	N813DE	McD Douglas MD-11	Delta Air Lines
	N813PA	Airbus A.310-324	Delta Air Lines
	N813UP	Douglas DC-8-73AF	United Parcel Service
	N814CK	Douglas DC-8-61F	American International Airways
	N814DE	McD Douglas MD-11	Delta Air Lines

Reg.	Type	Owner or Operator	Notes
N814PA	Airbus A.310-324	Delta Air Lines	
N814UP	Douglas DC-8-73AF	United Parcel Service	
N815DE	McD Douglas MD-11	Delta Air Lines	
N815EV	Douglas DC-8-73CF	Evergreen International Airlines	
N815PA	Airbus A.310-324	Delta Air Lines	
N816CK	Douglas DC-8-61F	American International Airways	
N816EV	Douglas DC-8-73CF	Evergreen International Airlines/TNT	
N816PA	Airbus A.310-324	Delta Air Lines	
N817CK	Douglas DC-8-61F	American International Airways	
N817EV	Douglas DC-8-62AF	Evergreen International Airlines	
N817PA	Airbus A.310-324	Delta Air Lines	
N818PA	Airbus A.310-324	Delta Air Lines	
N818UP	Douglas DC-8-73AF	United Parcel Service	
N819PA	Airbus A.310-324	Delta Air Lines	
N819UP	Douglas DC-8-73AF	United Parcel Service	
N820BX	Douglas DC-8-71AF	Burlington Express	
N820PA	Airbus A.310-324	Delta Air Lines	
N821BX	Douglas DC-8-71AF	Burlington Express	
N821PA	Airbus A.310-324	Delta Air Lines	
N822BX	Douglas DC-8-71AF	Burlington Express	
N822PA	Airbus A.310-324	Delta Air Lines	
N823PA	Airbus A.310-324	Delta Air Lines	
N824BX	Douglas DC-8-71AF	Burlington Express	
N824PA	Airbus A.310-324	Delta Air Lines	
N835AB	Airbus A.310-324	Delta Air Lines	
N836AB	Airbus A.310-324	Delta Air Lines	
N836UP	Douglas DC-8-73AF	United Parcel Service	
N837AB	Airbus A.310-324	Delta Air Lines	
N838AB	Airbus A.310-324	Delta Air Lines	
N839AD	Airbus A.310-324	Delta Air Lines	
N840AB	Airbus A.310-324	Delta Air Lines	
N840UP	Douglas DC-8-73AF	United Parcel Service	
N841AB	Airbus A.310-324	Delta Air Lines	
N842AB	Airbus A.310-324	Delta Air Lines	
N843AB	Airbus A.310-324	Delta Air Lines	
N851UP	Douglas DC-8-73AF	United Parcel Service	
N852UP	Douglas DC-8-73AF	United Parcel Service	
N863BX	Boeing 707-321C	Burlington Express	
N865F	Douglas DC-8-63AF	Emery Worldwide	
N866UP	Douglas DC-8-73AF	United Parcel Service	
N867BX	Douglas DC-8-63AF	Burlington Express	
N867UP	Douglas DC-8-73AF	United Parcel Service	
N868BX	Douglas DC-8-63AF	Burlington Express	
N868UP	Douglas DC-8-73AF	United Parcel Service	
N869BX	Douglas DC-8-63AF	Burlington Express	
N870BX	Douglas DC-8-63AF	Burlington Express	
N870SJ	Douglas DC-8-71AF	Southern Air Transport	
N870TV	Douglas DC-8-73AF	Emery Worldwide	
N871SJ	Douglas DC-8-71AF	Southern Air Transport	
N872SJ	Douglas DC-8-71AF	Southern Air Transport	
N873SJ	Douglas DC-8-73AF	Southern Air Transport	
N874UP	Douglas DC-8-73AF	United Parcel Service	
N875SJ	Douglas DC-8-71AF	Southern Air Transport	
N880UP	Douglas DC-8-73AF	United Parcel Service	
N891FS	Boeing 737-205	Braathens SAFE *Magnus Barfot*	
N894UP	Douglas DC-8-73AF	United Parcel Service	
N901SJ	L.100-30 Hercules	Southern Air Transport	
N905SJ	L.100-30 Hercules	Southern Air Transport	
N906R	Douglas DC-8-63AF	Emery Worldwide	
N906SJ	L.100-30 Hercules	Southern Air Transport	
N907SJ	L.100-30 Hercules	Southern Air Transport	
N908SJ	L.100-30 Hercules	Southern Air Transport	
N909SJ	L.100-30 Hercules	Southern Air Transport/Schreiner Airways	
N910SJ	L.100-30 Hercules	Southern Air Transport	
N912SJ	L.100-30 Hercules	Southern Air Transport	
N916SJ	L.100-30 Hercules	Southern Air Transport	
N918SJ	L.100-30 Hercules	Southern Air Transport	
N919SJ	L.100-30 Hercules	Southern Air Transport	
N920SJ	L.100-30 Hercules	Southern Air Transport	
N921R	Douglas DC-8-63AF	Emery Worldwide	
N921SJ	L.100-30 Hercules	Southern Air Transport	
N923SJ	L.100-30 Hercules	Southern Air Transport	
N929R	Douglas DC-8-63AF	Emery Worldwide	

Notes	Reg.	Type	Owner or Operator
	N950R	Douglas DC-8-63AF	Emery Worldwide
	N951R	Douglas DC-8-63AF	Emery Worldwide
	N952R	Douglas DC-8-63AF	Emery Worldwide
	N957R	Douglas DC-8-63AF	Emery Worldwide
	N959R	Douglas DC-8-63AF	Emery Worldwide
	N961R	Douglas DC-8-73AF	Emery Worldwide
	N964R	Douglas DC-8-63AF	Emery Worldwide
	N990CF	Douglas DC-8-62AF	Emery Worldwide
	N993CF	Douglas DC-8-62AF	Emery Worldwide
	N994CF	Douglas DC-8-62AF	Emery Worldwide
	N995CF	Douglas DC-8-62AF	Emery Worldwide
	N996CF	Douglas DC-8-62AF	Emery Worldwide
	N997CF	Douglas DC-8-62AF	Emery Worldwide
	N998CF	Douglas DC-8-62AF	Emery Worldwide
	N1309E	Boeing 747-306	K.L.M. *Admiral Richard E. Byrd*
	N1738D	L.1011-385 TriStar 250	Delta Air Lines
	N1739D	L.1011-385 TriStar 250	Delta Air Lines
	N1750B	McD Douglas MD-11	American Airlines
	N1751A	McD Douglas MD-11	American Airlines
	N1752K	McD Douglas MD-11 (1AC)	American Airlines
	N1753	McD Douglas MD-11 (1AD)	American Airlines
	N1754	McD Douglas MD-11 (1AE)	American Airlines
	N1755	McD Douglas MD-11	American Airlines
	N1756	McD Douglas MD-11	American Airlines
	N1757A	McD Douglas MD-11	American Airlines
	N1758B	McD Douglas MD-11	American Airlines
	N1759	McD Douglas MD-11	American Airlines
	N1760A	McD Douglas MD-11	American Airlines
	N1761R	McD Douglas MD-11	American Airlines
	N1762B	McD Douglas MD-11	American Airlines
	N1763	McD Douglas MD-11	American Airlines
	N1764B	McD Douglas MD-11	American Airlines
	N1765B	McD Douglas MD-11	American Airlines
	N1766A	McD Douglas MD-11	American Airlines
	N1767A	McD Douglas MD-11	American Airlines
	N1768D	McD Douglas MD-11	American Airlines
	N1804	Douglas DC-8-62AF	Arrow Air
	N1805	Douglas DC-8-62	Rich International Airways
	N1808E	Douglas DC-8-62AF	Arrow Air
	N2674U	Douglas DC-8-73AF	Emery Worldwide
	N3016Z	Douglas DC-10-30	Zambia Airways *Nkwazi*
	N3024W	Douglas DC-10-30	Nigeria Airways
	N3140D	L.1011-385 TriStar 500 (598)	B.W.I.A. *Sunjet St. Lucia*
	N4508H	Boeing 747SP-09	China Airlines
	N4522V	Boeing 747SP-09	China Airlines
	N4714U	Boeing 747-122	United Airlines
	N4716U	Boeing 747-122	United Airlines
	N4717U	Boeing 747-122	United Airlines *Edward E. Carlson*
	N4718U	Boeing 747-122	United Airlines *Thomas F. Gleed*
	N4719U	Boeing 747-122	United Airlines *Friendship Japan*
	N4720U	Boeing 747-122	United Airlines
	N4723U	Boeing 747-122	United Airlines *William A. Patterson*
	N4724U	Boeing 747-122	United Airlines
	N4727U	Boeing 747-122	United Airlines *Robert E. Johnson*
	N4728U	Boeing 747-122	United Airlines *Gardner Cowles*
	N4729U	Boeing 747-122	United Airlines
	N4732U	Boeing 747-122	United Airlines
	N4735U	Boeing 747-122	United Airlines
	N4935C	Douglas DC-8-63	Rich International Airways
	N7036T	L.1011-385 TriStar 100	Trans World Airlines
	N7251U	Boeing 727-222	United Airlines
	N7253U	Boeing 727-222	United Airlines
	N7256U	Boeing 727-222	United Airlines
	N7257U	Boeing 727-222	United Airlines
	N7375A	Boeing 767-323ER	American Airlines
	N7622U	Boeing 727-222	United Airlines
	N7638U	Boeing 727-222	United Airlines
	N7644U	Boeing 727-222	United Airlines
	N7646U	Boeing 727-222	United Airlines
	N7647U	Boeing 727-222	United Airlines
	N8034T	L.1011-385 TriStar 100	Trans World Airlines *(stored)*
	N8089U	Douglas DC-8-71AF	Southern Air Transport
	N8097U	Douglas DC-8-71AF	Southern Air Transport

Reg.	Type	Owner or Operator	Notes
N8228P	Douglas DC-10-30	Aeromexico *Castillo de Chapultepec*	
N8872Z	Boeing 727-225	Delta Air Lines	
N8875Z	Boeing 727-225	Delta Air Lines	
N8879Z	Boeing 727-225	Delta Air Lines	
N8887Z	Boeing 727-225	Delta Air Lines	
N8889Z	Boeing 727-225	Delta Air Lines	
N8890Z	Boeing 727-225	Delta Air Lines	
N8891Z	Boeing 727-225	Delta Air Lines	
N8892Z	Boeing 727-225	Delta Air Lines	
N8968U	Douglas DC-8-62AF	Arrow Air	
N8974U	Douglas DC-8-62	Rich International Airways	
N12061	Douglas DC-10-30	Continental Airlines *Richard M. Adams*	
N12064	Douglas DC-10-30	Continental Airlines	
N13066	Douglas DC-10-30	Continental Airlines	
N13067	Douglas DC-10-30	Continental Airlines	
N14062	Douglas DC-10-30	Continental Airlines	
N14063	Douglas DC-10-30	Continental Airlines	
N15069	Douglas DC-10-30	Continental Airlines	
N17010	Boeing 747-143	Continental Airlines	
N17011	Boeing 747-143	Continental Airlines	
N17025	Boeing 747-238B	Continental Airlines	
N19072	Douglas DC-10-30	Continental Airlines	
N31018	L.1011-385 TriStar 50	Trans World Airlines	
N31019	L.1011-385 TriStar 50	Trans World Airlines	
N31022	L.1011-385 TriStar 50	American Trans Air	
N31023	L.1011-385 TriStar 50	Trans World Airlines	
N31024	L.1011-385 TriStar 50	Trans World Airlines *(stored)*	
N31029	L.1011-385 TriStar 100	Trans World Airlines	
N31030	L.1011-385 TriStar 100	Trans World Airlines	
N31031	L.1011-385 TriStar 100	Trans World Airlines	
N31032	L.1011-385 TriStar 100	Trans World Airlines *(stored)*	
N33021	Boeing 747-243B	Continental Airlines	
N39356	Boeing 767-323ER	American Airlines	
N39364	Boeing 767-323ER	American Airlines	
N39365	Boeing 767-323ER	American Airlines	
N39367	Boeing 767-323ER	American Airlines	
N41020	L.1011-385 TriStar 50	Trans World Airlines *(stored)*	
N41068	Douglas DC-10-30	Continental Airlines	
N42086	Douglas DC-8-62AF	Arrow Air	
N50022	Boeing 747-238B	Continental Airlines	
N53110	Boeing 747-131	Trans World Airlines	
N53116	Boeing 747-131	Trans World Airlines *(stored)*	
N54325	Boeing 727-231	Trans World Airlines	
N54649	Douglas DC-10-30	Air France	
N68060	Douglas DC-10-30	Continental Airlines *Robert F. Six*	
N68065	Douglas DC-10-30	Continental Airlines *Robert P. Gallaway*	
N76073	Douglas DC-10-30	Continental Airlines	
N78019	Boeing 747-230B	Continental Airlines	
N81025	L.1011-385 TriStar 100	Trans World Airlines	
N81026	L.1011-385 TriStar 100	Trans World Airlines	
N81027	L.1011-385 TriStar 50	Trans World Airlines *(stored)*	
N81028	L.1011-385 TriStar 100	Trans World Airlines	
N83071	Douglas DC-10-30	Continental Airlines	
N87070	Douglas DC-10-30	Continental Airlines	
N93104	Boeing 747-131	Trans World Airlines	
N93105	Boeing 747-131	Trans World Airlines	
N93107	Boeing 747-131	Trans World Airlines	
N93108	Boeing 747-131	Trans World Airlines	
N93109	Boeing 747-131	Trans World Airlines	
N93117	Boeing 747-131	Trans World Airlines *(stored)*	
N93119	Boeing 747-131	Trans World Airlines	

OD (Lebanon)

OD-AFD	Boeing 707-3B4C	Middle East Airlines	
OD-AFE	Boeing 707-3B4C	Middle East Airlines	
OD-AFM	Boeing 720-023B	Middle East Airlines	
OD-AFZ	Boeing 720-023B	Middle East Airlines	
OD-AGB	Boeing 720-023B	Middle East Airlines	
OD-AGD	Boeing 707-323C	TMA of Lebanon	
OD-AGF	Boeing 720-047B	Middle East Airlines	

Notes	Reg.	Type	Owner or Operator
	OD-AGO	Boeing 707-321C	TMA of Lebanon
	OD-AGP	Boeing 707-321C	TMA of Lebanon
	OD-AGS	Boeing 707-331C	TMA of Lebanon
	OD-AGU	Boeing 707-347C	Middle East Airlines
	OD-AGV	Boeing 707-347C	Middle East Airlines
	OD-AGX	Boeing 707-327C	TMA of Lebanon
	OD-AGY	Boeing 707-327C	TMA of Lebanon
	OD-AHC	Boeing 707-323C	Middle East Airlines
	OD-AHD	Boeing 707-323C	Middle East Airlines
	OD-AHE	Boeing 707-323C	Middle East Airlines
	OD-AHF	Boeing 707-323B	Middle East Airlines

Note: MEA also uses the 747s N202AE, N203AE and N204AE when not on lease, two Airbus A.310s leased from KLM as PH-AGE and PH-AGF and another registered D-APOL.

OE (Austria)

	Reg.	Type	Owner or Operator
	OE-ILF	Boeing 737-3Z9	Lauda Air *Bob Marley*
	OE-ILG	Boeing 737-3Z9	Lauda Air *John Lennon*
	OE-LAA	Airbus A.310-324	Austrian Airlines *New York*
	OE-LAB	Airbus A.310-324	Austrian Airlines *Tokyo*
	OE-LAC	Airbus A.310-324	Austrian Airlines *Paris*
	OE-LAD	Airbus A.310-324	Austrian Airlines *Chicago*
	OE-LAU	Boeing 767-3Z9ER	Lauda Air *Johann Strauss*
	OE-LAW	Boeing 767-3Z9ER	Lauda Air *Franz Schubert*
	OE-LAX	Boeing 767-3Z9ER	Lauda Air *James Dean*
	OE-	Canadair Regional Jet 100ER	Lauda Air
	OE-	Canadair Regional Jet 100ER	Lauda Air
	OE-	Canadair Regional Jet 100ER	Lauda Air
	OE-	Canadair Regional Jet 100ER	Lauda Air
	OE-	Canadair Regional Jet 100ER	Lauda Air
	OE-	Canadair Regional Jet 100ER	Lauda Air
	OE-LDP	McD Douglas MD-81	Austrian Airlines *Niederösterreich*
	OE-LDR	McD Douglas MD-81	Austrian Airlines *Wien*
	OE-LDS	McD Douglas MD-81	Austrian Airlines *Burgenland*
	OE-LDT	McD Douglas MD-81	Austrian Airlines *Kärnten*
	OE-LDU	McD Douglas MD-81	Austrian Airlines *Steiermark*
	OE-LDV	McD Douglas MD-81	Austrian Airlines *Oberösterreich*
	OE-LDW	McD Douglas MD-81	Austrian Airlines *Salzburg*
	OE-LDX	McD Douglas MD-82	Austrian Airlines *Tirol*
	OE-LDY	McD Douglas MD-82	Austrian Airlines *Vorarlberg*
	OE-LDZ	McD Douglas MD-82	Austrian Airlines *Graz*
	OE-LEC	D.H.C.8-311 Dash Eight	Tyrolean Airways
	OE-LLF	D.H.C.8-106 Dash Eight	Tyrolean Airways
	OE-LLG	D.H.C.8-106 Dash Eight	Tyrolean Airways
	OE-LLH	D.H.C.8-103 Dash Eight	Tyrolean Airways *Stadt Kitzbühel*
	OE-LLK	D.H.C.8-103 Dash Eight	Tyrolean Airways *Stadt Salzburg*
	OE-LLL	D.H.C.8-103 Dash Eight	Tyrolean Airways *Stadt Graz*
	OE-LLM	D.H.C.8-103 Dash Eight	Tyrolean Airways *Stadt Klagenfurt*
	OE-LLN	D.H.C.8-103 Dash Eight	Tyrolean Airways *Stadt Linz*
	OE-LLP	D.H.C.8-103 Dash Eight	Tyrolean Airways
	OE-LLS	D.H.C.7-102 Dash Seven	Tyrolean Airways *Stadt Innsbruck*
	OE-LLU	D.H.C.7-102 Dash Seven	Tyrolean Airways *Stadt Wien*
	OE-LLV	D.H.C.8-314 Dash Eight	Tyrolean Airways *Land Tirol*
	OE-LLW	D.H.C.8-314 Dash Eight	Tyrolean Airways *Land Steiermark*
	OE-LLX	D.H.C.8-314 Dash Eight	Tyrolean Airways *Land Salzburg*
	OE-LMA	McD Douglas MD-82	Austrian Airlines *Linz*
	OE-LMB	McD Douglas MD-82	Austrian Airlines *Eisenstadt*
	OE-LMC	McD Douglas MD-82	Austrian Airlines *Baden*
	OE-LMD	McD Douglas MD-83	Austrian Airlines *Villach*
	OE-LME	McD Douglas MD-83	Austrian Airlines *Krems*
	OE-LMK	McD Douglas MD-87	Austrian Airlines *St Pölten*
	OE-LML	McD Douglas MD-87	Austrian Airlines *Salzburg*
	OE-LMM	McD Douglas MD-87	Austrian Airlines *Innsbruck*
	OE-LMN	McD Douglas MD-87	Austrian Airlines *Klagenfurt*
	OE-LMO	McD Douglas MD-87	Austrian Airlines *Bregenz*
	OE-LNH	Boeing 737-4Z9	Lauda Air *Elvis Presley*
	OE-LNI	Boeing 737-4Z9	Lauda Air *Janise Joplin*
	OE-LNK	Boeing 737-4Z9	Lauda Air

Reg.	Type	Owner or Operator	Notes

OH (Finland)

OH-LAA	Airbus A.300B4-203	Finnair
OH-LAB	Airbus A.300B4-203	Finnair
OH-LGA	McD Douglas MD-11	Finnair
OH-LGB	McD Douglas MD-11	Finnair
OH-LGC	McD Douglas MD-11	Finnair
OH-LGD	McD Douglas MD-11	Finnair
OH-LHA	Douglas DC-10-30ER	Finnair *Iso Antti*
OH-LHB	Douglas DC-10-30ER	Finnair
OH-LHD	Douglas DC-10-30ER	Finnair
OH-LHE	Douglas DC-10-30ER	Finnair
OH-LMA	McD Douglas MD-87	Finnair
OH-LMB	McD Douglas MD-87	Finnair
OH-LMC	McD Douglas MD-87	Finnair
OH-LMG	McD Douglas MD-83	Finnair
OH-LMH	McD Douglas MD-82	Finnair
OH-LMN	McD Douglas MD-82	Finnair
OH-LMO	McD Douglas MD-82	Finnair
OH-LMP	McD Douglas MD-82	Finnair
OH-LMR	McD Douglas MD-83	Finnair
OH-LMS	McD Douglas MD-83	Finnair
OH-LMT	McD Douglas MD-82	Finnair
OH-LMU	McD Douglas MD-83	Finnair
OH-LMV	McD Douglas MD-83	Finnair
OH-LMW	McD Douglas MD-82	Finnair
OH-LMX	McD Douglas MD-82	Finnair
OH-LMY	McD Douglas MD-82	Finnair
OH-LMZ	McD Douglas MD-82	Finnair
OH-LNB	Douglas DC-9-41	Finnair
OH-LNC	Douglas DC-9-41	Finnair
OH-LND	Douglas DC-9-41	Finnair
OH-LNE	Douglas DC-9-41	Finnair
OH-LNF	Douglas DC-9-41	Finnair
OH-LYN	Douglas DC-9-51	Finnair
OH-LYO	Douglas DC-9-51	Finnair
OH-LYP	Douglas DC-9-51	Finnair
OH-LYR	Douglas DC-9-51	Finnair
OH-LYS	Douglas DC-9-51	Finnair
OH-LYT	Douglas DC-9-51	Finnair
OH-LYU	Douglas DC-9-51	Finnair
OH-LYV	Douglas DC-9-51	Finnair
OH-LYW	Douglas DC-9-51	Finnair
OH-LYX	Douglas DC-9-51	Finnair
OH-LYY	Douglas DC-9-51	Finnair
OH-LYZ	Douglas DC-9-51	Finnair

Note: Finnair also operates a DC-10-30ER which retains its US registration N345HC.

OK (Czech Republic and Slovakia)

OK-BYZ	Ilyushin IL-62	Ensor Air (*stored*)
OK-CFH	Tupolev Tu-134A	Ceskoslovenske Aerolinie (CSA)
OK-EFJ	Tupolev Tu-134A	CSA
OK-EFK	Tupolev Tu-134A	CSA
OK-FBF	Ilyushin IL-62	EspeAir
OK-GBH	Ilyushin IL-62	EspeAir
OK-HFL	Tupolev Tu-134A	CSA
OK-HFM	Tupolev Tu-134A	CSA
OK-IFN	Tupolev Tu-134A	CSA
OK-JBI	Ilyushin IL-62M	CSA *Plzen*
OK-JBJ	Ilyushin IL-62M	CSA *Hradec Kralové*
OK-JGY	Boeing 727-230	Air Terrex
OK-KBK	Ilyushin IL-62M	CSA *Ceske Budejovice*
OK-KBN	Ilyushin IL-62M	CSA
OK-LCP	Tupolev Tu-154B-2	Ensor Air
OK-OBL	Ilyushin IL-62M	CSA *Ostrava*
OK-PBM	Ilyushin IL-62M	CSA
OK-TCD	Tupolev Tu-154M	CSA *Trencianské Teplic*
OF-TGX	Boeing 727-51	Air Terrex
OK-UCE	Tupolev Tu-154M	CSA *Marianské Lazne*
OK-UCF	Tupolev Tu-154M	CSA *Smokovec*

Notes	Reg.	Type	Owner or Operator
	OK-VCG	Tupolev Tu-154M	CSA *Luhacovice*
	OK-VCP	Tupolev Tu-154M	Ensor Air
	OK-WAA	Airbus A.310-304	CSA *Praha*
	OK-WAB	Airbus A.310-304	CSA *Bratislava*
	OK-XGA	Boeing 737-55S	CSA *Plzen*
	OK-XGB	Boeing 737-55S	CSA *Olomouc*
	OK-XGC	Boeing 737-55S	CSA *Ceske Budejovice*
	OK-XGD	Boeing 737-55S	CSA *Poprad*
	OK-XGE	Boeing 737-55S	CSA *Kosice*

OO (Belgium)

Notes	Reg.	Type	Owner or Operator
	OO-DHB	Convair Cv.580	European Air Transport (DHL)
	OO-DHC	Convair Cv.580	European Air Transport (DHL)
	OO-DHD	Convair Cv.580	European Air Transport (DHL)
	OO-DHE	Convair Cv.580	European Air Transport (DHL)
	OO-DHF	Convair Cv.580	European Air Transport (DHL)
	OO-DHG	Convair Cv.580	European Air Transport (DHL)
	OO-DHH	Convair Cv.580	European Air Transport (DHL)
	OO-DHI	Convair Cv.580	European Air Transport (DHL)
	OO-DHJ	Convair Cv.580	European Air Transport (DHL)
	OO-DHL	Convair Cv.580	European Air Transport (DHL)
	OO-DHM	Boeing 727-31C	European Air Transport (DHL)
	OO-DHN	Boeing 727-31C	European Air Transport (DHL)
	OO-DHO	Boeing 727-31C	European Air Transport (DHL)
	OO-DHP	Boeing 727-35F	European Air Transport (DHL)
	OO-DHQ	Boeing 727-35F	European Air Transport (DHL)
	OO-DJA	F.28 Fellowship 3000	Delta Air Transport
	OO-DJB	F.28 Fellowship 4000	Delta Air Transport
	OO-DJE	BAe 146-200	Delta Air Transport/SABENA
	OO-DJF	BAe 146-200	Delta Air Transport/SABENA
	OO-DJG	BAe 146-200	Delta Air Transport/SABENA
/	OO-DJH	BAe 146-200	Delta Air Transport/SABENA
	OO-DJJ	BAe 146-200	Delta Air Transport/SABENA
	OO-DJK	F.28 Fellowship 4000	Delta Air Transport
	OO-DTF	EMB-120ER Brasilia	Delta Air Transport
	OO-DTG	EMB-120ER Brasilia	Delta Air Transport
	OO-DTH	EMB-120RT Brasilia	Delta Air Transport
	OO-DTI	EMB-120RT Brasilia	Delta Air Transport
	OO-DTJ	EMB-120RT Brasilia	Delta Air Transport
	OO-DTK	EMB-120ER Brasilia	Delta Air Transport
	OO-DTL	EMB-120RT Brasilia	Delta Air Transport
	OO-DTN	EMB-120RT Brasilia	Delta Air Transport
	OO-DTO	EMB-120RT Brasilia	Delta Air Transport
	OO-D	EMB-120RT Brasilia	Delta Air Transport
	OO-FEL	F.27 Friendship Mk 500	Sky Freighters
	OO-HUB	Convair Cv.580	European Air Transport (DHL)
	OO-ILI	Boeing 757-23A	Air Belgium
	OO-ILJ	Boeing 737-46B	Air Belgium
	OO-ING	Airbus A.300B4-103	European Airlines
	OO-JPA	Swearingen SA226AT Merlin IVA	European Air Transport
	OO-JPI	Swearingen SA226TC Metro II	European Air Transport
	OO-LTE	Boeing 737-3M8	European Airlines
	OO-LTJ	Boeing 737-3M8	EBA EuroBelgian Airlines
	OO-LTL	Boeing 737-3M8	EBA EuroBelgian Airlines
	OO-LTM	Boeing 737-3M8	EBA EuroBelgian Airlines
	OO-LTP	Boeing 737-33A	EBA EuroBelgian Airlines
	OO-LTR	Boeing 737-4S3	EBA EuroBelgian Airlines
	OO-MJE	Boeing 146-200	DAT Air Meuse
	OO-MKO	Airbus A.300B4-103	European Airlines
	OO-MTD	EMB-120RT Brasilia	DAT Air Meuse
	OO-SBJ	Boeing 737-46B	Sobelair *Juliette*
	OO-SBM	Boeing 737-429	Sobelair
	OO-SBQ	Boeing 737-229	Sobelair
	OO-SBT	Boeing 737-229	Sobelair
	OO-SBZ	Boeing 737-329	Sobelair
	OO-SCA	Airbus A.310-222	SABENA
	OO-SCB	Airbus A.310-222	SABENA
	OO-SCC	Airbus A.310-322	SABENA
	OO-SCD	Airbus A.340-211	SABENA/Air France
	OO-SCE	Airbus A.340-211	SABENA/Air France
	OO-SCF	Airbus A.340-211	SABENA/Air France

Reg.	Type	Owner or Operator	Notes
OO-SCG	Airbus A.340-211	SABENA/Air France	
OO-SCH	Airbus A.340-211	SABENA/Air France	
OO-SDA	Boeing 737-229	Sobelair	
OO-SDD	Boeing 737-229	SABENA	
OO-SDE	Boeing 737-229	SABENA	
OO-SDF	Boeing 737-229	SABENA	
OO-SDG	Boeing 737-229	SABENA	
OO-SDJ	Boeing 737-229C	SABENA	
OO-SDK	Boeing 737-229C	SABENA	
OO-SDL	Boeing 737-229	SABENA	
OO-SDM	Boeing 737-229	SABENA	
OO-SDN	Boeing 737-229	SABENA/Sobelair	
OO-SDO	Boeing 737-229	SABENA	
OO-SDP	Boeing 737-229C	SABENA	
OO-SDR	Boeing 737-229C	SABENA	
OO-SDV	Boeing 737-329	SABENA	
OO-SDW	Boeing 737-329	SABENA	
OO-SDX	Boeing 737-329	SABENA	
OO-SDY	Boeing 737-329	SABENA	
OO-SGA	Boeing 747-129A (SCD)	SABENA	
OO-SGC	Boeing 747-329 (SCD)	SABENA	
OO-SGD	Boeing 747-329 (SCD)	SABENA	
OO-SLA	Douglas DC-10-30CF	SABENA	
OO-SLB	Douglas DC-10-30CF	SABENA	
OO-SYA	Boeing 737-329	SABENA	
OO-SYB	Boeing 737-329	SABENA	
OO-SYC	Boeing 737-429	SABENA	
OO-SYD	Boeing 737-429	SABENA	
OO-SYE	Boeing 737-529	SABENA	
OO-SYF	Boeing 737-429	SABENA	
OO-SYG	Boeing 737-429	SABENA	
OO-SYH	Boeing 737-529	SABENA	
OO-SYI	Boeing 737-529	SABENA	
OO-SYJ	Boeing 737-529	SABENA	
OO-SYK	Boeing 737-529	SABENA	
OO-VDO	Boeing 737-4Y0	Chartair *Ville de Charleroi*	
OO-VLC	Fokker 50	V.L.M.	
OO-VLM	Fokker 50	V.L.M.	
OO-VLN	Fokker 50	V.L.M. *Royal Antwerp F.C.*	

Note: SABENA also operates Dash Eights PH-SDI, PH-SDJ and PH-SDM on lease from Schreiner Airways and the Boeing 747-228B F-GCBB on lease from Air France.

OY (Denmark)

OY-AUO	Swearingen SA226TC Metro II	Jetair	
OY-AZW	Swearingen SA226TC Metro II	Newair of Denmark	
OY-BDD	Nord 262A-21	Cimber Air (*stored*)	
OY-BHT	EMB-110P2 Bandeirante	Muk Air	
OY-BJT	Swearingen SA226TC Metro II	Jetair	
OY-BNM	EMB-110P2 Bandeirante	Muk Air	
OY-BPB	Douglas DC-3C	Flyvende MuseumsFly	
OY-BPL	Swearingen SA227AC Metro III	Metro Airways	
OY-BVF	F.27 Friendship Mk 600	Aviation Assistance	
OY-BVH	F.27 Friendship Mk 200	Aviation Assistance	
OY-BYH	Swearingen SA226TC Metro II	Jetair	
OY-BYN	Swearingen SA226TC Metro II	Muk Air	
OY-CCL	F.27 Friendship Mk 600	Alkair	
OY-CCN	F.27 Friendship Mk 600	Alkair	
OY-CHA	Swearingen SA226AT Merlin IV	Jetair	
OY-CIB	Aérospatiale ATR-42-300	Cimber Air/Lufthansa CityLine	
OY-CIC	Aérospatiale ATR-42-300	Cimber Air/Lufthansa CityLine	
OY-CID	Aérospatiale ATR-42-300	Cimber Air/Lufthansa CityLine	
OY-CIE	Aérospatiale ATR-42-300	Cimber Air/Lufthansa CityLine	
OY-CIF	Aérospatiale ATR-42-300	Cimber Air/Lufthansa CityLine	
OY-CIG	Aérospatiale ATR-42-300	Cimber Air/Lufthansa CityLine	
OY-CIH	Aérospatiale ATR-42-300	Cimber Air	
OY-CLB	BAe Jetstream 3102	Newair of Denmark	
OY-CLC	BAe Jetstream 3102	Newair of Denmark	
OY-CNA	Airbus A.300B4	Premair	
OY-CND	Airbus A.320-231	Premair *Merkur*	
OY-CNE	Airbus A.320-231	Premair *Jupiter*/Saarland Airlines	
OY-CNF	Airbus A.320-231	Premair *Venus*	

Notes	Reg.	Type	Owner or Operator
	OY-CNG	Airbus A.320-231	Premair *Mars*
	OY-CNH	Airbus A.320-231	Premair *Sirius*
	OY-CNI	Airbus A.320-231	Premair *Spica*
	OY-CNK	Airbus A.300B4	Premair
	OY-CNL	Airbus A.300B4	Premair
	OY-CPG	EMB-110P1 Bandeirante	Sun-Air
	OY-CRR	H.P. 137 Jetstream 1	Newair of Denmark (*stored*)
	OY-CRT	H.P. 137 Jetstream 1	Newair of Denmark (*stored*)
	OY-EDA	BAe Jetstream 3103	Sun-Air
	OY-EDB	BAe Jetstream 3103	Sun-Air
	OY-	BAe Jetstream 4100	Sun-Air
	OY-EEC	BAe Jetstream 3101	Sun-Air
	OY-JEO	Swearingen SA226TC Metro II	Jetair
	OY-JER	Swearingen SA226TC Metro II	Jetair
	OY-KAE	Fokker 50	S.A.S. Commuter *Hans*
	OY-KAF	Fokker 50	S.A.S. Commuter *Sigvat*
	OY-KAG	Fokker 50	S.A.S. Commuter *Odensis*
	OY-KAH	Fokker 50	S.A.S. Commuter *Bjorn*
	OY-KAI	Fokker 50	S.A.S. Commuter *Skjold*
	OY-KAK	Fokker 50	S.A.S. Commuter *Turid*
	OY-KDH	Boeing 767-383ER	S.A.S.
	OY-KDL	Boeing 767-383ER	S.A.S. *Tjodhild Viking*
	OY-KDM	Boeing 767-383ER	S.A.S. *Inva Viking*
	OY-KDN	Boeing 767-383ER	S.A.S. *Ulf Viking*
	OY-KDO	Boeing 767-383ER	S.A.S. *Svea Viking*
	OY-KGD	Douglas DC-9-21	S.A.S. *Ubbe Viking*
	OY-KGE	Douglas DC-9-21	S.A.S. *Orvar Viking*
	OY-KGF	Douglas DC-9-21	S.A.S. *Rolf Viking*
	OY-KGL	Douglas DC-9-41	S.A.S. *Angantyr Viking*
	OY-KGM	Douglas DC-9-41	S.A.S. *Arnfinn Viking*
	OY-KGN	Douglas DC-9-41	S.A.S. *Gram Viking*
	OY-KGO	Douglas DC-9-41	S.A.S. *Holte Viking*
	OY-KGP	Douglas DC-9-41	S.A.S. *Torbern Viking*
	OY-KGR	Douglas DC-9-41	S.A.S. *Holger Viking*
	OY-KGS	Douglas DC-9-41	S.A.S. *Hall Viking*
	OY-KGY	McD Douglas MD-81	S.A.S. *Rollo Viking*
	OY-KGZ	McD Douglas MD-81	S.A.S. *Hagbard Viking*
	OY-KHC	McD Douglas MD-81	S.A.S. *Faste Viking*
	OY-KHF	McD Douglas MD-87	S.A.S. *Ragnar Viking*
	OY-KHG	McD Douglas MD-81	S.A.S. *Alle Viking*
	OY-KHI	McD Douglas MD-87	S.A.S. *Torkel Viking*
	OY-KHK	McD Douglas MD-81	S.A.S. *Roald Viking*
	OY-KHL	McD Douglas MD-81	S.A.S. *Knud Viking*
	OY-KHM	McD Douglas MD-81	S.A.S. *Mette Viking*
	OY-KHN	McD Douglas MD-81	S.A.S. *Dan Viking*
	OY-KHP	McD Douglas MD-81	S.A.S. *Arild Viking*
	OY-KHR	McD Douglas MD-81	S.A.S. *Torkild Viking*
	OY-KHT	McD Douglas MD-82	S.A.S. *Gorm Viking*
	OY-KHU	McD Douglas MD-81	S.A.S. *Ravn Viking*
	OY-KHW	McD Douglas MD-87	S.A.S. *Ingemund Viking*
	OY-KIA	Douglas DC-9-21	S.A.S. *Guttorm Viking*
	OY-KIB	Douglas DC-9-21	S.A.S. *Gunder Viking*
	OY-KID	Douglas DC-9-21	S.A.S. *Rane Viking*
	OY-KIE	Douglas DC-9-21	S.A.S. *Skate Viking*
	OY-KIF	Douglas DC-9-21	S.A.S. *Svipdag Viking*
	OY-MAC	Boeing 737-5L9	Maersk Air
	OY-MAD	Boeing 737-5L9	Maersk Air
	OY-MAE	Boeing 737-5L9	Maersk Air
	OY-MAN	Boeing 737-3L9	Maersk Air
	OY-MAO	Boeing 737-3L9	Maersk Air
	OY-MBK	Boeing 737-4Y0	Maersk Air
	OY-MMG	Fokker 50	Maersk Air
	OY-MMH	Fokker 50	Maersk Air
	OY-MMI	Fokker 50	Maersk Air
	OY-MMJ	Fokker 50	Maersk Air
	OY-MMO	Boeing 737-3L9	Maersk Air
	OY-MMS	Fokker 50	Maersk Air
	OY-MMT	Fokker 50	Maersk Air
	OY-MMU	Fokker 50	Maersk Air
	OY-MMV	Fokker 50	Maersk Air
	OY-MUA	EMB-110P1 Bandeirante	Muk Air
	OY-MUB	Short SD3-30	Muk Air
	OY-MUF	F.27 Friendship	Newair of Denmark

Reg.	Type	Owner or Operator	Notes
OY-SAT	Boeing 727-2J4	—	
OY-SBE	Boeing 727-2J4	—	
OY-SBF	Boeing 727-2J4	—	
OY-SBG	Boeing 727-2J4	—	
OY-SBH	Boeing 727-2B7	—	
OY-SBI	Boeing 727-270	—	
OY-SBN	Boeing 727-2B7	—	
OY-SBO	Boeing 727-2K3	—	
OY-SHA	Boeing 757-2J4	—	
OY-SHB	Boeing 757-2J4	—	
OY-SRA	F.27 Friendship Mk 600	Starair	
OY-SRB	F.27 Friendship Mk 600	Alkair	
OY-SRC	F.27 Friendship Mk 600	Starair	
OY-SRR	F.27 Friendship Mk 600	Starair	
OY-SRZ	F.27 Friendship Mk 600	Starair	
OY-STI	S.E.210 Caravelle 10B	Sun-Air	
OY-SVF	BAe Jetstream 3102	Sun-Air	
OY-SVJ	BAe Jetstream 3101	Sun-Air	
OY-SVS	BAe Jetstream 4100	Sun-Air	
OY-SVZ	BAe Jetstream 3102	Sun-Air	
OY-TOV	Nord 262A-30	Cimber Air (*stored*)	
OY-UPS	Boeing 727-31C	Starair/UPS	
OY-UPT	Boeing 727-22C	Starair/UPS	

PH (Netherlands)

Reg.	Type	Owner or Operator	Notes
PH-AGA	Airbus A.310-203	K.L.M. *Rembrandt*	
PH-AGB	Airbus A.310-203	K.L.M. *Jeroen Bosch*	
PH-AGC	Airbus A.310-203	K.L.M. *Albert Cuyp*	
PH-AGD	Airbus A.310-203	K.L.M. *Marinus Ruppert*	
PH-AGE	Airbus A.310-203	Middle East Airlines	
PH-AGF	Airbus A.310-203	Middle East Airlines	
PH-AGG	Airbus A.310-203	K.L.M. *Vincent van Gogh*	
PH-AGH	Airbus A.310-203	K.L.M. *Pieter de Hoogh*	
PH-AGI	Airbus A.310-203	K.L.M. *Jan Toorop*	
PH-AGK	Airbus A.310-203	K.L.M. *Johannes Vermeer*	
PH-AHE	Boeing 757-27BER	Air Holland Charter	
PH-AHI	Boeing 757-27BER	Air Holland Charter	
PH-BDA	Boeing 737-306	K.L.M. *Willem Barentsz*	
PH-BDB	Boeing 737-306	K.L.M. *Olivier van Noort*	
PH-BDC	Boeing 737-306	K.L.M. *Cornelis De Houteman*	
PH-BDD	Boeing 737-306	K.L.M. *Anthony van Diemen*	
PH-BDE	Boeing 737-306	K.L.M. *Abel J. Tasman*	
PH-BDG	Boeing 737-306	K.L.M. *Michiel A. de Ruyter*	
PH-BDH	Boeing 737-306	K.L.M. *Petrus Plancius*	
PH-BDI	Boeing 737-306	K.L.M. *Maarten H. Tromp*	
PH-BDK	Boeing 737-306	K.L.M. *Jan H. van Linschoten*	
PH-BDL	Boeing 737-306	K.L.M. *Piet Heyn*	
PH-BDN	Boeing 737-306	K.L.M. *Willem van Ruysbroeck*	
PH-BDO	Boeing 737-306	K.L.M. *Jacob van Heemskerck*	
PH-BDP	Boeing 737-306	K.L.M. *Jacob Rogeveen*	
PH-BDR	Boeing 737-406	K.L.M. *Willem C. Schouten*	
PH-BDS	Boeing 737-406	K.L.M. *Jorris van Spilbergen*	
PH-BDT	Boeing 737-406	K.L.M. *Gerrit de Veer*	
PH-BDU	Boeing 737-406	K.L.M. *Marco Polo*	
PH-BDW	Boeing 737-406	K.L.M. *Leifur Eiriksson*	
PH-BDY	Boeing 737-406	K.L.M. *Vasco da Gama*	
PH-BDZ	Boeing 737-406	K.L.M. *Christophorus Columbus*	
PH-BFA	Boeing 747-406	K.L.M. *City of Atlanta*	
PH-BFB	Boeing 747-406	K.L.M. *City of Bangkok*	
PH-BFC	Boeing 747-406 (SCD)	K.L.M. *City of Calgary*	
PH-BFD	Boeing 747-406 (SCD)	K.L.M. *City of Dubai*	
PH-BFE	Boeing 747-406 (SCD)	K.L.M. *City of Melbourne*	
PH-BFF	Boeing 747-406 (SCD)	K.L.M. *City of Freetown*	
PH-BFG	Boeing 747-406	K.L.M. *City of Guayaquil*	
PH-BFH	Boeing 747-406 (SCD)	K.L.M. *City of Hong Kong*	
PH-BFI	Boeing 747-406 (SCD)	K.L.M. *City of Jakarta*	
PH-BFK	Boeing 747-406 (SCD)	K.L.M. *City of Karachi*	
PH-BFL	Boeing 747-406	K.L.M. *City of Lima*	
PH-BFM	Boeing 747-406 (SCD)	K.L.M. *City of Mexico*	
PH-BFN	Boeing 747-406	K.L.M. *City of Nairobi*	
PH-BFO	Boeing 747-406 (SCD)	K.L.M. *City of Orlando*	

Notes	Reg.	Type	Owner or Operator
	PH-BFP	Boeing 747-406 (SCD)	K.L.M. *City of Paramaribo*
	PH-BFR	Boeing 747-406 (SCD)	K.L.M. *City of Rio de Janiero*
	PH-BTA	Boeing 737-406	K.L.M. *Fernao Magalhaes*
	PH-BTB	Boeing 737-406	K.L.M. *Henry Hudson*
	PH-BTC	Boeing 737-406	K.L.M. *David Livingstone*
	PH-BTD	Boeing 737-306	K.L.M. *James Cook*
	PH-BTE	Boeing 737-306	K.L.M. *Roald Amundsen*
	PH-BTF	Boeing 737-406	K.L.M. *Alexander von Humboldt*
	PH-BTG	Boeing 737-406	K.L.M.
	PH-BUH	Boeing 747-306 (SCD)	K.L.M. *Dr Albert Plesman*
	PH-BUI	Boeing 747-306 (SCD)	K.L.M. *Wilbur Wright*
	PH-BUK	Boeing 747-306 (SCD)	K.L.M. *Louis Blériot*
	PH-BUL	Boeing 747-306 (SCD)	K.L.M. *Charles A. Lindbergh*
	PH-BUM	Boeing 747-306 (SCD)	K.L.M. *Charles E. Kingsford-Smith*
	PH-BUN	Boeing 747-306 (SCD)	K.L.M. *Anthony H. G. Fokker*
	PH-BUO	Boeing 747-306	K.L.M. *Missouri*
	PH-BUP	Boeing 747-306	K.L.M. *The Ganges*
	PH-BUR	Boeing 747-306	K.L.M. *The Indus*
	PH-BUU	Boeing 747-306 (SCD)	K.L.M. *Sir Frank Whittle*
	PH-BUV	Boeing 747-306 (SCD)	K.L.M. *Sir Geoffrey de Havilland*
	PH-BUW	Boeing 747-306 (SCD)	K.L.M. *Leonardo da Vinci*
	PH-CHB	F.28 Fellowship 4000	K.L.M. CityHopper *Birmingham*
	PH-CHD	F.28 Fellowship 4000	K.L.M. CityHopper *Maastricht*
	PH-CHF	F.28 Fellowship 4000	K.L.M. CityHopper *Guernsey*
	PH-CHN	F.28 Fellowship 4000	K.L.M. CityHopper *Belfast*
	PH-DDA	Douglas DC-3	Dutch Dakota Association
	PH-DDZ	Douglas DC-3	Dutch Dakota Association
	PH-DTA	Douglas DC-10-30	K.L.M. *Johann Sebastian Bach*
	PH-DTB	Douglas DC-10-30	K.L.M. *Ludwig van Beethoven*
	PH-DTC	Douglas DC-10-30	K.L.M. *Frédéric François Chopin*
	PH-DTD	Douglas DC-10-30	K.L.M. *Maurice Ravel*
	PH-DTL	Douglas DC-10-30	African Safari Airways
	PH-FWS	EMB-110P1 Bandeirante	Freeway Air
	PH-FWT	EMB-110P1 Bandeirante	Freeway Air
	PH-FXA	Dornier Do.228-202K	Flexair
	PH-HVF	Boeing 737-3K2	Transavia *Johan Cruijff*
	PH-HVJ	Boeing 737-3K2	Transavia *Nelli Cooman*
	PH-HVM	Boeing 737-3K2	Transavia
	PH-HVN	Boeing 737-3K2	Transavia
	PH-HVT	Boeing 737-3K2	Transavia
	PH-HVV	Boeing 737-3K2	Transavia
	PH-JDV	PA-42 Cheyenne III	BASE Business Airlines
	PH-KCA	McD Douglas MD-11	K.L.M. *Amy Johnson*
	PH-KCB	McD Douglas MD-11	K.L.M. *Maria Montessori*
	PH-KCC	McD Douglas MD-11	K.L.M. *Marie Curie*
	PH-KCD	McD Douglas MD-11	K.L.M. *Florence Nightingale*
	PH-KCE	McD Douglas MD-11	K.L.M. *Audrey Hepburn*
	PH-KCF	McD Douglas MD-11	K.L.M. *Annie Romein*
	PH-KFG	F.27 Friendship Mk 200	F.27 Friendship Association
	PH-KJA	BAe Jetstream 3108	BASE Business Airlines
	PH-KJB	BAe Jetstream 3108	BASE Business Airlines
	PH-KJG	BAe Jetstream 3102	BASE Airlines
	PH-KLC	Fokker 100	K.L.M. CityHopper
	PH-KLD	Fokker 100	K.L.M. CityHopper
	PH-KLE	Fokker 100	K.L.M. CityHopper
	PH-KLG	Fokker 100	K.L.M. CityHopper
	PH-KLH	Fokker 100	K.L.M. CityHopper
	PH-KLI	Fokker 100	K.L.M. CityHopper
	PH-KSA	SAAB SF.340B	K.L.M. CityHopper *Straatsburg*
	PH-KSB	SAAB SF.340B	K.L.M. CityHopper *Bristol*
	PH-KSC	SAAB SF.340B	K.L.M. CityHopper *Cardiff*
	PH-KSD	SAAB SF.340B	K.L.M. CityHopper *Neurenberg*
	PH-KSE	SAAB SF.340B	K.L.M. CityHopper *Southampton*
	PH-KSF	SAAB SF.340B	K.L.M. CityHopper *Basel*
	PH-KSG	SAAB SF.340B	K.L.M. CityHopper *Mulhouse*
	PH-KSH	SAAB SF.340B	K.L.M. CityHopper *Hamburg*
	PH-KSI	SAAB SF.340B	K.L.M. CityHopper *Eindhoven*
	PH-KSK	SAAB SF.340B	K.L.M. CityHopper *Rotterdam*
	PH-KSL	SAAB SF.340B	K.L.M. CityHopper *Luxembourg*
	PH-KSM	SAAB SF.340B	K.L.M. CityHopper *Malmoe*
	PH-KVA	Fokker 50	K.L.M. CityHopper *Bremen*
	PH-KVB	Fokker 50	K.L.M. CityHopper *Brussels*
	PH-KVC	Fokker 50	K.L.M. CityHopper *Stavanger*

Reg.	Type	Owner or Operator	Notes
PH-KVD	Fokker 50	K.L.M. CityHopper *Dusseldorf*	
PH-KVE	Fokker 50	K.L.M. CityHopper *Amsterdam*	
PH-KVF	Fokker 50	K.L.M. CityHopper *Parijs*	
PH-KVG	Fokker 50	K.L.M. CityHopper *Stuttgart*	
PH-KVH	Fokker 50	K.L.M. CityHopper *Hannover*	
PH-KVI	Fokker 50	K.L.M. CityHopper *Bordeaux*	
PH-KVK	Fokker 50	K.L.M. CityHopper *London*	
PH-MBP	Douglas DC-10-30CF	Martinair *Hong Kong*	
PH-MBT	Douglas DC-10-30CF	Martinair	
PH-MCA	Airbus A.310-203	K.L.M.	
PH-MCB	Airbus A.310-203CF	Martinair *Prins Maurits*	
PH-MCE	Boeing 747-21AC (SCD)	Martinair *Prins van Oranje*	
PH-MCF	Boeing 747-21AC (SCD)	Martinair *Prins Claus*	
PH-MCG	Boeing 767-31AER	Martinair *Prins Johan Friso*	
PH-MCH	Boeing 767-31AER	Martinair *Prins Constantijn*	
PH-MCI	Boeing 767-31AER	Martinair	
PH-MCL	Boeing 767-31AER	Martinair *Koningin Beatrix*	
PH-MCM	Boeing 767-31AER	Martinair	
PH-MCN	Boeing 747-228F	Martinair	
PH-MCO	Douglas DC-10-30	Martinair	
PH-MCP	McD Douglas MD-11CF	Martinair	
PH-MCR	McD Douglas MD-11CF	Martinair	
PH-MCS	McD Douglas MD-11CF	Martinair	
PH-MCT	McD Douglas MD-11F	Martinair	
PH-OZA	Boeing 737-3L9	Air Holland Charter	
PH-SDH	D.H.C.8-102 Dash Eight	Schreiner Airways	
PH-SDI	D.H.C.8-311A Dash Eight	Schreiner Airways/SABENA	
PH-SDJ	D.H.C.8-311A Dash Eight	Schreiner Airways/SABENA	
PH-SDM	D.H.C.8-311 Dash Eight	Schreiner Airways/SABENA	
PH-SDP	D.H.C.8-311 Dash Eight	Schreiner Airways/SABENA	
PH-SEZ	McD Douglas MD-82	Meridiana	
PH-TKA	Boeing 757-2K2ER	Transavia	
PH-TKB	Boeing 757-2K2ER	Transavia	
PH-TKC	Boeing 757-2K2ER	Transavia	
PH-TKD	Boeing 757-2K2ER	Transavia	
PH-TVH	Boeing 737-222	Transavia	
PH-TVP	Boeing 737-2K2	Transavia	
PH-TVR	Boeing 737-2K2	Transavia	
PH-TVS	Boeing 737-2K2	Transavia	
PH-TVU	Boeing 737-2K2	Transavia	
PH-TVX	Boeing 737-2K2	Transavia/K.L.M.	
PH-XLA	EMB-120RT Brasilia	Exel Commuter	
PH-XLB	EMB-120RT Brasilia	Exel Commuter	

Note: K.L.M. also operates Boeing 747-306, N1309E.

PK (Indonesia)

PK-GIA	Douglas DC-10-30	Garuda Indonesian Airways	
PK-GIB	Douglas DC-10-30	Garuda Indonesian Airways	
PK-GIC	Douglas DC-10-30	Garuda Indonesian Airways	
PK-GID	Douglas DC-10-30	Garuda Indonesian Airways	
PK-GIE	Douglas DC-10-30	Garuda Indonesian Airways	
PK-GIF	Douglas DC-10-30	Garuda Indonesian Airways	
PK-GIG	McD Douglas MD-11	Garuda Indonesian Airways	
PK-GII	McD Douglas MD-11	Garuda Indonesian Airways	
PK-GSA	Boeing 747-2U3B	Garuda Indonesian Airways	
PK-GSB	Boeing 747-2U3B	Garuda Indonesian Airways	
PK-GSC	Boeing 747-2U3B	Garuda Indonesian Airways	
PK-GSD	Boeing 747-2U3B	Garuda Indonesian Airways	
PK-GSE	Boeing 747-2U3B	Garuda Indonesian Airways	
PK-GSF	Boeing 747-2U3B	Garuda Indonesian Airways	
PK-PLR	L.100-30 Hercules	HeavyLift Cargo Airlines	

Note: MD-11s EI-CDI, EI-CDJ, EI-CDK, EI-CDL, EI-CDM and EI-CDN are also operated by Garuda.

PP (Brazil)

PP-VMA	Douglas DC-10-30	VARIG	
PP-VMB	Douglas DC-10-30	VARIG	
PP-VMD	Douglas DC-10-30	VARIG	

Notes	Reg.	Type	Owner or Operator
	PP-VMQ	Douglas DC-10-30	VARIG
	PP-VMT	Douglas DC-10-30F	VARIG Cargo
	PP-VMU	Douglas DC-10-30F	VARIG Cargo
	PP-VMV	Douglas DC-10-30	VARIG
	PP-VMW	Douglas DC-10-30	VARIG
	PP-VMX	Douglas DC-10-30	VARIG
	PP-VMY	Douglas DC-10-30	VARIG
	PP-VNA	Boeing 747-2L5B (SCD)	VARIG
	PP-VNB	Boeing 747-2L5B (SCD)	VARIG
	PP-VNC	Boeing 747-2L5B (SCD)	VARIG
	PP-VNH	Boeing 747-341 (SCD)	VARIG
	PP-VNI	Boeing 747-341 (SCD)	VARIG
	PP-VNN	Boeing 767-241ER	VARIG
	PP-VNO	Boeing 767-241ER	VARIG
	PP-VNP	Boeing 767-241ER	VARIG
	PP-VNQ	Boeing 767-241ER	VARIG
	PP-VNR	Boeing 767-241ER	VARIG
	PP-VNS	Boeing 767-241ER	VARIG
	PP-VOA	Boeing 747-341	VARIG
	PP-VOB	Boeing 747-341	VARIG
	PP-VOC	Boeing 747-341	VARIG
	PP-VOI	Boeing 767-341ER	VARIG
	PP-VOJ	Boeing 767-341ER	VARIG
	PP-VOK	Boeing 767-341ER	VARIG
	PP-VOL	Boeing 767-341ER	VARIG
	PP-VPG	Boeing 747-441	VARIG
	PP-VPH	Boeing 747-441	VARIG
	PP-VPI	Boeing 747-475	VARIG

RA (Russia)

All aircraft were originally operated by Aeroflot/Russia International using registrations with the country code CCCP. Some have now been transferred to other operators using the RA prefix leaving Aeroflot with a much smaller fleet. Those known to be with new airlines are shown with a code letter in parenthesis after the type. AF – AirFoyle, HV – HeavyLift/Volga Dnepr, H – HeavyLift, L – Aviompex, M – Bosna Air/VB-Air, T – Transaero, U – Moscow Airways.

Notes	Reg.	Type	Notes	Reg.	Type
	65014	Tu-134A		65666	Tu-134A
	65020	Tu-134A		65667	Tu-134A
	65024	Tu-134A		65669	Tu-134A
	65027	Tu-134A		65680	Tu-134A-3
	65035	Tu-134A		65681	Tu-134A
	65054	Tu-134A		65697	Tu-134A
	65064	Tu-134A		65703	Tu-134A
	65073	Tu-134A		65717	Tu-134A-3
	65087	Tu-134A		65730	Tu-134A
	65107	Tu-134A		65739	Tu-134A
	65119	Tu-134A		65758	Tu-134A
	65139	Tu-134A		65770	Tu-134A-3
	65141	Tu-134A		65771	Tu-134A
	65550	Tu-134A		65781	Tu-134A-3
	65552	Tu-134A-3		65782	Tu-134A
	65555	Tu-134A		65783	Tu-134A-3
	65557	Tu-134A-3		65784	Tu-134A-3
	65602	Tu-134		65785	Tu-134A-3
	65603	Tu-134		65786	Tu-134A-3
	65604	Tu-134		65794	Tu-134A
	65644	Tu-134		65796	Tu-134A
	65646	Tu-134A		65801	Tu-134A
	65647	Tu-134A		65835	Tu-134A
	65649	Tu-134A		65863	Tu-134A
	65650	Tu-134A		65864	Tu-134A
	65655	Tu-134A		65888	Tu-134A
	65656	Tu-134A		65894	Tu-134A
	65657	Tu-134A		65904	Tu-134A-3
	65658	Tu-134A		65905	Tu-134A-3
	65659	Tu-134A		65911	Tu-134A-3
	65660	Tu-134A		65912	Tu-134A-3
	65661	Tu-134A		65916	Tu-134A
	65665	Tu-134A		65919	Tu-134A

Reg.	Type	Notes	Reg.	Type	Notes
65921	Tu-134A-3		76836	IL-76TD	
65923	Tu-134A		76839	IL-76TD	
65926	Tu-134A				
65935	Tu-134A		82007	An-124 (AF)	
65939	Tu-134A		82008	An-124 (AF)	
65951	Tu-134A		82009	An-124	
65955	Tu-134A		82027	An-124 (AF)	
65956	Tu-134A		82033	An-124	
65965	Tu-134A		82042	An-124 (HV)	
65976	Tu-134A		82043	An-124 (HV)	
65978	Tu-134A-3		82044	An-124 (HV)	
			82045	An-124 (HV)	
73000	Boeing 737-2C9 (T)		82046	An-124 (HV)	
73001	Boeing 737-2C9 (T)				
76450	IL-76TD		85001	Tu-154	
76454	IL-76TD		85002	Tu-154	
76460	IL-76TD		85004	Tu-154	
76466	IL-76TD		85005	Tu-154	
76467	IL-76TD		85006	Tu-154	
76468	IL-76TD		85007	Tu-154	
76469	IL-76TD		85008	Tu-154	
76470	IL-76TD		85009	Tu-154	
76471	IL-76TD		85010	Tu-154	
76472	IL-76TD		85011	Tu-154	
76473	IL-76TD		85012	Tu-154	
76474	IL-76TD		85013	Tu-154	
76475	IL-76TD		85014	Tu-154	
76476	IL-76TD		85015	Tu-154	
76477	IL-76TD		85016	Tu-154	
76478	IL-76TD		85017	Tu-154	
76479	IL-76TD		85018	Tu-154	
76482	IL-76TD		85021	Tu-154	
76484	IL-76TD		85022	Tu-154	
76485	IL-76TD		85024	Tu-154	
76486	IL-76TD		85025	Tu-154	
76487	IL-76TD		85029	Tu-154	
76488	IL-76TD		85030	Tu-154	
76489	IL-76TD		85031	Tu-154	
76491	IL-76TD		85034	Tu-154	
76493	IL-76TD		85037	Tu-154	
76494	IL-76TD		85039	Tu-154	
76496	IL-76TD		85040	Tu-154	
76497	IL-76TD		85041	Tu-154	
76498	IL-76TD		85042	Tu-154	
76499	IL-76TD		85043	Tu-154	
76522	IL-76TD		85049	Tu-154	
76750	IL-76TD		85051	Tu-154	
76751	IL-76TD		85052	Tu-154	
76752	IL-76TD		85055	Tu-154	
76754	IL-76TD		85056	Tu-154	
76756	IL-76TD		85057	Tu-154	
76757	IL-76TD		85060	Tu-154A	
76758	IL-76TD (H)		85061	Tu-154A	
76761	IL-76TD		85062	Tu-154C	
76764	IL-76TD		85063	Tu-154C	
76777	IL-76TD		85064	Tu-154A	
76780	IL-76TD		85065	Tu-154A	
76781	IL-76TD		85066	Tu-154A	
76784	IL-76TD		85067	Tu-154C	
76785	IL-76TD		85068	Tu-154B	
76786	IL-76TD		85069	Tu-154A	
76787	IL-76TD		85070	Tu-154A	
76788	IL-76TD		85071	Tu-154A	
76789	IL-76TD		85072	Tu-154A	
76792	IL-76TD		85074	Tu-154A	
76795	IL-76TD		85075	Tu-154B	
76800	IL-76TD		85076	Tu-154A	
76801	IL-76TD		85078	Tu-154A	
76806	IL-76TD		85079	Tu-154A	
76812	IL-76TD		85080	Tu-154A	
76814	IL-76TD		85081	Tu-154C	
76834	IL-76TD		85082	Tu-154A	
76835	IL-76TD		85083	Tu-154A	

Notes	Reg.	Type	Notes	Reg.	Type
	85084	Tu-154A		85187	Tu-154B
	85085	Tu-154A		85188	Tu-154B
	85086	Tu-154A		85190	Tu-154B
	85087	Tu-154A		85191	Tu-154B
	85088	Tu-154A		85193	Tu-154B
	85089	Tu-154A		85195	Tu-154B
	85090	Tu-154A		85197	Tu-154B
	85091	Tu-154A		85198	Tu-154B
	85092	Tu-154B-1		85201	Tu-154B
	85094	Tu-154A		85202	Tu-154B
	85096	Tu-154B-2		85203	Tu-154B
	85098	Tu-154A		85204	Tu-154B
	85099	Tu-154A		85205	Tu-154B
	85100	Tu-154A		85206	Tu-154B
	85101	Tu-154A		85207	Tu-154B
	85103	Tu-154A		85210	Tu-154B
	85105	Tu-154A		85212	Tu-154B
	85106	Tu-154B-2		85213	Tu-154B
	85107	Tu-154A		85215	Tu-154B
	85108	Tu-154A		85216	Tu-154B
	85109	Tu-154B-1		85217	Tu-154B
	85110	Tu-154A		85219	Tu-154B
	85111	Tu-154A		85220	Tu-154B
	85112	Tu-154A		85223	Tu-154B
	85114	Tu-154A		85226	Tu-154B
	85115	Tu-154A		85227	Tu-154B
	85117	Tu-154A		85228	Tu-154B
	85119	Tu-154A		85229	Tu-154B-1
	85120	Tu-154B		85230	Tu-154B-1
	85123	Tu-154B		85233	Tu-154B-1
	85124	Tu-154B		85235	Tu-154B-1
	85129	Tu-154B		85236	Tu-154B-1
	85130	Tu-154B		85237	Tu-154B-1
	85131	Tu-154B		85238	Tu-154B-1
	85134	Tu-154B		85241	Tu-154B-1
	85135	Tu-154B		85242	Tu-154B-1
	85137	Tu-154B		85243	Tu-154B-1
	85138	Tu-154B		85244	Tu-154B-1
	85139	Tu-154B		85246	Tu-154B-1
	85140	Tu-154B		85247	Tu-154B-1
	85141	Tu-154B		85251	Tu-154B-1
	85142	Tu-154B		85252	Tu-154B-1
	85143	Tu-154B		85253	Tu-154B-1
	85145	Tu-154B		85255	Tu-154B-1
	85146	Tu-154B		85256	Tu-154B-1
	85148	Tu-154B		85257	Tu-154B-1
	85149	Tu-154B		85259	Tu-154B-1
	85150	Tu-154B		85261	Tu-154B-1
	85151	Tu-154B		85263	Tu-154B-1
	85152	Tu-154B		85264	Tu-154B-1
	85153	Tu-154B		85265	Tu-154B-1
	85155	Tu-154B		85266	Tu-154B-1
	85156	Tu-154B		85267	Tu-154B-1
	85157	Tu-154B		85268	Tu-154B-1
	85158	Tu-154B		85270	Tu-154B-1
	85160	Tu-154B		85271	Tu-154B-1
	85165	Tu-154B		85273	Tu-154B-1
	85167	Tu-154B		85275	Tu-154B-1
	85169	Tu-154B		85276	Tu-154B-1
	85170	Tu-154B		85277	Tu-154B-1
	85171	Tu-154B		85279	Tu-154B-1
	85172	Tu-154B		85280	Tu-154B-1
	85173	Tu-154B		85283	Tu-154B-1
	85174	Tu-154B		85284	Tu-154B-1
	85176	Tu-154B		85285	Tu-154B-1
	85178	Tu-154B		85287	Tu-154B-1
	85180	Tu-154B		85288	Tu-154B-1
	85181	Tu-154B		85289	Tu-154B-1
	85182	Tu-154B		85290	Tu-154B-1
	85183	Tu-154B		85291	Tu-154B-1
	85184	Tu-154B		85292	Tu-154B-2
	85185	Tu-154B		85293	Tu-154B-1
	85186	Tu-154B		85294	Tu-154B-1

Reg.	Type	Notes	Reg.	Type	Notes
85295	Tu-154B-1		85409	Tu-154B-2	
85296	Tu-154B-1		85410	Tu-154B-2	
85298	Tu-154B-1		85412	Tu-154B-2	
85299	Tu-154B-1		85414	Tu-154B-2	
85300	Tu-154B-2		85417	Tu-154B-2	
85301	Tu-154B-2		85418	Tu-154B-2	
85302	Tu-154B-2		85421	Tu-154B-2	
85303	Tu-154B-2		85425	Tu-154B-2	
85304	Tu-154B-2		85426	Tu-154B-2	
85305	Tu-154B-2		85427	Tu-154B-2	
85306	Tu-154B-2		85429	Tu-154B-2	
85307	Tu-154B-2		85430	Tu-154B-2	
85308	Tu-154B-2		85432	Tu-154B-2	
85309	Tu-154B-2		85434	Tu-154B-2	
85310	Tu-154B-2		85435	Tu-154B-2	
85311	Tu-154B-2		85436	Tu-154B-2	
85312	Tu-154B-2		85437	Tu-154B-2	
85313	Tu-154B-2		85439	Tu-154B-2	
85314	Tu-154B-2		85440	Tu-154B-2	
85315	Tu-154B-2		85441	Tu-154B-2	
85318	Tu-154B-2		85443	Tu-154B-2	
85319	Tu-154B-2		85444	Tu-154B-2	
85321	Tu-154B-2		85446	Tu-154B-2	
85323	Tu-154B-2		85448	Tu-154B-2	
85327	Tu-154B-2		85450	Tu-154B-2	
85328	Tu-154B-2		85451	Tu-154B-2	
85330	Tu-154B-2		85452	Tu-154B-2	
85333	Tu-154B-2		85453	Tu-154B-2	
85334	Tu-154B-2		85454	Tu-154B-2	
85335	Tu-154B-2		85455	Tu-154B-2	
85336	Tu-154B-2		85456	Tu-154B-2	
85337	Tu-154B-2		85457	Tu-154B-2	
85340	Tu-154B-2		85458	Tu-154B-2	
85341	Tu-154B-2		85461	Tu-154B-2	
85343	Tu-154B-2		85462	Tu-154B-2	
85346	Tu-154B-2		85463	Tu-154B-2	
85347	Tu-154B-2		85466	Tu-154B-2	
85348	Tu-154B-2		85467	Tu-154B-2	
85349	Tu-154B-2		85468	Tu-154B-2	
85351	Tu-154B-2		85469	Tu-154B-2	
85353	Tu-154B-2		85470	Tu-154B-2	
85354	Tu-154B-2		85471	Tu-154B-2	
85355	Tu-154B-2		85472	Tu-154B-2	
85357	Tu-154B-2		85475	Tu-154B-2	
85358	Tu-154B-2		85476	Tu-154B-2	
85359	Tu-154B-2		85477	Tu-154B-2	
85360	Tu-154B-2		85479	Tu-154B-2	
85361	Tu-154B-2		85480	Tu-154B-2	
85363	Tu-154B-2		85481	Tu-154B-2	
85365	Tu-154B-2		85485	Tu-154B-2	
85366	Tu-154B-2		85486	Tu-154B-2	
85367	Tu-154B-2		85487	Tu-154B-2	
85369	Tu-154B-2		85489	Tu-154B-2	
85371	Tu-154B-2		85491	Tu-154B-2	
85373	Tu-154B-2		85494	Tu-154B-2	
85374	Tu-154B-2		85495	Tu-154B-2	
85375	Tu-154B-2		85497	Tu-154B-2	
85376	Tu-154B-2		85498	Tu-154B-2	
85377	Tu-154B-2		85500	Tu-154B-2	
85380	Tu-154B-2		85501	Tu-154B-2	
85381	Tu-154B-2		85502	Tu-154B-2	
85383	Tu-154B-2		85503	Tu-154B-2	
85385	Tu-154B-2		85504	Tu-154B-2	
85386	Tu-154B-2		85505	Tu-154B-2	
85387	Tu-154B-2		85506	Tu-154B-2	
85388	Tu-154B-2		85508	Tu-154B-2	
85389	Tu-154B-2		85510	Tu-154B-2	
85390	Tu-154B-2		85512	Tu-154B-2	
85392	Tu-154B-2		85514	Tu-154B-2	
85400	Tu-154B-2		85518	Tu-154B-2	
85402	Tu-154B-2		85519	Tu-154B-2	
85404	Tu-154B-2		85520	Tu-154B-2	
85406	Tu-154B-2		85521	Tu-154B-2	

Notes	Reg.	Type	Notes	Reg.	Type
	85522	Tu-154B-2		85634	Tu-154M
	85523	Tu-154B-2		85635	Tu-154M
	85525	Tu-154C-2		85636	Tu-154M
	85526	Tu-154B-2		85637	Tu-154M
	85527	Tu-154B-2		85638	Tu-154M
	85529	Tu-154B-2		85639	Tu-154M
	85530	Tu-154B-2		85640	Tu-154M
	85534	Tu-154B-2		85641	Tu-154M
	85537	Tu-154B-2		85642	Tu-154M
	85540	Tu-154B-2		85643	Tu-154M
	85550	Tu-154B-2		85644	Tu-154M
	85551	Tu-154B-2		85645	Tu-154M
	85552	Tu-154B-2		85646	Tu-154M
	85553	Tu-154B-2		85647	Tu-154M
	85554	Tu-154B-2		85648	Tu-154M
	85555	Tu-154B-2		85649	Tu-154M
	85557	Tu-154B-2		85650	Tu-154M
	85559	Tu-154B-2		85651	Tu-154M
	85561	Tu-154B-2		85652	Tu-154M
	85562	Tu-154B-2		85653	Tu-154M
	85563	Tu-154B-2		85654	Tu-154M
	85564	Tu-154B-2		85655	Tu-154M
	85566	Tu-154B-2		85657	Tu-154M
	85567	Tu-154B-2		85658	Tu-154M
	85568	Tu-154B-2		85659	Tu-154M
	85570	Tu-154B-2		85660	Tu-154M
	85571	Tu-154B-2		85661	Tu-154M
	85572	Tu-154B-2		85662	Tu-154M
	85573	Tu-154B-2		85663	Tu-154M
	85574	Tu-154B-2		85665	Tu-154M
	85577	Tu-154B-2		85666	Tu-154M
	85579	Tu-154B-2		85667	Tu-154M
	85584	Tu-154B-2		85668	Tu-154M
	85585	Tu-154B-2		85669	Tu-154M
	85586	Tu-154B-2		85670	Tu-154M
	85587	Tu-154B-2		85671	Tu-154M
	85588	Tu-154B-2		85672	Tu-154M
	85590	Tu-154B-2		85675	Tu-154M
	85592	Tu-154B-2		85676	Tu-154M
	85594	Tu-154B-2		85677	Tu-154M
	85595	Tu-154B-2		85678	Tu-154M
	85596	Tu-154B-2		85679	Tu-154M
	85597	Tu-154B-2		85680	Tu-154M
	85600	Tu-154B-2		85681	Tu-154M
	85601	Tu-154B-2		85682	Tu-154M
	85602	Tu-154B-2		85683	Tu-154M
	85603	Tu-154B-2		85684	Tu-154M
	85604	Tu-154B-2		85685	Tu-154M
	85605	Tu-154B-2		85686	Tu-154M
	85606	Tu-154B-2		85687	Tu-154M
	85607	Tu-154B-2		85688	Tu-154M
	85609	Tu-154M		85689	Tu-154M
	85610	Tu-154M		85690	Tu-154M
	85612	Tu-154M		85692	Tu-154M
	85613	Tu-154M		85693	Tu-154M
	85614	Tu-154M		85694	Tu-154M
	85616	Tu-154M		85695	Tu-154M
	85617	Tu-154M		85697	Tu-154M
	85618	Tu-154M		85698	Tu-154M
	85619	Tu-154M		85699	Tu-154M
	85621	Tu-154M (M)		85702	Tu-154M
	85622	Tu-154M		85708	Tu-154M
	85623	Tu-154M		85712	Tu-154M
	85624	Tu-154M (M)		85713	Tu-154M
	85625	Tu-154M		85714	Tu-154M
	85626	Tu-154M		85718	Tu-154M
	85627	Tu-154M		85722	Tu-154M
	85628	Tu-154M		85723	Tu-154M
	85629	Tu-154M		85724	Tu-154M
	85630	Tu-154M (L)		85725	Tu-154M
	85631	Tu-154M (L)		85731	Tu-154M
	85632	Tu-154M		85750	Tu-154M
	85633	Tu-154M		85751	Tu-154M

Reg.	Type	Notes	Reg.	Type	Notes
85752	Tu-154M		86105	IL-86	
85758	Tu-154M		86106	IL-86	
85769	Tu-154M		86107	IL-86	
85770	Tu-154M		86108	IL-86	
85779	Tu-154M		86109	IL-86	
85783	Tu-154M		86110	IL-86	
85785	Tu-154M		86111	IL-86	
85786	Tu-154M		86112	IL-86	
85801	Tu-154M		86113	IL-86	
			86114	IL-86	
86000	IL-86		86115	IL-86	
86002	IL-86		86116	IL-86	
86003	IL-86		86119	IL-86	
86004	IL-86		86120	IL-86	
86005	IL-86		86121	IL-86	
86006	IL-86		86122	IL-86	
86007	IL-86		86123	IL-86	
86008	IL-86		86124	IL-86 (T)	
86009	IL-86		86138	IL-86	
86010	IL-86		86146	IL-86	
86011	IL-86		86147	IL-86	
86013	IL-86		86148	IL-86	
86014	IL-86		86149	IL-86	
86015	IL-86		86450	IL-62	
86017	IL-86		86451	IL-62	
86018	IL-86		86452	IL-62M	
86050	IL-86		86453	IL-62M	
86051	IL-86		86454	IL-62M	
86054	IL-86		86455	IL-62M	
86055	IL-86		86457	IL-62M	
86058	IL-86		86458	IL-62M	
86059	IL-86		86459	IL-62M	
86060	IL-86		86460	IL-62	
86061	IL-86		86461	IL-62	
86062	IL-86		86462	IL-62M	
86063	IL-86		86463	IL-62M	
86065	IL-86		86464	IL-62M	
86066	IL-86		86465	IL-62M	
86067	IL-86		86466	IL-62MK	
86068	IL-86		86468	IL-62MK	
86069	IL-86		86469	IL-62M	
86070	IL-86		86471	IL-62M	
86071	IL-86		86472	IL-62M	
86073	IL-86		86473	IL-62M	
86074	IL-86		86474	IL-62M	
86075	IL-86		86475	IL-62M	
86076	IL-86		86476	IL-62M	
86077	IL-86		86477	IL-62M	
86078	IL-86		86478	IL-62M	
86079	IL-86		86479	IL-62M	
86080	IL-86		86480	IL-62M	
86081	IL-86		86481	IL-62M	
86082	IL-86		86482	IL-62M	
86084	IL-86		86483	IL-62M	
86085	IL-86		86484	IL-62M	
86086	IL-86		86485	IL-62M	
86087	IL-86		86486	IL-62M	
86088	IL-86		86487	IL-62M	
86089	IL-86		86488	IL-62M	
86091	IL-86		86489	IL-62M	
86092	IL-86		86490	IL-62M	
86093	IL-86		86491	IL-62M	
86094	IL-86		86492	IL-62M	
86095	IL-86		86493	IL-62M	
86096	IL-86		86494	IL-62M	
86097	IL-86		86495	IL-62M	
86098	IL-86		86496	IL-62M	
86099	IL-86		86497	IL-62M	
86100	IL-86		86498	IL-62M	
86101	IL-86		86499	IL-62M	
86102	IL-86		86500	IL-62M	
86103	IL-86		86501	IL-62M	
86104	IL-86				

Notes	Reg.	Type	Notes	Reg.	Type
	86502	IL-62M		86623	IL-62M
	86503	IL-62M		86624	IL-62M
	86504	IL-62M		86649	IL-62
	86505	IL-62M		86650	IL-62
	86506	IL-62M		86652	IL-62
	86507	IL-62M		86653	IL-62
	86508	IL-62M		86654	IL-62
	86509	IL-62M		86655	IL-62
	86510	IL-62M		86656	IL-62M
	86511	IL-62M		86657	IL-62
	86512	IL-62M		86661	IL-62
	86514	IL-62M		86662	IL-62
	86515	IL-62M (U)		86663	IL-62
	86516	IL-62M		86664	IL-62
	86517	IL-62MK		86665	IL-62
	86518	IL-62M		86666	IL-62
	86519	IL-62M		86668	IL-62
	86520	IL-62MK		86669	IL-62
	86521	IL-62M		86672	IL-62
	86522	IL-62M		86673	IL-62M
	86523	IL-62M		86674	IL-62
	86524	IL-62M		86675	IL-62
	86527	IL-62MK		86677	IL-62
	86528	IL-62MK		86678	IL-62
	86530	IL-62MK		86680	IL-62
	86531	IL-62M		86681	IL-62
	86532	IL-62MK		86682	IL-62
	86533	IL-62M		86683	IL-62
	86535	IL-62M		86684	IL-62
	86536	IL-62M		86685	IL-62
	86537	IL-62M		86686	IL-62
	86538	IL-62M		86687	IL-62
	86539	IL-62MK		86689	IL-62
	86540	IL-62M		86690	IL-62
	86554	IL-62M		86691	IL-62
	86555	IL-62M		86692	IL-62M
	86558	IL-62M		86693	IL-62M
	86560	IL-62M		86695	IL-62
	86563	IL-62M		86696	IL-62
	86565	IL-62M		86697	IL-62
	86605	IL-62		86698	IL-62
	86606	IL-62		86699	IL-62
	86608	IL-62		86700	IL-62M
	86611	IL-62		86701	IL-62M
	86612	IL-62		86702	IL-62M
	86614	IL-62		86703	IL-62M
	86615	IL-62		86705	IL-62M
	86616	IL-62		86706	IL-62M
	86617	IL-62		86707	IL-62M
	86618	IL-62M		86708	IL-62MK
	86619	IL-62M		86709	IL-62MK
	86620	IL-62M		86710	IL-62MK
	86621	IL-62M		86711	IL-62M
	86622	IL-62M		86712	IL-62M

Note: Aeroflot also operates Airbus A.310-308s registered F-OGQQ, F-OGQR, FOGQS, F-OGQT and F-OGQU.

Notes	Reg.	Type	Owner or Operator

RP (Philippines)

RP-C5746	Boeing 747-212B	Philippine Airlines
RP-C5751	Boeing 747-4F6	Philippine Airlines
RP-C5752	Boeing 747-4F6	Philippine Airlines

Note: Philippine Airlines operates four Boeing 747-2F6Bs which retain their U.S. identities N741PR, N742PR, N743PR and N744PR, three 747-283Bs registered EI-BTS, EI-BWF and EI-BZA and two 747-211Bs registered N207AE and N208AE.

S2 (Bangladesh)

S2-ACO	Douglas DC-10-30	Bangladesh Biman *The City of Hazrat-Shah Makhdoom (R.A.)*	
S2-ACP	Douglas DC-10-30	Bangladesh Biman *The City of Dhaka*	
S2-ACQ	Douglas DC-10-30	Bangladesh Biman *The City of Hz Shah Jalal (R.A.)*	
S2-ACR	Douglas DC-10-30	Bangladesh Biman *The New Era*	
S2-ADA	Douglas DC-10-30	Bangladesh Biman	
S2-ADB	Douglas DC-10-30	Bangladesh Biman	

S5 (Slovenia)

S5-AAA	Airbus A.320-231	Adria Airways/Cretan Airlines
S5-AAB	Airbus A.320-231	Adria Airways/Cretan Airlines
S5-AAC	Airbus A.320-231	Adria Airways
S5-ABA	McD Douglas MD-82	Adria Airways
S5-ABB	McD Douglas MD-82	Adria Airways
S5-ABC	McD Douglas MD-82	Adria Airways
S5-ABD	McD Douglas MD-82	Adria Airways
S5-ABE	McD Douglas MD-81	Adria Airways
S5-ABF	Douglas DC-9-32	Adria Airways
S5-ABG	Douglas DC-9-33RC	Adria Airways
S5-ABH	Douglas DC-9-32	Adria Airways

S7 (Seychelles)

S7-AAQ	Boeing 767-35H	Air Europe SpA (*to be I-AEJD*)
S7-AAS	Boeing 767-2Q8ER	Air Seychelles *Aldabra*
S7-AAV	Boeing 767-35H	Air Europe SpA (*to be I-AEJE*)
S7-AAX	Boeing 757-28A	Air Seychelles *Aride*

SE (Sweden)

SE-CFP	Douglas DC-3	Flygande Veteraner *Fridtjof Viking*
SE-DAK	Douglas DC-9-41	S.A.S. *Ragnvald Viking*
SE-DAR	Douglas DC-9-41	S.A.S. *Agnar Viking*
SE-DAS	Douglas DC-9-41	S.A.S. *Garder Viking*
SE-DAU	Douglas DC-9-41	S.A.S. *Hadding Viking*
SE-DAW	Douglas DC-9-41	S.A.S. *Gotrik Viking*
SE-DAX	Douglas DC-9-41	S.A.S. *Helsing Viking*
SE-DBM	Douglas DC-9-41	S.A.S. *Ossur Viking*
SE-DBO	Douglas DC-9-21	S.A.S. *Siger Viking*
SE-DDP	Douglas DC-9-41	S.A.S. *Brun Viking*
SE-DDR	Douglas DC-9-41	S.A.S. *Atle Viking*
SE-DDS	Douglas DC-9-41	S.A.S. *Alrik Viking*
SE-DDT	Douglas DC-9-41	S.A.S. *Amund Viking*
SE-DEI	BAe 146-200QT	City Air Scandinavia/TNT
SE-DFR	McD Douglas MD-81	S.A.S. *Ingjald Viking*
SE-DFS	McD Douglas MD-82	S.A.S. *Gaut Viking*
SE-DFT	McD Douglas MD-82	S.A.S. *Assur Viking*
SE-DFY	McD Douglas MD-81	S.A.S. *Ottar Viking*
SE-DGA	F.28 Fellowship 1000	S.A.S. *Alf Viking*
SE-DGB	F.28 Fellowship 1000	S.A.S. *Brage Viking*
SE-DGC	F.28 Fellowship 1000	S.A.S. *Dag Viking*
SE-DGE	F.28 Fellowship 4000	S.A.S. *Erik Viking*
SE-DGF	F.28 Fellowship 4000	S.A.S. *Egil Viking*
SE-DGG	F.28 Fellowship 4000	S.A.S. *Gunnhild Viking*
SE-DGH	F.28 Fellowship 4000	S.A.S. *Hjalmar Viking*
SE-DGI	F.28 Fellowship 4000	S.A.S. *Ingeborg Viking*
SE-DGK	F.28 Fellowship 4000	S.A.S. *Knut Viking*
SE-DGL	F.28 Fellowship 4000	S.A.S. *Loke Viking*
SE-DGM	F.28 Fellowship 4000	S.A.S. *Hild Viking*
SE-DGN	F.28 Fellowship 4000	S.A.S. *Gunnar Viking*
SE-DGO	F.28 Fellowship 4000	S.A.S. *Odd Viking*
SE-DGP	F.28 Fellowship 4000	S.A.S. *Steinar Viking*
SE-DGR	F.28 Fellowship 4000	S.A.S. *Randver Viking*
SE-DGS	F.28 Fellowship 4000	S.A.S. *Sigrun Viking*
SE-DGT	F.28 Fellowship 4000	S.A.S. *Tola Viking*
SE-DGU	F.28 Fellowship 4000	S.A.S. *Ulfljot Viking*

Notes	Reg.	Type	Owner or Operator
	SE-DGX	F.28 Fellowship 4000	S.A.S. *Vemund Viking*
	SE-DHC	McD Douglas MD-83	Transwede
	SE-DHG	McD Douglas MD-87	Transwede
	SE-DHI	McD Douglas MD-87	Transwede
	SE-DHN	McD Douglas MD-83	Transwede
	SE-DHS	Douglas DC-10-10	Premair *Baloo*
	SE-DHT	Douglas DC-10-10	Premair *Dumbo*
	SE-DHU	Douglas DC-10-10	Premair *Bamse*
	SE-DHX	Douglas DC-10-10	(leased to Sun Country)
	SE-DHY	Douglas DC-10-10	Premair *Snoopy*
	SE-DHZ	Douglas DC-10-10	(leased to Sun Country)
	SE-DIA	McD Douglas MD-81	S.A.S. *Ulvrik Viking*
	SE-DIB	McD Douglas MD-87	S.A.S. *Varin Viking*
	SE-DIC	McD Douglas MD-87	S.A.S. *Grane Viking*
	SE-DIF	McD Douglas MD-87	S.A.S. *Hjorulv Viking*
	SE-DIH	McD Douglas MD-87	S.A.S. *Slagfinn Viking*
	SE-DII	McD Douglas MD-81	S.A.S. *Sigtrygg Viking*
	SE-DIK	McD Douglas MD-82	S.A.S. *Stenkil Viking*
	SE-DIL	McD Douglas MD-81	S.A.S. *Tord Viking*
	SE-DIM	BAe 146-300QT	Malmö Aviation/TNT
	SE-DIN	McD Douglas MD-81	S.A.S. *Eskil Viking*
	SE-DIP	McD Douglas MD-87	S.A.S. *Jarl Viking*
	SE-DIR	McD Douglas MD-81	S.A.S. *Nora Viking*
	SE-DIS	McD Douglas MD-81	S.A.S. *Sigmund Viking*
	SE-DIT	BAe 146-300QT	Malmö Aviation/TNT
	SE-DIU	McD Douglas MD-87	S.A.S. *Torsten Viking*
	SE-DIX	McD Douglas MD-81	S.A.S. *Adils Viking*
	SE-DIY	McD Douglas MD-81	S.A.S. *Albin Viking*
	SE-DIZ	McD Douglas MD-82	S.A.S. *Sigyn Viking*
	SE-DKO	Boeing 767-383ER	S.A.S. *Ingegerd Viking*
	SE-DKU	Boeing 767-383ER	S.A.S. *Tor Viking*
	SE-DKX	Boeing 767-383ER	S.A.S. *Sven Viking*
	SE-DLC	Douglas DC-9-41	Nordic East *City of Stockholm*
	SE-DLD	Boeing 737-205	Air One
	SE-DLP	Boeing 737-205	Nordic East *K4 Jaegaren*
	SE-DLS	McD Douglas MD-83	Transwede
	SE-DLU	McD Douglas MD-83	Transwede
	SE-DLV	McD Douglas MD-83	Transwede
	SE-DLX	McD Douglas MD-83	Transwede
	SE-DMA	McD Douglas MD-87	S.A.S. *Lage Viking*
	SE-DMB	McD Douglas MD-81	S.A.S. *Bjarne Viking*
	SE-DMD	McD Douglas MD-81	S.A.S. *Holmfrid Viking*
	SE-DME	McD Douglas MD-81	S.A.S. *Kristen Viking*
	SE-DNA	Boeing 737-59D	S.A.S. *Agne Viking*
	SE-DNB	Boeing 737-59D	S.A.S. *Birger Viking*
	SE-DND	Boeing 737-59D	S.A.S. *Disa Viking*
	SE-DNF	Boeing 737-5Q8	S.A.S. *Frode Viking*
	SE-DNG	Boeing 737-5Q8	S.A.S. *Godfred Viking*
	SE-DNH	Boeing 737-5Q8	S.A.S. *Helge Viking*
	SE-DNK	Boeing 737-59D	S.A.S. *Katrin Viking*
	SE-DNL	Boeing 737-59D	S.A.S. *Arnljot Viking*
	SE-DNM	Boeing 737-59D	S.A.S. *Hjoerdis Viking*
	SE-DOB	Boeing 767-383ER	S.A.S. *Helga Viking*
	SE-DOC	Boeing 767-383ER	S.A.S. *Gudrun Viking*
	SE-DPA	Boeing 737-33A	Falcon Cargo
	SE-DPB	Boeing 737-33A	Falcon Cargo
	SE-DPC	Boeing 737-33A	Falcon Cargo
	SE-DPH	McD Douglas MD-83	S.A.S.
	SE-DPI	McD Douglas MD-83	S.A.S.
	SE-DPN	Boeing 737-3G7	—
	SE-DPU	McD Douglas MD-83	Transwede
	SE-DRA	BAe 146-200	Malmö Aviation
	SE-DRB	BAe 146-200	Malmö Aviation
	SE-DRC	BAe 146-200	Malmö Aviation
	SE-DRD	BAe 146-200	Malmö Aviation
	SE-DUA	Fokker 100	Transwede
	SE-DUB	Fokker 100	Transwede
	SE-DUC	Fokker 100	Transwede
	SE-DUD	Fokker 100	Transwede
	SE-DUE	Fokker 100	Transwede
	SE-KBP	FH.227E Friendship	Sweden Airways
	SE-KGA	FH.227B Friendship	Sweden Airways
	SE-KGB	FH.227B Friendship	Sweden Airways

Reg.	Type	Owner or Operator	Notes
SE-LFA	Fokker 50	S.A.S. Commuter *Jorund*	
SE-LFB	Fokker 50	S.A.S. Commuter *Sture*	
SE-LFC	Fokker 50	S.A.S. Commuter *Ylva*	
SE-LFK	Fokker 50	S.A.S. Commuter *Alvar*	
SE-LFN	Fokker 50	S.A.S. Commuter *Edmund*	
SE-LFO	Fokker 50	S.A.S. Commuter *Folke*	
SE-LFP	Fokker 50	S.A.S. Commuter *Ingemar*	
SE-LFR	Fokker 50	S.A.S. Commuter *Vagn*	
SE-LFS	Fokker 50	S.A.S. Commuter *Vigge*	

SP (Poland)

Reg.	Type	Owner or Operator	Notes
SP-LCA	Tupolev Tu-154M	Polskie Linie Lotnicze (LOT)	
SP-LCB	Tupolev Tu-154M	LOT	
SP-LCC	Tupolev Tu-154M	LOT	
SP-LCD	Tupolev Tu-154M	LOT	
SP-LCE	Tupolev Tu-154M	LOT	
SP-LCF	Tupolev Tu-154M	LOT	
SP-LCG	Tupolev Tu-154M	LOT	
SP-LCH	Tupolev Tu-154M	LOT	
SP-LCI	Tupolev Tu-154M	LOT	
SP-LCK	Tupolev Tu-154M	LOT	
SP-LCL	Tupolev Tu-154M	LOT	
SP-LCM	Tupolev Tu-154M	LOT	
SP-LCN	Tupolev Tu-154M	LOT	
SP-LCO	Tupolev Tu-154M	LOT	
SP-LHA	Tupolev Tu-134A	LOT	
SP-LHB	Tupolev Tu-134A	LOT	
SP-LHC	Tupolev Tu-134A	LOT	
SP-LHD	Tupolev Tu-134A	LOT	
SP-LHE	Tupolev Tu-134A	LOT	
SP-LHF	Tupolev Tu-134A	LOT	
SP-LHG	Tupolev Tu-134A	LOT	
SP-LKA	Boeing 737-55D	LOT	
SP-LKB	Boeing 737-55D	LOT	
SP-LKC	Boeing 737-55D	LOT	
SP-LKD	Boeing 737-55D	LOT	
SP-LKE	Boeing 737-55D	LOT	
SP-LLA	Boeing 737-45D	LOT	
SP-LLB	Boeing 737-45D	LOT	
SP-LLC	Boeing 737-45D	LOT	
SP-LLD	Boeing 737-45D	LOT	
SP-LOA	Boeing 767-25DER	LOT *Gneizao*	
SP-LOB	Boeing 767-25DER	LOT *Kracow*	
SP-LPA	Boeing 767-35DER	LOT *Warszawa*	

ST (Sudan)

Reg.	Type	Owner or Operator	Notes
ST-AFA	Boeing 707-3J8C	Sudan Airways	
ST-AFB	Boeing 707-3J8C	Sudan Airways	
ST-AIX	Boeing 707-369C	Sudan Airways	
ST-AKW	Boeing 707-330C	Transarabian Air Transport	
ST-AMF	Boeing 707-321C	Transarabian Air Transport	
ST-NSR	Boeing 707-330B	Sudan Airways	

Note: Sudan Airways also operates an A.310-304 which retains the registration F-OGQN and named *Khartoum*. The airline also leases the A.310-304 F-GKTD.

SU (Egypt)

Reg.	Type	Owner or Operator	Notes
SU-AOU	Boeing 707-366C	EgyptAir Cargo *Khopho*	
SU-APD	Boeing 707-366C	EgyptAir *Khafrah*	
SU-AVX	Boeing 707-366C	EgyptAir *Tutankhamun*	
SU-AVY	Boeing 707-366C	EgyptAir *Akhenaton*	
SU-AVZ	Boeing 707-366C	EgyptAir *Mena*	
SU-BCB	Airbus A.300B4	EgyptAir *Osiris*	
SU-BCC	Airbus A.300B4	EgyptAir *Nout*	
SU-BDF	Airbus A.300B4	EgyptAir *Hathor*	
SU-BDG	Airbus A.300B4	EgyptAir *Aton*	
SU-BLM	Boeing 737-4Y0	Transmed Airlines	
SU-DAA	Boeing 707-351C	ZAS Airline of Egypt	
SU-DAC	Boeing 707-336C	ZAS Airline of Egypt	

Notes	Reg.	Type	Owner or Operator
	SU-DAL	McD Douglas MD-83	ZAS Airline of Egypt
	SU-DAM	McD Douglas MD-83	ZAS Airline of Egypt
	SU-DAO	McD Douglas MD-87	ZAS Airline of Egypt
	SU-DAR	Airbus A.300B4-203	ZAS Airline of Egypt
	SU-DAS	Airbus A.300B4-203	ZAS Airline of Egypt
	SU-GAH	Boeing 767-266ER	EgyptAir *Nefertiti*
	SU-GAI	Boeing 767-266ER	EgyptAir *Nefertari*
	SU-GAJ	Boeing 767-266ER	EgyptAir *Tiye*
	SU-GAL	Boeing 747-366 (SCD)	EgyptAir *Hatshepsut*
	SU-GAM	Boeing 747-366 (SCD)	EgyptAir *Cleopatra*
	SU-GAO	Boeing 767-366ER	EgyptAir *Ramses II*
	SU-GAP	Boeing 767-366ER	EgyptAir *Thutmosis III*
	SU-GAR	Airbus A.300-622R	EgyptAir *Zoser*
	SU-GAS	Airbus A.300-622R	EgyptAir *Cheops*
	SU-GAT	Airbus A.300-622R	EgyptAir *Chephren*
	SU-GAU	Airbus A.300-622R	EgyptAir *Mycerinus*
	SU-GAV	Airbus A.300-622R	EgyptAir *Menes*
	SU-GAW	Airbus A.300-622R	EgyptAir *Ahmuse*
	SU-GAX	Airbus A.300-622R	EgyptAir *Tut-Ankh-Amun*
	SU-GAY	Airbus A.300-622R	EgyptAir *Seti I*
	SU-GAZ	Airbus A.300-622R	EgyptAir
	SU-GBA	Airbus A.320-231	EgyptAir *Aswan*
	SU-GBB	Airbus A.320-231	EgyptAir *Luxor*
	SU-GBC	Airbus A.320-231	EgyptAir *Hurghada*
	SU-GBD	Airbus A.320-231	EgyptAir *Taba*
	SU-GBE	Airbus A.320-231	EgyptAir *El Alamein*
	SU-GBF	Airbus A.320-231	EgyptAir *Sharm El Sheikh*
	SU-GBG	Airbus A.320-231	EgyptAir *Saint Catherine*
	SU-OAA	Ilyushin IL-76TD	Cairo Aviation
	SU-OAB	Ilyushin IL-76TD	Cairo Aviation
	SU-RAA	Airbus A.320-231	Shorouk Air
	SU-RAB	Airbus A.320-231	Shorouk Air
	SU-RAC	Boeing 757-29J	Shorouk Air
	SU-RAD	Boeing 757-29J	Shorouk Air
	SU-RAE	Boeing 757-29JPF	Shorouk Air
	SU-RAF	Boeing 757-29JPF	Shorouk Air
	SU-RAG	Airbus A.320-231	Shorouk Air

SX (Greece)

	Reg.	Type	Owner or Operator
	SX-BAQ	McD Douglas MD-83	Venus Airlines
	SX-BAS	Airbus A.320-231	Cretan Airlines (S5-AAA)
	SX-BAT	Airbus A.320-231	Cretan Airlines (S5-AAB)
	SX-BCA	Boeing 737-284	Olympic Airways *Apollo*
	SX-BCB	Boeing 737-284	Olympic Airways *Hermes*
	SX-BCC	Boeing 737-284	Olympic Airways *Hercules*
	SX-BCD	Boeing 737-284	Olympic Airways *Hephaestus*
	SX-BCE	Boeing 737-284	Olympic Airways *Dionysus*
	SX-BCF	Boeing 737-284	Olympic Airways *Poseidon*
	SX-BCG	Boeing 737-284	Olympic Airways *Phoebus*
	SX-BCH	Boeing 737-284	Olympic Airways *Triton*
	SX-BCI	Boeing 737-284	Olympic Airways *Proteus*
	SX-BCK	Boeing 737-284	Olympic Airways *Nereus*
	SX-BCL	Boeing 737-284	Olympic Airways *Isle of Thassos*
	SX-BEB	Airbus A.300B4	Olympic Airways *Odysseus*
	SX-BEC	Airbus A.300B4	Olympic Airways *Achilleus*
	SX-BED	Airbus A.300B4	Olympic Airways *Telemachus*
	SX-BEE	Airbus A.300B4	Olympic Airways *Nestor*
	SX-BEF	Airbus A.300B4	Olympic Airways *Ajax*
	SX-BEG	Airbus A.300B4	Olympic Airways *Diomedes*
	SX-BEH	Airbus A.300B4	Olympic Airways *Pileus*
	SX-BEI	Airbus A.300B4	Olympic Airways *Neoptolemos*
	SX-BEK	Airbus A.300-605R	Olympic Airways *Macedonia*
	SX-BEL	Airbus A.300-605R	Olympic Airways
	SX-BEM	Airbus A.300-605R	Olympic Airways
	SX-BEN	Airbus A.300-605R	Olympic Airways
	SX-BKA	Boeing 737-484	Olympic Airways *Vergina*
	SX-BKB	Boeing 737-484	Olympic Airways *Olynthos*
	SX-BKC	Boeing 737-484	Olympic Airways *Philipoli*
	SX-BKD	Boeing 737-484	Olympic Airways *Amphipoli*
	SX-BKE	Boeing 737-484	Olympic Airways *Stagira*
	SX-BKF	Boeing 737-484	Olympic Airways *Dion*

Reg.	Type	Owner or Operator	Notes
SX-BKG	Boeing 737-484	Olympic Airways	
SX-CBA	Boeing 727-284	Olympic Airways *Mount Olympus*	
SX-CBB	Boeing 727-284	Olympic Airways *Mount Pindos*	
SX-CBC	Boeing 727-284	Olympic Airways *Mount Parnassus*	
SX-CBD	Boeing 727-284	Olympic Airways *Mount Helicon*	
SX-CBE	Boeing 727-284	Olympic Airways *Mount Athos*	
SX-CBF	Boeing 727-284	Olympic Airways *Mount Taygetus*	
SX-CBG	Boeing 727-230	Olympic Airways *Mount Menalon*	
SX-CBH	Boeing 727-230	Olympic Airways *Mount Vermio*	
SX-CBI	Boeing 727-230	Greek Government (VIP)	
SX-OAB	Boeing 747-284B	Olympic Airways *Olympic Eagle*	
SX-OAC	Boeing 747-212B	Olympic Airways *Olympic Spirit*	
SX-OAD	Boeing 747-212B	Olympic Airways *Olympic Flame*	
SX-OAE	Boeing 747-212B	Olympic Airways *Olympic Peace*	
SX-XXX	Airbus A.320-231	South East European Airlines	

TC (Turkey)

TC-ACA	Boeing 737-4Y0	Istanbul Airlines	
TC-ADA	Boeing 737-4Y0	Istanbul Airlines	
TC-AFB	Boeing 727-228	Istanbul Airlines	
TC-AFC	Boeing 727-228	Istanbul Airlines	
TC-AFK	Boeing 737-4Y0	Pegasus Airlines	
TC-AFM	Boeing 737-4Q8	Pegasus Airlines	
TC-AFN	Boeing 727-230	Istanbul Airlines	
TC-AFO	Boeing 727-230	Istanbul Airlines	
TC-AFP	Boeing 727-230	Istanbul Airlines	
TC-AFR	Boeing 727-230	Istanbul Airlines	
TC-AFT	Boeing 727-230	Istanbul Airlines	
TC-AGA	Boeing 737-4Y0	Istanbul Airlines	
TC-APA	Boeing 737-4S3	Istanbul Airlines	
TC-AVA	Boeing 737-4S3	Istanbul Airlines	
TC-AYA	Boeing 737-4Y0	Istanbul Airlines	
TC-AYZ	Boeing 737-4Y0	Istanbul Airlines	
TC-AZA	Boeing 737-4Y0	Istanbul Airlines	
TC-BIR	Boeing 737-3M8	Birgenair	
TC-CYO	Boeing 737-3H9	Bosphorus Airways	
TC-GRA	Tupolev Tu-154M	Greenair *Cappadocia*	
TC-GRB	Tupolev Tu-154M	Greenair *Perestroika*	
TC-GRC	Tupolev Tu-154M	Greenair *Fenerbahce*	
TC-GUL	Boeing 757-225	Birgenair	
TC-IHO	Boeing 727-230	Bosphorus Airways	
TC-IKO	Boeing 727-230	Bosphorus Airways	
TC-JAB	Douglas DC-9-32	Türk Hava Yollari (THY) *Bogazici*	
TC-JAD	Douglas DC-9-32	Türk Hava Yollari (THY) *Anadolu*	
TC-JAE	Douglas DC-9-32	Türk Hava Yollari (THY) *Trakya*	
TC-JAF	Douglas DC-9-32	Türk Hava Yollari (THY) *Ege*	
TC-JAG	Douglas DC-9-32	Türk Hava Yollari (THY) *Akdeniz*	
TC-JAK	Douglas DC-9-32	Türk Hava Yollari (THY) *Karadeniz*	
TC-JAL	Douglas DC-9-32	Türk Hava Yollari (THY) *Halic*	
TC-JBF	Boeing 727-2F2	Türk Hava Yollari (THY) *Adana*	
TC-JBG	Boeing 727-2F2	Türk Hava Yollari (THY) *Besparmak*	
TC-JBJ	Boeing 727-2F2	Türk Hava Yollari (THY) *Yaruvatan*	
TC-JBK	Douglas DC-9-32	Türk Hava Yollari (THY) *Aydin*	
TC-JBL	Douglas DC-9-32	Türk Hava Yollari (THY) *Gediz*	
TC-JBM	Boeing 727-2F2	Türk Hava Yollari (THY) *Menderes*	
TC-JCA	Boeing 727-2F2	Türk Hava Yollari (THY) *Edirne*	
TC-JCB	Boeing 727-2F2	Türk Hava Yollari (THY) *Kars*	
TC-JCD	Boeing 727-2F2	Türk Hava Yollari (THY) *Sinop*	
TC-JCE	Boeing 727-2F2	Türk Hava Yollari (THY) *Hatay*	
TC-JCK	Boeing 727-243	Türk Hava Yollari (THY) *Erciyes*	
TC-JCL	Airbus A.310-203	Türk Hava Yollari (THY) *Seyhan*	
TC-JCM	Airbus A.310-203	Türk Hava Yollari (THY) *Ceyhan*	
TC-JCN	Airbus A.310-203	Türk Hava Yollari (THY) *Dicle*	
TC-JCO	Airbus A.310-203	Türk Hava Yollari (THY) *Firat*	
TC-JCR	Airbus A.310-203	Türk Hava Yollari (THY) *Kizilirmak*	
TC-JCS	Airbus A.310-203	Türk Hava Yollari (THY) *Yesilirmak*	
TC-JCU	Airbus A.310-203	Türk Hava Yollari (THY) *Sakarya*	
TC-JCV	Airbus A.310-304	Türk Hava Yollari (THY) *Aras*	
TC-JCY	Airbus A.310-304	Türk Hava Yollari (THY) *Coruh*	
TC-JCZ	Airbus A.310-304	Türk Hava Yollari (THY) *Ergene*	
TC-JDA	Airbus A.310-304ET	Türk Hava Yollari (THY) *Aksu*	
TC-JDB	Airbus A.310-304ET	Türk Hava Yollari (THY) *Goksu*	

Notes	Reg.	Type	Owner or Operator
	TC-JDC	Airbus A.310-304ET	Türk Hava Yollari (THY) *Meric*
	TC-JDD	Airbus A.310-304ET	Türk Hava Yollari (THY) *Dalaman*
	TC-JDE	Boeing 737-4Y0	Türk Hava Yollari (THY) *Kemer*
	TC-JDF	Boeing 737-4Y0	Türk Hava Yollari (THY) *Ayvalik*
	TC-JDG	Boeing 737-4Y0	Türk Hava Yollari (THY) *Marmaris*
	TC-JDH	Boeing 737-4Y0	Türk Hava Yollari (THY) *Amasra*
	TC-JDI	Boeing 737-4Q8	Türk Hava Yollari (THY)
	TC-JDJ	Airbus A.340-311	Türk Hava Yollari (THY) *Istanbul*
	TC-JDK	Airbus A.340-311	Türk Hava Yollari (THY)
	TC-JDT	Boeing 737-4Y0	Türk Hava Yollari (THY) *Istanbul*
	TC-JDU	Boeing 737-5Y0	Türk Hava Yollari (THY) *Bursa*
	TU-JDV	Boeing 737-5Y0	Türk Hava Yollari (THY) *Trabzon*
	TC-JDY	Boeing 737-4Y0	Türk Hava Yollari (THY) *Ankara*
	TC-JDZ	Boeing 737-4Y0	Türk Hava Yollari (THY) *Izmir*
	TC-JEA	Boeing 737-42J	Türk Hava Yollari (THY)
	TC-JEC	Boeing 727-228	Türk Hava Yollari (THY) *Yesilada*
	TC-JED	Boeing 737-4Q8	Türk Hava Yollari (THY) *Bodrum*
	TC-JEE	Boeing 737-4Q8	Türk Hava Yollari (THY) *Cesme*
	TC-JEF	Boeing 737-4Q8	Türk Hava Yollari (THY)
	TC-JEG	Boeing 737-4Q8	Türk Hava Yollari (THY)
	TC-JEH	Boeing 737-4Q8	Türk Hava Yollari (THY)
	TC-JEI	Boeing 737-4Q8	Türk Hava Yollari (THY)
	TC-JEJ	Boeing 737-4Q8	Türk Hava Yollari (THY)
	TC-JEK	Boeing 737-4Q8	Türk Hava Yollari (THY)
	TC-JEL	Boeing 737-4Q8	Türk Hava Yollari (THY)
	TC-JEM	Boeing 737-4Q8	Türk Hava Yollari (THY)
	TC-JER	Boeing 737-4Y0	Türk Hava Yollari (THY)
	TC-JES	Boeing 737-4Y0	Türk Hava Yollari (THY)
	TC-JET	Boeing 737-4Y0	Türk Hava Yollari (THY) *Canakkale*
	TC-JEU	Boeing 737-4Y0	Türk Hava Yollari (THY) *Samsun*
	TC-JEV	Boeing 737-4Y0	Türk Hava Yollari (THY)
	TC-JEY	Boeing 737-4Y0	Türk Hava Yollari (THY) *Side*
	TC-JEZ	Boeing 737-4Y0	Türk Hava Yollari (THY) *Bergama*
	TC-JFA	Boeing 727-264	Türk Hava Yollari (THY) *Ortaköy*
	TC-JFB	Boeing 727-264	Türk Hava Yollari (THY) *Vaniköy*
	TC-JUR	Boeing 737-205	Sultan Air
	TC-MAB	Douglas DC-8-61	Birgenair
	TC-MIO	Boeing 737-3H9	Bosphorus Airways *Kaan*
	TC-ONA	Airbus A.320-211	Onur Air
	TC-ONB	Airbus A.320-211	Onur Air *Ertug*
	TC-ONC	Airbus A.320-211	Onur Air *Aydin-Baf*
	TC-OND	Airbus A.320-211	Onur Air *Yeditepe*
	TC-RTU	McD Douglas MD-83	TUR European Airways
	TC-RUT	Boeing 727-230	TUR European Airways
	TC-SUN	Boeing 737-3Y0	Sun Express
	TC-SUP	Boeing 737-3Y0	Sun Express
	TC-SUR	Boeing 737-3Y0	Sun Express
	TC-SUS	Boeing 737-430	Sun Express
	TC-TCA	Boeing 727-230	TUR European Airways
	TC-TCB	Boeing 727-230	TUR European Airways
	TC-TRU	McD Douglas MD-83	TUR European Airways
	TC-TUR	Boeing 727-230	TUR European Airways
	TC-VAA	Boeing 737-248	Sultan Air *Kanuni Sultan Sueleyman*
	TC-VAB	Boeing 737-248	Sultan Air

TF (Iceland)

	TF-ABD	Boeing 737-204	Atlanta Icelandic
	TF-ABF	Boeing 737-205	Atlanta Icelandic
	TF-ABH	Boeing 737-222	Atlanta Icelandic
	TF-ABJ	Boeing 737-201C	Atlanta Icelandic
	TF-ABR	Boeing 747-133	Atlanta Icelandic
	TF-ABT	Boeing 737-205C	Atlanta Icelandic/Finnair Cargo *Spirit of Nome 1924 Alaska*
	TF-FIA	Boeing 737-408	Icelandair *Aldis*
	TF-FIB	Boeing 737-408	Icelandair *Eydis*
	TF-FIC	Boeing 737-408	Icelandair *Vedis*
	TF-FID	Boeing 737-408	Icelandair *Heiddis*
	TF-FIH	Boeing 757-208ER	Icelandair *Hafdis*
	TF-FII	Boeing 757-208ER	Icelandair *Fanndis*
	TF-FIJ	Boeing 757-208ER	Icelandair *Svandis*
	TF-FIK	Boeing 757-236	Icelandiar
	TF-FIR	Fokker 50	Icelandair *Asdis*

Reg.	Type	Owner or Operator	Notes
TF-FIS	Fokker 50	Icelandair *Sigdis*	
TF-FIT	Fokker 50	Icelandair *Freydis*	
TF-FIU	Fokker 50	Icelandair *Valdis*	

TJ (Cameroon)

TJ-CAB	Boeing 747-2H7B (SCD)	Cameroon Airlines *Mont Cameroun*

TR (Gabon)

Note: Air Gabon operates Boeing 747-2Q2B F-ODJG for which the registration TR-LXK has been reserved.

TS (Tunisia)

TS-IMA	Airbus A.300B4	Tunis-Air *Amilcar*
TS-IMB	Airbus A.320-211	Tunis-Air *Fahrat Hached*
TS-IMC	Airbus A.320-211	Tunis-Air *7 Novembre*
TS-IMD	Airbus A.320-211	Tunis-Air *Khereddine*
TS-IME	Airbus A.320-211	Tunis-Air *Tabarka*
TS-IMF	Airbus A.320-211	Tunis-Air *Jerba*
TS-IMG	Airbus A.320-211	Tunis-Air
TS-IMH	Airbus A.320-211	Tunis-Air
TS-IOC	Boeing 737-2H3	Tunis-Air *Salammbo*
TS-IOD	Boeing 737-2H3C	Tunis-Air *Bulla Regia*
TS-IOE	Boeing 737-2H3	Tunis-Air *Zarzis*
TS-IOF	Boeing 737-2H3	Tunis-Air *Sousse*
TS-IOG	Boeing 737-5H3	Tunis-Air *Sfax*
TS-IOH	Boeing 737-5H3	Tunis-Air *Hammamet*
TS-IOI	Boeing 737-5H3	Tunis-Air
TS-JHN	Boeing 727-2H3	Tunis-Air *Carthago*
TS-JHQ	Boeing 727-2H3	Tunis-Air *Tozeur-Nefta*
TS-JHR	Boeing 727-2H3	Tunis-Air *Bizerte*
TS-JHS	Boeing 727-2H3	Tunis-Air *Kairouan*
TS-JHT	Boeing 727-2H3	Tunis-Air *Sidi Bousaid*
TS-JHU	Boeing 727-2H3	Tunis-Air *Hannibal*
TS-JHW	Boeing 727-2H3	Tunis-Air *Ibn Khaldoun*

TU (Ivory Coast)

TU-TAC	Airbus A.310-304	Air Afrique
TU-TAD	Airbus A.310-304	Air Afrique
TU-TAE	Airbus A.310-304	Air Afrique
TU-TAF	Airbus A.310-304	Air Afrique
TU-TAG	Airbus A.310-304	Air Afrique
TU-TAL	Douglas DC-10-30	Air Afrique *Libreville*
TU-TAM	Douglas DC-10-30	Air Afrique *Cotonou*
TU-TAN	Douglas DC-10-30	Air Afrique *Niamey*
TU-TAO	Airbus A.300B4-203	Air Afrique *Nouackchott*
TU-TAS	Airbus A.300B4-203	Air Afrique *Bangui*
TU-TAT	Airbus A.300B4-203	Air Afrique

UK (Uzbekistan)

The following are operated by Uzbekistan Airways with registrations prefixed by UK.

76351	IL-76TD
76358	IL-76TD
76359	IL-76TD
76442	IL-76TD
76447	IL-76TD
76448	IL-76TD
76449	IL-76TD
76793	IL-76TD
76811	IL-76TD
76813	IL-76TD
76824	IL-76TD
85050	Tu-154B
85189	Tu-154B
85245	Tu-154B-1
85248	Tu-154B-1
85249	Tu-154B-1

Notes	Reg.	Type	Owner or Operator
	85272	Tu-154B-1	
	85286	Tu-154B-1	
	85322	Tu-154B-2	
	85344	Tu-154B-2	
	85356	Tu-154B-2	
	85370	Tu-154B-2	
	85397	Tu-154B-2	
	85398	Tu-154B-2	
	85401	Tu-154B-2	
	85416	Tu-154B-2	
	85423	Tu-154B-2	
	85433	Tu-154B-2	
	85438	Tu-154B-2	
	85459	Tu-154B-2	
	85575	Tu-154B-2	
	85578	Tu-154B-2	
	85611	Tu-154M	
	85711	Tu-154M	
	85764	Tu-154M	
	85776	Tu-154M	
	86012	IL-86	
	86016	IL-86	
	86052	IL-86	
	86053	IL-86	
	86056	IL-86	
	86057	IL-86	
	86064	IL-86	
	86072	IL-86	
	86083	IL-86	
	86090	IL-86	
	86534	IL-62M	
	86569	IL-62M	
	86573	IL-62M	
	86574	IL-62M	
	86575	IL-62M	
	86576	IL-62M	
	86577	IL-62M	
	86578	IL-62M	
	86610	IL-62M	
	86659	IL-62M	
	86704	IL-62M	
	86933	IL-62MK	
	86934	IL-62MK	

Note: Uzbekistan Airways also operates two Airbus A.310-324S registered F-OGQY and F-OGQZ.

UR (Ukraine)

UR-GAA	Boeing 737-4Y0	Ukraine International	
UR-GAB	Boeing 737-4Y0	Ukraine International	

The following are operated by Air Ukraine with registrations prefixed by UR.

65037	Tu-134A	
65048	Tu-134A-3	
65073	Tu-134A	
65076	Tu-134A-3	
65077	Tu-134A-3	
65089	Tu-134A	
65134	Tu-134A-3	
65135	Tu-134A-3	
65757	Tu-134A-3	
65761	Tu-134A	
65764	Tu-134A-3	
65765	Tu-134A	
65790	Tu-134A-3	
65841	Tu-134A	
65852	Tu-134A	
65864	Tu-134A	
76398	IL-76TD	
76707	IL-76TD	
85116	Tu-154A	
85132	Tu-154B	
85154	Tu-154B	
85179	Tu-154B	

Reg.	Type	Owner or Operator	Notes
85218	Tu-154B		
85232	Tu-154B-1		
85316	Tu-154B-2		
85350	Tu-154B-2		
85362	Tu-154B-2		
85368	Tu-154B-2		
85379	Tu-154B-2		
85395	Tu-154B-2		
85399	Tu-154B-2		
85424	Tu-154B-2		
85445	Tu-154B-2		
85460	Tu-154B-2		
85482	Tu-154B-2		
85499	Tu-154B-2		
85513	Tu-154B-2		
85526	Tu-154B-2		
85535	Tu-154B-2		
85700	Tu-154M		
85701	Tu-154M		
85707	Tu-154M		
85710	Tu-154M		
86132	IL-62M		
86133	IL-62M		
86134	IL-62M		
86135	IL-62M		
86580	IL-62M		
86581	IL-62M		
86582	IL-62M		

V2 (Antigua)

Note: Seagreen Air Transport operates two Boeing 707s registered N14AZ and N21AZ.

V5 (Namibia)

V5-SPF	Boeing 747SP-44	Air Namibia	

V8 (Brunei)

V8-HM1	Airbus A.310-304	Brunei Royal Flight	
V8-RBA	Boeing 757-2M6ER	Royal Brunei Airlines	
V8-RBB	Boeing 757-2M6ER	Royal Brunei Airlines	
V8-RBC	Boeing 757-2M6ER	Royal Brunei Airlines	
V8-RBE	Boeing 767-33AER	Royal Brunei Airlines	
V8-RBF	Boeing 767-33AER	Royal Brunei Airlines	
V8-RBG	Boeing 767-33AER	Royal Brunei Airlines	
V8-RBH	Boeing 767-33AER	Royal Brunei Airlines	
V8-RBJ	Boeing 767-33AER	Royal Brunei Airlines	
V8-RBK	Boeing 767-33AER	Royal Brunei Airlines	

VH (Australia)

VH-EBQ	Boeing 747-238B	QANTAS Airways City of Bunbury	
VH-EBR	Boeing 747-238B	QANTAS Airways City of Mt Gambier	
VH-EBS	Boeing 747-238B	QANTAS Airways City of Broken Hill	
VH-EBT	Boeing 747-338	QANTAS Airways City of Wagga Wagga	
VH-EBU	Boeing 747-338	QANTAS Airways City of Warrnambool	
VH-EBV	Boeing 747-338	QANTAS Airways Geraldton	
VH-EBW	Boeing 747-338	QANTAS Airways City of Tamworth	
VH-EBX	Boeing 747-338	QANTAS Airways City of Wodonga	
VH-EBY	Boeing 747-338	QANTAS Airways City of Mildura	
VH-OJA	Boeing 747-438	QANTAS Airways City of Canberra	
VH-OJB	Boeing 747-438	QANTAS Airways City of Sydney	
VH-OJC	Boeing 747-438	QANTAS Airways City of Melbourne	
VH-OJD	Boeing 747-438	QANTAS Airways City of Brisbane	
VH-OJE	Boeing 747-438	QANTAS Airways City of Adelaide	
VH-OJF	Boeing 747-438	QANTAS Airways City of Perth	
VH-OJG	Boeing 747-438	QANTAS Airways City of Hobart	
VH-OJH	Boeing 747-438	QANTAS Airways City of Darwin	
VH-OJI	Boeing 747-438	QANTAS Airways Longreach	
VH-OJJ	Boeing 747-438	QANTAS Airways Winton	

Notes	Reg.	Type	Owner or Operator
	VH-OJK	Boeing 747-438	QANTAS Airways *City of Newcastle*
	VH-OJL	Boeing 747-438	QANTAS Airways *City of Sale*
	VH-OJM	Boeing 747-438	QANTAS Airways *City of Gosford*
	VH-OJN	Boeing 747-438	QANTAS Airways *City of Dubbo*
	VH-OJO	Boeing 747-438	QANTAS Airways *City of Toowoomba*
	VH-OJP	Boeing 747-438	QANTAS Airways *City of Albury*
	VH-OJQ	Boeing 747-438	QANTAS Airways *City of Mandurah*
	VH-OJR	Boeing 747-438	QANTAS Airways *City of Bathurst*

VR-H (Hong Kong)

	VR-HIA	Boeing 747-267B	Cathay Pacific Airways
	VR-HIB	Boeing 747-267B	Cathay Pacific Airways
	VR-HIC	Boeing 747-267B	Cathay Pacific Airways
	VR-HID	Boeing 747-267B	Cathay Pacific Airways
	VR-HIE	Boeing 747-267B	Cathay Pacific Airways
	VR-HIF	Boeing 747-267B	Cathay Pacific Airways
	VR-HIH	Boeing 747-267B (SCD)	Cathay Pacific Cargo
	VR-HII	Boeing 747-367	Cathay Pacific Airways
	VR-HIJ	Boeing 747-367	Cathay Pacific Airways
	VR-HIK	Boeing 747-367	Cathay Pacific Airways
	VR-HKG	Boeing 747-267B	Cathay Pacific Airways
	VR-HKM	Boeing 747-132F	Air Hong Kong
	VR-HKN	Boeing 747-132F	Air Hong Kong
	VR-HOL	Boeing 747-367	Cathay Pacific Airways
	VR-HOM	Boeing 747-367	Cathay Pacific Airways
	VR-HON	Boeing 747-367	Cathay Pacific Airways
	VR-HOO	Boeing 747-467	Cathay Pacific Airways
	VR-HOP	Boeing 747-467	Cathay Pacific Airways
	VR-HOR	Boeing 747-467	Cathay Pacific Airways
	VR-HOS	Boeing 747-467	Cathay Pacific Airways
	VR-HOT	Boeing 747-467	Cathay Pacific Airways
	VR-HOU	Boeing 747-467	Cathay Pacific Airways
	VR-HOV	Boeing 747-467	Cathay Pacific Airways
	VR-HOW	Boeing 747-467	Cathay Pacific Airways
	VR-HOX	Boeing 747-467	Cathay Pacific Airways
	VR-HOY	Boeing 747-467	Cathay Pacific Airways
	VR-HOZ	Boeing 747-467	Cathay Pacific Airways
	VR-HUA	Boeing 747-467	Cathay Pacific Airways
	VR-HUB	Boeing 747-467	Cathay Pacific Airways
	VR-HUD	Boeing 747-467	Cathay Pacific Airways
	VR-HUE	Boeing 747-467	Cathay Pacific Airways
	VR-HUF	Boeing 747-467	Cathay Pacific Airways
	VR-HUG	Boeing 747-467	Cathay Pacific Airways
	VR-HUH	Boeing 747-467	Cathay Pacific Airways
	VR-HUJ	Boeing 747-467F	Cathay Pacific Airways
	VR-HVX	Boeing 747-267F (SCD)	Cathay Pacific Airways
	VR-HVY	Boeing 747-236F (SCD)	Cathay Pacific Airways *Hong Kong Jumbo*
	VR-HVZ	Boeing 747-267F (SCD)	Cathay Pacific Airways

VT (India)

	VT-EBE	Boeing 747-237B	Air-India *Shahjehan*
	VT-EBN	Boeing 747-237B	Air-India *Rajendra Chola*
	VT-EDU	Boeing 747-237B	Air-India *Akbar*
	VT-EFJ	Boeing 747-237B	Air-India *Chandragupta*
	VT-EFU	Boeing 747-237B	Air-India *Krishna Deva Raya*
	VT-EGA	Boeing 747-237B	Air-India *Samudra Gupta*
	VT-EGB	Boeing 747-237B	Air-India *Mahendra Varman*
	VT-EGC	Boeing 747-237B	Air-India *Harsha Vardhana*
	VT-EJG	Airbus A.310-304	Air-India *Vamuna*
	VT-EJH	Airbus A.310-304	Air-India *Tista*
	VT-EJI	Airbus A.310-304	Air-India *Saraswati*
	VT-EJJ	Airbus A.310-304	Air-India *Beas*
	VT-EJK	Airbus A.310-304	Air-India *Gomti*
	VT-EJL	Airbus A.310-304	Air-India *Sabarmati*
	VT-ENQ	Boeing 747-212B	Air-India *Himalaya*
	VT-EPW	Boeing 747-337 (SCD)	Air-India *Shivaji*
	VT-EPX	Boeing 747-337 (SCD)	Air-India *Narasimha Varman*
	VT-EQS	Airbus A.310-304	Air-India *Krishna*
	VT-EQT	Airbus A.310-304	Air-India *Narmada*
	VT-ESM	Boeing 747-437	Air-India

Reg.	Type	Owner or Operator	Notes
VT-ESN	Boeing 747-437	Air-India	
VT-ESO	Boeing 747-437	Air-India	
VT-ESP	Boeing 747-437	Air-India	

Note: Air-India Cargo operates Douglas DC-8s and Boeing 747s on lease from various airlines.

XA (Mexico)

XA-AMR	Douglas DC-10-30	Aeromexico	
XA-RIY	Douglas DC-10-30	Aeromexico *Jose Marie Morelos*	

Note: Aeromexico also operates DC-10-30s N8228P *Castillo de Chapultepec* and N417DG *Ciudad de Mexico.*

YA (Afghanistan)

YA-FAX	Boeing 727-228	Ariana Afghan Airlines	
YA-FAY	Boeing 727-228	Ariana Afghan Airlines	
YA-FAZ	Boeing 727-228	Ariana Afghan Airlines	

YI (Iraq)

YI-AGE	Boeing 707-370C	Iraqi Airways	
YI-AGF	Boeing 707-370C	Iraqi Airways	
YI-AGG	Boeing 707-370C	Iraqi Airways	
YI-AGK	Boeing 727-270	Iraqi Airways *Ninevah*	
YI-AGL	Boeing 727-270	Iraqi Airways *Basrah*	
YI-AGM	Boeing 727-270	Iraqi Airways *Al Habbania*	
YI-AGN	Boeing 747-270C (SCD)	Iraqi Airways *Tigris*	
YI-AGO	Boeing 747-270C (SCD)	Iraqi Airways *Euphrates*	
YI-AGP	Boeing 747-270C (SCD)	Iraqi Airways *Shat-al-Arab*	
YI-AGQ	Boeing 727-270	Iraqi Airways *Ataameem*	
YI-AGR	Boeing 727-270	Iraqi Airways *Babylon*	
YI-AGS	Boeing 727-270	Iraqi Airways	
YI-AKO	Ilyushin IL-76M	Iraqi Airways	
YI-AKQ	Ilyushin IL-76M	Iraqi Airways	
YI-AKT	Ilyushin IL-76M	Iraqi Airways	
YI-AKU	Ilyushin IL-76M	Iraqi Airways	
YI-AKV	Ilyushin IL-76M	Iraqi Airways	
YI-AKW	Ilyushin IL-76M	Iraqi Airways	
YI-AKX	Ilyushin IL-76M	Iraqi Airways	
YI-ALP	Ilyushin IL-76M	Iraqi Airways	
YI-ALR	Ilyushin IL-76MD	Iraqi Airways	
YI-ALS	Ilyushin IL-76MD	Iraqi Airways	
YI-ALT	Ilyushin IL-76MD	Iraqi Airways	
YI-ALU	Ilyushin IL-76MD	Iraqi Airways	
YI-ALV	Ilyushin IL-76MD	Iraqi Airways	
YI-ALW	Ilyushin IL-76MD	Iraqi Airways	
YI-ALX	Ilyushin IL-76MD	Iraqi Airways	
YI-ANA	Ilyushin IL-76MD	Iraqi Airways	
YI-ANB	Ilyushin IL-76MD	Iraqi Airways	
YI-ANC	Ilyushin IL-76MD	Iraqi Airways	
YI-AND	Ilyushin IL-76MD	Iraqi Airways	
YI-ANE	Ilyushin IL-76MD	Iraqi Airways	
YI-ANF	Ilyushin IL-76MD	Iraqi Airways	
YI-ANG	Ilyushin IL-76MD	Iraqi Airways	
YI-ANH	Ilyushin IL-76MD	Iraqi Airways	
YI-ANI	Ilyushin IL-76MD	Iraqi Airways	

YK (Syria)

YK-AGA	Boeing 727-294	Syrian Arab Airlines *October 6*	
YK-AGB	Boeing 727-294	Syrian Arab Airlines *Damascus*	
YK-AGC	Boeing 727-294	Syrian Arab Airlines *Palmyra*	
YK-AHA	Boeing 747SP-94	Syrian Arab Airlines *16 Novembre*	
YK-AHB	Boeing 747SP-94	Syrian Arab Airlines *Arab Solidarity*	
YK-AIA	Tupolev Tu-154M	Syrian Arab Airlines	
YK-AIB	Tupolev Tu-154M	Syrian Arab Airlines	
YK-AIC	Tupolev Tu-154M	Syrian Arab Airlines	
YK-ATA	Ilyushin IL-76M	Syrian Arab Airlines	
YK-ATB	Ilyushin IL-76M	Syrian Arab Airlines	
YK-ATC	Ilyushin IL-76M	Syrian Arab Airlines	
YK-ATD	Ilyushin IL-76M	Syrian Arab Airlines	

Notes	Reg.	Type	Owner or Operator

YL (Latvia)

YL-BAA	Douglas DC-9-15RC	Baltic International
YL-LAA	Tupolev Tu-154B	Latavio Latvian Airlines
YL-LAB	Tupolev Tu-154B-2	Latavio Latvian Airlines
YL-LAD	Tupolev Tu-154B-2	Latavio Latvian Airlines
YL-LAE	Tupolev Tu-154B-2	Baltic International
YL-LAF	Tupolev Tu-154B-2	Latavio Latvian Airlines
YL-LAG	Tupolev Tu-154B-2	Latavio Latvian Airlines
YL-LAH	Tupolev Tu-154B-2	Latavio Latvian Airlines
YL-LAI	Tupolev Tu-154M	Latavio Latvian Airlines
YL-LBA	Tupolev Tu-134B-3	Latavio Latvian Airlines
YL-LBC	Tupolev Tu-134B-3	Latavio Latvian Airlines
YL-LBD	Tupolev Tu-134B-3	Latavio Latvian Airlines
YL-LBE	Tupolev Tu-134B-3	Latavio Latvian Airlines
YL-LBF	Tupolev Tu-134B-3	Latavio Latvian Airlines
YL-LBG	Tupolev Tu-134B-3	Latavio Latvian Airlines
YL-LBH	Tupolev Tu-134B-3	LatCharter
YL-LBI	Tupolev Tu-134B-3	Latavio Latvian Airlines
YL-LBJ	Tupolev Tu-134B-3	Latavio Latvian Airlines
YL-LBK	Tupolev Tu-134B-3	Baltic International
YL-LBL	Tupolev Tu-134B-3	Latavio Latvian Airlines
YL-LBM	Tupolev Tu-134B-3	Baltic International
YL-LBN	Tupolev Tu-134B-3	Latavio Latvian Airlines

YR (Romania)

YR-ABA	Boeing 707-3K1C	Tarom
YR-ABC	Boeing 707-3K1C	Tarom
YR-ABN	Boeing 707-321C	Tarom
YR-BCI	BAC One-Eleven 525FT	Tarom
YR-BCJ	BAC One-Eleven 525FT	Tarom
YR-BCK	BAC One-Eleven 525FT	Tarom
YR-BCL	BAC One-Eleven 525FT	Tarom
YR-BCM	BAC One-Eleven 525FT	Tarom
YR-BCN	BAC One-Eleven 525FT	Tarom
YR-BCO	BAC One Eleven 525FT	Tarom
YR-BGA	Boeing 737-38J	Tarom *Alba Iulia*
YR-BGB	Boeing 737-38J	Tarom *Bucuresti*
YR-	Boeing 737-38J	Tarom
YR-	Boeing 737-38J	Tarom
YR-	Boeing 737-38J	Tarom
YR-BRA	RomBac One-Eleven 561RC	Tarom
YR-BRB	RomBac One-Eleven 561RC	Tarom
YR-BRC	RomBac One-Eleven 561RC	Tarom
YR-BRD	RomBac One-Eleven 561RC	Tarom
YR-BRF	RomBac One-Eleven 561RC	Tarom
YR-BRG	RomBac One-Eleven 561RC	Tarom
YR-IMF	Ilyushin IL-18V	Tarom
YR-IMG	Ilyushin IL-18V	Tarom
YR-IMJ	Ilyushin IL-18D	Tarom
YR-IML	Ilyushin IL-18D	Tarom
YR-IRC	Ilyushin IL-62	Tarom
YR-IRD	Ilyushin IL-62M	Tarom
YR-IRE	Ilyushin IL-62M	Tarom
YR-JBA	BAC One-Eleven 528FL	Jaro International
YR-JBB	BAC One-Eleven 528FL	Jaro International
YR-LCA	Airbus A.310-325	Tarom *Transilvania*
YR-LCB	Airbus A.310-325	Tarom *Moldova*
YR-LCC	Airbus A.310-325	Tarom
YR-TPB	Tupolev Tu-154B	Tarom
YR-TPD	Tupolev Tu-154B	Tarom
YR-TPE	Tupolev Tu-154B-1	Tarom
YR-TPF	Tupolev Tu-154B-1	Tarom
YR-TPG	Tupolev Tu-154B-1	Tarom
YR-TPI	Tupolev Tu-154B-2	Tarom
YR-TPK	Tupolev Tu-154B-2	Tarom
YR-TPL	Tupolev Tu-154B-2	Tarom

YU (Yugoslavia)

YU-AHN	Douglas DC-9-32	Jugoslovenski Aerotransport (JAT)
YU-AHU	Douglas DC-9-32	JAT

Reg.	Type	Owner or Operator	Notes
YU-AHV	Douglas DC-9-32	JAT	
YU-AJH	Douglas DC-9-32	JAT	
YU-AJI	Douglas DC-9-32	JAT	
YU-AJJ	Douglas DC-9-32	JAT	
YU-AJK	Douglas DC-9-32	JAT	
YU-AJL	Douglas DC-9-32	JAT	
YU-AJM	Douglas DC-9-32	JAT	
YU-AKB	Boeing 727-2H9	JAT/Air Commerce	
YU-AKD	Boeing 727-2L8	Aviogenex *Split*	
YU-AKE	Boeing 727-2H9	JAT	
YU-AKF	Boeing 727-2H9	JAT	
YU-AKG	Boeing 727-2H9	JAT	
YU-AKH	Boeing 727-2L8	Aviogenex *Dubrovnik*	
YU-AKI	Boeing 727-2H9	JAT	
YU-AKJ	Boeing 727-2H9	JAT	
YU-AKM	Boeing 727-243	Aviogenex *Pula*	
YU-AMB	Douglas DC-10-30	JAT *Edvard Rusijan*	
YU-AND	Boeing 737-3H9	JAT	
YU-ANF	Boeing 737-3H9	JAT	
YU-ANI	Boeing 737-3H9	JAT	
YU-ANK	Boeing 737-3H9	JAT	
YU-ANP	Boeing 737-2K3	Aviogenex *Zadar*	
YU-ANU	Boeing 737-2K3	Aviogenex *Tivat*	
YU-ANV	Boeing 737-3H9	JAT	
YU-AOF	Boeing 737-2K5	Aviogenex	
YU-AOG	Boeing 737-2K5	Aviogenex	

Note: Both JAT and Aviogenex have been affected by the war in Yugoslavia with aircraft grounded or leased out.

YV (Venezuela)

YV-134C	Douglas DC-10-30	VIASA	
YV-135C	Douglas DC-10-30	VIASA	
YV-136C	Douglas DC-10-30	VIASA	
YV-137C	Douglas DC-10-30	VIASA	
YV-138C	Douglas DC-10-30	VIASA	

Z (Zimbabwe)

Z-WKS	Boeing 707-330B	Air Zimbabwe	
Z-WKU	Boeing 707-330B	Air Zimbabwe	
Z-WMJ	Douglas DC-8-55F	Affretair *Captain Jack Malloch*	
Z-WPE	Boeing 767-2N0ER	Air Zimbabwe *Victoria Falls*	
Z-WPF	Boeing 767-2N0ER	Air Zimbabwe *Chimanimani*	
Z-WSB	Douglas DC-8-55F	Affretair	
Z-WZL	Douglas DC-8-71AF	Affretair	

ZK (New Zealand)

ZK-NBS	Boeing 747-419	Air New Zealand *Mataatua*	
ZK-NBT	Boeing 747-419	Air New Zealand	
ZK-NBU	Boeing 747-419	Air New Zealand	
ZK-NBV	Boeing 747-419	Air New Zealand	
ZK-NZV	Boeing 747-219B	Air New Zealand *Aotea*	
ZK-NZW	Boeing 747-219B	Air New Zealand *Tainui*	
ZK-NZX	Boeing 747-219B	Air New Zealand	
ZK-NZY	Boeing 747-219B	Air New Zealand *Te Arawa*	
ZK-NZZ	Boeing 747-219B	Air New Zealand	

ZP (Paraguay)

ZP-CCE	Boeing 707-321B	Lineas Aéreas Paraguayas	
ZP-CCF	Boeing 707-321B	Lineas Aéreas Paraguayas	
ZP-CCG	Boeing 707-321B	Lineas Aéreas Paraguayas	
ZP-CCH	Douglas DC-8-63	Lineas Aéreas Paraguayas	

ZS (South Africa)

ZS-SAL	Boeing 747-244B	South African Airways *Tafelberg*	
ZS-SAM	Boeing 747-244B	South African Airways *Drakensberg*	

Notes	Reg.	Type	Owner or Operator
	ZS-SAN	Boeing 747-244B	South African Airways *Lebombo*
	ZS-SAO	Boeing 747-244B	South African Airways *Magaliesberg*
	ZS-SAP	Boeing 747-244B	South African Airways *Swartberg*
	ZS-SAR	Boeing 747-244B (SCD)	South African Airways *Waterberg*
	ZS-SAT	Boeing 747-344	South African Airways *Johannesburg*
	ZS-SAU	Boeing 747-344	South African Airways *Cape Town*
	ZS-SAV	Boeing 747-444	South African Airways *Durban*
	ZS-SAW	Boeing 747-444	South African Airways *Bloemfontein*
	ZS-SAX	Boeing 747-444	South African Airways
	ZS-SAY	Boeing 747-444	South African Airways *Vulindlela*
	ZS-SPE	Boeing 747-SP44	South African Airways

3B (Mauritius)

	3B-NAG	Boeing 747SP-44	Air Mauritius *Chateau du Reduit*
	3B-NAJ	Boeing 747SP-44	Air Mauritius *Chateau Mon Plaisir*
	3B-NAK	Boeing 767-23BER	Air Mauritius *City of Curepipe*
	3B-NAL	Boeing 767-23BER	Air Mauritius *City of Port Louis*
	3B-NAQ	Boeing 747SP-27	Air Mauritius *Chateau Benares*

3D (Swaziland)

	3D-ADV	Douglas DC-8-54F	African International Airways
	3D-AFR	Douglas DC-8-54F	African International Airways
	3D-AFX	Douglas DC-8-54F	African International Airways
	3D-ASB	Boeing 707-323C	Air Swazi Cargo

4K (Azerbaijan)

The following are operated by Azerbaijan Airlines with the registrations prefixed by 4K.

65075	Tu-134A
65702	Tu-134A
65705	Tu-134B-3
65708	Tu-134B-3
65709	Tu-134A
65711	Tu-134B-3
65713	Tu-134B-3
65714	Tu-134B-3
65985	Tu-134B-3
85147	Tu-154B
85177	Tu-154B
85192	Tu-154B-1
85199	Tu-154B
85211	Tu-154B
85214	Tu-154B
85274	Tu-154B-1
85329	Tu-154B-2
85364	Tu-154B-2
85391	Tu-154B-2
85393	Tu-154B-2
85548	Tu-154B-2
85698	Tu-154M
85734	Tu-154M

4R (Sri Lanka)

	4R-ULA	L.1011-385 TriStar 500	Air Lanka *City of Jayewardenepura*
	4R-ULB	L.1011-385 TriStar 500	Air Lanka *City of Kandy*
	4R-ULC	L.1011-385 TriStar 100	Air Lanka *City of Anuradhapura*
	4R-ULE	L.1011-385 TriStar 50	Air Lanka *City of Ratnapura*
	4R-ULM	L.1011-385 TriStar 200	Air Lanka
	4R-ULN	L.1011-385 TriStar 200	Air Lanka
	4R-	Airbus A.340-311	Air Lanka
	4R-	Airbus A.340-311	Air Lanka
	4R-	Airbus A.340-311	Air Lanka

4X (Israel)

	4X-ABN	Boeing 737-258	El Al/Arkia
	4X-ABO	Boeing 737-258	El Al/Arkia
	4X-AXA	Boeing 747-258B	El Al

Reg.	Type	Owner or Operator
4X-AXB	Boeing 747-258B	El Al
4X-AXC	Boeing 747-258B	El Al
4X-AXD	Boeing 747-258C	El Al Cargo Air Lines
4X-AXF	Boeing 747-258C	El Al Cargo Air Lines
4X-AXH	Boeing 747-258B	El Al
4X-AXQ	Boeing 747-238B	El Al
4X-AXZ	Boeing 747-124F (SCD)	El Al
4X-BAF	Boeing 737-281	Arkia
4X-EAA	Boeing 767-258	El Al
4X-EAB	Boeing 767-258	El Al
4X-EAC	Boeing 767-258ER	El Al
4X-EAD	Boeing 767-258ER	El Al
4X-EBL	Boeing 757-258	El Al/Arkia
4X-EBM	Boeing 757-258	El Al/Arkia
4X-EBR	Boeing 757-258	El Al
4X-EBS	Boeing 757-258ER	El Al
4X-EBT	Boeing 757-258ER	El Al
4X-EBU	Boeing 757-258	El Al
4X-EBV	Boeing 757-258	El Al
4X-ELA	Boeing 747-458	El Al
4X-ELB	Boeing 747-458	El Al

5A (Libya)

Reg.	Type	Owner or Operator
5A-DAI	Boeing 727-224	Libyan Arab Airlines
5A-DAK	Boeing 707-3L5C	Libyan Arab Airlines
5A-DIB	Boeing 727-2L5	Libyan Arab Airlines
5A-DIC	Boeing 727-2L5	Libyan Arab Airlines
5A-DID	Boeing 727-2L5	Libyan Arab Airlines
5A-DIE	Boeing 727-2L5	Libyan Arab Airlines
5A-DIF	Boeing 727-2L5	Libyan Arab Airlines
5A-DIG	Boeing 727-2L5	Libyan Arab Airlines
5A-DIH	Boeing 727-2L5	Libyan Arab Airlines
5A-DII	Boeing 727-2L5	Libyan Arab Airlines
5A-DJM	Boeing 707-321B	Libyan Arab Airlines
5A-DJU	Boeing 707-351C	Libyan Arab Airlines

Note: Services to the UK suspended. Libyan Arab's two A.310-203 are operated as 7T-VJE and 7T-VJF with Air Algerie.

5B (Cyprus)

Reg.	Type	Owner or Operator
5B-CIO	Boeing 737-3Y0	TEA Cyprus
5B-DAG	BAC One Eleven 537GF	Cyprus Airways
5B-DAH	BAC One Eleven 537GF	Cyprus Airways
5B-DAJ	BAC One Eleven 537GF	Cyprus Airways
5B-DAQ	Airbus A.310-203	Cyprus Airways *Soli*
5B-DAR	Airbus A.310-203	Cyprus Airways *Aepia*
5B-DAS	Airbus A.310-203	Cyprus Airways *Salamis*
5B-DAT	Airbus A.320-231	Cyprus Airways *Praxandros*
5B-DAU	Airbus A.320-231	Cyprus Airways *Evethon*
5B-DAV	Airbus A.320-231	Cyprus Airways *Kinyras*
5B-DAW	Airbus A.320-231	Cyprus Airways *Agapinor*
5B-DAX	Airbus A.310-204	Cyprus Airways *Engomi*
5B-DAZ	Boeing 707-328C	Avistar
5B-DBA	Airbus A.320-231	Cyprus Airways *Evagoras*
5B-DBB	Airbus A.320-231	Eurocypria Airways *Akamas*
5B-DBC	Airbus A.320-231	Eurocypria Airways *Tefkros*
5B-DBD	Airbus A.320-231	Eurocypria Airways *Onosilos*

5N (Nigeria)

Reg.	Type	Owner or Operator
5N-ABK	Boeing 707-3F9C	Nigeria Airways
5N-ANN	Douglas DC-10-30	Nigeria Airways *Yunkari*
5N-AOQ	Boeing 707-355C	Okada Air
5N-ARQ	Boeing 707-338C	DAS Air Cargo
5N-ATY	Douglas DC-8-55F	Liberia World Airlines
5N-AUE	Airbus A.310-222	Nigeria Airways *River Yobe*
5N-AUF	Airbus A.310-222	Nigeria Airways
5N-AUG	Airbus A.310-222	Nigeria Airways *Lekki Peninsula*

Notes	Reg.	Type	Owner or Operator
	5N-AUH	Airbus A.310-222	Nigeria Airways *Rima River*
	5N-AWE	Douglas DC-8-55F	Kabo Air
	5N-AWO	Boeing 707-321C	G.A.S. Air
	5N-BBB	L.1011-385 TriStar 100	ADC Airlines
	5N-EDO	Boeing 747-146	Okada Air
	5N-OCL	Boeing 707-351C	Overnight Cargo
	5N-TAS	Boeing 707-321C	Thames Air
	5N-TTK	Boeing 727-264	Triax Airlines

Note: Nigeria Airways operates a DC-10-30 which retains its US identity N3024W (5N-AUI reserved)

5R (Madagascar)

5R-MFT	Boeing 747-2B2B (SCD)	Air Madagascar *Tolom Piavotana*

5X (Uganda)

5X-JON	Boeing 707-369C	DAS Air Cargo *Spirit of John*
5X-JEF	Boeing 707-379C	DAS Air Cargo
5X-UCF	L-100-30 Hercules	Uganda Air Cargo *The Silver Lady*

5Y (Kenya)

5Y-ANA	Boeing 707-328C	Yana Air Cargo
5Y-AXI	Boeing 707-330B	African Airlines International
5Y-AXM	Boeing 707-330B	African Airlines International
5Y-AXW	Boeing 707-321B	African Airlines International
5Y-BEL	Airbus A.310-304	Kenya Airways *Nyayo Star*
5Y-BEN	Airbus A.310-304	Kenya Airways *Harambee Star*
5Y-BFT	Airbus A.310-304	Kenya Airways *Uhuru Star*
5Y-BHG	Boeing 757-23A	Kenya Airways *Umoja Star*
5Y-ZEB	Douglas DC-8-63	African Safari Airways

Note: African Safari also operates DC-8-63 which carries the registration HB-IBF and DC-10-30 which retains PH-DTL.

6Y (Jamaica)

Note: Air Jamaica operates its UK services jointly with British Airways.

7O (Yemen)

7O-ACV	Boeing 727-2N8	Yemenia
7O-ACW	Boeing 727-2N8	Yemenia
7O-ACX	Boeing 727-2N8	Yemenia
7O-ACY	Boeing 727-2N8	Yemenia
7O-ADA	Boeing 727-2N8	Yemenia

Note: Alyemda operates the Airbus A.310-304 F-ODSV.

7T (Algeria)

7T-VEA	Boeing 727-2D6	Air Algerie *Tassili*
7T-VEB	Boeing 727-2D6	Air Algerie *Hoggar*
7T-VED	Boeing 737-2D6C	Air Algerie *Atlas Saharien*
7T-VEE	Boeing 737-2D6C	Air Algerie *Oasis*
7T-VEF	Boeing 737-2D6	Air Algerie *Saoura*
7T-VEG	Boeing 737-2D6	Air Algerie *Monts des Ouleds Neils*
7T-VEH	Boeing 727-2D6	Air Algerie *Lalla Khadidja*
7T-VEI	Boeing 727-2D6	Air Algerie *Djebel Amour*
7T-VEJ	Boeing 737-2D6	Air Algerie *Chrea*
7T-VEK	Boeing 737-2D6	Air Algerie *Edough*
7T-VEL	Boeing 737-2D6	Air Algerie *Akfadou*
7T-VEM	Boeing 727-2D6	Air Algerie *Mont du Ksall*
7T-VEN	Boeing 737-2D6	Air Algerie *La Soummam*
7T-VEO	Boeing 737-2D6	Air Algerie *La Titteri*
7T-VEP	Boeing 727-2D6	Air Algerie *Mont du Tessala*
7T-VEQ	Boeing 737-2D6	Air Algerie *Le Zaccar*
7T-VER	Boeing 737-2D6	Air Algerie *Le Souf*
7T-VES	Boeing 737-2D6C	Air Algerie *Le Tadmaït*
7T-VET	Boeing 727-2D6	Air Algerie *Georges du Rhumel*
7T-VEU	Boeing 727-2D6	Air Algerie *Djurdjura*
7T-VEV	Boeing 727-2D6	Air Algerie
7T-VEW	Boeing 727-2D6	Air Algerie
7T-VEX	Boeing 727-2D6	Air Algerie *Djemila*

Reg.	Type	Owner or Operator	Notes
7T-VEY	Boeing 737-2D6	Air Algerie *Rhoufi*	
7T-VEZ	Boeing 737-2T4	Air Algerie *Monts du Daia*	
7T-VJA	Boeing 737-2T4	Air Algerie *Monts des Babors*	
7T-VJB	Boeing 737-2T4	Air Algerie *Monts des Bibons*	
7T-VJC	Airbus A.310-203	Air Algerie	
7T-VJD	Airbus A.310-203	Air Algerie	
7T-VJE	Airbus A.310-203	Air Algerie/Libyan Arab	
7T-VJF	Airbus A.310-203	Air Algerie/Libyan Arab	
7T-VJG	Boeing 767-3D6	Air Algerie	
7T-VJH	Boeing 767-3D6	Air Algerie	
7T-VJI	Boeing 767-3D6	Air Algerie	

9A (Croatia)

9A-CTA	Boeing 737-230	Croatia Airlines	
9A-CTB	Boeing 737-230	Croatia Airlines	
9A-CTC	Boeing 737-230	Croatia Airlines	
9A-CTD	Boeing 737-230	Croatia Airlines	
9A-CTE	Boeing 737-230	Croatia Airlines	
9A-CTF	Boeing 737-230	Croatia Airlines	

9G (Ghana)

9G-ADM	Boeing 707-321C	Continental Cargo Airlines	
9G-ANA	Douglas DC-10-30	Ghana Airways	
9G-MKA	Douglas DC-8-55F	Cargo D'or Airlines	
9G-MKB	Douglas DC-8-55F	Cargo D'or Airlines	
9G-MKC	Douglas DC-8-55F	Cargo D'or Airlines	
9G-TWO	Boeing 707-336C	Phoenix Aviation	

9H (Malta)

9H-ABA	Boeing 737-2Y5	Air Malta *Manuel de Vilhena*	
9H-ABB	Boeing 737-2Y5	Air Malta *Philippe Villiers de L'isle Adam*	
9H-ABC	Boeing 737-2Y5	Air Malta *Claude de la Sengle*	
9H-ABE	Boeing 737-2Y5	Air Malta *Alof de Wignacourt*	
9H-ABF	Boeing 737-2Y5	Air Malta *Manuel Pinto*	
9H-ABG	Boeing 737-2Y5	Air Malta *Jean de Lavalette*	
9H-ABP	Airbus A.320-211	Air Malta *Nicholas de Cottoner*	
9H-ABQ	Airbus A.320-211	Air Malta *Hughes Loubenx de Verdelle*	
9H-ABR	Boeing 737-3Y5	Air Malta *Juan de Homedes*	
9H-ABS	Boeing 737-3Y5	Air Malta *Antoines de Paule*	
9H-ABT	Boeing 737-3Y5	Air Malta *Ferdinand von Hompesch*	

9J (Zambia)

9J-AFL	Douglas DC-8-71	Zambia Airways	

Note: Zambia Airways operates DC-10-30 N3016Z *Nkwazi* on lease.

9K (Kuwait)

9K-ADA	Boeing 747-269B (SCD)	Kuwait Airways *Al Sabahiya*	
9K-ADB	Boeing 747-269B (SCD)	Kuwait Airways *Al Jaberiya*	
9K-ADC	Boeing 747-269B (SCD)	Kuwait Airways *Al Murbarakiya*	
9K-ADD	Boeing 747-269B (SCD)	Kuwait Airways *Al Salmiya*	
9K-ADE	Boeing 747-469	Kuwait Airways	
9K-AIA	Boeing 767-269ER	Kuwait Airways *Al Riggah*	
9K-AIC	Boeing 767-269ER	Kuwait Airways *Garouh*	
9K-ALA	Airbus A.310-308	Kuwait Airways *Al-Jahra*	
9K-ALB	Airbus A.310-308	Kuwait Airways *Gharnada*	
9K-ALC	Airbus A.310-308	Kuwait Airways *Kadhma*	
9K-AMA	Airbus A.300-605R	Kuwait Airways	
9K-AMB	Airbus A.300-605R	Kuwait Airways	
9K-AMC	Airbus A.300-605R	Kuwait Airways *Burghan*	
9K-AMD	Airbus A.300-605R	Kuwait Airways	
9K-AME	Airbus A.300-605R	Kuwait Airways	

9M (Malaysia)

9M-MHI	Boeing 747-236B	Malaysian Airline System	
9M-MHJ	Boeing 747-236B	Malaysian Airline System	
9M-MHK	Boeing 747-3H6 (SCD)	Malaysian Airline System *Kota Kinabalu*	

Notes	Reg.	Type	Owner or Operator
	9M-MHL	Boeing 747-4H6 (SCD)	Malaysian Airline System *Kuala Lumpur*
	9M-MHM	Boeing 747-4H6 (SCD)	Malaysian Airline System *Penang*
	9M-MHN	Boeing 747-4H6	Malaysian Airline System *Malacca*
	9M-MHO	Boeing 747-4H6	Malaysian Airline System *Alor Setar*
	9M-MPA	Boeing 747-4H6	Malaysian Airline System *Ipoh*
	9M-MPB	Boeing 747-4H6	Malaysian Airline System
	9M-MPC	Boeing 747-4H6	Malaysian Airline System
	9M-MPD	Boeing 747-4H6	Malaysian Airline System
	9M-MPE	Boeing 747-4H6	Malaysian Airline System
	9M-MPF	Boeing 747-4H6	Malaysian Airline System
	9M-MPG	Boeing 747-4H6	Malaysian Airline System

9N (Nepal)

	9N-ACA	Boeing 757-2F8	Royal Nepal Airlines
	9N-ACB	Boeing 757-2F8C	Royal Nepal Airlines *Gandaki*

9Q (Zaïre)

	9Q-CBW	Boeing 707-329C	Scibe Airlift Zaïre
	9Q-CJW	Boeing 707-321C	New ACS
	9Q-CLI	Douglas DC-10-30	Air Zaïre *Mont Ngaliema*
	9Q-CLV	Douglas DC-8-54F	Transair Cargo (Zaïre)
	9Q-CMD	Boeing 707-441	Blue Airlines
	9Q-CSZ	Boeing 707-323C	Shabair
	9Q-CTK	Boeing 707-436	New ACS
	9Q-CVH	Douglas DC-8-55F	Transair Cargo (Zaïre)

9V (Singapore)

	9V-SFA	Boeing 747-412F	Singapore Airlines
	9V-SFB	Boeing 747-412F	Singapore Airlines
	9V-SKA	Boeing 747-312	Singapore Airlines
	9V-SKD	Boeing 747-312	Singapore Airlines
	9V-SKM	Boeing 747-312 (SCD)	Singapore Airlines
	9V-SKN	Boeing 747-312 (SCD)	Singapore Airlines
	9V-SKP	Boeing 747-312 (SCD)	Singapore Airlines
	9V-SKQ	Boeing 747-212F (SCD)	Singapore Airlines
	9V-SMA	Boeing 747-412	Singapore Airlines
	9V-SMB	Boeing 747-412	Singapore Airlines
	9V-SMC	Boeing 747-412	Singapore Airlines
	9V-SMD	Boeing 747-412	Singapore Airlines
	9V-SME	Boeing 747-412	Singapore Airlines
	9V-SMF	Boeing 747-412	Singapore Airlines
	9V-SMG	Boeing 747-412	Singapore Airlines
	9V-SMH	Boeing 747-412	Singapore Airlines
	9V-SMI	Boeing 747-412	Singapore Airlines
	9V-SMJ	Boeing 747-412	Singapore Airlines
	9V-SMK	Boeing 747-412	Singapore Airlines
	9V-SML	Boeing 747-412	Singapore Airlines
	9V-SMM	Boeing 747-412	Singapore Airlines
	9V-SMN	Boeing 747-412	Singapore Airlines
	9V-SMO	Boeing 747-412	Singapore Airlines
	9V-SMP	Boeing 747-412	Singapore Airlines
	9V-SMQ	Boeing 747-412	Singapore Airlines
	9V-SMR	Boeing 747-412	Singapore Airlines
	9V-SMS	Boeing 747-412	Singapore Airlines
	9V-SMT	Boeing 747-412	Singapore Airlines
	9V-SMU	Boeing 747-412	Singapore Airlines
	9V-SMV	Boeing 747-412	Singapore Airlines
	9V-SMW	Boeing 747-412	Singapore Airlines
	9V-SMX	Boeing 747-412	Singapore Airlines
	9V-SPB	Boeing 747-412	Singapore Airlines
	9V-SPC	Boeing 747-412	Singapore Airlines
	9V-SQP	Boeing 747-212B	Singapore Airlines
	9V-SQQ	Boeing 747-212B	Singapore Airlines
	9V-SQR	Boeing 747-212B	Singapore Airlines
	9V-SQS	Boeing 747-212B	Singapore Airlines
	9V-SQT	Boeing 747-245F (SCD)	Singapore Airlines
	9V-SQU	Boeing 747-245F (SCD)	Singapore Airlines
	9V-SQV	Boeing 747-249F	Singapore Airlines

Note: Singapore Airlines also operates Boeing 747-312 N116KB, N117KC, N119KE, N120KF, N121KG, N122KH, N123KJ, N124KK and N125KL.

9XR (Rwanda)

| 9XR-JA | Boeing 707-328C | Air Rwanda | |

9Y (Trinidad and Tobago)

9Y-TGJ	L.1011 TriStar 500 (595)	B.W.I.A. *Sunjet Trinidad*	
9Y-TGN	L.1011 TriStar 500 (596)	B.W.I.A. *Sunjet Barbados*	
9Y-THA	L.1011 TriStar 500 (597)	B.W.I.A. *Sunjet Antigua*	

Note: B.W.I.A. also operates a TriStar 500 which retains its US registration N3140D (598) and named *Sunjet St. Lucia*.

RA-76476, IL-76. *AJW*

Aircraft included in this section are those based in the UK but which retain their non-British identities.

Notes	Reg.	Type	Owner or Operator
	A40-AB	V.1103 VC10 ★	Brooklands Museum (G-ASIX)
	CF-EQS	Boeing-Stearman PT-17 ★	Imperial War Museum/Duxford
	CF-KCG	Grumman TBM-3E Avenger AS.3★	Imperial War Museum/Duxford
	D-692	Staaken Z-1 Flitzer	D. J. Evans & L. R. Williams (G-BVAW)
	D-HMQV	Bolkow Bo 102 ★	International Helicopter Museum (IHM)/Weston-s-Mare
	D-IFSB	D.H.104 Dove 6★	Mosquito Aircraft Museum
	F-BDRS	Boeing B-17G (231983) ★	Imperial War Museum/Duxford
	F-BMCY	Potez 840*	Sumburgh Fire Service
	N2FU	Learjet 35A	Motor Racing Developments Inc
	N12FU	Dassault Falcon 20C	Motor Racing Developments Inc
	N18E	Boeing 247D ★	Science Museum/Wroughton
	N18JC	H.295 Super Courier	Atlantic Bridge Aviation
	N18V	Beech D.17S Traveler (PB1)	R. Lamplough
	N27TS	Cessna 501 Citation	Eagle SP 147 Inc
	N33VC	Lockheed T-33A (54-21261)	Old Flying Machine Co/Duxford
	N36SF	Hawker Sea Fury FB.10 (361)	J. Bradshaw/Benson
	N47DD	Republic P-47D Thunderbolt (45-49192)★	Imperial War Museum/Duxford
	N47DD	Republic P-47D Thunderbolt (226671)	The Fighter Collection/Duxford
	N51RR	P-51D Mustang (474008)	D. Gilmour/North Weald
	N71AF	R. Commander 680W	Metropolitan Aviation
	N167F	P-51D Mustang (473877)	RLS 51 Ltd/Duxford
	N200GX	BAe 125 Srs 800A	Glaxo Aviation Inc
	N232J	Hawker Sea Fury FB.11	R. Lamplough/North Weald
	N260QB	Pitts S-2S Special	D. Baker
	N339BB	Sikorsky S-76A	Air Hanson Ltd/Blackbushe
	N444M	Grumman G.44 Widgeon (1411)	M. Dunkerley/Biggin Hill
	N500LN	Howard 500	D. Baker
	N513L	Vultee BT-15 Valiant (121821)	Aces High Ltd/North Weald
	N535SM	R. Commander 680	J. E. Tuberty
	N707TJ	Boeing Stearman A.75N1	V. S. E. Norman (Crunchie)
	N736GX	Cessna R.172K (tailwheel)	Mission Aviation Fellowship/Headcorn
	N999PJ	M.S.760 Paris 2	Aces High Ltd/North Weald
	N1009N	P-40N Kittyhawk (FR870)	B. J. Grey/Duxford
	N1042B	B-25J Mitchell (430823)	Aces High Ltd/North Weald
	N1051S	P-51D-25-NA Mustang (511371)	Myrick Aviation/Leavesden
	N1344	Ryan PT-22	H. Mitchell
	N1447Q	Cessna 150L	US Embassy Flying Club/Denham
	N2700	Fairchild C-119G	Aces High Ltd (G-BLSW)/North Weald
	N2929W	PA-28-151 Warrior	R. Lobell
	N3145X	P-38J Lightning	Fighter Collection/Duxford
	N3455	Douglas DC-3	Aces High Ltd (G-AMSN)/North Weald
	N3851Q	Cessna 172K	Bentwaters Aero Club/Woodbridge
	N3922B	Boeing Stearman E.75N1	P. Hoffman/Swanton Morley
	N4306Z	PA-28 -161 Warrior II	USAF Aero Club/Upper Heyford
	N4565L	Douglas DC.3	Hibernian Dakota Flight Ltd/Ipswich
	N4575C	G.21C Goose	Blue Arrow Challenge PLC
	N4596N	Boeing Stearman PT-13D	N. Mason & D. Gilmour/North Weald
	N4712V	Boeing Stearman PT-13D	Wessex Aviation & Transport Ltd
	N4727V	Spad S.VII (S4523)	Imperial War Museum/Duxford
	N4806E	Douglas A-26C Invader ★	R. & R. Cadman/Southend
	N4845V	FM-2 Wildcat (86711)	Fighter Collection/Duxford
	N5237V	Boeing B-17G (483868) ★	RAF Museum/Hendon
	N5824H	PA-38 Tomahawk	Lakenheath Aero Club
	N6268	Travel Air Model 2000	Personal Plane Services Ltd
	N6526D	P-51D Mustang (413573) ★	RAF Museum/Henlow
	N7614C	B-25J Mitchell	Imperial War Museum/Duxford
	N7777G	L.749A Constellation ★	Science Museum (G-CONI)/Wroughton
	N8389H	Beech C-45	Bar-Belle Aviation Ltd
	N9043	Stolp SA.301 Starduster Too	J. McTaggart
	N9089Z	TB-25J Mitchell (44-30861) ★	Aces High Ltd (G-BKXW)/North Weald
	N9115Z	TB-25N Mitchell (34037) ★	RAF Museum/Hendon
	N9606H	Fairchild M.62A Cornell ★	Rebel Air Museum/Earls Colne

Reg.	Type	Owner or Operator	Notes
N26634	PA-24 Comanche 250	P. Biggs (G-BFKR)	
N33600	Cessna L-19A Bird Dog (111989) ★	Museum of Army Flying/Middle Wallop	
N43069	PA-28-161 Warrior II	Lakenheath Aero Club	
N49272	Ryan PT-23 (23)	H. Mitchell	
N50755	Boeing Stearman PT-17 (40-1766)	E. Boulter/Swanton Morley	
N50993	Ryan PT-22	V. S. E. Norman	
N53091	Boeing Stearman A.75N1	Eastern Stearman Ltd	
N54426	Boeing Stearman A.75N1	R. Simpson	
N54922	Boeing Stearman N25-4	V. S. E. Norman (Crunchie)	
N56028	Ryan PT-22	V. S. E. Norman	
N56421	Ryan PT-22 (855)	PT Flight/Cosford	
N58566	BT-13 Valiant	PT Flight/Cosford	
N75664	Boeing Stearman E.75N1 (208)	—	
N88972	B-25D-30-ND Mitchell (KL161)	Fighter Collection/Duxford	
N91437	PA-38-112 Tomahawk	Lakenheath Aero Club	
N91457	PA-38-112 Tomahawk	Lakenheath Aero Club	
N91590	PA-38-112 Tomahawk	Lakenheath Aero Club	
N96240	Beech D.18S	Visionair Ltd (G-AYAH) (*derelict*)/Rochester	
N99153	T-28C Trojan ★	Norfolk & Suffolk Aviation Museum/Flixton	
NC5171N	Lockheed 10A Electra ★	Science Museum (G-LIOA)/Wroughton	
NC15214	Waco UKC-S	P. H. McConnell/White Waltham	
NC16403	Cessna C.34 Airmaster	Kennet Aircraft Ltd (G-BSEB)	
NL9494Z	TB-25N Mitchell (151632)	Visionair Ltd	
NX11SN	Yakovlev C-11	Old Flying Machine Co/Duxford	
NX55JP	FG-1D Corsair (N25648)	Old Flying Machine Co/Duxford	
NX700HL	F8F-2B Bearcat (121714)	B. J. S. Grey/Duxford	
VH-BRC	S.24 Sandringham ★	Southampton Hall of Aviation	
VH-SNB	D.H.84 Dragon ★	Museum of Flight/E. Fortune	
VH-UTH	GAL Monospar ST-12 ★	Newark Air Museum (*stored*)	
VR-BEP	WS.55 Whirlwind 3 ★	East Midlands Aeropark (G-BAMH)	
VR-BET	WS.55 Whirlwind 3 ★	IHM (G-ANJV)/Weston-s-Mare	
VR-BEU	WS.55 Whirlwind 3 ★	IHM (G-ATKV)/Weston-s-Mare	
VR-BKC	Boeing 727-1H2	USAL Inc	
VR-BKG	Dassault Falcon 50	Sioux Co Ltd/Cranfield	
VR-BKQ	Agusta A.109A-II	USAL Ltd/Fairoaks	
VR-BKY	H.S.125 Srs F.3B	Corporate Jet Services	
VR-BKZ	H.S.125 Srs 700A	Dennis Vanguard International	
VR-BLU	Learjet 35A	Contship Ltd/Stansted	
VR-BLX	F.27 Friendship Mk 400	BP Flight Operations Ltd	
VR-BLY	F.27 Friendship Mk 400	BP Flight Operations Ltd	
VR-BLZ	F.27 Friendship Mk 400	BP Flight Operations Ltd	
VR-BMF	Dassault Falcon 50	Glaxo (UK) Ltd/Heathrow	
VR-BNB	H.S.125 Srs 700A	Speedflight Ltd/Guernsey	
VR-BOO	McD Douglas MD-87	Ford Motor Co Ltd/Stansted	
VR-BOP	McD Douglas MD-87	Ford Motor Co Ltd/Stansted	
VR-BRS	H.S.125 Srs 600A	Speedflight Ltd/Guernsey	
VR-BUB	Cessna 500 Cltation	Midair Aviation Ltd/Bournemouth	
VR-BUL	Cessna 560 Citation IV	Fegotila Ltd/Staverton	
VR-BVI	H.S.125 Srs F400A	Group 4 Ltd/Staverton	
VR-BYE	Cessna 550 Citation II	Corporate Jet Services/Staverton	
VR-CAR	Canadair CL.601 Challenger	McClaren Motor Racing	
VR-CBW	G.1159C Gulfstream 4	Rolls-Royce PLC/Filton	
VR-CCK	Agusta A.109A-II	Tarmac PLC/E. Midlands	
VR-CCO	Agusta A.109A	Aerospace Finance Ltd/Fairoaks	
VC-CCQ	Dassault Falcon 50	Frank Williams Racing/Kidlington	
VR-CMF	G.1159C Gulfstream 4	Aravco Ltd/Heathrow	
VR-CMP	Agusta A.109A-II	Bola Ltd/Fairoaks	
VR-CSH	Beech 350 Super King Air	United Biscuits Ltd	
VR-CYM	G.1159C Gulfstream 4	Jet Fly Corporation/Heathrow	
5N-ABW	Westland Widgeon 2 ★	IHM (G-AOZE)/Weston-s-Mare	

Radio Frequencies

The frequencies used by the larger airfields/airports are listed below. Abbreviations used: TWR — Tower, APP — Approach, A/G — Air-ground advisory. It is possible for changes to be made from time to time with the frequencies allocated which are all quoted in Megahertz (MHz).

Airfield	TWR	APP	A/G	Airfield	TWR	APP	A/G
Aberdeen	118.1	120.4		Ingoldmells			130.45
Aldergrove	118.3	120.0		Inverness	122.6		
Alderney	125.35			Ipswich	118.325		
Andrewsfield			130.55	Jersey	119.45	120.3	
Audley End			122.35	Kidlington	118.875	125.325	
Barton			122.7	Land's End	130.7		
Barrow			123.2	Leavesden	122.15		
Belfast City	130.75	130.85		Leeds	120.3	123.75	
Bembridge			123.25	Leicester			122.25
Biggin Hill	134.8	129.4		Liverpool	118.1	119.85	
Birmingham	118.3	131.325		London City	118.075		
Blackbushe			122.3	Long Marston			130.1
Blackpool	118.4	135.95		Luton	120.2	128.75	
Bodmin			122.7	Lydd	120.7	131.3	
Booker			126.55	Manchester	118.625	119.4	
Bourn			129.8	Manston	128.775	126.35	
Bournemouth	125.6	119.625		Netherthorpe			123.275
Bristol	133.85	132.4		Newcastle	119.7	126.35	
Cambridge	122.2	123.6		North Denes			123.4
Cardiff	125.0	125.85		North Weald			123.525
Carlisle			123.6	Norwich	124.25	119.35	
Compton Abbas			122.7	Perth	119.8	122.3	
Conington			129.725	Plymouth	122.6	133.55	
Coventry	119.25			Popham			129.8
Cranfield	123.2	122.85		Prestwick	118.15	120.55	
Denham			130.725	Redhill	120.275		
Dundee	122.9			Rochester			122.25
Dunkeswell			123.475	Ronaldsway	118.9	120.85	
Dunsfold	124.325	119.825		Sandown			123.5
Duxford			122.075	Seething			122.6
East Midlands	124.0	120.125		Sherburn			122.6
Edinburgh	118.7	121.2		Shipdham			123.05
Elstree			122.4	Shobdon			123.5
Exeter	119.8	128.15		Shoreham	125.4	123.15	
Fairoaks			123.425	Sibson			122.3
Felthorpe			123.5	Sleap			122.45
Fenland			122.925	Southampton	118.2	131.0	
Filton	124.95	122.725		Southend	127.725	128.95	
Gamston			130.475	Stansted	123.8	125.55	
Gatwick	134.225	128.575		Stapleford			122.8
Glasgow	118.8	119.1		Staverton	122.9	126.65	
Goodwood	120.65	122.45		Sumburgh	118.25	123.15	
Guernsey	119.95	128.65		Swansea	119.7		
Halfpenny Green			123.0	Swanton Morley			123.5
Hatfield	130.8	123.35		Sywell			122.7
Haverfordwest			122.2	Teesside	119.8	118.85	
Hawarden	124.95	123.35		Thruxton			130.45
Hayes Heliport			123.65	Tollerton			122.8
Headcorn			122.0	Wellesbourne			130.45
Heathrow	118.7	119.72		White Waltham			122.6
	118.5	134.97		Wick	119.7		
Hethel			122.35	Wickenby			122.45
Hucknall			130.8	Woodford	126.925	130.05	
Humberside	118.55	124.675		Yeovil	125.4	130.8	

Airline Flight Codes

Three-letter flight codes are now in general use. Those listed below identify both UK and overseas carriers appearing in the book.

Code	Airline		Code	Airline		Code	Airline	
AAF	Aigle Azur	F	DAH	Air Algerie	7T	MEA	Middle East A/L	OD
AAG	Air Atlantique	G	DAL	Delta A/L	N	MNX	Manx A/L	G
AAL	American A/L	N	DAT	Delta Air Transport	OO	MON	Monarch A/L	G
AAN	Oasis	EC	DLH	Lufthansa	D	MOR	Morefly	LN
ABB	Air Belgium	OO	DMA	Maersk Air	OY	MPH	Martinair	PH
ABR	Hunting	G	DQI	Cimber Air	OY	NAW	Newair	OY
ACA	Air Canada	C	DYA	Alyemda	7O	NEX	Northern Executive	G
ACF	Air Charter Intl	F	EGY	Egypt Air	SU	NGA	Nigeria A/L	5N
ADR	Adria A/W	S5	EIA	Evergreen Intl	N	NWA	Northwest A/L	N
AEA	Air Europa	EC	EIN	Aer Lingus	EI	OAL	Olympic A/L	SX
AEF	Aero Lloyd	D	ELY	El Al	4X	PAL	Philippine A/L	RP
AFL	Aeroflot	RA	ETH	Ethiopian A/L	ET	PGA	Portugalia	CS
AFM	Affretair	Z	EUI	Euralair	F	PGT	Pegasus	TC
AFR	Air France	F	EWW	Emery	N	PIA	Pakistan Intl	AP
AGX	Aviogenex	YU	EXS	Channel Express	G	QFA	Qantas	VH
AHK	Air Hong Kong	VR-H	FDE	Federal Express	N	QSC	African Safaris	5Y
AIC	Air-India	VT	FIN	Finnair	OH	RAM	Royal Air Maroc	CN
AIH	Airtours (European)	G	FOB	Ford	G	RBA	Royal Brunei	V8
ALK	Air Lanka	4R	FOF	Fred Olsen	LN	RIA	Rich Intl	N
AMC	Air Malta	9H	FUA	Futura	EC	RJA	Royal Jordanian	JY
AMM	Air 2000	G	FXY	Flexair	PH	RNA	Royal Nepal A/L	9N
AMT	American Trans Air	N	GBL	GB Airways	G	ROT	Tarom	YR
ANA	All Nippon A/W	JA	GEC	German Cargo	D	RWD	Air Rwanda	9XR
ANZ	Air New Zealand	ZK	GFA	Gulf Air	A40	RYR	Ryanair	EI
AOM	AOM French A/L	F	GFG	Germania	D	SAA	South African A/W	ZS
APW	Arrow Air	N	GHA	Ghana A/W	9G	SAB	Sabena	OO
ARG	Argentine A/W	LV	GIA	Garuda	PK	SAS	SAS	SE OY LN
ATI	ATI	I	GIL	Gill Air	G	SAY	Suckling A/W	G
ATT	Aer Turas	EI	GNT	Business Air	G	SDI	Saudi	HZ
AUA	Austrian A/L	OE	GRN	Greenair	TC	SEY	Air Seychelles	S7
AUR	Aurigny A/S	G	HAL	Hawaiian Air	N	SIA	Singapore A/L	9V
AVA	Avianca	HK	HAS	Hamburg A/L	D	SJM	Southern AT	N
AWC	Titan A/W	G	HLA	HeavyLift	G	SLA	Sobelair	OO
AYC	Aviaco	EC	HLF	Hapag-Lloyd	D	SPP	Spanair	EC
AZA	Alitalia	I	IAW	Iraqi A/W	YI	SUD	Sudan A/W	ST
AZI	Air Zimbabwe	Z	IBE	Iberia	EC	SUT	Sultan Air	TC
AZR	Air Zaire	9Q	ICE	Icelandair	TF	SWE	Swedair	SE
BAC	BAC Leasing	G	INS	Instone A/L	G	SWR	Swissair	HB
BAL	Britannia A/L	G	IRA	Iran Air	EP	SXS	Sun Express	TC
BAW	British Airways	G	IST	Istanbul A/L	TC	SYR	Syrian Arab	YK
BBB	Balair CTA	HB	ITF	Air Inter	F	TAP	Air Portugal	CS
BBC	Bangladesh Biman	S2	JAL	Japan A/L	JA	TAR	Tunis Air	TS
BCS	European A/T	OO	JAT	JAT	YU	TAT	TAT	F
BER	Air Berlin	N	JEA	Jersey European A/W	G	TCT	TUR European	TC
BIH	British Intl Heli	G	KAC	Kuwait A/W	9K	THA	Thai A/W Intl	HS
BMA	British Midland	G	KAL	Korean Air	HL	THG	Thurston	G
BRA	Braathens	LN	KAR	Kar-Air	OH	THY	Turkish A/L	TC
BSP	Bosphorous A/W	TC	KIS	Contactair	D	TIH	Airtours (US)	G
BWA	BWIA	9Y	KLM	KLM	PH	TLA	TransLift	EI
BWD	British World	G	KQA	Kenya A/W	5Y	TLE	Air Toulouse	F
BZH	Brit Air	F	LAA	Libyan Arab A/L	5A	TMA	Trans Mediterranean	OD
CCA	Air China	B	LAZ	Bulgarian A/L	LZ	TOW	Tower Air	N
CDN	Canadian A/L Intl	C	LDA	Lauda Air	OE	TRA	Transavia	PH
CFE	City Flyer	G	LEI	Air UK Leisure	G	TSC	Air Transat	C
CFG	Condor	D	LGL	Luxair	LX	TSW	TEA Basle	HB
CKT	Caledonian	G	LIB	Air Liberte	F	TWA	TWA	N
CLH	Lufthansa CityLine	D	LIT	Air Littoral	F	TWE	Transwede	SE
CLX	Cargolux	LX	LKA	Alkair	OY	TYR	Tyrolean	OE
CMM	Canada 3000 A/L	C	LOG	Loganair	G	UAE	Emirates A/L	A6
CNB	Air Columbus	CS	LOT	Polish A/L (LOT)	SP	UAL	United A/L	N
COA	Continental A/L	N	LTE	LTE	EC	UGA	Uganda A/L	5X
CPA	Cathay Pacific	VR-H	LTS	LTU Sud	D	UKA	Air UK	G
CRL	Corse Air	F	LTU	LTU	D	UKR	Air Ukraine	UR
CRX	Crossair	HB	MAH	Malev	HA	ULE	Leisure Intl	G
CSA	Czech A/L	OK	MAS	Malaysian A/L	9M	UPA	Air Foyle	G
CTN	Croatia A/L	9A	MAU	Air Mauritius	3B	UPS	United Parcels	N
CYP	Cyprus A/W	5B	MDN	Meridiana	EC	USA	USAir	N

UTA	UTA	F	VIR	Virgin Atlantic	G	WOA	World A/W	N
UYC	Cameroon A/L	TJ	VIV	Viva Air	EC	ZAC	Zambia A/W	9J
UZB	Uzbekistan A/W	UK	VRG	Varig	PP	ZAS	ZAS A/L of Egypt	SU
VIA	Viasa	YV	WDL	WDL	D			

479766 (G-BKHG), Piper J-3C-65 Cub. *AJW*

EI-CIB, BAC One-Eleven 501EX. *AJW*

British Aircraft Preservation Council Register

The British Aircraft Preservation Council was formed in 1967 to co-ordinate the works of all bodies involved in the preservation, restoration and display of historical aircraft. Membership covers the whole spectrum of national, Service, commercial and voluntary groups, and meetings are held regularly at the bases of member organisations. The Council is able to provide a means of communication, helping to resolve any misunderstandings or duplication of effort. Every effort is taken to encourage the raising of standards of both organisation and technical capacity amongst the member groups to the benfit of everyone interested in aviation. To assist historians, the B.A.P.C. register has been set up and provides an identity for those aircraft which do not qualify for a Service serial or inclusion in the UK Civil Register.

Aircraft on the current B.A.P.C. Register are as follows:

Notes	Reg. Type	Owner or Operator
6	Roe Triplane Type IV (replica)	Greater Manchester Museum of Science & Technology
7	Southampton University MPA	Southampton Hall of Aviation
8	Dixon ornithopter	The Shuttleworth Collection
9	Humber Monoplane (replica)	Airport Terminal/Birmingham
10	Hafner R.II Revoplane	Museum of Army Flying/Middle Wallop
12	Mignet HM.14	Museum of Flight/E. Fortune
13	Mignet HM.14	Brimpex Metal Treatments
14	Addyman standard training glider	N. H. Ponsford
15	Addyman standard training glider	The Aeroplane Collection Ltd
16	Addyman ultra-light aircraft	N. H. Ponsford
17	Woodhams Sprite	The Aeroplane Collection Ltd
18	Killick MP Gyroplane	N. H. Ponsford
19	Bristol F.2b	Brussels Air Museum
20	Lee-Richards annular biplane (replica)	Newark Air Musem
21	Thruxton Jackaroo	M. J. Brett
22	Mignet HM.14 (G-AEOF)	Aviodome/Schiphol
25	Nyborg TGN-III glider	Midland Air Museum
27	Mignet HM.14	M. J. Abbey
28	Wright Flyer (replica)	Bygone Times Antique Warehouse/ Eccleston, Lancs
29	Mignet HM.14 (replica) (G-ADRY)	Brooklands Museum of Aviation/ Weybridge
32	Crossley Tom Thumb	Midland Air Museum
33	DFS.108-49 Grunau Baby IIb	Russavia Collection
34	DFS.108-49 Grunau Baby IIb	D. Elsdon
35	EoN primary glider	Russavia Collection
36	Fieseler Fi.103 (V-1) (replica)	Kent Battle of Britain Museum/Hawkinge
37	Blake Bluetit	The Shuttleworth Collection
38	Bristol Scout replica (A1742)	Stored/Wroughton
40	Bristol Boxkite (replica)	Bristol City Museum
41	B.E.2C (replica) (6232)	Historical Aircraft Museum/RAF St Athan
42	Avro 504 (replica) (H1968)	Historical Aircraft Museum/RAF St Athan
43	Mignet HM.14	Lincolnshire Aviation Museum
44	Miles Magister (L6906)	Museum of Berkshire Aviation (G-AKKY)/ Woodley
45	Pilcher Hawk (replica)	Stanford Hall Museum
46	Mignet HM.14	Alan McKechnie Racing Ltd
47	Watkins Monoplane	Historical Aircraft Museum/RAF St Athan
48	Pilcher Hawk (replica)	Glasgow Museum of Transport
49	Pilcher Hawk	Royal Scottish Museum/Edinburgh
50	Roe Triplane Type 1	Science Museum/S. Kensington
51	Vickers Vimy IV	Science Museum/S. Kensington
52	Lilienthal glider	Science Museum Store/Hayes
53	Wright Flyer (replica)	Science Museum/S. Kensington
54	JAP-Harding monoplane	Science Museum/S. Kensington
55	Levavasseur Antoinette VII	Science Museum/S. Kensington
56	Fokker E.III (210/16)	Science Museum/S. Kensington
57	Pilcher Hawk (replica)	Science Museum/S. Kensington
58	Yokosuka MXY7 Ohka II (15-1585)	F.A.A. Museum/Yeovilton
59	Sopwith Camel (replica) (D3419)	Historical Aircraft Museum/RAF St Athan
60	Murray M.1 helicopter	The Aeroplane Collection Ltd
61	Stewart man-powered ornithopter	Lincolnshire Aviation Museum
62	Cody Biplane (304)	Science Museum/S. Kensington
63	Hurricane (replica) (L1592)	Kent Battle of Britain Museum/Hawkinge
64	Hurricane (replica) (P3059)	Kent Battle of Britain Museum/Hawkinge

Notes	Reg.	Type	Owner or Operator
	65	Spitfire (replica) (N3289)	Kent Battle of Britain Museum/Hawkinge
	66	Bf 109 (replica) (1480)	Kent Battle of Britain Museum/Hawkinge
	67	Bf 109 (replica) (14)	Kent Battle of Britain Museum/Hawkinge
	68	Hurricane (replica) (H3426)	Midland Air Museum
	69	Spitfire (replica) (N3313)	Kent Battle of Britain Museum/Hawkinge
	70	Auster AOP.5 (TJ398)	Aircraft Preservation Soc of Scotland
	71	Spitfire (replica) (P8140)	Norfolk & Suffolk Aviation Museum
	72	Hurricane (replica) (V7767)	N. Weald Restoration Flight
	73	Hurricane (replica)	Queens Head/Bishop's Stortford
	74	Bf 109 (replica) (6357/6)	Kent Battle of Britain Museum/Hawkinge
	75	Mignet HM.14 (G-AEFG)	N. H. Ponsford
	76	Mignet HM.14 (G-AFFI)	Yorkshire Air Museum/Elvington
	77	Mignet HM.14 (replica) (G-ADRG)	Stratford Aircraft Collection
	79	Fiat G.46-4 (MM53211)	British Air Reserve/Lympne
	80	Airspeed Horsa (KJ351)	Museum of Army Flying/Middle Wallop
	81	Hawkridge Dagling	Russavia Collection
	82	Hawker Hind (Afghan)	RAF Museum/Hendon
	83	Kawasaki Ki-100-1b	Aerospace Museum/Cosford
	84	Nakajima Ki-46 (Dinah III)	Historical Aircraft Museum/RAF St Athan
	85	Weir W-2 autogyro	Museum of Flight/E. Fortune
	86	de Havilland Tiger Moth (replica)	Yorkshire Aircraft Preservation Soc
	87	Bristol Babe (replica) (G-EASQ)	Bomber County Museum/Hemswell
	88	Fokker Dr 1 (replica) (102/18)	F.A.A. Museum/Yeovilton
	89	Cayley glider (replica)	Greater Manchester Museum of Science & Technology
	90	Colditz Cock (replica)	Imperial War Museum/Duxford
	91	Fieseler Fi 103 (V.1)	Lashenden Air Warfare Museum
	92	Fieseler Fi 103 (V.1)	Historical Aircraft Museum/RAF St Athan
	93	Fieseler Fi 103 (V.1)	Imperial War Museum/Duxford
	94	Fieseler Fi 103 (V.1)	Aerospace Museum/Cosford
	95	Gizmer autogyro	F. Fewsdale
	96	Brown helicopter	NE Aircraft Museum
	97	Luton L.A.4A Minor	NE Aircraft Museum
	98	Yokosuka MXY7 Ohka II	Greater Manchester Museum of Science & Technology
	99	Yokosuka MXY7 Ohka II	Aerospace Museum/Cosford
	100	Clarke glider	RAF Museum/Hendon
	101	Mignet HM.14	Lincolnshire Aviation Museum
	103	Pilcher glider (replica)	Personal Plane Services Ltd
	105	Blériot XI (replica)	Aviodome/Schiphol
	106	Blériot XI	RAF Museum/Hendon
	107	Blériot XXVII	RAF Museum/Hendon
	108	Fairey Swordfish IV (HS503)	Cosford Aerospace Museum
	109	Slingsby Kirby Cadet TX.1	RAF Museum/Henlow store
	110	Fokker D.VII replica (static) (5125)	—
	111	Sopwith Triplane replica (static) (N5492)	F.A.A. Museum/Yeovilton
	112	D.H.2 replica (static) (5964)	Museum of Army Flying/Middle Wallop
	113	S.E.5A replica (static) (B4863)	—
	114	Vickers Type 60 Viking (static) (G-EBED)	Brooklands Museum of Aviation/Weybridge
	115	Mignet HM.14	Essex Aviation Group/Andrewsfield
	116	Santos-Dumont Demoiselle (replica)	Cornwall Aero Park/Helston
	117	B.E.2C (replica)	N. Weald Aircraft Restoration Flight
	118	Albatros D.V (replica) (C19/18)	S. Yorks Aviation Soc/Firbeck
	119	Bensen B.7	NE Aircraft Museum
	120	Mignet HM.14 (G-AEJZ)	Bomber County Museum/Hemswell
	121	Mignet HM.14 (G-AEKR)	S. Yorks Aviation Soc/Firbeck
	122	Avro 504 (replica)	British Broadcasting Corp
	123	Vickers FB.5 Gunbus (replica)	A. Topen (stored)/Cranfield
	124	Lilienthal Glider Type XI (replica)	Science Museum/S. Kensington
	125	Clay Cherub (G-BDGP)	B. R. Clay
	126	D.31 Turbulent (static)	Midland Air Museum store
	127	Halton Jupiter MPA	The Shuttleworth Collection
	128	Watkinson Cyclogyroplane Mk IV	International Helicopter Museum/Weston-s-Mare
	129	Blackburn 1911 Monoplane (replica)	Cornwall Aero Park/Helston store
	130	Blackburn 1912 Monoplane (replica)	Cornwall Aero Park/Helston store
	131	Pilcher Hawk (replica)	C. Paton
	132	Blériot XI (G-BLXI)	Musée de L'Automobile/France

Reg.	Type	Owner or Operator	Notes
133	Fokker Dr 1 (replica) (425/17)	Newark Air Museum	
134	Pitts S-2A static (G-CARS)	Toyota Ltd/Sywell	
135	Bristol M.1C (replica) (C4912)	—	
136	Deperdussin Seaplane (replica)	Reno/Nevada	
137	Sopwith Baby Floatplane (replica) (8151)	—	
138	Hansa Brandenburg W.29 Floatplane (replica) (2292)	—	
139	Fokker Dr 1 (replica) 150/17	—	
140	Curtiss R3C-2 Floatplane (replica)	Planes of Fame Museum/Chino, Ca	
141	Macchi M.39 Floatplane (replica)	Planes of Fame Museum/Chino, Ca	
142	SE-5A (replica) (F5459)	Cornwall Aero Park/Helston	
143	Paxton MPA	R. A. Paxton/Staverton	
144	Weybridge Mercury MPA	Cranwell Gliding Club	
145	Oliver MPA	D. Oliver (*stored*)/Warton	
146	Pedal Aeronauts Toucan MPA	The Shuttleworth Collection	
147	Bensen B.7	Norfolk & Suffolk Aviation Museum	
148	Hawker Fury II (replica) (K7271)	Aerospace Museum/Cosford	
149	Short S.27 (replica)	F.A.A. Museum (*stored*)/Yeovilton	
150	SEPECAT Jaguar GR.1 (replica) (XX718)	RAF Exhibition Flight	
151	SEPECAT Jaguar GR.1 (replica) (XZ363)	RAF Exhibition Flight	
152	BAe Hawk T.1 (replica) (XX263)	RAF Exhibition Flight	
153	Westland WG.33	IHM/Weston-s-Mare	
154	D.31 Turbulent	Lincolnshire Aviation Museum	
155	Panavia Tornado GR.1 (replica) (ZA446)	RAF Exhibition Flight	
156	Supermarine S-6B (replica) (S1595)	Planes of Fame Museum/Chino, Ca	
157	Waco CG-4A	Pennine Aviation Museum	
158	Fieseler Fi 103 (V.1)	Joint Bomb Disposal School/Chattenden	
159	Yokosuka MXY7 Ohka II	Joint Bomb Disposal School/Chattenden	
160	Chargus 108 hang glider	Museum of Flight/E. Fortune	
161	Stewart Ornithopter Coppelia	Bomber County Museum	
162	Goodhart Newbury Manflier MPA	Science Museum/Wroughton	
163	AFEE 10/42 Rotabuggy	Museum of Army Flying/Middle Wallop	
164	Wight Quadruplane Type 1 (replica)	Wessex Aviation Soc/Wimborne	
165	Bristol F.2b (E2466)	RAF Museum/Hendon	
167	S.E.5A replica	Newark Air Museum	
168	D.H.60G Moth static replica (G-AAAH)	Hilton Hotel/Gatwick	
169	SEPECAT Jaguar GR.1 (static replica) (XX110)	No 1 S. of T.T. RAF Halton	
170	Pilcher Hawk (replica)	A. Gourlay/Strathallan	
171	BAe Hawk T.1 (replica) (XX297)	RAF Exhibition Flight/Abingdon	
172	Chargus Midas Super 8 hang glider	Science Museum/Wroughton	
173	Birdman Promotions Grasshopper	Science Museum/Wroughton	
174	Bensen B.7	Science Museum/Wroughton	
175	Volmer VJ-23 Swingwing	Greater Manchester Museum of Science & Technology	
176	SE-5A (replica) (A4850)	S. Yorks Aviation Soc/Firbeck	
177	Avro 504K (replica) (G1381)	Brooklands Museum of Aviation/Weybridge	
178	Avro 504K (replica) (E373)	Bygone Times Antique Warehouse/Eccleston, Lancs	
179	Sopwith Pup (replica) (A7317)	Midland Air Museum/Coventry	
180	McCurdy Silver Dart (replica)	RAF Museum/Cardington store	
181	RAF B.E.2b (replica)	RAF Museum/Hendon	
182	Wood Ornithopter	Greater Manchester Museum of Science & Technology	
183	Zurowski ZP.1	Newark Air Museum	
184	Spitfire IX (replica) (EN398)	Aces High Ltd/North Weald	
185	Waco CG-4A (243809)	Museum of Army Flying/Middle Wallop	
186	D.H.82B Queen Bee (K3584)	Mosquito Aircraft Museum	
187	Roe Type 1 biplane (replica)	Brooklands Museum of Aviation/Weybridge	
188	McBroom Cobra 88	Science Museum/Wroughton	
189	Blériot XI (replica)	—	
190	Spitfire (replica) (K5054)	Biggin Hill Museum	
191	BAe Harrier GR.5 (replica) (ZD472)	RAF Exhibition Flight	
192	Weedhopper JC-24	The Aeroplane Collection/Warmingham, Cheshire	

Notes	Reg.	Type	Owner or Operator
	193	Hovey WD-11 Whing Ding	The Aeroplane Collection
	194	Santos Dumont Demoiselle (replica)	Brooklands Museum of Aviation/Weybridge
	195	Moonraker 77 hang glider	Museum of Flight/E. Fortune
	196	Sigma 2M hang glider	Museum of Flight/E. Fortune
	197	Cirrus III hang glider	Museum of Flight/E. Fortune
	198	Fieseler Fi.103 (V-1)	Imperial War Museum/Lambeth
	199	Fieseler Fi.103 (V-1)	Science Museum/S. Kensington
	200	Bensen B.7	K. Fern Collection/Stoke
	204	McBroom Hang Glider	The Aeroplane Collection
	208	SE-5A (replica) (D2700)	Prince's Mead Shopping Precinct/Farnborough
	209	Spitfire IX (replica)	Museum of D-Day Aviation/Appledram, West Sussex
	210	Avro 504J (replica)	Southampton Hall of Aviation
	211	Mignet HM.14 (replica)	Vintage & Rotary Wing Collection
	212	Bensen B.8	International Helicopter Museum/Weston-s-Mare
	213	Vertigo MPA	International Helicopter Museum/Weston-s-Mare
	214	Spitfire prototype (replica)	The Spitfire Soc
	215	Airwave hang-glider	Southampton Hall of Aviation
	216	D.H.88 Comet (replica) (G-ACSS)	Trout Lake Air Force
	217	Spitfire (replica) (K9926)	RAF Museum/Bentley Priory
	218	Hurricane (replica) (P3386)	RAF Museum/Bentley Priory
	219	Hurricane (replica) (L1710)	RAF Memorial Chapel/Biggin Hill
	220	Spitfire (replica) (N3194)	RAF Memorial Chapel/Biggin Hill
	221	Spitfire (replica) (MH777)	RAF Museum/Northolt
	222	Spitfire (replica) (BR600)	RAF Museum/Uxbridge
	223	Hurricane (replica) (V7467)	RAF Museum/Coltishall
	224	Spitfire V (replica)	—
	225	Spitfire (replica) (P8448)	RAF Museum/Swanton Manley
	226	Spitfire (replica) (EN343)	RAF Museum/Benson
	227	Spitfire (replica) (L1070)	RAF Museum/Turnhouse
	228	Olympus hang-glider	NE Aircraft Museum/Usworth
	229	Spitfire (replica) (L1096)	RAF Museum/Church Fenton
	230	Spitfire (replica) (AA908)	Eden Camp/Malton
	231	Mignet HM.14	—
	233	Broburn Wanderlust sailplane	Museum of Berkshire Aviation/Woodley
	234	Vickers FB.5 Gunbus (replica)	Macclesfield Historical Aviation Soc

Note: Registrations/Serials carried are mostly false identities. MPA = Man Powered Aircraft.

G-AFAX, B.A. Eagle 2. *AJW*

EC-EMD, Douglas DC-8-62F. *A/W*

OH-LAB, Airbus A.300B4-203, AJW

N306FE, Douglas DC-10-30AF. AJW

OY-CLB, BAe Jetstream 3102. AJW

PH-SDJ, D.H.C.8-311A Dash Eight. AJW

329

VR-HOS, Boeing 747-467 and B-2460, Boeing 747-4J6. AJW

Future Allocations Log (In-Sequence)

The grid provides the facility to record future in-sequence registrations as they are issued or seen. To trace a particular code, refer to the left hand column which contains the three letters following the G prefix. The final letter can be found by reading across the columns headed A to Z. For example, the box for G-BVLD is located five rows down (BVL) and then four across to the D column.

G-	A	B	C	D	E	F	G	H	I	J	K	L	M	N	O	P	R	S	T	U	V	W	X	Y	Z
BVH																									
BVI																									
BVJ																									
BVK																									
BVL																									
BVM																									
BVN																									
BVO																									
BVP																									
BVR																									
BVS																									
BVT																									
BVU																									
BVV																									
BVW																									
BVX																									
BVY																									
BVZ																									
BWA																									
BWB																									
BWC																									
BWD																									
BWE																									
BWF																									
BWG																									
BWH																									
BWI																									
BWJ																									
BWK																									
BWL																									
BWM																									
BWN																									
BWO																									
BWP																									
BWR	A	B	C	D	E	F	G	H	I	J	K	L	M	N	O	P	R	S	T	U	V	W	X	Y	Z

Future Allocations Log
(Out-of-Sequence)

This grid can be used to record out-of-sequence registrations as they are issued or seen. The first column is provided for the ranges prefixed with G-B, ie from G-BWxx to G-BZxx. The remaining columns cover the sequences from G-Cxxx to G-Zxxx and in this case it is necessary to insert the last three letters in the appropriate section.

G-B	G-C	G-E	G-G	G-J	G-L	G-N	G-O	G-P	G-S	G-U
											G-V
	G-D	G-F	G-H		G-M	G-O				
				G-K						
										G-W
								G-R		
									G-T	
										G-X
G-C	G-E	G-G	G-I	G-L	G-N					
										G-Y
										G-Z

Overseas Airliners Registration Log

This grid may be used to record airliner registrations not included in the main section

Reg.	Type	Operator

Addenda

New or restored British registrations

Notes	Reg.	Type	Owner or Operator
	G-AWYR	BAC One-Eleven 501EX	British Airways (*stored ex EI-CID*)
	G-AWYT	BAC One-Eleven 501EX	British Airways (*stored ex EI-CIE*)
	G-AWYU	BAC One-Eleven 501EX	British Airways (*stored ex EI-CIC*)
	G-AXJK	BAC One-Eleven 501EX	British Airways (*stored ex EI-CIB*)
	G-AYLZ	Super Aero 45 Srs 04	M. Emery
	G-BKNL	Cameron D-96 airship	Sport Promotion SRL/Italy
	G-FFHI	AS.355F-1 Twin Squirrel	Ford Farm Helicopters Ltd (G-GWHH/ G-BKUL)
	G-HUGO	Colt 260A balloon	Adventure Ballooning
	G-INDE	PA-44-180 Seminole	Standby One Flight Services Ltd (G-BHNM)
	G-IYAK	Yakovlev C-11	E. K. Coventry
	G-MUZO	Shaw Europa	J. T. Grant
	G-NEXT	AS.355F-1 Twin Squirrel	Bristow Helicopters Ltd (G-OAMV)
	G-NOCK	Cessna FR.182RG	R. J. Howard (G-BGTK)
	G-OEAA	EMB-110P1 Bandeirante	Euroair Transport Ltd/Knight Air Ltd (G-BTAA/G-BHJY)/Leeds
	G-OEAB	EMB-110P2 Bandeirante	Euroair Transport Ltd/Knight Air Ltd G-BKWB/G-CHEV)/Leeds
	G-OGAZ	SA.341G Gazelle 1	M. Wood Haulage (G-OCJR/G-BRGS)
	G-OLXX	Avro RJ70A	British Aerospace PLC
	G-OOTC	PA-28R-201T Turbo Arrow III	T. J. Caton (G-CLIV)
	G-SIVA	Hughes 369E	C. J. Siva-Jothy (G-TBIX)
	G-SOKO	Soko P-2 Kraguj	J. Mussell (G-BRXK)
	G-SSGS	Shaw Europa	SGS Partnership
	G-UORO	Shaw Europa	D. Dufton
	G-UILE	Lancair 320	R. J. Martin
	G-ZGBE	Beech 95-58PA	GB Express Ltd (G-BNKL)

Cancellations

G-AVXX, G-BDHL, G-BEBF, G-BFNU, G-BGJG, G-BGJK, G-BGJM, G-BGTK, G-BHNM, G-BKLT, G-BKWB, G-BLCV, G-BMGH, G-BNKL, G-BPWX, G-BPZT, G-BRXK, G-BTAA, G-BTXK, G-BUBF, G-BUUW, G-BVAK, G-BVAL, G-BVDX, G-CLIK, G-CLIV, G-GJCB, G-GWHH, G-KNDY, G-LAKD, G-MHIH, G-MONM, G-MTLE, G-OBMC, G-OJCR, G-OFRH, G-TBIX, G-THUR, G-WICK

New overseas registrations

Reg.	Type	Owner or Operator	Notes
EC-FUA	Boeing 757-256	Iberia	
EC-FUB	Boeing 757-256	Iberia	
F-GDXP	Douglas DC-3	Transvalair	
F-GNDC	Douglas DC-10-30	AOM French Airlines (*ex F-GDJK*)	
LN-RCH	Boeing 767-383ER	S.A.S. *Ingegerd Viking*	
LN-RCI	Boeing 767-383ER	S.A.S. *Helga Viking*	
LN-RCK	Boeing 767-383ER	S.A.S. *Tor Viking*	
LN-RCL	Boeing 767-383ER	S.A.S. *Sven Viking*	
N388AA	Boeing 767-323ER	American Airlines	
N389AA	Boeing 767-323ER	American Airlines	
N390AA	Boeing 767-323ER	American Airlines	
N751PR	Boeing 747-4F6	Philippine Airlines (*RP-C5751 not taken up*)	
N562US	Boeing 767-2B7ER	USAir/British Airways	
N746OU	Boeing 727-222	United Airlines	
TC-GEN	Boeing 757-225	Birgenair	
4K-AZI	Boeing 727-235	Azerbaijan Airlines	
5N-MAS	Boeing 707 321C	Trans Air Services	

Cancellations

C-FNXA, CS-TKA, CS-TKB, D-CDIZ, F-BPVA, F-BPVD, F-BPVN, F-BUAR, F-GATS, F-GDJK, F-GNBB, I-AEJD, I-AEJE, N762BE, N764BE, N765BE, N766BE, N7622U, N7644U, N31024, OY-MBK, PH-TVP, RP-C5751, SE-DKO, SE-DKU, SE-DKX, SE-DOB, TF-ABT, S7-AAQ

Monthly news & aircraft movements throughout the UK

Over 400 pages every year, packed with regular national UK movement reports, airfield and airline news. Add extensive Stansted and Heathrow movement lists, a full UK register update and illustrate with photographs and you have the best magazine of its type. All this for just £14.00 per year.

To commence your membership from January 1994 send £14.00 to Stansted Aviation Society (CAM offer), 271 Birchanger Lane, Birchanger, Bishop's Stortford, Herts CM23 5QP. Or to join during the year, simply send £1.20 per month of 1994 remaining. As well as postal subscription to the magazine you will also be entitled to discounts at the Society shop (open Sundays at Stansted Airport) which stocks a range of books, models, registers and magazines.

Stansted Aviation Society
NEWS 14/12
December 1993
Volume 14 Number 12

The essential magazine for the aircraft enthusiast

Just £14 p.a.

Stansted Aviation Society